CONCEPTUAL PHYSICS

The High School Physics Program

Written and illustrated by

Paul G. Hewitt

With contributions from

Christopher Chiaverina
New Trier High School

Kenneth W. Ford
Germantown Academy

Diane Riendeau
Deerfield High School

Phillip R. Wolf
Mt. San Antonio College

PEARSON

Boston, Massachusetts • Chandler, Arizona • Glenview, Illinois • Upper Saddle River, New Jersey

About the Author

Paul G. Hewitt's ability to communicate the concepts of physics through simple language, cartoon sketches, and thought-provoking demonstrations has made his courses at City College of San Francisco extremely popular. The American Association of Physics Teachers honored Professor Hewitt in 1982 with its Millikan Award for outstanding teaching, and the Exploratorium (San Francisco's innovative science museum) presented him with its Outstanding Educator Award in 2000.

Long before becoming a physicist, Paul at 17 years old was the New England Amateur Athletic Union silver-medalist flyweight boxing champion. He later became a uranium prospector in Colorado after a stint in the U.S. Army, then a commercial artist and sign painter. He entered college at the age of 27, receiving a bachelor's degree in physics from Lowell Technological Institute. He earned two master's degrees from Utah State University, one in physics and another in science education. His 36-year teaching career was mainly at City College of San Francisco, where for a decade he taught physics evenings at the Exploratorium. He guest taught at various high schools and universities, including the University of California, both Berkeley and Santa Cruz campuses, and the University of Hawaii, both Manoa and Hilo campuses. He is now retired and enjoying the good life in Florida and California.

Cover photograph: roller coaster, Jeremy Sutton-Hibbert/Alamy; background, Shutterstock.

13-digit ISBN 978-0-13-364749-5
10-digit ISBN 0-13-364749-8
12 13 14 15 16   V063   14 13 12

To students who wonder
and teachers who instill
in them a love of learning

Conceptual Physics Photo Album

Conceptual Physics is a very personal book, and this is reflected in the many photographs of family and friends throughout this edition. My wife Lillian and I demonstrate Newton's third law in Figure 7.16. Another photo of Lil is Figure 26.4, and more recently with our pet conure Sneezlee in Figure 28.13. Also illustrating Newton's third law on page 121 is my brother Steve and his daughter Gretchen. My other brother Dave Hewitt and his wife Barbara operate the water pump in Figure 20.9. My sister, Marjorie Hewitt Suchocki, an author and theologian at Claremont School of Theology, illustrates reflection on page 581. My favorite photo of my daughter Leslie is shown holding a molecular model in Figure 17.1. My son Paul illustrates adiabatic compression in Figure 24.3, and his wife Ludmila holds the polarizing filters in Figure 27.17. My late son James is shown illustrating gyroscopic motion in Figure 12.13b, and again as a tot in the magnifying glass in Figure 30.7. He left me my first grandson, Manuel, showing a catenary on page 352. My younger grandchildren, Megan and Emily Abrams, and Alexander and Grace Hewitt, are assembled for the photo of Figure 28.14.

Renowned physicist Ken Ford, a major contributor to this and previous editions, pursues his passion for teaching ninth graders in Figure 15.12. His other passion for flying is indicated in Figure 26.15. Tim and Elise, children of Diane Riendeau, another contributor to this book, are shown on pages 43 and 760. Frank Oppenheimer, who years ago invited me to teach at the Exploratorium in San Francisco, is featured in Figure 25.2.

Dear friends include Marshall Ellenstein, Figure 1.2, a major contributor to every edition I've written, and the producer of the DVD classroom lectures, *Conceptual Physics Alive!* and *The San Francisco Years*. Burl Grey, who stimulated my love of physics a half century ago, is shown in Figure 2.3. Will Maynez shows the airtrack he built for CCSF in Figure 8.13. Tenny Lim, former student and now a design engineer for Jet Propulsion Labs, puts energy into her bow in Figure 9.6, and shows balance with husband Mark in Figure 11.20. Back in the 1990s my physics student Helen Yan posed for a black and white photo of the same box she shows in Figure 22.14. Helen continued in physics and is now an orbit analyst for Lockhead Martin Corp. Howie Brand shows impulse and changes in momentum in Figure 8.9. Lori Patterson is electrified in Figure 33.18. Her son Ryan displays magnetic personality in Figure 36.9. Mona El Tawil-Nassar demonstrates a classroom capacitor in Figure 33.16. Tammy and Larry Tunison demonstrate radiation safety in Figure 39.14. Former student Cassy Cosme safely breaks bricks with her bare hand in Figure 8.7. I safely break a cement block above Paul Robinson in Figure 6.7, while he lies between beds of sharp nails. Robinson's children, David and Kristin, are on page 230.

The six unit openers are adorned with children of close friends and family members. Opening Unit I, Genichiro Nakada sits between Debbie and Natalie Limogan, children of my close friends, Hideko and Herman Limogan. Andrés Riveros Mendoza, son of David Riveros who is co-author of a Mexican version of *Conceptual Physics,* opens Unit II. The opening of Unit III features Terrence Jones, son of my niece Corine Jones. My grandson Alexander opens Unit IV, granddaughter Megan opens Unit V, and grandchildren Grace and Alexander open Unit VI.

These photographs of people very dear to me, all the more make *Conceptual Physics* a labor of love.

Contents

UNIT II PROPERTIES OF MATTER 322

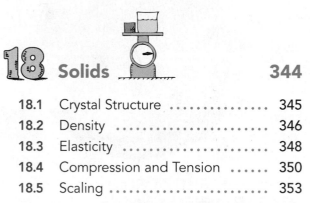

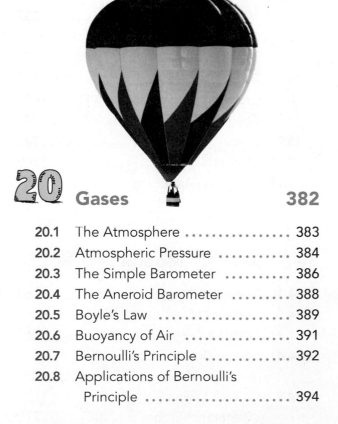

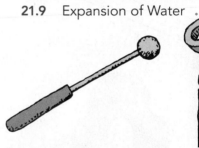 

UNIT IV SOUND AND LIGHT 488

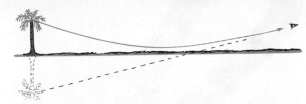

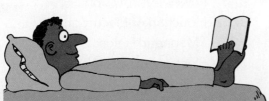

Activities and Features

discover!

Link to...

Physics on the Job

Physics of Sports

Physics in the Kitchen

Science, Technology, and Society

do the math!

CONCEPTS BEFORE COMPUTATION

An innovative approach pioneered by Paul Hewitt in Conceptual Physics

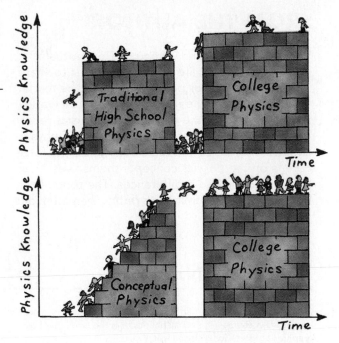

Only Conceptual Physics provides comprehensive content and a three-step learning sequence that builds conceptual understanding and offers computational reinforcement.

 EXPLORATION

Ignite interest with meaningful examples and hands-on activities.

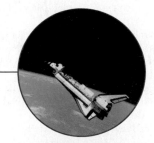

 CONCEPT DEVELOPMENT

Expand understanding with engaging narrative and visuals, multimedia presentations, and a wide range of concept-development questions and exercises.

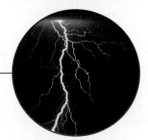

APPLICATION

Reinforce and apply key concepts with hands-on laboratory work, critical thinking, and problem solving.

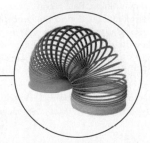

FROM THE AUTHOR

The teaching and writing of *Conceptual Physics* is my life's work. My aim is to share my passion for physics, to guide the reader to see physics as the rules of the physical world, and to teach how the equations of physics reveal the connections in nature. Whereas many physics courses emphasize the tools of physics, the focus here is on the physics concepts themselves, their similarities, and their differences. The tone of the book is friendly, illuminating rather than intimidating, and rich with analogies and clear explanations, with more qualitative questions than algebraic problems—all to help you discover that physics is fascinating, to provide a solid science foundation, and to see that a knowledge of physics is important to your overall education. The testimonials below are from some of the most prestigious professors of major universities in the United States—physicists who are familiar with this book and are willing to share their impressions of it.

Paul G. Hewitt

TESTIMONIALS

Conceptual Physics is not an "about physics" course, nor a physics appreciation course—it is REAL physics. It is the book that best prepares students for college-level physics.
Sumner P. Davis
Department of Physics - University of California at Berkeley

I find students who have had a conceptual physics course in high school are generally better prepared for university physics than those who have had a traditional problem-solving course.
Eric Mazur
Department of Physics - Harvard University

Turning high school students into proficient solvers of physics problems is, I suspect, the wrong approach. The emphasis should be on concepts, so vital and appealing that it should be unthinkable for any educated person in the twenty-first century not to have mastered their elements. **Conceptual Physics** is a welcome and bold step in transforming the way physics should be taught.
David L. Goodstein
Vice Provost, Professor of Physics and Applied Physics,
Frank G. Gilloon Distinguished Teaching and Service Professor
California Institute of Technology

The national workshop Comprehensive Conceptual Curriculum for Physics (C[3]P) enthusiastically endorses, advocates, and promotes the use of Hewitt's **Conceptual Physics** textbook. It is the only textbook that we endorse.
Richard P. Olenick
Professor of Physics, C[3]P Principal Investigator
Department of Physics - University of Dallas

In my opinion, Paul Hewitt's **Conceptual Physics** provides a wonderful introduction to the concepts and spirit of physics. His text, coupled with open-ended laboratories, encouragement for personal science hobbies, and further immersion in the formalism of physics, would prepare students well for a calculus-based introductory course at any university.
Edwin F. Taylor
Senior Research Scientist, Emeritus
Department of Physics - Massachusetts Institute of Technology

By stressing an understanding of the ideas of physics instead of rote computation, **Conceptual Physics**, together with its insightful Concept-Development Practice Book, not only provides a firm foundation for further study in science, but more importantly, nurtures a scientific outlook for everyday life.
Helen Quinn
Senior Research Physicist,
Assistant to Director for Education Programs
Stanford Linear Accelerator Center

For 14 years **Conceptual Physics** has been our fundamental physics course at Edison High, the highly successful science and computer magnet school that annually leads the central valley in the number of National Merit Finalists. Thanks to the solid foundation provided by **Conceptual Physics**, we have the largest offerings of AP science courses and the highest scores in the valley. We use it with gifted students in the ninth grade and sophomores through seniors in our non-AP courses. Its readability with focus on concepts couched in real-life applications makes it enormously successful, separating it from other physics programs.
Roger Lucido
Former Vice President, AAPT, Northern California
Center for Advanced Research and Technology (CART)

I have used **Conceptual Physics** with ninth grade and senior students, with great success in both basic and honors sections. **Conceptual Physics** gets hold of the big ideas and makes them understandable to students at all levels. While the calculations in standard texts look impressive to non-scientists, students learn to follow them and to solve similar problems without real understanding. My students, however, learn concepts first, which are more fundamental than calculations. Follow-up problems are then understood. Different ability levels are easily accommodated with the supplementary materials that come with the text and with additional numerical problems in the new appendix. Conceptual Physics is a text that all students read and profit from.
Craig B. Merow
Director, Academy Scholars Program
Germantown Academy
Fort Washington, Pennsylvania

TO THE STUDENT

You can't fully enjoy a game unless you know its rules. Whether it's a ball game, computer game, or party game—if you don't know the rules, it can be boring. You miss out on what others enjoy. Just as a musician hears what untrained ears can't, and just as a cook tastes in food what others miss, a person who knows nature's rules can better appreciate nature.

Learning that satellites follow the same rules as tossed baseballs changes the way you see orbiting astronauts on TV. Learning the rules of light changes the way you see blue skies, white clouds, and rainbows. Richness in life is not only seeing the world with wide open eyes, but knowing what to look for.

We begin by looking at some of nature's basic rules—physics. We treat physics conceptually in this book, which means concepts are presented in familiar English, with equations as "guides to thinking." Comprehension of concepts before calculation is the key to understanding.

Enjoy your physics!

Paul G. Hewitt

1 ABOUT SCIENCE

THE BIG IDEA : Science is the study of nature's rules.

What would it be like to live in outer space? At first thought, we might think this question is for astronauts. But on second thought, we realize this question is for everybody, for all of us are in outer space. At every moment we are riding on planet Earth, which has been in outer space for billions of years, hurtling completely out of human control in orbit around the sun. Although more than 130 objects beyond our solar system have recently been found, our small life-supporting planet is special to us—it is our home.

We can't control Earth's motion, but we have learned the rules by which it moves—rules that were painstakingly discovered by investigators throughout much of human history. The study of nature's rules is what this book is about. These rules in physics are surprisingly few in number, explaining such things as why Earth is round, why its rainbows are colorful arcs, and why skies are blue and sunsets are red. Understanding nature's rules adds richness to the way we see our world.

discover!

What is the Relationship Among Art, Science, and Technology?

1. Carefully place a drop of water on a television screen or computer monitor.
2. Look at the screen through the droplet.
3. How close to the screen must you be to see individual dots without looking through the droplet?
4. Use a magnifying glass to examine a color image in a newspaper.

Analyze and Conclude

1. **Observing** How are the color images you see on television and computer monitors, in newspapers, and in Pointillist paintings produced?
2. **Predicting** How do you suppose the images on outdoor electronic displays are produced?
3. **Making Generalizations** How do art, science, and technology converge to bring us the color images that are so much a part of our daily lives?

1.1 The Basic Science—Physics

Much of science today is what used to be called *natural philosophy*. Natural philosophy was the study of unanswered questions about nature. As the answers were found, they became part of what is now called science.

The study of science today branches into the study of living things and nonliving things—the life sciences and the physical sciences. The life sciences branch into areas such as biology, zoology, and botany. The physical sciences branch into areas such as geology, astronomy, chemistry, and physics.

Physics is more than a part of the physical sciences, it is the most basic of all the sciences. ☑ **Physics is about the nature of basic things such as motion, forces, energy, matter, heat, sound, light, and the composition of atoms.** Chemistry is about how matter is put together, how atoms combine to form molecules, and how the molecules combine to make up the many kinds of matter around us. Biology is still more complex and involves matter that is alive. So physics supports chemistry, which in turn supports biology. The ideas of physics are fundamental to these more complicated sciences. That's why physics is the most basic science. You can understand other sciences much better if you first understand physics. This book presents physics conceptually so that you can enjoy understanding it.

CONCEPT CHECK What is physics about?

Most new discoveries occur where science fields overlap—in biochemistry and biophysics, for example. Study more than one field of science!

1.2 Mathematics— The Language of Science

Science was transformed in the 1600s when it was learned that nature can be analyzed, modeled, and described mathematically. When the ideas of science are expressed in mathematical terms, they are unambiguous. The equations of science provide compact expressions of relationships between concepts. Physics equations are guides to thinking! They don't have the double meanings that so often confuse the discussion of ideas expressed in common language. ☑ **When scientific findings in nature are expressed mathematically, they are easier to verify or disprove by experiment.**[1.2] The methods of mathematics and experimentation have led to enormous successes in science.

CONCEPT CHECK Why is mathematics the language of science?

The superscript 1.2 refers to a note to the text. Notes are listed in Appendix G, which begins on page 891.

a

b

1.3 Scientific Methods

The Italian physicist Galileo Galilei (1564–1642) and the English philosopher Francis Bacon (1561–1626), shown in Figure 1.1, are usually credited as the founders of the scientific method. **Scientific methods** are extremely effective in gaining, organizing, and applying new knowledge. ✅ **Scientific methods generally include some, if not all, of the following:**

1. **Recognize a problem.**

2. **Make an educated guess—a hypothesis—about the answer.**

3. **Predict the consequences of the hypothesis.**

4. **Perform experiments to test predictions.**

5. **Formulate the simplest general rule that organizes the main ingredients: hypothesis, prediction, and experimental outcome.**

Although this method is popular, it is not the universal key to discoveries and advances in science. Trial and error, experimentation without guessing, and accidental discovery account for much of the progress in science. The success of science has more to do with an attitude common to scientists than with a particular method. This attitude is one of inquiry, experimentation, and humility.

CONCEPT CHECK What are the steps of a scientific method?

1.4 The Scientific Attitude

In science, a **fact** is a close agreement by competent observers who make a series of observations of the same phenomenon. A scientific **hypothesis** is an educated guess that is not fully accepted until demonstrated by experiment. When hypotheses about the relationship among natural quantities are tested over and over again and not contradicted, they may become **laws** or **principles.**

Physics is a way of finding knowledge, how things get to be known, what is not known, and to what extent things are known (for in science, nothing is known absolutely).

2

☑ **If a scientist finds evidence that contradicts a hypothesis, law, or principle, then the hypothesis, law, or principle must be changed or abandoned**. A scientist must be prepared to change or abandon an idea. The Greek philosopher Aristotle (384–322 B.C.) claimed that an object twice as heavy as another falls twice as fast. This false idea was held to be true for nearly 2000 years because of Aristotle's authority. In modern science, however, a single verifiable experiment to the contrary outweighs any authority, regardless of reputation.

Scientists must accept their findings even when they would like them to be different. They must distinguish between what they see and what they wish to see. Scientists, like most people, have a vast capacity for fooling themselves.[1.4] People have always tended to adopt and retain general rules, ideas, and hypotheses without thoroughly questioning their validity, even after they have been shown to be false. Most often when an idea is adopted, particular attention is given to cases that seem to support it, while cases that seem to refute it are distorted, belittled, or ignored.

Go Online
SciLINKS NSTA

For: Links on hypothesis
Visit: www.SciLinks.org
Web Code: csn – 0104

FACTS ARE REVISABLE DATA ABOUT THE WORLD

THEORIES INTERPRET FACTS

Scientific Theories Scientists use the word *theory* differently from the way it is used in everyday speech. In everyday speech, a theory is the same as a hypothesis—a supposition that has not been verified. A scientific **theory,** on the other hand, is a synthesis of a large body of information that encompasses well-tested and verified hypotheses about certain aspects of the natural world. For example, physicists speak of atomic theory; biologists speak of cell theory.

The theories of science are not fixed, but rather they evolve as they go through stages of redefinition and refinement. During the past hundred years, the theory of the atom has been refined as new evidence was gathered. Similarly, biologists have refined the cell theory.

The refinement of theories is a strength of science, not a weakness. Competent scientists must be experts at changing their minds when confronted with solid experimental evidence to the contrary of a theory, or when a conceptually simpler hypothesis forces them to a new point of view. More important than defending beliefs is improving upon them. Better hypotheses are made by those who are honest in the face of experimental evidence.

The scientific attitude accompanies a search for order, for uniformities, and for lawful relations among the events of nature. These enable us to make predictions. By better understanding nature, we can better control our destinies.

CONCEPT CHECK : When must a hypothesis, law, or principle be changed or abandoned?

1.5 Scientific Hypotheses

FIGURE 1.2 ▲
Experiments are conducted to test scientific hypotheses.

Before a hypothesis can be classified as scientific, it must link to a general understanding of nature and conform to a cardinal rule. The rule is that the hypothesis must be testable. It is more important that there be a way of proving a hypothesis *wrong* than there be a way of proving it correct. At first this may seem strange, for usually we concern ourselves with verifying that something is true. Scientific hypotheses are different. ⊘ **To determine whether a hypothesis is scientific or not, look to see if there is a test for proving it wrong.** If there is no test for its possible wrongness, then it is not scientific. Albert Einstein put it well when he stated, "No number of experiments can prove me right; a single experiment can prove me wrong."

Consider the hypothesis "The alignment of planets in the sky determines the best time for making decisions." Many people believe it, but this hypothesis is not scientific. It cannot be proven wrong, nor can it be proven right. It is *speculation.* Likewise, the hypothesis "Intelligent life exists on other planets somewhere in the universe" is not scientific. Although it can be proven correct by the verification of a single instance of intelligent life existing elsewhere in the universe, there is no way to prove it wrong if no life is ever found. If we searched the far reaches of the universe for eons and found no life, we would not prove that it doesn't exist "around the next corner." The hypothesis "Most people stop for red lights" is also outside of science, but for a different reason. Although it can easily be tested and shown to be right or wrong, the hypothesis doesn't link up to our general understanding of nature. It doesn't fit into the structure of science.

Here is a hypothesis that is scientific: "No material object can travel faster than light." Even if it were supported by a thousand other experiments, this hypothesis could be proven wrong by a single experiment. (So far, we find it to be true.) A hypothesis that has no test for its possible wrongness lies outside the domain of science.

Experiment is the test of truth in science.

CONCEPT CHECK : How do you know if a hypothesis is scientific?

think!

Which of these is a scientific hypothesis?
a. Atoms are the smallest particles of matter.
b. The universe is surrounded by a second universe, the existence of which cannot be detected by scientists.
c. Albert Einstein was the greatest physicist of the 1900s.
Answer: 1.5

1.6 Science, Technology, and Society

Science and technology are different. ⊘ **Science is a method of answering theoretical questions; technology is a method of solving practical problems.** Science has to do with discovering facts and relationships between observable phenomena in nature and with establishing theories that organize and make sense of these facts and relationships. Technology has to do with tools, techniques, and procedures for putting the findings of science to use.

Science and technology are human enterprises, but in different ways. In deciding what problems to work on, scientists are guided by their own interests, and sometimes by a desire to help other people or to serve their nation. Most often scientists are driven primarily by curiosity, the simple urge to know. They pursue knowledge, insofar as is possible, that is free of current fashion, beliefs, and value judgments. What scientists discover may shock or anger some people, as did Darwin's theory of evolution. But science by itself does not intrude on human life—technology does. Once developed, technology can hardly be ignored. Technologists specifically set out to design, create, or build something for the use and enjoyment of humans, often for the betterment of human life. Yet some technology can have adverse side effects or create other problems that must be solved. Although technology derives from science, it has to be judged on how it affects human life.

We are all familiar with the abuses of technology. Many people blame technology itself for widespread pollution, resource depletion, and even social decay. The blame placed on technology often obscures its promise. That promise is a cleaner and healthier world. It is much wiser to combat the dangers of technology with knowledge than with ignorance. Wise applications of science and technology can lead to a better world.

Science and technology make up a larger part of our everyday lives than ever before. Humans now have much influence over nature's delicate balance. With that power comes a responsibility to maintain that balance, and to do that, we must understand nature's basic rules. Citizens must be knowledgeable about how the world works in order to deal with issues such as acid rain, global warming, and toxic wastes. The scientific way of thinking becomes vital to society as new facts are discovered and new ideas for caring for the planet are needed.

CONCEPT CHECK What is the difference between science and technology?

Science is a way of learning how to tell the difference between what is known and what isn't known. It provides a way of thinking that allows us to make sound judgments.

SCIENCE IS ABOUT NATURAL ORDER

RELIGION IS ABOUT NATURE'S PURPOSE

1.7 Science, Art, and Religion

The search for order and meaning in the world takes different forms; one is science, another is art, and another is religion. Although the roots of all three go back thousands of years, the traditions of science are relatively recent. More important, the domains of science, art, and religion are different, even though they overlap. ✅ **Science is mostly concerned with discovering and recording natural phenomena, the arts are concerned with the value of human interactions as they pertain to the senses, and religion is concerned with the source, purpose, and meaning of everything.**

The principal values of science and the arts are comparable. Literature describes the human experience. It allows us to learn about emotions, even if we haven't yet experienced them. The arts do not necessarily give us those experiences, but they describe them to us and suggest what may be in store for us. Similarly, science tells us what is possible in nature. Scientific knowledge helps us to predict possibilities in nature even before these possibilities have been experienced. It provides us with a way of connecting things, of seeing relationships between and among them, and of making sense of the many natural events we find around us. Though science may not answer all questions, it widens our perspective of nature. A truly educated person is knowledgeable in both the arts and science.

Scientific disputes are settled by better evidence. No wars are fought over science.

Science and religion are different. The domain of science is natural order; the domain of religion is nature's purpose. Religious beliefs and practices usually involve faith in and worship of a supreme being and the creation of human community—not the practices of science. In this respect, science and religion are as different as apples and oranges and do not contradict each other. The two complement rather than contradict each other.

When we study the nature of light later in this book, we will treat light first as a wave and then as a particle. To the person who knows only a little physics, waves and particles are contradictory. Light can be only one or the other, and we have to choose between them. But to the enlightened physicist, waves and particles complement each other and provide a deeper understanding of light. Similarly, people who are either uninformed or misinformed about the deeper nature of both science and religion often feel they must choose between them. But if we have an understanding of science and religion, we can embrace both without contradiction. (Of course, this doesn't apply to certain extremists who steadfastly assert that one cannot embrace both their brand of religion and science.)

CONCEPT CHECK How are science, art, and religion different?

1.8 In Perspective

More than 3000 years ago, enormous human effort went into the construction of great pyramids in Egypt. They were the world's greatest monuments to a vision of the universe. The Pyramids testify to human genius, endurance, and thirst for deeper understanding. A few centuries ago, the then-modern world directed its brilliance to the building of great stone and marble structures. Cathedrals, synagogues, temples, and mosques were manifestations of people's vision. Some of these structures took more than a century to build, which means that nobody witnessed both the beginning and the end of construction. Even the architects and early builders who lived to a ripe old age never saw the finished results of their labors. Entire lifetimes were spent in the shadows of construction that must have seemed without beginning or end. This enormous focus of human energy was inspired by a vision that went beyond world concerns—a vision of the cosmos. To the people of these times, the structures they erected were their "spaceships of faith"—firmly anchored but pointing to the cosmos.

Doubt and uncertainty are hallmarks of science. Most physicists feel it is more interesting to live without knowing than to have answers that might be wrong.

Progress in our age is much quicker than it was thousands of years ago. Today the efforts of many of our most skilled scientists, engineers, and artisans are directed toward building the spaceships that orbit Earth, and others that will voyage beyond. The time required to build these spaceships is extremely brief compared with the time spent building the stone and marble structures of the past. Many people working on today's spaceships were alive before the first jetliner carried passengers. Where will younger lives lead in a comparable time?

We are at the dawn of a major change in human growth, not unlike the stage of a chicken embryo before it fully matures. When the chicken embryo exhausts the last of its inner-egg resources and before it pokes its way out of its shell, it may seem to be at its last moments. But what seems like an end is really only a beginning. Are we like the hatching chicks ready to poke through to a whole new range of possibilities? Are our space-faring efforts the early signs of a new human era?

Earth is our cradle and has served us well. But cradles, however comfortable, are outgrown one day. With inspiration similar to the inspiration of those who built the early cathedrals, synagogues, temples, and mosques, we aim for the cosmos. We live in a challenging and exciting time!

FIGURE 1.3 ▲
NASA astronauts may one day travel in this spaceship of the future.

CONCEPT CHECK : How does progress today differ from progress thousands of years ago?

1 REVIEW

Go Online
PHSchool.com

For: Self-Assessment
Visit: PHSchool.com
Web Code: csa – 0100

Concept Summary · · · · · ·

- Physics is about the nature of basic things such as motion, forces, energy, matter, heat, sound, light, and the composition of atoms.

- When scientific findings in nature are expressed mathematically, they are easier to verify or disprove by experiment.

- Scientific methods include some, if not all, of the following: recognizing a problem, making a hypothesis, predicting, performing experiments, and formulating rules.

- If a scientist finds evidence that contradicts a hypothesis, law, or principle then the hypothesis, law, or principle must be changed or abandoned.

- To determine whether a hypothesis is scientific or not, look to see if there is a test for proving it wrong.

- Science is a method of answering theoretical questions; technology is a method of solving practical problems.

- Science is mostly concerned with discovering and recording natural phenomena, the arts are concerned with the value of human interactions as they pertain to the senses, and religion is concerned with the source, purpose, and meaning of everything.

- Progress in our age is much quicker than it was thousands of years ago.

Key Terms · · · · · ·

scientific method (p. 2)   **law** (p. 2)

fact (p. 2)   **principle** (p. 2)

hypothesis (p. 2)   **theory** (p. 3)

think! Answers

1.5   Only (a) is a scientific hypothesis, because there is a test for its wrongness. The statement is not only *capable* of being proven wrong, but it *has* been proven wrong. Statement (b) has no test for possible wrongness and is therefore unscientific. Some pseudoscientists and other pretenders of knowledge will not even consider a test for the possible wrongness of their statements. Statement (c) is an assertion that has no test for possible wrongness. If Einstein was not the greatest physicist, how would we know? It is important to note that because the name Einstein is generally held in high esteem, it is a favorite of pseudoscientists.

1.7   All of them! In this book, we focus on science, an enchanting human activity shared by a wide variety of people. With present-day tools and know-how, we are reaching farther and finding out more about ourselves and our environment than people in the past were ever able to do. The more we know about science, the more passionate we feel toward our surroundings. There is physics in everything we see, hear, smell, taste, and touch!

1 ASSESS

Check Concepts ......

Section 1.1
1. Why is physics the most basic science?

Section 1.2
2. Why is mathematics important to science?

Section 1.3
3. What are the steps of the *scientific method*?

Section 1.4
4. Is a scientific fact something that is absolute and unchanging? Defend your answer.

5. Scientific theories undergo change. Is this a strength or a weakness of science? Defend your answer.

Section 1.5
6. What does it mean to say that if a hypothesis is scientific, then there must be a means of proving it wrong?

Section 1.6
7. How do science and technology differ?

Section 1.7
8. How are science and the arts similar?

9. How do science and religion differ?

10. Why do citizens have a responsibility to have some basic understanding of nature's rules?

Section 1.8
11. How does the rate of change of progress differ today from the rate in previous centuries?

Think and Explain ......

12. Why does science tend to be a "self-correcting" way of knowing about things?

13. What is likely being misunderstood by someone who says, "But that's only a scientific theory"?

14. **a.** Make an argument for halting the advances of technology.
    b. Make an argument for continuing advances in technology.
    c. Contrast your two arguments.

UNIT 1

MECHANICS

Go Online

SCIENCE NEWS

For: Articles on mechanics
Visit: PHSchool.com
Web Code: cse – 1000

IT'S A FACT!

Every time you catch a ball, ride a bike, or lift a bag, you are using physics to make predictions without realizing it. For example, you predict where obstacles will be at later times. You estimate how much force it will take to move an object. You prevent objects from rolling away or tipping over. Mechanics is the branch of physics that deals with the effects of forces and energy in a given situation. In this unit, you will learn many interesting facts about forces, motion, and energy.

An object is in a state of **equilibrium** if the sum of the forces acting on it is zero. [Ch. 2]

> You cannot touch without being touched—that's Newton's third law!!

10

Angular momentum is conserved when no external torque acts on an object. *[Ch. 12]*

A **satellite** travels fast enough to fall around another body rather than into it. *[Ch. 14]*

A windmill transforms the mechanical **energy** of wind into electrical energy. *[Ch. 9]*

A cheetah can move at the greatest **speed** of any land animal. *[Ch. 4]*

2 MECHANICAL EQUILIBRIUM

THE BIG IDEA : An object in mechanical equilibrium is stable, without changes in motion.

It's good when your personal life is stable—when things important to you are in balance. It's also nice when the needs of family and friends are in harmony. Financially, we prefer our expenses to be balanced by earnings. Economists are concerned with the balance between the inflow and outflow of goods. These examples illustrate the idea of *equilibrium*. In nature we see an energy equilibrium when energy radiated away from Earth is balanced by the input of solar energy from the sun. Whenever a glass thermometer acquires the same temperature as the object being measured, we have thermal equilibrium. There are many forms of equilibrium. In this chapter we will be concerned with *mechanical equilibrium*. Things in mechanical equilibrium are stable, without changes of motion. The rocks shown at right are in mechanical equilibrium. An unbalanced external force would be needed to change their resting state.

discover!

How Do You Know When an Object Is in Equilibrium?

1. Stretch a strong rope between another student and yourself.
2. With the two of you pulling hard on the rope, have a third person push down on the center of the rope with his or her little finger.
3. Try to make the rope straight while the person continues to push down on the center of the rope.

Analyze and Conclude

1. **Observing** Did the rope remain straight with the application of the small downward force on the center of the rope?
2. **Predicting** Is there any way to make the rope straight as long as someone is pushing down on the center of the rope?
3. **Making Generalizations** What do you think are the conditions necessary for equilibrium?

2.1 Force

A **force** is a push or a pull. A force of some kind is always required to change the state of motion of an object. The state of motion may be one of rest or of moving uniformly along a straight-line path. For example, a hockey puck at rest on ice remains at rest until a force is exerted on it. Once moving, a hockey puck sliding along the ice will continue sliding until a force slows it down. ⊘ **A force is needed to change an object's state of motion.**

Net Force Most often, more than one force acts on an object. The combination of all forces acting on an object is called the **net force**. The net force on an object changes its motion.

For example, suppose you pull horizontally on an object with a force of 10 pounds. If a friend assists you and also pulls in the same direction with a force of 5 pounds, then the net force is the sum of these forces, or 15 pounds. The object moves as if it were pulled with a single 15-pound force. However, if your friend pulls with a force of 5 pounds in the opposite direction, then the net force is the difference of these forces, or 5 pounds toward you. The resulting motion of the object is the same as if it were pulled with a single 5-pound force. This is shown in Figure 2.1, where instead of pounds, the scientific unit of force is used—the newton, abbreviated N.[2.1.1]

APPLIED FORCES	NET FORCE
5 N / 10 N	15 N
5 N / 10 N	5 N
5 N / 5 N	0 N

FIGURE 2.1 ▲
The net force depends on the magnitudes and directions of the applied forces.

The superscript 2.1.1 refers to a note to the text. Notes are listed in Appendix G.

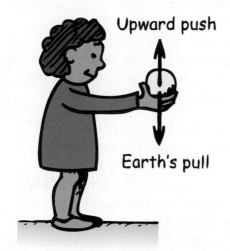
Upward push

Earth's pull

◀ **FIGURE 2.2**
When the girl holds the rock with as much force upward as gravity pulls downward, the net force on the rock is zero.

When you hold a rock at rest in your hand, you are pushing upward on it with as much force as Earth's gravity pulls down on it. If you push harder, it will move upward; if you push with less force, it will move downward. But just holding it at rest, as shown in Figure 2.2, means the upward and downward forces on it add to zero. The net force on the rock is zero.

FIGURE 2.3 ▶

a. The upward tension in the string has the same magnitude as the weight of the bag, so the net force on the bag is zero. **b.** Burl Grey, who first introduced the author to the concept of tension, shows a 2-lb bag producing a tension of 9 newtons. (The weight is actually slightly more than 2 lb, and the tension slightly more than 9 N.)

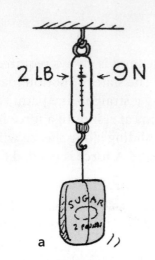

a

b

Scalars can be added, subtracted, multiplied, and divided like ordinary numbers. When 2 liters of water are added to 3 liters of water, the result is 5 liters. But when something is pulled by two forces, one 2 N and the other 3 N, the result may or may not be 5 N. With vector quantities, direction matters.

FIGURE 2.4 ▲
This vector, scaled so that 1 cm = 20 N, represents a force of 60 N to the right.

Tension and Weight If you tie a string around a 2-pound bag of sugar and suspend it from a scale, a spring in the scale stretches until the scale reads 2 pounds, as shown in Figure 2.3. The stretched spring is under a "stretching force" called *tension*. A scale in a science lab is likely calibrated to read this 2-pound force as 9 newtons. Both pounds and newtons are units of weight, which, in turn, are units of force. The bag of sugar is attracted to Earth with a gravitational force of 2 pounds—or, equivalently, 9 newtons. Suspend twice as much sugar from the scale and the reading will be 18 newtons.

There are two forces acting on the bag of sugar—tension force acting upward and weight acting downward. The two forces on the bag are equal and opposite, and they cancel to zero. The net force on the bag is zero, and it remains at rest.

Force Vectors In Figures 2.1 and 2.2, forces are represented by arrows. When the length of the arrow is scaled to represent the amount (magnitude) of the force and the direction of the arrow points in the direction of the force, we refer to the arrow as a vector.[2.1,2] A **vector** is an arrow that represents the magnitude and direction of a quantity. A **vector quantity** is a quantity that needs both magnitude and direction for a complete description. Force is an example of a vector quantity. By contrast, a **scalar quantity** is a quantity that can be described by magnitude only and has no direction. Time, area, and volume are scalar quantities. (We'll return to vectors in Chapter 5.)

CONCEPT CHECK : How can you change an object's state of motion?

When I was in high school, my counselor advised me not to enroll in science and math classes, but to instead focus on what seemed to be my gift for art. I took this advice. I was then interested in drawing comic strips and in boxing, neither of which earned me much success. After a stint in the U.S. Army, I tried my luck at sign painting, and the cold Boston winters drove me south to Miami, Florida. There, at age 26, I got a job painting billboards and met a new friend, Burl Grey, a sign painter with an active intellect. Burl, like me, had never studied physics in high school. But he was passionate about science in general. He shared that passion with me by asking many fascinating science questions as we painted together.

I remember Burl asking me questions about the tensions in the ropes that held up the scaffold we stood on. The scaffold was simply a heavy horizontal plank suspended by a pair of ropes at each end. Burl twanged the rope nearest his end of the scaffold and asked me to do the same with mine. He was comparing the tensions in the two ropes—to determine which was greater. Burl was heavier than I was, and he guessed that the tension in his rope was greater. Like a more tightly stretched guitar string, the rope with greater tension twangs at a higher pitch. That Burl's rope had a higher pitch seemed reasonable because his rope supported more of the load.

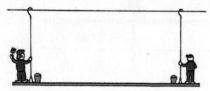

When I walked toward Burl to borrow one of his brushes, he asked if tensions in the ropes had changed. Did tension in his rope increase as I moved closer? We agreed that it should have because even more of the load was then supported by Burl's rope. How about my rope? Would its tension decrease? We agreed that it would, for it would be supporting less of the total load. I was unaware at the time that we were discussing physics.

Burl and I used exaggeration to bolster our reasoning (just as physicists do). If we both stood at an extreme end of the scaffold and leaned outward, it was easy to imagine the opposite end of the staging rising like the end of a seesaw, with the opposite rope going limp. Then there would be no tension in that rope. We then reasoned the tension in my rope would

gradually decrease as I walked toward Burl. It was fun posing such questions and seeing if we could answer them.

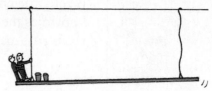

A question that we couldn't answer was whether or not the decrease of tension in my rope when I walked away from it would be *exactly* compensated by a tension increase in Burl's rope. For example, if the tension in my rope underwent a decrease of 50 newtons, would Burl's rope gain 50 newtons? (We talked pounds back then, but here we use the scientific unit of force, the *newton*—abbreviated N.) Would the gain be *exactly* 50 N? And if so, would this be a grand coincidence? I didn't know the answers until more than a year later, when Burl's stimulation resulted in my leaving full-time painting and going to college to learn more about science.[2.1.3]

At college I learned that any object at rest, such as the sign-painting scaffold that supported us, experiences no net force. It is said to be in *equilibrium*. That is, all the forces that act on it balance to zero ($\Sigma F = 0$). So the sum of the upward forces supplied by the supporting ropes do indeed add up to the downward forces of our weights plus the weight of the scaffold. A 50-N loss in one would be accompanied by a 50-N gain in the other.

I tell this true story to make the point that one's thinking is very different when there is a rule to guide it. Now when I look at any motionless object, I know immediately that all the forces acting on it cancel out. We view nature differently when we know its rules. It makes nature seem simpler and easier to understand. Without the rules of physics, we tend to be superstitious and see magic where there is none. Quite wonderfully, everything is beautifully connected to everything else by a surprisingly small number of rules. The rules of nature are what the study of physics is about.

Consider the gymnast above hanging from the rings. If she hangs with her weight evenly divided between the two rings, how would scale readings in both supporting ropes compare with her weight? Suppose she hangs with slightly more of her weight supported by the left ring. How would a scale on the right read?

Answer: 2.2

2.2 Mechanical Equilibrium

Mechanical equilibrium is a state wherein no physical changes occur; it is a state of steadiness. Whenever the net force on an object is zero, the object is said to be in mechanical equilibrium—this is known as the **equilibrium rule.**[2.2] ☑ **You can express the equilibrium rule mathematically as**

$$\Sigma F = 0$$

The symbol Σ stands for "the sum of" and F stands for "forces." (Please don't be intimidated by the expression $\Sigma F = 0$, which is physics shorthand that says a lot in so little space—that all the forces acting on something add vectorially to zero.) For a suspended object at rest, like the bag of sugar mentioned earlier, the rule states that the forces acting upward on the object must be balanced by other forces acting downward to make the vector sum equal zero. (Vector quantities take direction into account, so if upward forces are positive, downward ones are negative, and when summed they equal zero.)

FIGURE 2.5 ▲
The sum of the upward vectors equals the sum of the downward vectors. $\Sigma F = 0$, and the scaffold is in equilibrium.

In Figure 2.5 we see the forces of interest to Burl and Paul on their sign-painting scaffold. The sum of the upward tensions is equal to the sum of their weights plus the weight of the scaffold. Note how the magnitudes of the two upward vectors equal the magnitude of the three downward vectors. Net force on the scaffold is zero, so we say it is in mechanical equilibrium.

CONCEPT CHECK : How can you express the equilibrium rule mathematically?

If you look carefully at bridges and other structures around you, you'll see evidence of $\Sigma F = 0$.

2.3 Support Force

Consider a book lying at rest on a table, as shown in Figure 2.6a. The book is in equilibrium. What forces act on the book? One is the force due to gravity—the weight of the book. Since the book is in equilibrium, there must be another force acting on it to produce a net force of zero—an upward force opposite to the force of gravity.

Where is the upward force coming from? It is coming from the table that supports the book. We call this the **support force** —the upward force that balances the weight of an object on a surface. A support force is often called the *normal force*.[2.3.1] ☑ **For an object at rest on a horizontal surface, the support force must equal the object's weight.** So in this case, the support force must equal the weight of the book. We say the upward support force is positive and the downward weight is negative. The two forces add mathematically to zero. So the net force on the book is zero. Another way to say the same thing is $\Sigma F = 0$.

To better understand that the table pushes up on the book, compare the case of compressing a spring, shown in Figure 2.6b. If you push the spring down, you can feel the spring pushing up on your hand. Similarly, the book lying on the table compresses atoms in the table, which behave like microscopic springs. The weight of the book squeezes downward on the atoms, and they squeeze upward on the book. The compressed atoms produce the support force.

When you step on a bathroom scale, two forces act on the scale, as shown in Figure 2.7. One force is the downward pull of gravity, your weight, and the other is the upward support force of the floor. These forces compress a mechanism (in effect, a spring) that is calibrated to show your weight. So the scale shows the support force. When you're standing on a bathroom scale at rest, the support force and your weight have the same magnitude.[2.3.2]

CONCEPT CHECK: For an object at rest on a horizontal surface, what is the support force equal to?

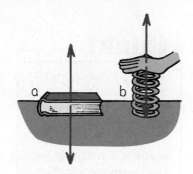

FIGURE 2.6 ▲
a. The table pushes up on the book with as much force as the downward weight of the book. **b.** The spring pushes up on your hand with as much force as you push down on the spring.

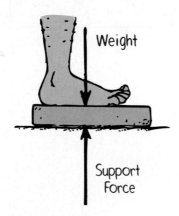

FIGURE 2.7 ▲
The upward support force is as much as the downward pull of gravity.

think!

What is the net force on a bathroom scale when a 110-pound person stands on it? *Answer: 2.3.1*

Suppose you stand on two bathroom scales with your weight evenly distributed between the two scales. What is the reading on each of the scales? What happens when you stand with more of your weight on one foot than the other?
Answer: 2.3.2

2.4 Equilibrium for Moving Objects

When an object isn't moving, it's in equilibrium. The forces on it add up to zero. But the state of rest is only one form of equilibrium. An object moving at constant speed in a straight-line path is also in a state of equilibrium. Once in motion, if there is no net force to change the state of motion, it's in equilibrium.

Equilibrium is a state of no change. A hockey puck sliding along slippery ice or a bowling ball rolling at constant velocity is in equilibrium—until either experiences a non-zero net force. Whether at rest or steadily moving in a straight-line path, the sum of the forces on both is zero: $\Sigma F = 0$.

Interestingly, an object under the influence of only one force cannot be in equilibrium. Net force in that case is not zero. Only when there is no force at all, or when two or more forces combine to zero, can an object be in equilibrium. We can test whether or not something is in equilibrium by noting whether or not it undergoes changes in motion.

Figure 2.8 shows a desk being pushed horizontally across a factory floor. If the desk moves steadily at constant speed, without change in its motion, it is in equilibrium. This tells us that more than one horizontal force acts on the desk—likely the force of friction between the bottom of the desk and the floor. Friction is a contact force between objects that slide or tend to slide against each other (more about friction in Chapter 6). The fact that the net force on the desk equals zero means that the force of friction must be equal in magnitude and opposite in direction to our pushing force.

FIGURE 2.8 ▶
When the push on the desk is as much as the force of friction between the desk and the floor, the net force is zero and the desk slides at an unchanging speed.

Types of equilibrium include static (at rest) and dynamic (moving at constant speed in a straight-line path).

⊘ **Objects at rest are said to be in static equilibrium; objects moving at constant speed in a straight-line path are said to be in dynamic equilibrium.** Both of these situations are examples of mechanical equilibrium. As mentioned at the beginning of this chapter, there are other types of equilibrium. In Chapter 11 we'll discuss another type of mechanical equilibrium—rotational equilibrium. Then in Chapter 21 when we study heat, we'll discuss thermal equilibrium, where temperature doesn't change.

The equilibrium rule, $\Sigma F = 0$, provides a reasoned way to view all things at rest—balanced rocks, objects in your room, or the steel beams in bridges. Whatever their configuration, if at rest, all acting forces always balance to zero. The same is true of objects that move steadily, not speeding up, slowing down, or changing direction. For such moving things, all acting forces also balance to zero. The equilibrium rule is one that allows you to see more than meets the eye of the casual observer. It's good to know the rule for the stability of things in our everyday world. Physics is everywhere.

CONCEPT CHECK : How are static and dynamic equilibrium different?

2.5 Vectors

Look at Figure 2.9. When gymnast Nellie Newton is suspended by a single vertical strand of rope (Figure 2.9a), the tension in the rope is 300 N, her weight. If she hangs by two vertical strands of rope (Figure 2.9b), the tension in each is 150 N, half her weight. Rope tensions pull her upward and gravity pulls her downward. In the figures, we see that the vectors representing rope tensions and weight balance out. $\Sigma F = 0$, and she is in equilibrium.

I was only a scalar until you came along and gave me direction!

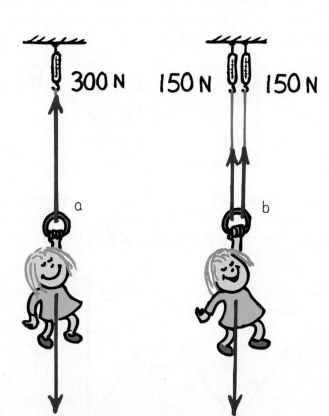

◄ FIGURE 2.9
a. The tension in the rope is 300 N, equal to Nellie's weight.
b. The tension in each rope is now 150 N, half of Nellie's weight. In each case, $\Sigma F = 0$.

FIGURE 2.10 ▲

When the ropes are at an angle to each other, you need to use the parallelogram rule to determine their tension.

Combining vectors is quite simple when they are parallel. If they are in the same direction, they add. If they are in opposite directions, they subtract. The sum of two or more vectors is called their **resultant.** But what about vectors that act at an angle to each other? Consider Nellie hanging by a pair of ropes, as shown in Figure 2.10. To find the resultant of nonparallel vectors, we use the parallelogram rule.[2.5]

The Parallelogram Rule ☑ **To find the resultant of two non-parallel vectors, construct a parallelogram wherein the two vectors are adjacent sides. The diagonal of the parallelogram shows the resultant.** Consider two vectors at right angles to each other, as shown below. The constructed parallelogram in this special case is a rectangle. The diagonal is the resultant R.

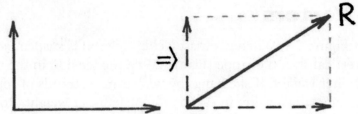

In the special case of two perpendicular vectors that are equal in magnitude, the parallelogram is a square. Since for any square the length of a diagonal is $\sqrt{2}$, or 1.414, times one of the sides, the resultant is $\sqrt{2}$ times one of the vectors. For example, the resultant of two equal vectors of magnitude 100 acting at a right angle to each other is 141.4.

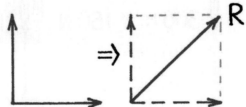

Now consider the vectors shown below, which represent the tensions of the ropes in Figure 2.10. Notice that the tension vectors form a parallelogram in which the resultant R is vertical.

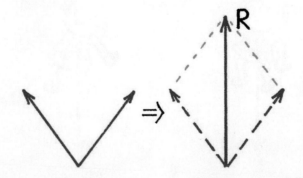

a   b   c

Applying the Parallelogram Rule When Nellie Newton is suspended at rest from the two non-vertical ropes shown in Figure 2.10, is the rope tension greater or less than tension in the vertical ropes? Note there are three forces acting on Nellie: a tension in the left rope, a tension in the right rope, and her weight. Figure 2.11 shows a step-by-step solution. Because Nellie is suspended in equilibrium, the resultant of rope tensions must have the same magnitude as her weight. Using the parallelogram rule, we find that the tension in each rope is more than half her weight.

In Figure 2.12, the ropes are at a greater angle from the vertical. Note that the tensions in both ropes are appreciably greater. As the angle between the supporting ropes increases, the tension increases. In terms of the parallelogram, as the angle increases, the vector lengths increase in order for the diagonal to remain the same. Remember, the upward diagonal must be equal and opposite to Nellie's weight. If it isn't, she won't be in equilibrium. By measuring the vectors, you'll see that for this particular angle the tension in each rope is twice her weight.

FIGURE 2.11 ▲
a. Nellie's weight is shown by the downward vertical vector. An equal and opposite vector is needed for equilibrium, shown by the dashed vector. **b.** This dashed vector is the diagonal of the parallelogram defined by the dotted lines. **c.** Both rope tensions are shown by the constructed vectors.

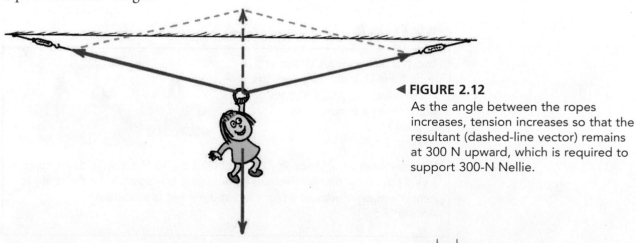

◄ **FIGURE 2.12**
As the angle between the ropes increases, tension increases so that the resultant (dashed-line vector) remains at 300 N upward, which is required to support 300-N Nellie.

FIGURE 2.13 ►

Here the ropes supporting Nellie have different angles. Note that tension is unequal in the two ropes.

In Figure 2.13, we see Nellie hanging by ropes at different angles from the vertical. Which rope has the greater tension? By the parallelogram rule, we see that the right rope bears most of the load and has the greater tension.

FIGURE 2.14 ►

You can safely hang from a clothesline hanging vertically, but you'll break the clothesline if it is strung horizontally.

If you understand this physics, you will understand why a vertical clothesline can support your weight while a horizontal clothesline cannot. The tension in the horizontal clothesline is much greater than the tension in the vertical clothesline, and so the horizontal one breaks.

CONCEPT CHECK : How can you find the resultant of two vectors?

think!

Two sets of swings are shown at right. If the children on the swings are of equal weights, the ropes of which swing are more likely to break?
Answer: 2.5.1

Consider what would happen if you suspended a 10-N object midway along a very tight, horizontally stretched guitar string. Is it possible for the string to remain horizontal without a slight sag at the point of suspension?
Answer: 2.5.2

REVIEW

Concept Summary · · · · · ·

- A force is needed to change an object's state of motion.

- You can express the equilibrium rule mathematically as $\Sigma F = 0$.

- For an object at rest on a horizontal surface, the support force must equal the object's weight.

- Objects at rest are said to be in static equilibrium; objects moving at constant speed in a straight-line path are said to be in dynamic equilibrium.

- To find the resultant of two nonparallel vectors, construct a parallelogram wherein the two vectors are adjacent sides. The diagonal of the parallelogram shows the resultant.

Key Terms · · · · · ·

force (p. 13)

net force (p. 13)

vector (p. 14)

vector quantity (p. 14)

scalar quantity (p. 14)

mechanical equilibrium (p. 16)

equilibrium rule (p.16)

support force (p. 17)

resultant (p. 20)

think! Answers

2.2   In the first case, the reading on each scale will be half her weight. In the second case, when more of her weight is supported by the left ring, the reading on the right reduces to less than half her weight. But in both cases, the sum of the scale readings equals her weight.

2.3.1 Zero, as the scale is at rest. The scale reads the support force (which has the same magnitude as weight), not the net force.

2.3.2 In the first case, the reading on each scale is half your weight. (The sum of the scale readings balances your weight, and the net force on you is zero.) In the second case, if you lean more on one scale than the other, more than half your weight will be read on that scale but less than half on the other. In this way they add up to your weight.

2.4   Neither, for both forces have the same strength. Call the thrust *positive*. Then the air resistance is *negative*. Since the plane is in equilibrium, the two forces combine to equal zero.

2.5.1 The tension is greater in the ropes hanging at an angle. The angled ropes are more likely to break than the vertical ropes.

2.5.2 No way! If the 10-N load is to hang in equilibrium, there must be a supporting 10-N upward resultant. The tension in each half of the guitar string must form a parallelogram with a vertically upward 10-N resultant. For a slight sag, the sides of the parallelogram are very, very long and the tension force is very large. To approach no sag is to approach an infinite tension.

ASSESS

Check Concepts ......

Section 2.1

1. What is the difference between force and net force on an object?

2. What is the net force on a box that is being pulled to the right with a force of 40 N and pulled to the left with a force of 30 N?

3. What name is given to the stretching force that occurs in a spring or rope being pulled?

4. What two quantities are necessary to determine a vector quantity?

5. How does a vector quantity differ from a scalar quantity?

6. Give an example of a vector quantity. Give an example of a scalar quantity.

Section 2.2

7. How much tension is in a rope that holds up a 20-N bag of apples at rest?

8. What does $\Sigma F = 0$ mean?

9. What is the net force on an object at rest?

10. When you do pull-ups and you hang at rest, how much of your weight is supported by each arm?

Section 2.3

11. What is the angle between a support force and the surface on object rests upon?

12. What two forces compress a spring inside a weighing scale when you weigh yourself?

13. When you are at rest and supported by a pair of weighing scales, how does the sum of the scale readings compare with your weight?

Section 2.4

14. Can an object be moving and still be in equilibrium? Defend your answer.

15. If you push a crate across a factory floor at constant speed in a constant direction, what is the magnitude of the force of friction on the crate compared with your push?

16. Distinguish between static equilibrium and dynamic equilibrium.

Section 2.5

17. According to the parallelogram rule for two vectors, what does the diagonal of a constructed parallelogram represent?

18. Consider the suspension of Nellie in Figure 2.11. Name the three forces that act on her. What is your evidence that they cancel to zero?

19. Consider Nellie in Figure 2.12. What changes in rope tension occur when the ropes make a greater angle with the vertical?

20. When Nellie hangs from ropes at different angles, as shown in Figure 2.13, how does the vector resultant of the two rope tensions compare with her weight?

Think and Rank ......

Rank each of the following sets of scenarios in order of the quantity or property involved. List them from left to right. If scenarios have equal rankings, then separate them with an equal sign. (e.g., A = B)

21. Blocks A and B are supported by the table. Block C is partly supported by the table and partly by the rope. Rank the support forces provided by the table from greatest to least.

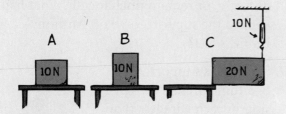

22. In the diagram below, identical blocks are suspended by ropes, each rope having a scale to measure the tension (stretching force) in the rope. Rank the scale readings from greatest to least.

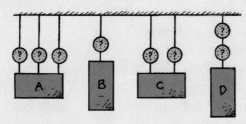

23. Burl and Paul stand on their sign-painting scaffold. Tension in the left rope is measured by a scale. Rank the tensions in that rope from greatest to least.

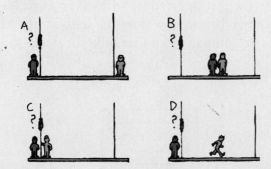

24. Percy does gymnastics, suspended by one rope in A and by two ropes in positions B, C, and D. Rank the tensions in the ropes from greatest to least.

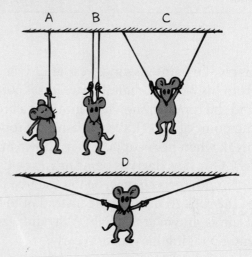

Think and Explain ......

25. A cat lies on the floor. Can you say that no force acts on the cat? Or is it correct to say that no *net* force acts on the cat? Explain.

26. Consider two forces, one having a magnitude of 20 N and the other a magnitude of 12 N. What is the maximum net force possible for these two forces? The minimum?

27. When a box of chocolate bars is in mechanical equilibrium, what can be correctly said about all the forces that act on it? Must the net force necessarily be zero?

28. Faina says that an object cannot be in mechanical equilibrium when only a single force acts on it. Do you agree or disagree?

29. Phyllis Physics hangs at rest from the ends of the rope, as shown at right. How does the reading on the scale compare to her weight?

30. Harry the painter swings year after year from his bosun's chair. His weight is 500 N and the rope, unknown to him, has a breaking point of 300 N. Why doesn't the rope break when he is supported as shown at the left? One day Harry is painting near a flagpole, and, for a change, he ties the free end of the rope to the flagpole instead of to his chair as shown at the right. Why did Harry end up taking his vacation early?

31. How many significant forces act on a your physics book when it is at rest on a table? Identify the forces.

32. Why doesn't the support force that acts on a book resting on a table cause the book to rise from the table?

33. Nicole stands on a bathroom scale and reads her weight. Does the reading change if she stands on one foot instead of both feet? Defend your answer.

34. Justin sets a hockey puck sliding across the ice at a constant speed. Is the puck in equilibrium? Why or why not?

35. Alyssa pulls horizontally on a crate with a force of 200 N, and it slides across the floor at a constant speed in a straight line. How much friction is acting on the crate?

36. Consider a heavy refrigerator at rest on a kitchen floor. When Anthony and Daniel start to lift it, does the support force on the refrigerator provided by the floor increase, decrease, or remain unchanged? What happens to the support force on Anthony's and Daniel's feet?

37. Sneezlee is supported by two thin wires. Is the tension in each wire less than, equal to, or more than half his weight? Use the parallelogram rule to defend your answer.

38. Sneezlee's wire supports are repositioned as shown. How does the tension in each wire compare with the tension of the previous question?

39. If a picture frame were supported by a pair of vertical wires, tension in each wire would be half the weight of the frame. When the frame is supported by wires at an angle, as shown below, how does the tension in each wire compare with that of vertical wires?

40. A monkey hangs by a strand of rope and holds onto the zoo cage as shown. Since her arm holding the cage is horizontal, only the rope supports her weight. How does the tension in the rope compare with her weight?

41. Why can't the strong man pull hard enough to make the chain perfectly straight?

Think and Solve ......

42. Two vertical chains are used to hold up a 1000-N log. One chain has a tension of 400 N. Find the tension in the other chain.

43. Lucy Lightweight stands with one foot on one bathroom scale and her other foot on a second bathroom scale. Each scale reads 300 N. What is Lucy's weight?

44. Harry Heavyweight, who weighs 1200 N, stands on a pair of bathroom scales so that one scale reads twice as much as the other. What are the scale readings?

45. The sketch shows a painter's staging in mechanical equilibrium. The person in the middle weighs 250 N, and the tensions in both ropes are 200 N. What is the weight of the staging?

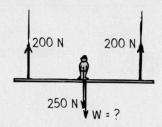

46. A staging that weighs 300 N supports two painters, one 250 N and the other 300 N. The tension in the left rope is 400 N. What is the tension in the right rope?

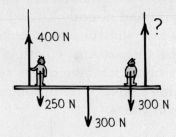

47. Two children push on a heavy crate that rests on a basement floor. One pushes horizontally with a force of 150 N and the other pushes in the same direction with a force of 180 N. The crate remains stationary. Show that the force of friction between the crate and the floor is 330 N.

48. Two children push on a crate. They find that when they push together horizontally with forces of 155 N and 187 N, respectively, the crate slides across the floor at a constant speed. Show that the force of friction between the crate and the floor is 342 N.

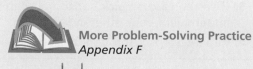

More Problem-Solving Practice
Appendix F

3 NEWTON'S FIRST LAW OF MOTION—INERTIA

 **THE BIG IDEA** : Forces cause changes in motion.

If you see a ball at rest in the middle of a flat field you know it's in equilibrium. No net force acts on it. But if you suddenly saw it begin to move across the ground, you'd look for forces that don't balance to zero. If there's no wind and nobody kicking it, you might look to see if someone was pulling the ball with a rope or pushing it with a stick. You would reason that something was causing it to move. We don't believe that changes in motion occur without cause.

discover!

Can You Snap a Card Out From Under a Coin?

1. Balance half of a 3" × 5" file card on the tip of an index finger.

2. Place a penny on the card just above your fingertip.

3. Give the card a quick horizontal snap with the fingernail of your other index finger.

4. Repeat Steps 1 through 3 using a quarter.

Analyze and Conclude

1. **Observing** What happened to the penny when the card was quickly removed? Did changing the coin affect results?

2. **Predicting** Do you think this would work with a card made of sandpaper?

3. **Making Generalizations** Why were you able to snap the card without moving the coin?

3.1 Aristotle on Motion

The idea that a force causes motion goes back to the fourth century B.C., when the Greeks were developing some of the ideas of science. ⊘ **Aristotle, the foremost Greek scientist, studied motion and divided it into two types: *natural motion* and *violent motion*.**

Natural motion on Earth was thought to be either straight up or straight down, such as a boulder falling toward the ground or a puff of smoke rising in the air. Objects would seek their natural resting places: boulders on the ground and smoke high in the air like the clouds. It was "natural" for heavy things to fall and for very light things to rise. Aristotle proclaimed circular motion was natural for the heavens, for he saw both circular motion and the heavens as being without beginning or end. Thus, the planets and stars moved in perfect circles around Earth. Since these motions were considered natural, they were not thought to be caused by forces.

Violent motion, on the other hand, was imposed motion. It was the result of forces that pushed or pulled. A cart moved because it was pulled by a horse; a tug-of-war was won by pulling on a rope; a ship was pushed by the force of the wind. The important thing about defining violent motion was that it had an external cause. Violent motion was imparted to objects. Objects in their natural resting places could not move by themselves; they had to be pushed or pulled.

FIGURE 3.1 ▲
Boulders do not move without cause.

Link to HISTORY

Aristotle (384–322 B.C.)
Aristotle was the most famous philosopher, scientist, and educator of ancient Greece. He was the son of a physician who personally served the king of Macedonia. At age 17, Aristotle entered the Academy of Plato, where he worked and studied for 20 years until Plato's death. He then became the tutor of young Alexander the Great. Eight years later, Aristotle formed his own school. His aim was to arrange existing knowledge in a system, just as Euclid had done earlier with geometry. Aristotle made careful observations, collected specimens, and gathered together and classified almost all existing knowledge of the physical world. His systematic approach became the method from which European science later arose. After his death, his voluminous notebooks were preserved in caves near his home and were later sold to the library at Alexandria. Scholarly activity came to a stop in most of Europe during the Dark Ages, and many of the works of Aristotle were forgotten and lost. Some of his texts, however, were reintroduced to Europe during the 1000s and 1100s and were translated into Latin. The Church, the dominant political and cultural force in Western Europe, at first prohibited the works of Aristotle. But soon thereafter the Church accepted them and incorporated them into Christian doctrine.

It was commonly thought for nearly 2000 years that if an object was moving "against its nature," then a force of some kind was responsible. Such motion was possible only because of an outside force. If there were no force there would be no motion (except in the vertical direction). So the proper state of objects was one of rest, unless they were being pushed or pulled, or were moving toward their natural resting place. Most thinkers before the 1500s considered it obvious that Earth must be in its natural resting place and assumed that a force large enough to move it was unthinkable. To them it was clear that Earth did not move.

CONCEPT CHECK : According to Aristotle, what were the two types of motion?

3.2 Copernicus and the Moving Earth

It was in this intellectual climate that the astronomer Nicolaus Copernicus (1473–1543), shown in Figure 3.2, formulated his theory of the moving Earth. ☑ **Copernicus reasoned that the simplest way to interpret astronomical observations was to assume that Earth and the other planets move around the sun.** This idea was extremely controversial at the time. People preferred to believe that Earth was at the center of the universe.

Copernicus worked on his ideas in secret to escape persecution. In the last days of his life and at the urging of close friends, he sent his ideas to the printer. The first copy of his work, *De Revolutionibus*, reached him on the day of his death, May 24, 1543.

CONCEPT CHECK : What did Copernicus state about Earth's motion?

3.3 Galileo on Motion

Galileo, the foremost scientist of late-Renaissance Italy, was outspoken in his support of Copernicus. As a result, he suffered a trial and house arrest. One of Galileo's great contributions to physics was demolishing the notion that a force is necessary to keep an object moving.

A force is any push or pull. **Friction** is the name given to the force that acts between materials that touch as they move past each other. Friction is caused by the irregularities in the surfaces of objects that are touching. Even very smooth surfaces have microscopic irregularities that obstruct motion. If friction were absent, a moving object would need no force whatever to remain in motion.

FIGURE 3.2 ▼
Nicolaus Copernicus proposed that Earth moved around the sun.

Galileo did all his work before the advent of mechanical clocks. He timed some of his experiments with his pulse, and others with the dripping of water drops. Einstein called Galileo the father of modern physics.

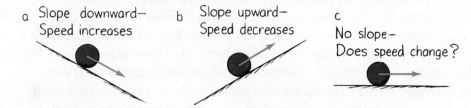

a Slope downward—
   Speed increases

b Slope upward—
   Speed decreases

c No slope—
   Does speed change?

◀ **FIGURE 3.3**
Galileo rolled balls along surfaces tilted at different angles. **a.** When the ball rolls downward, it moves with Earth's gravity, and its speed increases. **b.** When the ball rolls upward, it moves against gravity and loses speed. **c.** When the ball rolls on a level plane, it does not move with or against gravity.

⊘ **Galileo argued that only when friction is present—as it usually is—is a force needed to keep an object moving.** He tested his idea by rolling balls along plane surfaces tilted at different angles. He noted that a ball rolling down an inclined plane speeds up, as shown in Figure 3.3a. The ball is rolling partly in the direction of the pull of Earth's gravity. He also noted that a ball rolling up an inclined plane—in a direction opposed by gravity—slows down, as shown in Figure 3.3b. What about a ball rolling on a level surface, as shown in Figure 3.3c? That ball does not roll with or against gravity. Galileo found that a ball rolling on a smooth horizontal plane has almost constant velocity. He stated that if friction were entirely absent, a ball moving horizontally would move forever. No push or pull would be required to keep it moving once it is set in motion.

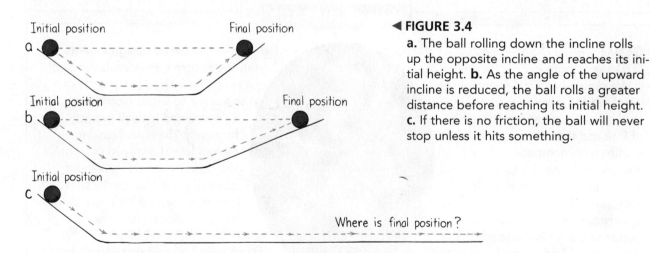

a Initial position   Final position

b Initial position   Final position

c Initial position

                         Where is final position?

◀ **FIGURE 3.4**
a. The ball rolling down the incline rolls up the opposite incline and reaches its initial height. **b.** As the angle of the upward incline is reduced, the ball rolls a greater distance before reaching its initial height. **c.** If there is no friction, the ball will never stop unless it hits something.

Galileo's conclusion was supported by another line of reasoning. He described two inclined planes facing each other, as in Figure 3.4. A ball released to roll down one plane would roll up the other to reach nearly the same height. The smoother the planes were, the more nearly equal would be the initial and final heights. He noted that the ball tended to attain the same height, even when the second plane was longer and inclined at a smaller angle than the first plane. Always, the ball went farther and tended to reach the same height.

think!

A ball is rolled across a counter top and rolls slowly to a stop. How would Aristotle interpret this behavior? How would Galileo interpret it? How would you interpret it?

Answer: 3.3

What if the angle of incline of the second plane were reduced to zero so that the plane was perfectly horizontal? How far would the ball roll? He realized that only friction would keep it from rolling forever. It was not the nature of the ball to come to rest as Aristotle had claimed. In the absence of friction, the moving ball would naturally keep moving. Galileo stated that this tendency of a moving body to keep moving is natural and that every material object resists change to its state of motion. The property of a body to resist changes to its state of motion is called **inertia.**

Galileo was concerned with *how* things move rather than *why* they move. He showed that experiment, not logic, is the best test of knowledge. Galileo's findings about motion and his concept of inertia discredited Aristotle's theory of motion. The way was open for Isaac Newton (1642–1727) to synthesize a new vision of the universe.

CONCEPT CHECK : According to Galileo, when is a force needed to keep an object moving?

Link to HISTORY

Galileo Galilei (1564–1642)
Galileo was born in Pisa, Italy, in the same year Shakespeare was born and Michelangelo died. He studied medicine at the University of Pisa and then changed his studies to mathematics. He developed an early interest in motion and was soon at odds with others around him, who held to Aristotelian ideas on falling bodies. He left Pisa to teach at the University of Padua and became an advocate of the new theory of the solar system advanced by Copernicus. Galileo was one of the first to build a telescope, and was the first to direct it to the nighttime sky. He discovered mountains on the moon and the moons of Jupiter. He published his findings in Italian instead of in Latin, the standard scholarly language of his time, and because of the recent invention of the printing press, his ideas reached many people.

He soon encountered disagreements with the Roman Catholic Church and was warned not to teach and not to adhere to Copernican views. He restrained himself publicly for nearly 15 years. Thinking he had found a way to present the Copernican views without contradicting Church doctrine, Galileo published his observations and conclusions. However, he was brought to trial and was found guilty, and he was forced to renounce his discoveries. By then an old man broken in health and spirit, he was sentenced to house arrest for the remainder of his life. Nevertheless, he completed his studies on motion and his writings were smuggled from Italy and published in Holland. Galileo had damaged his eyes years earlier by looking at the sun through a telescope, which led to blindness at the age of 74. He died 4 years later.

3.4 Newton's Law of Inertia

On Christmas day in the year Galileo died, Isaac Newton was born. By age 24, he had developed his famous laws of motion. They replaced the Aristotelian ideas that dominated the thinking of the best minds for most of the previous 2000 years. This chapter covers the first of Newton's three laws of motion. Newton's two other laws of motion are covered in following chapters.

Newton's first law, usually called the **law of inertia,** is a restatement of Galileo's idea that a force is not needed to keep an object moving. ☑ **Newton's first law states that every object continues in a state of rest, or of uniform speed in a straight line, unless acted on by a nonzero net force.**

think!

A force of gravity between the sun and its planets holds the planets in orbit around the sun. If that force of gravity suddenly disappeared, in what kind of path would the planets move?
Answer: 3.4.1

Objects at Rest Simply put, things tend to keep on doing what they're already doing. Dishes on a tabletop, for example, are in a state of rest. They tend to remain at rest, as is evidenced if you snap a tablecloth from beneath them, as shown in Figure 3.5. Try this at first with some unbreakable dishes. If you do it properly, you'll find the brief and small forces of friction are not significant enough to appreciably move the dishes (close inspection will show that brief friction between the dishes and the fast-moving tablecloth starts the dishes moving, but immediately after the tablecloth is removed friction between the dishes and table stops them). Objects in a state of rest tend to remain at rest. Only a force will change that state.

FIGURE 3.5 ▲
Objects at rest tend to remain at rest.

FIGURE 3.6 ▶
Blasts of air from many tiny holes provide a nearly friction-free surface on the air table.

Notice that Newton's law of inertia and the equilibrium rule of Chapter 2 say the same thing: When $\Sigma F = 0$, objects don't change their states of motion.

Objects in Motion Now consider an object in motion. If you slide a hockey puck along the surface of a city street, the puck quite soon comes to rest. If you slide it along ice, it slides for a longer distance. This is because the friction force is very small. If you slide it along an air table where friction is practically absent, such as the one shown in Figure 3.6, it slides with no apparent loss in speed. We see that in the absence of forces, a moving object tends to move in a straight line indefinitely. Toss an object from a space station located in the vacuum of outer space, and the object will move forever. It will move by virtue of its own inertia.

We see that the law of inertia provides a completely different way of viewing motion. Whereas the ancients thought continual forces were needed to maintain motion, we now know that objects continue to move by themselves. Forces are needed to overcome any friction that may be present and to set objects in motion initially. Once the object is moving in a force-free environment, it will move in a straight line indefinitely. In Chapter 6 we'll see that forces are needed to accelerate objects, but not to maintain motion if there is no friction.

CONCEPT CHECK What is Newton's first law of motion?

34

Isaac Newton (1642–1727)

On Christmas day in the year 1642, the year that Galileo died, Isaac Newton was born prematurely and barely survived. Newton's birthplace was his mother's farmhouse in Woolsthorpe, England. His father died several months before his birth, and Isaac grew up under the care of his mother and grandmother. As a child he showed no particular signs of brightness, and at the age of 14 he was taken out of school to work on his mother's farm. As a farmer he was a failure, preferring to read books he borrowed from a neighboring pharmacist. An uncle sensed the scholarly potential in young Isaac and prompted him to study at the University of Cambridge, which he did for 5 years, graduating without particular distinction.

A plague swept through England, and Newton retreated to his mother's farm—this time to continue his studies. At the farm, when he was 23 and 24 years old, he laid the foundations for the science of physics. Seeing an apple fall to the ground led him to consider the force of gravity extending to the moon and beyond. He formulated the law of universal gravitation. He invented the calculus, a very important mathematical tool in science. He extended Galileo's work and developed the three fundamental laws of motion. He also formulated a theory of the nature of light and showed, using prisms, that white light is composed of all colors of the rainbow. It was his experiments with prisms that first made him famous.

When the plague subsided, Newton returned to Cambridge and soon established a reputation for himself as a first-rate mathematician. His mathematics teacher resigned in his favor and Newton was appointed the Lucasian professor of mathematics. He held this post for 28 years. In 1672 he was elected to the Royal Society, where he exhibited the world's first reflector telescope. It can still be seen, preserved at the library of the Royal Society in London with the inscription: "The first reflecting telescope, invented by Sir Isaac Newton, and made with his own hands."

It wasn't until Newton was 42 that he began to write one of the greatest scientific books ever written, the *Principia Mathematica Philosophiae Naturalis*. He wrote the work in Latin and completed it in 18 months. It appeared in print in 1687 and wasn't printed in English until 1729, two years after his death. When asked how he was able to make so many discoveries, Newton replied that he solved his problems by continually thinking very long and hard about them—and not by sudden insight.

At the age of 46 he was elected a member of Parliament. He attended the sessions in Parliament for two years and never gave a speech. One day he rose and the House fell silent to hear the great man. Newton's "speech" was very brief; he simply requested that a window be closed because of a draft.

Although Newton's hair turned gray at 30, it remained full, long, and wavy all his life. Unlike others in his time, he did not wear a wig. He was a modest man, although very sensitive to criticism. He never married. He remained healthy in body and mind into old age. At 80, he still had all his teeth, his eyesight and hearing were sharp, and his mind was alert. In his lifetime he was regarded by his countrymen as the greatest scientist who ever lived. In 1705 he was knighted by Queen Anne. Newton died at the age of 85 and was buried in Westminster Abbey along with England's kings and heroes.

Newton "opened up" the universe, showing that the same natural laws that act on Earth govern the larger cosmos as well. For humankind this led to increased humility, but also to hope and inspiration because of the evidence of a rational order. Newton ushered in the Age of Reason. His ideas and insights truly changed the world and elevated the human condition.

FIGURE 3.7 ▲
You can tell how much matter is in a can when you kick it.

3.5 Mass—A Measure of Inertia

Kick an empty can, as shown in Figure 3.7, and it moves. Kick a can filled with sand and it doesn't move as much. Kick a can filled with steel nails and you'll hurt your foot. The nail-filled can has more inertia than the sand-filled can, which in turn has more inertia than the empty can. The amount of inertia an object has depends on its *mass*—which is roughly the amount of material present in the object. ✅ **The more mass an object has, the greater its inertia and the more force it takes to change its state of motion.** Mass is a measure of the inertia of an object.

Mass Is Not Volume Do not confuse mass and volume. They are entirely different concepts. Volume is a measure of space and is measured in units such as cubic centimeters, cubic meters, and liters. Mass is measured in the fundamental unit of **kilograms.** If an object has a large mass, it may or may not have a large volume. For example, equal-size bags of cotton and nails may have equal volumes, but very unequal masses. How many kilograms of matter an object contains and how much space the object occupies are two different things. (A liter of milk, juice, or soda—anything that is mainly water—has a mass of about one kilogram.)

Which has more mass, a feather pillow or a common automobile battery as shown in Figure 3.8? Clearly an automobile battery is more difficult to set into motion. This is evidence of the battery's greater inertia and hence its greater mass. The pillow may be bigger, that is, it may have a larger volume, but it has less mass. Mass is different from volume.

FIGURE 3.8 ▶
The pillow has a larger size (volume) but a smaller mass than the battery.

Mass Is Not Weight Mass is often confused with *weight*. We say a heavy object contains a lot of matter. We often determine the amount of matter in an object by measuring its gravitational attraction to Earth. However, mass is more fundamental than weight. Mass is a measure of the amount of material in an object and depends only on the number of and kind of atoms that compose it. Weight on the other hand is a measure of the gravitational force acting on the object. Weight depends on an object's location.

Mass is a property within the body. Weight is an outside force on the body.

Mass Is Inertia The amount of material in a particular stone is the same whether the stone is located on Earth, on the moon, or in outer space. Hence, the stone's mass is the same in all of these locations. This could be demonstrated by shaking the stone back and forth in these three locations. The same force would be required to shake the stone with the same rhythm whether the stone was on Earth, on the moon, or in a force-free region of outer space, as shown in Figure 3.9. The stone's inertia, or mass, is solely a property of the stone and not its location.

But the weight of the stone would be very different on Earth and on the moon, and still different in outer space. On the surface of the moon, the stone would have only one-sixth the weight it has on Earth. This is because the force of gravity on the moon is only one-sixth as strong as it is on Earth. If the stone were in a gravity-free region of space, its weight would be zero. Its mass, on the other hand, would not be zero. Mass is different from weight.

We can define mass and weight as follows:

Mass is the quantity of matter in an object. More specifically, mass is a measure of the inertia, or "laziness," that an object exhibits in response to any effort made to start it, stop it, or otherwise change its state of motion.

Weight is the force of gravity on an object.

While mass and weight are not the same, they are proportional to each other in a given place. Objects with great mass have great weight; objects with little mass have little weight. In the same location, twice the mass weighs twice as much. Mass and weight are proportional to each other, but they are not equal to each other. Remember that mass has to do with the amount of matter in the object, while weight has to do with how strongly that matter is attracted by gravity.

FIGURE 3.9 ▲
It's just as difficult to shake a stone in its weightless state in space as it is in its weighted state on Earth.

Link to SPACE SCIENCE

Inertia in Action
Pioneer and *Voyager* spacecraft launched in the late 1970s have gone beyond the orbits of Saturn, Uranus, and Pluto, and are still cruising beyond the solar system. Initially, force supplied by rockets sent the spacecraft on their journeys. However,  once in outer space these engines supplied no more force. Except for the gravitational effect of the stars and planets in the universe, the motion of the spacecraft will continue without change.

FIGURE 3.10 ▲
One kilogram of nails weighs 10 newtons, which is equal to 2.2 pounds.

One Kilogram Weighs 10 Newtons In the United States it is common to describe the amount of matter in an object by its gravitational pull to Earth, that is, by its weight. In the United States, the traditional unit of weight is the pound. In most parts of the world, however, the measure of matter is commonly expressed in units of mass. The SI[3.5.1] unit of mass is the kilogram; its symbol is kg. At Earth's surface, a 1-kg bag of nails has a weight of 2.2 pounds.

The SI unit of *force* is the **newton** (named after guess who?). One newton is equal to slightly less than a quarter pound, about the weight of a quarter-pound burger *after* it is cooked. The SI symbol for the newton is N and is written with a capital letter because it is named after a person. A 1-kg bag of nails weighs 10 N in SI units as shown in Figure 3.10. Away from Earth's surface, where the force of gravity is less, the bag of nails weighs less.

If you know the mass of something in kilograms and want its weight in newtons at Earth's surface, multiply the number of kilograms by 10. Or, if you know the weight in newtons, divide by 10 and you'll have the mass in kilograms. Once again, weight and mass are proportional to each other.[3.5.2]

CONCEPT CHECK What is the relationship between mass and inertia?

3.6 The Moving Earth Again

Copernicus announced the idea of a moving Earth in the sixteenth century. This controversial idea stimulated much argument and debate. One of the arguments against a moving Earth was as follows. Consider a bird sitting at rest in the top of a tall tree, as shown in Figure 3.11. On the ground below is a fat, juicy worm. The bird sees the worm, drops down vertically, and catches it. It was argued that this would not be possible if Earth moved as Copernicus suggested. If Copernicus were correct, Earth would have to travel at a speed of 107,000 km/h to circle the sun in one year. Convert this speed to kilometers per second and you'll get 30 km/s. Even if the bird could descend from its branch in one second, the worm would have been swept away by the moving Earth for a distance of 30 kilometers. For the bird to catch the worm under this circumstance would be an impossible task. The fact that birds *do* catch worms from high tree branches seemed to be clear evidence that Earth must be at rest.

FIGURE 3.11 ▶
Earth does not need to be at rest for the bird to catch the worm.

Objects Move With Earth Can you refute this argument? You can if you invoke the idea of inertia. You see, not only is Earth moving at 30 km/s, but so are the tree, the branch of the tree, the bird that sits on it, the worm below, and even the air in between. All are moving at 30 km/s. ⊘ **The law of inertia states that objects in motion remain in motion if no unbalanced forces act on them.** So objects on Earth move with Earth as Earth moves around the sun. When the bird drops from the branch, its initial sideways motion of 30 km/s remains unchanged. It catches the worm and is quite unaffected by the motion of its total environment.

Stand next to a wall. Jump up so that your feet no longer touch the floor. Does the 30-km/s wall slam into you? Why not? Because you are also traveling at 30 km/s, before, during, and after your jump. The 30 km/s is the speed of Earth relative to the sun, not the speed of the wall relative to you.

Objects Move With Vehicles Four hundred years ago, people had difficulty with ideas like these, not only because they failed to acknowledge the concept of inertia, but also because they were not accustomed to moving in high-speed vehicles. Slow, bumpy rides in horse-drawn carriages do not lend themselves to experiments that reveal inertia. Today, as shown in Figure 3.12, we flip a coin in a high-speed car, bus, or plane and catch the vertically moving coin as we would if the vehicle were at rest. We see evidence for the law of inertia when the horizontal motion of the coin before, during, and after the catch is the same. The coin keeps up with us. The vertical force of gravity affects only the vertical motion of the coin.

Our notions of motion today are very different from those of our distant ancestors. Aristotle did not recognize the idea of inertia, because he did not see that all moving things follow the same rules. He imagined different rules for motion in the heavens and motion on Earth. He saw horizontal motion as "unnatural," requiring a sustained force. Galileo and Newton, on the other hand, saw that all moving things follow the same rules. To them, moving things required *no* force to keep moving if friction was not present. We can only wonder how differently science might have progressed if Aristotle had recognized the unity of all kinds of motion and friction's effect on motion.

CONCEPT CHECK How does the law of inertia apply to objects in motion?

Go Online
SciLINKS NSTA

For: Links on inertia
Visit: www.SciLinks.org
Web Code: csn – 0306

◀ **FIGURE 3.12**
Flip a coin in a high-speed airplane, and it behaves as if the plane were at rest. The coin keeps up with you—inertia in action!

Inertia safety—the more than 3-million-kg steel ball hanging at the 87th floor of the tallest skyscraper in Taipei helps stabilize the 101-story building against vibrations caused by earthquakes or strong winds.

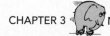

 **REVIEW**

Concept Summary ......

- Aristotle, the foremost Greek scientist, studied motion and divided it into two types: *natural motion* and *violent motion*.

- Copernicus reasoned that the simplest way to interpret astronomical observations was to assume that Earth and the other planets move around the sun.

- Galileo argued that only when friction is present—as it usually is—is a force needed to keep an object moving.

- Newton's first law states that every object continues in a state of rest, or of uniform speed in a straight line, unless acted on by a nonzero net force.

- The more mass an object has, the greater its inertia and the more force it takes to change its state of motion.

- The law of inertia states that objects in motion remain in motion if no unbalanced forces act on them.

Key Terms ......

friction (p. 30)

inertia (p. 32)

Newton's first law (p. 33)

law of inertia (p. 33)

kilograms (p. 36)

mass (p. 37)

weight (p. 37)

newton (p. 38)

think! Answers

3.3 Aristotle would probably say that the ball stops because it seeks its natural state of rest. Galileo would probably say that the friction between the ball and the table overcomes the ball's natural tendency to continue rolling—overcomes the ball's inertia—and brings it to a stop. Only you can answer the last question!

3.4.1 Each planet would move in straight lines at constant speed.

3.4.2 In a strict sense, no. We don't know the reason *why* objects persist in their motion when nothing acts on them, but we know that they do, and we call this property *inertia*. We understand many things, and we have labels for these things. There are also many things we do not understand, and we have labels for these things too. Education consists not so much in acquiring new labels, but in learning what is understood, what is not, and why.

3.5 Two kilograms of *anything* has twice the inertia and twice the mass of one kilogram of anything else. In the same location, where mass and weight are proportional, two kilograms of anything will weigh twice as much as one kilogram of anything. Except for volume, the answer to all the questions is yes. Bananas are much more dense than bread, so two kilograms of bananas must occupy less volume than one kilogram of bread.

40

ASSESS

Check Concepts ......

Section 3.1

1. What were the two classifications of motion, according to Aristotle?

2. According to Aristotle, what kinds of motion required no forces?

Section 3.2

3. What simple way of interpreting astronomical observations did Copernicus advocate?

Section 3.3

4. What were the consequences to Galileo for supporting the ideas of Copernicus?

5. Who relied on experiment, Aristotle or Galileo?

6. How did Galileo discredit Aristotle's assertion that a force is needed to keep objects moving?

7. Galileo let a ball roll down one incline and then up another. Compared with its initial height, how high did the ball roll up the second incline?

8. What name is given to the property of an object to resist changes in motion?

Section 3.4

9. Who was the first to consider the role of inertia, Galileo or Newton?

10. What is the tendency of an object at rest when no forces act on it?

11. What is the tendency of a moving object when no forces act on it?

Section 3.5

12. What relationship does mass have with inertia?

13. What does it mean to say mass and weight are proportional to each other?

14. When does an object with twice the mass of another weigh twice as much?

15. What do you feel when you shake something to and fro? What do you feel when you hold it against the pull of gravity?

16. What is the standard (or SI) unit of measurement for mass?

17. What is the standard (or SI) unit of measurement for weight?

18. What is the weight of a 1-kg brick?

Section 3.6

19. How fast are you moving relative to Earth when you are standing still? How fast are you moving relative to the sun?

20. If you're in a smooth-riding bus that is going at 40 km/h and you flip a coin vertically, how fast does the coin move horizontally while in midair?

Think and Rank ······

Rank each of the following sets of scenarios in order of the quantity or property involved. List them from left to right. If scenarios have equal rankings, then separate them with an equal sign. (e.g., A = B)

21. Different materials rest on a table.

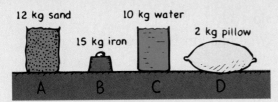

a. From greatest to least, rank them by how much they resist being set into motion.
b. From greatest to least, rank them by weight.
c. From greatest to least, rank them by the support (normal) force the table exerts on them.

22. The three pucks are sliding across ice at the noted speeds. Air resistance and ice friction are negligible.

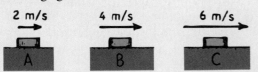

a. Rank them, from greatest to least, by the force needed to keep them going.
b. Rank them, from greatest to least, by the force needed to stop them in the same time interval.

Plug and Chug ······

23. If a woman has a mass of 50 kg, calculate her weight in newtons.

24. Calculate in newtons the weight of a 2000-kg elephant.

25. Calculate in newtons the weight of a 2.5-kg melon. What is its weight in pounds?

26. An apple weighs about 1 N. What is its mass in kilograms? What is its weight in pounds?

27. Susie Small finds she weighs 300 N. Calculate her mass.

Think and Explain ······

28. A bowling ball rolling along a lane gradually slows as it rolls. How would Aristotle interpret this observation? How would Galileo interpret it?

29. When a ball rolls down an inclined plane, it gains speed because of gravity. When rolling up it loses speed because of gravity. Why doesn't gravity play a role when it rolls on a horizontal surface?

30. Jacob gives his skateboard a push and it rolls across the classroom floor. Emily says that after it leaves Jacob's hand, his *force* remains with it, keeping it going. Sophia disagrees and says that Jacob's push gives the skateboard *speed*, not force, and that when his hand is no longer in contact the force is no more. Who do you agree with? Discuss this with your classmates.

31. A space probe can be carried by a rocket into outer space. Your friend asks what kind of force keeps the probe moving after it is released from the rocket and on its own. What is your answer?

32. In an orbiting spacecraft, you are handed two identical closed boxes, one filled with sand and the other filled with feathers. How can you tell which is which without opening the boxes?

33. Many automobile passengers suffer neck injuries when struck by cars from behind. How does Newton's law of inertia apply here? How do headrests help to guard against this type of injury?

34. Tim practices a demonstration before doing it for Sunday dinner. What concept is he illustrating, and why is he careful not to pull the tablecloth slightly upward?

35. Suppose you place a ball in the middle of a wagon that is at rest and then abruptly pull the wagon forward. Describe the motion of the ball relative to the ground and the wagon.

36. To pull a wagon across a lawn with constant velocity, you have to exert a steady force. Does this fact contradict Newton's first law, which tells us that motion with constant velocity indicates no force?

37. When a junked car is crushed into a compact cube, does its mass change? Its volume? Its weight?

38. If an elephant were chasing you, its enormous mass would be very threatening. But if you zigzagged, the elephant's mass would be to your advantage. Why?

39. When you compress a sponge, which quantity changes: mass, inertia, volume, or weight?

40. Which has more mass, a 2-kg fluffy pillow or a 3-kg small piece of iron? More volume? Why are your answers different?

41. Is it more accurate to say that a dieting person loses mass or loses weight?

42. A massive ball is suspended on a string and slowly pulled by another string attached to it from below, as shown.
    a. Is the string tension greater in the upper or the lower string? Which string is more likely to break? Which property, mass or weight, is more important here?
    b. If the string is instead snapped downward, which string is more likely to break? Is mass or weight more important this time?

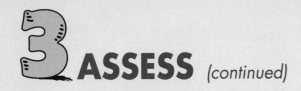

43. The head of a hammer is loose and you wish to tighten it by banging it against the top of a workbench. Why is it better to hold the hammer with the handle down, as shown below, rather than with the head down? Explain in terms of inertia.

44. As Earth rotates about its axis, it takes three hours for the United States to pass beneath a point above Earth that is stationary relative to the sun. What is wrong with the following scheme? To travel from Washington, D.C. to San Francisco using very little fuel, simply ascend in a helicopter high over Washington, D.C., and wait three hours until San Francisco passes below.

45. In which position is the compression the least in the arms of the weightlifters shown? The most?

46. A stone is shown at rest on the ground.
  a. The vector shows the weight of the stone. Complete the vector diagram showing another vector that results in zero net force on the stone.
  b. What is the conventional name of the vector you have drawn?

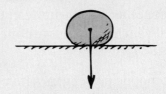

47. Here a stone is suspended at rest by a string.
  a. Draw force vectors for all the forces that act on the stone.
  b. Should your vectors have a zero resultant?
  c. Why, or why not?

48. Here a stone is being accelerated vertically upward.
  a. Draw force vectors to some suitable scale showing relative forces acting on the stone.
  b. Which is the longer vector, and why?

49. Suppose the string in the figure in Question 48 breaks and the stone slows in its upward motion.
   a. Draw a force vector diagram of the stone when it reaches the top of its path.
   b. Is the net force on the stone zero at the top?

50. Here is a stone sliding down a friction-free incline.
   a. Identify the forces that act on it and draw appropriate force vectors.
   b. By the parallelogram rule, construct the resultant force on the stone (carefully showing it has a direction parallel to the incline—the same direction as the stone's acceleration).

Think and Solve ······

51. Calculate your own mass in kilograms and your weight in newtons.

52. A medium-size American automobile has a weight of about 3000 pounds. What is its mass in kilograms?

53. What is the weight in newtons of an automobile with a mass of 1800 kg?

54. If a woman weighed 500 N on Earth, what would she weigh on Jupiter, where the acceleration of gravity is 26 m/s^2?

55. Gravitational force on the moon is only 1/6 that on Earth. What is the weight of a 10-kg object on the moon and on Earth? What is its mass on the moon and on Earth?

Activity ······

56. Grandparents are interested in the educational progress of their grandchildren. Many have little science background. It's possible that relatives far back in your family tree believed that Earth was stationary in the center of the universe. Write a letter to Grandma or Grandpa. Tell what you've learned about a moving Earth and how a person who might be unsure of it could be convinced.

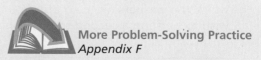

More Problem-Solving Practice
Appendix F

4 LINEAR MOTION

THE BIG IDEA : You can describe the motion of an object by its position, speed, direction, and acceleration.

More than 2000 years ago, the ancient Greek scientists were familiar with some of the ideas of physics that we study today. They had a good understanding of some of the properties of light, but they were confused about motion. Great progress in understanding motion occurred with Galileo and his study of balls rolling on inclined planes, as discussed in the previous chapter. In this chapter, we look at motion in more detail.

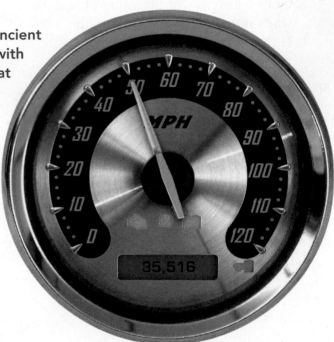

discover!

Do Objects Fall Faster the Longer They Fall?

1. Attach washers to a 3.5 m long string at the following distances from one end: 0.0 m, 0.11 m, 0.44 m, 0.99 m, 1.76 m and 2.76 m.

2. Stand on a chair or desk with the string and washers suspended over a piece of metal such as a pie tin. The washer tied to the end of the string should be just touching the metal surface.

3. Release the string and listen to the rate at which the washers hit the metal. You may wish to perform a second trial to confirm your observations.

Analyze and Conclude

1. **Observing** Describe the time intervals between sounds.

2. **Predicting** What would you hear if the washers were evenly spaced on the string?

3. **Making Generalizations** What can you say about the distance traveled by a falling object during each second of fall?

◀ FIGURE 4.1
Although you may be at rest relative to Earth's surface, you're moving about 100,000 km/h relative to the sun.

4.1 Motion Is Relative

Everything moves. Even things that appear to be at rest move. They move with respect to the sun and stars. When we describe the motion of one object with respect to another, we say that the object is moving **relative** to the other object. A book that is at rest, relative to the table it lies on, is moving at about 30 kilometers per second relative to the sun. The book moves even faster relative to the center of our galaxy. When we discuss the motion of something, we describe its motion relative to something else. ☑ **An object is moving if its position relative to a fixed point is changing.** When we say that a space shuttle moves at 8 kilometers per second, we mean its movement relative to Earth below. When we say a racing car in the Indy 500 reaches a speed of 300 kilometers per hour, of course we mean relative to the track. Unless stated otherwise, when we discuss the speeds of things in our environment, we mean speed with respect to the surface of Earth even though Earth moves around the sun, as shown in Figure 4.1. Motion is relative.

think!

A hungry mosquito sees you resting in a hammock in a 3-meter per second breeze. How fast and in what direction should the mosquito fly in order to hover above you for lunch?
Answer: 4.1

CONCEPT CHECK How can you tell if an object is moving?

◀ FIGURE 4.2
The racing cars in the Indy 500 move relative to the track.

4.2 Speed

think!

If a cheetah can maintain a constant speed of 25 m/s, it will cover 25 meters every second. At this rate, how far will it travel in 10 seconds? In 1 minute?

Answer: 4.2.1

Before the time of Galileo, people described moving things as simply "slow" or "fast." Such descriptions were vague. Galileo is credited as being the first to measure *speed* by considering the distance covered and the time it takes. **Speed** is how fast an object is moving. ⊘ **You can calculate the speed of an object by dividing the distance covered by time.**

$$\text{Speed} = \frac{\text{distance}}{\text{time}}$$

For example, if a cheetah, such as the one shown in Figure 4.3, covers 50 meters in a time of 2 seconds, its speed is 25 m/s.

FIGURE 4.3 ▶
A cheetah is the fastest land animal over distances less than 500 meters and can achieve peak speeds of 100 km/h.

Any combination of units for distance and time that are useful and convenient are legitimate for describing speed. Miles per hour (mi/h), kilometers per hour (km/h), centimeters per day (the speed of a sick snail?), or light-years per century are all legitimate units for speed. The slash symbol (/) is read as "per." Throughout this book, we'll primarily use the units *meters per second* (m/s) for speed. Table 4.1 shows some comparative speeds in different units.

Table 4.1	Approximate Speeds in Different Units
12 mi/h =	20 km/h = 6 m/s (bowling ball)
25 mi/h =	40 km/h = 11 m/s (very good sprinter)
37 mi/h =	60 km/h = 17 m/s (sprinting rabbit)
50 mi/h =	80 km/h = 22 m/s (tsunami)
62 mi/h =	100 km/h = 28 m/s (sprinting cheetah)
75 mi/h =	120 km/h = 33 m/s (batted softball)
100 mi/h =	160 km/h = 44 m/s (batted baseball)

Instantaneous Speed A car does not always move at the same speed. A car may travel down a street at 50 km/h, slow to 0 km/h at a red light, and speed up to only 30 km/h because of traffic. You can tell the speed of the car at any instant by looking at the car's speedometer, such as the one in Figure 4.4. The speed at any instant is called the **instantaneous speed.** A car traveling at 50 km/h may go at that speed for only one minute. If the car continued at that speed for a full hour, it would cover 50 km. If it continued at that speed for only half an hour, it would cover only half that distance, or 25 km. In one minute, the car would cover less than 1 km.

Average Speed In planning a trip by car, the driver often wants to know how long it will take to cover a certain distance. The car will certainly not travel at the same speed all during the trip. The driver cares only about the *average speed* for the trip as a whole. The **average speed** is the total distance covered divided by the time.

$$\text{average speed} = \frac{\text{total distance covered}}{\text{time interval}}$$

Average speed can be calculated rather easily. For example, if we drive a distance of 60 kilometers during a time of 1 hour, we say our average speed is 60 kilometers per hour (60 km/h). Or, if we travel 240 kilometers in 4 hours,

$$\text{average speed} = \frac{\text{total distance covered}}{\text{time interval}} = \frac{240 \text{ km}}{4 \text{ h}} = 60 \text{ km/h}$$

Note that when a distance in kilometers (km) is divided by a time in hours (h), the answer is in kilometers per hour (km/h).

Since average speed is the distance covered divided by the time of travel, it does not indicate variations in the speed that may take place during the trip. In practice, we experience a variety of speeds on most trips, so the average speed is often quite different from the instantaneous speed. Whether we talk about average speed or instantaneous speed, we are talking about the rates at which distance is traveled.

If we know average speed and travel time, the distance traveled is easy to find. A simple rearrangement of the definition above gives

$$\text{total distance covered} = \text{average speed} \times \text{travel time}$$

For example, if your average speed is 80 kilometers per hour on a 4-hour trip, then you cover a total distance of 320 kilometers.

CONCEPT CHECK How can you calculate speed?

FIGURE 4.4 ▲
The speedometer for a North American car gives readings of instantaneous speed in both mi/h and km/h. Odometers for the U.S. market give readings in miles; those for the Canadian market give readings in kilometers.

think!

The speedometer in every car also has an odometer that records the distance traveled. If the odometer reads zero at the beginning of a trip and 35 km a half hour later, what is the average speed?
Answer: 4.2.2

4.3 Velocity

Velocity is directed speed.

In everyday language, we can use the words *speed* and *velocity* interchangeably. In physics, we make a distinction between the two. Very simply, the difference is that **velocity** is speed in a given direction. When we say a car travels at 60 km/h, we are specifying its speed. But if we say a car moves at 60 km/h to the north, we are specifying its velocity. ✅ **Speed is a description of how fast an object moves; velocity is how fast and in what direction it moves.**

A quantity such as velocity that specifies direction as well as magnitude is called a vector quantity. Recall in Chapter 2 that quantities that require only magnitude for a description are scalar quantities. Speed is a scalar quantity. Velocity, like force, is a vector quantity.

Constant Velocity Constant speed means steady speed. Something with constant speed doesn't speed up or slow down. Constant velocity, on the other hand, means both constant speed *and* constant direction. Constant direction is a straight line—the object's path doesn't curve. So constant velocity means motion in a straight line at constant speed. The car in Figure 4.5 may have a constant speed, but its velocity is changing.

FIGURE 4.5 ▶
The car on the circular track may have a constant speed but not a constant velocity, because its direction of motion is changing every instant.

Changing Velocity If *either* the speed *or* the direction (or both) is changing, then the velocity is changing. Constant speed and constant velocity are not the same. A body may move at constant speed along a curved path, for example, but it does not move with constant velocity, because its direction is changing every instant.

In a car there are three controls that are used to change the velocity. One is the gas pedal, which is used to maintain or increase the speed. The second is the brake, which is used to decrease the speed. The third is the steering wheel, which is used to change the direction.

think!

The speedometer of a car moving northward reads 60 km/h. It passes another car that travels southward at 60 km/h. Do both cars have the same speed? Do they have the same velocity?
Answer: 4.3

CONCEPT CHECK How is velocity different from speed?

4.4 Acceleration

We can change the state of motion of an object by changing its speed, its direction of motion, or both. Any of these changes is a change in velocity. Sometimes we are interested in how fast the velocity is changing. A driver on a two-lane road who wants to pass another car would like to be able to speed up and pass in the shortest possible time. **Acceleration** is the rate at which the velocity is changing.[4.4.1] ✅ **You can calculate the acceleration of an object by dividing the change in its velocity by time.**

$$\text{acceleration} = \frac{\text{change of velocity}}{\text{time interval}}$$

We are familiar with acceleration in an automobile, such as the one shown in Figure 4.6. The driver depresses the gas pedal, which is appropriately called the accelerator. The passengers then experience acceleration, or "pickup" as it is sometimes called, as they are pressed into their seats. The key idea that defines acceleration is *change*. Whenever we change our state of motion, we are accelerating. A car that can accelerate well has the ability to change its velocity rapidly. A car that can go from zero to 60 km/h in 5 seconds has a greater acceleration than another car that can go from zero to 80 km/h in 10 seconds. So having good acceleration means being able to change velocity quickly and does not necessarily refer to how fast something is moving.

In physics, the term *acceleration* applies to decreases as well as increases in speed. The brakes of a car can produce large retarding accelerations, that is, they can produce a large decrease per second in the speed. This is often called *deceleration*. We experience deceleration when the driver of a bus or car slams on the brakes and we tend to hurtle forward.

think!

Suppose a car moving in a straight line steadily increases its speed each second, first from 35 to 40 km/h, then from 40 to 45 km/h, then from 45 to 50 km/h. What is its acceleration?
Answer: 4.4.1

Can you see that the gas pedal (accelerator), brakes, and steering wheel in an automobile are all controls for acceleration?

FIGURE 4.6 ▲
A car is accelerating whenever there is a *change* in its state of motion.

Mathematics is the
language of nature.

Change in Direction Acceleration also applies to changes in *direction*. If you ride around a curve at a constant speed of 50 km/h, you feel the effects of acceleration as your body tends to move toward the outside of the curve. You may round the curve at constant speed, but your velocity is not constant, because your direction is changing every instant. Your state of motion is changing: you are accelerating. It is important to distinguish between speed and velocity. Acceleration is defined as the rate of change in *velocity*, rather than *speed*. Acceleration, like velocity, is a vector quantity because it is directional. The acceleration vector points in the direction the velocity is changing, as shown in Figure 4.7. If we change speed, direction, or both, we change velocity and we accelerate.

FIGURE 4.7 ▶
When you accelerate in the direction of your velocity, you speed up; against your velocity, you slow down; at an angle to your velocity, your direction changes.

Change in Speed When straight-line motion is considered, it is common to use speed and velocity interchangeably. When the direction is not changing, acceleration may be expressed as the rate at which *speed* changes.

$$\text{acceleration (along a straight line)} = \frac{\text{change in speed}}{\text{time interval}}$$

Speed and velocity are measured in units of distance per time. Since acceleration is the change in velocity or speed per time interval, its units are those of speed per time. If we speed up, without changing direction, from zero to 10 km/h in 1 second, our change in speed is 10 km/h in a time interval of 1 s. Our acceleration along a straight line is

$$\text{acceleration} = \frac{\text{change in speed}}{\text{time interval}} = \frac{10 \text{ km/h}}{1 \text{ s}} = 10 \text{ km/h·s}$$

The acceleration is 10 km/h·s, which is read as "10 kilometers per hour-second." [4.4.2.] Note that a unit for time appears twice: once for the unit of speed and again for the interval of time in which the speed is changing.

CONCEPT CHECK How do you calculate acceleration?

think!

In 5 seconds a car moving in a straight line increases its speed from 50 km/h to 65 km/h, while a truck goes from rest to 15 km/h in a straight line. Which undergoes greater acceleration? What is the acceleration of each vehicle?
Answer: 4.4.2

4.5 Free Fall: How Fast

An apple falls from a tree. Does it accelerate while falling? We know it starts from a rest position and gains speed as it falls. We know this because it would be safe to catch if it fell a meter or two, but not if it fell from a high-flying balloon. Thus, the apple must gain more speed during the time it drops from a great height than during the shorter time it takes to drop a meter. This gain in speed indicates that the apple does accelerate as it falls.

Falling Objects Gravity causes the apple to accelerate downward once it begins falling. In real life, air resistance affects the acceleration of a falling object. Let's imagine there is no air resistance and that gravity is the only thing affecting a falling object. An object moving under the influence of the gravitational force only is said to be in **free fall.** Freely falling objects are affected only by gravity. Table 4.2 shows the instantaneous speed at the end of each second of fall of a freely falling object dropped from rest. The **elapsed time** is the time that has elapsed, or passed, since the beginning of any motion, in this case the fall.

Note in Table 4.2 the way the speed changes. During each second of fall, the instantaneous speed of the object increases by an additional 10 meters per second. This gain in speed per second is the acceleration.

$$\text{acceleration} = \frac{\text{change in speed}}{\text{time interval}} = \frac{10 \text{ m/s}}{1 \text{ s}} = 10 \text{ m/s}^2$$

Note that when the change in speed is in m/s and the time interval is in s, the acceleration is in m/s², which is read as "meters per second squared." The unit of time, the second, occurs twice—once for the unit of speed and again for the time interval during which the speed changes.

Table 4.2	Free Fall Speeds of Objects
Elapsed Time (seconds)	**Instantaneous Speed (meters/second)**
0	0
1	10
2	20
3	30
4	40
5	50
t	10t

> Free fall to a sky diver means fall before the parachute is opened, usually with lots of air resistance. Physics terms and everyday terms often mean different things.

think!

During the span of the second time interval in Table 4.2, the object begins at 10 m/s and ends at 20 m/s. What is the average speed of the object during this 1-second interval? What is its acceleration?
Answer: 4.5.1

CHAPTER 4   LINEAR MOTION   **53**

☑ **The acceleration of an object in free fall is about 10 meters per second squared (10 m/s²).** For free fall, it is customary to use the letter *g* to represent the acceleration because the acceleration is due to gravity. Although *g* varies slightly in different parts of the world, its average value is nearly 10 m/s². More accurately, *g* is 9.8 m/s², but it is easier to see the ideas involved when it is rounded off to 10 m/s². Where accuracy is important, the value of 9.8 m/s² should be used for the acceleration during free fall. Note in Table 4.2 that the instantaneous speed of an object falling from rest is equal to the acceleration multiplied by the amount of time it falls, the elapsed time.

$$\text{instantaneous speed} = \text{acceleration} \times \text{elapsed time}$$

The instantaneous speed *v* of an object falling from rest after an elapsed time *t* can be expressed in equation form[4.5]

$$v = gt$$

The letter *v* symbolizes both speed and velocity. Take a moment to check this equation with Table 4.2. You will see that whenever the acceleration *g* = 10 m/s² is multiplied by the elapsed time in seconds, the result is the instantaneous speed in meters per second.

The average speed of any object moving in a straight line with constant acceleration is calculated the way we find the average of any two numbers: add them and divide by 2. For example, the average speed of a freely-falling object in its first second of fall is the sum of its initial and final speed, divided by 2. So, adding the initial speed of zero and the final speed of 10 m/s, and then dividing by 2, we get 5 m/s. Average speed and instantaneous speed are usually very different.

think!

What would the speedometer reading on the falling rock shown in Figure 4.8 be 4.5 seconds after it drops from rest? How about 8 seconds after it is dropped?
Answer: 4.5.2

FIGURE 4.8 ▶
If a falling rock were somehow equipped with a speedometer, in each succeeding second of fall its reading would increase by the same amount, 10 m/s. Table 4.2 shows the speed we would read at various seconds of fall.

In Figure 4.8 we imagine a freely-falling boulder with a speedometer attached. As the boulder falls, the speedometer shows that the boulder acquires 10 m/s of speed each second. This 10 m/s gain each second is the boulder's acceleration.

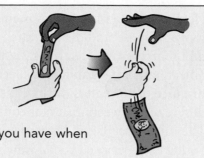

Rising Objects So far, we have been looking at objects moving straight downward due to gravity. Now consider an object thrown straight up. It continues to move upward for a while, then it comes back down. At the highest point, when the object is changing its direction of motion from upward to downward, its instantaneous speed is zero. It then starts downward just as if it had been dropped from rest at that height.

During the upward part of this motion, the object slows from its initial upward velocity to zero velocity. We know the object is accelerating because its velocity is changing. How much does its speed decrease each second? It should come as no surprise that the speed decreases at the same rate it increases when moving downward—at 10 meters per second each second. So as Figure 4.9 shows, the *instantaneous speed* at points of equal elevation in the path is the same whether the object is moving upward or downward. The *velocities* are different of course, because they are in opposite directions. During each second, the speed or the velocity changes by 10 m/s. The acceleration is 10 m/s² downward the entire time, whether the object is moving upward or downward.

CONCEPT CHECK: What is the acceleration of an object in free fall?

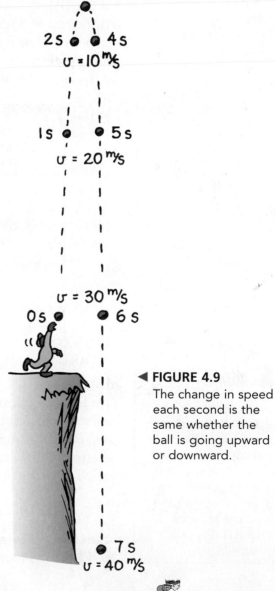

◀ **FIGURE 4.9**
The change in speed each second is the same whether the ball is going upward or downward.

FIGURE 4.10 ▲

Pretend that a falling rock is somehow equipped with an *odometer*. The readings of distance fallen increase with time and are shown in Table 4.3.

4.6 Free Fall: How Far

How *fast* something moves is entirely different from how *far* it moves—speed and distance are not the same thing. To understand the difference, return to Table 4.2. At the end of the first second, the falling object has an instantaneous speed of 10 m/s. Does this mean it falls a distance of 10 meters during this first second? No. Here's where the difference between instantaneous speed and average speed comes in. The initial speed of fall is zero and takes a full second to get to 10 m/s. So the average speed is half way between zero and 10 m/s—that's 5 m/s, as discussed earlier. So during the first second, the object has an average speed of 5 m/s and falls a distance of 5 m.

Table 4.3 shows the total distance moved by a freely falling object dropped from rest. At the end of one second, it has fallen 5 meters. At the end of 2 seconds, it has dropped a total distance of 20 meters. At the end of 3 seconds, it has dropped 45 meters altogether. ☑ **For each second of free fall, an object falls a greater distance than it did in the previous second.** These distances form a mathematical pattern[4.6.1]: at the end of time t, the object has fallen a distance d of $\frac{1}{2}gt^2$.

Table 4.3	Free Fall Distances of an Object
Elapsed Time (seconds)	**Distance Fallen (meters)**
0	0
1	5
2	20
3	45
4	80
5	125
t	$\frac{1}{2}gt^2$

We used freely falling objects to describe the relationship between distance traveled, acceleration, and velocity acquired. In our examples, we used the acceleration of gravity, $g = 10$ m/s². But accelerating objects need not be freely falling objects. A car accelerates when we step on the gas or the brake pedal. Whenever an object's initial speed is zero and the acceleration a is constant, that is, steady and "non-jerky," the equations[4.6.2] for the velocity and distance traveled are

$$v = at \text{ and } d = \frac{1}{2}at^2$$

CONCEPT CHECK: For a falling object, how does the distance per second change?

think!

An apple drops from a tree and hits the ground in one second. What is its speed upon striking the ground? What is its average speed during the one second? How high above ground was the apple when it first dropped?

Answer: 4.6

4.7 Graphs of Motion

Equations and tables are not the only way to describe relationships such as velocity and acceleration. Another way is to use graphs that visually describe relationships. Since you'll develop basic graphing skills in the laboratory, we won't make a big deal of graphs. Here we'll simply show the graphs for Tables 4.2 and 4.3.

Speed-Versus-Time Figure 4.11 is a graph of the speed-versus-time data in Table 4.2. Note that speed v is plotted on the vertical axis and time t is plotted on the horizontal axis. In this case, the "curve" that best fits the points forms a straight line. The straightness of the curve indicates a "linear" relationship between speed and time. For every increase of 1 s, there is the same 10 m/s increase in speed. Mathematicians call this *linearity,* and the graph shows why—the curve is a straight line. Since the object is dropped from rest, the line starts at the origin, where both v and t are zero. If we double t, we double v; if we triple t, we triple v; and so on. This particular linearity is called a *direct proportion,* and we say that time and speed are directly proportional to each other.

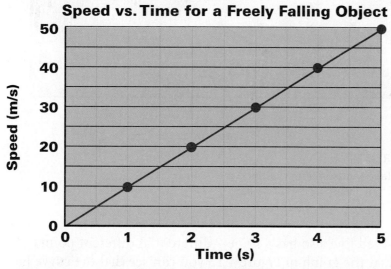

◀ FIGURE 4.11
A speed-versus-time graph of the data from Table 4.2 is linear.

The curve is a straight line, so its slope is constant—like an inclined plane. *Slope* is the vertical change divided by the horizontal change for any part of the line. ☑ **On a speed-versus-time graph the slope represents speed per time, or acceleration.** Note that for each 10 m/s of vertical change there is a corresponding horizontal change of 1 s. We see the slope is 10 m/s divided by 1 s, or 10 m/s^2. The straight line shows the acceleration is constant. If the acceleration were greater, the slope of the graph would be steeper. For more information about slope, see Appendix C.

The slope of a line on a graph is RISE/RUN.

Distance-Versus-Time Figure 4.12 is a graph of the distance-versus-time data in Table 4.3. Distance *d* is plotted on the vertical axis, and time *t* is on the horizontal axis. The result is a curved line. The curve shows that the relationship between distance traveled and time is *nonlinear*. The relationship shown here is *quadratic* and the curve is *parabolic*—when we double *t*, we do not double *d*; we quadruple it. Distance depends on time *squared!*

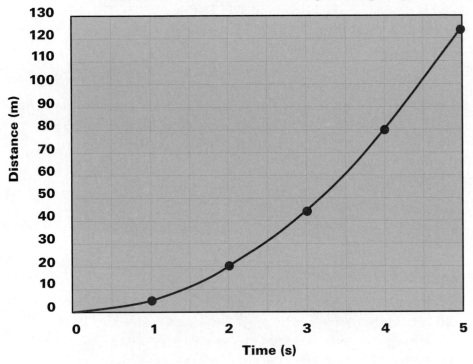

FIGURE 4.12 ▲
A distance-versus-time graph of the data from Table 4.3 is parabolic.

How fast something falls is entirely different than how far it falls. From rest, how fast is given by $v = gt$; how far by $d = \frac{1}{2}gt^2$.

A curved line also has a slope—different at different points. If you look at the graph in Figure 4.12 you can see that the curve has a certain slant or "steepness" at every point. This slope changes from one point to the next. The slope of the curve on a distance-versus-time graph is very significant. It is speed, the *rate* at which distance is covered per unit of time. In this graph the slope steepens (becomes greater) as time passes. This shows that speed increases as time passes. In fact, if the slope could be measured accurately, you would find it increases by 10 meters per second each second.

CONCEPT CHECK : What does a slope of a speed-versus-time graph represent?

4.8 Air Resistance and Falling Objects

Drop a feather and a coin and we notice the coin reaches the floor far ahead of the feather. Air resistance is responsible for these different accelerations. This fact can be shown quite nicely with a closed glass tube connected to a vacuum pump. The feather and coin are placed inside. When the tube is inverted with air inside, the coin falls much more rapidly than the feather. The feather flutters through the air. But if the air is removed with a vacuum pump and the tube is quickly inverted, the feather and coin fall side by side with the same acceleration, g, as shown in Figure 4.13.

⊘ **Air resistance noticeably slows the motion of things with large surface areas like falling feathers or pieces of paper. But air resistance less noticeably affects the motion of more compact objects like stones and baseballs.** In many cases the effect of air resistance is small enough to be neglected. With negligible air resistance, falling objects can be considered to be falling freely. Air resistance will be covered in more detail in Chapter 6.

FIGURE 4.13 ▲
A feather and a coin accelerate equally when there is no air around them.

CONCEPT CHECK : How does air resistance affect falling objects?

4.9 How Fast, How Far, How Quickly How Fast Changes

Some of the confusion that occurs in analyzing the motion of falling objects comes about from mixing up "how fast" with "how far." When we wish to specify how fast something freely falls from rest after a certain elapsed time, we are talking about speed or velocity. The appropriate equation is $v = gt$. When we wish to specify how far that object has fallen, we are talking about distance. The appropriate equation is $d = \frac{1}{2}gt^2$. Velocity or speed (how fast) and distance (how far) are entirely different from each other.

One of the most confusing concepts encountered in this book is acceleration, or "how quickly does speed or velocity change." What makes acceleration so complex is that it is *a rate of a rate*. It is often confused with velocity, which is itself a rate (the rate at which distance is covered). Acceleration is not velocity, nor is it even a change in velocity. ⊘ **Acceleration is the rate at which velocity itself changes.**

Please be patient with yourself if you find that you require several hours to achieve a clear understanding of motion. It took people nearly 2000 years from the time of Aristotle to Galileo to achieve as much!

CONCEPT CHECK : What is the relationship between velocity and acceleration?

Hang time can be several seconds in the sport of sail surfing—quite a bit different when the air plays a major role!

Physics of Sports

Hang Time

Some people are gifted with great jumping ability. Leaping straight up, they seem to hang in the air. Ask your friends to estimate the "hang time" of the great jumpers—the amount of time a jumper is airborne (feet off the ground). One or two seconds? Several? Nope. Surprisingly, the hang time of the greatest jumpers is almost always less than 1 second! Our perception of a longer hang time is one of many illusions we have about nature.

Jumping ability is best measured by a standing vertical jump. Stand facing a wall, and with feet flat on the floor and arms extended upward, make a mark on the wall at the top of your reach. Then make your jump, and at the peak, make another mark. The distance between these two marks measures your vertical leap.

Here's the physics. When you leap upward, jumping force is applied only as long as your feet are still in contact with the ground. The greater the force, the greater your launch speed and the higher the jump is. It is important to note that as soon as your feet leave the ground, whatever upward speed you attain immediately decreases at the steady rate of g, 10 m/s². Maximum height is attained when your upward speed decreases to zero. You then begin falling, gaining speed at exactly the same rate, g. If you land as you took off, upright with legs extended, then time rising equals time falling. Hang time is the sum of rising and falling times.

The relationship between rising or falling time and vertical height is given by

$$d = \frac{1}{2}gt^2$$

If we know the vertical height, we can rearrange this expression to read

$$t = \sqrt{\frac{2d}{g}}$$

No basketball player is known to have exceeded a jump of 1.25 meters (4 feet). Setting d equal[4.9] to 1.25 m, and using the more precise 9.8 m/s² for g, we find that t, half the hang time, is

$$t = \sqrt{\frac{2d}{g}} = \sqrt{\frac{2(1.25 \text{ m})}{9.8 \text{ m/s}^2}} = 0.50 \text{ s}$$

Doubling this, we see such a record hang time would be 1 second!

We've only been talking about vertical motion. How about running jumps? We'll learn in Chapter 5 that hang time depends only on the jumper's vertical speed at launch; it does not depend on horizontal speed. While airborne, the jumper's horizontal speed remains constant but the vertical speed undergoes acceleration. Interesting physics!

60

REVIEW

Concept Summary ・・・・・・

- An object is moving if its position relative to a fixed point is changing.

- You can calculate the speed of an object by dividing the distance covered by time.

- Speed is a description of how fast an object moves; velocity is how fast and in what direction it moves.

- You can calculate the acceleration of an object by dividing the change in its velocity by time.

- The acceleration of an object in free fall is about 10 meters per second squared (10 m/s²).

- For each second of free fall, an object falls a greater distance than it did in the previous second.

- On a speed-versus-time graph the slope represents speed per time, or acceleration.

- Air resistance noticeably slows the motion of things with large surface areas like falling feathers or pieces of paper. But air resistance less noticeably affects the motion of more compact objects like stones and baseballs.

- Acceleration is the rate at which velocity itself changes.

Key Terms ・・・・・・

relative (*p. 47*)

speed (*p. 48*)

instantaneous speed (*p. 49*)

average speed (*p. 49*)

velocity (*p. 50*)

acceleration (*p. 51*)

free fall (*p. 53*)

elapsed time (*p. 53*)

think! Answers

4.1 The mosquito should fly toward you into the breeze. When above you it should fly at 3 meters per second in order to hover at rest above you. Unless its grip on your skin is strong enough after landing, it must continue flying at 3 meters per second to keep from being blown off. That's why a breeze is an effective deterrent to mosquito bites.

4.2.1 In 10 s the cheetah will cover 250 m, and in 1 minute (or 60 s) it will cover 1500 m.

4.2.2
$$\text{average speed} = \frac{\text{total distance covered}}{\text{time interval}} =$$
$$\frac{35 \text{ km}}{0.5 \text{ h}} = 70 \text{ km/h.}$$

At some point, the speedometer would have to exceed 70 km/h.

4.3 Both cars have the same speed, but they have opposite velocities because they are moving in opposite directions.

4.4.1 We see that the speed increases by 5 km/h during each 1-s interval. The acceleration is therefore 5 km/h·s during each interval.

4.4.2 The car and truck both increase their speed by 15 km/h during the same time interval, so their acceleration is the same.

4.5.1 The average speed will be 15 m/s. The acceleration will be 10 m/s².

4.5.2 The speedometer readings would be 45 m/s and 80 m/s, respectively.

4.6 When it hits the ground, the apple's speed will be 10 m/s. Its average speed is 5 m/s, and it starts 5 m above the ground.

ASSESS

Check Concepts ......

Section 4.1

1. How can you be both at rest and also moving about 107,000 km/h at the same time?

2. You cover 10 meters in a time of 1 second. Is your speed the same if you cover 20 meters in 2 seconds?

Section 4.2

3. Does the speedometer of a car read instantaneous speed or average speed?

4. Average speed = distance covered divided by travel time. Do some algebra and multiply both sides of this relation by travel time. What does the result say about distance covered?

Section 4.3

5. Which is a vector quantity, speed or velocity? Defend your answer.

6. What two controls on a car cause a change in speed? What control causes only a change in velocity?

Section 4.4

7. What is the acceleration of a car moving along a straight-line path that increases its speed from zero to 100 km/h in 10 s?

8. By how much does the speed of a vehicle moving in a straight line change each second when it is accelerating at 2 km/h·s? At 4 km/h·s? At 10 km/h·s?

9. Why does the unit of time enter twice in the unit of acceleration?

Section 4.5

10. What is the meaning of *free fall*?

11. For a freely falling object dropped from rest, what is the instantaneous speed at the end of the fifth second of fall? The sixth second?

12. For a freely falling object dropped from rest, what is the *acceleration* at the end of the fifth second of fall? The sixth second? At the end of any elapsed time *t*?

Section 4.6

13. How far will a freely falling object fall from rest in five seconds? Six seconds?

14. How far will an object move in one second if its average speed is 5 m/s?

15. How far will a freely falling object have fallen from a position of rest when its instantaneous speed is 10 m/s?

Section 4.7

16. What does the slope of the curve on a distance-versus-time graph represent?

17. What does the slope of the curve on a velocity-versus-time graph represent?

Section 4.8

18. Does air resistance increase or decrease the acceleration of a falling object?

Section 4.9

19. What is the appropriate equation for how fast an object freely falls from a position of rest? For how far that object falls?

Think and Rank ......

Rank each of the following sets of scenarios in order of the quantity or property involved. List them from left to right. If scenarios have equal rankings, then separate them with an equal sign. (e.g., A = B)

20. Jogging Jake runs along a train flatcar that moves at the velocities shown. From greatest to least, rank the relative velocities of Jake as seen by an observer on the ground. (Call the direction to the right positive.)

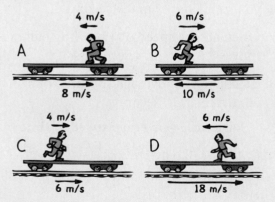

21. Below we see before and after snapshots of a car's velocity. The time interval between before and after for each is the same.

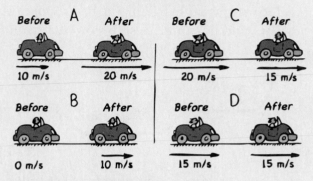

a. Rank the cars in terms of the change in velocity, from most positive to most negative. (Negative numbers rank lower than positive ones, and remember, tie scores can be part of your ranking.)

b. Rank them in terms of acceleration, from greatest to least.

22. These are drawings of same-size balls of different masses thrown straight downward. The speeds shown occur immediately after leaving the thrower's hand. Ignore air resistance. Rank their *accelerations* from greatest to least. Or are the accelerations the same for each?

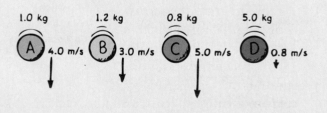

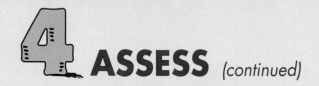

23. A track is made of a piece of channel metal bent as shown. A ball is released from rest at the left end of the track and continues past the various points. Rank the ball at points A, B, C, and D, from fastest to slowest. (Again, watch for tie scores.)

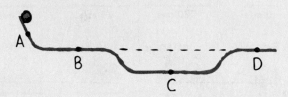

24. A ball is released from rest at the left end of three different tracks. The tracks are bent from pieces of metal of the same length.

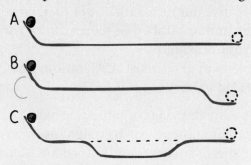

a. From fastest to slowest, rank the tracks in terms of the *speed* of the ball at the end. Or, do all balls have the same speed there?

b. From longest to shortest, rank the tracks in terms of the *time* for the ball to reach the end. Or do all balls reach the end in the same time?

c. From greatest to least, rank the tracks in terms of the *average speed* of the ball. Or do the balls all have the same average speed on all three tracks?

25. In the speed versus time graphs, all times *t* are in s and all speeds *v* are in m/s.

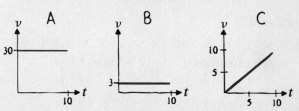

a. From greatest to least, rank the graphs in terms of the greatest *speed* at 10 seconds.

b. From greatest to least, rank the graphs in terms of the greatest *acceleration*.

c. From greatest to least, rank the graphs in terms of the greatest *distance* covered in 10 seconds.

Plug and Chug ······

These are to familiarize you with the central equations of the chapter.

$$\text{Average speed} = \frac{\text{total distance covered}}{\text{time interval}}$$

26. Calculate your average walking speed when you step 1 meter in 0.5 second.

27. Calculate the speed of a bowling ball that moves 8 meters in 4 seconds.

28. Calculate your average speed if you run 50 meters in 10 seconds.

$$\text{Distance} = \text{average speed} \times \text{time}$$

29. Calculate the distance (in km) that Charlie runs if he maintains an average speed of 8 km/h for 1 hour.

30. Calculate the distance you will travel if you maintain an average speed of 10 m/s for 40 seconds.

31. Calculate the distance (in km) you will travel if you maintain an average speed of 10 km/h for 1/2 hour.

$$\text{Acceleration} = \frac{\text{change of velocity}}{\text{time interval}}$$

32. Calculate the acceleration of a car (in km/h/s) that can go from rest to 100 km/h in 10 s.

33. Calculate the acceleration of a bus that goes from 10 km/h to a speed of 50 km/h in 10 seconds.

34. Calculate the acceleration of a ball that starts from rest and rolls down a ramp and gains a speed of 25 m/s in 5 seconds.

From a rest position:

$$\text{Instantaneous speed} = \text{acceleration} \times \text{time}$$

$$v = at$$

35. Calculate the instantaneous speed (in m/s) at the 10-second mark for a car that accelerates at 2 m/s² from a position of rest.

36. Calculate the speed (in m/s) of a skateboarder who accelerates from rest for 3 seconds down a ramp at an acceleration of 5 m/s².

Velocity acquired in free fall, from rest:

$$v = gt$$

37. Calculate the instantaneous speed of an apple 8 seconds after being dropped from rest.

38. On a distant planet a freely-falling object has an acceleration of 20 m/s². Calculate the speed an object dropped from rest on this distant planet acquires in 1.5 s.

39. A sky diver steps from a high-flying helicopter. If there were no air resistance, how fast would she be falling at the end of a 12-second jump?

Distance fallen in free fall, from rest:

$$d = \tfrac{1}{2}gt^2$$

40. Calculate the vertical distance an object dropped from rest would cover in 12 seconds if it fell freely without air resistance.

41. An apple drops from a tree and hits the ground in 1.5 seconds. Calculate how far it falls.

Think and Explain ······

42. Light travels in a straight line at a constant speed of 300,000 km/s. What is the light's acceleration?

43. a. If a freely falling rock were equipped with a speedometer, by how much would its speed readings increase with each second of fall?
    b. Suppose the freely falling rock were dropped near the surface of a planet where *g* = 20 m/s². By how much would its speed readings change each second?

44. Which has more acceleration when moving in a straight line—a car increasing its speed from 50 to 60 km/h, or a bicycle that goes from zero to 10 km/h in the same time? Defend your answer.

45. Correct your friend who says, "The dragster rounded the curve at a constant velocity of 100 km/h."

46. What is the acceleration of a car that moves at a steady velocity of 100 km/h due north for 100 seconds? Explain your answer and state why this question is an exercise in careful reading as well as physics.

47. Tiffany stands at the edge of a cliff and throws a ball straight up at a certain speed and another ball straight down with the same initial speed. Neglect air resistance.
    a. Which ball is in the air for the longest time?
    b. Which ball has the greater speed when it strikes the ground below?

48. A ball is thrown straight up. What will be the instantaneous velocity at the top of its path? What will be its acceleration at the top? Why are your answers different?

49. Two balls are released simultaneously from rest at the left ends of the equal-length tracks A and B as shown. Which ball reaches the end of its track first?

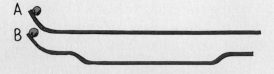

50. Refer to the tracks in the previous problem.
    a. Does the ball on B roll faster in the dip than the ball rolling along track A?
    b. On track B, is the speed gained going down into the dip equal to the speed lost going up the dip? If so, do the balls then have the same speed at the ends of both tracks?
    c. Is the average speed of the ball on the lower part of track B greater than the average speed of the ball on A during the same time?
    d. So overall, which ball has the greater *average* speed? (Do you wish to change your answer to the previous exercise?)

Think and Solve ••••••

51. A dragster going at 15 m/s north increases its velocity to 25 m/s north in 4 seconds. What is its acceleration during this time interval?

52. An apple drops from a tree and hits the ground in 1.5 s. What is its speed just before it hits the ground?

53. On a distant planet a freely falling object has an acceleration of 20 m/s^2. What vertical distance will an object dropped from rest on this planet cover in 1.8 s?

54. If you throw a ball straight upward at a speed of 10 m/s, how long will it take to reach zero speed? How long will it take to return to its starting point? How fast will it be going when it returns to its starting point?

55. Hanna tosses a ball straight up with enough speed to remain in the air for several seconds.
  a. What is the velocity of the ball when it reaches its highest point?
  b. What is its velocity 1 s before it reaches its highest point?
  c. What is the change in its velocity during this 1-s interval?
  d. What is its velocity 1 s after it reaches its highest point?
  e. What is the change in velocity during this 1-s interval?
  f. What is the change in velocity during the 2-s interval? (Caution: velocity, not speed!)
  g. What is the acceleration of the ball during any of these time intervals and at the moment the ball has zero velocity?

56. Kenny Klutz drops his physics book off his aunt's high-rise balcony. It hits the ground below 1.5 s later.
  a. With what speed does it hit?
  b. How high is the balcony?
    Ignore air drag.

57. Calculate the hang time of an athlete who jumps a vertical distance of 0.75 meter.

Activities ••••••

58. By any method you choose, determine your average speed of walking. How do your results compare with those of your classmates?

59. You can compare your reaction time with that of a friend by catching a ruler that is dropped between your fingers. Let your friend hold the ruler as shown in the figure.

Snap your fingers together as soon as you see the ruler released. On what does the number of centimeters that pass through your fingers depend? You can calculate your reaction time in seconds by solving $d = \frac{1}{2}gt^2$ for time: $t = \sqrt{2d/g}$. If you express d in meters (likely a fraction of a meter), then $t = 0.45\sqrt{d}$; if you express d in centimeters, then $t = 0.045\sqrt{d}$. Compare your reaction time with those of your classmates.

60. Calculate your personal "hang time," the time your feet are off the ground during a vertical jump.

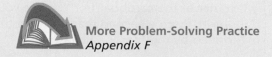

More Problem-Solving Practice
Appendix F

 # PROJECTILE MOTION

 **THE BIG IDEA** :⋮ Projectile motion can be described by the horizontal and vertical components of motion.

I n the previous chapter, we studied simple straight-line motion—linear motion. We distinguished between motion with constant velocity, such as a bowling ball rolling horizontally, and accelerated motion, such as an object falling vertically under the influence of gravity. Now we extend these ideas to nonlinear motion—motion along a curved path. Throw a baseball and the path it follows is a curve. This curve is a combination of constant-velocity horizontal motion and accelerated vertical motion. We'll see that the velocity of a thrown ball at any instant has two independent "components" of motion—what happens horizontally is not affected by what happens vertically.

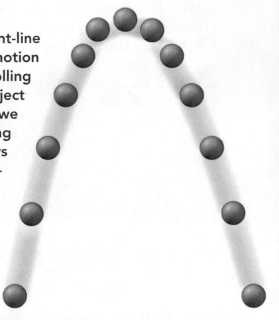

discover!

How Should You Aim to Hit a Falling Target?

1. On one corner of a rectangular piece of rigid cardboard, tape two 5-cm lengths of soda straws so they form a trough. Angle the straws to point toward the diagonal corner of the cardboard.

2. Draw a straight line passing through the center of the soda straws and extending to the top of the cardboard.

3. Tilt the cardboard so that Marble 1 will roll downhill. Hold Marble 1 in the upper right corner of the cardboard on the line you've drawn. Place a second marble in the trough formed by the two soda straws.

4. At the same time, release Marble 1 and launch Marble 2 by giving it a flick with your finger.

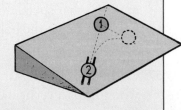

Analyze and Conclude

1. **Observing** Did you hit Marble 1? If so, what determined the point of collision?

2. **Predicting** What would happen if you used marbles with different masses?

3. **Making Generalizations** Why do the two marbles fall the same vertical distance from the line in the same amount of time?

5.1 Vector and Scalar Quantities

It is often said that a picture is worth a thousand words. Sometimes a picture explains a physics concept better than an equation does. Physicists love sketching doodles and equations to explain ideas. Their doodles often include arrows, where each arrow represents the magnitude and the direction of a certain quantity. The quantity might be the tension in a stretched rope, the compressive force in a squeezed spring, or the change in velocity of an airplane flying in the wind.

A quantity that requires both magnitude and direction for a complete description is a vector quantity. Recall from Chapter 4 that velocity differs from speed in that velocity includes direction in its description. Velocity is a vector quantity, as is acceleration. In later chapters we'll see that other quantities, such as momentum, are also vector quantities. For now we'll focus on the vector nature of velocity.

Recall from Chapter 2 that a quantity that is completely described by magnitude only is a scalar quantity. Scalars can be added, subtracted, multiplied, and divided like ordinary numbers. ⊘ **A vector quantity includes both magnitude and direction, but a scalar quantity includes only magnitude.** When 3 kg of sand is added to 1 kg of cement, the resulting mixture has a mass of 4 kg. When 5 liters of water are poured from a pail that has 8 liters of water in it, the resulting volume is 3 liters. If a scheduled 60-minute trip has a 15-minute delay, the trip takes 75 minutes. In each of these cases, no direction is involved. We see that descriptions such as 10 kilograms north, 5 liters east, or 15 minutes south have no meaning.

CONCEPT CHECK How does a scalar quantity differ from a vector quantity?

Physics on the Job

Air-Traffic Controller

Busy airports have many aircraft landing or taking off every minute. Air-traffic controllers are responsible for guiding pilots to their destinations. Using an understanding of vectors, air-traffic controllers determine the proper speed and direction of an aircraft by taking into account the velocity of the wind, path of the aircraft, and local air traffic. They use radar equipment as well as their view from the control tower to follow the motion of all aircraft flying near the airport.

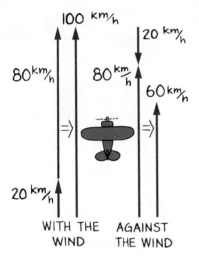

FIGURE 5.1 ▲
This vector, scaled so that
1 cm = 20 km/h, represents
60 km/h to the right.

5.2 Velocity Vectors

The vector in Figure 5.1 is scaled so that 1 centimeter represents 20 kilometers per hour. It is 3 centimeters long and points to the right; therefore it represents a velocity of 60 kilometers per hour to the right, or 60 km/h east.

The velocity of something is often the result of combining two or more other velocities. For example, an airplane's velocity is a combination of the velocity of the airplane relative to the air and the velocity of the air relative to the ground, or the wind velocity. Consider a small airplane slowly flying north at 80 km/h relative to the surrounding air. Suppose there is a tailwind blowing north at a velocity of 20 km/h. This example is represented with vectors in Figure 5.2. Here the velocity vectors are scaled so that 1 cm represents 20 km/h. Thus, the 80-km/h velocity of the airplane is shown by the 4-cm vector, and the 20-km/h tailwind is shown by the 1-cm vector. With or without vectors we can see that the resulting velocity is going to be 100 km/h. Without the tailwind, the airplane travels 80 kilometers in one hour relative to the ground below. With the tailwind, it travels 100 kilometers in one hour relative to the ground below.

Now suppose the airplane makes a U-turn and flies *into* the wind. The velocity vectors are now in opposite directions. The resulting speed of the airplane is 80 km/h − 20 km/h = 60 km/h. Flying against a 20-km/h wind, the airplane travels only 60 kilometers in one hour relative to the ground.

We didn't have to use vectors to answer questions about tailwinds and headwinds, but we'll now see that vectors are useful for combining velocities that are not parallel.

Consider an 80-km/h airplane flying north caught in a strong crosswind of 60 km/h blowing from west to east. Figure 5.3 shows vectors for the airplane velocity and wind velocity. The scale is 1 cm = 20 km/h. The sum of these two vectors, called the *resultant*, is the diagonal of the rectangle described by the two vectors.

FIGURE 5.2 ▲
The airplane's velocity relative to the ground depends on the airplane's velocity relative to the air and on the wind's velocity.

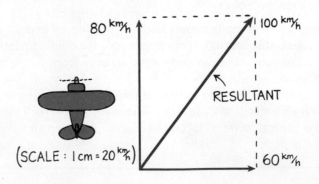

FIGURE 5.3 ▶
An 80-km/h airplane flying in a 60-km/h crosswind has a resultant speed of 100 km/h relative to the ground.

FIGURE 5.4 ▼
The 3-unit and 4-unit vectors add to produce a resultant vector of 5 units, at 37° from the horizontal.

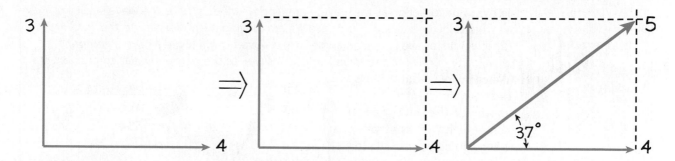

☑ **The resultant of two perpendicular vectors is the diagonal of a rectangle constructed with the two vectors as sides.** We learned this in Chapter 2. Here, the diagonal of the constructed rectangle measures 5 cm, which represents 100 km/h. So relative to the ground, the airplane moves 100 km/h northeasterly.[5.2.1]

In Figure 5.4 we see a 3-unit vector at right angles to a 4-unit vector. Can you see that they make up the sides of a rectangle, and when added vectorially they produce a resultant of magnitude of 5? (Note that $5^2 = 3^2 + 4^2$.)

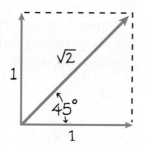

◄ FIGURE 5.5
The diagonal of a square is $\sqrt{2}$, or 1.414, times the length of one of its sides.

In the special case of adding a pair of equal-magnitude vectors that are at right angles to each other, we construct a square, as shown in Figure 5.5. For any square, the length of its diagonal is $\sqrt{2}$, or 1.414, times either of its sides. Thus, the resultant is $\sqrt{2}$ times either of the vectors. For instance, the resultant of two equal vectors of magnitude 100 acting at right angles to each other is 141.4.[5.2.2]

CONCEPT CHECK : What is the resultant of two perpendicular vectors?

think!

Suppose that an airplane normally flying at 80 km/h encounters wind at a right angle to its forward motion—a crosswind. Will the airplane fly faster or slower than 80 km/h?
Answer: 5.2

Surfing Surfing nicely illustrates component and resultant vectors. (1) When surfing in the same direction as the wave, our velocity is the same as the wave's velocity, $v_\perp$. This velocity is called $v_\perp$ because we are moving perpendicular to the wave front. (2) To go faster, we surf at an angle to the wave front. Now we have a component of velocity parallel to the wave front, $v_\parallel$, as well as the perpendicular component $v_\perp$.

We can vary $v_\parallel$, but $v_\perp$ stays relatively constant as long as we ride the wave. Adding components, we see that when surfing at an angle to the wave front, our resultant velocity, v_r, exceeds $v_\perp$. (3) As we increase our angle relative to the wave front, the resultant velocity also increases.

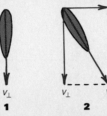

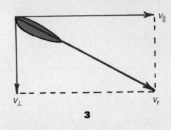

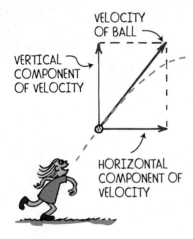

VELOCITY OF BALL

VERTICAL COMPONENT OF VELOCITY

HORIZONTAL COMPONENT OF VELOCITY

FIGURE 5.6 ▲

A ball's velocity can be resolved into horizontal and vertical components.

5.3 Components of Vectors

Often we will need to change a single vector into an equivalent set of two *component* vectors at right angles to each other. Any vector can be "resolved" into two component vectors at right angles to each other, as shown in Figure 5.6. Two vectors at right angles that add up to a given vector are known as the **components** of the given vector they replace. The process of determining the components of a vector is called **resolution.** Any vector drawn on a piece of paper can be resolved into vertical and horizontal components that are perpendicular. ⊘ **The perpendicular components of a vector are independent of each other.**

Vector resolution is illustrated in Figure 5.7. Vector *V* represents a vector quantity. First, vertical and horizontal lines are drawn from the tail of the vector (top). Second, a rectangle is drawn that encloses the vector *V* as its diagonal (bottom). The sides of this rectangle are the desired components, vectors *X* and *Y*.

CONCEPT CHECK How do components of a vector affect each other?

FIGURE 5.7 ▶

Vectors *X* and *Y* are the horizontal and vertical components of a vector *V*.

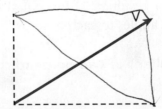

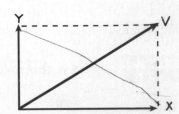

FIGURE 5.8 ▼
Projectile motion can be separated into components.

a. Roll a ball along a horizontal surface, and its velocity is constant because no component of gravitational force acts horizontally.

b. Drop it, and it accelerates downward and covers a greater vertical distance each second.

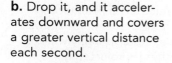

5.4 Projectile Motion

A cannonball shot from a cannon, a stone thrown into the air, a ball rolling off the edge of a table, a spacecraft circling Earth—all of these are examples of *projectiles*. A **projectile** is any object that moves through the air or space, acted on only by gravity (and air resistance, if any). Projectiles near the surface of Earth follow a curved path that at first seems rather complicated. However, these paths are surprisingly simple when we look at the horizontal and vertical components of motion separately.

   ⊘ **The horizontal component of motion for a projectile is just like the horizontal motion of a ball rolling freely along a level surface without friction.** When friction is negligible, a rolling ball moves at constant velocity. The ball covers equal distances in equal intervals of time as shown in Figure 5.8a. With no horizontal force acting on the ball there is no horizontal acceleration. The same is true for the projectile—when no horizontal force acts on the projectile, the horizontal component of velocity remains constant.

   ⊘ **The vertical component of a projectile's velocity is like the motion for a freely falling object.** Gravity acts vertically downward. Like a ball dropped in midair, a projectile accelerates downward as shown on the right in Figure 5.8b. Its vertical component of velocity changes with time. The increasing speed in the vertical direction causes a greater distance to be covered in each successive equal time interval. Or, if the ball is projected upward, the vertical distances of travel decrease with time on the way up.

   Most important, the horizontal component of motion for a projectile is completely independent of the vertical component of motion. Each component is independent of the other. Their combined effects produce the variety of curved paths that projectiles follow.

CONCEPT CHECK Describe the components of projectile motion.

FIGURE 5.9 ▶

A strobe-light photo of two balls released simultaneously from a mechanism that allows one ball to drop freely while the other is projected horizontally. Notice that in equal times both balls fall the same vertical distance.

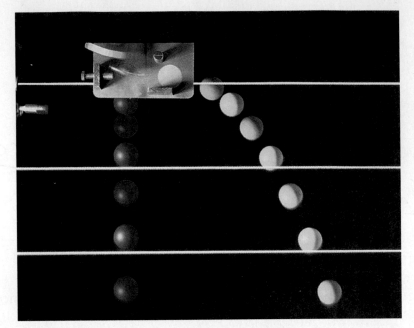

The curved path shown in Figure 5.9 is the combination of constant horizontal motion and vertical motion that undergoes acceleration due to gravity.

5.5 Projectiles Launched Horizontally

Projectile motion is nicely analyzed in the multiple-flash exposure in Figure 5.9. The photo shows equally timed successive positions for two balls. One ball is projected horizontally while the other is simply dropped. Study the photo carefully, for there's a lot of good physics here. Analyze the curved path of the ball by considering the horizontal and vertical velocity components separately. There are two important things to notice. The first is that the ball's horizontal component of motion remains constant. The ball moves the same horizontal distance in the equal time intervals between each flash, because no horizontal component of force is acting on it. Gravity acts only downward, so the only acceleration of the ball is downward. The second thing to note is that both balls fall the same vertical distance in the same time. The vertical distance fallen has nothing to do with the horizontal component of motion. ☑ **The downward motion of a horizontally launched projectile is the same as that of free fall.**

The path traced by a projectile accelerating only in the vertical direction while moving at constant horizontal velocity is a *parabola*. When air resistance is small enough to neglect—usually for slow-moving or very heavy projectiles—the curved paths are parabolic.

Toss a stone from a cliff and its path curves as it accelerates toward the ground below. Figure 5.10a shows how the trajectory is a combination of constant horizontal motion and accelerated vertical motion.

think!

At the instant a horizontally pointed cannon is fired, a cannonball held at the cannon's side is released and drops to the ground. Which cannonball strikes the ground first, the one fired from the cannon or the one dropped?
Answer: 5.5

CONCEPT CHECK : Describe the downward motion of a horizontally launched projectile.

discover!

Which Coin Hits the Ground First?

1. Place a coin at the edge of a table so that it hangs over slightly. Place a second coin on the table some distance from the first coin.

2. Slide the second coin so it hits the first one and both coins fall to the floor below. Which coin hits the ground first?

3. **Think** Does your answer depend on the speed of the coin? Explain.

5.6 Projectiles Launched at an Angle

In Figure 5.10, we see the paths of stones thrown horizontally and at angles upward and downward. The dashed straight lines show the ideal trajectories of the stones if there were no gravity. Notice that the vertical distance that the stone falls beneath the idealized straight-line paths is the same for equal times. This vertical distance is independent of what's happening horizontally.

A projectile's path is called its *trajectory*.

FIGURE 5.10 ▼
No matter the angle at which a projectile is launched, the vertical distance of fall beneath the idealized straight-line path is the same for equal times.

a. The trajectory of the stone combines horizontal motion with the pull of gravity.

b. The trajectory of the stone combines the upward motion with the pull of gravity.

c. The trajectory of the stone combines downward motion with the pull of gravity.

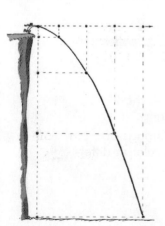

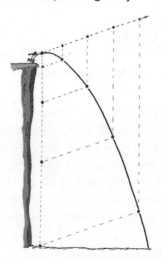

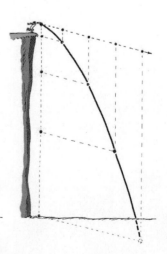

FIGURE 5.11 ▼

With no gravity, the projectile would follow the straight-line path (dashed line). But because of gravity, it falls beneath this line the same vertical distance it would fall if it were released from rest. Compare the distances fallen with those in Table 4.3.

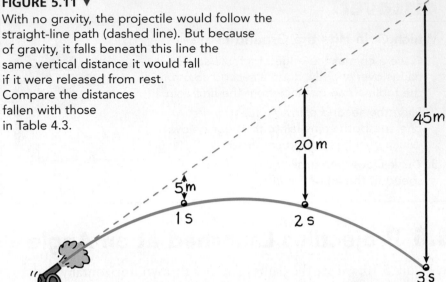

think!

A projectile is launched at an angle into the air. Neglecting air resistance, what is its vertical acceleration? Its horizontal acceleration?

Answer: 5.6.1

Figure 5.11 shows specific vertical distances for a cannonball shot at an upward angle. If there were no gravity, the cannonball would follow the straight-line path shown by the dashed line. But there is gravity, so this doesn't occur. What happens is that the cannonball continuously falls beneath the imaginary line until it finally strikes the ground. The vertical distance it falls *beneath any point on the dashed line* is the same vertical distance it would fall if it were dropped from rest and had been falling for the same amount of time. This distance, introduced in Chapter 4, is given by $d = \frac{1}{2}gt^2$, where t is the elapsed time. Using the value of 10 m/s² for g in the equation yields $d = 5t^2$ meters.

discover!

How Can You Model Projectile Motion?

1. Mark a ruler at five equal spaces. From the first mark, hang a bead on a 1-cm long string. At the next mark, hang a bead on a 4-cm long string.

2. Hang beads on the next three marks with strings of lengths 9 cm, 16 cm, and 25 cm. Hold the ruler at different angles and see where the beads hang.

3. **Think** Why is this model accurate?

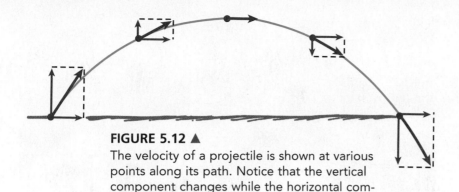

FIGURE 5.12 ▲
The velocity of a projectile is shown at various points along its path. Notice that the vertical component changes while the horizontal component does not. Air resistance is neglected.

Height We can put this another way. Toss a projectile skyward at some angle and pretend there is no gravity. After so many seconds t, it should be at a certain point along a straight-line path. But due to gravity, it isn't. Where is it? The answer is, it's directly below that point. How far below? The answer is $5t^2$ meters below that point. How about that? ☑ **The vertical distance a projectile falls below an imaginary straight-line path increases continually with time and is equal to $5t^2$ meters.**

Note also from Figure 5.11 that since there is no horizontal acceleration, the cannonball moves equal horizontal distances in equal time intervals. That's because there is no horizontal acceleration. The only acceleration is vertical, in the direction of Earth's gravity.

Figure 5.12 shows vectors representing both the horizontal and vertical components of velocity for a projectile on a parabolic path. Notice that the horizontal component is always the same and that only the vertical component changes. Note also that the actual resultant velocity vector is represented by the diagonal of the rectangle formed by the vector components. At the top of the path the vertical component shrinks to zero, so the velocity there *is* the same as the horizontal component of velocity at all other points. Everywhere else the magnitude of velocity is greater, just as the diagonal of a rectangle is greater than either of its sides.

Range Figure 5.13 shows the path traced by a projectile with the same launching speed but at a steeper angle. Notice that the initial velocity vector has a greater vertical component than when the projection angle is less. This greater component results in a higher path. However, since the horizontal component is less, the range is less.

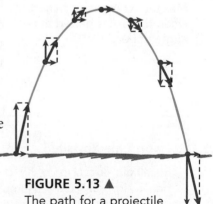

FIGURE 5.13 ▲
The path for a projectile fired at a steep angle. Again, air resistance is neglected.

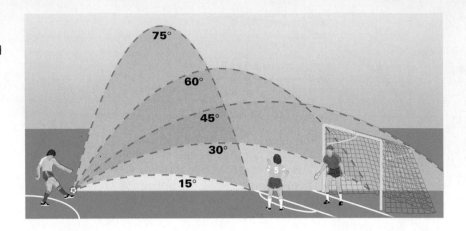

FIGURE 5.14 ▶

The paths of projectiles launched at the same speed but at different angles. The paths neglect air resistance.

FIGURE 5.15 ▲

Maximum range is attained when the ball is batted at an angle of nearly 45°.

Horizontal Ranges Figure 5.14 shows the paths of several projectiles all having the same initial speed but different projection angles. The figure neglects the effects of air resistance, so the paths are all parabolas. Notice that these projectiles reach different heights (altitude) above the ground. They also travel different horizontal distances, that is, they have different *horizontal ranges.*

The remarkable thing to note from Figure 5.14 is that the same range is obtained for two different projection angles—angles that add up to 90 degrees! For example, an object thrown into the air at an angle of 60 degrees will have the same range as if it were thrown at 30 degrees with the same speed. Of course, for the smaller angle the object remains in the air for a shorter time. Maximum range is usually attained at an angle of 45°. For a thrown javelin, on the other hand, maximum range is achieved for an angle quite a bit less than 45°, because the force of gravity on the relatively heavy javelin is significant during launch. Just as you can't throw a heavy rock as fast upward as sideways, so it is that the javelin's launch speed is reduced when thrown upward.

Physics of Sports

Hang Time Revisited

Recall our discussion of hang time in Chapter 4. We stated that the time one is airborne during a jump is independent of horizontal speed. Now we see why this is so—horizontal and vertical components of motion are independent of each other. The rules of projectile motion apply to jumping. Once the feet are off the ground, if we neglect air resistance, the only force acting on the jumper is gravity. Hang time depends only on the vertical component of liftoff velocity. It turns out that jumping force can be somewhat increased by the action of running, so hang time for a running jump usually exceeds that for a standing jump. However, once the feet are off the ground, only the vertical component of liftoff velocity determines hang time.

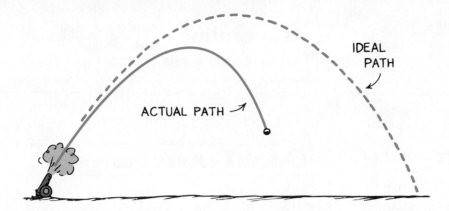

◀ **FIGURE 5.16**
In the presence of air resistance, the path of a high-speed projectile falls below the idealized parabola and follows the solid curve.

Speed We have emphasized the special case of projectile motion for negligible air resistance. As we can see in Figure 5.16, when the effect of air resistance is significant, the range of a projectile is diminished and the path is not a true parabola.

If air resistance is negligible, a projectile will rise to its maximum height in the same time it takes to fall from that height to the ground. This is due to the constant effect of gravity. The deceleration due to gravity going up is the same as the acceleration due to gravity coming down. The speed it loses going up is therefore the same as the speed it gains coming down, as shown in Figure 5.17. So the projectile hits the ground with the same speed it had originally when it was projected upward from the ground.

For short-range projectile motion such as a batted ball in a baseball game, we usually assume the ground is flat. However, for very long range projectiles the curvature of Earth's surface must be taken into account. We'll see that if an object is projected fast enough, it will fall all the way around Earth and become an Earth satellite! More about satellites in Chapter 14.

CONCEPT ⋮ Describe how far below an imaginary straight-line
CHECK ⋮ path a projectile falls.

think!

At what point in its path does a projectile have minimum speed?
Answer: 5.6.2

The longest time a jumper is airborne for a standing jump (hang time) is 1 second, for a record 1.25 meters (4 ft) height. Can anyone in your school jump that high, raising their center of gravity 1.25 meters above the ground? Not likely!

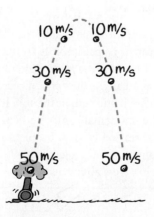

◀ **FIGURE 5.17**
Without air resistance, the speed lost while the cannonball is going up equals the speed gained while it is coming down. The time to go up equals the time to come down.

Go Online

PHSchool.com

For: Self-Assessment
Visit: PHSchool.com
Web Code: csa – 0500

Concept Summary ......

- A vector quantity includes both magnitude and direction, but a scalar quantity includes only magnitude.

- The resultant of two perpendicular vectors is the diagonal of a rectangle constructed with the two vectors as sides.

- The perpendicular components of a vector are independent of each other.

- The horizontal component of motion for a projectile is just like the horizontal motion of a ball rolling freely along a level surface without friction. The vertical component of a projectile's velocity is like the motion for a freely falling object.

- The downward motion of a horizontally launched projectile is the same as that of free fall.

- The vertical distance a projectile falls below an imaginary straight-line path increases continually with time and is equal to $5t^2$ meters.

Key Terms ......

components *(p. 72)*   **projectile** *(p. 73)*
resolution *(p. 72)*

think! Answers

5.2   A crosswind would increase the speed of the airplane and blow it off course by a predictable amount.

5.5   Both cannonballs fall the same vertical distance with the same acceleration g and therefore strike the ground at the same time. Do you see that this is consistent with our analysis of Figure 5.9? Ask which cannonball strikes the ground first when the cannon is pointed at an upward angle. In this case, the cannonball that is simply dropped hits the ground first. Now consider the case when the cannon is pointed downward. The fired cannonball hits first. So upward, the dropped cannonball hits first; downward, the fired cannonball hits first. There must be some angle where both hit at the same time. Do you see it would be when the cannon is pointing neither upward nor downward, that is, when it is pointing horizontally?

5.6.1   Its vertical acceleration is g because the force of gravity is downward. Its horizontal acceleration is zero because no horizontal force acts on it.

5.6.2   The minimum speed of a projectile occurs at the top of its path. If it is launched vertically, its speed at the top is zero. If it is projected at an angle, the vertical component of velocity is still zero at the top, leaving only the horizontal component. So the speed at the top is equal to the horizontal component of the projectile's velocity at any point. How about that?

ASSESS

Check Concepts • • • • • •

Section 5.1

1. How does a vector quantity differ from a scalar quantity?

2. Why is speed classified as a scalar quantity and velocity classified as a vector quantity?

Section 5.2

3. If a vector that is 1 cm long represents a velocity of 10 km/h, what velocity does a vector 2 cm long drawn to the same scale represent?

4. When a rectangle is constructed in order to add perpendicular velocities, what part of the rectangle represents the resultant vector?

Section 5.3

5. Will a vector at 45° to the horizontal be larger or smaller than its horizontal and vertical components? By how much?

Section 5.4

6. Why does a bowling ball move without acceleration when it rolls along a bowling alley?

7. In the absence of air resistance, why does the horizontal component of velocity for a projectile remain constant while the vertical component changes?

8. How does the downward component of the motion of a projectile compare with the motion of free fall?

Section 5.5

9. At the instant a ball is thrown horizontally over a level range, a ball held at the side of the first is released and drops to the ground. If air resistance is neglected, which ball strikes the ground first?

Section 5.6

10. **a.** How far below an initial straight-line path will a projectile fall in one second?

    b. Does your answer depend on the angle of launch or on the initial speed of the projectile? Defend your answer.

11. Neglecting air resistance, if you throw a ball straight up with a speed of 20 m/s, how fast will it be moving when you catch it?

12. **a.** Neglecting air resistance, if you throw a baseball at 20 m/s to your friend who is on first base, will the catching speed be greater than, equal to, or less than 20 m/s?

    b. Does the speed change if air resistance is a factor?

13. What do we call a projectile that continually "falls" around Earth?

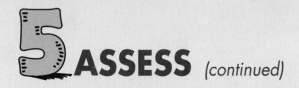
Think and Rank ......

Rank each of the following sets of scenarios in order of the quantity or property involved. List them from left to right. If scenarios have equal rankings, then separate them with an equal sign. (e.g., A = B)

14. The vectors represent initial velocities of projectiles launched at ground level.

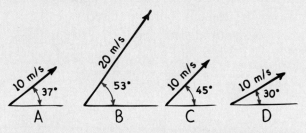

  a. Rank them by their vertical components of velocity from greatest to least.
  b. Rank them by their horizontal components of velocity from greatest to least.

15. A toy car rolls off tables of various heights at different speeds as shown.

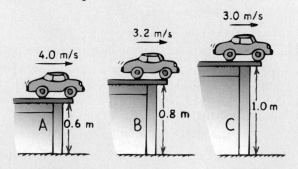

  a. Rank them for the time in the air, from greatest to least.
  b. Rank them for horizontal range, from greatest to least.

16. Water balloons of different masses are launched by slingshots at different launching velocities *v*. All have the same vertical component of launching velocities.

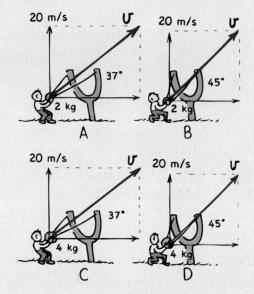

  a. Rank by the *time* in the air, from longest to shortest.
  b. Rank by the maximum *height* reached, from highest to lowest.
  c. Rank by the maximum *range*, from greatest to least.

17. The airplane is blown off course by wind in the directions shown. Use the parallelogram rule and rank from highest to lowest the resulting speed across the ground.

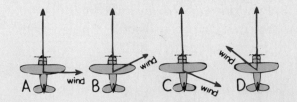

Plug and Chug ••••••

For Questions 18–19, recall that when two vectors in the same or exactly opposite directions are added, the magnitude of their resultant is the sum or difference of their original magnitudes.

18. Calculate the resultant velocity of an airplane that normally flies at 200 km/h if it encounters a 50-km/h tailwind. If it encounters a 50-km/h headwind.

19. Calculate the magnitude of the resultant of a pair of 100-km/h velocity vectors that are at right angles to each other.

For Questions 20–21, recall that the resultant V of two vectors A and B at right angles to each other is found using the Pythagorean theorem:

$$V = \sqrt{A^2 + B^2}$$

20. Calculate the resulting speed of an airplane with an airspeed of 120 km/h pointing due north when it encounters a wind of 90 km/h directed from the west. (Recall, speed is the magnitude of velocity.)

21. Calculate the speed of raindrops hitting your face when they fall vertically at 3 m/s while you're running horizontally at 4 m/s.

Think and Explain ••••••

22. Whenever you add 3 and 4, the result is 7. This is true if the quantities being added are scalar quantities. If 3 and 4 are the magnitudes of vector quantities, when will the magnitude of their sum be 5?

23. Christopher can paddle a canoe in still water at 8 km/h. How successful will he be at canoeing upstream in a river that flows at 8 km/h?

24. How does the vertical distance a projectile falls below an otherwise straight-line path compare with the vertical distance it would fall from rest in the same time?

25. The speed of falling rain is the same 10 m above ground as it is just before it hits the ground. What does this tell you about whether or not the rain encounters air resistance?

26. Marshall says that when a pair of vectors are at right angles to each other, the magnitude of their resultant is greater than the magnitude of either vector alone. Renee says he is speaking in generalities and that what he says isn't always true. With whom do you agree?

27. How is the horizontal component of velocity for a projectile affected by the vertical component?

28. Rain falling vertically will make vertical streaks on a car's side window. However, if the car is moving, the streaks are slanted. If the streaks from a vertically falling rain make 45° streaks, how fast is the car moving compared with the speed of the falling rain?

29. An airplane encounters a wind that blows in a perpendicular direction to the direction its nose is pointing. Does the effect of this wind increase or decrease speed across the ground below? Or does it have no effect on ground speed?

30. A projectile is launched vertically at 50 m/s. If air resistance can be neglected, at what speed will it return to its initial level? Where in its trajectory will it have minimum speed?

31. A batted baseball follows a parabolic path on a day when the sun is directly overhead. How does the speed of the ball's shadow across the field compare with the ball's horizontal component of velocity?

32. When air resistance acts on a projectile, does it affect the horizontal component of velocity, the vertical component of velocity, or both? Defend your answer.

33. You're driving behind a car and wish to pass, so you turn to the left and pull into the passing lane without changing speed. Why does the distance increase between you and the car you're following?

34. Brandon launches a projectile at an angle of 75° above the horizontal, which strikes the ground a certain distance down range. For what other angle of launch at the same speed would the projectile land just as far away?

35. When you jump up, your hang time is the time your feet are off the ground. Does hang time depend on your vertical component of velocity when you jump, your horizontal component of velocity, or both? Defend your answer.

36. The hang time of a basketball player who jumps a vertical distance of 2 feet (0.6 m) is 2/3 second. What will be the hang time if the player reaches the same height while jumping a horizontal distance of 4 feet (1.2 m)?

Think and Solve ......

37. Sneezlee flies at a speed of 10 m/s in still air.

a. If he flies into a 2-m/s headwind, how fast will he be traveling relative to the ground below?

b. Relative to the ground below, how fast will he travel when he experiences a 2-m/s tailwind?

c. While flying at 10 m/s, suppose that he encounters a 10-m/s cross wind (coming at a right angle to his heading). What is his speed relative to the ground below?

38. A boat is rowed at 8 km/h directly across a river that flows at 6 km/h, as shown in the figure.

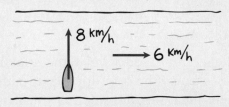

a. What is the resultant speed of the boat?

b. How fast and in what direction can the boat be rowed to reach a destination directly across the river?

39. If a 14-unit vector makes an angle of 45° with the horizontal, what are its horizontal and vertical components?

40. Harry accidentally falls out of a helicopter that is traveling at 15 m/s. He plunges into a swimming pool 2 seconds later. Assuming no air resistance, what was the horizontal distance between Harry and the swimming pool when he fell from the helicopter?

41. Refer to the previous problem.

 a. What are the horizontal and vertical components of Harry's velocity just as he hits the water?
 b. Show that Harry hits the water at a speed of 25 m/s.

42. Harry and Angela look from their balcony to a swimming pool below that is 15 m from the bottom of their building. They estimate the balcony is 45 m high and wonder how fast they would have to jump horizontally to succeed in reaching the pool. What is your answer?

43. A girl throws a slingshot pellet directly at a target that is far enough away to take one-half second to reach. How far below the target does the pellet hit? How high above the target should she aim?

44. The boy on the tower in the figure below throws a ball a distance of 60 m, as shown. At what speed, in m/s, is the ball thrown?

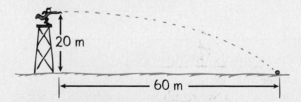

45. A cannonball launched with an initial velocity of 141 m/s at an angle of 45° follows a parabolic path and hits a balloon at the top of its trajectory. Neglecting air resistance, how fast is it going when it hits the balloon? What is the acceleration of the cannonball just before it hits the balloon?

46. Joshua throws a stone horizontally from a cliff at a speed of 20 m/s, which strikes the ground 2.0 seconds later.

 a. Use your knowledge of vectors and show that the stone strikes the ground at a speed of about 28 m/s.
 b. At what angle does the ball strike the ground?

47. On a bowling alley, Isabella rolls a bowling ball that covers a distance of 10 meters in 1 second. The speed of the ball is 10 m/s. If the ball were instead dropped from rest off the edge of a building, what would be its speed at the end of 1 second?

48. A bowling ball is moving at 10 m/s when it rolls off the edge of a tall building. What is the ball's speed one second later? (*Hint:* think vectors!)

49. Calculate Hotshot Harry's hang time if he moves horizontally 3 m during a 1.25-m high jump. What is his hang time if he moves 6 m horizontally during this jump?

50. Megan rolls a ball across a lab bench y meters high and the ball rolls off the edge of the bench with horizontal speed v.

 a. From the equation $y = \frac{1}{2}gt^2$, which gives the vertical distance y an object falls from rest, derive an equation that shows the time t taken for the ball to reach the floor.
 b. Write an equation showing how far the ball will land from a point on the floor directly below the edge of the bench.
 c. Calculate the time in the air and the landing location for $v = 1.5$ m/s and a bench height of 1.2 m.

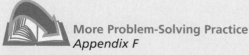

More Problem-Solving Practice
Appendix F

6 NEWTON'S SECOND LAW OF MOTION—FORCE AND ACCELERATION

 **THE BIG IDEA** : An object accelerates when a net force acts on it.

In Chapter 2, we discussed the concept of mechanical equilibrium, $\Sigma F = 0$, which means that forces are balanced. In Chapter 3, we extended this idea to the law of inertia, again with balanced forces. In this chapter we consider what happens when forces aren't balanced—when the net force is *not* zero—when an object is not in equilibrium. The net force on a kicked football, for example, is greater than zero, and the ball accelerates. Its path through the air is not a straight line but curves downward due to gravity—again an acceleration. Most of the motion we see undergoes change. This chapter covers *changes* in motion—accelerated motion.

We learned that acceleration describes how quickly velocity changes. Specifically, it is the change in velocity per unit of time. Recall the definition of acceleration:

$$\text{acceleration} = \frac{\text{change in velocity}}{\text{time interval}}$$

We will now focus on the *cause* of acceleration: *force*.

---

discover!

What Effect Does Air Resistance Have on Falling Objects?

1. Use a stopwatch to determine the time required for a single coffee filter to fall one meter.
2. Determine the time required for four coffee filters nested inside one another to fall two meters.
3. Determine the time required for nine nested filters to fall a distance of three meters.
4. If possible, measure the time of fall for sixteen nested filters dropped from a height of four meters.

Analyze and Conclude

1. **Observing** What did you observe about the motion of a single filter as it fell? Did it appear to accelerate or did it move with a constant velocity? How did the time of fall compare for each of the four trials?
2. **Predicting** How long do you think it would take for twenty-five nested coffee filters to fall through a distance of five meters?
3. **Making Generalizations** What determines the speed of similarly shaped objects falling under the influence of gravity and air resistance?

6.1 Force Causes Acceleration

Consider an object at rest, such as a hockey puck on perfectly smooth ice. The forces on it (gravity and the support force) are balanced, so the puck is in equilibrium. Hit the puck (that is, apply an unbalanced force to it) and the puck experiences a change in motion—it accelerates. When the hockey stick is no longer pushing it, there are no unbalanced forces and the puck moves at constant velocity. Apply another force by striking the puck again, and the puck's motion changes again. ⊘ **Unbalanced forces acting on an object cause the object to accelerate.**

Most often, the force we apply is not the only force acting on an object. For example, after the boy kicks the football in Figure 6.1, both gravity and air resistance act on the football. Recall from the previous chapter that the combination of forces acting on an object is the *net force*. Acceleration depends on the *net force*. To increase the acceleration of an object, you must increase the net force acting on it. Double the force on an object and its acceleration doubles. If you triple the force, its acceleration triples. We say an object's acceleration is directly proportional to the net force acting on it. We write

$$\text{acceleration} \sim \text{net force}$$

The symbol ~ stands for "is directly proportional to."

CONCEPT CHECK What causes an object to accelerate?

FIGURE 6.1 ▲
Kick a football and it neither remains at rest nor moves in a straight line.

6.2 Mass Resists Acceleration

Push on an empty shopping cart. Then push equally hard on a heavily loaded shopping cart, as shown in Figure 6.2. The loaded shopping cart will accelerate much less than the empty cart. Acceleration depends on the mass being pushed. ⊘ **For a constant force, an increase in the mass will result in a decrease in the acceleration.** The same force applied to twice as much mass results in only half the acceleration. For three times the mass, one-third the acceleration results. In other words, for a given force, the acceleration produced is *inversely proportional* to the mass. This relationship can be written as an equation:

$$\text{acceleration} \sim \frac{1}{\text{mass}}$$

Inversely means that the two values change in opposite directions. Mathematically we see that as the denominator increases, the whole quantity decreases by the same factor.

CONCEPT CHECK How does an increase in mass affect acceleration?

FIGURE 6.2 ▲
The acceleration produced depends on the mass that is pushed.

Here's directly proportional.

Here's inversely proportional.

6.3 Newton's Second Law

Newton was the first to realize that the acceleration produced when we move something depends not only on how hard we push or pull, but also on the object's mass. He came up with one of the most important rules of nature ever proposed, his second law of motion. **Newton's second law** describes the relationship among an object's mass, an object's acceleration, and the net force on an object.

⊘ **Newton's second law states that the acceleration produced by a net force on an object is directly proportional to the magnitude of the net force, is in the same direction as the net force, and is inversely proportional to the mass of the object.**

This relationship can be written as an equation:

$$\text{acceleration} \sim \frac{\text{net force}}{\text{mass}}$$

By using consistent units, such as newtons (N) for force, kilograms (kg) for mass, and meters per second squared (m/s^2) for acceleration, we get the exact equation

$$\text{acceleration} = \frac{\text{net force}}{\text{mass}}$$

In briefest form, where a is acceleration, F is net force, and m is mass,

$$a = \frac{F}{m}$$

The acceleration is equal to the net force divided by the mass. From this relationship we see that doubling the net force acting on an object doubles its acceleration. Suppose instead that the mass is doubled. Then acceleration will be halved. If both the net force and the mass are doubled, the acceleration will be unchanged.

CONCEPT CHECK: What is the relationship among an object's mass, an object's acceleration, and the net force on an object?

---

discover!

Acceleration, Which Way?

1. Pull a spool of thread horizontally to the right by the thread. The thread should be at the bottom of the spool. Which direction does the spool roll?

2. Repeat step one with the thread at the top of the spool. Which direction does the spool roll?

3. Are the net force on an object and an object's acceleration always in the same direction? Why?

FIGURE 6.3 ▲
The great acceleration of the racing car is due
to its ability to produce large forces.

think!

If a car can accelerate at
2 m/s², what acceleration
can it attain if it is tow-
ing another car of equal
mass?
Answer: 6.3

do the math!

**A car has a mass of 1000 kg. What is the
acceleration produced by a force of 2000 N?**

You can use Newton's second law to solve for
the car's acceleration.

$$a = \frac{F}{m} = \frac{2000 \text{ N}}{1000 \text{ kg}} = \frac{2000 \text{ kg·m/s}^2}{1000 \text{ kg}} = 2 \text{ m/s}^2$$

**If the force is 4000 N, what is the
acceleration?**

$$a = \frac{F}{m} = \frac{4000 \text{ N}}{1000 \text{ kg}} = \frac{4000 \text{ kg·m/s}^2}{1000 \text{ kg}} = 4 \text{ m/s}^2$$

Doubling the force on the same mass simply
doubles the acceleration.

Physics problems are often more complicated
than these. We don't focus on solving complicated problems in this book. Instead we emphasize equations as guides to thinking about the
relationships of basic physics concepts. The Plug
and Chug problems at the ends of many chapters familiarize you with equations, and the Think
and Solve problems go a step or two further for
more challenge. Solving problems is an important skill in physics. But first, learn the concepts!
Then problem solving will be more meaningful.

**How much force, or thrust, must a 30,000-kg
jet plane develop to achieve an acceleration
of 1.5 m/s²?**

If you know the mass of an object in kilograms
(kg) and its acceleration in meters per second
(m/s²), then the force will be expressed in newtons (N). One newton is the force needed to
give a mass of one kilogram an acceleration of
one meter per second squared. You can arrange
Newton's second law to read

$$\text{force} = \text{mass} \times \text{acceleration}$$
$$F = ma$$
$$= (30{,}000 \text{ kg})(1.5 \text{ m/s}^2)$$
$$= 45{,}000 \text{ kg·m/s}^2$$
$$= 45{,}000 \text{ N}$$

The dot between kg and m/s² means that the
units are multiplied together.

FIGURE 6.4 ▲
A concrete road divider has a better design than a steel road divider for slowing an out-of-control, sideswiping car.

think!

Two forces act on a book resting on a table: its weight and the support force from the table. Does a force of friction act as well?
Answer: 6.4

6.4 Friction

Friction is a force like any other force and affects motion. Friction acts on materials that are in contact with each other, and it always acts in a direction to oppose relative motion. When two solid objects come into contact, the friction is mainly due to irregularities in the two surfaces. When one object slides against another, it must either rise over the irregular bumps or else scrape them off. Either way requires force.

⊘ **The force of friction between the surfaces depends on the kinds of material in contact and how much the surfaces are pressed together.** For example, rubber against concrete produces more friction than steel against steel. That's why concrete road dividers have replaced steel rails. The friction produced by a tire rubbing against the concrete is more effective in slowing the car than the friction produced by a steel car body sliding against a steel rail. Notice in Figure 6.4 that the concrete divider is wider at the bottom to ensure that the tire of a sideswiping car will make contact with the divider before the steel car body does.

Friction is not restricted to solids sliding or tending to slide over one another. Friction also occurs in liquids and gases. Both liquids and gases are called **fluids** because they flow. Fluid friction occurs as an object pushes aside the fluid it is moving through. Have you ever tried running a 100-m dash through waist-deep water? The friction of liquids is appreciable, even at low speeds. **Air resistance** is the friction acting on something moving through air. Air resistance is a very common form of fluid friction. You usually don't notice air resistance when walking or jogging, but you do notice it at the higher speeds that occur when riding a bicycle or skiing downhill.

Link to TECHNOLOGY

Automobile Design The first automobiles were little more than horse carriages with engines. Over time, engineers came to realize that by reducing the frontal surface of cars and eliminating parts that stick out, the air resistance force on a car could be reduced. When a car cruises at a constant speed, the net force on the car is zero. By lowering the air resistance force at any speed, the amount of force needed by the engine is reduced, meaning better fuel economy. Over the years, cars have gotten sleeker, with teardrop-shaped bodies, and teardrop shapes around side mirrors. Door handles are set into the doors. Even wheel wells and the undersides of cars have been smoothed. Automotive engineers use computers to design cars with less air resistance and use wind tunnels to measure the cars' air resistance.

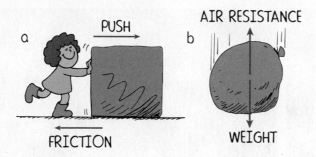

a PUSH

FRICTION

b AIR RESISTANCE

WEIGHT

◀ FIGURE 6.5
The direction of the force of friction always opposes the direction of motion. **a.** Push the crate to the right and friction acts toward the left. **b.** The sack falls downward and air friction acts upward.

When friction is present, an object may move with a constant velocity even when an outside force is applied to it. In such a case, the friction force just balances the applied force. The net force is zero, so there is no acceleration. For example, in Figure 6.5 the crate moves with a constant velocity when the force pushing it just balances the force of friction. The sack will also fall with a constant velocity once the force due to air resistance balances the sack's weight. A diagram showing all the forces acting on an object is called a **free-body diagram.**

CONCEPT CHECK : What factors affect the force of friction between surfaces?

6.5 Applying Force—Pressure

Look at Figure 6.6. No matter how you place a book on a table, the force of the book on the table is the same. You can check this by placing a book in any position on a bathroom scale. You'll read the same weight in all cases. Balance a book in different positions on the palm of your hand. Although the force is always the same, you'll notice differences in the way the book presses against your palm. These differences are due to differences in the area of contact for each case. ✅ **For a constant force, an increase in the area of contact will result in a decrease in the pressure.** The amount of force *per unit of area* is called **pressure.** More precisely, when the force is perpendicular to the surface area,

$$\text{pressure} = \frac{\text{force}}{\text{area of application}}$$

In equation form,

$$P = \frac{F}{A}$$

where P is the pressure and A is the area over which the force acts. Force, which is measured in newtons, is different from pressure. Pressure is measured in newtons per square meter, or **pascals** (Pa). One newton per square meter is equal to one pascal.

FIGURE 6.6 ▲
The upright book exerts the same force, but greater pressure, against the supporting surface.

think!

In attempting to do the demonstration shown in Figure 6.7, would it be wise to begin with a few nails and work upward to more nails?
Answer: 6.5

You exert more pressure against the ground when you stand on one foot than when you stand on both feet. This is due to the decreased area of contact. Stand on one toe like a ballerina and the pressure is huge. The smaller the area supporting a given force, the greater the pressure on that surface.

You can calculate the pressure you exert on the ground when you are standing. One way is to moisten the bottom of your foot with water and step on a clean sheet of graph paper. Count the number of squares on the graph paper contained within your footprint. Divide your weight by this area and you have the average pressure you exert on the ground when standing on one foot. How will this pressure compare with the pressure you exert when you stand on two feet?

A dramatic illustration of pressure is shown in Figure 6.7. The author applies appreciable force when he breaks the cement block with the sledgehammer. Yet his friend (the author of the lab manual) sandwiched between two beds of sharp nails is unharmed. The friend is unharmed because much of the force is distributed over the more than 200 nails that make contact with his body. The combined surface area of this many nails results in a tolerable pressure that does not puncture the skin. **CAUTION:** *This demonstration is quite dangerous. Do not attempt it on your own.*

CONCEPT CHECK : How does the area of contact affect the pressure a force exerts on an object?

6.6 Free Fall Explained

Recall that free fall occurs when a falling object encounters no air resistance. Also recall that Galileo showed that falling objects accelerate equally, regardless of their masses. This is *strictly* true if air resistance is negligible, that is, if the objects are in free fall. It is *approximately* true when air resistance is very small compared with the mass of the falling object. For example, a 10-kg cannonball and a 1-kg stone dropped

◀ FIGURE 6.8
In Galileo's famous demonstration, a 10-kg cannonball and a 1-kg stone strike the ground at practically the same time.

from an elevated position at the same time will fall together and strike the ground at practically the same time. This experiment, said to be done by Galileo from the Leaning Tower of Pisa and shown in Figure 6.8, demolished the Aristotelian idea that an object that weighs ten times as much as another should fall ten times faster than the lighter object. Galileo's experiment and many others that showed the same result were convincing. But Galileo couldn't say *why* the accelerations were equal. The explanation is a straightforward application of Newton's second law and is the topic of the cartoon "Backyard Physics." Let's treat it separately here.

Recall that mass (a quantity of matter) and weight (the force due to gravity) are proportional. A 2-kg bag of nails weighs twice as much as a 1-kg bag of nails. So a 10-kg cannonball experiences 10 times as much gravitational force (weight) as a 1-kg stone. The followers of Aristotle believed that the cannonball should accelerate at a rate ten times that of the stone, because they considered only the cannonball's ten-times-greater weight. However, Newton's second law tells us to consider the mass as well. A little thought will show that ten times as much force acting on ten times as much mass produces the same acceleration as the smaller force acting on the smaller mass. In symbolic notation,

Remember that only a single force acts on something in free fall— the force due to gravity.

$$\frac{F}{m} = \frac{F}{m}$$

where F stands for the force (weight) acting on the cannonball, and m stands for the correspondingly large mass of the cannonball. The small F and m stand for the smaller weight and smaller mass of the stone. As Figure 6.9 shows, the *ratio* of weight to mass is the same for these or any objects. All freely falling objects undergo the same acceleration at the same place on Earth. In Chapter 4 we introduced the symbol g for the acceleration.

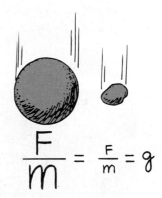

$$\frac{F}{m} = \frac{F}{m} = g$$

FIGURE 6.9 ▲
The ratio of weight (F) to mass (m) is the same for the 10-kg cannonball and the 1-kg stone.

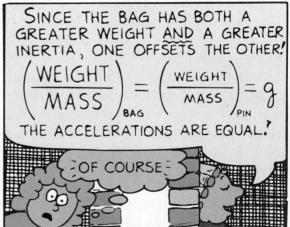

We can show the same result with numerical values. The weight of a 1-kg stone is 10 N at Earth's surface. The weight of a 10-kg cannonball is 100 N at Earth's surface. The force acting on a falling object is the force due to gravity—the object's weight. Using Newton's second law, the acceleration of the stone is

$$a = \frac{F}{m} = \frac{weight}{m} = \frac{10 \text{ N}}{1 \text{ kg}} = \frac{10 \text{ kg·m/s}^2}{1 \text{ kg}} = 10 \text{ m/s}^2 = g$$

and the acceleration of the cannonball is

$$a = \frac{F}{m} = \frac{weight}{m} = \frac{100 \text{ N}}{10 \text{ kg}} = \frac{100 \text{ kg·m/s}^2}{10 \text{ kg}} = 10 \text{ m/s}^2 = g$$

In the famous coin-and-feather-in-a-vacuum-tube demonstration discussed in Chapter 4, the reason for the equal accelerations was not discussed. Now we know why the acceleration of the coin and the feather are the same. ☑ **All freely falling objects fall with the same acceleration because the net force on an object is only its weight, and the ratio of weight to mass is the same for all objects.**

CONCEPT CHECK: Why do all freely falling objects fall with the same acceleration?

When the forces of gravity and air resistance act on a falling object, it is *not* in free fall.

6.7 Falling and Air Resistance

The feather and coin fall with equal accelerations in a vacuum, but very unequally in the presence of air. When falling in air, the coin falls quickly while the feather flutters to the ground. The force due to air resistance diminishes the net force acting on the falling objects.

Speed and Area The force due to air resistance is experienced when you stick your hand out of the window of a moving car. If the car moves faster, the force on your hand increases, indicating that air resistance force depends on speed. If instead of just your hand, you hold your physics book out the window with the large side facing forward, exposing maximum frontal area for the book, the air resistance force is much larger than it was on your hand at the same speed. You find that the force of air resistance is also proportional to the frontal area of the moving object. ☑ **The air resistance force an object experiences depends on the object's speed and area.** An expression describes the relationship between speed, area, and air resistance:

$$\text{Air resistance force} \sim \text{speed} \times \text{frontal area}$$

The expression shows that the air resistance force is directly proportional to the speed and frontal area of an object.

Go Online

SciLINKS NSTA

For: Links on Air-Resistance
Visit: www.SciLinks.org
Web Code: csn – 0607

think!

Which experiences a greater air resistance force, a falling piece of paper or a falling elephant?
Answer: 6.7.1

It's important to emphasize that zero acceleration does not mean zero velocity. Zero acceleration means that the object will maintain the velocity it happens to have, neither speeding up nor slowing down nor changing direction.

Terminal Speed When the air resistance force on a falling object, like the sky divers shown in Figure 6.10, builds up to the point where it equals the weight of the object, then the net force on the object is zero and the object stops accelerating. We say that the object has reached its terminal speed. **Terminal speed** is the speed at which the acceleration of a falling object is zero because friction balances the weight. If we are concerned with direction, which is down for falling objects, we say it has reached its terminal velocity. **Terminal velocity** is terminal speed together with the direction of motion.

A falling feather reaches its terminal speed quite quickly. Its area is large relative to its very small weight. Even at small speeds the air resistance has a large effect on the feather's motion. A coin, however, has a relatively small area compared to its weight, so the coin will have to fall faster than a feather to reach its terminal speed.

The terminal speed for a sky diver varies from about 150 to 200 km/h, depending on the weight and orientation of the body. A heavier person will attain a greater terminal speed than a lighter person. The greater weight is more effective in "plowing through" air. Body orientation also makes a difference. More air is encountered when the body is spread out and surface area is increased, like that of the flying squirrel in Figure 6.11.

FIGURE 6.11 ▲
The flying squirrel increases its area by spreading out. This increases air resistance and decreases the speed of its fall.

Link to LIFE SCIENCE

Terminal Velocity Skydivers and flying squirrels are not alone in increasing their surface areas when falling. When the paradise tree snake (Chysopelea paradisi) jumps from a tree branch it doubles its width by flattening itself. It acquires a slightly concave shape and maneuvers itself by undulating in a graceful S-shape, traveling more than 20 meters in a single leap.

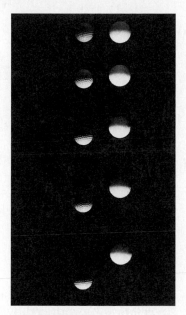

FIGURE 6.12 ▲
This stroboscopic photo shows a golf ball and a foam ball falling in air. The heavier golf ball is more effective in overcoming air resistance, so its acceleration is greater.

Terminal speed can be controlled by variations in body orientation. A heavy sky diver and a light sky diver can remain in close proximity to each other if the heavy person spreads out like a flying squirrel while the light person falls head or feet first. A parachute greatly increases air resistance, and cuts the terminal speed down to 15 to 25 km/h, slow enough for a safe landing.

If you hold a baseball and tennis ball at arm's length and release them at the same time, you'll see them strike the floor at the same time. But if you drop them from the top of a building, you'll notice the heavier baseball strikes the ground first. This is due to the buildup of air resistance at higher speeds. At low speeds, air resistance is often negligible, but at high speeds, it can make quite a difference. The effect of air resistance is more pronounced on the lighter tennis ball than on the heavier baseball, so the acceleration of the fall is less for the tennis ball. The tennis ball behaves more like a parachute than the baseball does. Figure 6.12 shows that a golf ball has a greater acceleration falling in air than a foam ball.

When Galileo reportedly dropped the objects of different weights from the Leaning Tower of Pisa, the heavier object *did* get to the ground first. However, the time difference was only a split second, rather than the pronounced time difference expected by the followers of Aristotle. The behavior of falling objects was never really understood until Newton announced his second law of motion.

Isaac Newton truly changed our way of seeing the world by showing how concepts connect to one another. The connection between acceleration, force, and mass, discovered by Newton in the 1600s, led to men landing on the moon in the 1900s. Newton's second law was primarily responsible for this feat.

CONCEPT CHECK : What factors determine the air resistance force on an object?

think!

If a heavy person and a light person open their parachutes together at the same altitude and each wears the same size parachute, who will reach the ground first?
Answer: 6.7.2

6 REVIEW

Concept Summary ······

- Unbalanced forces acting on an object cause the object to accelerate.

- For a constant force, an increase in the mass will result in a decrease in the acceleration.

- Newton's second law states that the acceleration produced by a net force on an object is directly proportional to the magnitude of the net force, is in the same direction as the net force, and is inversely proportional to the mass of the object.

- The force of friction between two surfaces depends on the kinds of material in contact and how much the surfaces are pressed together.

- For a constant force, an increase in the area of contact will result in a decrease in the pressure.

- All freely falling objects fall with the same acceleration because the net force on an object is only its weight, and the ratio of weight to mass is the same for all objects.

- The air resistance force on an object depends on the object's speed and area.

Key Terms ······

inversely (p. 87)

Newton's
  second law (p. 88)

fluid (p. 90)

air resistance (p. 90)

free-body diagram (p. 91)

pressure (p. 91)

pascal (p. 91)

terminal speed
  (p. 96)

terminal velocity
  (p. 96)

think! Answers

6.3 The same force on twice the mass produces half the acceleration, or 1 m/s².

6.4 No, not unless the book tends to slide or does slide across the table. For example, if it is pushed toward the left by another force, then friction between the book and table will act toward the right. Friction forces occur only when an object tends to slide or is sliding. (More about this in the Concept-Development Practice Book.)

6.5 No, no, no! There would be one less physics teacher if the demonstration were performed with fewer nails. The resulting greater pressure would cause harm.

6.7.1 The elephant! It has a greater frontal area and falls faster than a piece of paper—both of which mean the elephant pushes more air molecules out of the way. The effect of the air resistance force on each, however, is another story!

6.7.2 The heavy person will reach the ground first. Like a feather, the light person reaches terminal speed sooner, while the heavy person continues to accelerate until a greater terminal speed is reached. The heavy person moves ahead of the light person, and the separation continues to increase as they descend.

Check Concepts ● ● ● ● ● ●

Section 6.1

1. What produces acceleration?

2. In Chapter 4 we defined acceleration as the time rate of change of velocity. What other equation for acceleration is given in this chapter?

Section 6.2

3. Is acceleration directly proportional to mass, or is it inversely proportional to mass?

4. If two quantities are inversely proportional to each other, does that mean as one increases the other increases also?

Section 6.3

5. If the net force acting on a sliding block is tripled, what happens to the acceleration?

6. If the mass of a sliding block is tripled at the same time the net force on it is tripled, how does the resulting acceleration compare with the original acceleration?

Section 6.4

7. Motion is affected by solid objects in contact. In what other situations does friction affect motion?

8. Suppose you exert a horizontal push on a crate that rests on a level floor, and it doesn't move. How much friction acts compared with your push?

9. How great is the air resistance that acts on a 10-N sack that falls in air at constant velocity?

Section 6.5

10. Distinguish between force and pressure.

11. When do you produce more pressure on the ground, standing or lying down?

12. Why is it important that many nails are in the boards of Figure 6.7?

Section 6.6

13. What is meant by *free fall*?

14. The ratio of circumference/diameter for all circles is π. What is the ratio of force/mass for all freely-falling bodies?

15. Why doesn't a heavy object accelerate more than a light object when both are freely falling?

6 ASSESS (continued)

Section 6.7

16. Does air resistance on a falling object increase or does it decrease with increasing speed?

17. If two objects of the same size fall through air at different speeds, which encounters the greater air resistance?

18. What is the acceleration of a falling object that has reached its terminal velocity?

19. What, besides speed, affects the air resistance on a skydiver?

20. How much air resistance acts on a falling 100-N box of nails when it reaches terminal velocity?

Think and Rank ······

Rank each of the following sets of scenarios in order of the quantity or property involved. List them from left to right. If scenarios have equal rankings, then separate them with an equal sign. (e.g., A = B)

21. Each diagram shows a ball traveling from left to right. The position of the ball each second is indicated by the second. Rank the net forces from greatest to least required to produce the motion indicated in each diagram. Right is positive and left is negative.

22. Boxes of various masses are on a friction-free level table.

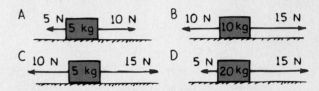

Rank each of the following from greatest to least.
a. the net forces on the boxes
b. the accelerations of the boxes

23. Each block on the friction-free lab bench is connected by a string and pulled by a second falling block.

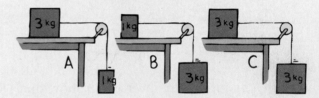

Rank each of the following from greatest to least.
a. the acceleration of the two-block systems
b. the tension in the strings

24. All the aluminum blocks have the same mass and are gently lowered onto a gelatin surface, which easily supports them. All have square bottom surfaces. Rank them by how much they dent into the surface, from greatest to least depth.

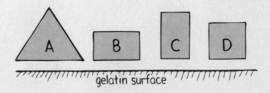

100

Plug and Chug ......

These questions are to familiarize you with the key equations of the chapter.

$$\text{Acceleration} = \frac{\text{net force}}{\text{mass}}$$

$$a = \frac{F}{m}$$

25. Calculate the acceleration of a 40-kg crate of softball gear when pulled sideways with a net force of 200 N.

26. Calculate the acceleration of a 2000-kg, single-engine airplane as it begins its takeoff with an engine thrust of 500 N.

27. Calculate the acceleration of a 300,000-kg jumbo jet just before takeoff when the thrust for each of its four engines is 30,000 N.

28. Calculate the acceleration if you push with a 20-N horizontal force against a 2-kg block on a horizontal friction-free air table.

$$F = ma$$

29. Calculate the horizontal force that must be applied to a 1-kg puck to make it accelerate on a horizontal friction-free air table with the same acceleration it would have if it were dropped and fell freely.

30. Calculate the horizontal force that must be applied to produce an acceleration of 1.8g for a 1.2-kg puck on a horizontal friction-free air table.

Think and Explain ......

31. If you push horizontally on your book with a force of 1 N to make the book slide at constant velocity, how much is the force of friction on the book?

32. Terry says that if an object has no acceleration, then no forces are exerted on it. Sherry doesn't agree, but can't provide an explanation. They both look to you. What do you say?

33. When a car is moving in reverse, backing from a driveway, the driver applies the brakes. In what direction is the car's acceleration?

34. The auto in the sketch moves forward as the brakes are applied. A bystander says that during the interval of braking, the auto's velocity and acceleration are in opposite directions. Do you agree or disagree?

35. What is the difference between saying that one quantity is proportional to another and saying it is equal to another?

36. What is the acceleration of a rock at the top of its trajectory when thrown straight upward? Explain whether or not the answer is zero by using the equation $a = F/m$ as a guide to your thinking.

37. When blocking in football, why does a defending lineman often attempt to get his body under that of his opponent and push upward? What effect does this have on the friction force between the opposing lineman's feet and the ground?

38. An aircraft gains speed during takeoff due to the constant thrust of its engines. When is the acceleration during takeoff greatest—at the beginning of the run along the runway or just before the aircraft lifts into the air? Think, then explain.

39. A rocket becomes progressively easier to accelerate as it travels through outer space. Why is this so? (*Hint*: About 90 percent of the mass of a newly launched rocket is fuel.)

40. A common saying goes, "It's not the fall that hurts you; it's the sudden stop." Translate this into Newton's laws of motion.

41. On which of these hills does the ball roll down with increasing speed and decreasing acceleration along the path? (Use this example if you wish to explain to someone the difference between speed and acceleration.)

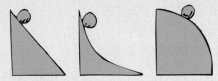

42. Why does a sharp knife cut better than a dull knife?

43. When Helen lifts one foot and remains standing on a bathroom scale, pressure on the scale is doubled. Does the weight reading change?

44. Aristotle claimed the speed of a falling object depends on its weight. We now know that objects in free fall, whatever their weights, gain speed at the same rate. Why does weight not affect acceleration?

45. After learning why objects of different mass have the same acceleration in free fall, Erik wonders if objects tied to equal lengths of string would swing together in unison. Lisa wonders if objects of different masses would slide at equal speeds down a friction-free inclined plane. What is your thinking on these hypotheses?

46. In a vacuum, a coin and a feather fall side by side. Would it be correct to say that in a vacuum equal forces of gravity act on both the coin and the feather?

47. As a sky diver falls faster and faster through the air (before reaching terminal speed), does the net force on her increase, decrease, or remain unchanged? Does her acceleration increase, decrease, or remain unchanged? Defend your answers.

48. After she jumps, a sky diver reaches terminal speed after 10 seconds. Does she gain more speed during the first second of fall or the ninth second of fall? Compared with the first second of fall, does she fall a greater or a lesser distance during the ninth second?

49. Can you think of a reason why the acceleration of an object thrown downward through the air would actually be less than 10 m/s²?

50. How does the weight of a falling body compare with the air resistance it encounters just before it reaches terminal velocity? Just after it reaches terminal velocity?

51. Why does a cat that falls from a 50-story building hit the safety net with no more speed than if it fell from the 20th story?

52. A regular tennis ball and another one filled with sand are dropped at the same time from the top of a high building. Your friend says that even though air resistance is present, both balls should hit the ground at the same time because they are the same size and pass through the same amount of air. What do you say?

53. If you drop an object, its acceleration toward the ground is 10 m/s². If you throw it downward instead, will its acceleration after throwing be greater than 10 m/s²? Why or why not? (Ignore air resistance.)

54. Suzy Skydiver, who has mass m, steps from the basket of a high-flying balloon of mass M and does a sky dive.
    a. What is the net force on Suzy at the moment she steps from the basket?
    b. What is the net force on her when air resistance builds up to equal *half* her weight?
    c. What is the net force on her when she reaches terminal speed v?
    d. What is the net force on her after she opens her parachute and reaches a new terminal speed $0.1v$?

Think and Solve ......

55. What is the acceleration during takeoff of a jumbo jet with a mass of 30,000 kg when the thrust for each of its *four* engines is 30,000 N?

56. A net force on a 2-kg cart accelerates the cart at 3 m/s². How much acceleration will the same net force produce on a 4-kg cart?

57. A net force of 10.0 N is exerted by Irene on a 6.7-kg cart for 3.0 seconds. Show that the cart will have an acceleration of 1.5 m/s².

58. Toby Toobad, who has a mass of 100 kg, is skateboarding at 9.0 m/s when he smacks into a brick wall and comes to a dead stop in 0.2 s. Show that his deceleration is 45 m/s² (that's 4.5 times *g*—ouch!).

59. A net force of 10.0 N on a box of plastic foam causes it to accelerate at 2.0 m/s². Show that the mass of the box is 5.0 kg.

60. Austin's truck has a mass of 2000 kg. When traveling at 22.0 m/s, it brakes to a stop in 4.0 s. Show that the magnitude of the braking force acting on the truck is 11,000 N.

61. If a loaded truck that can accelerate at 1 m/s² loses its load and has three-fourths of its original mass, what acceleration can it attain if the same driving force acts on it?

62. An occupant of a car can survive a crash if the deceleration during the crash is less than 30*g*. Calculate the force on a 70-kg person decelerating at this rate.

63. What is the pressure on a table when a 20-N book with a 0.05-m² cover lies flat on it? What is the pressure when the book stands on its end (area 0.01 m²)?

64. A falling 50-kg parachutist experiences an upward acceleration of 6.2 m/s² when she opens her parachute. Show that the drag force is 810 N when this occurs.

65. A 10-kg mass on a horizontal friction-free air track is accelerated by a string attached to another 10-kg mass hanging vertically from a pulley as shown. What is the force due to gravity, in newtons, on the hanging 10-kg mass? What is the acceleration of the system of both masses?

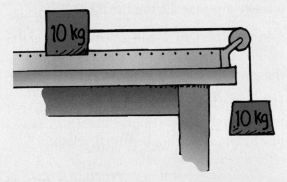

66. Suppose the masses described in problem 65 are 1 kg and 100 kg, respectively. Compare the accelerations when they are interchanged, that is, for the case where the 1-kg mass dangles over the pulley, and then for the case where the 100-kg mass dangles over the pulley. What does this indicate about the maximum acceleration of such a system of masses?

67. Skelly the skater is propelled by rocket power. Skelly and the rocket together have a mass of 25 kg. The thrusting force is 100 N and friction is 20 N.

a. What is Skelly's acceleration?

b. How far does he go in 5 s if he starts from rest?

Activities ······

68. Drop a sheet of paper and a coin at the same time. Which reaches the ground first? Why? Now crumple the paper into a small, tight wad and again drop it with the coin. Explain the difference observed. Will the coin and paper fall together if dropped from a second-, third-, or fourth-story window? Try it and explain your observations.

69. Glue a penny to a string. When in a moving automobile, hang the string and penny out a window. It will be swept backward due to air resistance. When the string makes an angle of 45°, easily seen with a protractor, the air resistance on the coin equals the weight of the coin. A look at the speedometer tells you the coin's terminal speed in air! Do you see why the angle makes a difference?

70. The net force acting on an object and the resulting acceleration are always in the same direction. You can demonstrate this with a spool. If the spool is gently pulled horizontally to the right, in which direction will it roll?

71. Write a letter to a friend who has not yet studied physics and tell what you've learned about Galileo introducing the concepts of acceleration and inertia. Tell of how Galileo was also familiar with forces, but didn't see the connection among these three concepts. Tell how Isaac Newton did see the connection, revealed in his second law of motion. Explain with the second law why heavy and light objects in free fall gain the same speed in the same time. In this letter, it's okay to use an equation or two, making it clear that you see equations as a shorthand notation of explanations.

More Problem-Solving Practice
Appendix F

7 NEWTON'S THIRD LAW OF MOTION—ACTION AND REACTION

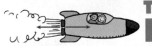

THE BIG IDEA : For every force, there is an equal and opposite force.

I f you lean over too far, you'll fall. But if you lean over with your hand out-stretched and make contact with a wall, you can do so without falling. When you push against the wall, it pushes back on you. That's why you are supported. Ask your friends why you don't topple over. How many will answer, "Because the wall is pushing on you and holding you in place"? Probably not very many people, unless they're physics types, realize that walls can push on us every bit as much as we push on them.[7.0] Similarly, kayak paddles that push water backward are pushed forward by the water.

discover!

Can There Be Only One Force In an Interaction?

1. Connect the hooks of two spring balances. Have a tug-of-war with a classmate. Observe the reading on the scales during the tug-of-war. (Caution: Don't pull too hard!)

2. Try to have one person pull harder than the other. Note the scale readings again.

3. With your classmate, hold two bathroom scales back to back. Now push on the scales and share scale readings.

Analyze and Conclude

1. **Observing** How did readings on the spring balances compare throughout your tug-of-war?

2. **Predicting** Is there some way for one person to exert a force without causing the other person to interact? Explain.

3. **Making Generalizations** Why do we say forces occur only in pairs?

FIGURE 7.1 ▲
When you push on the wall, the wall pushes on you.

FIGURE 7.2 ▲
The interaction that drives the nail is the same as the one that halts the hammer.

7.1 Forces and Interactions

In the simplest sense, a force is a push or a pull. Looking closer, however, Newton realized that a force is not a thing in itself. ☑ **A force is always part of a mutual action that involves another force.** A mutual action is an **interaction** between one thing and another. For example, consider the interaction between a hammer and a nail, as shown in Figure 7.2. A hammer exerts a force on the nail and drives it into a board. But this force is only half the story, for there must also be a force exerted on the hammer to halt it in the process. What exerts this force? The nail does! Newton reasoned that while the hammer exerts a force on the nail, the nail exerts a force on the hammer. So, in the interaction between the hammer and the nail, there are a pair of forces, one acting on the nail and the other acting on the hammer. Such observations led Newton to his third law: the law of action and reaction.

think!
Does a stick of dynamite contain force? Explain.
Answer: 7.1

CONCEPT CHECK Why do forces always occur in pairs?

Link to BIOLOGY

Action–Reaction in Action Why do migrating birds, such as geese, fly in a V formation? The answer is simple, physics! The bird's wings deflect air downward and the air pushes the bird upward. But the story doesn't end there. The downward-moving air meets the air below and swirls upward.

This upward-swirling air creates an updraft, which is strongest off to the side of the bird. A trailing bird positions itself to get added lift from the updraft, thus conserving its energy. This bird, in turn, creates an updraft for a following bird, and so on. The result is a flock flying in a V formation.

FIGURE 7.3 ▲
When the girl jumps to shore, the boat moves backward.

FIGURE 7.4 ▲
The dog wags the tail and the tail wags the dog.

think!

We know that Earth pulls on the moon. Does the moon also pull on Earth? If so, which pull is stronger?
Answer: 7.3

7.2 Newton's Third Law

Newton's third law describes the relationship between two forces in an interaction. ⊘ **Newton's third law states that whenever one object exerts a force on a second object, the second object exerts an equal and opposite force on the first object.** One force is called the **action force.** The other force is called the **reaction force.** It doesn't matter which force we call *action* and which we call *reaction*. The important thing is that they are partners in a single interaction and that neither force exists without the other. They are equal in strength and opposite in direction. Newton's third law is often stated: "To every action there is always an equal opposing reaction."

Look at Figures 7.3 and 7.4. In every interaction, the forces always occur in pairs. For example, you interact with the floor when you walk on it. You push against the floor, and the floor simultaneously pushes against you. Likewise, the tires of a car interact with the road to produce the car's motion. The tires push against the road, and the road simultaneously pushes back on the tires. When swimming, you interact with the water. You push the water backward, and the water pushes you forward. Notice that the interactions in these examples depend on friction. For example, a person trying to walk on ice, where friction is minimal, may not be able to exert an action force against the ice. Without the action force there cannot be a reaction force, and thus there is no resulting forward motion.

CONCEPT CHECK: What happens when an object exerts a force on another object?

7.3 Identifying Action and Reaction

Sometimes the identity of the pair of action and reaction forces in an interaction is not immediately obvious. For example, what are the action and reaction forces in the case of a falling boulder? You might say that Earth's gravitational force on the boulder is the action force, but can you identify the reaction force? Is it the weight of the boulder? No, weight is simply another name for the force of gravity. Is it caused by the ground where the boulder lands? No, the ground does not act on the boulder until the boulder hits it.

There is a simple recipe for treating action and reaction forces. First identify the interaction. Let's say one object, A, interacts with another object, B. The action and reaction forces are stated in this form:

Action: Object A exerts a force on object B.

Reaction: Object B exerts a force on object A.

Look at Figure 7.5. ✅ **To identify a pair of action–reaction forces, first identify the interacting objects A and B, and if the action is A on B, the reaction is B on A.** So, in the case of the falling boulder, the interaction during the fall is the gravitational attraction between the boulder and Earth. If we call the *action* Earth exerting a force on the boulder, then the *reaction* is the boulder simultaneously exerting a force on Earth.

You can't pull on something unless that something simultaneously pulls on you. That's the law!

CONCEPT CHECK : How do you identify the acton–reaction forces in an interaction?

ACTION : TIRE PUSHES ROAD   REACTION : ROAD PUSHES TIRE

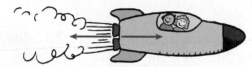

ACTION : ROCKET PUSHES GAS   REACTION : GAS PUSHES ROCKET

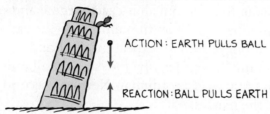

ACTION : EARTH PULLS BALL

REACTION : BALL PULLS EARTH

FIGURE 7.5 ▲
In the force-pair between object A and object B, note that when action is *A exerts force on B*, the reaction is simply *B exerts force on A*.

discover!

What are the action–reaction pairs?

1. Each of the drawings below shows the action force on an object. Recopy each of the drawings in your notebook.

2. Draw the appropriate vectors showing the reaction forces.

3. **Think** Specify the action–reaction pairs in each example.

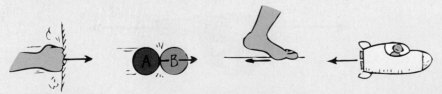

Go Online
*Sci*LINKS™ NSTA

For: Links on action and reaction
Visit: www.SciLinks.org
Web Code: csn – 0703

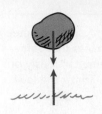

FIGURE 7.6 ▲
Earth is pulled up by the boulder with just as much force as the boulder is pulled down by Earth.

7.4 Action and Reaction on Different Masses

Interestingly enough, in the interaction between the boulder and Earth, shown in Figure 7.6, the boulder pulls up on Earth with as much force as Earth pulls down on the boulder. The forces are equal in strength and opposite in direction. We say the boulder falls to Earth. Could we also say Earth falls to the boulder? The answer is yes, but the distance Earth falls is much less. Although the pair of forces between the boulder and Earth are the same, the masses are quite unequal. Recall that Newton's second law states that acceleration is not only proportional to the net force, but it is also inversely proportional to the mass. Because Earth has a huge mass, we don't sense its infinitesimally small acceleration. Although Earth's acceleration is negligible, strictly speaking it does move up toward the falling boulder. So when you step off a curb, the street actually comes up a tiny bit to meet you!

Force and Mass A similar example occurs during the firing of a cannon, as shown in Figure 7.7. When the cannon is fired, there is an interaction between the cannon and the cannonball. The force the cannon exerts on the cannonball is exactly equal and opposite to the force the cannonball exerts on the cannon, so the cannon "kicks." On first consideration, you might expect the cannon to kick more than it does, or you might wonder why the cannonball moves so fast compared with the cannon. According to Newton's second law, we must also consider the masses.

Let F represent both the action and reaction forces; m, the mass of the cannon; and m, the mass of the cannonball. Different-sized symbols indicate the differences in masses and the accelerations. The acceleration of the cannonball and cannon are

$$\text{Cannonball:} \quad \frac{F}{m} = a \qquad \text{Cannon:} \quad \frac{F}{m} = a$$

Do you see why the change in the velocity of the cannonball is great compared with the change in velocity of the cannon?
☑ A given force exerted on a small mass produces a greater acceleration than the same force exerted on a large mass.

FIGURE 7.7 ▶
The cannonball undergoes more acceleration than the cannon because its mass is much smaller.

If we extend the basic idea of a cannon recoiling from the cannonball it launches, we can understand rocket propulsion. Consider air escaping from an untied, blown-up balloon. If the balloon is released and allowed to move as shown in Figure 7.8, it accelerates as the air comes out. A rocket accelerates in much the same way—it continually recoils from the exhaust gases ejected from its engine. Each molecule of exhaust gas acts like a tiny molecular cannonball shot downward from the rocket.

A common misconception is that a rocket, like the one shown in Figure 7.9, is propelled by the impact of exhaust gases against the atmosphere. In fact, before the advent of rockets, it was commonly thought that sending a rocket to the moon was impossible because of the absence of an atmosphere for the rocket to push against. This is like saying a cannon won't recoil unless the cannonball has air to push against. This is not true! Both the rocket and recoiling cannon accelerate because of the reaction forces created by the "cannonballs" they fire—air or no air. In fact, rockets work better above the atmosphere where there is no air resistance.

FIGURE 7.8 ▲
The balloon recoils from the escaping air and climbs upward.

Lift Using Newton's third law, we can understand how a helicopter gets its lifting force. The whirling blades are shaped to force air particles downward (action), and the air forces the blades upward (reaction). This upward reaction force is called lift. When lift equals the weight of the craft, the helicopter hovers in midair. When lift is greater, the helicopter climbs upward.

Birds and airplanes also fly because of action and reaction forces. When a bird is soaring, the shape of its wings deflects air downward. The air in turn pushes the bird up. The slightly tilted wings of an airplane also deflect oncoming air downward and produce lift. Airplanes must continuously push air downward to maintain lift and remain airborne. This continuous supply of air is produced by the forward motion of the aircraft, which results from jets or propellers that push air backward. When the engines push air back, the air in turn pushes the engines and the plane forward. We will learn later how the curved surface of an airplane wing enhances the lifting force.

CONCEPT CHECK : Why do objects that experience the same amount of force accelerate at different rates?

think!

A tug of war occurs between boys and girls on a polished floor that's somewhat slippery. If the boys are wearing socks and the girls are wearing rubber-soled shoes, who will surely win, and why?
Answer: 7.4

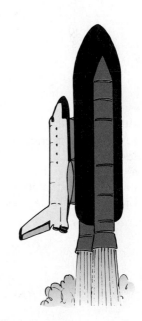

FIGURE 7.9 ▲
The rocket recoils from the "molecular cannonballs" it fires and climbs upward.

7.5 Defining Systems

An interesting question often arises: since action and reaction forces are equal and opposite, why don't they cancel to zero? To answer this question, we must consider the system involved. Consider, for example, a system consisting of a single orange, as in Figure 7.10. The dashed line surrounding the orange encloses and defines the system. The vector that pokes outside the dashed line represents an external force on the system. The system (that is, the orange) accelerates in accord with Newton's second law.

FIGURE 7.10 ▶

A force acts on the orange, and the orange accelerates to the right.

In Figure 7.11 we see that this force is provided by an apple, which doesn't change our analysis. The apple is outside the system. The fact that the orange simultaneously exerts a force on the apple, which is external to the system, may affect the apple (another system), but not the orange. You can't cancel a force on the orange with a force on the apple. So in this case the action and reaction forces don't cancel. ✓ **Action and reaction forces do not cancel each other when either of the forces is external to the system being considered.**

FIGURE 7.11 ▶

The force on the orange, provided by the apple, is not cancelled by the reaction force on the apple. The orange still accelerates.

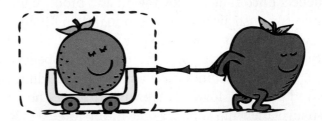

Now let's consider a larger system, enclosing both the orange and the apple. We see the system bounded by the dashed line in Figure 7.12a. Notice that the force pair is internal to the orange–apple system. Therefore these forces do cancel each other. They play no role in accelerating the system. A force external to the system is needed for acceleration. That's where friction with the floor comes in, as in Figure 7.12b. When the apple pushes against the floor, the floor simultaneously pushes on the apple—an external force on the system. The system accelerates to the right.

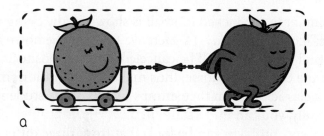

◀ **FIGURE 7.12**
Consider the larger system of orange + apple. **a.** Action and reaction forces cancel. **b.** When the floor pushes on the apple (reaction to the apple's push on the floor), the orange–apple system accelerates.

Inside a baseball are trillions and trillions of interatomic forces at play. They hold the ball together but play no role in accelerating the ball. Although every one of the interatomic forces is part of an action–reaction pair within the ball, they combine to zero, no matter how many of them there are. A force external to the ball, such as a swinging bat provides, is needed to accelerate the ball. If the action–reaction forces are internal to the system, then they cancel and the system does not accelerate.

Consider the football in Figure 7.13a. There is one interaction between the foot and the football, and the ball accelerates. But when two kicks act on the ball as in Figure 7.13b, no acceleration occurs. In this case there are two interactions occurring. If the two kicks on the ball are simultaneous, equal, and opposite, then the net force on the ball is zero. It is important to notice that the opposing forces act on the same object, not on different objects, so they do not make up an action–reaction pair.[7.5]

CONCEPT CHECK : Why don't action–reaction forces cancel each other?

think!

Suppose a friend who hears about Newton's third law says that you can't move a football by kicking it because the reaction force by the kicked ball would be equal and opposite to your kicking force. The net force would be zero, so no matter how hard you kick, the ball won't move! What do you say to your friend?
Answer: 7.5

FIGURE 7.13 ▲
A football is kicked. **a.** A acts on B and B accelerates. **b.** Both A and C act on B. They can cancel each other so B does not accelerate.

FIGURE 7.14 ▲

All the pairs of forces that act on the horse and cart are shown. The acceleration of the horse–cart system is due to the net force $F - f$, while an equal and opposite force acts on the ground.

think!

What is the net force that acts on the cart in Figure 7.14? On the horse? On the horse–cart system?

Answer: 7.6

7.6 The Horse–Cart Problem

A situation similar to the kicked football is shown in the comic strip "Horse Sense." Look at Figure 7.14. Here we think of the horse as believing its pull on the cart will be canceled by the opposite and equal pull by the cart on the horse, thus making acceleration impossible. This is a classic problem that stumps many college students. By thinking carefully, you can understand it.

The horse–cart problem can be looked at from three different points of view. First, consider the point of view of the farmer, who is concerned with getting his cart (the cart system) to market. Then, there is the point of view of the horse (the horse system). Finally, there is the point of view of the horse and cart together (the horse–cart system).

From the farmer's point of view, the only concern is with the force that is exerted on the cart system. The net force on the cart, divided by the mass of the cart, will produce a very real acceleration. The farmer doesn't care about the reaction on the horse.

Now look at the horse system. It's true that the opposite reaction force by the cart on the horse restrains the horse. Without this force, the horse could freely gallop to the market. This force tends to hold the horse back. So how does the horse move forward? The horse moves forward by interacting with the ground. When the horse pushes backward on the ground, the ground simultaneously pushes forward on the horse. ⊘ **If the horse in the horse–cart system pushes the ground with a greater force than it pulls on the cart, there is a net force on the horse, and the horse–cart system accelerates.** When the cart is up to speed, the horse need only push against the ground with enough force to offset the friction between the cart wheels and the ground.

Finally, look at the horse–cart system as a whole. From this viewpoint, the pull of the horse on the cart and the reaction of the cart on the horse are internal forces, or forces that act and react within the system. They contribute nothing to the acceleration of the horse–cart system. They cancel and can be neglected. To move across the ground, there must be an interaction between the horse–cart system and the ground. For example, if your car is stalled, you can't get it moving by sitting inside and pushing on the dashboard. You must interact with the ground outside. You must get outside and make the ground push the car. The horse–cart system is similar. It is the outside reaction by the ground that pushes the system.

CONCEPT CHECK How does a horse–cart system accelerate?

HONESTLY, THE WALL HIT MY HAND AND SPRAINED MY WRIST!

FIGURE 7.15 ▲
If you hit the wall, it will hit you equally hard.

7.7 Action Equals Reaction

This chapter began with a discussion of how a wall pushes back on you when you push against it. Suppose that for some reason, you punch the wall. Bam! Your hand is hurt. Look at the cartoon in Figure 7.15. Your friends see your damaged hand and ask what happened. What can you say truthfully? You can say that the wall hit your hand. How hard did the wall hit your hand? It hit just as hard as you hit the wall. You cannot hit the wall any harder than the wall can hit you back.

Hold a sheet of paper in midair and tell your friends that the heavyweight champion of the world could not strike the paper with a force of 200 N (45 pounds). You are correct, because a 200-N interaction between the champ's fist and the sheet of paper in midair isn't possible. The paper is not capable of exerting a reaction force of 200 N, and you cannot have an action force without a reaction force. Now, if you hold the paper against the wall, that's a different story. The wall will easily assist the paper in providing 200 N of reaction force, and more if needed!

⊘ **For every interaction between things, there is always a pair of oppositely directed forces that are equal in strength.** If you push hard on the world, for example, the world pushes hard on you. If you touch the world gently, the world will touch you gently in return. The way you touch others is the way others touch you, as shown in Figure 7.16.

**CONCEPT : What must occur in every interaction
CHECK : between things?**

FIGURE 7.16 ▶
The author and his wife demonstrate that you cannot touch without being touched—Newton's third law.

REVIEW

Concept Summary ......

- A force is always part of a mutual action that involves another force.

- Newton's third law states, that whenever one object exerts a force on a second object, the second object exerts an equal and opposite force on the first object.

- To identify a pair of action–reaction forces, first identify the interacting objects A and B, and if the action is A on B, the reaction is B on A.

- A given force exerted on a small mass produces a greater acceleration than the same force exerted on a large mass.

- Action and reaction forces do not cancel each other when either of the forces is external to the system being considered.

- If the horse in the horse–cart system pushes on the ground with a greater force than it pulls on the cart, there is a net force on the horse, and the horse–cart system accelerates.

- For every interaction between things, there is always a pair of oppositely directed forces that are equal in strength.

Key Terms ......

interaction (p.107)   action force (p.108)

Newton's third   reaction
   law (p.108)   force (p.108)

think! Answers

7.1 No. Force is not something an object has, like mass. Force is an interaction between one object and another. An object may possess the capability of exerting a force on another object, but it cannot possess force as a thing in itself. Later we will see that something like a stick of dynamite possesses *energy*.

7.3 Asking which pull is stronger is like asking which distance is greater—between New York and San Francisco, or between San Francisco and New York. The distances either way are the same. It is the same with force pairs. Both Earth and moon pull on each other with equal and opposite forces.

7.4 The girls will win. The force of friction is greater between the girls' feet and the floor than between the boys' feet and the floor. When both the girls and the boys exert action forces on the floor, the floor exerts a greater reaction force on the girls' feet. As a result, the girls stay at rest and the boys slide towards the girls.

7.5 Tell your friend that if you kick a football, it will accelerate. No other force has been applied to the ball. What about the reaction force? Aha! That force doesn't act on the ball; it acts on your foot. Tell your friend that you can't cancel a force on the ball with a force on your foot.

7.6 The net force on the cart is $P - f$; on the horse, $F - P$; on the horse–cart system, $F - f$.

7 ASSESS

Check Concepts ······

Section 7.1

1. Can an action force exist without a reaction force?

2. When a hammer exerts a force on a nail, how does this amount of force compare with that of the nail on the hammer?

Section 7.2

3. When you walk on a floor, what pushes you along?

4. State Newton's third law of motion.

Section 7.3

5. Consider hitting a baseball with a bat. If we call the force the bat exerts against the ball the action force, identify the reaction force.

6. If a bat hits a ball with 1000 N of force, can the ball exert less than 1000 N of force on the bat? More than 1000 N?

Section 7.4

7. If the world pulls you downward against your chair, what is the reaction force?

8. When a cannon is fired, are the forces on the cannonball and on the cannon equal in magnitude? Are the accelerations of the two equal?

9. When a cannon is fired, why do the cannonball and cannon have very different accelerations?

10. Identify the force that propels a rocket.

11. How does a helicopter get its lifting force?

Section 7.5

12. True or false: When a net force is exerted on a system, the system will accelerate, but when an applied force and its reaction are within a system, the system as a whole does not accelerate.

13. When can two kicks on a soccer ball produce a net force of zero on the ball?

14. Why don't the enormous number of interatomic forces inside a baseball accelerate the baseball?

Section 7.6

15. Referring to Figure 7.14, how many horizontal forces are exerted on the cart? What is the horizontal net force on the cart?

16. How many horizontal forces are exerted on the horse in Figure 7.14? What is the horizontal net force on the horse?

17. How many horizontal forces are exerted on the horse–cart system in Figure 7.14? What is the horizontal net force on the horse–cart system?

Section 7.7

18. If you hit a wall with a force of 200 N, how much force does the wall exert on you?

19. Can you physically touch another person without that person touching you with the same magnitude of force?

20. Fill in the blanks: Newton's first law is often called the law of _____; Newton's second law highlights the concepts of force, mass, and _____; and Newton's third law is the law of _____ and _____.

Think and Rank ······

Rank each of the following sets of scenarios in order of the quantity or property involved. List them from left to right. If scenarios have equal rankings, then separate them with an equal sign. (e.g., A = B)

21. Three sets of double boxes rest on a table.

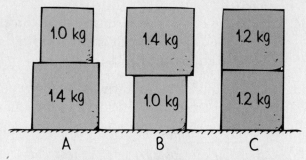

Rank the following from greatest to least.
a. the normal force that the table exerts on the sets
b. the normal force exerted by the bottom block on the top block

22. A van exerts a force on trailers of different masses *m*. All velocities *v* are constant. Compared with the force exerted on the trailer, rank the magnitude of force the trailer exerts on the van. Or are all pairs of forces equal in magnitude?

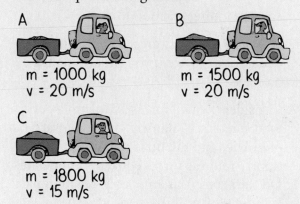

23. Each of these boxes is pulled by the same force *F* to the left. All boxes have the same mass and slide on a friction-free surface.

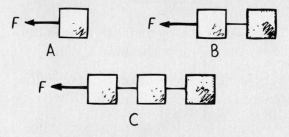

Rank the following from greatest to least.
a. the acceleration of the boxes
b. the tension in the rope connected to the boxes on the right in B and in C

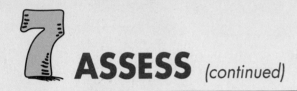

Think and Explain · · · · · ·

24. When you rub your hands together, can you push harder on one hand than the other?

25. Your weight is the result of the gravitational force of Earth on your body. What is the corresponding reaction force?

26. Why can you exert greater force on the pedals of a bicycle if you pull up on the handlebars?

27. Consider the two forces acting on a person who stands still, namely, the downward pull of gravity and the upward support of the floor. Are these forces equal and opposite? Do they comprise an action–reaction pair? Why or why not?

28. If you walk on a log that is floating in the water, the log moves backward. Why?

29. Why is it easier to walk on a carpeted floor than on a smooth, polished floor?

30. If you step off a ledge, you accelerate noticeably toward Earth. Does Earth accelerate toward you as well? Explain.

31. When a racquet hits a tennis ball, action and reaction forces occur between the racquet and ball. What other action–reaction pair of forces occur for the ball both before and after interaction with the racquet? Neglect air resistance.

32. Suppose you're weighing yourself while standing next to the bathroom sink. Using the idea of action and reaction, explain why the scale reading will be less when you push down on the top of the sink. Why will the scale reading be more if you pull up on the bottom of the sink?

33. When a high jumper leaves the ground, what is the source of the upward force that accelerates her? What force acts after her feet are no longer in contact with the ground?

34. What is the reaction force to an action force of 1000 N exerted by Earth on an orbiting communications satellite?

35. If action equals reaction, why isn't Earth pulled into orbit around a communications satellite?

36. A small car bumps into a van at rest in a parking lot. Upon which vehicle is the force of impact greater? Which vehicle undergoes the greater change in acceleration? Defend your answer.

37. Does your answer to question 36 depend on the relative speeds of the vehicles?

38. A speeding bus makes contact with a bug that splatters onto the windshield. Because of the sudden force, the unfortunate bug undergoes a sudden deceleration. Is the corresponding force that the bug exerts against the windshield greater, less, or the same? Is the resulting deceleration of the bus greater than, less than, or the same as that of the bug?

39. Consider two carts, one twice as massive as the other, that fly apart when the compressed spring squeezed between them is released. How fast does the heavier cart roll compared with the lighter cart?

40. Some people used to think that a rocket could not travel to the moon because it would have no air to push against once it left Earth's atmosphere. We now know that idea was mistaken. What force propels a rocket when it is in a vacuum?

41. Since the force that acts on a cannonball when a cannon is fired is equal and opposite to the force that acts on the cannon, does this imply a zero net force and therefore the impossibility of an accelerating cannonball? Explain.

42. Suppose you exert 200 N on your refrigerator and push it across the kitchen floor at constant velocity. What friction force acts between the refrigerator and the floor? Is the friction force equal and opposite to your 200-N push? Does the friction force make up the reaction force to your push?

43. The photo shows Steve Hewitt and his daughter Gretchen. Is Gretchen touching Steve, or is Steve touching her? Explain.

44. Hold your hand like a flat wing outside the window of a moving vehicle. Then tilt it slightly upward and your hand will rise. Explain this in terms of Newton's third law.

45. Your teacher challenges you and your best friend to each pull on a pair of scales attached to the ends of a horizontal rope, in tug-of-war fashion, so that the readings on the scales will differ. Can this be done? Explain.

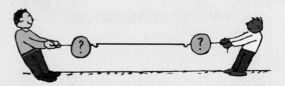

46. A pair of 50-N weights are attached to a spring scale as shown. Does the spring scale read 0, 50, or 100 N? (*Hint:* Would it read any differently if one of the strings were held by your hand instead of being attached to the 50-N weight?)

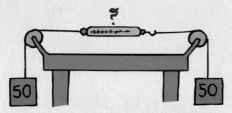

47. The strong man can withstand the tension force exerted by the two horses pulling in opposite directions. How would the tension compare if only one horse pulled and the left rope were tied to a tree? How would the tension compare if the two horses pulled in the same direction, with the left rope tied to the tree?

48. A balloon floats motionless in the air. A balloonist begins climbing up the supporting cable. In which direction does the balloon move as the balloonist climbs? Explain.

49. When you get up from a sitting position, do your feet push against the floor with a force equal to, more than, or less than your weight? Explain.

50. When a weightlifter jerks a barbell over his head, is the force exerted on the barbell more than, less than, or equal to the barbell's weight? Explain.

51. Identify two pairs of action-reaction forces that exist when you stand on a scale.

52. A car of mass m cruises along the highway at a constant velocity v. The tires push backward on the road with a force f. The reaction to this force provides the forward force on the car. Wind resistance against the car is R.
    a. Using symbols, what is the net force on the car?
    b. Using symbols, what is the acceleration of the car?
    c. A friend says that since the car is moving forward, there must be a net forward force, which means f must be greater than R, even at constant velocity. What do you say to enlighten your friend?

Think and Solve ......

53. What will be the acceleration of recoil when a 60-kg person on rollerskates pushes against a wall with a force of 30 N?

54. Two people attempt a tug-of-war on low-friction ice. One person has four times the mass of the other. Relative to the acceleration of the heavier person, what will be the acceleration of the lighter person?

55. Two blocks, one three times as massive as the other, are connected by a compressed spring. When the spring is released, both blocks fly apart. Relative to the acceleration of the heavier block, what is the acceleration of the lighter block?

56. What is the net force on a falling 100-N barrel hitting a pavement with 5000 N of force?

57. Amanda looks at a 1.0-kg bag of jellybeans resting on a table.
   a. Calculate the amount of force that the table exerts on the bag of jellybeans.
   b. How does this compare with the force that the bag of jellybeans exerts on the table?

58. When 56-kg Diane on rollerskates pushes against a wall with a force of 28 N, she accelerates away from the wall. Show that Diane's recoil acceleration is 0.50 m/s².

59. A 7.00-kg bowling ball moving at 8.0 m/s strikes a 1.0-kg bowling pin and slows to 7.0 m/s in 0.040 s.
   a. Show that the force of impact on the bowling ball is 175 N.
   b. How much force acts on the bowling pin?

60. A 70-kg skydiver is falling at her terminal speed. Show that she exerts a 700-N downward force on the air as she falls.

61. Gymnast Gracie of weight *mg* is suspended by a pair of vertical ropes attached to the ceiling.
   a. In terms of Gracie's weight, what is the tension in each rope?
   b. If Gracie's mass is 30 kg, show that the tension in each rope is 150 N.

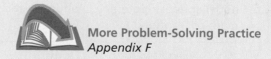

More Problem-Solving Practice
Appendix F

8 MOMENTUM

Momentum is conserved for all collisions as long as external forces don't interfere.

Have you ever wondered how a tae kwon do expert can break a stack of cement bricks with the blow of a bare hand? Or why falling on a wooden floor hurts less than falling on a cement floor? Or why follow-through is important in golf, baseball, and boxing? To understand these things, you need to recall the concept of inertia introduced and developed when we discussed Newton's laws of motion. Inertia was discussed both in terms of objects at rest and objects in motion. In this chapter we are concerned only with the concept of inertia in motion—momentum.

discover!

How Does a Collision Affect the Motion of Marbles?

1. Place five marbles, all identical in size and shape, in the center groove of a ruler. Launch a sixth marble toward the five stationary marbles. Note any changes in the marbles' motion.

2. Now launch two marbles at four stationary marbles. Then launch three marbles at three stationary marbles, and so on. Note any changes in the marbles' motion.

3. Remove all but two marbles from the groove. Roll these two marbles at each other with equal speeds. Note any changes in the marbles' motion.

Analyze and Conclude

1. **Observing** How did the approximate speed of the marbles before each collision compare to after each collision?

2. **Drawing Conclusions** What factors determine how the speed of the marbles changes in a collision?

3. **Predicting** What do you think would happen if three marbles rolling to the right and two marbles rolling to the left with the same speed were to collide?

8.1 Momentum

We know that it's harder to stop a large truck than a small car when both are moving at the same speed. We say the truck has more momentum than the car. By momentum, we mean *inertia in motion*. More specifically, **momentum** is the mass of an object multiplied by its velocity.

$$\text{momentum} = \text{mass} \times \text{velocity}$$

or, in abbreviated notation,

$$\text{momentum} = mv$$

When direction is not an important factor, we can say

$$\text{momentum} = \text{mass} \times \text{speed}$$

which we still abbreviate mv.

⊘ **A moving object can have a large momentum if it has a large mass, a high speed, or both.** A moving truck has more momentum than a car moving at the same speed because the truck has more mass. But a fast car can have more momentum than a slow truck. And a truck at rest has no momentum at all. Figure 8.1 compares the momentum of a truck to that of a roller skate.

CONCEPT CHECK What factors affect an object's momentum?

8.2 Impulse Changes Momentum

If the momentum of an object changes, either the mass or the velocity or both change. If the mass remains unchanged, as is most often the case, then the velocity changes and acceleration occurs. What produces acceleration? We know the answer is *force*. The greater the force acting on an object, the greater its change in velocity, and hence, the greater its change in momentum.

think!

Can you think of a case where the roller skate and the truck shown in Figure 8.1 would have the same momentum?
Answer: 8.1

The derivation of $Ft = \Delta(mv)$ is given in Appendix G, Note 8.2.

Impulse ☑ **The change in momentum depends on the force that acts and the length of time it acts.** As Figure 8.2 shows, apply a brief force to a stalled automobile, and you produce a change in its momentum. Apply the same force over an extended period of time and you produce a greater change in the automobile's momentum. A force sustained for a long time produces more change in momentum than does the same force applied briefly. So both force and time are important in changing an object's momentum.

FIGURE 8.2 ▶
When you push with the same force for twice the time, you impart twice the impulse and produce twice the change in momentum.

The quantity *force × time interval* is called **impulse.** In shorthand notation,

$$\text{impulse} = Ft$$

The greater the impulse exerted on something, the greater will be the change in momentum. The exact relationship[8.2] is

$$\text{impulse} = \text{change in momentum}$$

$$\text{or}$$

$$Ft = \Delta(mv)$$

The impulse–momentum relationship helps us to analyze a variety of situations where the momentum changes. Consider the familiar examples of impulse in the following cases of increasing and decreasing momentum.

Increasing Momentum To increase the momentum of an object, it makes sense to apply the greatest force possible for as long as possible. A golfer teeing off and a baseball player trying for a home run do both of these things when they swing as hard as possible and follow through with their swing.

The forces involved in impulses usually vary from instant to instant. Look at Figure 8.3. A golf club that strikes a golf ball exerts zero force on the ball until it comes in contact with it; then the force increases rapidly as the ball becomes distorted. The force then diminishes as the ball comes up to speed and returns to its original shape. So when we speak of such forces in this chapter, we mean the *average* force.

FIGURE 8.3 ▲
The force of impact on a golf ball varies throughout the duration of impact.

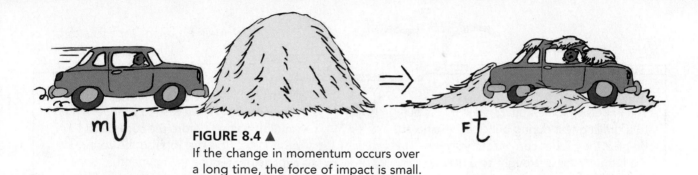

FIGURE 8.4 ▲
If the change in momentum occurs over a long time, the force of impact is small.

Decreasing Momentum If you were in a car that was out of control and had to choose between hitting a haystack, as in Figure 8.4 or a concrete wall as in Figure 8.5, you wouldn't have to call on your knowledge of physics to make up your mind. Common sense tells you to choose the haystack. But knowing the physics helps you to understand *why* hitting a soft object is entirely different from hitting a hard one.

In the case of hitting either thc wall or the haystack and coming to a stop, your momentum is decreased by the same impulse. The same impulse does not mean the same amount of force or the same amount of time; rather it means the same *product* of force and time. By hitting the haystack instead of the wall, you extend the contact time—*the time during which your momentum is brought to zero.* A longer contact time reduces the force and decreases the resulting deceleration. For example, if the time is extended 100 times, the force of impact is reduced 100 times. Whenever we wish the force to be small, we extend the time.

We know that a padded dashboard in a car is safer than a rigid metal one and that airbags save lives. You also know that to catch a fast-moving ball safely with your bare hand—you extend your hand forward so there's plenty of room for it to move backward after making contact with the ball. When you extend the time of contact, you reduce the force of the catch.

think!

When a dish falls, will the impulse be less if it lands on a carpet than if it lands on a hard floor?
Answer: 8.2.1

FIGURE 8.5 ▲
If the change in momentum occurs over a short time, the force of impact is large.

Bungee Jumping

The impulse–momentum relationship is put to a thrilling test during bungee jumping. Be glad the rubber cord stretches when the jumper's fall is brought to a halt, because the cord has to apply an impulse equal to the jumper's momentum in order to stop the jumper—hopefully above ground level.

Note how $Ft = \Delta(mv)$ applies here. The momentum, mv, we wish to change is the amount gained before the cord begins stretching. Ft is the impulse the cord supplies to reduce the momentum to zero. Because the rubber cord stretches for a long time, a large time interval t ensures that a small average force F acts on the jumper. Elastic cords typically stretch to twice their original length during the fall.

Whether body A acts on body B, or body B acts on body A, in accordance with Newton's third law, both have the same amount of impulse Ft.

When jumping from an elevated position down to the ground, you should bend your knees when your feet make contact with the ground. By doing so you extend the time during which your momentum decreases by 10 to 20 times that of a stiff-legged, abrupt landing. The resulting force on your bones is reduced by 10 to 20 times. A wrestler thrown to the floor tries to extend his time of hitting the mat by relaxing his muscles and spreading the impulse into a series of smaller ones as his foot, knee, hip, ribs, and shoulder successively hit the mat. Of course, falling on a mat is preferable to falling on a solid floor because the mat also increases the stopping time.

When a boxer gets punched, the impulse provided by the boxer's jaw must counteract the momentum of the punch. As Figure 8.6a shows, when the boxer moves away from the punch, he increases the time of contact and reduces the force. When the boxer moves toward the punch, as in Figure 8.6b, the time of contact is reduced and the force is increased.

think!

If the boxer in Figure 8.6 is able to make the contact time five times longer by "riding" with the punch, how much will the force of the punch impact be reduced?

Answer: 8.2.2

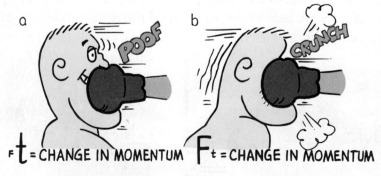

Ft = CHANGE IN MOMENTUM Ft = CHANGE IN MOMENTUM

FIGURE 8.6 ▲

The impulse provided by a boxer's jaw counteracts the momentum of the punch. **a.** The boxer moves away from the punch. **b.** The boxer moves toward the punch. Ouch!

We know a glass dish is more likely to survive if it is dropped on a carpet rather than a sidewalk because the carpet has more "give" than the sidewalk. Ask why a surface with more give makes for a safer fall and you will get a puzzled response from most people. They may simply say, "Because it gives more." However, your question is, "*Why* is a surface with more give safer for the dish?" In this case, a common explanation isn't enough. A deeper explanation is needed.

To bring the dish or its fragments to rest, the carpet or the sidewalk must provide an impulse, which you know involves two variables—force and time. Since time is longer hitting the carpet than hitting the sidewalk, a smaller force results. The shorter time hitting the sidewalk results in a greater stopping force. The safety net used by circus acrobats is a good example of how to achieve the impulse needed for a safe landing. The safety net reduces the stopping force on a fallen acrobat by substantially increasing the time interval of the contact.

Sometimes a difference in time is important even if you can't notice the give in a surface. For example, a wooden floor and a concrete floor may both seem rigid, but the wooden floor can have enough give to make quite a difference in the forces that these two surfaces exert.

A flower pot dropped onto your head bounces quickly. Ouch! If bouncing took a longer time, as with a safety net, then the force of the bounce would be much smaller.

CONCEPT CHECK : What factors affect how much an object's momentum changes?

8.3 Bouncing

If a flower pot falls from a shelf onto your head, you may be in trouble. If it bounces from your head, you may be in more serious trouble. Why? Because impulses are greater when an object bounces. **The impulse required to bring an object to a stop and then to "throw it back again" is greater than the impulse required merely to bring the object to a stop.** Suppose, for example, that you catch the falling pot with your hands. You provide an impulse to reduce its momentum to zero. If you throw the pot upward again, you have to provide additional impulse. It takes a greater impulse to catch the pot *and* throw it back up than merely to catch it. This increased amount of impulse is supplied by your head if the pot bounces from it. The karate expert in Figure 8.7 strikes the bricks in such a way that her hand is made to bounce back, yielding as much as twice the impulse to the bricks.

FIGURE 8.7 ▲
Cassy imparts a large impulse to the bricks in a short time and produces considerable force.

IMPULSE

FIGURE 8.8 ▶
The curved blades of the Pelton Wheel cause water to bounce and make a U-turn, producing a large impulse that turns the wheel.

The fact that impulses are greater when bouncing takes place was used with great success during the California Gold Rush. The waterwheels used in gold mining operations were not very effective. A man named Lester A. Pelton saw that the problem had to do with the flat paddles on the waterwheel. He designed the curve-shaped paddle that is shown in Figure 8.8. This paddle caused the incoming water to make a U-turn upon impact with the paddle. Because the water "bounced," the impulse exerted on the waterwheel was increased. Pelton patented his idea and probably made more money from his invention, the Pelton Wheel, than any of the gold miners earned. Physics can indeed make you rich!

CONCEPT CHECK How does the impulse of a bounce compare to stopping only?

8.4 Conservation of Momentum

From Newton's second law you know that to accelerate an object, a net force must be applied to it. This chapter says much the same thing, but in different language. If you wish to change the momentum of an object, exert an impulse on it.

In either case, the force or impulse must be exerted on the object by something outside the object. Internal forces won't work. For example, the molecular forces within a basketball have no effect on the momentum of the basketball, just as a push against the dashboard of a car you're sitting in does not affect the momentum of the car. Molecular forces within the basketball and a push on the dashboard are internal forces. They come in balanced pairs that cancel within the object. To change the momentum of the basketball or the car, an outside push or pull is required. If no outside force is present, no change in momentum is possible.

FIGURE 8.9 ▲
Teacher Howie Brand shows that the block topples when the swinging dart bounces from it. When he removes the rubber head of the dart so it doesn't bounce when it hits the block, no toppling occurs.

Consider the cannon being fired in Figure 8.10. The force on the cannonball inside the cannon barrel is equal and opposite to the force causing the cannon to recoil. Recall Newton's third law about action and reaction forces. These forces are internal to the system comprising the cannon and the cannonball, so they don't change the momentum of the cannon–cannonball system. Before the firing, the system is at rest and the momentum is zero. After the firing the net momentum, or total momentum, is *still* zero. Net momentum is neither gained nor lost. Let's consider the effects of internal and external forces carefully.

Most of the cannonball's momentum is in speed; most of the recoiling cannon's momentum is in mass. So $mV = Mv$.

FIGURE 8.10 ▶
The momentum before firing is zero. After firing, the net momentum is still zero because the momentum of the cannon is equal and opposite to the momentum of the cannonball.

Momentum, like the quantities velocity and force, has both direction and magnitude. It is a *vector quantity*. Like velocity and force, momentum can be canceled. So, although the cannonball in the preceding example gains momentum when fired and the recoiling cannon gains momentum in the opposite direction, the cannon–cannonball *system* gains none. The momenta (plural form of momentum) of the cannonball and the cannon are equal in magnitude and opposite in direction. Therefore, these momenta cancel each other out for the system as a whole. No external force acted on the system before or during firing. Since no net force acts on the system, there is no net impulse on the system and there is no net change in the momentum.

In every case, the momentum of a system cannot change unless it is acted on by external forces. A system will have the same momentum before some internal interaction as it has after the interaction occurs. When momentum, or any quantity in physics, does not change, we say it is *conserved*. The **law of conservation of momentum** describes the momentum of a system. ☑ **The law of conservation of momentum states that, in the absence of an external force, the momentum of a system remains unchanged.** If a system undergoes changes wherein all forces are internal as for example in atomic nuclei undergoing radioactive decay, cars colliding, or stars exploding, the net momentum of the system before and after the event is the same.

CONCEPT CHECK : What does the law of conservation of momentum state?

Go Online
SciLINKS NSTA

For: Links on momentum
Visit: www.SciLinks.org
Web Code: csn – 0804

think!

Newton's second law states that if no net force is exerted on a system, no acceleration occurs. Does it follow that no change in momentum occurs?
Answer: 8.4

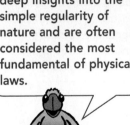

A conservation law is constancy during change. Conservation laws are a source of deep insights into the simple regularity of nature and are often considered the most fundamental of physical laws.

discover!

How Are Motion and Conservation of Momentum Related?

1. Stand at rest on a skateboard and throw a massive object forward or backward. What do you notice?
2. Repeat the throwing motion in Step 1, but this time don't let go of the object. What do you notice?
3. **Think** How is the difference in your motion in Steps 1 and 2 related to conservation of momentum?

8.5 Collisions

The collision of objects clearly shows the conservation of momentum. ✅ **Whenever objects collide in the absence of external forces, the net momentum of both objects before the collision equals the net momentum of both objects after the collision.**

$$\text{net momentum}_{\text{before collision}} = \text{net momentum}_{\text{after collision}}$$

Elastic Collisions When a moving billiard ball collides head-on with a ball at rest, the first ball comes to rest and the second ball moves away with a velocity equal to the initial velocity of the first ball. We see that momentum is transferred from the first ball to the second ball. When objects collide without being permanently deformed and without generating heat, the collision is said to be an **elastic collision.** Colliding objects bounce perfectly in perfect elastic collisions, as shown in Figure 8.11. Note that the sum of the momentum vectors is the same before and after each collision.

FIGURE 8.11 ▼
Colliding objects bounce perfectly in elastic collisions. **a.** A moving ball strikes a ball at rest. **b.** Two moving balls collide head-on. **c.** Two balls moving in the same direction collide.

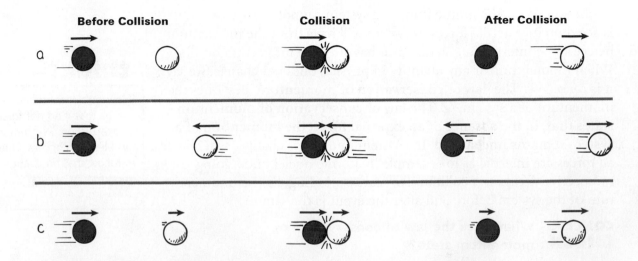

132

Inelastic Collisions A collision in which the colliding objects become distorted and generate heat during the collision is an **inelastic collision.** Momentum conservation holds true even in inelastic collisions. Whenever colliding objects become tangled or couple together, a totally inelastic collision occurs. The freight train cars in Figure 8.12 provide an example. Suppose the freight cars are of equal mass m, and that one car moves at 4 m/s toward the other car that is at rest. Can you predict the velocity of the coupled cars after impact? From the conservation of momentum,

net momentum $_{\text{before collision}}$ = net momentum $_{\text{after collision}}$

or, in equation form,

$$(\text{net } mv)_{\text{before}} = (\text{net } mv)_{\text{after}}$$

$$(m)(4 \text{ m/s}) + (m)(0 \text{ m/s}) = (2m)(v_{\text{after}})$$

Momentum is conserved for all collisions, elastic and inelastic (when there are no external forces to provide net impulse).

Since twice as much mass is moving after the collision, can you see that the velocity, v_{after}, must be one half of 4 m/s? Solving for the velocity after the collision, we find $v_{\text{after}} = 2$ m/s in the same direction as the velocity before the collision, v_{before}. The initial momentum is shared by both cars without loss or gain. Momentum is conserved.

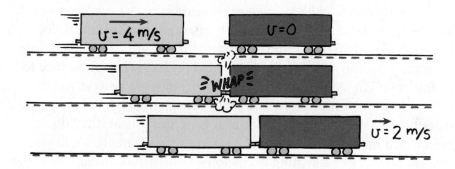

◄ **FIGURE 8.12**
In an inelastic collision between two freight cars, the momentum of the freight car on the left is shared with the freight car on the right.

Most collisions usually involve some external force. Billiard balls do not continue indefinitely with the momentum imparted to them. The moving balls encounter friction with the table and the air. These external forces are usually negligible during the collision, so the net momentum does not change during collision. The net momentum of two colliding trucks is the same before and just after the collision. As the combined wreck slides along the pavement, friction provides an impulse to decrease its momentum. Similarly, a pair of space vehicles docking in orbit have the same net momentum just before and just after contact. Since there is no air resistance in space, the combined momentum of the space vehicles after docking is then changed only by gravity.

FIGURE 8.13 ▲
An air track nicely demonstrates conservation of momentum. Many small air jets provide a nearly frictionless cushion of air for the gliders to slide on.

Pucks and carts ride nearly free of friction on cushions of air on air tracks like the one shown in Figure 8.13. Galileo worked hard to produce smooth surfaces to minimize friction. How he would have loved to experiment with today's air tracks!

Perfectly elastic collisions are not common in the everyday world. We find in practice that some heat is generated during collisions. Drop a ball and after it bounces from the floor, both the ball and the floor are a bit warmer. Even a dropped superball will not bounce to its initial height. At the microscopic level, however, perfectly elastic collisions are commonplace. For example, electrically charged particles bounce off one another without generating heat; they don't even touch in the classic sense of the word. Later chapters will show that the concept of touching needs to be considered differently at the atomic level.

CONCEPT : How does conservation of momentum
CHECK : apply to collisions?

think!

Suppose one of the gliders in Figure 8.13 is loaded so it has three times the mass of the other glider. The loaded glider is initially at rest. The unloaded glider collides with the loaded glider and the two gliders stick together. Describe the motion of the gliders after the collision. *Answer: 8.5*

do the math!

Consider a 6-kg fish that swims toward and swallows a 2-kg fish that is at rest. If the larger fish swims at 1 m/s, what is its velocity immediately after lunch?

Momentum is conserved from the instant before lunch until the instant after (in so brief an interval, water resistance does not have time to change the momentum), so we can write

$$\text{net momentum}_{\text{before lunch}} = \text{net momentum}_{\text{after lunch}}$$

$$(\text{net } mv)_{\text{before}} = (\text{net } mv)_{\text{after}}$$

$$(6 \text{ kg})(1 \text{ m/s}) + (2 \text{ kg})(0 \text{ m/s}) = (6 \text{ kg} + 2 \text{ kg})(v_{\text{after}})$$

$$6 \text{ kg·m/s} = (8 \text{ kg})(v_{\text{after}})$$

$$v_{\text{after}} = \frac{6 \text{ kg·m/s}}{8 \text{ kg}}$$

$$v_{\text{after}} = \frac{3}{4} \text{ m/s}$$

We see that the small fish has no momentum before lunch because its velocity is zero. Using simple algebra we see that after lunch the combined mass of the two-fish system is 8 kg and its speed is $\frac{3}{4}$ m/s in the same direction as the large fish's direction before lunch.

Suppose the small fish is not at rest but is swimming toward the large fish at 2 m/s. What is the velocity of the larger fish immediately after lunch?

If we consider the direction of the large fish as positive, then the velocity of the small fish is −2 m/s.

$$(\text{net } mv)_{\text{before}} = (\text{net } mv)_{\text{after}}$$

$$(6 \text{ kg})(1 \text{ m/s}) + (2 \text{ kg})(-2 \text{ m/s}) = (6 \text{ kg} + 2 \text{ kg})(v_{\text{after}})$$

$$(6 \text{ kg·m/s}) + (-4 \text{ kg·m/s}) = (8 \text{ kg})(v_{\text{after}})$$

$$\frac{2 \text{ kg·m/s}}{8 \text{ kg}} = v_{\text{after}} = \frac{1}{4} \text{ m/s}$$

The negative momentum of the small fish is very effective in slowing the large fish. If the small fish were swimming at −3 m/s, then both fish would have equal and opposite momenta. Zero momentum before lunch would equal zero momentum after lunch, and both fish would come to a halt.

More interestingly, suppose the small fish swims at −4 m/s.

$$(\text{net } mv)_{\text{before}} = (\text{net } mv)_{\text{after}}$$

$$(6 \text{ kg})(1 \text{ m/s}) + (2 \text{ kg})(-4 \text{ m/s}) = (6 \text{ kg} + 2 \text{ kg})(v_{\text{after}})$$

$$(6 \text{ kg·m/s}) + (-8 \text{ kg·m/s}) = (8 \text{ kg})(v_{\text{after}})$$

$$\frac{-2 \text{ kg·m/s}}{8 \text{ kg}} = v_{\text{after}} = -\frac{1}{4} \text{ m/s}$$

The minus sign tells us that after lunch the two-fish system moves in a direction opposite to the large fish's direction before lunch.

8.6 Momentum Vectors

Momentum is conserved even when interacting objects don't move along the same straight line. To analyze momentum in any direction, we use the vector techniques we've previously learned. ✅ **The vector sum of the momenta is the same before and after a collision.** We'll look at momentum conservation involving angles by briefly considering the three following examples.

FIGURE 8.14 ▶
Momentum is a vector quantity. The momentum of the wreck is equal to the vector sum of the momenta of car A and car B before the collision.

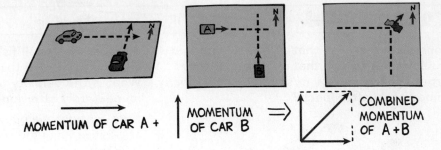

MOMENTUM OF CAR A + MOMENTUM OF CAR B ⟹ COMBINED MOMENTUM OF A + B

Notice in Figure 8.14 that the momentum of car A is directed due east and that of car B is directed due north. If their momenta are equal in magnitude, after colliding their combined momentum will be in a northeast direction with a magnitude $\sqrt{2}$ times the momentum either vehicle had before the collision (just as the diagonal of a square is $\sqrt{2}$ times the length of a side).

FIGURE 8.15 ▶

When the firecracker bursts, the vector sum of the momenta of its fragments add up to the firecracker's momentum just before bursting.

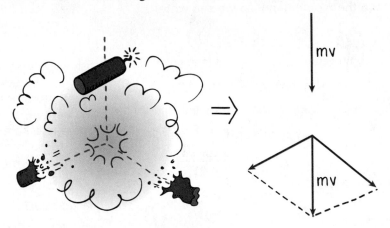

mv

mv

Figure 8.15 shows a falling firecracker that explodes into two pieces. The momenta of the fragments combine by vector rules to equal the original momentum of the falling firecracker.

Figure 8.16 shows tracks made by subatomic particles in a bubble chamber. The mass of these particles can be computed by applying both the conservation of momentum and conservation of energy laws—the conservation of energy law will be discussed in the next chapter. The conservation laws are extremely useful to experimenters in the atomic and subatomic realms. A very important feature of their usefulness is that forces do not show up in the equations. Forces in collisions, however complicated, are not a concern.

Conservation of momentum and, as the next chapter will discuss, conservation of energy are the two most powerful tools of mechanics. Their application yields detailed information that ranges from understanding the interactions of subatomic particles to entire galaxies.

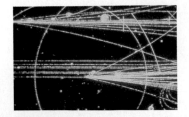

FIGURE 8.16 ▲

Momentum is conserved for the high-speed elementary particles, as shown by the tracks they leave in a bubble chamber.

CONCEPT CHECK: What is true about the vector sum of momenta in a collision?

REVIEW

Concept Summary ······

- A moving object can have a large momentum if it has a large mass, a high speed, or both.

- The change in momentum depends on the force that acts and the length of time it acts.

- The impulse required to bring an object to a stop and then to "throw it back again" is greater than the impulse required merely to bring the object to a stop.

- The law of conservation of momentum states that in the absence of an external force, the momentum of a system remains unchanged.

- Whenever objects collide in the absence of external forces, the net momentum of both objects before collision equals the net momentum of both objects after collision.

- The vector sum of the momenta is the same before and after a collision.

Key Terms ·····

momentum (p. 125)

impulse (p. 126)

law of conservation of momentum (p. 131)

elastic collision (p. 132)

inelastic collision (p. 133)

think! Answers

8.1   The roller skate and truck can have the same momentum if the speed of the roller skate is much greater than the speed of the truck. How much greater? As many times greater as the truck's mass is greater than the roller skate's mass. Get it? For example, a 1000-kg truck backing out of a driveway at 0.01 m/s has the same momentum as a 1-kg skate going 10 m/s. Both have momentum = 10 kg m/s.

8.2.1   No. The impulse would be the same for either surface because the same momentum change occurs for each. It is the *force* that is less for the impulse on the carpet because of the greater time of momentum change.

8.2.2   Since the time of impact increases five times, the force of impact will be reduced five times.

8.4   Yes, because no acceleration means that no change occurs in velocity or in momentum (mass × velocity). Another line of reasoning is simply that no net force means there is no net impulse and thus no change in momentum.

8.5   The mass of the stuck-together gliders is four times that of the unloaded glider. Thus, the postcollision velocity of the stuck-together gliders is one-fourth of the unloaded glider's velocity before collision. This velocity is in the same direction as before, since the direction as well as the amount of momentum is conserved.

Check Concepts ......

Section 8.1

1. Distinguish between *mass* and *momentum.* Which is inertia and which is inertia in motion?

2. **a.** Which has the greater mass, a heavy truck at rest or a rolling skateboard?
   b. Which has greater momentum?

3. Distinguish between *force* and *impulse.*

Section 8.2

4. Distinguish between *impact* and *impulse.* Which designates a force and which is force multiplied by time?

5. When the force of impact on an object is extended in time, does the impulse increase or decrease?

6. Distinguish between *impulse* and *momentum.* Which is force × time and which is inertia in motion?

7. Does impulse equal momentum, or a *change* in momentum?

8. For a constant force, suppose the duration of impact on an object is doubled.
   a. How much is the impulse increased?
   b. How much is the resulting change in momentum increased?

9. In a car crash, why is it advantageous for an occupant to extend the time during which the collision takes place?

10. If the time of impact in a collision is extended by four times, how much does the force of impact change?

11. Why is it advantageous for a boxer to ride with the punch? Why should he avoid moving into an oncoming punch?

Section 8.3

12. Visualize yourself on a skateboard.
    a. When you throw a ball, do you experience an impulse?
    b. Do you experience an impulse when you catch a ball of the same speed?
    c. Do you experience an impulse when you catch it and then throw it out again?
    d. Which impulse is greatest?

13. Why is more impulse delivered during a collision when bouncing occurs than during one when it doesn't?

14. Why is the Pelton Wheel an improvement over paddle wheels with flat blades?

Section 8.4

15. In terms of momentum conservation, why does a cannon recoil when fired?

16. What does it mean to say that momentum is conserved?

Section 8.5

17. Distinguish between an elastic and an inelastic collision.

18. Imagine that you are hovering next to the space shuttle in an Earth orbit. Your buddy of equal mass, who is moving at 4 km/h with respect to the shuttle, bumps into you. If he holds onto you, how fast do you both move with respect to the ship?

Section 8.6

19. Is momentum conserved for colliding objects that are moving at angles to one another? Explain.

Think and Rank ......

Rank each of the following sets of scenarios in order of the quantity or property involved. List them from left to right. If scenarios have equal rankings, then separate them with an equal sign. (e.g., A = B)

20. The balls have different masses and speeds.

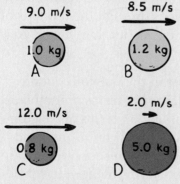

Rank the following from greatest to least.
a. momentum
b. the impulse needed to stop them

21. Below are before-and-after pictures of a car's speed. The mass of the car doesn't change.

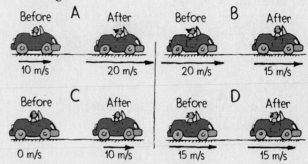

Rank the following from greatest to least.
a. the magnitude of momentum change
b. the magnitude of the impulse producing the momentum change

22. Jogging Jake runs along a train flatcar that moves at the velocities shown. In each case, Jake's velocity is given relative to the car.

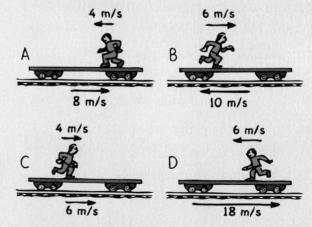

Rank the following from greatest to least.
a. the magnitude of Jake's momentum relative to the car
b. Jake's momentum to the right relative to an observer at rest on the ground

23. Rick pushes crates starting at rest across a floor for 3 seconds with a net force as shown.

For each crate, rank the following from greatest to least.
a. change in momentum
b. final speed
c. momentum in 3 seconds

Plug and Chug ······

The key equations of the chapter are shown below in bold type.

Momentum = $m \times v$

24. Calculate the momentum of a 10-kg bowling ball rolling at 2 m/s.

25. Calculate the momentum of a 50-kg carton that slides at 4 m/s across an icy surface.

Impulse = Ft

26. Calculate the impulse when an average force of 10 N is exerted on a cart for 2.5 s.

27. Calculate the impulse when an average force of 10 N acts on a cart for 5.0 s.

Think and Explain ······

For answers to Think and Explains and Think and Solves, you may express momentum with the symbol p. Then $p = mv$.

28. A lunar vehicle is tested on Earth at a speed of 10 km/h. When it travels as fast on the moon, is its momentum more, less, or the same?

29. When you ride a bicycle at full speed and the bike stops suddenly, why do you have to push hard on the handlebars to keep from flying forward?

30. Can Andrew produce a net impulse on an automobile by sitting inside and pushing on the dashboard? Can the internal forces within a soccer ball produce an impulse on the soccer ball that will change its momentum?

31. Brian tries to jump from his canoe to the dock. He lands in the water, delighting his companions. What's your explanation for his mishap?

32. Jason throws a ball horizontally while standing on roller skates. He rolls backward with a momentum that matches that of the ball. Will he end up rolling backward if he goes through the motions of throwing the ball, but does not let go of it? Explain.

33. The example in the previous question can be explained in terms of momentum conservation and in terms of Newton's third law. Assuming you've answered it in terms of momentum conservation, answer it also in terms of Newton's third law (or vice versa if you answered already via Newton's third law).

34. In the previous chapter, rocket propulsion was explained in terms of Newton's third law. That is, the force that propels a rocket is from the exhaust gases pushing against the rocket, the reaction to the force the rocket exerts on the exhaust gases. Explain rocket propulsion in terms of momentum conservation.

35. In terms of impulse and momentum, why are air bags in automobiles a good idea?

36. Why do gymnasts use floor mats that are very thick?

37. When jumping from a significant height, why is it advantageous to land with your knees slightly bent?

38. In terms of impulse and momentum, why are nylon ropes, which stretch considerably under tension, favored by mountain climbers?

39. Would it be a dangerous mistake for a bungee jumper to use a steel cable rather than an elastic cord?

40. When catching a foul ball at a baseball game, why is it important to extend your bare hands upward so they can move downward as the ball is being caught?

41. Why would it be a poor idea to have the back of your hand up against the outfield wall when you catch a long fly ball?

42. Many years ago, automobiles were manufactured to be as rigid as possible. Today's autos are designed to crumple upon impact. Why?

43. Why is it difficult for a firefighter to hold a hose that ejects large amounts of water at high speed?

44. You can't throw a raw egg against a wall without breaking the shell, but you can throw it at the same speed into a sagging sheet without breaking it. Explain.

45. Why can Muhammad exert a greater punching force with his bare fist than he can while wearing a boxing glove?

46. Why do 6-ounce boxing gloves hit harder than 16-ounce gloves?

47. Suppose you roll a bowling ball into a pillow and the ball stops. Now suppose you roll it against a spring and it bounces back with an equal and opposite momentum.
   a. Which object exerts a greater impulse, the pillow or the spring?
   b. If the time it takes the pillow to stop the ball is the same as the time of contact of the ball with the spring, how do the average forces exerted on the ball compare?

48. If you topple from your treehouse, you'll continuously gain momentum as you fall to the ground below. Doesn't this violate the law of conservation of momentum? Defend your answer.

49. If a fully loaded shopping cart and an empty one traveling at the same speed have a head-on collision, which cart will experience the greater force of impact? The greater impulse? The greater change in momentum? The greater acceleration?

50. A bug and the windshield of a fast-moving car collide. Indicate whether each of the following statements is true or false.
    a. The forces of impact on the bug and on the car are the same size.
    b. The impulses on the bug and on the car are the same size.
    c. The changes in speed of the bug and of the car are the same.
    d. The changes in momentum of the bug and of the car are the same size.

51. What difference in recoil would you expect in firing a solid ball versus firing a hollow ball from the same cannon? Explain.

52. A group of playful astronauts, each with a bag full of balls, form a circle as they free-fall in space. Describe what happens when they begin tossing balls simultaneously to one another.

53. A proton from an accelerator strikes an atom. An electron is observed flying forward in the same direction the proton was moving and at a speed much greater than the speed of the proton. What conclusion can you draw about the relative mass of a proton and an electron?

Think and Solve ••••••

54. Using units, show that kg·m/s is equivalent to N·s.

55. A 1000-kg car moving at 20 m/s slams into a building and comes to a halt. Which of the following questions can be answered using the given information, and which one *cannot* be answered? Explain.
    a. What impulse acts on the car?
    b. What is the force of impact on the car?

56. A car with a mass of 1000 kg moves at 20 m/s. What braking force is needed to bring the car to a halt in 10 s?

57. A 2-kg blob of putty moving at 3 m/s slams into a 2-kg blob of putty at rest.
    a. Calculate the speed of the two stuck-together blobs of putty immediately after colliding.
    b. Calculate the speed of the two blobs if the one at rest was 4 kg.

58. A 1-kg dart moving horizontally at 10 m/s strikes and sticks to a wood block of mass 9 kg, which slides across a friction-free level surface. What is the speed of the block and the dart after the collision?

59. Assume an 8-kg bowling ball moving at 2 m/s bounces off a spring at the same speed that it had before bouncing.
  a. What is its momentum of recoil?
  b. What is its change in momentum? (*Hint:* What is the change in temperature when something goes from 1° to −1°?)
  c. If the interaction with the spring occurs in 0.5 s, calculate the average force the spring exerts on it.

60. Brakes are applied in bringing a 1200-kg car moving at 25 m/s to rest in 20.0 s. Show that the amount of braking force is 1500 N.

61. A 20.0-kg mass moving at a speed of 3.0 m/s is stopped by a constant force of 15.0 N. Show that the stopping time required is 4.0 s.

62. A 1-kg ostrich egg is thrown at 2 m/s at a bed sheet and is brought to rest in 0.2 s. Show that the average amount of force on the egg is 10 N.

63. A railroad diesel engine weighs four times as much as a freight car. If the diesel engine coasts at 5 km/h into a freight car that is at rest, how fast do the two coast after they couple?

64. A comic-strip superhero meets an asteroid in outer space and hurls it at 100 m/s. The asteroid is a thousand times more massive than the superhero is. In the strip, the superhero is seen at rest after the throw. Taking physics into account, what would be his recoil speed? What is this in miles per hour?

65. A 5-kg fish swimming 1 m/s swallows an absent-minded 1-kg fish at rest. What is the speed of the large fish immediately after lunch? What would its speed be if the small fish were swimming toward it at 4 m/s?

Activity • • • • • •

66. Visit your local pool or billiards parlor and bone up on momentum conservation. Note that no matter how complicated the collision of balls, the momentum along the line of action of the cue ball before impact is the same as the combined momentum of all the balls along this direction after impact. Also, the components of momenta perpendicular to this line of action add to zero after impact, the same value as before impact in this direction. When rotational skidding, English, is imparted by striking the cue ball off center, rotational momentum, which is also conserved, somewhat complicates the analysis. But regardless of how the cue ball is struck, in the absence of external forces, both linear and rotational momentum are always conserved. Pool or billiards offers a first-rate exhibition of momentum conservation in action.

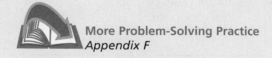

More Problem-Solving Practice
Appendix F

9 ENERGY

THE BIG IDEA : Energy can change from one form to another without a net loss or gain.

E nergy is the most central concept underlying all of science. Surprisingly, the idea of energy was unknown to Isaac Newton, and its existence was still being debated in the 1850s. Even though the concept of energy is relatively new, today we find it ingrained not only in all branches of science, but in nearly every aspect of human society. We are all quite familiar with energy. Energy comes to us from the sun in the form of sunlight, it is in the food we eat, and it sustains life. Energy may be the most familiar concept in science, yet it is one of the most difficult to define. Persons, places, and things have energy, but we observe only the effects of energy when something is happening—only when energy is being transferred from one place to another or transformed from one form to another. We begin our study of energy by observing a related concept, *work*.

discover!

Where Does a Popper Toy Get Its Energy?

1. Turn a popper (slice of a hollow rubber ball) inside out and place it on a table or floor. Observe what happens to the popper toy.

2. Once again compress the popper and drop it onto a table or floor. Observe what happens to the popper.

Analyze and Conclude

1. **Observing** What propelled the popper into the air?

2. **Predicting** Will dropping the popper from greater heights make the popper jump higher? Explain.

3. **Making Generalizations** Describe where the popper got the energy to move upward and downward through the air.

9.1 Work

The previous chapter showed that the change in an object's motion is related to both force and how long the force acts. "How long" meant time. Remember, the quantity *force × time* is called *impulse*. But "how long" need not always mean time. It can mean distance also. When we consider the quantity *force × distance*, we are talking about the concept of work. **Work** is the product of the net force on an object and the distance through which the object is moved.

We do work when we lift a load against Earth's gravity. The heavier the load or the higher we lift it, the more work we do.
⊘ **Work is done when a force acts on an object and the object moves in the direction of the force.**

Let's look at the simplest case, in which the force is constant and the motion takes place in a straight line in the direction of the force. Then the work done on an object by an applied force is the product of the force and the distance through which the object is moved.[9.1]

$$\text{work} = \text{net force} \times \text{distance}$$

In equation form,

$$W = Fd$$

If we lift two loads up one story, we do twice as much work as we would in lifting one load the same distance, because the *force* needed to lift twice the weight is twice as great. Similarly, if we lift one load two stories instead of one story, we do twice as much work because the *distance* is twice as great.

Notice that the definition of work involves both a force *and* a distance. The weight lifter in Figure 9.1 is holding a barbell weighing 1000 N over his head. He may get really tired holding it, but if the barbell is not moved by the force he exerts, he does no work on the barbell. Work may be done on the muscles by stretching and squeezing them, which is force times distance on a biological scale, but this work is not done on the barbell. Lifting the barbell, however, is a different story. When the weight lifter raises the barbell from the floor, he is doing work on it.

Work generally falls into two categories. One of these is the work done against another force. When an archer stretches her bowstring, she is doing work against the elastic forces of the bow. Similarly, when the ram of a pile driver is raised, work is required to raise the ram against the force of gravity. When you do push-ups, you do work against your own weight. You do work on something when you force it to move against the influence of an opposing force—often friction.

think!

Suppose that you apply a 60-N horizontal force to a 32-kg package, which pushes it 4 meters across a mailroom floor. How much work do you do on the package?
Answer: 9.1

FIGURE 9.1 ▲

Work is done in lifting the barbell but not in holding it steady. If the barbell could be lifted twice as high, the weight lifter would have to do twice as much work.

The physics of a weightlifter holding a stationary barbell overhead is no different than the physics of a table supporting a barbell's weight. No net force acts on the barbell, no work is done on it, and no change in its energy occurs.

The other category of work is work done to change the speed of an object. This kind of work is done in bringing an automobile up to speed or in slowing it down. In both categories, work involves a transfer of energy between something and its surroundings.

The unit of measurement for work combines a unit of force, N, with a unit of distance, m. The resulting unit of work is the newton-meter (N·m), also called the **joule** (rhymes with cool) in honor of James Joule. One joule (J) of work is done when a force of 1 N is exerted over a distance of 1 m, as in lifting an apple over your head. For larger values, we speak of kilojoules (kJ)—thousands of joules—or megajoules (MJ)—millions of joules. The weight lifter in Figure 9.1 does work on the order of kilojoules. To stop a loaded truck going at 100 km/h takes megajoules of work.

CONCEPT CHECK : When is work done on an object?

9.2 Power

The definition of work says nothing about how long it takes to do the work. When carrying a load up some stairs, you do the same amount of work whether you walk or run up the stairs. So why are you more tired after running upstairs in a few seconds than after walking upstairs in a few minutes? To understand this difference, we need to talk about how fast the work is done, or power. **Power** is the rate at which work is done. ✅ **Power equals the amount of work done divided by the time interval during which the work is done.**

$$\text{power} = \frac{\text{work done}}{\text{time interval}}$$

A high-power engine does work rapidly. An automobile engine that delivers twice the power of another automobile engine does not necessarily produce twice as much work or go twice as fast as the less powerful engine. Twice the power means the engine can do twice the work in the same amount of time or the same amount of work in half the time. A powerful engine can get an automobile up to a given speed in less time than a less powerful engine can.

The unit of power is the joule per second, also known as the **watt,** in honor of James Watt, the eighteenth-century developer of the steam engine. One watt (W) of power is expended when one joule of work is done in one second. One kilowatt (kW) equals 1000 watts. One megawatt (MW) equals one million watts. The space shuttle in Figure 9.2 uses 33,000 MW of power.

FIGURE 9.2 ▼

The three main engines of the space shuttle can develop 33,000 MW of power when fuel is burned at the enormous rate of 3400 kg/s. This is like emptying an average-size swimming pool in 20 seconds!

In the United States, we customarily rate engines in units of horsepower and electricity in kilowatts, but either may be used. In the metric system of units, automobiles are rated in kilowatts. One horsepower (hp) is the same as 0.75 kW, so an engine rated at 134 hp is a 100-kW engine.

CONCEPT CHECK How can you calculate power?

think!

If a forklift is replaced with a new forklift that has twice the power, how much greater a load can it lift in the same amount of time? If it lifts the same load, how much faster can it operate? *Answer: 9.2*

9.3 Mechanical Energy

When work is done by an archer in drawing back a bowstring, the bent bow acquires the ability to do work on the arrow. When work is done to stretch a rubber band, the rubber band acquires the ability to do work on an object when it is released. When work is done to wind a spring mechanism, the spring acquires the ability to do work on various gears to run a clock, ring a bell, or sound an alarm.

In each case, something has been acquired that enables the object to do work. It may be in the form of a compression of atoms in the material of an object; a physical separation of attracting bodies; or a rearrangement of electric charges in the molecules of a substance. The property of an object or system that enables it to do work is **energy**. [9.3] Like work, energy is measured in joules. It appears in many forms that will be discussed in the following chapters. For now we will focus on mechanical energy. **Mechanical energy** is the energy due to the position of something or the movement of something. ☑ **The two forms of mechanical energy are kinetic energy and potential energy.**

CONCEPT CHECK What are the two forms of mechanical energy?

---

discover!

What Happens When You Do Work on Sand?

1. Pour a handful of dry sand into a can.
2. Measure the temperature of the sand with a thermometer.
3. Remove the thermometer and cover the can.
4. Shake the can vigorously for a minute or so. Now remove the cover and measure the temperature of the sand again.
5. Describe what happened to the temperature of the sand after you shook it.
6. **Think** How can you explain the change in temperature of the sand in terms of work and energy?

9.4 Potential Energy

An object may store energy by virtue of its position. Energy that is stored and held in readiness is called **potential energy** (PE) because in the stored state it has the potential for doing work. ⊘ **Three examples of potential energy are elastic potential energy, chemical energy, and gravitational potential energy.**

Elastic Potential Energy A stretched or compressed spring, for example, has a potential for doing work. This type of potential energy is *elastic potential energy*. When a bow is drawn back, energy is stored in the bow. The bow can do work on the arrow. A stretched rubber band has potential energy because of its position. If the rubber band is part of a slingshot, it is also capable of doing work.

Chemical Energy The chemical energy in fuels is also potential energy. It is actually energy of position at the submicroscopic level. This energy is available when the positions of electric charges within and between molecules are altered, that is, when a chemical change takes place. Any substance that can do work through chemical reactions possesses chemical energy. Potential energy is found in fossil fuels, electric batteries, and the food we eat.

Gravitational Potential Energy Work is required to elevate objects against Earth's gravity. The potential energy due to elevated positions is *gravitational potential energy*. Water in an elevated reservoir and the raised ram of a pile driver have gravitational potential energy.

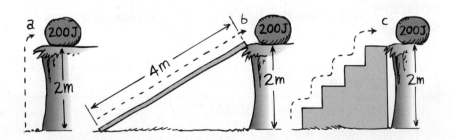

FIGURE 9.3 ▲
The potential energy of the 100-N boulder with respect to the ground below is 200 J in each case because the work done in elevating it 2 m is the same whether the boulder is **a.** lifted with 100 N of force, **b.** pushed up the 4-m incline with 50 N of force, or **c.** lifted with 100 N of force up each 0.5-m stair. No work is done in moving it horizontally, neglecting friction.

The amount of gravitational potential energy possessed by an elevated object is equal to the work done against gravity in lifting it. The work done equals the force required to move it upward times the vertical distance it is moved (remember $W = Fd$). The upward force required while moving at constant velocity is equal to the weight, mg, of the object, so the work done in lifting it through a height h is the product mgh.

Go Online
SCi LINKS™ NSTA

For: Links on potential energy
Visit: www.SciLinks.org
Web Code: csn – 0904

$$\text{gravitational potential energy} = \text{weight} \times \text{height}$$

$$PE = mgh$$

Note that the height is the distance above some arbitrarily chosen reference level, such as the ground or the floor of a building. The gravitational potential energy, mgh, is relative to that level and depends only on mg and h. For example, if you're in a third-story classroom and a ball rests on the floor, you can say the ball is at height 0. Lift it and it has positive PE relative to the floor. Toss it out the window and it has negative PE relative to the floor. We can see in Figure 9.3 that the potential energy of the boulder at the top of the ledge does not depend on the path taken to get it there.

Hydroelectric power stations make use of gravitational potential energy. When a need for power exists, water from an upper reservoir flows through a long tunnel to an electric generator. Gravitational potential energy of the water is converted to electrical energy. Most of this energy is delivered to consumers during daylight hours. A few power stations *buy* electricity at night, when there is much less demand. They use this electricity to pump water from a lower reservoir back up to the upper reservoir. This process, called *pumped storage,* is practical when the cost of electricity is less at night. Then electrical energy is transformed to gravitational potential energy. Although the pumped storage system doesn't generate any overall net energy, it helps to smooth out differences between energy demand and supply.

When h is below a reference point, PE is negative relative to that reference point.

CONCEPT CHECK Name three examples of potential energy.

think!

You lift a 100-N boulder 1 m.
a. How much work is done on the boulder?
b. What power is expended if you lift the boulder in a time of 2 s?
c. What is the gravitational potential energy of the boulder in the lifted position? *Answer: 9.4*

Refer to Note 9.5 in Appendix G for the derivation of the equation $W = \Delta KE$.

9.5 Kinetic Energy

Push on an object and you can set it in motion. If an object is moving, then it is capable of doing work. It has energy of motion, or **kinetic energy** (KE). The kinetic energy of an object depends on the mass of the object as well as its speed. It is equal to half the mass multiplied by the square of the speed.

$$\text{kinetic energy} = \tfrac{1}{2}\text{mass} \times \text{speed}^2$$

$$KE = \tfrac{1}{2}mv^2$$

When you throw a ball, you do work on it to give it speed as it leaves your hand. The moving ball can then hit something and push it, doing work on what it hits. ✅ **The kinetic energy of a moving object is equal to the work required to bring it to its speed from rest, or the work the object can do while being brought to rest.** [9.5]

$$\text{net force} \times \text{distance} = \text{kinetic energy}$$

$$Fd = \tfrac{1}{2}mv^2$$

Note that the speed is squared, so if the speed of an object is doubled, its kinetic energy is quadrupled ($2^2 = 4$). Consequently, it takes four times the work to double the speed. Also, an object moving twice as fast takes four times as much work to stop. Whenever work is done, energy changes.

CONCEPT CHECK: How are work and the kinetic energy of a moving object related?

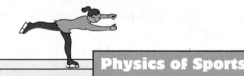

Physics of Sports

The Sweet Spot

The sweet spot of a softball bat or a tennis racquet is the place where the ball's impact produces minimum vibrations in the racquet or bat. Strike a ball at the sweet spot and it goes faster and farther. Strike a ball in another part of the bat or racquet, and vibrations can occur that sting your hand! From an energy point of view, there is energy in the vibrations of the bat or racquet. There is energy in the ball after being struck. Energy that is not in vibrations is energy available to the ball. Do you see why a ball will go faster and farther when struck at the sweet spot?

a

b

◀ **FIGURE 9.4**
Due to friction, energy is transferred both into the floor and into the tire when the bicycle skids to a stop. **a.** An infrared camera reveals the heated tire track on the floor. **b.** The warmth of the tire is also revealed.

9.6 Work-Energy Theorem

So we see that to increase the kinetic energy of an object, work must be done on it. Or if an object is moving, work is required to bring it to rest. In either case, the change in kinetic energy is equal to the net work done. The **work-energy theorem** describes the relationship between work and energy. ✅ **The work-energy theorem states that whenever work is done, energy changes.** We abbreviate "change in" with the delta symbol, Δ, and say

$$\text{Work} = \Delta KE$$

Work equals change in kinetic energy. The work in this equation is the *net* work—that is, the work based on the net force.

The work-energy theorem emphasizes the role of *change*. If there is no change in an object's kinetic energy, then we know no net work was done on it. Push against a box on a floor. If it doesn't slide, then you are not doing work on the box. Put the box on a very slippery floor and push again. If there is no friction at all, the work of your push times the distance of your push appears as kinetic energy of the box. If there is some friction, it is the *net* force of your push minus the frictional force that is multiplied by distance to give the gain in kinetic energy. If the box moves at a constant speed, you are pushing just hard enough to overcome friction. Then the net force and net work are zero, and, according to the work-energy theorem, $\Delta KE = 0$. The kinetic energy doesn't change.

The work-energy theorem applies to decreasing speed as well. The more kinetic energy something has, the more work is required to stop it. Twice as much kinetic energy means twice as much work. When we apply the brakes to slow a car, or the bike in Figure 9.4, we do work on it. This work is the friction force supplied by the brakes multiplied by the distance over which the friction force acts.

think!

A friend says that if you do 100 J of work on a moving cart, the cart will gain 100 J of KE. Another friend says this depends on whether or not there is friction. What is your opinion of these statements? *Answer: 9.6.1*

Interestingly, the maximum friction that the brakes can supply is nearly the same whether the car moves slowly or quickly. In a panic stop with antilock brakes, the only way for the brakes to do more work is to act over a longer distance. A car moving at twice the speed of another has four times ($2^2 = 4$) as much kinetic energy, and will require four times as much work to stop. Since the frictional force is nearly the same for both cars, the faster one takes four times as much distance to stop. The same rule applies to older-model brakes that can lock the wheels. The force of friction on a skidding tire is also nearly independent of speed. So, as accident investigators are well aware, an automobile going 100 kilometers per hour, with four times the kinetic energy it would have at 50 kilometers per hour, skids four times as far with its wheels locked as it would with a speed of 50 kilometers per hour. Figure 9.5 shows the skid distances for a car moving at 45 km/h, 90 km/h, and 180 km/h. The distances would be even greater if the driver's reaction time were taken into account. Kinetic energy depends on speed *squared*.

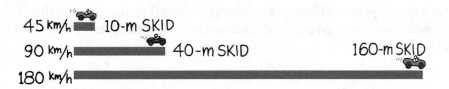

45 km/h 10-m SKID
90 km/h 40-m SKID
180 km/h 160-m SKID

FIGURE 9.5 ▲
Typical stopping distances for cars equipped with antilock brakes traveling at various speeds. The work done to stop the car is friction force × distance of slide.

Kinetic energy often appears hidden in different forms of energy, such as heat, sound, light, and electricity. Random molecular motion is sensed as heat. Sound consists of molecules vibrating in rhythmic patterns. Even light energy originates in the motion of electrons within atoms. Electrons in motion make electric currents. We see that kinetic energy plays a role in other energy forms.

CONCEPT CHECK What is the work-energy theorem?

---

think!

When the brakes of a car are locked, the car skids to a stop. How much farther will the car skid if it's moving 3 times as fast?
Answer: 9.6.2

9.7 Conservation of Energy

More important than knowing *what energy is*, is understanding how it behaves—*how it transforms*. We can understand nearly every process that occurs in nature if we analyze it in terms of a transformation of energy from one form to another.

As you draw back the arrow in a bow, as shown in Figure 9.6, you do work stretching the bow. The bow then has potential energy. When released, the arrow has kinetic energy equal to this potential energy. It delivers this energy to its target. The small distance the arrow moves multiplied by the average force of impact doesn't quite match the kinetic energy of the target. But if you investigate further, you'll find that both the arrow and target are a bit warmer. By how much? By the energy difference. Energy changes from one form to another without a net loss or a net gain.

The study of the various forms of energy and the transformations from one form into another is the **law of conservation of energy.** ⊘ **The law of conservation of energy states that energy cannot be created or destroyed. It can be transformed from one form into another, but the total amount of energy never changes.**

FIGURE 9.6 ▲
When released, potential energy will become the kinetic energy of the arrow.

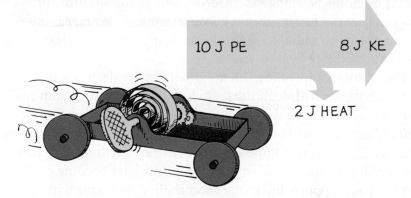

10 J PE   8 J KE

2 J HEAT

◄ **FIGURE 9.7**
Part of the PE of the wound spring changes into KE. The remaining PE goes into heating the machinery and the surroundings due to friction. No energy is lost.

Figures 9.7 and 9.8 demonstrate conservation of energy in two different systems. When you consider any system in its entirety, whether it is as simple as the swinging pendulum or as complex as an exploding galaxy, there is one quantity that does not change: energy. Energy may change form, but the total energy score stays the same.

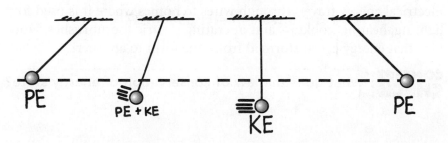

PE   PE + KE   KE   PE

◄ **FIGURE 9.8**
Everywhere along the path of the pendulum bob, the sum of PE and KE is the same. Because of the work done against friction, this energy will eventually be transformed into heat.

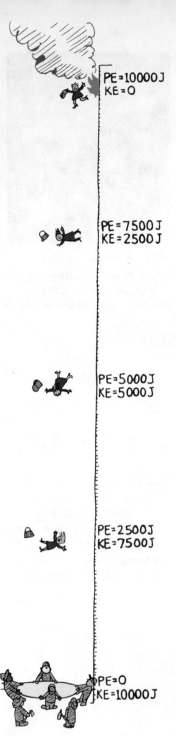

PE = 10000 J
KE = 0

PE = 7500 J
KE = 2500 J

PE = 5000 J
KE = 5000 J

PE = 2500 J
KE = 7500 J

PE = 0
KE = 10000 J

FIGURE 9.9 ▲
When the woman in distress leaps from the burning building, note that the sum of her PE and KE remains constant at each successive position all the way down to the ground.

Link to CHEMISTRY

Reactions What process provides energy for rockets that lift the space shuttle into orbit? What process releases energy from the food we eat? The answer is *chemical reactions.* During a chemical reaction the bonds between atoms *break* and then reform. Breaking bonds requires energy, and forming bonds releases it. Pulling atoms apart is like pulling apart two magnets stuck together; it takes energy to do it. And when atoms join, it is like two separated magnets that slam together; energy is released. Rapid energy release can produce flames. Slow energy release occurs during the digestion of food. The conservation of energy rules chemical reactions. The amount of energy required to break a chemical bond is the same amount released when that bond is formed.

This energy score takes into account the fact that each atom that makes up matter is a concentrated bundle of energy. When the nuclei (cores) of atoms rearrange themselves, enormous amounts of energy can be released. The sun shines because some of its nuclear energy is transformed into radiant energy. In nuclear reactors, nuclear energy is transformed into heat.

Enormous compression due to gravity in the deep hot interior of the sun causes hydrogen nuclei to fuse and become helium nuclei. This high-temperature welding of atomic nuclei is called *thermonuclear fusion* and will be covered later, in Chapter 40. This process releases radiant energy, some of which reaches Earth. Part of this energy falls on plants, and some of the plants later become coal. Another part supports life in the food chain that begins with microscopic marine animals and plants, and later gets stored in oil. Part of the sun's energy is used to evaporate water from the ocean. Some water returns to Earth as rain that is trapped behind a dam. By virtue of its elevated position, the water behind the dam has potential energy that is used to power a generating plant below the dam. The generating plant transforms the energy of falling water into electrical energy. Electrical energy travels through wires to homes where it is used for lighting, heating, cooking, and operating electric toothbrushes. How nice that energy is transformed from one form to another!

CONCEPT CHECK What does the law of conservation of energy state?

9.8 Machines

A **machine** is a device used to multiply forces or simply to change the direction of forces. The concept that underlies every machine is the conservation of energy. A machine cannot put out more energy than is put into it. A machine cannot create energy. ☑ **A machine transfers energy from one place to another or transforms it from one form to another.**

Levers Consider one of the simplest machines, the lever, shown in Figure 9.10. A **lever** is a simple machine made of a bar that turns about a fixed point. At the same time we do work on one end of the lever, the other end does work on the load. We see that the direction of force is changed. If we push *down*, the load is lifted *up*. If the heat from friction is small enough to neglect, the work input will be equal to the work output.

$$\text{work input} = \text{work output}$$

Since work equals force times distance, we can say

$$(\text{force} \times \text{distance})_{\text{input}} = (\text{force} \times \text{distance})_{\text{output}}$$

A little thought will show that the pivot point, or **fulcrum,** of the lever can be relatively close to the load. Then a small input force exerted through a large distance will produce a large output force over a correspondingly short distance. In this way, a lever can multiply forces. However, no machine can multiply work or energy. That's a conservation of energy no-no!

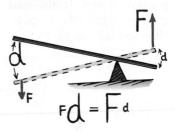

FIGURE 9.11 ▼

The output force (80 N) is eight times the input force (10 N), while the output distance (1/8 m) is one-eighth of the input distance (1 m).

80 N

10 N

1m

⅛m

Consider the ideal weightless lever in Figure 9.11. The child pushes down 10 N and lifts an 80-N load. The ratio of output force to input force for a machine is called the **mechanical advantage.** Here the mechanical advantage is (80 N)/(10 N), or 8. Notice that the load moves only one-eighth of the distance the input force moves. Neglecting friction, the mechanical advantage can also be determined by the ratio of input distance to output distance.

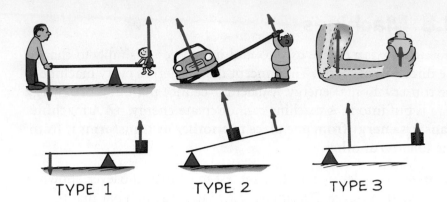

TYPE 1   TYPE 2   TYPE 3

Three common ways to set up a lever are shown in Figure 9.12. A type 1 lever has the fulcrum between the force and the load, or between input and output. This kind of lever is commonly seen in a playground seesaw with children sitting on each end of it. Push down on one end and you lift a load at the other. You can increase force at the expense of distance. Note that the directions of input and output are opposite.

For a type 2 lever, the load is between the fulcrum and the input force. To lift a load, you *lift* the end of the lever. One example is placing one end of a long steel bar under an automobile frame and lifting on the free end to raise the automobile. Again, force on the load is increased at the expense of distance. Since the input and output forces are on the same side of the fulcrum, the forces have the same direction.

In the type 3 lever, the fulcrum is at one end and the load is at the other. The input force is applied between them. Your biceps muscles are connected to the bones in your forearm in this way. The fulcrum is your elbow and the load is in your hand. The type 3 lever increases distance at the expense of force. When you move your biceps muscles a short distance, your hand moves a much greater distance. The input and output forces are on the same side of the fulcrum and therefore they have the same direction.

Pulleys A **pulley** is basically a kind of lever that can be used to change the direction of a force. Properly used, a pulley or system of pulleys can multiply forces.

The single pulley in Figure 9.13a behaves like a type 1 lever. The axis of the pulley acts as the fulcrum, and both lever distances (the radius of the pulley) are equal so the pulley does not multiply force. It simply changes the direction of the applied force. In this case, the mechanical advantage equals 1. Notice that the input distance equals the output distance the load moves.

A machine can multiply force, but never energy. No way!

In Figure 9.13b, the single pulley acts as a type 2 lever. Careful thought will show that the fulcrum is at the left end of the "lever" where the supporting rope makes contact with the pulley. The load is suspended halfway between the fulcrum and the input end of the lever, which is on the right end of the "lever." Each newton of input will support two newtons of load, so the mechanical advantage is 2. This number checks with the distances moved. To raise the load 1 m, the woman will have to pull the rope up 2 m. We can say the mechanical advantage is 2 for another reason: the load is now supported by two strands of rope. This means each strand supports half the load. The force the woman applies to support the load is therefore only half of the weight of the load.

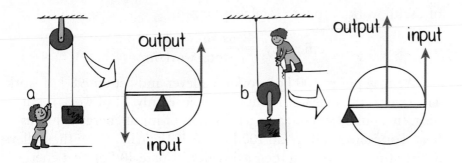

The mechanical advantage for simple pulley systems is the same as the number of strands of rope that actually support the load. In Figure 9.13a, the load is supported by one strand and the mechanical advantage is 1. In Figure 9.13b, the load is supported by two strands and the mechanical advantage is 2. Can you use this rule to state the mechanical advantage of the pulley system in Figure 9.13c?[9.8]

The mechanical advantage of the simple system in Figure 9.13c is 2. Notice that although three strands of rope are shown, only two strands actually support the load. The upper pulley serves only to change the direction of the force. Actually experimenting with a variety of pulley systems is much more beneficial than reading about them in a textbook, so try to get your hands on some pulleys, in or out of class. They're fun.

The pulley system shown in Figure 9.14 is a bit more complex, but the principles of energy conservation are the same. When the rope is pulled 5 m with a force of 100 N, a 500-N load is lifted 1 m. The mechanical advantage is (500 N)/(100 N), or 5. Force is multiplied at the expense of distance. The mechanical advantage can also be found from the ratio of distances: (input distance)/(output distance) = 5.

CONCEPT CHECK : How does a machine use energy?

FIGURE 9.13 ▲
A pulley is useful.
a. A pulley can change the direction of a force.
b. A pulley multiplies force. **c.** Two pulleys can change the direction and multiply force.

FIGURE 9.14 ▲
A complex pulley system is shown here.

9.9 Efficiency

The previous examples of machines were considered to be *ideal*. All the work input was transferred to work output. An ideal machine would have 100% efficiency. No real machine can be 100% efficient. ⊘ **In any machine, some energy is transformed into atomic or molecular kinetic energy—making the machine warmer.** We say this wasted energy is dissipated as heat.[9.9.1]

When a simple lever rocks about its fulcrum, or a pulley turns about its axis, a small fraction of input energy is converted into thermal energy. The **efficiency** of a machine is the ratio of useful energy output to total energy input, or the percentage of the work input that is converted to work output. Efficiency can be expressed as the ratio of useful work output to total work input.

$$\text{efficiency} = \frac{\text{useful work output}}{\text{total work input}}$$

We may put in 100 J of work on a lever and get out 98 J of work. The lever is then 98% efficient and we lose only 2 J of work input as heat. In a pulley system, a larger fraction of input energy is lost as heat. For example, if we do 100 J of work, the friction on the pulleys as they turn and rub on their axle can dissipate 40 J of heat energy. So the work output is only 60 J and the pulley system has an efficiency of 60%. The lower the efficiency of a machine, the greater is the amount of energy wasted as heat.

FIGURE 9.15 ▶
Pushing the block of ice 5 times farther up the incline than the vertical distance it's lifted requires a force of only one-fifth its weight. Whether pushed up the plane or simply lifted, the ice gains the same amount of PE.

5 m   1 m

Inclined Planes An inclined plane is a machine. Sliding a load up an incline requires less force than lifting it vertically. Figure 9.15 shows a 5-m inclined plane with its high end elevated by 1 m. Using the plane to elevate a heavy load, we push the load five times farther than we lift it vertically. If friction is negligible, we need apply only one-fifth of the force required to lift the load vertically. The inclined plane shown has a *theoretical* mechanical advantage of 5.

An icy plank used to slide a block of ice up to some height might have an efficiency of almost 100%. However, when the load is a wooden crate sliding on a wooden plank, both the actual mechanical advantage and the efficiency will be considerably less. Friction will require you to exert more force (a greater work input) without any increase in work output.

Efficiency can also be expressed as the ratio of actual mechanical advantage to theoretical mechanical advantage.

$$\text{efficiency} = \frac{\text{actual mechanical advantage}}{\text{theoretical mechanical advantage}}$$

Efficiency will always be a fraction less than 1. To convert efficiency to percent, we simply express it as a decimal and multiply by 100%. For example, an efficiency of 0.25 expressed in percent is $0.25 \times 100\%$, or 25%.

Energy is nature's way of keeping score.

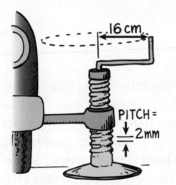

◄ **FIGURE 9.16**
The auto jack is like an inclined plane wrapped around a cylinder. Every time the handle is turned one revolution, the load is raised a distance of one pitch.

16 cm

PITCH = 2 mm

Complex Machines The auto jack shown in Figure 9.16 is actually an inclined plane wrapped around a cylinder. You can see that a single turn of the handle raises the load a relatively small distance. If the circular distance the handle is moved is 500 times greater than the pitch, which is the distance between ridges, then the theoretical mechanical advantage of the jack is 500.[9.9.2] No wonder a child can raise a loaded moving van with one of these devices! In practice there is a great deal of friction in this type of jack, so the efficiency might be about 20%. Thus the jack actually multiplies force by about 100 times, so the actual mechanical advantage approximates an impressive 100. Imagine the value of one of these devices if it had been available when the great pyramids were being built!

An automobile engine is a machine that transforms chemical energy stored in fuel into mechanical energy. The molecules of the gasoline break up as the fuel burns. Burning is a chemical reaction in which atoms combine with the oxygen in the air. Carbon atoms from the gasoline combine with oxygen atoms to form carbon dioxide, hydrogen atoms combine with oxygen, and energy is released. The converted energy is used to run the engine.

think!

A child on a sled (total weight 500 N) is pulled up a 10-m slope that elevates her a vertical distance of 1 m. What is the theoretical mechanical advantage of the slope?

Answer: 9.9

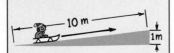

As physicists learned in the nineteenth century, transforming 100% of thermal energy into mechanical energy is not possible. Some heat must flow from the engine. Friction adds more to the energy loss. Even the best-designed gasoline-powered automobile engines are unlikely to be more than 35% efficient. Some of the heat energy goes into the cooling system and is released through the radiator to the air. Some of it goes out the tailpipe with the exhaust gases, and almost half goes into heating engine parts as a result of friction.

On top of these contributors to inefficiency, the fuel does not burn completely. A certain amount of it goes unused. We can look at inefficiency in this way: In any transformation there is a dilution of the amount of *useful energy*. Useful energy ultimately becomes thermal energy. Energy is not destroyed, it is simply degraded. Through heat transfer, thermal energy is the graveyard of useful energy.

CONCEPT CHECK Why can't a machine be 100% efficient?

9.10 Energy for Life

Every living cell in every organism is a machine. Like any machine, living cells need an energy supply. Most living organisms on this planet feed on various hydrocarbon compounds that release energy when they react with oxygen. There is more energy stored in gasoline than in the products of its combustion. ✔ **There is more energy stored in the molecules in food than there is in the reaction products after the food is metabolized. This energy difference sustains life.**[9.10]

The same principle of combustion occurs in the metabolism of food in the body and the burning of fossil fuels in mechanical engines. The main difference is the rate at which the reactions take place. During metabolism, the reaction rate is much slower and energy is released as it is needed by the body. Like the burning of fossil fuels, the reaction is self-sustaining once it starts. In metabolism, carbon combines with oxygen to form carbon dioxide.

The reverse process is more difficult. Only green plants and certain one-celled organisms can make carbon dioxide combine with water to produce hydrocarbon compounds such as sugar. This process is *photosynthesis* and requires an energy input, which normally comes from sunlight. Sugar is the simplest food. All other foods, such as carbohydrates, proteins, and fats, are also synthesized compounds containing carbon, hydrogen, oxygen, and other elements. Because green plants are able to use the energy of sunlight to make food that gives us and all other organisms energy, there is life.

In biology, you'll learn how the body takes energy from the food you eat to build molecules of adenosine triphosphate, or ATP, and how this supply of ATP is used to run all the chemical reactions that sustain life.

CONCEPT CHECK What role does energy play in sustaining life?

9.11 Sources of Energy

✔ **The sun is the source of practically all our energy on Earth.**
(Exceptions are nuclear and geothermal energy.) The energy from
burning wood comes from the sun. Even the energy we obtain from
Earth's compost of the past—fossil fuels such as petroleum, coal, and
natural gas—comes from the sun. These fuels are created by *photosynthesis,* the process by which plants trap solar energy and store it
as plant tissue.

Solar Power Sunlight is directly transformed into electricity by
photovoltaic cells, like those found in solar-powered calculators, or
more recently, in the flexible solar shingles on the roof of the building in Figure 9.17. We use the energy in sunlight to generate electricity indirectly as well. Sunlight evaporates water, which later falls as
rain; rainwater flows into rivers and turns water wheels, or it flows
into modern generator turbines as it returns to the sea.

Wind, caused by unequal warming of Earth's surface, is another
form of solar power. The energy of wind can be used to turn generator turbines within specially equipped windmills. Because wind
is not steady, wind power cannot by itself provide all of our energy
needs. But because the wind is always blowing somewhere, windmills
spread out over a large geographical area and integrated into a power
grid can make a substantial contribution to the overall energy mix.
Harnessing the wind is very practical when the energy it produces is
stored for future use, such as in the form of hydrogen.

◀ **FIGURE 9.17**
Solar shingles look like
traditional asphalt shingles
but they are hooked into
a home's electrical system.

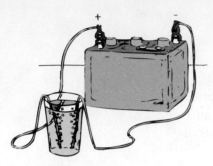

FIGURE 9.18 ▲

When electric current passes through water, bubbles of hydrogen form at one wire and bubbles of oxygen form at the other. In a fuel cell, the reverse process occurs: hydrogen and oxygen combine to produce water and electricity.

Fuel Cells Hydrogen, the least polluting of all fuels, holds much promise for the future. Because it takes energy to make hydrogen (to extract it from water and carbon compounds), it is not a *source* of energy. A simple method to extract hydrogen from water is shown in Figure 9.18. Place two platinum wires that are connected to the terminals of an ordinary battery into a glass of water (with an electrolyte dissolved in the water for conductivity). Be sure the wires don't touch each other. Bubbles of hydrogen form on one wire, and bubbles of oxygen form on the other. Electricity splits water into its constituent parts.

If you make the electrolysis process run backward, you have a fuel cell. In a **fuel cell,** hydrogen and oxygen gas are compressed at electrodes to produce water and electric current. The space shuttle uses fuel cells to meet its electrical needs while producing drinking water for the astronauts. Here on Earth, fuel-cell researchers are developing fuel cells for buses, automobiles, and trains.

Nuclear and Geothermal Energy The most concentrated form of usable energy is stored in uranium and plutonium, which are nuclear fuels. Interestingly, Earth's interior is kept hot by producing a form of nuclear power, radioactivity, which has been with us since the Earth was formed.

A byproduct of radioactivity in Earth's interior is geothermal energy. Geothermal energy is held in underground reservoirs of hot water. Geothermal energy is a practical energy source in areas of volcanic activity, such as Iceland, New Zealand, Japan, and Hawaii. In these places, heated water near Earth's surface is tapped to provide steam for running turbogenerators.

Energy sources such as nuclear, geothermal, wind, solar, and water power are environmentally friendly. The combustion of fossil fuels, on the other hand, leads to increased atmospheric concentrations of carbon dioxide, sulfur dioxide, and other pollutants.

As the world population increases, so does our need for energy. With the rules of physics to guide them, technologists are now researching newer and cleaner energy sources. But they race to keep up with world population and greater demand in the developing world.

CONCEPT CHECK : What is the source of practically all of our energy on Earth?

Watch for the growth of fuel-cell technology. The major hurdle for this technology is not the device itself, but with acquiring hydrogen fuel economically. One way is via solar cells.

Energy Conservation Most energy consumed in America comes from fossil fuels. Oil, natural gas, and coal supply the energy for almost all our industry and technology. About 70% of electrical power in the United States comes from fossil fuels, with about 21% from nuclear power. Worldwide, fossil fuels also account for most energy consumption. We have grown to depend on fossil fuels because they have been plentiful and inexpensive. Until recently, our consumption was small enough that we could ignore their environmental impact.

But things have changed. Fossil fuels are being consumed at a rate that threatens to deplete the entire world supply. Locally and globally, our fossil fuel consumption is measurably polluting the air we breathe and the water we drink. Yet, despite these problems, many people consider fossil fuels to be as inexhaustible as the sun's glow and as acceptable as Mom's apple pie, because these fuels lasted and nurtured us through the 1900s. Financially, fossil fuels are still a bargain, but this is destined to change. Environmentally, the costs are already dramatic. Some other fuel must take the place of fossil fuels if we are to maintain the industry and technology to which we are accustomed. The French have chosen nuclear, with about 74% of their electricity coming from nuclear power plants. What energy source would you choose as an alternative?

In the meantime, we shouldn't waste energy. As individuals, we should limit the consumption of useful energy by such measures as turning off unused electrical appliances, using less hot water, going easy on heating and air conditioning, and driving energy-efficient automobiles. By doing these things, we are conserving useful energy.

Critical Thinking In how many reasonable ways can we reduce energy consumption?

REVIEW

Concept Summary ······

- Work is done when a force acts on an object and the object moves in the direction of the force.

- Power equals work divided by the time.

- The two forms of mechanical energy are kinetic energy and potential energy.

- Three examples of potential energy are elastic potential energy, chemical energy, and gravitational potential energy.

- The kinetic energy of a moving object is equal to the work done on it.

- The work-energy theorem states that whenever work is done, energy changes.

- Energy cannot be created or destroyed.

- A machine transfers energy from one place to another or transforms it from one form to another.

- In a machine, some energy is transformed into atomic kinetic energy.

- There is more energy stored in the molecules in food than there is in the reaction products after the food is metabolized. The energy difference sustains life.

- The sun supplies most of Earth's energy.

think! Answers

9.1 $W = Fd = 60 \text{ N} \times 4 \text{ m} = 240 \text{ J}$

9.2   The forklift that delivers twice the power will lift twice the load in the same time, or the same load in half the time.

9.4   **a.** $W = Fd = 100 \text{ N·m} = 100 \text{ J}$

      b. Power $= \dfrac{100 \text{ J}}{2 \text{ s}} = 50 \text{ W}$

      c. It depends. Relative to its starting position, the boulder's PE is 100 J. Relative to some other reference level, its PE would be some other value.

9.6.1   Careful. Although you do 100 J of work on the cart, this may not mean the cart gains 100 J of KE. How much KE the cart gains depends on the net work done on it.

9.6.2   Nine times farther. The car has nine times as much kinetic energy when it travels three times as fast:

      $\frac{1}{2}m(3v)^2 = 9(\frac{1}{2}mv^2)$

9.9   The ideal, or theoretical, mechanical advantage is

      $\dfrac{\text{input distance}}{\text{output distance}} = \dfrac{10 \text{ m}}{1 \text{ m}} = 10$

Key Terms ······

work *(p. 145)*
joule *(p. 146)*
power *(p. 146)*
watt *(p. 146)*
energy *(p. 147)*

mechanical energy *(p. 147)*
potential energy *(p. 148)*
kinetic energy *(p. 150)*

work-energy theorem *(p. 151)*
law of conservation of energy *(p. 153)*
machine *(p. 155)*
lever *(p. 155)*

fulcrum *(p. 155)*
mechanical advantage *(p. 155)*
pulley *(p. 156)*
efficiency *(p. 158)*
fuel cell *(p. 162)*

ASSESS

Check Concepts · · · · · ·

Section 9.1

1. A force sets an object in motion. When the force is multiplied by the time of its application, we call the quantity *impulse*, which changes the *momentum* of that object. What do we call the quantity *force × distance*, and what quantity can this change?

2. Work is required to lift a barbell. How many times more work is required to lift the barbell three times as high?

3. Which requires more work, lifting a 10-kg load a vertical distance of 2 m or lifting a 5-kg load a vertical distance of 4 m?

4. How many joules of work are done on an object when a force of 10 N pushes it a distance of 10 m?

Section 9.2

5. How much power is required to do 100 J of work on an object in a time of 0.5 s? How much power is required if the same work is done in 1 s?

Section 9.3

6. What are the two main forms of mechanical energy?

Section 9.4

7. a. If you do 100 J of work to elevate a bucket of water, what is its gravitational potential energy relative to its starting position?
   b. What would the gravitational potential energy be if the bucket were raised twice as high?

Section 9.5

8. A boulder is raised above the ground so that its potential energy relative to the ground is 200 J. Then it is dropped. What is its kinetic energy just before it hits the ground?

Section 9.6

9. Suppose you know the amount of work the brakes of a car must do to stop a car at a given speed. How much work must they do to stop a car that is moving four times as fast? How will the stopping distances compare?

10. How does speed affect the friction between a road and a skidding tire?

Section 9.7

11. What will be the *kinetic* energy of an arrow having a *potential* energy of 50 J after it is shot from a bow?

12. What does it mean to say that in any system the total energy score stays the same?

13. In what sense is energy from coal actually solar energy?

14. How does the amount of work done on an automobile by its engine relate to the energy content of the gasoline?

Section 9.8

15. In what two ways can a machine alter an input force?

16. In what way is a machine subject to the law of energy conservation? Is it possible for a machine to multiply energy or work input?

17. What does it mean to say that a machine has a certain mechanical advantage?

18. In which type of lever is the output force smaller than the input force?

Section 9.9

19. What is the efficiency of a machine that requires 100 J of energy to do 35 J of work?

20. Distinguish between theoretical mechanical advantage and actual mechanical advantage. How would these compare if a machine were 100% efficient?

21. What is the efficiency of her body when a cyclist expends 1000 W of power to deliver mechanical energy to the bicycle at the rate of 100 W?

Section 9.10

22. In what sense are our bodies machines?

Section 9.11

23. What is the ultimate source of the energy derived from the burning of fossil fuels, from dams, and from windmills?

24. What is the ultimate source of geothermal energy?

25. Can we correctly say that a new source of energy is hydrogen? Why or why not?

Think and Rank ······

Rank each of the following sets of scenarios in order of the quantity or property involved. List them from left to right. If scenarios have equal rankings, then separate them with an equal sign. (e.g., A = B)

26. The mass and speed of three vehicles are shown below.

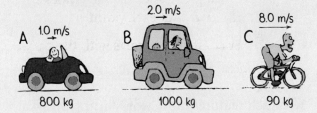

a. Rank the vehicles by momentum from greatest to least.
b. Rank the vehicles by kinetic energy from greatest to least.

27. Consider these four situations.

(A) a 3-kg ball at rest atop a 5-m-tall hill
(B) a 4-kg ball at rest atop a 5-m-tall hill
(C) a 3-kg ball moving at 2 m/s atop a 5-m-tall hill
(D) a 4-kg ball moving at 2 m/s at ground level

a. Rank from greatest to least the potential energy of each ball.
b. Rank from greatest to least the kinetic energy of each ball.
c. Rank from greatest to least the total energy of each ball.

28. A ball is released at the left end of the metal track shown below. Assume it has only enough friction to roll, but not to lessen its speed.

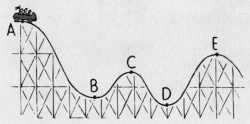

   a. Rank from greatest to least the ball's momentum at each point.
   b. Rank from greatest to least the ball's kinetic energy at each point.
   c. Rank from greatest to least the ball's potential energy at each point.

29. The roller coaster ride starts with the car at rest at point A.

   a. Rank from greatest to least the car's speed at each point.
   b. Rank from greatest to least the car's kinetic energy at each point.
   c. Rank from greatest to least the car's potential energy at each point.

30. Rank the efficiency of these machines from highest to lowest.
   (A) energy in 100 J; energy out 60 J
   (B) energy in 100 J; energy out 50 J
   (C) energy in 200 J; energy out 80 J
   (D) energy in 200 J; energy out 120 J

31. Carts moving along the lab floor run up short inclines. Friction effects are negligible.

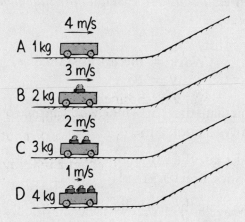

   a. Rank the carts by kinetic energy before they meet the incline.
   b. Rank the carts by how high they go up the incline.
   c. Rank the carts by potential energy when they reach the highest point on the incline.
   d. Why are your answers different for b and c?

32. Rank the scale readings from greatest to least. (Ignore friction.)

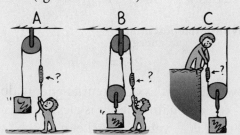

Plug and Chug ······

The key equations of the chapter are shown below in bold type.

$$\text{Work} = \text{force} \times \text{distance}$$
$$W = Fd$$

33. Calculate the work done when a force of 1 N moves a book 2 m.

34. Calculate the work done when a 20-N force pushes a cart 3.5 m.

35. Calculate the work done in lifting a 500-N barbell 2.2 m above the floor. (What is the potential energy of the barbell when it is lifted to this height?)

$$\text{Power} = \frac{\text{work done}}{\text{time interval}}$$

36. Calculate the watts of power expended when a force of 1 N moves a book 2 m in a time interval of 1 s.

37. Calculate the power expended when a 20-N force pushes a cart 3.5 m in a time of 0.5 s.

$$\frac{\text{Gravitational potential}}{\text{energy}} = \text{weight} \times \text{height}$$
$$PE = mgh$$

38. How many joules of potential energy does a 1-kg book gain when it is elevated 4 m? When it is elevated 8 m? (Let $g = 10$ N/kg.)

39. Calculate the increase in potential energy when a 20-kg block of ice is lifted a vertical distance of 2 m.

$$\text{Kinetic energy} = \frac{1}{2}\,\text{mass} \times \text{speed}^2$$
$$KE = \frac{1}{2}mv^2$$

40. Calculate the number of joules of kinetic energy a 1-kg book has when tossed across the room at a speed of 2 m/s.

$$\text{Work} = \Delta KE$$

41. How much work is required to increase the kinetic energy of a car by 5000 J?

42. What change in kinetic energy does an airplane experience on takeoff if it is moved a distance of 500 m by a sustained net force of 5000 N?

Think and Explain ······

43. Which requires more work: stretching a strong spring a certain distance or stretching a weak spring the same distance? Defend your answer.

44. Two people who weigh the same amount climb a flight of stairs. The first person climbs the stairs in 30 s, while the second person climbs them in 40 s. Which person does more work? Which uses more power?

45. A physics teacher demonstrates energy conservation by releasing a heavy pendulum bob, as shown in the sketch, allowing it to swing to and fro. What would happen if, in his exuberance, he gave the bob a slight shove as it left his nose? Explain.

46. Consider the kinetic energy of a fly in the cabin of a fast-moving train. Does it have the same or different kinetic energies relative to the train? Relative to the ground outside?

47. When a driver applies brakes to keep a car going downhill at constant speed and constant kinetic energy, the potential energy of the car decreases. Where does this energy go? Where does most of it go in a hybrid vehicle?

48. What is the theoretical mechanical advantage for each of the three lever systems shown?

49. Dry-rock geothermal power can be a major contributor to power with no pollution. The bottom of a hole drilled down into Earth's interior is fractured, making a large-surfaced hot cavity. Water is introduced from the top by a second hole. Superheated water rising to the surface then drives a conventional turbine to produce electricity. What is the source of this energy?

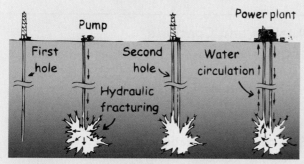

Think and Solve · · · · · ·

50. A stuntman on a cliff has a PE of 10,000 J. Show that when his potential energy is 2000 J, his kinetic energy is 8000 J.

51. Relative to the ground below, how many joules of PE does a 1000-N boulder have at the top of a 5-m ledge? If it falls, with how much KE will it strike the ground? What will be its speed on impact?

52. A hammer falls off a rooftop and strikes the ground with a certain KE. If it fell from a roof that was four times higher, how would its KE of impact compare? Its speed of impact? (Neglect air resistance.)

53. A car can go from 0 to 100 km/h in 10 s. If the engine delivered twice the power, how many seconds would it take?

54. If a car traveling at 60 km/h will skid 20 m when its brakes lock, how far will it skid if it is traveling at 120 km/h when its brakes lock? (This question is typical on some driver's license exams.)

Activity · · · · · ·

55. Place a small rubber ball on top of a basketball and drop them together. How high does the smaller ball bounce? (Perhaps this is best done in the gym, or outdoors.) Can you reconcile this result with energy conservation?

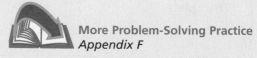

More Problem-Solving Practice
Appendix F

10 CIRCULAR MOTION

THE BIG IDEA : Centripetal force keeps an object in circular motion.

Which moves faster on a merry-go-round, a horse near the outside rail or one near the inside rail? If you swing a tin can at the end of a string in a circle over your head and the string breaks, does the can fly directly outward, or does it continue its motion without changing its direction? While a hamster rotates its cage about an axis, does the hamster rotate or does it revolve about the same axis? These questions indicate the flavor of this chapter. We begin by discussing the difference between rotation and revolution.

---

discover!

Why Do Objects Move in Circles?

1. Roll a marble around the rim of a paper plate.
2. Using a pair of scissors, cut a 90° wedge-shaped piece from the plate.
3. Roll the marble around the rim of the modified plate.

Analyze and Conclude

1. **Observing** Describe the motion of the marble before and after a section of the plate was removed.
2. **Predicting** What could you do to keep the marble moving in a circle?
3. **Making Generalizations** What is required to keep any object moving in a circle?

10.1 Rotation and Revolution

Both the Ferris wheel shown in Figure 10.1 and an ice skater doing a pirouette turn around an axis. An **axis** is the straight line around which rotation takes place.

◀ **FIGURE 10.1**
The Ferris wheel turns about an axis.

✅ **Two types of circular motion are rotation and revolution.** When an object turns about an *internal* axis—that is, an axis located within the body of the object—the motion is called **rotation,** or *spin.* Both the Ferris wheel and the skater rotate. When an object turns about an *external* axis, the motion is called **revolution.** Although the Ferris wheel rotates, the riders *revolve* about its axis.

Earth undergoes both types of rotational motion. It revolves around the sun once every $365\frac{1}{4}$ days,[10.1.1] and it rotates around an axis passing through its geographical poles once every 24 hours.[10.1.2]

You rotate about an internal axis when you spin. You revolve around an external axis when you circle about that axis.

CONCEPT CHECK What are two types of circular motion?

10.2 Rotational Speed

We began this chapter by asking which moves faster on a merry-go-round, a horse near the outside rail or one near the inside rail. Similarly, which part of a turntable moves faster? On the pre-CD record player shown in Figure 10.2, which part of the record moves faster under the stylus—the outer part where the ladybug sits or a part near the orange center? If you ask people these questions you'll probably get more than one answer, because some people will think about linear speed while others will think about rotational speed.

FIGURE 10.2 ▲
The turntable *rotates* around its axis while a ladybug sitting at its edge *revolves* around the same axis.

think!

At an amusement park, you and a friend sit on a large rotating disk. You sit at the edge and have a rotational speed of 4 RPM and a linear speed of 6 m/s. Your friend sits halfway to the center. What is her rotational speed? What is her linear speed?
Answer: 10.2.1

Types of Speed **Linear speed,** which we simply called speed in Chapter 4, is the distance traveled per unit of time. A point on the outer edge of a merry-go-round or turntable travels a greater distance in one complete rotation than a point near the center. So the linear speed is greater on the outer edge of a rotating object than it is closer to the axis. The speed of something moving along a circular path can be called **tangential speed** because the direction of motion is always tangent to the circle. For circular motion, we can use the terms linear speed and tangential speed interchangeably.

Rotational speed (sometimes called angular speed) is the number of rotations per unit of time. All parts of the rigid merry-go-round and the turntable rotate about their axis *in the same amount of time.* Thus, all parts have the same rate of rotation, or the same *number of rotations per unit of time.* It is common to express rotational speed in revolutions per minute (RPM).[10.2.1] For example, phonograph turntables that were common in the past rotate at $33\frac{1}{3}$ RPM. A ladybug sitting anywhere on the surface of the turntable in Figure 10.3 revolves at $33\frac{1}{3}$ RPM.

FIGURE 10.3 ▶

All parts of the turntable rotate at the same rotational speed. **a.** A point farther away from the center travels a longer path in the same time and therefore has a greater tangential speed. **b.** A ladybug sitting twice as far from the center moves twice as fast.

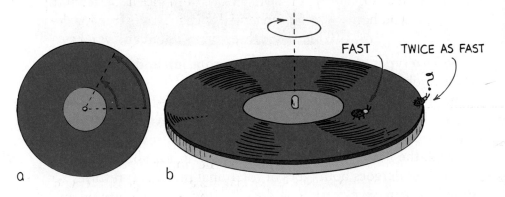

Tangential and Rotational Speed Tangential speed and rotational speed are related. Have you ever ridden on a giant rotating platform in an amusement park? The faster it turns, the faster your tangential speed is. Tangential speed is directly proportional to the rotational speed and the radial distance from the axis of rotation. So we state[10.2.2]

$$\text{Tangential speed} \sim \text{radial distance} \times \text{rotational speed}$$

In symbol form,

$$v \sim r\omega$$

where v is tangential speed and ω (pronounced oh MAY guh) is rotational speed. You move faster if the rate of rotation increases (bigger ω). You also move faster if you are farther from the axis (bigger r).

We use the symbol ~ to mean directly proportional.

At the axis of the rotating platform, you have no tangential speed, but you do have rotational speed. You rotate in one place. As you move away from the center, your tangential speed increases while your rotational speed stays the same. Move out twice as far from the center, and you have twice the tangential speed. This is true for the ladybugs in Figure 10.3. Move out three times as far, and you have three times as much tangential speed.

To summarize: In any rigidly rotating system, all parts have the same rotational speed. However, the linear or tangential speed can vary. ⊘ **Tangential speed depends on rotational speed and the distance from the axis of rotation.**

Railroad Train Wheels Why does a moving freight train stay on the tracks? Most people assume that flanges at the edge of the wheel prevent the wheels from rolling off the tracks. However, these flanges are only in use in emergency situations or when they follow slots that switch the train from one set of tracks to another. So how do the wheels of a train stay on the tracks? They stay on the tracks because their rims are slightly tapered.

A curved path occurs when a tapered cup rolls, as shown in Figure 10.4. The wider part of the cup travels a greater distance per revolution. As illustrated in Figure 10.5, if you fasten a pair of cups together at their wide ends and roll the pair along a pair of parallel tracks, the cups will remain on the track and center themselves whenever they roll off center. This occurs because when the pair rolls to the left of center, for example, the wider part of the left cup rides on the left track while the narrow part of the right cup rides on the right track. This steers the pair toward the center. If it "overshoots" toward the right, the process repeats, this time toward the left, as the wheels tend to center themselves.

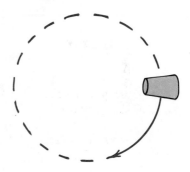

FIGURE 10.4 ▲
A tapered cup rolls in a curve because the wide part of the cup rolls faster than the narrow part.

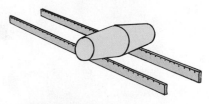

FIGURE 10.5 ▲
A pair of cups fastened together will stay on the tracks as they roll.

FIGURE 10.6 ▼
The tapered shape of railroad train wheels
(shown exaggerated here) is essential on
the curves of railroad tracks.

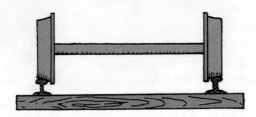

think!

Train wheels ride on a pair
of tracks. For straight-
line motion, both tracks
are the same length. But
which track is longer for
a curve, the one on the
outside or the one on the
inside of the curve?
Answer: 10.2.2

The wheels of railroad trains are similarly tapered, as shown in
Figure 10.6. This tapered shape is essential on the curves of railroad
tracks. On any curve, the distance along the outer part is longer than
the distance along the inner part, as illustrated in Figure 10.3a. So
whenever a vehicle follows a curve, its outer wheels travel faster than
its inner wheels. For an automobile, this is no problem because the
wheels roll independent of each other. For a train, however, pairs of
wheels are firmly connected like the pair of fastened cups, so they
rotate together. Opposite wheels have the same RPM at any time. But
due to the slightly tapered rim of the wheel, when a train rounds a
curve, wheels on the outer track ride on the wider part of the tapered
rims (and cover a greater distance in the same time) while opposite
wheels ride on their narrower parts (covering a smaller distance in
the same time). This is illustrated in Figure 10.7. In this way, the
wheels have different linear speeds for the same rotational speed. This
is $v \sim r\omega$ in action! Can you see that if the wheels were not tapered,
scraping would occur and the wheels would squeal when a train
rounded a curve on the tracks?

CONCEPT
CHECK : What is the relationship among tangential speed,
rotational speed, and radial distance?

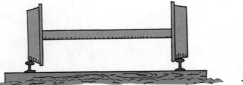

a Narrow part of left wheel goes
   slower, so wheels curve to left.

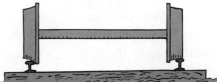

b Wide part of left wheel goes
   faster, so wheels curve to right.

FIGURE 10.7 ▲
When a train rounds a curve, the wheels have different linear speeds for the same rotational speed.

10.3 Centripetal Force

Velocity involves both speed and direction. When an object moves in a circle, even at constant speed, the object still undergoes an acceleration because its direction is changing. This change in direction is due to a net force (otherwise the object would continue to go in a straight line).

Any object moving in a circle undergoes an acceleration that is directed to the center of the circle—a *centripetal acceleration*.[10.3.1] Centripetal means "toward the center." Correspondingly, the force directed toward a fixed center that causes an object to follow a circular path is called a **centripetal force.** The force you feel from the wall while on a rotating carnival centrifuge is a centripetal force. It forces you into a circular path. If it ceased to act, you'd move in a straight line, in accord with the law of inertia.

Examples of Centripetal Forces If you whirl a tin can on the end of a string, as shown in Figure 10.8, you find you must keep pulling on the string—exerting a centripetal force. The string transmits the centripetal force, pulling the can from a straight-line path into a circular path. Centripetal forces can be exerted in a variety of ways. The "string" that holds the moon on its almost circular path, for example, is gravity. Electrical forces provide the centripetal force acting between an orbiting electron and the atomic nucleus in an atom. Anything that moves in a circular path is acted on by a centripetal force.

Centripetal force is not a basic force of nature, but is simply the label given to any force, whether string tension, gravitation, electrical force, or whatever, that is directed toward a fixed center. If the motion is circular and executed at constant speed, this force acts at right angles (perpendicular) to the path of the moving object.

When an automobile rounds a corner, for example, friction between the tires and the road provides the centripetal force that holds the car in a curved path. This is illustrated in Figure 10.9a. If friction is insufficient (due to an oily surface, gravel, etc.), the tires slide sideways and the car fails to make the curve. As shown in Figure 10.9b, the car tends to skid tangentially off the road.

Go Online

SciLINKS

NSTA

For: Links on centripetal force
Visit: www.SciLinks.org
Web Code: csn – 1003

FIGURE 10.8 ▲
The force exerted on a whirling can is toward the center. No outward force acts on the can.

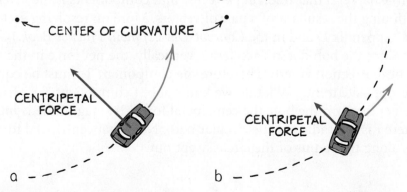

CENTER OF CURVATURE

CENTRIPETAL FORCE

CENTRIPETAL FORCE

a

b

◀ **FIGURE 10.9**
Centripetal force holds a car in a curved path.
a. For the car to go around a curve, there must be sufficient friction to provide the required centripetal force.
b. If the force of friction is not great enough, skidding occurs.

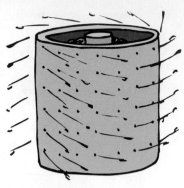

FIGURE 10.10 ▲
The clothes in a washing machine are forced into a circular path, but the water is not, and it flies off tangentially.

Centripetal force plays the main role in the operation of a centrifuge, which you may use in a biology lab to separate particles in a liquid. A household example is the spinning tub in an automatic washer like the one shown in Figure 10.10. In its spin cycle, the tub rotates at high speed and the tub's wall produces a centripetal force on the wet clothes, forcing them into a circular path. The holes in the tub's wall prevent the tub from exerting the same force on the water in the clothes. The water escapes tangentially out the holes. Strictly speaking, the clothes are forced away from the water; the water is not forced away from the clothes. Think about that.

Calculating Centripetal Forces ☑ **The centripetal force on an object depends on the object's tangential speed, its mass, and the radius of its circular path.** Greater speed and greater mass require greater centripetal force. Traveling in a circular path with a smaller radius of curvature requires a greater centripetal force. In equation form,[10.3.2]

$$\text{Centripetal force} = \frac{\text{mass} \times \text{speed}^2}{\text{radius of curvature}}$$

$$F_c = \frac{mv^2}{r}$$

Centripetal force, F_c, is measured in newtons when m is expressed in kilograms, v in meters/second, and r in meters.

Adding Force Vectors Figure 10.11 is a sketch of a conical pendulum—a bob held in a circular path by a string attached above. This arrangement is called a conical pendulum because the string sweeps out a cone. Only two forces act on the bob: **mg,** the force due to gravity, and tension **T** in the string. Both are vectors. Figure 10.12 shows vector **T** resolved into two perpendicular components, **T**$_x$ (horizontal), and **T**$_y$ (vertical). (We show these vectors as dashed to distinguish them from the tension vector **T**). Interestingly, if vector **T** were replaced with forces represented by these component vectors, the bob would behave just as it does when it is supported only by **T**. (Recall from Chapter 5 that resolving a vector into components is the reverse of finding the resultant of a pair of vectors. More on resolving vectors is in Appendix D and in the *Concept-Development Practice Book*.)

Since the bob doesn't accelerate vertically, the net force in the vertical direction is zero. Therefore the component **T**$_y$ must be equal and opposite to **mg**. What do we know about component **T**$_x$? That's the net force on the bob, the centripetal force! Its magnitude is mv/r^2, where r is the radius of the circular path. Note that centripetal force lies along the radius of the circle swept out.

Mixtures are separated in a centrifuge according to their *densities*. That's how cream is separated from milk, and lighter plasma is separated from heavier blood corpuscles.

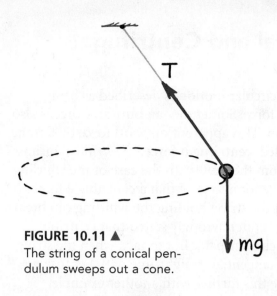

FIGURE 10.11 ▲
The string of a conical pendulum sweeps out a cone.

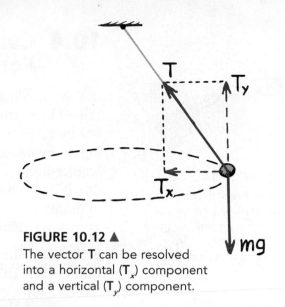

FIGURE 10.12 ▲
The vector **T** can be resolved into a horizontal (**T**$_x$) component and a vertical (**T**$_y$) component.

As another example, consider a vehicle rounding a banked curve, as illustrated in Figure 10.13. Suppose its speed is such that the vehicle has no tendency to slide down the curve or up the curve. At that speed, friction plays no role in keeping the vehicle on the track (interestingly, the angle of banked curves are chosen for zero friction at the designated speed). Only two forces act on the vehicle, one **mg,** and the other the normal force **n** (the support force of the surface). Note that **n** is resolved into **n**$_x$ and **n**$_y$ components. Again, **n**$_y$ is equal and opposite to **mg**, and **n**$_x$ is the centripetal force that keeps the vehicle in a circular path.

Whenever you want to identify the centripetal force that acts on a circularly moving object, it will be the net force that acts exactly along the radial direction—toward the center of the circular path.

CONCEPT : What factors affect the centripetal force acting on
CHECK : an object?

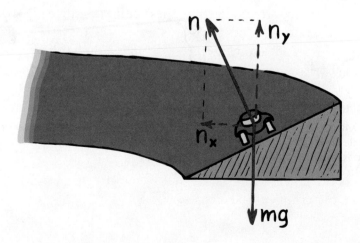

◀ **FIGURE 10.13**
Centripetal force keeps the vehicle in a circular path as it rounds a banked curve.

FIGURE 10.14 ▲
When the string breaks, the whirling can moves in a straight line, tangent to—not outward from the center of—its circular path.

If you bang against a door (action), the door bangs against you (reaction).

10.4 Centripetal and Centrifugal Forces

In the preceding examples, circular motion is described as being caused by a center-directed force. Sometimes an outward force is also attributed to circular motion. This apparent outward force on a rotating or revolving body is called **centrifugal force.** *Centrifugal* means "center-fleeing," or "away from the center." In the case of the whirling can, it is a common misconception to state that a centrifugal force pulls outward on the can. If the string holding the whirling can breaks, as shown in Figure 10.14, it is often wrongly stated that centrifugal force pulls the can from its circular path. But in fact, when the string breaks the can goes off in a tangential straight-line path because *no* force acts on it. We illustrate this further with another example.

Suppose you are the passenger in a car that suddenly stops short. If you're not wearing a seat belt you pitch forward toward the dashboard. When this happens, you don't say that something forced you forward. You know that you pitched forward because of the *absence* of a force, which a seat belt provides. Similarly, if you are in a car that rounds a sharp corner to the left, you tend to pitch outward against the right door. Why? Not because of some outward or centrifugal force, but rather because there is no centripetal force holding you in circular motion. The idea that a centrifugal force bangs you against the car door is a misconception.

So when you swing a tin can in a circular path, as shown in Figure 10.15, there is *no* force pulling the can outward. Only the force from the string acts on the can to pull the can inward. The outward force is *on the string,* not on the can.

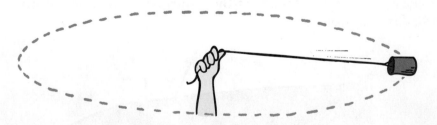

FIGURE 10.15 ▲
The only force that is exerted on the whirling can (neglecting gravity) is directed *toward* the center of circular motion. This is a *centripetal* force. No outward force acts on the can.

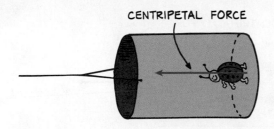
CENTRIPETAL FORCE

◀ **FIGURE 10.16**
The can provides the centripetal force necessary to hold the ladybug in a circular path.

Now suppose there is a ladybug inside the whirling can, as shown in Figure 10.16. The can presses against the bug's feet and provides the centripetal force that holds it in a circular path. The ladybug in turn presses against the floor of the can. Neglecting gravity, the *only* force exerted *on the ladybug* is the force of the can on its feet. From our outside stationary frame of reference, we see there is no centrifugal force exerted on the ladybug. ☑ **The "centrifugal-force effect" is attributed not to any real force but to inertia—the tendency of the moving body to follow a straight-line path.**

CONCEPT CHECK : What causes the "centrifugal-force effect"?

discover!

Why Doesn't the Water Fall Out of the Bucket?

1. Fill a bucket halfway with water.
2. Swing the bucket of water in a vertical circle fast enough that the water won't fall out at the top.
3. **Think** Why does the water stay in the bucket?

10.5 Centrifugal Force in a Rotating Reference Frame

Our view of nature depends on the frame of reference from which we view it. For instance, when sitting in a fast-moving vehicle, we have no speed at all relative to the vehicle, but we have an appreciable speed relative to the reference frame of the stationary ground outside. From one frame of reference we have speed; from another we have none—likewise with force. Recall the ladybug inside the whirling can. From a stationary frame of reference outside the whirling can, we see there is *no* centrifugal force acting on the ladybug inside the whirling can. However, we do see centripetal force acting on the can and the ladybug, producing circular motion.

Go Online
*sci*LINKS NSTA

For: Links on centrifugal force
Visit: www.SciLinks.org
Web Code: csn – 1005

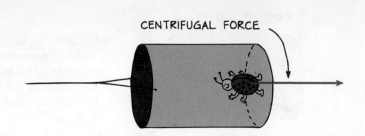

CENTRIFUGAL FORCE

FIGURE 10.17 ▶
From the reference frame of the ladybug inside the whirling can, the ladybug feels as if she is being held to the bottom of the can by a force that is directed away from the center of circular motion.

think!

A heavy iron ball is attached by a spring to a rotating platform, as shown in the sketch. Two observers, one in the rotating frame and one on the ground at rest, observe its motion. Which observer sees the ball being pulled outward, stretching the spring? Which observer sees the spring pulling the ball into circular motion?
Answer: 10.5

But nature seen from the reference frame of the rotating system is different. In the rotating frame of reference of the whirling can, shown in Figure 10.17, both centripetal force (supplied by the can) *and* centrifugal force act *on the ladybug.* To the ladybug, the centrifugal force appears as a force in its own right, as real as the pull of gravity. However, if she were to stop rotating, she would feel no such force. Thus, there is a fundamental difference between the gravity-like centrifugal force and actual gravitational force. Gravitational force is always an interaction between one mass and another. The gravity we feel is due to the interaction between our mass and the mass of Earth. However, in a rotating reference frame the centrifugal force has no agent such as mass—there is no interaction counterpart.

⊘ **Centrifugal force is an effect of rotation. It is not part of an interaction and therefore it cannot be a true force.** For this reason, physicists refer to centrifugal force as a *fictitious force,* unlike gravitational, electromagnetic, and nuclear forces. Nevertheless, to observers who are in a rotating system, centrifugal force is very real. Just as gravity is ever present at Earth's surface, centrifugal force is ever present within a rotating system.

CONCEPT CHECK : Why is centrifugal force not considered a true force?

Physics on the Job

Roller Coaster Designer
Since 1884, when the first American roller coaster was constructed, roller coasters have evolved into thrilling machines that rise over 100 meters high and reach speeds of over 150 km/h. Roller coaster designers, or mechanical design engineers, use the laws of physics to create rides that are both exciting and safe. In particular, designers must understand how roller coasters can safely navigate tall loops without exerting too much force on the riders. Designers of modern roller coasters first test their designs on computers to identify any problems before construction begins. Many private companies design roller coasters for amusement parks throughout the world.

10 REVIEW

Go Online
PHSchool.com

For: Self-Assessment
Visit: PHSchool.com
Web Code: csa – 1000

Concept Summary · · · · · ·

- Two types of circular motion are rotation and revolution.

- Tangential speed depends on rotational speed and the distance from the axis of rotation.

- The centripetal force on an object depends on the object's tangential speed, its mass, and the radius of its circular path.

- The "centrifugal-force effect" is attributed not to any real force but to inertia—the tendency of the moving body to follow a straight-line path.

- Centrifugal force is an effect of rotation. It is not part of an interaction and therefore it cannot be a true force.

Key Terms · · · · · ·

axis (p. 171)
rotation (p. 171)
revolution (p. 171)
linear speed (p. 172)
tangential speed (p. 172)
rotational speed (p. 172)
centripetal force (p. 175)
centrifugal force (p. 178)

---

think! Answers

10.2.1 Her rotational speed is also 4 RPM, and her linear speed is 3 m/s.

10.2.2 Similar to Figure 10.3a, the outer track is longer—just as a circle with a greater radius has a greater circumference.

10.5 The observer in the reference frame of the rotating platform states that centrifugal force pulls radially outward on the ball, which stretches the spring. The observer in the rest frame states that centripetal force supplied by the stretched spring pulls the ball into circular motion. (Only the observer in the rest frame can identify an action–reaction pair of forces; where action is spring-on-ball, reaction is ball-on-spring. The rotating observer can't identify a reaction counterpart to the centrifugal force because there isn't any.)

10 ASSESS

Check Concepts ......

Section 10.1

1. Distinguish between a rotation and a revolution.

2. Does a child on a merry-go-round revolve or rotate around the merry-go-round's axis?

Section 10.2

3. Distinguish between linear speed and rotational speed.

4. What is linear speed called when something moves in a circle?

5. At a given distance from the axis, how does linear (or tangential) speed change as rotational speed changes?

6. At a given rotational speed, how does linear (or tangential) speed change as the distance from the axis changes?

7. When you roll a cylinder across a surface it follows a straight-line path. A tapered cup rolled on the same surface follows a circular path. Why?

Section 10.3

8. When you whirl a can at the end of a string in a circular path, what is the direction of the force that acts on the can?

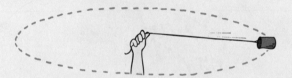

9. Does an inward force or an outward force act on the clothes during the spin cycle of an automatic washer?

Section 10.4

10. When a car makes a turn, do seat belts provide you with a centripetal force or centrifugal force?

11. If the string that holds a whirling can in its circular path breaks, what causes the can to move in a straight-line path—centripetal force, centrifugal force, or a lack of force? What law of physics supports your answer?

Section 10.5

12. Identify the action and reaction forces in the interaction between the ladybug and the whirling can in Figure 10.17.

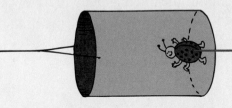

13. A ladybug in the bottom of a whirling tin can feels a centrifugal force pushing it against the bottom of the can. Is there an outside source of this force? Can you identify this as the action force of an action–reaction pair? If so, what is the reaction force?

14. Why is the centrifugal force the ladybug feels in the rotating frame called a fictitious force?

Think and Rank ......

Rank each of the following sets of scenarios in order of the quantity or property involved. List them from left to right. If scenarios have equal rankings, then separate them with an equal sign. (e.g., A = B)

15. Three locations on our rotating world are shown. Rank these locations from greatest to least for the following quantities.

    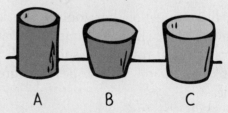

    a. rotational speed about Earth's polar axis
    b. tangential speed

16. Biker Bob rides his bicycle inside the rotating space station at the speeds and directions given. The tangential speed of the floor of the station is 10 m/s clockwise.

    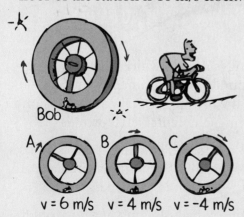

    a. Rank his speeds from highest to lowest relative to the stars.
    b. Rank the normal forces on Bob from largest to smallest.

17. Inside Biker Bob's space station is a ladder that extends from the inner surface of the rim to the central axis. Bob climbs the ladder (toward the center). Point A is at the floor, point B is halfway to the center, and point C is at the central axis.

    a. Rank the linear speeds of Bob relative to the center of the station, from highest to lowest. Or are the speeds the same at all parts of the ladder?
    b. Rank the support forces Bob experiences on the ladder rungs, from greatest to least. Or are the support forces the same in all locations?

18. The three cups shown below are rolled on a level surface. Rank the cups by the amount they depart from a straight-line path (most curved to least curved).

    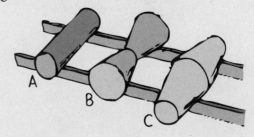

19. Three types of rollers are placed on slightly inclined parallel meter stick tracks, as shown below. Rank the rollers, in terms of their ability to remain stable as they roll, from greatest to least.

20. A meterstick is mounted horizontally above a turntable as shown. Identical metal washers are hung at the positions shown. The turntable and meterstick are then spun. Rank from greatest to least, the following quantities for the washers.

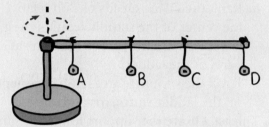

a. rotational speed
b. linear speed
c. angle the string makes with the vertical
d. inward force on each
e. outward force on each

21. A ball is swung in a horizontal circle as shown below. The ball swings from various lengths of rope at the speeds indicated. Rank the tension in the ropes from greatest to least.

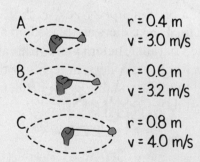

A   r = 0.4 m
     v = 3.0 m/s

B   r = 0.6 m
     v = 3.2 m/s

C   r = 0.8 m
     v = 4.0 m/s

22. Paula flies a loop-the-loop maneuver at constant speed. Two forces act on Paula, the force due to gravity and the normal force of the seat pressing on her (which provides the sensation of weight). Rank from largest to smallest the normal forces on Paula at points A, B, and C.

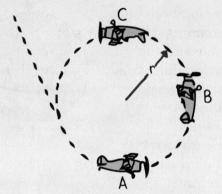

Plug and Chug ......

The equation for centripetal force is shown below.

$$F_c = \frac{mv^2}{r}$$

23. A string is used to whirl a 2-kg toy in a horizontal circle of radius 2.5 m. Show that when the toy moves at 3 m/s the tension in the string (the centripetal force) is 7.2 N.

24. A 60-kg ice skater moving at 5 m/s grabs a 6-m rope and is swept into a circular path. Find the tension in the rope.

25. A 2-kg iron ball is swung in a horizontal circular path at the end of a 1.6-m length of rope. Assume the rope is very nearly horizontal and the ball's speed is 10 m/s. Calculate the tension in the rope.

26. A 70-kg person sits on the edge of a horizontal rotating platform 2 m from the center of the platform and has a tangential speed of 3 m/s. Calculate the force of friction that keeps the person in place.

Think and Explain ......

27. Dan and Sue cycle at the same speed. The tires on Dan's bike are larger in diameter than those on Sue's bike. Which wheels, if either, have the greater rotational speed?

28. A large wheel is coupled to a wheel with half the diameter as shown.

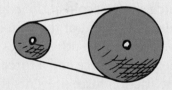

   a. How does the rotational speed of the smaller wheel compare with that of the larger wheel?
   b. How do the tangential speeds at the rims compare (assuming the belt doesn't slip)?

29. Use the equation $v = r\omega$ to explain why the end of a fly swatter moves much faster than your wrist when swatting a fly.

30. The wheels of railroad trains are tapered, a feature especially important on curves. For sharp curves, should the wheels be less tapered or more tapered?

31. If you lose your grip on a rapidly spinning merry-go-round and fall off, in which direction will you fly?

32. Consider the pair of cups taped together as shown. Will this design correct its motion and keep the pair of cups on the track? Predict before you try it and see!

33. Which state in the United States has the greatest tangential speed as Earth rotates around its axis?

34. The speedometer in a car is driven by a cable connected to the shaft that turns the car's wheels. Will speedometer readings be more or less than actual speed when the car's wheels are replaced with smaller ones?

35. Keeping in mind the concept from the previous question, a taxi driver wishes to increase his fares by adjusting the size of his tires. Should he change to larger tires or smaller tires?

36. A motorcyclist is able to ride on the vertical wall of a bowl-shaped track, as shown. Does centripetal force or centrifugal force act on the motorcycle? Defend your answer.

37. When a soaring eagle turns during its flight, what is the source of the centripetal force acting on it?

38. A car resting on a level road has two forces acting on it: its weight (down) and the normal force (up). Recall from Chapter 4 that the normal force is the support force, which is always perpendicular to the supporting surface. If the car makes a turn on a level road, the normal force is still straight up. Friction between the wheels and road is the only centripetal force providing curved motion. Suppose the road is banked so the normal force has a component that provides centripetal force as shown in the sketch. Do you think the road could be banked so that for a given speed and a given radius of curvature, a vehicle could make the turn without friction? Explain.

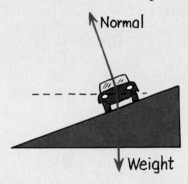

39. Friction is needed for a car rounding a curve. But if the road is banked, friction may not be required at all. What, then, supplies the needed centripetal force?

40. Under what conditions could a car remain on a banked track covered with slippery ice?

41. A racing car on a flat circular track needs friction between the tires and the track to maintain circular motion. How much more friction is required for twice the speed?

42. Can an object move along a curved path if no force acts on it?

43. When you are in the front passenger seat of a car turning left, you may find that you feel pressed against the right door. Why do you press against the door? Why does the door press on you? Does your explanation involve a centrifugal force or Newton's laws?

44. As a car speeds up when rounding a curve, does centripetal acceleration also increase? Use an equation to defend your answer.

45. Explain why a centripetal force does not do work on a circularly moving object.

46. The sketch shows a coin at the edge of a turntable. The weight of the coin is shown by the vector **W**. Two other forces act on the coin, the normal force and a force of friction. The friction force prevents the coin from sliding off the edge. Draw in force vectors for both of these.

47. The sketch shows a conical pendulum. The bob swings in a circular path. The tension **T** and weight **W** are shown by vectors. Draw a parallelogram with these vectors and show that their resultant lies in the plane of the circle (recall the parallelogram rule in Chapter 5). What name do we use for this resultant force?

Think and Solve ••••••

48. Consider a bicycle that has wheels with a circumference of 2 m. Solve for the linear speed of the bicycle when its wheels rotate at 1 revolution per second.

49. Solve for the tangential speed of a passenger on a Ferris wheel that has a radius of 10 m and rotates once in 30 s.

50. A wheel of radius r meters rolls across a floor at 2 rotations per second. Begin with speed = distance/time and show that the speed of the wheel rolling across the floor is $4\pi r$ m/s.

51. Megan rides a horse at the outer edge of a merry-go-round. She is located 6 m from the central axis and is a bit frightened of the speed. So her parents place her on a horse 3 m from the axis. While on the inner horse, how will her linear speed compare with her speed on the outer horse?

52. Emily rides on a horizontal rotating platform of radius r at an amusement park and moves at speed v one-third the way from the center to the outer edge.
   a. If the rotation rate of the platform remains constant, what will be her linear speed when she moves to the outer edge?
   b. If Emily's linear speed was 1.0 m/s at one-third the radius from the center, show that she would move at 3.0 m/s at the outer edge.

53. From the equation $F = \dfrac{mv^2}{r}$, calculate the tension in a 2-m length of string that whirls a 1-kg mass at 2 m/s in a horizontal circle.

54. Answer the previous question for each of the following cases.
   a. twice the mass
   b. twice the speed
   c. twice the length of string (radial distance)
   d. twice the mass, twice the speed, and twice the distance all at the same time

55. A turntable that turns 10 revolutions each second is located on top of a mountain. Mounted on the turntable is a laser that emits a bright beam of light. As the turntable and laser rotate, the beam also rotates and sweeps across the sky. On a dark night the beam reaches some clouds 10 km away.
   a. How fast does the spot of laser light sweep across the clouds?
   b. How fast does the spot of laser light sweep across clouds that are 20 km away?
   c. At what distance will the laser beam sweep across the sky at the speed of light (300,000 km/s)?

56. Harry Hotrod rounds a corner in his sports car at 50 km/h. Fortunately, a force of friction holds him on the road. If he rounds the corner at twice the speed, how much greater must the force of friction be to prevent him from skidding off the road? (You can solve this by using a simple proportion.)

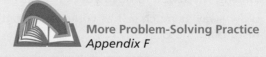

More Problem-Solving Practice
Appendix F

11 ROTATIONAL EQUILIBRIUM

THE BIG IDEA

An object remains in rotational equilibrium if its center of mass is above the area of support.

Push on an object that is free to move, and you set it in motion. Some objects will move without rotating, some will rotate without moving, and others will do both. For example, a kicked football often tumbles end over end. What determines whether an object will rotate when a force acts on it? Why doesn't the Leaning Tower of Pisa rotate and topple over? This chapter is about the factors that affect rotational equilibrium. We will see that these factors explain most of the techniques used by gymnasts, ice skaters, skateboarders, and divers.

discover!

How Far Can Objects Be Tipped Before They Topple Over?

1. Pour a teaspoon of salt onto a flat surface.
2. Place the base of a small beaker or flat-bottomed drinking glass on the salt.
3. While tilting the beaker to the side, gently work the base of the beaker into the salt.
4. With a little finesse, the beaker will remain leaning when you remove your hand.
5. Blow away as much salt as you can without disturbing the beaker.

Analyze and Conclude

1. **Observing** What prevents the beaker from toppling over?
2. **Predicting** What do you think would be the least amount of salt needed to support the beaker?
3. **Making Generalizations** How can you ensure an object won't topple over?

11.1 Torque

Every time you open a door, turn on a water faucet, or tighten a nut with a wrench, you exert a turning force. These everyday movements are shown in Figure 11.1. **Torque** is produced by this turning force and tends to produce rotational acceleration. Torque is different from force. If you want to make an object move, apply a force. Unbalanced forces make things accelerate. ✅ **To make an object turn or rotate, apply a torque.** Torques produce rotation.

In Chapter 2 we learned that systems are in mechanical equilibrium when $\Sigma F = 0$. The other condition for mechanical equilibrium is the rotational part: Σtorques = 0.

FIGURE 11.1 ▲
A torque produces rotation.

A torque is produced when a force is applied with "leverage." You use leverage when you use a claw hammer to pull a nail from a piece of wood. The longer the handle of the hammer, the greater the leverage and the easier the task. The longer handle of a crowbar provides even more leverage. You use leverage when you use a screwdriver or a table knife to open the lid of a paint can.

A torque is used when opening a door. A doorknob is placed far away from the turning axis at its hinges to provide more leverage when you push or pull on the doorknob. The direction of your applied force is important. In opening a door, you'd never push or pull the doorknob sideways to make the door turn. As shown in Figure 11.2, you push *perpendicular* to the plane of the door. Experience has taught you that a perpendicular push or pull gives more rotation for less effort.

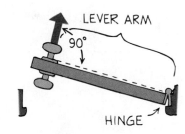

FIGURE 11.2 ▲
When a perpendicular force is applied, the lever arm is the distance between the doorknob and the edge with the hinges.

think!

If you cannot exert enough torque to turn a stubborn bolt, would more torque be produced if you fastened a length of rope to the wrench handle as shown?
Answer: 11.1

If you have used both short- and long-handled wrenches, you also know that less effort and more leverage result with a long handle. When the force is perpendicular, the distance from the turning axis to the point of contact is called the **lever arm.** If the force is not at a right angle to the lever arm, then only the perpendicular component of the force, $F_\perp$, will contribute to the torque. Torque is defined as[11.1]

$$\text{torque} = \text{force}_\perp \times \text{lever arm}$$

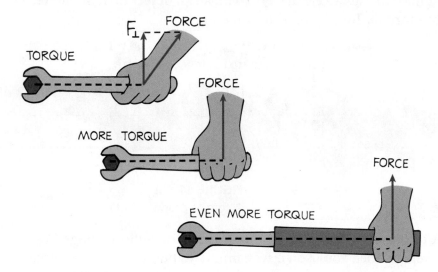

FIGURE 11.3 ▶
Although the magnitudes of the applied forces are the same in each case, the torques are different.

So the same torque can be produced by a large force with a short lever arm, or a small force with a long lever arm. Similarly, as shown in Figure 11.3, the same force can produce different amounts of torque. Greater torques are produced when both the force and lever arm are large.

CONCEPT CHECK How do you make an object turn or rotate?

discover!

Can You Pull a String Without Producing Torque?

1. Place a spool of string or thread on a table. For best results, use a spool with rims noticeably wider than its axle.

2. Pull gently on the string or thread so that the spool rolls without skidding and its gain in rotational speed is directly proportional to the torque.

3. Predict the effect of pulling the string both ways—with the string on the top and with the string on the bottom.

4. **Think** Is there an angle at which the string can be pulled that will produce no torque?

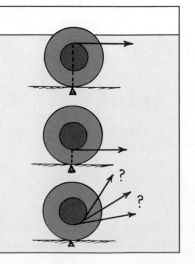

11.2 Balanced Torques

Torques are intuitively familiar to youngsters playing on a seesaw. Children can balance a seesaw even when their weights are not equal. Weight alone does not produce a change in rotation—torque does. Children soon learn that the distance they sit from the pivot point is as important as their weight. In Figure 11.4, the heavier boy sits a shorter distance from the fulcrum (turning axis) while the lighter girl sits farther away. Balance is achieved if the torque that tends to produce clockwise rotation by the boy equals the torque that tends to produce counterclockwise rotation by the girl. ✅ **When balanced torques act on an object, there is no change in rotation.**

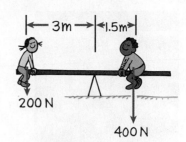

FIGURE 11.4 ▲
A pair of torques can balance each other.

---

do the math!

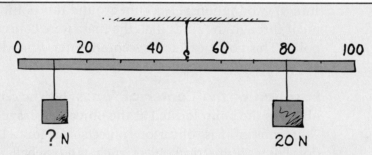

What is the weight of the block hung at the 10-cm mark?

The meterstick is supported at the center, and a 20-N block is hung at the 80-cm mark. The block hung at the 10-cm mark just balances the system. You can compute the unknown weight by applying the principle of balanced torques. The block of unknown weight tends to rotate the system of blocks and stick *counterclockwise* (ccw), and the 20-N block tends to rotate the system *clockwise* (cw). The system is in balance when the two torques are equal:

counterclockwise torque = clockwise torque

$$(F_\perp d)_{ccw} = (F_\perp d)_{cw}$$

Rearrange the equation to solve for the unknown weight:

$$F_{\perp ccw} = \frac{(F_\perp)_{cw} \times (d)_{cw}}{(d)_{ccw}}$$

The lever arm for the unknown weight is 40 cm, because the distance between the 10-cm mark and the pivot point at the 50-cm mark is 40 cm. Similarly, the lever arm for the 20-N block is 30 cm because its distance from the pivot point is 30 cm. Substituting these values into the equation, we determine the unknown weight:

$$F_{\perp ccw} = \frac{(20\ N) \times (30\ cm)}{(40\ cm)} = 15\ N$$

The unknown weight is thus 15 N. This makes sense. You can tell that the weight is less than 20 N because its lever arm is greater than that of the block of known weight. In fact, the unknown weight's lever arm is (40 cm) ÷ (30 cm) or $\frac{4}{3}$ that of the first block, so its weight is $\frac{3}{4}$ as much. Anytime you use physics to compute something, consider whether or not your answer makes sense. Computation without comprehension is not conceptual physics!

FIGURE 11.5 ▲
This scale relies on balanced torques.

Scale balances that work with sliding weights, such as the one shown in Figure 11.5, are based on balanced torques, not balanced masses. The sliding weights are adjusted until the counterclockwise torque just balances the clockwise torque. Then the arm remains horizontal. We say the scale is in rotational equilibrium.

CONCEPT CHECK : What happens when balanced torques act on an object?

11.3 Center of Mass

Throw a baseball into the air, and it follows a smooth parabolic path. Throw a baseball bat into the air and its path is not smooth. The bat seems to wobble all over the place. But it wobbles about a special point. As shown in Figure 11.6, this point stays on a parabolic path, even though the rest of the bat does not. The motion of the bat is the sum of two motions: (1) a spin around this point and (2) a movement through the air as if all the mass were concentrated at this point. This point, called the **center of mass,** is where all the mass of an object can be considered to be concentrated.

Location of the Center of Mass ⊘ **The center of mass of an object is the point located at the object's average position of mass**. The center of mass of various objects in Figure 11.7 is shown by a dot. For a symmetrical object, such as a baseball, this point is at the geometric center of the object. But an irregularly shaped object, such as a baseball bat, has more mass at one end than the other end, so the center of mass is toward the heavier end. The center of mass of a piece of tile cut into the shape of a triangle is located on the line passing through the center and the apex, one-third of the way up from the base. A solid cone's center of mass is one-fourth of the way up from its base.

FIGURE 11.6 ▶
The centers of mass of the baseball and of the spinning baseball bat each follow parabolic paths.

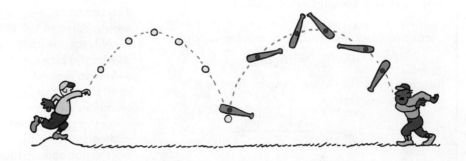

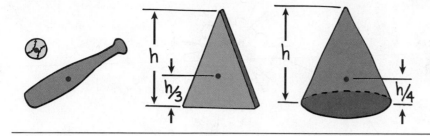

Objects not made of the same material throughout (that is, objects of varying density) may have the center of mass quite far from the geometric center. Consider a hollow ball half filled with lead. The center of mass would not be at the geometric center; rather, it would be located somewhere within the lead part. The ball will always roll to a stop with its center of mass as low as possible. Make the ball the body of a lightweight toy clown, and whenever it is pushed over, it will come back right-side up as illustrated in Figure 11.8.

◀ **FIGURE 11.8**
The center of mass of the toy is below its geometric center.

LEAD
BOTTOM

CENTER
OF MASS

Motion About the Center of Mass The multiple-flash photograph in Figure 11.9 shows the top view of a wrench sliding across a smooth horizontal surface. Notice that its center of mass, marked by the white dot, follows a straight-line path. Other parts of the wrench rotate about this point as the wrench moves across the surface. The motion of the wrench is a combination of straight-line motion of its center of mass and rotation around its center of mass.

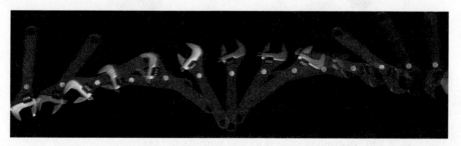

◀ **FIGURE 11.9**
The center of mass of the rotating wrench follows a straight-line path.

FIGURE 11.10 ▶

The center of mass of the fireworks rocket and its fragments move along the same path before and after the explosion.

If the wrench were instead tossed into the air, no matter how it rotated, its center of mass would follow a smooth parabola. The same is true even for an exploding projectile, such as the fireworks rocket shown in Figure 11.10. The internal forces during the explosion do not change the projectile's center of mass. Interestingly enough, if air resistance is negligible, the center of mass of the dispersed fragments as they fly through the air will be at any time where the center of mass would have been if the explosion had never occurred.

Go Online

SciLINKS NSTA

For: Links on center of mass
Visit: www.SciLinks.org
Web Code: csn – 1103

Applying Spin to an Object When you throw a ball and apply spin to it, or when you launch a plastic flying disk, a force must be applied to the edge of the object. This produces a torque that adds rotation to the projectile. If you wish to kick a football so that it sails through the air without tumbling, kick it in the middle, as illustrated in Figure 11.11a. If you want it to tumble end over end in its trajectory, kick it above or below the middle, as shown in Figure 11.11b. Then you apply torque as well as force to the ball. A skilled pool player similarly strikes the cue ball below its center to put backspin on the ball.

CONCEPT CHECK Where is an object's center of mass located?

FIGURE 11.11 ▲

a. If the football is kicked in line with its center, it will move without rotating. **b.** If it is kicked above or below its center, it will rotate.

11.4 Center of Gravity

Center of mass is often called **center of gravity,** which is the average position of all the particles of *weight* that make up an object. For almost all objects on and near Earth, these terms are interchangeable. There can be a small difference between center of gravity and center of mass when an object is large enough for gravity to vary from one part to another. For example, the center of gravity of the Sears Tower in Chicago is about 1 millimeter below its center of mass. This is due to the lower stories being pulled a little more strongly by Earth's gravity than the upper stories. ☑ **For everyday objects, the center of gravity is the same as the center of mass.**

Wobbling If you threw a wrench so that it rotated as it moved through the air, you'd see it wobble about its center of gravity. The center of gravity itself would follow a parabolic path. Now suppose you threw a lopsided ball—one with its center of gravity off-center. You'd see it wobble also. The sun itself wobbles for a similar reason. As shown in Figure 11.12, the center of gravity of the solar system can lie outside the massive sun, not at the sun's geometric center. Why? Because the masses of the planets contribute to the overall mass of the solar system. As the planets orbit at their respective distances, the sun actually wobbles off-center. Astronomers look for similar wobbles in nearby stars—the wobble is an indication of a star with a planetary system.

FIGURE 11.12 ▼
If all the planets were lined up on one side of the sun, the center of gravity of the solar system would lie outside the sun.

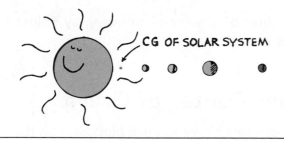

Locating the Center of Gravity The center of gravity (called the CG from here on) of a uniform object (such as a meterstick) is at the midpoint, its geometric center. The CG is the balance point. Supporting that single point supports the whole object. In Figure 11.13 the many small vectors represent the force of gravity along the meterstick. All of these can be combined into a resultant force that acts at the CG. The effect is as if the weight of the meterstick were concentrated at this point. That's why you can balance the meterstick with a single upward force directed at this point.

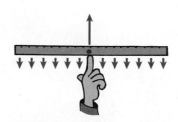

FIGURE 11.13 ▲
The weight of the entire stick behaves as if it were concentrated at its center.

FIGURE 11.14 ▼

You can use a plumb bob to find the CG for an irregularly shaped object.

If you suspend any object (a pendulum, for example) at a single point, the CG of the object will hang directly below (or at) the point of suspension. To locate the object's CG, construct a vertical line beneath the point of suspension. The CG lies somewhere along that line. Figure 11.14 shows how a plumb line and bob can be used to construct a line that is exactly vertical. You can locate the CG by suspending the object from some other point and constructing a second vertical line. The CG is where the two lines intersect.

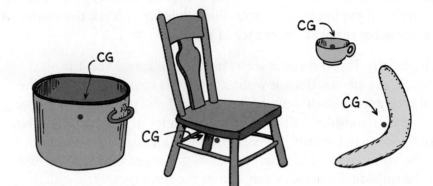

FIGURE11.15 ▶

There is no material at the CG of these objects.

The CG of an object may be located where no actual material exists, as illustrated in Figure 11.15. The CG of a ring lies at the geometric center where no matter exists. The same holds true for a hollow sphere such as a basketball. The CG of even half a ring or half a hollow ball is still outside the physical structure. There is no material at the CG of an empty cup, bowl, or boomerang.

think!

Where is the CG of a donut located?
Answer: 11.4.1

Can an object have more than one CG?
Answer: 11.4.2

CONCEPT CHECK : How is the center of gravity of an everyday object related to its center of mass?

11.5 Torque and Center of Gravity

Pin a plumb line to the center of a heavy wooden block and tilt the block until it topples over as shown in Figure 11.16. You can see that the block will begin to topple when the plumb line extends beyond the supporting base of the block.

FIGURE 11.16 ▶

The block topples when the CG extends beyond its support base.

The Rule For Toppling ✅ **If the center of gravity of an object is above the area of support, the object will remain upright.** If the CG extends outside the area of support, an unbalanced torque exists, and the object will topple. This principle is dramatically employed in Figure 11.17. The bus must not topple when the chassis is tilted 28° with the top deck fully loaded and only the driver and conductor on the lower deck. Because so much of the weight of the vehicle is in the lower part, the load of the passengers on the upper deck raises the CG only a little, so the bus can be tilted well beyond this 28° limit without toppling.

The Leaning Tower of Pisa does not topple because its CG does not extend beyond its base. As shown in Figure 11.18, a vertical line below the CG falls inside the base, and so the Leaning Tower has stood for centuries. If the tower leaned far enough that the CG extended beyond the base, an unbalanced torque would topple the tower.

The support base of an object does not have to be solid. The four legs of a chair bound a rectangular area that is the support base for the chair, as shown in Figure 11.19. Practically speaking, supporting props could be erected to hold the Leaning Tower up if it leaned too far. Such props would create a new support base. An object will remain upright if the CG is above its base of support.

FIGURE 11.18 ▲
The Leaning Tower of Pisa does not topple over because its CG lies above its base.

◀ **FIGURE 11.19**
The shaded area bounded by the bottom of the chair legs defines the support base of the chair.

FIGURE 11.20 ▶

Gyroscopes and computer-assisted motors in the self-balancing electric scooter make continual adjustments to keep the combined CGs of Mark, Tenny, and the vehicles above the support base.

Balancing Try balancing a broom upright on the palm of your hand. The support base is quite small and relatively far beneath the CG, so it's difficult to maintain balance for very long. After some practice, you can do it if you learn to make slight movements of your hand to exactly respond to variations in balance. You learn to avoid under-responding or over-responding to the slightest variations in balance. A self-balancing electric scooter, like the one shown in Figure 11.20, does much the same. Variations in balance are quickly sensed and an internal high-speed computer regulates a motor to keep the vehicle upright. The computer regulates corrective adjustments of the wheel speed, in a way quite similar to the way your brain coordinates the adjustments you make when balancing a broom on the palm of your hand. Both feats are truly amazing.

FIGURE 11.21 ▶

The moon is slightly football-shaped due to Earth's gravitational pull.

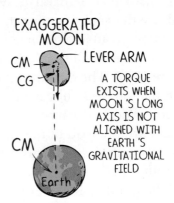

The Moon's CG Center of gravity and torque explain the fact that only one side of the moon continually faces Earth. Because the side of the moon nearest Earth is gravitationally tugged toward Earth a bit more than farther parts, the moon's CG is slightly closer to Earth than its center of mass. While the moon rotates about its center of mass, Earth pulls on its CG. This produces a torque when the moon's CG is not on the line between the moon's and Earth's centers, as illustrated in Figure 11.21. This torque keeps one hemisphere of the moon facing Earth, just as torque aligns a magnetic compass in a magnetic field.

CONCEPT CHECK : What is the rule for toppling?

◀ **FIGURE 11.22**
A high jumper executes a "Fosbury flop" to clear the bar while his CG nearly passes beneath the bar.

11.6 Center of Gravity of People

⊘ **The center of gravity of a person is not located in a fixed place, but depends on body orientation.** When you stand erect with your arms hanging at your sides, your CG is within your body. It is typically 2 to 3 cm below your navel, and midway between your front and back. The CG is slightly lower in women than in men because women tend to be proportionally larger in the pelvis and smaller in the shoulders. In children, the CG is approximately 5% higher because of their proportionally larger heads and shorter legs.

Raise your arms vertically overhead. Your CG rises 5 to 8 cm. Bend your body into a U or C shape and your CG may be located outside your body altogether. This fact is nicely employed by the high jumper in Figure 11.22, who clears the bar while his CG nearly passes beneath the bar.

As shown in Figure 11.23, when you stand, your CG is somewhere above your support base, the area bounded by your feet. In unstable situations, as in standing in the aisle of a bumpy-riding bus, you place your feet farther apart to increase this area. Standing on one foot greatly decreases this area. In learning to walk, a baby must learn to coordinate and position the CG above a supporting foot. Many birds, pigeons for example, do this by jerking their heads back and forth with each step.

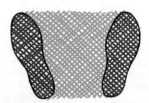

FIGURE 11.23 ▲
When you stand, your CG is somewhere above the area bounded by your feet.

Link to BIOLOGY

Tails You can bend over only so far when trying to extend your horizontal reach. How far you can extend depends on keeping your CG within your support base. A monkey can reach proportionally much farther than you can without toppling. How? By extending its tail, thus keeping its CG above its feet. A tail gives an animal the ability to shift its CG and increase stability. The massive tails of dinosaurs tell us that they were able to extend their heads considerably beyond the support base of their feet.

FIGURE 11.24 ▶
You can lean over and touch your toes without toppling only if your CG is above the area bounded by your feet.

You can probably bend over and touch your toes without bending your knees. In doing so, you unconsciously extend the lower part of your body, as shown in Figure 11.24. In this way your CG, which is now outside your body, is nevertheless above your supporting feet. If you try it while standing with your heels to a wall, you may be in for a surprise. You cannot do it! This is because you are unable to adjust your body, and your CG protrudes beyond your feet. You are off balance and torque topples you over.

CONCEPT CHECK: On what does the location of a person's center of gravity depend?

11.7 Stability

It is nearly impossible to balance a pen upright on its point, while it is rather easy to stand it upright on its flat end, because the base of support is inadequate for the point and adequate for the flat end. But there is a second reason. Consider a solid wooden cone on a level table. As you can see in Figure 11.25a, you cannot stand it on its tip. Even if you position it so that its CG is exactly above its tip, the slightest vibration or air current will cause the cone to topple.

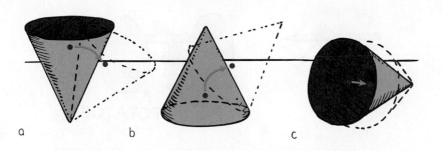

Change in the Location of the CG Upon Toppling

⊘ **When an object is toppled, the center of gravity of that object is raised, lowered, or unchanged.** What happens to the CG of the cone in Figure 11.25a when it topples? The answer to this question provides the second reason for stability. A little thought will show that the CG is lowered by *any* movement. We say that an object balanced so that any displacement lowers its center of mass is in **unstable equilibrium.**

A cone balances easily on its base, as shown in Figure 11.25b. To make it topple, its CG must be raised. This means the cone's potential energy must be increased, which requires work. We say an object that is balanced so that any displacement raises its center of mass is in **stable equilibrium.**

An object that is balanced so that any small movement neither raises nor lowers its center of gravity is in **neutral equilibrium.** A cone lying on its side, such as the one shown in Figure 11.25c, is in neutral equilibrium.

Like the cone, the pen is in unstable equilibrium when it is on its point. When the pen is on its flat end, as in Figure 11.26, it is in stable equilibrium because the CG must be raised slightly to topple it over.

Consider the upright book and the book lying flat in Figure 11.27. Both are in stable equilibrium. But you know the flat book is more stable. Why? Because it would take considerably more work to raise its CG to the point of toppling than to do the same for the upright book. An object with a low CG is usually more stable than an object with a relatively high CG.

FIGURE 11.26 ▲
For the pen to topple when it is on its flat end, it must rotate over one edge. During the rotation, the CG rises slightly and then falls.

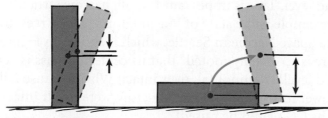

FIGURE 11.27 ▲
Toppling the upright book requires only a slight raising of its CG. Toppling the flat book requires a relatively large raising of its CG.

FIGURE 11.28 ▶
A pencil balanced on the edge of a hand is in unstable equilibrium. **a.** The CG of the pencil is lowered when it tilts. **b.** When the ends of the pencil are stuck into long potatoes that hang below, it is stable because its new CG rises when it is tipped.

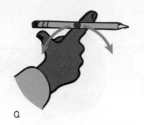
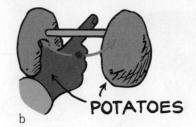

a

b

POTATOES

Objects in Stable Equilibrium The horizontally balanced pencil in Figure 11.28a is in unstable equilibrium. Its CG is lowered when it tilts. But suspend a potato from each end and the pencil becomes stable, as shown in Figure 11.28b. Why? Because the CG is below the point of support, and is raised when the pencil is tilted.

Some well-known balancing toys depend on this principle. Their secret is that they have been weighted so that the CG lies vertically underneath the point of support while most of the remainder of the toy is above it. See the example in Figure 11.29. A toy that hangs with its CG below its point of support is in stable equilibrium because the CG rises when the toy tilts.

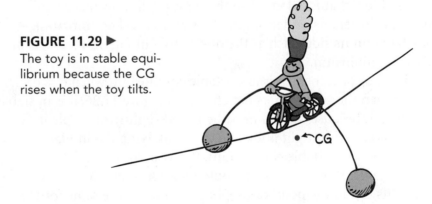

FIGURE 11.29 ▶

The toy is in stable equilibrium because the CG rises when the toy tilts.

CG

FIGURE 11.30 ▲

The Seattle Space Needle can no more fall over than can a floating iceberg.

The CG of a building is lowered if much of the structure is below ground level. This is important for tall, narrow structures. An extreme example is the state of Washington's tallest freestanding structure, the Space Needle in Seattle, which is shown in Figure 11.30. This structure is so "deeply rooted" that its center of mass is actually below ground level. It cannot fall over intact. Why? Because falling would not lower its CG at all. If the structure were to tilt intact onto the ground, its CG would be raised!

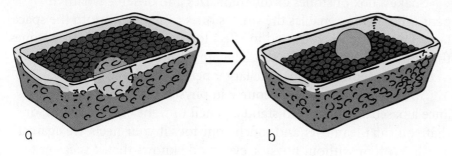

◀ FIGURE 11.31
The CG of an object has a tendency to take the lowest position available. **a.** A table tennis ball is placed at the bottom of a container of dried beans. **b.** When the container is shaken from side to side, the ball is nudged to the top.

Lowering the CG of an Object The tendency for the CG to take the lowest position available is illustrated in Figure 11.31. Place a very light object, such as a table tennis ball, at the bottom of a box of dried beans or small stones. Shake the box, and the beans or stones tend to go to the bottom and force the ball to the top. By this process the CG of the whole system takes a lower position.

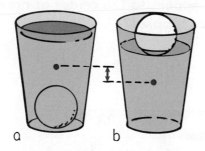

◀ FIGURE 11.32
The CG of the glass of water is affected by the position of the table tennis ball. **a.** The CG is higher when the ball is anchored to the bottom. **b.** The CG is lower when the ball floats.

As shown in Figure 11.32, the same thing happens in water when an object rises to the surface and floats. If the object weighs less than an equal volume of water, the CG of the whole system will be lowered when the object is forced to the surface. This is because the heavier (more dense) water can then occupy the available lower space. If the object is heavier than an equal volume of water, it will be more dense than water and sink. In either case, the CG of the whole system is lowered. In the case where the object weighs the same as an equal volume of water (same density), the CG of the system is unchanged whether the object rises or sinks. The object can be at any level beneath the surface without affecting the CG. You can see that a fish must weigh the same as an equal volume of water (have the same density); otherwise it would be unable to remain at different levels in the water. We will return to these ideas in Chapter 19, where liquids are treated in more detail.

The CG of an iceberg is very far below the surface of the water it floats upon.

Shake a box of stones of different sizes and observe what happens. The shaking enables the small stones to slip down into the spaces between the larger stones and in effect lower the CG. The larger stones therefore tend to rise to the top. The same thing happens when a tray of berries is gently shaken—the larger berries tend to come to the top.

You don't need to take a course in physics to know where to balance a baseball bat, how to stand a pencil upright on its flat end, or that you can't lean over and touch your toes if your heels are against a wall. With or without physics, everybody knows that it is easier to hang by your hands below a supporting rope than it is to stand on your hands above a supporting floor. And you don't need a formal study of physics to balance like a gymnast. But maybe it's nice to know that physics is at the root of many things you already know about.

Knowing about things is not always the same as understanding things. Understanding begins with knowledge. So we begin by knowing about things, and then progress deeper to an understanding of things. That's where a knowledge of physics is very helpful.

CONCEPT CHECK : What happens to the center of gravity when an object is toppled?

Science, Technology, and Society

Science and Pseudoscience Science uses a powerful method of combining logic, observation, and experiment to find correlations, sometimes leading to a cause-and-effect relationship between things. It involves asking the kinds of questions science can handle, and searching for answers via careful, controlled experimentation. Only when repeated experiments produce consistent results and objective evidence is provided, is an idea scientifically valid. Such ideas reliably explain and predict many types of events.

A pseudoscience is a false science. It claims the power of science to explain and predict events, but it is not based on the careful methods of science. Often, "evidence" cited by a pseudoscientist to "prove" his or her case is subjective. Also, in pseudoscience, cause-and-effect relationships may be claimed, but no detailed logical connections can be provided.

The danger of pseudoscience is that it can lead us to believe things that aren't true, or make us think we know things we don't. Thus, we may make unwise decisions. Nevertheless, pseudosciences appeal to many people. They can excite the imagination, simplify complex issues, and soothe anxiety about the unknown.

Critical Thinking Are horoscopes that are seen frequently in newspapers and magazines an example of science or pseudoscience? Explain. How can you identify pseudoscience?

 **REVIEW**

Go **Online**
PHSchool.com
For: Self-Assessment
Visit: PHSchool.com
Web Code: csa – 1100

Concept Summary ......

- To make an object turn or rotate, apply a torque.

- When balanced torques act on an object, there is no change in rotation.

- The center of mass of an object is the point located at the object's average position of mass.

- For everyday objects, the center of gravity is the same as the center of mass.

- If the CG of an object is above the area of support, the object will remain upright.

- The CG of a person is not located in a fixed place, but depends on body orientation.

- When an object is toppled, the CG of that object is raised, lowered, or unchanged.

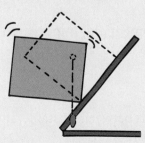

Key Terms ......

torque (*p. 189*)

lever arm (*p. 190*)

center of mass (*p. 192*)

center of gravity (*p. 195*)

unstable equilibrium (*p. 201*)

stable equilibrium (*p. 201*)

neutral equilibrium (*p. 201*)

think! Answers

11.1   No, because the lever arm is the same. To increase the lever arm, a better idea would be to use a pipe that extends upward.

11.4.1   In the center of the hole!

11.4.2   No. A rigid object has one CG. If it is non-rigid, such as a piece of clay or putty, and is distorted into different shapes, then its CG may change as its shape is changed. Even then, it has one CG for any given shape.

11.6   You tend to hold your free arm out-stretched to shift the CG of your body away from the load so your combined CG will more easily be above the base of support. To really help matters, divide the load in two if possible, and carry half in each hand. Or, carry the load on your head!

11 ASSESS

Check Concepts • • • • • •

Section 11.1

1. How does torque differ from force?

2. In what direction should a force be applied to produce maximum torque?

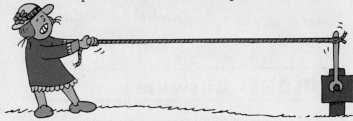

Section 11.2

3. How do clockwise and counterclockwise torques compare when a system is balanced?

4. For two kids of different masses balancing on a seesaw, should the heavier kid sit closer or farther from the fulcrum compared with the lighter kid?

Section 11.3

5. What part of an object follows a smooth path when the object is made to spin through the air or across a flat smooth surface?

6. Why is the center of mass of a baseball bat not at its midpoint?

7. To kick a football so that it doesn't rotate through the air, where should it be kicked relative to its center of mass?

8. Describe the motion of the center of mass of a fireworks projectile, before and after it explodes in midair.

Section 11.4

9. When are the center of gravity and center of mass of an object the same? Give an example of when they can be different.

10. Where is the center of gravity of an object that hangs in equilibrium? For an object that stands in equilibrium?

Section 11.5

11. Why does the Leaning Tower of Pisa not topple?

12. How far can an object be tipped before it topples over?

Section 11.6

13. In terms of center of gravity, support base, and torque, why can you not stand with your heels and back to a wall and then bend over to touch your toes and return to your stand-up position?

14. Why do some high jumpers arch their bodies into a U shape when passing over the high bar?

Section 11.7

15. Distinguish between unstable, stable, and neutral equilibrium.

16. Is the gravitational potential energy more, less, or unchanged when the CG of an object is raised?

17. What is the "secret" of balancing toys that exhibit stable equilibrium while appearing to be unstable?

18. What accounts for the stability of the Space Needle in Seattle?

19. If a container of dried beans with a table tennis ball at the bottom is shaken, what happens to the CG of the container?

Think and Rank ······

Rank each of the following sets of scenarios in order of the quantity or property involved. List them from left to right. If scenarios have equal rankings, then separate them with an equal sign. (e.g., A = B)

20. You hold a meterstick with the same suspended masses at the angles shown. Rank the torque needed to keep the stick steady from largest to smallest.

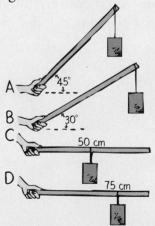

21. In a physics lab you find four different vertically mounted cart wheels that are *not* free to rotate. Each has a block that hangs from a string wrapped around the wheel. Rank the torques these blocks produce about the wheel axes from greatest to least.

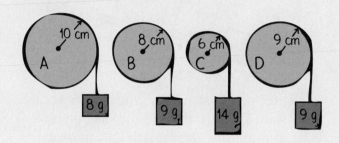

22. Perky (left) and Sneezlee (right) have the same mass and nicely balance at opposite ends of a seesaw. For the three positions, rank the length of the lever arm between Perky and the center of the seesaw from longest to shortest.

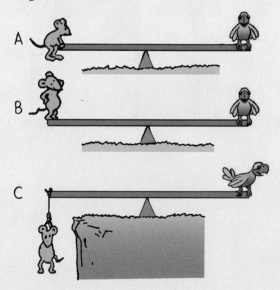

23. When Suzie gradually increases the angle of the incline, the uniform blocks of wood begin to topple (there is enough friction to keep them from sliding). Rank the order in which the blocks tip from first to last.

24. Three people stand with their backs against a wall. They are all agile and in good physical condition. Their task is to lean over and touch their toes without toppling over. Rank their chances for success from highest to lowest.

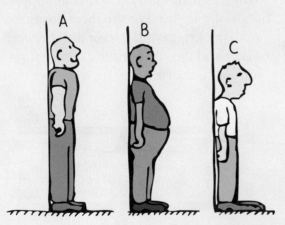

Plug and Chug ••••••

25. a. Calculate the individual torques produced by the weights of the girl and boy on the seesaw in the figure. What is the net torque?

   b. Calculate the distance a 600-N boy should sit from the fulcrum.

   c. Calculate the distance a 300-N girl should sit when the boy weighs 400 N.

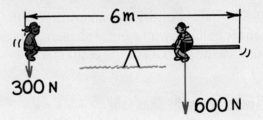

Think and Explain ••••••

26. Which is better for prying open a stuck cover from a can of paint—a screwdriver with a thick handle or one with a long handle? Which is better for turning stubborn screws? Explain.

27. The spool is pulled in three ways, as shown below. There is sufficient friction for rotation. In what direction will the spool roll in each case?

28. If you know your own weight and have a seesaw and a meterstick available, how can you determine the approximate weight of a friend?

29. Is the net torque changed when a partner on a seesaw stands or hangs from her end instead of sitting? (Does the lever arm change?)

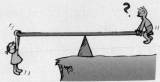

30. You cannot stand with your heels and back to the wall and then lean over and touch your toes without toppling. Would either stronger legs or longer feet help you to do this? Defend your answer.

31. Explain why a long pole is more beneficial to a tightrope walker if the pole droops.

32. When a bowling ball leaves your hand it may not spin. But farther along the alley it does spin. What produces the spinning?

33. Using the ideas of torque and center of gravity, explain why a ball rolls down a hill.

34. How do you throw a football so that it spins about its long axis when traveling through the air?

35. When you pedal a bicycle, maximum torque is produced when the pedal sprocket arms are in the horizontal position, and no torque is produced when they are in the vertical position. Explain.

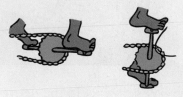

36. To balance automobile wheels, particularly when tires have worn unevenly, lead weights are fastened to their edges. Where should the CG of the balanced wheel be located?

37. Why does a washing machine vibrate violently if the clothes are not evenly distributed in the tub?

38. A bottle rack that seems to defy common sense is shown in the figure. Where is the CG of the rack and bottle?

39. Which glass in the figure is unstable and will topple?

40. Which balancing act in the figure is in stable equilibrium? In unstable equilibrium? Nearly at neutral equilibrium?

41. How can the three bricks in the figure be stacked so that the top brick has maximum horizontal overhang above the bottom brick? For example, stacking them as the dotted lines suggest would be unstable and the bricks would topple. (*Hint:* Start with the top brick and think your way down. At every interface the CG of the bricks above must not extend beyond the end of the supporting brick.)

42. Why is the middle seating most comfortable in a bus traveling along a bumpy road?

43. Why does a hiker carrying a heavy backpack lean forward?

44. Why is it easier to carry the same amount of water in two buckets, one in each hand, than in a single bucket?

45. A long track balanced like a seesaw supports a golf ball and a more massive billiard ball with a compressed spring between the two as shown in the figure. The CG of the two-ball system is therefore directly above the point of support (the triangular fulcrum). When the spring is released, the balls move away from each other. As the balls roll outward, will the track remain in balance, or will it tip? What principles do you use for your explanation?

46. How does a heavy tail enable a monkey standing on a branch to reach to farther branches?

47. Where is the center of mass of Earth's atmosphere?

48. As of 2007 more than 225 planets outside our solar system have been found (including an Earthlike one, not too hot and not too cold, likely with liquid water, orbiting about the star Gliese 581). Most of these planets were discovered by tiny wobbles of their parent stars. Why do stellar wobbles indicate the presence of planets?

Think and Solve • • • • • •

49. To tighten a bolt, you push with a force of 80 N at the end of a wrench handle that is 0.25 m from the axis of the bolt.
   a. What torque are you exerting?
   b. If you move your hand inward to be only 0.10 m from the bolt, what force do you have to exert to achieve the same torque?
   c. Do your answers depend on the direction of your push relative to the direction of the wrench handle?

The diagram below shows a ruler balanced with the fulcrum at the 50-cm mark. Copy the diagram onto a sheet of paper and answer Questions 50–52 below.

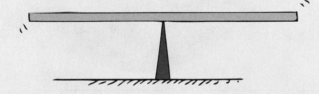

50. If a 200-g mass is placed at the 20-cm mark (30 cm from the fulcrum), at what mark should a 500-g mass be placed so that the system balances?

51. If a 100-g mass was placed at the 25-cm mark, and a 20-g mass at the 10-cm mark, where should a 500-g mass be placed to balance the system?

52. Find an arrangement of a 50-g, a 100-g, a 200-g, and a 500-g mass that balances. Show all the calculations and indicate the positions the masses should occupy (as in Questions 50 and 51).

53. The rock has a mass of 1 kg. What is the mass of the measuring stick if it is balanced by a support force at the one-quarter mark?

Activities • • • • • •

54. Suspend a belt from a piece of stiff wire that is bent as shown. Why does the belt balance as it does?

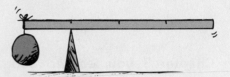

55. Hang a hammer on a loose ruler as shown. Then explain why it doesn't fall.

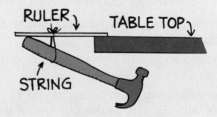

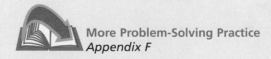

More Problem-Solving Practice
Appendix F

12 ROTATIONAL MOTION

THE BIG IDEA : Rotating objects tend to keep rotating while non-rotating objects tend to remain non-rotating.

In Chapter 3 you learned about inertia: An object at rest tends to stay at rest, and an object in motion tends to remain moving in a straight line—Newton's first law of motion. In Chapter 8 this concept was extended when you learned about momentum. In the absence of an external force, the momentum of an object remains unchanged—conservation of momentum. In this chapter we extend the law of momentum conservation to rotation.

discover!

What Makes an Object Easy to Rotate?

1. Try balancing a 12" ruler upright on the tip of your finger.
2. Mold a large ball of clay around one end of the ruler.
3. Try balancing the ruler on the tip of your finger with the clay at the top end of the ruler.
4. Now try balancing a pencil and then a meterstick on your fingertip.

Analyze and Conclude

1. **Observing** How did the addition of the clay affect your ability to balance the ruler on your fingertip? Which was easier to balance, the pencil or the meterstick?

2. **Predicting** Which would be easier to rotate back and forth, a meterstick held at its center with balls of clay at the ends or a meterstick with balls of clay near the 40 cm and 60 cm marks?

3. **Making Generalizations** How does the distribution of mass in an object that is easy to balance affect its tendency to remain balanced?

12.1 Rotational Inertia

Newton's first law, the law of inertia, also applies to rotating objects. In every case in which an object is rotating about an internal axis, the object tends to keep rotating about that axis. Rotating objects tend to keep rotating, while non-rotating objects tend to remain non-rotating. The resistance of an object to changes in its rotational motion is called **rotational inertia** (sometimes called the *moment of inertia*). **The greater an object's rotational inertia, the more difficult it is to change the rotational speed of the object.**

Just as it takes a force to change the linear state of motion of an object, a torque is required to change the rotational state of motion of an object. In the absence of a net torque, a rotating top keeps rotating, while a non-rotating top stays non-rotating.

think!

When swinging your leg from your hip, why is the rotational inertia of the leg less when it is bent?
Answer: 12.1

EASY TO ROTATE   DIFFICULT TO ROTATE

◀ **FIGURE 12.1**
Rotational inertia depends on the distance of mass from the axis of rotation.

Rotational Inertia and Mass Like inertia in the linear sense, rotational inertia depends on mass. But unlike inertia, rotational inertia depends on the *distribution* of the mass. As illustrated in Figure 12.1, the greater the distance between an object's mass concentration and the axis of rotation, the greater the rotational inertia. The tightrope walker shown in Figure 12.2 increases his rotational inertia by holding a long pole, allowing him to resist rotation.

ROTATIONAL INERTIA SIGH

◀ **FIGURE 12.2**
By holding a long pole, the tightrope walker increases his rotational inertia.

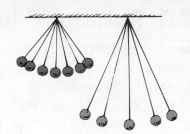

FIGURE 12.3 ▶
The short pendulum will swing back and forth more frequently than the long pendulum.

FIGURE 12.4 ▲
For similar mass distributions, short legs have less rotational inertia than long legs.

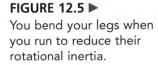

A long baseball bat held near its thinner end has more rotational inertia than a short bat of the same mass. Once moving, it has a greater tendency to keep moving, but it is harder to bring it up to speed. A short bat has less rotational inertia than a long bat, and is easier to swing. Baseball players sometimes "choke up" on a bat by grasping it closer than normal to the more massive end. Choking up on the bat reduces its rotational inertia and makes it easier to bring up to speed. A bat held at its end, or a long bat, doesn't "want" to swing as readily. Similarly, as illustrated in Figure 12.3, the short pendulum has less rotational inertia and therefore swings back and forth more frequently than the long pendulum. Long-legged animals such as giraffes, horses, and ostriches normally run with a slower gait than hippos, dachshunds, and mice. The chihuahua shown in Figure 12.4 runs with quicker strides than his longer-legged friend.

It is important to note that the rotational inertia of an object is not necessarily a fixed quantity. It is greater when the mass within the object is extended from the axis of rotation. Figure 12.5 illustrates how you can try this with your outstretched legs. Swing your outstretched leg back and forth from the hip. Now do the same with your leg bent. In the bent position it swings back and forth more easily. To reduce the rotational inertia of your legs, simply bend them. That's an important reason for running with your legs bent—bent legs are easier to swing back and forth.

FIGURE 12.5 ▶
You bend your legs when you run to reduce their rotational inertia.

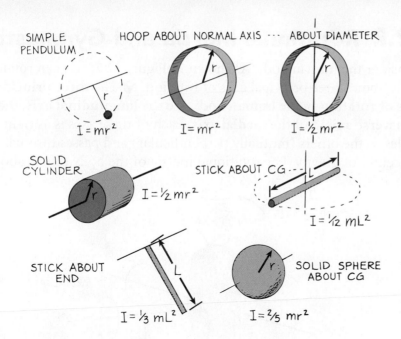

SIMPLE PENDULUM
$I = mr^2$

HOOP ABOUT NORMAL AXIS
$I = mr^2$

ABOUT DIAMETER
$I = \frac{1}{2}mr^2$

SOLID CYLINDER
$I = \frac{1}{2}mr^2$

STICK ABOUT CG
$I = \frac{1}{12}mL^2$

STICK ABOUT END
$I = \frac{1}{3}mL^2$

SOLID SPHERE ABOUT CG
$I = \frac{2}{5}mr^2$

◀ **FIGURE 12.6**
Rotational inertias of various objects are different.

Formulas for Rotational Inertia When all the mass m of an object is concentrated at the same distance r from a rotational axis (as in a simple pendulum bob swinging on a string about its pivot point, or a thin wheel turning about its center), then the rotational inertia $I = mr^2$. When the mass is more spread out, as in your leg, the rotational inertia is less and the formula is different. Figure 12.6 compares rotational inertias for various shapes and axes. (It is not important for you to learn these values, but you can see how they vary with the shape and axis.)

Rotational inertia depends very much on the location of the axis of rotation. A meterstick rotated about one end, for example, has four times the rotational inertia that it has when rotated about its center.

CONCEPT CHECK How does rotational inertia affect how easily the rotational speed of an object changes?

---

discover!

What is the Easiest Way to Rotate Your Pencil?

1. Flip your pencil back and forth between your fingers.

2. Compare the ease of rotation when you flip it about its midpoint versus flipping it about one of its ends.

3. For a third comparison, rotate the pencil between your thumb and forefinger about the pencil's long axis (so the lead is the axis).

4. Study the three cases shown in Figure 12.6.

5. **Think** In which case is rotation easiest? In this case, is the small rotational inertia consistent with the small r?

12.2 Rotational Inertia and Gymnastics

There's plenty of physics in sports!

Consider the human body. As shown in Figure 12.7, you can rotate freely about three principal axes of rotation. ✓ **The three principal axes of rotation in the human body are the longitudinal axis, the transverse axis, and the medial axis.** Each of these axes is at right angles to the others (mutually perpendicular) and passes through the center of gravity. The rotational inertia of the body differs about each axis.

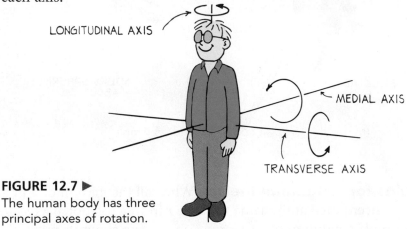

LONGITUDINAL AXIS

MEDIAL AXIS

TRANSVERSE AXIS

FIGURE 12.7 ▶
The human body has three principal axes of rotation.

Longitudinal Axis Rotational inertia is least about the *longitudinal axis*, which is the vertical head-to-toe axis, because most of the mass is concentrated along this axis. Thus, a rotation of your body about your longitudinal axis is the easiest rotation to perform. An ice skater executes this type rotation when going into a spin. Rotational inertia is increased by simply extending a leg or the arms. The skater has the least amount of rotational inertia when her arms are tucked in, as shown in Figure 12.8a. The rotational inertia when both arms are extended, as in Figure 12.8b, is about three times more than in the tucked position, so if you go into a spin with outstretched arms, you will triple your spin rate when you draw your arms in. With your leg extended as well, as in Figures 12.8c and 12.8d, you can vary your spin rate by as much as six times. (We will see *why* this happens in Section 12.5.)

FIGURE 12.8 ▼

An ice skater rotates around her longitudinal axis when going into a spin.

a   b   c   d

Transverse Axis

You rotate about your *transverse axis* when you perform a somersault or a flip. Figure 12.9 shows the rotational inertia of different positions, from the least (when your arms and legs are drawn inward in the tuck position) to the greatest (when your arms and legs are fully extended in a line). The relative magnitudes of rotational inertia stated in the caption are with respect to the body's center of gravity.

Rotational inertia is greater when the axis is through the hands, such as when doing a somersault on the floor or swinging from a horizontal bar with your body fully extended. In Figure 12.10, the rotational inertia of a gymnast is up to 20 times greater when she is swinging in a fully extended position from a horizontal bar than after dismount when she somersaults in the tuck position. Rotation transfers from one axis to another, from the bar to a line through her center of gravity, and she automatically increases her rate of rotation by up to 20 times. This is how she is able to complete two or three somersaults before contact with the ground.

FIGURE 12.9 ▲
A flip involves rotation about the transverse axis. **a.** Rotational inertia is least in the tuck position. **b.** Rotational inertia is 1.5 times greater than in the tuck position. **c.** Rotational inertia is 3 times greater than in the tuck position. **d.** The gymnast's rotational inertia is 5 times greater than in the tuck position.

◀ **FIGURE 12.10**
The rotational inertia of a body is with respect to the rotational axis. **a.** The gymnast has the greatest rotational inertia when she pivots about the bar. **b.** The axis of rotation changes from the bar to a line through her center of gravity when she somersaults in the tuck position.

Medial Axis

The third axis of rotation for the human body is the front-to-back axis, or *medial axis*. This is a less common axis of rotation and is used in executing a cartwheel. Like rotations about the other axes, rotational inertia can be varied with different body configurations.

CONCEPT CHECK : What are the three principal axes of rotation in the human body?

12.3 Rotational Inertia and Rolling

In Figure 12.11, which will roll down the incline with greater acceleration, the hollow cylinder or the solid cylinder of the same mass and radius? The answer is the cylinder with the smaller rotational inertia. Why? Because the cylinder with the greater rotational inertia requires more time to get rolling. Remember that inertia of any kind is a measure of "laziness." Which has the greater rotational inertia—the hollow or the solid cylinder? The answer is, the one with its mass concentrated farthest from the axis of rotation—the hollow cylinder. So a hollow cylinder has a greater rotational inertia than a solid cylinder of the same radius and mass and will be more "lazy" in gaining speed. The solid cylinder will roll with greater acceleration.

FIGURE 12.11 ▶
A solid cylinder rolls down an incline faster than a hollow one, whether or not they have the same mass or diameter.

Interestingly enough, any solid cylinder will roll down an incline with more acceleration than any hollow cylinder, regardless of mass or radius. A hollow cylinder has more "laziness per mass" than a solid cylinder. ✅ **Objects of the same shape but different sizes accelerate equally when rolled down an incline.** You should experiment and see this for yourself. If started together, the smaller shape, whether it be a ball, disk, or hoop, rotates more times than the larger shape, but both reach the bottom of the incline in the same time. Why? Because all objects of the same shape have the same "laziness per mass" ratio. Similarly, recall from Chapter 6 how the same "weight per mass" ratio of all freely falling objects accounted for their equal acceleration: $a = F/m$.

Just as objects of any mass in free fall have equal accelerations, round objects of any mass having the same shape roll down an incline with the same acceleration.

CONCEPT
CHECK : What happens when objects of the same shape but different sizes are rolled down an incline?

think!

A heavy iron cylinder and a light wooden cylinder, similar in shape, roll down an incline. Which will have more acceleration?
Answer: 12.3.1

Would you expect the rotational inertia of a hollow sphere about its center to be greater or less than the rotational inertia of a solid sphere? Defend your answer.
Answer: 12.3.2

12.4 Angular Momentum

Anything that rotates, whether it be a cylinder rolling down an incline or an acrobat doing a somersault, keeps on rotating until something stops it. A rotating object has a "strength of rotation." Recall from Chapter 8 that all moving objects have "inertia of motion," or momentum. This kind of momentum, which is called **linear momentum,** is the product of the mass and the velocity of an object. Rotating objects have angular momentum.[12.4]

Angular momentum is defined as the product of rotational inertia, I, and rotational velocity, ω.

angular momentum = rotational inertia (I) × rotational velocity (ω)

Like linear momentum, angular momentum is a vector quantity and has direction as well as magnitude. When a direction is assigned to rotational speed, we call it **rotational velocity.** Rotational velocity is a vector whose magnitude is the rotational speed. (By convention, the rotational velocity vector, as well as the angular momentum vector, have the same direction and lie along the axis of rotation.)

In this book, we won't treat the vector nature of angular momentum (or even of torque, which also is a vector) except to acknowledge the remarkable action of the gyroscope. Low-friction swivels can be turned in any direction without exerting a torque on the whirling gyroscope shown in Figure 12.13a. As a result, it stays pointed in the same direction. Similarly, the rotating bicycle wheel in Figure 12.13b shows what happens when a torque by Earth's gravity acts to change the direction of the bicycle wheel's angular momentum (which is along the wheel's axle). The pull of gravity that acts to topple the wheel over and change its rotational axis causes it instead to *precess* in a circular path about a vertical axis. You must do this yourself while standing on a turntable to fully *believe* it. Full *understanding* will likely not come until a later time.

FIGURE 12.12 ▲
The turntable has more angular momentum when it is turning at 45 RPM than at $33\frac{1}{3}$ RPM. It has even more angular momentum if a load is placed on it so its rotational inertia is greater.

FIGURE 12.13 ▼
The gyroscope is a remarkable device. **a.** The operation of a gyroscope relies on the vector nature of angular momentum. **b.** Angular momentum keeps the wheel axle almost horizontal when a torque supplied by Earth's gravity acts on it.

a

b

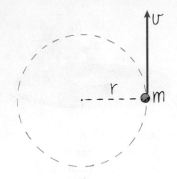

FIGURE 12.14 ▲

An object of concentrated mass *m* whirling in a circular path of radius *r* with a speed *v* has angular momentum *mvr*.

Figure 12.14 illustrates the case of an object that is small compared with the radial distance to its axis of rotation. In such cases as a tin can swinging from a long string or a planet orbiting in a circle around the sun, the angular momentum is simply equal to the magnitude of its linear momentum, *mv*, multiplied by the radial distance, *r*. In equation form,

$$\text{angular momentum} = mvr$$

Just as an external net force is required to change the linear momentum of an object, an external net torque is required to change the angular momentum of an object. ⊘ **Newton's first law of inertia for rotating systems states that an object or system of objects will maintain its angular momentum unless acted upon by an unbalanced external torque.**

FIGURE 12.15 ▶

The lightweight wheels on racing bikes have less angular momentum than those on recreational bikes, so it takes less effort to get them turning.

We know it is easier to balance on a moving bicycle than on one at rest. The spinning wheels, such as those shown on the bikes in Figure 12.15, have angular momentum. When our center of gravity is not above a point of support, a slight torque is produced. When the wheels are at rest, we fall over. But when the bicycle is moving, the wheels have angular momentum, and a greater torque is required to change the direction of the angular momentum. The moving bicycle is easier to balance than a stationary bike.

CONCEPT CHECK : How does Newton's first law apply to rotating systems?

12.5 Conservation of Angular Momentum

Just as the linear momentum of any system is conserved if no net force acts on the system, angular momentum is conserved for systems in rotation. The **law of conservation of angular momentum** states that if no unbalanced external torque acts on a rotating system, the angular momentum of that system is constant. This means that with no net external torque, the product of rotational inertia and rotational velocity at one time will be the same as at any other time. ⊘ **Angular momentum is conserved when no net external torque acts on an object.**

An interesting example of angular momentum conservation is shown in Figure 12.16. The man stands on a low-friction turntable with weights extended. Because of the extended weights his overall rotational inertia is relatively large in this position. As he slowly turns, his angular momentum is the product of his rotational inertia and rotational velocity. When he pulls the weights inward, his overall rotational inertia is considerably decreased. What is the result? His rotational speed increases! This is best appreciated by the turning person who feels changes in rotational speed that seem to be mysterious. But it's straight physics! This procedure is used by a figure skater who starts to whirl with her arms and perhaps a leg extended, and then draws her arms and leg in to obtain a greater rotational speed. Whenever a rotating body contracts, its rotational speed increases.

Go Online

SciLINKS NSTA

For: Links on rotational motion

Visit: www.SciLinks.org

Web Code: csn – 1205

◀ **FIGURE 12.16**
When the man pulls his arms and the whirling weights inward, he decreases his rotational inertia, and his rotational speed correspondingly increases.

Similarly, when a gymnast is spinning freely, as shown in Figure 12.17, angular momentum does not change. However, rotational speed can be changed by making variations in rotational inertia. This is done by moving some part of the body toward or away from the axis of rotation.

FIGURE 12.17 ▲
Rotational speed is controlled by variations in the body's rotational inertia as angular momentum is conserved during a forward somersault.

The cat shown in Figure 12.18 is held upside down and dropped but is able to execute a twist and land upright even if it has no initial angular momentum. Zero-angular-momentum twists and turns are performed by turning one part of the body against the other. While falling, the cat rearranges its limbs and tail. Repeated reorientations of the body configuration result in the head and tail rotating one way and the feet the other, so that the feet are downward when the cat reaches the ground. During this maneuver the total angular momentum remains zero. When it is over, the cat is not turning. This maneuver rotates the body through an angle, but does not create continuing rotation. To do so would violate angular momentum conservation.

Humans can perform similar twists without difficulty, though not as fast as a cat can. Astronauts have learned to make zero-angular-momentum rotations about any principal axis to orient their bodies in any preferred direction when floating in space.

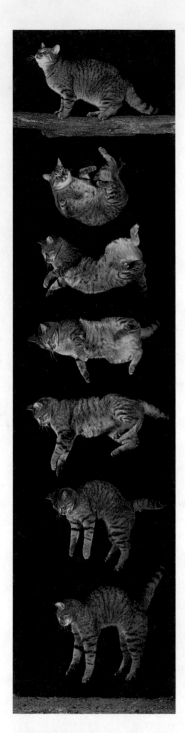

FIGURE 12.18 ▲
After being dropped upside down, the cat rotates so it can land on its feet.

CONCEPT CHECK : What happens to angular momentum when no net external torque acts on an object?

12.6 Simulated Gravity

In Chapter 10, we considered a ladybug in a rotating frame of reference. Now consider a colony of ladybugs living inside a bicycle tire, as shown in Figure 12.19 below. If we toss the wheel through the air or drop it from an airplane high in the sky, the ladybugs will be in a weightless condition and seem to float freely while the wheel is in free fall. Now spin the wheel. The ladybugs will feel themselves pressed to the outer part of the tire's inner surface. If the wheel is spun at just the right speed, the ladybugs will experience *simulated gravity* that feels like the gravity they are accustomed to. ☑ **From within a rotating frame of reference, there seems to be an outwardly directed centrifugal force, which can simulate gravity.** Gravity is simulated by centrifugal force. To the ladybugs, the direction "up" is toward the center of the wheel. The "down" direction to the ladybugs is what we call "radially outward," away from the center of the wheel.

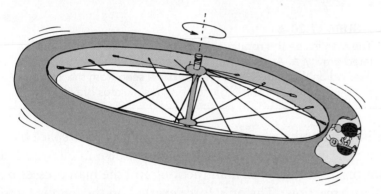

◀ **FIGURE 12.19**
If the spinning wheel freely falls, the ladybugs inside will experience a centrifugal force that feels like gravity when the wheel spins at the appropriate rate.

Need for Simulated Gravity Today we live on the outer surface of our spherical planet, held here by gravity. Earth has been the cradle of humankind. But we will not stay in the cradle forever. We are on our way to becoming a spacefaring people. In the years ahead many people will likely live in huge lazily rotating space stations where simulated gravity will be provided so the people can function normally.

Link to ASTRONOMY

Spiral Galaxies The shapes of galaxies such as our Milky Way have much to do with the conservation of angular momentum. Consider a globular mass of gas in space that begins to contract under the influence of its own gravity. If it has even the slightest rotation about some axis, it has some angular momentum, which must be conserved. As the gas contracts, its rotational inertia decreases. Then, like a spinning ice skater who draws her arms inward, the ball of gas spins faster. As it does so, it is flattened, just as our spinning Earth is flattened at its poles. If the glob has enough angular momentum, it turns into a flat pancake with a diameter far greater than its thickness, and may become a spiral galaxy.

Support Force Occupants in today's space vehicles feel weightless because they lack a support force. They're not pressed against a supporting floor by gravity, nor do they experience a centrifugal force due to spinning. But future space travelers need not be subject to weightlessness. Their space habitats will probably spin, like the ladybugs' spinning bicycle wheel, effectively supplying a support force and nicely simulating gravity.

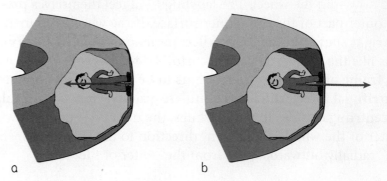

FIGURE 12.20 ▲

The man inside this rotating space habitat experiences simulated gravity. **a.** As seen from the outside, the only force exerted on the man is by the floor. **b.** As seen from the inside, there is a fictitious centrifugal force that simulates gravity.

The interaction between the man and the floor of a space habitat, as seen at rest outside the rotating system, is shown in Figure 12.20a. The floor presses against the man (action) and the man presses back on the floor (reaction). The only force exerted on the man is by the floor. It is directed toward the center and is a centripetal force. As seen from inside the rotating system, in Figure 12.20b, in addition to the man-floor interaction there is a centrifugal force exerted on the man at his center of mass. It seems as real as gravity. Yet, unlike gravity, it has no reaction counterpart—there is nothing out there that he can pull back on. Centrifugal force is not part of an interaction, but results from rotation. It is therefore called a fictitious force.

Challenges of Simulated Gravity The comfortable 1 *g* we experience at Earth's surface is due to gravity. Inside a rotating spaceship the acceleration experienced is the centripetal/centrifugal acceleration due to rotation. The magnitude of this acceleration is directly proportional to the radial distance and the square of the rotational speed. For a given RPM, the acceleration, like the linear speed, increases with increasing radial distance. Doubling the distance from the axis of rotation doubles the centripetal/centrifugal acceleration. At the axis where radial distance is zero, there is no acceleration due to rotation.

Small-diameter structures would have to rotate at high speeds to provide a simulated gravitational acceleration of 1 g. Sensitive and delicate organs in our inner ears sense rotation. Although there appears to be no difficulty at a single revolution per minute (1 RPM) or so, many people have difficulty adjusting to rotational rates greater than 2 or 3 RPM (although some people easily adapt to 10 or so RPM). To simulate normal Earth gravity at 1 RPM requires a large structure—one almost 2 km in diameter. This is an immense structure compared with the size of today's space shuttle vehicles. Economics will probably dictate that the size of the first inhabited structures be small. If these structures also do not rotate, the inhabitants will have to adjust to living in a seemingly weightless environment. Larger rotating habitats with simulated gravity will likely follow later. Imagine yourself living in a rotating space colony such as the one shown in Figure 12.21.

The idea of a rotating space station to keep astronauts' feet on the floor, wonderfully shown in the 1968 movie *2001: A Space Odyssey*, and in Arthur C. Clarke's 1973 book *Rendezvous with Rama*, is credited to the Russian scientist Konstantin Tsiolkovsky in 1920.

◀ **FIGURE 12.21**
This NASA depiction of a rotational space colony may be a glimpse into the future.

If the structure rotates so that inhabitants on the inside of the outer edge experience 1 g, then halfway between the axis and the outer edge they would experience only 0.5 g. At the axis itself they would experience weightlessness at 0 g. The possible variations of g within the rotating space habitat holds promise for a most different and as yet unexperienced environment. We could perform ballet at 0.5 g; acrobatics at 0.2 g and lower g states; three-dimensional soccer and sports not yet conceived in very low g states. People will explore possibilities never before available to them. This time of transition from our earthly cradle to new vistas is an exciting time in which to live—especially for those who will be prepared to play a role in these new adventures.[12.6]

CONCEPT CHECK How is gravity simulated?

 **REVIEW**

Go Online
PHSchool.com

For: Self-Assessment
Visit: PHSchool.com
Web Code: csa – 1200

Concept Summary ......

- The greater an object's rotational inertia, the more difficult it is to change the rotational speed of the object.

- The three principal axes of rotation in the human body are the longitudinal axis, the transverse axis, and the medial axis.

- Objects of the same shape but different sizes accelerate equally when rolled down an incline.

- Newton's first law of inertia for rotating systems states that an object or system of objects will maintain its angular momentum unless acted upon by an unbalanced external torque.

- Angular momentum is conserved when no net external torque acts on an object.

- From within a rotating frame of reference, there seems to be an outwardly directed centrifugal force, which can simulate gravity.

Key Terms ......

rotational inertia *(p. 213)*

linear momentum *(p. 219)*

angular momentum *(p. 219)*

rotational velocity *(p. 219)*

law of conservation of angular momentum *(p. 221)*

think! Answers

12.1   The rotational inertia of any object is less when its mass is concentrated closer to the axis of rotation. Can you see that a bent leg satisfies this requirement?

12.3.1   The cylinders have different masses, but the *same rotational inertia per mass,* so both will accelerate equally down the incline. Their different masses make no difference, just as the acceleration of free fall is not affected by different masses. All objects of the same shape have the same "laziness per mass" ratio.

12.3.2   Greater. Just as the value mr^2 for a hoop's rotational inertia is greater than a solid cylinder's ($\frac{1}{2}mr^2$), the rotational inertia of a hollow sphere would be greater than that of a same-mass solid sphere for the same reason: the mass of the hollow sphere is farther from the center. A thin spherical shell has a rotational inertia of $\frac{2}{3}mr^2$, or 1.66 times greater than a solid sphere's $\frac{2}{5}mr^2$.

12 ASSESS

Check Concepts ......

Section 12.1

1. What is the law of inertia for rotation?

2. Does the rotational inertia of an object differ for different axes of rotation?

3. Which is easier to get swinging, a baseball bat held at the end, or one held closer to the massive end (choked up)?

4. Which has a greater rotational inertia, a cylinder about its axis or a sphere about a diameter if the two have the same mass and radius?

5. Which will swing to and fro more often, a short pendulum or a long pendulum?

Section 12.2

6. Why does bending your legs when running enable you to swing your legs to and fro more rapidly?

7. What are the three principal axes of rotation for the human body?

8. How does a skater decrease his or her rotational inertia while spinning?

Section 12.3

9. Which will have the greater acceleration rolling down an incline—a hoop or a solid disk?

Section 12.4

10. Distinguish between linear momentum and angular momentum.

11. The text says that angular momentum is $I\omega$, then says it is mvr. Which is it?

12. Momentum is conserved when there is no net external force. When is angular momentum conserved?

Section 12.5

13. What does it mean to say that angular momentum is conserved?

14. If a skater who is spinning pulls her arms in so as to reduce her rotational inertia to half, by how much will her angular momentum increase?

15. If a skater who is spinning pulls her arms in so as to reduce her rotational inertia to half, by how much will her rate of spin increase?

16. Why are your answers different to the previous two questions?

Section 12.6

17. How can gravity be simulated in an orbiting space station?

18. How will the value of g vary at different distances from the hub of a rotating space station?

Think and Rank ......

Rank each of the following sets of scenarios in order of the quantity or property involved. List them from left to right. If scenarios have equal rankings, then separate them with an equal sign. (e.g., A = B)

19. Three iron shapes of the same mass rotate about the axis shown by the circle with the dot inside. Rank them, from greatest to least, in terms of the rotational inertia about this axis.

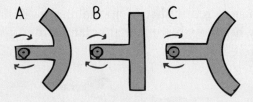

20. Beginning from a rest position, a solid disk A, a solid ball B, and a hoop C, race down an incline. Rank them in order of finishing: winner, second place, and third place.

21. Perky rides at different radial distances from the center of a turntable that rotates at a fixed rate. His distances and tangential speeds at three different locations are as follows.

(A) $r = 15$ cm, $v = 7.5$ cm/s
(B) $r = 10$ cm, $v = 5.0$ cm/s
(C) $r = 5.0$ cm, $v = 2.5$ cm/s

a. Rank from greatest to least, Perky's angular momenta.
b. Rank from greatest to least, the amounts of friction needed to keep Perky from sliding off.

22. Students Art, Bart, Cis, and Dot sit on a rotating turntable at different distances from the center as indicated.

(A) Art, $m = 60$ kg, sits at $\frac{1}{4}r$.

(B) Bart, $m = 25$ kg, sits at $\frac{1}{2}r$.

(C) Cis, $m = 50$ kg, sits at $\frac{3}{4}r$.

(D) Dot, $m = 20$ kg, sits at r.

From greatest to least, rank the angular momenta of the four students.

Think and Explain ......

23. Mei Fan says that a basketball has greater rotational inertia than a solid ball of the same size and mass because most of a basketball's mass is far from its center. Ashley says no, that the center of mass of any uniform ball is at its center, and mass distribution doesn't matter. Whom do you agree with?

24. Stand two metersticks against the wall and let them topple over. Now put a wad of clay on top of one of the sticks and let them topple again. Which reaches the floor first?

25. Why is a stick with a wad of clay at the top easier to balance on the palm of your hand than an empty stick?

26. At the circus, a performer balances his friends at the top of a vertical pole. Why is this feat easier for the performer than balancing an empty pole?

27. If you walked along the top of a fence, why would holding your arms out help you to balance?

28. Which will have the greater acceleration rolling down an incline—a bowling ball or a volleyball? Defend your answer.

29. Any rolling object takes more time to roll down an inclined plane than a non-rolling object sliding without friction. Jim says this is because all the PE of the non-rolling object goes into translational KE, with none "wasted" as rotational KE. John doesn't think a sliding object slides down an incline faster than a rolling object. With whom do you agree?

30. Jim says that in a race between a can of water and a can of ice rolling down an incline, the water filled can will win because the water inside "slides" down the incline, while the ice is made to rotate, slowing its movement down the incline. John now agrees. Do you agree?

31. Consider two rotating bicycle wheels, one filled with air and the other filled with water. Which would be more difficult to stop rotating? Explain.

32. You sit in the middle of a large, freely rotating turntable at an amusement park. If you crawled toward the outer rim, would your rotational speed increase, decrease, or remain unchanged? What law of physics supports your answer?

33. A sizable quantity of soil is washed down the Mississippi River and deposited in the Gulf of Mexico each year. What effect does this tend to have on the length of a day? (*Hint:* Relate this to a spinning skater who extends her arms outward.)

34. If all of Earth's inhabitants moved to the equator, how would this affect Earth's rotational inertia? How would it affect the length of a day?

35. If the world's populations move to the North and South Poles, would the length of a day increase, decrease, or stay the same?

36. If the polar ice caps of Earth were to melt, the oceans everywhere would be deeper by about 30 m. What effect would this have on Earth's rotation?

37. A toy train is initially at rest on a track fastened to a bicycle wheel, which is free to rotate. How does the wheel respond when the train moves clockwise? When the train backs up? Does the angular momentum of the wheel-train system change during these maneuvers? How would the resulting motions be affected if the train were much more massive than the track? If the track were much more massive?

38. Why does a typical small helicopter with a single main rotor have a second small rotor on its tail? Describe the consequence if the small rotor fails in flight.

39. We believe our galaxy was formed from a huge cloud of gas. The original cloud was far larger than the present size of the galaxy, more or less spherical, and rotating very much more slowly than the galaxy is now. In this sketch we see the original cloud and the galaxy as it is now (seen edgewise). Explain how the law of gravitation and the conservation of angular momentum contribute to the galaxy's present shape and why it rotates faster now than when it was a larger, spherical cloud.

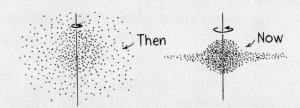

Then   Now

40. An occupant inside a rotating space habitat of the future will feel pulled by artificial gravity against the outer wall of the habitat (which becomes the "floor"). What physics provides an explanation?

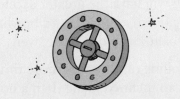

41. Explain why the faster Earth spins, the less a person weighs, whereas the faster a space station spins, the more a person weighs.

Think and Solve ......

42. What happens to the rotational inertia of a simple pendulum when the mass of the bob is doubled and the length of the pendulum is halved? (See Figure 12.6.)

43. What happens to the rotational inertia of a simple pendulum when both the mass of the bob and the length of the pendulum are doubled?

44. What happens to the rotational inertia of a simple pendulum when both the mass of the bob and the length of the pendulum are halved?

45. A pair of identical 1000-kg space pods in outer space are connected to each other by a 900-m-long cable. They rotate about a common point like a spinning dumbbell as shown in the figure. Calculate the rotational inertia of each pod about the axis of rotation. What is the rotational inertia of the two-pod system about its midpoint? Express your answers in kg·m².

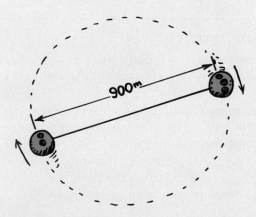

46. The two-pod system in the previous question rotates 1.2 RPM to provide artificial gravity for its occupants. If one of the pods pulls in 100 m of cable (bringing the pods closer together), what will be the system's new rotation rate?

47. Gretchen moves at a speed of 6.0 m/s when sitting on the edge of a horizontal rotating platform of diameter 4.0 m. Her mass is 45 kg. Show that her angular momentum about the center of the platform will be 540 kg·m²/s.

48. If a trapeze artist rotates twice each second while sailing through the air, and contracts to reduce her rotational inertia to one-third, how many rotations per second will result?

49. A 0.60-kg puck revolves at 2.4 m/s at the end of a 0.90-m string on a frictionless air table. Show that when the string is shortened to 0.60 m the speed of the puck will be 3.6 m/s.

Activity ......

50. Gather a selection of canned foods. Predict which will roll faster down an incline. Compare liquids (which slide or slosh rather than roll inside the can) and solids. Roll the cans to test your predictions. Describe your results.

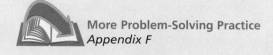

More Problem-Solving Practice
Appendix F

13 UNIVERSAL GRAVITATION

THE BIG IDEA : Everything pulls on everything else.

Objects such as leaves, rain, and satellites fall because of gravity. Gravity is what holds tea in a cup and what makes bubbles rise. It made Earth round, and it builds up the pressures that kindle every star that shines. These are things that gravity does. But what is gravity? Contrary to what some people think, gravity was not discovered by Isaac Newton. That discovery dates back to earlier times when Earth dwellers experienced the consequences of tripping and falling. What Newton discovered, prompted by a falling apple, was that gravity is a universal force—that it is not unique to Earth, as others of his time assumed.

discover!

How Does the Surface Area of a Balloon Vary With Diameter?

1. Inflate a round balloon to a diameter of 8 cm. Use a marker to draw a rectangle the size of a postage stamp on the balloon. Do not tie the end of the balloon.

2. Now inflate the balloon to a diameter of 16 cm. How many postage stamps will fit in the square you drew?

3. If possible, increase the diameter of the balloon to 24 cm and once again determine how many stamps will fit in the square.

Analyze and Conclude

1. **Observing** Describe how the area of the square grew as you increased the diameter of the balloon.

2. **Predicting** If you could increase the diameter of the balloon to 32 cm, how many postage stamps would fit in the expanded square?

3. **Making Generalizations** How does the area of the square drawn on the balloon's surface increase with increasing balloon diameter?

13.1 The Falling Apple

According to popular legend, the idea that gravity extends through-out the universe occurred to Newton while he was sitting under-neath an apple tree on his mother's farm pondering the forces of nature. This scene is illustrated in Figure 13.1. Newton understood the concept of inertia developed earlier by Galileo; he knew that without an outside force, moving objects continue to move at constant speed in a straight line. He knew that if an object undergoes a change in speed or direction, then a force is responsible.

A falling apple triggered what was to become one of the most far-reaching generalizations of the human mind. Newton saw the apple fall, or maybe even felt it fall on his head—the story about this is not clear. Perhaps he looked up through the apple tree branches and noticed the moon. Newton was probably puzzled by the fact that the moon does not follow a straight-line path, but instead circles about Earth. He knew that circular motion is accelerated motion, which requires a force. But what was this force? Newton had the insight to see that the moon is falling toward Earth, just as the apple is.

⊘ **Newton reasoned that the moon is falling toward Earth for the same reason an apple falls from a tree—they are both pulled by Earth's gravity.**

CONCEPT CHECK : What was Newton's reasoning about the apple falling from the tree?

FIGURE 13.1 ▲
According to legend, Newton discovered that gravity extends to the moon (and beyond) while sitting under an apple tree.

13.2 The Falling Moon

Newton developed this idea further. He compared the falling apple with the falling moon. Newton realized that if the moon did not fall, it would move off in a straight line and leave its orbit, as suggested in Figure 13.2. His idea was that the moon must be falling *around* Earth.

Thus the moon falls in the sense that it *falls beneath the straight line it would follow if no force acted on it.* He hypothesized that the moon was simply a projectile circling Earth under the attraction of gravity.

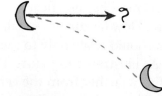

Oh no, the moon is falling!

FIGURE 13.2 ▶
If the moon did not fall, it would follow a straight-line path.

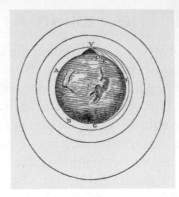

FIGURE 13.3 ▶

This original drawing by Isaac Newton shows how a projectile fired fast enough would fall around Earth and become an Earth satellite.

Newton's Hypothesis Newton compared the motion of the moon to a cannonball fired from the top of a high mountain. If the mountaintop was above Earth's atmosphere, air resistance would not impede the motion of the cannonball. If a cannonball were fired with a small horizontal speed, it would follow a parabolic path and soon hit Earth below. If it were fired faster, its path would be less curved and it would hit Earth farther away. If the cannonball were fired fast enough, its path would become a circle and the cannonball would circle indefinitely. Newton illustrated this in the drawing in Figure 13.3.

Both the orbiting cannonball and the moon have a component of velocity parallel to Earth's surface. This sideways or *tangential velocity*, as illustrated in Figure 13.4, is sufficient to ensure nearly circular motion *around* Earth rather than *into* it. ☑ **The moon is actually falling toward Earth but has great enough tangential velocity to avoid hitting Earth.** If there is no resistance to reduce its speed, the moon will continue "falling" around and around Earth indefinitely.

Newton's Test For Newton's idea to advance from hypothesis to scientific theory, it would have to be tested. Newton's test was to see if the moon's "fall" beneath its otherwise straight-line path was in correct proportion to the fall of an apple or any object at Earth's surface. He reasoned that the mass of the moon should not affect how it falls, just as mass has no effect on the acceleration of freely falling objects on Earth. How far the moon falls, and how far an apple at Earth's surface falls, should relate only to their respective *distances* from Earth's center.

As illustrated in Figure 13.5, the moon was already known to be 60 times farther from the center of Earth than an apple at Earth's surface. The apple will fall 5 m in its first second of fall—or more precisely, 4.9 m. Newton reasoned that gravitational attraction to Earth must be "diluted" by distance. Does this mean the force of Earth's gravity would reduce to $\frac{1}{60}$ at the moon's distance? No, as we shall soon see, the influence of gravity should be diluted to $\frac{1}{60}$ of $\frac{1}{60}$, or to $\frac{1}{(60)^2}$. So in one second the moon should fall $\frac{1}{(60)^2}$ of 5 m, which is 1.4 millimeters.[13.2.1]

FIGURE 13.4 ▲

Tangential velocity is the "sideways" velocity—the component of velocity parallel to the surface of Earth and perpendicular to the pull of gravity.

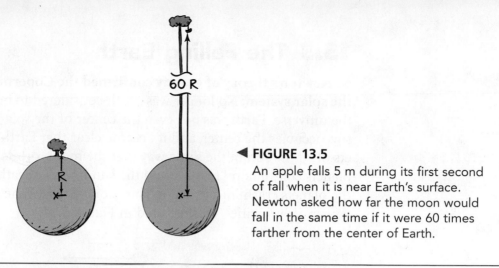

◀ **FIGURE 13.5**
An apple falls 5 m during its first second of fall when it is near Earth's surface. Newton asked how far the moon would fall in the same time if it were 60 times farther from the center of Earth.

Newton's Calculation Using geometry, Newton calculated how far the circle of the moon's orbit lies below the straight-line distance the moon otherwise would travel in one second. His value turned out to be about the 1.4-mm distance accepted today, as shown in Figure 13.6. But he was unsure of the exact Earth–moon distance, and whether or not the correct distance to use was the distance between their centers. At this time he hadn't proved mathematically that the gravity of the spherical Earth (and moon) is the same as if all its mass were concentrated at its center.

Because of this uncertainty, and also because of criticisms he had experienced in publishing earlier findings in optics, he placed his papers in a drawer, where they remained for nearly 20 years. During this period he laid the foundation and developed the field of geometrical optics for which he first became famous.

Newton finally returned to the moon problem at the prodding of his astronomer friend Edmund Halley (of Halley's comet fame). It wasn't until after Newton invented a new branch of mathematics, calculus, to prove his center-of-gravity hypothesis, that he published what is one of the greatest achievements of the human mind—the law of universal gravitation.[13.2.2] Newton generalized his moon finding to all objects, and stated that all objects in the universe attract each other.

CONCEPT CHECK Why doesn't the moon hit Earth?

FIGURE 13.6 ▶
If the force that pulls apples off trees also pulls the moon into orbit, the circle of the moon's orbit should fall 1.4 mm below a point along the straight line where the moon would otherwise be one second later.

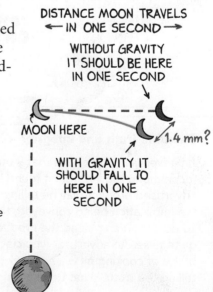

DISTANCE MOON TRAVELS
← IN ONE SECOND →

WITHOUT GRAVITY IT SHOULD BE HERE IN ONE SECOND

MOON HERE

1.4 mm?

WITH GRAVITY IT SHOULD FALL TO HERE IN ONE SECOND

13.3 The Falling Earth

☑ **Newton's theory of gravity confirmed the Copernican theory of the solar system.** No longer was Earth considered to be the center of the universe. Earth was not even the center of the solar system. The sun occupies the center, and it became clear that Earth and the planets orbit the sun in the same way that the moon orbits Earth. The planets continually "fall" around the sun in closed paths. Why don't the planets crash into the sun? They don't because the planets have tangential velocities, as illustrated in Figure 13.7.

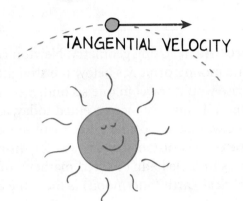

TANGENTIAL VELOCITY

FIGURE 13.7 ▶
The tangential velocity of Earth about the sun allows it to fall around the sun rather than directly into it.

What would happen if the tangential velocities of the planets were reduced to zero? The answer is simple enough: Their motion would be straight toward the sun and they would indeed crash into it. Any objects in the solar system with insufficient tangential velocities have long ago crashed into the sun; what remains is the harmony we observe.

CONCEPT CHECK : What theory of the solar system did Newton's theory of gravity confirm?

Science, Technology, and Society

Scientific Truth and Integrity

An advertiser who claims that 9 out of 10 doctors recommend the ingredient found in his or her advertised product may be telling the truth. But the implication being conveyed, that 9 out of 10 doctors recommend the product itself, may be quite false. An advertiser who claims that a certain brand of cooking oil will not soak through foods is telling the truth. What the advertiser doesn't say is that no other brands of cooking oil soak through foods either—at least not at ordinary temperatures and pressures. While the facts stated are true, the implications conveyed are not. There is a difference between truthfulness and integrity.

Critical Thinking Do you think advertisers have a responsibility to be completely truthful about their products? Explain why or why not.

13.4 Newton's Law of Universal Gravitation

Newton did not discover gravity. ☑ **Newton discovered that gravity is universal. Everything pulls on everything else in the universe in a way that involves only mass and distance.**

Newton's **law of universal gravitation** states that every object attracts every other object with a force. For any two objects, this force is directly proportional to the mass of each object. The greater the masses, the greater the force of attraction between them.[13.4.1] Newton also deduced that this force decreases as the square of the distance between the centers of the objects. The farther away the objects are from each other, the less the force of attraction between them.

The law can be expressed as

$$\text{Force} \sim \frac{\text{mass}_1 \times \text{mass}_2}{\text{distance}^2}$$

or in symbol notation, as

$$F \sim \frac{m_1 m_2}{d^2}$$

where m_1 is the mass of one object, m_2 is the mass of the other, and d is the distance between their centers.

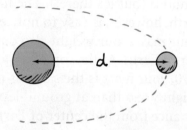

◀ **FIGURE 13.8**
The force of gravity between objects depends on the distance between their centers.

The Universal Gravitational Constant, G The law of universal gravitation can be expressed as an exact equation when a proportionality constant is introduced. In the equation for universal gravitation, the **universal gravitational constant,** G, describes the strength of gravity. Then the equation is

$$F = G\frac{m_1 m_2}{d^2}$$

In words, the force of gravity between two objects is found by multiplying their masses, dividing by the square of the distance between their centers, and then multiplying this result by G. The magnitude of G is given by the magnitude of the force between two masses of 1 kilogram each, 1 meter apart: 0.0000000000667 newton. For these masses, this is an extremely weak force. The units of G are such as to make the force come out in newtons. In scientific notation,[13.4.2]

$$G = 6.67 \times 10^{-11} \text{ N·m}^2/\text{kg}^2$$

Just as sheet music guides a musician playing music, equations guide a physics student to see how concepts are connected.

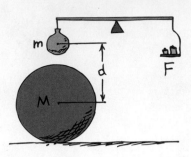

FIGURE 13.9 ▲
Philipp von Jolly developed a method of measuring the gravitational attraction between two masses.

Just as π relates circumference and diameter for circles, G relates gravitational force to a combination of mass and distance. G, like π, is a constant of proportionality.

Measuring G G was first measured 150 years after Newton's discovery of universal gravitation by an English physicist, Henry Cavendish. Cavendish accomplished this by measuring the tiny force between lead masses with an extremely sensitive torsion balance. A simpler method was later developed by Philipp von Jolly, who attached a spherical flask of mercury to one arm of a sensitive balance, as shown in Figure 13.9. After the balance was put in equilibrium, a 6-ton lead sphere was rolled beneath the mercury flask. The flask was pulled slightly downward. In effect, the gravitational force F between the lead mass and the mercury was equal to the weight that had to be placed on the opposite end of the balance to restore equilibrium. Since the quantities F, m_1, m_2, and d were all known, the value of G could be calculated:

$$G = \frac{F}{m_1 m_2/d^2} = 6.67 \times 10^{-11} \frac{N}{kg^2/m^2} = 6.67 \times 10^{-11} \, N \cdot m^2/kg^2$$

The value of G tells us that the force of gravity is a very weak force. It is the weakest of the presently known four fundamental forces. (The other three are the electromagnetic force and two kinds of nuclear forces.) We sense gravitation only when masses like that of Earth are involved. The force of attraction between you and a classmate is too weak to notice (but it's there!). The force of attraction between you and Earth, however, is easy to notice. It is your weight.

In addition to your mass, your weight also depends on your distance from the center of Earth. At the top of a mountain, like the one shown in Figure 13.10, your mass is the same as it is anywhere else, but your weight is slightly less than at ground level. Your weight is less because your distance from the center of Earth is greater.

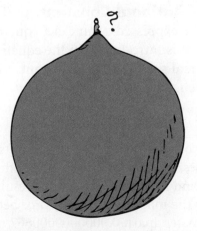

FIGURE 13.10 ▲
Your weight is less at the top of a mountain because you are farther from the center of Earth.

Interestingly, Cavendish's first measure of G was called the "Weighing the Earth" experiment, because once the value of G was known, the mass of Earth was easily calculated. The force that Earth exerts on a mass of 1 kilogram at its surface is 10 newtons. The distance between the 1-kilogram mass and the center of Earth is Earth's radius, 6.4×10^6 meters. Therefore, from $F = (Gm_1m_2/d^2)$, where m_1 is the mass of Earth,

$$10\text{ N} = 6.67 \times 10^{-11}\text{ N} \cdot \text{m}^2/\text{kg}^2 \times \frac{m_1 \times 1\text{ kg}}{(6.4 \times 10^6\text{ m})^2}$$

Rearranging to solve for m_1 gives

$$m_1 = \frac{10 \times (6.4 \times 10^6\text{ m})^2}{1\text{ kg} \times (6.67 \times 10^{-11}\text{ N} \cdot \text{m}^2/\text{kg}^2)}$$

from which the mass of Earth $m_1 = 6 \times 10^{24}$ kilograms.

CONCEPT CHECK What did Newton discover about gravity?

FIGURE 13.11 ▲

When G was first measured in the 1700s, newspapers everywhere announced the discovery as one that measured the mass of Planet Earth. This was particularly exciting at a time when a great portion of Earth's surface was still undiscovered.

do the math!

How can you express very large and very small numbers in scientific notation?

Very large and very small numbers are conveniently expressed in a mathematical format called *scientific notation*. An example of a large number is the equatorial radius of Earth: 6,370,000 m. This number can be obtained by multiplying 6.37 by 10, and again by 10, and so on until 10 has been used as a multiplier six times. So 6,370,000 can be written as 6.37×10^6. That's 6.37 million meters. A thousand million is a billion, 10^9. To better comprehend the size of a billion:

▶ A billion meters is slightly more than the Earth–moon distance.

▶ A billion kilograms is the mass of about 120 Eiffel Towers.

▶ A billion Earths would equal the mass of about three suns.

▶ A billion seconds is 31.7 years.

▶ A billion minutes is 1903 years.

▶ A billion years ago there were no humans on Earth.

▶ A billion people live in China.

▶ A billion atoms make up the dot over this i.

Small numbers are expressed in scientific notation by dividing by 10 successive times. A millimeter (mm) is $\frac{1}{1000}$ m, or 1 m divided by 10 three times. In scientific notation, 1 mm = 10^{-3} m. The gravitational constant G is a very small number, 0.000000000066726 N·m²/kg². By dividing 6.6726 by 10 eleven times, and rounding off, it is 6.67×10^{-11} N·m²/kg².

13.5 Gravity and Distance: The Inverse-Square Law

We can understand how gravity is reduced with distance by considering an imaginary "butter gun" used in a busy restaurant for buttering toast. Imagine melted butter sprayed through a square opening in a screen. The opening is exactly the size of one piece of square toast. And imagine that a spurt from the gun deposits an even layer of butter 1 mm thick. Consider the consequences of holding the toast twice as far from the butter gun. You can see in Figure 13.12 that the butter would spread out for twice the distance and would cover twice as much toast vertically and twice as much toast horizontally. A little thought will show that the butter would now spread out to cover four pieces of toast. How thick will the butter be on each piece of toast? Since it has been diluted to cover four times as much area, its thickness will be one-quarter as much, or 0.25 mm.

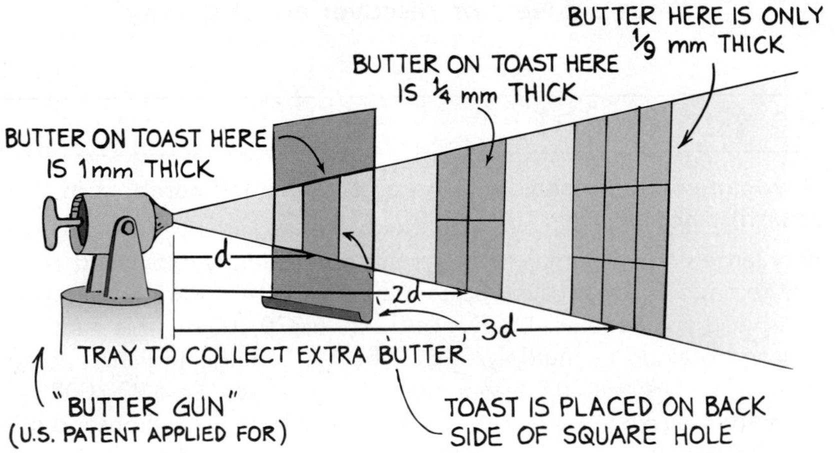

FIGURE 13.12 ▶

Butter spray travels outward from the nozzle of the butter gun in straight lines. Like gravity, the "strength" of the spray obeys an inverse-square law.

BUTTER HERE IS ONLY $\frac{1}{9}$ mm THICK

BUTTER ON TOAST HERE IS $\frac{1}{4}$ mm THICK

BUTTER ON TOAST HERE IS 1mm THICK

d

$2d$

$3d$

TRAY TO COLLECT EXTRA BUTTER

"BUTTER GUN" (U.S. PATENT APPLIED FOR)

TOAST IS PLACED ON BACK SIDE OF SQUARE HOLE

Note what has happened. When the butter gets twice as far from the gun, it is only $\frac{1}{4}$ as thick. More thought will show that if it gets 3 times as far, it will spread out to cover 3×3, or 9, pieces of toast. How thick will the butter be then? Can you see it will be $\frac{1}{9}$ as thick? And can you see that $\frac{1}{9}$ is the inverse *square* of 3? (The inverse of 3 is simply $\frac{1}{3}$; the inverse square of 3 is $(\frac{1}{3})^2$, or $\frac{1}{9}$.) When a quantity varies as the inverse square of its distance from its source, it follows an **inverse-square law**. ✔ **Gravity decreases according to the inverse-square law. The force of gravity weakens as the square of distance.** This law applies not only to the spreading of butter from a butter gun, and the weakening of gravity with distance, but to all cases where the effect from a localized source spreads evenly throughout the surrounding space. More examples are light, radiation, and sound.

Saying that *F* is inversely proportional to the **square** of *d* means, for example, that if *d* increases by a factor of 3, *F* decreases by a factor of 9.

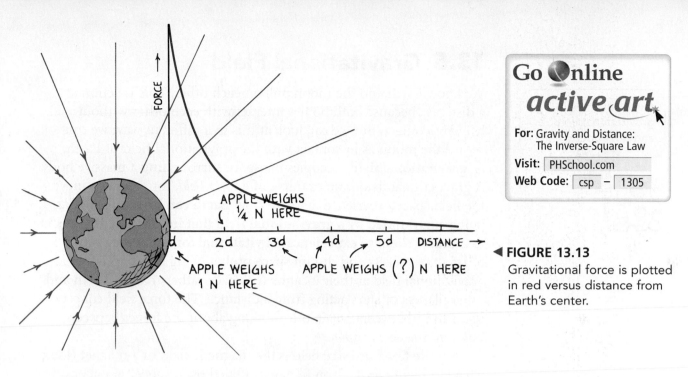

Go Online
active art

For: Gravity and Distance:
The Inverse-Square Law
Visit: PHSchool.com
Web Code: csp – 1305

◀ **FIGURE 13.13**
Gravitational force is plotted in red versus distance from Earth's center.

Figure 13.13 shows how the greater the distance from Earth's center, the less an object will weigh. An apple that weighs 1 N at Earth's surface weighs only 0.25 N when located twice as far from Earth's center because the pull of gravity is only $\frac{1}{4}$ as strong. When it is 3 times as far, it weighs only $\frac{1}{9}$ as much, or 0.11 N. If your little sister weighs 300 N at sea level, she will weigh only 299 N atop Mt. Everest. But no matter how great the distance, Earth's gravity does not drop to zero. Even if you were transported to the far reaches of the universe, the gravitational influence of Earth would be with you. It may be overwhelmed by the gravitational influences of nearer and more massive objects, but it is there. The gravitational influence of every object, however small or far away, is exerted through all space. That's impressive!

Myth: There is no gravity in space.
Fact: Gravity is everywhere!

CONCEPT CHECK How does the force of gravity change with distance?

think!

Suppose that an apple at the top of a tree is pulled by Earth's gravity with a force of 1 N. If the tree were twice as tall, would the force of gravity on the apple be only $\frac{1}{4}$ as strong? Explain your answer.
Answer: 13.5

13.6 Gravitational Field

Earth has a gravitational field and a magnetic field.

We know Earth and the moon pull on each other. This is action at a distance, because both bodies interact with each other without being in contact. But we can look at this in a different way: we can regard the moon as in contact with the gravitational field of Earth. A **gravitational field** occupies the space surrounding a massive body. A gravitational field is an example of a *force field,* for any mass in the field space experiences a force.[13.6] ⊘ **Earth can be thought of as being surrounded by a gravitational field that interacts with objects and causes them to experience gravitational forces.** It is common to think of rockets and distant space probes being influenced by the gravitational field at their locations in space rather than by Earth and other planets or stars acting from a distance. The force field concept plays an in-between role in our thinking about the forces between different masses.

A more familiar force field is the magnetic field of a magnet (look ahead to Figure 36.4). Iron filings sprinkled over a sheet of paper on top of a magnet reveal the shape of the magnet's magnetic field. The pattern of filings shows the strength and direction of the magnetic field at different locations around the magnet. Where the filings are close together, the field is strong. The direction of the filings shows the direction of the field at each point. Planet Earth is a giant magnet, and like all magnets, is surrounded in a magnetic field. Evidence of the field is easily seen by the orientation of a magnetic compass.

FIGURE 13.14 ▶
Field lines represent the gravitational field about Earth.

Field lines can also represent the pattern of Earth's gravitational field. Like the iron filings around a magnet, the field lines are closer together where the gravitational field is stronger. The arrows in Figure 13.14 show the field direction. A particle, astronaut, spaceship, or any mass in the vicinity of Earth will be accelerated in the direction of the field lines at that location. The strength of Earth's gravitational field, like the strength of its force on objects, follows the inverse-square law. Earth's gravitational field is strongest near Earth's surface and weaker at greater distances from Earth.

Another example of a force field is the one that surrounds electrical charges—the electric field, which we shall study in Chapter 33. In Chapter 36 we'll learn how magnets align with the magnetic fields of Earth to become compasses. In Chapter 11 we've already learned how the moon similarly aligns with Earth's gravitational field, resulting in the same side of the moon facing us. Force fields have far-reaching effects.

CONCEPT CHECK What kind of field surrounds Earth and causes objects to experience gravitational forces?

Physics on the Job

Astronaut

Three. Two. One. The Space Shuttle leaves Earth with its crew of seven astronauts. An astronaut pilots, or works on a spacecraft, or conducts experiments during spaceflights. Astronauts understand how the force of gravity will change throughout their trip. They apply physics to control the direction of a spacecraft, conduct experiments in space, and move outside the spacecraft. Astronauts usually have flight experience along with degrees in scientific disciplines such as physics or chemistry. The United States astronaut program is managed by the National Aeronautics and Space Administration (NASA).

13.7 Gravitational Field Inside a Planet

think!

If you stepped into a hole bored completely through Earth and made no attempt to grab the edges at either end, what kind of motion would you experience?

Answer: 13.7

The gravitational field of Earth exists inside Earth as well as outside. To investigate the gravitational field beneath the surface, imagine a hole drilled completely through Earth, say from the North Pole to the South Pole, as shown in Figure 13.15. Forget about impracticalities such as lava and high temperatures, and consider the kind of motion you would undergo if you fell into such a hole.

If you started at the North Pole end, you'd fall and gain speed all the way down to the center, and then overshoot and lose speed all the way to the South Pole. You'd gain speed moving toward the center, and lose speed moving away from the center. Without air drag, the trip would take nearly 45 minutes. If you failed to grab the edge, you'd fall back toward the center, overshoot, and return to the North Pole in the same amount of time.

Suppose you had some way to measure your acceleration during this trip. At the beginning of the fall, your acceleration would be *g*, but you'd find acceleration progressively decreasing as you continue toward the center of Earth.[13.7] Why? Because as you are being pulled "downward" toward Earth's center, you are also being pulled "upward" by the part of Earth that is "above" you. In fact, as illustrated in Figure 13.16, when you get to the center of Earth, the pull "down" is balanced by the pull "up." You are pulled in every direction equally, so the net force on you is zero. There is no acceleration as you whiz with maximum speed past the center of Earth. ✓ **The gravitational field of Earth at its center is zero!**

CONCEPT CHECK Describe the gravitational field of Earth at its center.

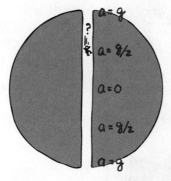

FIGURE 13.15 ▲
As you fall faster and faster into a hole bored through Earth, your acceleration diminishes because the pull of the mass above you partly cancels the pull below.

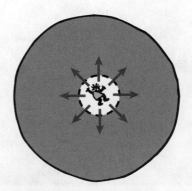

FIGURE 13.16 ▲
In a cavity at the center of Earth, your weight would be zero, because you would be pulled equally by gravity in all directions.

13.8 Weight and Weightlessness

The force of gravity, like any force, causes acceleration. Objects under the influence of gravity are pulled toward each other and accelerate (as long as nothing prevents the acceleration). We are almost always in contact with Earth. For this reason, we think of gravity primarily as something that presses us against Earth rather than as something that accelerates us. ⊘ **Force against Earth is the sensation we interpret as weight.**

Stand on a bathroom scale that is supported on a stationary floor. The gravitational force between you and Earth pulls you against the supporting floor and scale. By Newton's third law, the floor and scale in turn push upward on you. Located between you and the supporting floor is a spring-like gauge inside the bathroom scale. This pair of forces compresses the gauge. The weight reading on the scale is linked to the amount of compression.

◀ **FIGURE 13.17**
The sensation of weight is equal to the force that you exert against the supporting floor.

If you repeated this weighing procedure in a moving elevator, as shown in Figure 13.17, you would find your weight reading would vary—not during steady motion, but during accelerated motion. If the elevator accelerated upward, the bathroom scale and floor would push harder against your feet, and the gauge inside the scale would be compressed even more. The scale would show an increase in your weight.

If the elevator accelerated downward, the support force of the floor would be less and the scale would show a decrease in your weight. If the elevator cable broke and the elevator fell freely, the scale reading would register zero. According to the scale, you would be weightless. And you would feel weightless, for your insides would no longer be supported by your legs and pelvic region. Your organs would respond as though gravity were absent. But gravity is not absent, so would you really be weightless? The answer to this question depends on your definition of weight.

Rather than define your weight as the force of gravity that acts on you, it is more practical to define weight as the force you exert against a supporting floor (or weighing scales). According to this definition, you are as heavy as you feel. Thus, the condition of **weightlessness** is not the absence of gravity; rather, it is the absence of a support force. That queasy feeling you get when you are in a car that seems to leave the road momentarily when it goes over a hump, or worse, off a cliff, as shown in Figure 13.18, is not the absence of gravity. It is the absence of a support force.

Astronauts in orbit are without a support force and are in a sustained state of weightlessness. Astronauts sometimes experience "space sickness" until they get used to a state of sustained weightlessness. Future space travelers, however, need not be subjected to weightlessness. As mentioned in the previous chapter, lazily rotating giant wheels will likely supplant today's non-rotating space habitats. Rotation effectively supplies a support force and nicely provides weight.

CONCEPT CHECK : What sensation do we interpret as weight?

13.9 Ocean Tides

Seafaring people have always known there was a connection between the ocean tides and the moon, but no one could offer a satisfactory theory to explain why there are two high tides per day. You may have noticed this rise and fall of seawater, as shown in Figure 13.19, on visits to the ocean. ⊘ **Newton showed that the ocean tides are caused by *differences* in the gravitational pull of the moon on opposite sides of Earth.** The moon's attraction is stronger on Earth's oceans closer to the moon, and weaker on the oceans farther from the moon because the gravitational force is weaker with increased distance.

This difference in pulls across Earth slightly elongates it. Through a similar effect of Earth on the moon, the moon is slightly elongated, too. Rather than being spherical, both Earth and moon are pulled into a shape that slightly resembles a football.

FIGURE 13.19 ▶
The ocean tides are caused by differences in the gravitational pull of the moon on opposite sides of Earth.

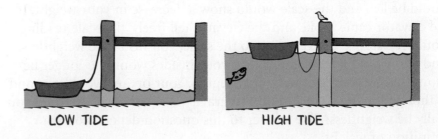

LOW TIDE   HIGH TIDE

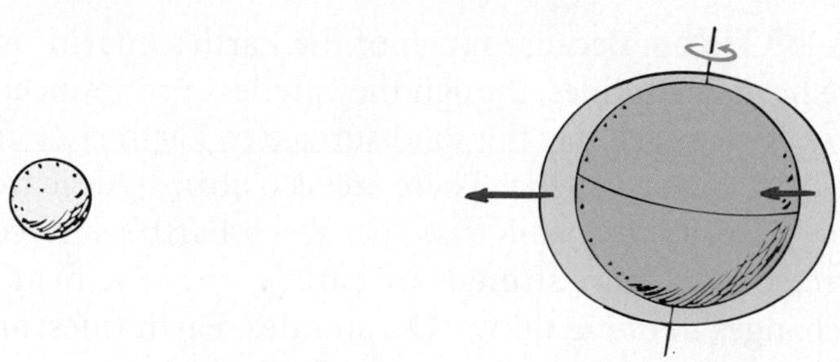

◀ **FIGURE 13.20**
The two tidal bulges remain relatively fixed with respect to the moon while Earth spins daily beneath them.

For Earth, the elongation is mainly in the most pliable part—the oceans. The oceans bulge out about 1 meter on average, on opposite sides of Earth. Because Earth spins once per day, a fixed point on Earth passes beneath both of these bulges each day, as illustrated in Figure 13.20. This produces two sets of ocean tides per day—two high tides and two low tides.[13.9]

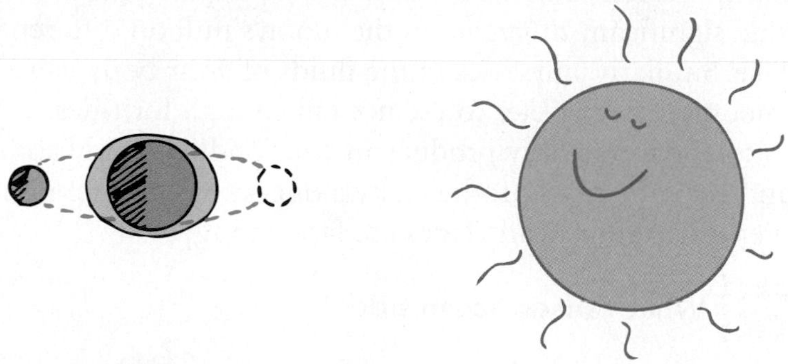

◀ **FIGURE 13.21**
When the sun, the moon, and Earth are aligned, spring tides occur.

Factors Affecting Ocean Tides The sun also contributes to ocean tides, about half as much as the moon—even though its pull on Earth is 180 times greater than the moon's pull on Earth. Then why aren't tides due to the sun 180 times greater than lunar tides? Because the *difference* in gravitational pulls by the sun on opposite sides of Earth is very small (only about 0.017 percent, compared to 6.7 percent for the moon's gravitation).

Figure 13.21 illustrates the configuration of the sun, Earth, and moon that produces spring tides. A **spring tide** is a high or low tide that occurs when the sun, Earth, and moon are all lined up. The tides due to the sun and the moon coincide, making the high tides higher than average and the low tides lower than average. Spring tides occur at the times of a new or full moon (and have nothing to do with the spring season).

A **neap tide** occurs when the moon is halfway between a new moon and a full moon, in either direction. As illustrated in Figure 13.22, the pulls of the moon and sun are perpendicular to each other. As a result, the solar and lunar tides do not overlap, so the high tides are not as high and low tides are not as low.

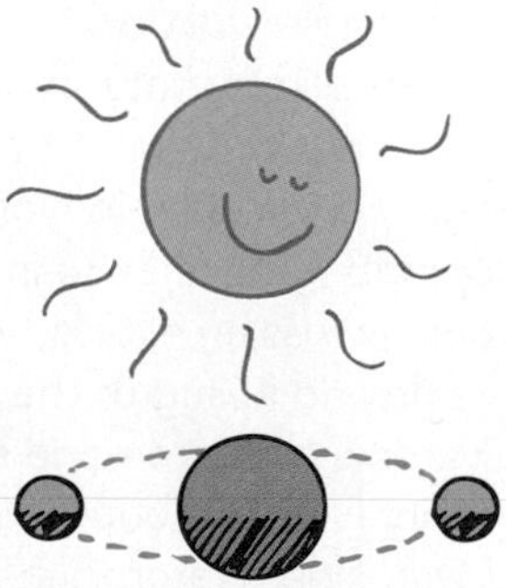

FIGURE 13.22 ▲
When the attractions of the sun and the moon are at right angles to each other (at the time of a half moon), neap tides occur.

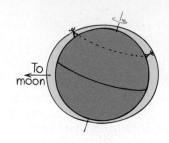

FIGURE 13.23 ▲
Earth's tilt causes the two daily high tides to be unequal.

Atmospheric tides influence the number of cosmic rays reaching Earth's surface. Like ocean tides, atmospheric tides are greatest when the moon, sun, and Earth are aligned.

Other Types of Tides Because much of the Earth's interior is deformable, we have Earth tides, though they are less pronounced than ocean tides. Twice each day the solid surface of Earth rises and falls as much as one-quarter meter. There are also atmospheric tides, which affect the intensity of cosmic rays that reach Earth's surface. These rays, affected even more strongly by Earth's magnetic field, induce subtle changes in living things. Ocean tides, Earth tides, and atmospheric tides are greatest when the sun, Earth, and moon are aligned—at the time of a full or new moon. The tilt of Earth's axis, interfering landmasses, friction with the ocean bottom, and other factors complicate tidal motions. Figure 13.23 illustrates the effect of the tilt of Earth's axis on the tides.

Although the moon produces considerable tides in Earth's oceans, which are thousands of kilometers across, it produces scarcely any tides in a lake. That's because no part of the lake is significantly closer to the moon than any other part—this means there is no significant *difference* in the moon's pull on different parts of the lake. Similarly, any tides in the fluids of your body caused by the moon are negligible. You're not tall enough for tides. What micro-tides the moon may produce in your body are only about one two-hundredth the tides produced by a one-kilogram melon held one meter above your head! Tides are fascinating.

CONCEPT CHECK What causes ocean tides?

Science, Technology, and Society

Power Production
Power plants that run on tidal power are numerous throughout the world. The first modern tidal power plant in North America has been operating since 1984 in Nova Scotia, Canada. A dam across an estuary gets its power from the rising and falling of the daily ocean tide. First the water is higher on one side of the dam, and is maintained at about 1.6 meters higher than the lower side. Water then flows through a series of gates to the lower side, turning a huge turbine in the process. When the tide changes, the flow of water is in the reverse direction, again turning the turbine. The dam produces more than 20 MW of power—enough to meet the electricity needs for 4500 homes. The largest tidal power plant produces 240 MW of electric power in Brittany,

France. Watch for the growth of this green technology.

Critical Thinking What are the advantages of using ocean tides to produce electricity?

13.10 Black Holes

There are two main processes going on continuously in stars like our sun. Figure 13.24 illustrates these two processes. One process is gravitation, which tends to crush all solar material toward the center. The other process is thermonuclear fusion consisting of reactions similar to those in a hydrogen bomb. These hydrogen bomb-like reactions tend to blow solar material outward. When the processes of gravitation and thermonuclear fusion balance each other, the result is the sun of a given size.

For: Links on black holes
Visit: www.SciLinks.org
Web Code: csn – 1310

Formation of Black Holes If the fusion rate increases, the sun will get hotter and bigger; if the fusion rate decreases, the sun will get cooler and smaller. What will happen when the sun runs out of fusion fuel (hydrogen)? The answer is, gravitation will dominate and the sun will start to collapse. For our sun, this collapse will ignite the nuclear ashes of fusion (helium) and fuse them into carbon. During this fusion process, the sun will expand to become the type of star known as a *red giant*. It will be so big that it will extend beyond Earth's orbit and swallow Earth. Fortunately, this won't take place until some 5 billion years from now. When the helium is all "burned," the red giant will collapse and die out. It will no longer give off heat and light. It will then be the type of star called a *black dwarf*—a cool cinder among billions of others.

The story is a bit different for stars more massive than the sun. For a heavy star, one that is at least two to three times more massive than our sun,[13.10] once the flame of thermonuclear fusion is extinguished, gravitational collapse takes over—and it doesn't stop! The star not only caves in on itself, but the atoms that compose the stellar material also cave in on themselves until there are no empty spaces. According to theory, the collapse never stops and the density becomes literally infinite. Gravitation near these shrunken configurations, which are called **black holes,** is so enormous that nothing can get back out. Even light cannot escape a black hole. They have crushed themselves out of visible existence.

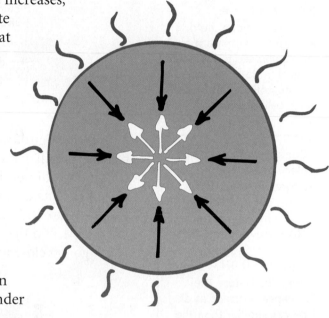

FIGURE 13.24 ▲
The size of the sun is the result of a "tug of war" between two opposing processes: nuclear fusion and gravitational contraction.

Gravitational Field Near Black Holes Perhaps surprisingly, a black hole is no more massive than the star from which it collapsed. ☑ **When a massive star collapses into a black hole, there is no change in the gravitational field at any point beyond the original radius of the star.** The gravitational field near the black hole may be enormous, but, as shown in Figure 13.25, the field beyond the original radius of the star is no different after collapse than before. The amount of mass has not changed, so there is no change in the field at any point beyond this distance. Black holes will be formidable only to future astronauts who venture too close.

FIGURE 13.25 ▶
The gravitational field strength near a giant star that collapses to become a black hole is the same before collapse (left) and after collapse (right).

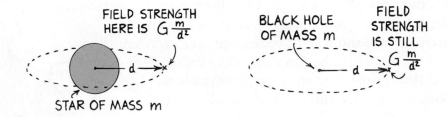

FIELD STRENGTH HERE IS $G\frac{m}{d^2}$

STAR OF MASS m

BLACK HOLE OF MASS m

FIELD STRENGTH IS STILL $G\frac{m}{d^2}$

Contrary to stories about black holes, they're non-aggressive and don't reach out to swallow innocents at a distance. Their gravitational fields are no stronger than the original fields about the stars before their collapse—except at distances smaller than the radius of the original star. Black holes shouldn't worry future astronauts, unless they get too close.

The configuration of the gravitational field about a black hole represents the collapse of space itself. The field is usually represented as a warped two-dimensional surface, as shown in Figure 13.26.

Astronauts could enter the fringes of this warp and, with a powerful spaceship, still escape. After a certain distance, however, they could not escape, and they would disappear from the observable universe. Don't go too close to a black hole!

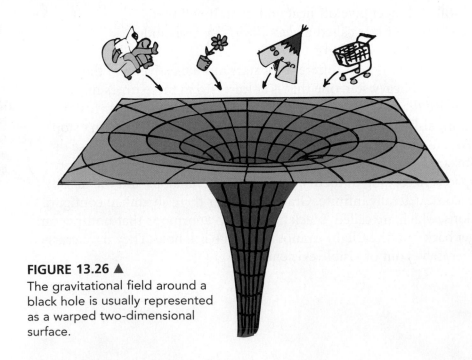

FIGURE 13.26 ▲
The gravitational field around a black hole is usually represented as a warped two-dimensional surface.

Effects of Black Holes Although black holes can't be seen, their effects can be. Many stars in the sky occur as binaries—pairs that orbit around each other. Sometimes only one star of a binary pair is seen. Matter streams from this visible star toward its invisible companion, emitting X-rays as it accelerates toward the "nothingness" that is probably a black hole. And near the centers of most galaxies are immensely massive yet very small centers of force that cause stars near them to speed around in tight orbits. These black holes, if that's what they are, are more massive than a million suns.

CONCEPT CHECK : What happens to the gravitational field of a star that has collapsed into a black hole?

13.11 Universal Gravitation

We all know that Earth is round. But *why* is Earth round? It is round because of gravitation. Since everything attracts everything else, Earth had attracted itself together before it became solid. Any "corners" of Earth have been pulled in so that Earth is a giant sphere. The sun, the moon, and Earth are all fairly spherical because they have to be (rotational effects make them somewhat wider at their equators). Figure 13.27 shows how gravity played a role in the formation of the solar system. A slightly rotating ball of interstellar gas, which is illustrated in Figure 13.27a, contracted due to mutual gravitation, which is shown in Figure 13.27b. To conserve angular momentum, the rotational speed of the ball of gas increased. The increased momentum of the individual particles and clusters of particles caused them to sweep in wider paths about the rotational axis, producing an overall disk shape, as shown in Figure 13.27c. The greater surface area of the disk promoted cooling and clusters of swirling matter—the birthplace of the planets.

FIGURE 13.27 ▼
Gravity played an important role in the formation of the solar system.

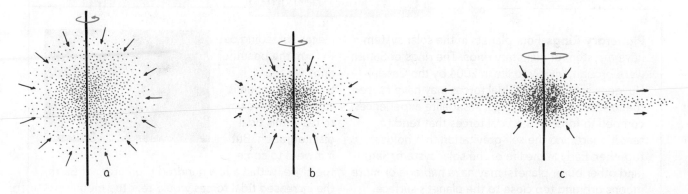

Perturbations in the Solar System If everything pulls on everything else, then the planets must pull on each other. The net force that controls Jupiter, for example, is not just from the sun, but from the planets also. Their effect is small compared with the pull of the more massive sun, but it still shows. When the planet Saturn is near Jupiter, for example, its pull disturbs the otherwise smooth path of Jupiter. Both planets deviate from their normal orbits. The deviation of an orbiting object from its path around a center of force caused by the action of an additional center of force is called a **perturbation.**

Until the middle of the last century astronomers were puzzled by unexplained perturbations of the planet Uranus. Even when the influences of the other planets were taken into account, Uranus was behaving strangely. Either the law of gravitation was failing at this great distance from the sun, or some unknown influence such as another planet was perturbing Uranus.

The source of Uranus's perturbation was uncovered in 1845 and 1846 by two astronomers, John Adams in England and Urbain Leverrier in France. With only pencil and paper and the application of Newton's law of gravitation, both astronomers independently arrived at the same conclusion: A disturbing body beyond the orbit of Uranus was the culprit. They sent letters to their local observatories with instructions to search a certain part of the sky. The request by Adams was delayed by misunderstandings at Greenwich, England, but Leverrier's request to the director of the Berlin Observatory was heeded right away. The planet Neptune was discovered within a half hour.

Link to ASTRONOMY

Planetary Rings Four planets in the solar system have a system of planetary rings. The rings of Saturn were brought vividly to life in 2004 by the Cassini-Huygens space probe. Tidal forces may have caused the formation of these rings. A satellite experiences competing forces—the tidal forces that tend to tear it apart, and the self-gravitation that holds it together. Early in the life of the solar system, Saturn (and other outer planets) may have had one or more moons orbiting too close to the planet's surface. Powerful tidal forces could have stretched them and torn them apart. During billions of years fragments could have separated into billions of still smaller

pieces spreading out to form the beautiful rings we see today. Our moon is sufficiently far away to resist this tidal disintegration. But if it were to come too close, within a few hundred kilometers of Earth, the increased tidal forces would tear the moon apart. Then Earth, like Saturn, Jupiter, Uranus, and Neptune, would have a system of planetary rings!

discover!

Which Hand Is Bigger?

1. Hold your hands outstretched, one twice as far from your eyes as the other.
2. Make a casual judgment about which hand looks bigger.
3. Now, overlap your hands slightly and carefully view them with one eye closed.
4. **Think** Why does one hand appear bigger than the other?

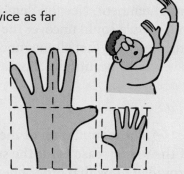

Subsequent tracking of the orbits of both Uranus and Neptune led to the prediction of another massive body beyond Neptune. In 1930, at the Lowell Observatory in Arizona, Pluto was discovered. Whatever you may have learned in your early schooling, astronomers now regard Pluto as a dwarf planet and not a full-fledged planet. Pluto takes 248 years to make a single revolution about the sun, so no one will see it in its discovered position again until the year 2178.

The Expanding Universe The shapes of distant galaxies provide further evidence that the law of gravity applies to larger distances. According to current scientific understanding, the universe origi- nated and grew from the explosion of a primordial fireball some 13.7 billion years ago. This is the "Big Bang" theory of the origin of the universe. All the matter of the universe was hurled outward from this event and continues in an outward expansion. Evidence for this includes precise measurements of the earliest remnant of the Big Bang: its cosmic microwave background.

More recent evidence suggests the universe is not only expanding, but *accelerating* outward. It is pushed by an anti-gravity *dark energy* that makes up an estimated 73 percent of the universe. Twenty-three percent of the universe is composed of the yet-to-be discovered par- ticles of exotic *dark matter*. Ordinary matter—the stuff of stars, cab- bages, and kings—makes up only 4 percent. The concepts of dark matter and dark energy will continue to inspire exciting research throughout this century. They may hold clues to how the cosmos began and where it is headed, and may be the key to understanding the fate of the universe. Our present view of the universe has pro- gressed appreciably beyond the universe as Newton perceived it.

Scientists' usage of the term theory differs from common usage. The theory of gravity, for example, is universally accepted by scientists, based on the preponder- ance of evidence and the success of the model. The term *theory* does not imply fundamental doubts about a phenom- enon's existence.

Your author wonders about readers of this book who will continue in their study of physics and help to decipher the nature of dark matter, dark energy, and other wonders of the universe yet to be discovered.

Newton's Impact on Science Few theories have affected science and civilization as much as Newton's theory of gravity. The successes of Newton's ideas ushered in the Age of Reason, or Century of Enlightenment. Newton demonstrated that by observation and reason, people could uncover the workings of the physical universe. How profound it is that all the moons and planets and stars and galaxies have such a beautifully simple rule to govern them, namely,

$$F = G\frac{m_1 m_2}{d^2}$$

☑ **The formulation of the law of universal gravitation is one of the major reasons for the success in science that followed, for it provided hope that other phenomena of the world might also be described by equally simple and universal laws.**

This hope nurtured the thinking of many scientists, artists, writers, and philosophers of the 1700s. One of these was the English philosopher John Locke, who argued that observation and reason, as demonstrated by Newton, should be our best judge and guide in all things. Locke urged that all of nature and even society should be searched to discover any "natural laws" that might exist. Using Newtonian physics as a model of reason, Locke and his followers modeled a system of government that found adherents in the 13 British colonies across the Atlantic. These ideas culminated in the Declaration of Independence and the Constitution of the United States of America.

CONCEPT CHECK : How did the formulation of the law of universal gravitation affect science?

Physics on the Job

Astronomer
Astronomers study the physics of nature's extremes—from the coldness of empty space to the fiery hotness of exploding stars, and from tiny elementary particles of matter to the vastness of the universe itself. Astronomers work mainly for university and government observatories. Whereas most of the efforts of early astronomers were in cataloging objects in the sky, astronomers today employ much physics as they study the history of the universe from the Big Bang to the present and seek to understand black holes, "dark matter" and "dark energy." It can truly be said that astronomers are far-out people.

REVIEW

Go Online
PHSchool.com

For: Self-Assessment
Visit: PHSchool.com
Web Code: csa – 1300

Concept Summary ......

- Newton reasoned that the moon is falling toward Earth for the same reason an apple falls from a tree—they are both pulled by Earth's gravity.

- The moon is actually falling toward Earth but has great enough tangential velocity to avoid hitting Earth.

- Newton's theory of gravity confirmed the Copernican theory of the solar system.

- Newton discovered that gravity is universal.

- Gravity decreases according to the inverse-square law.

- Earth can be thought of as being surrounded by a gravitational field that causes objects to experience gravitational forces.

- The gravitational field of Earth at its center is zero.

- Force against Earth is the sensation we interpret as weight.

- The ocean tides are caused by *differences* in the gravitational pull of the moon on opposite sides of Earth.

- When a massive star collapses into a black hole, there is no change in the gravitational field at any point beyond the original radius of the star.

- The formulation of the law of universal gravitation provided hope that other phenomena of the world might also be described by equally simple and universal laws.

Key Terms ......

law of universal gravitation *(p. 237)*

universal gravitational constant *(p. 237)*

inverse-square law *(p. 240)*

gravitational field *(p. 242)*

weightlessness *(p. 246)*

spring tide *(p. 247)*

neap tide *(p. 247)*

black hole *(p. 249)*

perturbation *(p. 252)*

think! Answers

13.5   No, because the twice-as-tall apple tree is not twice as far from Earth's center. The taller tree would have to have a height equal to the radius of Earth (6370 km) before the weight of the apple would reduce to $\frac{1}{4}$N. Before its weight decreases by 1%, an apple or any object must be raised 32 km—nearly four times the height of Mt. Everest, the tallest mountain in the world. So as a practical matter we disregard the effects of everyday changes in elevation.

13.7   You would oscillate back and forth, approximating *simple harmonic motion*. A round trip would take nearly 90 minutes. Interestingly enough, we will see in the next chapter that an Earth satellite in close orbit about Earth also takes the same 90 minutes to make a complete round trip. This is not a coincidence, but a feature of simple harmonic motion (Chapter 25).

13 ASSESS

Check Concepts ......

Section 13.1

1. In Newton's insight, what did a falling apple have in common with the moon?

Section 13.2

2. In what sense does the moon "fall"?

Section 13.3

3. How does the tangential velocity of a planet relate to it orbiting around the sun?

Section 13.4

4. What is the gravitational force between two 1-kilogram bodies that are 1 meter apart?

5. When *G* was first measured in the 1700s, how did newspapers report the experiment?

6. In what way does the force of gravity between two objects depend on their masses?

Section 13.5

7. How does the force of gravity depend on the distance between two objects?

8. How does the force of gravity between two bodies change when the distance between them is doubled?

9. How does the intensity of light, radiation, and sound change when a point source is twice as far away?

10. Do you escape from Earth's gravity if you're above the atmosphere? By being on the moon? Defend your answers.

11. At what distance away from Earth is Earth's gravitational force on an object zero?

Section 13.6

12. True or false: The strength of a gravitational field equals the gravitational force per mass on a particle in the field.

Section 13.7

13. What is the value of Earth's gravitational field at the center of Earth?

14. If you stepped into a hole that passed completely through Earth, you'd oscillate down and up. How long would a one-way trip take? How long would a round trip take?

Section 13.8

15. Would the gauge inside a bathroom scale be more compressed or less compressed if you weighed yourself in an elevator that accelerated upward? Downward?

Section 13.9

16. Do tides depend more on the strength of gravitational pull or on the *difference* in strengths? Explain.

17. Why are ocean tides higher at the time of a full moon?

Section 13.10

18. What two competing effects determine the size of a star?

19. Why are black holes black?

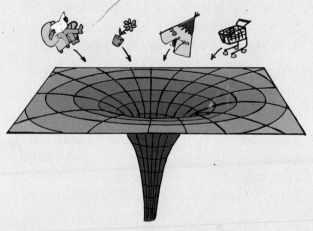

Section 13.11

20. What was the cause of perturbations discovered in the orbit of Planet Uranus?

Think and Rank ......

Rank each of the following sets of scenarios in order of the quantity or property involved. List them from left to right. If scenarios have equal rankings, then separate them with an equal sign. (e.g., A = B)

21. The planet and its moon gravitationally attract each other. Rank gravitational attractions between them from greatest to least.

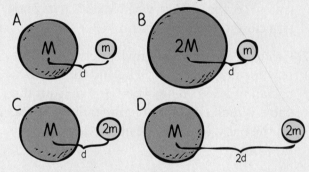

Plug and Chug ......

The equation for gravitational force between two bodies separated by a distance is shown below.

$$F = G\frac{m_1 m_2}{d^2}$$

22. Calculate the force of gravity on a 1-kg mass at Earth's surface. The mass of Earth is 6×10^{24} kg, and its radius is 6.4×10^6 m.

23. Calculate the force of gravity on the same 1-kg mass if it were 6.4×10^6 m above Earth's surface (that is, if it were 2 Earth radii from Earth's center).

24. Calculate the force of gravity between Earth (mass = 6.0×10^{24} kg) and the moon (mass = 7.4×10^{22} kg). The average Earth–moon distance is 3.8×10^{8} m.

25. Calculate the force of gravity between Earth and the sun (sun's mass = 2.0×10^{30} kg; average Earth–sun distance = 1.5×10^{11} m).

26. Calculate the force of gravity between a newborn baby (mass = 4 kg) and the planet Mars (mass = 6.4×10^{23} kg), when Mars is at its position closest to Earth (distance = 8×10^{10} m).

27. Calculate the force of gravity between a newborn baby of mass 4 kg and the obstetrician of mass 75 kg, who is 0.3 m from the baby. Which exerts more gravitational force on the baby, Mars or the obstetrician? By how much?

Think and Explain ......

28. Comment on whether or not this label on a consumer product should be cause for concern. *CAUTION: The mass of this product affects every other mass in the universe, with an attractive force that is proportional to the product of the masses and inversely proportional to the square of the distance between them.*

29. Gravitational force acts on all objects in proportion to their masses. Why, then, doesn't a heavy object fall faster than a lighter one? (Is the answer something you learned much earlier?)

30. Irene says that Earth's force of gravity is stronger on a piece of iron than on a piece of wood of the same mass. Do you agree? Defend your answer.

31. Stephan says that the force of gravity is stronger on a piece of paper after it's crumpled. His classmates disagree, so Stephan "proves" his point by dropping two pieces of paper, one crumpled and the other not. Sure enough, the crumpled piece falls faster. Has Stephan proven his point? Explain.

32. Earth and the moon are gravitationally attracted to each other. Does the more massive Earth attract the moon with a greater force, the same force, or less force than the moon attracts Earth?

33. What is the magnitude and direction of the gravitational force that acts on a woman who weighs 500 N at the surface of Earth?

34. If the gravitational forces of the sun on the planets suddenly disappeared, in what kind of paths would the planets move?

35. The moon "falls" 1.4 mm each second. Does this mean that it gets 1.4 mm closer to Earth each second? Would it get closer if its tangential velocity were reduced? Explain.

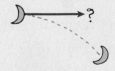

36. If the moon were twice as massive, would the attractive force of Earth on the moon be twice as large? Of the moon on Earth?

37. The weight of an apple near the surface of Earth is 1 N. What is the weight of Earth in the gravitational field of the apple?

38. A friend proposes an idea for launching space probes that consists of boring a hole completely through Earth. Your friend reasons that a probe dropped into such a hole would accelerate all the way through and shoot like a projectile out the other side. Defend or oppose the reasoning of your friend.

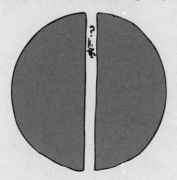

39. If you stand on a shrinking planet, so that in effect you get closer to its center, your weight will increase. But if you instead burrow into the planet and get closer to its center, your weight will decrease. Explain.

40. If you were unfortunate enough to be in a freely falling elevator, you might notice the bag of groceries you were carrying hovering in front of you, apparently weightless. Cite the frames of reference in which the groceries would be falling, and those in which they would not be falling.

41. What two forces act on you in a moving elevator? When are these forces equal in magnitude, and when are they not?

42. A friend says that astronauts in orbit are weightless because they're beyond the pull of Earth's gravity. Correct your friend's ignorance.

43. The sun exerts almost 200 times more force on the oceans of Earth than the moon does. Why then, is the moon more effective in raising tides?

44. From a point of view at the sun, does the moon circle Earth, or does Earth circle the moon?

45. What would be the effect on Earth's tides if the diameter of Earth were larger than it is? If Earth were as it presently is, but the moon were larger—with the same mass?

46. Whenever the ocean tide is unusually high, will the following low tide be unusually low? Defend your answer in terms of "conservation of water." (If you slosh water in a tub so that it is extra deep at one end, will water at the other end be extra s

47. The human body is more than 50% water. Is it likely that the moon's gravitational pull causes any significant biological tides—cyclic changes in water flow among the body's fluid compartments? (*Hint:* Is any part of your body appreciably closer to the moon than any other part? Is there a *difference* in lunar pulls?)

48. A black hole is no more massive than the star from which it collapsed. Why then, is gravitation so intense near a black hole?

49. Which requires more fuel—a rocket going from Earth to the moon, or a rocket coming from the moon to Earth? Why?

50. Recent evidence indicates that the present expansion of the universe is accelerating. Is this consistent with, or contrary to, the law of gravity? Explain.

51. The planet Jupiter is about 300 times as massive as Earth, but an object on its surface would weigh only 2.5 times as much as it would on Earth. Can you come up with an explanation? (*Hint:* Let the terms in the equation for gravitational force guide your thinking.)

52. Some people dismiss the validity of scientific theories by saying they are "only" theories. The law of universal gravitation is a theory. Does this mean that scientists still doubt its validity? Explain.

Think and Solve ······

53. Equate your weight *mg* to Newton's equation for gravitational force,

$$G\,\frac{mM}{R^2}$$

where *M* is the mass of Earth and *R* is Earth's radius. Show that acceleration of free fall is

$$g = \frac{GM}{R^2}$$

54. Isabella drops a chunk of iron of mass *m* from the roof of her high school and it accelerates at *g*. Then she ties two chunks of iron together, of mass 2*m*. Show that when she drops the double chunk, the acceleration of fall is also *g*.

55. The symbol *g* can mean acceleration due to gravity or gravitational field strength. Show that the units of *g* can be expressed as either m/s^2 or N/kg.

56. By what factor would your weight change if the Earth's diameter were doubled and its mass were also doubled?

57. Find the change in the force of gravity between two objects when both masses are doubled and the distance between them is also doubled.

58. If you stood atop a ladder that was so tall that you doubled your distance from Earth's center, how would your weight compare with its present value?

59. Suppose you stood atop a ladder that was so tall that you were three Earth radii from Earth's center. Show that your weight would be one ninth its present value.

60. Consider a pair of planets that both somehow double in mass while keeping their same distance apart. By what factor does the force of gravity change between them?

61. By what factor does the force of gravity between two planets change when masses remain the same but the distance between them is increased by four?

62. By what factor does the force of gravity between two planets change when the masses remain the same, but the distance between them is *decreased* by four?

63. By what factor does the force of gravity between two planets change when the masses of the planets remain unchanged, but the distance between them is *decreased* by five?

64. Many people mistakenly believe that the astronauts that orbit the Earth are "above gravity." Earth's mass is 6×10^{24} kg, and its radius is 6.38×10^6 m (6380 km). Use the inverse-square law to show that in space-shuttle territory, 200 kilometers above Earth's surface, the force of gravity on a shuttle is about 94% that at Earth's surface.

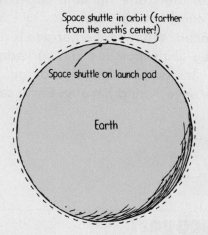

Space shuttle in orbit (farther from the earth's center!)

Space shuttle on launch pad

Earth

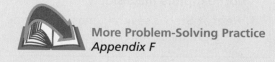

More Problem-Solving Practice
Appendix F

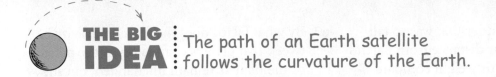

14 SATELLITE MOTION

THE BIG IDEA : The path of an Earth satellite follows the curvature of the Earth.

If you drop a stone, it will fall in a straight-line path to the ground below. If you move your hand horizontally as you drop the stone, it will follow a curved path to the ground. If you move your hand faster, the stone will land farther away and the curvature of the path will be less pronounced. What would happen if the curvature of the path matched the curvature of Earth? The answer is simple enough: Without air resistance, you'd have an Earth satellite!

discover!

What Happens When You Disturb the Path of a Pendulum?

1. Make a pendulum from a mass and a 1-m long string. Tie the free end of the string to a support.

2. Set the pendulum swinging. It should move back and forth only and not side-to-side.

3. While the pendulum is swinging back and forth, tap the mass sideways.

4. Repeat Step 3 several times, each time tapping the mass with a different force.

Analyze and Conclude

1. **Observing** Describe the original shape of the path of the mass.

2. **Drawing Conclusions** What effect does tapping the mass with different forces have on the shape of the path?

3. **Predicting** How might changing the amount of mass affect the nature of the path?

14.1 Earth Satellites

Simply put, an Earth **satellite** is a projectile moving fast enough to fall continually *around* Earth rather than *into* it. Imagine yourself on a planet that is smaller than Earth as shown in Figure 14.2. Because of the planet's small size and low mass, you would not have to throw the stone very fast to make its curved path match the surface curvature of the planet. If you threw the stone just right, it would follow a circular orbit.

◀ **FIGURE 14.2**
If you toss the stone horizontally with the proper speed, its path will match the surface curvature of the small planet.

How fast would the stone have to be thrown horizontally for it to orbit Earth? The answer depends on the rate at which the stone falls and the rate at which Earth curves. Recall from Chapter 4 that a stone dropped from rest accelerates downward (or toward the center of Earth) at 10 m/s² and falls a vertical distance of 5 meters during the first second. Also recall from Chapter 5 that the same is true of any projectile as it starts to fall. Recall that in the first second a projectile will fall a vertical distance of 5 meters below the straight-line path it would have taken without gravity as shown in Figure 14.3. (It may be helpful to refresh your memory and review Figure 5.11.)

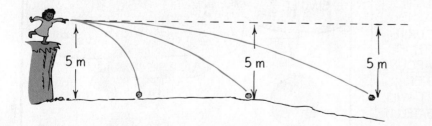

◀ **FIGURE 14.3**
Throw a stone at any speed and one second later it will have fallen 5 m below where it would have been without gravity.

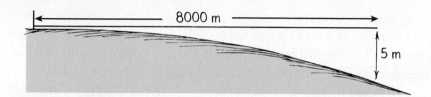

8000 m

5 m

A geometric fact about the curvature of our Earth is that its surface drops a vertical distance of nearly 5 meters for every 8000 meters tangent to its surface as shown in Figure 14.4.

☑ **A stone thrown fast enough to go a horizontal distance of 8000 meters during the time (1 second) it takes to fall 5 meters, will orbit Earth.** Isn't this speed simply 8000 meters per second? So we see that the orbital speed for close orbit about Earth is 8000 m/s (or 8 km/s). If this doesn't seem to be very fast, convert it to kilometers per hour; you'll see it is an impressive 29,000 km/h (or 18,000 mi/h). At that speed, atmospheric friction would burn an object to a crisp. That's why a satellite must stay about 150 kilometers or more above Earth's surface—to keep from burning due to the friction of the atmosphere.

The 5-meter drop for each 8000-meter tangent means that if you were floating in a calm ocean you'd be able to see only the top of a 5-meter mast on a boat 8000 meters away.

CONCEPT CHECK: Near the surface of Earth, how fast does a stone have to be thrown to orbit Earth?

14.2 Circular Orbits

Interestingly, in circular orbit the speed of a circling satellite is not changed by gravity. We can understand this by comparing a satellite in circular orbit to a bowling ball rolling along a bowling alley as shown in Figure 14.5. Why doesn't the gravity that acts on the bowling ball change its speed? The answer is that gravity is pulling neither forward nor backward—it pulls straight downward, perpendicular to the ball's motion. The bowling ball has no component of gravitational force along the direction of the alley.

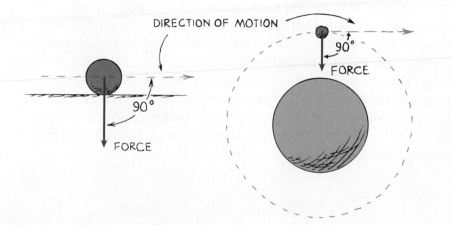

DIRECTION OF MOTION

90°

FORCE

90°

FORCE

◀ FIGURE 14.5
The speeds of the bowling ball and the satellite are not affected by the force of gravity because there is no horizontal component of the gravitational force.

The same is true for a satellite in circular orbit. Here a satellite is always moving at a right angle (perpendicular) to the force of gravity. It doesn't move in the direction of gravity, which would increase its speed, nor does it move in a direction against gravity, which would decrease its speed. Instead, the satellite exactly "criss-crosses" gravity, so that no change in speed occurs—only a change in direction. ☑ **A satellite in circular orbit around Earth is always moving perpendicular to gravity and parallel to Earth's surface at constant speed.**

For a satellite close to Earth, the time for a complete orbit around Earth, its **period,** is about 90 minutes. For higher altitudes, the orbital speed is less and the period is longer. Communications satellites are located in orbit 6.5 Earth radii from Earth's center, so that their period is 24 hours. This period matches Earth's daily rotation. They are launched to orbit in the plane of Earth's equator, so they are always above the same place on the equator. The moon is farther away, and has a 27.3-day period. The higher the orbit of a satellite, the slower its speed and the longer its period.[14.2]

FIGURE 14.6 ▶

The ISS and its inhabitants circle 360 km above the Earth, well above its atmosphere, in a state of continual free fall.

The international space station (ISS), shown in Figure 14.6, orbits at 360 kilometers above Earth's surface. Like all satellites, tangential velocity assures that it falls around Earth rather than into it. Acceleration toward Earth is somewhat less than 1 *g* because of altitude. This acceleration, however, is not sensed by the astronauts; relative to the station, they experience zero *g*. Over extended periods of time this causes loss of muscle strength and other detrimental changes in the body. Future space travelers, however, can avoid this when space stations rotate (recall our discussion of rotating space habitats in Chapter 12). Rotation effectively supplies a support force and can nicely provide Earth-normal weight.

Think of the International Space Station as Earth's lifeboat.

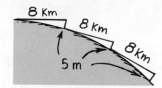

◀ **FIGURE 14.7**
A satellite in circular orbit close to Earth moves tangentially at 8 km/s. Each second, it falls 5 m beneath each successive 8-km tangent.

Recall from Chapter 13 that Isaac Newton understood satellite motion from his investigation of the moon's motion. He thought about the launching of artificial satellites, for he reasoned that without air resistance, a cannonball could circle Earth and coast indefinitely if it had sufficient speed. As Figure 14.7 demonstrates, he calculated this speed to be the same as 8 km/s. Since such speed was impossible then, he was not optimistic about people launching satellites. What Newton did not consider was multistage rockets—the idea of rockets carried piggyback style on other rockets to reach orbital speed by a succession of rocket firings.

CONCEPT CHECK : Describe the motion of a satellite in relation to Earth's surface and gravity.

When a spacecraft enters the atmosphere at too steep an angle, more than about 6 degrees, it can burn up. If it comes in too shallow it could bounce back into space like a pebble skipped across water.

14.3 Elliptical Orbits

☑ **A satellite in orbit around Earth traces an oval-shaped path called an ellipse.** An **ellipse** is the closed path taken by a point that moves in such a way that the sum of its distances from two fixed points is constant. The two fixed points in an ellipse are called **foci.** For a satellite orbiting a planet, the center of the planet is at one focus and the other focus could be inside or outside the planet. An ellipse can be easily constructed by using a pair of tacks, one at each focus, a loop of string, and a pencil, as shown in Figure 14.8. The closer the tacks, the closer the ellipse is to a circle. When the foci are together, the ellipse *is* a circle. A circle is a special case of an ellipse.

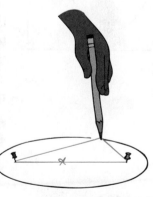

FIGURE 14.8 ▲
A simple method of constructing an ellipse is shown here.

discover!

How Do You Draw Different Ellipses?

1. Draw an ellipse with a loop of string, two tacks, and a pen or pencil, as shown in Figure 14.8.

2. Try different tack spacings for a variety of ellipses. Or draw an ellipse by tracing the edge of the shadow cast by a circular disk on a flat surface.

3. **Think** How can you move the disk to get different ellipses?

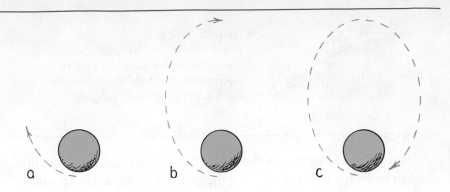

FIGURE 14.9 ▶
A satellite moves in an elliptical orbit. **a.** When the satellite exceeds 8 km/s, it overshoots a circle. **b.** At its maximum separation, it starts to come back toward Earth. **c.** The cycle repeats itself.

a   b   c

think!

The orbit of a satellite is shown in the sketch. In which of the positions *A* through *D* does the satellite have the greatest speed? The least speed?
Answer: 14.3

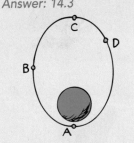

Satellite speed, which is constant in a circular orbit, *varies* in an elliptical orbit. When the initial speed is more than 8 km/s, the satellite overshoots a circular path and moves away from Earth, against the force of gravity. It therefore loses speed. Like a rock thrown into the air, the satellite slows to a point where it no longer recedes, and begins falling back toward Earth. The speed lost in receding is regained as it falls back. The satellite then rejoins its path with the same speed it had initially. The procedure repeats over and over, and an ellipse is traced each cycle as shown in Figure 14.9.

Quite interestingly, the apparently parabolic paths of projectiles such as cannonballs are actually tiny segments of a thin ellipse that extends within and just beyond the center of Earth. Figure 14.10 shows that for speeds less than orbital speeds, the center of Earth is the far focus of the elliptical path. In this case the near focus is close to the launching site and varies for different speeds. When the projectile traces a circular orbit, both foci are together at Earth's center. For elliptical orbits, the near focus is Earth's center and the location of the far focus varies for different speeds.

CONCEPT CHECK : What is the shape of the path of a satellite in an orbit around Earth?

FIGURE 14.10 ▶
The parabolic paths of projectiles are actually segments of ellipses. **a.** For relatively low speeds, the center of Earth is the far focus. **b.** For greater speeds, the near focus is Earth's center.

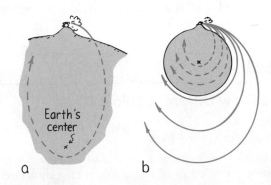

Earth's center

a   b

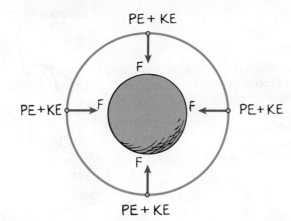

PE + KE

F

PE + KE ○→ F   F ←○ PE + KE

F

PE + KE

For a satellite in circular orbit, no component of force acts along the direction of motion. The speed, and thus the KE, cannot change.

14.4 Energy Conservation and Satellite Motion

Recall from Chapter 9 that moving objects have kinetic energy (KE). An object above Earth's surface has potential energy (PE) due to its position. Everywhere in its orbit, a satellite has both KE and PE.

⊘ **The sum of the KE and PE of a satellite is constant at all points along an orbit.**

In a circular orbit, the distance between a planet's center and the satellite's center is constant, as shown in Figure 14.11. This means that the PE of the satellite is the same everywhere in orbit. So, by the law of conservation of energy, the KE is also constant. Thus, the speed is constant in any circular orbit.

In an elliptical orbit the situation is different. Both speed and distance vary. The **apogee** is the point in a satellite's orbit farthest from the center of Earth. The **perigee** is the point in a satellite's orbit closest to the center of Earth. The PE is greatest when the satellite is at the apogee and least when the satellite is at the perigee. Correspondingly, the KE will be least when the PE is most; and the KE will be most when the PE is least, as Figure 14.12 shows. At every point in the orbit, the sum of the KE and PE is constant.

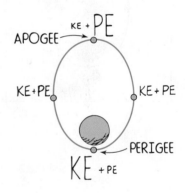

FIGURE 14.12 ▲
The sum of KE and PE for a satellite is a constant at all points along an elliptical orbit.

Physics on the Job

Satellite Design Engineer Satellites play an important role in conducting scientific research, obtaining environmental data, and providing communications services. Satellite design engineers are employed by the United States government through NASA and by commercial communications companies. The goal of a satellite design engineer is to design satellites that will orbit at specific distances from Earth, carry the necessary equipment, and withstand the conditions to which they will be exposed—all of this within a controlled monetary budget.

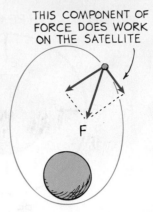

THIS COMPONENT OF FORCE DOES WORK ON THE SATELLITE

FIGURE 14.13 ▶

In an elliptical orbit, a component of force exists along the direction of the satellite's motion. This component changes the speed and, thus, the KE.

think!

The orbital path of a satellite is shown below. In which of the positions *A* through *D* does the satellite have the most KE? Most PE? Most total energy? *Answer: 14.4*

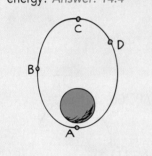

At all points on the orbit—except at the apogee and perigee—there is a component of gravitational force parallel to the direction of satellite motion, as Figure 14.13 shows. This component changes the speed of the satellite. Or we can say: (this component of force) × (distance moved) = change in KE. Either way we look at it, when the satellite gains altitude and moves against this component, its speed and KE decrease. The decrease continues to the apogee. Once past the apogee, the satellite moves in the same direction as the component, and the speed and KE increase. The increase continues until the satellite whips past the perigee and repeats the cycle.

CONCEPT CHECK : What is the relationship between the KE and PE of a satellite in motion?

14.5 Kepler's Laws Of Planetary Motion

Newton's law of gravitation was preceded by Kepler's laws of planetary motion. **Kepler's laws of planetary motion** are three important discoveries about planetary motion that were made by the German astronomer Johannes Kepler in the beginning of the 1600s. Kepler's career as an astronomer began with a junior assistantship with the famed Danish astronomer Tycho Brahe. Brahe headed the world's first great observatory in Denmark, just prior to the advent of the telescope. Using huge brass protractor-like instruments called *quadrants*, Brahe measured the positions of planets over twenty years so accurately that his measurements are still valid today. Brahe entrusted his data to Kepler. After Brahe's death, Kepler devoted many years of his life to the analysis of Brahe's measurements.

a. Tycho Brahe

b. Johannes Kepler

◀ FIGURE 14.14
a. Tycho Brahe (1546–1601) measured the positions of planets over 20 years so accurately that his measurements are still valid today.
b. Johannes Kepler (1571–1630) devoted many years of his life to the analysis of Brahe's measurements.

Kepler's First Law Kepler's expectation that the planets would move in perfect circles around the sun was shattered after years of effort. He found the paths to be ellipses. ☑ **Kepler's first law states that the path of each planet around the sun is an ellipse with the sun at one focus.**

Kepler's Second Law Kepler also found that the planets do not go around the sun at a uniform speed but move faster when they are nearer the sun and more slowly when they are farther from the sun. They accomplish this in such a way that an imaginary line or spoke joining the sun and the planet sweeps out equal areas of space in equal intervals of time. The triangular-shaped areas swept out during a month when a planet is orbiting far from the sun and when a planet is orbiting closer to the sun are shown in Figure 14.15. These two areas are equal. ☑ **Kepler's second law states that each planet moves so that an imaginary line drawn from the sun to any planet sweeps out equal areas of space in equal intervals of time.**

Kepler was the first to coin the word *satellite*. He had no clear idea *why* the planets moved as he discovered. He lacked a conceptual model. Kepler didn't see that a satellite is simply a projectile under the influence of a gravitational force directed toward the body around which the satellite orbits. You know that if you toss a rock upward, it goes slower the higher it rises because it's going against Earth gravity. And you know that when it returns it's going with gravity and its speed increases. Kepler never realized that a satellite behaves in the same way. Going away from the sun, it slows down. Returning toward the sun, it speeds up. A satellite, whether a planet orbiting the sun, or one of today's satellites orbiting Earth, is slowed going against the gravitational field and sped up going with the field. Kepler wasn't aware of this simplicity, and instead fabricated complex systems of geometrical figures to find sense in his discoveries. These proved futile.

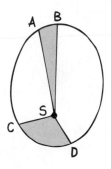

FIGURE 14.15 ▲
Equal areas of space are swept out in equal intervals of time.

Kepler's second law is a consequence of the conservation of angular momentum. And his third law is the result of equating Newton's law of gravitation to centripetal force. The connections of concepts—yum!

The mass of any celestial body can be found if it has one or more satellites, for the body's mass is directly proportional to r^3/T^2.

Kepler's Third Law After ten years of searching by trial and error for a connection between the time it takes a planet to orbit the sun and its distance from the sun, Kepler discovered a third law. From Brahe's data, Kepler found that the square of any planet's period (T) is directly proportional to the cube of its average orbital radius (r). ☑ **Kepler's third law states that the square of the orbital period of a planet is directly proportional to the cube of the average distance of the planet from the sun.** This means that the ratio T^2/r^3 is the same for all planets. So if a planet's period is known, its average orbital radial distance is easily calculated (or vice versa). Kepler's laws apply not only to planets but also to moons or any satellite in orbit around any body. The elliptical orbits of the planets are very nearly circular. Only the precise measurements of Brahe showed the slight differences.

It is interesting to note that Kepler was familiar with Galileo's concepts of inertia and accelerated motion, but he failed to apply them to his own work. Like Aristotle, he thought that the force on a moving body would be in the same direction as the body's motion. Kepler never appreciated the concept of inertia. Galileo, on the other hand, never appreciated Kepler's work and held to his conviction that the planets move in circles.[14.6] Further understanding of planetary motion required someone who could integrate the findings of these two great scientists. The rest is history, for as we have seen, this task was later taken up by Isaac Newton.

CONCEPT CHECK What are Kepler's three laws of planetary motion?

14.6 Escape Speed

When a payload is put into Earth-orbit by a rocket, the speed and direction of the rocket are very important. For example, what would happen if the rocket were launched vertically and quickly achieved a speed of 8 km/s? Everyone had better get out of the way, because it would soon come crashing back at 8 km/s. As Figure 14.16 shows, to achieve orbit, the payload must be launched *horizontally* at 8 km/s once above air resistance. Launched vertically, the old saying "What goes up must come down" becomes a sad fact of life.

Earth But isn't there some vertical speed that is sufficient to ensure that what goes up will escape and not come down? The answer is yes. Neglecting air resistance, fire anything at any speed greater than 11.2 km/s, and it will leave Earth, going more and more slowly, but never stopping.[14.6.1] Let's look at this from an energy point of view.

FIGURE 14.16 ▲
The initial thrust of the rocket lifts it vertically. Another thrust tips it from its vertical course. When it is moving horizontally, it is boosted to the required speed for orbit.

How much work is required to move a payload against the force of Earth's gravity to a distance very, very far ("infinitely far") away? The PE is not infinite because the distance is infinite. But gravity diminishes rapidly with distance via the inverse-square law. Most of the work done in launching a rocket, for example, occurs near Earth. It turns out that the value of PE for a 1-kilogram mass infinitely far away is 62 million joules (MJ). So to put a payload infinitely far from Earth's surface requires at least 62 MJ of energy per kilogram of load. A KE per unit mass of 62 MJ/kg corresponds to a speed of 11.2 km/s. This is the value of the escape speed from the surface of Earth.[14.6.2] The **escape speed** is the minimum speed necessary for an object to escape permanently from a gravitational field that holds it.

✅ **If we give a payload any more energy than 62 MJ/kg at the surface of Earth or, equivalently, any greater speed than 11.2 km/s, then, neglecting air resistance, the payload will escape from Earth never to return.** As it continues outward, its PE increases and its KE decreases. Its speed becomes less and less, though it is never reduced to zero. The payload outruns the gravity of Earth. It escapes.

The Solar System The escape speeds of various bodies in the solar system are shown in Table 14.1. Note that the escape speed from the sun is 620 km/s at the surface of the sun. Even at a distance equaling that of Earth's orbit, the escape speed from the sun is 42.2 km/s. The escape speed values in the table ignore the forces exerted by other bodies. A projectile fired from Earth at 11.2 km/s, for example, escapes Earth but not necessarily the moon, and certainly not the sun.

Table 14.1	Escape Speeds at the Surface of Bodies in the Solar System		
Astronomical Body	Mass (Earth masses)	Radius (Earth radii)	Escape Speed (km/s)
Sun	333,000	109	620
Sun (at a distance of Earth's orbit)	333,000	23,500	42.2
Jupiter	318	11	60.2
Saturn	95.2	9.2	36.0
Neptune	17.3	3.47	24.9
Uranus	14.5	3.7	22.3
Earth	1.00	1.00	11.2
Venus	0.82	0.95	10.4
Mars	0.11	0.53	5.0
Mercury	0.055	0.38	4.3
Moon	0.0123	0.28	2.4

FIGURE 14.17 ▶

Pioneer 10, launched from Earth in 1972, escaped from the solar system in 1984 and is wandering in interstellar space.

The first probe to escape the solar system, *Pioneer 10*, shown in Figure 14.17, was launched from Earth in 1972 with a speed of only 15 km/s. The escape was accomplished by directing the probe into the path of oncoming Jupiter. It was whipped about by Jupiter's great gravitational field, picking up speed in the process—just as the speed of a ball encountering an oncoming bat is increased when it departs from the bat. Its speed of departure from Jupiter was increased enough to exceed the sun's escape speed at the distance of Jupiter. *Pioneer 10* passed the orbit of Pluto in 1984. Unless it collides with another body, it will continue indefinitely through interstellar space. Like a note in a bottle cast into the sea, *Pioneer 10* contains information about Earth that might be of interest to extraterrestrials, in hopes that it will one day wash up and be found on some distant "seashore."

It is important to point out that the escape speeds for different bodies refer to the initial speed given by a brief thrust, after which there is no force to assist motion. But we could escape Earth at any *sustained* speed greater than zero, given enough time. Suppose a rocket is going to a destination such as the moon. If the rocket engines burn out while still close to Earth, the rocket will need a minimum speed of 11.2 km/s. But if the rocket engines can be sustained for long periods of time, the rocket could go to the moon without ever attaining 11.2 km/s.

It is interesting to note that the accuracy with which an unpiloted rocket reaches its destination is accomplished not by staying on a preplanned path, or by getting back on that path if it strays off course. No attempt is made to return the rocket to its planned path. Instead, by communication with the control center, the rocket in effect asks, "Where am I now, and where do I want to go? What is the best way to get there from here, given my present situation?" With the aid of high-speed computers, the answers to these questions are used to find a *new* path. Corrective thrusters put the rocket on this new path. This process is repeated continuously along the way until the rocket reaches its destination.

Go Online

sci LINKS™ **NSTA**

For: Links on satellite motion
Visit: PHSchool.com
Web Code: csn – 1406

Is there a lesson to be learned here? Suppose you find in your personal life that you are "off course." You may, like the rocket, find it better to take a newer course that leads to your goal as best plotted from your present position and circumstances, rather than try to get back on the course you plotted from a previous position and in, perhaps, different circumstances. So many ideas in physics, it seems, have a moral.

The mind that encompasses the universe is as marvelous as the universe that encompasses the mind.

CONCEPT CHECK What condition is necessary for a payload to escape Earth's gravity?

Science, Technology, and Society

Communications Satellites The electromagnetic signals that are broadcast into space to carry television programs or telephone conversations travel in straight lines. In times past these straight-line (often called line-of-sight) communications required tall receiving antenna towers and signal-boosting relay stations on high buildings or mountains. Today many television and telephone signals bounce to us from satellites. These communications satellites are in equatorial orbits with 24-hour periods. Because they revolve once each time Earth rotates once, they appear stationary when we look up at them. These satellites are said to be in geosynchronous orbits.

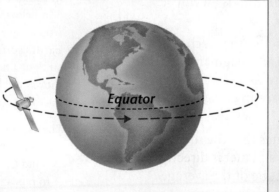

Equator

Dish-shaped antennas almost anywhere on Earth are on a line of sight from one or more communications satellites. Because communications satellites are in equatorial orbit, dish antennas on the equator may tilt east or west, but they don't tilt north or south. An equatorial dish right under a communications satellite is looking straight up. If it held water, it would resemble a birdbath filled to the brim.

Antennas north of the equator must be tilted to the south (and perhaps east or west, too). Those south of the equator must be tilted to the north, and likely east or west as well. Unless you live on the equator, all of the antennas that you see look like partly emptied bowls. In Antarctica or near the North Pole, a dish antenna is tipped so far over that it could hold no water at all.

The fact that geosynchronous satellites remain in one place overhead means it is possible for them to drop vertical cables to Earth's surface where they could be attached. Cables composed of very strong and lightweight carbon-based materials are currently being researched. Rather than being rocketed to the satellite, supplies could be lifted in elevator fashion. Watch for such space elevators in the future!

Critical Thinking Explain why it is not possible for a single communications satellite to serve all parts of Earth.

REVIEW

Go Online
PHSchool.com

For: Self-Assessment
Visit: PHSchool.com
Web Code: csa – 1400

Concept Summary ......

- A stone thrown fast enough to go a horizontal distance of 8000 meters during the time (1 second) it takes to fall 5 meters will orbit Earth.

- A satellite in circular orbit around Earth is always moving perpendicular to gravity and parallel to Earth's surface at constant speed.

- A satellite in orbit around Earth traces and oval-shaped path called an ellipse.

- The sum of the KE and PE of a satellite is constant at all points along an orbit.

- Kepler's first law states that the path of each planet around the sun is an ellipse with the sun at one focus.

- Kepler's second law states that each planet moves so that an imaginary line drawn from the sun to any planet sweeps out equal areas of space in equal intervals of time.

- Kepler's third law states that the square of the orbital period of a planet is directly proportional to the cube of the average distance of the planet from the sun. ($T^2 \sim r^3$ for all planets)

- If we give a payload any more energy than 62 MJ/kg at the surface of Earth or, equivalently, any greater speed than 11.2 km/s, then, neglecting air resistance, the payload will escape from Earth never to return.

Key Terms ......

satellite (p. 263)

period (p. 266)

ellipse (p. 267)

focus (pl. **foci**) (p. 267)

apogee (p. 269)

perigee (p. 269)

Kepler's laws of planetary motion (p. 270)

escape speed (p. 273)

think! Answers

14.2 In each second, the satellite falls about 5 m below the straight-line tangent it would have taken if there were no gravity. Earth's surface curves 5 m below an 8-km straight-line tangent. Since the satellite moves at 8 km/s, it "falls" at the same rate Earth "curves."

14.3 The satellite has its greatest speed as it whips around A. It has its least speed at C. Beyond C, it gains speed as it falls back to A to repeat its cycle.

14.4 The KE is maximum at A; the PE is maximum at C; the total energy is the same anywhere in the orbit.

Check Concepts ••••••

Section 14.1

1. If we drop a ball from rest, how far will it fall vertically in the first second? If we instead move our hand horizontally and drop it (throw it), how far will it fall vertically in the first second?

2. What do the distances 8000 m and 5 m have to do with a line tangent to Earth's surface?

Section 14.2

3. How does the direction of motion of a satellite in circular orbit compare with the curve of Earth's surface?

4. Why doesn't gravitational force change the speed of a satellite in circular orbit?

5. Does the period of a satellite in a circular orbit increase or decrease as its distance from Earth increases?

Section 14.3

6. Describe an ellipse.

Section 14.4

7. Why does gravitational force change the speed of a satellite in elliptical orbit?

8. a. Where in an elliptical orbit is the speed of a satellite maximum?
   b. Where is it minimum?

9. The sum of PE and KE for a satellite in a circular orbit is constant. Is this sum also constant for a satellite in an elliptical orbit?

10. Why does the force of gravity do no work on a satellite in circular orbit, but does do work on a satellite in an elliptical orbit?

Section 14.5

11. What scientist gathered accurate data on planetary paths around the sun? What scientist discovered that the paths are ellipses? What scientist explained the ellipses?

12. When is the speed of a satellite greatest, when closer to Earth or farther from Earth?

13. What is the mathematical relationship between how long it takes a planet to orbit the sun and its distance from the sun?

Section 14.6

14. **a.** What is the minimum speed for circling Earth in close orbit?

b. What is the maximum speed in an orbit that comes close to Earth at one point?

c. What happens to a satellite traveling faster than the maximum speed described in part (b)?

15. Neglecting air resistance, what will happen to a projectile that is fired vertically at 8 km/s? At 12 km/s?

16. **a.** How fast would a particle have to be ejected from the sun to leave the solar system?

b. What speed would be needed if an ejected particle started at a distance from the sun equal to Earth's distance from the sun?

17. What is the escape speed on the moon?

18. Although the escape speed from the surface of Earth is 11.2 km/s, couldn't a rocket with enough fuel escape at any speed? Why or why not?

19. How was *Pioneer 10* able to escape the solar system with an initial speed less than escape speed?

Think and Rank ......

Rank each of the following sets of scenarios in order of the quantity or property involved. List them from left to right. If scenarios have equal rankings, then separate them with an equal sign. (e.g., A = B)

20. The dashed lines show three circular orbits about Earth.

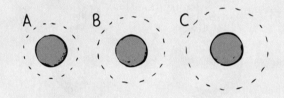

Rank the following quantities for these orbits from greatest to least.
a. orbital speed
b. time for orbiting Earth

21. Four satellites in circular orbit about Earth have the following characteristics:

(A) m = 4000 kg; height 300 km
(B) m = 5000 kg; height 350 km
(C) m = 4000 kg; height 400 km
(D) m = 5000 kg; height 500 km

a. Rank the satellites' orbital speeds from greatest to least.
b. Rank the satellites' times for orbiting Earth from greatest to least.
c. Does mass affect your answers to parts (a) and (b)?

22. The positions of a satellite in elliptical orbit are indicated.

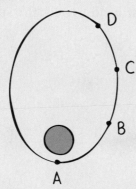

Rank these quantities from greatest to least.
a. gravitational force
b. speed
c. momentum
d. KE
e. PE
f. total energy (KE + PE)
g. acceleration

23. Kepler tells us that a planet sweeps out equal areas in equal intervals of time. Four such equal-area "triangles" are shown.

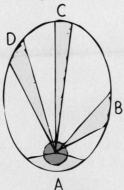

Rank these quantities from greatest to least.
a. average speed during the time interval
b. acceleration during the time interval

Think and Explain ......

24. A satellite can orbit at 5 km above the moon, but not at 5 km above Earth. Why?

25. Does the speed of a satellite around Earth depend on its mass? Its distance from Earth? The mass of Earth?

26. If a cannonball is fired from a tall mountain, gravity changes its speed all along its trajectory. But if it is fired fast enough to go into circular orbit, gravity does not change its speed at all. Why?

27. Does gravity do any *net* work on a satellite in an elliptical orbit during one full orbit? Explain your answer.

28. A geosynchronous Earth satellite can remain almost directly overhead in Singapore, but not San Francisco, Chicago, or New York City. Why?

29. If you stopped an Earth satellite dead in its tracks, it would simply crash into Earth. Why, then, don't the communications satellites that hover motionless above the same spot on Earth crash into Earth?

30. In an accidental explosion, a satellite breaks in half while in circular orbit about Earth. One half is brought momentarily to rest. What is the fate of the half brought to rest? What is the speed of the other half? (*Hint:* Think momentum conservation.)

31. Would you expect the speed of a satellite in close circular orbit about the moon to be less than, equal to, or greater than 8 km/s? Why?

32. Why do you suppose that sites close to the equator are preferred for launching satellites? (*Hint:* Look at the spinning Earth from above either pole and compare it to a spinning turntable.)

33. Why do you suppose that a space shuttle is sent into orbit by firing it in an easterly direction (the direction in which Earth spins)?

34. Consider two planets: Mercury, close to the sun, and Uranus, far from the sun. Which of these planets has a period shorter than Earth's period around the sun? Which has a period longer than Earth's?

35. What is the maximum possible speed of impact upon Earth's surface for a faraway object initially at rest that falls to Earth due only to Earth's gravity?

36. Why does most of the work done in launching a rocket take place when the rocket is still close to Earth's surface?

37. If Pluto were somehow stopped short in its orbit, it would fall into the sun rather than around it. About how fast would it be moving when it hit the sun?

38. If an astronaut in an orbiting space shuttle wished to drop something to Earth, how could this be accomplished?

39. If Earth somehow acquired more mass, with no change in its radius, would escape speed be less than, equal to, or more than 11.2 km/s? Why?

Think and Solve ••••••

40. Calculate the speed in m/s at which Earth revolves around the sun. Note: The orbit is nearly circular.

41. A spaceship in circular orbit about the moon is 2.0×10^6 m from its center.
   a. Show that the period of the spaceship is 2.2 h.
   b. Show that the speed of the spaceship relative to the moon is about 5800 km/h.

42. Calculate the speed in m/s at which the moon revolves around Earth. Note: The orbit is nearly circular.

43. At a particular point, a satellite in an elliptical orbit has a gravitational potential energy of 5000 MJ with respect to Earth's surface and a kinetic energy of 4500 MJ. At another point in its orbit, the satellite's potential energy is 6000 MJ. What is its kinetic energy at that point?

44. An orbiting satellite of mass m is pulled toward Earth by a force ma. Equate ma to the force in Newton's equation for universal gravitation and show that the satellite's acceleration is $a = \dfrac{GM}{d^2}$.

45. The force of gravity between Earth and an Earth satellite is given by $F = G\dfrac{mM}{d^2}$, where m is the mass of the satellite, M is the mass of Earth, and d is the distance between the satellite and the center of Earth. If the satellite follows a circular orbit, the force keeping it in orbit must be the centripetal force, given by $F = \dfrac{mv^2}{r}$. Equate the two expressions for force to show that the speed is $v = \sqrt{\dfrac{GM}{d}}$.

46. Use the result of Question 45 (now with the sun instead of Earth as the center of force) to calculate the speed in m/s at which Earth revolves about the sun. Assume Earth's orbit is nearly circular.

47. In 1610, Galileo discovered four moons of Jupiter. (Today we know that there are more than 60!) Io, the innermost of the moons observed by Galileo, is 4.2×10^8 m from Jupiter's center and has a period of 1.5×10^5 s. Calculate Jupiter's mass.

48. A planet in a circular orbit takes a time T to orbit its sun at a radial distance r. In terms of r and T, how fast is the planet moving in its orbit?

49. The speed of a satellite in a circular orbit is given by the equation $v = \sqrt{\dfrac{GM}{r}}$, where G is the gravitational constant, M is the mass of Earth, and r is the radial distance between the satellite and the center of Earth. Equate this to the other expression for speed, $v = \dfrac{d}{t}$. Find the equation for the time the satellite takes to completely orbit Earth—the period T. Use the circumference of the complete orbit, $2\pi r$, for the distance traveled, and T for the period of rotation.

50. Use the equation $T = 2\pi\sqrt{\dfrac{r^3}{GM}}$ to show that the period of the space shuttle 200 km (200,000 m) above Earth's surface is about 90 minutes. The radius of Earth is 6370 km (6,370,000 m).

More Problem-Solving Practice
Appendix F

CHAPTER 14 ⬤ SATELLITE MOTION **281**

15 SPECIAL RELATIVITY— SPACE AND TIME

THE BIG IDEA : Motion through space is related to motion in time.

Everyone knows that we move in time, at the rate of 24 hours per day. And everyone knows that we can move through space, at rates ranging from a snail's pace to those of supersonic aircraft and space shuttles. But relatively few people know that motion through space is related to motion in time.

The first person to understand the relationship between space and time was Albert Einstein.[15.0] Einstein went beyond common sense when he stated in 1905 that in moving through space we also change our rate of proceeding into the future—time itself is altered. This view was introduced to the world in his *special theory of relativity*. Ten years later Einstein announced a similar theory, called the *general theory of relativity* (discussed in the next chapter), that shows how gravity is related to space and time. These theories have enormously changed the way scientists view the workings of the universe.

discover!

How are Speed and Length Contraction Related?

1. Obtain six soda straws and determine the length of a single soda straw in centimeters.

2. Multiply the length of a soda straw by the following factors: 1, 0.9999999999999978, 0.999999944, 0.995, 0.5, and 0.045.

3. Use scissors to cut soda straw segments to the lengths determined in Step 2. If you find it impossible to cut the straws to the required lengths, simply leave them uncut.

4. Compare the lengths of the soda straws by placing them one above the other.

Analyze and Conclude

1. **Observing** The cut lengths represent the effects of length contraction you would observe if a soda straw were moving past you at the following speeds (c represents the speed of light, or roughly 3×10^8 m/s): 0, 20 m/s, 100,000 m/s, 0.1c, 0.87c, and 0.999c.

2. **Predicting** What fraction of a soda straw's length would you see if you were moving past a soda straw at a speed of 0.87c?

3. **Making Generalizations** When do length contraction effects become noticeable?

15.1 Space-Time

Newton and other investigators before Einstein thought of space as an infinite expanse in which all things exist. It was never clear whether the universe exists in space, or space exists within the universe. Is there space outside the universe? Or is space only within the universe? The same question could be raised for time. Does the universe exist in time, or does time exist only within the universe? Einstein's answer to these questions is that both space and time exist only within the universe. There is no time or space "outside." Einstein reasoned that space and time are two parts of one whole called **space-time.**

◀ **FIGURE 15.1**
The universe does not exist in a certain part of infinite space, nor does it exist during a certain era in time. It is the other way around: space and time exist within the universe.

Einstein's **special theory of relativity** describes how time is affected by motion in space at constant velocity, and how mass and energy are related. ☑ **From the viewpoint of special relativity, you travel through a combination of space and time. You travel through space-time.** The colorful cloud of gas and dust particles in Figure 15.1 moves through space-time. To begin to understand this, consider your present knowledge that you are moving through time at the rate of 24 hours per day. This is only half the story. To get the other half, convert your thinking from "moving through time" to "moving through space-time." When you stand still, like the girl in Figure 15.2, then all your traveling is through time. When you move a bit, then some of your travel is through space and most of it is still through time. If you were somehow able to travel through space at the speed of light, all your traveling would be through space, with no travel through time![15.1] You would be as ageless as light, for light travels through space only and is timeless. From the frame of reference of a photon traveling from one part of the universe to another, the journey takes no time at all!

FIGURE 15.2 ▲
When you stand still, you are traveling at the maximum rate in time: 24 hours per day. If you traveled at the maximum rate through space (the speed of light), time would stand still.

Motion in space affects motion in time. Whenever we move through space, we to some degree alter our rate of moving into the future. This is known as *time dilation*, or the stretching of time. If spacecraft of the future reach sufficient speed, people will be able to travel noticeably in time. They will be able to jump centuries ahead, just as today people can jump from Earth to the moon. The special theory of relativity that Einstein developed rests on two fundamental assumptions, or **postulates.**

CONCEPT CHECK : How can you describe a person's travel from the viewpoint of special relativity?

15.2 The First Postulate of Special Relativity

Einstein reasoned that there is no stationary hitching post in the universe relative to which motion should be measured. Instead, all motion is relative and all frames of reference are arbitrary. A spaceship, for example, cannot measure its speed relative to empty space, but only relative to other objects. Look at Figure 15.3. If spaceship A drifts past spaceship B in empty space, spaceman A and spacewoman B will each observe only the relative motion. From this observation each will be unable to determine who is moving and who is at rest, if either.

FIGURE 15.3 ▲
Spaceman A considers himself at rest and sees spacewoman B pass by. But spacewoman B considers herself at rest and sees spaceman A pass by. Spaceman A and spacewoman B will both observe only the relative motion.

This is a familiar experience to a passenger in a car at rest waiting for the traffic light to change. If you look out the window and see the car in the next lane begin moving backward, you may be surprised to find that the car you're observing is really at rest—your car is moving forward. If you could not see out the windows, there would be no way to determine whether your car was moving with constant velocity or was at rest.

In the cabin of a high-speed jetliner, we flip a coin and catch it just as we would if the plane were at rest. If we swing a pendulum, it will move no differently when the plane is moving uniformly (constant velocity) than when not moving at all. There is no physical experiment we can perform to determine our state of uniform motion. Of course, we can look outside and see Earth whizzing by, or send a radar signal out. However, no experiment confined within the cabin itself can determine whether or not there is uniform motion. The laws of physics within the uniformly moving cabin are the same as those in a stationary laboratory. The person playing pool in Figure 15.4 does not have to make adjustments to his game as long as the ship moves at a constant velocity.

◀ **FIGURE 15.4**

A person playing pool on a smooth and fast-moving ocean liner does not have to make adjustments to compensate for the speed of the ship. The laws of physics are the same for the ship whether it is moving uniformly or is at rest.

Einstein's **first postulate of special relativity** assumes our inability to detect a state of uniform motion. ☑ **The first postulate of special relativity states that all the laws of nature are the same in all uniformly moving frames of reference.** Many experiments can detect *accelerated* motion, but none can, according to Einstein, detect the state of uniform motion. No experiment can be performed that will determine whether a closed cabin is at rest or moving at constant velocity.

CONCEPT CHECK: What does the first postulate of special relativity state?

The postulates themselves don't have to make "common" sense. As with all postulates in science, the test of their validity is that they lead to predictions that we can test.

15.3 The Second Postulate of Special Relativity

One of the questions that Einstein as a youth asked himself was, "What would a light beam look like *if* you traveled along beside it?" According to classical physics, the beam would be at rest to such an observer. The more Einstein thought about this, the more convinced he became of its impossibility. He came to the conclusion that *if* an observer could travel *close* to the speed of light, he would measure the light as moving away from him at 300,000 km/s.[15.3]

FIGURE 15.5 ▼

The speed of light is constant regardless of the speed of the flashlight or observer.

Einstein's **second postulate of special relativity** assumes that the speed of light is constant. ✅ **The second postulate of special relativity states that the speed of light in empty space will always have the same value regardless of the motion of the source or the motion of the observer.** As Figure 15.5 shows, the speed of light is constant regardless of the speed of the flashlight or the source.

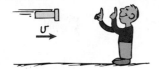  

The speed of light in all reference frames is always the same. Consider, for example, a spaceship departing from the space station shown in Figure 15.6. A flash of light is emitted from the station at 300,000 km/s—a speed we'll simply call *c*. No matter what the speed of the spaceship relative to the space station is, an observer on the spaceship will measure the speed of the flash of light passing her as *c*. If she sends a flash of her own to the space station, observers on the station will measure the speed of these flashes as *c*. The speed of the flashes will be no different if the spaceship stops or turns around and approaches. All observers who measure the speed of light will find it has the same value, *c*.

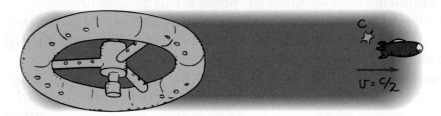

FIGURE 15.6 ▲

The speed of a light flash emitted by either the spaceship or the space station is measured as *c* by observers on the ship or the space station. Everyone who measures the speed of light will get the same value *c*.

$$\frac{\text{SPACE}}{\text{TIME}} = \frac{\text{SPACE}}{\text{TIME}} = c$$

FIGURE 15.7 ▲

All space and time measurements of light are unified by *c*.

As Figure 15.7 shows, the constancy of the speed of light is what unifies space and time. And for any observation of motion through space, there is a corresponding passage of time. The ratio of space to time for light is the same for all who measure it. The speed of light is a constant.

CONCEPT CHECK : What does the second postulate of special relativity state?

15.4 Time Dilation

Einstein proposed that time can be stretched depending on the motion between the observer and the events being observed. The stretching of time is **time dilation.** ☑ **Time dilation occurs ever so slightly for everyday speeds, but significantly for speeds approaching the speed of light.**

We measure time with a clock. A clock can be any device that measures periodic intervals, such as the swings of a pendulum, the oscillations of a balance wheel, or the vibrations of a quartz crystal. We are going to consider a "light clock," a rather impractical device, but one that will help to describe time dilation.

A Moving Light Clock Imagine an empty tube with a mirror at each end as shown in Figure 15.8. A flash of light bounces back and forth between the parallel mirrors. The mirrors are perfect reflectors, so the flash bounces indefinitely. If the tube is 300,000 km in length, each bounce will take 1 s in the frame of reference of the light clock. If the tube is 3 km long, each bounce will take 0.00001 s.

Suppose we view the light clock as it whizzes past us in a high-speed spaceship as shown in Figure 15.9. We see the light flash bouncing up and down along a longer diagonal path.

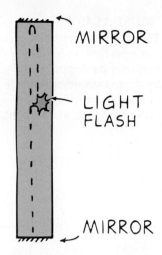

FIGURE 15.8 ▲
A stationary light clock is shown here. Light bounces between parallel mirrors and "ticks off" equal intervals of time.

FIGURE 15.9 ▲
The moving ship contains a light clock. **a.** An observer moving with the spaceship observes the light flash moving vertically. **b.** An observer who is passed by the moving ship observes the flash moving along a diagonal path.

But remember the second postulate of relativity: The speed will be measured by *any* observer as c. Since the speed of light will not increase, we must measure more time between bounces! For us, looking in from the outside, one tick of the light clock takes longer than it takes for occupants of the spaceship. The spaceship's clock, according to our observations, has slowed down—although, for occupants of the spaceship, it has not slowed at all!

think!

Does time dilation mean that time really passes more slowly in moving systems or that it only seems to pass more slowly? Explain.
Answer: 15.4.1

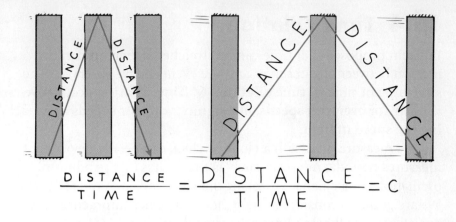

FIGURE 15.10 ▶

The longer distance taken by the light flash in following the diagonal path must be divided by a correspondingly longer time interval to yield an unvarying value for the speed of light.

$$\frac{DISTANCE}{TIME} = \frac{DISTANCE}{TIME} = c$$

Einstein showed that the relation between the time t_0 (proper time) in the observer's own frame of reference and the relative time t measured in another frame of reference is

$$t = \frac{t_0}{\sqrt{1-\left(\frac{v}{c}\right)^2}}$$

where v represents the relative velocity between the observer and the observed and c is the speed of light. As the equation for time and Figure 15.10 show, the speed of the light clock has no effect on the speed of light.

The slowing of time is not peculiar to the light clock. It is time itself in the moving frame of reference, as viewed from our frame of reference, that slows. The heartbeats of the spaceship occupants will have a slower rhythm. All events on the moving ship will be observed by us as slower. We say that time is stretched—it is dilated.

How do the occupants on the spaceship view their own time? Time for them is the same as when they do not appear to us to be moving at all. Recall Einstein's first postulate: All laws of nature are the same in all uniformly moving frames of reference. There is no way the spaceship occupants can tell uniform motion from rest. They have no clues that events on board are seen to be dilated when viewed from other frames of reference.

---

think!

If you were moving in a spaceship at a high speed relative to Earth, would you notice a difference in your pulse rate? In the pulse rate of the people back on Earth? Explain.

Answer: 15.4.2

FIGURE 15.11 ▶

A light clock moves to the right at a constant speed, v.

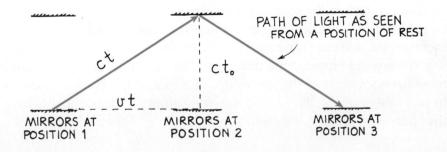

PATH OF LIGHT AS SEEN FROM A POSITION OF REST

ct

ct_0

vt

MIRRORS AT POSITION 1

MIRRORS AT POSITION 2

MIRRORS AT POSITION 3

How do occupants on the spaceship view *our* time? From *their* frame of reference, it appears that *we* are the ones who are moving. They see our time running slow, just as we see their time running slow. There is no contradiction here. It is physically impossible for observers in different frames of reference to refer to one and the same realm of space-time. The measurements in one frame of reference need not agree with the measurements made in another reference frame. There is only one measurement they will always agree on: the speed of light.

FIGURE 15.12 ▲
Physicist Ken Ford emphasizes the meaning of the time dilation equation with his ninth-grade high school students.

do the math!

How Can You Derive the Time Dilation Equation?[15.4]

Figure 15.11 shows three successive positions of the light clock as it moves to the right at constant speed v. The diagonal lines represent the path of the light flash as it starts from the lower mirror at position 1, moves to the upper mirror at position 2, and then back to the lower mirror at position 3.

The symbol t_o represents the time it takes for the flash to move between the mirrors as measured from a frame of reference fixed to the light clock. Since the speed of light is always c, the light flash is observed to move a vertical distance ct_o in the frame of reference of the light clock. This is the distance between mirrors. This vertical distance is the same in both reference frames.

The symbol t represents the time it takes the flash to move from one mirror to the other as measured from a frame of reference in which the light clock moves to the right with speed v. Since the speed of the flash is c and the time to go from position 1 to position 2 is t, the diagonal distance traveled is ct. During this time t, the clock moves a horizontal distance vt from position 1 to position 2.

These three distances make up a right triangle in the figure, in which ct is the hypotenuse, and ct_o and vt are legs. A well-known theorem of geometry (the Pythagorean theorem) states that the square of the hypotenuse is equal to the sum of the squares of the other two sides. If we apply this to the figure, we obtain

$$(ct)^2 = (ct_o)^2 + (vt)^2$$

$$(ct)^2 - (vt)^2 = (ct_o)^2$$

$$t^2[1 - (v^2/c^2)] = t_o^2$$

$$t^2 = \frac{t_o^2}{1 - (v^2/c^2)}$$

$$t = \frac{t_o}{\sqrt{1 - (v^2/c^2)}}$$

The mathematical derivation of this equation for time dilation is included here mainly to show that it involves only a bit of geometry and elementary algebra. It is not expected that you master it!

The Twin Trip A dramatic illustration of time dilation is afforded by identical twins, one an astronaut who takes a high-speed round-trip journey while the other stays home on Earth. As Figure 15.13 shows, when the traveling twin returns, he is younger than the stay-at-home twin. How much younger depends on the relative speeds involved. If the traveling twin maintains a speed of 50% the speed of light for one year (according to clocks aboard the spaceship), 1.15 years will have elapsed on Earth. If the traveling twin maintains a speed of 87% the speed of light for a year, then 2 years will have elapsed on Earth. At 99.5% the speed of light, 10 Earth years would pass in one spaceship year. At this speed the traveling twin would age a single year while the stay-at-home twin ages 10 years.

The question arises, since motion is relative, why isn't it just as well the other way around—why wouldn't the traveling twin return to find his stay-at-home twin younger than himself? Aha, there's a fundamental difference here. The space-traveling twin experiences two frames of reference in his round trip—one receding from Earth, and the other approaching Earth. He has been in two realms of space-time, separated by the event of turning around. The stay-at-home twin, on the other hand, experiences a single frame of reference—one realm of space-time.

Please do the practice pages on *The Twin Trip* in the *Concept Development Practice Book*. You'll see that the twins can meet again at the same place in space only at the expense of time.

FIGURE 15.13 ▲
The traveling twin does not age as fast as the stay-at-home twin.

Clockwatching on a Trolley-Car Ride Pretend you are Einstein in a trolley car that provided the high-speed travel back then. Suppose the trolley car, like the one shown in Figure 15.14, is moving in a direction away from a huge clock displayed in a village square. The clock reads 12 noon. To say it reads 12 noon is to say that light carrying the information "12 noon" is reflected by the clock and travels toward you along your line of sight. If you suddenly move your head to the side, instead of meeting your eye, the light carrying the information continues past, presumably out into space. Out there an observer who later receives the light says, "Oh, it's 12 noon on Earth now" (or more correctly, "light left the clock at 12 noon on Earth"). You and the distant observer will see 12 noon at different times. You wonder more about this idea. If the trolley car traveled as fast as the light, then it would keep up with the information that says "12 noon." Traveling at the speed of light, then, tells the time is always 12 noon at the village square. Time at the village square is frozen!

If the trolley car is not moving, you see the village-square clock move into the future at the rate of 60 seconds per minute; if you move at the speed of light, you see seconds on the clock taking infinite time. These are the two extremes. What's in between? What happens for speeds less than the speed of light?

A little thought will show that you will receive the message "1 o'clock" anywhere from 60 minutes to an infinity of time after you receive the message "12 noon," depending on what your speed is between the extremes of zero and the speed of light. From your high-speed (but less than c) moving frame of reference, you see all events taking place in the reference frame of the clock on Earth as happening in slow motion. As Figure 15.15 shows, 1 second on a stationary clock is stretched out, as measured on a moving clock. If you reverse direction and travel at high-speed back toward the clock, you'll see all events occurring in the clock's frame of reference as being speeded up. When you return and are once again sitting in the square, will the effects of going and coming compensate each other? Amazingly, no! Time will be stretched. The wristwatch you were wearing the whole time and the *village* clock will disagree. This is time dilation.

CONCEPT : How does time dilation at everyday speeds compare
CHECK : with time dilation at light speed?

FIGURE 15.14 ▲
Light that carries the information "12 noon" is reflected by the clock and travels toward the trolley.

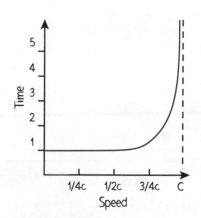

FIGURE 15.15 ▲
The graph shows how 1 second on a stationary clock is stretched out, as measured on a moving clock.

─ **think!** ─────────────────────

Will observers A and B agree on measurements of time if A moves at half the speed of light relative to B? If both A and B move together at 0.5c relative to Earth? Explain. *Answer: 15.4.3*

If traveling backward in time were possible, wouldn't we have tourists from the future?

15.5 Space and Time Travel

Before the theory of special relativity was introduced, it was argued that humans would never be able to venture to the stars. It was thought that our life span is too short to cover such great distances—at least for the distant stars. Alpha Centauri is the nearest star to Earth, after the sun, and it is 4 light-years away.[15.5] It was therefore thought that a round-trip even at the speed of light would require 8 years. The center of our galaxy is some 30,000 light-years away, so it was reasoned that a person traveling even at the speed of light would have to survive for 30,000 years to make such a voyage! But these arguments fail to take into account time dilation. Time for a person on Earth and time for a person in a high-speed spaceship are not the same.

A person's heart beats to the rhythm of the realm of time it is in. One realm of time seems the same as any other realm of time to the person, but not to an observer who is located outside the person's frame of reference—for she sees the difference. As an example, astronauts traveling at 99% the speed of light could go to the star Procyon (11.4 light-years distant) and back in 23.0 years in Earth time. It would take light itself 22.8 years in Earth time to make the same round trip. Because of time dilation, it would seem that only 3 years had gone by for the astronauts. All their clocks would indicate this, and biologically they would be only 3 years older. It would be the space officials greeting them on their return who would be 23 years older.

At higher speeds the results are even more impressive. At a speed of 99.99% the speed of light, travelers could travel slightly more than 70 light-years in a single year of their own time. At 99.999% the speed of light, this distance would be pushed appreciably farther than 200 years. A 5-year trip for them would take them farther than light travels in 1000 Earth-time years.

Link to TECHNOLOGY

Relativistic Clocks

In 1971 atomic clocks were carried around Earth in jet planes. Upon landing, the traveling clocks were a few billionths of a second "younger" than twin clocks that stayed behind. Atomic clocks now cruise overhead at even greater speeds in the satellites that are part of the global positioning system (GPS). In designing this system, which can pinpoint positions on Earth to within meters, scientists and engineers had to accommodate for relativistic time dilation. If they didn't, GPS could not precisely locate positions on Earth. Time dilation is a fact of everyday life to scientists and engineers—especially those who design equipment for global navigation work.

Such journeys seem impossible to us today. ☑ **The amounts of energy required to propel spaceships to relativistic speeds are billions of times the energy used to put the space shuttles into orbit.** The problems of shielding radiation induced by these high speeds seems formidable. The practicalities of such space journeys are prohibitive, so far. For the present, interstellar space travel must be relegated to science fiction. This is not because of scientific fantasy, but simply because of the impracticality of space travel. Traveling close to the speed of light in order to take advantage of time dilation is completely consistent with the laws of physics.

If these problems are ever overcome and space travel becomes routine, people might have the option of taking a trip and returning in future centuries of their choosing. For example, one might depart from Earth in a high-speed ship in the year 2150, travel for 5 years or so, and return in the year 2500. One might live among Earthlings of that period for a while and depart again to try out the year 3000 for style. People could keep jumping into the future with some expense of their own time, but they could not travel into the past. They could never return to the same era on Earth that they bid farewell to.

Time, as we know it, travels only one way—forward. Here on Earth we constantly move into the future at the steady rate of 24 hours per day. An astronaut leaving on a deep-space voyage must live with the fact that, upon her return, much more time will have elapsed on Earth than she has experienced on her voyage. Star travelers will not bid "so long, see you later" to those they leave behind but, rather, a permanent "good-bye."

CONCEPT CHECK : Why does space travel at relativistic speeds seem impossible?

You can see into the past, but you cannot go into the past. When you look at stars or galaxies at night, you're looking at light that's been on its way to you for dozens, hundreds, even millions of years. You can only see the universe as it was in the past.

FIGURE 15.17 ▲

A meterstick traveling at 87% the speed of light relative to an observer would be measured as only half as long as normal.

Link to BIOLOGY

Muons and Mutations

When cosmic rays bombard atoms at the top of the atmosphere, new particles are made. Some are muons, radio-active particles that streak downward toward Earth's surface. A muon's average lifetime is only two millionths of a second, seemingly too brief to reach the ground below before decay-ing. But because muons move at nearly the speed of light, length contraction dramatically shortens their distance to Earth. You are hit by hundreds of muons every second! Muon impact, like that of all high-speed elementary particles, causes bio-logical mutations. So we see a link between the effects of relativity and the evolution of living creatures on Earth.

15.6 Length Contraction

For moving objects, space as well as time undergoes changes. ⊘ **When an object moves at a very high speed relative to an observer, its measured length in the direction of motion is contracted.** The observable shortening of objects moving at speeds approaching the speed of light is **length contraction.** The amount of contraction is related to the amount of time dilation. For everyday speeds, the amount of contraction is much too small to be measured. For relativistic speeds, the contraction would be noticeable. As Figure 15.17 shows, a meterstick aboard a spaceship whizzing past you at 87% the speed of light, for example, would appear to you to be only 0.5 meter long. If it whizzed past at 99.5% the speed of light, it would appear to you to be contracted to one tenth its original length. The width of the stick, perpendicular to the direction of travel, doesn't change. As relative speed gets closer and closer to the speed of light, the measured lengths of objects contract closer and closer to zero.

Do people aboard the spaceship also see their metersticks—and everything else in their environment—contracted? The answer is no. People in the spaceship see nothing at all unusual about the lengths of things in their own reference frame. If they did, it would violate the first postulate of relativity. Recall that all the laws of physics are the same in all uniformly moving reference frames. Besides, there is no relative speed between the people on the spaceship and the things they observe in their own reference frame. However, there is a relative speed between themselves and *our* frame of reference, so they will see *our* metersticks contracted—and us as well. As Figure 15.18 shows, a rule of relativity is that changes due to alterations of space-time are always seen in the frame of reference of the "other guy."

FIGURE 15.18 ▲

In the frame of reference of the meterstick on the spaceship, its length is 1 meter. Observers from this frame see our metersticks contracted. The effects of relativity are always attributed to "the other guy."

The contraction of speeding objects is the contraction of space itself. Space contracts in only one direction, the direction of motion. Lengths along the direction perpendicular to this motion are the same in the two frames of reference. So if an object, like the baseball in Figure 15.19, is moving horizontally, no contraction takes place vertically.

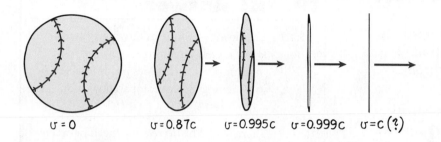

◀ **FIGURE 15.19**

As relative speed increases, contraction in the direction of motion increases. Lengths in the perpendicular direction do not change.

Relativistic length contraction is stated mathematically:

$$L = L_0 \sqrt{1 - \left(\frac{v^2}{c^2}\right)}$$

In this equation, v is the speed of the object relative to the observer, c is the speed of light, L is the length of the moving object as measured by the observer, and L_0 is the measured length of the object at rest.[15.6]

Suppose that an object is at rest, so that $v = 0$. When 0 is substituted for v in the equation, we find $L = L_0$, as we would expect. It was stated earlier that if an object were moving at 87% the speed of light, it would contract to half its length. When $0.87c$ is substituted for v in the equation, we find $L = 0.5L_0$. Or when $0.995c$ is substituted for v, we find $L = 0.1L_0$, as stated earlier. If the object could reach the speed c, its length would contract to zero. This is one of the reasons that the speed of light is the upper limit for the speed of any object.

Einstein's theory of relativity has raised many philosophical questions. What, exactly, is time? Can we say it is nature's way of seeing to it that everything does not all happen at once? And why does time seem to move in one direction? Has it always moved forward? Are there other parts of the universe where time moves backward? Perhaps these unanswered questions will be answered by the physicists of tomorrow. How exciting!

CONCEPT CHECK : How does the length of an object change when it is moving at a very high speed relative to an observer?

think!

A spacewoman travels by a spherical planet so fast that it appears to her to be an ellipsoid (egg shaped). If she sees the short diameter as half the long diameter, what is her speed relative to the planet?
Answer: 15.6

In summary—Time dilation: moving clocks run slowly. Length contraction: moving objects are shorter (in the direction of motion).

REVIEW

Go Online

PHSchool.com

For: Self-Assessment

Visit: PHSchool.com

Web Code: csa – 1500

Concept Summary

- From the viewpoint of special relativity, you travel through a combination of space and time. You travel through space-time.

- The first postulate of special relativity states that all the laws of nature are the same in all uniformly moving frames of reference.

- The second postulate of special relativity states that the speed of light in empty space will always have the same value regardless of the motion of the source or the motion of the observer.

- Time dilation occurs ever so slightly for everyday speeds, but significantly for speeds approaching the speed of light.

- The amounts of energy required to propel spaceships to relativistic speeds are billions of times the energy used to put the space shuttles into orbit.

- When an object moves at a very high speed relative to an observer, its measured length in the direction of motion is contracted.

Key Terms

space-time (p. 283)

special theory of relativity (p. 283)

postulate (p. 284)

first postulate of special relativity (p. 285)

second postulate of special relativity (p. 286)

time dilation (p. 287)

length contraction (p. 294)

think! Answers

15.4.1 The slowing of time in moving systems is not merely an illusion resulting from motion. Time really does pass more slowly in a moving system compared with one at relative rest.

15.4.2 There would be no relative speed between you and your own pulse, so no relativistic effects would be noticed. There would be a relativistic effect between you and people back on Earth. You would find their pulse rate slower than normal (and they would find your pulse rate slower than normal). Relativity effects are always attributed to "the other guy."

15.4.3 When A and B have different motions relative to each other, each will observe a slowing of time in the frame of reference of the other. So they will not agree on measurements of time. When they are moving in unison, they share the same frame of reference and will agree on measurements of time. They will see each other's time as passing normally, and each one will see events on Earth in the same slow motion.

15.6 The spacewoman passes the spherical planet at 87% the speed of light.

15 ASSESS

Check Concepts • • • • • •

Section 15.1

1. What is space-time?

2. Can you travel while remaining in one place in space? Explain.

3. Does light travel through space? Through time? Through both space and time?

4. What is time dilation?

Section 15.2

5. What is the first postulate of special relativity?

Section 15.3

6. What is the second postulate of special relativity?

7. The ratio of velocity gain to time for a freely falling body is *g*. Similarly, what is the ratio of distance to time for light waves?

Section 15.4

8. The path of light in a vertical "light clock" in a high-speed spaceship is seen to be longer when viewed from a stationary frame of reference. Why, then, does the light not appear to be moving faster?

9. If we view a passing spaceship and see that the inhabitants' time is running slow, how do they see our time running?

10. If you were traveling in a high-speed rocket ship, would clocks on board appear to you to be running slow? Defend your answer.

11. Is it possible for a person with a 70-year life span to travel farther than light travels in 70 years? Explain.

Section 15.5

12. What are the present-day obstacles to interstellar space travel?

Section 15.6

13. How long would a meterstick appear if it were thrown like a spear at 99.5% the speed of light?

14. How long would a meterstick appear if it were traveling at 99.5% the speed of light, but with its length perpendicular to its direction of motion? (Why are your answers to this question and the last question different?)

15. If you were traveling in a high-speed space-ship, would metersticks on board appear contracted to you? Defend your answer.

Think and Rank ......

Rank each of the following sets of scenarios in order of the quantity or property involved. List them from left to right. If scenarios have equal rankings, then separate them with an equal sign. (e.g., A = B)

16. A spaceship emits brief flashes of light at 1-second intervals. The circles represent light already emitted by the spaceship.

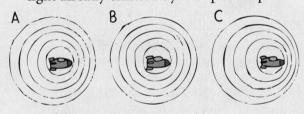

Rank the following quantities from greatest to least.
a. the speeds at which the flashes reach an observer to the right, in front of the approaching spaceship
b. how frequently the flashes reach the same observer
c. the speeds of the spaceship as seen by you, an Earth observer

17. Three spaceships shoot space probes at the speeds shown.

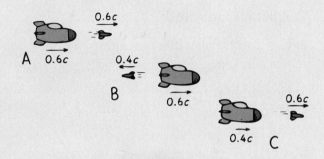

Rank the following quantities from greatest to least.
a. the speeds of the probes as seen by an Earth observer
b. the speed of light reflected from the de-parting probes as seen by the spaceship

Plug and Chug ......

18. If a spaceship moves away from you at half the speed of light and fires a rocket away from you at half the speed of light relative to the spaceship, common sense may tell you the rocket moves at the speed of light relative to you. But it doesn't! The relativistic addition of velocities (not covered in the chapter) is given by

$$v = \frac{v_1 + v_2}{1 + \frac{v_1 v_2}{c^2}}$$

Substitute $0.5c$ for both v_1 and v_2 and show that the velocity, v, of the rocket relative to you is $0.8c$.

19. If the spaceship in question 18 somehow travels at c relative to you, and it somehow fires its rocket at c relative to itself, use the equation to show that the speed of the rocket relative to you is still c!

20. Substitute small values of v_1 and v_2 in the preceding equation and show for everyday speeds that v is practically equal to $v_1 + v_2$.

Think and Explain ••••••

21. If you were in a smooth-riding train with no windows, could you sense the difference between uniform motion and rest? Between accelerated motion and rest? Explain how you could do this with a bowl filled with water.

22. Suppose you're playing catch with a friend in a moving train. When you toss the ball in the direction the train is moving, how does the speed of the ball appear to an observer standing at rest outside the train? (Does it increase or appear the same as if the observer were riding on the train?)

23. Suppose you're shining a light while riding on a train. When you shine the light in the direction the train is moving, how would the speed of light appear to an observer standing at rest outside the train? (Does it increase or appear the same as if the observer were riding with the train?)

24. People who ride in a bus all know they're moving through space. But you know that they're also moving through something else. What else are they moving through?

25. Light travels a certain distance in, say, 10,000 years. Can an astronaut travel more slowly than the speed of light and yet travel the same distance in a 10-year trip? Explain.

26. Can you get younger by traveling at speeds near the speed of light? Explain.

27. Explain why it is that when we look out into the universe, we see into the past.

28. One of the fads of the future might be "century hopping," where occupants of high-speed spaceships would depart from Earth for a few years and return centuries later. What are the present-day obstacles to such a practice?

29. If you were in a high-speed spaceship traveling away from Earth at a speed close to that of light, would you measure your normal pulse to be slower, the same, or faster? How would your measurements of pulses of friends back on Earth be if you could monitor them from your ship? Explain.

30. Is it possible for a person to be biologically older than his or her parents? Explain.

31. If stationary observers measure the shape of an emblem on fast-moving rocket ship as exactly circular, then what is the shape according to observers on the rocket ship?

32. The two-mile-long linear accelerator at Stanford University in California is less than a meter long to the electrons that travel in it. Explain.

Think and Solve ······

33. Joe Burpy is 30 years old and has a daughter who is 6 years old. Joe leaves on a space bus and takes a 5-year (space-bus time) round-trip at $0.99c$. How old will he and his daughter be when he returns?

34. Assume that your heart normally beats once every second, and that you are in a spaceship that moves past Earth at $0.6c$.
  a. What time do you measure between your own heartbeats?
  b. Show that your heartbeats are measured by someone on Earth to be 1.25 s apart.
  c. As you and the spaceship whiz past Earth, you make similar measurements on Earthlings who measure their own heartbeats to be 1 s apart. How much time do you measure between their heartbeats?

35. Thomas, a rhino, is 2.5 meters long when at rest.
  a. How long will you measure him to be when he's running by at $0.80c$?
  b. Show that you would measure a time of 6.3 ns for the length of his body to pass you.

36. A ship whizzes by you at 0.60c. Someone aboard is making a 3-minute egg for breakfast.

a. What cooking time will you measure for the egg?

b. Why should you not be surprised when the egg turns out to be perfectly cooked, rather than overcooked?

37. Before leaving the planet Hislaurels for a starship voyage, you pack a meterstick in your luggage. After the ship has settled down to a steady speed of 0.50c, you take the meterstick out of your bag.

a. How long will you measure the meterstick to be?

b. If the meterstick is moving parallel to an observer resting on Hislaurels, how long will the observer measure the meterstick?

38. You are standing facing forward on the floor of your starship, which is moving at 0.80c relative to Earth. Before you left Earth, you measured your feet to be 25 cm long.

a. People on Earth will now measure your feet to be how long?

b. Do you need to be concerned now that the shoes that you packed for the trip will be too big?

39. Pinocchio is concerned that Gepetto will see his long nose and realize that he has been lying. So Pinocchio decides to run past Gepetto fast enough that his 10-inch long nose will be seen by Gepetto to be only 2 inches long.

a. How fast must Pinocchio run?

b. When running past Gepetto, will Pinocchio see Gepetto's nose shortened?

40. Lizzie is scooting down the Interstate at 17 percent of the speed of light and measures the distance between mileposts to be less than 5,280 feet.

a. What distance does she measure?

b. What distance would she measure at 32 percent the speed of light?

 16 RELATIVITY—MOMENTUM, MASS, ENERGY, AND GRAVITY

THE BIG IDEA : According to special relativity, mass and energy are equivalent. According to general relativity, gravity causes space to become curved and time to undergo changes.

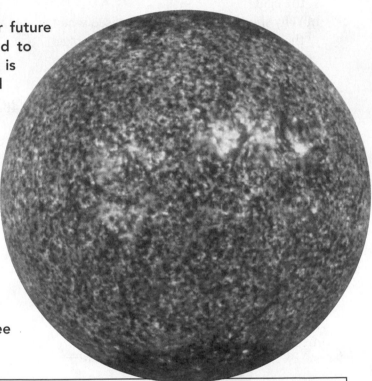

No material object, particle or future spaceship, can be accelerated to the speed of light. Why this is so has to do with momentum and energy, which, in relativity theory, have new definitions. One of the most celebrated outcomes of special relativity is the discovery that mass and energy are one and the same thing—as described by $E = mc^2$. Einstein's *general theory of relativity*, developed a decade after his special theory of relativity, offers another celebrated outcome, an alternative to Newton's theory of gravity. Both theories of relativity have changed the way we see the universe.

discover!

How Can Space-Time be Modeled?

1. Stretch a plastic garbage bag tightly across the top of a trash can. Tape the edges of the bag to the side of the can.
2. Place a pool ball or other heavy sphere in the center of the garbage bag. This should cause the bag to sag in the center.
3. Launch a marble by giving it a velocity tangent to the circumference of the can.
4. Try launching the marble with a variety of initial velocities.

Analyze and Conclude

1. **Observing** Describe the motion of the marble. What effect does changing the initial speed and direction of the marble have on the shape of the orbit?
2. **Predicting** How might changing the mass of the heavy central sphere affect the motion of the marble?
3. **Making Generalizations** How closely does this model represent the motion of Earth satellites?

302

16.1 Momentum and Inertia in Relativity

If we push an object that is free to move, it will accelerate. If we maintain a steady push, it will accelerate to higher and higher speeds. If we push with a greater and greater force, we expect the acceleration in turn to increase. It might seem that the speed should increase without limit, but there is a speed limit in the universe—the speed of light. In fact, we cannot accelerate any material object enough to reach the speed of light, let alone surpass it.

At least one thing reaches the speed of light—light itself! But a particle of light has no rest mass. A material particle can never be brought to the speed of light. Light can never be brought to rest.

Newtonian and Relativistic Momentum We can understand this from Newton's second law, which Newton originally expressed in terms of momentum: $F = \Delta mv/\Delta t$ (which reduces to the familiar $F = ma$, or $a = F/m$). The momentum form, interestingly, remains valid in relativity theory. Recall from Chapter 8 that the change of momentum of an object is equal to the impulse applied to it. Apply more impulse and the object acquires more momentum. Double the impulse and the momentum doubles. Apply ten times as much impulse and the object gains ten times as much momentum. Does this mean that momentum can increase without any limit, even though speed cannot? Yes, it does.

We learned that momentum equals mass times velocity. In equation form, $p = mv$ (we use p for momentum). To Newton, infinite momentum would mean infinite speed. Not so in relativity. Einstein showed that a new definition of momentum is required. It is

$$ p = \frac{mv}{\sqrt{1 - \dfrac{v^2}{c^2}}} $$

where v is the speed of an object and c is the speed of light. This is **relativistic momentum,** which is noticeable at speeds approaching the speed of light. Notice that the square root in the denominator looks just like the one in the formula for time dilation in Chapter 15. It tells us that the relativistic momentum of an object of mass m and speed v is larger than mv by a factor of $1/\sqrt{1 - (v^2/c^2)}$.

⊘ **As an object approaches the speed of light, its momentum increases dramatically.** As v approaches c, the denominator of the equation approaches zero. This means that the momentum approaches infinity! An object pushed to the speed of light would have infinite momentum and would require an infinite impulse, which is clearly impossible. So nothing that has mass can be pushed to the speed of light, much less beyond it. Hence, we see that c is the speed limit in the universe.

FIGURE 16.1 ▶

If the momentum of the electrons were equal to the Newtonian value *mv*, the beam would follow the dashed line. But because the relativistic momentum, or inertia in motion, is greater, the beam follows the "stiffer" trajectory shown by the solid line.

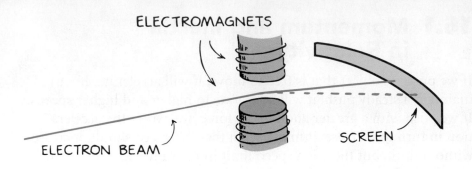

ELECTROMAGNETS

ELECTRON BEAM

SCREEN

What if *v* is much less than *c*? Then the denominator of the equation is nearly equal to 1 and *p* is nearly equal to *mv*. Newton's definition of momentum is valid at low speed.

Trajectory of High-Speed Particles We often say that a particle pushed close to the speed of light acts *as if* its mass were increasing, because its momentum—its "inertia in motion"—increases more than its speed increases. The **rest mass** of an object, represented by *m* in the equation on the previous page, is a true constant, a property of the object no matter what speed it has.

Subatomic particles are routinely pushed to nearly the speed of light. The momenta of such particles may be thousands of times more than the Newton expression *mv* predicts. One way to look at the momentum of a high-speed particle is in terms of the "stiffness" of its trajectory. The more momentum it has, the harder it is to deflect it—the "stiffer" is its trajectory. If it has a lot of momentum, it more greatly resists changing course.

This can be seen when a beam of electrons is directed into a magnetic field, as shown in Figure 16.1. Charged particles moving in a magnetic field experience a force that deflects them from their normal paths. For a particle with a small momentum, the path curves sharply. For a particle with a large momentum, the path curves only a little—its trajectory is "stiffer." Even though one particle may be moving only a little faster than another one—say 99.9% of the speed of light instead of 99% of the speed of light—its momentum will be considerably greater and it will follow a straighter path in the magnetic field. Through such experiments, physicists working with subatomic particles at atomic accelerators verify every day the correctness of the relativistic definition of momentum and the speed limit imposed by nature.

CONCEPT CHECK How does an object's momentum change as it approaches the speed of light?

At ordinary speeds, an object's momentum is simply its classical value, *mv*. For example, at 30 m/s (0.0000001c), the relativistic momentum differs from the classical value by less than one trillionth of a percent. Newton's definition of momentum is valid at low speeds.

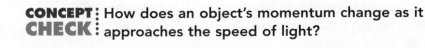

16.2 Equivalence of Mass and Energy

A remarkable insight of Einstein's special theory of relativity is his conclusion that mass is simply a form of energy. A piece of matter, even if at rest and even if not interacting with anything else, has an "energy of being" called its **rest energy.** Einstein concluded that it takes energy to make mass and that energy is released when mass disappears. Rest mass is, in effect, a kind of potential energy. Mass stores energy, just as a boulder rolled to the top of a hill stores energy. When the mass of something decreases, as it can do in nuclear reactions, energy is released, just as the boulder rolling to the bottom of the hill releases energy.

$E = mc^2$ says that mass is congealed energy. Mass and energy are two sides of the same coin.

Conversion of Mass to Energy The amount of rest energy E is related to the mass m by the most celebrated equation of the twentieth century,

$$E = mc^2$$

where c is again the speed of light. This equation gives the total energy content of a piece of stationary matter of mass m. ☑ **Mass and energy are equivalent—anything with mass also has energy.**

In ordinary units of measurement, the speed of light c is a large quantity and its square is even larger. This means that a small amount of mass stores a large amount of energy. The quantity c^2 is a "conversion factor." It converts the measurement of mass to the measurement of equivalent energy. It is the ratio of rest energy to mass: $E/m = c^2$. Its appearance in either form of this equation has nothing to do with light and nothing to do with motion. The magnitude of c^2 is 90 quadrillion (9×10^{16}) joules per kilogram. One kilogram of matter has an "energy of being" equal to 90 quadrillion joules. Even a speck of matter with a mass of only 1 milligram has a rest energy of 90 billion joules. (This is equivalent to the kinetic energy of a 3-ton truck moving at over 20 times the speed of sound!)

Examples of Mass-Energy Conversions Rest energy, like any form of energy, can be converted to other forms. When we strike a match, for example, a chemical reaction occurs and heat is released. Phosphorus atoms in the match head rearrange themselves and combine with oxygen in the air to form new molecules. The resulting molecules have very slightly less mass than the separate phosphorus and oxygen molecules. From a mass standpoint, the whole is slightly less than the sum of its parts, but not by very much—by only about one part in a billion. For all chemical reactions that give off energy, there is a corresponding decrease in mass.

think!

Can we look at the equation $E = mc^2$ in another way and say that matter transforms into pure energy when it is traveling at the speed of light squared?
Answer: 16.2

FIGURE 16.2 ▼

In one second, 4.5 million tons of rest mass are converted to radiant energy in the sun.

In nuclear reactions, the decrease in rest mass is considerably more than in chemical reactions—about one part in a thousand. This decrease of mass in the sun by the process of thermonuclear fusion bathes the solar system with radiant energy and nourishes life. The sun is so massive that in a million years only one ten-millionth of the sun's rest mass will have been converted to radiant energy. The present stage of thermonuclear fusion in the sun has been going on for the past 5 billion years, and there is sufficient hydrogen fuel for fusion to last another 5 billion years. It is nice to have such a big sun! Nuclear power plants, such as the one shown in Figure 16.3, make use of the equivalence of mass and energy to produce enormous amounts of energy.

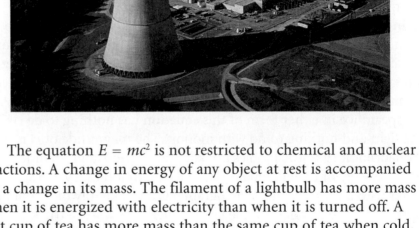

FIGURE 16.3 ▶

Saying that a power plant delivers 90 million megajoules of energy to its consumers is equivalent to saying that it delivers 1 gram of energy to its consumers, because mass and energy are equivalent.

The equation $E = mc^2$ is not restricted to chemical and nuclear reactions. A change in energy of any object at rest is accompanied by a change in its mass. The filament of a lightbulb has more mass when it is energized with electricity than when it is turned off. A hot cup of tea has more mass than the same cup of tea when cold. A wound-up spring clock has more mass than the same clock when unwound. But these examples involve incredibly small changes in mass—too small to be measured by conventional methods. No wonder the fundamental relationship between mass and energy was not discovered until the 1900s.

The equation $E = mc^2$ is more than a formula for the conversion of rest mass into other kinds of energy, or vice versa. It states that energy and mass are the *same thing*. Mass is simply congealed energy. If you want to know how much energy is in a system, measure its mass. For an object at rest, its energy *is* its mass. Shake a massive object back and forth; it is energy itself that is hard to shake.

CONCEPT CHECK : **What is the relationship between mass and energy?**

16.3 The Correspondence Principle

If a new theory is to be valid, it must account for the verified results of the old theory. The **correspondence principle** states that new theory and old must overlap and agree in the region where the results of the old theory have been fully verified. It was advanced as a principle by the Danish physicist Niels Bohr early in the twentieth century when Newtonian mechanics was being challenged by both quantum theory and relativity. ◯ **According to the correspondence principle, if the equations of special relativity (or any other new theory) are to be valid, they must correspond to those of Newtonian mechanics—classical mechanics—when speeds much less than the speed of light are considered.**

Equations remind us that you can never change only one thing. Change a term on one side of an equation and you change something on the other side.

The relativity equations for time dilation, length contraction, and momentum are

$$t = \frac{t_0}{\sqrt{1 - \dfrac{v^2}{c^2}}}$$

$$L = L_0 \sqrt{1 - \frac{v^2}{c^2}}$$

$$p = \frac{mv}{\sqrt{1 - \dfrac{v^2}{c^2}}}$$

We can see that each of these equations reduces to a Newtonian value for speeds that are very small compared with c. Then, the ratio $(v/c)^2$ is very small, and for everyday speeds may be taken to be zero. The relativity equations become

$$t = \frac{t_0}{\sqrt{1 - 0}} = t_0$$

$$L = L_0 \sqrt{1 - 0} = L_0$$

$$p = \frac{mv}{\sqrt{1 - 0}} = mv$$

Much of nature is built on patterns, and looking for those patterns is the primary preoccupation of both artists and scientists. We connect things that were always there but never put together in our thinking.

So for everyday speeds, the time scales and length scales of moving objects are essentially unchanged. Also, the Newtonian equation for momentum holds true (and so does the Newtonian equation for kinetic energy). But when the speed of light is approached, things change dramatically. Near the speed of light Newtonian mechanics change completely. The equations of special relativity hold for all speeds, although they are significant only for speeds near the speed of light.

So we see that advances in science take place not by discarding the current ideas and techniques, but by extending them to reveal new implications. Einstein never claimed that accepted laws of physics were wrong, but instead showed that the laws of physics implied something that hadn't before been appreciated.

The special theory of relativity is about motion observed in uniformly moving frames of reference, which is why it is called special. Einstein's conviction that the laws of nature should be expressed in the same form in *every* frame of reference, accelerated as well as non-accelerated, was the primary motivation that led him to develop the **general theory of relativity** —a new theory of gravitation, in which gravity causes space to become curved and time to slow down.

CONCEPT CHECK: How does the correspondence principle apply to special relativity?

16.4 General Relativity

Einstein was led to a new theory of gravity by thinking about observers in accelerated motion. He imagined himself in a spaceship far away from gravitational influences, as shown in Figure 16.4. In such a spaceship at rest or in uniform motion relative to the distant stars, Einstein and everything within the ship would float freely; there would be no "up" and no "down." But if rocket motors were activated to accelerate the ship, things would be different; phenomena similar to gravity would be observed. The wall adjacent to the rocket motors (the "floor") would push up against any occupants and give them the sensation of weight. If the acceleration of the spaceship were equal to g, the occupants could well be convinced the ship was not accelerating, but was at rest on the surface of Earth.

Einstein actually imagined himself in elevators, certainly more common at the time than spaceships.

FIGURE 16.4 ▶

Imagine being on a spaceship far away from gravitational influences. **a.** Everything inside is weightless when the spaceship isn't accelerating. **b.** When the spaceship accelerates, an occupant inside feels "gravity."

The Principle of Equivalence Einstein concluded, in what is now called the **principle of equivalence,** that gravity and accelerated motion through space-time are related. ✓ **The principle of equivalence states that local observations made in an accelerated frame of reference cannot be distinguished from observations made in a Newtonian gravitational field.** There is no way you can tell whether you are being pulled by gravity or being accelerated. The effects of gravity and the effects of acceleration are equivalent.

To examine this new "gravity" in the accelerating spaceship, Einstein considered the consequence of dropping two balls, say one of wood and the other of lead. Figure 16.5 shows that when released, the balls would continue to move upward side by side with the velocity that the ship had at the moment of release. If the ship were moving at *constant velocity* (zero acceleration), the balls would appear to remain suspended in the same place since both the ship and the balls move the same amount. But if the ship were accelerating, the floor would move upward faster than the balls, which would soon be intercepted by the floor. Both balls, regardless of their masses, would meet the floor at the same time. Occupants of the spaceship might attribute their observations to the force of gravity.

◄ **FIGURE 16.5**
To an observer inside the accelerating ship, a lead ball and a wood ball accelerate downward together when released, just as they would if pulled by gravity.

Both interpretations of the falling balls are equally valid. Einstein incorporated this equivalence, or impossibility of distinguishing between gravitation and acceleration, in the foundation of his general theory of relativity. The principle of equivalence would be interesting but not revolutionary if it applied only to mechanical phenomena. But Einstein went further and stated that the principle holds for all natural phenomena, including optical, electromagnetic, and mechanical phenomena.

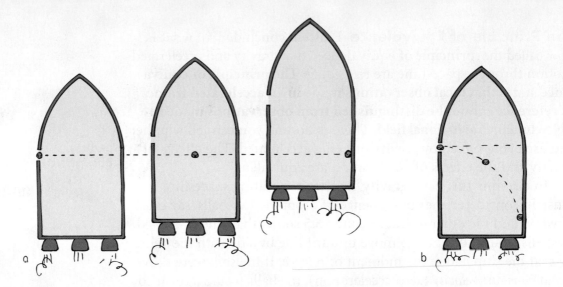

FIGURE 16.6 ▲
A ball is thrown sideways
in an accelerating spaceship
in the absence of gravity.
a. An outside observer sees
the ball travel in a straight
line. **b.** To an inside
observer, the ball follows
a parabolic path as if in a
gravitational field.

Bending of Light by Gravity Just as a tossed ball curves in a
gravitational field, so does a light beam. Consider a ball thrown sideways in a stationary spaceship in the absence of gravity. The ball will
follow a straight-line path relative to both an observer inside the ship
and to a stationary observer outside the spaceship. But if the ship is
accelerating, the floor overtakes the ball and it hits the wall below the
level at which it was thrown. An observer outside the ship still sees
a straight-line path, as illustrated in Figure 16.6a, but to an observer
in the accelerating ship, the path is curved; it is a parabola, as shown
in Figure 16.6b. Figure 16.7 illustrates that the same holds true for a
beam of light. The only difference is in the amount of path curvature.
As shown in Figure 16.8, if a ball were thrown at nearly the speed of
light, the curvature of its path would be nearly the same as that of the
light beam.

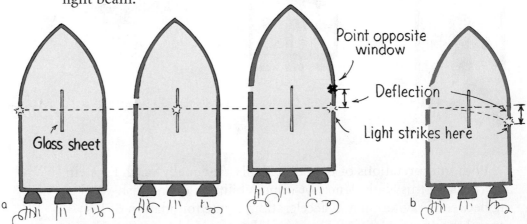

FIGURE 16.7 ▲
A light ray enters the spaceship horizontally through a side
window. **a.** Like the ball in Figure 16.6, light appears, to an
outside observer, to be travelling horizontally in a straight
line. **b.** To an inside observer, the light appears to bend.

Using his principle of equivalence, Einstein took another giant step that led him to the general theory of relativity. He reasoned that since acceleration (a space-time effect) can mimic gravity (a force), perhaps gravity is not a separate force after all; perhaps it is nothing but a manifestation of space-time. From this bold idea he derived the mathematics of gravity as being a result of curved space-time.

According to Newton, tossed balls curve because of a force of gravity. According to Einstein, tossed balls and light don't curve because of any force, but because the space-time in which they travel is curved.

FIGURE 16.8 ▲
The trajectory of a baseball tossed at nearly the speed of light closely follows the trajectory of a light beam.

CONCEPT CHECK What does the principle of equivalence state?

16.5 Gravity, Space, and a New Geometry

Space-time has four dimensions—three space dimensions (such as length, width, and height) and one time dimension (past to future). Einstein perceived a gravitational field as a geometrical warping of four-dimensional space-time. Four-dimensional geometry is altogether different from the three-dimensional geometry introduced by Euclid centuries earlier. Euclidean geometry (the ordinary geometry taught in school) is no longer valid when applied to objects in the presence of strong gravitational fields.

Four-Dimensional Geometry The familiar rules of Euclidean geometry pertain to various figures that can be drawn on a flat surface. In Euclidean geometry, the ratio of the circumference of a circle to its diameter is equal to π; all the angles in a triangle add up to 180°; and the shortest distance between two points is a straight line. The rules of Euclidean geometry are valid in flat space, but if you draw circles or triangles on a curved surface like a sphere or a saddle-shaped object, as shown in Figure 16.9, the Euclidean rules no longer hold. If you measure the sum of the angles for a triangle drawn on the outside of a ball (positive curvature), the sum of the angles is greater than 180°. For a triangle drawn on a "saddle" (negative curvature), the sum is less than 180°.

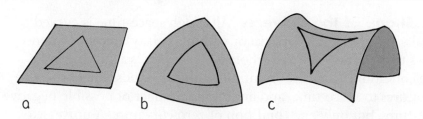

a   b   c

◄ FIGURE 16.9
The sum of the angles of a triangle is not always 180°. **a.** On a flat surface, the sum is 180°. **b.** On a spherical surface, the sum is greater than 180°. **c.** On a saddle-shaped surface, the sum is less than 180°.

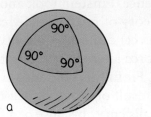
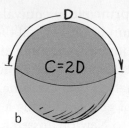

FIGURE 16.10 ▶
The geometry of Earth's two-dimensional curved surface differs from the Euclidean geometry of a flat plane.

Look at an airplane's flight path drawn on a flat map and you'll see that the line is curved. The same line drawn on the surface of a globe would be a geodesic—a "straight" (shortest-distance-between-two-points) line on Earth's curved surface.

FIGURE 16.11 ▶
The light rays joining the three planets form a triangle. Since the sun's gravity bends the light rays, the sum of the angles of the resulting triangle is greater than 180°.

Similarly, the geometry of Earth's two-dimensional curved surface differs from the Euclidean geometry of a flat plane. As shown in Figure 16.10a, the sum of the angles for an equilateral triangle (the one here has the sides equal $\frac{1}{4}$ Earth's circumference) is greater than 180°. Earth's circumference is only twice its diameter, as illustrated in Figure 16.10b, instead of 3.14 times its diameter.

Of course, the lines forming the triangles in Figures 16.9 and 16.10 are not "straight" from the three-dimensional view, but are the "straightest" or *shortest* distances between two points if we are confined to the curved surface. These lines of shortest distance are called **geodesics.**

The path of a light beam follows a geodesic. Suppose three experimenters on planets Earth, Venus, and Mars measure the angles of a triangle formed by light beams traveling between them. The light beams bend when passing the sun, resulting in the sum of the three angles being larger than 180°, as illustrated in Figure 16.11. So the three-dimensional space around the sun is positively curved. The planets that orbit the sun travel along *four*-dimensional geodesics in this positively curved space-time. Freely falling objects, satellites, and light rays all travel along geodesics in four-dimensional space-time.

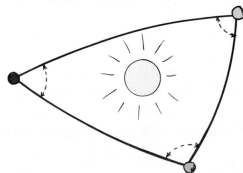

The Shape of the Universe Although space-time is curved "locally" (within a solar system or within a galaxy), recent evidence shows that the universe as a whole is "flat." This is a striking knife-edge condition. There are an infinite number of possible positive curvatures to space-time, and an infinite number of possible negative curvatures, but only one condition of zero curvature. A universe of zero or negative curvature is open-ended and extends without limit.

If the universe had positive curvature, it would close in on itself, just as the surface of Earth closes in on itself. If you march straight ahead on Earth, never turning, you will eventually return to your starting point. And if you shine a flashlight into a space of positive curvature, the light will eventually illuminate the back of your head (if you wait long enough!). No one knows why the universe is actually flat or nearly flat. The leading theory is that this is the result of an incredibly large and near-instantaneous inflation that took place as part of the Big Bang some 13.7 billion years ago.

General relativity, then, calls for a new geometry: a geometry not only of curved space but of curved time as well—a geometry of curved four-dimensional space-time.[16.5.1] Even if the universe at large has no average curvature, there's very much curvature near massive bodies. ⊘ **The presence of mass produces a curvature or warping of space-time; conversely, a curvature of space-time reveals the presence of mass.** Instead of visualizing gravitational forces between masses, we abandon altogether the idea of force and think of masses responding in their motion to the curvature or warping of the space-time they inhabit. General relativity tells us that the bumps, depressions, and warpings of geometrical space-time *are* gravity.[16.5.2]

We cannot visualize the four-dimensional bumps and depressions in space-time because we are three-dimensional beings. We can get a glimpse of this warping by considering a simplified analogy in two dimensions: a heavy ball resting on the middle of a waterbed, which is illustrated in Figure 16.12. The more massive the ball, the more it dents or warps the two-dimensional surface. A marble rolled across such a surface may trace an oval curve and orbit the ball. The planets that orbit the sun similarly travel along four-dimensional geodesics in the warped space-time about the sun.

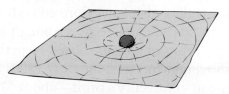

Gravitational Waves Every object has mass, and therefore makes a bump or depression in the surrounding space-time. When an object moves, the surrounding warp of space and time moves to readjust to the new position. These readjustments produce ripples in the overall geometry of space-time, similar to moving a ball that rests on the surface of a waterbed. A disturbance ripples across the waterbed surface in waves; if we move a more massive ball, then we get a greater disturbance and the production of even stronger waves. The ripples that travel outward from the gravitational sources at the speed of light are **gravitational waves.**

think!

Whoa! We learned previously that the pull of gravity is an interaction between masses. And we learned that light has no mass. Now we say that light can be bent by gravity. Isn't this a contradiction?
Answer: 16.5

◀ **FIGURE 16.12**
Space-time near a star is curved in a way similar to the surface of a waterbed when a heavy ball rests on it.

Any accelerating object produces a gravitational wave. In general, the more massive the object and the greater its acceleration, the stronger the resulting gravitational wave. But even the strongest waves produced by ordinary astronomical events are the weakest known in nature. For example, the gravitational waves emitted by a vibrating electric charge are a trillion-trillion-trillion times weaker than the electromagnetic waves emitted by the same charge. Detecting gravitational waves is enormously difficult, but physicists think they may be able to do it, and searches are under way at present.

CONCEPT CHECK : What is the relationship between the presence of mass and the curvature of space-time?

16.6 Tests of General Relativity

⊘ **Upon developing the general theory of relativity, Einstein predicted that the elliptical orbits of the planets precess about the sun, starlight passing close to the sun is deflected, and gravitation causes time to slow down.** Later, his predictions were successfully tested and confirmed.

Precession of the Planetary Orbits Using four-dimensional field equations, Einstein recalculated the orbits of the planets about the sun. Planets and comets travel along curved paths because of the curvature of space-time. With only one minor exception, his theory gave almost exactly the same results as Newton's law of gravity. The exception was that Einstein's theory predicted that the elliptical orbits of the planets should precess independent of the Newtonian influence of other planets, as shown in Figure 16.13. This precession would be very slight for distant planets and more pronounced close to the sun. Mercury is the only planet close enough to the sun for the curvature of space to produce an effect big enough to measure.

Precession in the orbits of planets caused by perturbations of other planets was well known. Since the early 1800s astronomers measured a precession of Mercury's orbit—about 574 seconds of arc per century. Perturbations by the other planets were found to account for the precession—except for 43 seconds of arc per century. Even after all known corrections due to possible perturbations by other planets had been applied, the calculations of scientists failed to account for the extra 43 seconds of arc. Either Venus was extra massive or a never-discovered other planet (called Vulcan) was pulling on Mercury. And then came the explanation of Einstein, whose general relativity equations applied to Mercury's orbit predict the extra 43 seconds of arc per century!

FIGURE 16.13 ▲
Einstein's theory predicted that elliptical orbits of the planets should precess.

Deflection of Starlight As a second test of his theory, Einstein predicted that starlight passing close to the sun would be deflected by an angle of 1.75 seconds of arc—large enough to be measured. This deflection of starlight can be observed during an eclipse of the sun. (Measuring this deflection has become a standard practice at every total eclipse since the first measurements were made during the total eclipse of 1919.) A photograph taken of the darkened sky around the eclipsed sun reveals the presence of the nearby bright stars. The positions of the stars are compared with those in other photographs of the same part of the sky taken at night with the same telescope. In every instance, the deflection of starlight, which is illustrated in Figure 16.14, has supported Einstein's prediction. More support is provided by "gravitational lensing," a phenomenon in which light from a distant galaxy is bent as it passes by a nearer galaxy in such a way that multiple images of the distant galaxy appear.

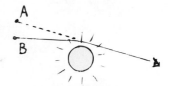

FIGURE 16.14 ▲
Starlight bends as it grazes the sun. Point A shows the apparent position; point B shows the true position. (The deflection is exaggerated.)

Gravitational Red Shift Einstein made a third prediction—that gravity causes clocks to run slow. He predicted that clocks on the first floor of a building should tick slightly more slowly than clocks on the top floor, which are farther from Earth and at a higher gravitation potential energy. As shown in Figure 16.15, if you move from a distant point down to the surface of Earth, you move in the direction that the gravitational force acts—toward lower potential energy, where clocks run more slowly. From the top to the bottom of the tallest sky-scraper, the difference is very small—only a few millionths of a second per decade—because the difference in Earth's gravitation at the bot-tom and top of the skyscraper is very small. For larger differences, like those at the surface of the sun compared with the surface of Earth, the clock-slowing effect is more pronounced. A clock in the deeper "potential well" at the sur-face of the sun should run measurably slower than a clock at the surface of Earth. Einstein suggested a way to measure this.

◀ FIGURE 16.15
Gravity causes clocks to run slow. A clock at the surface of Earth runs slower than a clock farther away.

Newton's and Einstein's Gravity Compared From Newton's law, one can calculate the orbits of comets and asteroids and even predict the existence of undiscovered planets. Even today, when computing the trajectories of space probes throughout the solar system and beyond, only ordinary Newtonian theory is used. This is because the gravitational fields of these bodies are very weak, and from the viewpoint of general relativity, the surrounding space-time is essentially flat. But for regions of more intense gravitation, where space-time is more appreciably curved, Newtonian theory cannot adequately account for various phenomena—like the precession of Mercury's orbit close to the sun and, in the case of stronger fields, the gravitational red shift and other apparent distortions of space and time. These distortions reach their limit in the case of a star that collapses to a black hole, where space-time completely folds over on itself. Only Einsteinian gravitation reaches into this domain.

think!

Why do we not notice the bending of light by gravity in our everyday environment?
Answer: 16.6

Light traveling "against gravity" is observed to have a slightly lower frequency due to an effect called the **gravitational red shift.** Because red light is at the low-frequency end of the visible spectrum, a lowering of frequency shifts the color of the emitted light toward the red. Although this effect is weak in the gravitational field of the sun, it is stronger in more compact stars with greater surface gravity. An experiment confirming Einstein's prediction was performed in 1960 with high-frequency gamma rays sent between the top and bottom floors of a laboratory building at Harvard University.[16.6] Incredibly precise measurements confirmed the gravitational slowing of time.

So measurements of time depend not only on relative motion, as we learned in special relativity, but also on gravity. In special relativity, time dilation depends on the *speed* of one frame of reference relative to another one. In general relativity, the gravitational red shift depends on the *location* of one point in a gravitational field relative to another one. It is important to note the relativistic nature of time in both special relativity and general relativity. In both theories, however, there is no way that you can extend the duration of your own experience. Others moving at different speeds or in different gravitational fields may see you aging slowly, but your aging is seen from *their* frame of reference—never your own. As mentioned earlier, changes in time and other relativistic effects are always attributed to "the other guy."

The medieval philosopher William of Occam said that when deciding between two competing theories, choose the simpler explanation—don't make more assumptions than are necessary when describing phenomena.

CONCEPT CHECK What three predictions did Einstein make based on his general theory of relativity?

Go Online
PHSchool.com

For: Self-Assessment
Visit: PHSchool.com
Web Code: csa – 1600

Concept Summary ......

- As an object approaches the speed of light, its momentum increases dramatically.

- Mass and energy are equivalent—anything with mass also has energy.

- According to the correspondence principle, if the equations of special relativity (or any other new theory) are to be valid, they must correspond to those of Newtonian mechanics—when speeds much less than the speed of light are considered.

- The principle of equivalence states that local observations made in an accelerated frame of reference cannot be distinguished from observations made in a Newtonian gravitational field.

- The presence of mass produces a curvature or warping of space-time; conversely, a curvature of space-time reveals the presence of mass.

- Upon developing the general theory of relativity, Einstein predicted that the elliptical orbits of the planets precess about the sun, starlight passing close to the sun is deflected, and gravitation causes time to slow down.

Key Terms ......

relativistic momentum *(p. 303)*

rest mass *(p. 304)*

rest energy *(p. 305)*

correspondence principle *(p. 307)*

general theory of relativity *(p. 308)*

principle of equivalence *(p. 309)*

geodesic *(p. 312)*

gravitational wave *(p. 313)*

gravitational red shift *(p. 316)*

think! Answers

16.2   No, no, no! Matter cannot be made to move at the speed of light, let alone the speed of light squared (which is not a speed!). The equation $E = mc^2$ simply means that energy and mass are "two sides of the same coin."

16.5   There is no contradiction when the mass-energy equivalence is understood. It's true that light is massless, but it is not "energy-less." The fact that gravity deflects light is evidence that gravity pulls on the energy of light. Energy indeed is equivalent to mass!

16.6   Earth's gravity is too weak to produce a measurable bending. Even the sun produces only a tiny deflection. It takes a whole galaxy to bend light appreciably.

16ASSESS

Check Concepts ......

Section 16.1

1. What would be the momentum of an object if it were pushed to the speed of light?

2. What is meant by rest mass?

3. What relativistic effect is evident when a beam of high-speed charged particles bends in a magnetic field?

Section 16.2

4. What is meant by the equivalence of mass and energy? That is, what does the equation $E = mc^2$ mean?

5. What is the numerical quantity of the ratio rest energy/rest mass?

6. Does the equation $E = mc^2$ apply only to reactions that involve the atomic nucleus? Explain.

7. What evidence is there for the equivalence of mass and energy?

8. When the mass of something decreases, does it emit or absorb energy?

9. Compare the relative amounts of mass lost in nuclear reactions and in chemical reactions.

Section 16.3

10. What is the correspondence principle?

11. What results when low everyday speeds are used in the relativistic equations for time and length?

12. Do the equations of Newton and Einstein overlap, or is there a sharp break between them?

Section 16.4

13. State the principle of equivalence.

14. Compare the bending of the paths of baseballs and of photons by a gravitational field.

Section 16.5

15. What is a *geodesic*?

16. According to general relativity, in what paths do planets travel as they orbit the sun?

Section 16.6

17. What is the evidence for light bending near the sun?

18. Which runs faster, a clock at the top of the Sears Tower in Chicago or a clock on the shore of Lake Michigan?

19. Moving "downhill" in a gravitational field has what effect on the frequency of light?

20. Does Einstein's theory of gravitation invalidate Newton's theory of gravitation? Explain.

Think and Rank • • • • • •

Rank each of the following sets of scenarios in order of the quantity or property involved. List them from left to right. If scenarios have equal rankings, then separate them with an equal sign. (e.g., A = B)

21. Electrons are fired at different speeds through a magnetic field and are bent from their straight-line paths to hit the detector at the points shown. Rank the speeds of the electrons from highest to lowest.

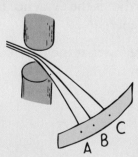

22. To an Earth observer, metersticks on three spaceships are seen to have these lengths. Rank the speeds of the spaceships relative to Earth from highest to lowest.

$$\underset{A}{\rule{2cm}{2pt}} = \underset{B}{\rule{1.5cm}{2pt}} = \underset{C}{\rule{1cm}{2pt}}$$

Think and Explain • • • • • •

23. What happens to the momentum of a massive object as its speed gets closer and closer to the speed of light?

24. When a charged particle moves through a magnetic field, what is the evidence that its momentum is greater than the value *mv*?

25. According to $E = mc^2$, how does the amount of energy in a kilogram of feathers compare with the amount of energy in a kilogram of iron?

26. Does a fully charged flashlight battery weigh more than the same battery when dead? Defend your answer.

27. Two safety pins, identical except that one is latched and one is unlatched, are placed in identical acid baths. After the pins are dissolved, what, if anything, is different about the two acid baths?

28. A friend says that the equation $E = mc^2$ has relevance to nuclear power plants, but not to fossil-fuel power plants. Another friend looks to see if you agree. What do you say?

29. Is this label on a consumer product cause for alarm? *CAUTION: The mass of this product contains the energy equivalent of 3 million tons of TNT per gram.*

30. An astronaut awakes in her closed capsule, which actually sits on the moon. Can she tell whether her weight is the result of gravitation or of accelerated motion? Explain.

31. An astronaut is provided "gravity" when the ship's engines are activated to accelerate the ship. This requires the use of fuel. Is there a way to accelerate and provide "gravity" without the sustained use of fuel? (*Hint:* Recall simulated gravity in Chapter 12.)

32. What happens to the separation distance between two people if they both walk north at the same rate from two locations on Earth's equator?

33. Your friend whimsically says that at the North Pole, a step in any direction is a step south. Do you agree?

34. We readily note the bending of light by reflection and refraction, but why are we not aware of the bending of light by gravity?

35. Light *does* bend in a gravitational field. Why is this bending not taken into consideration by surveyors who use laser beams as straight lines?

36. Your friend says that light passing the sun is bent whether or not Earth experiences a solar eclipse. Do you agree or disagree, and why?

37. In 2004 when Mercury passed between the sun and Earth, light was not appreciably bent as it passed Mercury. Why?

38. During the first second of its flight, a bullet fired horizontally drops a vertical distance of 4.9 m from its otherwise straight-line path in a gravitational field of 1 *g*. By what distance would a beam of light drop from its otherwise straight-line path if it traveled in a uniform field of 1 *g* for 1 s? For 2 s?

39. A photon changes its energy when it "falls" in a gravitational field. This change in energy is not evidenced by a change in speed, however. What is the evidence for this change in energy?

40. Do you age faster at the top of a mountain or at sea level?

41. Should a person who worries about growing old live at the top or at the bottom of a tall apartment building?

42. Is light emitted from the surface of a massive star red-shifted or blue-shifted by gravity?

43. From our frame of reference on Earth, objects slow to a stop as they approach black holes in space because time gets infinitely stretched by the strong gravity near the black hole. If astronauts accidentally falling into a black hole tried to signal back to Earth by flashing a light, what kind of wavelengths of light would best be looked for in Earth-based telescopes?

44. Gravitational waves are difficult to detect. Is this due to having long wavelengths or short ones? High energy or low energy?

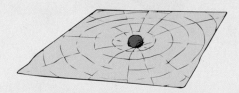

Think and Solve ......

45. A 100-watt light bulb consumes 100 joules of energy every second. How long could you burn that light bulb from the energy in one penny, which has a mass of 0.003 kg? (Assume all the penny's mass is converted to energy.)

46. The fractional change of mass to energy in a fission reactor is about 0.1 percent, or 1 part in a thousand.
   a. For each kilogram of uranium that undergoes fission, how much energy is released?
   b. If energy costs three cents per megajoule, how much is this energy worth in dollars?

Activity ......

47. Write a letter to your grandparents explaining how Einstein's theories of relativity concern the fast and the big—that relativity is not only "out there," but affects this world. Tell them how these ideas stimulate your quest for more knowledge.

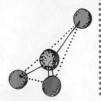

PROPERTIES OF MATTER

IT'S A FACT!

Most matter is made from only about 100 different kinds of atoms. Atoms can combine to form larger particles called molecules. Particles of matter that are held together in an orderly arrangement form solids. Particles that flow freely by sliding over one another form liquids. Particles that move freely between collisions form gases. In this unit, you will learn many interesting facts about atomic structure and the properties of solids, liquids, and gases.

An immersed object is held up by a **buoyant** force equal to the weight of the fluid it displaces. [Ch. 20]

Atoms are so tiny that I inhale billions of trillions with each breath, nearly a trillion times more atoms than the total population of people since time began! Every time I breathe in, I inhale atoms exhaled by every person **who ever lived,** except for other babies far away. Every time I breathe out, or sweat, I release atoms into the air that spread everywhere and become part of everybody else. New babies and all who follow will be made of the atoms that are now part of me. So we're all one!

Even irregularly shaped minerals are made up of regular geometric shapes called **crystals.** [Ch. 18]

Earth is the only planet in the solar system covered mostly by a **liquid**–water. [Ch. 19]

Go Online
SCIENCE NEWS

For: Articles on properties of matter
Visit: PHSchool.com
Web Code: cse – 2000

Nearly all the **elements** on Earth are remnants of stars that exploded long ago. [Ch. 17]

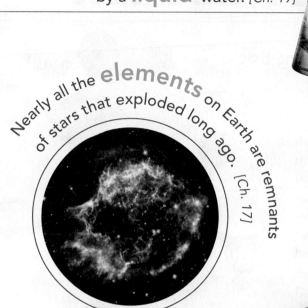

If an elephant did not have large ears, it would not have enough **surface area** to cool its large mass. [Ch. 18]

THE ATOMIC NATURE OF MATTER

THE BIG IDEA : Atoms are the building blocks of most matter.

Suppose you break apart a large boulder with a heavy sledgehammer. You break the boulder into rocks. Then you break the rocks into stones, and the stones into gravel. You keep going and break the gravel into sand, and the sand into a powder of fine crystals. Each fine crystal is composed of many billions of smaller particles called atoms. Atoms are the building blocks of most matter. Everything you see, hear, taste, feel, or smell in the world around you is made of atoms. Shoes, ships, mice, lead, and people are all made of atoms.[17.0]

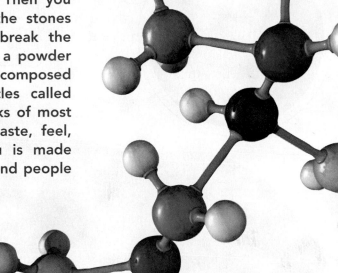

discover!

How Do We Know That Atoms Exist?

1. Place a drop of water on a microscope slide.
2. Add a drop of whole milk to the water drop using a wire or needle and stir.
3. Place a cover slip on the slide.
4. Insert the slide into a microscope and wait a while for the milk to settle.
5. Focus on fat globules in the milk. Start with a low magnification and then switch to a higher one.

Analyze and Conclude

1. **Observing** What did you see when you viewed the fat droplets under the microscope?
2. **Predicting** What would happen if you replaced the fat globules with chalk dust?
3. **Making Generalizations** What does the motion of the milk fat droplets tell you about the surrounding water?

17.1 Elements

Just as dots of light of only three colors combine to form almost every conceivable color on a television screen, only about 100 distinct kinds of atoms combine to form all the materials we know about. **Atoms** are the building blocks of matter. A material composed of only one kind of atom is called an **element.**

To date about 115 elements are known. Of these, about 90 occur in nature. The others are made in the laboratory with high-energy atomic accelerators and nuclear reactors. These laboratory-produced elements are too unstable (radioactive) to occur naturally in appreciable amounts.

☑ **Every simple, complex, living, or nonliving substance in the known universe is put together from a pantry containing less than 100 elements.** More than 99% of the material on Earth is formed from only about a dozen of the elements. The other elements are relatively rare. Living things, for example, are composed primarily of five elements: oxygen (O), carbon (C), hydrogen (H), nitrogen (N), and calcium (Ca). The letters in parentheses represent the chemical symbols for these elements. Table 17.1 lists the 16 most common elements on Earth. Most of these elements, not just the five most common ones, are critical for life.

Table 17.1	The 16 Most Common Elements on Earth		
Aluminum (Al)	Fluorine (F)	Nitrogen (N)	Silicon (Si)
Calcium (Ca)	Hydrogen (H)	Oxygen (O)	Sodium (Na)
Carbon (C)	Iron (Fe)	Phosphorus (P)	Sulfur (S)
Chlorine (Cl)	Magnesium (Mg)	Potassium (K)	Titanium (Ti)

The lightest element of all is hydrogen. In the universe at large, it is the most abundant element—over 90% of the atoms in the known universe are hydrogen. Helium, the second-lightest element, makes up most of the remaining atoms in the universe, although it is rare on Earth. The heavier, naturally formed atoms that we find around us were manufactured by fusion reactions in the hot, high-pressure cauldrons deep within stars. Elements heavier than iron are formed when huge stars implode and then explode—an event called a supernova. The heaviest elements are formed when pairs of neutron stars, the super-dense cores of supernovas, collide. Nearly all the atoms on Earth are remnants of stars that exploded long before the solar system came into being.

Just as we don't own the atoms in our bodies, we don't own energy—we rent it. Much of the energy we receive from the sun is eventually radiated back into space.

FIGURE 17.1 ▶

Both Leslie and you are made of stardust—in the sense that the carbon, oxygen, nitrogen, and other atoms that make up your body originated in the deep interior of ancient stars, which have long since exploded.

All of the matter that we encounter in our daily lives, as well as matter in the sun and other stars, is made up of elements. But not all matter in the universe is composed of elements. In the closing years of the twentieth century, astrophysicists found that gravitational forces within galaxies were far greater than visible matter could account for. Only in this twenty-first century has it been confirmed that some twenty-three percent of the matter in the universe is composed of an unseen dark matter. Astrophysicists believe this dark matter is made up of particles not yet detected, and that much of the rest of the universe is *dark energy* (briefly mentioned in Chapter 9). Indeed, the nature of dark matter, which gravitationally affects ordinary matter, and dark energy, which pushes outward on the expanding universe, is the focus of enormous present-day research.

CONCEPT CHECK What do all substances have in common?

If a typical atom were expanded to a diameter of 3 km, about the size of a medium-sized airport, the nucleus would be about the size of a basketball. Atoms are mostly empty space.

---

discover!

How fast do atoms migrate?

1. Put some drops of food coloring into a small container of water. How long does it take for the colored drops to spread to all parts of the water?

2. Repeat, using hot water. What happened to the migration rate of the drops?

3. **Think** Why did the rate change?

17.2 Atoms Are Small

⚗ **Atoms are so small that there are about 10^{23} atoms in a gram of water (a thimbleful).** The number 10^{23} is an enormous number, more than the number of drops of water in all the lakes and rivers of the world. So there are more atoms in a thimbleful of water than there are drops of water in the world's lakes and rivers. Atoms are so small that there are about as many atoms in the air in your lungs at any moment as there are breathfuls of air in the atmosphere of the whole world.

Atoms are perpetually moving. They also migrate from one location to another. In solids the rate of migration is low, in liquids it is greater, and in gases migration is greatest. Drops of food coloring in a glass of water soon spread to color the entire glass of water. Likewise, a cupful of toxic material thrown into an ocean spreads around and is eventually found in every part of the world's oceans. The same is true of materials released into the atmosphere.

It takes about six years for one of your exhaled breaths, such as the one in Figure 17.2, to become evenly mixed in the atmosphere. At that point, every person in the world inhales an average of one of your exhaled atoms in a single breath. And this occurs for *each* breath you exhale! When you take into account the many thousands of breaths that people exhale, at any time—like right now—you have hordes of atoms in your lungs that were once in the lungs of every person who ever lived. We are literally breathing one another's breaths.

Atoms are too small to be seen—at least with visible light. You could connect an array of optical microscopes atop one another and never "see" an atom. This is because light is made up of waves, and atoms are smaller than the wavelengths of visible light. The size of a particle visible under the highest magnification must be larger than the wavelengths of visible light. This is better understood by an analogy with water waves. A ship is much larger than the water waves that roll on by it. As Figure 17.3 shows, water waves can reveal features of the ship. They *diffract* as they pass the ship. In contrast, diffraction is nil for waves that pass the anchor chain, revealing little or nothing about it. Similarly, waves of visible light are too coarse compared with the size of an atom to show details of the atom's size and shape. Atoms are incredibly small. (More about this in Chapter 31.)

CONCEPT CHECK How small are atoms?

FIGURE 17.2 ▲
There are as many atoms in a normal breath of air as there are breathfuls of air in the atmosphere of the world.

think!

Does your brain contain atoms that were once part of Albert Einstein? Explain.
Answer: 17.2

FIGURE 17.3 ▲
Information about the ship is revealed by passing waves, because the distance between wave crests is small compared with the size of the ship. The passing waves reveal nothing about the chain.

think!

World population grows each year. Does this mean the mass of Earth increases each year? Explain.

Answer: 17.3

17.3 Atoms Are Recyclable

Atoms are ageless and are much older than the materials they compose. Some atoms are nearly as old as the universe itself. Most atoms that make up our world are at least as old as the sun and Earth.

⬙ **Atoms in your body have been around since long before the solar system came into existence, more than 4.6 billion years ago.** They cycle and recycle among innumerable forms, both living and nonliving. Every time you breathe, for example, only some of the atoms that you inhale are exhaled in your next breath. The remaining atoms are taken into your body to become part of you, and most leave your body sooner or later—to become part of everything else.

Strictly speaking, you don't "own" the atoms that make up your body—you're simply their present caretaker. There will be many others who later will care for the atoms that presently compose you. We all share from the same atom pool, as atoms migrate around, within, and throughout us. So some of the atoms in the ear you scratch today may have been part of your neighbor's breath yesterday!

Most people know we are all made of the same *kinds* of atoms. But what most people don't know is that we are made of the *same* atoms—atoms that cycle from person to person and creature to creature as we breathe and perspire.

CONCEPT CHECK: For how long have the atoms in your body been around?

17.4 Evidence for Atoms

The idea that matter is made of atoms goes back to the Greeks in the 400s B.C. It was revived in the early 1800s by an English meteorologist and school teacher, John Dalton. He explained the nature of chemical reactions by proposing that all matter is made of atoms, but he had no direct evidence for their existence. The first fairly direct evidence for the existence of atoms was unknowingly discovered in 1827. A Scottish botanist, Robert Brown, was looking through a microscope to study pollen grains floating in water. He noticed that the grains were in a constant state of agitation, always jiggling about. At first, Brown thought that the grains were some sort of moving life forms. Later, he found that inanimate dust particles and grains of soot floating in water also showed this kind of motion. **Brownian motion** is the perpetual jiggling of particles that are just large enough to be seen.

The jittery motion of a huge balloon in the midst of a soccer field filled with jostling people would look like Brownian motion from a high-flying aircraft. The people may be too small to see, but not the larger balloon.

Brownian motion is evidence that atoms exist, as it results from the motion of neighboring atoms and molecules. They bump into the larger particles we can see. More direct evidence for the existence of atoms is available today. An image of individual atoms is shown in Figure 17.4. The image was made not with visible light but with an electron beam. A familiar example of an electron beam is the one that sprays the picture on some television screens. Although an electron beam is a stream of tiny particles (electrons), it has wave properties, with a wavelength more than a thousand times smaller than the wavelength of visible light. With such a beam, atomic detail can be seen. The historic (1970) image in Figure 17.4 was taken with a very thin electron beam in a scanning electron microscope. It is the first such image of clearly distinguishable atoms.

In the mid-1980s, researchers developed a different kind of microscope—the scanning tunneling microscope, small enough to be held in your hand. In Figure 17.5, you can see individual atoms. Even greater detail is possible with newer types of imaging devices that are presently revolutionizing microscopy.

We can't see inside atoms, but images with today's devices help us to construct better models of the atom. From these models we can make predictions about unseen portions of the natural world.

CONCEPT
CHECK : How does Brownian motion provide evidence for the existence of atoms?

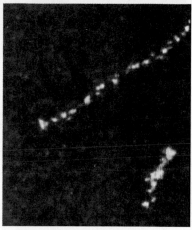

FIGURE 17.4 ▲
The strings of dots are chains of thorium atoms imaged with a scanning electron microscope by researchers at the University of Chicago's Enrico Fermi Institute.

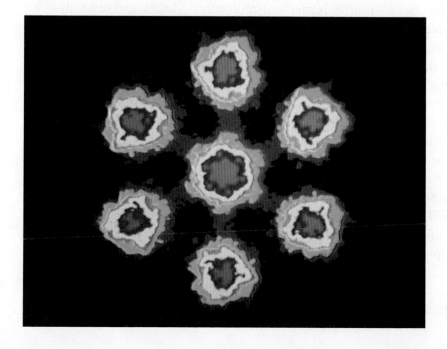

Atoms are in a state of perpetual motion—moving all the time.

◀ **FIGURE 17.5**
A scanning tunneling microscope created this image of uranium atoms.

17.5 Molecules

Atoms can combine to form larger particles called *molecules*. A **molecule** is the smallest particle of a substance consisting of two or more atoms that bond together by sharing electrons. ☑ **Molecules can be made up of atoms of the same element or of different elements.** For example, two atoms of hydrogen (H) combine with a single atom of oxygen (O) to form a water molecule (H_2O). The gases nitrogen and oxygen, which make up most of the atmosphere, are both made of simple two-atom molecules (N_2 and O_2). In contrast, the double helix of deoxyribonucleic acid (DNA), the blueprint of life, is composed of millions of atoms.

FIGURE 17.6 ▶

Models of the simple molecules O_2 (oxygen gas), NH_3 (ammonia), and CH_4 (methane) show their structure. The atoms that compose a molecule are not just mixed together, but are bonded in a well-defined way.

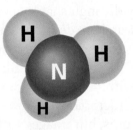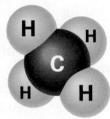

Matter that is a gas or liquid at room temperature is usually made of molecules. Matter made of molecules may contain all the same kind of molecule, or it may be a mixture of different kinds of molecules, as shown in Figure 17.6. Purified water contains almost entirely H_2O molecules, whereas clean air contains molecules belonging to several different substances.

But not all matter is made of molecules. Metals and crystalline minerals (including common table salt) are made of atoms that are not joined in molecules.

Like atoms, individual molecules are too small to be seen with optical microscopes.[17.5] More direct evidence of tiny molecules is seen in electron microscope photographs. The photograph in Figure 17.7 is of virus molecules, each composed of thousands of atoms. These giant molecules are visible with a short-wavelength electron beam, but are still too small to be seen with visible light.

We are able to detect some molecules through our sense of smell. Noxious gases such as sulfur dioxide, ammonia, and ether are clearly sensed by the organs in our nose. The smell of perfume is the result of molecules that rapidly evaporate from the liquid and jostle around completely haphazardly in the air until some of them accidentally get close enough to our noses to be inhaled. The perfume molecules are certainly not attracted to our noses! They wander aimlessly in all directions from the liquid perfume to become a small fraction of the randomly jostling molecules in the air.

FIGURE 17.7 ▲

A scientist used an electron microscope to take this photograph of rubella virus molecules. The white dots are the virus erupting on the surface of an infected cell.

CONCEPT CHECK : What are molecules made of?

17.6 Compounds

A **compound** is a substance that is made of atoms of different elements combined in a fixed proportion. The **chemical formula** of the compound tells the proportions of each kind of atom. For example, in the gas carbon dioxide, the formula CO_2 indicates that for every carbon (C) atom there are two oxygen (O) atoms. Water, table salt, and carbon dioxide are all compounds. Air, wood, and salty water are not compounds, because the proportions of their atoms vary.

A compound may or may not be made of molecules. Water and carbon dioxide are made of molecules. On the other hand, table salt (NaCl) is made of different kinds of atoms arranged in a regular pattern. (We'll soon see that the atoms in NaCl are actually *ions*.) Every chlorine atom is surrounded by six sodium atoms, as shown in Figure 17.8. In turn, every sodium atom is surrounded by six chlorine atoms. As a whole, there is one sodium atom for each chlorine atom, but there are no separate groups that can be labeled molecules.

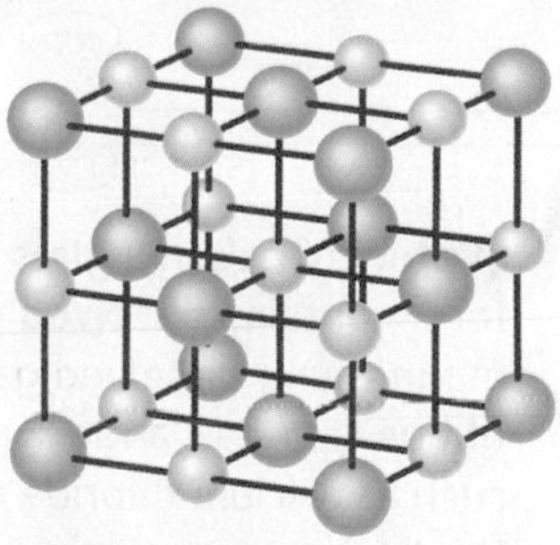

☑ **Compounds have properties different from those of the elements of which they are made.** At ordinary temperatures, water is a liquid, whereas hydrogen and oxygen are both gases. Table salt is an edible solid, whereas chlorine is a poisonous gas.

CONCEPT CHECK: How are compounds different from their component elements?

FIGURE 17.8 ▲
Table salt (NaCl) is a compound that is not made of molecules. The sodium and chlorine ions are arranged in a repeating pattern. Each ion is surrounded by six ions of the other kind.

17.7 The Atomic Nucleus

An atom is mostly empty space. Almost all of an atom's mass is packed into the dense central region called the **nucleus.** The New Zealander physicist Ernest Rutherford discovered this in 1911 in his now-famous gold foil experiment. Rutherford's group shot a beam of charged particles (alpha particles) from a radioactive source through a thin gold foil. They measured the angles at which the particles were deflected from their straight-line paths when they emerged. This was accomplished by noting spots of light on a zinc-sulfide screen that nearly surrounded the gold foil as shown in Figure 17.9.

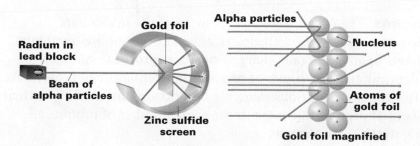

◀ **FIGURE 17.9**
The occasional large-angle scattering of alpha particles from the gold atoms led Rutherford to the discovery of the small, very massive nuclei at their centers.

Water What's in a glass of water? Tap water is far from being pure H_2O, for it contains dissolved compounds of metals such as iron, potassium, and magnesium; dissolved gases such as oxygen and nitrogen; trace amounts of heavy metals and organic compounds; and other chemical compounds such as calcium fluoride and chlorine disinfectants. Now don't panic and go thirsty. You probably wouldn't like the taste of pure water, for some dissolved substances give water a pleasing taste and promote good health. As much as 10% of our daily requirement of iron, potassium, calciuum, and magnesium is obtained from ordinary drinking water. Bottoms up!

Atoms were a philosophical concept with ancient Greeks and became a scientific concept with the experiments of the chemist John Dalton in the early 1800s. Atoms weren't fully validated until the work of Albert Einstein in the early 1900s.

Most particles continued in a more or less straight-line path through the thin foil. But, surprisingly, some particles were widely deflected. Some were even scattered back almost along their incoming path. It was as surprising, Rutherford said, as firing a 15-inch artillery shell at a piece of tissue paper and having it come back and hit you.

Rutherford reasoned that within the atom there had to be a positively charged object with two special properties. It had to be very small compared with the size of the atom, and it had to be massive enough to resist being shoved aside by heavy alpha particles. Rutherford had discovered the atomic nucleus.

✓ **The mass of an atom is primarily concentrated in the nucleus.** However, the nucleus occupies less than a trillionth of the volume of an atom. Atomic nuclei (plural of nucleus) are extremely compact and extremely dense. If bare atomic nuclei could be packed against one another into a lump 1 cm in diameter (about the size of a small grape), the lump would weigh about a billion tons!

Huge electrical forces of repulsion prevent such close packing of atomic nuclei because each nucleus is electrically charged and repels the other nuclei. Only under special circumstances are the nuclei of two or more atoms squashed into contact. When this happens, the violent reaction known as nuclear fusion takes place. Fusion occurs in the core of stars and in a hydrogen bomb.

Nucleons The principal building blocks of the nucleus are **nucleons.** [17.7] Nucleons in an electrically neutral state are **neutrons.** Nucleons in an electrically charged state are **protons.** All neutrons are identical; they are copies of one another. Similarly, all protons are identical. Atoms of various elements differ from one another by their numbers of protons. Atoms with the same number of protons all belong to the same element.

Go Online

SciLINKS

For: Links on atoms
Visit: www.SciLinks.org
Web Code: csn – 1707

Isotopes For a given element, however, the number of neutrons will vary. Atoms of the same element having different numbers of neutrons are called **isotopes** of that element. The nucleus of the common hydrogen atom has a single proton. When this proton is accompanied by a neutron, we have *deuterium*, an isotope of hydrogen. When two neutrons are in a hydrogen nucleus, we have the isotope *tritium*. Every element has a variety of isotopes. Lighter elements usually have an equal number of protons and neutrons, and heavier elements usually have more neutrons than protons.

Atomic Number Atoms are classified by their **atomic number,** which is the number of protons in the nucleus. The nucleus of a hydrogen atom has one proton, so its atomic number is 1. Helium has two protons, so its atomic number is 2. Lithium has three protons, so its atomic number is 3, and so on, in sequence up to the heaviest elements.

Electric Charge Electric charge comes in two kinds, positive and negative. Protons in the atom's nucleus are positive, and electrons orbiting the nucleus are negative. Positive and negative refer to a basic property of matter—electric *charge.* (Much more about electric charge in Unit V.) Like kinds of charge repel one another and unlike kinds attract one another. Protons repel protons but attract electrons. Electrons repel electrons but attract protons. Inside the nucleus, protons are held to one another by a *strong nuclear force.* This force is extremely intense but acts only across tiny distances. (More about the strong nuclear force in Chapter 39.)

How long would it take to count to one million (10^6)? If each count takes one second, counting nonstop to a million would take 11.6 days. Counting to a billion (10^9) would take 31.7 years. Counting to a trillion (10^{12}) would take 31,700 years, and to a trillion trillion (10^{24}) would take about 2 million times the estimated age of the universe.

CONCEPT CHECK Where is the mass of an atom primarily concentrated?

Physics on the Job

Chemist Many of the products you use every day—from shampoo to vitamins to some foods—were developed by chemists. A chemist uses an understanding of atoms and elements to isolate and identify unknown chemicals, synthesize chemicals in the laboratory, and perform tests to maintain quality standards in industrial processes. Chemists work for government and university laboratories as well as for research departments of private corporations. Most chemists hold undergraduate degrees in chemistry along with advanced degrees in more specific fields such as biochemistry, nuclear chemistry, or analytical chemistry.

17.8 Electrons in the Atom

Electrons that orbit the atomic nucleus are identical to the electrons that flow in the wires of electric circuits. They are negatively charged subatomic particles. The electron's mass is less than $\frac{1}{1800}$ the mass of a proton or neutron, so electrons do not significantly contribute to the atom's overall mass.

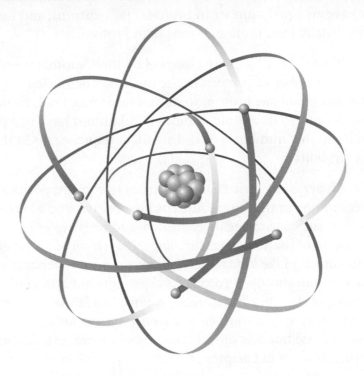

FIGURE 17.10 ▶
The classic model of the atom consists of a tiny nucleus surrounded by orbiting electrons.

In an electrically neutral atom, such as the one shown in Figure 17.10, the number of negatively charged electrons always equals the number of positively charged protons in the nucleus. When the number of electrons in an atom differs from the number of protons, the atom is no longer neutral and has a net charge. An atom with a net charge is an **ion.**

Attraction between a proton and an electron can cause a *bond* between atoms to form a molecule. For example, two atoms can be held together by the sharing of electrons (a covalent bond). Atoms also stick to each other when ions of opposite charge are formed, and these ions are held together by simple electric forces (an ionic bond).

Just like our solar system, the atom is mostly empty space. The nucleus and surrounding electrons occupy only a tiny fraction of the atomic volume. Yet the electrons, because of their wave nature, form a kind of cloud around the nucleus. Compressing this electron cloud takes great energy and means that when two atoms come close together, they repel each other. If it were not for this repulsive force between atoms, solid matter would be much more dense than it is.

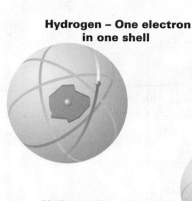
Hydrogen – One electron in one shell

Lithium –Three electrons in two shells

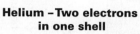
Helium –Two electrons in one shell

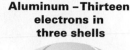
Aluminum –Thirteen electrons in three shells

FIGURE 17.11 ▲
The shell model of the atom pictures the electrons orbiting in concentric, spherical shells around the nucleus.

We and the solid floor upon which we stand are mostly empty space, because the atoms making up these and all materials are themselves mostly empty space. But we don't fall through the floor. The forces of repulsion keep atoms from caving in on one another under pressure.

Scientists use a model to explain how atoms of different elements interact to form compounds. In the **shell model of the atom,** electrons are pictured as orbiting in spherical shells around the nucleus, as shown in Figure 17.11. There are seven different shells, and each shell has its own capacity for electrons. ☑ **The arrangement of electrons in the shells around the atomic nucleus dictates the atom's chemical properties.** These properties include melting and freezing temperatures, electrical conductivity, and the taste, texture, appearance, and color of substances. The arrangement of electrons quite literally gives life and color to the world.

The **periodic table** is a chart that lists atoms by their atomic number and by their electron arrangements as shown in Figure 17.12 on the next page. As you read across from left to right, each element has one more proton and electron than the preceding element. As you go down, each element has one more shell filled to its capacity than the element above.

Elements in the same column have similar chemical properties, reacting with other elements in similar ways to form new compounds and materials. Elements in the same column are said to belong to the same *group* or family of elements. Elements of the same group have similar chemical properties because their outermost electrons are arranged in a similar fashion.

The periodic table is a chemist's road map.

**CONCEPT
CHECK :** What does the arrangement of electrons around the nucleus determine?

FIGURE 17.12 ▲

The periodic table of the elements. The atomic number, above the chemical symbol, is equal to the number of protons in the nucleus (and equivalently, the number of electrons that surround the nucleus in a neutral atom). The number below is the atomic mass. Each row in the periodic table corresponds to a different number of electron shells in the atom.

Note that the uppermost row consists of only two elements, hydrogen and helium. The electrons of helium complete the innermost shell. Elements are arranged vertically on the basis of similarity in the arrangement of outer electrons, which dictates similarities in physical and chemical properties of the elements and their compounds.

1A	IIA	IIIB	IVB	VB	VIB	VIIB	VIII			IB	IIB	IIIA	IVA	VA	VIA	VIIA	0
1 **H** Hydrogen 1.008																	2 **He** Helium 4.003
3 **Li** Lithium 6.94	4 **Be** Beryllium 9.012											5 **B** Boron 10.81	6 **C** Carbon 12.011	7 **N** Nitrogen 14.007	8 **O** Oxygen 15.999	9 **F** Fluorine 18.998	10 **Ne** Neon 20.17
11 **Na** Sodium 22.990	12 **Mg** Magnesium 24.305											13 **Al** Aluminum 26.98	14 **Si** Silicon 28.09	15 **P** Phosphorus 30.974	16 **S** Sulfur 32.06	17 **Cl** Chlorine 35.453	18 **Ar** Argon 39.948
19 **K** Potassium 39.098	20 **Ca** Calcium 40.08	21 **Sc** Scandium 44.956	22 **Ti** Titanium 47.90	23 **V** Vanadium 50.942	24 **Cr** Chromium 51.996	25 **Mn** Manganese 54.938	26 **Fe** Iron 55.847	27 **Co** Cobalt 58.933	28 **Ni** Nickel 58.71	29 **Cu** Copper 63.546	30 **Zn** Zinc 65.38	31 **Ga** Gallium 69.735	32 **Ge** Germanium 72.59	33 **As** Arsenic 74.992	34 **Se** Selenium 78.96	35 **Br** Bromine 79.904	36 **Kr** Krypton 83.80
37 **Rb** Rubidium 85.467	38 **Sr** Strontium 87.62	39 **Y** Yttrium 88.906	40 **Zr** Zirconium 91.22	41 **Nb** Niobium 92.906	42 **Mo** Molybdenum 95.94	43 **Tc** Technetium (98)	44 **Ru** Ruthenium 101.07	45 **Rh** Rhodium 102.91	46 **Pd** Palladium 106.4	47 **Ag** Silver 107.868	48 **Cd** Cadmium 112.41	49 **In** Indium 114.82	50 **Sn** Tin 118.69	51 **Sb** Antimony 121.75	52 **Te** Tellurium 127.60	53 **I** Iodine 126.904	54 **Xe** Xenon 131.30
55 **Cs** Cesium 132.905	56 **Ba** Barium 137.33	71 **Lu** Lutetium 174.967	72 **Hf** Hafnium 178.49	73 **Ta** Tantalum 180.947	74 **W** Tungsten 183.85	75 **Re** Rhenium 186.207	76 **Os** Osmium 190.02	77 **Ir** Iridium 192.22	78 **Pt** Platinum 195.09	79 **Au** Gold 196.967	80 **Hg** Mercury 200.59	81 **Tl** Thallium 204.37	82 **Pb** Lead 207.2	83 **Bi** Bismuth 208.98	84 **Po** Polonium (209)	85 **At** Astatine (210)	86 **Rn** Radon (222)
87 **Fr** Francium (233)	88 **Ra** Radium (226)	103 **Lr** Lawrencium (262)	104 **Rf** Rutherfordium (261)	105 **Db** Dubnium (262)	106 **Sg** Seaborgium (263)	107 **Bh** Bohrium (264)	108 **Hs** Hassium (265)	109 **Mt** Meitnerium (268)	110 **Ds** Darmstadtium (269)	111 **Rg** Roentgenium (272)	112 **Uub** Ununbium (272)		114 **Uuq** Ununquadium				

Rare Earths (Lanthanide series)

57 **La** Lanthanum 139.91	58 **Ce** Cerium 140.12	59 **Pr** Praseodymium 140.91	60 **Nd** Neodymium 144.24	61 **Pm** Promethium (145)	62 **Sm** Samarium 150.36	63 **Eu** Europium 151.96	64 **Gd** Gadolinium 157.25	65 **Tb** Terbium 158.93	66 **Dy** Dysprosium 162.50	67 **Ho** Holmium 164.93	68 **Er** Erbium 167.26	69 **Tm** Thulium 168.93	70 **Yb** Ytterbium 173.04

Actinide series

89 **Ac** Actinium (227)	90 **Th** Thorium 232.038	91 **Pa** Proactinium 231.036	92 **U** Uranium 238.029	93 **Np** Neptunium (237)	94 **Pu** Plutonium (244)	95 **Am** Americium (243)	96 **Cm** Curium (247)	97 **Bk** Berkelium (247)	98 **Cf** Californium (251)	99 **Es** Einsteinium (252)	100 **Fm** Fermium (257)	101 **Md** Mendelevium (258)	102 **No** Nobelium (259)

17.9 The Phases of Matter

⊘ **Matter exists in four phases: solid, liquid, gaseous, and plasma.** In the **plasma** phase, matter consists of positive ions and free electrons. These charged particles make plasma a great conductor of electricity. The plasma phase exists only at high temperatures. Although plasma is less common to our everyday experience, it is the predominant phase of matter in the universe. The sun and other stars as well as much of the intergalactic matter are in the plasma phase. Closer to home, the glowing gas in a fluorescent tube is a plasma, as are the gases of the aurora borealis, shown in Figure 17.13.

In all phases of matter, the atoms are constantly in motion. In the solid phase, the atoms and molecules vibrate about fixed positions. If the rate of molecular vibration is increased enough, molecules will shake apart and wander throughout the material, jostling in nonfixed positions. The shape of the material is no longer fixed but takes the shape of its container. This is the liquid phase. If more energy is put into the material so that the molecules move about at even greater rates, they may break away from one another and become a gas.

All substances can be transformed from one phase to another. We often observe this changing of phase in the compound H_2O. When solid, it is ice. If we heat the ice, the increased molecular motion jiggles the molecules out of their fixed positions, and we have liquid water. If we heat the water, we can reach a stage where the continued increase in molecular motion results in a separation between water molecules, and we have steam. Continued heating causes the molecules to separate into atoms. If we heat these to temperatures exceeding 2000°C, the atoms themselves will be shaken apart, making a gas of ions and free electrons. Then we have a plasma.

Watch for superheated plasma torches that create more electricity than they consume as they incinerate trash, making today's landfills history.

CONCEPT CHECK What are the four phases of matter?

◀ **FIGURE 17.13**
The aurora borealis is light given off by glowing plasma. High-altitude gases in the northern sky are transformed into glowing plasmas by the bombardment of charged particles from the sun. Less spectacular plasmas are found in glowing fluorescent tubes and advertising signs.

Go **O**nline
PHSchool.com

For: Self-Assessment
Visit: PHSchool.com
Web Code: csa – 1700

Concept Summary ......

- Every simple, complex, living, or nonliving substance is put together from a pantry containing less than 100 elements.

- Atoms are so small that there are about 10^{23} in a gram of water (a thimbleful).

- Atoms in your body have been around since long before the solar system came into existence, more than 4.6 billion years ago.

- Brownian motion is evidence that atoms exist, as it results from the motion of neighboring atoms and molecules. They bump into the larger particles we can see.

- Molecules can be made up of atoms of the same elements or of different elements.

- Compounds have properties different from those of the elements of which they are made.

- The mass of an atom is primarily concentrated in the nucleus.

- The arrangement of electrons in the shells around the atomic nucleus dictates the atom's chemical properties.

- Matter exists in four phases: solid, liquid, gaseous, and plasma.

Key Terms ......

atoms (*p. 325*)

element (*p. 325*)

Brownian motion (*p. 328*)

molecule (*p. 330*)

compound (*p. 331*)

chemical formula (*p. 331*)

nucleus (*p. 331*)

nucleons (*p. 332*)

neutrons (*p. 332*)

protons (*p. 332*)

isotopes (*p. 333*)

atomic number (*p. 333*)

ion (*p. 334*)

shell model of the atom (*p. 335*)

periodic table (*p. 335*)

plasma (*p. 337*)

think! Answers

17.2 Yes, and of physicist Richard Feynman too. However, these atoms are combined differently than they were before. The next time you feel insignificant, take comfort in the thought that many of the atoms that compose you will be part of the bodies of all the people on Earth who are yet to be! In this sense, our atoms at least, *are* immortal.

17.3 The mass of Earth does increase by the addition of roughly 40,000 tons of interplanetary dust each year. But the increasing number of people does not increase the mass of the Earth. The atoms that make up our body are the same atoms that were here before we were born. The atoms that make up a baby forming in the mother's womb must be supplied by the food she eats. And those atoms were formed in the stars that have long since exploded.

Check Concepts ......

Section 17.1

1. Approximately how many elements are known today?

2. Which element has the lightest atoms?

Section 17.2

3. How does the approximate number of atoms in the air in your lungs compare with the number of breaths of air in the atmosphere of the whole world?

4. From where did the heaviest elements originate?

5. How do the sizes of atoms compare with the wavelengths of visible light?

Section 17.3

6. How does the age of most atoms compare with the age of the solar system?

7. What is meant by the statement that you don't "own" the atoms that make up your body?

Section 17.4

8. What causes dust particles to move with Brownian motion?

9. Individual atoms cannot be seen with visible light; yet there is an image of individual atoms in Figure 17.4. Explain.

10. What is the purpose of a model in science?

Section 17.5

11. Distinguish between an atom and a molecule.

12. a. How many elements compose pure water?
    b. How many individual atoms are there in a water molecule?

13. a. Cite an example of a substance that is made of molecules.
    b. Cite a substance that is made of atoms rather than molecules.

14. True or false: We smell things because certain molecules are attracted to our noses.

Section 17.6

15. a. What is a compound?
    b. Cite the chemical formulas for at least three compounds.

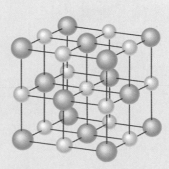

ASSESS (continued)

Section 17.7

16. What did Rutherford discover when his group bombarded a thin foil of gold with subatomic particles?

17. How does the mass of an atomic nucleus compare with the mass of the whole atom?

18. How does the size of an atomic nucleus compare with the size of the whole atom?

19. What are the two kinds of nucleons?

20. a. What is an isotope?
b. Give two examples of isotopes.

21. How does the atomic number of an element compare with the number of protons in its nucleus?

22. How does the atomic number of an element compare with the number of electrons that normally surround the nucleus?

Section 17.8

23. How does the mass of an electron compare with the mass of a nucleon?

24. a. What is an ion?
b. Give two examples of ions.

25. At the atomic level, a solid block of iron is mostly empty space. Explain.

26. What is the periodic table of the elements?

27. What does the atomic number of an element tell you about the element?

28. According to the shell model of the atom, how many electron shells are there in the hydrogen atom? The lithium atom? The aluminum atom?

Section 17.9

29. What are the four phases of matter?

30. In terms of electrical conduction, how does a plasma differ from a gas?

31. How many types of atoms can you expect to find in a pure sample of any element?

32. How many individual atoms are in a water molecule?

Think and Explain ······

33. Which of these formulas represent pure elements? H_2, H_2O, He, Na, NaCl, Au, U

34. Which are older, the atoms in the body of an elderly person, or those in a baby?

35. A cat strolls across your backyard. An hour later, a dog with his nose to the ground follows the trail of the cat. Explain this occurrence from a molecular point of view.

36. Suppose you smell the shaving lotion your brother is wearing almost immediately after he walks into the room. From an atomic point of view, exactly what is happening?

37. If no molecules in a body could escape, would the body have any odor?

38. A kitten will add several kilograms to its mass as it grows into a full-sized cat. From where do the atoms that make up this added mass originate?

39. Where were the atoms that make up a new-born baby manufactured?

40. Although you can't see an atom through a microscope, at some point a clump of atoms is large enough to see as a "dot" through a microscope. What determines when the clump of atoms is big enough to be seen?

41. Why is Brownian motion apparent only for microscopic particles?

42. Atoms are mostly empty space, and structures such as a floor are composed of atoms and are therefore also mostly empty space. Why don't you fall through the floor?

43. What element will result if a proton is added to the nucleus of carbon? (See periodic table.)

44. If two protons and two neutrons are removed from the nucleus of an oxygen atom, what nucleus remains?

45. What element results if you add a pair of protons to the nucleus of mercury? (See periodic table.)

46. What element results if one of the neutrons in a nitrogen nucleus is converted by radioactive decay into a proton?

47. What element will result if two protons and two neutrons are ejected from a uranium nucleus?

48. In what way does the number of protons in an atomic nucleus dictate the chemical properties of the element?

49. What element results if two protons and two neutrons are ejected from a radium nucleus?

50. You could swallow a capsule of the element germanium without harm. But if a proton were added to each of the germanium nuclei, you would not want to swallow the capsule. Why?

51. A particular atom contains 29 electrons, 34 neutrons, and 29 protons. What is the identity of this element and what is its atomic number?

52. The atomic masses of two isotopes of cobalt are 59 and 60.
    a. What is the number of protons and neutrons in each?
    b. What is the number of orbiting electrons in each when the isotopes are electrically neutral?

53. When an atom loses an electron and becomes a positively charged ion, how significant is the change in the atom's mass?

54. One isotope of lead has 82 protons and 124 neutrons in its nucleus. What can you say about the number of protons in the nucleus of any other isotope of lead?

55. Which contributes more to an atom's mass—electrons or protons? Which contributes more to an atom's size?

56. An ozone molecule and an oxygen molecule are pure oxygen. How are they different?

57. Is it possible to have a molecule that isn't a compound? Give an example.

58. Is it possible to have a compound that isn't made up of molecules? Give an example.

59. If you eat metallic sodium or inhale chlorine gas, you run a great risk of dying. When these two elements combine, however, you can safely sprinkle the resulting compound on your popcorn for better taste. What is going on?

60. To become a negative ion, does an atom lose or gain an electron?

61. To become a positive ion, does an atom lose or gain an electron?

62. Helium is an inert gas, meaning that it doesn't readily combine with other elements. What five other elements would you also expect to be inert gases? (See the periodic table.)

63. Why don't equal masses of golf balls and table-tennis balls contain the same number of balls? Also, why don't equal masses of pure carbon and oxygen contain the same number of atoms?

64. Which contains more atoms: 1 kg of lead or 1 kg of aluminum?

65. In a gaseous mixture of hydrogen and oxygen molecules, both with the same average kinetic energy, which molecules move faster on average?

66. A hydrogen atom and a carbon atom have the same speed. Which has the greater kinetic energy?

67. In what sense is it correct to say that much of a tree is solidified air?

68. The phases of matter are solid, liquid, gas, and plasma. What does the addition or subtraction of heat have to do with changes of phase?

69. Write a letter to your grandparents that discusses the importance of the periodic table of elements. Also tell them what you've learned about the differences among atoms, elements, and molecules.

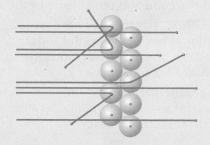

Think and Solve ......

70. Show that there are 16 grams of oxygen in 18 grams of water.

71. Show that there are 4 grams of hydrogen in 16 grams of methane gas. (The chemical formula for methane is CH_4.)

72. A typical atom is around 2×10^{-10} m in diameter, while a baby's hair is about 2×10^{-5} m in thickness. How many atoms thick is a typical baby's hair?

73. A typical atom is around 2×10^{-10} m in diameter, while a typical bacterium is about 10^{-6} m in diameter. How many atoms thick is the typical bacterium?

74. Gas A is composed of diatomic molecules (two atoms to a molecule) of a pure element. Gas B is composed of monatomic molecules (one atom to a molecule) of another pure element. Gas A has three times the mass of an equal volume of gas B at the same temperature and pressure. How do the atomic masses of elements A and B compare?

SOLIDS

THE BIG IDEA Solids can be described in terms of crystal structure, density, and elasticity.

Humans have been classifying and using solid materials for many thousands of years. The names Stone Age, Bronze Age, and Iron Age tell us the importance of solid materials in the development of civilization. Wood and clay were perhaps the first materials important to early peoples, and gems were put to use for art and adornment.

Not until recent times has the discovery of atoms and their interactions made it possible to understand the structure of materials. We have progressed from being finders and assemblers of materials to actual makers of materials. In today's laboratories chemists, metallurgists, and materials scientists routinely design and produce new materials to meet specific needs.

discover!

How Does Size Affect the Relationship Between Surface Area and Volume?

1. Place a single sugar cube on your desk.
2. Using additional sugar cubes, construct the next largest cube possible—that is, a cube with two sugar cubes on a side.
3. Now construct a cube with three sugar cubes on a side.

Analyze and Conclude

1. **Observing** What happened to the surface area of the cube and the volume of the cube as the length of a side increased?
2. **Predicting** What would be the surface area and volume of a cube with four sugar cubes on a side? Five sugar cubes on a side?
3. **Making Generalizations** What happens to the ratio of surface area to volume as an object's linear dimensions increase?

18.1 Crystal Structure

When we look at samples of minerals such as quartz, mica, or galena, we see many smooth, flat surfaces at angles to one another within the mineral. The mineral samples are made of **crystals,** or regular geometric shapes whose component particles are arranged in an orderly, repeating pattern. ⊘ **The shape of a crystal mirrors the geometric arrangement of atoms within the crystal.** The mineral samples themselves may have very irregular shapes, as if they were tiny cubes or other small units stuck together to make a free-form solid sculpture.

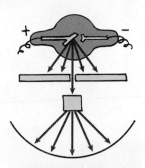

Not all crystals are evident to the naked eye. Their existence in many solids was not discovered until X-rays became a tool of research early in the twentieth century. The X-ray pattern caused by X-rays passing through the crystal structure of common table salt (sodium chloride) is shown in Figure 18.1. Rays from the X-ray tube are blocked by a lead screen except for a narrow beam that hits the crystal of sodium chloride. The radiation that penetrates the crystal produces the pattern shown on the photographic film beyond the crystal. The white spot in the center is caused by the main unscattered beam of X-rays. The size and arrangement of the other spots indicate the arrangement of sodium and chlorine atoms in the crystal. All crystals of sodium chloride produce this same design.

FIGURE 18.1 ▲
When X-rays pass through a crystal of common table salt (sodium chloride), they produce a distinctive pattern on photographic film.

The patterns made by X-rays on photographic film show that the atoms in a crystal have an orderly arrangement. Every crystalline structure has its own unique X-ray pattern. For example, in a sodium chloride crystal, the atoms are arranged like a three-dimensional chess board or a child's jungle gym, as shown in Figure 18.2.

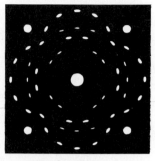

◀ **FIGURE 18.2**
In this model of a sodium chloride crystal, the large spheres represent chloride ions, and the small ones represent sodium ions.

Metals such as iron, copper, and gold have relatively simple crystal structures. Tin and cobalt are only slightly more complex. You can see metal crystals if you look carefully at a metal surface that has been cleaned (etched) with acid.

You can also see them on the surface of galvanized iron that has been exposed to the weather, or on brass doorknobs that have been etched by the perspiration of hands.

CONCEPT CHECK: What determines the shape of a crystal?

FIGURE 18.3 ▶
When the loaf of bread is squeezed, its volume decreases and its density increases.

18.2 Density

One of the properties of solids, as well as liquids and even gases, is the measure of how tightly the material is packed together: density. **Density** is a measure of how much matter occupies a given space; it is the amount of mass per unit volume:

$$\text{density} = \frac{\text{mass}}{\text{volume}}$$

The symbol for density is the Greek letter ρ.

Density is not mass and it is not volume. Density is a ratio; it is the amount of mass per unit volume. Density is a property of a material; it doesn't matter how much you have. A pure iron nail has the same density as a pure iron frying pan. The frying pan may have 100 times as many iron atoms and have 100 times as much mass, but its atoms will take up 100 times as much space. The mass per unit volume for the iron nail and the iron frying pan is the same.

 ⊘ **The density of a material depends upon the masses of the individual atoms that make it up, and the spacing between those atoms.** Iridium, a hard, brittle, silvery-white metal in the platinum family, is the densest substance on Earth, even though an individual iridium atom is less massive than individual atoms of gold, mercury, lead, or uranium. The close spacing of iridium atoms in an iridium crystal gives it the greatest density. A cubic centimeter of iridium contains more atoms than a cubic centimeter of gold or uranium.

Table 18.1 lists the densities of a few materials in units of grams per cubic centimeter.[18.2.1] Density varies somewhat with temperature and pressure, so, except for water, densities are given at 0°C and atmospheric pressure. Note that water at 4°C has a density of 1.00 g/cm³. The gram was originally defined as the mass of a cubic centimeter of water at a temperature of 4°C. A gold brick, with a density of 19.3 g/cm³, is 19.3 times more massive than an equal volume of water.

think!

Which has greater density—1 kg of water or 10 kg of water? 5 kg of lead or 10 kg of aluminum?
Answer: 18.2.1

Table 18.1	Densities of a Few Substances		
Solids	Density (g/cm³)	Liquids	Density (g/cm³)
Iridium	22.7	Mercury	13.6
Osmium	22.6	Glycerin	1.26
Platinum	21.4	Sea water	1.03
Gold	19.3	Water at 4°C	1.00
Uranium	19.0	Benzene	0.90
Lead	11.3	Ethyl alcohol	0.81
Silver	10.5		
Copper	8.9		
Brass	8.6		
Iron	7.8		
Steel	7.8		
Tin	7.3		
Diamond	3.5		
Aluminum	2.7		
Graphite	2.25		
Ice	0.92		
Pine wood	0.50		
Balsa wood	0.12		

Go Online
SciLINKS NSTA

For: Links on density
Visit: www.SciLinks.org
Web Code: csn – 1802

A quantity known as **weight density** can be expressed by the amount of *weight* a body has per unit volume:

$$\text{weight density} = \frac{\text{weight}}{\text{volume}}$$

Weight density is commonly used when discussing liquid pressure (see next chapter).[18.2.2]

A standard measure of density is **specific gravity** —the ratio of the mass (or weight) of a substance to the mass (or weight) of an equal volume of water. For example, if a substance weighs five times as much as an equal volume of water, its specific gravity is 5. Or put another way, specific gravity is a ratio of the density of a material to the density of water. So specific gravity has no units (density units divided by density units cancel). If you want to know the specific gravity of any material listed in Table 18.1, it's there. The magnitude of its density is its specific gravity.

think!

The density of gold is 19.3 g/cm³. What is its specific gravity?
Answer: 18.2.2

CONCEPT CHECK: What determines the density of a material?

do the math!

Suppose you have a gold nugget with a mass of 57.9 g and a volume of 3.00 cm³. How can you determine if the nugget is pure gold?

One of the reasons gold was used as money was that it is one of the densest of all substances and could therefore be easily identified. A merchant suspicious that gold was diluted with a less valuable substance had only to compute its density by measuring its mass and dividing by its volume. The merchant would then compare this value with the density of gold, 19.3 g/cm³.

Compute its density as follows:

$$\text{density} = \frac{\text{mass}}{\text{volume}} = \frac{57.9 \text{ g}}{3.00 \text{ cm}^3} = 19.3 \text{ g/cm}^3$$

Its density matches that of gold, so the nugget can be presumed to be pure gold. (It is possible to get the same density by mixing gold with a platinum alloy, but this is unlikely since platinum has several times the value of gold.)

18.3 Elasticity

When we hang a weight on a spring, the spring stretches. When we add additional weights, the spring stretches still more. When we remove the weights, the spring returns to its original length. A material that returns to its original shape after it has been stretched or compressed is said to be **elastic.**

When a batter hits a baseball, the bat temporarily changes the ball's shape. When an archer shoots an arrow, he first bends the bow, which springs back to its original form when the arrow is released. The spring, the baseball, and the bow are examples of elastic objects.

⊘ **A body's elasticity describes how much it changes shape when a deforming force acts on it, and how well it returns to its original shape when the deforming force is removed.**

Not all materials return to their original shape when a deforming force is applied and then removed. Materials that do not resume their original shape after being distorted are said to be **inelastic.** Clay, putty, and dough are inelastic materials. Lead is also inelastic, since it is easy to distort it permanently.

FIGURE 18.4 ▼

The bow is elastic. When the deforming force is removed, the bow returns to its original shape.

When you hang a weight on a spring, the weight applies a force to the spring. It is found that the stretch is directly proportional to the applied force, as shown in Figure 18.5.

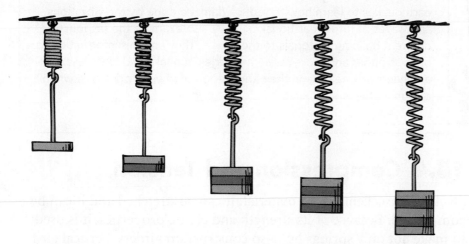

◀ **FIGURE 18.5**
The stretch of the spring is directly proportional to the applied force. When the weight is doubled, the spring stretches twice as much.

This relationship was noted by the British physicist Robert Hooke, a contemporary of Isaac Newton, in the mid-seventeenth century. According to **Hooke's law,** the amount of stretch (or compression), x, is directly proportional to the applied force F. Double the force and you double the stretch; triple the force and you get three times the stretch, and so on. In equation form,

$$F \sim \Delta x$$

If an elastic material is stretched or compressed more than a certain amount, it will not return to its original state. Instead, it will remain distorted. The distance at which permanent distortion occurs is called the **elastic limit.** Hooke's law holds only as long as the force does not stretch or compress the material beyond its elastic limit.

In lab, you'll learn that the ratio of force to stretch for a spring is called the spring constant (k), and Hooke's law can be written as $F = k\Delta x$, where k is expressed in N/m.

CONCEPT : What characteristics are described by an
CHECK : object's elasticity?

think!

A certain tree branch is found to obey Hooke's law. When a 20-kg load is hung from the end of it, the branch sags a distance of 10 cm. If, instead, a 40-kg load is hung from the same place, by how much will the branch sag? What would you find if a 60-kg load were hung from the same place? (Assume that none of these loads makes the branch sag beyond its elastic limit.)
Answer: 18.3.1

If a force of 10 N stretches a certain spring 4 cm, how much stretch will occur for an applied force of 15 N?
Answer: 18.3.2

Civil Engineer Devastating earthquakes strike in many parts of the world. Civil engineers study the collapsed structures left by earthquakes to learn how to reduce damage done by the vibrations and waves of future earthquakes. They also examine the responses of different building materials to the quake. They use this information to build stronger and more resilient bridges, tunnels, and highways. Civil engineers rely heavily on their knowledge of physics principles when designing these structures.

18.4 Compression and Tension

A beam in the position of the one below in Figure 18.6 is known as a cantilever beam.

Steel is an excellent elastic material. It can be stretched and it can be compressed. Because of its strength and elastic properties, it is used to make not only springs but also construction girders. Vertical girders of steel used in the construction of tall buildings undergo only slight compression. A typical 25-meter-long vertical girder used in high-rise construction is compressed about a millimeter when it carries a 10-ton load. Most deformation occurs when girders are used horizontally, where the tendency is to sag under heavy loads.

☑ **A horizontal beam supported at one or both ends is under stress from the load it supports, including its own weight. It undergoes a stress of both compression and tension (stretching).** Consider the beam supported at one end in Figure 18.6. It sags because of its own weight and because of the load it carries at its end.

FIGURE 18.6 ▶
The top part of the beam is stretched and the bottom part is compressed. The middle portion is neither stretched nor compressed.

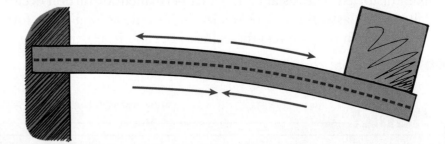

Neutral Layer Can you see that the top part of the beam is stretched? Atoms are tugged away from one another. The top part is slightly longer. And can you see that the bottom part of the beam is compressed? Atoms there are pushed toward one another, making the bottom part slightly shorter. So the top part of the beam is stretched, and the bottom part is compressed. A little thought will show that somewhere in between the top and bottom, there will be a region that is neither stretched nor compressed. This is the *neutral layer* (indicated by the red dashed line in the figure).

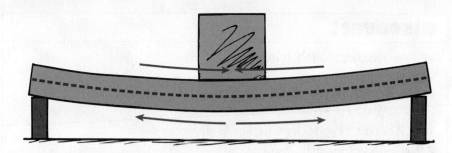

Consider the beam shown in Figure 18.7. It is supported at both ends, and carries a load in the middle. This time the top of the beam is in compression and the bottom is in tension. Again, there is a neutral layer along the middle portion of the length of the beam where neither tension nor compression occurs.

I-Beams Have you ever wondered why the cross section of many steel girders has the form of the letter I, as shown in Figure 18.8? Most of the material in these I-beams is concentrated in the top and bottom parts, called the *flanges*. The piece joining the bars, called the *web*, is thinner. Why is it shaped like this?

The answer is that the stress is predominantly in the top and bottom flanges when the beam is used horizontally in construction. One flange tends to be stretched while the other tends to be compressed. The web between the top and bottom flanges is a region of low stress that acts principally to hold the top and bottom flanges apart. Heavier loads are supported by farther-apart flanges. For this purpose, comparatively little material is needed. An I-beam is nearly as strong as a solid bar, and its weight is considerably less.

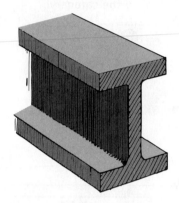

FIGURE 18.8 ▲
An I-beam is like a solid bar with some of the steel scooped from its middle where it is needed least. The beam is therefore lighter for nearly the same strength.

CONCEPT : How is a horizontal beam affected by the
CHECK : load it supports?

---

think!

If you had to make a hole horizontally through the tree branch shown, in a location that would weaken it the least, would you bore it through the top, the middle, or the bottom?

Answer: 18.4

discover!

Why construct with triangles?

You have probably noticed triangular shapes in steel bridges and sports domes. You can verify for yourself the structural merits of the triangle.

1. Nail or bolt three sticks together as shown below.
2. Nail or bolt four sticks together.
3. **Think** How well do the two shapes resist collapse when you apply pressure on them?

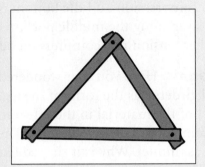

Link to ARCHITECTURE

The Catenary Tension in a stretched rope lies along the direction of the rope, and likewise for a taut chain. Tension between chain links lie along the direction of the chain, even when the chain sags. The curved shape of a rope or chain that sags under its own weight is a catenary. In the photo at the right, both the curve of the sagging chain and the Gateway Arch in the background are catenaries.

In a free-standing stone arch, stones press against one another, producing compression between them. An arch that takes the shape of an inverted catenary is extremely stable because compression within it occurs exactly along the curve. Even a catenary arch made of slippery blocks of ice is stable, for compression only presses the blocks firmly together with no side components of force. The same is true for the catenary arch that graces the city of St. Louis.

If you twirl an arch through a complete circle, you have a dome. The weight of the dome, like that of the arch, produces compression. The catenary shape applied to domes was not appreciated by those who built early domes such as the Notre Dame Cathedral in Paris, which required elaborate buttressing. One of the first successful domes without buttressing was St. Paul's Cathedral in London, designed by Christopher Wren. Its curved shape, a catenary, was suggested by Robert Hooke. Modern domes since then, such as the Astrodome in Houston, employ the catenary shape.

18.5 Scaling

Did you ever notice how strong an ant is for its size? An ant can carry the weight of several ants on its back, whereas a strong elephant could not even carry one elephant on its back. How strong would an ant be if it were scaled up to the size of an elephant? Would this "super ant" be several times stronger than an elephant? Surprisingly, the answer is no. Such an ant would not be able to lift its own weight off the ground. Its legs would be too thin for its greater weight and would likely break.

Ants have thin legs and elephants have thick legs for a reason. The proportions of things in nature are in accord with their size. The study of how size affects the relationship between weight, strength, and surface area is known as **scaling.** As the size of a thing increases, it grows heavier much faster than it grows stronger. You can support a toothpick horizontally at its ends, and you'll notice no sag. But support a tree of the same kind of wood horizontally at its ends and you'll see a noticeable sag. The tree is not as strong per unit mass as the toothpick is.

Galileo studied scaling and described the different bone sizes of various creatures.

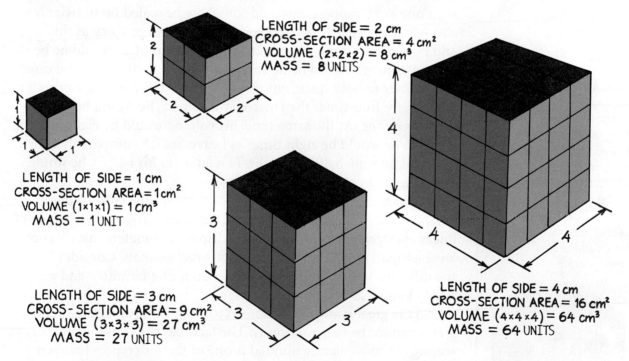

LENGTH OF SIDE = 2 cm
CROSS-SECTION AREA = 4 cm²
VOLUME (2×2×2) = 8 cm³
MASS = 8 UNITS

LENGTH OF SIDE = 1 cm
CROSS-SECTION AREA = 1 cm²
VOLUME (1×1×1) = 1 cm³
MASS = 1 UNIT

LENGTH OF SIDE = 3 cm
CROSS-SECTION AREA = 9 cm²
VOLUME (3×3×3) = 27 cm³
MASS = 27 UNITS

LENGTH OF SIDE = 4 cm
CROSS-SECTION AREA = 16 cm²
VOLUME (4×4×4) = 64 cm³
MASS = 64 UNITS

FIGURE 18.9 ▲

If the linear dimensions of an object are multiplied by some number, then the area will grow by the square of the number, and the volume (and mass and weight) will grow by the cube of the number. If the linear dimensions of the cube grow by 2, the area will grow by $2^2 = 4$, and the volume will grow by $2^3 = 8$. If the linear dimensions grow by 3, the area will grow by $3^2 = 9$, and the volume will grow by $3^3 = 27$.

think!

Suppose a cube 1 cm long on each side were scaled up to a cube 10 cm long on each edge. What would be the volume of the scaled-up cube? What would be its cross-sectional surface area? Its total surface area?

Answer: 18.5

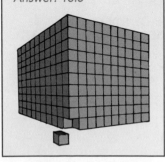

How Scaling Affects Strength Weight depends on volume, and strength comes from the area of the cross section of limbs—tree limbs or animal limbs. To understand this weight-strength relationship, let's consider the simple case of a solid cube of matter, 1 centimeter on a side.

A 1-cubic-centimeter cube has a cross section of 1 square centimeter. That is, if we sliced through the cube parallel to one of its faces, the sliced area would be 1 square centimeter. Compare this to a cube made of the same material that has double the linear dimensions, a cube 2 centimeters on each side. Its cross-sectional area will be 2×2 (or 4) square centimeters, and its volume will be $2 \times 2 \times 2$ (or 8) cubic centimeters. It will be eight times more massive.

☑ **When linear dimensions are enlarged, the cross-sectional area (as well as the total surface area) grows as the square of the enlargement, whereas volume and weight grow as the cube of the enlargement.** These relationships are illustrated in Figure 18.9.

The volume (and weight) increases much faster than the corresponding enlargement of cross-sectional area. Although the figure demonstrates the simple example of a cube, the principle applies to an object of any shape. Consider an athlete who can lift his weight with one arm. Suppose he could somehow be scaled up to twice his size—that is, twice as tall, twice as broad, his bones twice as thick, and every linear dimension enlarged by a factor of 2. Would he be twice as strong? Would he be able to lift himself with twice the ease? The answer to both questions is no. Since his twice-as-thick arms would have four times the cross-sectional area, he would be four times as strong. At the same time, his volume would be eight times as great, so he would be eight times as heavy. So, for comparable effort, he could lift only half his weight. *In relation to his weight*, he would be weaker than before.

The fact that volume (and weight) grows as the cube of linear enlargement, while strength (and surface area) grows as the square of linear enlargement is evident in the disproportionately thick legs of large animals compared with those of small animals. Consider the different legs of an elephant and a deer, or a tarantula and a daddy longlegs.

So the great strengths attributed to King Kong and other fictional giants cannot be taken seriously. The fact that the consequences of scaling are conveniently omitted is one of the differences between science and science fiction.

CONCEPT CHECK: If the linear dimensions of an object double, by how much will the cross-sectional area grow?

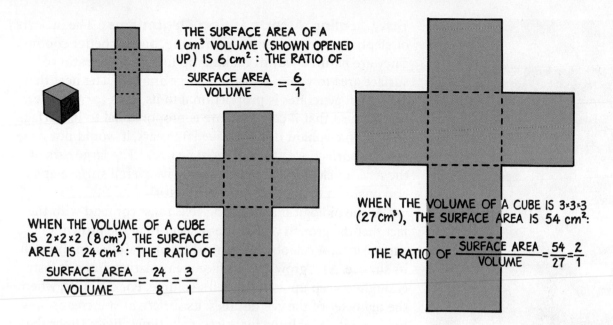

THE SURFACE AREA OF A 1 cm³ VOLUME (SHOWN OPENED UP) IS 6 cm² : THE RATIO OF

$$\frac{SURFACE\ AREA}{VOLUME} = \frac{6}{1}$$

WHEN THE VOLUME OF A CUBE IS 2×2×2 (8 cm³) THE SURFACE AREA IS 24 cm² : THE RATIO OF

$$\frac{SURFACE\ AREA}{VOLUME} = \frac{24}{8} = \frac{3}{1}$$

WHEN THE VOLUME OF A CUBE IS 3×3×3 (27 cm³), THE SURFACE AREA IS 54 cm²:

THE RATIO OF $\frac{SURFACE\ AREA}{VOLUME} = \frac{54}{27} = \frac{2}{1}$

FIGURE 18.10 ▲
As an object grows proportionally in all directions, there is a greater increase in volume than in surface area. As a result, the ratio of surface area to volume decreases.

How Scaling Affects Surface Area vs. Volume Important also is the comparison of total surface area with volume. Look at Figure 18.10. ✅ **As the linear size of an object increases, the volume grows faster than the total surface area.** (Volume grows as the cube of the enlargement, and both cross-sectional area and total surface area grow as the square of the enlargement.) So as an object grows, the surface area to volume ratio *decreases*. The following examples may be helpful.

An experienced cook knows that more skin results when peeling 5 kg of small potatoes than when peeling 5 kg of large potatoes. Smaller objects have more surface area per kilogram. Since cooling occurs at the surfaces of objects, crushed ice will cool a drink much faster than a single ice cube of the same mass. This is because crushed ice presents more surface area to the beverage.

The rusting of iron is also a surface phenomenon. The greater the amount of surface exposed to the air, the faster rusting takes place. That's why small filings and iron in the form of "steel wool," which have large surfaces compared with their volumes, are soon eaten away. The same mass of iron packed in a solid cube or sphere would undergo little rusting in comparison.

Chunks of coal burn, while coal dust explodes when ignited. Thin French fries cook faster in oil than fat fries. Flat hamburgers cook faster than meatballs of the same mass. Large raindrops fall faster than small raindrops, and large fish move faster than small fish. These are all consequences of the fact that volume and area are not in direct proportion to each other.

A sphere has less surface area per volume of material than any other shape. When a fat ball-shaped burger is flattened, its surface area increases—which allows greater heat transfer from the grill to the burger.

FIGURE 18.11 ▲
The African elephant has less surface area compared with its weight than other animals. It compensates for this with its large ears, which significantly increase the surface area through which heat is dissipated, and promote cooling.

How Scaling Affects Living Organisms   The big ears of elephants are not for better hearing, but for better cooling. They are nature's way of making up for the small ratio of surface area to volume for these large animals. The heat that an animal generates is proportional to its mass (or volume), but the heat that it can dissipate is proportional to its surface area. If an elephant did not have large ears, it would not have enough surface area to cool its huge mass. The large ears of the African elephant greatly increase its overall surface area, and enable it to cool off in hot climates.

At the biological level, living cells must contend with the fact that the growth of volume is faster than the growth of surface area. A cell obtains nourishment by diffusion through its surface. As it grows, its surface area enlarges, but not fast enough to keep up with the cell's volume. For example, when the diameter of the cell doubles, its surface area increases four times, while its volume increases eight times. Eight times the mass must be sustained by only four times the access to nourishment. This puts a limit on the growth of a living cell. So cells divide, and there is life as we know it. That's nice.

Not so nice is the fate of large animals when they fall. The statement "the bigger they are, the harder they fall" holds true and is a consequence of the small ratio of surface area to weight. Air resistance to movement through the air depends on the surface area of the moving object. If you fell off a cliff, even with air resistance, for a short time your speed would increase at the rate of very nearly 1 *g*. You would have too little surface area relative to your weight—unless you wore a parachute. Small animals need no parachute. They have plenty of surface area relative to their small weights. An insect can fall from the top of a tree to the ground below without harm. The surface-area-to- weight ratio is in the insect's favor—in a sense, the insect is its own parachute.

It is interesting to note that the rate of heartbeat in a mammal is related to the size of the mammal. The heart of a tiny shrew beats about twenty times as fast as the heart of an elephant. In general, small mammals live fast and die young; larger animals live at a leisurely pace and live longer. Don't feel bad about a pet hamster that doesn't live as long as a dog. All warm-blooded animals have about the same life span—not in terms of years, but in the average number of heartbeats (about 800 million). Humans are the exception: we live two to three times longer than other mammals of our size.

CONCEPT CHECK : If the linear dimensions of an object double, by how much will the volume grow?

REVIEW

Go Online
PHSchool.com

For: Self-Assessment
Visit: PHSchool.com
Web Code: csa – 1800

Concept Summary ······

- The shape of a crystal mirrors the geometric arrangement of atoms within the crystal.

- The density of a material depends upon the masses of its individual atoms and the spacing between those atoms.

- A body's elasticity describes how much it changes shape when a deforming force acts on it, and how well it returns to its original shape when the deforming force is removed.

- A horizontal beam supported at one or both ends is under stress from the load it supports, including its own weight. It undergoes stresses of both compression and tension (stretching).

- When linear dimensions are enlarged, the cross-sectional area (as well as the total surface area) grows as the square of the enlargement, whereas volume and weight grow as the cube of the enlargement. As the linear size of an object increases, the volume grows faster than the total surface area.

Key Terms ······

crystal (p. 345)

density (p. 346)

weight density (p. 347)

specific gravity (p. 347)

elastic (p. 348)

inelastic (p. 348)

Hooke's law (p. 349)

elastic limit (p. 349)

scaling (p. 353)

think! Answers

18.2.1   The density of *any* amount of water (at 4°C) is 1.00 g/cm^3. Any amount of lead always has a greater density than any amount of aluminum; the amount of material is irrelevant.

18.2.2 $\dfrac{\text{density of gold}}{\text{density of water}} = \dfrac{19.3 \text{ g/cm}^3}{1.0 \text{ g/cm}^3} = 19.3$

18.3.1   A 40-kg load has twice the weight of a 20-kg load. In accord with Hooke's law, $F \sim \Delta x$, two times the applied force will result in two times the stretch, so the branch should sag 20 cm. The weight of the 60-kg load will make the branch sag three times as much, or 30 cm.

18.3.2   The spring will stretch 6 cm. By ratio and proportion:

$$\frac{10 \text{ N}}{4 \text{ cm}} = \frac{15 \text{ N}}{x}$$

Then $x = (15 \text{ N}) \times (4 \text{ cm})/(10 \text{ N}) = 6 \text{ cm}$.

18.4   Drill the hole through the middle. Wood fibers in the top part of the branch are stretched, and if you drill the hole there, tension in that part may pull the branch apart. Fibers in the lower part are compressed, and a hole there might crush under compression. In between, in the neutral layer, the hole will not affect the strength of the branch because fibers there are neither stretched nor compressed.

18.5   Volume of the scaled-up cube is (10 cm)^3, or 1000 cm^3. Its cross-sectional surface area is (10 cm)^2, or 100 cm^2. Its total surface area = 6 × 100 cm^2 = 600 cm^2.

Check Concepts · · · · · ·

Section 18.1

1. How does the arrangement of atoms differ in a crystalline and a noncrystalline substance?

2. What evidence do we have for the microscopic crystal nature of some solids?

3. What evidence do we have for the visible crystal nature of some solids?

Section 18.2

4. What happens to the density of a uniform piece of wood when we cut it in half?

5. Uranium is the heaviest atom found in nature. Why isn't uranium metal the most dense material?

6. Which has the greater density—a heavy bar of pure gold or a pure gold ring?

7. **a.** Does the mass of a loaf of bread change when you squeeze it?
   b. Does its volume change?
   c. Does its density change?

8. What is the difference between mass density and weight density?

Section 18.3

9. **a.** What is the evidence for the claim that steel is elastic?
   b. That putty is inelastic?

10. What is Hooke's law?

11. What is an elastic limit?

12. A 2-kg mass stretches a spring 3 cm. How far does the spring stretch when it supports 6 kg? (Assume the spring has not reached its elastic limit.)

Section 18.4

13. Is a steel beam slightly shorter when it stands vertically? Explain.

14. Where is the neutral layer in a horizontal beam that supports a load?

15. Why is the cross section of a metal beam I-shaped and not rectangular?

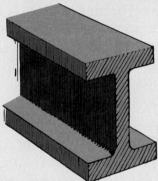

Section 18.5

16. What is the weight–strength relationship in scaling?

17. **a.** If the linear dimensions of an object are doubled, how much does the total area increase?
    b. How much does the volume increase?

18. True or false: As the volume of an object increases, its surface area also increases, but the *ratio* of surface area to volume decreases. Explain.

19. Which will cool a drink faster—a 10-gram ice cube or 10 grams of crushed ice?

20. a. Which has more skin—an elephant or a mouse?
   b. Which has more skin *per unit of body weight*—an elephant or a mouse?

Think and Explain ......

21. You take 1000 milligrams of a vitamin. Your friend takes 1 gram of the same vitamin. Who takes more?

22. Your friend says that the primary difference between a solid and a liquid is the kind of atoms in the material. Do you agree or disagree, and why?

23. How does the density of a 100-kg iron block compare with the density of an iron filing?

24. Which has more volume—a kilogram of lead or a kilogram of aluminum?

25. Which has more weight—a liter of ice or a liter of water?

26. A certain spring stretches 1 cm for each kilogram it supports.
   a. If the elastic limit is not reached, how far will it stretch when it supports a load of 8 kg?
   b. Suppose the spring is placed next to an identical spring so the two side-by-side springs equally share the 8-kg load. How far will each spring stretch?

27. A thick rope is stronger than a thin rope of the same material. Is a long rope stronger than a short rope?

28. When you bend a meterstick, one side is under tension, and the other is under compression. Which side is which?

29. Compression and tension stress occurs in a beam that supports a load (even when the load is its own weight). Show by means of a simple sketch an example where a horizontal load-carrying beam is in tension at the top and compression at the bottom. Then show a case where the opposite occurs: compression at the top and tension at the bottom.

30. Consider a model steel bridge that is 1/100 the exact scale of the real bridge that is to be built.
   a. If the model bridge weighs 50 N, what will the real bridge weigh?
   b. If the model bridge doesn't appear to sag under its own weight, is this evidence that the real bridge, built exactly to scale, will not appear to sag either? Explain.

31. Only with great difficulty can you crush an egg when squeezing it along its long axis, but it breaks easily if you squeeze it sideways. Why?

32. Archie designs an arch to serve as an outdoor sculpture in a park. The arch is to be a certain width and a certain height. To achieve the size and shape for the strongest arch, Archie suspends a chain from two supports of equal heights that are as far apart as the arch is wide. Archie allows the chain to hang as low as the arch is high. He builds the arch to have exactly the shape of the hanging chain, but inverted. Explain why.

33. Why is cement not needed between the stone blocks of an arch that has the shape of an inverted catenary?

34. If you use a batch of cake batter for cupcakes instead of a cake and bake them for the time suggested for baking a cake, what will be the result?

35. If you were trapped on a cold mountain, why would it make sense for you to sit in a crouched position and grab your knees? (*Hint:* A piece of wire will cool faster when stretched out than when rolled up into a ball.)

36. Animals lose heat through the surface areas of their skin. A small animal, such as a mouse, uses a much larger proportion of its energy to keep warm than does a large animal, such as an elephant. Why is the rate of heat loss per unit area greater in a small animal than a large one?

37. Why is heating more efficient in large apartment buildings than in single-family dwellings?

38. Some environmentally conscious people build their homes in the shape of domes. Why is less heat lost in a dome-shaped dwelling?

39. Why does crushed ice melt faster than the same mass of ice cubes?

40. Which fall faster, large or small raindrops?

Think and Solve ······

41. A one-cubic-centimeter cube has sides 1 cm in length. What is the length of the sides of a cube of volume two cubic centimeters?

42. A solid cube has sides 4.0 cm long and a mass of 672.0 g.
    a. What is the volume of the cube?
    b. What is the total surface area of the cube?
    c. What is the density of the cube?

43. A solid sphere has a radius of 2.0 cm and a mass of 352.0 g.
  a. What is the volume of the sphere?
  b. What is the surface area of the sphere? (A useful way to remember the formula for the area of a sphere is that it is 4 times the area of a circle of the same radius: $4\pi r^2$.)
  c. What is the density of the sphere?
  d. What can you say about the material used to make this sphere and the cube of the previous problem?

44. A solid 5.0-kg cylinder is 10 cm tall with a radius of 3.0 cm. Show that its density is 18 g/cm³.

45. A cube of metal 0.30 m to a side is said to be pure gold. Gold has a density of 1.93×10^4 kg/m³.
  a. What is the volume of the gold cube?
  b. Calculate the mass of the cube.
  c. Calculate the weight of the cube in newtons, and then in pounds (recall that 1 N = 0.22 lb). Could you lift it?

46. What is the weight of a cubic meter of cork? Could you lift it? (For the density of cork, use 400 kg/m³.)

47. A certain spring stretches 3 cm when a load of 15 N is suspended from it. How much will the spring stretch if 45 N is suspended from it (and the spring doesn't reach its elastic limit)?

48. If a certain spring stretches 4 cm when a load of 10 N is suspended from it, how much will the spring stretch if it is cut in half and 10 N is suspended from it?

49. Consider eight one-cubic-centimeter sugar cubes stacked two-by-two to form a single bigger cube. What will be the volume of the combined cube? How does its surface area compare to the total surface area of the eight separate cubes?

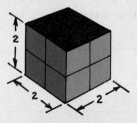

50. Consider eight little spheres of mercury, each with a diameter of 1 millimeter. When they coalesce to form a single sphere, how big will it be? How does its surface area compare to the total surface area of the previous eight little spheres?

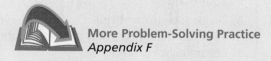

More Problem-Solving Practice
Appendix F

19 LIVE LIQUIDS

THE BIG IDEA : In the liquid phase, molecules can flow freely from position to position by sliding over one another. A liquid takes the shape of its container.

We live on the only planet in the solar system covered mostly by a liquid. Earth's oceans are made of H_2O in the liquid phase. If Earth were a little closer to the sun, the oceans would turn to vapor. If Earth were a little farther away, most of its surface, not just its polar regions, would be solid ice. It's nice that Earth is where it is.

In the liquid phase, molecules can flow freely from position to position by sliding over one another. A liquid takes the shape of its container.

discover!

When Does a Liquid Behave Like a Solid?

1. Put one cup of cornstarch in bowl.
2. While stirring, add ½ cup of water.
3. Try pushing on the mixture hard, then softly then stir the mixture quickly, then very slowly.
4. After pouring some of the mixture on the table, push on the puddle with the side of your hand.
5. Try to pick up mixture. Once you have it in your hands, try to keep it in solid form by continually kneading it.

Analyze and Conclude

1. **Observing** What is unusual about the mixture of cornstarch and water?
2. **Predicting** What do you suppose would happen if you were to try to play catch with the mixture?
3. **Making Generalizations** Can you think of other substances that change from a liquid to a solid state, or vice versa, when stressed?

19.1 Liquid Pressure

A liquid in a container exerts forces on the walls and bottom of the container. To investigate the interaction between the liquid and a surface, it is useful to discuss the concept of *pressure*. Recall from Chapter 6 that pressure is defined as the force per unit area on which the force acts.[19.1.1]

$$\text{pressure} = \frac{\text{force}}{\text{area}}$$

The pressure that a block exerts on a table is simply the weight of the block divided by its area of contact. Similarly, for a liquid in a cylindrical container like the one shown in Figure 19.1, the pressure the liquid exerts against the bottom of the container is the weight of the liquid divided by the area of the container bottom. (We'll ignore for now the additional atmospheric pressure.) ⊘ **The pressure of a liquid at rest depends only on gravity and the density and depth of the liquid.**

Density How much a liquid weighs, and thus how much pressure it exerts, depends on its density. Consider two identical containers, one filled with mercury and the other filled to the same depth with water. For the same depth, the denser liquid exerts more pressure. Mercury is 13.6 times as dense as water. So for the same volume of liquid, the weight of mercury is 13.6 times the weight of water. Thus, the pressure of mercury on the bottom is 13.6 times the pressure of water.

Depth For any given liquid, the pressure on the bottom of the container will be greater if the liquid is deeper. Consider the two containers in Figure 19.2a. The liquid in the first container is twice as deep as the liquid in the second container. As with the two blocks on top of each other in Figure 19.2b, liquid pressure at the bottom of the first container will be twice that of the second container.

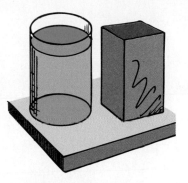

FIGURE 19.1 ▲
The liquid exerts a pressure against the bottom of its container, just as the block exerts a pressure against the table.

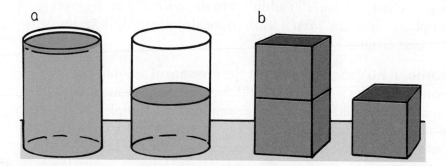

◀ **FIGURE 19.2**
Liquid pressure depends on depth. **a.** The liquid in the first container is twice as deep, so the pressure on the bottom is twice that exerted by the liquid in the second container. **b.** Similarly, the two blocks exert twice as much pressure on the table as one block.

Liquid pressure = ρgh

The pressure of a liquid at rest does not depend on the shape of the container or the size of its bottom surface. Liquids are practically incompressible, so except for changes in temperature, the density of a liquid is normally the same at all depths. The pressure created by a liquid[19.1.2] is

$$\text{pressure due to liquid } = \text{ density} \times g \times \text{depth}$$

At a given depth, a given liquid exerts the same pressure against *any* surface—the bottom or sides of its container, or even the surface of an object submerged in the liquid to that depth. The pressure a liquid exerts depends on its density and depth.

If you press your hand against a surface, and somebody else presses against your hand in the same direction, then the pressure against the surface is greater than if you pressed alone. Likewise with the atmospheric pressure that presses on the surface of a liquid. The total pressure of a liquid, then, is density × g × depth *plus* the pressure of the atmosphere. When this distinction is important we will use the term *total pressure.* Otherwise, our discussions of liquid pressure refer to pressure in addition to the normally ever-present atmospheric pressure. (You'll learn more about atmospheric pressure in the next chapter.)

Volume It may surprise you that the pressure of a liquid does not depend on the amount of liquid. Neither the volume nor even the total weight of liquid matters. For example, if you sampled water pressure at 1 meter beneath the surface of a large lake and 1 meter beneath the surface of a small pool, the pressures would be the same.[19.1.3] The dam that must withstand the greater pressure is the dam with the deepest water behind it, not the most water as shown in Figure 19.3.

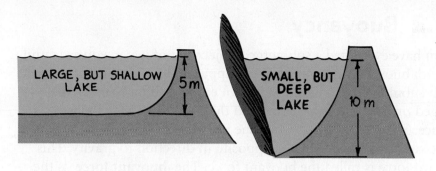

The water pressure is greater at the bottom of the deeper lake, not the lake with more water. The dam holding back water twice as deep must withstand greater average water pressure, regardless of the total volume of water.

The fact that water pressure depends on depth and not on volume is nicely illustrated with the "Pascal's vases" shown in Figure 19.4. Note that the water's surface in each of the connected vases is at the same level. This occurs because the pressures at equal depths beneath the surfaces are the same. At the bottom of all four vases, for example, the presures are equal. If they were not, liquid would flow until the pressures were equalized. This is why we say "water seeks its own level."

FIGURE 19.4 ▼
The pressure of the liquid is the same at any given depth below the surface, regardless of the shape of the container.

FIGURE 19.5 ▼
The forces in a liquid produce pressure. **a.** The forces against a surface add up to a net force that is perpendicular to the surface. **b.** Liquid escaping through a hole initially moves perpendicular to the surface.

At any point within a liquid, the forces that produce pressure are exerted equally in all directions. For example, when you are swimming under water, no matter which way you tilt your head, you feel the same amount of water pressure on your ears.

When the liquid is pressing against a surface, there is a force from the liquid directed perpendicular to the surface as shown in Figure 19.5a. If there is a hole in the surface, the liquid initially will move perpendicular to the surface. Gravity, of course, causes the path of the liquid to curve downward as shown in Figure 19.5b. At greater depths, the net force is greater, and the velocity of the escaping liquid is greater.

a

b

CONCEPT CHECK What determines the pressure of a liquid?

FIGURE 19.6 ▲
The upward forces against the bottom of a submerged object are greater than the downward forces against the top. There is a net upward force, the buoyant force.

Stick your foot in a swimming pool and your foot is immersed. Jump in and sink below the surface and immersion is total—you're submerged.

19.2 Buoyancy

If you have ever lifted a submerged object out of water, you are familiar with buoyancy. **Buoyancy** is the apparent loss of weight of objects when submerged in a liquid. It is a lot easier to lift a boulder submerged on the bottom of a riverbed than to lift it above the water's surface. The reason is that when the boulder is submerged, the water exerts an upward force that is opposite in direction to gravity. This upward force is called the buoyant force. The **buoyant force** is the net upward force exerted by a fluid on a submerged or immersed object.

To understand where the buoyant force comes from, look at Figure 19.6. The arrows represent the forces within the liquid that produce pressure against the submerged boulder. The forces are greater at greater depth. The forces acting horizontally against the sides cancel each other, so the boulder is not pushed sideways. But the forces acting upward against the bottom are greater than those acting downward against the top because the bottom of the boulder is deeper. The difference in upward and downward forces is the buoyant force.

⊘ **When the weight of a submerged object is greater than the buoyant force, the object will sink. When the weight is less than the buoyant force, the object will rise to the surface and float.** When the weight is equal to the buoyant force, the submerged object will remain at any level, like a fish.

To further understand buoyancy, it helps to think more about what happens when an object is placed in water. If a stone is placed in a container of water, the water level will rise as shown in Figure 19.7. Water is said to be displaced, or pushed aside, by the stone. A little thought will tell us that the volume—that is, the amount of space taken up, or the number of cubic centimeters—of water displaced is equal to the volume of the stone. *A completely submerged object always displaces a volume of liquid equal to its own volume.*

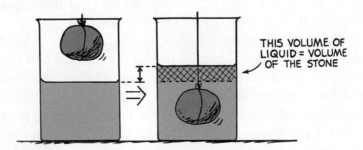

THIS VOLUME OF
LIQUID = VOLUME
OF THE STONE

FIGURE 19.7 ▲
When an object is submerged, it displaces a volume of water equal to the volume of the object itself.

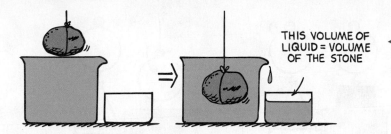

THIS VOLUME OF LIQUID = VOLUME OF THE STONE

As Figure 19.8 shows, this gives us a good way to determine the volume of an irregularly shaped object. Simply submerge it in water in a measuring cup and note the apparent increase in volume of the water. That increase is equal to the volume of the submerged object. You'll find this technique handy whenever you want to determine the density of things like rocks that have irregular shapes.

For: Links on buoyancy
Visit: www.SciLinks.org
Web Code: csn – 1902

CONCEPT CHECK What determines if an object will sink or float?

19.3 Archimedes' Principle

Archimedes' principle describes the relationship between buoyancy and displaced liquid. It was discovered in ancient times by the Greek philosopher Archimedes (third century B.C.). ☑ **Archimedes' principle states that the buoyant force on an immersed object is equal to the weight of the fluid it displaces.** Archimedes' principle is true for liquids and gases, which are both fluids.

Immersed means "either completely or partially submerged." For example, if we immerse a sealed 1-liter container like the one shown in Figure 19.9 halfway into water, it will displace half a liter of water and be buoyed up by the weight of half a liter of water. If we immerse it all the way (submerge it), it will be buoyed up by the weight of a full liter of water (10 newtons). Unless the completely submerged container becomes compressed, the buoyant force will equal the weight of 1 liter of water at *any* depth.[19.3] Why? Because the container will displace the same volume of water, and hence the same weight of water, at any depth. The weight of this displaced water (not the weight of the submerged object!) is the buoyant force.

think!

A 1-liter (L) container filled with mercury has a mass of 13.6 kg and weighs 136 N. When it is submerged in water, what is the buoyant force on it?
Answer: 19.3.1

◀ **FIGURE 19.9**
A liter of water occupies 1000 cubic centimeters, has a mass of 1 kilogram, and weighs 10 N. Any object with a volume of 1 liter will experience a buoyant force of 10 N when fully submerged in water.

FIGURE 19.10 ▶

A brick weighs less in water than in air. The buoyant force on the submerged brick is equal to the weight of the water displaced.

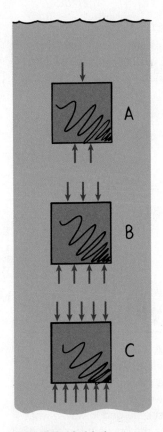

FIGURE 19.11 ▲

The difference in the upward force and the downward force acting on the submerged block is the same at any depth.

A 300-gram brick weighs about 3 N in air. Suppose as shown in Figure 19.10, the brick displaces 2 N of water when it is submerged. The buoyant force on the submerged brick will also equal 2 N. The brick will seem to weigh less under water than above water. The apparent weight of a submerged object is its weight in air minus the buoyant force. In the water, the block's apparent weight will be 3 N minus the 2-N buoyant force, or 1 N. So the block's appears lighter under water by an amount equal to the weight of water (2 N) that has spilled into the smaller container.

For any submerged block, the upward force due to water pressure on the bottom of the block, minus the downward force due to water pressure on the top, equals the weight of liquid displaced. As long as the block is submerged, depth makes no difference. Why? Because although there is more pressure at greater depths, the *difference* in pressures on the bottom and top of the block is the same at any depth as shown in Figure 19.11. Whatever the shape of a submerged object, the buoyant force equals the weight of liquid displaced.

CONCEPT CHECK What does Archimedes' principle state?

┌─ **think!** ─────────────────────────────────

A solid block is held suspended beneath the water in the three positions, A, B, and C, shown in Figure 19.11. In which position is the buoyant force on it greatest?
Answer: 19.3.2

A stone is thrown into a deep lake. As it sinks deeper and deeper into the water, does the buoyant force on it increase, decrease, or remain unchanged?
Answer: 19.3.3

19.4 Does It Sink, or Does It Float?

We have learned that the buoyant force on a submerged object depends on the object's volume. A smaller object displaces less water, so a smaller buoyant force acts on it. A larger object displaces more water, so a larger buoyant force acts on it. The submerged object's *volume*—not its *weight*—determines buoyant force. (A misunderstanding of this idea is at the root of a lot of confusion that you or your friends may have about buoyancy!)

So far we've focused on the weight of displaced fluid, not the weight of the submerged object. Now we consider its role.

Whether an object sinks or floats (or does neither) depends on both its buoyant force (up) and its weight (down)—how great the buoyant force is compared *with the object's weight*. Careful thought will show that when the buoyant force exactly equals the weight of a completely submerged object, then the object's weight must equal the weight of displaced water. Since the volumes of the object and of the displaced water are the same, the density of the object must equal the density of water.

Look at Figure 19.12. The fish is "at one" with the water—it doesn't sink or float. The density of the fish equals the density of water. If the fish were somehow bloated up, it would be less dense than water, and would float to the top. If the fish swallowed a stone and became more dense than water, it would sink to the bottom.

FIGURE 19.12 ▼
The wood floats because it is less dense than water. The rock sinks because it is more dense than water. The fish neither rises nor sinks because it has the same density as water.

Cans of diet drinks float in water, while sugared drinks sink! Diet drinks are less dense than water. Sugared drinks are denser than water.

☑ **Sinking and floating can be summed up in three simple rules.**

1. **An object more dense than the fluid in which it is immersed sinks.**
2. **An object less dense than the fluid in which it is immersed floats.**
3. **An object with density equal to the density of the fluid in which it is immersed neither sinks nor floats.**

From these rules, what do we say about people who, try as they may, cannot float?[19.4] They're simply too dense! To float more easily, you must reduce your density. Since density is mass divided by volume, you must either reduce your mass or increase your volume. Taking in a lung full of air can increase your volume (temporarily!). A life jacket does the job better. It increases volume while adding little to your mass.

The density of a submarine is controlled by the flow of water into and out of its ballast tanks. In this way the weight of the submarine can be varied to achieve the desired average density. A fish regulates its density by expanding or contracting an air sac that changes its volume. The fish can move upward by increasing its volume (which decreases density) and downward by contracting its volume (which increases density). A crocodile increases its density when it swallows stones. From 4 to 5 kg of stones have been found lodged in the front part of the stomach in large crocodiles. With its increased density, a crocodile like the one in Figure 19.13, swims lower in the water and exposes less of itself to its prey.

think!

We know that if a fish makes itself more dense, it will sink; if it makes itself less dense, it will rise. In terms of buoyant force, why is this so?
Answer: 19.4

CONCEPT CHECK : What are the three rules of sinking and floating?

FIGURE 19.13 ▲
The crocodile on the left is less dense than the crocodile on the right because its belly is not full of stones.

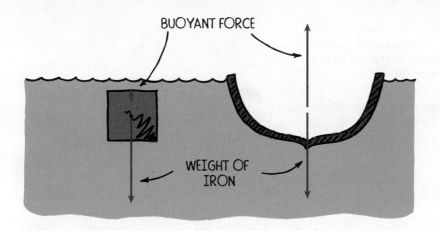

19.5 Flotation

Primitive peoples made their boats of wood. Could they have conceived of an iron ship? We don't know. The idea of floating iron might have seemed strange. Today it is easy for us to understand how a ship made of iron can float.

Consider a solid 1-ton block of iron. Iron is nearly eight times as dense as water, so when it is submerged, it will displace only 1/8 ton of water. The buoyant force will be far from enough to keep it from sinking. Suppose we reshape the same iron block into a bowl shape, as shown in Figure 19.14. The iron bowl still weighs 1 ton. If you lower the bowl into a body of water, it displaces a greater volume of water than before. The deeper the bowl is immersed, the more water is displaced and the greater is the buoyant force exerted on the bowl. When the weight of the displaced water equals the weight of the bowl, it will sink no farther. It will float because the buoyant force now equals the weight of the bowl. This is an example of the principle of flotation.

Only in the special case of floating does the buoyant force acting on an object equal the object's weight.

Link to GEOLOGY

Floating Mountains Just as most of a floating iceberg is below the water's surface, most of a mountain is below ground level. Mountains "float" too! About 15% of a mountain is above the surrounding ground level. The rest extends deep into Earth, resting on the dense semiliquid mantle. If we could shave off the top of an iceberg, the iceberg would be lighter and float higher. Similarly, when mountains erode they float higher. That's why it takes so long for mountains to weather away. As the mountain wears away, it floats higher, pushed up from below. When a mile of mountain erodes away, 85% of it comes back.

FIGURE 19.15 ▼
The weight of the floating canoe equals
the weight of the water displaced by
the submerged part of the canoe.

FIGURE 19.16 ▲
A floating object displaces
a weight of liquid equal to
its own weight.

☑ **The principle of flotation states that a floating object displaces a weight of fluid equal to its own weight.**[19.5] Figure 19.16 demonstrates a simple experiment you can do to test the principle of flotation.

Every ship must be designed to displace a weight of water equal to its own weight. Thus, a 10,000-ton ship must be built wide enough to displace 10,000 tons of water before it sinks too deep below the surface. The canoe in Figure 19.15 and the ship in Figure 19.17 float lower in the water when they are loaded. The weight of the load equals the weight of the extra water displaced.

Think about a submarine beneath the surface. If it displaces a weight of water greater than its own weight, it will rise. If it displaces less, it will go down. If it displaces exactly its weight, it will remain at constant depth. Water has slightly different densities at different temperatures, so a submarine must make periodic adjustments as it moves through the ocean. As the next chapter shows, a hot-air balloon obeys the same rules.

CONCEPT CHECK : What does the principle of flotation state?

FIGURE 19.17 ▲
The same ship is shown empty and loaded. The
weight of the ship's load equals the weight of
extra water displaced.

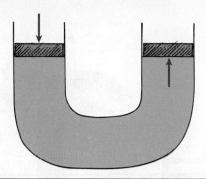

◀ **FIGURE 19.18**
The force exerted on the left piston increases the pressure in the liquid and is transmitted to the right piston.

19.6 Pascal's Principle

Push a stick against a wall and you can exert pressure at a distance. Interestingly enough, we can do the same with a fluid. Whenever we change the pressure in one part of a fluid, this change is transmitted to other parts. For example, if the pressure of city water is increased at the pumping station by 10 units of pressure, the pressure everywhere in the pipes of the connected system will be increased by 10 units of pressure (when water is not moving). **Pascal's principle** describes how changes in a pressure are transmitted in a fluid.

ⓥ **Pascal's principle states that changes in pressure at any point in an enclosed fluid at rest are transmitted undiminished to all points in the fluid and act in all directions.**

Pascal's principle was discovered in the seventeenth century by Blaise Pascal, for whom the SI unit of pressure is named. Pascal's principle is employed in a hydraulic press. If you fill a U-shaped tube with water and place pistons at each end, as shown in Figure 19.18, pressure exerted against the left piston will be transmitted throughout the liquid and against the bottom of the right piston. (The pistons are simply "plugs" that fit snugly but can freely slide inside the tube.) The pressure the left piston exerts against the water will be exactly equal to the pressure the water exerts against the right piston if the levels are the same.

This is nothing to get excited about. But suppose you make the tube on the right side wider and use a piston of larger area; then the result is impressive. In Figure 19.19 the piston on the left has an area of 1 square centimeter, and the piston on the right has an area fifty times as great, 50 square centimeters. Suppose there is a 1-newton load on the left piston. Then an additional pressure of 1 newton per square centimeter (1 N/cm^2) is transmitted throughout the liquid and up against the larger piston. Here is where the difference between force and pressure comes in. The additional pressure of 1 N/cm^2 is exerted against *every* square centimeter of the larger piston. Since there are 50 square centimeters, the total extra force exerted on the larger piston is 50 newtons. Thus, the larger piston will support a 50-newton load. This is 50 times the load on the smaller piston!

FIGURE 19.19 ▼
A 1-N load on the left piston will support 50 N on the right piston.

$$\frac{F}{A} = P = \frac{F}{A}$$

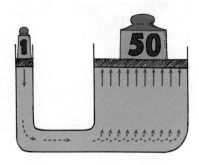

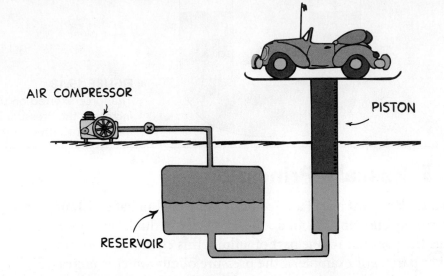

FIGURE 19.20 ▶
The automobile lift in a service station is an application of Pascal's Principle. A low-pressure exerted over a relatively large area produces a large force.

think!

As the automobile in Figure 19.20 is being lifted, how does the change in oil level in the reservoir compare with the distance the automobile moves?
Answer: 19.6

Although water covers two-thirds of the planet, oceans are the least understood ecosystems and likely the most at risk.

This is quite remarkable, for we can multiply forces with such a device—1 newton input, 50 newtons output. By further increasing the area of the larger piston (or reducing the area of the smaller piston), we can multiply forces to any amount. Pascal's principle underlies the operation of the hydraulic press.

The hydraulic press does not violate energy conservation, for the increase in force is compensated for by a decrease in distance moved. When the small piston in the last example is moved downward 10 cm, the large piston will be raised only one-fiftieth of this, or 0.2 cm. Very much like a mechanical lever, the input force multiplied by the distance it moves is equal to the output force multiplied by the distance it moves. The hydraulic press is a "machine," much like those discussed in Section 9.8.

Pascal's principle applies to all fluids (gases and liquids). A typical application of Pascal's principle for gases and liquids is the automobile lift shown in Figure 19.20. The automobile lift is in many service stations. Compressed air exerts pressure on the oil in an underground reservoir. The oil in turn transmits the pressure to a cylinder, which lifts the automobile. The relatively low pressure that exerts the lifting force against the piston is about the same as the air pressure in the tires of the automobile, because a low pressure exerted over a relatively large area produces a considerable force. It's important to note that the oil surface doesn't act like the input pistons of Figures 19.18 and 19.19. Whatever air pressure the compressor supplies to the reservoir, regardless of the oil's surface area, is transmitted through the oil to the piston that raises the car.

CONCEPT CHECK : What does Pascal's principle state?

19 REVIEW

Go Online
PHSchool.com

For: Self-Assessment
Visit: PHSchool.com
Web Code: csa – 1900

Concept Summary • • • • • •

- The pressure of a liquid at rest depends only on gravity and the density and depth of the liquid.

- When the weight of a submerged object is greater than the buoyant force, the object will sink. When the weight is less than the buoyant force, the object will rise to the surface and float.

- Archimedes's principle states that the buoyant force on an immersed object is equal to the weight of the fluid it displaces.

- Sinking and floating can be summed up in three simple rules:

  1. An object more dense than the fluid in which it is immersed sinks.

  2. An object less dense than the fluid in which it is immersed floats.

  3. An object with density equal to the density of the fluid in which it is immersed neither sinks nor floats.

- The principle of flotation states that a floating object displaces a weight of fluid equal to its own weight.

- Pascal's principle states that changes in pressure at any point in an enclosed fluid at rest are transmitted undiminished to all points in the fluid and act in all directions.

Key Terms • • • • • •

buoyancy (*p. 366*)

buoyant force
(*p. 366*)

Archimedes' principle (*p. 367*)

Pascal's principle (*p. 373*)

think! Answers

19.1 To measure the same height, the brick mason can extend a garden hose that is open at both ends from the front to the back of the house, and fill it with water until the water level reaches the height of bricks in the front. Since water seeks its own level, the level of water in the other end of the hose will be the same!

19.3.1 The buoyant force equals the weight of 1 L of water (about 10 N) because the *volume* of displaced water is 1 L.

19.3.2 The buoyant force is the same at all three positions, because the amount of water displaced is the same in A, B, and C.

19.3.3 The volume of displaced water is the same at any depth. Water is practically incompressible, so its density is the same at any depth, and equal volumes of water weigh the same. The buoyant force on the stone remains unchanged as it sinks deeper and deeper.

19.4 When the fish increases its density by decreasing its volume, it displaces less water, so the buoyant force decreases. When the fish decreases its density by expanding, it displaces more water, and the buoyant force increases.

19.6 The car moves up a greater distance than the oil level drops, since the area of the piston is smaller than the surface area of the oil in the reservoir.

19 ASSESS

Check Concepts ......

Section 19.1

1. Distinguish between *pressure* and *force*.

2. What is the relationship between liquid pressure and depth of a liquid? Between liquid pressure and density?

3. a. By how much does the water pressure on a submarine change when the submarine dives to double its previous depth (neglect the very real effect of atmospheric pressure above)?
   b. If the submarine operated in fresh water, would the pressure it feels be greater or less than at the same depth in salt water?

4. How does water pressure 1 meter below the surface of a small pond compare with water pressure 1 meter below the surface of a huge lake?

5. If you immerse a tin can with a small hole in it in water so that water spurts through the hole, what will be the direction of water flow where the hole is?

Section 19.2

6. Why does the buoyant force act upward for an object submerged in water?

7. How does the buoyant force that acts on a fish compare with the weight of the fish?

8. Why does the buoyant force on submerged objects not act sideways?

9. How does the volume of a completely submerged object compare with the volume of water displaced?

Section 19.3

10. When an object is said to be immersed in water, does this mean it is completely submerged? Does it mean it is partially submerged? Does the word *immersed* apply to either case?

11. What is the mass of 1 liter of water in kilograms? What is its weight in newtons?

12. a. Does the buoyant force on a submerged object depend on the weight of the object itself or on the weight of the fluid displaced by the object?
    b. Does it depend on the weight of the object itself or on its volume? Defend your answer.

Section 19.4

13. When the buoyant force on a submerged object is equal to the weight of the object, how do the densities of the object and water compare?

14. When the buoyant force on a submerged object is more than the weight of the object, how do the densities of the object and water compare?

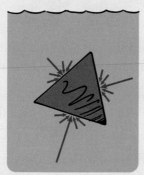

15. When the buoyant force on a submerged object is less than the weight of the object, how do the densities of the object and water compare?

16. a. How is the density of a submarine controlled?
    b. How is the density of a fish controlled?

Section 19.5

17. Does the buoyant force on a floating object depend on the weight of the object itself or on the weight of the fluid displaced by the object? Or are these both the same for the special case of floating?

18. What is the buoyant force that acts on a 100-ton ship? (To make things simple, give your answer in tons.)

Section 19.6

19. According to Pascal's principle, what happens to the pressure in all parts of a confined fluid when you produce an increase in pressure in one part?

20. When the pressure in a hydraulic press is increased by an additional 10 N/cm², how much extra load will the output piston support when its cross-sectional area is 50 square centimeters?

Plug and Chug ······

Use the following equations to help you answer Questions 21–25.

$$\text{Density: } \rho = m/V$$
$$\text{Pressure: } P = F/A$$
$$\text{Liquid pressure: } P = \rho gh$$

21. Calculate the amount of pressure you experience when you balance a 5-kg ball on the tip of your finger, say of area 1 cm².

22. Calculate the water pressure at the base of Hoover Dam. The depth of water behind the dam is 220 m. (Neglect the pressure due to the atmosphere.)

23. Calculate the water pressure in the pipes at the bottom of a high-rise building that is fed by a reservoir 30 m above on the roof.

24. An 8.6-kg piece of metal displaces 1 liter of water when submerged. Calculate its density.

25. A 4.7-kg piece of metal displaces 0.6 liter of water when submerged. Calculate its density.

Think and Explain ......

26. Stand on a bathroom scale and read your weight. When you lift one foot up so you're standing on the other foot, does the reading change? Does a scale read force or pressure?

27. Which is more likely to hurt—being stepped on by a man wearing loafers or being stepped on by a half-as-heavy woman wearing spike heels? Defend your answer.

28. Why are persons who are confined to bed less likely to develop bedsores on their bodies if they use a waterbed rather than an ordinary mattress?

29. The sketch shows a reservoir that supplies water to a farm. It is made of wood and is reinforced with metal hoops.
   a. Why is it elevated?
   b. Why are the hoops closer together near the bottom part of the tank?

30. If water faucets upstairs and downstairs are turned fully on, will more water per second flow out the downstairs faucet? Or will the water flowing from the faucets be the same?

31. In a deep dive, a whale is appreciably compressed by the pressure of the surrounding water. What happens to the whale's density?

32. Which teapot holds more liquid?

33. What physics principle accounts for the observation that water seeks its own level?

34. When you are bathing on a stony beach, why do the stones hurt your feet less when you step in deep water?

35. If liquid pressure were the same at all depths, would there be a buoyant force on an object submerged in the liquid? Explain.

36. If a 1-L container is immersed halfway in water, what volume of water is displaced? What is the buoyant force on the container?

37. How much force is needed to push a nearly weightless but rigid 1-L carton beneath a surface of water?

38. Why will a volleyball held beneath the surface of water have more buoyant force than if it is floating?

39. A barge filled with scrap iron is in a canal lock. If the iron is thrown overboard, does the water level at the side of the lock rise, fall, or remain unchanged? Explain.

40. Would the water level in a canal lock go up or down if a ship in the lock were to sink?

41. A ship sailing from the ocean into a fresh-water harbor sinks slightly deeper into the water. Does the buoyant force on it change? If so, does the force increase or decrease?

42. Suppose you have two life preservers that are identical in size, the first a light one filled with foam and the second a very heavy one filled with lead pellets. If you submerge these life preservers in water, upon which will the buoyant force be greater? Upon which will the buoyant force be ineffective? Why are your answers different?

43. When the block of wood is placed in the beaker, what happens to the scale reading? Answer the same question for an iron block.

44. When an ice cube in a glass of water melts, does the water level in the glass rise, fall, or remain unchanged? Does your answer change if the ice cube contains many air bubbles? Does your answer change if the ice cube contains many grains of heavy sand?

45. In the hydraulic arrangement shown, the larger piston has an area that is 50 times that of the smaller piston. The strong man hopes to exert enough force on the large piston to raise the 10 kg that rests on the small piston. Do you think he will be successful? Explain.

46. Hydraulic devices multiply forces. Why does this not violate the law of conservation of energy?

Think and Solve ......

You may need the following information for some of the Think and Solve problems that follow.

The density ρ of fresh water is 1000 kg/m³, or equivalently, 1.00 kg/liter. Weight density ρ_w is 9800 N/m³, or equivalently, 9.80 N/liter. For sea water, these values are 1030 kg/m³, or 1.03 kg/liter, and 10,094 N/m³, or 10.094 N/liter.

47. Which produces more pressure on the ground, an elephant or a woman balancing on high heels? Assume an elephant weighs 500 times more than the woman, and the cross-sectional area of its feet is 10,000 times greater than that of the woman's heels.

48. A hole of area 12 cm² is made in the bottom of a barge 1.5 m below the freshwater surface. A board is held over the hole from inside the barge to stop water from leaking in. Show that the force necessary to hold the board in position is 18 N.

49. The water level at the top of a water tower is 50 m above ground level.
   a. Show that the gravitational potential energy (*mgh*) of each kilogram of water at the water surface in the tower is 500 J relative to ground level.
   b. Show that the water pressure at the base of the tower is 500,000 N/m².

50. A dike in Holland springs a leak through a hole of area 1 cm² at a depth of 2 m below the water surface. With what force would a boy have to push on the hole with his thumb to stop the leak? Could he do it?

51. When a 1.8-kg wrench is suspended in water from a spring scale, the scale reading is 1.6 kg. What is the density of the wrench?

52. A 13.5-kg block of metal displaces 5 liters of water when submerged. What kind of metal is likely to compose the block?

53. Phil can support 100 N of iron ($\rho = 7{,}800$ kg/m³) in water. How many newtons can he support in air?

54. A 1-kg rock suspended above water weighs 10 N. When the rock is suspended beneath the surface of the water, the scale reads 8 N.

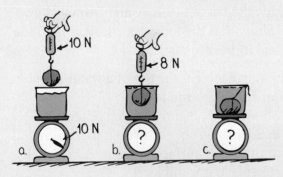

a. What is the buoyant force on the rock?
b. If a container of water on a bathroom-type scale weighs 10 N, what is the scale reading when the rock is suspended beneath the surface of the water?
c. What is the scale reading when the rock is released and rests at the bottom of the container?

55. A merchant in Katmandu sells you a solid gold 1.000-kg statue for a very reasonable price. You wonder whether or not you got a bargain, so you lower the statue into a measuring cup and measure its volume. What volume will verify that it's pure gold?

56. A prospector desires to know if a nugget is pure gold. The nugget has a mass of 380 grams on a balance. When immersed in water its mass appears as 350 grams. Is the nugget pure gold?

57. Consider a friend of mass 100 kg who can just barely float in fresh water. Show that the volume of your friend is about 0.1 m³.

58. A gravel barge, rectangular in shape, is 4 m wide and 10 m long. When loaded, it sinks 2 m in the water. Show that the weight of gravel in the barge is 800,000 N.

59. A rectangular barge 5 m long and 2 m wide floats in fresh water.
a. Show that the barge will sink 5 cm lower when loaded with 500 kg of sand.
b. If the barge can only be pushed 10 cm deeper into the water before water overflows to sink it, how many kilograms of sand can it carry?

60. A circus elephant weighing 18,800 N is taken on board a barge of length 6.2 m and breadth 3.0 m, which floats in a river. Show that the barge sinks 10 cm when the elephant gets on board.

61. In the hydraulic pistons shown in the sketch, the small piston has a diameter of 2 cm and the large piston has a diameter of 6 cm. How much force can the larger piston exert compared with the force applied to the smaller piston?

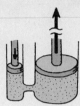

Activities ......

62. Try to float an egg in water. Then dissolve salt in the water until the egg floats. How does the density of an egg compare with the density of tap water? Salt water? How do you know?

63. Punch a couple of holes in the bottom of a water-filled container, and water will spurt out because of water pressure (left of figure). Now drop the container and watch what happens. Explain your observations. (*Hint:* What happens to *g*, and hence weight, and hence pressure in the reference frame of the falling container?)

64. Make a Cartesian diver like the one shown below. Completely fill a large, pliable plastic bottle with water. Partially fill a small pill bottle so that it just barely floats when capped, turned upside down, and placed in the large bottle. (You may have to experiment to get it just right.) Once the pill bottle is barely floating, secure the lid or cap on the large bottle so that it is airtight. When you press the sides of the large bottle, the pill bottle sinks; when you release it, the bottle returns to the top. Experiment by squeezing the bottle different ways to get different results. Explain the behavior you see.

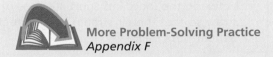

More Problem-Solving Practice
Appendix F

20 GASES

THE BIG IDEA : Gas molecules are far apart and can move freely between collisions.

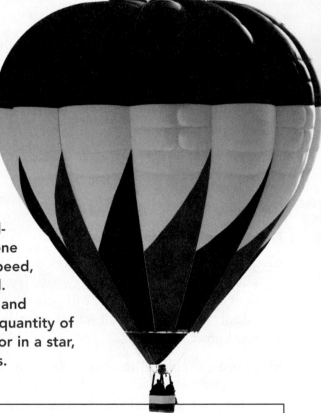

Gases are similar to liquids in that they flow; hence both are called *fluids*. The primary difference between gases and liquids is the distance between molecules. In a liquid, the molecules are close together, where they continually experience attractive forces from the surrounding molecules. These forces strongly affect the motion of the molecules. In a gas, the molecules are far apart, allowing them to move freely between collisions. When two molecules in a gas collide, if one gains speed in the collision, the other loses speed, such that their total kinetic energy is unchanged.

A gas expands to fill all space available to it and takes the shape of its container. Only when the quantity of gas is very large, such as in Earth's atmosphere or in a star, does gravitation determine the shape of the gas.

discover!

How Can You Levitate an Object?

1. Bend the elbow of a flexible straw approximately 90°.
2. Place the long section of the straw in your mouth and hold a table tennis ball a few centimeters above the short section.
3. Blow steadily through the straw as you release the ball. Keep trying until the ball levitates.
4. While still blowing, increase the angle between the long and short sections of the straw so that the air stream is not directly beneath the ball.

Analyze and Conclude

1. **Observing** What happened when the air stream was no longer directly beneath the ball?
2. **Predicting** How large can the angle between the two sections of the straw be if the ball is to remain suspended?
3. **Making Generalizations** What keeps the ball suspended when the air stream is not directly beneath the ball?

20.1 The Atmosphere

We don't have to look far to find a sample of gas. We live in an ocean of gas, our atmosphere. ⊘ **Earth's atmosphere consists of molecules that occupy space and extends many kilometers above Earth's surface.** The molecules are energized by sunlight and kept in continual motion like the gas molecules shown in Figure 20.1. Without Earth's gravity, they would fly off into outer space. And without the sun's energy, the molecules would eventually cool and just end up as matter on the ground. Fortunately, because of an energizing sun and because of gravity, we have an atmosphere.

Unlike the ocean, which has a very definite upper surface, Earth's atmosphere has no definite upper surface. And unlike the ocean's uniform density at any depth, the density of the atmosphere decreases with altitude. Molecules in the atmosphere are closer together at sea level than at higher altitudes. The atmosphere is like a huge pile of feathers, where those at the bottom are more squashed than those nearer to the top. The air gets thinner and thinner (less dense) the higher one goes; it eventually thins out into space.

Even in the vacuous regions of interplanetary space there is a gas density of about one molecule per cubic centimeter. This is primarily hydrogen, the most plentiful element in the universe.

Figure 20.2 shows how thin our atmosphere is. Note that 50% of the atmosphere is below 5.6 kilometers (18,000 ft), 75% of the atmosphere is below 11 kilometers (56,000 ft), 90% of the atmosphere is below 17.7 kilometers, and 99% of the atmosphere is below an altitude of about 30 kilometers. Compared with Earth's radius, 30 kilometers is very small. To give you an idea of how small, the "thickness" of the atmosphere relative to the size of the world is like the thickness of the skin of an apple relative to the size of the apple. Our atmosphere is a delicate and finite life-sustaining thin shell of air; that's why we should care for it.

CONCEPT CHECK What is the atmosphere?

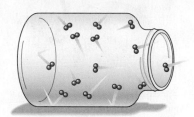

FIGURE 20.1 ▲
Molecules in the gaseous state are in continuous motion.

FIGURE 20.2 ▼
The temperature of the atmosphere drops as one goes higher (until it rises again at very high altitudes).

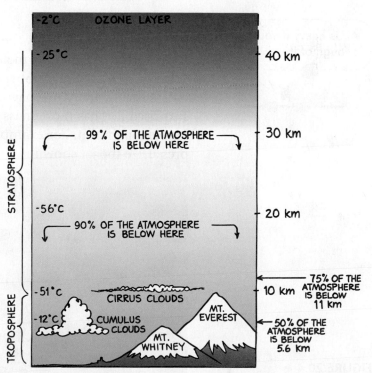

FIGURE 20.3 ▲

You don't notice the weight of a bag of water while you're submerged in water. Similarly, you don't notice the weight of air as you walk around in it.

20.2 Atmospheric Pressure

We live at the bottom of an ocean of air. The atmosphere, much like water in a lake, exerts pressure. ✅ **Atmospheric pressure is caused by the weight of air, just as water pressure is caused by the weight of water.** We are so accustomed to the invisible air around us that we sometimes forget it has weight. Perhaps a fish "forgets" about the weight of water in the same way. Figure 20.3 illustrates this point.

Table 20.1	Densities of Various Gases
Gas	**Density (kg/m³)***
Dry air	
0° C	1.29
10° C	1.25
20° C	1.21
30° C	1.16
Helium	0.178
Hydrogen	0.090
Oxygen	1.43

* At sea level atmospheric pressure and at 0° C (unless otherwise specified)

Air is heavy if you have enough of it.

Table 20.1 shows how the density of air changes with temperature. At sea level, 1 cubic meter of air at 20°C has a mass of about 1.2 kg. Calculate the number of cubic meters in your room, multiply by 1.2 kg/m³, and you'll have the mass of air in your room. Don't be surprised if it has more mass than your kid sister. Air is heavy if you have enough of it. For example, it takes more than 1800 kg of air to pressurize the jet shown in Figure 20.4.

FIGURE 20.4 ▶

Fully pressurizing a 777 jumbo jet adds 1800 kg to its mass.

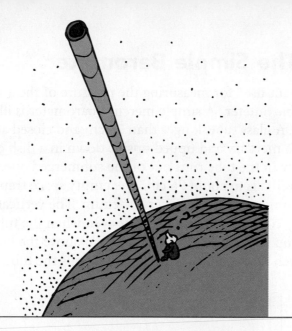

The mass of air that would occupy a bamboo pole that extends to the "top" of the atmosphere is about 1 kg. This air has a weight of 10 N.

If your kid sister doesn't believe air has weight, maybe it's because she's surrounded by air all the time. Hand her a plastic bag of water and she'll tell you it has weight. But hand her the same bag of water while she's submerged in a swimming pool, and she won't feel its weight because the bag is surrounded by water.

Consider a superlong hollow bamboo pole, like the one shown in Figure 20.5, that reaches up through the atmosphere for 30 kilometers. Suppose the inside cross-sectional area of the pole is 1 square centimeter. If the density of air inside the pole matches the density of air outside, the enclosed mass of air would be about 1 kilogram. The weight of this much air is about 10 newtons. So air pressure at the bottom of the bamboo pole would be about 10 newtons per square centimeter (10 N/cm²). Of course, the same is true without the bamboo pole.

There are 10,000 square centimeters in 1 square meter. So a column of air 1 square meter in cross section that extends up through the atmosphere, as illustrated in Figure 20.6, has a mass of about 10,000 kilograms. The weight of this air is about 100,000 newtons (10^5 N). This weight produces a pressure of 100,000 newtons per square meter, or equivalently, 100,000 pascals, or 100 kilopascals. More exactly, the average atmospheric pressure at sea level is 101.3 kilopascals (101.3 kPa).[20.2]

The pressure of the atmosphere is not uniform. Aside from variations with altitude, there are variations in atmospheric pressure at any one locality due to moving air currents and storms. Measurement of changing air pressure is important to meteorologists in predicting weather.

think!

About how many kilograms of air occupy a classroom that has a 200-square-meter floor area and a 4-meter-high ceiling?
Answer: 20.2

FIGURE 20.6 ▲
The weight of air that bears down on a 1-square-meter surface at sea level is about 100,000 newtons.

CONCEPT CHECK : What causes atmospheric pressure?

20.3 The Simple Barometer

An instrument used for measuring the pressure of the atmosphere is called a **barometer.** A simple mercury barometer is illustrated in Figure 20.7. A glass tube, longer than 76 cm and closed at one end, is filled with mercury and tipped upside down in a dish of mercury. The mercury in the tube runs out of the submerged open bottom until the level falls to about 76 cm. The empty space trapped above, except for some mercury vapor, is a vacuum. The vertical height of the mercury column remains constant even when the tube is tilted, unless the top of the tube is less than 76 cm above the level in the dish, in which case the mercury completely fills the tube.

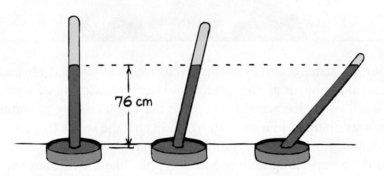

FIGURE 20.7 ▶

In a simple mercury barometer, variations above and below the average column height of 76 cm are caused by variations in atmospheric pressure.

76 cm

Why does mercury behave this way? The explanation is similar to the reason a simple see-saw balances when the weights of people at its two ends are equal. The barometer "balances" when the weight of liquid in the tube exerts the same pressure as the atmosphere outside. Whatever the width of the tube, a 76-cm column of mercury weighs the same as the air that would fill a supertall 30-km tube of the same width. If the atmospheric pressure increases, then it will push the mercury column higher than 76 cm. The mercury is literally pushed up into the tube of a barometer by atmospheric pressure. ✅ **The height of the mercury in the tube of a simple barometer is a measure of the atmospheric pressure.**

Could water be used to make a barometer? The answer is yes, but the glass tube would have to be much longer—13.6 times as long, to be exact. You may recognize this number as the density of mercury relative to that of water. A volume of water 13.6 times that of mercury is needed to provide the same weight as the mercury in the tube (or in the imaginary tube of air outside). So the height of the tube would have to be at least 13.6 times taller than the mercury column. A water barometer would have to be 13.6 × (0.76 m), or 10.3 m high—too tall to be practical.

The operation of a barometer is similar to the process of drinking through a straw, which is shown in Figure 20.8. By sucking, you reduce the air pressure in the straw that is placed in a drink. Atmospheric pressure on the liquid's surface pushes liquid up into the reduced-pressure region. Strictly speaking, the liquid is not *sucked* up; it is *pushed* up the straw by the pressure of the atmosphere. If the atmosphere is prevented from pushing on the surface of the drink, as in the party trick bottle with the straw through the airtight cork stopper, one can suck and suck and get no drink.

◀ **FIGURE 20.8**
You cannot drink soda through the straw unless the atmosphere exerts a pressure on the surrounding liquid.

If you understand these ideas, you can understand why there is a 10.3-meter limit on the height water can be lifted with vacuum pumps. The old-fashioned farm-type pump shown in Figure 20.9 operates by producing a partial vacuum in a pipe that extends down into the water below. The atmospheric pressure exerted on the surface of the water simply pushes the water up into the region of reduced pressure inside the pipe. Can you see that even with a perfect vacuum, the maximum height to which water can be lifted is 10.3 meters?

CONCEPT CHECK : How does a simple mercury barometer show pressure?

FIGURE 20.9 ▲
The atmosphere pushes water from below up into a pipe that is evacuated of air by the pumping action.

FIGURE 20.10 ▶
Atmospheric pressure is used to crush a can. **a.** The can is heated until steam forms. **b.** The can is capped and removed from the heat. **c.** When the can cools, the air pressure inside is reduced.

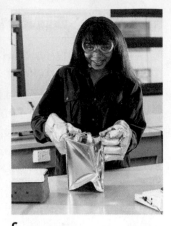

a   b   c

20.4 The Aneroid Barometer

Figure 20.10 shows a popular classroom demonstration used to illustrate atmospheric pressure. A can containing a little water is heated until steam forms. Then the can is capped securely and removed from the source of heat. There is now less air inside the can than before it was heated. (Why? Because when the water boils and changes to steam, the steam pushes air out of the can.) When the sealed can cools, the pressure inside is reduced because steam inside the can condenses to a liquid when it cools. The greater pressure of the atmosphere outside the can then proceeds to crush the can. The pressure of the atmosphere is even more dramatically shown when a 50-gallon drum is crushed by the same procedure.

A much more subtle application of atmospheric crushing is used in an aneroid barometer. An **aneroid barometer** is an instrument that measures variations in atmospheric pressure without a liquid. An example of an aneroid barometer is shown in Figure 20.11. This small portable instrument is more prevalent than the mercury barometer. ⊘ **An aneroid barometer uses a small metal box that is partially exhausted of air. The box has a slightly flexible lid that bends in or out as atmospheric pressure changes.** The pressure difference between the inside and outside is less drastic than that of the crushed can of Figure 20.10. Motion of the lid is indicated on a scale by a mechanical spring-and-lever system. Since atmospheric pressure decreases with increasing altitude, a barometer can be used to determine elevation. An aneroid barometer calibrated for altitude is called an *altimeter* ("altitude meter"). Some of these instruments are sensitive enough to indicate changes in elevation of less than a meter.

a

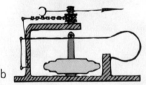

b

FIGURE 20.11 ▲
Aneroid barometers work without liquids. **a.** Variations in atmospheric pressure are indicated on the face of the instrument. **b.** The spring-and-lever system can be seen in this cross-sectional diagram.

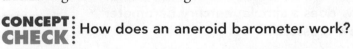

CONCEPT CHECK How does an aneroid barometer work?

20.5 Boyle's Law

The air pressure inside the inflated tires of an automobile is considerably more than the atmospheric pressure outside. The density of air inside is also more than that of the air outside. To understand the relationship between pressure and density, think of the molecules inside the tire.[20.5.1]

Inside the tire, the molecules behave like tiny table tennis balls, perpetually moving helter-skelter and banging against the inner walls. Their impacts on the inner surface of the tire produce a jittery force that appears to our coarse senses as a steady push. This pushing force averaged over a unit of area provides the pressure of the enclosed air.

Suppose there are twice as many molecules in the same volume. As illustrated in Figure 20.12, the air density is then doubled. If the molecules move at the same average speed—or, equivalently, if they have the same temperature—then to a close approximation, the number of collisions will double. This means the pressure is doubled. So pressure is proportional to density.

◄ FIGURE 20.12
When the density of the air in the tire is increased, the pressure is increased.

The density of the air can also be doubled by simply compressing the air to half its volume. We increase the density of air in a balloon when we squeeze it, and likewise increase air density in the cylinder of a tire pump when we push the piston downward. Consider the cylinder with the movable piston in Figure 20.13. If the piston is pushed downward so that the volume is half the original volume, the density of molecules will be doubled, and the pressure will correspondingly be doubled. Decrease the volume to a third its original value, and the pressure will be increased by three, and so on.

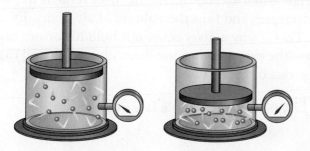

◄ FIGURE 20.13
When the volume of gas is decreased, the density—and therefore pressure—are increased.

think!

If you squeeze a balloon to one-third its volume, by how much will the pressure inside increase?
Answer: 20.5.1

FIGURE 20.14 ▶

A scuba diver must be aware of Boyle's law when ascending to the surface.

Or Boyle's law can look like this: $PV = Pv$, or $PV = pV$.

Notice from these examples that the product of pressure and volume is the same for any given quantity of a gas. For example, a doubled pressure multiplied by a halved volume gives the same value as a tripled pressure multiplied by a one-third volume. **Boyle's law** describes the relationship between the pressure and volume of a gas. ⊘ **Boyle's law states that the product of pressure and volume for a given mass of gas is a constant as long as the temperature does not change.** "Pressure × volume" for a sample of gas at one time is equal to any "different pressure × different volume" of the same sample of gas at any other time. In equation form,

$$P_1V_1 = P_2V_2$$

where P_1 and V_1 represent the original pressure and volume, respectively, and P_2 and V_2 the second, or final, pressure and volume. Boyle's law is named after Robert Boyle, the seventeenth-century physicist who is credited with its discovery.[20.5.2]

Scuba divers, such as the one in Figure 20.14, must be aware of Boyle's law when ascending. As the diver returns to the surface, pressure decreases and thus the volume of air in the diver's lungs increases. This is why a diver must not hold his or her breath while ascending—the expansion of the diver's lungs beyond capacity can be very dangerous or even fatal.

think!

A scuba diver 10.3 m deep breathes compressed air. If she holds her breath while returning to the surface, by how much does the volume of her lungs tend to increase?

Answer: 20.5.2

CONCEPT CHECK : What does Boyle's law state?

FIGURE 20.15 ▲
The dirigible and the fish both hover at a given level for the same reason.

think!

Two rubber balloons are inflated to the same size, one with air and the other with helium. Which balloon experiences the greater buoyant force? Why does the air-filled balloon sink and the helium-filled balloon float?
Answer: 20.6

20.6 Buoyancy of Air

In the last chapter you learned about buoyancy in liquids. All the rules for buoyancy were stated in terms of *fluids* rather than liquids. The reason is simple enough: the rules hold for gases as well as liquids. Consider the dirigible and the fish in Figure 20.15. The physical laws that explain a dirigible aloft in the air are the same that explain a fish "aloft" in water. Archimedes' principle for air states that an object surrounded by air is buoyed up by a force equal to the weight of the air displaced.

Recall that a cubic meter of air at ordinary atmospheric pressure and room temperature has a mass of about 1.2 kg, so its weight is about 12 N. Therefore any 1-cubic-meter object in air is buoyed up with a force of 12 N. If the mass of the 1-cubic-meter object is greater than 1.2 kg (so that its weight is greater than 12 N), it will fall to the ground when released. If a 1-cubic-meter object has a mass less than 1.2 kg, it will rise in the air. Any object that has a mass less than the mass of an equal volume of surrounding air will rise. ☑ **Any object less dense than the air around it will rise.** A gas-filled balloon, such as the one shown in Figure 20.16, rises in the air because it is less dense than the surrounding air.

When you next see a large dirigible airship aloft in the air, think of it as a giant fish. Both remain aloft as they swim through their fluids for the same reason: they both displace their own weights of fluid. When in motion, the dirigible may be raised or lowered by means of horizontal rudders or "elevators."

CONCEPT CHECK : What causes an object to rise?

FIGURE 20.16 ▲
Everything is buoyed up by a force equal to the weight of the air it displaces.

FIGURE 20.17 ▶
Because the flow is continuous, water speeds up when it flows through the narrow or shallow part of the brook.

20.7 Bernoulli's Principle

The discussion of fluid pressure thus far has been confined to stationary fluids. Motion produces an additional influence.

Relationship Between Fluid Pressure and Speed Most people think that atmospheric pressure increases in a gale, tornado, or hurricane. Actually, the opposite is true. High-speed winds may blow the roof off your house, but the pressure within air that gains speed is actually less than for still air of the same density. As strange as it may first seem, when the speed of a fluid increases, its pressure decreases. This is true for all fluids—liquids and gases alike.

Consider a continuous flow of water through a pipe. Because water doesn't "bunch up," the amount of water that flows past any given section of the pipe is the same as the amount that flows past any other section of the same pipe. This is true whether the pipe widens or narrows. As a consequence of continuous flow, the water in the wide parts will slow down, and in the narrow parts, it will speed up. You can observe this when you put your finger over the outlet of a water hose. As shown in Figure 20.17, this is also apparent when water flows through a narrow part of a brook.

Daniel Bernoulli, a Swiss scientist of the eighteenth century, advanced the theory of water flowing through pipes. The relationship between the speed of a fluid and the pressure in the fluid is described by **Bernoulli's principle.** He found that the greater the speed of flow, the less is the force of the water at right angles (sideways) to the direction of flow. The pressure at the walls of the pipes decreases when the speed of the water increases. Bernoulli found this to be a principle of both liquids and gases. ☑ **Bernoulli's principle in its simplest form states that when the speed of a fluid increases, pressure in the fluid decreases.**

A fluid continues to move at *constant volume per unit of time* through different cross sections of a pipe or confined regions. This is called the "principle of continuity."

Bernoulli's principle is a consequence of the conservation of energy, although, surprisingly, he developed it long before the concept of energy was formalized.[20.7] The full energy picture for a fluid in motion is quite complicated. Simply stated, higher speed means lower pressure, and lower speed means higher pressure.

The decrease of fluid pressure with increasing speed may at first seem surprising, particularly if we fail to distinguish between the pressure within the fluid and the pressure exerted by the fluid on something that interferes with its flow. The pressure within the fast-moving water in a fire hose is relatively low, whereas the pressure that the water can exert on anything in its path to slow it down may be huge.

Pressure inside a fluid is different from the pressure it can exert on anything that changes its momentum!

Streamlines In steady flow, one small bit of fluid follows along the same path as a bit of fluid in front of it. The motion of a fluid in steady flow follows streamlines, which are represented by thin lines in Figure 20.18 and later figures. **Streamlines** are the smooth paths, or trajectories, of the bits of fluid. The lines are closer together in the narrower regions, where the flow is faster and pressure is less.

Pressure differences are nicely evident when liquid contains air bubbles. The volume of an air bubble depends on the pressure of the surrounding liquid. Where the liquid gains speed, pressure is lowered and bubbles are bigger. As Figure 20.18b indicates, bubbles are squeezed smaller in slower higher-pressure liquid.

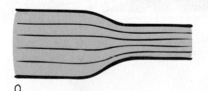
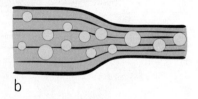

a b

FIGURE 20.18 ▲
Water speeds up when it flows into the narrower pipe.
a. The close together streamlines indicate increased speed and decreased internal pressure. **b.** The bubbles are bigger in the narrow part because internal pressure there is less.

Bernoulli's principle holds only for steady flow. If the flow speed is too great, the flow may become turbulent and follow a changing, curling path known as an **eddy.** In that case, Bernoulli's principle does not hold.

CONCEPT CHECK What does Bernoulli's principle state?

The paper rises when you blow air across the top of it.

20.8 Applications of Bernoulli's Principle

Bernoulli's principle partly accounts for the flight of birds and aircraft. Try blowing air across the top of a sheet of paper, as shown in Figure 20.19. The paper rises because air passes faster over the top of the sheet than below it.

Lift Similarly, the shape and orientation of airplane wings ensure that air passes somewhat faster over the top surface of the wing than beneath the lower surface. As shown by the streamlines in Figure 20.20, pressure above the wing is less than pressure below the wing. **Lift** is the upward force created by the difference between the air pressure above and below the wing.[20.8] Even a small pressure difference multiplied by a large wing area can produce a considerable force. ⊘ **When lift equals weight, horizontal flight is possible.** The lift is greater for higher speeds and larger wing areas. Hence, low-speed gliders have very large wings relative to the size of the fuselage. The wings of faster-moving aircraft are relatively small.

FIGURE 20.20 ▶

Air pressure above the wing is less than the pressure below the wing.

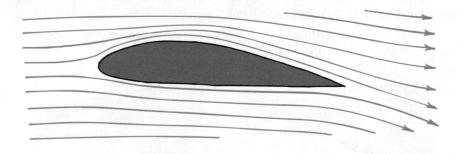

Atmospheric pressure decreases in a strong wind. As Figure 20.21 shows, air pressure above a roof is less than air pressure inside the building when a wind is blowing. This produces a lift that may result in the roof being blown off. Roofs are usually constructed to withstand increased downward loads, the weight of snow for example, but not always for increased upward forces. Unless the building is well vented, the stagnant air inside can push the roof off.

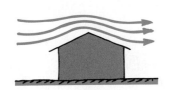

FIGURE 20.21 ▲

In high winds, air pressure above a roof can drastically decrease.

Curve Balls Bernoulli's principle is partly involved in the curved path of spinning balls. When a moving baseball, or any kind of ball spins, unequal air pressures are produced on opposite sides of the ball. In Figure 20.22b, the streamlines are closer together at B than at A for the direction of spin shown. Air pressure is greater at A, and the ball curves as indicated.

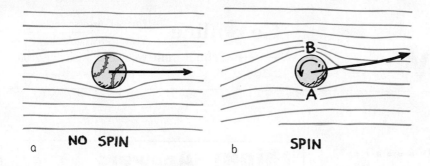

a NO SPIN   b SPIN

◄ FIGURE 20.22
Bernoulli's principle is partly
involved in the curved path
of a spinning ball. **a.** The
streamlines are the same
on either side of a nonspin-
ning ball. **b.** A spinning ball
produces a crowding of
streamlines.

Boat Collisions Bernoulli's principle explains why passing ships run the risk of a sideways collision. Water flowing between the ships travels faster than water flowing past the outer sides. Streamlines are closer together between the ships than outside. Hence, water pressure acting against the hulls is reduced between the ships. Unless the ships are steered to compensate for this, the greater pressure against the outer sides of the ships forces them together. Figure 20.23 shows a demonstration of this, which you can do in your kitchen sink. Loosely moor a pair of toy boats side by side. Then direct a stream of water between them. The boats will draw together and collide.

Go Online
SciLINKS NSTA

For: Links on
Bernoulli's principle
Visit: www.SciLinks.org
Web Code: csn – 2008

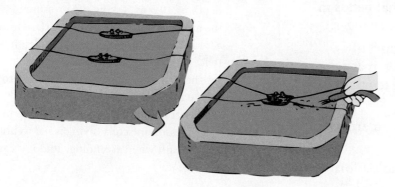

◄ FIGURE 20.23
Try this experiment in
your sink and watch
Bernoulli's principle in
action!

Shower Curtains A similar thing happens to a bathroom shower curtain when the shower water is turned on full blast. Air near the water stream flows into the lower-pressure stream and is swept downward with the falling water. Air pressure inside the curtain is thus reduced, and the atmospheric pressure outside pushes the curtain inward (providing an escape route for the downward-swept air). This effect is small compared with the convection produced by temperature differences, but nevertheless, the next time you're taking a shower and the curtain swings in against your legs, think of Daniel Bernoulli!

CONCEPT CHECK How is horizontal flight possible?

REVIEW

Go Online

For: Self-Assessment
Visit: PHSchool.com
PHSchool.com Web Code: csa – 2000

Concept Summary ......

- Earth's atmosphere consists of molecules that occupy space and extends many kilometers above Earth's surface.

- Atmospheric pressure is caused by the weight of air, just as water pressure is caused by the weight of water.

- The height of the mercury in the tube of a simple barometer is a measure of the atmospheric pressure.

- An aneroid barometer uses a small metal box that is partially exhausted of air. The box has a slightly flexible lid that bends in or out as atmospheric pressure changes.

- Boyle's law states that the product of pressure and volume for a given mass of gas is a constant as long as the temperature does not change.

- Any object less dense than the air around it will rise.

- Bernoulli's principle in its simplest form states that when the speed of a fluid increases, pressure in the fluid decreases.

- When lift equals weight, horizontal flight is possible.

Key Terms ....

barometer (p. 386)   **streamline** (p. 393)

aneroid   **eddy** (p. 393)
  barometer (p. 388)   **lift** (p. 394)

Boyle's law (p. 390)

Bernoulli's
  principle (p. 392)

think! Answers

20.2   960 kg. The volume of air is $(200 \text{ m}^2) \times (4 \text{ m}) = 800 \text{ m}^3$. Each cubic meter of air has a mass of about 1.2 kg, so $(800 \text{ m}^3) \times (1.2 \text{ kg/m}^3) = 960$ kg (about a ton).

20.5.1   The pressure in the balloon is increased three times. No wonder balloons break when you squeeze them!

20.5.2   Atmospheric pressure can support a column of water 10.3 m high, so the pressure in water due to the weight of the water alone equals atmospheric pressure at a depth of 10.3 m. Taking the pressure of the atmosphere at the water's surface into account, the total pressure at this depth is twice atmospheric pressure. Unfortunately for the scuba diver, her lungs will tend to inflate to twice their normal size if she holds her breath while rising to the surface. A first lesson in scuba diving is *not* to hold your breath when ascending. To do so can be fatal.

20.6   Both balloons are buoyed upward with the same buoyant force because they displace the same weight of air. The reason the air-filled balloon sinks in air is because it is heavier than the buoyant force that acts on it. The helium-filled balloon is lighter than the buoyant force that acts on it. Or put another way, the air-filled balloon is slightly more dense than the surrounding air (principally because it is filled with *compressed* air). Helium, even somewhat compressed, is much less dense than air.

20 ASSESS

Check Concepts ......

Section 20.1

1. **a.** What is the energy source for the motion of gases in the atmosphere?
   b. What prevents atmospheric gases from flying off into space?

2. How does the density of gases at different elevations in the atmosphere differ from the density of liquids at different depths?

Section 20.2

3. What causes atmospheric pressure?

4. Why doesn't the pressure of the atmosphere break windows?

5. What is the mass of a cubic meter of air at 20°C at sea level?

6. **a.** What is the mass of a column of air that has a cross-sectional area of 1 square centimeter and that extends from sea level to the top of the atmosphere?
   b. What is the weight of this air column?
   c. What is the pressure at the bottom of this column?

7. Is the value for atmospheric pressure at the surface of Earth a constant? Explain.

Section 20.3

8. How does the pressure at the bottom of the 76-cm column of mercury in a barometer compare with the pressure due to the weight of the atmosphere?

9. When you drink liquid through a straw, it is more accurate to say the liquid is *pushed* up the straw rather than *sucked* up the straw. What exactly does the pushing? Explain.

10. Why will a vacuum pump not operate for a well that is deeper than 10.3 m?

Section 20.4

11. The atmosphere does not ordinarily crush cans. Yet it will crush a can after it has been heated, capped, and cooled. Why?

12. What property of atmospheric pressure is used by an aneroid barometer?

Section 20.5

13. When air is compressed, what happens to its density?

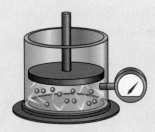

14. A piston in an airtight pump is withdrawn so that the volume of the air chamber is increased five times. What is the change in pressure?

15. When you squeeze an air-filled toy balloon to half size, how does the air pressure inside change?

Section 20.6

16. **a.** How much buoyant force acts on a 1-N balloon suspended at rest in air?
    b. What happens if the buoyant force decreases?
    c. What happens if the buoyant force increases?

Section 20.7

17. When the speed of a fluid flowing in a horizontal pipe increases, what happens to the internal pressure in the fluid?

18. **a.** What are streamlines?
    b. Is the pressure greater or less in regions where streamlines are crowded?

Section 20.8

19. In addition to Bernoulli's principle, what other physics explains the lift produced by an airplane wing?

20. Why does a spinning ball curve in flight?

Plug and Chug ••••••

The key equations of the chapter are shown below in bold type.

$$\rho = \frac{m}{V}$$

21. Calculate the density of a gas with a mass of 4.29 kg and a volume of 3.0 cubic meters. Express your answer in kg/m³.

22. Calculate the density of a gas with a mass of 0.00020 kg and a volume of 1.0 liter. Express your answer in kg/m³.

$$P_1 V_1 = P_2 V_2$$

23. An inflated balloon has internal pressure P_1. Use Boyle's law to calculate the pressure P_2 when the balloon is compressed to half its volume.

24. Use Boyle's law to calculate the pressure on the same balloon if it instead expands to twice its volume.

$$P = \frac{F}{A}$$

25. Calculate the lift on a model airplane wing with an area on one side of 100 cm² and a difference in air pressure above and below the wing of 0.01 N/cm².

Think and Explain ......

26. We can understand how pressure in water depends on depth by considering a stack of bricks. The pressure below the bottom brick is determined by the weight of the entire stack. Halfway up the stack, the pressure is half as great as it is at the bottom because the weight of the bricks above is half as great. To explain atmospheric pressure, we should consider compressible bricks, like foam rubber. Why is this so?

27. The "pump" in a vacuum cleaner is merely a high-speed fan. Would a vacuum cleaner pick up dust from a rug on the moon? Explain.

28. Which would weigh more—a bottle filled with helium gas, or the same bottle evacuated?

29. A steel tank filled with helium gas doesn't rise in air, but a balloon containing the same helium easily rises. Why?

30. From Table 20.1, which filling would be more effective in making a balloon rise—helium or hydrogen? Why?

31. A helium-filled balloon pulls upward on its string. Your friend says the upward force is evidence that atmospheric pressure is greater at the bottom of the balloon than on the top. Another friend says such a small difference in altitude wouldn't make a difference in atmospheric pressure. They both look to you for an answer. What do you tell them?

32. Two identical balloons of the same volume are pumped up with air to more than atmospheric pressure and suspended on the ends of a horizontal stick that is balanced. One of the balloons is then punctured. Is there a change in the stick's balance? If so, which way does it tip?

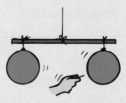

33. How would the density of air at the bottom of a deep mine shaft compare to the density of the atmosphere at the surface of the ground?

34. Atmospheric pressure is nicely demonstrated with the pair of hemispheres shown below. When placed together, the hemispheres make up a hollow sphere. After a vacuum pump evacuates much of the air inside, a considerable force is needed to separate the hemispheres. Suppose two people find they must pull with 150 N each to separate them. If instead, one end of the sphere is attached to a wall and only one person pulls the other end, how much force would the one person have to supply to separate the hemispheres?

35. Relative to sea level, would it be slightly more difficult or somewhat easier to drink through a straw at the bottom of a deep mine? At the top of a high mountain? Explain.

36. If there were a liquid twice as dense as mercury, and if it were used to make a barometer, how tall would the column be?

37. Before boarding an airplane, you buy a bag of chips (or any item sealed in an airtight foil package) and, while in flight, you notice that the bag is puffed up. Explain why this occurs.

38. Why do you suppose that airplane windows are smaller than bus windows?

39. Why do your ears "pop" when you ascend to higher altitudes?

40. Small bubbles of air are released by a scuba diver deep in the water. As the bubbles rise, do they become larger, smaller, or stay about the same size? Explain.

41. When you squeeze an air-filled toy balloon, its volume decreases. Your friend says that the mass and the density of air inside increase. Do you agree with your friend? Defend your response.

42. Consider a huge, lazily rotating space habitat, carrying its own atmosphere. Would a helium-filled balloon "rise" in such a setting? Defend your answer.

43. It is easy to breathe when snorkeling with only your face beneath the surface of the water, but quite difficult to breathe when you are submerged nearly a meter, and nearly impossible when you are more than a meter deep (even if your snorkel tube reaches to the surface). Figure out why, and explain carefully.

44. An inflated balloon sufficiently weighted with rocks will sink in water.
  a. What will happen to the size of the balloon as it sinks?
  b. Compared with its volume at the surface, what volume will it have when it is 10.3 m below the surface?

45. a. Would a balloon rise in an atmosphere where the pressure was somehow the same at all altitudes?
  b. Would a balloon rise in the complete absence of atmospheric pressure (for example, at the surface of the moon)?

46. The buoyant force of air is considerably greater on an elephant than on a small helium-filled balloon. Why, then, does the elephant remain on the ground, while the balloon rises?

47. Why is it that when cars pass each other at high speeds on the road, they tend to be drawn to each other?

48. In a department store, an air stream from a hose connected to the exhaust of a vacuum cleaner blows upward at an angle and supports a beach ball in midair. Which is more effective in keeping the ball up—air blowing across the top or air blowing across the bottom of the ball?

49. What physics principle underlies the following three observations? When passing an oncoming truck on the highway, your car tends to swerve toward the truck. The canvas roof of a convertible automobile bulges upward when the car is traveling at high speeds. The windows of older passenger trains sometimes break when a high-speed train passes by on the next track.

50. When a steadily flowing gas flows from a larger-diameter pipe to a smaller-diameter pipe, what happens to each of the following?
  a. its speed
  b. its pressure
  c. the spacing between its streamlines

51. The diameter of a fire hose varies with the flow rate of water inside. The hose may be relatively narrow, and at another time puffed up like a fat snake. In which case is water flowing fast, and when is water hardly flowing at all?

52. You overhear a conversation between two physics types. One says that birds couldn't fly before the time of Bernoulli. The other says that it was not so. Birds could fly before the time of Bernoulli but couldn't fly before the time of Newton. Humor aside, what points are they making?

53. Explain how an airplane is able to fly upside down.

Think and Solve ......

54. A typical school gym is about 60.0 m × 30.0 m × 10.0 m. Show that the mass of air in the gym on a 20°C day is around 22,000 kg.

55. The "height" of the atmosphere is about 30 km. The radius of Earth is 6400 km. What percentage of Earth's radius is the height of the atmosphere?

56. The weight of the atmosphere above 1 square meter of Earth's surface is about 100,000 newtons. If the density of the atmosphere were a *constant* 1.2 kg/m^3, calculate where the top of the atmosphere would be.

57. Average atmospheric pressure at Earth's surface is 1.01×10^5 N/m^2. Earth's radius is 6.37×10^6 m. Show that the total weight of Earth's atmosphere is about 5.15×10^{19} N.

58. A party balloon is squeezed to 2/3 of its initial volume. Show that the pressure in the balloon is increased by 1.5 times.

59. An automobile is supported by four tires inflated to a gauge pressure of 180 kPa. The area of contact of each of the tires (ignoring the effects of tread thickness) is 190 cm^2 (which means the total area of tire contact is 0.076 m^2). Estimate the mass of the car in kilograms.

60. Suppose you have a syringe that contains air but has no needle. You put your thumb over the opening and then squeezed the plunger of the syringe from the 15 mL mark to the 6 mL mark. Show that the pressure in the syringe will then be 250 kPa.

61. A mercury barometer reads 760 mm at sea level. When it is carried to an altitude of 5.6 km, the height of the mercury column is reduced to half its initial value, or 380 mm.

   a. What is the air pressure at this altitude relative to sea-level pressure?

   b. If the barometer is taken up another 5.6 km to an altitude of 11.2 km, will the height of its mercury column fall another 380 mm and be zero? Why or why not?

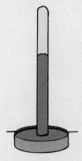

62. On a perfect fall day, you are hovering at low altitude in a hot-air balloon, accelerating neither upward nor downward. The total weight of the balloon, including its load and the hot air in it, is 20,000 N. Find the weight of the displaced air.

63. Referring to the previous problem, find the volume of the displaced air.

64. In 1982 Larry Walters ascended from his home in Long Beach, California, to an altitude of 4900 m (16,000 ft) after tying 42 helium-filled, 1.9-m diameter weather balloons to his patio chair. Show that the buoyant force on these balloons at sea level would be 1800 N.

65. How many newtons of lift are exerted on the wings of an airplane that have a total area of 100 m² when the difference in air pressure below and above the wings is 5% of atmospheric pressure?

Activities ······

66. Try this in the bathtub or while washing dishes. Lower a glass, mouth downward, over a small floating object as shown. What happens? How deep would the glass have to be pushed to compress the enclosed air to half its volume? (*Hint:* You can't do this in your bathtub unless it's 10.3 m deep!)

67. Place a card over the open top of a glass filled to the brim with water, and invert it. What happens? Why? Try turning the glass sideways as shown below.

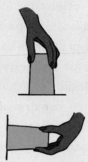

68. Fill a bottle with water and hold it partially under water so that its mouth is beneath the surface. What happens to the water in the bottle? Explain. How tall would the bottle have to be before water ran out? (*Hint:* You can't do this indoors unless you have a ceiling 10.3 m high!)

69. Hold a spoon in a stream of water, as shown. Describe and explain the effect in terms of the differences in pressure.

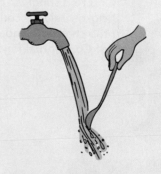

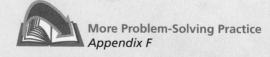

More Problem-Solving Practice
Appendix F

UNIT III HEAT

IT'S A FACT!

Heat is a form of energy. When a substance absorbs heat, its particles move faster. The absorption leads to a rise in temperature or a change in phase—from solid to liquid, or liquid to gas. A hotter substance can transfer heat to a colder substance through direct contact, through movement (such as wind), or through radiation. In this unit, you will learn many interesting facts about thermodynamics, the study of heat.

The **greenhouse effect** explains how air in a greenhouse becomes appreciably hotter than outside air on a sunny day. [Ch. 22]

Although the temperature of these sparks exceeds 2000°C, the heat they impart when striking my skin is very small—which illustrates that **temperature** and **heat** are different concepts. Learning to distinguish between closely related concepts is the challenge and essence of *Conceptual Physics*.

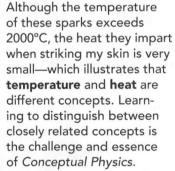

Evaporation keeps animals cool and helps maintain a stable body temperature. [Ch. 23]

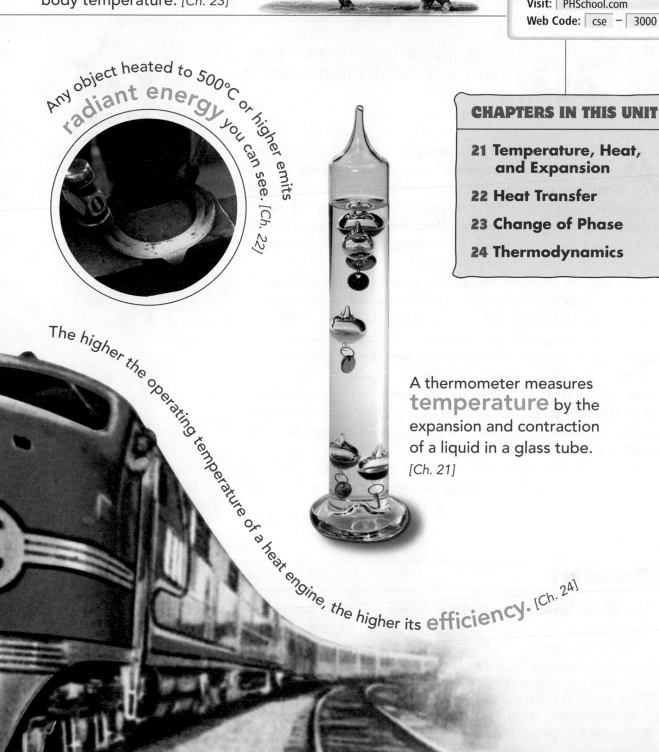

Go Online
SCIENCE NEWS

For: Articles on heat
Visit: PHSchool.com
Web Code: cse – 3000

Any object heated to 500°C or higher emits radiant energy you can see. [Ch. 22]

A thermometer measures temperature by the expansion and contraction of a liquid in a glass tube. [Ch. 21]

The higher the operating temperature of a heat engine, the higher its efficiency. [Ch. 24]

21 TEMPERATURE, HEAT, AND EXPANSION

THE BIG IDEA : When matter gets warmer, the atoms or molecules in the matter move faster.

All matter—solid, liquid, and gas—is composed of continually jiggling atoms or molecules. Because of this random motion, the atoms and molecules in matter have kinetic energy. The average kinetic energy of these individual particles causes an effect we can sense—warmth. Whenever something becomes warmer, the kinetic energy of its atoms or molecules has increased.

It's easy to increase the kinetic energy in matter. You can warm a penny by striking it with a hammer—the blow causes the molecules in the penny to jostle faster. If you put a flame to a liquid, the liquid also becomes warmer. Rapidly compress air in a tire pump and the air becomes warmer. When the atoms or molecules in matter move faster, the matter gets warmer. Its atoms or molecules have more kinetic energy. For brevity in this chapter, rather than saying *atoms and molecules*, we'll simply say molecules—by which we mean either.

So when you warm up by a fire on a cold winter night, you are increasing the molecular kinetic energy in your body.

---

discover!

How Much Heat Can a Balloon Hold?

1. Fill a balloon with air and fill a second, similar balloon with water.

2. Hold a lighted match close to the bottom of the air-filled balloon. **CAUTION!** Do not touch the match to the balloon. Remove the match if the balloon looks as if it is about to rupture.

3. Now hold a lighted match near the bottom of the water-filled balloon.

Analyze and Conclude

1. **Observing** What happened to each of the balloons when exposed to the flame?

2. **Predicting** How long do you think it would take for the water-filled balloon to rupture if the flame were not removed?

3. **Making Generalizations** What role does water play in preventing the rupture of the balloon?

21.1 Temperature

The quantity that tells how hot or cold something is compared with a standard is **temperature.** We express temperature by a number that corresponds to a degree mark on some chosen scale.

Nearly all matter expands when its temperature increases and contracts when its temperature decreases. A common thermometer measures temperature by showing the expansion and contraction of a liquid—usually mercury or colored alcohol—in a glass tube using a scale. Temperature is generally measured on one of three different scales.

Celsius Scale On the most widely used temperature scale, the **Celsius scale,** the number 0 is assigned to the temperature at which water freezes, and the number 100 to the temperature at which water boils (at standard atmospheric pressure).[21.1] The gap between freezing and boiling is divided into 100 equal parts, called *degrees.*

Fahrenheit Scale On the temperature scale used commonly in the United States, the **Fahrenheit scale,** the number 32 designates the temperature at which water freezes, and the number 212 is assigned to the temperature at which water boils (at 1 atm). The Fahrenheit scale will become obsolete if and when the United States goes metric.

Kelvin Scale The scale used in scientific research is the SI scale—the *Kelvin scale.* Its degrees are the same size as the Celsius degree and are called "kelvins." On the **Kelvin scale,** the number 0 is assigned to the lowest possible temperature—*absolute zero.* At **absolute zero,** a substance has no kinetic energy to give up. Zero on the Kelvin scale, or absolute zero, corresponds to –273°C on the Celsius scale. We will learn more about the Kelvin scale in Chapter 24.

Scale Conversion Arithmetic formulas can be used for converting from one temperature scale to another and are often popular in classroom exams. Such arithmetic exercises are not really physics, so we will not be concerned with them here. Besides, a conversion from Celsius to Fahrenheit, or vice versa, can be very closely approximated by simply reading the corresponding temperature from the side-by-side scales in Figure 21.1.

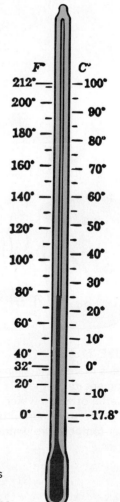

FIGURE 21.1 ▶
This thermometer measures temperature on both Fahrenheit and Celsius scales.

Desert Ants
The surface temperatures of some deserts in Africa and central Asia reach 60°C (140°F). This is hot, but not too hot for a species of ant (*Cataglyphis*) that thrives at this searing temperature. These desert ants can forage for food at temperatures too high for lizards who eat them. Resistant to heat, these ants can withstand higher temperatures than any other creatures in the desert. They scavenge the desert surface for corpses of those who did not find cover in time, touching the hot sand as little as possible while often sprinting on four legs with two high in the air. Although their foraging paths zigzag over the desert floor, their return paths are almost straight lines to their nest holes. They attain speeds of 100 body lengths per second. During an average six-day life, most of these ants retrieve 15 to 20 times their weight in food.

FIGURE 21.2 ▲
There is more molecular kinetic energy in the bucketful of warm water than in the small cupful of higher-temperature water.

Temperature and Kinetic Energy Temperature is related to the random motions of the molecules in a substance. In the simplest case of an ideal gas, temperature is proportional to the *average* kinetic energy of molecular translational motion (that is, motion along a straight or curved path). In solids and liquids, where molecules are more constrained and have potential energy, temperature is more complicated. But it is still true that temperature is closely related to the average kinetic energy of translational motion of molecules.

⊘ **The higher the temperature of a substance, the faster is the motion of its molecules.** So the warmth you feel when you touch a hot surface is the kinetic energy transferred by molecules in the surface to molecules in your fingers.

Note that temperature is *not* a measure of the *total* kinetic energy of all the molecules in a substance. There is twice as much kinetic energy in 2 liters of boiling water as in 1 liter. But the temperatures of both liters of water are the same because the average kinetic energy of molecules in each is the same. Figure 21.2 shows that a bucket of warm water can contain more molecular kinetic energy than a cup of hot water.

CONCEPT CHECK : What is the relationship between the temperature of a substance and the speed of its molecules?

21.2 Heat

If you touch a hot stove, energy enters your hand from the stove because the stove is warmer than your hand. But if you touch ice, energy passes from your hand into the colder ice. The direction of spontaneous energy transfer is always from a warmer to a cooler substance. The energy that transfers from one object to another because of a temperature difference between them is called **heat.**

It is common—but incorrect with physics types—to think that matter *contains* heat. Matter contains energy in several forms, but it does not contain heat. Heat is energy *in transit,* moving from a body of higher temperature to one of lower temperature. Once transferred, the energy ceases to be heat.[21.2] In Chapter 9, we called the energy resulting from heat flow *thermal energy,* to make clear its link to heat and temperature. In this and following chapters, we will use the term that scientists prefer, *internal energy.*

When heat flows from one object or substance to another one it is in contact with, the objects or substances are in **thermal contact.** Figure 21.3 uses an analogy to show how heat flows between two objects in thermal contact. ✅ **When two substances of different temperatures are in thermal contact, heat flows from the higher-temperature substance into the lower-temperature substance.** However, heat will not necessarily flow from a substance with more total molecular kinetic energy to a substance with less. For example, there is more total molecular kinetic energy in a large bowl of warm water than there is in a red-hot thumbtack. Yet, if the tack is immersed in the water, heat does not flow from the water to the tack. It flows from the hot tack to the cooler water. Heat flows according to temperature differences—that is, average molecular kinetic energy differences. Heat never flows on its own from a cooler substance into a hotter substance.

A cool lake has more internal energy than a red-hot tack, even though the tack is at a higher temperature.

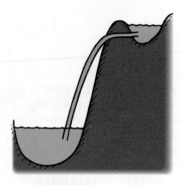

FIGURE 21.3 ▲
Just as water will not flow uphill by itself, regardless of the relative amounts of water in the reservoirs, heat will not flow from a cooler substance into a hotter substance by itself.

CONCEPT CHECK ⋮ What causes heat to flow?

---

discover!

Can You Trust Your Senses?

1. Put some hot water, some warm water, and some cold water in three open containers.

2. Place a finger in the hot water and a finger of the other hand in the cold water. How do they feel?

3. After a few seconds, place both fingers in the warm water. How do they feel now?

4. **Think** Why is a thermometer better for measuring temperature?

21.3 Thermal Equilibrium

After objects in thermal contact with each other reach the same temperature, we say the objects are in **thermal equilibrium.** When objects are in thermal equilibrium, no heat flows between them.

To read a thermometer we wait until it reaches thermal equilibrium with the substance being measured. ⊘ **When a thermometer is in contact with a substance, heat flows between them until they have the same temperature.** The temperature of the thermometer is also the temperature of the substance. So a thermometer, interestingly enough, shows only its own temperature. This is shown in Figure 21.4.

FIGURE 21.4 ▶

Somewhat like water in the pipes seeking a common level (for which the pressures at equal elevations are the same), the thermometer and its immediate surroundings reach a common temperature (at which the average kinetic energy per particle is the same for both).

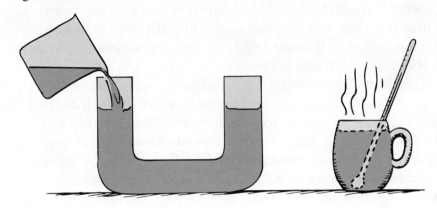

A thermometer should be small enough that it does not appreciably alter the temperature of the substance being measured. If you are measuring the temperature of room air, then the heat absorbed by the thermometer will not lower the air temperature noticeably. But if you are trying to measure the temperature of a drop of water, the temperature of the drop after thermal contact may be quite different from its initial temperature.

CONCEPT CHECK ⋮ How does a thermometer measure temperature?

think!

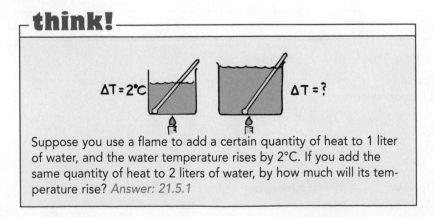

Suppose you use a flame to add a certain quantity of heat to 1 liter of water, and the water temperature rises by 2°C. If you add the same quantity of heat to 2 liters of water, by how much will its temperature rise? *Answer: 21.5.1*

21.4 Internal Energy

In addition to the translational kinetic energy of jostling molecules in a substance, there is energy in other forms. There is rotational kinetic energy of molecules and kinetic energy due to internal movements of atoms within molecules. There is also potential energy due to the forces between molecules. The grand total of all energies inside a substance is called **internal energy.** A substance does not contain heat—it has internal energy.

⊘ **When a substance takes in or gives off heat, its internal energy changes.** Absorbed heat may make the molecules of a substance jostle faster. In other cases, as when ice is melting, a substance absorbs heat without an increase in temperature. The substance changes phase, the subject of Chapter 23.

No matter how cold an object is, it always has some internal energy.

CONCEPT : What happens to the internal energy of a substance
CHECK : that takes in or gives off heat?

21.5 Measurement of Heat

So we see that heat is energy transferred from one substance to another by a temperature difference. ⊘ **The amount of heat transferred can be determined by measuring the temperature change of a known mass of a substance that absorbs the heat.**

When a substance absorbs heat, the resulting temperature change depends on more than just the mass of the substance, as shown in Figure 21.5. The quantity of heat that brings a cupful of soup to a boil might raise the temperature of a pot of soup by only a few degrees. To quantify heat, we must specify the *mass* and *kind* of substance affected.

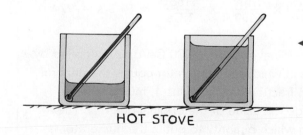

HOT STOVE

◀ **FIGURE 21.5**
Although the same quantity of heat is added to both containers, the temperature of the container with less water increases more.

The unit of heat is defined as the heat necessary to produce some standard, agreed-on temperature change for a specified mass of material. The most commonly used unit for heat is the *calorie*. The **calorie** is defined as the amount of heat required to raise the temperature of 1 gram of water by 1°C.

think!

Which will raise the temperature more, adding 1 calorie or 4.186 joules?

Answer: 21.5.2

The **kilocalorie** is 1000 calories (the heat required to raise the temperature of 1 kilogram of water by 1°C). The heat unit used in rating foods is actually a kilocalorie, although it's often referred to as the calorie. To distinguish it from the smaller calorie, the food unit is sometimes called a Calorie (written with a capital C).

It is important to remember that the calorie and the Calorie are units of energy. In the International System of Units (SI), quantity of heat is measured in joules, the SI unit for all forms of energy. The relationship between calories and joules is that 1 calorie equals 4.186 J. In this book, we'll learn about heat with the conceptually simpler calorie—but in the lab, you may use the joule equivalent, where an input of 4.186 joules raises the temperature of 1 gram of water by 1°C.[21.5]

The energy value in food is determined by burning the food and measuring the energy that is released as heat. Food and other fuels are rated by how much energy a certain mass of the fuel gives off as heat when burned.

CONCEPT CHECK : How can you determine the amount of heat transferred to a substance?

FIGURE 21.6 ▲
To the weight watcher, the peanut contains 10 Calories; to the physicist, it releases 10,000 calories (or 41,860 joules) of energy when burned or digested.

---

do the math!

A woman with an average diet consumes and expends about 2000 Calories per day. The energy used by her body is eventually given off as heat. How many joules per second does her body give off?

We find this by converting 2000 Calories per day to joules per second. We use the information that 1 Calorie equals 4186 joules, 1 day equals 24 hours, and 1 hour equals 3600 seconds. The conversion is then set up as follows:

$$\frac{2000 \ \cancel{Cal}}{1 \ \cancel{d}} \times \frac{1 \ \cancel{d}}{24 \ \cancel{h}} \times \frac{1 \ \cancel{h}}{3600 \ s} \times \frac{4186 \ J}{1 \ \cancel{Cal}} = 97 \ J/s = 97 \ W$$

Notice that the original quantity (2000 Cal/d) is multiplied by a set of fractions in which the numerator equals the denominator. Since each fraction has the value 1, multiplying by it does not change the value of the original quantity. The rule for choosing which quantity to put in the numerator is that the units should cancel and reduce to those of the end result. (We call this technique "dimensional analysis.") On the average, the woman emits heat at the rate of 97 J/s, which is 97 watts. This is nearly the same as a glowing 100-W lamp! It's easy to see why a crowded room soon becomes warm!

21.6 Specific Heat Capacity

Almost everyone has noticed that some foods remain hot much longer than others. Boiled onions and moist squash on a hot dish, for example, are often too hot to eat while mashed potatoes may be just right. The filling of hot apple pie can burn your tongue while the crust will not, even when the pie has just been taken out of the oven. The aluminum covering on a frozen dinner can be peeled off with your bare fingers as soon as it is removed from the oven, as shown in Figure 21.7. (But be careful of the food beneath it!)

Different substances have different capacities for storing internal energy, or heat. ⊘ **The capacity of a substance to store heat depends on its chemical composition.** If we heat a pot of water on a stove, we may find that it requires 15 minutes to raise it from room temperature to its boiling temperature. But if we were to put an equal mass of iron on the same flame, we would find that it would rise through the same temperature range in only about 2 minutes. For silver, the time would be less than a minute. A specific material requires a specific amount of heat to raise the temperature of a given mass of the material by a specified number of degrees. The **specific heat capacity** of a material is the quantity of heat required to raise the temperature of a unit mass of the material by 1 degree.

FIGURE 21.7 ▲
You can touch the aluminum pan of the frozen dinner soon after it has been taken from the hot oven, but you'll burn your fingers if you touch the food it contains.

Table 21.1	Specific Heat Capacities	
Material	**(J/g°C)**	**(cal/g°C)**
Water	4.186	1.00
Aluminum	0.900	0.215
Clay	1.4	0.33
Copper	0.386	0.092
Lead	0.128	0.031
Olive Oil	1.97	0.471
Silver	0.23	0.056
Steel (iron)	0.448	0.107

We can think of specific heat capacity as thermal inertia. Recall that *inertia* is a term used in mechanics to signify the resistance of an object to change in its state of motion. Specific heat capacity is like a thermal inertia since it signifies the resistance of a substance to change in its temperature.

> If you add 1 calorie (4.186 joules) of heat to 1 gram of water, you'll raise its temperature by 1 Celsius degree.

think!

Which has a higher specific heat capacity—water or sand? Explain.
Answer: 21.6

Go Online
SciLINKS™ NSTA

For: Links on specific heat capacity
Visit: www.SciLinks.org
Web Code: csn – 2106

Absorbed energy can affect substances in different ways. Absorbed energy that increases the translational speed of molecules is responsible for increases in temperature. Absorbed energy may also increase the rotation of molecules, increase the internal vibrations within molecules, or stretch intermolecular bonds and be stored as potential energy. These kinds of energy, however, are not measured by a substance's temperature. Temperature is a measure only of the kinetic energy of translational motion. Generally, only part of the energy absorbed by a substance raises its temperature.

Whereas a gram of water requires 1 calorie of energy to raise the temperature 1°C, it takes only about one eighth as much energy to raise the temperature of a gram of iron by the same amount. Iron atoms in the iron lattice primarily shake back and forth in translational fashion, while water molecules soak up a lot of energy in rotations, internal vibrations, and bond stretching. So water absorbs more heat per gram than iron for the same change in temperature. Water has a higher specific heat capacity (sometimes simply called *specific heat*) than iron has.

CONCEPT CHECK: Why do different substances have different capacities to store heat?

---

do the math!

How many calories are needed to raise the temperature of 1 liter of water by 15°C?

When we know the specific heat capacity, *c*, for a particular substance, then the quantity of heat, *Q*, involved when the mass, *m*, of the substance undergoes a temperature change, ΔT, is $Q = mc\Delta T$. Heat transferred = mass × specific heat capacity × temperature change.

The specific heat capacity for water, *c*, is 1 cal/g°C, and the mass of 1 liter of water is 1 kilogram, which is 1000 grams. Since *c* is expressed in calories per *gram* °C, we express the mass of water, *m*, in grams. Then,

$$Q = mc\Delta T$$

$$Q = (1000 \text{ g})(1 \text{ cal/g°C})(15°) = 15{,}000 \text{ calories}$$

Suppose we deliver this energy to the water with a 1000-watt immersion heater. How long will it take to heat the water?

We know that 1000 watts delivers energy at the rate 1000 joules per second. Converting calories to joules,

$$15{,}000 \text{ cal} \times 4.186 \text{ J/cal} = 63{,}000 \text{ joules}$$

At the rate of 1000 joules per second, the time required for heating the water by 15°C is 63 seconds, a little more than a minute.

21.7 The High Specific Heat Capacity of Water

Water has a much higher capacity for storing energy than most common materials. A relatively small amount of water absorbs a great deal of heat for a correspondingly small temperature rise. Because of this, water is a very useful cooling agent, and is used in cooling systems in automobiles and other engines. If a liquid of lower specific heat capacity were used in cooling systems, its temperature would rise higher for a comparable absorption of heat. (Of course, if the temperature of the liquid rises to the temperature of the engine, no further cooling will take place.) Water also takes longer to cool, a useful fact to your great-grandparents, who on cold winter nights likely used foot-warming hot-water bottles in their beds.

Water's capacity to store heat also affects the global climate. As shown in Figure 21.8, water takes more energy to heat up than land does. ✅ **The property of water to resist changes in temperature improves the climate in many places.** Europe and the west coast of the United States both benefit from this property of water.

> Water is king when it comes to specific heat capacity!

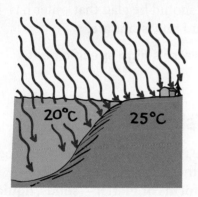

◀ **FIGURE 21.8**
Water has a high specific heat and is transparent, so it takes more energy to heat up than land does.

Climate of Europe The next time you are looking at a world globe, notice the high latitude of Europe. If water did not have a high heat capacity, the countries of Europe would be as cold as the northeastern regions of Canada, for both Europe and Canada get about the same amount of the sun's energy per square kilometer. The Atlantic current known as the Gulf Stream brings warm water northeast from the Caribbean. It holds much of its internal energy long enough to reach the North Atlantic off the coast of Europe, where it then cools. The energy released (one calorie per degree for each gram of water that cools) is carried by the prevailing westerly winds over the European continent.

Climate of America Similarly, the climates differ on the east and west coasts of North America. The prevailing winds in the latitudes of North America are westerly. On the west coast, air moves from the Pacific Ocean to the land. Because of water's high heat capacity, ocean temperature does not vary much from summer to winter. The water is warmer than the air in the winter, and cooler than the air in the summer. In winter, the water warms the air that moves over it and warms the western coastal regions of North America. In summer, the water cools the air and the western coastal regions are cooled. On the east coast, air moves from the land to the Atlantic Ocean. Land, with a lower specific heat capacity, gets hot in summer but cools rapidly in winter. As a result of water's high heat capacity and the wind directions, the west coast city of San Francisco is warmer in the winter and cooler in the summer than the east coast city of Washington, D.C., which is at about the same latitude.

The central interior of a large continent usually experiences extremes of temperature. For example, the high summer and low winter temperatures common in Manitoba and the Dakotas are largely due to the absence of large bodies of water. Europeans, islanders, and people living near ocean air currents should be glad that water has such a high specific heat capacity. San Franciscans are!

CONCEPT CHECK: What is the effect of water's high specific heat capacity on climate?

think!

Why is it advisable to allow telephone lines to sag when stringing them between poles in summer?
Answer: 21.8

21.8 Thermal Expansion

When the temperature of a substance is increased, its molecules jiggle faster and normally tend to move farther apart. This results in an *expansion* of the substance. **Most forms of matter—solids, liquids, and gases—expand when they are heated and contract when they are cooled.** You can see an example of this in Figure 21.9. For comparable pressures and comparable changes in temperature, gases generally expand or contract much more than liquids, and liquids expand or contract more than solids.[21.8] This thermal expansion of solids must be accounted for in construction. It also has applications in certain electronic devices.

FIGURE 21.9 ▶
The extreme heat of a July day in Asbury Park, New Jersey, caused the buckling of these railroad tracks.

Expansion Joints If concrete sidewalks and highway paving were laid down in one continuous piece, cracks would appear due to the expansion and contraction brought about by the difference between summer and winter temperatures. To prevent this, the surface is laid in small sections, each one being separated from the next by a small gap that is filled in with a substance such as tar. On a hot summer day, expansion often squeezes this material out of the joints.

◄ FIGURE 21.10
This gap is called an *expansion joint,* and it allows the bridge to expand and contract.

The *expansion* of materials must be allowed for in the construction of structures and devices of all kinds. Different materials expand at different rates. A dentist uses filling material that has the same rate of expansion as teeth. The aluminum pistons of an automobile engine are enough smaller in diameter than the steel cylinders to allow for the much greater expansion rate of aluminum. A civil engineer uses steel having the same expansion rate as concrete for reinforcing concrete. Long steel bridges often have one end fixed while the other rests on rockers that allow for expansion. The roadway itself is segmented with tongue-and-groove-type gaps called expansion joints, as shown in Figure 21.10.

Bimetallic Strips In a **bimetallic strip,** two strips of different metals, say one of brass and the other of iron, are welded or riveted together, as shown in Figure 21.11. When the strip is heated, the difference in the amounts of expansion of brass and iron shows up easily. One side of the double strip becomes longer than the other, causing the strip to bend into a curve. On the other hand, when the strip is cooled, it bends in the opposite direction, because the metal that expands the most also contracts the most. The movement of the strip may be used to turn a pointer, regulate a valve, or operate a switch.

FIGURE 21.11 ▼
In a bimetallic strip, brass expands (or contracts) more when heated (or cooled) than does iron, so the strip bends as shown.

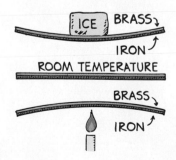

do the math!

Consider the expansion of a make-believe snugly fitting steel pipe that completely encircles Earth. How much longer would this 40-million-meter long pipe be if its temperature increased by 1°C?

Steel changes in length about 1 part in 100,000 for each Celsius degree change in temperature. This is a *ratio*,

$$\frac{1}{100,000}$$

Thermal expansion and contraction account for the creaky noises often heard in the attics of old houses on cold nights.

For different lengths of steel, expansion follows the same proportion. For short lengths of steel, expansion may be negligible.

For the pipe, the ratio of its change in length X to its full size is the same as the ratio above. For a 1°C temperature change:

$$\frac{1}{100,000} = \frac{X\,\text{m}}{40,000,000\,\text{m}}$$

A little computation will show that the change in length X is 400 m. Here's the interesting part: If such a pipe were elongated by this 400 m, then there would be a gap between it and Earth's surface. Would the gap be big enough to put this book under? To crawl under? To drive a truck under? How big would this gap be?

We can find the gap by ratio and proportion. The ratio of circumference C to diameter D for any circle is equal to π (about 3.14). The ratio of the change in circumference ΔC to the change in diameter ΔD also has the same value:

$$\frac{\Delta C}{\Delta D} = \frac{400\,\text{m}}{\Delta D} = 3.14$$

Solve for ΔD:

$$\Delta D = \frac{400\,\text{m}}{3.14} = 127.4\,\text{m}$$

This 127.4 m is the increase in *diameter* of the circular pipe. The size of the gap between Earth's surface and the expanded pipe is equal to the increase in radius, which is half the increase in diameter, or 63.7 m.

So if a steel pipe that fits snugly against Earth were increased in temperature by 1°C, perhaps by people all along its length breathing hard on it, the pipe would expand and stand an amazing 63.7 m off the ground! Using ratio and proportion is a straightforward way to solve many problems. Another way to solve for the expansion of a material involves a formula ($\Delta L = \alpha L_0 \Delta T$). You will encounter this formula in the lab part of your course.

Thermostats A **thermostat**, such as the one in Figure 21.12, is a practical application of a bimetallic strip that is used to control temperature. As the temperature of a room changes, the back-and-forth bending of the bimetallic coil opens and closes an electric circuit. When the room becomes too cold, the coil bends toward the brass side, and in so doing it closes an electric switch that turns on the heat. When the room becomes too warm, the coil bends toward the iron side, which opens the switch and turns off the heating unit. Refrigerators are equipped with special thermostats to prevent them from becoming too hot or too cold. Bimetallic strips are used in oven thermometers, electric toasters, and other devices.

Glass How much a substance expands depends on its change in temperature. If one part of a piece of glass is heated or cooled more rapidly than adjacent parts, the expansion or contraction that results may break the glass. This is especially true for thick glass. Borosilicate glass is formulated to expand very little with increasing temperature.

CONCEPT CHECK How does matter change when heated or cooled?

FIGURE 21.12 ▲
When the bimetallic coil expands in a thermostat, the mercury rolls away from the electrical contacts and breaks the circuit. When the coil contracts, the mercury rolls against the contacts and completes the electric circuit.

---

discover!

How Can You Open a Tightly Closed Jar?

1. Find a glass jar with a metal lid that is difficult to open.

2. Heat the lid by placing it in a stream of hot water or momentarily placing it on a hot stove. Try to unscrew the lid. What happens?

3. **Think** Why is the jar easier to open after the metal lid is heated?

21.9 Expansion of Water

Almost all liquids will expand when they are heated. Ice-cold water, however, does just the opposite! Water at the temperature of melting ice, 0°C (or 32°F), *contracts* when the temperature is increased. This is most unusual. As the water is heated and its temperature rises, it continues to contract until it reaches a temperature of 4°C. With further increase in temperature, the water then begins to *expand*; the expansion continues all the way to the boiling point, 100°C. This odd behavior is shown graphically in Figure 21.13 on the next page.

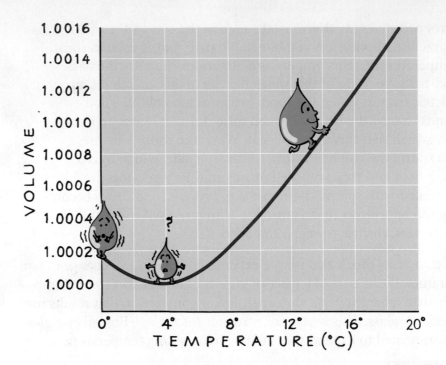

FIGURE 21.13 ▶
The graph shows the
change in volume of water
with increasing temperature.

A given amount of water has its smallest volume—and thus its
greatest density—at 4°C. The same amount of water has its largest
volume—and smallest density—in its solid form, ice. (Remember, ice
floats in water, so it must be less dense than water.) The volume of ice
at 0°C is not shown in Figure 21.13. (If it were plotted to the same exaggerated scale, the graph would extend far beyond the top of the page.)
After water has turned to ice, further cooling causes it to contract.

The explanation for this behavior of water has to do with the odd
crystal structure of ice. The crystals of most solids are structured so
that the solid state occupies a smaller volume than the liquid state.
Ice, however, has open-structured crystals, as shown in Figure 21.14.
These crystals result from the angular shape of the water molecules,
plus the fact that the forces binding water molecules together are
strongest at certain angles. Water molecules in this open structure
occupy a greater volume than they do in the liquid state. ✅ **At 0°C,
ice is less dense than water, and so ice floats on water.**

FIGURE 21.14 ▶
Water molecules in their
crystal form have an open-
structured, six-sided
arrangement. As a result,
water expands upon
freezing, and ice is less
dense than water.

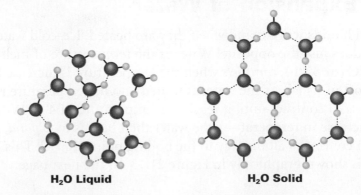

H₂O Liquid   H₂O Solid

◄ **FIGURE 21.15**
The six-sided structure of
a snowflake is a result of
the six-sided ice crystals
that make it up.

Melting Ice When ice melts, not all the open-structured crystals collapse. Some crystals remain in the ice-water mixture, which makes up a microscopic slush that slightly "bloats" the water (increasing its volume slightly). Ice water is therefore less dense than slightly warmer water. With an increase in temperature, more of the remaining ice crystals collapse. The melting of these crystals further decreases the volume of the water.

While crystals are collapsing as the temperature increases between 0°C and 10°C, increased molecular motion results in expansion. This effect is shown in the center graph in Figure 21.16. Whether ice crystals are in the water or not, increased vibrational motion of the molecules increases the volume of the water.

When we combine the effects of contraction and expansion, the curve looks like the right-hand graph in Figure 21.16 (or Figure 21.13). This behavior of water is of great importance in nature. Suppose that the greatest density of water were at its freezing point, as is true of most liquids. Then the coldest water would settle to the bottom, and ponds would freeze from the bottom up. Pond organisms would then be destroyed in winter months. Fortunately, this does not happen. The densest water, which settles at the bottom of a pond, is 4 degrees above the freezing temperature. Water at the freezing point, 0°C, is less dense and floats, so ice forms at the surface while the pond remains liquid below the ice.

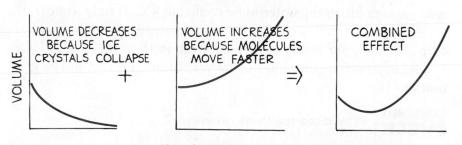

◄ **FIGURE 21.16**
The collapsing of
ice crystals (left) plus increased molecular motion
with increasing tempera-
ture (center) combine to
make water most dense at
4°C (right).

Freezing Water Let's examine this in more detail. Most of the cooling in a pond takes place at its surface, when the surface air is colder than the water. As the surface water is cooled, it becomes denser and sinks to the bottom. Water will "float" at the surface for further cooling only if it is as dense or less dense than the water below.

Consider a pond that is initially at, say, 10°C. It cannot possibly be cooled to 0°C without first being cooled to 4°C. And water at 4°C cannot remain at the surface for further cooling unless all the water below has at least an equal density—that is, unless all the water below is at 4°C. If the water below the surface is any temperature other than 4°C, any surface water at 4°C will be denser and sink before it can be further cooled. So before any ice can form, all the water in a pond must be cooled to 4°C. Only when this condition is met can the surface water be cooled to 3°, 2°, 1°, and 0°C without sinking. Then ice can form, as shown in Figure 21.17.

FIGURE 21.17 ▶

As water is cooled at the surface, it sinks until the entire lake is 4°C. Only then can the surface water cool to 0°C without sinking.

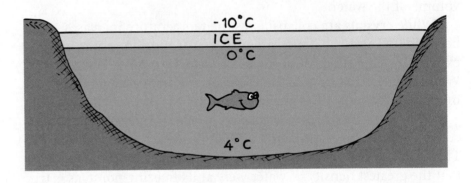

Thus, the water at the surface is first to freeze. Continued cooling of the pond results in the freezing of the water next to the ice, so a pond freezes from the surface downward. In a cold winter the ice will be thicker than in a milder winter.

Very deep bodies of water are not ice-covered even in the coldest of winters. This is because all the water in a lake must be cooled to 4°C before lower temperatures can be reached, and the winter is not long enough for all the water to be cooled to 4°C. If only some of the water is 4°C, it will lie on the bottom. Because of water's high specific heat and poor ability to conduct heat, the bottom of deep lakes in cold regions is a constant 4°C the year round. Fish should be glad that this is so.

CONCEPT CHECK Why does ice float on water?

21 REVIEW

Go Online
PHSchool.com

For: Self-Assessment
Visit: PHSchool.com
Web Code: csa – 2100

Concept Summary ......

- The higher the temperature of a substance, the faster is the motion of its molecules.

- When two substances are in thermal contact, heat flows from the higher-temperature substance into the lower-temperature one.

- When a thermometer is in contact with a substance, heat flows between them until they have the same temperature.

- When a substance takes in or gives off heat, its internal energy changes.

- Heat transferred can be found by measuring the temperature change of a known mass of substance that absorbs the heat.

- The capacity of a substance to store heat depends on its chemical composition.

- The property of water to resist changes in temperature improves the climate.

- Most forms of matter expand when they are heated and contract when they are cooled.

- At 0°C, ice is less dense than water, and so ice floats on water.

Key Terms ......

temperature (p. 407)

Celsius scale (p. 407)

Fahrenheit scale (p. 407)

Kelvin scale (p. 407)

absolute zero (p. 407)

heat (p. 409)

thermal contact (p. 409)

thermal equilibrium (p. 410)

internal energy (p. 411)

calorie (p. 411)

kilocalorie (p. 412)

specific heat capacity (p. 413)

bimetallic strip (p. 417)

thermostat (p. 419)

think! Answers

21.5.1   Its temperature will rise by 1°C because there are twice as many molecules in 2 liters of water and each molecule receives only half as much energy on average. So average kinetic energy, and temperature, increase by half as much.

21.5.2   Both are the same. This is like asking which is longer, a 1-mile-long track or a 1.6-kilometer-long track. They're the same quantity expressed in different units.

21.6   Water has a greater heat capacity than sand. Water is much slower to warm in the hot sun and slower to cool in the cold night. Water has more thermal inertia. Sand's low heat capacity, as evidenced by how quickly the surface warms in the morning sun and how quickly it cools at night, affects local climates.

21.8   Telephone lines are longer in summer, when they are warmer, and shorter in winter, when they are cooler. They therefore sag more on hot summer days than in winter. If the telephone lines are not strung with enough sag in summer, they might contract too much and snap during the winter.

21 ASSESS

Check Concepts ......

Section 21.1

1. What is the connection between temperature and kinetic energy?

2. How many degrees are between the melting point of ice and boiling point of water on the Celsius scale? Fahrenheit scale?

3. Why does 2 liters of boiling water not have twice as great a temperature as 1 liter of boiling water?

Section 21.2

4. Why is it incorrect to say that matter *contains* heat?

5. In terms of differences in temperature between objects in thermal contact, in what direction does heat flow?

Section 21.3

6. What is meant by saying that a thermometer measures its own temperature?

7. What is thermal equilibrium?

Section 21.4

8. What is internal energy?

Section 21.5

9. What is the difference between a calorie and a Calorie?

10. What is the difference between a calorie and a joule?

Section 21.6

11. What does it mean to say that a material has a high or low specific heat capacity?

12. Do substances that heat up quickly normally have high or low specific heat capacities?

Section 21.7

13. How does the specific heat capacity of water compare with that of other common substances?

14. Why is the North American west coast warmer in winter months and cooler in summer months than the east coast?

Section 21.8

15. Why does a bimetallic strip curve when it is heated (or cooled)?

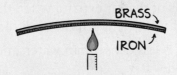

16. Which expands most for increases in temperature: solids, liquids, or gases?

Section 21.9

17. At what temperature is the density of water greatest?

18. Ice is less dense than water because of its open crystalline structure. But why is water at 0°C less dense than water at 4°C?

19. Why do lakes and ponds freeze from the top down rather than from the bottom up?

20. Why do shallow lakes freeze quickly in winter, and deep lakes not at all?

Think and Rank ••••••

Rank each of the following sets of scenarios in order of the quantity or property involved. List them from left to right. If scenarios have equal rankings, then separate them with an equal sign. (e.g., A = B)

21. The four plastic-foam soup bowls contain the same amount of water at 20°C. You also have a batch of 100-g copper cylinders that have initial temperatures as shown. The cylinders are submerged in the bowls.

Rank the bowls according to the maximum temperature of the water after the cylinders are added.

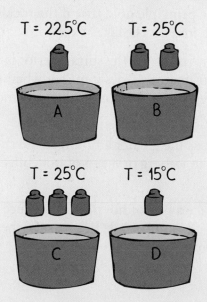

22. Four plastic-foam soup bowls contain the same amount of water at 20°C. You dunk cylinders of different metals, but of equal masses, in the bowls. All four cylinders have been in a hot oven and have the same temperature. (See Table 21.1 for specific heat capacities of these metals.)

Rank the bowls according to the maximum temperature of the water after the cylinders are added.

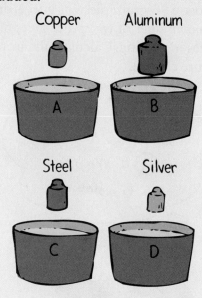

Plug and Chug ••••••

Heat transfer in calories is given by $Q = mc\Delta T$, where m is mass in grams, c is specific heat capacity in cal/g°C, and ΔT is in °C.

23. Calculate the number of calories of heat needed to change 500 grams of water by 50 Celsius degrees.

24. Calculate the number of calories given off by 500 grams of water cooling from 50°C to 20°C.

25. A 30-gram piece of iron is heated to 100°C and then dropped into cool water where the iron's temperature drops to 30°C. How many calories does it lose to the water? (The specific heat capacity of iron is 0.11 cal/g°C.)

26. Suppose a 30-gram piece of iron is dropped into a container of water and gives off 165 calories in cooling. Calculate the iron's temperature change.

27. What mass of water will give up 240 calories when its temperature drops from 80°C to 68°C?

28. When a 50-gram piece of aluminum at 100°C is placed in water, it loses 735 calories of heat while cooling to 30°C. Calculate the specific heat capacity of the aluminum.

Think and Explain ••••••

29. In your room, there are things such as tables, chairs, other people, and so forth. Which of these things has a temperature
   a. lower than room temperature?
   b. greater than room temperature?
   c. equal to room temperature?

30. Which is greater, an increase in temperature of 1°C or an increase of 1°F?

31. If you drop a hot rock into a pail of water, the temperature of the rock and the water will change until both are equal. The rock will cool and the water will warm. Does the same principle hold true if the rock is dropped into a large lake? Explain.

32. The temperature of the sun's interior is about 10^7 degrees. Does it matter whether this is degrees Celsius or kelvins? Defend your answer.

33. Which has the greater amount of internal energy, an iceberg or a cup of hot coffee? Explain.

34. If you take a bite of hot pizza, the sauce may burn your mouth while the crust, at the same temperature, will not. Explain.

35. In the old days, on a cold winter night it was common to bring a hot object to bed with you. Which would be better—a 10-kilogram iron brick or a 10-kilogram jug of hot water at the same temperature? Explain.

36. In addition to the overall motion of molecules that is associated with temperature, some molecules can absorb large amounts of energy in the form of internal vibrations and rotations of the molecules themselves. Would you expect materials composed of such molecules to have a high or a low specific heat capacity? Why?

37. Desert sand is very hot in the day and very cool at night. What does this tell you about its specific heat?

38. Why does adding the same amount of heat to two different objects not necessarily produce the same increase in temperature?

39. When a 1-kg metal pan containing 1 kg of cold water is removed from the refrigerator and set on a table, which absorbs more heat from the room—the pan or the water? Defend your answer.

40. On a hot day, you remove from a picnic cooler a chilled watermelon and some chilled sandwiches. Which will remain cool for a longer time? Why?

41. Why is it important to protect water pipes so they don't freeze?

42. Iceland, so named to discourage conquest by expanding empires, is not at all ice-covered like Greenland and parts of Siberia, even though it is nearly on the Arctic Circle. The average winter temperature of Iceland is considerably higher than regions at the same latitude in eastern Greenland and central Siberia. Why is this so?

43. A metal ball is just able to pass through a metal ring. When the ball is heated, thermal expansion will not allow it to pass through the ring. What would happen if the ring, rather than the ball, were heated? Would the ball pass through the heated ring? Does the size of the hole in the ring increase, decrease, or stay the same?

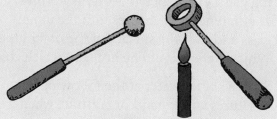

44. After a machinist slips a hot, snugly fitting iron ring over a cold brass cylinder, the ring becomes "locked" in position and can't be removed even by subsequent heating. This procedure is called "shrink fitting." How does it occur? Can you conclude anything about the thermal expansion rates of iron and brass?

45. Suppose you cut a small gap in a metal ring, as shown. If you heat the ring, will the gap become wider or narrower?

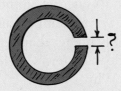

46. Would a bimetallic strip function if the two different metals happened to have the same rates of expansion? Is it important that they expand at different rates? Explain.

47. Cite an exception to the claim that all substances expand when heated.

48. An old remedy for a pair of nested drinking glasses that stick together is to run water at different temperatures into the inner glass and over the surface of the outer glass. Which water should be hot, and which cold?

49. State whether water at the following temperatures will expand or contract when warmed: 0°C; 4°C; 6°C.

50. Suppose that water is used in a thermometer instead of mercury. If the temperature is at 4°C and then changes, why can't the thermometer indicate whether the temperature is rising or falling?

51. If water had a lower specific heat capacity, would lakes be more likely or less likely to freeze in the winter?

52. How does the combined volume of the billions and billions of hexagonal open spaces in the crystals in a piece of ice compare with the portion of ice that floats above the surface of the water?

Think and Solve ......

53. People in the pioneering days placed hot potatoes in their pockets on cold winter days to keep their hands warm. Assuming that a potato is mostly water, Andrew calculates 24,000 calories of heat are released by a 350-g potato that cools from 85°C to 15°C. Alexis calculates that 102,000 joules of heat are released. Whose answer do you agree with, and why?

54. If you wished to warm 100 kg of water by 15°C for your bath, how much heat would be required? (Give your answer in calories and joules.)

55. Anthony's thin plastic water bottle holds 500 mL of water at temperature 28°C. He puts it into the refrigerator. Show that the refrigerator removes 50,000 J of heat from the water to cool it to 4°C.

56. Samantha decides to try the "Ice-Water Diet." She drinks water at 0°C, and it must warm up to her body temperature, 37°C.
   a. How much ice water must she drink to "burn" 3500 Calories (the approximate energy content of one pound of fat)? Each Calorie is 1000 calories.
   b. Why would she recommend, or not recommend, this diet for losing weight?

57. What would be the final temperature of the mixture of 50 g of 20°C water and 50 g of 40°C water?

58. What would be the final temperature if you mixed a liter of 20°C water with 2 liters of 40°C water?

59. What would be the final temperature if you mixed a liter of 40°C water with 2 liters of 20°C water?

60. What would be the final temperature when 100 g of 25°C water is mixed with 75 g of 40°C water?

61. What will be the final temperature of 100 g of 20°C water when 100 g of 40°C iron nails are submerged in it? (The specific heat of iron is 0.12 cal/g°C.)

62. What is the specific heat capacity of a 50-gram piece of 100°C metal that will change 400 grams of 20°C water to 22°C?

63. Taylor finds that a certain amount of heat raises the temperature of a sample of iron by 10°C. Show that the same amount of heat will raise the temperature of an equal mass of lead by 35°C.

64. Suppose that a metal bar 1 m long expands 0.5 cm when it is heated. How much would it expand if it were 100 m long?

65. Steel expands 1 part in 100,000 for each Celsius degree increase in temperature. If the 1.5-km main span of a steel suspension bridge had no expansion joints, how much longer would it be for a temperature increase of 20°C?

66. A cook pours 1 L of ice water at 0°C into a pan of hot water at 80°C and finds that the mixture reaches a temperature of 60°C. How much hot water was in the pan?

67. Your (perfectly insulated) bathtub has 82 liters of water in it, but it has cooled down to a temperature of 39°C. You'd like to add just the right amount of 50°C water to the tub to make your bathwater the perfect temperature of 42°C. Show that adding 31 liters of 50°C water to the tub will accomplish this goal.

More Problem-Solving Practice
Appendix F

HEAT TRANSFER

THE BIG IDEA : Heat can be transferred by conduction, by convection, and by radiation.

The spontaneous transfer of heat is always from warmer objects to cooler objects. If several objects near one another have different temperatures, then those that are warm become cooler and those that are cool become warmer, until all have a common temperature. This equalization of temperatures is brought about in three ways: by *conduction*, by *convection*, and by *radiation*.

discover!

Does White Ever Appear Black?

1. Using a paper punch or sharp pencil, make a small hole in the center of a black sheet of construction paper.
2. Place the paper on top of a polystyrene coffee cup or any cup that is all white inside.

Analyze and Conclude

1. **Observing** Which is darker, the construction paper or the hole?
2. **Predicting** What do you think will happen if you enlarge the hole?
3. **Making Generalizations** Why do openings such as the pupil of the eye and doorways of distant houses appear black even in the daytime?

22.1 Conduction

If you hold one end of an iron rod in a flame, as shown in Figure 22.1, before long the rod will become too hot to hold. Heat has transferred through the metal by *conduction*. **Conduction** of heat is the transfer of energy within materials and between different materials that are in direct contact. Materials that conduct heat well are known as heat **conductors.** Metals are the best conductors. Among the common metals, silver is the most conductive, followed by copper, aluminum, and iron.

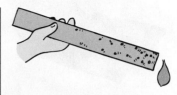

FIGURE 22.1 ▲
Heat from the flame causes atoms and free electrons in the end of the metal to move faster and jostle against others. Those particles do the same and increase the energy of vibrating atoms along the length of the rod.

Conduction is explained by collisions between atoms or molecules, and the actions of loosely bound electrons. ⊘ **In conduction, collisions between particles transfer thermal energy, without any overall transfer of matter.** When the end of an iron rod is held in a flame, the atoms at the heated end vibrate more rapidly. These atoms vibrate against neighboring atoms, which in turn do the same. More important, free electrons that can drift through the metal are made to jostle and transfer energy by colliding with atoms and other free electrons within the rod.

Conductors Materials composed of atoms with "loose" outer electrons are good conductors of heat (and electricity also). Because metals have the "loosest" outer electrons, they are the best conductors of heat and electricity.

◀ **FIGURE 22.2**
The tile floor feels cold to the bare feet, while the carpet at the same temperature feels warm. This is because tile is a better conductor than carpet.

Touch a piece of metal and a piece of wood in your immediate vicinity. Which one *feels* colder? Which is *really* colder? Your answers should be different. If the materials are in the same vicinity, they should have the same temperature, room temperature. Thus neither is really colder. Yet, the metal *feels* colder because it is a better conductor, like the tile in Figure 22.2; heat easily moves out of your warmer hand into the cooler metal. Wood, on the other hand, is a poor conductor. Little heat moves out of your hand into the wood, so your hand does not sense that it is touching something cooler. Wood, wool, straw, paper, cork, and polystyrene are all poor heat conductors. Instead, they are called good *insulators*.

think!

If you hold one end of a metal bar against a piece of ice, the end in your hand will soon become cold. Does cold flow from the ice to your hand?
Answer: 22.1.1

FIGURE 22.3 ▲
A "warm" blanket does not provide you with heat; it simply slows the transfer of your body heat to the surroundings.

FIGURE 22.4 ▶
Snow lasts longest on the roof of a well-insulated house. Thus, the snow patterns reveal the conduction, or lack of conduction, of heat through the roof. The houses with more snow on the roof are better insulated.

think!

You can place your hand into a hot pizza oven for several seconds without harm, whereas you'd never touch the metal inside surfaces for even a second. Why?
Answer: 22.1.2

Insulators Liquids and gases generally make poor conductors—they are good insulators. An **insulator** is any material that is a poor conductor of heat and that delays the transfer of heat. Air is a very good insulator. Porous materials having many small air spaces are good insulators. The good insulating properties of materials such as wool, fur, and feathers are largely due to the air spaces they contain. Birds vary their insulation by fluffing their feathers to create air spaces. Be glad that air is a poor conductor, for if it were not, you'd feel quite chilly on a 25°C (77°F) day!

Snowflakes imprison a lot of air in their crystals and are good insulators. Snow slows the escape of heat from Earth's surface, shields Eskimo dwellings from the cold, and provides protection from the cold to animals on cold winter nights. Snow, like the blanket in Figure 22.3, is not a source of heat; it simply prevents any heat from escaping too rapidly.

Heat is energy and is tangible. Cold is not; cold is simply the absence of heat. Strictly speaking, there is no "cold" that passes through a conductor or an insulator. Only heat is transferred. We don't insulate a home, such as some of those in Figure 22.4, to keep the cold out; we insulate to keep the heat in. If the home becomes colder, it is because heat flows out.

It is important to note that no insulator can totally prevent heat from getting through it. An insulator just reduces the rate at which heat penetrates. Even the best-insulated warm homes in winter will gradually cool. Insulation slows down heat transfer.

CONCEPT CHECK How does conduction transfer heat?

22.2 Convection

Conduction involves the transfer of energy from molecule to molecule. Energy moves from one place to another, but the molecules themselves do not. Another means of heat transfer is by movement of the hotter substance. Air in contact with a hot stove rises and warms the region above. Water heated in a boiler in the basement rises to warm the radiators in the upper floors. This is **convection,** a means of heat transfer by movement of the heated substance itself, such as by currents in a fluid.

think!

You can hold your fingers beside the candle flame without harm, but not above the flame. Why?
Answer: 22.2

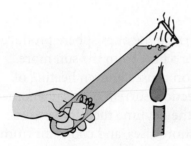

◄ **FIGURE 22.5**
When the test tube is heated at the top, convection is prevented and heat can reach the ice by conduction only. Since water is a poor conductor, the top water will boil without melting the ice.

 In convection, heat is transferred by movement of the hotter substance from one place to another. A simple demonstration illustrates the difference between conduction and convection. With a bit of steel wool, trap a piece of ice at the bottom of a test tube nearly filled with water. Hold the tube by the bottom with your bare hand and place the top in the flame of a Bunsen burner, as shown in Figure 22.5. The water at the top will come to a vigorous boil while the ice below remains unmelted. The hot water at the top is less dense and remains at the top. Any heat that reaches the ice must be transferred by conduction, and we see that water is a poor conductor of heat. If you repeat the experiment, only this time holding the test tube at the top by means of tongs and heating the water from below while the ice floats at the surface, the ice will melt quickly. Heat gets to the top by convection, for the hot water rises to the surface, carrying its energy with it to the ice.

Convection ovens are simply ovens with a fan inside, which speeds up cooking by circulating the warmed air.

discover!

Can You See Convection?

1. Bring a beaker full of water to a boil.

2. Drop a small amount of dark dye or food coloring into the water. What path does it take as it flows through the water?

3. **Think** Give three other examples of where you can see the paths of convection.

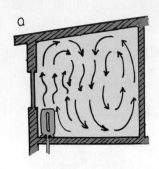

Convection occurs in all fluids. **a.** Convection currents transfer heat in air. **b.** Convection currents transfer heat in liquid.

Convection occurs in all fluids, whether liquid or gas. Whether we heat water in a pan or heat air in a room, the process is the same, as shown in Figure 22.6. When the fluid is heated, it expands, becomes less dense, and rises. Warm air or warm water rises for the same reason that a block of wood floats in water and a helium-filled balloon rises in air. In effect, convection is an application of Archimedes' principle, for the warmer fluid is buoyed upward by denser surrounding fluid. Cooler fluid then moves to the bottom, and the process continues. In this way, convection currents keep a fluid stirred up as it heats. Convection currents also have a large influence on the air in the atmosphere.

Moving Air Convection currents stirring the atmosphere produce winds. Some parts of Earth's surface absorb heat from the sun more readily than others. The uneven absorption causes uneven heating of the air near the surface and creates convection currents. This phenomenon is often evident at the seashore. In the daytime the shore warms more easily than the water. Air over the shore rises, and cooler air from above the water takes its place. The result is a sea breeze, as shown in Figure 22.7.

At night the process reverses as the shore cools off more quickly than the water—the warmer air is now over the sea. If you build a fire on the beach you'll notice that the smoke sweeps inward in the day and seaward at night.

FIGURE 22.7 ▼
Convection currents are produced by uneven heating.

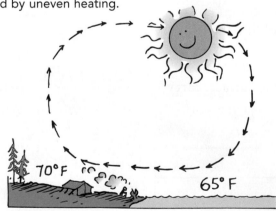

a. During the day, the land is warmer than the air, and a sea breeze results.

b. At night, the land is cooler than the water, so the air flows in the other direction.

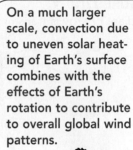

On a much larger scale, convection due to uneven solar heating of Earth's surface combines with the effects of Earth's rotation to contribute to overall global wind patterns.

Cooling Air Rising warm air, like a rising balloon, expands. Why? Because less atmospheric pressure squeezes on it at higher altitudes. As the air expands, it cools—just the opposite of what happens when air is compressed. If you've ever compressed air with a tire pump, you probably noticed that the air and pump became quite hot. The opposite happens when air expands. Expanding air cools.

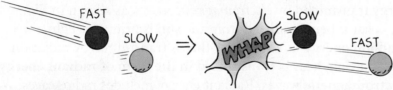

FIGURE 22.8 ▲
When a molecule collides with a target molecule that is receding, its rebound speed after the collision is less than it was before the collision.

We can understand the cooling of expanding air by thinking of molecules of air as tiny balls bouncing against one another. Speed is picked up by a ball when it is hit by another that approaches with a greater speed. When a ball collides with one that is receding, its rebound speed is reduced, as shown in Figure 22.8. Likewise for a table-tennis ball moving toward a paddle; it picks up speed when it hits an approaching paddle, but loses speed when it hits a receding paddle. This also applies to a region of air that is expanding; molecules collide, on the average, with more molecules that are receding than are approaching, as shown in Figure 22.9. Thus, in expanding air, the average speed of the molecules decreases and the air cools.[22.2]

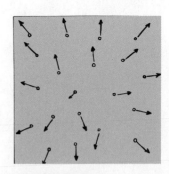

FIGURE 22.9 ▲
Molecules in a region of expanding air collide more often with receding molecules than with approaching ones.

CONCEPT CHECK How does convection transfer heat?

FIGURE 22.10 ▼
Radiant energy is transmitted as electromagnetic waves.

a. Radio waves send signals through the air.

b. You feel infrared waves as heat.

c. A visible form of radiant energy is light waves.

FIGURE 22.11 ▲

Most of the heat from a fireplace goes up the chimney by convection. The heat that warms us comes to us by radiation.

22.3 Radiation

How does the sun warm Earth's surface? It can't be through conduction, because there is 150 million kilometers of virtually nothing between Earth and the sun. Nor can it be by convection, because there is nothing between the sun and Earth to expand and rise. The sun's heat is transmitted by another process—by *radiation*.[22.3.1] **Radiation** is energy transmitted by *electromagnetic waves*, as shown in Figure 22.10. What is being radiated from the sun is primarily light.

Radiant energy is any energy that is transmitted by radiation. ⊘ **In radiation, heat is transmitted in the form of radiant energy, or electromagnetic waves.** Radiant energy includes radio waves, microwaves, infrared radiation (such as the heat from the fireplace in Figure 22.11), visible light, ultraviolet radiation, X-rays, and gamma rays. These types of radiant energy are listed in order of wavelength, from longest to shortest.[22.3.2]

CONCEPT CHECK How does radiation transmit heat?

discover!

Why Do Glasses Keep You Cool?

1. Sit close to a fire in a fireplace and feel the heat on your closed eyelids.

2. Now slip a pair of glasses over your eyes. How do your eyes feel?

3. **Think** Why did the glasses cause your eyes to feel a different temperature?

22.4 Emission of Radiant Energy

⊘ **All substances continuously emit radiant energy in a mixture of wavelengths.** Objects at low temperatures emit long waves, just as long, lazy waves are produced when you shake a rope with little energy as shown in Figure 22.12. Higher-temperature objects emit waves of shorter wavelengths. Objects of everyday temperatures emit waves mostly in the long-wavelength end of the infrared region, which is between radio and light waves. Shorter-wavelength infrared waves absorbed by our skin produce the sensation of heat. Thus, when we speak of heat radiation, we are speaking of infrared radiation.

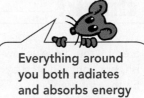

Everything around you both radiates and absorbs energy continuously!

◀ **FIGURE 22.12**
Shorter wavelengths are produced when the rope is shaken more rapidly.

The fact that all objects in our environment continuously emit infrared radiation underlies infrared thermometers such as the one in Figure 22.13. How nice it is that you simply point the thermometer at something whose temperature you want, press a button, and a digital temperature reading appears. The radiation emitted by the object whose temperature you wish to know provides the reading. Typical classroom infrared thermometers operate in the range of about −30°C to 200°C.

The average frequency $\overline{f}$ of radiant energy is directly proportional to the Kelvin temperature T of the emitter:

$$\overline{f} \sim T$$

People, with a surface temperature of 310 K, emit light in the low-frequency infrared part of the spectrum, which is why we can't see each other in the dark. If an object is hot enough, some of the radiant energy it emits is in the range of visible light. At a temperature of about 500°C an object begins to emit the longest waves we can see, red light. Higher temperatures produce a yellowish light. At about 1500°C all the different waves to which the eye is sensitive are emitted and we see an object as "white hot." You can see this relationship in the temperatures of the stars. A blue-hot star is hotter than a white-hot star, and a red-hot star is less hot. Since the color blue has nearly twice the frequency of red, a blue-hot star has nearly twice the surface temperature of a red-hot star. The radiant energy emitted by the stars is called **stellar radiation.**

FIGURE 22.13 ▼
An infrared thermometer measures the infrared radiant energy emitted by a body and converts it to temperature.

think!

Why is it that light radiated by the sun is yellowish, but light radiated by Earth is infrared?
Answer: 22.4

The surface of the sun has a high temperature (5500°C) and therefore emits radiant energy at a high frequency—much of it in the visible portion of the electromagnetic spectrum. The surface of Earth, by comparison, is relatively cool, and so the radiant energy it emits consists of frequencies lower than those of visible light. Radiant energy that is emitted by Earth is called **terrestrial radiation,** which is in the form of infrared waves—below our threshold of sight. The source of the sun's radiant energy involves thermonuclear fusion in its deep interior. In contrast, much of Earth's supply of energy is fueled by radioactive decay in its interior. So we see that both the sun and Earth glow—the sun at high visible frequencies and Earth at low infrared frequencies. And both glows are related to nuclear processes in their interiors. (We'll treat radioactive decay in Chapter 39 and thermonuclear fusion in Chapter 40.)

When radiant energy encounters objects, it is partly reflected and partly absorbed. The part that is absorbed increases the internal energy of the objects.

CONCEPT CHECK What substances emit radiant energy?

22.5 Absorption of Radiant Energy

If everything is emitting energy, why doesn't everything finally run out of it? The answer is that everything also absorbs energy from its environment.

Absorption and Emission For example, a book sitting on your desk is both absorbing and radiating energy at the same rate. It is in *thermal equilibrium* with its environment. Imagine that you move the book out into the bright sunshine. If the book's temperature doesn't change, it radiates the same amount of energy as before. But because the sun shines on it, the book absorbs more energy than it radiates. Its temperature increases. As the book gets hotter, it radiates more energy, eventually reaching a *new* thermal equilibrium. Then it radiates as much energy as it receives. In the sunshine the book remains at this new higher temperature.

If you move the book back indoors, the opposite process occurs. The hot book initially radiates more energy than it receives from its surroundings. So it cools. In cooling, it radiates less energy. At a sufficiently lowered temperature it radiates no more energy than it receives from the room. It stops cooling. It has reached thermal equilibrium again.

A hot pizza placed outside on a winter day is a net emitter. The same pizza placed in a hotter oven is a net absorber.

☑ **Good emitters of radiant energy are also good absorbers; poor emitters are poor absorbers.** For example, a radio antenna constructed to be a good emitter of radio waves is also, by its very design, a good receiver (absorber) of them. A poorly designed transmitting antenna is also a poor receiver.

A blacktop pavement and dark automobile body may remain hotter than their surroundings on a hot day. But at nightfall these dark objects cool faster! Sooner or later, all objects in thermal contact come to thermal equilibrium. So a dark object that absorbs radiant energy well emits radiation equally well.[22.5]

think!

If a good absorber of radiant energy were a poor emitter, how would its temperature compare with its surroundings?
Answer: 22.5

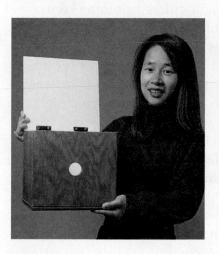

◀ **FIGURE 22.14**
Even though the interior of the box has been painted white, the hole looks black.

Absorption and Reflection Absorption and reflection are opposite processes. Therefore, a good absorber of radiant energy reflects very little radiant energy, including the range of radiant energy we call light. So a good absorber appears dark. A perfect absorber reflects no radiant energy and appears perfectly black. The pupil of the eye, for example, allows radiant energy to enter with no reflection and appears perfectly black. (The red "pupils" that appear in some flash portraits are from direct light reflected off the retina at the back of the eyeball.)

Look at the open ends of pipes in a stack. The holes appear black. Look at open doorways or windows of distant houses in the daytime, and they too look black. Openings appear black, as in Figure 22.14, because the radiant energy that enters is reflected from the inside walls many times and is partly absorbed at each reflection until very little or none remains to come back out. You can see this illustrated in Figure 22.15.

FIGURE 22.15 ▶
Radiant energy that enters an opening has little chance of leaving before it is completely absorbed.

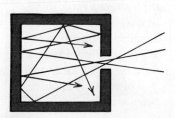

◀ FIGURE 22.16
Anything with a mirrorlike surface reflects most of the radiant energy it encounters. That's why it is a poor absorber of radiant energy.

Good reflectors, on the other hand, are poor absorbers, like the toaster in Figure 22.16. Light-colored objects reflect more light and heat than dark-colored ones. In summer, light-colored clothing keeps people cooler.

On a sunny day Earth's surface is a net absorber. At night it is a net emitter. On a cloudless night its "surroundings" are the frigid depths of space and cooling is faster than on a cloudy night, where the surroundings are nearby clouds. Record-breaking cold nights occur when the skies are clear.

The next time you're in the direct light of the sun, step in and out of the shade. You'll note the difference in the radiant energy you receive. Then think about the enormous amount of energy the sun emits to reach you some 150,000,000 kilometers distant. Is the sun unusually hot? Not as hot as some welding torches in auto shops. You feel the sun's heat not because it is hot (which it is), but primarily because it is *big*. Really big!

CONCEPT CHECK: How does an object's emission rate compare with its absorption rate?

22.6 Newton's Law of Cooling

An object hotter than its surroundings eventually cools to match the surrounding temperature. When considering how quickly (or slowly) something cools, we speak of its *rate* of cooling—how many degrees change per unit of time.

The rate of cooling of an object depends on how much hotter the object is than the surroundings. ☑ **The colder an object's surroundings, the faster the object will cool.** The temperature change per minute of a hot apple pie will be more if the hot pie is put in a cold freezer than if put on the kitchen table because the temperature difference is greater. A warm home will lose heat to the cold outside at a greater rate when there is a larger difference between the inside and outside temperatures. Keeping the inside of your home at a high temperature on a cold day is more costly than keeping it at a lower temperature. If you keep the temperature difference small, the rate of cooling will be correspondingly low.

think!

Since a hot cup of tea loses heat more rapidly than a lukewarm cup of tea, would it be correct to say that a hot cup of tea will cool to room temperature before a lukewarm cup of tea will? Explain.
Answer: 22.6

This principle is known as *Newton's law of cooling.* (Guess who is credited with discovering this?) **Newton's law of cooling** states that the rate of cooling of an object—whether by conduction, convection, or radiation—is approximately proportional to the temperature difference ΔT between the object and its surroundings:

$$\text{rate of cooling} \sim \Delta T$$

Newton's law of cooling also holds for heating. If an object is cooler than its surroundings, its rate of warming up is also proportional to ΔT. Frozen food warms up faster in a warmer room.

CONCEPT CHECK What causes an object to cool faster?

Newton's law of cooling is an empirical relationship and not a fundamental law like Newton's laws of motion.

22.7 Global Warming and the Greenhouse Effect

An automobile sitting in the bright sun on a hot day with its windows rolled up can get very hot inside—appreciably hotter than the outside air. This is an example of the *greenhouse effect,* so named for the same temperature-raising effect in florists' glass greenhouses. The **greenhouse effect** is the warming of a planet's surface due to the trapping of radiation by the planet's atmosphere. Understanding the greenhouse effect requires knowing about two concepts.

Causes of the Greenhouse Effect The first concept has been previously stated—that all things radiate, and the frequency and wavelength of radiation depends on the temperature of the object emitting the radiation. High-temperature objects radiate short waves; low-temperature objects radiate long waves. The second concept we need to know is that the transparency of things such as air and glass depends on the wavelength of radiation. Air is transparent to both infrared (long) waves and visible (short) waves, unless the air contains excess carbon dioxide and water vapor, in which case it absorbs infrared waves. Glass is transparent to visible light waves but absorbs infrared waves. (This is discussed later, in Chapter 27.)

Now to why that car gets so hot in bright sunlight: Compared with the car, the sun's temperature is very high. This means the wavelengths of waves the sun radiates are very short. These short waves easily pass through both Earth's atmosphere and the glass windows of the car. So energy from the sun gets into the car interior, where, except for some reflection, it is absorbed. The interior of the car warms up.

Physics on the Job

Ecologist

The greenhouse effect is of particular concern to the ecologist. Ecologists study the relationship between the living and nonliving factors in an ecosystem. Ecologists need to use physics when they analyze changes in atmospheric temperatures over time. Understanding the relationships between energy, temperature, and greenhouse gases enables ecologists to identify processes that interfere with Earth's natural processes. Ecologists can find opportunities in government and privately funded projects.

The car interior radiates its own waves, but since it is not as hot as the sun, the radiated waves are longer. The reradiated long waves encounter glass windows that aren't transparent to them. So most of the reradiated energy remains in the car, which makes the car's interior even warmer. (That is why leaving your pet in a car on a hot sunny day is a no-no.) As hot as the interior gets, it won't be hot enough to radiate waves that can pass through glass (unless it glows red or white hot!).

The same effect occurs in Earth's atmosphere, which is transparent to solar radiation, as shown in Figure 22.17. The surface of Earth absorbs this energy, and reradiates part of this at longer wavelengths, as shown in Figure 22.18. Energy that Earth radiates is called terrestrial radiation. Atmospheric gases (mainly water vapor, carbon dioxide, and methane) absorb and re-emit much of this long-wavelength terrestrial radiation back to Earth. So the long-wavelength radiation that cannot escape Earth's atmosphere warms Earth. This global warming process is very nice, for Earth would be a frigid −18°C otherwise. Our present environmental concern is that increased levels of carbon dioxide and other atmospheric gases in the atmosphere may further increase the temperature and produce a new thermal balance unfavorable to the biosphere.[22.7]

Consequences of the Greenhouse Effect Averaged over a few years, the amount of solar radiation that strikes Earth exactly balances the terrestrial radiation Earth emits into space. This balance results in the average temperature of Earth—a temperature that presently supports life as we know it. We now see that over a period of decades, Earth's average temperature can be changed—by natural causes and also by human activity.

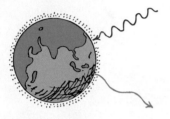

FIGURE 22.17 ▲
Earth's temperature depends on the energy balance between incoming solar radiation and outgoing terrestrial radiation.

FIGURE 22.18 ▶
Earth's atmosphere acts as a sort of one-way valve. It allows visible light from the sun in, but because of its water vapor and carbon dioxide content, it prevents terrestrial radiation from leaving.

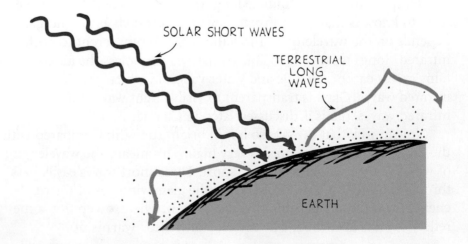

SOLAR SHORT WAVES

TERRESTRIAL LONG WAVES

EARTH

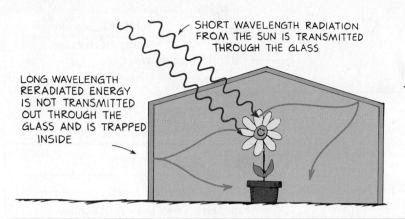

SHORT WAVELENGTH RADIATION FROM THE SUN IS TRANSMITTED THROUGH THE GLASS

LONG WAVELENGTH RERADIATED ENERGY IS NOT TRANSMITTED OUT THROUGH THE GLASS AND IS TRAPPED INSIDE

◀ **FIGURE 22.19**

Shorter-wavelength radiant energy from the sun enters through the glass roof of the greenhouse. The soil emits long-wavelength radiant energy, which is unable to pass through the glass. Income exceeds outgo, so the interior is warmed.

Adding materials such as those from the burning of fossil fuels to the atmosphere changes the absorption and reflection of solar radiation. Except where the source of energy is solar, wind, or water, increased energy consumption on Earth adds heat. These activities can change the radiative balance and change Earth's average temperature.

⊘ **The near unanimous view of climate scientists is that human activity is a main driver of global warming and climate change.** This view is the outcome of a long, painstaking road of successively more sophisticated climate models.

Confidence in the models, run by more and more sophisticated computers, is bolstered by an intriguing outcome: data gathered earlier about Earth and its atmosphere that were fed into the models successfully "predicted" the recent climate of the past twenty years.

Although water vapor is the main greenhouse gas, CO_2 is the gas most rapidly increasing in the atmosphere. Concern doesn't stop there, for further warming by CO_2 can produce more water vapor as well. The greater concern is the combination of growing amounts of both these greenhouse gases.

An important credo is "You can never change only one thing." Change one thing, and you change another. Burn fossil fuels and you warm the planet. Increase global temperature and you increase storm activity. Changed climate means changed rainfall patterns, changed coastal boundaries, and changes in insect breeding patterns. How these changes upon changes will play out, we don't know.

What we do know is that energy consumption is related to population size. We are seriously questioning the idea of continued growth. (Please take the time to read Appendix E, "Exponential Growth and Doubling Time"—very important stuff.)

Volcanoes put more particulate matter into the atmosphere than industries and all human activity. But when it comes to carbon dioxide, the impact of humans is big enough to affect climate.

Go Online
SciLINKS NSTA

For: Links on global warming
Visit: www.SciLinks.org
Web Code: csn – 2207

CONCEPT CHECK : How does human activity affect climate change?

22 REVIEW

Go Online

PHSchool.com

For: Self-Assessment
Visit: PHSchool.com
Web Code: csa – 2200

Concept Summary

- In conduction, collisions between particles transfer thermal energy, without any overall transfer of matter.

- In convection, heat is transferred by movement of the hotter substance from one place to another.

- In radiation, heat is transmitted in the form of radiant energy, or electromagnetic waves.

- All substances continuously emit radiant energy in a mixture of wavelengths.

- Good emitters of radiant energy are also good absorbers; poor emitters are poor absorbers.

- The colder an object's surroundings, the faster the object will cool.

- The near unanimous view of climate scientists is that human activity is a main driver of global warming and climate change.

Key Terms

conduction (p. 431)

conductors (p. 431)

insulator (p. 432)

convection (p. 433)

radiation (p. 436)

radiant energy (p. 436)

stellar radiation (p. 437)

terrestrial radiation (p. 438)

Newton's law of cooling (p. 441)

greenhouse effect (p. 441)

think! Answers

22.1.1 Cold does not flow from the ice to your hand. Heat flows from your hand to the ice. The metal is cold to your touch because you are transferring heat to the metal.

22.1.2 Air is a poor conductor, so the rate of heat flow from the hot air to your relatively cool hand is low. But touching the metal parts is a different story. Metal conducts heat very well, and a lot of heat in a short time is conducted into your hand when thermal contact is made.

22.2 Heat travels upward by convection. Air is a poor conductor, so very little heat travels sideways.

22.4 The answer is that the sun has a higher temperature than Earth. Earth radiates in the infrared because its temperature is relatively low compared to the sun.

22.5 If a good absorber were not also a good emitter, there would be a net absorption of radiant energy and the temperature of a good absorber would remain higher than the temperature of the surroundings. Things around us approach a common temperature only because good absorbers are, by their very nature, also good emitters.

22.6 No! Although the rate of cooling is greater for the hotter cup, it has farther to cool to reach thermal equilibrium. The extra time is equal to the time the hotter cup takes to cool to the initial temperature of the lukewarm cup of tea. Cooling rate and cooling time are not the same.

444

22 ASSESS

Check Concepts ......

Section 22.1

1. What is the role of "loose" electrons in heat conductors?

2. Why does a piece of room-temperature metal feel cooler to the touch than paper, wood, or cloth?

3. What is the difference between a conductor and an insulator?

4. Why are materials such as wood, fur, feathers, and even snow good insulators?

5. What is meant by saying that cold is not a tangible thing?

Section 22.2

6. How does Archimedes' principle relate to convection?

7. Why does the direction of coastal winds change from day to night?

8. How does the temperature of a gas change when it is compressed? When it expands?

Section 22.3

9. Dominoes are placed upright in a row, one next to another. When one is tipped over, it knocks against its neighbor, which does the same in cascade fashion until the whole row collapses. Which of the three types of heat transfer is this most similar to?

10. What is radiant energy?

Section 22.4

11. How does the predominant frequency of radiant energy vary with the absolute temperature of the radiating source?

12. Is a good absorber of radiation a good emitter or a poor emitter?

13. Which will normally cool faster, a black pot of hot tea or a silvered pot of hot tea?

Section 22.5

14. Why does a good absorber of radiant energy appear black?

15. Why do eye pupils appear black?

Section 22.6

16. Which will undergo the greater rate of cooling, a red-hot poker in a warm oven or a red-hot poker in a cold room (or do both cool at the same rate)?

17. Does Newton's law of cooling apply to warming as well as to cooling?

Section 22.7

18. What is terrestrial radiation?

19. Solar radiant energy is composed of short waves, yet terrestrial radiation is composed of relatively longer waves. Why?

20. a. What does it mean to say that the greenhouse effect is like a one-way valve?
b. Is the greenhouse effect more pronounced for florists' greenhouses or for Earth's surface?

Think and Explain ······

21. At what common temperature will both a block of wood and a piece of metal feel neither hot nor cool when you touch them with your hand?

22. If you stick a metal rod in a snowbank, the end in your hand will soon become cold. Does cold flow from the snow to your hand?

23. Wood is a better insulator than glass. Yet fiberglass is commonly used as an insulator in wooden buildings. Explain.

24. Visit a snow-covered cemetery and note that the snow does not slope upward against the gravestones but, instead, forms depressions around them, as shown. Make a hypothesis explaining why this is so.

25. Wood is a poor conductor, which means that heat is slow to transfer—even when wood is very hot. Why can firewalkers safely walk barefoot on red-hot wooden coals, but not safely walk barefoot on red-hot pieces of iron?

26. When a space shuttle is in orbit and there appears to be no gravity in the cabin, why can a candle not stay lit?

27. A friend says that, in a mixture of gases in thermal equilibrium, the molecules have the same average kinetic energy. Do you agree or disagree? Defend your answer.

28. A friend says that, in a mixture of gases in thermal equilibrium, the molecules have the same average speed. Do you agree or disagree? Defend your answer.

29. In a mixture of hydrogen and oxygen gases at the same temperature, which molecules move faster? Why?

30. Which atoms have the greater average speed in a mixture, U-238 or U-235? How would this affect diffusion through a porous membrane of otherwise identical gases made from these isotopes?

31. Notice that a desk lamp often has small holes near the top of the metal lampshade. How do these holes keep the lamp cool?

32. Turn an incandescent lamp on and off quickly while you are standing near it. You feel its heat, but you find when you touch the bulb that it is not hot. Explain why you felt heat from the lamp.

33. In Montana, the state highway department spreads coal dust on top of snow. When the sun comes out, the snow rapidly melts. Why?

34. Suppose that a person at a restaurant is served coffee before he or she is ready to drink it. In order that the coffee be hottest when the person is ready for it, should cream be added to it right away or just before it is drunk?

35. Will a can of beverage cool just as fast in the regular part of the refrigerator as it will in the freezer compartment? (What physical law do you think about in answering this?)

36. Is it important to convert temperatures to the Kelvin scale when we use Newton's law of cooling? Why or why not?

37. If you wish to save fuel on a cold day, and you're going to leave your warm house for a half hour or so, should you turn your thermostat down a few degrees, down all the way, or leave it at room temperature?

38. Why is whitewash sometimes applied to the glass of florists' greenhouses? Would you expect this practice to be more prevalent in winter or summer months?

39. If the composition of the upper atmosphere were changed so that it permitted a greater amount of terrestrial radiation to escape, what effect would this have on Earth's climate? Conversely, what would be the effect if the upper atmosphere reduced the escape of terrestrial radiation?

Think and Solve ......

40. An automobile cooling system holds 12 liters of water. Show that when its temperature rises from 20°C to 70°C, it absorbs 60 kilocalories.

41. Austin places a 50-g aluminum ball into an insulated cup containing 75 g of water at 20°C. The ball and water reach an equilibrium temperature of 37°C. Austin makes some calculations and reports that the initial temperature of the ball must have been slightly more than 155°C. Do your calculations agree? (Ignore heat transfer to the cup.)

42. Decay of radioactive isotopes of thorium and uranium in granite and other rocks in Earth's interior provides sufficient energy to keep the interior molten, heat lava, and provide warmth to natural hot springs. This is due to the average release of about 0.03 J per kilogram each year. Show that 13.3 million years are required for a chunk of thermally insulated granite to increase 500°C in temperature. (Use 800 J/kg°C for the specific heat capacity of granite.)

43. In a lab you burn a 0.6-g peanut beneath 50 g of water. Heat from the peanut increases the water temperature from 22°C to 50°C.
  a. Assuming 40% efficiency, show that the food value of the peanut is 3500 calories (3.5 Calories).
  b. What is the food value in Calories per gram?

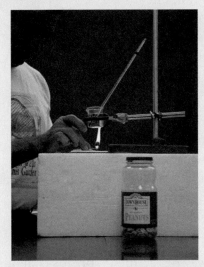

44. Pounding a nail into wood makes the nail warmer. Suppose a hammer exerts an average force of 500 N on a 6-cm nail whose mass is 5 grams when it drives into a piece of wood. Work is done on the nail and it becomes hotter. If all the heat goes to the nail, show that its increase in temperature is slightly more than 13°C. (Use 450 J/kg°C for the specific heat capacity of the nail.)

45. At a certain location, the solar power per unit area reaching Earth's surface is 200 W/m², averaged over a 24-hour day. Consider a house with an average power requirement of 3 kW with solar panels on the roof that convert solar power to electric power with 25 percent efficiency. Show that a solar collector area of 60 square meters will meet the 3 kW requirement.

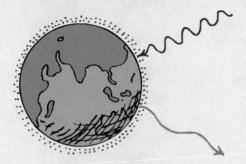

Activities ● ● ● ● ● ●

46. Hold the bottom end of a test tube full of cold water in your hand. Heat the top part in a flame until the water boils. The fact that you can still hold the bottom shows that water is a poor conductor of heat. This is even more dramatic when you wedge chunks of ice at the bottom; then the water above can be brought to a boil without melting the ice. Try it and see.

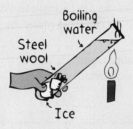

Boiling water

Steel wool

Ice

47. If you live where there is snow, do as Benjamin Franklin did more than two centuries ago and lay samples of light and dark cloth on the snow. (If you don't live in a snowy area, try this using ice cubes.) Describe differences in the rate of melting beneath the cloths.

48. Wrap a piece of paper around a thick metal bar and place it in a flame. Note that the paper will not catch fire. Can you figure out why? (*Hint:* Paper generally will not ignite until its temperature reaches about 230°C.)

Tightly rolled paper

Iron bar

More Problem-Solving Practice
Appendix F

23 CHANGE OF PHASE

THE BIG IDEA : Changes of phase involve a transfer of energy.

The four possible forms of matter—solid, liquid, gas, and plasma—are called **phases.** Matter can change from one phase (or *state*, as it is also sometimes called) to another. Ice, for example, is the solid phase of H_2O. Add energy, and the rigid molecular structure breaks down to the liquid phase, water. Add more energy, and the liquid changes to the gaseous phase as the water boils to become steam.

The phase of matter depends on its temperature and the pressure that is exerted upon it. Changes of phase involve a transfer of energy.

discover!

How Do Clouds Form?
1. Cover the bottom of a gallon jar with a thin layer of water.
2. Drop a lit match into the jar.
3. Quickly place the fingers of a rubber glove inside the jar and stretch the open end of the glove over the jar's mouth.
4. Put your fingers in the glove and quickly pull the glove out of the jar.

Analyze and Conclude
1. **Observing** What did you observe when you pulled the glove out of the jar?
2. **Predicting** What do you suppose would happen if you were to pull the glove out of the jar more slowly?
3. **Making Generalizations** What factors are necessary for cloud formation?

23.1 Evaporation

Water in an open container will eventually evaporate, or dry up. The liquid that disappears becomes water vapor in the air. **Evaporation** is a change of phase from liquid to gas that takes place at the surface of a liquid.

The temperature of anything is related to the average kinetic energy of its molecules. Molecules in the liquid phase continuously move about in all directions and bump into one another at different speeds. Some of the molecules gain kinetic energy while others lose kinetic energy. Those molecules at the surface of the liquid that gain kinetic energy by being bumped from below may have enough energy to break free of the liquid. They can leave the surface and fly into the space above the liquid. They now comprise a *vapor*, molecules in the gaseous phase.

The increased kinetic energy of molecules bumped free of the liquid comes from molecules remaining in the liquid. This is "billiard-ball physics": When balls bump into one another and some gain kinetic energy, the other balls lose this same amount of kinetic energy. So the average kinetic energy of the molecules remaining behind in the liquid is lowered. ✓ **Evaporation is a process that cools the liquid left behind.**

A canteen, such as the one in Figure 23.1, keeps cool by evaporation when the cloth covering on the sides is kept wet. As the faster-moving water molecules leave the cloth, the temperature of the cloth decreases. The cool cloth in turn cools the metal canteen by conduction, which in turn cools the water inside.

FIGURE 23.1 ▲
The cloth covering on the sides of the canteen promotes cooling when it is wet.

◄ FIGURE 23.2
Pigs lack sweat glands. They wallow in mud to cool themselves.

When the human body overheats, sweat glands produce perspiration. As the sweat evaporates, it cools us and helps us maintain a stable body temperature. Animals that lack sweat glands, such as the pig in Figure 23.2, must cool themselves in other ways. For example, dogs cool themselves by panting.

CONCEPT CHECK How does evaporation affect a liquid's temperature?

23.2 Condensation

The process opposite to evaporation is *condensation*. **Condensation** is the changing of a gas to a liquid. The formation of droplets of water on the outside of a cold soda can is an example. Water vapor molecules collide with the slower-moving molecules of the cold can surface. The vapor molecules give up so much kinetic energy that they can't stay in the gaseous phase. They condense.

Condensation also occurs when gas molecules are captured by liquids. In their random motion, gas molecules may hit a liquid and lose kinetic energy. The attractive forces exerted on them by the liquid may hold them. Gas molecules become liquid molecules.[23.2.1]

☑ **Condensation warms the area where the liquid forms.** Kinetic energy lost by condensing gas molecules warms the surface they strike. A steam burn, for example, is more damaging than a burn from boiling water of the same temperature. Steam gives up energy when it condenses to the liquid that wets the skin. The radiator in Figure 23.3 also works by condensation of steam.

The effects of condensation can be seen in the atmosphere. The air always contains some water vapor. This water vapor can make the air feel humid, or it can lead to the formation of fog and clouds.

Relative Humidity At any given temperature and pressure, there is a limit to the amount of water vapor in the air. When any substance contains the maximum amount of another substance, the first substance is **saturated.** The ratio of how much water vapor is in the air to the maximum amount that *could* be in the air at the same temperature is the **relative humidity**. Relative humidity is *not* a measure of how much water vapor is in the air. On a hot day with a low relative humidity, there may be more water vapor in the air than on a cold day with high relative humidity.

At a relative humidity of 100%, the air is saturated. More water vapor is required to saturate high-temperature air than low-temperature air. The warm air of tropical regions is capable of containing much more moisture than cold Arctic air.

For saturation, there must be water vapor molecules in the air undergoing condensation. When slow-moving molecules collide, some stick together—they condense. To understand this, think of a fly making grazing contact with flypaper. At low speed it would surely get stuck, whereas at high speed it is more able to rebound into the air. Similarly, when water vapor molecules collide, they are more likely to stick together and become part of a liquid if they are moving slowly as shown in Figure 23.4. At higher speeds, they can bounce apart and remain in the gaseous phase. The faster the water molecules move, the less able they are to condense to form droplets.

FIGURE 23.3 ▲
Heat is given up by steam when it condenses inside the radiator.

A camel's best source of water is its over-sized nose, with an inside structure that recaptures most of the moisture in water-saturated air coming from its lungs. So it withdraws water from its own exhaled breath.

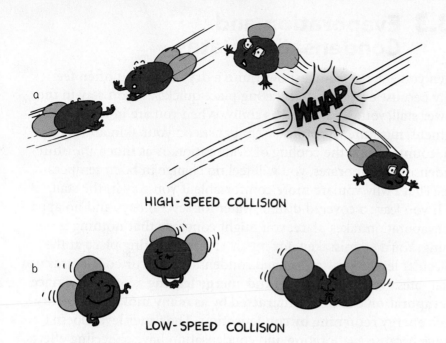

HIGH-SPEED COLLISION

LOW-SPEED COLLISION

◀ **FIGURE 23.4**
a. At high speeds, molecules of water vapor bounce apart and remain a gas.
b. At lower speeds, molecules of water vapor are more likely to stick together and form a liquid.

Although condensation in the air occurs more readily at low temperatures, it can occur at high temperatures also. Recall that temperature is a measure of *average* kinetic energy. There are always some molecules moving faster than average, and some moving slower. Even at high temperature, there will be enough slow molecules to cause condensation—provided there is enough water vapor present. Whatever the temperature, it is the slower molecules that are more likely to stick.

Fog and Clouds Warm air rises. As it rises, it expands. As it expands, it cools. As it cools, water vapor molecules begin sticking together after colliding, rather than bouncing off one another. If there are larger and slower-moving particles or ions present, water vapor condenses upon these particles, and we have a cloud.

Fog is basically a cloud that forms near the ground. Flying through a cloud is much like driving through fog. Fog occurs in areas where moist air near the ground cools. For example, moist air that has blown in from over an ocean or lake may pass over cooler land. Some of the water vapor condenses out of the air as it cools, and we have fog.[23.2.2] A key feature of fog and cloud formation is a slowing down of water vapor molecules in air.

CONCEPT CHECK How does condensation affect temperature?

---

think!

Is it correct to say that relative humidity is a measure of the amount of water vapor in the air at a particular temperature? Explain.
Answer: 23.2

Cloud formation can be stimulated by "seeding" the air with appropriate particles or ions.

23.3 Evaporation and Condensation Rates

FIGURE 23.5 ▲
If you feel chilly outside the shower stall, step back inside and be warmed by the condensation of the excess water vapor there.

When you emerge from a shower into a dry room, you often feel chilly because evaporation is taking place quickly. If you stay in the shower stall, you will not feel as chilly. When you are in a moist environment, moisture from the air condenses on your skin and warms you, counteracting the cooling of evaporation. If as much moisture condenses as evaporates, you will feel no change in body temperature. That's why you are more comfortable if you stay in the stall.

If you leave a covered dish of water for several days and no apparent evaporation takes place, you might conclude that nothing is happening. You'd be mistaken, for much activity is taking place at the molecular level. Evaporation *and* condensation occur continuously at equal rates. ☑ **The molecules and energy leaving a liquid's surface by evaporation can be counteracted by as many molecules and as much energy returning by condensation.** The water level doesn't change because evaporation and condensation have canceling effects.

Evaporation and condensation normally take place at the same time. If evaporation exceeds condensation, the liquid is cooled. If condensation exceeds evaporation, the liquid is warmed.

CONCEPT CHECK : How can evaporation and condensation take place at the same time?

23.4 Boiling

Evaporation takes place at the surface of a liquid. A change of phase from liquid to gas can also take place beneath the surface of a liquid, causing bubbles. The bubbles are buoyed upward to the surface, where they escape into the surrounding air. The change of phase from liquid to gas beneath a liquid's surface is called **boiling.**

The pressure of the vapor within the bubbles in a boiling liquid must be great enough to resist the pressure of the surrounding water. Unless the vapor pressure is great enough, the surrounding pressures will collapse any bubbles that may form. At temperatures below the boiling point, the vapor pressure is not great enough. Bubbles do not form until the boiling point is reached.

As the atmospheric pressure is increased, the molecules in the vapor are required to move faster to exert increased pressure within the bubble in order to counteract the additional atmospheric pressure. ☑ **Increasing the pressure on the surface of a liquid raises the boiling point of the liquid.** Conversely, lowered pressure (as at high altitudes) decreases the boiling point. Thus, boiling depends not only on temperature but on pressure also.

PRESSURE OF ATMOSPHERE

FIGURE 23.6 ▲
The motion of molecules in the bubble of steam (much enlarged) creates a gas pressure that counteracts the water pressure against the bubble.

High Pressure A pressure cooker is based on this fact. A pressure cooker has a tight-fitting lid that does not allow vapor to escape until it reaches a certain pressure greater than normal air pressure. As the evaporating vapor builds up inside the sealed pressure cooker, pressure on the surface of the liquid is increased, which prevents boiling. A pressure cooker reaches a higher temperature because the increased pressure forces the water to reach a higher temperature before boiling can occur. The increased temperature of the water cooks the food faster.

Low Pressure It is important to note that it is the high temperature of the water that cooks the food, not the boiling process itself. At high altitudes, water boils at a lower temperature. In Denver, Colorado, the "mile-high city," for example, water boils at 95°C, instead of the 100°C boiling temperature characteristic of sea level. If you try to cook food in boiling water of a lower temperature, you must wait a longer time for proper cooking. A "three-minute" boiled egg in Denver is runny. If the temperature of the boiling water were very low, food would not cook at all.

Boiling, like evaporation, is a process that cools the liquid left behind. Heating water is one thing; boiling is another. When 100°C water at atmospheric pressure is boiling, heat is taken away as fast as it is added. Figure 23.7 shows the water is being cooled by boiling as fast as it is being heated by energy from the heat source. If cooling did not take place, continued application of heat to a pot of boiling water would result in a continued increase in temperature.

CONCEPT CHECK What is the effect of pressure on the boiling temperature of a liquid?

FIGURE 23.7 ▼
Heating and boiling are two distinct processes. Heating warms the water, and boiling cools it.

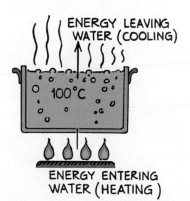

ENERGY LEAVING WATER (COOLING)

100°C

ENERGY ENTERING WATER (HEATING)

23.5 Freezing

When energy is continually withdrawn from a liquid, molecular motion slows until the forces of attraction between the molecules cause them to get closer to one another. The molecules then vibrate about fixed positions and form a solid. Water provides a good example of this process. When energy is extracted from water at a temperature of 0°C and at atmospheric pressure, ice is formed. The liquid water gives way to the solid ice phase. The change in phase from liquid to solid is called **freezing.** Figure 23.8 shows the open six-sided structure of an ice crystal.

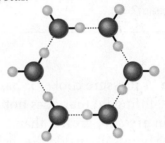

FIGURE 23.8 ▶
Pure ice crystals have an open, hexagonal structure.

Although streams can freeze over in cold weather, most often they don't. Why? Because streams are usually fed with warmer groundwater.

Interestingly enough, if sugar or salt is dissolved in the water, the freezing temperature will be lowered. These "foreign" molecules or ions get in the way of water molecules that ordinarily would join together. As ice crystals do form, the hindrance is intensified, for the proportion of foreign molecules or ions among liquid water molecules that remain increases. Connections become more difficult. ⊘ **In general, dissolving anything in a liquid lowers the liquid's freezing temperature.** Antifreeze in an automobile engine is a practical application of this process.

CONCEPT CHECK: What effect does dissolving anything in a liquid have on the liquid's freezing temperature?

23.6 Boiling and Freezing at the Same Time

Suppose that a dish of water at room temperature is placed in a vacuum jar, as shown in Figure 23.9. If the pressure in the jar is slowly reduced by a vacuum pump, the vapor pressure of the molecules within the water will be high enough to form bubbles, and the water will start to boil. The boiling process takes higher-energy molecules away from the water left in the dish, which cools to a lower temperature. As the pressure is further reduced, more and more of the faster remaining slow-moving molecules boil away.

Continued boiling results in a lowering of temperature until the freezing point of approximately 0°C is reached. Continued cooling by boiling causes ice to form over the surface of the bubbling water. ☑ **Lowering the pressure can cause boiling and freezing to take place at the same time!** This must be witnessed to be appreciated. Frozen bubbles of boiling water are a remarkable sight.

If some drops of coffee are sprayed into a vacuum chamber, they too will boil until they freeze. Even after they are frozen, the water molecules will continue to evaporate until little crystals of coffee solids are left. This is how freeze-dried coffee is made. The low temperature of this process tends to keep the chemical structure of coffee solids from changing. When hot water is added, much of the original flavor of the coffee is preserved.

CONCEPT CHECK : What can cause boiling and freezing to take place at the same time?

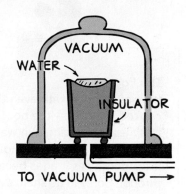

FIGURE 23.9 ▲
The apparatus shown can be used to demonstrate that water will freeze and boil at the same time in a vacuum. A gram or two of water is placed in a dish that is insulated from the base by a polystyrene cup.

23.7 Regelation

The open-structured crystals of ice can be crushed by the application of pressure. Whereas ice normally melts at 0°C, the application of pressure lowers the melting point. The crystals are simply crushed to the liquid phase. At twice standard atmospheric pressure, the melting point is lowered to −0.007°C. Quite a bit more pressure must be applied for an observable effect.

When the pressure is removed, refreezing occurs. The phenomenon of melting under pressure and freezing again when the pressure is reduced is called **regelation**. It is one of the properties of water that make it different from other substances. ☑ **Regelation can occur only in substances that expand when they freeze.**

You can see regelation if you suspend a fine wire that supports heavy weights over an ice block, as shown in Figure 23.10. The wire will slowly cut its way through the ice, but its track will refill with ice. You will see the wire and weights fall to the floor, leaving the ice in a single solid piece!

To make a snowball, you use regelation. When you compress the snow, you cause a slight melting, which helps to bind the snow into a ball. Making snowballs is difficult in very cold weather, because the pressure you can apply may not be enough to melt the snow.

Once, it was thought that an ice skate's pressure lowered the freezing point of ice. Now, we know that this is not sufficient to explain ice-skating. Ice has a thin layer of liquid on its surface even at very low temperatures.

CONCEPT CHECK : Why do so few substances undergo regelation?

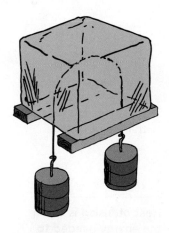

FIGURE 23.10 ▲
Regelation allows the wire to cut through the ice, but leaves the ice in a single solid piece.

The Egg Test

Physics can help with even the simplest of all cooked creations—the boiled egg. Test the egg for freshness by placing it in water. If it sinks and lies on its side, it's fresh. If it floats, it's rotten. An egg loses density as it ages because it loses moisture through pores in its shell, eventually becoming less dense than water. To test that the egg is raw, spin it on a tabletop. If it wobbles, it's uncooked. The wobbling indicates that the yolk is moving within the egg, thus changing the egg's center of gravity. Eggs sometimes crack while boiling due to an air pocket inside. With heat, the air pressure in the pocket increases enough to crack the shell. If you carefully pierce the egg's big end with a small, clean pin before boiling, it won't crack. Finally be sure you actually boil the water. You can heat an egg indefinitely at lower temperatures, but it doesn't cook. Cooking requires exceeding a threshold temperature so that the long-stranded molecules of the egg become cross-linked. That's why an egg won't cook by boiling at very high altitudes—the boiling water is not hot enough to cook the egg.

23.8 Energy and Changes of Phase

If you heat a solid sufficiently, it will melt and become a liquid. If you heat the liquid, it will vaporize and become a gas. ⊘ **Energy must be put into a substance to change its phase from solid to liquid to gas. Conversely, energy must be extracted from a substance to change its phase from gas to liquid to solid.** Figure 23.11 shows the flow of energy.

FIGURE 23.11 ▶

The change in the internal energy of a substance causes the change of phase.

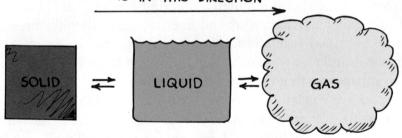

ENERGY IS ABSORBED WHEN CHANGE OF PHASE IS IN THIS DIRECTION

SOLID ⇌ LIQUID ⇌ GAS

ENERGY IS RELEASED WHEN CHANGE OF PHASE IS IN THIS DIRECTION

Heat of fusion is either the energy needed to separate molecules from the solid phase, or the energy released when bonds form in a liquid and change it to the solid phase.

Examples of Phase Changes The general behavior of many substances can be illustrated with a description of the changes of phase of H_2O. To make the numbers simple, suppose we have a 1-gram piece of ice at a temperature of –50°C in a closed container, and it is put on a stove to heat. A thermometer in the container reveals a slow increase in temperature up to 0°C. (It takes about half of a calorie to raise the temperature of the gram of ice by 1°C.) Once it reaches 0°C, the temperature of the ice remains at 0°C even though heat input continues. Rather than getting warmer, the ice melts.

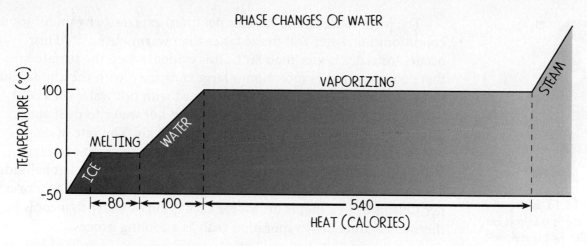

PHASE CHANGES OF WATER

FIGURE 23.12 ▲
The graph shows the energy involved in the heating and the change of phase of 1 gram of H_2O.

In order for the whole gram of ice to melt, 80 calories (335 joules) of heat energy must be absorbed by the ice. Not until all the ice melts does the temperature again begin to rise. Each additional calorie absorbed by the gram of water increases its temperature by 1°C until it reaches its boiling temperature, 100°C. Again, as heat is added, the temperature remains constant while more of the gram of water is boiled away and becomes steam. The water must absorb 540 calories (2255 joules) of heat to vaporize the whole gram.[23.8.1] Finally, when all the water has become steam at 100°C, the temperature begins to rise once more. It continues to rise as long as heat is added (again taking about a half calorie per gram for each 1°C rise in temperature). This process is shown graphed in Figure 23.12.

Reversibility of Phase Changes The phase change sequence is reversible. When the molecules in a gram of steam condense to form boiling water, they liberate 540 calories (2255 joules) of heat to the environment. When the water is cooled from 100°C to 0°C, 100 additional calories are liberated to the environment. When ice water fuses to become solid ice, 80 more calories (335 joules) of energy are released by the water.

The 540 calories (2255 joules) required to vaporize a gram of water is a relatively large amount of energy—much more than is required to change a gram of ice at absolute zero to boiling water at 100°C. Although the molecules in steam and boiling water at 100°C have the same average kinetic energy, steam has more potential energy, because the molecules are free of each other and are not bound together in the liquid. Steam contains a vast amount of energy that can be released during condensation.

think!

How much energy is released when a gram of steam at 100°C condenses to water at 100°C?
Answer: 23.8.1

Water's heat of vaporization is huge. The energy needed to vaporize a quantity of boiling water is nearly seven times the energy needed to melt the same amount of ice.

FIGURE 23.13 ▲

When a car is washed on a cold day, hot water will freeze more readily than warm water because of the energy that the rapidly evaporating water takes with it.

The large value of 540 calories per gram explains why under some conditions hot water will freeze faster than warm water.[23.8.2] This occurs for water hotter than 80°C. It is evident when the surface area that cools by rapid evaporation is large compared with the amount of water involved. Examples are a car washed with hot water on a cold winter day, and a skating rink flooded with hot water to melt and smooth out the rough spots and refreeze quickly. The rate of cooling by rapid evaporation is very high because each gram of water that evaporates draws at least 540 calories from the water left behind. This is an enormous quantity of energy compared with the 1 calorie per Celsius degree that is drawn for each gram of water that cools by thermal conduction. Evaporation truly is a cooling process.

Applications of Phase Changes A refrigerator's cooling cycle is a good example of the energy interchanges that occur with the changes of phase of the refrigeration fluid (not water!). The liquid is pumped into the cooling unit, where it is forced through a tiny opening to evaporate and draw heat from the things stored in the food compartment. The gas is then directed outside the cooling unit to coils located in the back. As the gas condenses in the coils, appropriately called condensation coils, heat is given off to the surrounding air. The liquid returns to the cooling unit, and the cycle continues. A motor pumps the fluid through the system, where it enters the cyclic processes of vaporization and condensation. The next time you're near a refrigerator, place your hand near the condensation coils in the back (or bottom), and you will feel the heat that has been extracted from the inside.

An air conditioner employs the same principles. It simply pumps heat from one part of the unit to another. When the roles of vaporization and condensation are reversed, the air conditioner becomes a heater. A device that moves heat is called a **heat pump.**

FIGURE 23.14 ▶

The refrigeration cycle in a common refrigerator keeps the inside cool.

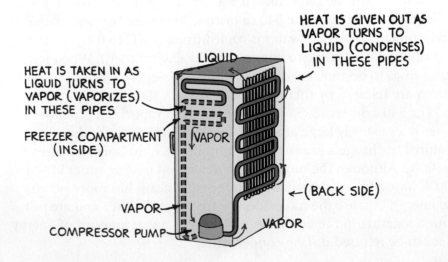

HEAT IS TAKEN IN AS LIQUID TURNS TO VAPOR (VAPORIZES) IN THESE PIPES

FREEZER COMPARTMENT (INSIDE)

HEAT IS GIVEN OUT AS VAPOR TURNS TO LIQUID (CONDENSES) IN THESE PIPES

LIQUID

VAPOR

(BACK SIDE)

VAPOR

VAPOR

COMPRESSOR PUMP

A way that some people judge the hotness of a clothes iron is to touch it briefly with a finger. This is also a way to burn the finger—unless it is first moistened. Energy that ordinarily would go into burning the finger goes, instead, into changing the phase of the moisture on it. The energy converts the moisture to a vapor, which additionally provides an insulating layer between the finger and the hot surface.

Similarly, you may have seen news photos or heard stories about people walking barefoot without harm over red-hot coals from firewood. (**CAUTION!** Never try this on your own; even experienced "firewalkers" have received bad burns when the conditions were not just right.) The primary factor here is the low conductivity of wood—even red-hot wood. Although its temperature is high, relatively little heat is conducted to the feet, just as little heat is conducted by air when you put your hand briefly into a hot pizza oven (because air is a poor conductor). But if you touch metal in the hot oven, OUCH! Similarly, a firewalker who steps on a hot piece of metal or another good conductor will be burned. A secondary factor is skin moisture. Perspiration on the soles of the feet decreases heat transfer to the feet. Much of the heat that would go to the feet instead goes to vaporizing the moisture—again, like touching a hot clothes iron with a wetted finger. Temperature is one thing; heat transfer is another.

In brief, a solid absorbs energy when it melts; a liquid absorbs energy when it vaporizes. Conversely, a gas emits energy when it liquefies; a liquid releases energy when it solidifies.

CONCEPT
CHECK : How is energy related to phase changes?

A refrigerator is a "heat pump." It transfers heat out of a cold environment and into a warm environment. When the process is reversed, the heat pump is an air conditioner. In both cases, external energy operates the device.

think!

When H_2O in the vapor phase condenses, is the surrounding air warmed or cooled?
Answer: 23.8.2

Physics on the Job

Fire Fighting
Firefighters regularly enter burning buildings to save lives and property. In order to perform their job effectively and safely, firefighters must be knowledgeable about the physics of heat. The most common fire control is dousing a flame with water. In some cases, a fine mist is more effective in quenching a fire. Why? Because the fine mist readily turns to steam, and in so doing quickly absorbs energy and cools the burning material. Properly dealing with flames saves lives, including their own. To firefighters, the physics of heat is much more than a classroom assignment. It's a matter of staying alive. Job opportunities exist for firefighters with city or county fire departments and the National Forest Service.

# REVIEW

Go Online
PHSchool.com
For: Self-Assessment
Visit: PHSchool.com
Web Code: csa – 2300

Concept Summary

- Evaporation cools the liquid left behind.
- Condensation warms the area where the liquid forms.
- The molecules and energy leaving a liquid's surface by evaporation can be counteracted by as many molecules and as much energy returning by condensation.
- Increasing the pressure on the surface of a liquid raises the boiling point of the liquid.
- In general, dissolving anything in a liquid lowers the liquid's freezing temperature.
- Lowering the pressure can cause boiling and freezing to take place at the same time.
- Regelation can occur only in substances that expand when they freeze.
- Energy must be put into a substance to change its phase from solid to liquid to gas. Conversely, energy must be extracted from a substance to change its phase from gas to liquid to solid.

Key Terms

phases *(p. 450)*

evaporation *(p. 451)*

condensation *(p. 452)*

saturated *(p. 452)*

relative humidity *(p. 452)*

boiling *(p. 454)*

freezing *(p. 456)*

regelation *(p. 457)*

heat pump *(p. 460)*

think! Answers

23.2   No. Humidity is a measure of the amount of water vapor *per volume of air,* whatever the temperature. Relative humidity, on the other hand, is the amount of vapor in the air compared with the amount for saturation at a particular temperature. Relative humidity is a ratio, expressed as a percent. Air with 60% of the vapor contained by saturated air at the same temperature has a relative humidity of 60%.

23.4   No, no, no! When we say boiling is a cooling process, we mean that the *water* (not your hands!) is being cooled. A dip in 100°C water would be most uncomfortable for your hands!

23.8.1   One gram of steam at 100°C releases 540 calories of energy when it condenses to become water at the same temperature.

23.8.2   The surrounding air is warmed because the change of phase is from vapor to liquid, which releases energy.

23 ASSESS

Check Concepts ......

Section 23.1

1. Do all the molecules or atoms in a liquid have about the same speed, or much different speeds?

2. What is evaporation, and why is it also a cooling process?

3. Why does a hot dog pant?

Section 23.2

4. What is condensation, and why is it also a warming process?

5. Why is being burned by steam more damaging than being burned by boiling water of the same temperature?

6. Which usually contains more water vapor—warm air or cool air?

7. Why does warm moist air form clouds when it rises?

Section 23.3

8. How can you tell if the rate of evaporation equals the rate of condensation?

9. Why do you feel less chilly if you dry yourself inside the shower stall after taking a shower?

Section 23.4

10. What is the difference between evaporation and boiling?

11. Why does the temperature at which a liquid boils depend on atmospheric pressure?

12. Why is a pressure cooker even more useful when cooking food in the mountains than when cooking at sea level?

Section 23.5

13. Why does antifreeze or any soluble substance put in water lower its freezing temperature?

Section 23.6

14. How can water be made to both boil and freeze at the same time?

Section 23.7

15. What is regelation, and what does it have to do with the open-structured crystals in ice?

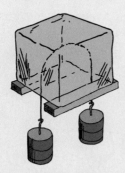

Section 23.8

16. a. How many calories are needed to raise the temperature of 1 gram of water by 1°C?
   b. How many calories are needed to melt 1 gram of ice at 0°C?
   c. How many calories are needed to vaporize 1 gram of boiling water at 100°C?

17. When a vapor turns to a liquid, does it give off energy or does it absorb energy?

18. What is the effect of rapid evaporation on the temperature of water?

19. In a refrigerator, does the food cool when a vapor turns to a liquid, or vice versa?

20. Why is it important that a finger be wet before it is touched to a hot clothes iron?

Plug and Chug ......

Use the following information to help you answer Questions 21–26.

Quantity of heat energy required for change of phase = (mass) × (heat of fusion or heat of vaporization), or in equation form, $Q = mL$.

Quantity of heat energy responsible for a temperature change = (mass) × (specific heat) × (change in temperature), or in equation form, $Q = mc\Delta T$.

For water, heat of fusion = 80 cal/g; heat of vaporization = 540 cal/g.

21. Calculate the energy absorbed by 20 grams of water that warms from 30°C to 90°C.

22. Calculate the energy needed to melt 50 grams of 0°C ice.

23. Calculate the energy needed to melt 100 grams of 0°C ice and then heat it to 30°C.

24. Calculate the energy absorbed by 20 grams of 100°C water that is turned into 100°C steam.

25. Calculate the energy released by 20 grams of 100°C steam that condenses to 100°C water.

26. Calculate the total energy released when 20 grams of steam condenses to water, cools, and then turns to ice at 0°C.

Think and Explain • • • • •

27. a. Evaporation is a cooling process. What cools and what warms during evaporation?

   b. Condensation is a warming process. What warms and what cools during condensation?

28. You're not chilly when swimming in warm water. But when emerging from warm water on a warm summer day, you feel chilly if the wind is blowing. Explain.

29. Classmate Matthew says that if all the molecules in a particular liquid had the same speed, and some were able to evaporate, the remaining liquid would not undergo cooling. Do you agree or disagree, and what is your explanation?

30. You can determine wind direction if you wet your finger and hold it up into the air. Explain.

31. Give two reasons why pouring a hot cup of coffee into a saucer results in faster cooling.

32. At a picnic, why would wrapping a bottle in a wet cloth be a better method of cooling than placing the bottle in a bucket of cold water?

33. Why does dew form on the surface of a cold soft-drink can?

34. Air-conditioning units contain no water whatever, yet it is common to see water dripping from them when they're running on a hot day. Explain.

35. Why do clouds often form above mountain peaks? (*Hint:* Consider the updrafts.)

36. Sometimes moisture forms on the inside of your windows at home. And sometimes it forms on the outside. What is your explanation?

37. If a large tub of water is kept in a small unheated room, even on a very cold day the temperature of the room will not go below 0°C. Why not?

38. On a clear night, why does more dew form in an open field than under a tree or beneath a park bench?

39. Machines used for making snow at ski areas blow a mixture of compressed air and water through a nozzle. The temperature of the mixture may initially be well above the freezing temperature of water, yet crystals of snow are formed as the mixture is ejected from the nozzle. Explain how this happens.

40. People who live where snowfall is common will attest to the fact that air temperatures are generally higher on snowy days than on clear days. Some people get cause and effect mixed up when they say that snowfall cannot occur on very cold days. Explain.

41. A piece of metal and an equal mass of wood are both removed from a hot oven at equal temperatures and dropped onto blocks of ice. The metal has a lower specific heat capacity than the wood. Which will melt more ice before cooling to 0°C?

42. Why is it that, in cold winters, a tub of water placed in a farmer's canning cellar helps prevent canned food from freezing?

43. Why will spraying fruit trees with water before a frost help to protect the fruit from freezing?

44. Andrew says that potatoes will cook faster in vigorously boiling water than in gently boiling water. Madison disagrees. Whom do you agree with, and why?

45. Why is the constant temperature of boiling water on a hot stove evidence that boiling is a cooling process? (What would happen to its temperature if boiling were not a cooling process?)

46. How can water be brought to a boil without heating it?

47. Elizabeth says that the boiling temperature of water decreases when the water is under reduced pressure. Austin says the opposite is true—that reduced pressure increases the boiling point. Whom do you agree with and why?

48. Nick suspends a small jar of water in a saucepan, careful that the bottom of the jar doesn't rest on the bottom of the saucepan. Nick then puts water in the pan, surrounding the jar. He puts the saucepan on a hot stove and is puzzled to see that although the water in the pan comes to a boil, the water in the jar doesn't. He looks to you for an explanation. Explain.

49. Room-temperature water will boil spontaneously in a vacuum—on the moon, for example. Could you cook an egg in this boiling water? Defend your answer.

50. Your inventor friend proposes a design for cookware that will allow boiling to take place at a temperature of less than 100°C so that food can be cooked with the consumption of less energy. Comment on this idea.

51. Hydrothermal vents are openings in the ocean floor that discharge very hot water. Water emerging at nearly 280°C from one such vent off the Oregon coast, some 2400 m beneath the surface, is not boiling. Provide an explanation.

52. In the power plant of a nuclear submarine, the temperature of the water in the reactor is above 100°C. How is this possible?

Think and Solve ......

53. The specific heat capacity of ice is 0.48 cal/g°C. Make the assumption that it remains at that value all the way to absolute zero (at very low temperatures it's lower, which we'll ignore here).

a. Show that the heat required to change a 1-gram ice cube at absolute zero (−273°C) to 1 gram of boiling water is about 310 calories.
b. Show that more energy is needed to turn 100°C water to 100°C steam.

54. How much steam at 100°C must be condensed in order to melt 1 gram of 0°C ice and have the resulting ice water remain at 0°C? (The answer is *not* 0.148 grams!)

55. How many calories are given off by 1 gram of 100°C steam that changes phase to 1 gram of ice at 0°C?

56. If 20 grams of hot water at 80°C is poured into a cavity in a very large block of ice at 0°C, what will be the final temperature of the water in the cavity? How much ice must melt in order to cool the hot water down to this temperature?

Answer Questions 57–61 in terms of joules rather than calories.

57. How much energy is needed to melt 5 kg of ice at 0°C?

58. How much energy is given to your body when 0.5 kg of steam condenses on your skin?

59. If that same amount of energy (answer to question 58) were used to warm 4 kg of water (8 times as much!) initially at 0° C, what would be the final temperature of the water?

60. The heat of vaporization of ethyl alcohol is 8.5×10^5 J/kg. If 2 kg of it were allowed to vaporize in a refrigerator, how much energy would be drawn from the air molecules?

61. How much energy is needed to change 1 kg of ice at –10°C to steam at 120°C?

Activity ......

62. Boil some water in a pan and note that bubbles form at particular regions of the pan. These are nucleation sites—scratched or flawed regions of the pan, or simply bits of dirt. When water reaches the boiling point these sites provide havens where microscopic bubbles can collect long enough to become big bubbles. Nucleation sites are also important for phase changes of condensation and solidification. Snowflakes and raindrops typically form around dust particles, for example.

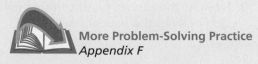

More Problem-Solving Practice
Appendix F

24 THERMODYNAMICS

THE BIG IDEA ⋮ Heat normally flows from hot to cold.

The study of heat and its transformation into mechanical energy is called **thermodynamics.** The word *thermodynamics* stems from Greek words meaning "movement of heat." The science of thermodynamics was developed in the mid-1800s, before the atomic and molecular nature of matter was understood. So far, our study of heat has been concerned with the microscopic behavior of jiggling atoms and molecules. Now we will see that thermodynamics bypasses the molecular details of systems and focuses on the macroscopic level—mechanical work, pressure, temperature, and their roles in energy transformation. The foundation of thermodynamics is the conservation of energy and the fact that heat flows from hot to cold, and not the other way around. It provides the basic theory of heat engines, from steam turbines to fusion reactors, and the basic theory of refrigerators and heat pumps. We begin our study of thermodynamics with a look at one of its early concepts—a lowest limit of temperature.

discover!

Can Temperature Change Without Heat Transfer?

1. Place a rubber band, loosely looped over your index fingers, in contact with your upper lip.
2. Quickly stretch the rubber band.
3. Now let the rubber band contract quickly. Do not snap the rubber band.

Analyze and Conclude

1. **Observing** Describe what you felt when the rubber band was stretched and then allowed to contract rapidly.
2. **Predicting** What do you think you would feel if the rubber band were stretched and allowed to contract more slowly?
3. **Making Generalizations** Why do you think the rate of performing a process may affect the outcome of the process?

24.1 Absolute Zero

As thermal motion of atoms increases, temperature increases. There seems to be no upper limit of temperature. In contrast, there is a definite limit at the other end of the temperature scale. If we continually decrease the thermal motion of atoms in a substance, the temperature will drop. ◉ **As the thermal motion of atoms in a substance approaches zero, the kinetic energy of the atoms approaches zero, and the temperature of the substance approaches a lower limit.** This limit is the *absolute zero* of temperature. **Absolute zero** is the temperature at which no more energy can be extracted from a substance and no further lowering of its temperature is possible. This limiting temperature is 273 degrees below zero on the Celsius scale. This value was found in the 1800s by experimenters who discovered that all gases contract by the same proportion when temperature is decreased.[24.1]

Absolute zero corresponds to zero degrees on the Kelvin, or thermodynamic, scale and is written 0 K (short for "zero kelvin"). Unlike the Celsius scale, there are no negative numbers on the thermodynamic scale. Degrees on the Kelvin scale are the same size as those on the Celsius scale. Thus, ice melts at 0°C, or 273 K, and water boils at 100°C, or 373 K. The Kelvin scale was named after the British physicist Lord Kelvin, who coined the word *thermodynamics* and first suggested such a scale.

Figure 24.1 shows the temperature of various objects and phenomena with respect to absolute zero. At very high temperatures, the measurements of temperature on the Kelvin and Celsius scales are close to identical.

CONCEPT CHECK: What happens to a substance's temperature as the motion of its atoms approaches zero?

think!

A sample of hydrogen gas has a temperature of 0°C. If the gas is heated until its molecules have doubled their average kinetic energy (the gas has twice the absolute temperature), what will be its temperature in degrees Celsius? *Answer: 24.1*

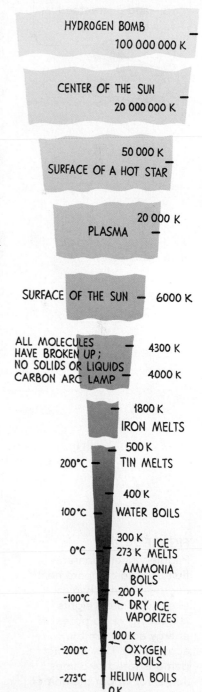

FIGURE 24.1 ▶
The figure shows the absolute temperatures of various objects and phenomena.

HYDROGEN BOMB
100 000 000 K

CENTER OF THE SUN
20 000 000 K

50 000 K
SURFACE OF A HOT STAR

20 000 K
PLASMA

SURFACE OF THE SUN — 6000 K

ALL MOLECULES HAVE BROKEN UP; NO SOLIDS OR LIQUIDS — 4300 K
CARBON ARC LAMP — 4000 K

1800 K
IRON MELTS

500 K
200°C — TIN MELTS

400 K
100°C — WATER BOILS

300 K ICE
0°C — 273 K MELTS
AMMONIA BOILS

200 K
-100°C — DRY ICE VAPORIZES

100 K
-200°C — OXYGEN BOILS

-273°C — HELIUM BOILS
0 K

24.2 First Law of Thermodynamics

In the eighteenth century, heat was thought to be an invisible fluid called *caloric,* which flowed like water from hot objects to cold objects. Caloric was conserved in its interactions, a discovery that led to the law of conservation of energy. In the 1840s, using the apparatus shown in Figure 24.2, scientist James Joule demonstrated that the flow of heat was nothing more than the flow of energy itself. The caloric theory of heat was gradually abandoned.[24.2.1] Today we view heat as a form of energy. Energy can neither be created nor destroyed.

The **first law of thermodynamics** is the law of conservation of energy applied to thermal systems. ✓ **The first law of thermodynamics states that whenever heat is added to a system, it transforms to an equal amount of some other form of energy.**

Heat By *system,* we mean any group of atoms, molecules, particles, or objects we wish to deal with. The system may be the steam in a steam engine, the whole Earth's atmosphere, or even the body of a living creature. It is important to define what is contained within the system as well as what is outside of it. If we add heat energy to the steam in a steam engine, to Earth's atmosphere, or to the body of a living creature, these systems will be able to do work on external things. This added energy does one or both of two things: (1) increases the internal energy of the system if it remains in the system and (2) does external work if it leaves the system. So, the first law of thermodynamics states

$$\text{Heat added} = \frac{\text{increase in}}{\text{internal energy}} + \frac{\text{external work done}}{\text{by the system}}$$

Let's say you put an air-filled, rigid, airtight can on a hotplate and add a certain amount of energy to the can. **Caution:** *Do not actually do this.* Since the can has a fixed volume, the walls of the can don't move, so no work is done. All of the heat going into the can increases the internal energy of the enclosed air, so its temperature rises.

FIGURE 24.2 ▶
Paddle-wheel apparatus first used to compare heat energy with mechanical energy. As the weights fall, they give up potential energy and warm the water accordingly. This was first demonstrated by James Joule, for whom the unit of energy is named.

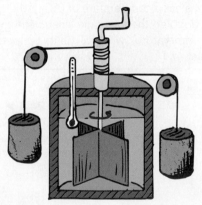

Now suppose instead that we replace the can with a balloon. This time, as the air is heated it expands, exerting a force for some distance on the surrounding atmosphere. Since some of the heat added to the air goes into doing work, less of the added heat goes into increasing the enclosed air's internal energy. Can you see that in this second situation the temperature of the enclosed air will be lower because some of the energy added to the system goes to work outside the system? The first law of thermodynamics makes good sense.

When a given quantity of heat is supplied to a steam engine, some of this heat increases the internal energy of the steam and the rest is transformed into mechanical work as the steam pushes a piston outward. That is, heat input equals the increase in internal energy plus the work output. The first law of thermodynamics is simply the thermal version of the law of conservation of energy.

Work Adding heat is not the only way to increase the internal energy of a system. If we set the "heat added" part of the first law to zero, we will see that changes in internal energy are equal to the work done on or by the system.[24.2.2] If work is done on a system—compressing it, for example—the internal energy will increase. The temperature of the system rises without any heat input. On the other hand, if work is done *by* the system—expanding against its surroundings, for example—the system's internal energy will decrease. With no heat extracted, the system cools.

Consider a bicycle pump. When we pump on the handle, the pump becomes hot. Why? Because we are putting mechanical work into the system and raising its internal energy. If the process happens quickly enough, so that very little heat is conducted from the system during compression, then nearly all of the work input will go into increasing internal energy, significantly raising the air's temperature.

CONCEPT CHECK What does the first law of thermodynamics state?

think!

If 10 J of energy is added to a system that does no external work, by how much will the internal energy of that system be raised?
Answer: 24.2

24.3 Adiabatic Processes

When a gas is compressed or expanded so that no heat enters or leaves a system, the process is said to be **adiabatic** (Greek for "impassible"). Adiabatic changes of volume can be achieved by performing the process rapidly so that heat has little time to enter or leave (as with the bicycle pump in Figure 24.3), or by thermally insulating a system from its surroundings (with polystyrene foam, for example).

A common example of a near adiabatic process is the compression and expansion of gases in the cylinders of an automobile engine, shown in Figure 24.4. Compression and expansion occur in only a few hundredths of a second, too short a time for appreciable heat energy to leave the combustion chamber. For very high compressions, like those in a diesel engine, the temperatures achieved are high enough to ignite a fuel mixture without the use of a spark plug. Diesel engines have no spark plugs.

FIGURE 24.3 ▲
Do work on a pump by pressing down on the piston and the air is warmed.

   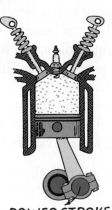 

INTAKE COMPRESSION IGNITION POWER STROKE EXHAUST

a. A fuel–air mixture fills the cylinder as the piston moves down.

b. The piston moves up and compresses the mixture—adiabatically, since no heat transfer occurs.

c. The spark plug fires, ignites the mixture, and raises its temperature.

d. Adiabatic expansion pushes the piston downward—the power stroke.

e. The burned gases are pushed out the exhaust valve, and the cycle repeats.

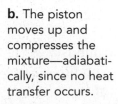

FIGURE 24.4 ▲
One cycle of a four-stroke internal combustion engine is shown above.

◉ **When work is done on a gas by adiabatically compressing it, the gas gains internal energy and becomes warmer.** When a gas adiabatically expands, it does work on its surroundings and gives up internal energy, and thus becomes cooler. Recall the activity in Chapter 22 of blowing on your hand with puckered lips so your breath expands as it leaves your mouth, repeated here in Figure 24.5. Your breath is considerably cooler than when blown without expanding from your wide-open mouth.

Heat and Temperature Air temperature may be changed by adding or subtracting heat, by changing the pressure of the air, or by both. Heat may be added by solar radiation, by long-wave Earth radiation, by moisture condensation, or by contact with the warm ground. Heat may be subtracted by radiation to space, by evaporation of rain falling through dry air, or by contact with cold surfaces.

There are many atmospheric processes, usually involving time scales of a day or less, in which the amount of heat added or subtracted is very small—small enough that the process is nearly adiabatic. In this case, an increase in pressure will cause an increase in temperature, and vice versa. We then have the adiabatic form of the first law:

$$\text{Change in air temperature} \sim \text{pressure change}$$

FIGURE 24.5 ▲
Blow warm air onto your hand from your wide-open mouth. Now reduce the opening between your lips so the air expands as you blow. Adiabatic expansion— the air is cooled.

Pressure and Temperature Adiabatic processes in the atmosphere occur in large masses of air that have dimensions on the order of kilometers. We'll call these large masses of air *blobs*. Due to their large size, mixing of different temperatures or pressures of air occurs only at their edges and doesn't appreciably alter the overall composition of the blobs. A blob behaves as if it were enclosed in a giant, tissue-light garment bag. As a blob of air flows up the side of a mountain, its pressure lessens, allowing it to expand and cool. The reduced pressure results in reduced temperature, as shown in Figure 24.6. Measurements show that the temperature of a blob of dry air drops by 10°C for each 1-kilometer increase in altitude (or for a decrease in pressure due to a 1-kilometer increase in altitude). Air flowing over tall mountains or rising in thunderstorms or cyclones may change elevation by several kilometers. So if a blob of dry air at ground level with a comfortable temperature of 25°C rose to 6 kilometers, its temperature would be a frigid –35°C. On the other hand, if air at a typical temperature of –20°C at an altitude of 6 kilometers descended to the ground, its temperature would be a roasting 40°C.

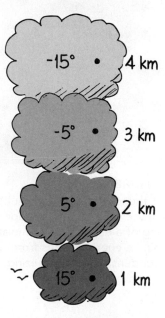

FIGURE 24.6 ▲
The temperature of a blob of dry air that expands adiabatically changes by about 10°C for each kilometer of elevation.

---

think!

If a blob of air initially at 0°C expands adiabatically while flowing upward alongside a mountain a vertical distance of 1 km, what will its temperature be? When it has risen 5 km?
Answer: 24.3.1

Imagine a giant dry-cleaner's garment bag full of air at a temperature of –10°C floating like a balloon with a string hanging from it 6 km above the ground. If you were able to yank it suddenly to the ground, what would its approximate temperature be?
Answer: 24.3.2

FIGURE 24.7 ▶

Chinooks, warm dry winds, occur when high-altitude air descends and is adiabatically warmed.

A dramatic example of this adiabatic warming is the *chinook*—a wind that blows down from the Rocky Mountains across the Great Plains. Cold air moving down the slopes of the mountains is compressed by the atmosphere into a smaller volume and is appreciably warmed, as shown in Figure 24.7. In this way communities in the paths of chinooks experience relatively warm weather in midwinter. The effect of expansion or compression on gases is quite impressive.[24.3] It can even create thunderheads like the one in Figure 24.8.

CONCEPT CHECK What is the effect of adiabatic compression on a gas?

24.4 Second and Third Laws of Thermodynamics

FIGURE 24.8 ▲

A thunderhead is the result of the rapid adiabatic cooling of a rising mass of moist air. Its energy comes from condensation and freezing of water vapor.

If we place a hot brick next to a cold brick, heat flows from the hot brick to the cold brick until both bricks arrive at a common temperature: thermal equilibrium. No energy will be destroyed, in accord with the first law of thermodynamics. But pretend the hot brick takes heat from the cold brick and becomes hotter. Would this violate the first law of thermodynamics? No, because energy is still conserved in the process. But it would violate the *second law of thermodynamics*. The **second law of thermodynamics** describes the direction of heat flow in natural processes. ⊘ **The second law of thermodynamics states that heat will never of itself flow from a cold object to a hot object.**

Heat flows one way, from hot to cold. In winter, heat flows from inside a warm heated home to the cold air outside. In summer, heat flows from the hot air outside into the home's cooler interior. Heat can be made to flow the other way, but only by imposing external effort—as occurs with heat pumps that move heat from cooler outside air into a home's warmer interior, or air conditioners that remove heat from a cool interior to warmer air outside. Without external effort, the direction of heat flow is from hot to cold.

There is a huge amount of internal energy in the ocean, but all this energy cannot be used to light a single flashlight lamp without external effort. Energy will not of itself flow from the lower-temperature ocean to the higher-temperature lamp filament.

There is also a *third law of thermodynamics,* which restates what we've learned about the lowest limit of temperature: *no system can reach absolute zero.*

As investigators attempt to reach this lowest temperature, it becomes more difficult to get closer to it. Physicists have been able to record temperatures that are less than a millionth of 1 kelvin—but never as low as 0 K.

> Absolute zero isn't the coldest you can reach. It's the coldest you can hope to approach. (Researchers have been within a billionth of a degree of absolute zero.)

CONCEPT CHECK: What does the second law of thermodynamics state about heat flow?

24.5 Heat Engines and the Second Law

It is easy to change work completely into heat—simply rub your hands together briskly. Or push a crate at constant speed along a floor. All the work you do in overcoming friction is completely converted to heat. But the reverse process, changing heat completely into work, can never occur. The best that can be done is the conversion of some heat to mechanical work. The first heat engine to do this was the steam engine, invented in about 1700.

Heat Engine Mechanics A **heat engine** is any device that changes internal energy into mechanical work. The basic idea behind a heat engine, whether a steam engine, internal combustion engine, or jet engine, is that mechanical work can be obtained only when heat flows from a high temperature to a low temperature. In every heat engine only some of the heat can be transformed into work.

In considering heat engines, we talk about *reservoirs.* We picture a "high-temperature reservoir" as vast, something from which we can extract heat without cooling it down. Likewise we picture a "low-temperature reservoir" as something that can absorb heat without itself warming up. Heat flows out of a high-temperature reservoir, into the heat engine, and then into a low-temperature reservoir, as shown in Figure 24.9. Every heat engine will (1) increase its internal energy by absorbing heat from a reservoir of higher temperature, (2) convert some of this energy into mechanical work, and (3) expel the remaining energy as heat to some lower-temperature reservoir. In a gasoline engine, for example, (1) the burning fuel in the combustion chamber is the high-temperature reservoir, (2) mechanical work is done on the piston, and (3) the expelled energy goes out as exhaust.

FIGURE 24.9 ▼
When heat energy flows in any heat engine from a high-temperature place to a low-temperature place, part of this energy is transformed into work output.

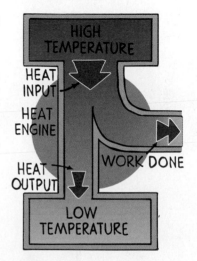

⊘ **According to the second law of thermodynamics, no heat engine can convert all heat input to mechanical energy output.** Only some of the heat can be transformed into work, with the remainder expelled in the process. Applied to heat engines, the second law states that when work is done by a heat engine running between two temperatures, T_{hot} and T_{cold}, only some of the input heat at T_{hot} can be converted to work, and the rest is expelled as heat at T_{cold}.

There is always heat exhaust, which may be desirable or undesirable. Hot steam expelled in a laundry on a cold winter day may be quite desirable, while the same steam on a hot summer day is something else. When expelled heat is undesirable, we call it *thermal pollution*.

Heat Engine Efficiency Before the second law was understood, it was thought that a very-low-friction heat engine could convert nearly all the input energy to useful work. But not so. In 1824 the French engineer Sadi Carnot carefully analyzed the cycles of compression and expansion in a heat engine and made a fundamental discovery. He showed that the upper fraction of heat that can be converted to useful work, even under ideal conditions, depends on the temperature difference between the hot reservoir and the cold sink. The **Carnot efficiency,** or ideal efficiency, of a heat engine is the ideal maximum percentage of input energy that the engine can convert to work. The equation for the ideal efficiency is given as follows:

$$\text{Ideal efficiency} = \frac{T_{hot} - T_{cold}}{T_{hot}}$$

T_{hot} is the temperature of the hot reservoir and T_{cold} is the temperature of the cold. Ideal efficiency depends only on the temperature difference between input and exhaust. Whenever ratios of temperatures are involved, the absolute temperature scale must be used.

Link to TECHNOLOGY

Fuel Cells and Electric Vehicles One of the attractions of fuel cells, and of electric vehicles in general, is that they are *not* heat engines—their efficiencies are not limited by the Carnot cycle constraints of the second law. While the efficiency of an engine that burns (combusts) fuel will always be limited by the temperature difference between the cylinder and the exhaust, fuel cells and batteries have no such thermal constraints. Fuel cells running on pure hydrogen can be as much as 80% efficient in converting chemical energy to electrical energy. Watch the growth of fuel-cell technology and electric automobiles.

So T_{hot} and T_{cold} are expressed in kelvins. For example, when the hot reservoir in a steam turbine is 400 K (127°C) and the sink is 300 K (27°C), the ideal efficiency is

$$\frac{(400\ K - 300\ K)}{400\ K} = \frac{1}{4}$$

This means that even under *ideal* conditions, only 25% of the internal energy of the steam can be converted into work, while the remaining 75% is expelled as waste. This is why steam is superheated to high temperatures in steam engines and power plants. The higher the steam temperature driving a motor or turbogenerator, the higher the efficiency of power production. (Increasing operating temperature in the example to 600 K yields an efficiency of (600 K − 300 K)/600 K = 1/2, twice the efficiency at 400 K.)

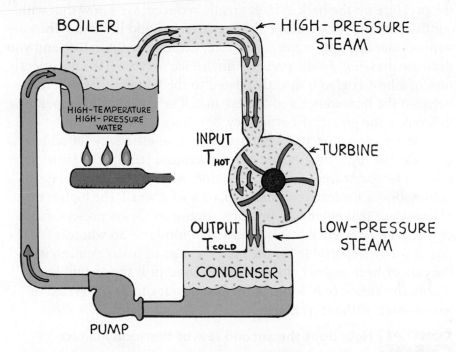

◀ **FIGURE 24.10**
A steam turbine turns because high-temperature steam from the boiler exerts more pressure on the front side of the turbine blades than the low-temperature steam exerts on the back side of the blades. Without a pressure difference, the turbine would not turn.

Heat Engine Physics We can see the role of temperature difference between heat reservoir and sink in the operation of the steam-turbine engine in Figure 24.10. Steam from the boiler is the hot reservoir while the sink is the exhaust region after the steam passes through the turbine. The hot steam exerts pressure and does work on the turbine blades when it pushes on their front sides. This is nice. But steam pressure is not confined to the front sides of the blades; steam pressure is also exerted on the *back sides* of the blades—countereffective and not so nice. A pressure *difference* across the blades is vital, for it causes the turbine to keep spinning, allowing it to do work. (If pressures were the same on both the front and the back of the blades, no work would be done.)

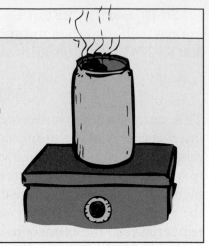

What Can Air Do to a Can?

1. Put a small amount of water in an aluminum soft drink can and heat it on the stove until steam issues from the opening.

2. With a pair of tongs, invert the can into a pan of water. Observe what happens to the can.

3. **Think** What role did condensation play in what happened to the can?

Biological systems are enormously complex, and while living, never reach thermal equilibrium.

How do you get a pressure difference? By condensing the steam, the pressure on the back sides is greatly reduced. We know that with confined steam, temperature and pressure go hand in hand—increase temperature and you increase pressure; decrease temperature and you decrease pressure. So the pressure difference necessary for the operation of a heat engine is directly related to the temperature difference between the heat source and the exhaust. The greater the temperature difference, the greater the efficiency.[24.5.1]

Carnot's equation states the upper limit of efficiency for all heat engines. The higher the operating temperature (compared with exhaust temperature) of any heat engine, whether in an ordinary automobile, a nuclear-powered ship, or a jet aircraft, the higher the efficiency of that engine. In practice, friction is always present in all engines, and efficiency is always less than ideal.[24.5.2] So whereas friction is solely responsible for the inefficiencies of many devices, in the case of heat engines, the overriding concept is the second law of thermodynamics; only some of the heat input can be converted to work—even without friction.

CONCEPT CHECK: How does the second law of thermodynamics apply to heat engines?

FIGURE 24.11 ▶

Try to push a heavy crate across a rough floor and all your work will go into heating the floor and crate. Work against friction turns into disorganized energy.

24.6 Order Tends to Disorder

The first law of thermodynamics states that energy can be neither created nor destroyed. The second law adds that whenever energy transforms, some of it degenerates into waste heat, unavailable to do work. Another way to say this is that organized, usuable energy degenerates into disorganized, nonusable energy. The energy of gasoline is in an organized and usable form. When gasoline burns in an automobile engine, part of its energy does useful work such as moving the pistons, part of the energy heats the engine and surroundings, and part of the energy goes out the exhaust. Useful energy degenerates to nonuseful forms and is unavailable for doing the same work again.

Organized energy in the form of electricity that goes into electric lights in homes and office buildings degenerates to heat energy. This is a principal source of heating in many office buildings in moderate climates, such as the Transamerica Pyramid in San Francisco. All of the electrical energy in the lamps, even the part that briefly exists in the form of light, turns into heat energy, which is used to warm the buildings (that explains why the lights are on most of the time). This energy is degenerated and has no further use.

We see that the quality of energy is lowered with each transformation. Organized energy tends to disorganized forms. In this broader regard, the second law can be stated another way: ✔ **Natural systems tend to proceed toward a state of greater disorder.**

Imagine that in a corner of a room sits a closed jar filled with argon gas atoms. When the lid is removed, the argon atoms move in haphazard directions, eventually mixing with the air molecules in the room. This is what we would expect—the system moves from a more ordered state (argon atoms concentrated in the jar) to a more disordered state (argon atoms spread evenly throughout the room).

You would not expect the argon atoms to spontaneously order themselves back into the jar to return to the more ordered containment. This is because compared with the immense number of ways the argon atoms can randomly move, the chance of them returning to such an ordered state is practically zero.

Disordered energy can be changed to ordered energy only at the expense of work input. For example, plants can assemble sugar molecules from less organized carbon dioxide and water molecules only by using energy input from sunlight. But without some imposed work input, no increase in order occurs.

In the broadest sense, the message of the second law is that the tendency of the universe, and all that is in it, tends to disorder.

CONCEPT CHECK: What happens to the orderly state of any natural system?

FIGURE 24.12 ▲
The Transamerica® Pyramid and some other buildings are heated by electric lighting, which is why the lights are on most of the time.

FIGURE 24.13 ▲
Argon gas goes from the jar to the air and not the other way around.

24.7 Entropy

The idea of ordered energy tending to disordered energy is embodied in the concept of *entropy*.[24.7.1] **Entropy** is the measure of the amount of disorder in a system. Disorder increases; entropy increases.

⊘ **According to the second law of thermodynamics, in the long run, the entropy of a system always increases for natural processes.** Gas molecules escaping from a bottle move from a relatively orderly state to a disorderly state. Organized structures in time become disorganized messes. Things left to themselves run down, such as the house in Figure 24.14. Whenever a physical system is allowed to distribute its energy freely, it always does so such that entropy increases while the available energy of the system for doing work decreases.

Entropy normally increases in physical systems. However, when there is work input, as in living organisms, entropy decreases. All living things, from bacteria to trees to human beings, extract energy from their surroundings and use it to increase their own organization. This order in life forms is maintained by increasing entropy elsewhere, so for the system "life forms plus their waste products" there is still a net increase in entropy.[24.7.2] Energy must be transformed into the living system to support life. When it is not, the organism soon dies and tends toward disorder.

FIGURE 24.14 ▶
This run-down house demonstrates entropy. Without continual maintenance, the house will eventually fall apart.

The first law of thermodynamics is a universal law of nature for which no exceptions have been observed. The second law, however, is a probability statement. Disordered states are much more probable than ordered states. Given enough time, even the most improbable states may occur; entropy may sometimes spontaneously decrease. Although theoretically the haphazard motions of air molecules could momentarily become harmonious in a corner of the room, or a barrelful of pennies dumped on the floor could all come up heads, or a breeze might come into a messy room and make it organized, the odds of these things actually occurring are infinitesimally small.

These situations are possible—but so highly improbable that they are never observed. The second law tells us the most probable course of events—not the only possible one.

The laws of thermodynamics are sometimes put this way: You can't win (because you can't get any more energy out of a system than you put in), you can't break even (because you can't even get as much energy out as you put in), and you can't get out of the game (entropy in the universe is always increasing).

CONCEPT CHECK What always happens to the entropy of systems?

Science, Technology, and Society

Thermodynamics and Thermal Pollution

A modern electric power plant, though large and complex, can be approximated as a simple heat engine. The power plant uses heat from the burning of coal, oil, gas, or heat from nuclear fission to do work turning electric generators. In this process, it also produces waste heat as an inevitable consequence of the second law of thermodynamics. This waste heat is sometimes called *thermal pollution* because, like chemical wastes, it pollutes the environment.

Waste heat discharged into waterways can raise temperatures of aquatic environments enough to kill organisms and disrupt ecosystems. Waste heat

discharged into the air can contribute to weather changes. Thermal pollution is unlike chemical pollution, since chemical pollution can be reduced by various methods. The only way to manage thermal pollution is to spread waste heat over areas large enough to absorb it without significantly increasing temperatures. Conservation and efficient technology are absolutely crucial to the health of our planet.

Critical Thinking Explain how the second law of thermodynamics tells us that it is impossible to produce usable energy with zero environmental impact.

 **REVIEW**

Concept Summary · · · · · ·

- As the thermal motion of atoms in a substance approaches zero, the kinetic energy of the atoms approaches zero, and the temperature of the substance approaches a lower limit.

- The first law of thermodynamics states that whenever heat is added to a system, it transforms to an equal amount of some other form of energy.

- When work is done on a gas by adiabatically compressing it, the gas gains internal energy and becomes warmer.

- The second law of thermodynamics states that heat will never of itself flow from a cold object to a hot object.

- According to the second law of thermodynamics, no heat engine can convert all heat input to mechanical energy output.

- Natural systems tend to proceed toward a state of greater disorder.

- According to the second law of thermodynamics, in the long run, entropy always increases for natural processes.

Key Terms · · · · · ·

thermodynamics
   (p. 468)
absolute zero
   (p. 469)
first law of thermodynamics (p. 470)
adiabatic (p. 472)

second law of thermodynamics
   (p. 474)
heat engine (p. 475)
Carnot efficiency
   (p. 476)
entropy (p. 480)

think! Answers

24.1 At 0°C the gas has an absolute temperature of 273 K. Twice as much average kinetic energy means it has twice the absolute temperature, or two times 273 K. This would be 546 K, or 273°C. Do you and your classmates agree?

24.2 10 J.

24.3.1 At 1 km elevation, its temperature will be −10°C; at 5 km, −50°C.

24.3.2 If it were pulled down so quickly that heat conduction was negligible, it would be adiabatically compressed by the atmosphere and its temperature would rise to a piping hot 50°C (122°F), just as compressed air gets hot in a bicycle pump.

24.5 Zero efficiency; (400 K − 400 K)/400 K = 0. This means no work output is possible for any heat engine unless a temperature difference exists between the reservoir and the sink.

24 ASSESS

Check Concepts ......

Section 24.1

1. What is the meaning of the Greek words from which we get the word *thermodynamics*?

2. Is the study of thermodynamics concerned primarily with microscopic or macroscopic processes?

3. What is the lowest possible temperature on the Celsius scale? On the Kelvin scale?

4. What is the temperature of melting ice in kelvins? Of boiling water?

Section 24.2

5. How does the law of the conservation of energy relate to the first law of thermodynamics?

6. What happens to the internal energy of a system when work is done on it? What happens to its temperature?

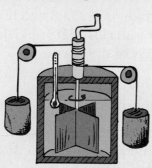

7. What is the relationship between heat added to a system and the internal energy and external work done by the system?

8. If work is done adiabatically on a system, will the internal energy of the system increase or decrease? If work is done by a system, will the internal energy of the system increase or decrease?

Section 24.3

9. What condition is necessary for a process to be adiabatic?

10. What happens to the temperature of air when it is adiabatically compressed? When it adiabatically expands?

11. What generally happens to the temperature of rising air?

12. What generally happens to the temperature of sinking air?

Section 24.4

13. How does the second law of thermodynamics relate to the direction of heat flow?

Section 24.5

14. What three processes occur in every heat engine?

15. What is thermal pollution?

16. If all friction could be removed from a heat engine, would it be 100% efficient? Explain.

17. What is the ideal efficiency of a heat engine that operates with its hot reservoir at 500 K and its sink at 300 K?

18. Why are heat engines intentionally run at high operating temperatures?

Section 24.6

19. Give at least two examples to distinguish between organized energy and disorganized energy.

20. How much of the electrical energy transformed by a common lightbulb becomes heat energy?

21. With respect to orderly and disorderly states, what do natural systems tend to do? Can a disorderly state ever transform to an orderly state? Explain.

Section 24.7

22. What is the physicist's term for a measure of messiness?

23. Under what condition can entropy decrease in a system?

24. What is the relationship between the second law of thermodynamics and entropy?

25. Distinguish between the first, second, and third laws of thermodynamics in terms of whether or not exceptions occur.

Plug and Chug ······

Use the following equation to help you answer Questions 26–29.

$$\text{Ideal efficiency} = \frac{T_{\text{hot}} - T_{\text{cold}}}{T_{\text{hot}}}$$

26. Calculate the *ideal* efficiency of a heat engine that takes in energy at 800 K and expels heat to a reservoir at 300 K.

27. Calculate the ideal efficiency of a ship's boiler when steam comes out at 530 K, pushes through a steam turbine, and exits into a condenser that is kept at 290 K by circulating seawater.

28. Calculate the ideal efficiency of a steam turbine that has a hot reservoir of 112°C high-pressure steam and a sink at 27°C.

29. In a heat engine driven by ocean temperature differences, the heat source (water near the surface) is at 293 K and the heat sink (deeper water) is at 283 K. Calculate the ideal efficiency of the engine.

Think and Explain ······

30. On which temperature scale does the average kinetic energy of molecules double when the temperature doubles?

31. On a 10°C day, your friend who likes cold weather says she wishes it were twice as cold. Taking this to mean she wishes the air had half the internal energy, what temperature would this be?

32. A friend said the temperature inside a certain oven is 600 and the temperature inside a certain star is 60,000. You're unsure about whether your friend meant kelvins or degrees Celsius. How much difference does it make in each case?

33. Maria vigorously shakes a can of liquid back and forth for more than a minute. Does the temperature of the liquid increase? Why or why not? (Try it and see.)

34. When you pump a tire with a bicycle pump, the cylinder of the pump becomes hot. Give two reasons why this is so.

35. What happens to the gas pressure within a sealed gallon can when it is heated? When it is cooled?

36. We know that warm air rises. So it might seem that the air temperature should be higher at the top of mountains than down below. But the opposite is most often the case. Why?

37. The combined molecular kinetic energies of molecules in a very large container of cold water are greater than the combined molecular kinetic energies in a cup of hot tea. Pretend you partially immerse the teacup in the cold water and that the tea absorbs 10 joules of energy from the water and becomes hotter, while the water that gives up 10 joules of energy becomes cooler. Would this energy transfer violate the first law of thermodynamics? The second law of thermodynamics? Explain.

38. Is it possible to entirely convert a given amount of heat into mechanical energy? Is it possible to entirely convert a given amount of mechanical energy into heat? Cite examples to illustrate your answers.

39. Suppose one wishes to cool a kitchen by leaving the refrigerator door open and closing the kitchen door and windows. What will happen to the room temperature? Why?

40. Will the efficiency of a car engine increase, decrease, or remain the same if the muffler is removed? If the car is driven on a very cold day? Defend your answers.

41. Consider the inverted soft drink can placed in a pan of water, as featured in the Discover! box in Section 24.5. The can is crushed by atmospheric pressure. Would crushing occur if the water were hot but not boiling? Would it be crushed in boiling water? (Try it and see!)

42. A mixture of fuel and air is burned rapidly in a combustion engine to push a piston in the engine that in turn propels the vehicle. In a jet engine, a mixture of fuel and air is burned rapidly and, instead of pushing pistons, pushes the aircraft itself. Which do you suppose is more efficient?

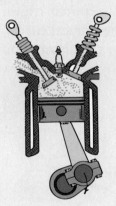

43. In buildings that are being heated electrically, is it wasteful to turn on all the lights? Is turning on all the lights wasteful if the building is being cooled by air conditioning? Defend your answers.

44. Why is "thermal pollution" a relative term?

45. Is it possible to construct a heat engine that produces no thermal pollution? Defend your answer.

46. What happens to the efficiency of a heat engine when the temperature of the reservoir into which heat energy is ejected is lowered?

47. Water put into a freezer compartment in your refrigerator goes to a state of less molecular disorder when it freezes. Is this an exception to the entropy principle? Explain.

48. Carlos says that perpetual motion machines are impossible to construct. John says that perpetual motion is common in nature— the motion of molecules, for example. Do you agree with Carlos, John, or both?

Think and Solve ••••••

49. Helium has the special property that its internal energy is directly proportional to its absolute temperature. Consider a flask of helium with a temperature of 10°C. If it is heated until it has twice the internal energy, what will its temperature be?

50. Imagine a giant dry-cleaner's bag full of air at a temperature of −35°C floating like a balloon with a string hanging from it 10 km above the ground. Estimate its temperature if you were able to yank it suddenly to Earth's surface.

51. What is the ideal efficiency of an automobile engine wherein fuel is heated to 2700 K and the outdoor air is 300 K?

52. Dr. Knute C. Cuckoo claims to have invented a heat engine that will revolutionize life as we know it. It runs between a hot source at 300°C and cold heat "sink" at 25°C. Dr. C. claims that his engine is 92% efficient.

   a. What is the actual maximum efficiency of his heat engine?
   b. What error did he make in his choice of temperature scales?

53. Which heat engine has greater ideal efficiency, one that operates between the temperatures 600 K and 400 K or one that operates between 500 K and 400 K? Explain how your answer conforms to the idea that a higher operating temperature yields higher efficiency.

54. To increase the efficiency of a heat engine, would it be better to increase the temperature of the reservoir while holding the temperature of the sink constant, or to decrease the temperature of the sink while holding the temperature of the reservoir constant? Show your work.

55. A heat engine takes in 100 kJ of energy from a source at 800 K and expels 50 kJ to a reservoir at 300 K. Calculate the ideal efficiency and the actual efficiency of the engine.

56. A certain heat engine takes in 25 kJ of heat and exhausts 17 kJ. Chris says that the efficiency of the engine is 0.32. Confirm his findings.

57. During one cycle, an ideal heat engine exhausts 3800 J of heat while performing 1200 J of useful work. Anthony says the efficiency of the engine is 0.24. Show that he is correct.

58. A heat engine operates between $T_{hot} = 750°C$ and $T_{cold} = 35°C$. Michael says that the theoretical maximum efficiency is about 70%. Do you agree? If so, show why. If not, show why not.

59. A college physics exam states that a power plant generating 420 MW of electricity runs between 540°C and 30°C, and asks for the minimum amount power input required for such a plant. The answer key reveals that the answer is 670,000 kJ each second, or 670 MW. Show how this figure comes about.

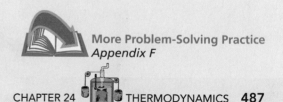

More Problem-Solving Practice
Appendix F

IT'S A FACT!

Both light and sound travel as waves. Sound waves must be transmitted through some kind of medium, whether it is a solid, liquid, or gas. Light does not need a medium to propagate. Thus, in the vacuum of outer space, you can see but not hear. In this unit, you will learn many interesting facts about waves, sound, and light.

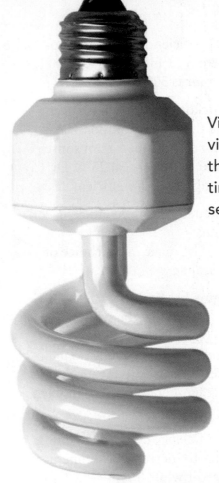

Visible light vibrates more than 100 trillion times per second. [Ch. 27]

Isn't this disc the pits? I mean, there are billions of them, carefully inscribed in an array that is scanned at millions of pits per second by a laser beam. Digitized music! Or a whole encyclopedia! But the beauty of a CD is more than what it holds—just look at the brilliant spectrum of colors diffracted by the evenly spaced rows of pits. I find it even more beautiful when I know **why** it's so colorful and **why** it holds so much music or information. That's the physics of it all!

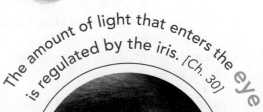

The amount of light that enters the eye is regulated by the iris. [Ch. 30]

The **colors** of most objects depend on the way the objects reflect light. [Ch. 28]

Go Online
SCIENCE NEWS

For: Articles on sound and light

Visit: PHSchool.com

Web Code: cse – 4000

Diffraction in feathers produces beautiful iridescent colors. [Ch. 31]

A **prism** separates white light into colors arranged according to their frequencies. [Ch. 29]

Sound travels about four times faster in water than in air. [Ch. 26]

25 VIBRATIONS AND WAVES

THE BIG IDEA : Waves transmit energy through space and time.

All around us we see things that wiggle and jiggle. Even things too small to see, such as atoms, are constantly wiggling and jiggling. A repeating, back-and-forth motion about an equilibrium position is a **vibration.** A vibration cannot exist in one instant. It needs time to move back and forth. Strike a bell and the vibrations will continue for some time before they die down.

A disturbance that is transmitted progressively from one place to the next with no actual transport of matter is a **wave.** A wave cannot exist in one place but must extend from one place to another. Light and sound are both forms of energy that move through space as waves. This chapter is about vibrations and waves, and the following chapters continue with the study of sound and light.

discover!

What Are Standing Waves?

1. Fill a foam cup nearly to the top with water. Place the cup on a smooth, dry surface.
2. While applying a moderate downward pressure, drag the cup across the surface.
3. Adjust the downward pressure on the cup until a pattern of waves, called standing waves, appears on the surface of the water.
4. Now try to change the pattern by altering both the speed of the cup and the downward pressure.

Analyze and Conclude

1. **Observing** Describe the patterns that you produced on the surface of the water.
2. **Predicting** What do you think might happen if you were to drag the cup on a different kind of surface?
3. **Making Generalizations** Do you think standing waves can be produced in other media? Explain.

25.1 Vibration of a Pendulum

Suspend a stone at the end of a string and you have a simple pendulum. Pendulums like the one in Figure 25.1 swing back and forth with such regularity that they have long been used to control the motion of clocks. Galileo discovered that the time a pendulum takes to swing back and forth through small angles depends only on the length of the pendulum—the mass has no effect. The time of a back-and-forth swing of the pendulum is called the **period.** ⊘ **The period of the pendulum depends only on the length of a pendulum and the acceleration of gravity.** [25.1]

A long pendulum has a longer period than a shorter pendulum; that is, it swings back and forth more slowly—less frequently—than a short pendulum. When walking, we allow our legs to swing with the help of gravity, like a pendulum. In the same way that a long pendulum has a greater period, a person with long legs tends to walk with a slower stride than a person with short legs. This is most noticeable in long-legged animals such as giraffes and horses, which run with a slower gait than do short-legged animals such as hamsters and mice.

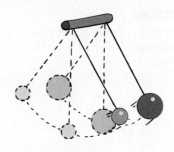

FIGURE 25.1 ▲
Two pendulums of the same length have the same period regardless of mass.

CONCEPT CHECK What determines the period of a pendulum?

25.2 Wave Description

The back-and-forth vibratory motion (often called oscillatory motion) of a swinging pendulum is called **simple harmonic motion.** [25.2] The pendulum bob filled with sand in Figure 25.2 exhibits simple harmonic motion above a conveyor belt. When the conveyor belt is stationary, the sand traces out a straight line. More interestingly, when the conveyor belt is moving at constant speed, the sand traces out a special curve known as a sine curve. A **sine curve** is a pictorial representation of a wave. ⊘ **The source of all waves is something that vibrates.**

think!

What is the frequency in vibrations per second of a 100-Hz wave?
Answer: 25.2.1

◀ **FIGURE 25.2**
Frank Oppenheimer, founder of the Exploratorium® science museum in San Francisco, demonstrates that a pendulum swinging back and forth traces out a straight line over a stationary surface and a sine curve when the surface moves at constant speed.

FIGURE 25.3 ▶
A sine curve is a pictorial representation of a wave.

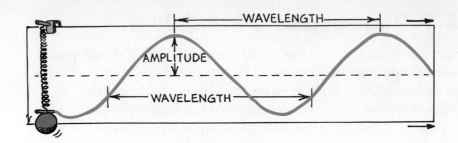

The Parts of a Wave A weight attached to a spring undergoes vertical simple harmonic motion as shown in Figure 25.3. A marking pen attached to the bob traces a sine curve on a sheet of paper that is moving horizontally at constant speed. Like a water wave, the high points on a wave are called **crests.** The low points on a wave are called **troughs.** The straight dashed line represents the "home" position, or midpoint of the vibration. The term **amplitude** refers to the distance from the midpoint to the crest (or trough) of the wave. So the amplitude equals the maximum displacement from equilibrium.

The **wavelength** of a wave is the distance from the top of one crest to the top of the next one. Or equivalently, the wavelength is the distance between successive identical parts of the wave. The wavelengths of waves at the beach are measured in meters, the wavelengths of ripples in a pond in centimeters, and the wavelengths of light in billionths of a meter (nanometers).

Be clear about the distinction between *frequency* and *speed.* How frequently a wave vibrates is altogether different from how fast it moves from one location to another.

Frequency The number of vibrations an object makes in a unit of time is an object's **frequency.** The frequency of a vibrating pendulum, or object on a spring, specifies the number of back-and-forth vibrations it makes in a given time (usually one second). A complete back-and-forth vibration is one cycle. If it occurs in one second, the frequency is one vibration per second or one cycle per second. If two vibrations occur in one second, the frequency is two vibrations or two cycles per second. The frequency of the vibrating source and the frequency of the wave it produces are the same.

The unit of frequency is called the **hertz** (Hz). A frequency of one cycle per second is 1 hertz, two cycles per second is 2 hertz, and so on. Higher frequencies are measured in kilohertz (kHz—thousands of hertz), and still higher frequencies in megahertz (MHz—millions of hertz) or gigahertz (GHz—billions of hertz). AM radio waves are broadcast in kilohertz, while FM radio waves are broadcast in megahertz; radar and microwave ovens operate at gigahertz. A station at 960 kHz broadcasts radio waves that have a frequency of 960,000 hertz. A station at 101 MHz broadcasts radio waves with a frequency of 101,000,000 hertz. As Figure 25.4 shows, these radio-wave frequencies are the frequencies at which electrons vibrate in the transmitting antenna of a radio station.

FIGURE 25.4 ▲
Electrons in the transmitting antenna of a radio station at 960 kHz on the AM dial vibrate 960,000 times each second and produce 960-kHz radio waves.

If the frequency of a vibrating object is known, its period can be calculated, and vice versa. Suppose, for example, that a pendulum makes two vibrations in one second. Its frequency is 2 Hz. The time needed to complete one vibration—that is, the period of vibration—is 1/2 second. Or if the vibration period is 3 Hz, then the period is 1/3 second. As you can see below, frequency and period are inverses of each other:

$$\text{frequency} = \frac{1}{\text{period}} \text{ or period} = \frac{1}{\text{frequency}}$$

think!

The Sears Tower in Chicago sways back and forth at a frequency of about 0.1 Hz. What is its period of vibration?

Answer: 25.2.2

CONCEPT CHECK : What is the source of all waves?

25.3 Wave Motion

Most of the information around us gets to us in some form of wave. Sound is energy that travels to our ears in the form of a wave. Light is energy that comes to our eyes in the form of a different kind of wave (an electromagnetic wave). The signals that reach our radio and television sets also travel in the form of electromagnetic waves.

When energy is transferred by a wave from a vibrating source to a distant receiver, there is no transfer of matter between the two points. To see this, think about the very simple wave produced when one end of a horizontally stretched string is shaken up and down as shown in Figure 25.5. After the end of the string is shaken, a rhythmic disturbance travels along the string. Each part of the string moves up and down while the disturbance moves horizontally along the length of the string. It is the disturbance that moves along the length of the string, not parts of the string itself.

FIGURE 25.5 ▲
When the string is shaken up and down, a disturbance moves along the string.

Link to ENTOMOLOGY

Noisy Bugs Big bumblebees flap their wings at about 130 flaps per second, and produce sound of 130 Hz. A honeybee flaps its wings at 225 flaps per second and produces a higher-pitched sound of 225 Hz. The annoying high-pitched whine of a mosquito results from its wings flapping at 600 Hz. These sounds are produced by pressure variations in the air caused by vibrating wings.

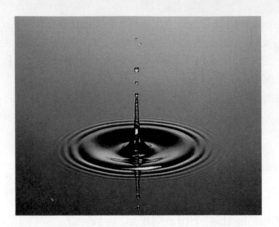

FIGURE 25.6 ▶
A circular water wave in a still
pond moves out from the center
in an expanding circle.

Go Online

SCi LINKS™ NSTA

For: Links on wave motion
Visit: www.SciLinks.org
Web Code: csn – 2503

Drop a stone in a quiet pond and you'll produce a wave that
moves out from the center in an expanding circle as shown in Figure
25.6. It is the disturbance that moves, not the water, for after the disturbance passes, the water is where it was before the wave passed.

When someone speaks to you from across the room, the sound wave
is a disturbance in the air that travels across the room. The air molecules
themselves do not move along, as they would in a wind. The air, like the
rope and the water in the previous examples, is the medium through
which wave energy travels. ☑ **The energy transferred by a wave from
a vibrating source to a receiver is carried by a disturbance in a
medium.** Energy is not transferred by matter moving from one place to
another within the medium.

CONCEPT CHECK ⁝ How does a wave transfer energy?

---

discover!

Making Waves

Part 1

1. Oscillate a marking pen back and forth across a piece of paper
   as you slowly pull the paper in a direction perpendicular to your
   oscillation.
2. Repeat Step 1, but pull the paper faster this time.
3. **Think** What happens to the wavelength of the curves when you
   pull the paper faster?

Part 2

1. Repeatedly dip your finger into a wide pan of water to make
   circular waves on the surface.
2. Repeat Step 1, but dip your finger more frequently.
3. **Think** What happens to the wavelength of the waves when you dip
   your finger more frequently?

25.4 Wave Speed

The speed of a wave depends on the medium through which the wave moves. Sound waves, for example, move at speeds of about 330 m/s to 350 m/s in air (depending on temperature), and about four times faster in water. Whatever the medium, the speed, wavelength, and frequency of the wave are related. Consider the simple case of water waves, as shown in Figure 25.7. Imagine that you fix your eyes at a stationary point on the surface of water and observe the waves passing by this point. If you observe the distance between crests (the wavelength) and also count the number of crests that pass each second (the frequency), then you can calculate the horizontal distance a particular crest moves each second. For example, in Figure 25.7, one crest passes by the bird every second. The waves therefore move at 1 meter per second.

⊘ **You can calculate the speed of a wave by multiplying the wavelength by the frequency.** For example, if the wavelength is 3 meters and if two crests pass a stationary point each second, then 3 meters × 2 waves pass by in 1 second. The waves therefore move at 6 meters per second. In equation form, this relationship is written as

$$v = \lambda f$$

where v is wave speed, λ (Greek letter lambda) is wavelength, and f is wave frequency. This relationship holds for all kinds of waves, whether they are water waves, sound waves, radio waves, or light waves.

The equation $v = \lambda f$ makes sense: During each vibration, a wave travels a distance of one wavelength.

FIGURE 25.7 ▼
If the wavelength is 1 meter, and one wavelength per second passes the pole, then the speed of the wave is 1 m/s.

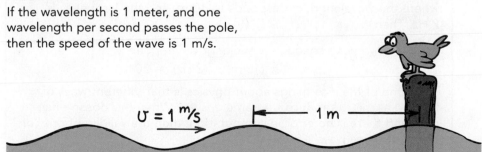

Table 25.1	Sound Waves	
Wavelength (m)	Frequency (Hz)	Wave Speed (m/s)
2.13	160	340
1.29	264	340
0.86	396	340
0.64	528	340

think!

What is the wavelength of a 340-Hz sound wave when the speed of sound in air is 340 m/s?

Answer: 25.4.2

Table 25.1 shows some wavelengths and corresponding frequencies of sound in air at the same temperature. Notice that the product of wavelength and frequency is the same for each example—340 m/s in this case. During a concert, you do not hear the high notes in a chord before you hear the low notes. The sounds of all instruments reach you at the same time. Notice that long wavelengths have low frequencies, and short wavelengths have high frequencies. Wavelength and frequency vary inversely to produce the same wave speed for all sounds.

CONCEPT CHECK How do you calculate the speed of a wave?

do the math!

If a train of freight cars, each 10 m long, rolls by you at the rate of 2 cars each second, what is the speed of the train?

You can look at this problem in two ways, the Chapter 4 way and the Chapter 25 way.

From Chapter 4 recall:

$$v = \frac{d}{t} = \frac{2 \times 10 \text{ m}}{1 \text{ s}} = 20 \text{ m/s}$$

Note that d is the length of that part of the train that passes you in time t.

Here in Chapter 25 we compare the train to wave motion, where the wavelength corresponds to 10 m, and the frequency is 2 Hz. Then

$$\text{wave speed} = \text{wavelength} \times \text{frequency}$$
$$= (10 \text{ m}) \times (2 \text{ Hz}) = 20 \text{ m/s}$$

One of the nice things about physics is that different ways of looking at things produce the same answer. When this doesn't happen, and there is no error in computation, then the validity of one (or both!) of those ways is suspect.

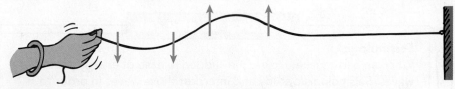

◀ FIGURE 25.8
A person creates a trans-
verse wave by shaking
the free end of a rope up
and down. The arrows
represent the motion of
the rope.

25.5 Transverse Waves

Suppose you create a wave along a rope by shaking the free end up
and down, as shown in Figure 25.8. The motion of the rope is at right
angles to the direction in which the wave is moving. Whenever the
motion of the medium is at right angles to the direction in which
a wave travels, the wave is a **transverse wave.** ☑ **Waves in the
stretched strings of musical instruments and the electromagnetic
waves that make up radio waves and light are transverse.**

CONCEPT
CHECK What are some examples of transverse waves?

25.6 Longitudinal Waves

Not all waves are transverse. Sometimes the particles of the
medium move back and forth in the same direction in which the
wave travels. When the particles oscillate parallel to or *along* the
direction of the wave rather than at right angles to it, the wave is
a **longitudinal wave.** ☑ **Sound waves are longitudinal waves.**

Both transverse and longitudinal waves can be demonstrated with
a loosely-coiled spring, as shown in Figure 25.9. A transverse wave is
demonstrated by shaking the end of a coiled spring up and down. A
longitudinal wave is demonstrated by shaking the end of the coiled
spring in and out. In this case we see that the medium vibrates parallel to the direction of energy transfer.

CONCEPT
CHECK What is an example of a longitudinal wave?

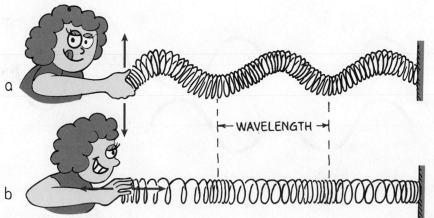

◀ FIGURE 25.9
Transverse and longitudi-
nal waves transfer energy
from left to right.
a. When the end of a
coiled spring is shaken up
and down, a transverse
wave is produced.
b. When it is shaken in
and out, a longitudinal
wave is produced.

25.7 Interference

A material object such as a rock will not share its space with another rock. But more than one vibration or wave can exist at the same time in the same space. If you drop two rocks in water, the waves produced by each can overlap and form an interference pattern. An **interference pattern** is a regular arrangement of places where wave effects are increased, decreased, or neutralized. ✅ **Interference patterns occur when waves from different sources arrive at the same point—at the same time.**

In **constructive interference,** the crest of one wave overlaps the crest of another and their individual effects add together. The result is a wave of increased amplitude. As Figure 25.10a shows, this is called reinforcement. In **destructive interference,** the crest of one wave overlaps the trough of another and their individual effects are reduced. The high part of one wave simply fills in the low part of another. As Figure 25.10b shows, this is called cancellation.

Sound, a longitudinal wave, requires a medium. It can't travel in a vacuum because there's nothing to compress and stretch.

FIGURE 25.10 ▶

There are two types of wave interference. **a.** In constructive interference, the waves reinforce each other to produce a wave of increased amplitude. **b.** In destructive interference, the waves cancel each other and no wave is produced.

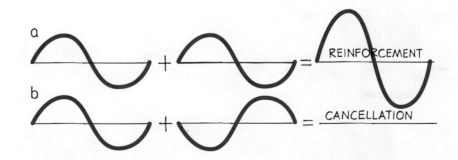

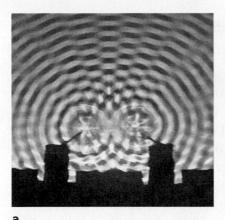

a

b

◀ **FIGURE 25.11**
a. Two overlapping water waves produce an interference pattern.
b. Overlapping concentric circles produce a pictorial representation of an interference pattern.

Wave interference is easiest to see in water. Figure 25.11a shows the interference pattern made when two vibrating objects touch the surface of water. The gray "spokes" are regions where waves cancel each other out. At points along these regions, the waves from the two objects arrive "out of step," or out of phase, with one another. When waves are **out of phase,** the crests of one wave overlap the troughs of another to produce regions of zero amplitude. The dark and light-striped regions are where the waves are "in step," or in phase, with each other. When waves are **in phase,** the crests of one wave overlap the crests of the other, and the troughs overlap as well.

Interference patterns are nicely illustrated by the overlapping of concentric circles printed on a pair of clear sheets, as shown in Figures 25.11b and 25.12. When the sheets overlap with their centers slightly apart, a so-called *moiré pattern* is formed that is very similar to the interference pattern of water waves (or any kind of waves). A slight shift in either of the sheets produces noticeably different patterns. If a pair of such sheets is available, be sure to try this and see the variety of patterns for yourself.

Interference is characteristic of all wave motion, whether the waves are water waves, sound waves, or light waves. The interference of sound is discussed in the next chapter, and the interference of light in Chapter 31.

FIGURE 25.12 ▼
A moiré pattern is very similar to an interference pattern.

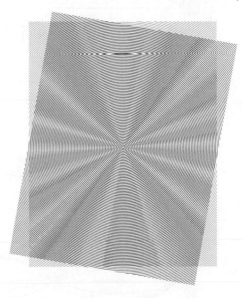

CONCEPT CHECK What causes interference patterns?

25.8 Standing Waves

If you tie a rope to a wall and shake the free end up and down, you will produce a wave in the rope. The wall is too rigid to shake, so the wave is reflected back along the rope to you. By shaking the rope just right, you can cause the incident (original) and reflected waves to form a standing wave. A **standing wave** is a wave that appears to stay in one place—it does not seem to move through the medium. Certain parts of a standing wave remain stationary. **Nodes** are the stationary points on a standing wave.

Interestingly enough, you could hold your fingers on either side of the rope at a node, and the rope would not touch them. Other parts of the rope would make contact with your fingers. The positions on a standing wave with the largest amplitudes are known as **antinodes.** Antinodes occur halfway between nodes.

Standing waves are the result of interference. When two waves of equal amplitude and wavelength pass through each other in opposite directions, the waves are always out of phase at the nodes. As Figure 25.13 shows, the nodes are stable regions of destructive interference.

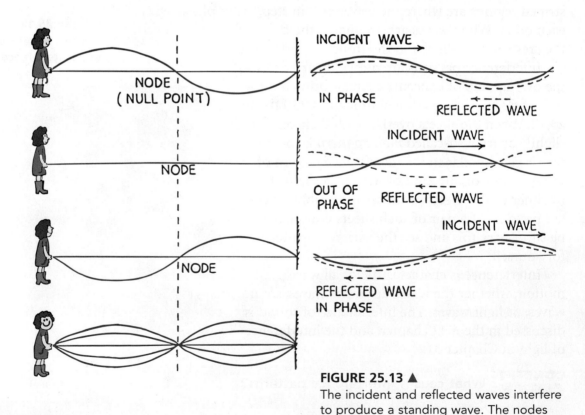

FIGURE 25.13 ▲
The incident and reflected waves interfere to produce a standing wave. The nodes are places that remain stationary.

You can produce a variety of standing waves by shaking the rope at different frequencies. Once you find a frequency that produces a standing wave, doubling or tripling the frequency will also produce a standing wave. ⊘ **A standing wave forms only if half a wavelength or a multiple of half a wavelength fits exactly into the length of the vibrating medium.** In Figure 25.14a, the rope length equals half a wavelength. In Figure 25.14b, the rope length equals one wavelength. In Figure 25.14c, the rope length equals one and one-half wavelengths. If you keep increasing the frequency, you'll produce more interesting waves.

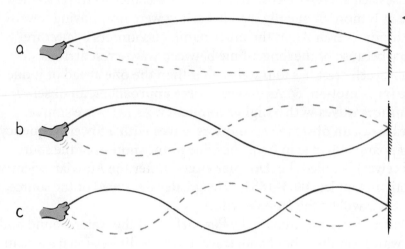

◀ **FIGURE 25.14**
You can produce a variety of standing waves.
a. Shake the rope until you set up a standing wave of $\frac{1}{2}$ wavelength.
b. Shake with twice the frequency and produce a standing wave of 1 wavelength.
c. Shake with three times the frequency and produce a standing wave of $1\frac{1}{2}$ wavelengths.

Standing waves are set up in the strings of musical instruments that are struck. They are set up in the air in an organ pipe and the air of a soda-pop bottle when air is blown over the top. Standing waves can be produced in either transverse or longitudinal waves.

CONCEPT CHECK At what wavelengths can a standing wave form in a vibrating medium?

25.9 The Doppler Effect

Imagine a bug jiggling its legs and bobbing up and down in the middle of a quiet puddle, as shown in Figure 25.15. Suppose the bug is not going anywhere but is merely treading water in a fixed position. The crests of the wave it makes are concentric circles, because the wave speed is the same in all directions. If the bug bobs in the water at a constant frequency, the distance between wave crests (the wavelength) will be the same for all successive waves. Waves encounter point A as frequently as they encounter point B. This means that the frequency of wave motion is the same at points A and B, or anywhere in the vicinity of the bug. This wave frequency is the same as the bobbing frequency of the bug.

Go Online
active art

For: Doppler Effect activity
Visit: www.PHSchool.com
Web Code: csp – 4259

FIGURE 25.15 ▼
A stationary bug jiggling
in still water produces a
circular water wave.

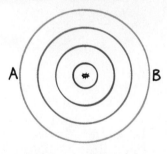

FIGURE 25.16 ▼
A bug swimming in still
water produces a wave
pattern that is no longer
concentric.

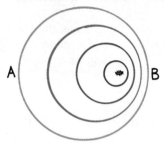

Suppose the jiggling bug moves across the water at a speed less than the wave speed. In effect, the bug chases part of the crests it has produced. The wave pattern is distorted and is no longer concentric, as shown in Figure 25.16. The center of the outer crest was made when the bug was at the center of that circle. The center of the next smaller crest was made when the bug was at the center of that circle, and so forth. The centers of the circular crests move in the direction of the swimming bug. Although the bug maintains the same bobbing frequency as before, an observer at B would encounter the crests more often. The observer would encounter a *higher* frequency. This is because each successive crest has a shorter distance to travel so they arrive at B more frequently than if the bug were not moving toward B.

An observer at A, on the other hand, encounters a *lower* frequency because of the longer time between wave-crest arrivals. To reach A, each crest has to travel farther than the one ahead of it due to the bug's motion. ☑ **As a wave source approaches, an observer encounters waves with a higher frequency. As the wave source moves away, an observer encounters waves with a lower frequency.** This apparent change in frequency due to the motion of the source (or receiver) is called the **Doppler effect** (after the Austrian scientist Christian Doppler, 1803–1853). The greater the speed of the source, the greater will be the Doppler effect.

Water waves spread over the flat surface of the water. Sound and light waves, on the other hand, travel in three-dimensional space in all directions like an expanding balloon. Just as circular wave crests are closer together in front of the swimming bug, spherical sound or light wave crests ahead of a moving source are closer together than those behind the source and encounter a receiver more frequently.

Physics on the Job

Police Officer
Police officers are responsible for protecting people. While that involves catching criminals and solving crimes, it also requires that police officers prevent drivers from speeding. In this way, police officers protect pedestrians and people in vehicles. One way that police officers prevent speeding is by using radar equipment. Radar equipment sends waves toward a moving vehicle and uses the Doppler effect to determine the speed of the vehicle. By knowing how to operate the device, police officers can determine when a driver is not obeying the speed limit.

Sound The Doppler effect is evident when you hear the changing pitch of a siren as a firetruck passes you. Look at Figure 25.17. When the firetruck approaches, the pitch sounds higher than normal. This occurs because the sound wave crests are encountering you more frequently. When the firetruck passes and moves away, you hear a drop in pitch because the wave crests are encountering you less frequently.

Police make use of the Doppler effect of radar waves in measuring the speeds of cars on the highway. Radar waves are electromagnetic waves, lower in frequency than light and higher in frequency than radio waves. Police bounce them off moving cars as shown in Figure 25.18. A computer built into the radar system calculates the speed of the car relative to the radar unit by comparing the frequency of the radar with the frequency of the reflected waves.

Bats hunt moths in darkness by echo location and the Doppler effect. Some moths are protected by a thick covering of fuzzy scales that deaden the echoes.

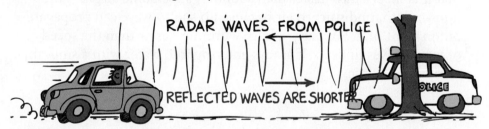

◀ **FIGURE 25.18**
The police calculate a car's speed by measuring the Doppler effect of radar waves.

Light The Doppler effect also occurs for light. When a light source approaches, there is an increase in its measured frequency, and when it recedes, there is a decrease in its frequency. An increase in frequency is called a **blue shift,** because the increase is toward the high-frequency, or blue, end of the color spectrum. A decrease in frequency is called a **red shift,** referring to the low-frequency, or red, end of the color spectrum. Distant galaxies, for example, show a red shift in the light they emit. A measurement of this shift enables astronomers to calculate their speeds of recession. A rapidly spinning star shows a red shift on the side turning away from us and a blue shift on the side turning toward us. This enables a calculation of the star's spin rate.

CONCEPT CHECK How does the apparent frequency of waves change as a wave source moves?

think!
When a source moves toward you, do you measure an increase or decrease in wave speed?
Answer: 25.9

25.10 Bow Waves

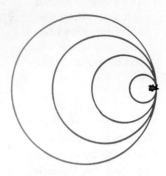

When the speed of the source in a medium is as great as the speed of the waves it produces, something interesting happens. The waves pile up. Consider the bug in the previous example when it swims as fast as the wave speed. Can you see that the bug will keep up with the wave crests it produces? Instead of the crests getting ahead of the bug, they pile up or superimpose on one another directly in front of the bug, as suggested in Figure 25.19. The bug moves right along with the leading edge of the waves it is producing.

The same thing happens when an aircraft travels at the speed of sound. In the early days of jet aircraft, it was believed that this pileup of sound waves in front of the airplane imposed a "sound barrier" and that to go faster than the speed of sound, the plane would have to "break the sound barrier." What actually happens is that the overlapping wave crests disrupt the flow of air over the wings, so that it is harder to control the plane when it is flying close to the speed of sound. But the barrier is not real. Just as a boat can easily travel faster than the speed of water waves, an airplane with sufficient power can easily travel faster than the speed of sound. Then we say that it is *supersonic*—faster than sound. A supersonic airplane flies into smooth, undisturbed air because no sound wave can propagate out in front of it. Similarly, a bug swimming faster than the speed of water waves finds itself always entering into water with a smooth, unrippled surface.

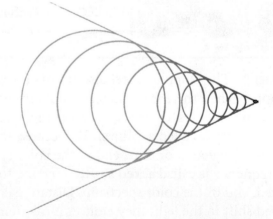

FIGURE 25.20 ▶
A bug swimming faster than the wave speed produces a wave pattern in which the wave crests overlap at the edges.

When the bug swims faster than wave speed, ideally it produces a wave pattern as shown in Figure 25.20. It outruns the wave crests it produces. The crests overlap at the edges, and the pattern made by these overlapping crests is a V shape, called a **bow wave,** which appears to be dragging behind the bug. ⊘ **A bow wave occurs when a wave source moves faster than the waves it produces.** The familiar bow wave generated by a speedboat knifing through the water is produced by the overlapping of many circular wave crests.

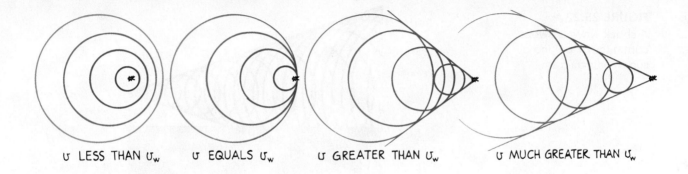

Figure 25.21 shows some wave patterns made by sources moving at various speeds. After the speed of the source exceeds the wave speed, increased speed produces a bow wave with a narrower V shape.

CONCEPT CHECK : What causes a bow wave?

FIGURE 25.21 ▲
The wave patterns made by a bug swimming at successively greater speeds change. Overlapping at the edges occurs only when the source travels faster than wave speed.

25.11 Shock Waves

A speedboat knifing through the water generates a two-dimensional bow wave. A supersonic aircraft similarly generates a shock wave. A **shock wave** is a three-dimensional wave that consists of overlapping spheres that form a cone. ✓ **A shock wave occurs when an object moves faster than the speed of sound.** Just as the bow wave of a speedboat spreads until it reaches the shore of a lake, the conical shock wave generated by a supersonic craft spreads until it reaches the ground, as shown in Figure 25.22.

The bow wave of a speedboat that passes by can splash and douse you if you are at the water's edge. In a sense, you can say that you are hit by a "water boom." In the same way, a conical shell of compressed air sweeps behind a supersonic aircraft. The sharp crack heard when the shock wave that sweeps behind a supersonic aircraft reaches the listeners is called a **sonic boom.**

We don't hear a sonic boom from a slower-than-sound, or subsonic, aircraft, because the sound wave crests reach our ears one at a time and are perceived as a continuous tone. Only when the craft moves faster than sound do the crests overlap and encounter the listener in a single burst. The sudden increase in pressure has much the same effect as the sudden expansion of air produced by an explosion. Both processes direct a burst of high-pressure air to the listener. The ear cannot distinguish between the high pressure from an explosion and the high pressure from many overlapping wave crests.

Don't confuse *supersonic* with *ultrasonic*. Supersonic has to do with speed—faster than sound. Ultrasonic involves frequency—higher than we can hear.

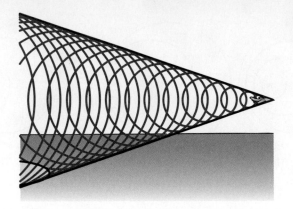

Watch for the advent of newly designed aircraft that fly 1.8 times the speed of sound and produce sonic booms only one-hundredth the strength of the supersonic Concorde, which was grounded following a fatal accident in 2000.

A common misconception is that sonic booms are produced at the moment that an aircraft flies through the "sound barrier"—that is, just as the aircraft surpasses the speed of sound. This is equivalent to saying that a boat produces a bow wave only when it first overtakes its own waves. This is not so. The fact is that a shock wave and its resulting sonic boom are swept continuously behind an aircraft traveling faster than sound, just as a bow wave is swept continuously behind a speedboat. In Figure 25.23, listener B is in the process of hearing a sonic boom. Listener A has already heard it, and listener C will hear it shortly. The aircraft that generated this shock wave may have broken through the sound barrier hours ago!

It is not necessary that the moving source emit sound for it to produce a shock wave. Once an object is moving faster than the speed of sound, it will *make* sound. A supersonic bullet passing overhead produces a crack, which is a small sonic boom. If the bullet were larger and disturbed more air in its path, the crack would be more boomlike. When a lion tamer cracks a circus whip, the cracking sound is actually a sonic boom produced by the tip of the whip when it travels faster than the speed of sound. Snap a towel and the end can exceed the speed of sound and produce a mini sonic boom. The bullet, whip, and towel are not in themselves sound sources, but when traveling at supersonic speeds they produce their own sound as waves of air are generated to the sides of the moving objects.

On the matter of sound in general: You know that you'll damage your eyes if you stare at the sun. What many people don't know is that you'll similarly damage your ears if you overexpose them to loud sounds. Do as your author does when in a room with very loud music—leave. If for any reason you don't want to leave—really enjoyable music or good camaraderie with friends—stay, but use ear plugs of some kind! You're not being a wimp when you give the same care to your ears that you give to your eyes.

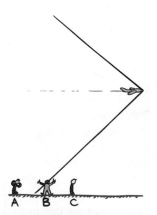

FIGURE 25.23 ▲
The shock wave has not yet encountered listener C, but is now encountering listener B, and has already passed listener A.

CONCEPT CHECK What causes a shock wave?

25 REVIEW

Concept Summary

- The period of a pendulum depends only on the length of the pendulum and the acceleration of gravity.
- The source of all waves is a vibration.
- The energy in waves is carried by a disturbance in a medium.
- Calculate the wave speed by multiplying the wavelength and the frequency.
- Waves in the stretched strings of musical instruments and electromagnetic waves are transverse. Sound waves are longitudinal.
- Interference patterns occur when waves from different sources arrive at the same point—at the same time.
- A standing wave forms if a multiple of half a wavelength fits into the length of the medium.
- As a wave source approaches, an observer encounters waves with a higher frequency. As a wave source moves away, an observer encounters waves with a lower frequency.
- A bow wave occurs when a wave source moves faster than the waves it produces.
- A shock wave occurs when an object moves faster than the speed of sound.

Key Terms

vibration (p. 490)
wave (p. 490)
period (p. 491)
simple harmonic motion (p. 491)
sine curve (p. 491)

crest (p. 492)
trough (p. 492)
amplitude (p. 492)
wavelength (p. 492)
frequency (p. 492)
hertz (p. 492)
transverse wave (p. 497)
longitudinal wave (p. 497)
interference pattern (p. 498)
constructive interference (p. 498)

destructive interference (p. 498)
out of phase (p. 499)
in phase (p. 499)
standing wave (p. 500)
node (p. 500)
antinodes (p. 500)
Doppler effect (p. 502)
blue shift (p. 503)
red shift (p. 503)
bow wave (p. 504)
shock wave (p. 505)
sonic boom (p. 505)

think! Answers

25.2.1   A 100-Hz wave vibrates 100 times/s.

25.2.1   The period is $= \frac{1 \text{ vib}}{0.1 \text{ Hz}} = \frac{1 \text{ vib}}{0.1 \text{ vib/s}} = 10$ s.

25.4.1   The frequency of the wave is 2 Hz; its wavelength is 1.5 m; and its wave speed is $\lambda \times f = (1.5 \text{ m}) \times (2 \text{ Hz}) = 3$ m/s.

25.4.2   The wavelength must be 1 m. Then wave speed $= (1 \text{ m}) \times (340 \text{ Hz}) \times 340$ m/s.

25.8   Yes. This is called destructive interference. In a standing wave, for example, parts of the wave have no amplitude—the nodes.

25.9   Neither! It is the *frequency* of a wave that undergoes a change, not the wave *speed*.

25 ASSESS

Check Concepts ......

Section 25.0

1. Does a vibration or a wave spread out through space?

Section 25.1

2. What is the period of a pendulum that takes one second to make a complete back-and-forth vibration?

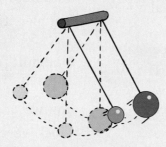

3. Suppose that a pendulum has a period of 1.5 seconds. How long does it take to make a complete back-and-forth vibration?

4. Is a pendulum with a 1.5-second period longer or shorter in length than a pendulum with a 1-second period?

Section 25.2

5. How is a sine curve related to a wave?

6. Distinguish among these different parts of a wave: amplitude, crest, trough, and wavelength.

7. Distinguish between the *period* and the *frequency* of a vibration or a wave. How do they relate to one another?

Section 25.3

8. Does the medium in which a wave travels move along with the wave itself? Defend your answer.

Section 25.4

9. How does the speed of a wave relate to its wavelength and frequency?

10. As the frequency of sound is increased, does the wavelength increase or decrease? Give an example.

Sections 25.5 and 25.6

11. Distinguish between a *transverse* wave and a *longitudinal* wave.

Section 25.7

12. Distinguish between *constructive* interference and *destructive* interference.

13. Is interference a property of only some types of waves or of all types of waves?

Section 25.8

14. What causes a standing wave?

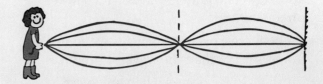

Section 25.9

15. When a wave source moves toward a receiver, does the receiver encounter an increase in wave frequency, wave speed, or both?

16. Does the Doppler effect occur for only some types of waves or all types of waves?

Section 25.10

17. Compared with the speed of water waves how fast must a bug swim to keep up with the waves it produces? How fast must a boat move to produce a bow wave?

18. Distinguish a *bow* wave from a *shock* wave.

Section 25.11

19. a. What is a sonic boom?
   b. How fast must an aircraft fly in order to produce a sonic boom?

20. If you encounter a sonic boom, is that evidence that an aircraft just exceeded the speed of sound to become supersonic?

Think and Rank ......

Rank each of the following sets of scenarios in order of the quantity or property involved. List them from left to right. If scenarios have equal rankings, then separate them with an equal sign. (e.g., A = B)

21. A fire engine's siren emits a certain frequency. Rank from greatest to least the *apparent* frequency heard by the stationary listener in each scenario.

   (A) The fire engine is traveling toward a listener at 30 m/s.
   (B) The fire engine is traveling away from a listener at 5 m/s.
   (C) The fire engine is traveling toward a listener at 5 m/s.
   (D) The fire engine is traveling away from a listener at 30 m/s.

22. Shown below are four different pairs of transverse wave pulses that move toward each other. At some point in time the pulses meet and interact (interfere) with each other. Rank the four cases from greatest to least on the basis of the height of the peak that results when the centers of the pairs coincide.

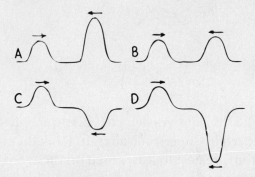

23. All the waves below have the same speed in the same medium. Use a ruler and rank these waves from greatest to least according to amplitude, wavelength, frequency, and period.

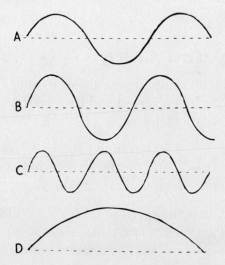

24. The four sets of waves below are a top view of circular wave patterns made by a bug jiggling on the surface of water. Rank them from greatest to least based on the speed of the bug.

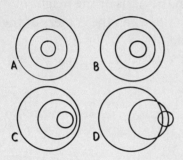

25. The shock waves depicted below are produced by supersonic aircraft. Rank them from greatest to least based on the speed of the aircraft.

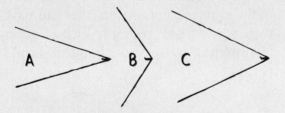

Plug and Chug ......

26. A nurse counts 76 heartbeats in one minute. What are the period and frequency of the heart's oscillations?

27. New York's 300-m high Citicorp® Tower oscillates in the wind with a period of 6.80 s. Calculate its frequency of vibration.

28. Calculate the speed of waves in a puddle that are 0.15 m apart and made by tapping the water surface twice each second.

29. Calculate the speed of waves in water that are 0.4 m apart and have a frequency of 2 Hz.

30. The lowest frequency we can hear is about 20 Hz. Calculate the wavelength associated with this frequency for sound that travels at 340 m/s. How long is this in feet?

Think and Explain ......

31. Does the period of a pendulum depend of the mass of the bob? On the length of the string?

32. If a pendulum is shortened, does the frequency increase or decrease? What about its period?

33. Carmelita swings to and fro in a sitting position on a playground swing. William says that if she stands while swinging, a longer time will occur between back-and-forth swings. Carlos says no, that the to-and-fro time of the swing will be unaffected. Who, if either, do you agree with?

34. You dip your finger repeatedly into a puddle of water and make waves. What happens to the wavelength if you dip your finger more frequently?

35. If you double the frequency of a vibrating object, what happens to its period?

36. How does the frequency of vibration of a small object floating in water compare to the number of waves passing it each second?

37. If you triple the frequency of a vibrating object, what will happen to its period?

38. Red light has a longer wavelength than violet light. Which has the greater frequency?

39. How far, in terms of wavelength, does a wave travel in one period?

40. If a wave vibrates up and down twice each second and travels a distance of 20 m each second, what is its frequency? Its wave speed? (Why is this question best answered by careful reading of the question rather than searching for a formula?)

41. The wave patterns seen in Figure 25.6 are composed of circles. What does this tell you about the speed of the waves in different directions?

42. Sound from Source A has a frequency twice as great as the frequency of sound from Source B. Compare the wavelengths of sound from the two sources.

43. What kind of motion should you impart to a stretched coiled spring to produce a transverse wave? A longitudinal wave?

44. Would it be correct to say that the Doppler effect is the apparent change in the speed of a wave due to the motion of the source? (Why is this question a test of reading comprehension as well as a test of physics knowledge?)

45. In the Doppler effect, does frequency change? Does wavelength change? Does wave speed change?

46. Can the Doppler effect be observed with longitudinal waves, with transverse waves, or with both?

47. A railroad locomotive is at rest with its whistle shrieking, and then it starts moving toward you.
  a. Does the frequency that you hear increase, decrease, or stay the same?
  b. Does the wavelength that reaches your ear increase, decrease, or stay the same?
  c. How about the speed of sound in the air between you and the locomotive?

48. When a driver blows his horn while approaching a stationary listener, the listener hears an increase in the frequency of the horn. Would the listener hear an increase in the frequency of the horn if she were also in a car traveling at the same speed in the same direction as the first driver? Explain.

49. Astronomers find that light coming from point A at the edge of the sun has a slightly higher frequency than light from point B at the opposite side. What do these measurements tell us about the sun's motion?

50. Does a boat moving through the water always produce a bow wave? Defend your answer.

51. Whenever you watch a high-flying aircraft overhead, it seems that its sound comes from behind the craft rather than from where you see it. Why is this?

52. How does the angle of the V shape of a bow wave depend on the speed of the wave source?

53. Why is it that a subsonic aircraft, no matter how loud it may be, cannot produce a sonic boom?

54. True or false: A sonic boom occurs only when an aircraft is breaking through the sound barrier. Defend your answer.

55. Consider an earthquake caused by a single disturbance, which sends out both transverse and longitudinal waves that travel with distinctly different speeds in the ground. How can earth scientists in different locations determine the earthquake origin?

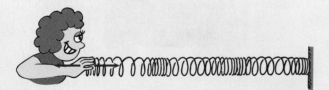

Think and Solve ······

56. The period of a simple pendulum is given by $T = 2\pi\sqrt{\frac{L}{g}}$, where g is the acceleration of gravity and L is the length of the pendulum. In a lab, you want to double the period of a certain pendulum. Your friend says you'll have to make the pendulum twice as long. Do you agree with your friend?

57. Maria shows her friends a simple 31-cm-long pendulum. Her teacher, looking on, asks if she can predict the period of the pendulum before she demonstrates it. What's your prediction?

58. The Foucault pendulum in the rotunda of the Griffith Observatory in Los Angeles has a 110-kg brass ball at the end of a 12.2-m-long cable. What is the period of this pendulum?

59. You are looking through your grandparents' window and notice a hummingbird feeder hanging by a rope. You can't see the top of the rope, but you notice that in a gentle breeze the feeder moves back and forth with a period of 4.0 seconds. You make a calculation and announce to your grandparents that the rope is 4 m long. Your grandparents go outside and measure the rope. Should they be impressed with you?

60. For your science fair project you decide to make a simple pendulum for a grandfather clock, such that the period of the pendulum is 2.00 seconds. Show that the length of your pendulum should be just slightly less than the length of a meterstick. (Use $g = 9.8$ m/s^2 here.)

61. Melanie is new to the nursing program. With a patient she counts 84 heartbeats in one minute. She calculates that the period and frequency of the heartbeats are 0.71 s and 1.4 Hz respectively. Is she correct?

62. A design engineer figures that a proposed new skyscraper will swing to and fro in strong winds at a frequency of 0.15 Hz. A new assistant asks how much time a person in the skyscraper will experience during each complete swing. What's your answer?

63. In lab you strike a tuning fork that has a frequency of 340 Hz. For a speed of sound of 340 m/s, how does the wavelength of the resulting sound wave compare with the length of a meter stick?

64. If a wave vibrates back and forth three times each second, and its wavelength is 2 meters, what is its frequency? Its period? Its speed?

65. While watching ocean waves at the dock of the bay, Otis notices that 10 waves pass beneath him in 30 seconds. He also notices that the crests of successive waves exactly coincide with the posts that are 5 meters apart. What are the period, frequency, wavelength, and speed of the ocean waves?

66. The crests on a long surface water wave are 20 m apart, and in 1 minute 10 crests pass by. What is the speed of this wave?

67. Radio waves are electromagnetic waves that travel at the speed of light, 300,000 kilometers per second. What is the wavelength of FM radio waves received at 100 megahertz on your radio dial?

68. The wavelength of red light is about 700 nanometers, or 7×10^{-7} m. The frequency of the red light reflected from a metal surface and the frequency of the vibrating electron that produces it are the same. What is this frequency?

69. The half-angle of the shock-wave cone generated by a supersonic aircraft is 45°. What is the speed of the plane relative to the speed of sound?

Activity ••••••

70. Tie a rubber tube, a spring, or a rope to a fixed support and produce standing waves, as Figure 25.14 suggests. How many nodes can you produce? How can you change the number of nodes?

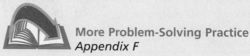

More Problem-Solving Practice
Appendix F

26 SOUND

THE BIG IDEA : Sound is a form of energy that spreads out through space.

When a singer sings, the vocal chords in the singer's throat vibrate to and fro, causing adjacent air molecules to vibrate. This air, in turn, vibrates against neighboring air molecules. A series of ripples in the form of a longitudinal wave travels through the air. The frequency of the ripples matches the frequency of the singer's vibrating vocal chords. When the ripples hit your eardrum, the eardrum is pushed and then pulled with the same frequency as the singer's vibrating vocal chords. Vibrations in the eardrum send rhythmic electrical impulses into your brain. And you hear the voice of the singer.

Molecules of air behave like tiny table-tennis balls. If you place a tuning fork in the middle of a room and then strike the tuning fork with a rubber hammer, the prongs of the vibrating tuning fork set the surrounding air molecules into motion in the same way that the moving paddle sets the table-tennis balls into motion.

---

discover!

What Is Acoustical Interference?

1. Strike a tuning fork with a rubber hammer or on the heel of your shoe. (Do not strike the tuning fork on the edge of the table.)
2. Place the vibrating tuning fork near your ear.
3. Slowly rotate the vibrating tuning fork. Make certain that you rotate the tuning fork through 360 degrees.

Analyze and Conclude

1. **Observing** What do you hear as you rotate the tuning fork?
2. **Predicting** What do you think you would hear if you were to use a tuning fork with a higher pitch? A lower pitch?
3. **Making Generalizations** What causes the changes in sound intensity produced by rotating a tuning fork?

514

26.1 The Origin of Sound

⊘ **All sounds originate in the vibrations of material objects.** In a piano, violin, or guitar, a sound wave is produced by vibrating strings; in a saxophone, by a vibrating reed; in a flute, by a fluttering column of air at the mouthpiece. The prongs of the tuning fork in Figure 26.1 vibrate when the fork is struck. Your voice results from the vibration of your vocal chords.

In each of these cases, the original vibration stimulates the vibration of something larger or more massive—the sounding board of a stringed instrument, the air column within a reed or wind instrument, or the air in the throat and mouth of a singer. This vibrating material then sends a disturbance through a surrounding medium, usually air, in the form of longitudinal waves. Under ordinary conditions, the frequency of the sound waves produced equals the frequency of the vibrating source.

We describe our subjective impression about the frequency of sound by the word **pitch.** A high-pitched sound like that from a piccolo has a high vibration frequency, while a low-pitched sound like that from a foghorn has a low vibration frequency.

A young person can normally hear pitches with frequencies from about 20 to 20,000 hertz. As we grow older, our hearing range shrinks, especially at the high-frequency end. Sound waves with frequencies below 20 hertz are called **infrasonic,** and those with frequencies above 20,000 hertz are called **ultrasonic.** We cannot hear infrasonic or ultrasonic sound waves. Dogs can hear frequencies of 40,000 Hz or more. Bats can hear sounds at over 100,000 Hz.

CONCEPT CHECK What is the source of all sound?

FIGURE 26.1 ▲
The source of all sound waves is vibration.

26.2 Sound in Air

Clap your hands and you produce a sound pulse that goes out in all directions. The pulse vibrates the air somewhat as a similar pulse would vibrate the coiled spring shown in Figure 26.2. Each particle moves back and forth along the direction of motion of the expanding wave.

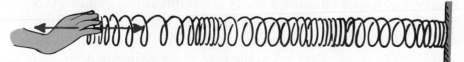

◀ **FIGURE 26.2**
A compression travels along the spring.

For a clearer picture of this process, consider the long room shown in Figure 26.3. At one end is an open window with a curtain over it. At the other end is a door.

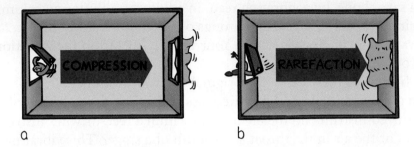

a   b

When you quickly open the door as in Figure 26.3a, you can imagine the door pushing the molecules next to it away from their initial positions, and into their neighbors. Neighboring molecules, in turn, push into their neighbors, and so on, like a compression wave moving along a spring, until the curtain flaps out the window. A pulse of compressed air has moved from the door to the curtain. This pulse of compressed air is called a **compression.**

When you quickly close the door as in Figure 26.3b, the door pushes neighboring air molecules out of the room. This produces an area of low pressure next to the door. Neighboring molecules then move into it, leaving a zone of lower pressure behind them. We say the air in this zone of lower pressure is *rarefied*. Other molecules farther from the door, in turn, move into these rarefied regions, resulting in a pulse of rarefied air moving from the door to the curtain. This is evident when the lower-pressure air reaches the curtain, which flaps inward. This pulse of low-pressure air is called a **rarefaction.**

For all wave motion, it is not the medium that travels across the room, but a *pulse* that travels. In both cases the pulse travels from the door to the curtain. We know this because in both cases the curtain moves *after* the door is opened or closed.

If you swing the door open and closed in periodic fashion, you can set up a wave of periodic compressions and rarefactions that will make the curtain swing in and out of the window. On a much smaller but more rapid scale, this is what happens when a tuning fork is struck or when the speaker in Figure 26.4 produces music. ✅ **As a source of sound vibrates, a series of compressions and rarefactions travels outward from the source.** The vibrations of the tuning fork and the waves it produces are considerably higher in frequency and lower in amplitude than in the case of the swinging door. You don't notice the effect of sound waves on the curtain, but you are well aware of them when they meet your sensitive eardrums.

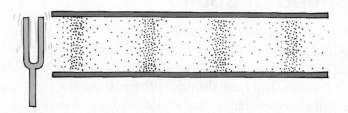

Consider sound waves in the tube shown in Figure 26.5. For simplicity, only the waves that travel in the tube are shown. When the prong of the tuning fork next to the tube moves toward the tube, a compression enters the tube. When the prong swings away, in the opposite direction, a rarefaction follows the compression. It is like the table-tennis paddle moving back and forth in a room packed with table-tennis balls. As the source vibrates, a series of compressions and rarefactions is produced.

CONCEPT CHECK How does a sound wave travel through air?

26.3 Media That Transmit Sound

Most sounds you hear are transmitted through the air, but put your ear to the ground as Native Americans did, and you can hear the hoofbeats of distant horses through the ground before you can hear them through the air. More practically, put your ear to a metal fence and have a friend tap it far away. The sound is transmitted louder and faster by the metal than by the air. ☑ **Sound travels in solids, liquids, and gases.**

Or click two rocks together underwater while your ear is submerged. You'll hear the clicking sound very clearly. If you've ever been swimming in the presence of motorized boats, you've probably noticed that you can hear the boats' motors much more clearly under water than above water. Solids and liquids are generally good conductors of sound—much better than air. The speed of sound differs in different materials. In general, sound is transmitted faster in liquids than in gases, and still faster in solids.

The boy in Figure 26.6 cannot hear the ringing bell when air is removed from the jar because sound cannot travel in a vacuum. The transmission of sound requires a medium. If there is nothing to compress and expand, there can be no sound. There may still be vibrations, but without a medium there is no sound.

CONCEPT CHECK What media transmit sound?

FIGURE 26.6 ▲
Sound can be heard from the ringing bell when air is inside the jar, but not when the air is removed.

26.4 Speed of Sound

think!

How far away is a storm if you note a 3-second delay between a lightning flash and the sound of thunder? *Answer: 26.4*

Have you ever watched a distant person chopping wood or hammering, and noticed that the sound of the blow takes time to reach your ears? You see the blow before you hear it. This is most noticeable in the case of lightning. You hear thunder *after* you see the lightning. These experiences are evidence that sound is much slower than light.

⊘ **The speed of sound in a gas depends on the temperature of the gas and the mass of the particles in the gas.** The speed of sound in dry air at 0°C is about 330 meters per second, or about 1200 kilometers per hour, about one-millionth the speed of light. Water vapor in the air and increased temperatures increase this speed slightly. This makes sense, for the faster-moving molecules in warm air bump into each other more often and therefore can transmit a pulse in less time. For each degree increase in air temperature above 0°C, the speed of sound in air increases by about 0.60 m/s. So in air at a normal room temperature of about 20°C, sound travels at about 340 m/s. The speed of sound in a gas also depends on the mass of its particles. Lighter particles such as hydrogen molecules and helium atoms move faster and transmit sound much more quickly than heavier gases such as oxygen and nitrogen, found in air.

The speed of sound in a solid material depends not on the material's density, but on its elasticity. Elasticity is the ability of a material to change shape in response to an applied force, and then resume its initial shape once the distorting force is removed. ⊘ **The speed of sound in a material depends on the material's elasticity.** Steel is very elastic; putty is inelastic.[26.4] In elastic materials, the atoms are relatively close together and respond quickly to each other's motions, transmitting energy with little loss. Sound travels about fifteen times faster in steel than in air, and about four times faster in water than in air.

CONCEPT CHECK What determines the speed of sound in a medium?

Link to TECHNOLOGY

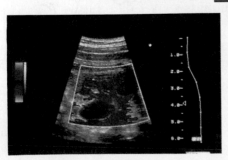

Ultrasound Imaging A technique for harmlessly "seeing" inside a body uses high-frequency sound (ultrasound) instead of X-rays. Ultrasound that enters the body is reflected more strongly from the outside of an organ than from its inside, and we get a picture of the outline of the organ. When ultrasound is incident upon a moving object, the reflected sound has a slightly different frequency. Using this Doppler effect, a physician can "see" the beating heart of a developing fetus that is only 11 weeks old.

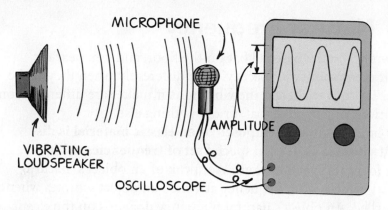

MICROPHONE

VIBRATING
LOUDSPEAKER

AMPLITUDE

OSCILLOSCOPE

◀ **FIGURE 26.7**

The loudspeaker at the left is a paper cone that vibrates in rhythm with an electric signal. The sound sets up similar vibrations in the microphone, which are displayed on the screen of an oscilloscope. The wave on the oscilloscope reveals information about the sound.

26.5 Loudness

The intensity of a sound is proportional to the square of the amplitude of a sound wave. ✔ **Sound intensity is objective and is measured by instruments. Loudness, on the other hand, is a physiological sensation sensed in the brain.** It differs for different people. Loudness is subjective but is related to sound intensity. The unit of intensity for sound is the decibel (dB), after Alexander Graham Bell, inventor of the telephone. The oscilloscope shown in Figure 26.7 measures sound.

Some common sources and sound levels are given in Table 26.1. Starting with zero at the threshold of hearing for a normal ear, an increase of each 10 dB means that sound intensity increases by a factor of 10. A sound of 10 dB is 10 times as intense as sound of 0 dB; 20 dB is not twice but 10 times as intense as 10 dB, or 100 times as intense as the threshold of hearing. A 60-dB sound is 100 times as intense as a 40-dB sound.

Roughly, the sensation of loudness follows this decibel scale. We hear a 100-dB sound to be about as much louder than a 70-dB sound as the 70-dB sound is louder than a 40-dB sound because there is a 30-dB difference between the pairs of sound each time.

Physiological hearing damage begins at exposure to 85 decibels. The extent of damage depends on the length of exposure and on frequency characteristics. A single burst of sound can produce vibrations intense enough to tear apart the organ of Corti, the receptor organ in the inner ear. Less intense, but severe, noise can interfere with cellular processes in the organ and cause its eventual breakdown. Unfortunately, the cells of the Corti do not regenerate.

The decibel scale for loudness is logarithmic.

Table 26.1	Sound Levels
Source of Sound	**Level (dB)**
Jet engine, at 30 m	140
Threshold of pain	120
Loud rock music	115
Old subway train	100
Average factory	90
Busy street traffic	70
Normal speech	60
Library	40
Close whisper	20
Normal breathing	10
Hearing threshold	0

CONCEPT CHECK: What is the difference between sound intensity and loudness?

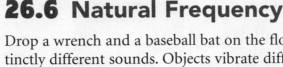

26.6 Natural Frequency

Drop a wrench and a baseball bat on the floor, and you hear distinctly different sounds. Objects vibrate differently when they strike the floor. Tap a wrench, and the vibrations it makes are different from the vibrations of a baseball bat, or of anything else.

☑ **When any object composed of an elastic material is disturbed, it vibrates at its own special set of frequencies, which together form its special sound.** We speak of an object's **natural frequency,** which is the frequency at which an object vibrates when it is disturbed. An object's natural frequency depends on the elasticity and shape of the object. The bells shown in Figure 26.8 and tuning forks vibrate at their own characteristic frequencies. Interestingly enough, most things—from planets to atoms and almost everything else in between—have a springiness to them and vibrate at one or more natural frequencies. A natural frequency is one at which minimum energy is required to produce forced vibrations. It is also the frequency that requires the least amount of energy to continue this vibration.

FIGURE 26.8 ▲
The natural frequency of the smaller bell is higher than that of the big bell, and it rings at a higher pitch.

CONCEPT CHECK What happens when an elastic material is disturbed?

26.7 Forced Vibration

When you strike an unmounted tuning fork, the sound it makes is faint. Strike a tuning fork while holding its base on a tabletop, and the sound is relatively loud. Why? It is because the table is forced to vibrate, and its larger surface sets more air in motion. The tabletop becomes a sounding board, and can be forced into vibration with forks of various frequencies. This is a case of a forced vibration. A **forced vibration** occurs when an object is made to vibrate by another vibrating object that is nearby.

The washtub in Figure 26.9 serves as a sounding board. ☑ **Sounding boards are an important part of all stringed musical instruments because they are forced into vibration and produce the sound.** The vibration of guitar strings in an acoustical guitar would be faint if they weren't transmitted to the guitar's wooden body. The mechanism in a music box is mounted on a sounding board. Without the sounding board, the sound the music box mechanism makes is barely audible.

FIGURE 26.9 ▲
When the string is plucked, the washtub is set into forced vibration and serves as a sounding board.

CONCEPT CHECK Why are sounding boards an important part of stringed instruments?

26.8 Resonance

Resonance is a phenomenon that occurs when the frequency of a vibration forced on an object matches the object's natural frequency and a dramatic increase in amplitude occurs. Resonance means to re-sound, or sound again. Putty doesn't resonate because it isn't elastic, and a dropped handkerchief is too limp. ☑ **An object resonates when there is a force to pull it back to its starting position and enough energy to keep it vibrating.**

A common experience illustrating resonance occurs on a swing like the one shown in Figure 26.10. When pumping a swing, you pump in rhythm with the natural frequency of the swing. More important than the force with which you pump is the timing. Even small pumps, or even small pushes from someone else, if delivered in rhythm with the natural frequency of the swinging motion, produce large amplitudes.

FIGURE 26.10 ▲
Pumping a swing in rhythm with its natural frequency produces larger amplitudes.

FIGURE 26.11 ▼
The stages of resonance are shown for a tuning fork. **a.** The first compression meets the fork and gives it a tiny and momentary push. **b.** The fork bends. **c.** The fork returns to its initial position just at the time a rarefaction arrives. **d.** It keeps moving and overshoots in the opposite direction. **e.** When it returns to its initial position, the next compression arrives to repeat the cycle.

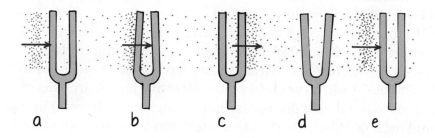

a   b   c   d   e

A common classroom demonstration of resonance uses a pair of tuning forks adjusted to the same frequency and spaced about a meter apart. When one of the forks is struck, it sets the other fork into vibration as shown in Figure 26.11. This is a small-scale version of pushing a friend on a swing—it's the timing that's important. When a sound wave impinges on the fork, each compression gives the prong a tiny push. Since the frequency of these pushes corresponds to the natural frequency of the fork, the pushes successively increase the amplitude of the fork's vibration. This is because the pushes occur at the right time and are repeatedly in the same direction as the instantaneous motion of the fork.

> Like humans, we parrots use our tongues to craft and shape sound. Tiny changes in the position of my tongue produce big differences in the sound I make.

FIGURE 26.12 ▲
In 1940, four months after being completed, the Tacoma Narrows Bridge in the state of Washington was destroyed by a 40-mile-per-hour wind.

Go Online
PHSchool.com

For: Links on interference
Visit: www.SciLinks.org
Web Code: csn – 2609

If the forks are not adjusted for matched frequencies, the timing of pushes will be off and resonance will not occur. When you tune your radio set, you are similarly adjusting the natural frequency of the electronics in the set to match one of the many incoming signals. The set then resonates to one station at a time, instead of playing all the stations at once.

Resonance occurs whenever successive impulses are applied to a vibrating object in rhythm with its natural frequency. English infantry troops marching across a footbridge in 1831 inadvertently caused the bridge to collapse when they marched in rhythm with the bridge's natural frequency. Since then, it is customary for troops to "break step" when crossing bridges. The Tacoma Narrows Bridge disaster in 1940, shown in Figure 26.12, is attributed to wind-generated resonance. A mild 40-mile-per-hour wind gale produced a fluctuating force that resonated with the natural frequency of the bridge, steadily increasing the amplitude over several hours until the bridge collapsed.

CONCEPT CHECK What causes resonance?

26.9 Interference

Sound waves, like any waves, can be made to interfere. A comparison of interference for transverse waves and longitudinal waves is shown in Figure 26.13. For sound, the crest of a wave corresponds to a compression, and the trough of a wave corresponds to a rarefaction. In either case, when the crests of one wave overlap the crests of another wave, there is constructive interference and an increase in amplitude. Or when the crests of one wave overlap the troughs of another wave, there is destructive interference and a decrease in amplitude. ☑ **When constructive interference occurs with sound waves, the listener hears a louder sound. When destructive interference occurs, the listener hears a fainter sound or no sound at all.** The listener in Figure 26.14a is equally distant from two sound speakers that simultaneously trigger identical sound waves of constant frequency. The listener hears a louder sound because the waves add. The compressions and rarefactions arrive in phase, that is, in step.

In Figure 26.14b, the listener moved to the side so that paths from the speakers differ by a half wavelength. The rarefactions from one speaker reach the listener at the same time as compressions from the other. It's like the crest of one water wave exactly filling in the trough of another water wave—destructive interference. (If the speakers emit many frequencies, not all wavelengths destructively interfere for a given difference in path lengths.)

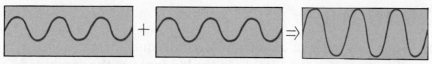

a. Two identical transverse waves in phase produce a wave of increased amplitude.

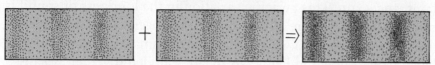

b. Two identical longitudinal waves in phase produce a wave of increased amplitude.

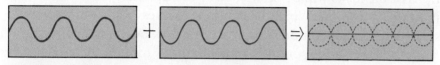

c. Two identical transverse waves that are out of phase destroy each other.

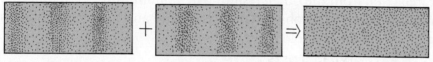

d. Two identical longitudinal waves that are out of phase destroy each other.

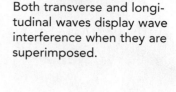

◄ FIGURE 26.13
Both transverse and longitudinal waves display wave interference when they are superimposed.

Destructive interference of sound waves is usually not a problem because there is usually enough reflection of sound to fill in canceled spots. Nevertheless, "dead spots" are sometimes evident in poorly designed theaters and gymnasiums, where sound waves reflected off walls interfere with unreflected waves to form zones of low amplitude. Often, moving your head a few centimeters in either direction can make a noticeable difference.

Destructive sound interference is a useful property in antinoise technology. Noisy devices such as jackhammers are being equipped with microphones that send the sound of the device to electronic microchips. The microchips create mirror-image wave patterns of the sound signals. For the jackhammer, this mirror-image sound signal is fed to earphones worn by the operator. Sound compressions (or rarefactions) from the hammer are neutralized by mirror-image rarefactions (or compressions) in the earphones. The combination of signals neutralizes the jackhammer noise. Noise-canceling earphones, shown in Figure 26.15, are already common for pilots. Some automobiles enjoy quiet riding due to noise cancellation. Noise-detecting microphones inside the car pick up engine or road noise. Speakers in the car then emit an opposite signal that cancels out those noises, so the human ear can't detect them. Similarly, the cabins of some airplanes are now quieted with antinoise technology.

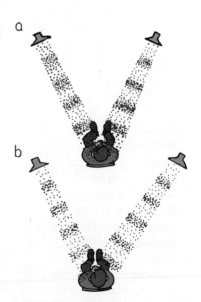

FIGURE 26.14 ▲
The sound waves from two speakers interfere. **a.** Waves arrive in phase. **b.** Waves arrive out of phase.

CONCEPT CHECK : What are the effects of constructive and destructive interference?

26.10 Beats

☑ **When two tones of slightly different frequency are sounded together, a regular fluctuation in the loudness of the combined sounds is heard.** The sound is loud, then faint, then loud, then faint, and so on. This periodic variation in the loudness of sound is called **beats.** Beats are an interesting and special case of interference.

Beats can be heard when two slightly mismatched tuning forks, like the ones shown in Figure 26.16, are sounded together. Because one fork vibrates at a frequency different from the other, the vibrations of the forks will be momentarily in step, then out of step, then in again, and so on. When the combined waves reach your ears in step—say when a compression from one fork overlaps a compression from the other—the sound is a maximum. A moment later, when the forks are out of step, a compression from one fork is met with a rarefaction from the other, resulting in a minimum. The sound that reaches your ears throbs between maximum and minimum loudness and produces a tremolo effect.

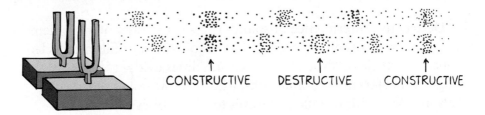

CONSTRUCTIVE   DESTRUCTIVE   CONSTRUCTIVE

FIGURE 26.16 ▲
The interference of two sound sources of slightly different frequencies produces beats.

A sound wave traveling through the ear canal vibrates the eardrum, which vibrates three tiny bones, which vibrate the fluid-filled cochlea. Inside the cochlea, tiny hair cells convert the pulse into an electrical signal to the brain. Ear plugs typically reduce noise by about 30 dB.

If you walk side by side with someone who has a different stride, there will be times when you are both in step, and times when you are both out of step. Suppose, for example, that you take exactly 70 steps in one minute and your friend takes 72 steps in the same time. Your friend gains two steps per minute on you. A little thought will show that you two will be momentarily in step twice each minute. In general, when two people with different strides walk together, the number of times they are in step in each unit of time is equal to the difference in the frequencies of their steps. This applies also to a pair of tuning forks. When one fork vibrates 264 times per second, and the other fork vibrates 262 times per second, they are in step twice each second. A beat frequency of 2 hertz is heard.

Beats can be nicely displayed on an oscilloscope. When sound signals of slightly different frequencies are fed into an oscilloscope, graphical representations of their pressure patterns can be displayed both individually and when the sounds overlap. Figure 26.17 shows the wave forms for two waves separately, and superposed. Although the separate waves are of constant amplitude, we see amplitude variations in the superposed wave form. Careful inspection of the figure shows this variation is produced by the interference of the two superposed waves. Maximum amplitude of the composite wave occurs when both waves are in phase, and minimum amplitude occurs when both waves are completely out of phase. Like the walkers in the previous example, the waves are in step twice each second, producing a beat frequency of 2 Hz. The 10- and 12-Hz waves, chosen for convenience here, are infrasonic, so they and their beats are inaudible. Higher-frequency audible waves behave exactly the same way and can produce audible beats.

If you overlap two combs of different teeth spacings as shown in Figure 26.18, you'll see a moiré pattern that is related to beats. The number of beats per length will equal the difference in the number of teeth per length for the two combs.

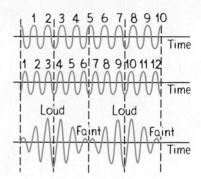

FIGURE 26.17 ▲
Sinusoidal representations of a 10-Hz sound wave and a 12-Hz sound wave during a 1-second time interval. When the two waves overlap, they produce a composite wave with a beat frequency of 2 Hz.

FIGURE 26.18 ▲
The unequal spacings of the combs produce a moiré pattern that is similar to beats.

Beats can occur with any kind of wave and are a practical way to compare frequencies. To tune a piano, a piano tuner listens for beats produced between a standard tuning fork and a particular string on the piano. When the frequencies are identical, the beats disappear. The members of an orchestra tune up by listening for beats between their instruments and a standard tone produced by an oboe.

CONCEPT CHECK : What causes beats?

think!

What is the beat frequency when a 262-Hz and a 266-Hz tuning fork are sounded together? A 262-Hz and a 272-Hz?
Answer: 26.10

Noise and Your Health

Most of us try to protect our eyes from excess light, but few give the same care to our ears. Near loudspeakers during her first time at a concert, Allison was alarmed at the pain in her ears. Her friends meant to reassure her when they told her she'd get used to it. But what they didn't tell her was that after the fine tuning of her ears was blasted, she wouldn't know the difference.

Industrial noise is even more damaging to the ears than amplified music because of its sudden high-energy peaks. Loud motorcycles, jackhammers, chain saws, and power tools not only produce steady high-volume sound, but also produce sporadic peaks of energy that can destroy tiny hair cells in the inner ear. When these tiny sensory cells in the inner ear are destroyed they can *never* be restored. Noise-induced hearing loss is insidious.

Fortunately for music devotees, damage caused by energetic peaks is somewhat limited by an inadequate response of electronic amplifiers and loudspeakers. Similarly for live music where most of the sound comes from amplifying equipment. If amplifying equipment were more responsive to sudden sound bursts, hearing loss at concerts would be more severe.

The impact of hearing loss isn't fully apparent until compounded by age. Today's young people will be tomorrow's old people—probably the hardest of hearing ever. Start now to care for your ears and prevent further hearing loss!

Critical Thinking Describe some situations you might find yourself in that could cause hearing loss. What can you do to protect your hearing?

 **REVIEW**

Go Online
PHSchool.com

For: Self-Assessment
Visit: PHSchool.com
Web Code: csa – 2600

Concept Summary ······

- All sounds originate in the vibrations of material objects.
- As a source of sound vibrates, a series of compressions and rarefactions travels outward from the source.
- Sound travels in solids, liquids, and gases.
- The speed of sound in a gas depends on the temperature of the gas and the mass of the particles in the gas.
- The speed of sound in a material depends on the material's elasticity.
- Sound intensity is objective and is measured by instruments. Loudness, on the other hand, is a physiological sensation sensed in the brain.
- When an object composed of an elastic material is disturbed, it vibrates at its own special set of frequencies, which together form its special sound.
- Sounding boards are an important part of all stringed musical instruments because they are forced into vibration and produce the sound.
- An object resonates when there is a force to pull it back to its starting position and enough energy to keep it vibrating.
- When constructive interference occurs with sound waves, the listener hears a louder sound. When destructive interference occurs, the listener hears a fainter sound or no sound at all.
- When two tones of slightly different frequency are sounded together, a fluctuation in the loudness of the combined sounds is heard; the sound is loud, then faint, then loud, then faint, and so on.

Key Terms ······

pitch (*p. 515*)

infrasonic (*p. 515*)

ultrasonic (*p. 515*)

compression (*p. 516*)

rarefaction (*p. 516*)

natural frequency (*p. 520*)

forced vibration (*p. 520*)

resonance (*p. 521*)

beats (*p. 524*)

think! Answers

26.4 For a speed of sound in air of 340 m/s, the distance is (340 m/s) × (3 s) = about 1000 m or 1 km. Time for the light is negligible, so the storm is about 1 km away.

26.10 The 262-Hz and 266-Hz forks will produce 4 beats per second, that is, 4 Hz (266 Hz minus 262 Hz). The tone heard will be halfway between, at 264 Hz, as the ear averages the frequencies. The 262-Hz and 272-Hz forks will sound like a tone at 267 Hz beating 10 times per second, or 10 Hz, which some people cannot hear. Beat frequencies greater than 10 Hz are normally too rapid to be heard.

26 ASSESS

Check Concepts · · · · ·

Section 26.1

1. What is the source of all sounds?

2. How does pitch relate to frequency?

3. What is the average frequency range of a young person's hearing?

4. Distinguish between *infrasonic* and *ultrasonic* sound.

Section 26.2

5. **a.** Distinguish between *compressions* and *rarefactions* of a sound wave.
   b. How are compressions and rarefactions produced?

Section 26.3

6. Light can travel through a vacuum, as is evidenced when you see the sun or the moon. Can sound travel through a vacuum also? Explain why or why not.

Section 26.4

7. **a.** How fast does sound travel in dry air at room temperature?
   b. How does air temperature affect the speed of sound?

8. How does the speed of sound in air compare with its speed in water and in steel?

9. Why does sound travel faster in solids and liquids than in gases?

Section 26.5

10. Is sound intensity subjective or is loudness subjective? Why?

Section 26.6

11. Why do different objects make different sounds when dropped on a floor?

12. What does it mean to say that everything has a natural frequency of vibration?

Section 26.7

13. Why is sound louder when a vibrating source is held to a sounding board?

Section 26.8

14. What is the relationship between forced vibration and resonance?

15. Why can a tuning fork or bell be set into resonance, while tissue paper cannot?

16. How is resonance produced in a vibrating object?

17. What does tuning in a radio station have to do with resonance?

Section 26.9

18. Is it possible for one sound wave to cancel another? Explain.

19. Why does destructive interference occur when the path lengths from two identical sources differ by half a wavelength?

Section 26.10

20. How does interference of sound relate to beats?

21. What is the beat frequency when a 494-Hz tuning fork and a 496-Hz tuning fork are sounded together?

528

Think and Rank · · · · · ·

Rank each of the following sets of scenarios in order of the quantity or property involved. List them from left to right. If scenarios have equal rankings, then separate them with an equal sign. (e.g., A = B)

22. The three waves below have the same frequency and travel in different media. Rank their speeds from greatest to least.

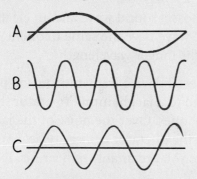

23. A pair of tuning forks of frequencies f_1 and f_2 are sounded together.

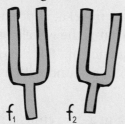

Rank from greatest to least the beat frequencies produced by the following pairs of tuning forks.

(A) $f_1 = 650$ Hz; $f_2 = 654$ Hz
(B) $f_1 = 300$ Hz; $f_2 = 305$ Hz
(C) $f_1 = 200$ Hz; $f_2 = 208$ Hz
(D) $f_1 = 800$ Hz; $f_2 = 801$ Hz

Think and Explain · · · · · ·

24. If the moon blew up, why wouldn't we be able to hear it?

25. When watching at a baseball game, we often hear the bat hitting the ball after we actually see the hit. Why?

26. In the stands of a racetrack, you notice smoke from the starter's gun before you hear it fire. Explain.

27. In an Olympic competition, a microphone picks up the sound of the starter's gun and sends it electrically to speakers at every runner's starting block. Why?

28. Why will marchers at the end of a long parade following a band be out of step with marchers nearer the band?

29. You watch a distant farmer driving a stake into the ground with a sledgehammer. He hits the stake at a regular rate of one stroke per second. You hear the sound of the blows exactly synchronized with the blows you see. And then you hear one more blow after you see him stop hammering. How far away is the farmer?

30. When a sound wave propagates past a point in the air, what are the changes that occur in the pressure of air at this point?

31. If the speed of sound depended on its frequency, would you enjoy a concert sitting in the second balcony?

32. If the frequency of sound is doubled, what change will occur in its speed? What change will occur in its wavelength?

33. Why is an echo weaker than the original sound?

34. How much more intense is a close whisper than a sound at the threshold of hearing?

35. The signal-to-noise ratio for a tape recorder is listed at 50 dB, meaning that when music is played back, the intensity level of the music is 50 dB greater than that of the noise from tape hiss and so forth. By what factor is the sound intensity of the music greater than that of the noise?

36. If the handle of a tuning fork is held solidly against a table, the sound becomes louder. Why? How will this affect the length of the time the fork keeps vibrating? Explain, using the law of energy conservation.

37. The sitar, an Indian musical instrument, has a set of strings that vibrate and produce music, even though they are never plucked by the player. These "sympathetic strings" are identical to the plucked strings and are mounted below them. What is your explanation?

38. Suppose a piano tuner hears 2 beats per second when listening to the combined sound from her tuning fork and the piano note being tuned. After slightly tightening the string, she hears 1 beat per second. Should she loosen or should she further tighten the string?

39. Why is it dangerous for people in the balcony of an auditorium to stamp their feet in a steady rhythm?

40. Why is the sound of a harp soft in comparison with the sound of a piano?

41. What physics principle is used by Laura when she pumps in rhythm with the natural frequency of the swing?

42. Suppose a sound wave and an electromagnetic wave have the same frequency. Which has the longer wavelength?

43. A special device transmits out-of-phase sound to a jackhammer operator through earphones. Over the noise of the jackhammer, the operator can easily hear your voice while you are unable to hear his. Explain.

Think and Solve

44. Sound waves travel at approximately 340 m/s. What is the wavelength of a sound with a frequency of 20 Hz? What is the wavelength of a sound with a frequency of 20 kHz?

45. A bat flying in a cave emits a sound and receives its echo 0.10 s later. Show that the distance to the wall of the cave is 17 m.

46. An oceanic depth-sounding vessel surveys the ocean bottom with ultrasonic sound that travels 1530 m/s in seawater. Find the depth of the water if the time delay of the echo to the ocean floor and back is 8 seconds.

47. On a field trip to Echo Cave, you clap your hands and receive an echo 1 second later. How far away is the cave wall?

48. Susie hammers on a block of wood when she is 85 m from a large brick wall. Each time she hits the block, she hears an echo 0.5 s later. With this information, show that the speed of sound is 340 m/s.

49. On a keyboard, you strike middle C, which has a frequency of 256 Hz.
a. Show that the period of one vibration of this tone is 0.00391 s.
b. As the sound leaves the instrument at a speed of 340 m/s, show that its wavelength in air is 1.33 m.

50. Suppose your friend is foolish enough to play his keyboard instrument underwater, where the speed of sound is 1,500 m/s.
a. Show that the wavelength of the middle-C tone in water would be 5.86 m.
b. Explain why middle C (or any other tone) has a longer wavelength in water than in air.

51. Two sounds, one at 240 Hz and the other at 243 Hz, occur at the same time. What beat frequency do you hear?

52. Two notes are sounding, one of which is 440 Hz. If a beat frequency of 5 Hz is heard, what is the other note's frequency?

53. What beat frequencies are possible with tuning forks of frequencies 256, 259, and 261 Hz?

Activities · · · · ·

54. Suspend the wire grill of a refrigerator or oven shelf from a string, the ends of which you hold to your ears. Let a friend gently stroke the grill with pieces of broom straw and other objects. The effect is best appreciated if you are in a relaxed condition with your eyes closed. Describe and explain your observations.

55. Wet your finger and rub it slowly around the rim of a thin-rimmed stemmed glass while you hold its base firmly against a tabletop with your other hand. Describe and explain your observations.

56. Blow over the tops of two identical empty bottles and see if the tone produced is of the same pitch. Then put one in a freezer and try the procedure again. Sound will travel more slowly in the colder denser air of the cold bottle and the note will be lower. Try it and see.

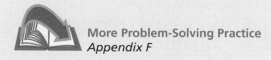

More Problem-Solving Practice
Appendix F

27 LIGHT

THE BIG IDEA : Light is the ONLY thing you see! All visible objects either emit or reflect light.

The only thing we can *really* see is light. But what *is* light? During the day the primary source of light is the sun, and the secondary source is the brightness of the sky. Other common sources are flames, white-hot filaments in lamps, and glowing gases in glass tubes. Almost everything we see, such as this page, is made visible by the light it reflects from such sources. Some materials, such as air, water, or window glass, allow light to pass through. Other materials, such as thin paper or frosted glass, allow the passage of light in diffused directions so that we can't see objects through them. Most materials do not allow the passage of any light, except through a very thin layer.

Why do things such as water and glass allow light to pass through, while things such as wood and steel block it? To answer these questions, you must know something about light itself.

discover!

Is "Black Light" Really Light?

1. Using a marker, write a message on a piece of colored paper. On a separate piece of colored paper, write a message with an "invisible ink" pen.
2. Turn off the lights and exchange papers with your neighbor.
3. Try to read the messages on the papers using only a flashlight.
4. Now try to read the messages using a "black" light.

Analyze and Conclude

1. **Observing** Which message was visible under the flashlight? Which message was visible under the black light?
2. **Predicting** Do you think you could see either message in the dark without the black light?
3. **Making Generalizations** How would you define light?

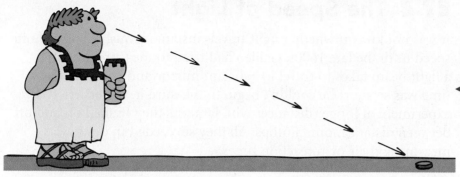

27.1 Early Concepts of Light

Light has been studied for thousands of years. Some of the ancient Greek philosophers thought that light consisted of tiny particles, which could enter the eye to create the sensation of vision. Others, including Socrates and Plato, thought that vision resulted from streamers or filaments emitted by the eye making contact with an object, as shown in Figure 27.1. This view was supported by Euclid, who explained why we do not see a needle on the floor until our eyes fall upon it.

Up until the time of Newton and beyond, most philosophers and scientists thought that light consisted of particles. However, one Greek, Empedocles, taught that light traveled in waves. One of Newton's contemporaries, the Dutch scientist Christian Huygens, also argued that light was a wave.

The particle theory was supported by the fact that light seemed to move in straight lines instead of spreading out as waves do. Huygens provided evidence that under some circumstances light does spread out. (This is known as *diffraction*, which you will learn about in Chapter 31.) Other scientists later found more evidence to support the wave theory. The wave theory became the accepted theory in the nineteenth century.

Then in 1905 Einstein published a theory explaining the *photoelectric effect*. According to this theory, light consists of particles called photons. **Photons** are massless bundles of concentrated electromagnetic energy. ✅ **Scientists now agree that light has a dual nature, part particle and part wave.** This chapter discusses only the wave nature of light and leaves the particle nature of light to Chapter 38.

Go Online

SciLINKS
NSTA

For: Links on Light
Visit: www.SciLink.org
Web Code: csn – 2701

CONCEPT CHECK What is the nature of light?

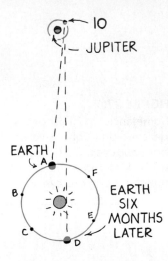

FIGURE 27.2 ▲

Light coming from Jupiter's moon Io takes a longer time to reach Earth at position D than at position A. The extra distance that the light travels divided by the extra time it takes gives the speed of light.

Light travels a million times faster than sound.

27.2 The Speed of Light

It was not known whether light travels instantaneously or with finite speed until the late 1600s. Galileo had tried to measure the time a light beam takes to travel to a distant mirror and back, but the time was so short he couldn't begin to measure it. Others tried the experiment at longer distances with lanterns they flashed on and off between distant mountaintops. All they succeeded in doing was measuring their own reaction times.

Olaus Roemer The first demonstration that light travels at a finite speed was supplied by the Danish astronomer Olaus Roemer about 1675. Roemer made very careful measurements of the periods of Jupiter's moons. The innermost moon, Io, is visible through a small telescope and was measured to revolve around Jupiter in 42.5 hours. Io disappears periodically into Jupiter's shadow, so this period could be measured with great accuracy. Roemer was puzzled to find an irregularity in the measurements of Io's observed period. He found that while Earth was moving away from Jupiter, say from position B to C in Figure 27.2, the measured periods of Io were all somewhat longer than average. When Earth was moving toward Jupiter, say from position E to F, the measured periods were shorter than average. Roemer estimated that the cumulative discrepancy between positions A and D amounted to about 22 minutes. That is, when Earth was at position D, Io would pass into Jupiter's shadow 22 minutes late, compared with observations at position A.[27.2]

Christian Huygens Christian Huygens correctly interpreted this discrepancy. When Earth was farther away from Jupiter, it was the *light* that was late, not the *moon*. Io passed into Jupiter's shadow at the predicted time, but the light carrying the message did not reach Roemer until it had traveled the extra distance across the diameter of Earth's orbit. There is some doubt as to whether Huygens knew the value of this distance. In any event, this distance is now known to be 300,000,000 km. Using the correct travel time of 1000 s for light to move across Earth's orbit makes the calculation of the speed of light quite simple:

$$\text{speed of light} = \frac{d}{t} = \frac{\text{extra distance traveled}}{\text{extra time measured}}$$

$$= \frac{300{,}000{,}000 \text{ km}}{1000 \text{ s}} = 300{,}000 \text{ km/s}$$

The speed of light is 300,000 km/s.

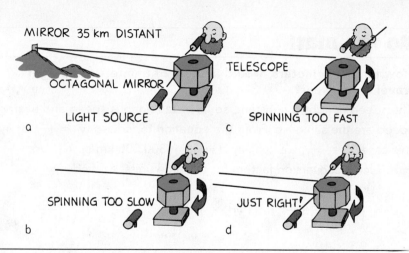

Albert Michelson The most famous experiment measuring the speed of light was performed by the American physicist Albert Michelson in 1880. Figure 27.3 shows how light from an intense source was directed by a lens to an octagonal mirror initially at rest. The mirror was adjusted so that a beam of light was reflected to a stationary mirror located on a mountain 35 km away and then reflected back to the octagonal mirror and into the eye of an observer. The distance the light had to travel to the distant mountain was known, so Michelson had to find only the time it took to make a round trip.

When the mirror was spun, short bursts of light reached the mountain mirror and were reflected back to the spinning octagonal mirror. If the rotating mirror made exactly one eighth rotation in the time the light made the trip to the distant mountain and back, the mirror was in a position to reflect light to the observer. If the mirror was rotated too slowly or too quickly, it would not be in a position to reflect light. When the light entered the eyepiece, Michelson knew that the time for the light to make the round trip and the time for the octagonal mirror to make one eighth of a rotation was the same. He divided the 70-km round trip distance by this time. ⊘ **Michelson's experimental value for the speed of light was 299,920 km/s, which is usually rounded to 300,000 km/s.** Michelson received the 1907 Nobel Prize in physics for this experiment. He was the first American scientist to receive this prize.

We now know that the speed of light in a vacuum is a universal constant. Light is so fast that if a beam of light could travel around Earth, it would make 7.5 trips in one second. Light takes 8 minutes to travel from the sun to Earth and 4 years from the next nearest star, Alpha Centauri. The distance light travels in one year is called a **light-year.**

CONCEPT CHECK : What was Michelson's experimental value for the speed of light?

think!

Light entered the eyepiece when Michelson's octagonal mirror made exactly one eighth of a rotation during the time light traveled to the distant mountain and back. Would light enter the eyepiece if the mirror turned one quarter of a rotation in this time?
Answer: 27.2

do the math!

How far, in kilometers, would a beam of uninterrupted light travel in one year?

The speed of light is constant, so its instantaneous speed and average speed are the same—c. From the equation for speed, $v = \dfrac{d}{t}$, or in this case, $c = \dfrac{d}{t}$, we can say $d = ct = (300{,}000 \text{ km/s}) \times (1 \text{ yr})$. Introducing conversion factors for the time units, we find

$$d = \left(\frac{300{,}000 \text{ km}}{1 \text{ s}}\right) \times (1 \text{ yr}) \times \left(\frac{365 \text{ d}}{1 \text{ yr}}\right) \times \left(\frac{24 \text{ h}}{1 \text{ d}}\right) \times \left(\frac{3600 \text{ s}}{1 \text{ h}}\right)$$

$$= 9.5 \times 10^{12} \text{ km}$$

This distance, 9.5×10^{12} km, is one light-year.

27.3 Electromagnetic Waves

Light is energy that is emitted by accelerating electric charges—often electrons in atoms. This energy travels in a wave that is partly electric and partly magnetic. Such a wave is an **electromagnetic wave.** Light is a small portion of the broad family of electromagnetic waves that includes such familiar forms as radio waves, microwaves, and X-rays. The range of electromagnetic waves, the **electromagnetic spectrum,** is shown in Figure 27.4. ✅ **The electromagnetic spectrum consists of radio waves, microwaves, infrared, light, ultraviolet rays, X-rays, and gamma rays.**

The lowest frequency of light we can see with our eyes appears red. The highest visible frequencies are nearly twice the frequency of red and appear violet. Electromagnetic waves of frequencies lower than the red of visible light are called **infrared.** Heat lamps give off infrared waves. Electromagnetic waves of frequencies higher than those of violet are called **ultraviolet.** These higher-frequency waves are responsible for sunburns.

CONCEPT CHECK What are the waves of the electromagnetic spectrum?

FIGURE 27.4 ▼

The electromagnetic spectrum is a continuous range of waves extending from radio waves to gamma rays.

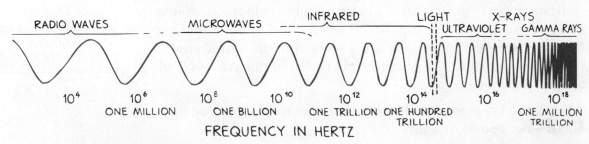

RADIO WAVES   MICROWAVES   INFRARED   LIGHT   X-RAYS   ULTRAVIOLET   GAMMA RAYS

10^4 10^6 ONE MILLION 10^8 10^{10} ONE BILLION 10^{12} ONE TRILLION 10^{14} ONE HUNDRED TRILLION 10^{16} 10^{18} ONE MILLION TRILLION

FREQUENCY IN HERTZ

536

27.4 Light and Transparent Materials

Light is energy carried in an electromagnetic wave that is generated by vibrating electric charges. When light strikes matter, electrons in the matter are forced into vibration. In effect, vibrations in an emitter are transferred to vibrations in a receiver. This is similar to the way sound is received by a receiver, as shown in Figure 27.5.

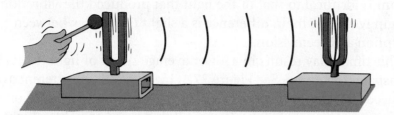

◀ **FIGURE 27.5**
Just as a sound wave can force a sound receiver into vibration, a light wave can force charged particles in materials into vibration.

Exactly how a receiving material responds when light is incident upon it depends on the frequency of the light and the natural frequency of electrons in the material. Visible light vibrates at a very high rate, more than 100 trillion times per second (10^{14} hertz). If a charged object is to respond to these ultrafast vibrations, it must have very little inertia. Electrons have a small enough mass to vibrate this fast.

⊘ **Light passes through materials whose atoms absorb the energy and immediately reemit it as light.** Materials that transmit light are **transparent.** Glass and water are transparent. Visualize the electrons in an atom as connected by imaginary springs, as shown in Figure 27.6. When light hits the electrons, they vibrate.

Materials that are springy (elastic) respond more to vibrations at some frequencies than at others. Bells ring at a particular frequency, tuning forks vibrate at a particular frequency, and so do the electrons in matter. The natural vibration frequencies of an electron depend on how strongly it is attached to a nearby nucleus. Different materials have different electric "spring strengths."

Electrons in glass have a natural vibration frequency in the ultraviolet range. When ultraviolet light shines on glass, resonance occurs as the wave builds and maintains a large vibration between the electron and the atomic nucleus, just as a large vibration is built when pushing someone at the resonant frequency on a swing. The energy received by the atom can be either passed on to neighboring atoms by collisions or reemitted as light. If ultraviolet light interacts with an atom that has the same natural frequency, the vibration amplitude of its electrons becomes unusually large. The atom typically holds on to this energy for about 1 million vibrations or 100 millionths of a second.

During this time the atom makes many collisions with other atoms and gives up its energy in the form of heat. That's why glass is not transparent to ultraviolet.

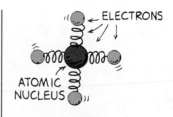

FIGURE 27.6 ▲
The electrons of atoms in glass can be imagined to be bound to the atomic nucleus as if connected by springs.

But when the electromagnetic wave has a lower frequency than ultraviolet, as visible light does, the electrons are forced into vibration with smaller amplitudes. The atom holds the energy for less time, with less chance of collision with neighboring atoms, and less energy is transferred as heat. The energy of the vibrating electrons is reemitted as transmitted light. Glass is transparent to all the frequencies of visible light. The frequency of the reemitted light passed from atom to atom is identical to that of the light that produced the vibration to begin with. The main difference is a slight time delay between absorption and reemission.

This time delay results in a lower average speed of light through a transparent material. See Figure 27.7. Light travels at different average speeds through different materials. In a vacuum, the speed of light is a constant 300,000 km/s; we call this speed of light c. Light travels at a speed a very small amount less than c in the atmosphere, but its speed there is usually rounded off to c. In water, light travels at 75% of its speed in a vacuum, or $0.75c$. In glass, light travels at about $0.67c$, depending on the type of glass. In a diamond, light travels at only $0.40c$, less than half its speed in a vacuum. When light emerges from these materials into the air, it travels at its original speed, c.

Infrared waves, which have frequencies lower than visible light, vibrate not only the electrons, but also the entire structure of the glass. This vibration of the structure increases the internal energy of the glass and makes it warmer. As Figure 27.8 shows, glass is transparent to visible light, but not to ultraviolet and infrared light.

Atoms are like optical tuning forks that resonate at certain frequencies.

CONCEPT CHECK : What kind of materials does light pass through?

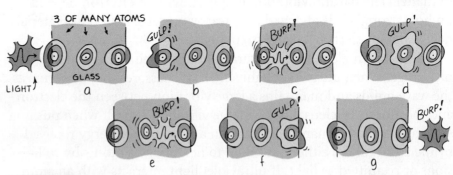

FIGURE 27.7 ▲
A light wave incident upon a pane of glass sets up vibrations in the atoms. Because of the time delay between absorptions and reemissions, the average speed of light in glass is less than c.

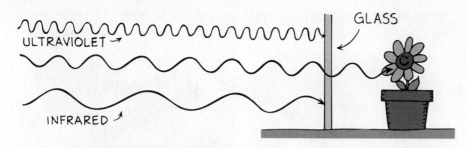

◀ **FIGURE 27.8**
Glass blocks both infrared and ultraviolet but is transparent to all the frequencies of visible light.

27.5 Opaque Materials

Materials that absorb light without reemission and thus allow no light through them are **opaque.** Wood, stone, and people are opaque. ⊘ **In opaque materials, any coordinated vibrations given by light to the atoms and molecules are turned into random kinetic energy— that is, into internal energy.** The materials become slightly warmer.

Metals are also opaque. Interestingly enough, in metals, the outer electrons of atoms are not bound to any particular atom. They are free to wander with very little restraint throughout the material. That's why metal conducts electricity and heat so well. When light shines on metal and sets these free electrons into vibration, their energy does not "spring" from atom to atom in the material but is reemitted as visible light. This reemitted light is seen as a reflection. That's why metals are shiny.

Our atmosphere is transparent to visible light and some infrared, but fortunately, it is almost opaque to high-frequency ultraviolet waves. The small amount of ultraviolet that does get through is responsible for sunburns. If it all got through, we wouldn't dare go out in the sun without protection. Clouds are semitransparent to ultraviolet, which is why you can get a sunburn on a cloudy day. Ultraviolet also reflects from sand and water, which is why you can sometimes get a sunburn while in the shade of a beach umbrella.

think!

Why is glass transparent to visible light but opaque to ultraviolet and infrared?
Answer: 27.5

CONCEPT
CHECK Why does light not pass through opaque materials?

discover!

Why is wetter darker?

1. Note the color of a surface and then wet it.
2. How did wetting the surface change its appearance?
3. **Think** What happens with each bounce as light bounces around inside the transparent wet region?

FIGURE 27.9 ▶
A large light source
produces a softer shadow
than a smaller source.

27.6 Shadows

A thin beam of light is often called a **ray.** Any beam of light—no matter how wide—can be thought of as made of a bundle of rays. ☑ **When light shines on an object, some of the rays may be stopped while others pass on in a straight-line path.** Look at Figure 27.9. A **shadow** is formed where light rays cannot reach. Sharp shadows are produced by a small light source nearby or by a larger source farther away. However, most shadows are somewhat blurry. There is usually a dark part on the inside and a lighter part around the edges. A total shadow is called an **umbra.** A partial shadow is called a **penumbra.** A penumbra appears where some of the light is blocked but where other light fills in. This can happen where light from one source is blocked and light from another source fills in, as in Figure 27.10. Or a penumbra occurs where light from a broad source is only partially blocked.

a   b   c

FIGURE 27.10 ▲
The sharpness of a shadow depends on the distance between the object and the wall. **a.** An object held close to a wall casts a sharp shadow. **b.** As the object is moved farther away, penumbras are formed and cut down on the umbra. **c.** When it is very far away, all the penumbras mix together into a big blur.

540

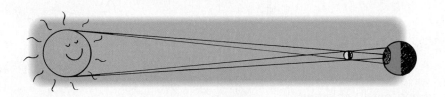

◀ **FIGURE 27.11**
An eclipse of the sun occurs when the moon's shadow falls on Earth.

A dramatic example of a penumbra occurs when the moon passes between Earth and the sun—during a solar eclipse. Look at Figure 27.11. Because of the large size of the sun, the rays taper to provide an umbra and a surrounding penumbra. The moon's shadow barely reaches Earth. If you stand in the umbra part of the shadow, you experience brief darkness during the day. If you stand in the penumbra, you experience a partial eclipse. The sunlight is dimmed, and the sun appears as a crescent. [27.6]

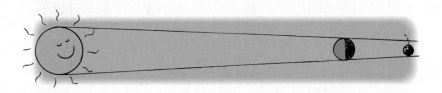

◀ **FIGURE 27.12**
An eclipse of the moon occurs when Earth's shadow falls on the moon.

Now look at Figure 27.12. Earth, like most objects in sunlight, casts a shadow. This shadow extends into space, and sometimes the moon passes into it. When this happens, we have a lunar eclipse. Whereas a solar eclipse can be observed only in a small region of Earth at a given time, a lunar eclipse can be seen by all observers on the nighttime half of Earth.

Shadows also occur when light is bent in passing through a transparent material such as water. In Figure 27.13 shadows are cast by turbulent, rising warm water. Light travels at slightly different speeds in warm and in cold water. The change in speed causes light to bend, just as layers of warm and cool air in the night sky bend starlight and cause the twinkling of stars. Some of the light gets deflected a bit and leaves darker places on the wall. The shapes of the shadows depend on how the light is bent. You will learn more about the bending of light in Chapter 29.

think!

Why are lunar eclipses more commonly seen than solar eclipses?
Answer: 27.6

◀ **FIGURE 27.13**
A heater at the tip of this submerged J-tube produces convection currents in the water. They are revealed by shadows cast by light that is deflected differently by the water of different temperatures.

CONCEPT CHECK : **What causes the formation of shadows?**

FIGURE 27.14 ▶
A vertically polarized
wave is on the left and
a horizontally polarized
wave is on the right.

27.7 Polarization

Light travels in waves. The fact that the waves are transverse—
and not longitudinal—is demonstrated by the phenomenon of
polarization. If you shake the end of a horizontal rope, as in Figure
27.14, a transverse wave travels along the rope. The vibrations are
back and forth in one direction, and the wave is said to be polarized. If the rope is shaken up and down, a vertically polarized wave is
produced; that is, the waves traveling along the rope are confined to
a vertical plane. If the rope is shaken from side to side, a horizontally
polarized wave is produced.

FIGURE 27.15 ▶

Polarized light lies along the
same plane as that of the
vibrations of the electron
that emits it.

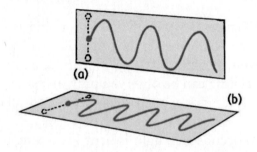

A single vibrating electron emits an electromagnetic wave that is
polarized. A vertically vibrating electron emits light that is vertically
polarized, while a horizontally vibrating electron emits light that is
horizontally polarized, as shown in Figure 27.15.

A common light source, such as an incandescent or fluorescent
lamp, a candle flame, or the sun, emits light that is not polarized. This
is because the vibrating electrons that produce the light vibrate in
random directions. When light from these sources shines on a polarizing filter, such as that from which Polaroid® sunglasses are made,
the light that is transmitted is polarized. The filter is said to have a
polarization axis that is in the direction of the vibrations of the polarized light wave.

Light will pass through a pair of polarizing filters when their
polarization axes are aligned but not when they are crossed at right
angles. This behavior is very much like the filtering of a vibrating rope
that passes through a pair of picket fences, as shown in Figure 27.16.

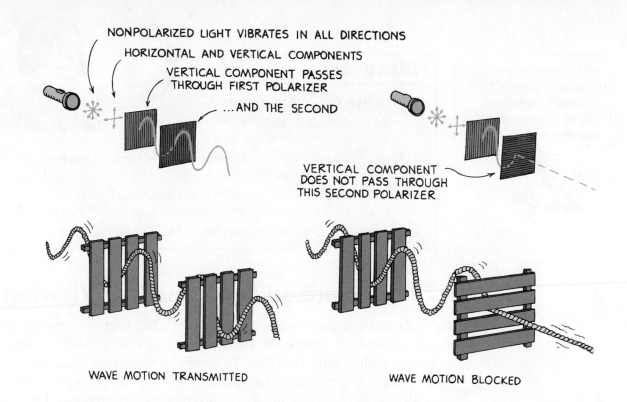

NONPOLARIZED LIGHT VIBRATES IN ALL DIRECTIONS

HORIZONTAL AND VERTICAL COMPONENTS

VERTICAL COMPONENT PASSES THROUGH FIRST POLARIZER

...AND THE SECOND

VERTICAL COMPONENT DOES NOT PASS THROUGH THIS SECOND POLARIZER

WAVE MOTION TRANSMITTED

WAVE MOTION BLOCKED

When you skip flat stones across the surface of a pond, stones with flat sides parallel to the water bounce ("reflect"), but stones with flat sides at right angles to the surface penetrate the water ("refract"). Light behaves similarly. The flat side of a stone is like the plane of vibration of polarized light. ✓ **Light that reflects at glancing angles from nonmetallic surfaces, such as glass, water, or roads, vibrates mainly in the plane of the reflecting surface.** So glare from a horizontal surface is horizontally polarized. The axes of Polaroid sunglasses are vertical so that glare from horizontal surfaces is eliminated. Figure 27.17 demonstrates the effect the orientation of polarizing filters has on the transmission of light.

CONCEPT : Why is glare from a horizontal surface horizontally
CHECK : polarized?

FIGURE 27.16 ▲
A rope analogy illustrates the effect of crossed sheets of polarizing material.

◀ **FIGURE 27.17**
a. Light is transmitted when the axes of the polarizing filters are aligned. **b.** Light is absorbed when they are at right angles to each other. **c.** Surprisingly, when a third filter is sandwiched between the two crossed ones, light is transmitted.

a

b

c

discover!

Which eye do you use more?

1. Hold a finger up at arm's length. With both eyes open, look past your finger to a distant object.
2. Now close your right eye. Does your finger jump to the right? If so, then you use your right eye more.
3. Check this by repeating with your left eye. Check with your friends. Is a left-handed person more likely to be left-eyed?
4. **Think** Is a right-handed person more likely to be right-eyed?

27.8 Polarized Light and 3-D Viewing

Vision in three dimensions depends on the fact that both eyes give impressions simultaneously (or nearly so), each eye viewing a scene from a slightly different angle. To convince yourself of this, hold an upright finger at arm's length and see how it switches position relative to the background as you alternately close each eye. The view seen by each eye is different. The combination of views in the eye-brain system gives depth. Look at Figure 27.18. ✅ **A pair of photographs or movie frames, taken a short distance apart (about average eye spacing), can be seen in 3-D when the left eye sees only the left view and the right eye sees only the right view.** Slide shows or movies accomplish this by projecting the pair of views through polarization filters onto a screen. Their polarization axes are at right angles to each other, as shown in Figure 27.19. The overlapping pictures look blurry to the naked eye.

think!

Which pair of glasses is best suited for automobile drivers? (The polarization axes are shown by the straight lines.)
Answer: 27.8

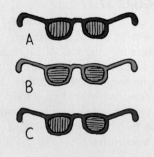

Life success is not acquiring
all the things you want,
but becoming the kind of person
you'd like to be.

Life success is not acquiring
all the things you want,
but becoming the kind of person
you'd like to be.

FIGURE 27.18 ▲
When your left eye looks at the left view of the statement while your right eye looks at the right view, your eye-brain system combines them to produce depth. The second and fourth lines appear farther away. To see this, place your face to the book with your nose touching the page. Now very slowly, without trying to focus your eyes at any one point, move away from the figure. If you've moved 30 centimeters and still haven't seen the stereo effect, start over. It may take a few tries.

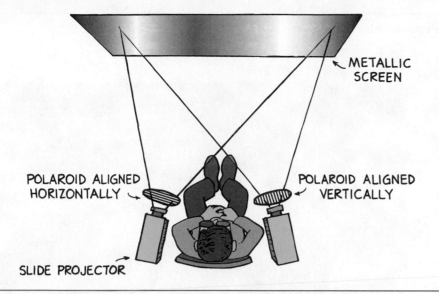

◀ **FIGURE 27.19**
A 3-D slide show uses polarizing filters. The left eye sees only polarized light from the left projector; the right eye sees only polarized light from the right projector. Both views merge in the brain to produce an image with depth.

METALLIC SCREEN

POLAROID ALIGNED HORIZONTALLY

POLAROID ALIGNED VERTICALLY

SLIDE PROJECTOR

To see in 3-D, the viewer wears polarizing eyeglasses with the lens axes also at right angles. In this way each eye sees a separate picture, just as in real life. The brain interprets the two pictures as a single picture with a feeling of depth. (Hand-held stereo viewers produce the same effect.)

Depth is also seen in computer-generated stereograms, as in Figure 27.20. Here, the slightly different patterns are hidden from a casual view. You can view the message of the figure (what this book is about!) with the procedure for viewing Figure 27.18. Once you've mastered the viewing technique, head for the local mall and check the variety of stereograms in posters and books.

CONCEPT CHECK: How can you see photographs or movies in 3-D?

FIGURE 27.20 ▲
Read the message in this computer-generated stereogram.

FIGURE 27.21 ▼ Try each of the optical Illusions below.

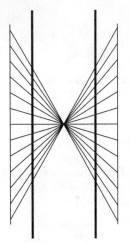

Are the vertical lines parallel?

Both rectangles are equally bright. Cover the boundary between them with a pencil and see.

Are the tiles really crooked?

Is the hat taller than the brim is wide?

Do these lines move?

Could you make this in the shop?

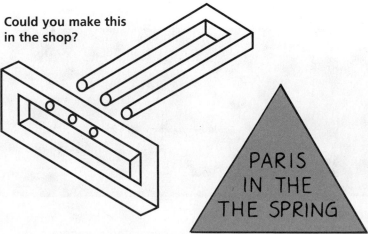

What does this sign read?

REVIEW

Go Online
PHSchool.com

For: Self-Assessment
Visit: PHSchool.com
Web Code: csa – 2700

Concept Summary ......

- Light has a dual nature, part particle and part wave.

- Michelson's experimental value for the speed of light was 299,920 km/s, usually rounded to 300,000 km/s.

- The electromagnetic spectrum consists of radio waves, microwaves, infrared, light, ultraviolet rays, X-rays, and gamma rays.

- Light passes through materials whose atoms absorb the energy and immediately reemit it as light.

- In opaque materials, any coordinated vibrations given by light to the atoms and molecules are turned into internal energy.

- When light shines on an object, some of the rays may be stopped while others pass on in a straight-line path.

- Light that reflects at glancing angles from nonmetallic surfaces vibrates mainly in the plane of the reflecting surface.

- A pair of images can be seen in 3-D when the left eye sees only the left view and the right eye sees only the right view.

Key Terms ......

photon (p. 533)

light-year (p. 535)

electromagnetic wave (p. 536)

electromagnetic spectrum (p. 536)

infrared (p. 536)

ultraviolet (p. 536)

transparent (p. 537)

opaque (p. 539)

ray (p. 540)

shadow (p. 540)

umbra (p. 540)

penumbra (p. 540)

polarization (p. 542)

think! Answers

27.2 Yes, light would enter the eyepiece whenever $\frac{1}{8}$ rotation—$\frac{1}{4}$, $\frac{1}{2}$, 1, etc.—in the time the the octagonal mirror turned in multiples of light made its round trip. What is required is that any of the eight faces be in place when the reflected flash returns from the mountain. Michelson did not spin the mirror fast enough, however, for these other possibilities to occur.

27.5 The natural frequency of vibration for electrons in glass matches the frequency of ultraviolet light, so resonance in the glass occurs when ultraviolet waves shine on it. These energetic vibrations of electrons generate heat instead of wave reemission, so the glass is opaque to ultraviolet. In the range of visible light, the forced vibrations of electrons in the glass are more subtle, and reemission of light rather than the generation of heat occurs, so the glass is transparent. Lower-frequency infrared causes entire atomic structures, not just electrons, to resonate, so heat is generated, and the glass is opaque to infrared.

27.6 There are usually two of each every year. However, the shadow of the moon on Earth is very small compared with the shadow of Earth on the moon. Only a relatively few people are in the shadow of the moon (solar eclipse), while everybody who views the nighttime sky can see the shadow of Earth on the moon (lunar eclipse).

27.8 Pair A is best suited because the vertical axes blocks horizontally polarized light that composes much of the glare from horizontal surfaces. (Pair C is suited for viewing 3-D movies.)

Check Concepts ......

Section 27.1

1. **a.** What is a photon?
   b. Which theory of light is the photon more consistent with—the wave theory or the particle theory?

Section 27.2

2. How long does it take for light to travel across the diameter of Earth's orbit around the sun?

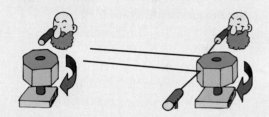

3. How did a spinning octagonal mirror help Michelson calculate the time that light took to make the round trip to the distant mountain?

4. How long does light take to travel from the sun to Earth? From the star Alpha Centauri to Earth?

5. How long does light take to travel a distance of one light-year?

Section 27.3

6. What is the source of electromagnetic waves?

7. Is light simply a small segment of the electromagnetic spectrum? Defend your answer.

8. How do the frequencies of infrared and ultraviolet light compare?

Section 27.4

9. How does the role of inertia relate to the rate at which electric charges can be forced into vibration?

10. Different bells and tuning forks have their own natural vibrations and emit their own tones when struck. How is this analogous to atoms, molecules, and light?

11. Light incident upon a pane of glass slows down in passing through the glass. Does it emerge at a slower speed or at its initial speed? Explain.

12. Will glass be transparent to light with frequencies that match its own natural frequencies?

13. Does the time delay between the absorption and reemission of light affect the average speed of light in a material? Explain.

14. When light encounters a material, it can build up vibrations in the electrons of certain atoms that may be intense enough to last over a long period of time. Will the energy of these vibrations tend to be absorbed and turned into heat or absorbed and reemitted as light?

15. Why would you expect the speed of light to be slightly less in the atmosphere than in a vacuum?

Section 27.5

16. What happens to the energy of light when it encounters an opaque material?

17. Why are metals shiny in appearance?

Section 27.6

18. Distinguish between an umbra and a penumbra.

19. a. Distinguish between a solar eclipse and a lunar eclipse.
    b. Which type of eclipse is dangerous to your eyes if viewed directly?

Section 27.7

20. What is the difference between light that is polarized and light that is not?

21. Why is light from a common lamp or from a candle flame nonpolarized?

22. In what direction is the polarization of the glare that reflects from a horizontal surface?

Section 27.8

23. How do polarizing filters allow each eye to see separate images in the projection of three-dimensional slides or movies?

Think and Explain ......

24. When you look at a distant galaxy through a telescope, how is it that you're looking backward in time?

25. When we look at the sun, we are seeing it as it was 8 minutes ago. So we can only see the sun "in the past." When you look at the back of your own hand, do you see it now or in the past?

26. What evidence can you cite to support the idea that light can travel through a vacuum?

27. Which have the longest wavelengths—light waves, X-rays, or radio waves?

28. Which has the shorter wavelengths, ultraviolet or infrared? Which has the higher frequencies?

29. Your friend says that microwaves and ultraviolet light have different wavelengths but travel through space at the same speed. Do you agree or disagree? Explain.

30. Your friend says that any radio wave travels appreciably faster than any sound wave. Do you agree or disagree, and why?

31. Are the wavelengths of radio and television signals longer or shorter than waves detectable by the human eye?

32. A helium-neon laser emits light of wavelength 6.33×10^{-7} m. Light from an argon laser has a wavelength of 5.15×10^{-7}m. Which laser emits the higher-frequency light?

33. If the octagonal mirror in the Michelson apparatus were spun at twice the speed that produced light in the eyepiece, would light still be seen? Would light be seen if the mirror spun 2.1 times the speed? Explain.

34. If the mirror in Michelson's apparatus had had six sides instead of eight, would it have had to spin faster or more slowly to measure the speed of light? Explain.

35. If a one-side-silvered plane mirror were used in the Michelson apparatus, how much faster would it have had to spin so reflected light would be seen in the telescope?

36. You can get a sunburn on a sunny day and on an overcast day. But you cannot get a sunburn if you are behind glass. Explain.

37. Short wavelengths of visible light interact more frequently with the atoms in glass than do longer wavelengths. Does this interaction time tend to speed up or slow down the average speed of short-wavelength light in glass?

38. Imagine that a person can walk only at a certain pace—no faster and no slower. If you time her uninterrupted walk across a room of known length, you can calculate her walking speed. If, however, she stops momentarily along the way to greet others in the room, the extra time spent in her brief interactions gives an average speed across the room that is less than her walking speed. How is this like light passing through glass? How is it different?

39. If you fire a ball through a pile of sand, it will slow down in the sand and emerge at less than its initial speed. But when light shines on a pane of glass, even though it slows down inside, its speed upon emerging is the same as its initial speed. Explain.

40. Short wavelengths of visible light interact more frequently with the atoms in glass than do longer wavelengths. Which do you suppose takes the longer time to get through glass—red light or blue light?

41. Suppose that sunlight is incident upon both a pair of reading glasses and a pair of sunglasses. Which pair would you expect to be warmer, and why?

42. Why does a high-flying plane cast little or no shadow on the ground, while a low-flying plane casts a sharp shadow?

43. The intensity of light decreases as the inverse square of the distance from the source. Does this mean that light energy is lost? Explain.

44. Only some of the people on the daytime side of Earth can witness a solar eclipse when it occurs, whereas all the people on the nighttime side of Earth can witness a lunar eclipse when it occurs. Why is this so?

45. Lunar eclipses are always eclipses of a full moon. That is, the moon is always seen full just before and after Earth's shadow passes over it. Why can we never have a lunar eclipse when the moon is in its crescent or half-moon phase?

46. Why do Polaroid sunglasses reduce glare, whereas unpolarized sunglasses simply cut down on the total amount of light reaching our eyes?

47. An ideal polarizing filter transmits 50% of the incident nonpolarized light. Why is this so?

48. What percentage of light would be transmitted by two ideal polarizing filters, one atop the other, with their axes aligned? With their axes crossed at right angles?

Think and Solve ······

To answer Questions 49–69, you need to know the following information.

The speed of light c is equal to the product of its wavelength λ and its frequency f.

$$c = \lambda f$$

The wavelengths of visible light range from 400 nm in the violet to 700 nm in the red.

$$1 \text{ nm} = 10^{-9} \text{ m}; \ 1 \ \mu\text{m} = 10^{-6} \text{ m}$$

49. Light with wavelength λ and frequency f in air slows to a speed v when transmitted through a piece of plastic.
   a. What is the light's frequency in the plastic?
   b. What is the light's wavelength in the plastic?

50. An atom emits violet light of wavelength 450 nm for a period of 1.0×10^{-10} seconds. Find the number of cycles the wave train contains.

51. About 150 years ago Armand Fizeau used a toothed wheel to measure the speed of light. One particular wheel had 150 teeth with 150 spaces (gaps) between them—the teeth and the gaps were of equal width. Light travels through the gap and is reflected back along its path by a mirror 8 km away. At what speed must the wheel rotate in order for the light to arrive back at the wheel and pass through the gap next to the one through which it first passed?

52. A common wavelength designation is the nanometer (nm), where 1 nm = 10^{-9} m. Express the wavelength of the red light from a helium-neon laser, 0.000000633 m, in nanometers.

53. Express the wavelength of infrared light from an argon laser, 0.00000109 m, in nanometers.

54. Laser scientists use as a rule of thumb that the laser light running around their labs covers 1 foot in a nanosecond. Verify the correctness of this rule.

55. The nearest star beyond the sun is Alpha Centauri, which is 4.2×10^{16} meters away. If we were to receive a radio message from this star today, show that it would have been sent 4.4 years ago.

56. The Hydra galaxy is moving away from Earth at 6.0×10^7 m/s. What fraction of the speed of light is this?

57. When listening to a radio station broadcasting at 101 MHz (101 million wave vibrations per second), you wonder how long the wavelength of these waves is. What is the answer, and how does it compare to your height?

58. Blue-green light has a frequency of about 6×10^{14} Hz.
   a. Using the relationship $c = \lambda f$, show that its wavelength in air is 5×10^{-7} m.
   b. How much larger is this wavelength than the diameter of an atom, which is about 10^{-10} m?

59. Some laser pointers emit light waves with a wavelength of 533 nm.
   a. What is the frequency of this light?
   b. Find the color of this light.

60. The wavelength of light emitted by a CO_2 laser is 10.6 μm. What frequency light is this, and in what part of the electromagnetic spectrum is it?

61. Atmospheric carbon dioxide strongly absorbs light in the 12.5 μm to 18 μm range. What frequency range does this correspond to, and in what part of the electromagnetic spectrum is it?

62. Solar eclipses appear as crescent-shaped spots of light on the ground beneath trees. The small openings between leaves act as pinhole cameras, casting images of the sun on the ground. Just before and after an eclipse, the spots are circular. It so happens that a spot 10 cm in diameter is cast by an opening 100 times higher. So a 10-cm spot is cast by an opening 10 m above the ground. How high above the ground is an opening that casts a spot 15 cm in diameter?

63. A satellite TV company broadcasts its signals from its earthbound broadcast station to a satellite in geosynchronous orbit 36,000 km away and from there back to Earth's surface.
   a. How much time elapses between the time the signal leaves the station and the time it is received by someone's satellite dish?
   b. Explain why the answer doesn't depend very much on exactly where the TV company and the customer are located on Earth.

64. Consider a pulse of laser light aimed at the moon that bounces back to Earth. The distance between Earth and the moon is 3.8×10^8 m.
  a. Show that the round-trip time for the light is 2.5 seconds.
  b. Why does an astronaut on the moon have to be patient in talking with Mission Control on Earth?

65. Stephen uses his cell phone to talk to Fiona, who is reading downstairs, 12 meters away. The phone signal leaves Stephen's phone, travels 6.0 km to a cell tower, and then is immediately sent to Fiona's phone. When Stephen speaks, how long does the signal take to get from his phone to Fiona's phone? How does this time compare with the time it would take for the sound to travel to Fiona if Stephen instead just yelled downstairs?

66. A light wave has wavelength λ.
  a. Write an equation for the frequency of this light.
  b. Convert the following wavelengths to frequencies in Hz: 400 nm, 500 nm, 600 nm, and 700 nm.
  c. What happens to the frequency of the light as the wavelength increases?

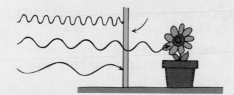

67. Linsey's favorite radio station broadcasts at a frequency f.
  a. Write an equation for the wavelength of these radio waves.
  b. What is the ratio of ceiling height h to wavelength λ for this wave?
  c. Calculate the answers for parts (a) and (b) above for a frequency of 97.3 MHz and a ceiling height of 2.4 meters.

68. At some point in its solar orbit, Mars is a distance d away from Earth.
  a. How long, in terms of distance d and the speed of light c, would it take for a radio wave sent by a video camera mounted on a Mars rover to tell people on Earth that the rover is about to go over a cliff?
  b. How long would it take for a radio signal from Earth to reach the Rover telling it to stop?
  c. Suppose that Mars is 144 million kilometers from Earth. Calculate the time that elapses between the moment the Mars rover sends a signal to Earth and the time the stop signal returns to the rover?

69. The wavelength of a particular color of visible light is λ. A thumbnail has an approximate thickness x.
  a. How many wavelengths of light thick is the thumbnail?
  b. Green light has a wavelength of about 500 nm. A thumbnail is about 0.40 mm thick. Calculate how many wavelengths thick the thumbnail is.

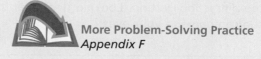

More Problem-Solving Practice
Appendix F

28 COLOR

**THE BIG IDEA** : The colors of objects depend on the color of the light that illuminates them.

Roses are red and violets are blue; colors intrigue artists and physics types, too. To the physicist, the colors of things are not in the substances of the things themselves. Color is in the eye of the beholder and is provoked by the frequencies of light emitted or reflected by things. We see red in a rose when light of certain frequencies reaches our eyes. Other frequencies will provoke the sensations of other colors. Whether or not these frequencies of light are actually perceived as colors depends on the eye–brain system. Many organisms, including people with defective color vision, see no red in a rose.

---

discover!

How Can Color Be Used To Identify Elements?

1. View an incandescent bulb through a diffraction grating and record what you see using crayons or colored pencils.

2. View a fluorescent lamp through a diffraction grating. Record your observations.

3. View a light source of your choice using the diffraction grating and record your observations. **Caution:** Never view the sun through the diffraction grating. Looking directly at the sun can damage your eyes.

Analyze and Conclude

1. **Observing** In what ways were the colors you viewed the same? In what ways were the spectra different?

2. **Predicting** Do two incandescent bulbs of different brightness have the same colors?

3. **Making Generalizations** How may color be used to identify elements found both here on Earth and in space?

28.1 The Color Spectrum

Isaac Newton, shown in Figure 28.1, was the first to make a systematic study of color. ✓ **By passing a narrow beam of sunlight through a triangular-shaped glass prism, Newton showed that sunlight is composed of a mixture of all the colors of the rainbow.** The prism cast the sunlight into an elongated patch of colors on a sheet of white paper. Newton called this spread of colors a **spectrum** and noted that the colors were formed in the order red, orange, yellow, green, blue, and violet, as shown in Figure 28.2.

Sunlight is an example of what is called white light. **White light** is a combination of all the colors. Under white light, white objects appear white and colored objects appear in their individual colors. Newton showed that the colors in the spectrum were a property not of the prism but of white light itself. He demonstrated this when he recombined the colors with a second prism to produce white light again. In other words, all the colors, one atop the other, combine to produce white light. Strictly speaking, white is not a color but a combination of all colors.

FIGURE 28.1 ▲
Newton passed sunlight through a glass prism to form the color spectrum.

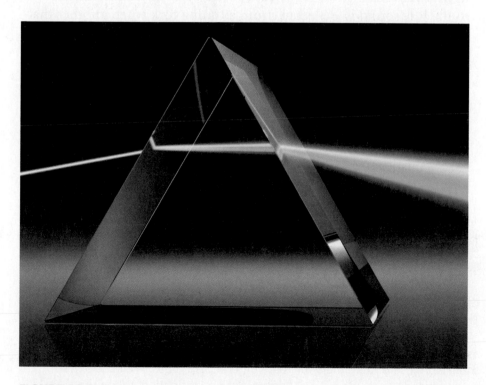

FIGURE 28.2 ▲
When sunlight passes through a prism, it separates into a spectrum of all the colors of the rainbow.

FIGURE 28.3 ▲
When a stack of razor blades bolted together is viewed end on, the edges appear black. Light that enters the wedge-shaped spaces between the blades is reflected so many times that most of it is absorbed.

Black is similarly not a color itself, but is the absence of light. Objects appear black when they absorb light of all visible frequencies. Carbon soot is an excellent absorber of light and looks very black. The dull finish of black velvet is an excellent absorber also. But even a polished surface may look black under some conditions. For example, highly polished razor blades are not black, but when stacked together and viewed end on as in Figure 28.3, they appear quite black. Most of the light that gets between the closely spaced edges of the blades gets trapped and is absorbed after being reflected many times.

Black objects that you can see do not absorb all light that falls on them, for there is always some reflection at the surface. If not, you wouldn't be able to see them.

CONCEPT CHECK : How did Isaac Newton show that sunlight is composed of a mixture of all colors of the rainbow?

28.2 Color by Reflection

The colors of most objects around you are due to the way the objects reflect light. ⊘ **The color of an opaque object is the color of the light it reflects.** Light is reflected from objects in a manner similar to the way sound is "reflected" from a tuning fork when another that is nearby sets it into vibration. A tuning fork can be made to vibrate even when the frequencies are not matched, although at significantly reduced amplitudes. The same is true of atoms and molecules. We can think of atoms and molecules as three-dimensional tuning forks with electrons that behave as tiny oscillators that whirl in orbits around the nuclei. Electrons can be forced temporarily into larger orbits by the vibrations of electromagnetic waves (such as light). Like acoustical tuning forks, once excited to more vigorous motion, electrons send out their own energy waves in all directions.

Link to ZOOLOGY

Chameleons
The chameleon can change its color to blend into its background or to suit its mood. Its skin consists of stacks of cells with red, yellow, and blue pigments, as well as brown melanin. The chameleon expands cells of one color while shrinking those of the others to create different skin hues. A chameleon's color depends on whether it is lounging, flirting, or fighting. When the chameleon is angry, melanin levels go up, masking the other colors, and the skin looks dark.

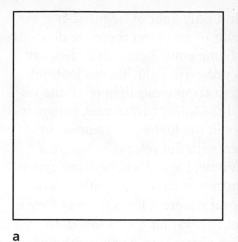

a. This square *reflects* all the colors illuminating it. In sunlight it is white. When illuminated with blue light, it is blue.
b. This square *absorbs* all the colors illuminating it. In sunlight it is warmer than the white square.

a   b

Differences Among Materials Different materials have different natural frequencies for absorbing and emitting radiation. In one material, electrons oscillate readily at certain frequencies; in another material, they oscillate readily at different frequencies. At the resonant frequencies where the amplitudes of oscillation are large, light is absorbed (recall from the previous chapter that glass absorbs ultraviolet light for this reason). But at frequencies below and above the resonant frequencies, light is reemitted. If the material is transparent, the reemitted light passes through it. If the material is opaque, the light passes back into the medium from which it came. This is reflection.

Most materials absorb light of some frequencies and reflect the rest. If a material absorbs light of most visible frequencies and reflects red, for example, the material appears red. If it reflects light of all the visible frequencies, as shown in Figure 28.4a, it will be the same color as the light that shines on it. If a material absorbs all the light that shines on it, as shown in Figure 28.4b, it reflects none and is black.

When white light falls on a flower, light of some frequencies is absorbed by the cells in the flower and some light is reflected. Cells that contain chlorophyll absorb light of most frequencies incident upon them and reflect the green part, so they appear green. The petals of a red rose, on the other hand, reflect primarily red light, with a lesser amount of blue. Interestingly enough, the petals of most yellow flowers, such as daffodils, reflect red and green as well as yellow. Yellow daffodils reflect light of a broad band of frequencies. The reflected colors of most objects are not pure single-frequency colors, but are composed of a spread of frequencies. So something yellow, for example, may simply be a mixture of colors without blue and violet—or it can be built of red and green together.

think!

When red light shines on a red rose, why do the leaves become warmer than the petals?
Answer: 28.2.1

When green light shines on a red rose, why do the petals look black?
Answer: 28.2.2

Light Sources An object can reflect only light of frequencies present in the illuminating light. The color of an object therefore depends on the kind of light used. A candle flame emits light that is deficient in the higher frequencies; it emits a yellowish light. Things look yellowish in candlelight. An incandescent lamp emits light of all the visible frequencies, but is richer toward the lower frequencies, enhancing the reds. A fluorescent lamp is richer in the higher frequencies, so blues are enhanced when illuminated with fluorescent lamps. In a fabric with a little bit of red, for example, the red will be more apparent when illuminated with an incandescent lamp than with a fluorescent lamp. Colors in daylight appear different from the way they appear when illuminated with either of these lamps, as shown in Figure 28.5. The perceived color of an object is subjective, although color differences between two objects are most easily detected in bright sunlight.

CONCEPT CHECK What determines the color of an opaque object?

28.3 Color by Transmission

⌾ **The color of a transparent object is the color of the light it transmits.** A red piece of glass appears red because it absorbs all the colors that compose white light, except red, which it transmits. The blue piece of glass in Figure 28.6 appears blue because it transmits primarily blue and absorbs the other colors that illuminate it.

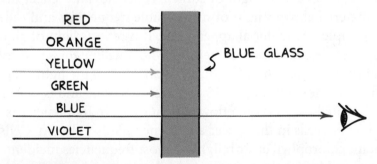

The material in the glass that selectively absorbs colored light is known as a **pigment.** From an atomic point of view, electrons in the pigment atoms selectively absorb light of certain frequencies in the illuminating light. Light of other frequencies is reemitted from atom to atom in the glass. The energy of the absorbed light increases the kinetic energy of the atoms, and the glass is warmed. Ordinary window glass is colorless because it transmits light of all visible frequencies equally well.

CONCEPT CHECK What determines the color of a transparent object?

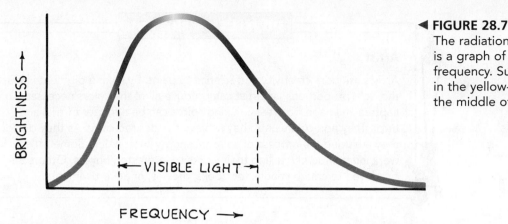

28.4 Sunlight

White light from the sun is a composite of all the visible frequencies. The brightness of solar frequencies is uneven, as indicated in the graph of brightness versus frequency in Figure 28.7. The graph indicates that the lowest frequencies of sunlight, in the red region, are not as bright as those in the middle-range yellow and green region.

✅ **Yellow-green light is the brightest part of sunlight.** Since humans evolved in the presence of sunlight, it is not surprising that we are most sensitive to yellow-green. That is why it is more and more common for new fire engines to be painted yellow-green, particularly at airports where visibility is vital. This also explains why at night we are able to see better under the illumination of yellow sodium-vapor lamps than we are under tungsten lamps of the same brightness. The blue portion of sunlight is not as bright, and the violet portion is even less bright.

The graphical distribution of brightness versus frequency in Figure 28.7 is called the *radiation curve* of sunlight. Most whites produced from reflected sunlight have this frequency distribution.

CONCEPT CHECK Which visible frequencies make up the brightest part of sunlight?

---

discover!

What is the Color of a Candle's Reflection?

1. Hold a candle flame, match flame, or any small source of white light in between you and a piece of colored glass. How many reflections do you see?

2. What is the color of the flame reflected from the front surface? From the back surface?

3. **Think** Explain why the flame's reflections are the color(s) that they are.

Artist

Artists use both creativity and science to paint. By mixing pigments in just the right proportions, an artist can produce all of the colors necessary to capture an image. To artists, mixing colors can be a matter of trial and error. They add colors until they achieve the desired color. As they do so, they are using the process of color mixing by subtraction. Some artists work independently, selling their works to interested buyers. Others are employed to create images for books, movies, or advertisements.

28.5 Mixing Colored Light

think!

What color does red light plus blue light make?
Answer: 28.5

Light of all the visible frequencies mixed together produces white. Interestingly enough, white also results from the combination of only red, green, and blue light. When a combination of only red, green, and blue light of equal brightness is overlapped on a screen, as shown in Figure 28.8, it appears white. Where red and green light alone overlap, the screen appears yellow. Red and blue light alone produce the bluish red color called *magenta.* Green and blue light alone produce the greenish blue color called *cyan.*

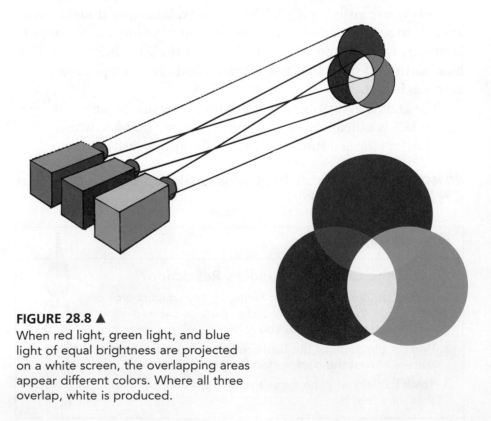

FIGURE 28.8 ▲
When red light, green light, and blue light of equal brightness are projected on a white screen, the overlapping areas appear different colors. Where all three overlap, white is produced.

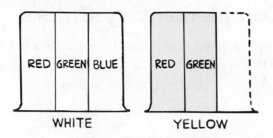

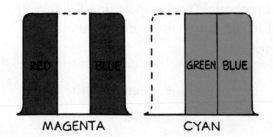

WHITE   YELLOW

MAGENTA   CYAN

◀ **FIGURE 28.9**
The low-frequency, middle-frequency, and high-frequency parts of white light appear *red, green,* and *blue.* To the human eye, red + green = yellow; red + blue = magenta; green + blue = cyan.

This can be understood if the frequencies of white light are divided into three regions as shown in Figure 28.9: the lower-frequency red end, the middle-frequency green part, and the higher-frequency blue end. The low and middle frequencies combined appear yellow to the human eye. The middle and high frequencies combined appear greenish blue (cyan). The low and high frequencies combined appear bluish red (magenta).

✅ **You can make almost any color at all by overlapping red, green, and blue light and adjusting the brightness of each color of light.** This amazing phenomenon is due to the way the human eye works. The three colors do not have to be red, green, and blue, although those three produce the highest number of different colors. For this reason red, green, and blue are called the **additive primary colors.**

Color television is based on the ability of the human eye to see combinations of three colors as a variety of different colors. A close examination of the picture on most color television tubes will reveal that the picture is made up of an assemblage of tiny spots, each less than a millimeter across. When the screen is lit, some of the spots are red, some green, and some blue. At a distance the mixtures of these colors provide a complete range of colors, plus white.[28.5]

CONCEPT CHECK : Which three visible frequencies combine to form almost any color?

Go Online
SciLINKS NSTA

For: Links on color
Visit: www.SciLinks.org
Web Code: csn – 2805

All the colors added together produce white. The absence of all color is black.

28.6 Complementary Colors

think!

What color does white light minus yellow light appear? *Answer: 28.6.1*

What color does white light minus green light appear? *Answer: 28.6.2*

What happens when two of the three additive primary colors are combined?

$$red + green = yellow$$

$$red + blue = magenta$$

$$blue + green = cyan$$

Now, a little thought and inspection of Figure 28.8 will show that when we add in the third color, we get white.

$$yellow + blue = white$$

$$magenta + green = white$$

$$cyan + red = white$$

When two colors are added together to produce white, they are called **complementary colors.** For example, we see that yellow and blue are complementary because yellow, after all, is the combination of red and green. And red, green, and blue light together appear white. By similar reasoning we see that magenta and green are complementary colors, as are cyan and red. ✓ **Every color has some complementary color that when added to it will produce white.** Figure 28.10 shows how six blocks and their shadows appear different colors under light of different colors.

FIGURE 28.10 ▼
Six blocks and their shadows appear as different colors depending on the color of light that illuminates them.

a. The blocks are lit by white light.

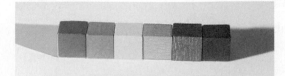

b. The blocks are lit by blue light.

c. The blocks are lit by red light from the right and green light from the left.

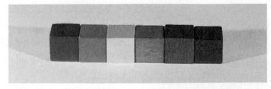

d. The blocks are lit by blue light from the left and red light from the right.

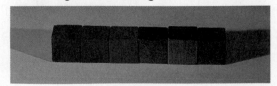

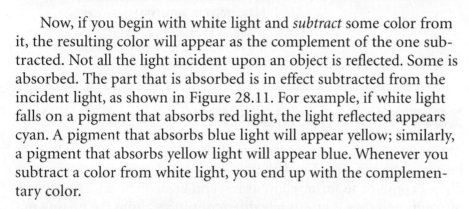
Now, if you begin with white light and *subtract* some color from it, the resulting color will appear as the complement of the one subtracted. Not all the light incident upon an object is reflected. Some is absorbed. The part that is absorbed is in effect subtracted from the incident light, as shown in Figure 28.11. For example, if white light falls on a pigment that absorbs red light, the light reflected appears cyan. A pigment that absorbs blue light will appear yellow; similarly, a pigment that absorbs yellow light will appear blue. Whenever you subtract a color from white light, you end up with the complementary color.

CONCEPT CHECK What happens when you combine any color with its complementary color?

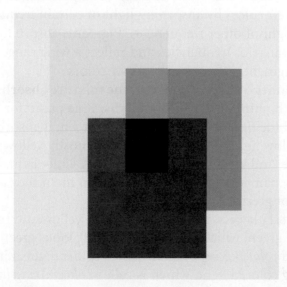

◀ **FIGURE 28.11**
When white light passes through all three transparencies, light of all frequencies is blocked (subtracted) and we have black. Where only yellow and cyan overlap, light of all frequencies except green is subtracted.

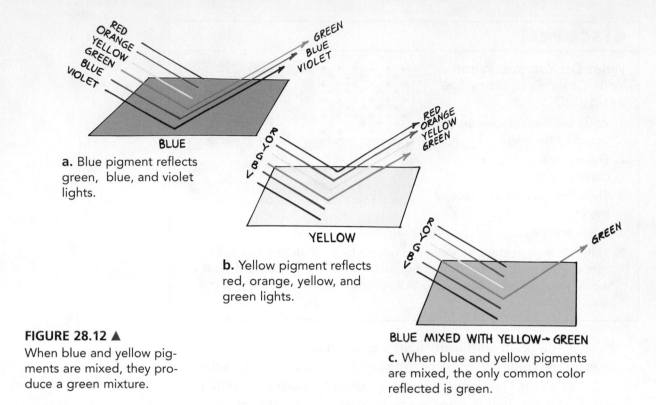

a. Blue pigment reflects green, blue, and violet lights.

b. Yellow pigment reflects red, orange, yellow, and green lights.

BLUE MIXED WITH YELLOW → GREEN

c. When blue and yellow pigments are mixed, the only common color reflected is green.

FIGURE 28.12 ▲
When blue and yellow pigments are mixed, they produce a green mixture.

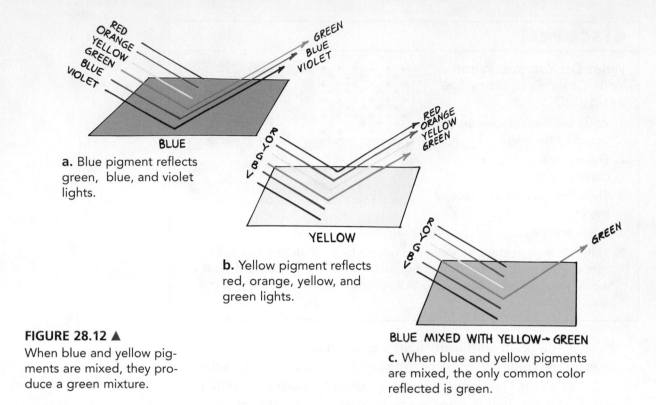

FIGURE 28.13 ▲
Sneezlee's rich colors represent many frequencies of light. The photo, however, is a mixture of only yellow, magenta, cyan, and black.

28.7 Mixing Colored Pigments

Artists know that if we mix red, green, and blue paint, the result will be not white but a muddy dark brown. Red and green paint certainly do not combine to form yellow as red and green light do. The mixing of paints and dyes is an entirely different process from the mixing of colored light.

Paints and dyes contain finely divided solid particles of pigment that produce their colors by absorbing light of certain frequencies and reflecting light of other frequencies. Pigments absorb light of a relatively wide range of frequencies and reflect a wide range as well. In this sense, pigments reflect a mixture of colors.

⊘ **When paints or dyes are mixed, the mixture absorbs all the frequencies each paint or dye in it absorbs.** Blue paint, for example, reflects mostly blue light, but also violet and green; it absorbs red, orange, and yellow light. Yellow paint reflects mostly yellow light, but also red, orange, and green; it absorbs blue and violet light. When blue and yellow paints are mixed, then between them they absorb all the colors except green.

As Figure 28.12 shows, the only color both yellow and blue pigments reflect is green, which is why the mixture looks green. This process is called *color mixing by subtraction*, to distinguish it from the effect of mixing colored light, which is called *color mixing by addition*.

So when you cast lights on the stage at a school play, you use the rules of color addition to produce various colors. But when you mix paint, you use the rules of color subtraction.

You may have learned as a child that you can make any color with paints of three so-called primary colors: red, yellow, and blue. Actually, the three paint or dye colors that are most useful in color mixing by subtraction are magenta (bluish red), yellow, and cyan (greenish blue). Magenta, yellow, and cyan are the **subtractive primary colors,** used in printing illustrations in full color.[28.7]

Table 28.1	Color Subtractions	
Pigment	Absorbs	Reflects
red	blue, green	red
green	blue, red	green
blue	red, green	blue
yellow	blue	red, green
cyan	red	green, blue
magenta	green	red, blue

Color printing is done on a press that prints each page with four differently colored inks (magenta, yellow, cyan, and black) in succession. Each color of ink comes from a different plate, which transfers the ink to the paper. The ink deposits are regulated on different parts of the plate by tiny dots. Examine the colored pictures in this book, or in any magazine, with a magnifying glass and see how the overlapping dots of three colors plus black give the appearance of many colors. Figure 28.14 shows how to reproduce a photograph.

CONCEPT CHECK: Which visible frequencies are absorbed by a mixture of paints or dyes?

a. magenta

b. yellow

c. cyan

d. magenta + yellow + cyan

e. black

f. magenta + yellow + cyan + black

FIGURE 28.14 ▲
Only four colors of ink are used to print color illustrations and photographs—magenta, yellow, cyan, and black. The addition of black produces the finished result.

28.8 Why the Sky Is Blue

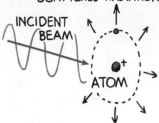

FIGURE 28.15 ▲
A beam of light falls on an atom and causes the electrons in the atom to move temporarily in larger orbits. The more vigorously oscillating electrons reemit light in various directions. Light is scattered.

If a sound beam of a particular frequency is directed to a tuning fork of similar frequency, the tuning fork will be set into vibration and effectively redirect the beam in multiple directions. The tuning fork scatters the sound. **Scattering** is a process in which sound or light is absorbed and reemitted in all directions. Figure 28.15 illustrates how an atom can scatter a beam of light. In the atmosphere, light is scattered by molecules and larger specks of matter that are far apart from one another.

The Sky We know that atoms and molecules behave like tiny optical tuning forks and reemit light waves that shine on them. Very tiny particles do the same. The tinier the particle, the higher the frequency of light it will scatter. This is similar to small bells ringing with higher notes than larger bells. The nitrogen and oxygen molecules and the tiny particles that make up the atmosphere are like tiny bells that "ring" with high frequencies when energized by sunlight. Like the sound from bells, the reemitted light is sent in all directions. It is scattered.

FIGURE 28.16 ▶
The sky is blue because its tiny particles scatter high-frequency light. The blue "sky" between the viewer and the distant mountains produces bluish mountains.

Most of the ultraviolet light from the sun is absorbed by a protective layer of ozone gas in the upper atmosphere. The remaining ultraviolet sunlight passing through the atmosphere is scattered by atmospheric particles and molecules. ☑ **The sky is blue because its component particles scatter high-frequency light.** Of the visible frequencies, violet light is scattered the most, followed by blue, green, yellow, orange, and red, in that order. Red light is scattered only a tenth as much as violet. Although violet light is scattered more than blue, our eyes are not very sensitive to violet light. Our eyes are more sensitive to blue, so we see a blue sky, as shown in Figure 28.16.

The droplets that compose a cloud come in a wide variety of sizes. Hence a wide variety of colors are scattered, which is why the cloud is white.

The blue of the sky varies in different places under different conditions. Where there are a lot of particles of dust and other particles larger than oxygen and nitrogen molecules, the lower frequencies of light are scattered more. This makes the sky less blue, and it takes on a whitish appearance. After a heavy rainstorm, when the particles have been washed away, the sky becomes a deeper blue.

The higher that one goes into the atmosphere, the fewer molecules there are in the air to scatter light. The sky appears darker. When there are no molecules, as on the moon for example, the "sky" is black.

The Clouds Water droplets in a variety of sizes—some of them microscopic—make up clouds. The different-size droplets result in a variety of frequencies for scattered light: low frequencies from larger droplets and high frequencies from tinier droplets of water molecules. The overall result is a white cloud, as shown in Figure 28.17. The electrons in a tiny droplet vibrate together and in step, which results in the scattering of a greater amount of energy than when the same number of electrons vibrate separately. Hence, clouds are bright!

Larger assortment of droplets absorb much of the light incident upon them, and so the intensity of the scattered light is less. This contributes to the darkness of clouds composed of larger droplets. Further increase in the size of the droplets causes them to fall as raindrops, and we have rain.

CONCEPT CHECK : Why is the sky blue?

There are no blue pigments in the feathers of a blue jay. Instead there are tiny alveolar cells in the barbs of its feather that scatter light—mainly high-frequency light. So a blue jay is blue for the same reason the sky is blue—scattering.

28.9 Why Sunsets Are Red

The lower frequencies of light are scattered the least by nitrogen and oxygen molecules. Therefore red, orange, and yellow light are transmitted through the atmosphere more readily than violet and blue. Red light, which is scattered the least, passes through more atmosphere without interacting with matter than light of any other color. Therefore, when light passes through a thick atmosphere, light of the lower frequencies is transmitted while light of the higher frequencies is scattered. At dawn and at sunset, sunlight reaches us through a longer path through the atmosphere than at noon.

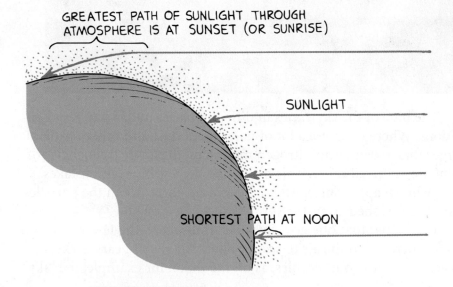

GREATEST PATH OF SUNLIGHT THROUGH ATMOSPHERE IS AT SUNSET (OR SUNRISE)

SUNLIGHT

SHORTEST PATH AT NOON

FIGURE 28.18 ▲
By the time a beam of sunlight gets to the ground at sunset, only the lower frequencies survive, producing a red sunset.

At noon sunlight travels through the least amount of atmosphere to reach Earth's surface, as shown in Figure 28.18. Then a relatively small amount of light is scattered from sunlight. As the day progresses and the sun is lower in the sky, the path through the atmosphere is longer, and more blue is scattered from the sunlight. Less and less blue remains in the sunlight that reaches Earth. The sun appears progressively redder, going from yellow to orange. **By the time a beam of light gets to the ground at sunset, all of the high-frequency light has already been scattered. Only the lower frequencies remain, resulting in a red sunset.** (The sequence is reversed between dawn and noon.)

The colors of the sun and sky are consistent with our rules for color mixing. When blue is subtracted from white light, the complementary color that is left is yellow. The subtraction of violet leaves orange. When green is subtracted, magenta is left. The relative amounts of scattering depend on atmospheric conditions, which change from day to day and give us a variety of sunsets.

The next time you find yourself admiring a crisp blue sky, or delighting in the shapes of bright clouds, or watching a beautiful sunset, such as the one shown in Figure 28.19, think about all those ultra-tiny optical tuning forks vibrating; you'll appreciate these everyday wonders of nature even more!

Why do you see the scattered blue when the background is dark, but not when the background is bright? Because the scattered blue is faint. A faint color will show itself against a dark background, but not against a bright background. For example, when you look from Earth's surface at the atmosphere against the darkness of space, the atmosphere is sky blue. But astronauts above who look below through the same atmosphere to the bright surface of Earth do not see the same blueness.

Isn't it true that knowing why the sky is blue and why sunsets are red *adds* to their beauty? Knowledge doesn't subtract.

CONCEPT CHECK Why are sunsets red?

think!

If molecules in the sky scattered low-frequency light more than high-frequency light, how would the colors of the sky and sunsets appear?
Answer: 28.9.1

Distant dark mountains are bluish in color. What is the source of this blueness? (Hint: What is between you and the mountains you see?)
Answer: 28.9.2

28.10 Why Water Is Greenish Blue

We often see a beautiful deep blue when we look at the surface of a lake or the ocean, as shown in Figure 28.20. But that is not the color of water. It is the reflected color of the sky. The color of water itself, as you can see by looking at a piece of white material under water, is a pale greenish blue.

FIGURE 28.20 ▶
Ocean water is cyan because it absorbs red. The froth in the waves is white because its droplets of many sizes scatter many colors.

Water is transparent to nearly all the visible frequencies of light. Water molecules absorb infrared waves because they resonate to the frequencies of infrared. The energy of the infrared waves is transformed into kinetic energy of the water molecules. Infrared is a strong component of the sunlight that warms water.

Water molecules resonate somewhat to the visible-red frequencies. This causes a gradual absorption of red light by water. A 15-m layer of water reduces red light to a quarter of its initial brightness. There is very little red light in the sunlight that penetrates below 30 m of water. When red is taken away from white light, what color remains? This question can be asked in another way: What is the complementary color of red? The complementary color of red is cyan—a greenish blue color. In seawater, the color of everything at these depths looks greenish blue.

It is interesting to note that many crabs and other sea animals that appear black in deep water are found to be red when they are raised to the surface. At great depths, black and red look the same. So both black and red sea animals are hardly seen by predators and prey in deep water. They have survived an evolutionary history while more visible varieties have not.

think!

Distant snow-covered mountains reflect a lot of light and are bright. But they sometimes look yellowish, depending on how far away they are. Why are they yellow? (*Hint:* What happens to the reflected white light as it travels from the mountain to you?) *Answer: 28.9.3*

In summary, the sky is blue because blue from sunlight is reemitted in all directions by molecules in the atmosphere. ☑ **Water is greenish blue because water molecules absorb red.** The colors of things depend on what colors are reflected by molecules, and also by what colors are absorbed by molecules.

CONCEPT CHECK Why is water greenish blue?

28.11 The Atomic Color Code— Atomic Spectra

When made to emit light, every element has its own characteristic color. The color is a blend of various frequencies of light. Light of each frequency is emitted when the electrons in an atom change energy states. These energy states are related to the orbits of electrons in the atom. Electrons surrounding the atomic nucleus have well-defined orbits. Another way of saying this is they have well-defined energy levels—lower energy near the atomic nucleus and higher energy farther from the nucleus. When an atom absorbs external energy, one or more of its electrons is boosted to a higher energy level. We say such an energized atom is in an excited state. An **excited state** is a state with greater energy than the atom's lowest energy state. The excited stage is only momentary, for the electron is quickly drawn back to its original or a lower level. When this electron transition occurs, the atom emits a throbbing pulse of light—a photon. Figures 28.21 and 28.22 model this process. ☑ **After an excited atom emits light, it returns to its normal state.**

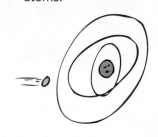

FIGURE 28.21 ▼
Light is emitted by excited atoms.

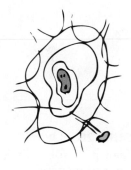

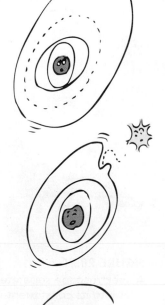

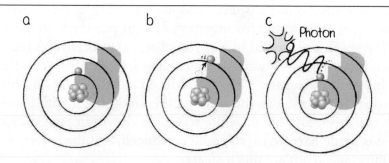

FIGURE 28.22 ▲
a. The different electron orbits in an atom are like steps in energy levels. **b.** When an electron is raised to a higher level, the atom is excited. **c.** When the electron returns to its original level, it releases energy in the form of light.

Relating Frequency and Energy The frequency of the emitted photon, or its color, is directly proportional to the energy transition of the electron. In shorthand notation,[28.11.1]

$$f \sim E$$

A photon carries an amount of energy that corresponds to its frequency. Red light from neon gas, for example, carries a certain amount of energy. A photon of twice the frequency has twice as much energy and is found in the ultraviolet part of the spectrum. When many atoms in a material are excited, many photons with many different frequencies are emitted, all corresponding to transitions of electrons between many different levels.

So measuring the frequencies of light in a spectrum is also measuring the relative energy levels in the atom emitting that light. Hence, the frequencies, or colors, of light emitted by elements are the "fingerprints" of the elements.

FIGURE 28.23 ▶

A fairly pure spectrum is produced by passing white light through a thin slit, two lenses, and a prism.

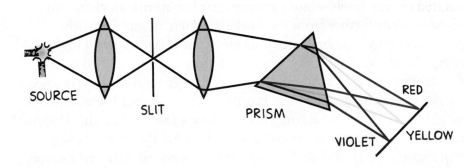

Analyzing Light The light from glowing elements can be analyzed with an instrument called a **spectroscope.** This chapter began with a brief account of Newton's investigation of light passing through a prism. The spectrum formed in Newton's first experiment was blurry because it was formed by overlapping circular images of the circular hole in his window shutter. He later produced a better spectrum by first passing light through a thin slit and then focusing it with lenses through the prism and onto a white screen, as shown in Figure 28.23. If the slit is made narrow, overlapping is reduced, and the colors in the resulting spectrum are much clearer.

FIGURE 28.24 ▲

A spectroscope separates light into its constituent frequencies. Light illuminates the thin slit at the left, and then it is focused by lenses onto either a diffraction grating (shown) or a prism on the rotating table in the middle.

This arrangement of thin slit, lenses, and a prism (or a diffraction grating) is the basis for the spectroscope.[28.11.2] A simple spectroscope with a diffraction grating is shown in Figure 28.24. A spectroscope displays the spectra of the light from hot gases and other light sources. (*Spectra* is the plural of *spectrum*.) The spectra of light sources are viewed through a magnifying eyepiece.

a. sunlight

b. hydrogen

c. sodium

d. mercury

FIGURE 28.25 ▲
a. Sunlight has a continuous spectrum. Each of the three elements **b.** hydrogen, **c.** sodium, and **d.** mercury has a different line spectrum.

When light from a glowing element is analyzed through a spectroscope, it is found that the colors are the composite of a variety of different frequencies of light. The spectrum of an element appears not as a continuous band of color but as a series of lines, as shown in Figure 28.25. Such a spectrum is known as a line spectrum. A **line spectrum** is a pattern of distinct lines of color, with each line corresponding to a frequency of light. The spectral lines seen in the spectroscope are images of the slit through which the light passes. Note that each colored line appears in the same position as that color in the continuous spectrum. A clear spectrum is produced when atoms are made to glow in the gaseous phase. In the solid phase, as in a lamp filament, where atoms are crowded together, the characteristic colors of the atoms are smudged to produce a continuous spectrum.

Much of the information that physicists have about atomic structure is from the study of atomic spectra. The atomic composition of common materials, the sun, and distant galaxies is revealed in the spectra of these sources. Even the element helium, the second most common element in the universe, was discovered through its "fingerprint" in sunlight. The spectrometer is a very useful and powerful tool.

CONCEPT CHECK : What happens to an excited atom after it emits light?

Most elements found on Earth, and even organic molecules, complex and simple, are found in spectra of interstellar gases.

28 REVIEW

Go Online
PHSchool.com

For: Self-Assessment
Visit: PHSchool.com
Web Code: csa – 2800

Concept Summary ......

- Sunlight is composed of a mixture of all the colors of the rainbow.

- The color of an opaque object is the color of light it reflects.

- The color of a transparent object is the color of the light it transmits.

- Yellow-green light is the brightest part of sunlight.

- You can make almost any color at all by overlapping red, green, and blue light and adjusting the brightnesses.

- Every color has a complementary color that when added to it will produce white.

- When paints or dyes are mixed, the mixture absorbs all the frequencies each paint or dye in it absorbs.

- The sky is blue because its component particles scatter high-frequency light.

- A beam of light at sunset contains only the lower frequencies, resulting in a red sunset.

- Water is greenish blue because water molecules absorb red.

- After an excited atom emits light, it returns to its normal state.

think! Answers

28.2.1 The leaves absorb rather than reflect red light, so the leaves become warmer.

28.2.2 The petals absorb rather than reflect the green light. So, the rose appears to have no color at all—black.

28.5 Magenta

28.6.1 Blue

28.6.2 Magenta

28.9.1 If low frequencies were scattered more, red light would be scattered out of the sunlight on its long path through the atmosphere at sunset, and the sunlight to reach your eye would be predominantly blue and violet.

28.9.2 If you look at distant dark mountains, very little light from them reaches you, and the blueness of the atmosphere between you and the mountains predominates. The blueness is of the low-altitude "sky" between you and the mountains.

28.9.3 Distant snow-covered mountains often appear a pale yellow because the blue in the white light from the snowy mountains is scattered on its way to you. The complementary color left is yellow.

Key Terms ......

spectrum *(p. 555)*

white light *(p. 555)*

pigment *(p. 558)*

additive primary colors *(p. 561)*

complementary colors *(p. 562)*

subtractive primary colors *(p. 565)*

scattering *(p. 566)*

excited state *(p. 571)*

spectroscope *(p. 572)*

line spectrum *(p. 573)*

ASSESS

Check Concepts ......

Section 28.1

1. List the order of colors in the color spectrum.

2. Are black and white real colors, in the sense that red and green are? Explain.

Section 28.2

3. What is emitted by the vibrating electrons of atoms?

4. What happens to light of a certain frequency that encounters atoms of the same resonant frequency?

5. Why does the color of an object look different under a fluorescent lamp from the way it looks under an incandescent lamp?

Section 28.3

6. a. What color(s) of light does a transparent red object *transmit*?
   b. What color(s) does it *absorb*?

7. What is the function of a pigment?

Section 28.4

8. Why are more and more fire engines being painted yellow-green instead of red?

Section 28.5

9. How can yellow be produced on a screen if only red light and green light are available?

10. What is the name of the color produced by a mixture of green and blue light?

11. What colors of spots are lit on a television tube to give full color?

Section 28.6

12. What are complementary colors?

13. What color is the complement of blue?

Section 28.7

14. The process of producing a color by mixing pigments is called color *mixing by subtraction*. Why do we say "subtraction" instead of "addition" in this case?

15. What colors of ink are used to print full-color pictures in books and magazines?

Section 28.8

16. What is light scattering?

17. Do tiny particles in the air scatter high or low frequencies of light?

18. Why is the sky blue?

19. Why are clouds white?

Section 28.9

20. Why are sunsets red?

Section 28.10

21. Why is water greenish blue?

Section 28.11

22. What is the function of a spectroscope?

23. Does the red light from glowing neon gas have only one frequency or a mixture of frequencies?

24. Why might atomic spectra be considered the "fingerprints" of atoms?

Think and Explain ......

25. What is the color of tennis balls and why?

26. Why are the interiors of optical instruments painted black?

27. On a TV screen, what dots are activated to produce yellow? Magenta? White?

28. Suppose two beams of white light are shone on a white screen, one beam through a pane of red glass and the other through a pane of green glass. What color appears on the screen where the two beams overlap? What occurs if instead the two panes of glass are placed in the path of a single beam?

29. In a dress shop that has only fluorescent lighting, a customer insists on taking a garment into the daylight at the doorway. Is she being reasonable? Explain.

30. What color would a yellow cloth appear to have if illuminated with sunlight? With yellow light? With blue light?

31. A spotlight is coated so that it won't transmit blue from its white-hot filament. What color is the emerging beam of light?

32. How could you use the spotlights at a play to make the yellow clothes of the performers suddenly change to black?

33. A stage performer stands where beams of red and green light cross.
    a. What is the color of her white shirt under this illumination?
    b. What are the colors of the shadows she casts on the stage floor?

34. What colors of ink do color ink-jet printers use to produce the colors you see?

35. On a photographic print, your dearest friend is seen wearing a red sweater. What color is the sweater on the negative?

36. Your friend says that red and cyan light produce white light because cyan is green + blue, and so red + green + blue = white. Do you agree or disagree, and why?

37. In which of these cases will a ripe banana appear black: when illuminated with red, yellow, green, or blue light?

38. When white light is shone on red ink dried on a glass plate, the color that is transmitted is red. What is the color that is reflected?

39. Why can't we see a laser beam going across the room unless there is fog, chalk dust, or a mist in the air?

40. Very big particles, such as droplets of water, absorb more radiation than they scatter. How does this fact help to explain why rain clouds appear dark?

41. If the sky on a certain planet in the solar system were normally orange, what color would sunsets be?

42. What causes the beautiful colors seen in the burning of materials in a fireplace?

43. What is the evidence for the claim that iron exists in the atmosphere of the sun?

44. The only light to reach very far beneath the surface of the ocean is greenish blue. Objects at these depths either reflect greenish blue or reflect no color at all. If a ship that is painted red, green, and white sinks to the bottom of the ocean, how will these colors appear?

45. A lamp filament is made of tungsten. When made to glow, it emits a continuous spectrum—all the colors of the rainbow. When tungsten gas is made to glow, however, the light is a composite of very discrete colors. Why is there a difference in spectra?

46. If we double the frequency of light, we double the energy of each of its photons. If we instead double the wavelength of light, what happens to the photon energy?

47. We can heat a piece of metal to red hot, and to white hot. Can we heat it until the metal glows blue hot?

48. We see a "green-hot" star not green, but white. Why? (*Hint:* Consider the width of the radiation curve in Figure 28.7.)

49. If you see a red-hot star, you can be certain that its peak intensity is in the infrared region. Why is this? And if you see a "violet-hot" star, you can be certain its peak intensity is in the ultraviolet range. Why is this?

Activities ••••••

50. If you have a computer with a color monitor and a color-controlled program available, try the following. Add full-strength red and full-strength green. Note that you produce yellow. Add about two-thirds strength blue and you get a lighter (not darker) yellow. Try full-strength red, blue, and green, and you get white. Can you see that the more light you shed on something, the brighter (that is, closer to white) it gets?

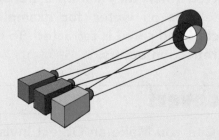

51. Simulate your own sunset: Add a few drops of milk to a glass of water and look through it to a lit incandescent bulb. The bulb appears to be red or pale orange, while light scattered to the side appears blue. Explain why this happens.

29 REFLECTION AND REFRACTION

THE BIG IDEA : When waves interact with matter, they can be reflected, transmitted, or a combination of both. Waves that are transmitted can be refracted.

When you shine a beam of light on a mirror, the light doesn't travel through the mirror, but is returned by the mirror's surface back into the air. When sound waves strike a canyon wall, they bounce back to you as an echo. When a wave transmitted along a spring reaches a wall, it reverses direction. In all these situations, waves remain in one medium rather than enter a new medium. These waves are *reflected*.

In other situations, such as when light passes from air into a transparent medium like water, waves travel from one medium into another. When waves strike the surface of a medium at an angle, their direction changes as they enter the second medium. These waves are *refracted*. This is evident when a pencil in a glass of water appears to be bent.

Usually waves are partly reflected and partly refracted when they fall on a transparent medium. When light shines on water, for example, some of the light is reflected and some is refracted. To understand this, let's see how reflection occurs.

discover!

How Can You Make an Object Invisible?

1. Obtain two small heat-resistant beakers, one smaller than the other.
2. Place the smaller beaker inside the larger beaker.
3. Pour light vegetable oil or baby oil into both beakers until the smaller beaker is completely submerged.

Analyze and Conclude

1. **Observing** What did you observe when the oil filled both beakers?
2. **Predicting** Do you think you would observe the same results if the beakers were filled with other clear liquids?
3. **Making Generalizations** What makes an object visible?

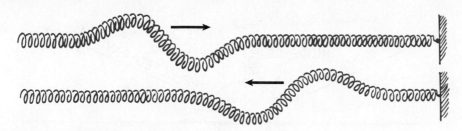

29.1 Reflection

☑ **When a wave reaches a boundary between two media, usually some or all of the wave bounces back into the first medium.** The return of a wave back into its original medium is called **reflection.** Suppose you fasten a spring to a wall and send a pulse along the spring's length, as illustrated in Figure 29.1. The wall is a very rigid medium compared with the spring. As a result, all the wave energy is reflected back along the spring rather than transmitted into the wall. Waves that travel along the spring are almost *totally reflected* at the wall.

If the wall is replaced with a less rigid medium, such as the heavy spring shown in Figure 29.2, some energy is transmitted into the new medium. Some of the wave energy is still reflected. The incoming wave is *partially reflected.*

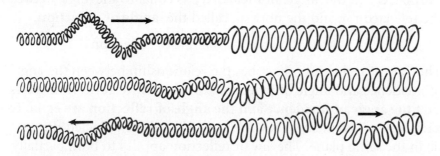

◀ **FIGURE 29.2**
When the wave reaches the heavy spring, it is partially reflected and partially transmitted.

A metal surface is rigid to light waves that shine upon it. Light energy does not propagate into the metal, but instead is returned in a reflected wave. The wave reflected from a metal surface has almost the full intensity of the incoming wave, apart from small energy losses due to the friction of the vibrating electrons in the surface. This is why metals such as silver and aluminum are so shiny. They reflect almost all the frequencies of visible light.

Other materials such as glass and water are not as rigid to light waves. When light shines perpendicularly on the surface of still water, about 2% of its energy is reflected and the rest is transmitted. When light strikes glass perpendicularly, about 4% of its energy is reflected. Except for slight losses, the rest is transmitted.

For: Links on reflection
Visit: www.SciLinks.org
Web Code: csn – 2901

CONCEPT : What happens when a wave reaches a boundary
CHECK : between two media?

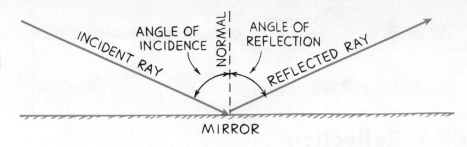

FIGURE 29.3 ▶

In reflection, the angle between the incident ray and the normal is equal to the angle between the reflected ray and the normal.

29.2 The Law of Reflection

In one dimension, reflected waves travel back in the direction from which they came. Let a ball drop to the floor, and it bounces straight up along its initial path. In two dimensions, the situation is a little different. A pool ball hitting the side of a pool table at an angle bounces back at the same angle in a new direction. Likewise with light.

The direction of incident and reflected waves is best described by straight-line *rays*. Incident rays and reflected rays make equal angles with a line perpendicular to the surface, called the **normal,** as shown in Figure 29.3. The angle between the incident ray and the normal, called the **angle of incidence,** is equal to the angle between the reflected ray and the normal, called the **angle of reflection.**

$$\text{angle of incidence} = \text{angle of reflection}$$

The **law of reflection** describes the relationship between the angle of incidence and angle of reflection. ✅ **The law of reflection states that the angle of incidence and the angle of reflection are equal to each other.** The incident ray, the normal, and the reflected ray all lie in the same plane. The law of reflection applies to both partially reflected and totally reflected waves.

CONCEPT CHECK ⦂ What is the law of reflection?

think!

If you look at your blue shirt in a mirror, what is the color of its image? What does this tell you about the frequency of light incident upon a mirror compared with the frequency of the light after it is reflected?
Answer: 29.2

29.3 Mirrors

Consider a candle flame placed in front of a plane (flat) mirror. Rays of light leaving the candle are reflected from the mirror surface in all directions. The number of rays is infinite, and every one obeys the law of reflection. Figure 29.4 shows only two rays that originate at the tip of the candle flame and reflect from the mirror to your eye. Note that the rays diverge (spread apart) from the tip of the flame, and continue diverging from the mirror upon reflection. These divergent rays *appear* to originate from a point located behind the mirror.

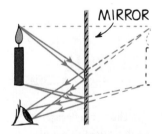

FIGURE 29.4 ▲

A virtual image is formed behind the plane mirror and is located at the position where the extended reflected rays (broken lines) converge.

Your experience is that light travels in straight lines. Therefore, you perceive the candle flame to be located behind the mirror. A **virtual image** is an image that appears to be in a location where light does not really reach. ✅ **Plane mirrors produce only virtual images.**

Your eye cannot ordinarily tell the difference between an object and its virtual image because the light that enters your eye is entering in exactly the same manner as it would without the mirror if there really were an object where you see the image. Notice that the image is as far behind the mirror as the object is in front of the mirror, and the image and object are the same size. As illustrated in Figure 29.5, when you view yourself in a mirror, your image is the same size your identical twin would appear if located as far behind the mirror as you are in front— as long as the mirror is flat.

Note in Figure 29.6a that Marjorie and her image have the same color of clothing—evidence that the light doesn't change frequency upon reflection. Interestingly, her left-right axis is no more reversed than her up-down axis. The axis that is reversed, as shown in Figure 29.6b is front-back. That's why it seems her left hand faces the right hand of her image.

FIGURE 29.5 ▼
For reflection in a plane mirror, object size equals image size and object distance equals image distance.

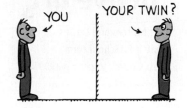

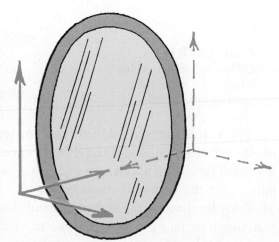

◄ FIGURE 29.6
a. Marjorie's image is as far behind the mirror as she is in front. **b.** Her front-back axis is the only axis that is reversed.

a   b

FIGURE 29.7 ▶
The law of reflection
holds for curved mirrors.
a. The image formed
by a convex mirror is
smaller than the object.
b. When the object is
close to a concave
mirror, the image can be
larger than the object.

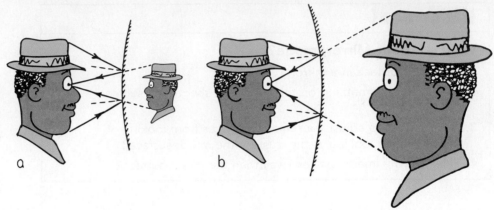

a

b

Go Online
active art

For: Mirrors and Lenses
Visit: PHSchool.com
Web Code: csp – 2903

The law of reflection still holds for curved mirrors, as illustrated in Figure 29.7. However, when the mirror is curved, the sizes and distances of object and image are no longer equal. The virtual image formed by a *convex* mirror (a mirror that curves outward) is smaller and closer to the mirror than the object is. When the object is close to a *concave* mirror (a mirror that curves inward like a "cave"), the virtual image can be larger and more distant than the object.

CONCEPT CHECK : What kind of images do mirrors produce?

29.4 Diffuse Reflection

☑ **When light is incident on a rough surface, it is reflected in many directions. Diffuse reflection,** as shown in Figure 29.8, is the reflection of light from a rough surface. Although each ray obeys the law of reflection, the many different angles that incident light rays encounter at the surface cause reflection in many directions.

FIGURE 29.8 ▶
Diffuse reflection occurs
when light is incident
on a rough surface.

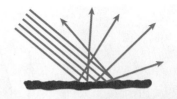

What constitutes a rough surface for some rays may be a polished surface for others. If the differences in elevations in a surface are small (less than about one-eighth the wavelength of the light that falls on it), the surface is considered polished. A surface may be polished for long wavelengths, but not polished for short wavelengths. Whether a surface is a diffuse reflector or a polished reflector depends on the wavelength of the waves it reflects.

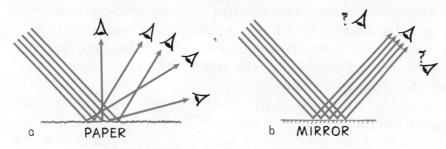

FIGURE 29.9 ▲
Diffuse reflection allows us to see most things around us. **a.** Light is diffusely reflected from paper in many directions. **b.** Light incident on a smooth mirror is only reflected in one direction.

Light that reflects from this page is diffuse. The page may be smooth to a long radio wave, but to the short wavelengths of visible light, it is rough. Rays of light incident on this page encounter millions of tiny flat surfaces facing in all directions, so they are reflected in all directions, as illustrated in Figure 29.9. A microscopic view of an ordinary paper surface is shown in Figure 29.10. Diffuse reflection allows us to read the page from any direction or position. We see most of the things around us by diffuse reflection.

CONCEPT CHECK: What happens when light is incident on a rough surface?

FIGURE 29.10 ▲
Ordinary paper, like this textbook page, has a rough surface that can be viewed with a microscope.

29.5 Reflection of Sound

An echo is reflected sound. The fraction of sound energy reflected from a surface is more when the surface is rigid and smooth, and less when the surface is soft and irregular. ☑ **Sound energy that is not reflected is absorbed or transmitted.**

Sound reflects from all surfaces—the walls, ceiling, floor, furniture, and people—of a room. People who design the interiors of buildings, whether office buildings, factories, or auditoriums, need to understand the reflective properties of surfaces. The study of sound is called *acoustics*.

When the walls of a room, auditorium, or concert hall are too reflective, the sound becomes garbled. This is due to multiple reflections of sound waves called **reverberations.** But when the reflective surfaces are more absorbent, the sound level is lower, and the hall sounds dull and lifeless. Reflection of sound in a room makes it sound lively and full, as you have probably found out while singing in the shower. In the design of an auditorium or concert hall, a balance between reverberation and absorption is desired.

The walls of concert halls are often designed with grooves so that the sound waves are diffused. This is illustrated in Figure 29.11a. In this way a person in the audience receives a small amount of reflected sound from many parts of the wall, rather than a larger amount of sound from one part of the wall.

Highly reflective surfaces are often placed behind and above the stage to direct sound out to an audience. The large shiny plastic plates in Figure 29.12 also reflect light. A listener can look up at these reflectors and see the reflected images of the members of the orchestra. (The plastic reflectors are somewhat curved, which increases the field of view.) Both sound and light obey the same law of reflection, so if a reflector is oriented so that you can *see* a particular musical instrument, rest assured that you will *hear* it also. Sound from the instrument will follow the line of sight to the reflector and then to you.

CONCEPT CHECK **What happens to sound energy that is not reflected?**

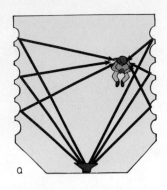
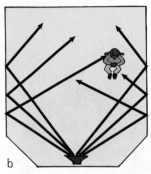

FIGURE 29.11 ▲
The walls of a concert hall are carefully designed.
a. With grooved walls, sound reflects from many small sections of the wall to a listener.
b. With flat walls, an intense reflected sound comes from only one part of the wall.

◄ FIGURE 29.12
The shiny plates above the orchestra in Davies Symphony Hall in San Francisco reflect both light and sound.

Go Online
SciLINKS NSTA

For: Links on refraction
Visit: www.SciLinks.org
Web Code: csn – 2906

29.6 Refraction

Suppose you take a rear axle with its wheels attached off an old toy cart and let it roll along a pavement that slopes gently downward and onto a downward-sloping mowed lawn. It rolls more slowly on the lawn because of the interaction of the wheels with the blades of grass. If you roll it at an angle, as shown in Figure 29.13, it will be deflected from its straight-line course. The direction of the axle and rolling wheels is shown in the illustration. Note that the wheel that first meets the lawn slows down first—because it interacts with the grass while the opposite wheel is still rolling on the pavement. The axle pivots, and the path bends toward the normal (the thin dashed line perpendicular to the grass-pavement boundary). The axle then continues across the lawn in a straight line at reduced speed.

☑ **When a wave that is traveling at an angle changes its speed upon crossing a boundary between two media, it bends.** Water waves bend, or refract, when one part of each wave is made to travel slower (or faster) than another part. **Refraction** is the bending of a wave as it crosses the boundary between two media at an angle. Water waves travel faster in deep water than in shallow water. Figure 29.14a shows a view from above of straight wave crests (the bright lines) moving toward the right edge of the photo. They are moving from deep water across a diagonal boundary into shallow water. At the boundary, the wave speed and direction of travel are abruptly altered. Since the wave moves more slowly in shallow water, the crests are closer together. If you look carefully, you'll see some reflection from the boundary.

In drawing a diagram of a wave, it is convenient to draw lines, called **wave fronts**, [29.6] that represent the positions of different crests. At each point along a wave front, the wave is moving perpendicular to the wave front. The direction of motion of the wave can thus be represented by rays that are perpendicular to the wave fronts. The ray in Figure 29.14b shows how the water wave changes direction after it crosses the boundary between deep and shallow water. Sometimes we analyze waves in terms of wave fronts, and at other times in terms of rays. Both are useful models for understanding wave behavior.

CONCEPT CHECK : What causes a wave to bend?

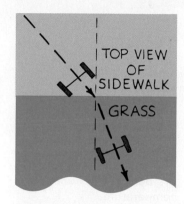

FIGURE 29.13 ▲
The direction of the rolling wheels changes when one wheel slows down before the other one.

Although wave speed and wavelength change when undergoing refraction, frequency remains unchanged.

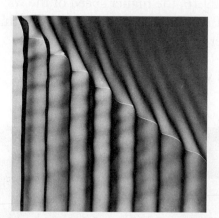

a

b

FIGURE 29.14 ▲
Water waves travel faster in deep water than in shallow water. **a.** The wave refracts at the boundary where the depth changes. **b.** The sample ray is perpendicular to the wave front it intersects.

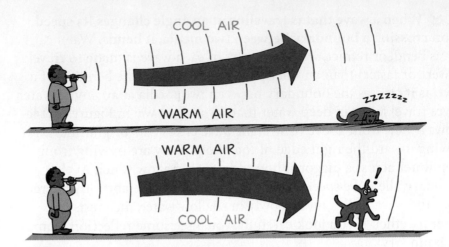

FIGURE 29.15 ▶
The wave fronts of sound are bent in air of uneven temperature.

29.7 Refraction of Sound

⊘ **Sound waves are refracted when parts of a wave front travel at different speeds.** This happens in uneven winds or when sound is traveling through air of uneven temperature. On a warm day the air near the ground may be appreciably warmer than the air above. Since sound travels faster in warmer air, the speed of sound near the ground is increased. The refraction is not abrupt but gradual, as shown in Figure 29.15. Sound waves therefore tend to bend away from warm ground, making it appear that the sound does not carry well.

On a cold day or at night, when the layer of air near the ground is colder than the air above, the speed of sound near the ground is reduced. As illustrated in Figure 29.16, the higher speed of the wave fronts above cause a bending of the sound toward Earth. When this happens, sound can be heard over considerably longer distances.

CONCEPT CHECK What causes sound waves to refract?

think!

Suppose you are downwind from a factory whistle. In which case will the whistle sound louder—if the wind speed near the ground is more than the wind speed several meters above the ground, or if it is less?
Answer: 29.7

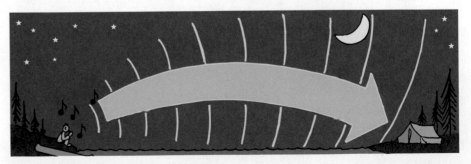

FIGURE 29.16 ▲
At night, when the air is cooler over the surface of the lake, sound is refracted toward the ground and carries unusually well.

29.8 Refraction of Light

Ponds or swimming pools appear shallower than they actually are. A pencil in a glass of water appears bent, the air above a hot stove seems to shimmer, and stars twinkle. These effects are due to the refraction of light. ☑ **Changes in the speed of light as it passes from one medium to another, or variations in the temperatures and densities of the same medium, cause refraction**. The directions of the light rays change because of refraction.[29.8]

Figure 29.17 shows rays and wave fronts of light refracted as they pass from air into water. (The wave fronts would be curved if the source of light were close, just as the wave fronts of water waves near a stone thrown into the water are curved. If we assume that the source of light is the sun, then it is so far away that the wave fronts are practically straight lines.) Note that the left portions of the wave fronts are the first to slow down when they enter the water (or right portion if you look along the direction of travel). The refracted ray of light, which is at right angles to the refracted wave fronts, is closer to the normal than is the incident ray.

Compare the refraction in this case to the bending of the axle's path in Figure 29.13. When light rays enter a medium in which their speed decreases, as when passing from air into water, the rays bend toward the normal. But when light rays enter a medium in which their speed increases, as when passing from water into air, the rays bend away from the normal.

Figure 29.18 shows a laser beam entering a container of water at the left and exiting at the right. The path would be the same if the light entered from the right and exited at the left. The light paths are reversible for both reflection and refraction. If you can see somebody by way of a reflective or refractive device, such as a mirror or a prism, then that person can see you (or your eyes) by looking through the device also.

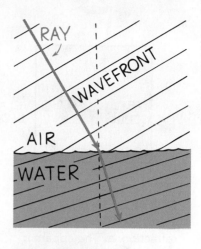

FIGURE 29.17 ▲
As a light wave passes from air into water, its speed decreases.

A light ray is always at right angles to its wave front.

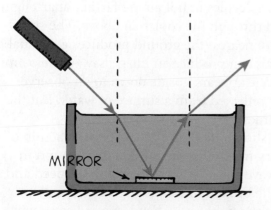

◄ **FIGURE 29.18**
The laser beam bends toward the normal when it enters the water, and away from the normal when it leaves.

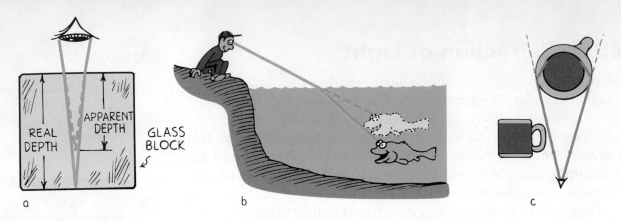

a
REAL DEPTH
APPARENT DEPTH
GLASS BLOCK

b

c

FIGURE 29.19 ▲
There are many effects of refraction. **a.** The apparent depth of the glass block is less than the real depth. **b.** The fish appears to be nearer than it actually is. **c.** The full glass mug appears to hold more root beer than it actually does.

As Figure 29.19a shows, a thick pane of glass appears to be only two-thirds its real thickness when viewed straight on. (For clarity, the diameter of the eye pupil is made larger than true scale.) Similarly, water in a pond or pool appears to be only three-quarters its true depth. In Figure 29.19b, the fish in the water appears to be nearer to the surface than it really is. It also seems closer. Another illusion is shown in Figure 29.19c. Light from the root beer is refracted through the sides of the thick glass, making the glass appear thinner than it is. The eye, accustomed to perceiving light traveling along straight lines, perceives the root beer to be at the outer edge of the glass, along the broken lines. These effects are due to the refraction of light whenever it crosses a boundary between air and another transparent medium.

CONCEPT CHECK : What causes the refraction of light?

29.9 Atmospheric Refraction

Although the speed of light in air is only 0.03% less than its speed in a vacuum, in some situations atmospheric refraction is quite noticeable. One interesting example is the appearance of a distorted image called a **mirage**. ⊘ **A mirage is caused by the refraction of light in Earth's atmosphere.** On hot days there may be a layer of very hot air in contact with the ground. Since molecules in hot air are farther apart, light travels faster through it than through the cooler air above. The speeding up of the part of the wave nearest the ground produces a gradual bending of the light rays. This can produce an image, say, of the palm tree in Figure 29.20. The image appears upside down to an observer at the right, just as if it were reflected from a surface of water. But the light is not reflected; it is refracted.

Wave fronts of light are shown in Figure 29.21. The refraction of light in air in this case is very much like the refraction of sound in Figure 29.15. Undeflected wave fronts would travel at one speed and in the direction shown by the broken lines. Their greater speed near the ground, however, causes the light ray to bend upward as shown.

think!

If the speed of light were the same for the various temperatures and densities of air, would there still be mirages?
Answer: 29.9

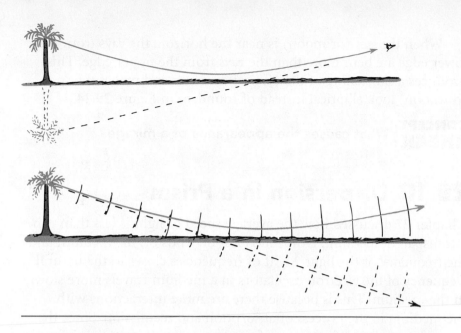

◀ FIGURE 29.20
The refraction of
light in air produces
a mirage.

◀ FIGURE 29.21
Wave fronts of light
travel faster in the hot air
near the ground, thereby
bending the rays of light
upward.

A motorist experiences a similar situation when driving along a hot road that appears to be wet ahead. The sky appears to be reflected from a wet surface but, in fact, light from the sky is being refracted through a layer of hot air. A mirage is not, as some people mistakenly believe, a "trick of the mind." As Figure 29.22 illustrates, a mirage is formed by real light and can be photographed.

◀ FIGURE 29.22
A driver might see a
mirage on a hot day.
The "wet" street is
actually dry.

When you watch the sun set, you see the sun for several minutes after it has really sunk below the horizon. This is because light is refracted by Earth's atmosphere, as shown in Figure 29.23. Since the density of the atmosphere changes gradually, the refracted rays bend gradually to produce a curved path. The same thing occurs at sunrise, so our daytimes are about 5 minutes longer because of atmospheric refraction.

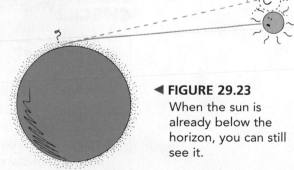

◀ FIGURE 29.23
When the sun is
already below the
horizon, you can still
see it.

FIGURE 29.24 ▲
Atmospheric refraction produces a "pumpkin" sun.

When the sun (or moon) is near the horizon, the rays from the lower edge are bent more than the rays from the upper edge. This produces a shortening of the vertical diameter and makes the sun (or moon) look elliptical instead of round, as in Figure 29.24.

CONCEPT CHECK What causes the appearance of a mirage?

29.10 Dispersion in a Prism

Chapter 27 discussed how the average speed of light is less than *c* in a transparent medium. How much less depends on the medium and the frequency of the light. Light of frequencies closer to the natural frequency of the electron oscillators in a medium travels more slowly in the medium. This is because there are more interactions with the medium in the process of absorption and reemission. Since the natural or resonant frequency of most transparent materials is in the ultraviolet part of the spectrum, visible light of higher frequencies travels more slowly than light of lower frequencies. Violet light travels about 1% slower in ordinary glass than red light. Light waves of colors between red and violet travel at their own intermediate speeds.

FIGURE 29.25 ▶
Dispersion through a prism occurs because different frequencies of light travel at different speeds.

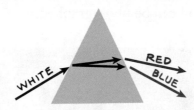

☑ **Since different frequencies of light travel at different speeds in transparent materials, they will refract differently and bend at different angles.** When light is bent twice at nonparallel boundaries, as in a prism, the separation of the different colors of light is quite apparent. This separation of light into colors arranged according to their frequency, as illustrated in Figure 29.25, is called **dispersion.**

CONCEPT CHECK What causes dispersion of light?

---

discover!

Why Do Stars Twinkle?

1. Look across a hot stove or hot pavement. Describe what you observe. What is a possible explanation for what you are seeing?

2. The next time you are outside on a clear night try to notice the twinkling of stars in the nighttime sky. What causes this twinkling?

3. **Think** Why are many observatories located atop mountains?

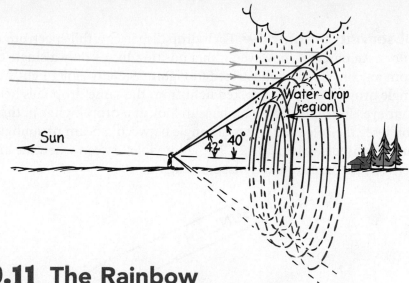

29.11 The Rainbow

A spectacular illustration of dispersion is the rainbow. ☑ **In order for you to see a rainbow, the sun must be shining in one part of the sky, and the water droplets in a cloud or in falling rain must be in the opposite part of the sky.** When you turn your back to the sun, you see the spectrum of colors in a bow. As illustrated in Figure 29.26, all rainbows would be completely round if the ground were not in the way.

Dispersion by a Raindrop Consider an individual spherical raindrop, as shown in Figure 29.27. Follow the ray of sunlight as it enters the drop near its top surface. Some of the light here is reflected (not shown), and the rest is refracted into the drop. At this first refraction, the light is dispersed into its spectral colors. Violet is bent the most and red the least. The rays reach the opposite part of the drop to be partly refracted out into the air (not shown) and partly reflected back into the water. Part of the rays that arrive at the lower surface of the drop are refracted into the air. This second refraction is similar to that of a prism, where refraction at the second surface increases the dispersion already produced at the first surface. This twice-refracted, once-reflected light is concentrated in a narrow range of angles.

think!

If light traveled at the same speed in raindrops as it does in air, would we still have rainbows?
Answer: 29.11.1

FIGURE 29.27 ▶
Dispersion of sunlight by a water drop produces a rainbow.

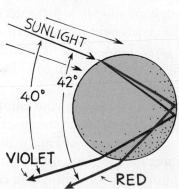

Observing a Rainbow Each drop disperses a full spectrum of colors. An observer, however, is in a position to see only a single color from any one drop, as illustrated in Figure 29.28. If violet light from a single drop enters your eye, red light from the same drop falls below your eye. To see red light you have to look at a drop higher in the sky. You'll see the color red when the angle between a beam of sunlight and the dispersed light is 42°. The color violet is seen when the angle between the sunbeam and dispersed light is 40°.

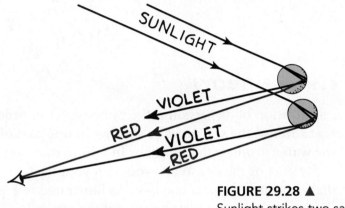

FIGURE 29.28 ▲
Sunlight strikes two sample drops and emerges as dispersed light.

You don't need to look only upward at 42° to see dispersed red light. You can see red by looking sideways at the same angle or anywhere along a circular arc swept out at a 42° angle. The dispersed light of other colors is along similar arcs, each at their own slightly different angle. Altogether, the arcs for each color form the familiar rainbow shape.

If you rotate the triangle shown in Figure 29.29, you sweep out the portion of a cone, with your eye at the apex. The raindrops that disperse light to you lie at the far edges of such a cone. The thicker the region of water drops, the thicker the conical edge you look through, and the more vivid the rainbow.

Your cone of vision that intersects the raindrops creating your rainbow is different from that of a person next to you. So when a friend says, "Look at the beautiful rainbow," you can reply, "Okay, move aside so I can see it too." Everybody sees his or her own personal rainbow.

So when you move, your rainbow moves with you. This means you can never approach the side of a rainbow, or see it end-on as in the exaggerated view of Figure 29.26. You *can't* get to its end. Hence the expression "looking for the pot of gold at the end of the rainbow" means pursuing something you can never reach.

FIGURE 29.29 ▲
Only raindrops along the dashed arc disperse red light to the observer at a 42° angle.

◀ FIGURE 29.30
Light from droplets inside the rainbow form a bright disk with the colored rainbow at its edge. The sky appears darker outside the rainbow because there is no light exiting raindrops in the way that produces the main rainbow. Notice the dimmer secondary bow.

Often a larger, secondary bow with colors reversed can be seen arching at a greater angle around the primary bow. You can see the secondary bow in Figure 29.30. The secondary bow is formed by similar circumstances and is a result of double reflection within the raindrops, as illustrated in Figure 29.31. Because most of the light is refracted out the back of the water drop during the extra reflection, the secondary bow is much dimmer.

CONCEPT CHECK : What are the conditions necessary for seeing a rainbow?

FIGURE 29.31 ▲
Double reflection in a water drop produces a secondary bow that is much dimmer than the primary bow.

think!

Point to a wall with your arm extended to approximate a 42° angle to the normal of the wall. Rotate your arm in a full circle while keeping the same 42° angle. What shape does your arm describe? What shape on the wall does your finger sweep out?
Answer: 29.11.2

29.12 Total Internal Reflection

When you're in a physics mood and you're going to take a bath, fill the tub extra deep and bring a waterproof flashlight into the tub with you. Turn the bathroom light off. Shine the submerged light straight up and then slowly tip it and note how the intensity of the emerging beam diminishes and how more light is reflected from the water surface to the bottom of the tub.

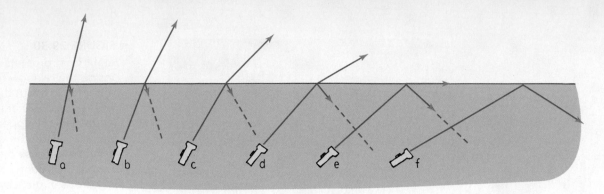

FIGURE 29.32 ▲
You can observe total
internal reflection in your
bathtub. **a–d.** Light emitted in the water at angles
below the critical angle is
partly refracted and partly
reflected at the surface.
e. At the critical angle,
the emerging beam skims
the surface. **f.** Past the
critical angle, there is total
internal reflection.

The Critical Angle At a certain angle, called the critical angle, you'll notice that the beam no longer emerges into the air above the surface. The **critical angle** is the angle of incidence that results in the light being refracted at an angle of 90° with respect to the normal. As a result, the intensity of the emerging beam reduces to zero. When the flashlight is tipped beyond the critical angle (48° from the normal in water), the beam cannot enter the air; it is only reflected. The beam is experiencing **total internal reflection,** which is the complete reflection of light back into its original medium. ☑ **Total internal reflection occurs when the angle of incidence is larger than the critical angle.** The only light emerging from the water surface is that which is diffusely reflected from the bottom of the bathtub.

This procedure is shown in Figure 29.32. The proportions of light refracted and reflected are indicated by the relative lengths of the solid arrows. The light reflected beneath the surface obeys the law of reflection: The angle of incidence is equal to the angle of reflection.

The critical angle for glass is about 43°, depending on the type of glass. This means that within the glass, rays of light that are more than 43° from the normal to a surface will be totally internally reflected at that surface. Rays of light in the glass prisms shown in Figure 29.33, for example, meet the back surface at 45° and are totally internally reflected. They will stay inside the glass until they meet a surface at an angle between 0° (straight on) and 43° to the normal.

Total internal reflection is as the name implies: total—100%. Silvered or aluminized mirrors reflect only 90 to 95% of incident light, and are marred by dust and dirt; prisms are more efficient. This is the main reason prisms are used instead of mirrors in many optical instruments. Figure 29.33 illustrates how prisms can be used to reflect light.

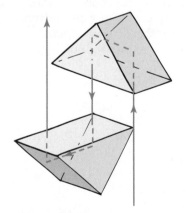

FIGURE 29.33 ▲
Prisms are more effi-
cient at reflecting light
than mirrors because of
total internal reflection.

Total Internal Reflection in Diamonds The critical angle for a diamond is 24.6°, smaller than in other common substances. This small critical angle means that light inside a diamond is more likely to be totally internally reflected than to escape. All light rays more than 24.6° from the normal to a surface in a diamond are kept inside by total internal reflection.

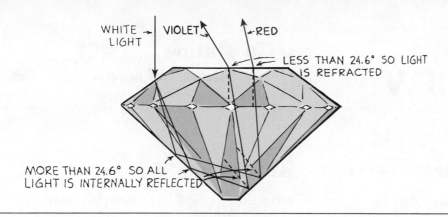

WHITE LIGHT → VIOLET ← RED

LESS THAN 24.6° SO LIGHT IS REFRACTED

MORE THAN 24.6° SO ALL LIGHT IS INTERNALLY REFLECTED

◀ FIGURE 29.34
The brilliance of diamonds is a result of total internal reflection.

As shown in Figure 29.34, when a diamond is cut as a gemstone, light that enters at one facet is usually totally internally reflected several times, without any loss in intensity, before exiting from another facet in another direction. A small critical angle, plus the pronounced refraction because of the unusually low speed of light in diamond, produces wide dispersion and a wide array of brilliant colors.

Light travels slowly in a diamond, but even more slowly in a silicon carbide crystal called *carborundum.*

Optical Fibers **Optical fibers,** sometimes called *light pipes,* are transparent fibers that pipe light from one place to another. As illustrated in Figure 29.35, they do this by a series of total internal reflections. Optical fibers are useful for getting light to inaccessible places. Mechanics and machinists use them to look at the interiors of engines, and physicians use them to look inside a patient's body. Light that shines down some of the fibers illuminates the scene and is reflected back along others.

Optical fibers are important in communications and have been replacing bulky and expensive copper cables to carry telephone messages between major switching centers. More information can be carried in the high frequencies of visible light than in the lower frequencies of electric current.

CONCEPT CHECK What causes total internal reflection to occur?

FIGURE 29.35 ▼
In an optical fiber, light is piped from one end to the other by a succession of total internal reflections.

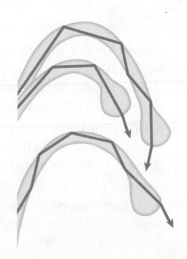

REVIEW

Go **O**nline
PHSchool.com

For: Self-Assessment
Visit: PHSchool.com
Web Code: csa – 2900

Concept Summary · · · · · ·

- When a wave reaches a boundary between two media, usually some or all of the wave bounces back into the first medium.

- The law of reflection states that the angle of incidence and the angle of reflection are equal to each other.

- Plane mirrors produce only virtual images.

- When light is incident on a rough surface, it is reflected in many directions.

- Sound energy that is not reflected is absorbed or transmitted.

- When a wave that is traveling at an angle changes its speed upon crossing a boundary between two media, it bends.

- Sound waves are refracted when parts of a wave front travel at different speeds.

- Changes in the speed of light as it passes from one medium to another, or variations in the temperatures and densities of the same medium, cause refraction.

- A mirage is caused by the refraction of light in Earth's atmosphere.

- Since different frequencies of light travel at different speeds in transparent materials, they will refract differently.

- In order for you to see a rainbow, the sun must be shining in one part of the sky, and water droplets must be in the opposite part of the sky.

- Total internal reflection occurs when the angle of incidence is larger than the critical angle.

Key Terms · · · · · ·

reflection (p. 579)

normal (p. 580)

angle of incidence (p. 580)

angle of reflection (p. 580)

law of reflection (p. 580)

virtual image (p. 581)

diffuse reflection (p. 582)

reverberation (p. 583)

refraction (p. 585)

wave front (p. 585)

mirage (p. 588)

dispersion (p. 590)

critical angle (p. 594)

total internal reflection (p. 594)

optical fiber (p. 595)

think! Answers

29.2   The color of the image will be the same as the color of the object because the frequency of light is not changed by reflection.

29.7   You'll hear the whistle better if the wind speed near the ground is less than the wind speed higher up. For this condition, the sound will be refracted toward the ground.

29.9   No! There would be no refraction if light traveled at the same speed in air of different temperatures and densities.

29.11.1 No. If there is no change in speed, there is no refraction. If there is no refraction, there is no dispersion of light and hence, no rainbow!

29.11.2 Your arm describes a cone, and your finger sweeps out a circle. Likewise with rainbows.

Check Concepts ......

Section 29.1

1. What becomes of a wave's energy when the wave is totally reflected at a boundary? When it is partially reflected at a boundary?

2. Why do smooth metal surfaces make good mirrors?

3. When light strikes perpendicular to the surface of a pane of glass, how much light is reflected and how much is transmitted at the first surface?

Section 29.2

4. What is meant by the normal to a surface?

5. What is the law of reflection?

Section 29.3

6. When you view your image in a plane mirror, how far behind the mirror is your image compared with your distance in front of the mirror?

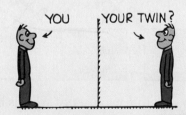

7. In what way does the law of reflection hold for *curved* mirrors?

Section 29.4

8. In what way does the law of reflection hold for diffuse reflection? Explain.

9. What is meant by the idea that a surface may be polished for some waves and rough for others?

Section 29.5

10. Distinguish between an echo and a reverberation.

11. Does the law of reflection hold for both sound waves and light waves?

Section 29.6

12. Distinguish between reflection and refraction.

13. When a wave crosses a surface at an angle from one medium into another, why does it change directions as it moves across the boundary into the new medium?

14. What is the orientation of a ray in relation to the wave front of a wave?

Section 29.7

15. Give an example where refraction is abrupt, and another where refraction is gradual.

Section 29.8

16. Does refraction occur for both sound waves and light waves?

17. If light had the same speed in air and in water, would light be refracted in passing from air into water?

18. If you can see the face of a friend who is underwater, can she also see you?

19. Does refraction tend to make objects submerged in water seem shallower or deeper than they really are?

Section 29.9

20. Is a mirage a result of refraction or reflection? Explain.

21. Is daytime a bit longer or is it a bit shorter because of atmospheric refraction?

Section 29.10

22. As light passes through a transparent medium, it undergoes an absorption-reemission process (discussed earlier, in Figure 27.7). Which interacts more with the medium, light of high frequencies or light of low frequencies? (Do high frequencies or low frequencies lag behind?)

23. Why does blue light refract at greater angles than red light in transparent materials?

Section 29.11

24. What conditions are necessary for viewing a rainbow in the sky?

25. How is a raindrop similar to a prism?

Section 29.12

26. What is the *critical angle* in terms of refraction and total internal reflection?

27. Why are optical fibers often called *light pipes*?

Think and Rank ······

Rank each of the following sets of scenarios in order of the quantity or property involved. List them from left to right. If scenarios have equal rankings, then separate them with an equal sign. (e.g., A = B)

28. Wheels from a toy cart are rolled from a concrete sidewalk onto the following surfaces.
  (A) a paved driveway
  (B) a grass lawn
  (C) close-cropped grass (like that on a golf-course putting green)

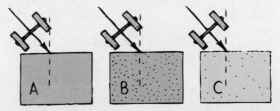

Due to slowing, each set of wheels bends at the boundary and is deflected from its original course. Rank the surfaces according to the amount each set of wheels bends at the boundary, from greatest amount of bending to least amount of bending.

29. Identical rays of light enter three transparent blocks composed of different materials. Light slows upon entering the blocks. Rank the blocks according to the speed light travels in each, from highest speed to lowest speed.

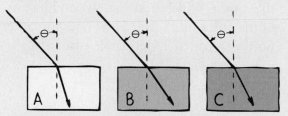

30. Identical rays of light in air are refracted upon entering three transparent materials.
(A) water, where speed slows to $0.75c$
(B) ethyl alcohol (speed $0.74c$)
(C) crown glass (speed $0.66c$)

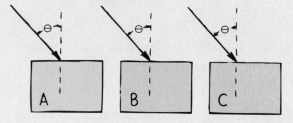

Rank the materials according to how much the light ray bends toward the normal, from most bending to least bending.

Think and Explain ••••••

31. On a steamy mirror, wipe an area just large enough to allow you to see your full face. How tall will the wiped area be compared with the vertical dimension of your face?

32. Suppose that a mirror and three lettered cards are set up as in the figure. If a person's eye is at point P, which of the lettered cards will be seen reflected in the mirror? Explain.

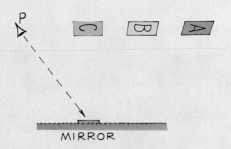

33. In the photograph below we see the bird and its reflection. Why don't we see the bird's feet in the reflection?

34. Contrast the types of reflection from a rough road and from the smooth surface of a wet road to explain why it is difficult for a motorist to see the roadway ahead when driving on a rainy night.

35. Cameras with automatic focus bounce a sonar (sound) beam from the object being photographed and compute distance from the time interval between sending and receiving the signal. Why will these cameras not focus properly for photographs of mirror images?

36. In the photograph below, Peter Hopkinson is standing astride a large mirror and boosts class interest with this zany demonstration. How does he accomplish his apparent levitation in midair?

37. Why is an echo weaker than the original sound?

38. Suppose you are standing downwind from a barking dog on a windy day. The wind blows faster well above the ground than close to the ground. Refraction will change the sound of the dog's bark. Will the sound of the bark be somewhat louder or somewhat diminished? Defend your answer.

39. Does the reflection of a scene in calm water look exactly the same as the scene itself only upside down? (*Hint:* Place a mirror on the floor between you and a table. Do you see the top of the table in the reflected image?)

40. If you were spearing a fish with a spear, would you aim above, below, or directly at the observed fish to make a direct hit? Would your answer be the same if you used laser light to "spear" the fish? Defend your answer.

41. The photo below shows two identical cola bottles, each with the *same* amount of cola. The right bottle is in air, and the left bottle is encased in solid plastic that has nearly the same index of refraction as glass (the speed of light in the plastic and in glass are nearly the same). Which bottle shows an illusion of the amount of cola? How does the other bottle give a truer view of its contents?

42. How do the different speeds of light in thin air and dense air affect the length of daylight?

43. Very short pulses of red light and blue light enter a glass block normal to its surface at the same time. Which pulse exits first?

44. When you stand with your back to the sun, you see a rainbow as a circular arc. Could you move off to one side and then see the rainbow as the segment of an ellipse rather than the segment of a circle (such as Figure 29.26 suggests)? Defend your answer.

45. A rainbow viewed from an airplane may form a complete circle. Will the shadow of the airplane appear at the center of the circle? Explain with the help of Figure 29.26.

46. Two observers standing apart from each other do not see the same rainbow. Explain.

47. Why is a secondary rainbow dimmer than the primary bow?

Think and Solve ......

48. When light strikes glass perpendicularly, about 4% of the light is reflected at each surface. Show that the amount of light transmitted through a pane of window glass is approximately 92%.

49. Suppose you walk toward a mirror at 1 m/s. How fast do you and your image approach each other? (The answer is *not* 1 m/s.)

50. A radio wave sent into space strikes an asteroid and is reflected back to Earth 1 second after being emitted. How far away is the asteroid?

51. A spider hangs by a strand of silk at eye level 20 cm in front of a plane mirror. You are behind the spider, 50 cm from the mirror. Show that the distance between your eye and the image of the spider in the mirror is 70 cm.

52. The average speed of light slows to $0.75c$ when it enters a particular piece of plastic.
  a. What change occurs in the frequency of light in the plastic?
  b. What change occurs in the wavelength?

Activities ......

53. Stand in front of a mirror and put two pieces of tape on the glass: one piece where you see the top of your head, and the other where you see the bottom of your feet. Compare the distance between the pieces of tape with your height. If a full-length mirror is not handy, use a smaller mirror and find the minimum length of mirror to see your face. Mark where you see the top of your head and the bottom of your chin. Then compare the distance between the marks with the length of your face. What must be the minimum length of a plane mirror in order for you to see a full view of yourself?

54. What effect does your distance from the mirror have on the answer to Activity 53? (*Hint:* Move closer and farther from your initial position. Be sure the top of your head lines up with the top piece of tape. At greater distances, is your image smaller than, larger than, or the same size as the space between the pieces of tape?) Are you surprised?

55. Look at a diamond under bright light. Turn the stone and note the flashes of color that refract, reflect, and refract toward you. When the flash encounters only one eye instead of two, your brain registers it differently than for both eyes. The one-eyed flash is a sparkle! What causes the brilliant sparkle of a diamond?

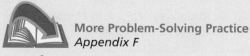

More Problem-Solving Practice
Appendix F

30 LENSES

THE BIG IDEA : Lenses change the paths of light.

A light ray bends as it enters glass and bends again as it leaves. The bending (refraction) is due to the difference between the average speed of light in glass and the average speed in air. Light passing through glass of a certain shape can form an image that appears larger, smaller, closer, or farther than the object being viewed. For example, magnifying glasses have been used for centuries and were well known to the early Greeks and medieval Arabs. Today, eyeglasses allow millions of people to read in comfort, and cameras, telescopes, and microscopes widen our view of the world.

discover!

What Types of Images Are Formed by Convex and Concave Lenses?

1. Cut off a one-centimeter length from the end of a drinking straw.
2. Cover one end of the short straw segment with a piece of transparent tape.
3. Place the taped end of the straw over a small object such as a letter or numeral in a newspaper.
4. Use an eyedropper, or the longer segment of the straw, to fill the short piece of the straw with water. Add water until the surface bulges outward above the top of the straw.
5. View the object through the straw from the time the water forms a convex surface until, as the water leaks out, the surface of the water becomes concave.

Analyze and Conclude

1. **Observing** Describe the appearance of the image of the object as seen through the water when the surface of the water was convex and when it was concave.
2. **Predicting** How would the image appear if the surface were flat, that is, neither convex nor concave?
3. **Making Generalizations** What types of images do you think are formed by convex and concave lenses?

30.1 Converging and Diverging Lenses

A **lens** is a piece of transparent material, such as glass, that refracts light. ⊘ **A lens forms an image by bending rays of light that pass through it.**

Learning about lenses is a hands-on activity. Not manipulating lenses while learning about them is like taking swimming lessons out of water.

Shapes of Lenses The shape of a lens can be understood by considering a lens to be a large number of portions of prisms, as shown in Figure 30.1. When arranged in certain positions, the prisms bend incoming parallel rays so they converge to (or diverge from) a single point. The arrangement shown in Figure 30.1a is thicker in the middle; it converges the light. The arrangement in Figure 30.1b is thinner in the middle; it diverges the light.

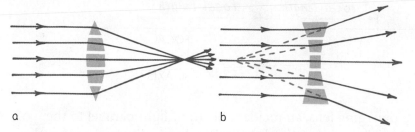

a   b

◄ **FIGURE 30.1**
A lens may be thought of as a set of prisms. **a.** Incoming parallel rays converge to a single point. **b.** Incoming rays seem to diverge from a single point.

In both arrangements, the most net bending of rays occurs at the outermost prisms, for they have the greatest angle between the two refracting surfaces. No net bending occurs in the middle "prism," for its glass faces are parallel and rays emerge in their original direction.

Real lenses are made not of prisms, of course, but of solid pieces of glass or plastic with surfaces that are usually ground to a spherical shape. Figure 30.2 shows how smooth lenses refract rays of light and form wave fronts. The lens in Figure 30.2a is a converging lens. A **converging lens,** also known as a **convex lens,** is thicker in the middle, causing rays of light that are initially parallel (straight wave fronts) to meet at a single point called the *focal point*. The lens in Figure 30.2b is a diverging lens. A **diverging lens,** also known as a **concave lens,** is thinner in the middle, causing the rays of light to appear to originate from a single point.

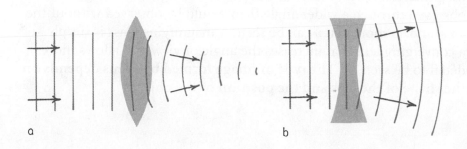

a   b

◄ **FIGURE 30.2**
Wave fronts travel more slowly in glass than in air. **a.** In the converging lens, the wave fronts are retarded more through the center of the lens, and the light converges. **b.** In the diverging lens, the waves are retarded more at the edges, and the light diverges.

Key Features of Lenses Figure 30.3 illustrates some important features of a lens. The **principal axis** of a lens is the line joining the centers of curvature of its surfaces. The **focal point** for a converging lens is the point at which a beam of light parallel to the principal axis converges. The **focal plane** is a plane perpendicular to the principal axis that passes through either focal point of a lens. For a converging lens, any incident parallel beam converges to a point on the focal plane. A lens affects light coming from the right in the same way as light coming from the left (*or* has the same effect on light incident from either side). Therefore, a lens has two focal points and two focal planes. When the lens of a camera is set for distant objects, the film is in the focal plane behind the lens in the camera.

FIGURE 30.3 ▶

The key features of a converging lens include the principal axis, focal point, and focal plane.

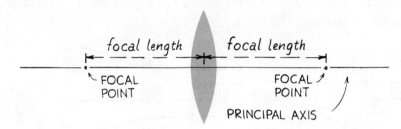

For a diverging lens, an incident beam of light parallel to the principal axis is not converged to a point, but is diverged so that the light appears to originate from a single point. The **focal length** of a lens, whether converging or diverging, is the distance between the center of the lens and its focal point. When the lens is thin, the focal lengths on either side are equal, even when the curvatures on the two sides are not.

CONCEPT CHECK How does a lens form an image?

30.2 Image Formation by a Lens

With unaided vision, an object far away is seen through a relatively small angle of view, as shown in Figure 30.4a. When you are closer, the same object is seen through a larger angle of view, as illustrated in Figure 30.4b. This wider angle allows the perception of more detail. Magnification occurs when the use of a lens allows an image to be observed through a wider angle than would be observed without the lens, and so more detail can be seen. A magnifying glass is simply a converging lens that increases the angle of view and allows more detail to be seen. ⊘ **The type of image formed by a lens depends on the shape of the lens and the position of the object.**

Go Online

SCi LINKS NSTA

For: Links on lenses
Visit: www.SciLinks.org
Web Code: csn – 3002

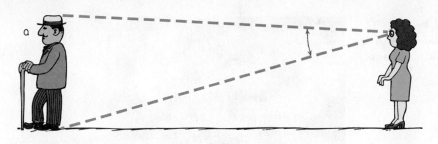

FIGURE 30.4 ▲

With unaided vision, the size of an object appears to change depending on your distance to the object. **a.** A distant object is viewed through a narrow angle. **b.** When the same object is viewed from a closer distance and thus through a wider angle, more detail is seen.

Images Formed by Converging Lenses When you use a magnifying glass, you hold it close to the object you wish to see magnified. This is because a converging lens will magnify only when the object is between the focal point and the lens, as shown in Figure 30.5. The magnified image will be farther from the lens than the object and right-side up (erect). If a screen were placed at the image distance, no image would appear on the screen because no light is actually directed to the image position. The rays that reach your eye, however, behave *as if* they came from the image position, so the image is a virtual image. Recall from Chapter 29 that a virtual image originates from a location where light does not actually reach.

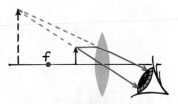

FIGURE 30.5 ▲

A converging lens can be used as a magnifying glass to produce a virtual image of a nearby object.

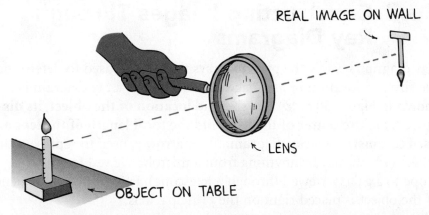

REAL IMAGE ON WALL

LENS

OBJECT ON TABLE

◀ **FIGURE 30.6**

A converging lens forms a real, upside-down image of a more distant object.

When the object is far enough away to be beyond the focal point of a converging lens, light originating from the object and passing through the lens converges and can be focused on a screen, as illustrated in Figure 30.6. An image formed by converging light is called a **real image.** A real image formed by a single converging lens is upside down (inverted). Converging lenses are used for projecting motion pictures onto a screen.

FIGURE 30.7 ▶

A diverging lens always produces a virtual image.

Images Formed by Diverging Lenses When a diverging lens is used alone, the image is always virtual, right-side up, and smaller than the object, as can be seen in Figure 30.7. It makes no difference how far or how near the object is. A diverging lens is often used for the viewfinder on a camera. When you look at the object to be photographed through the viewfinder, you see a right-side up virtual image that approximates the same proportions as the photograph to be taken.

┌─ **think!** ───────

Why is the greater part of the photograph in Figure 30.7 out of focus?
Answer: 30.2

CONCEPT : What determines the type of image
CHECK : formed by a lens?

30.3 Constructing Images Through Ray Diagrams

Ray diagrams show the principal rays that can be used to determine the size and location of an image. An example of a ray diagram is shown in Figure 30.8. ☑ **The size and location of the object, its distance from the center of the lens, and the focal length of the lens are used to construct a ray diagram.**[30.3] An arrow is used to represent the object (which may be anything from a microbe viewed in a microscope to a galaxy viewed through a telescope). For simplicity, one end of the object is placed right on the principal axis.

FIGURE 30.8 ▼

In a ray diagram, the three useful rays from the object converge on the image.

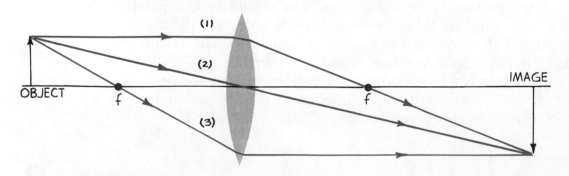

The Three Principal Rays To locate the position of the image, you only have to know the paths of two rays from a point on the object, represented by the vertical arrow. Any point except for the point on the principal axis will work, but it is customary to choose a point at the tip of the arrow.

The path of one refracted ray is known from the definition of the focal point. A ray parallel to the principal axis will be refracted by the lens to the focal point, as shown in Figure 30.8.

Another path is known: through the center of the lens where the faces are parallel to each other. A ray of light will pass through the center with no appreciable change in direction. Therefore, a ray from the tip of the arrowhead proceeds in a straight line through the center of the lens.

A third path is known: A ray of light that passes through the focal point in front of the lens emerges from the lens and proceeds parallel to the principal axis.

All three paths are shown in Figure 30.8, which is a typical ray diagram. The image is located where the three rays intersect. Any two of these three rays is sufficient to locate the relative size and location of the image.

We use these particular rays only because their paths through the lens are easy to predict. You should know that *all* light passing through a lens contributes to image formation.

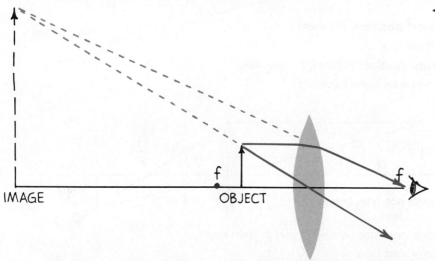

◀ **FIGURE 30.9**
The ray diagram for a magnifying glass shows that when the object is less than one focal length from the lens the image is virtual, right-side up, and magnified.

IMAGE

OBJECT

The ray diagram for a converging lens used as a magnifying glass is shown in Figure 30.9. In this case, where the distance from the lens to the object is less than the focal length, the rays diverge as they leave the lens. The rays of light appear to come from a point in front of the lens (same side of the lens as the object). The location of the image is found by extending the rays backward to the point where they converge. The virtual image that is formed is magnified and right-side up.

FIGURE 30.10 ▶

The ray diagrams illustrate the formation of an image when the object is at various positions in relation to a converging lens of focal length f.

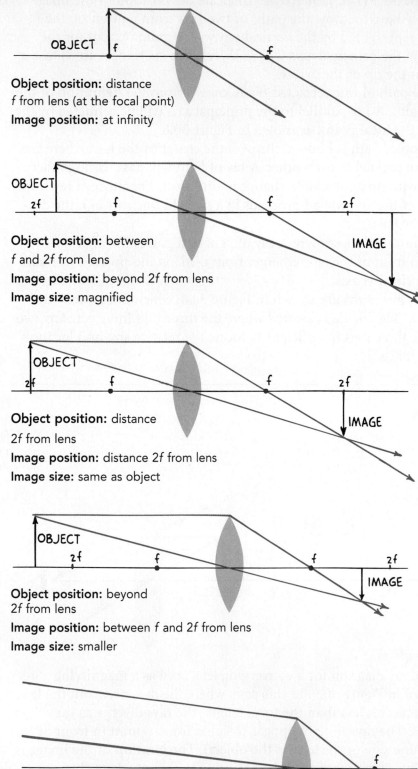

Object position: distance f from lens (at the focal point)
Image position: at infinity

Object position: between f and $2f$ from lens
Image position: beyond $2f$ from lens
Image size: magnified

Object position: distance $2f$ from lens
Image position: distance $2f$ from lens
Image size: same as object

Object position: beyond $2f$ from lens
Image position: between f and $2f$ from lens
Image size: smaller

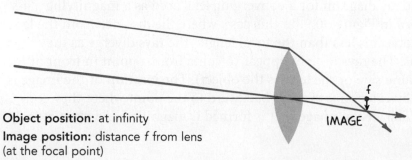

Object position: at infinity
Image position: distance f from lens (at the focal point)

The three rays useful for the construction of a ray diagram are summarized:

1. A ray parallel to the principal axis that passes through the focal point on the opposite side.

2. A ray passing through the center of the lens that is undeflected.

3. A ray through the focal point in front of the lens that emerges parallel to the principal axis after refraction by the lens.

Ray Diagrams for Converging and Diverging Lenses

The ray diagrams in Figure 30.10 show image formation by a converging lens as an object initially at the focal point is moved away from the lens along the principal axis. Since the object is not located between the focal point and the lens, all the images that are formed are real and inverted.

As illustrated in Figure 30.11, the method of drawing ray diagrams applies also to diverging lenses. A ray parallel to the principal axis from the tip of the arrow will be bent by the lens as if it had come from the focal point. A ray through the center goes straight through. A ray heading for the focal point on the far side of the lens is bent so that it emerges parallel to the axis of the lens.

Interestingly, when half a lens is covered, half as much light forms the image. This does not mean half the *image* is formed! Even a piece of broken lens can form a complete image on a screen. Try it and see.

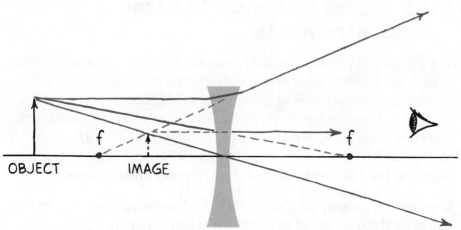

◀ **FIGURE 30.11**
The ray diagram shows how a virtual image is formed by a diverging lens.

On emerging from the lens, the three rays appear to come from a point on the same side of the lens as the object, which defines the position of the virtual image. The image is nearer to the lens than the object, smaller than the object, and right-side up. The image formed by a diverging lens is always virtual, reduced, and right-side up.

CONCEPT CHECK : What information is used to construct a ray diagram?

30.4 Image Formation Summarized

think!

Where must an object be located so that the image formed by a converging lens will be (a) at infinity? (b) as near the object as possible? (c) right-side up? (d) the same size? (e) inverted and enlarged?

Answer: 30.4

☑ **A converging lens forms either a real or a virtual image. A diverging lens always forms a virtual image.**

A converging lens is a simple magnifying glass when the object is within one focal length of the lens. The image is then virtual, magnified, and right-side up. When the object is beyond one focal length, a converging lens produces a real, inverted image. The location of the image depends on how close the object is to the focal point. If it is close to (but slightly beyond) the focal point, the image is far away (as with a slide projector or movie projector). If the object is far from the focal point, the image is nearer (as with a camera). In all cases where a real image is formed, the object and the image are on opposite sides of the lens.

When the object is viewed with a diverging lens, the image is virtual, reduced, and right-side up. This is true for all locations of the object. In all cases where a virtual image is formed, the object and the image are on the same side of the lens.

CONCEPT CHECK What types of images are produced by lenses?

30.5 Some Common Optical Instruments

The advent of eyeglasses probably occurred in Italy in the late 1200s. If anybody at the time or before viewed objects through a pair of lenses held far apart, one in front of the other, there is no record of it, for curiously enough, the telescope wasn't invented until some 300 years later. Today, lenses are used in many optical instruments. ☑ **Optical instruments that use lenses include the camera, the telescope (and binoculars), and the compound microscope.**

Camera A camera consists of a lens and sensitive film (or light-detecting chip) mounted in a light-tight box. In many cameras, the lens is mounted so that it can be moved back and forth to adjust the distance between the lens and film. The lens forms a real, inverted image on the film or chip. Figure 30.12 shows a camera with a single simple lens. In practice, most cameras make use of compound lenses to minimize distortions called *aberrations*.

The amount of light that gets to the film is regulated by a shutter and a diaphragm. The shutter controls the length of time that the film is exposed to light. The diaphragm controls the opening that light passes through to reach the film. Varying the size of the opening (aperture) varies the amount of light that reaches the film at any instant.

FIGURE 30.12 ▼

In a simple camera, the lens forms a real, inverted image on the film.

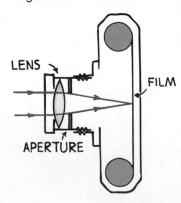

Telescope A simple telescope uses a lens to form a real image of a distant object. The real image is not caught on film but is projected in space to be examined by another lens used as a magnifying glass. The second lens, called the **eyepiece,** is positioned so that the image produced by the first lens is within one focal length of the eyepiece. The eyepiece forms an enlarged virtual image of the real image. When you look through a telescope, you are looking at an image of an image.

Figure 30.13 shows the lens arrangement for an *astronomical telescope.* The image is inverted, and thus the image of the man on the moon would appear upside down.

FIGURE 30.13 ▼
An astronomical telescope forms an inverted image. (For simplification, the image is shown close here; it is actually located at infinity.)

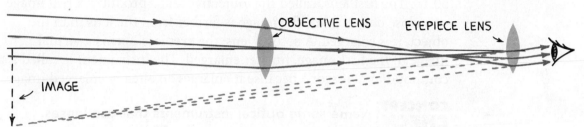

A third lens or a pair of reflecting prisms is used in the *terrestrial telescope,* which produces an image that is right-side up. A pair of these telescopes side by side, each with a pair of prisms, makes up a pair of *binoculars* like those shown in Figure 30.14.

Since no lens transmits 100% of the light incident upon it, astronomers prefer the brighter, inverted images of a two-lens telescope to the less bright, right-side-up images that a third lens or prisms would provide. For non-astronomical uses, such as viewing distant landscapes or sporting events, right-side-up images are more important to the viewer than brightness, so the additional lens or prisms are used.

FIGURE 30.14 ▼
Each side of a pair of binoculars uses a pair of prisms that flip the image right-side up.

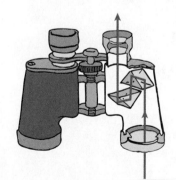

Link to TECHNOLOGY

The Digital Camera Rather than focusing an image onto film, the lens in a digital camera focuses light onto an array of millions of tiny light-sensitive semi-conductor photocells. Each cell produces an electrical signal in proportion to the amount of light hitting it. Usually, red, green, and blue filters on the different photocells make them sensitive to a particular color of light. All of the intensity and color information is relayed from the photocell array to a computer chip. Software processes the raw information to produce an image.

FIGURE 30.15 ▶

A compound microscope
uses two converging lenses.

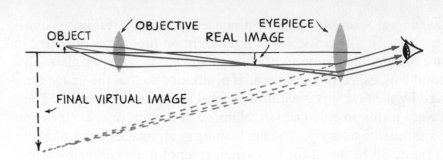

OBJECT / OBJECTIVE   EYEPIECE
REAL IMAGE

FINAL VIRTUAL IMAGE

Compound Microscope A compound microscope uses two converging lenses of short focal length, arranged as shown in Figure 30.15. The first lens, called the **objective lens,** produces a real image of a close object. Since the image is farther from the lens than the object, it is enlarged. A second lens, the eyepiece, forms a virtual image of the first image, further enlarged. The instrument is called a compound microscope because it enlarges an already enlarged image.

CONCEPT CHECK Name some optical instruments that use lenses.

30.6 The Eye

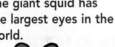

The giant squid has the largest eyes in the world.

In many respects, the human eye is similar to the camera. A diagram of the eye is shown in Figure 30.16. ✅ **The main parts of the eye are the cornea, the iris, the lens, and the retina.** Light enters through the transparent covering called the **cornea.** The amount of light that enters is regulated by the **iris,** the colored part of the eye that surrounds the pupil. The **pupil** is the opening in the iris through which light passes.[30.6] Light passes through the pupil and lens and is focused on a layer of tissue at the back of the eye—the **retina** —that is extremely sensitive to light. Different parts of the retina receive light from different directions.

FIGURE 30.16 ▶

Light enters the human eye through the cornea, passes through the pupil and lens, and is focused on the retina.

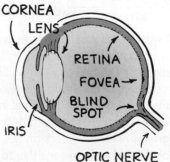

CORNEA
LENS
RETINA
FOVEA
BLIND SPOT
IRIS
OPTIC NERVE

The retina is not of uniform sensitivity. There is a small region in the center of our field of view where vision is most distinct. This spot is called the *fovea.* Much greater detail can be seen at the fovea than off to the side.

The Blind Spot There is also a spot in the retina where the nerves carrying all the information leave the eye in a narrow bundle. This is the *blind spot.* You can demonstrate that you have a blind spot in each eye if you hold this book at arm's length, close your left eye, and look at the round dot in Figure 30.17 with only your right eye. You can see both the round dot and the X at this distance. If you now move the book slowly toward your face, with your right eye still fixed upon the dot, you'll reach a position about 20 to 25 cm from your eye where the X disappears. To establish the blind spot in your left eye, close your right eye and similarly look at the X with your left eye so that the dot disappears. With both eyes opened, you'll find no position where either the X or the dot disappears because one eye "fills in" the part of the object to which the other eye is blind. Repeat the exercise of Figure 30.17 with small objects on various backgrounds.

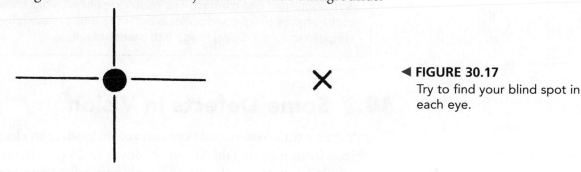

◀ **FIGURE 30.17**
Try to find your blind spot in each eye.

The Camera and the Eye In both the camera and the eye, the image is upside down, and this is compensated for in both cases. You simply turn the camera film around to look at it. Your brain has learned to turn around images it receives from your retina!

A principal difference between a camera and the human eye has to do with focusing. In a camera, focusing is accomplished by altering the distance between the lens and the film or chip. In the human eye, most of the focusing is done by the cornea, the transparent membrane at the outside of the eye. Adjustments in focusing of the image on the retina are made by changing the thickness and shape of the lens to regulate its focal length, as shown in Figure 30.18. This is called *accommodation* and is brought about by the action of the *ciliary muscle,* which surrounds the lens.

CONCEPT CHECK Name the main parts of the human eye.

NORMAL DISTANT VISION

NORMAL CLOSE VISION

◀ **FIGURE 30.18**
The shape of the lens changes to focus light on the retina.

Photographer

Photography blends art with physics. A photographer's ideas are based on artistry, but the execution relies on a savvy use of physics and, for most photographers now, computer technology. A photographer knows that a camera seldom records just what the eye sees.

Our eyes can discern detail simultaneously both in dark shadows and in light that is millions of times brighter; neither film nor digital image sensors can do this. Hence, the photographer experiments with brightness and contrast. The photographer who has knowledge of the physics of light and optics is better able to use available software to turn a digital image into a work of art.

30.7 Some Defects in Vision

If you have normal vision, your eye can accommodate to clearly see objects from infinity (the *far point*) down to 25 cm (the *near point*, which normally recedes for all people with advancing age). Unfortunately, not everyone has normal vision. ☑ **Three common vision problems are farsightedness, nearsightedness, and astigmatism.**

Farsightedness A **farsighted** person has trouble focusing on nearby objects because the eyeball is too short or the cornea is too flat so that images form behind the retina. As Figure 30.19 illustrates, farsighted people have to hold things more than 25 cm away to be able to focus them. The remedy is to increase the converging effect of the eye. This is done by wearing eyeglasses or contact lenses with converging lenses. Converging lenses will converge the rays that enter the eye sufficiently to focus them on the retina instead of behind it.

FIGURE 30.19 ▶
The eyeball of the farsighted eye is too short. A converging lens moves the image closer and onto the retina.

FARSIGHTED

 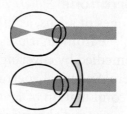

NEARSIGHTED

Nearsightedness A **nearsighted** person can see nearby objects clearly, but does not see distant objects clearly because they are focused too near the lens, in front of the retina. As depicted in Figure 30.20, the eyeball is too long or the surface of the cornea is too curved. A remedy is to wear corrective lenses that diverge the rays from distant objects so that they focus on the retina instead of in front of it.

Astigmatism **Astigmatism** of the eye is a defect that results when the cornea is curved more in one direction than the other, somewhat like the side of a barrel. Because of this defect, the eye does not form sharp images. The remedy is cylindrical corrective lenses that have more curvature in one direction than in another.

CONCEPT : Name and describe the three common
CHECK : vision problems.

30.8 Some Defects of Lenses

No lens gives a perfect image. The distortions in an image are called **aberrations.** By combining lenses in certain ways, aberrations can be minimized. For this reason, most optical instruments use compound lenses, each consisting of several simple lenses, instead of single lenses. ☑ **Two types of aberration are spherical aberration and chromatic aberration.**

Go Online
SciLINKS NSTA

For: Links on abnormalities of the eye
Visit: www.SciLinks.org
Web Code: csn – 3008

discover!

Can a Pinhole Improve Your Vision?

1. Poke a tiny hole in a piece of paper or cardboard.
2. Hold the pinhole in front of your eye and close to this page. Can you see the print clearly?
3. Why is bright light needed?
4. **Think** What advice do you have for someone who wears glasses and misplaces them, and can't see the small print in a telephone book?

Aberrations *Spherical aberration* results when light passes through the edges of a lens, as in Figure 30.21a, and focuses at a slightly different place from light passing through the center of the lens. This can be remedied by covering the edges of a lens, as with a diaphragm in a camera. Spherical aberration is corrected in good optical instruments by a combination of lenses.

Chromatic aberration is the result of the different speeds of light of various colors and hence the different refractions they undergo, as shown in Figure 30.21b. In a simple lens red light and blue light bend by different amounts (as in a prism), so they do not come to focus in the same place. *Achromatic lenses,* which combine simple lenses of different kinds of glass, correct this defect.

FIGURE 30.21 ▶
a. Spherical aberration occurs when light passes through the edges of a lens. **b.** Chromatic aberration occurs because different colors of light travel at different speeds.

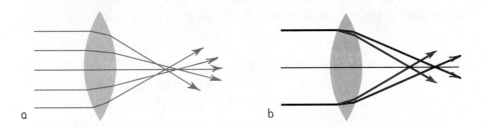

In the eye, vision is sharpest when the pupil is smallest because light then passes through only the center of the eye's lens, where spherical and chromatic aberrations are minimal. Also, light bends the least through the center of a lens, so minimal focusing is required for a sharp image. You see better in bright light because your pupils are smaller.

Methods for Correcting Vision An alternative to wearing eyeglasses for correcting vision is contact lenses. A more recent option is LASIK (acronym for *laser-assisted in-situ keratomileusis*), the procedure of reshaping the cornea using pulses from a laser. Another recent procedure is PRK (*photorefractive keratectomy*). Still another is IntraLase, where intraocular lenses are implanted in the eye like a contact lens, a procedure of choice for extremely nearsighted or farsighted people and for those who can't have laser surgery. The wearing of eyeglasses and contact lenses may soon be a thing of the past.

CONCEPT : Name the types of aberrations that can occur in
CHECK : images formed by lenses.

think!
Why is chromatic aberration a problem for lenses but not for mirrors?
Answer: 30.8

REVIEW

Concept Summary · · · · · ·

- A lens forms an image by bending rays of light that pass through it.

- The type of image formed by a lens depends on the shape of the lens and the position of the object.

- The size and location of the object, its distance from the center of the lens, and the focal length of the lens are used to construct a ray diagram.

- A converging lens forms either a real or a virtual image. A diverging lens always forms a virtual image.

- Optical instruments that use lenses include the camera, the telescope (and binoculars), and the compound microscope.

- The main parts of the eye are the cornea, the iris, the lens, and the retina.

- Three common vision problems are farsightedness, nearsightedness, and astigmatism.

- Two types of aberrations are spherical aberration and chromatic aberration.

think! Answers

30.2 Both Jamie and his cat and the virtual image of Jamie and his cat are "objects" for the lens of the camera that took this photograph. Since the objects are at different distances from the camera lens, their respective images are at different distances with respect to the film in the camera. So only one can be brought into focus.

30.4 The object should be (a) at one focal length from the lens (at the focal point) (see Figure 30.10); (b) and (c) within one focal length of the lens (see Figure 30.9); (d) at two focal lengths from the lens (see Figure 30.10); (e) between one and two focal lengths from the lens (see Figure 30.10).

30.8 Different frequencies travel at different speeds in a transparent medium, and therefore refract at different angles. This produces chromatic aberration. Light reflection, on the other hand, has nothing to do with the frequency of light. One color reflects the same as any other.

Key Terms · · · · · ·

lens *(p. 603)*

converging lens *(p. 603)*

convex lens *(p. 603)*

diverging lens *(p. 603)*

concave lens *(p. 603)*

principal axis *(p. 604)*

focal point *(p. 604)*

focal plane *(p. 604)*

focal length *(p. 604)*

real image *(p. 605)*

ray diagram *(p. 606)*

eyepiece *(p. 611)*

objective lens *(p. 612)*

cornea *(p. 612)*

iris *(p. 612)*

pupil *(p. 612)*

retina *(p. 612)*

farsighted *(p. 614)*

nearsighted *(p. 615)*

astigmatism *(p. 615)*

aberration *(p. 615)*

Check Concepts ••••••

Section 30.1

1. Distinguish between a *converging lens* and a *diverging lens.*

2. Distinguish between the focal *point* and focal *plane* of a lens.

Section 30.2

3. Distinguish between a *virtual* image and a *real* image.

Section 30.3

4. There are three convenient rays commonly used in ray diagrams to estimate the position of an image. Describe these three rays in terms of their orientation with respect to the principal axis and focal points.

5. How many of the rays in Question 4 are necessary for estimating the position of an image?

6. Do ray diagrams apply only to converging lenses, or to diverging lenses also?

Section 30.4

7. What types of images are formed by converging lenses?

8. What types of images are formed by diverging lenses?

Section 30.5

9. Explain what is meant by saying that in a telescope one looks at the image of an image.

10. What is the function of the eyepiece in an astronomical telecsope?

11. What type of lenses are used in a compound microscope?

Section 30.6

12. Which instrument—a telescope, a compound microscope, or a camera—is most similar to the eye?

13. Why do you not normally notice a blind spot when you look at your surroundings?

Section 30.7

14. Distinguish between *farsighted* and *nearsighted* vision.

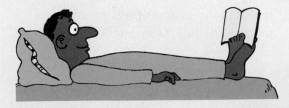

15. What is astigmatism, and how can it be corrected?

Section 30.8

16. Distinguish between *spherical* aberration and *chromatic* aberration, and cite a remedy for each.

Think and Rank ......

Rank each of the following sets of scenarios in order of the quantity or property involved. List them from left to right. If scenarios have equal rankings, then separate them with an equal sign. (e.g., A = B)

17. Percy stands at different distances from a lens with a focal length of 30 cm. Rank the image distance from farthest to Percy to closest to Percy.

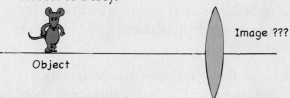

   (A) Object is at 10 cm.
   (B) Object is at 35 cm.
   (C) Object is at 60 cm.
   (D) Object is at 90 cm.

18. Depending on the location of Percy relative to the focal point of the converging lens (only one of the symmetrical focal points is shown here), the image may be real or virtual. The size of the image varies for object positions A, B, and C. Rank the image sizes from largest to smallest. (You may want to draw ray diagrams on a separate piece of paper.)

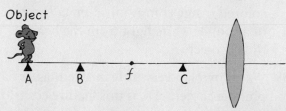

19. Here Percy is in front of a diverging lens. Virtual images are seen by viewing from the right side of the lens. For object positions A, B, and C, rank the sizes of the virtual images from largest to smallest.

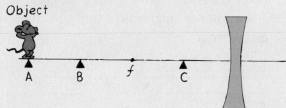

Think and Explain ......

20. When you cover the top half of a camera lens, what effect does this have on the pictures taken?

21. What will happen to the image projected onto a screen by a lens when you cover most of the lens?

22. **a.** What condition must exist for a converging lens to produce a virtual image?
    b. What condition must exist for a diverging lens to produce a real image?

23. How could you demonstrate that an image was indeed a real image?

24. Why do you suppose that a magnifying glass has often been called a "burning glass"?

25. In terms of focal length, how far is the camera lens from the film or chip when very distant objects are being photographed?

26. Can you photograph yourself in a mirror and focus the camera on both your image and the mirror frame? Explain.

27. If you take a photograph of your image in a plane mirror, how many meters away should you set your focus if you are 2 m in front of the mirror?

28. Copy the three drawings in the figure. Then use ray diagrams to find the image of each arrow.

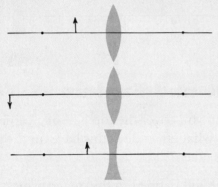

29. Maps of the moon are actually upside down. Why is this so?

30. The real image produced by a converging lens is inverted. Our eyes have converging lenses. Does this mean the images you see are upside down on your retinas? Explain.

31. In which case does light undergo the greater change in speed—traveling in air and entering a glass lens, or traveling in water and entering a glass lens?

32. In which case is refraction greater, light in water entering a glass lens, or light in air entering a glass lens?

33. From water to glass, the change in the speed of light is less than from air to glass. Does this mean a magnifying glass submerged in water will magnify more or less than in air?

34. A whale's eye uses hydraulics to move the lens of its eye closer or farther from the retina. When a whale dives after having had a look around in the air, in which direction should the lens be moved?

35. Focal-length variations in birds and reptiles are accomplished by eye muscles that change lens thickness and curvature. For near vision, should the lens be made thicker and more curved or thinner and less curved?

36. Would telescopes and microscopes magnify if light had the same speed in glass as in air? Explain.

37. If you have ever watched a water strider or other insect upon the surface of water, you may have noticed a large shadow cast by the contact point where the thin legs touch the water surface. Then around the shadow is a bright ring. What accounts for this?

38. What is responsible for the rainbow-colored fringe commonly seen at the edges of a spot of white light from the beam of a slide projector?

39. Waves overlap very little in the image of a pinhole camera. Does this feature contribute to sharpness or to a blurry image?

Activities • • • • • •

40. Look at the reflection of overhead lights from the two surfaces of eyeglasses, and you will see two fascinatingly different images. Why are they different?

41. Note the shapes of light spots that reach the ground in the shade of a tree. Most of them are circular, or elliptical if the sun is low in the sky. Interestingly, the spots of light are images of something very special to all who live on Earth. Identify this special something.

42. Determine the magnification power of a lens by focusing on the lines of a ruled piece of paper. Count the spaces between the lines that fit into one magnified space, and you have the magnification power of the lens. For example, if three spaces fit into one magnified space, then the magnification power of the lens is 3. Describe how you can do the same with binoculars and a distant brick wall.

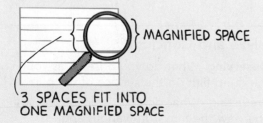

MAGNIFIED SPACE

3 SPACES FIT INTO ONE MAGNIFIED SPACE

43. Make a pinhole camera, as illustrated in the figure. Cut out one end of a small cardboard box, and cover the end with tissue paper. Make a clean-cut pinhole at the other end. Aim the camera at a bright object in a darkened room, and you will see an upside-down image on the translucent tissue paper. In a dark, windowless room, if you replace the tissue paper with unexposed photographic film, cover the back so it is light-tight, and cover the pinhole with a removable flap, you will be ready to take a picture.

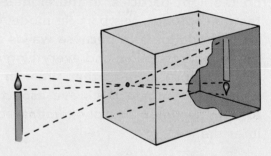

Exposure times differ, depending mostly on the kind of film and the amount of light. Try different exposure times, starting with about 3 seconds. Also try boxes of various lengths. You'll find everything in focus in your photographs, but the pictures will not have clear-cut, sharp outlines. The principal difference between your pinhole camera and a commercial one is the glass lens, which is larger than the pinhole and therefore admits more light in less time.

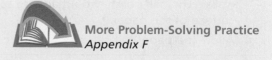

More Problem-Solving Practice
Appendix F

31 DIFFRACTION AND INTERFERENCE

THE BIG IDEA : The wave model of light explains diffraction and interference.

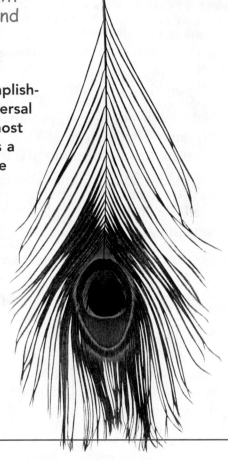

Today Isaac Newton is most famous for his accomplishments in mechanics—his laws of motion and universal gravitation. Early in his career, however, he was most famous for his work on light. Newton pictured light as a beam of ultra-tiny material particles. With this model he could explain reflection as a bouncing of the particles from a surface, and he could explain refraction as the result of deflecting forces from the surface acting on the light particles. In the eighteenth and nineteenth centuries, this particle model gave way to a wave model of light because waves could explain reflection, refraction, and everything else that was known about light at that time. In this chapter we will investigate the wave aspects of light to explain two important phenomena—diffraction and interference.

discover!

What Produces Iridescent Colors in Thin Films?

1. Submerge a piece of construction paper in a container of water.

2. Apply one drop of clear nail polish to the surface of the water and watch it spread out over the surface of the water.

3. After the nail polish has stopped spreading, slowly lift the construction paper out of the water. The nail polish should adhere to the surface of the paper.

4. Allow the paper to dry.

Analyze and Conclude

1. **Observing** What do you observe as you view the dried film on the surface of the paper?

2. **Predicting** What do you think you will see if you view the film from various angles?

3. **Making Generalizations** How would you explain the colors produced by thin films?

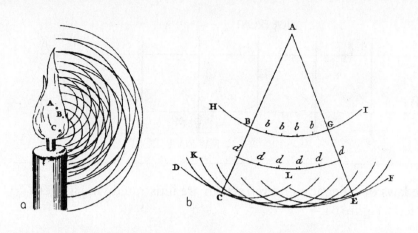

◀ FIGURE 31.1

These drawings are from Huygens' book *Treatise on Light*. **a.** Light from point A expands in wave fronts. **b.** Every point behaves as if it were a new source of waves.

31.1 Huygens' Principle

In the late 1600s a Dutch mathematician-scientist, Christian Huygens, proposed a very interesting idea about light. ⊘ **Huygens stated that light waves spreading out from a point source may be regarded as the overlapping of tiny secondary wavelets, and that every point on any wave front may be regarded as a new point source of secondary waves.** We see this in Figure 31.1. The idea that wave fronts are made up of tinier wave fronts is called **Huygens' principle.**

Wave Fronts Look at the spherical wave front in Figure 31.2. Each point along the wave front *AA′* is the source of a new wavelet that spreads out in a sphere from that point. Only a few of the infinite number of wavelets are shown in the figure. The new wave front *BB′* can be regarded as a smooth surface enclosing the infinite number of overlapping wavelets that started from *AA′* a short time earlier.

As a wave front spreads, it appears less curved. Very far from the original source, the wave fronts seem to form a plane. A good example is the plane waves that arrive from the sun. A Huygens' wavelet construction for plane waves is shown in Figure 31.3. (In a two-dimensional drawing, the planes are shown as straight lines.)

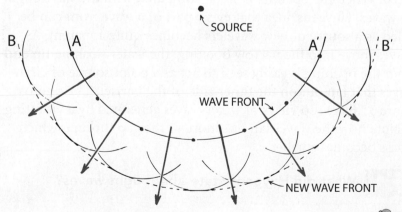

◀ FIGURE 31.2

Every point along the spherical wave front *AA′* is the source of a new wavelet.

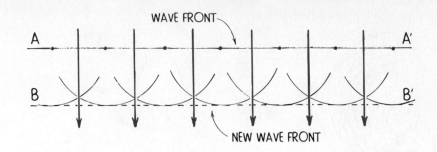

FIGURE 31.3 ▶

Far away from the source, the wave fronts appear to form a plane.

WAVE FRONT

A ⎯ A′

B ⎯ B′

NEW WAVE FRONT

The laws of reflection and refraction are illustrated via Huygens' principle in Figure 31.4.

Huygens' Principle in Water Waves You can observe Huygens' principle in water waves that are made to pass through a narrow opening. A wave with straight wave fronts can be generated in water by repeatedly dipping a stick lengthwise into the water, as shown in Figure 31.5. When the straight wave fronts pass through the opening in a barrier, interesting wave patterns result.

FIGURE 31.4 ▶

Each point along a wave front is the source of a new wave. **a.** The law of reflection can be proven using Huygens' principle. **b.** Huygens' principle can also illustrate refraction.

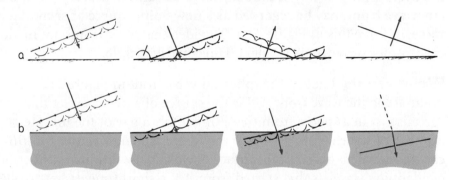

When the opening is wide, you'll see the straight wave fronts pass through without change—except at the corners, where the wave fronts are bent into the "shadow region" in accord with Huygens' principle. As you narrow the width of the opening, less of the wave gets through, and the spreading into the shadow region is more pronounced. When the opening is small compared with the wavelength of the waves, Huygens' idea that every part of a wave front can be regarded as a source of new wavelets becomes quite apparent. As the waves move into the narrow opening, the water sloshing up and down in the opening is easily seen to act as a point source of circular waves that fan out on the other side of the barrier. The photos in Figure 31.6 are top views of water waves generated by a vibrating stick. Note how the waves fan out more as the gap through which they pass becomes smaller.

FIGURE 31.5 ▲

When plane waves are created in a tank of water, they produce a pattern as they pass through an opening in a barrier.

CONCEPT CHECK What did Huygens state about light waves?

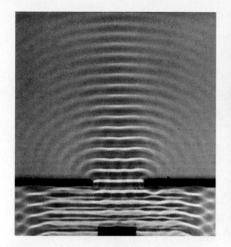
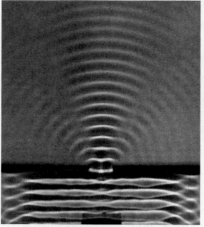
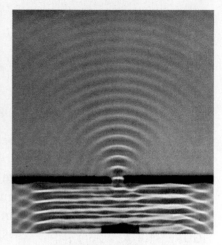

31.2 Diffraction

Any bending of a wave by means other than reflection or refraction is called **diffraction.** Figure 31.6 shows the diffraction of straight water waves through various openings. When the opening is wide compared with the wavelength, the spreading effect is small. As the opening becomes narrower, the diffraction becomes more pronounced. The same occurs for all kinds of waves, including light waves.

Diffraction of Visible Light When light passes through an opening that is large compared with the wavelength of light, as shown in Figure 31.7a, it casts a rather sharp shadow. When light passes through a small opening, such as a thin razor slit in a piece of opaque material, it casts a fuzzy shadow, for the light fans out like the water through the narrow opening, as shown in Figure 31.7b. The light is diffracted by the thin slit.

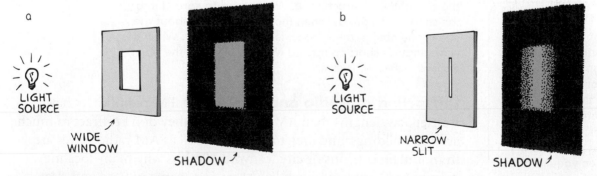

FIGURE 31.7 ▲
Diffraction occurs when light waves pass through an opening. **a.** Light casts a sharp shadow with some fuzziness at its edges when the opening is large compared with the wavelength of the light. **b.** Because of diffraction, it casts a fuzzier shadow when the opening is extremely narrow.

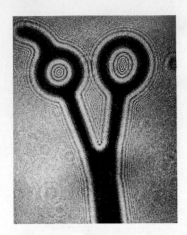

FIGURE 31.8 ▲
Diffraction fringes around the scissors are evident in the shadows of laser light, which is of a single frequency.

Diffraction is not confined to the spreading of light through narrow slits or other openings. Diffraction occurs to some degree for all shadows. Even the sharpest shadow is blurred at the edge. When light is of a single color, diffraction can produce sharp *diffraction fringes* at the edge of the shadow, as shown in Figure 31.8. In white light, the fringes merge together to create a fuzzy blur at the edge of a shadow.

Factors That Affect Diffraction ☑ **The extent of diffraction depends on the relative size of the wavelength compared with the size of the obstruction that casts the shadow.** This is illustrated in Figure 31.9. When the wavelength is long compared with the obstruction, the wave diffracts more. Long waves are better at filling in shadows. This is why foghorns emit low-frequency (long-wavelength) sound waves—to fill in "blind spots." Likewise for radio waves of the standard AM broadcast band. These are very long compared with the size of most objects in their path. Long waves don't "see" relatively small buildings in their path. They diffract, or bend, readily around buildings and reach more places than shorter wavelengths do.[31.2.1]

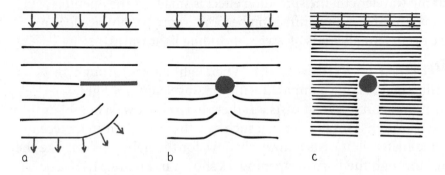

FIGURE 31.9 ▲
The amount of diffraction depends on the wavelength and the size of the obstruction. **a.** Waves tend to spread into the shadow region. **b.** When the wavelength is about the size of the object, the shadow is soon filled in. **c.** When the wavelength is short compared with the width of the object, a sharper shadow is cast.

Diffraction of Radio and TV Waves FM radio waves have shorter wavelengths than AM waves do, so they don't diffract as much around buildings, and aren't received as well as AM radio waves are in mountain canyons or city "canyons." This is why many localities have poor FM reception while AM stations come in loud and clear. TV waves, which are also electromagnetic waves, behave much like FM waves.[31.2.2] Both FM and TV transmission are "line of sight," meaning that obstacles between the transmission tower and antennas for receiving TV broadcasts can cause reception problems.

Cable TV avoids "line-of-sight" transmission problems by sending the signal through a cable or optical fiber rather than "over the air." Satellite TV is line of sight, but normally without a mountain between you and the satellite!

Diffraction in Microscopy Diffraction is not so helpful when we wish to see very small objects with microscopes. If the size of the object is the same as the wavelength of light, the image of the object will be blurred by diffraction. If the object is smaller than the wavelength of light, no structure can be seen. This is why the bacteria you look at in a biology lab just appear as little dots or rods. The internal details are too small to be seen with visible light. No amount of magnification can defeat this fundamental diffraction limit.

To see smaller details, you have to use shorter wavelengths. A beam of electrons has a wavelength associated with it that can be a thousand times shorter than the wavelengths of visible light. Microscopes that use beams of electrons to illuminate tiny things are called *electron microscopes*. Because of the shorter wavelength used, the diffraction limit of an electron microscope is much less than that of an optical microscope.

think!

Why is blue light used to view tiny objects in an optical microscope?
Answer: 31.2

Diffraction and Dolphins Smaller details can be better seen with smaller wavelengths. This is cleverly employed by the dolphin in scanning its environment with high-frequency sound—ultrasound.[31.2.3] The echoes of long-wavelength sound give the dolphin, like the one pictured in Figure 31.10, an overall image of objects in its surroundings. To examine more detail, the dolphin emits sounds of shorter wavelengths. With these sound waves, skin, muscle, and fat are almost transparent to dolphins, but bones, teeth, and gas-filled cavities are clearly apparent. Physical evidence of cancers, tumors, heart attacks, and even emotional states can all be "seen" by the dolphins. The dolphin has always done naturally what humans in the medical field have only recently been able to do with ultrasound devices.

FIGURE 31.10 ▲
A dolphin emits ultrashort-wavelength sounds to locate and identify objects in its environment.

CONCEPT CHECK What affects the extent of diffraction?

---

discover!

Can You See Diffraction in the Sky?

1. Hold two fingers close together between your eye and an illuminated source such as the sky.

2. Look carefully at the narrow opening. Do you see diffraction fringes?

3. Vary the width of the opening, and the distance of your fingers from your eye.

4. Cut a thin slit in a piece of cardboard and repeat the experiment. (Vary the size of the slit by bending the cardboard slightly.)

5. **Think** How do the diffraction fringes change with the width of the slit?

31.3 Interference

If you drop two stones into water at the same time, the two sets of waves that result cross each other and produce what is called an *interference pattern.* ⊘ **Within an interference pattern, wave amplitudes may be increased, decreased, or neutralized.** When the crest of one wave overlaps the crest of another, their individual effects add together; this is *constructive interference.* When the crest of one wave overlaps the trough of another, their individual effects are reduced; this is *destructive interference.* Constructive and destructive interference of waves is illustrated in Figure 31.11.

+ = REINFORCEMENT   + = CANCELLATION   + = PARTIAL CANCELLATION

FIGURE 31.11 ▲

Waves can interfere with each other constructively or destructively.

Water waves can be produced in shallow tanks of water known as *ripple tanks* under more carefully controlled conditions. Interesting patterns are produced when two sources of waves are placed side by side. Small spheres are made to vibrate at a controlled frequency in the water while the wave patterns are photographed from above. The gray "spokes" are regions of destructive interference. The dark and light striped regions are regions of constructive interference. The greater the frequency of the vibrating spheres, the closer together the stripes (and the shorter the wavelength). Note in Figure 31.12 how the number of regions of destructive interference depends on the wavelength and on the distance between the wave sources.

CONCEPT CHECK How does interference affect wave amplitudes?

FIGURE 31.12 ▶

You can observe interference from overlapping water waves from two vibrating sources. **a–b.** The separation between the sources is the same but the wavelength in (b) is shorter than the wavelength in (a). **b–c.** The wavelengths are the same but the sources are closer together in (c) than in (b).

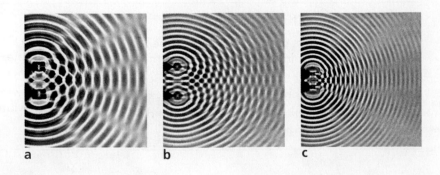

a   b   c

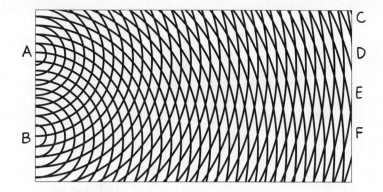

31.4 Young's Interference Experiment

In 1801 the British physicist and physician Thomas Young performed an experiment that was to make him famous.[31.4] Young discovered that when **monochromatic** light—light of a single color—was directed through two closely spaced pinholes, fringes of brightness and darkness were produced on a screen behind. He realized that the bright fringes of light resulted from light waves from both holes arriving crest to crest (constructive interference—more light). Similarly, the dark areas resulted from light waves arriving trough to crest (destructive interference—no light). Young described the interference pattern by drawing a sketch similar to Figure 31.13.

✅ **Young's interference experiment convincingly demonstrated the wave nature of light originally proposed by Huygens.**

Double Slit Experiment Young's experiment is now done with two closely spaced slits instead of pinholes, so the fringes are straight lines. A sodium vapor lamp provides a good source of monochromatic light, and a laser is even better. The experimental arrangement is shown in Figure 31.14a. The pattern of fringes that results is shown in Figure 31.14b.

FIGURE 31.14 ▼
Young's interference experiment demonstrated the wave nature of light.
a. The arrangement for the experiment includes two closely spaced slits and a monochromatic light source.
b. The interference fringes produced are straight lines.

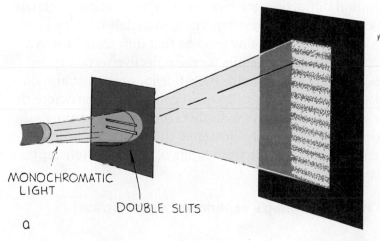

INTERFERENCE PATTERN

MONOCHROMATIC LIGHT

DOUBLE SLITS

a

b

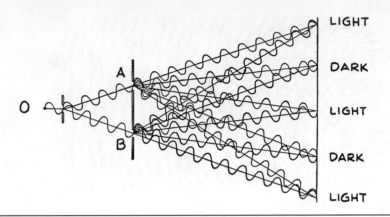

FIGURE 31.15 ▶
Light from *O* passes through slits *A* and *B* and produces an interference pattern on the screen at the right.

LIGHT
DARK
LIGHT
DARK
LIGHT

┌─ **think!** ────────

Why is it important that monochromatic (single-frequency) light be used in Young's interference experiment?
Answer: 31.4

└────────────────

Figure 31.15 shows how the series of bright and dark lines results from the different path lengths from the slits to the screen. A bright fringe occurs when waves from both slits arrive in phase. Dark regions occur when waves arrive out of phase.

Diffraction Gratings Interference patterns are not limited to double-slit arrangements. A multitude of closely spaced parallel slits makes up what is called a **diffraction grating.** Many spectrometers use diffraction gratings rather than prisms to disperse light into colors. Whereas a prism separates the colors of light by refraction, a diffraction grating, such as the one shown in Figure 31.16, separates colors by interference.

FIGURE 31.16 ▶
A diffraction grating disperses light into colors by interference among light beams diffracted by many slits or grooves.

FIGURE 31.17 ▲
Diffraction from ridges in a peacock's feathers produces beautiful iridescent colors.

More common diffraction gratings are seen in reflective materials used in items such as costume jewelry. These materials have hundreds or thousands of close-together, tiny grooves that diffract light into a brilliant spectrum of colors. The pits on the reflective surface of an audio compact disc not only provide high-fidelity music but also diffract light spectacularly into its component colors. But long before the advent of these high-tech items, the feathers of birds were nature's diffraction gratings, as is beautifully illustrated in Figure 31.17. Similarly, the striking colors of opals come from layers of tiny silica spheres that act as diffraction gratings.

CONCEPT CHECK : **What did Young's experiment demonstrate?**

31.5 Interference From Thin Films

Everyone who has seen soap bubbles or gasoline spilled on a wet street, as in Figure 31.18, has noticed the beautiful spectrum of colors reflected from them. Some types of bird feathers have colors that seem to change hue as the bird moves. ✅ **The colors seen in thin films are produced by the interference in the films of light waves of mixed frequencies.** The phenomenon in which the interference of light waves of mixed frequencies produces a spectrum of colors is known as **iridescence.**

A thin film, such as a soap bubble, has two closely spaced surfaces. Light that reflects from one surface may cancel light that reflects from the other surface. For example, the film may be just the right thickness in one place to cause the destructive interference of, say, blue light. If the film is illuminated with white light, then the light that reflects to your eye will have no blue in it. What happens when blue is taken away from white light? The answer is, the complementary color will appear. And for the cancellation of blue, we get yellow. So the soap bubble will appear yellow wherever blue is canceled.

In a thicker part of the film, where green is canceled, the bubble will appear magenta. The different colors correspond to the cancellations of their complementary colors by different thicknesses of the film.

Figure 31.19 illustrates interference for a thin layer of gasoline on a layer of water. Light reflects from both the upper gasoline–air surface and the lower gasoline–water surface. Suppose that the incident beam is monochromatic blue, as in the illustration. If the gasoline layer is just the right thickness to cause cancellation of light of that wavelength, then the gasoline surface appears dark to the eye. On the other hand, if the incident beam is white sunlight, the gasoline surface appears yellow to the eye. Blue is subtracted from the white, leaving the complementary color, yellow.

FIGURE 31.18 ▲
The intriguing colors of gasoline on a wet street correspond to different thicknesses of the thin film.

think!

What color will reflect from a soap bubble in sunlight when its thickness is such that red light is canceled?
Answer: 31.5

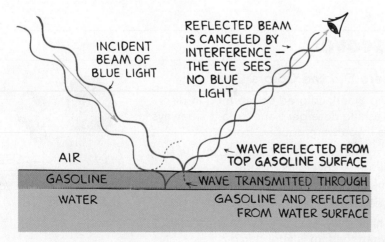

INCIDENT BEAM OF BLUE LIGHT

REFLECTED BEAM IS CANCELED BY INTERFERENCE — THE EYE SEES NO BLUE LIGHT

← WAVE REFLECTED FROM TOP GASOLINE SURFACE

← WAVE TRANSMITTED THROUGH GASOLINE AND REFLECTED FROM WATER SURFACE

AIR
GASOLINE
WATER

◄ **FIGURE 31.19**
The thin film of gasoline is just the right thickness that monochromatic blue light reflected from the top surface of the gasoline is canceled by light of the same wavelength reflected from the water.

FIGURE 31.20 ▶
Physicist and author Bob Greenler shows interference colors with *big* bubbles.

Soap-bubble colors come from interference of reflected light from inside and outside surfaces of the bubble.

The beautiful colors reflected from some types of seashells are produced by interference of light in their thin transparent coatings. So are the sparkling colors from fractures within opals. Interference colors can even be seen in the thin film of detergent left when dishes are not properly rinsed.

Interference provides the principal method for measuring the wavelengths of light. Wavelengths of other regions of the electromagnetic spectrum are also measured with interference techniques. Extremely small distances (millionths of a centimeter) are measured with instruments called *interferometers,* which make use of the principle of interference. These instruments are sensitive enough to detect the displacement at the end of a long, several-centimeters-thick solid steel bar when you gently apply opposite twists to opposite ends with your hands. They are among the most accurate measuring instruments known.

CONCEPT CHECK How are the colors seen in thin films produced?

---

discover!

Where Did the Colors Go?

1. Dip a dark-colored coffee mug in dishwashing detergent and hold it sideways as if you were pouring from it.
2. Look at the reflected light from the soap film that covers its mouth.
3. What do you observe when the film becomes very thin—just before it pops?
4. **Think** Why does the top appear black when the film is very thin?

31.6 Laser Light

Light emitted by a common lamp is incoherent. In **incoherent** light, the crests and troughs of the light waves don't line up with one another (and there are many different frequencies as well). As shown in Figure 31.21, incoherent light is chaotic. Interference within a beam of incoherent light is rampant, and a beam spreads out after a short distance, becoming wider and wider and less intense with increased distance.

◀ **FIGURE 31.21**
Incoherent white light contains waves of many frequencies and wavelengths that are out of phase with one another.

Even if a beam is filtered so that it is monochromatic (has a single frequency), as illustrated in Figure 31.22, it is still incoherent because the waves are out of phase and interfere with one another. The slightest differences in their directions result in a spreading with increased distance.

◀ **FIGURE 31.22**
Light of a single frequency and wavelength can still be out of phase.

Coherent Light A beam of light that has the same frequency, phase, and direction is said to be **coherent.** Figure 31.23 illustrates coherent light waves. There is no interference of waves within the beam. Only a beam of coherent light will not spread and diffuse.

Coherent light is produced by a **laser** (whose name comes from *light amplification by stimulated emission of radiation*).[31.6] ☑ **Laser light is emitted when excited atoms of a solid, liquid, or gas are stimulated to emit photons in phase.** Within a laser, a light wave emitted from one atom stimulates the emission of light from a neighboring atom so that the crests of each wave coincide. These waves stimulate the emission of others in cascade fashion, and a beam of coherent light is produced. This is very different from the random emission of light from atoms in common sources.

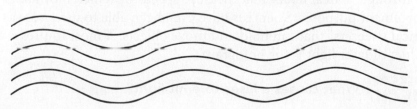

◀ **FIGURE 31.23**
Coherent light consists of identical waves that are all in phase.

Operation of Lasers A laser is not a source of energy. It is simply a converter of energy, taking advantage of the process of stimulated emission to concentrate a certain fraction of the energy input (commonly much less than 1%) into a thin beam of coherent light. Like all devices, a laser can put out no more energy than it takes in.

In a helium-neon laser, which is shown in Figure 31.24, a high voltage applied to a mixture of helium and neon gas energizes helium atoms to a state of high energy. Before the helium can emit light, it gives up its energy by collision with neon, which is boosted to an otherwise hard-to-come-by matched energy state. Light emitted by neon stimulates other energized neon atoms to emit matched-frequency light. The process cascades, and a coherent beam of light is produced. The output remains steady because the helium is constantly reenergized.

FIGURE 31.24 ▶
A helium-neon laser emits a steady output of coherent light.

Applications of Lasers Lasers come in many types and have broad applications in diverse fields. Surveyors and construction workers use them as "chalk lines," surgeons use them as scalpels, and garment manufacturers use them as cloth-cutting saws. They are used to read product codes, like the one shown in Figure 31.25, into cash registers, to read the music and video signals in CDs and DVDs, and to read the bar code on the cover of your *Conceptual Physics* textbook. Lasers are now being used to cut metals, transmit information through optical fibers, and measure speeds of vehicles for law enforcement purposes. Scientists have even been able to use lasers as "optical tweezers" that can hold and move objects. A most impressive product of laser light is the hologram.

780201 286526

FIGURE 31.25 ▲
A product code is read by laser light that reflects from the bar pattern and is converted to an electrical signal that is fed into a computer. The signal is high when light is reflected from the white spaces and low when reflected from a dark bar.

CONCEPT CHECK What causes a laser to emit light?

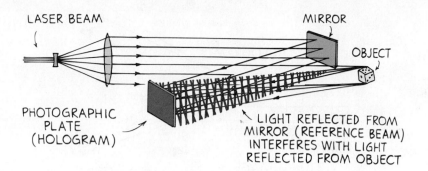

◄ **FIGURE 31.26**

In this simplified arrangement for making a hologram, the laser light that exposes the photographic film is made up of two parts: one part is reflected from the object, and one part is reflected from the mirror.

31.7 The Hologram

A **hologram** is a three-dimensional version of a photograph that contains the whole message or entire picture in every portion of its surface. To the naked eye, it appears to be an imageless piece of transparent film, but on its surface is a pattern of microscopic interference fringes. Light diffracted from these fringes produces an image that is extremely realistic. Holograms are also difficult to reproduce—hence their use on credit cards.

Producing a Hologram ✅ **A hologram is produced by the interference between two laser light beams on photographic film.** The two beams are part of one beam. One part illuminates the object and is reflected from the object to the film. The second part, called the *reference beam,* is reflected from a mirror to the film, as shown in Figure 31.26. Interference between the reference beam and light reflected from the different points on the object produces a pattern of microscopic fringes on the film. Light from nearer parts of the object travels shorter paths than light from farther parts of the object. The different distances traveled will produce slightly different interference patterns with the reference beam. In this way information about the depth of an object is recorded.

Holograms viewed with white light are common on credit cards. Watch for them on money.

Link to VISION

Spiky Stars All through the ages stars in the night sky have been drawn with pointed spikes. Ever wonder why? The reason doesn't have to do with the stars, which are point sources of light in the night sky, but rather with poor eyesight and diffraction. The surface of our eyes becomes scratched by a variety of causes and acts like a sort of diffraction grating. Instead of seeing point sources of light, we sometimes see spikes that may shimmer and twinkle due to temperature differences in the atmosphere. In a windy desert region where sandstorms are frequent, our corneas are even more scratched and we see more vivid star spikes. Stars don't really have pointed spikes. They just appear spiked because of scratches on the surfaces of our eyes.

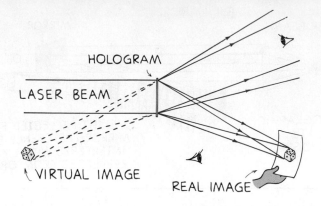

Viewing a Hologram

When light falls on a hologram, it is diffracted by the fringed pattern to produce wave fronts identical in form to the original wave fronts reflected by the object. The diffracted wave fronts produce the same effect as the original reflected wave fronts. As illustrated in Figure 31.27, when you look through a hologram, you see a three-dimensional virtual image. Looking through a hologram is like looking through a window. You refocus your eyes to see near and far parts of the image, just as you do when viewing a real object. Converging diffracted light produces a real image in front of the hologram, which can be projected on a screen. Since the image has depth, you cannot see near and far parts of the image in sharp focus for any single position on a flat screen. Parallax is evident when you move your head to the side and see down the sides of the object, or when you lower your head and look underneath the object. Holographic pictures appear to be three-dimensional, and therefore, are extremely realistic.

Interestingly enough, if the hologram is made on film, you can cut it in half and still see the entire image on each half. And you can cut one of the pieces in half again and again and see the entire image, just as you can put your eye to any part of a window to see outdoors. Every part of the hologram has received and recorded light from the entire object.

Even more interesting is holographic magnification. If holograms are made using short-wavelength light and viewed with light of a longer wavelength, the resulting image is magnified in the same proportion as the wavelengths. Holograms made with X-rays would be magnified thousands of times when viewed with visible light and appropriate viewing arrangements.

Light is interesting—especially when it is diffracted through the interference fringes of that supersophisticated diffraction grating, the hologram!

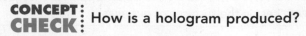 **CONCEPT CHECK** How is a hologram produced?

31 REVIEW

Go Online
PHSchool.com
For: Self-Assessment
Visit: PHSchool.com
Web Code: csa – 3100

Concept Summary ······

- Huygens stated that light waves spreading out from a point source may be regarded as the overlapping of tiny secondary wavelets, and that every point on any wave front may be regarded as a new point source of secondary waves.

- The extent of diffraction depends on the relative size of the wavelength compared with the size of the obstruction that casts the shadow.

- Within an interference pattern, wave amplitudes may be increased, decreased, or neutralized.

- Young's interference experiment convincingly demonstrated the wave nature of light originally proposed by Huygens.

- The colors seen in thin films are produced by the interference in the films of light waves of mixed frequencies.

- Laser light is emitted when excited atoms of a solid, liquid, or gas are stimulated to emit photons in phase.

- A hologram is produced by the interference between two laser light beams on photographic film.

Key Terms ······

Huygens' principle (p. 623)
diffraction (p. 625)
monochromatic (p. 629)
diffraction grating (p. 630)
iridescence (p. 631)
incoherent (p. 633)
coherent (p. 633)
laser (p. 633)
hologram (p. 635)

think! Answers

31.2 Blue light has a shorter wavelength than most of the other wavelengths of visible light, so there's less diffraction. More details of the object will be visible under blue light.

31.4 If light of a variety of wavelengths were diffracted by the slits, dark fringes for one wavelength would be filled in with bright fringes for another, resulting in no distinct fringe pattern. If the path difference equals one-half wavelength for one frequency, it cannot also equal one-half wavelength for any other frequency. Different frequencies will "fill in" the fringes.

31.5 You will see the color cyan, which is the complementary color of red.

31 ASSESS

Check Concepts ......

Section 31.1

1. What is Huygens' principle?

Section 31.2

2. a. Waves spread out when they pass through an opening. Does spreading become more or less pronounced for narrower openings?

b. What is this spreading called?

3. Does diffraction aid or hinder radio reception?

4. Does diffraction aid or hinder the viewing of images in a microscope?

Section 31.3

5. Is it possible for a wave to be canceled by another wave? Defend your answer.

Section 31.4

6. Does wave interference occur for waves in general, or only for light waves? Give examples to support your answer.

7. What was Thomas Young's discovery?

8. What is the cause of the fringes of light in Young's experiment?

9. What is a diffraction grating?

Section 31.5

10. What is required for part of the light reflected from a surface to be canceled by another part reflected from a second surface?

11. What is iridescence, and to what phenomenon is it related?

12. If a soap bubble is thick enough to cancel yellow by interference, what color will it appear if illuminated by white light?

13. Why is gasoline that is spilled on a wet surface so colorful?

14. What is an interferometer, and on what physics principle is it based?

Section 31.6

15. How does light from a laser differ from light from an ordinary lamp?

16. Can a laser put out more energy than is put in? (Would you have to know more about lasers to answer this question? Why?)

Section 31.7

17. What is a hologram, and on what physics principle is it based?

18. How does the image of a hologram differ from that of a common photograph?

19. What would be the advantage of making holograms with X-rays?

Think and Rank ••••••

Rank each of the following sets of scenarios in order of the quantity or property involved. List them from left to right. If scenarios have equal rankings, then separate them with an equal sign. (e.g., A = B)

20. The diagram of Thomas Young's experiment shows identical wave sources at points A and B. Points C and D mark regions of destructive interference where crests overlap troughs.

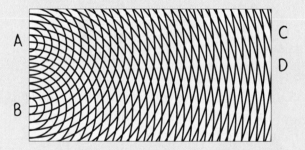

In the following scenarios, a change is made to wave sources A and B. Rank them by the distance between points C and D, from greatest to least.
(A) Distance between sources A and B is reduced to 0.9 as far.
(B) Distance between sources A and B is increased to 1.1 as far.
(C) Wavelength of waves is reduced to half.

21. Dark and light fringes on the screen are produced by interference. In the following scenarios, a change is made to either the light source or the spacing d between slits A and B. Rank them by the distance between fringes, from greatest to least.

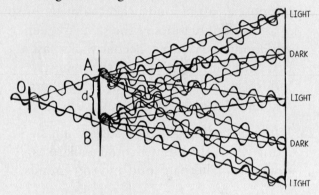

(A) Slit spacing d between A and B is reduced to $0.9d$.
(B) Slit spacing d between A and B is increased to $1.1d$.
(C) Wavelength of light is doubled.

Think and Explain ••••••

22. Suppose the speakers at an open-air rock concert are pointed forward. You move about and notice that the sounds of female vocalists can be heard in front of the stage, but very little off to the sides. By comparison you notice that bass sounds can be heard quite well both in front and off to the sides. What is your explanation?

23. In our everyday environment, diffraction is much more evident for sound waves than for light waves. Why is this so?

24. Why do radio waves diffract around buildings while light waves do not?

25. Suppose a pair of loudspeakers a meter or so apart emit pure tones of the same frequency and loudness. When a listener walks past in a path parallel to the line that joins the loudspeakers, the sound is heard to alternate from loud to soft. What is going on?

26. In the preceding question, suggest a path along which the listener could walk so as not to hear alternate loud and soft sounds.

27. When monochromatic light illuminates a pair of thin slits, an interference pattern is produced on a wall behind. How will the distance between the fringes of the pattern for red light differ from that for blue light?

28. Seashells, butterfly wings, and the feathers of some birds often change color as you look at them from different positions. Explain this phenomenon in terms of light interference.

29. When Thomas Young performed his interference experiment, monochromatic light passed through a single narrow opening before it reached the double openings. Explain why this made the fringes clear. (*Hint*: What would be the result if light reaching the double openings came from several different directions?)

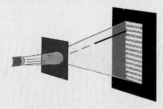

30. If you notice the interference patterns of a thin film of oil or gasoline on water, you'll note that the colors form complete rings. How are these rings similar to the lines of equal elevation on a contour map?

31. Figure 31.19 shows destructive interference of blue light waves reflected from the top gasoline surface and from the top water surface. If white light is incident at the same angle, the eye sees yellow light. Would changing the viewing angle still produce yellow light? Would changing the thickness of the gasoline layer still show yellow? Defend your answers.

32. Suppose the thickness of a soap film is just right for canceling yellow light.
    a. What color does the eye see?
    b. Why will this color change when the surface is viewed at a grazing angle?

33. The interference colors seen in soap bubbles are not reds, greens, and blues, but instead are magentas, yellows, and cyans. Why?

34. The left column lists some colored objects. Match them to the various ways that light may produce that color from the choices in the right column.
    a. yellow bananas
    b. blue sky
    c. rainbow
    d. peacock feathers
    e. soap bubble

    1. interference
    2. diffraction
    3. selective reflection
    4. refraction
    5. scattering

Activity · · · · · ·

35. Make some slides for a slide projector by sticking crumpled cellophane onto pieces of slide-sized polarizing material. Also try strips of cellophane tape, overlapping at different angles. (Experiment with different brands of tape.) Project the slides onto a large screen or white wall and rotate a second, slightly larger piece of polarizing material in front of the projector lens. The colors are vivid! Do this in rhythm with your favorite music, and you'll have your own light and sound show. Write a detailed description of how you put together your show.

More Problem-Solving Practice
Appendix F

UNIT V ELECTRICITY AND MAGNETISM

IT'S A FACT!

Electricity is a form of energy represented by the movement of electric charge from one position to another. An electric charge can exert a force on other charged objects without even touching them, similar to the way a magnet can attract or repel other objects without touching them. In this unit, you will learn many interesting facts about electricity and magnetism.

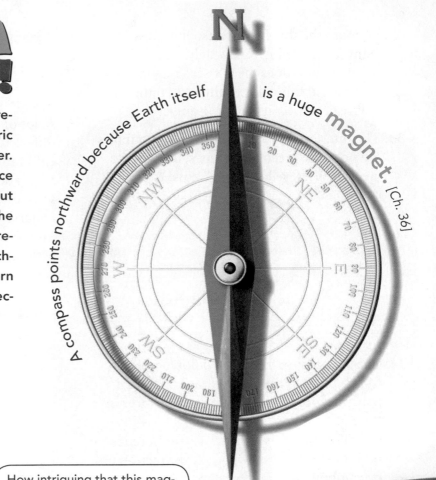

A compass points northward because Earth itself is a huge magnet. [Ch. 36]

How intriguing that this magnet outpulls the whole world when it lifts these nails. The pull between the nails and Earth I call a **gravitational force,** and the pull between the nails and the magnet I call a **magnetic force.** I can name these forces, but I don't yet understand them. My learning begins by realizing there's a big difference in knowing the names of things and really understanding those things.

The energy stored in a **capacitor** comes from the work required to charge it. [Ch. 33]

Go Online
SCIENCE NEWS

For: Articles on electricity and magnetism
Visit: PHSchool.com
Web Code: cse – 5000

A step-up **transformer** can increase voltage in order to power a neon sign. [Ch. 37]

Electric outlets are not a source of electrons. They are a source of **electrical energy.** [Ch. 34]

Any path along which electrons can flow is a **circuit.** [Ch. 35]

 32 ELECTROSTATICS

THE BIG IDEA : Electrostatics involves electric charges, the forces between them, and their behavior in materials.

Electricity in one form or another underlies just about everything around you. It's in the lightning from the sky; it's in the spark beneath your feet when you scuff across a rug; and it's what holds atoms together to form molecules. This chapter is about **electrostatics,** or electricity at rest. Electrostatics involves electric charges, the forces between them, and their behavior in materials.

An understanding of electricity requires a step-by-step approach, for one concept is the building block for the next. So please study this material with extra care. It is a good idea at this time to lean more heavily on the laboratory part of your course, for *doing* physics is better than only studying physics.

---

discover!

How Can an Object Become Electrically Charged?

1. Obtain an electrophorus and rub the insulating plate with a piece of wool, fur, or cloth.

2. Lower the pie pan onto the plate.

3. Touch the pie pan with your finger. The pan should now be charged.

4. Bring the pan in contact with an electroscope or hold it near a thin stream of water or small pieces of paper.

Analyze and Conclude

1. **Observing** What evidence do you have that the pie pan was actually charged?

2. **Predicting** How many times do you think you can charge the pie pan without having to once again rub the insulating plate?

3. **Making Generalizations** Based on your experimentation with the electrophorus, how would you define electric charge?

32.1 Electrical Forces and Charges

You are familiar with the force of gravity. It attracts you to Earth, and you call it your weight. Now consider a force acting on you that is billions upon billions of times stronger. Such a force could compress you to a size about the thickness of a piece of paper. But suppose that in addition to this enormous force there is a repelling force that is also billions upon billions of times stronger than gravity. The two forces acting on you would balance each other and have no noticeable effect at all, as shown in Figure 32.1. It so happens that there is a pair of such forces acting on you all the time—electrical forces.

The Atom **Electrical forces** arise from particles in atoms. In the simple model of the atom proposed in the early 1900s by Ernest Rutherford and Niels Bohr, a positively charged nucleus is surrounded by electrons, as illustrated in Figure 32.2. The protons in the nucleus attract the electrons and hold them in orbit. Electrons are attracted to protons, but electrons repel other electrons. The fundamental electrical property to which the mutual attractions or repulsions between electrons or protons is attributed is called **charge.** [32.1] By convention (general agreement), electrons are *negatively* charged and protons *positively* charged. Neutrons have no charge, and are neither attracted nor repelled by charged particles.

Here are some important facts about atoms:

1. Every atom has a positively charged nucleus surrounded by negatively charged electrons.

2. All electrons are identical; that is, each has the same mass and the same quantity of negative charge as every other electron.

3. The nucleus is composed of protons and neutrons. (The common form of hydrogen, which has no neutrons, is the only exception.) All protons are identical; similarly, all neutrons are identical. A proton has nearly 2000 times the mass of an electron, but its positive charge is equal in magnitude to the negative charge of an electron. A neutron has slightly greater mass than a proton and has no charge.

4. Atoms have as many electrons as protons, so a neutral atom has zero *net* charge.

Attraction and Repulsion Just *why* electrons repel electrons and are attracted to protons is beyond the scope of this book. We simply say that this electric behavior is fundamental, or basic. ✅ **The fundamental rule at the base of all electrical phenomena is that like charges repel and opposite charges attract.**

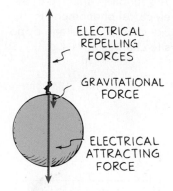

FIGURE 32.1 ▲
The enormous attractive and repulsive electrical forces between the charges in Earth and the charges in your body balance out, leaving the relatively weaker force of gravity, which only attracts. Hence your weight is due only to gravity.

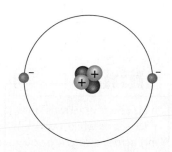

FIGURE 32.2 ▲
The helium nucleus is composed of two protons and two neutrons. The positively charged protons attract two negative electrons.

FIGURE 32.3 ▶

The fundamental rule of all electrical phenomena is that like charges repel and opposite charges attract.

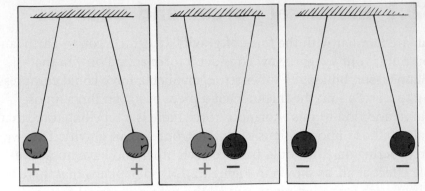

Negative and *positive* are just the **names** given to opposite charges. The names chosen could just as well have been "east and west" or "top and down" or "Mary and Larry."

The old saying that opposites attract, usually referring to people, was first popularized by public lecturers who traveled about by horse and wagon to entertain people by demonstrating the scientific marvels of electricity. An important part of these demonstrations was the charging and discharging of pith balls. Pith is a light, spongy plant tissue. Balls of pith were coated with aluminum paint so their surfaces would conduct electricity. When suspended from a silk thread, such a ball would be attracted to a rubber rod just rubbed with cat's fur, but when the two made contact, the force of attraction would change to a force of repulsion. Thereafter, the ball would be repelled by the rubber rod but attracted to a glass rod that had just been rubbed with silk. Figure 32.3 shows how a pair of pith balls charged in different ways exhibits both attraction and repulsion forces. The lecturer pointed out that nature provides two kinds of charge, just as it provides two sexes.

CONCEPT CHECK : What is the fundamental rule at the base of all electrical phenomena?

32.2 Conservation of Charge

Electrons and protons have electric charge. In a neutral atom, there are as many electrons as protons, so there is no net charge. The total positive charge balances the total negative charge exactly. If an electron is removed from an atom, the atom is no longer neutral. The atom has one more positive charge (proton) than negative charge (electron) and is said to be positively charged.

A charged atom is called an *ion*. A *positive ion* has a net positive charge; it has lost one or more electrons. A *negative ion* has a net negative charge; it has gained one or more extra electrons.

think!

If you scuff electrons onto your shoes while walking across a rug, are you negatively or positively charged?

Answer: 32.2

Electrically Charged Objects Matter is made of atoms, and atoms are made of electrons and protons (and neutrons as well). An object that has equal numbers of electrons and protons has no net electric charge. But if there is an imbalance in the numbers, the object is then electrically charged. An imbalance comes about by adding or removing electrons.

Although the innermost electrons in an atom are bound very tightly to the oppositely charged atomic nucleus, the outermost electrons of many atoms are bound very loosely and can be easily dislodged. How much energy is required to tear an electron away from an atom varies for different substances. The electrons are held more firmly in rubber than in fur, for example. Hence, when a rubber rod is rubbed by a piece of fur, as illustrated in Figure 32.4, electrons transfer from the fur to the rubber rod. The rubber then has an excess of electrons and is negatively charged. The fur, in turn, has a deficiency of electrons and is positively charged. If you rub a glass or plastic rod with silk, you'll find that the rod becomes positively charged. The silk has a greater affinity for electrons than the glass or plastic rod. Electrons are rubbed off the rod and onto the silk.

⊘ **An object that has unequal numbers of electrons and protons is electrically charged.** If it has more electrons than protons, the object is negatively charged. If it has fewer electrons than protons, it is positively charged.

FIGURE 32.4 ▲
When electrons are transferred from the fur to the rod, the rod becomes negatively charged.

Principle of Conservation of Charge The principle that electrons are neither created nor destroyed but are simply transferred from one material to another is known as **conservation of charge.** In every event, whether large-scale or at the atomic and nuclear level, the principle of conservation of charge applies. No case of the creation or destruction of net electric charge has ever been found. The conservation of charge is a cornerstone in physics, ranking with the conservation of energy and momentum.

Any object that is electrically charged has an excess or deficiency of some whole number of electrons—electrons cannot be divided into fractions of electrons. This means that the charge of the object is a whole-number multiple of the charge of an electron. It cannot have a charge equal to the charge of 1.5 or 1000.5 electrons, for example.[32.2] All charged objects to date have a charge that is a whole-number multiple of the charge of a single electron.

Conservation of charge is another of the physics conservation principles. Recall, from previous chapters, conservation of momentum and conservation of energy.

**CONCEPT
CHECK** : What causes an object to become electrically charged?

The Threat of Static Charge

Today electronics technicians in high-technology firms that build, test, and repair electronic circuit components follow procedures to guard against static charge, to prevent damage to delicate circuits. Some circuit components are so sensitive that they can be "fried" by static electric sparks. So electronics technicians work in environments free of high-resistance surfaces where static charge can accumulate and wear clothing of special fabric with ground wires between their sleeves and their socks. Some wear

special wrist bands that are clipped to a grounded surface, so that any charge that builds up, by movement on a chair for example, is discharged. As electronic components become smaller and circuit elements are placed closer together, the threat of electric sparks producing short circuits becomes greater and greater.

Critical Thinking What effects on your daily life are caused by static charge? What can you do to minimize these effects?

Coulomb's law is like Newton's law of gravity. But unlike gravity, electric forces can be attractive or repulsive.

32.3 Coulomb's Law

Recall from Newton's law of gravitation that the gravitational force between two objects of mass m_1 and mass m_2 is proportional to the product of the masses and inversely proportional to the square of the distance d between them:

$$F = G\frac{m_1 m_2}{d^2}$$

where G is the universal gravitational constant.

Force, Charges, and Distance The electrical force between any two objects obeys a similar inverse-square relationship with distance. The relationship among electrical force, charges, and distance, now known as **Coulomb's law,** was discovered by the French physicist Charles Coulomb (1736–1806) in the eighteenth century. ☑ **Coulomb's law states that for charged particles or objects that are small compared with the distance between them, the force between the charges varies directly as the product of the charges and inversely as the square of the distance between them.** Coulomb's law can be expressed as

$$F = k\frac{q_1 q_2}{d^2}$$

where d is the distance between the charged particles; q_1 represents the quantity of charge of one particle and q_2 the quantity of charge of the other particle; and k is the proportionality constant.

The SI unit of charge is the **coulomb,** abbreviated C. Common sense might say that it is the charge of a single electron, but it isn't. For historical reasons, it turns out that a charge of 1 C is the charge of 6.24 billion billion (6.24×10^{18}) electrons. This might seem like a great number of electrons, but it represents only the amount of charge that passes through a common 100-W lightbulb in about one second.

The Electrical Proportionality Constant The proportionality constant k in Coulomb's law is similar to G in Newton's law of gravitation. Instead of being a very small number like G, the electrical proportionality constant k is a very large number. Rounded off, it equals

$$k = 9,000,000,000 \ \text{N·m}^2/\text{C}^2$$

or, in scientific notation, $k = 9.0 \times 10^9 \ \text{N·m}^2/\text{C}^2$. The units N·m²/C² convert the right side of the equation to the unit of force, the newton (N), when the charges are in coulombs (C) and the distance is in meters (m). Note that if a pair of charges of 1 C each were 1 m apart, the force of repulsion between the two charges would be 9 billion newtons.[32.3.1] That would be more than 10 times the weight of a battleship! Obviously, such amounts of *net* charge do not exist in our everyday environment.

As can be seen in Figure 32.5, Newton's law of gravitation for masses is similar to Coulomb's law for electric charges.[32.3.2] Whereas the gravitational force of attraction between a pair of one-kilogram masses is extremely small, the electrical force between a pair of one-coulomb charges is extremely large. The greatest difference between gravitation and electrical forces is that while gravity only attracts, electrical forces may either attract or repel.

Go Online

SciLINKS NSTA

For: Links on Coulomb's law
Visit: www.SciLinks.org
Web Code: csn – 3203

think!

What is the chief significance of the fact that G in Newton's law of gravitation is a small number and k in Coulomb's law is a large number when both are expressed in SI units?
Answer: 32.3.1

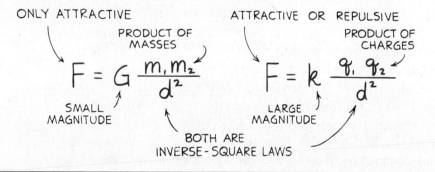

◀ **FIGURE 32.5**
Newton's law of gravitation is similar to Coulomb's law.

Electrical Forces in Atoms Because most objects have almost exactly equal numbers of electrons and protons, electrical forces usually balance out. Between Earth and the moon, for example, there is no measurable electrical force. In general, the weak gravitational force, which only attracts, is the predominant force between astronomical bodies.

think!

a. If an electron at a certain distance from a charged particle is attracted with a certain force, how will the force compare at twice this distance?
b. Is the charged particle in this case positive or negative?
Answer: 32.3.2

Although electrical forces balance out for astronomical and everyday objects, at the atomic level this is not always true. Often two or more atoms, when close together, share electrons. The negative electrons of one atom may at times be closer to the neighboring atom's positive nucleus than they are to the average location of the neighbor's electrons. Then the attractive force between these charges is greater than the repulsive force. This is called bonding and leads to the formation of molecules. It would be wise for anyone planning to study chemistry or biology to know something about electricity.

CONCEPT CHECK What does Coulomb's law state?

do the math!

How does the electrical force between the proton and the electron in a hydrogen atom compare to the gravitational force between these two particles?

The hydrogen atom's nucleus is a proton (mass 1.7×10^{-27} kg), outside of which there is a single electron (mass 9.1×10^{-31} kg) at an average separation distance (d) of 5.3×10^{-11} m.

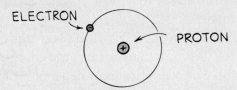

To solve for the electrical force, use Coulomb's law, where both the electron charge q_e and the proton charge q_p have the same magnitude (1.6×10^{-19} C).

$$F_e = k \frac{q_e q_p}{d^2} = (9.0 \times 10^9 \text{ N·m}^2/\text{C}^2) \frac{(1.6 \times 10^{-19} \text{ C})^2}{(5.3 \times 10^{-11} \text{ m})^2} = 8.2 \times 10^{-8} \text{ N}$$

The gravitational force F_g between them is $F_g = G \frac{m_e m_p}{d^2}$

$$= (6.7 \times 10^{-11} \text{ N·m}^2/\text{kg}^2) \frac{(9.1 \times 10^{-31} \text{ kg})(1.7 \times 10^{-27} \text{ kg})}{(5.3 \times 10^{-11} \text{ m})^2}$$

$$= 3.7 \times 10^{-47} \text{ N}$$

A comparison of the two forces is best shown by their ratio:

$$\frac{F_e}{F_g} = \frac{8.2 \times 10^{-8} \text{ N}}{3.7 \times 10^{-47} \text{ N}} = 2.2 \times 10^{39}$$

The electrical force between the particles is more than 10^{39} times greater than the gravitational force. In other words, the electric forces that subatomic particles exert on one another are so much stronger than their mutual gravitational forces that gravitation can be completely neglected.

32.4 Conductors and Insulators

Electrons are more easily moved in some materials than in others. Outer electrons of the atoms in a metal are not anchored to the nuclei of particular atoms, but are free to roam in the material. Materials through which electric charge can flow are called **conductors.** Metals are good conductors for the motion of electric charges for the same reason they are good conductors of heat: Their electrons are "loose."

Electrons in other materials—rubber and glass, for example—are tightly bound and remain with particular atoms. They are not free to wander about to other atoms in the material. These materials, known as **insulators,** are poor conductors of electricity, for the same reason they are generally poor conductors of heat.

Go Online
SciLINKS NSTA

For: Links on conductors and insulators
Visit: www.SciLinks.org
Web Code: csn – 3204

◄ **FIGURE 32.6**
It is easier for electric charge to flow through hundreds of kilometers of metal wire than through a few centimeters of insulating material.

Whether a substance is classified as a conductor or an insulator depends on how tightly the atoms of the substance hold their electrons. ⊘ **Electrons move easily in good conductors and poorly in good insulators.** All substances can be arranged in order of their ability to conduct electric charges. Those at the top of the list are the conductors, and those at the bottom are the insulators. The ends of the list are very far apart. The conductivity of a metal, for example, can be more than a million trillion times greater than the conductivity of an insulator such as glass. In power lines, such as those shown in Figure 32.6, charge flows much more easily through hundreds of kilometers of metal wire than through the few centimeters of insulating material that separates the wire from the supporting tower. In a common appliance cord, charges will flow through several meters of wire to the appliance, and then through its electrical network, and then back through the return wire rather than flow directly across from one wire to the other through the tiny thickness of rubber insulation.

Materials that don't hold electrons tightly lose them to materials that hold electrons more tightly.

Some materials, such as germanium and silicon, are good insulators in their pure crystalline form but increase tremendously in conductivity when even one atom in ten million is replaced with an impurity that adds or removes an electron from the crystal structure. **Semiconductors** are materials that can be made to behave sometimes as insulators and sometimes as conductors. Atoms in a semiconductor hold their electrons until given small energy boosts. This occurs in photovoltaic cells that convert solar energy into electrical energy. Thin layers of semiconducting materials sandwiched together make up *transistors,* which are used in digital media players, computers, and a variety of electrical applications. Transitors amplify electric signals and act as electric switches to control current in circuits—with very little power.

CONCEPT CHECK : What is the difference between a good conductor and a good insulator?

32.5 Charging by Friction and Contact

✅ **Two ways electric charge can be transferred are by friction and by contact.** We are all familiar with the electrical effects produced by friction. We can stroke a cat's fur and hear the crackle of sparks that are produced, or comb our hair in front of a mirror in a dark room and see as well as hear the sparks of electricity. We can scuff our shoes across a rug and feel the tingle as we reach for the doorknob, or do the same when sliding across seats while parked in an automobile, as illustrated in Figure 32.7. In all these cases electrons are being transferred by friction when one material rubs against another.

FIGURE 32.7 ▲
If you slide across a seat in an automobile you are in danger of being charged by friction.

Electrons can also be transferred from one material to another by simply touching. When a charged rod is placed in contact with a neutral object, some charge will transfer to the neutral object. This method of charging is simply called *charging by contact.* If the object is a good conductor, the charge will spread to all parts of its surface because the like charges repel each other. If it is a poor conductor, the extra charge will stay close to where the object was touched.

CONCEPT CHECK : What are two ways electric charge can be transferred?

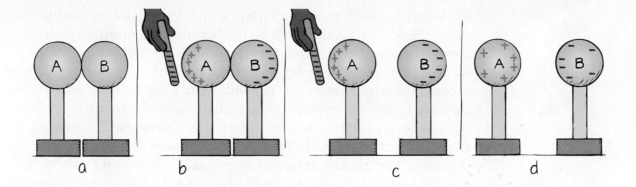

32.6 Charging by Induction

☑ **If a charged object is brought *near* a conducting surface, even without physical contact, electrons will move in the conducting surface.** In Figure 32.8a, the uncharged insulated metal spheres touch each other, so in effect they form a single noncharged conductor. In Figure 32.8b, a negatively charged rod is held near sphere A. Electrons in the metal are repelled by the rod, and excess negative charge has moved onto sphere B, leaving sphere A with excess positive charge. The charge on the two spheres has been redistributed, or **induced.** In Figure 32.8c, the spheres are separated while the rod is still present. In Figure 32.8d, the rod has been removed, and the spheres are charged equally and oppositely. They have been charged by **induction,** which is the charging of an object without direct contact. Since the charged rod never touched them, it retains its initial charge.

A single sphere can be charged similarly by induction. Consider a metal sphere that hangs from a nonconducting string. In Figure 32.9a, the net charge on the metal sphere is zero. In Figure 32.9b, a charge redistribution is induced by the presence of the charged rod. The net charge on the sphere is still zero. In Figure 32.9c, touching the sphere removes electrons by contact. In Figure 32.9d, the sphere is left positively charged. In Figure 32.9e, the sphere is attracted to the negative rod; it swings over to it and touches it. Now electrons move onto the sphere from the rod. The sphere has been negatively charged by contact. In Figure 32.9f, the negative sphere is repelled by the negative rod.

FIGURE 32.8 ▲
Charging by induction can be illustrated using two insulated metal spheres.

FIGURE 32.9 ▼
Charge induction by grounding can be illustrated using a metal sphere hanging from a nonconducting string.

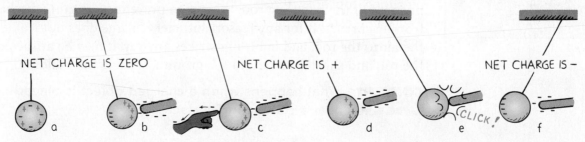

When we touch the metal surface with a finger, as illustrated in Figure 32.9c, charges that repel each other have a conducting path to a practically infinite reservoir for electric charge—the ground. When we allow charges to move off (or onto) a conductor by touching it, it is common to say that we are **grounding** it. Chapter 34 returns to this idea of grounding in the discussion of electric currents.

Charging by induction occurs during thunderstorms. The negatively charged bottoms of clouds induce a positive charge on the surface of Earth below, as seen in Figure 32.10. Benjamin Franklin was the first to demonstrate this in his famous kite-flying experiment, in which he proved that lightning is an electrical phenomenon.[32.6] Most lightning is an electrical discharge between oppositely charged parts of clouds. The kind of lightning we are most familiar with is the electrical discharge between the clouds and the oppositely charged ground below.

FIGURE 32.10 ▲
The bottom of the negatively charged cloud induces a positive charge at the surface of the ground below.

think!

Why does the negative rod in Figure 32.8 have the same charge before and after the spheres are charged, but not when charging takes place as in Figure 32.9?
Answer: 32.6

Franklin also found that charge flows readily to or from sharp points, and fashioned the first lightning rod. If the rod is placed above a building connected to the ground, the point of the rod collects electrons from the air, preventing a large buildup of positive charge on the building by induction. This continual "leaking" of charge prevents a charge buildup that might otherwise lead to a sudden discharge between the cloud and the building. The primary purpose of the lightning rod, then, is to prevent a lightning discharge from occurring. If for any reason sufficient charge does not leak from the air to the rod, and lightning strikes anyway, it may be attracted to the rod and short-circuited to the ground, sparing the building.

CONCEPT CHECK : What happens when a charged object is placed near a conducting surface?

32.7 Charge Polarization

Charging by induction is not restricted to conductors. ☑ **Charge polarization can occur in insulators that are *near* a charged object.** When a charged rod is brought near an insulator, there are no free electrons to migrate throughout the insulating material. Instead, as shown in Figure 32.11a, there is a rearrangement of the positions of charges within the atoms and molecules themselves. One side of the atom or molecule is induced to be slightly more positive (or negative) than the opposite side, and the atom or molecule is said to be **electrically polarized.** If the charged rod is negative, say, then the positive side of the atom or molecule is toward the rod, and the negative side of the atom or molecule is away from it. The atoms or molecules near the surface all become aligned this way, as seen in Figure 32.11b.

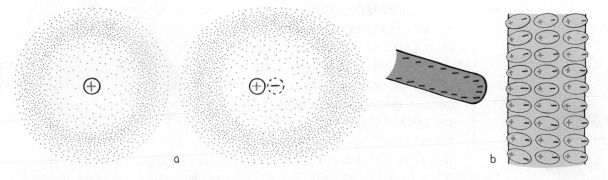

FIGURE 32.11 ▲
a. When an external negative charge is brought closer from the left, the charges within a neutral atom or molecule rearrange.
b. All the atoms or molecules near the surface of the insulator become electrically polarized.

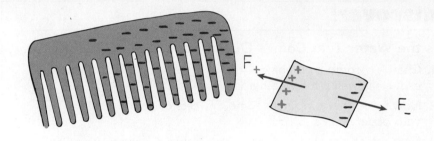

FIGURE 32.12 ▲
A charged comb attracts an uncharged piece of paper because the force of attraction for the closer charge is greater than the force of repulsion for the farther charge.

If you rub a balloon on your hair, you will find that the balloon will stick to a wall.

Examples of Charge Polarization This explains why electrically neutral bits of paper are attracted to a charged object, such as the comb shown in Figure 32.12. Molecules are polarized in the paper, with the oppositely charged sides of molecules closest to the charged object. Closeness wins, and the bits of paper experience a net attraction. Sometimes they will cling to the charged object and suddenly fly off. This indicates that charging by contact has occurred; the paper bits have acquired the same sign of charge as the charged object and are then repelled.

Rub an inflated balloon on your hair and it becomes charged. Place the balloon against the wall and it sticks. As shown in Figure 32.13, the charge on the balloon induces an opposite surface charge on the wall. Closeness wins, for the charge on the balloon is slightly closer to the opposite induced charge than to the charge of the same sign.

FIGURE 32.13 ▶
The negatively charged balloon polarizes molecules in the wooden wall and creates a positively charged surface, so the balloon sticks to the wall.

FIGURE 32.14 ▲
An H_2O molecule is an electric dipole.

Electric Dipoles Many molecules—H_2O, for example—are electrically polarized in their normal states. The distribution of electric charge is not perfectly even. As illustrated in Figure 32.14, there is a little more negative charge on one side of the molecule than on the other. Such molecules are said to be *electric dipoles*.

In summary, objects are electrically charged in three ways.

1. **By friction**, when electrons are transferred by friction from one object to another.

2. **By contact**, when electrons are transferred from one object to another by direct contact without rubbing. A charged rod placed in contact with an uncharged piece of metal, for example, will transfer charge to the metal.

3. **By induction**, when electrons are caused to gather or disperse by the presence of nearby charge (even without physical contact). A charged rod held near a metal surface, for example, repels charges of the same sign as those on the rod and attracts opposite charges. The result is a redistribution of charge on the object without any change in its net charge. If the metal surface is discharged by contact, with a finger for example, then a net charge will be left.

If the object is an insulator, on the other hand, then a realignment of charge rather than a migration of charge occurs. This is charge polarization, in which the surface near the charged object becomes oppositely charged. This occurs when you stick a charged balloon to a wall.

CONCEPT CHECK: What happens when an insulator is in the presence of a charged object?

Be glad that water is an electric dipole. If its opposite ends didn't attract different ions, almost all the chemistry that occurs in aqueous solutions would be impossible. Three cheers for the electric dipole nature of the water molecule!

Physics in the Kitchen

Microwave Cooking

Imagine an enclosure filled with table-tennis balls among a few batons, all at rest. Now imagine the batons suddenly flipping back and forth like semi-rotating propellers, striking neighboring table-tennis balls. Almost immediately most table-tennis balls are energized, vibrating in all directions. A microwave oven works similarly. The batons are water molecules that flip back and forth in rhythm with microwaves in the enclosure. The table-tennis balls are nonwater molecules that make up the bulk of material being cooked.

H_2O molecules are polar, with opposite charges on opposite sides. When an electric field is imposed on them, they align with the field like a compass aligns with a magnetic field. Microwaves are an electric field that oscillates, so H_2O molecules oscillate also—and quite energetically. Food is cooked by a sort of "kinetic friction" as flip-flopping H_2O molecules increase the thermal motion of surrounding food molecules.

A microwave oven wouldn't work without the presence of the electric dipoles in the food (usually, but not always, water). That's why microwaves pass through foam, paper, or ceramic plates with no effect. Microwaves also reflect and bounce off conductors with no effect. They do, however, energize water molecules.

 REVIEW

Concept Summary ······

- Like charges repel and opposite charges attract.
- An object that has unequal numbers of electrons and protons is electrically charged.
- Coulomb's law states that for charged particles or objects that are small compared with the distance between them, the force between the charges varies directly as the product of the charges and inversely as the square of the distance between them.
- Electrons move easily in good conductors and poorly in good insulators.
- Electric charge can be transferred by friction and by contact.
- If a charged object is brought *near* a conducting surface, electrons will move in the conducting surface.
- Charge polarization can occur in insulators that are *near* a charged object.

Key Terms ······

electrostatics (p. 644)

electrical forces (p. 645)

charge (p. 645)

conservation of charge (p. 647)

Coulomb's law (p. 648)

coulomb (p. 649)

conductor (p. 651)

insulator (p. 651)

semiconductor (p. 652)

induced (p. 653)

induction (p. 653)

grounding (p. 654)

electrically polarized (p. 655)

think! Answers

32.2   When your rubber- or plastic-soled shoes drag across the rug, they pick up electrons from the rug in the same way you charge a rubber or plastic rod by rubbing it with a cloth. You have more electrons after you scuff your shoes, so you are negatively charged (and the rug is positively charged).

32.3.1   The small value of G indicates that gravity is a weak force; the large value of k indicates that the electrical force is enormous in comparison.

32.3.2   **a.** In accord with the inverse-square law, at twice the distance the force will be one-fourth as much.
    b. Since there is a force of attraction, the charges must be opposite in sign, so the charged particle is positive.

32.6   In the charging process of Figure 32.8, no contact was made between the negative rod and either of the spheres. In the charging process of Figure 32.9, however, the rod touched the sphere when it was positively charged. A transfer of charge by contact reduced the negative charge on the rod.

32 ASSESS

Check Concepts ••••••

Section 32.1

1. Which force—gravitational or electrical—repels as well as attracts?

2. Gravitational forces depend on the property called *mass*. What comparable property underlies electrical forces?

3. How do protons and electrons differ in their electric charge?

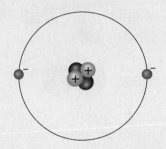

4. Is an electron in a hydrogen atom the same as an electron in a uranium atom?

5. Which has more mass—a proton or an electron?

6. In a normal atom, how many electrons are there compared with protons?

7. **a.** How do like charges behave toward each other?
   b. How do unlike charges behave toward each other?

Section 32.2

8. How does a negative ion differ from a positive ion?

9. What does it mean to say that charge is conserved?

10. **a.** If electrons are rubbed from cat's fur onto a rubber rod, does the rod become positively or negatively charged?
    b. How about the cat's fur?

Section 32.3

11. **a.** How is Coulomb's law similar to Newton's law of gravitation?
    b. How are the two laws different?

12. The SI unit of mass is the kilogram. What is the SI unit of charge?

13. The proportionality constant k in Coulomb's law is huge in ordinary units, whereas the proportionality constant G in Newton's law of gravity is tiny. What does this mean in terms of the relative strengths of these two forces?

Section 32.4

14. **a.** Why are metals good conductors?
    b. Why are materials such as rubber and glass good insulators?

15. What is a semiconductor?

Section 32.5

16. Which two methods of charging objects involve touching?

Section 32.6

17. Which method of charging objects involves no touching?

18. What is lightning?

19. What is the function of a lightning rod?

Section 32.7

20. What does it mean to say an object is electrically polarized?

21. When a charged object polarizes another, why is there an attraction between the objects?

22. What is an electric dipole?

Think and Rank ······

Rank each of the following sets of scenarios in order of the quantity or property involved. List them from left to right. If scenarios have equal rankings, then separate them with an equal sign. (e.g., A = B)

23. The three pairs of metal spheres below are all the same size and have different charges on their surfaces, as indicated. The pairs of spheres are brought into contact with each other. After several moments the spheres are separated. Rank from greatest to least the total amount of charge on the pairs of spheres after separation.

A

B   C
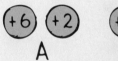

24. Three separate pairs of uncharged metal spheres are in contact. A (positively or negatively) charged rod is brought up to the same distance from each set of spheres. Rank the resulting charge on each sphere from greatest positive to greatest negative.

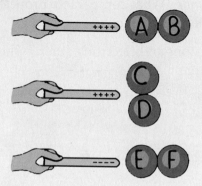

25. Indicated below are pairs of electric charges in three different arrangements. In each figure, a test charge is located at the point labeled P. The other, much larger, charges all have the same magnitude and lie on a line that passes through P. Note some charges are positive and some are negative. Rank the arrangements on the basis of the strength of the electric force on the test charge, from strongest to weakest.

A   B   C

26. Shown below are three separate pairs of point charges, pairs A, B, and C. Assume the pairs interact only with each other. Rank the magnitudes of the force between the pairs, from largest to smallest.

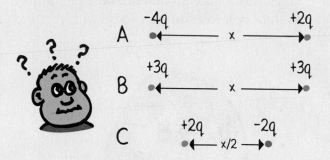

Think and Explain ......

27. Electrical forces between charges are enormous relative to gravitational forces. Yet, we normally don't sense electrical forces between us and our environment, while we do sense our gravitational interaction with Earth. Why is this so?

28. Two equally charged particles exert equal forces on each other. Suppose that the charge on one of the particles is doubled. The charge on the other remains the same.
a. How much stronger is the force between them?
b. How does the force change if the charges of both particles are doubled?

29. How will the forces between two charged particles compare when one particle has ten times as much charge as the other? Defend your answer.

30. If electrons were positive and protons negative, would Coulomb's law be written the same or differently?

31. If you scuff electrons from your hair onto a comb, are you positively or negatively charged? How about the comb?

32. The five thousand billion billion freely moving electrons in a penny repel one another. Why don't they fly out of the penny?

33. If a glass rod that is rubbed with a plastic dry cleaner's bag acquires a certain charge, why does the plastic bag have exactly the same amount of opposite charge?

34. Why do clothes often cling together after tumbling in a clothes dryer?

35. Why will dust be attracted to a CD wiped with a dry cloth?

36. When one material is rubbed against another, electrons jump readily from one to the other, but protons do not. Why is this? (Think in atomic terms.)

37. Plastic wrap becomes electrically charged when pulled from its container. Does the charged wrap stick better to glass bowls or metal bowls?

38. Explain how an object that is electrically neutral can be attracted to an object that is charged.

39. An electroscope is a simple device. It consists of a metal ball that is attached by a conductor to two fine gold leaves that are protected from air disturbances in a jar, as shown in the sketch. When the ball is touched by a charged object, the leaves that normally hang straight down spring apart. Why? (Electroscopes are useful not only as charge detectors, but also for measuring the amount of charge: the more charge transferred to the ball, the more the leaves diverge.)

40. Would it be necessary for a charged object to actually touch the leaves of an electroscope (see Question 39) for the leaves to diverge? Defend your answer.

41. Figure 32.12 shows a negatively charged plastic comb attracting bits of paper with no net charge. If the comb were positively charged, would it attract the same bits of paper? Defend your answer.

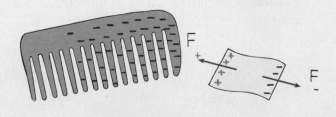

42. When a car is moved into a painting chamber, a mist of paint is sprayed around it. When the body of the car is given a sudden electric charge and the mist of paint is attracted to it, presto—the car is quickly and uniformly painted. What does the phenomenon of polarization have to do with this?

43. Imagine a proton at rest a certain distance from a negatively charged plate. It is released and collides with the plate. Then imagine the similar case of an electron at rest the same distance away from a plate of equal and opposite charge. In which case would the moving particle have the greater speed when the collision occurs? Why?

44. Consider a pair of particles with equal charges. When released, they fly apart from each other. Your teacher asks how the speeds will compare when they are ten times farther apart than when first released. Jess says that since the force on the particles decreases with distance, their speeds will be less. Marie says no, the speed of the repelled particles increases as long as they interact with each other. With whom do you agree or disagree, and why?

45. A pair of isolated protons will fly apart from each other. The same is true for a pair of isolated electrons. Your teacher asks which has the greater initial acceleration if the initial distance between the particles is the same. Sophia says the initial accelerations will be equal because the forces are equal. Sandra says no, that the electrons will accelerate more—but can't explain why. Both look to you for your input. What is your thinking?

Think and Solve ······

46. The charge on an electron is 1.6×10^{-19} C. How many electrons make a charge of 1 C?

47. By how much is the electrical force between a pair of ions reduced when their separation distance is doubled? Tripled?

48. Two pellets, each with a charge of 1 μC, are separated by a distance of 0.30 m. Show that the electric force between them is 0.1 N.

49. Two identical metal spheres are brought together into contact. Originally one had a charge of $+40$ μC and the other a charge of -10 μC. What is the charge on each after contact?

50. Consider two small charged objects, one with a charge of 15 μC and the other of unknown charge. When they are separated by a distance of 1.2 m, each exerts a force of 2.8 N on the other. What is the charge of the second object?

51. Proportional reasoning: Consider a pair of electrically charged coins suspended from insulating threads, a certain distance from each other. There is a specific amount of electrostatic force between them.
  a. If the charge on one coin were halved, what would happen to the force between them?
  b. If the charges on both coins were doubled, what would happen to the force between them?
  c. If the distance between the coins were tripled, what would happen to the force between them?
  d. If the distance between them were reduced to one-fourth the original distance, what would happen to the force between them?
  e. If the charge on each object were doubled and the distance between them were doubled, what would happen to the force between them?

52. Two spherical inflated rubber balloons each have the same amount of charge spread uniformly on their surfaces. If the repelling force is 2.5 N and the distance between the balloon centers is 0.30 m, find how much charge is on each balloon.

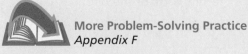

More Problem-Solving Practice
Appendix F

ELECTRIC FIELDS AND POTENTIAL

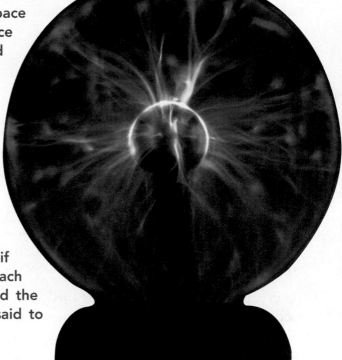

THE BIG IDEA : An electric field is a storehouse of energy.

The space around a strong magnet is different from how it would be if the magnet were not there. Put a paper clip in the space and you'll see the paper clip move. The space around the sun is different from how it would be if the sun were not there. The sun's gravitational influence affects the motions of the planets around it. Similarly, the space around a concentration of electric charge is different from how it would be if the charge were not there. If you walk by the charged dome of an electrostatic machine—a Van de Graaff generator, for example—you can sense the charge. Hair on your body stands out—just a tiny bit if you're more than a meter away, and more if you're closer. The space that surrounds each of these things—the magnet, the sun, and the electric charge—is altered. The space is said to contain a *force field*.

discover!

What Is Electric Shielding?

1. Wrap a cellular phone completely in aluminum foil.
2. Make a call to the wrapped phone.
3. Unwrap the cell phone, and now cover only part of it with foil. Make a call to the partly wrapped cell phone.
4. Repeat Step 3 a few more times, covering different parts of the phone.

Analyze and Conclude

1. **Observing** What effect did completely wrapping the phone have on reception? Did wrapping only part of the phone block the incoming signal? If so, which part of the phone needed to be covered in order to block the signal?
2. **Predicting** What other materials do you think could be used to shield a cellular phone?
3. **Making Generalizations** What is electric shielding, and why does it work?

33.1 Electric Fields

The force field that surrounds a mass is a gravitational field. If you throw a ball into the air, it follows a curved path. Earlier chapters showed that it curves because there is an interaction between the ball and Earth—between their centers of gravity, to be exact. Their centers of gravity are quite far apart, so this is "action at a distance."

The idea that things not in contact could exert forces on one another bothered Isaac Newton and many others. The concept of a force field explains how Earth can exert a force on things without touching them, like a tossed ball. The ball is in contact with the field all the time. The ball curves because it interacts with Earth's gravitational field. You can think of distant space probes as interacting with gravitational fields rather than with the masses of Earth and other astronomical bodies that are responsible for the fields.

Just as the space around Earth and every other mass is filled with a gravitational field, the space around every electric charge is filled with an electric field. An **electric field** is a force field that surrounds an electric charge or group of charges. In Figure 33.2, a gravitational force holds a satellite in orbit about a planet, and an electrical force holds an electron in orbit about a proton. In both cases there is no contact between the objects, and the forces are "acting at a distance." In terms of the field concept, the satellite and electron interact with the force fields of the planet and the proton and are everywhere in contact with these fields. Just as in the gravitational case, the force that one electric charge exerts on another can be described as the interaction between one charge and the electric field set up by the other.

FIGURE 33.1 ▲
You can sense the force field that surrounds a charged Van de Graaff generator.

The force on a charged particle gives electric field strength E. In equation form, $E = F/q$.

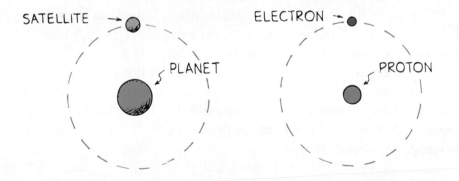

◄ FIGURE 33.2
The satellite and the electron both experience forces; they are both in force fields.

An electric field has both magnitude and direction. ☑ **The magnitude (strength) of an electric field can be measured by its effect on charges located in the field.** Imagine a small positive "test charge" that is placed in an electric field. Where the force is greatest on the test charge, the field is strongest. Where the force on the test charge is weak, the field is small.[33.1]

☑ **The direction of an electric field at any point, by convention, is the direction of the electrical force on a small *positive* test charge placed at that point.** Thus, if the charge that sets up the field is positive, the field points away from that charge. If the charge that sets up the field is negative, the field points toward that charge. (Be sure to distinguish between the hypothetical small test charge and the charge that sets up the field.)

CONCEPT: How are the magnitude and direction of an electric
CHECK: field determined?

33.2 Electric Field Lines

Since an electric field has both magnitude and direction, it is a *vector quantity* and can be represented by vectors. The negatively charged particle in Figure 33.3a is surrounded by vectors that point toward the particle. (If the particle were positively charged, the vectors would point away from the particle. The vectors always point in the direction of the force that would act on a positive test charge.) The magnitude of the field is indicated by the length of the vectors. The electric field is greater where the vectors are long than it is where the vectors are short. To represent a complete electric field by vectors, you would have to show a vector at every point in the space around the charge. Such a diagram would be totally unreadable!

A more useful way to describe an electric field is shown in Figure 33.3b. ☑ **You can use electric field lines (also called lines of force) to represent an electric field. Where the lines are farther apart, the field is weaker.** For an isolated charge, the lines extend to infinity, while for two or more opposite charges, the lines emanate from a positive charge and terminate on a negative charge. Some electric field configurations are shown in Figure 33.4.

The photographs in Figure 33.5 show bits of thread that are suspended in an oil bath surrounding charged conductors. The ends of the bits of thread line up end-to-end with the electric field lines. In Figures 33.5a and 33.5b, we see the field lines are characteristic of a single pair of point charges.

FIGURE 33.3 ▼
a. In a vector representation of an electric field, the length of the vectors indicates the magnitude of the field. **b.** In a lines-of-force representation, the distance between field lines indicates magnitudes.

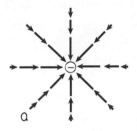

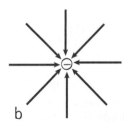

FIGURE 33.4 ▶
a. The field lines around a single positive charge extend to infinity. **b.** For a pair of equal but opposite charges, the field lines emanate from the positive charge and terminate on the negative charge. **c.** Field lines are evenly spaced between two oppositely charged capacitor plates.

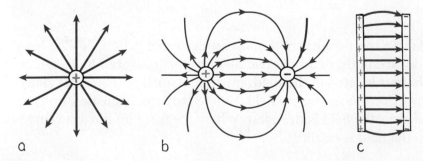

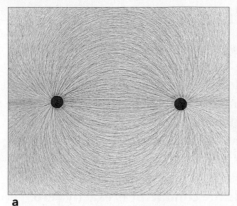
a

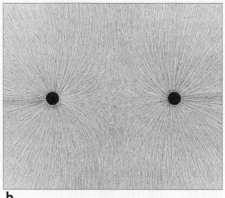
b

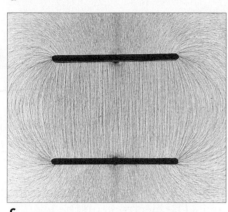
c

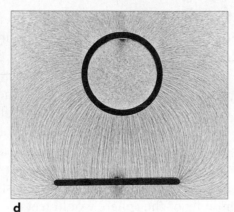
d

◀ **FIGURE 33.5**
Bits of fine thread suspended in an oil bath surrounding charged conductors line up end to end along the direction of the field. The photos illustrate field patterns for **a.** equal and opposite charges; **b.** equal like charges; **c.** oppositely charged plates; and **d.** oppositely charged cylinder and plate.

The oppositely charged parallel plates in Figure 33.5c produce nearly parallel field lines between the plates. Except near the ends, the field between the plates has a constant strength. Notice that in Figure 33.5d, there is no electric field inside the charged cylinder. The conductor shields the space from the field outside.

CONCEPT CHECK How can you represent an electric field?

think!

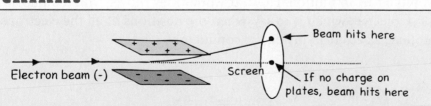

Beam hits here

Electron beam (-)

Screen

If no charge on plates, beam hits here

A beam of electrons is produced at one end of a glass tube and lights up a phosphor screen at the other end. When the beam is straight, it produces a spot in the middle of the screen. If the beam passes through the electric field of a pair of oppositely charged plates, it is deflected upward as shown. If the charges on the plates are reversed, in what direction will the beam deflect?
Answer: 33.2

FIGURE 33.6 ▲

Electrons from the lightning bolt mutually repel and spread over the outer metal surface. The overall electric field inside the car practically cancels to zero.

33.3 Electric Shielding

The dramatic photo in Figure 33.6 shows a car being struck by lightning. Yet, the occupant inside the car is completely safe. This is because the electrons that shower down upon the car are mutually repelled and spread over the outer metal surface, finally discharging when additional sparks jump from the car's body to the ground. The configuration of electrons on the car's surface at any moment is such that the electric fields inside the car practically cancel to zero. This is true of any charged conductor. ⊘ **If the charge on a conductor is not moving, the electric field inside the conductor is exactly zero.**

Charged Conductors The absence of electric field within a conductor holding static charge does not arise from the inability of an electric field to penetrate metals. It comes about because free electrons within the conductor can "settle down" and stop moving only when the electric field is zero. So the charges arrange themselves to ensure a zero field with the material.

Consider the charged metal sphere shown in Figure 33.7. Because of mutual repulsion, the electrons spread as far apart from one another as possible. They distribute themselves uniformly over the surface of the sphere. A positive test charge located exactly in the middle of the sphere would feel no force. The electrons on the left side of the sphere would tend to pull the test charge to the left, but the electrons on the right side of the sphere would tend to pull the test charge to the right equally hard. The net force on the test charge would be zero. Thus, the electric field is also zero. Interestingly enough, complete cancellation will occur *anywhere* inside the sphere.

If the conductor is not spherical, then the charge distribution will not be uniform. The remarkable thing is this: The exact charge distribution over the surface is such that the electric field everywhere inside the conductor is zero. Look at it this way: If there were an electric field inside a conductor, then free electrons inside the conductor would be set in motion. How far would they move? Until equilibrium is established, which is to say, when the positions of all the electrons produce a zero field inside the conductor.

FIGURE 33.7 ▲

The forces on a test charge located inside a charged hollow sphere cancel to zero.

FIGURE 33.8 ▶

Static charges are distributed on the surface of all conductors in such a way that the electric field inside the conductors is zero.

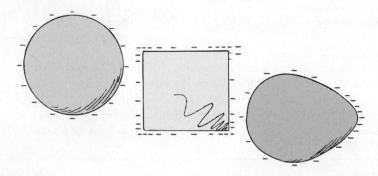

How to Shield an Electric Field There is no way to shield gravity, because gravity only attracts. There are no repelling parts of gravity to offset attracting parts. Shielding electric fields, however, is quite simple. Surround yourself or whatever you wish to shield with a conducting surface. Put this surface in an electric field of whatever field strength. The free charges in the conducting surface will arrange themselves on the surface of the conductor in a way such that all field contributions inside cancel one another. That's why certain electronic components are encased in metal boxes, and why certain cables have a metal covering—to shield them from all outside electrical activity.

FIGURE 33.9 ▲
The metal-lined cover shields the internal electrical components from external electric fields. Similarly, a metal cover shields the coaxial cable.

CONCEPT CHECK : How can you describe the electric field within a conductor holding static charge?

think!

It is said that a gravitational field, unlike an electric field, cannot be shielded. But the gravitational field at the center of Earth cancels to zero. Isn't this evidence that a gravitational field *can* be shielded?
Answer: 33.3

33.4 Electrical Potential Energy

Recall the relationship between work and potential energy. Work is done when a force moves something in the direction of the force. An object has potential energy by virtue of its location, say in a force field. For example, if you lift an object, you apply a force equal to its weight. When you raise it through some distance, you are doing work on the object. You are also increasing its gravitational potential energy. The greater the distance it is raised, the greater is the increase in its gravitational potential energy. Doing work increases its gravitational potential energy, as shown in Figure 33.10a.

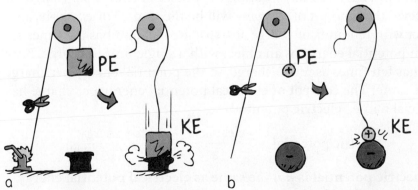

◀ **FIGURE 33.10**
a. Work is done to lift the mass against the gravitational field of Earth. In an elevated position, the mass has gravitational potential energy. When released, this energy is transferred to the piling below.
b. Similar energy transfer occurs for electric charges.

FIGURE 33.11 ▲
The small positive charge has more potential energy when it is closer to the positively charged sphere because work is required to move it to the closer location.

In a similar way, a charged object can have potential energy by virtue of its location in an electric field. Just as work is required to lift an object against the gravitational field of Earth, work is required to push a charged particle against the electric field of a charged body. (It may be more difficult to visualize, but the physics of both the gravitational case and the electrical case is the same.) ⊘ **The electrical potential energy of a charged particle is increased when work is done to push it against the electric field of something else that is charged.**

Figure 33.11a shows a small positive charge located at some distance from a positively charged sphere. If we push the small charge closer to the sphere (Figure 33.11b), we will expend energy to overcome electrical repulsion. Just as work is done in compressing a spring, work is done in pushing the charge against the electric field of the sphere. This work is equal to the energy gained by the charge. The energy a charge has due to its location in an electric field is called **electrical potential energy.** If the charge is released, it will accelerate in a direction away from the sphere, and its electrical potential energy will transform into kinetic energy.

CONCEPT : How can you increase the electrical potential energy
CHECK : of a charged particle?

33.5 Electric Potential

If in the preceding discussion we push two charges instead, we do twice as much work. The two charges in the same location will have twice the electrical potential energy as one; a group of ten charges will have ten times the potential energy; and so on.

Rather than deal with the total potential energy of a group of charges, it is convenient when working with electricity to consider the *electrical potential energy per charge.* The electrical potential energy per charge is the total electrical potential energy divided by the amount of charge. At any location the potential energy *per charge*—whatever the amount of charge—will be the same. For example, an object with ten units of charge at a specific location has ten times as much potential energy as an object with a single unit of charge. But it also has ten times as much charge, so the potential energy per charge is the same. The concept of electrical potential energy per charge has a special name, **electric potential.**

$$\text{electric potential} = \frac{\text{electrical potential energy}}{\text{charge}}$$

⊘ **Electric potential is *not* the same as electrical potential energy. Electric potential is electrical potential energy per charge.**

Distinguishing between *electrical potential energy* and *electric potential* is high-level physics!

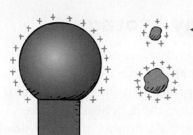

◄ FIGURE 33.12
An object of greater charge has more electrical potential energy in the field of the charged dome than an object of less charge, but the *electric potential* of any amount of charge at the same location is the same.

The SI unit of measurement for electric potential is the **volt,** named after the Italian physicist Allesandro Volta (1745–1827). The symbol for volt is V. Since potential energy is measured in joules and charge is measured in coulombs,

$$1 \text{ volt } = 1 \frac{\text{joule}}{\text{coulomb}}$$

Thus, a potential of 1 volt equals 1 joule of energy per coulomb of charge; 1000 volts equals 1000 joules of energy per coulomb of charge. If a conductor has a potential of 1000 volts, it would take 1000 joules of energy per coulomb to bring a small charge from very far away and add it to the charge on the conductor.[33.5] (Since the small charge would be much less than one coulomb, the energy required would be much less than 1000 joules. For example, to add the charge of one proton to the conductor, 1.6×10^{-19} C, it would take only 1.6×10^{-16} J of energy.)

Since electric potential is measured in volts, it is commonly called **voltage.** In this book the names will be used interchangeably. The significance of voltage is that once the location of zero voltage has been specified, a definite value for it can be assigned to a location whether or not a charge exists at that location. We can speak about the voltages at different locations in an electric field whether or not any charges occupy those locations.

Rub a balloon on your hair and the balloon becomes negatively charged, perhaps to several thousand volts! If the charge on the balloon were one coulomb, it would take several thousand joules of energy to give the balloon that voltage. However, one coulomb is a very large amount of charge; the charge on a balloon rubbed on hair is typically much less than a millionth of a coulomb. Therefore, the amount of energy associated with the charged balloon is very, very small—about a thousandth of a joule. A high voltage requires great energy only if a great amount of charge is involved. This example highlights the difference between electrical potential energy and electric potential.

think!

If there were twice as much charge on one of the charged objects near the charged sphere in Figure 33.12, would the electrical potential energy of the object in the field of the charged sphere be the same or would it be twice as great? Would the electrical potential of the object be the same or would it be twice as great? *Answer: 33.5*

FIGURE 33.13 ▲
Although the voltage of the charged balloon is high, the electrical potential energy is low because of the small amount of charge.

CONCEPT CHECK : What is the difference between electric potential and electrical potential energy?

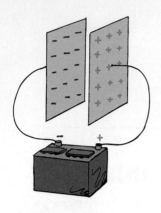

33.6 Electrical Energy Storage

Electrical energy can be stored in a common device called a **capacitor.** Capacitors are found in nearly all electronic circuits. Computer memories use very tiny capacitors to store the 1's and 0's of the binary code. Some keyboards have them beneath each key. Capacitors in photoflash units store larger amounts of energy slowly and release it rapidly during the short duration of the flash. Similarly, but on a grander scale, enormous amounts of energy are stored in banks of capacitors that power giant lasers in national laboratories.

The simplest capacitor is a pair of conducting plates separated by a small distance, but not touching each other. When the plates are connected to a charging device such as the battery shown in Figure 33.14, charge is transferred from one plate to the other. This occurs as the positive battery terminal pulls electrons from the plate connected to it. These electrons in effect are pumped through the battery and through the negative terminal to the opposite plate. The capacitor plates then have equal and opposite charges—the positive plate is connected to the positive battery terminal, and the negative plate is connected to the negative battery terminal. The charging process is complete when the potential difference between the plates equals the potential difference between the battery terminals—the battery voltage. The greater the battery voltage and the larger and closer the plates, the greater the charge that is stored.

In practice, the plates may be thin metallic foils separated by a thin sheet of paper. This "paper sandwich" is then rolled up to save space and may be inserted into a cylinder. Such a practical capacitor is shown with others in Figure 33.15. (We will consider the role of capacitors in circuits in the next chapter.)

FIGURE 33.14 ▲

A simple capacitor consists of two closely spaced metal parallel plates. When connected to a battery, the plates become equally and oppositely charged.

FIGURE 33.15 ▶

In these capacitors, the plates consist of thin metallic foils that have been rolled up into a cylinder.

Capacitors store and hold electric charges until discharged. A charged capacitor is discharged when a conducting path is provided between the plates. Note that a capacitor might store charge even after the electricity to a device has been turned off—for seconds, minutes, or even longer. Discharging a capacitor can be a shocking experience if you happen to be the conducting path. The energy transfer can be fatal where high voltages are present. That's the main reason for the warning labels on devices such as TV sets.

⊘ **The energy stored in a capacitor comes from the work done to charge it.** The energy is in the form of the electric field between its plates. Between parallel plates the electric field is uniform, as indicated in Figures 33.4c and 33.5c on previous pages. So the energy stored in a capacitor is energy stored in the electric field.

Electric fields are storehouses of energy. We will see in the next chapter that energy can be transported over long distances by electric fields, which can be directed through and guided by metal wires or directed through empty space. In Chapter 37 we will see how energy from the sun is radiated in the form of electric and magnetic fields. The fact that energy is contained in electric fields is truly far-reaching.

FIGURE 33.16 ▲
Mona El Tawil-Nassar adjusts demonstration capacitor plates.

CONCEPT : Where does the energy stored in a capacitor
CHECK : come from?

Link to TECHNOLOGY

Ink-Jet Printers The printhead of an ink-jet printer typically ejects a thin, steady stream of thousands of tiny ink droplets each second as it shuttles back and forth across the paper. As the stream flows between electrodes that are controlled by the computer, selective droplets are charged. The uncharged droplets then pass undeflected in the electric field of a parallel plate capacitor and form the image on the page; the charged droplets are deflected and do not reach the page. Thus, the image produced on the paper is made from ink droplets that are *not* charged. The blank spaces correspond to deflected ink that never made it to the paper.

33.7 The Van de Graaff Generator

A common laboratory device for building up high voltages is the *Van de Graaff generator.* This is the lightning machine often used by "evil scientists" in old science fiction movies. A simple model of the Van de Graaff generator is shown in Figure 33.17.

FIGURE 33.17 ▶
In a Van de Graaff generator,
a moving rubber belt carries
electrons from the voltage
source to a conducting sphere.

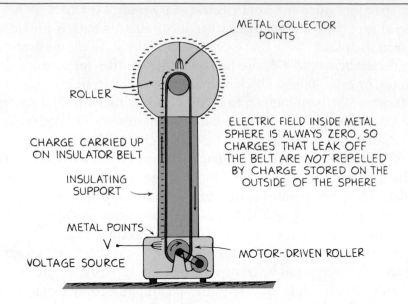

METAL COLLECTOR POINTS

ROLLER

ELECTRIC FIELD INSIDE METAL SPHERE IS ALWAYS ZERO, SO CHARGES THAT LEAK OFF THE BELT ARE *NOT* REPELLED BY CHARGE STORED ON THE OUTSIDE OF THE SPHERE

CHARGE CARRIED UP ON INSULATOR BELT

INSULATING SUPPORT

METAL POINTS

V

VOLTAGE SOURCE

MOTOR-DRIVEN ROLLER

An electric field is nature's storehouse of electrical energy.

A large hollow metal sphere is supported by a cylindrical insulating stand. A motor-driven rubber belt inside the support stand moves past a comblike set of metal needles that are maintained at a high electric potential. A continuous supply of electrons is deposited on the belt through electric discharge by the points of the needles and is carried up into the hollow metal sphere. The electrons leak onto metal points (which act like tiny lightning rods) attached to the inner surface of the sphere. Because of mutual repulsion, the electrons move to the outer surface of the conducting sphere. (Remember, static charge on any conductor is on the outside surface.) This leaves the inside surface uncharged and able to receive more electrons as they are brought up the belt. The process is continuous, and the charge builds up to a very high electric potential—on the order of millions of volts. Touching a Van de Graaff generator can be a hair-raising experience, as shown in Figure 33.18.

A sphere with a radius of 1 m can be raised to a potential of 3 million volts before electric discharge occurs through the air (because breakdown occurs in air when the electric field strength is about 3×10^6 V/m).[33.7] ⊘ **The voltage of a Van de Graaff generator can be increased by increasing the radius of the sphere or by placing the entire system in a container filled with high-pressure gas.** Van de Graaff generators in pressurized gas can produce voltages as high as 20 million volts. These devices accelerate charged particles used as projectiles for penetrating the nuclei of atoms.

FIGURE 33.18 ▲
The physics enthusiast and the dome of the Van de Graaff generator are charged to a high voltage.

CONCEPT CHECK: How can the voltage of a Van de Graaff generator be increased?

REVIEW

Concept Summary ······

- The magnitude (strength) of an electric field can be measured by its effect on charges located in the field. The direction of an electric field at any point is the direction of the electrical force on a small *positive* test charge.

- You can use electric field lines (also called lines of force) to represent an electric field. Where the lines are farther apart, the field is weaker.

- If the charge on a conductor is not moving, the electric field inside the conductor is exactly zero.

- The electrical potential energy of a charged particle is increased when work is done to push it against the electric field of something else that is charged.

- Electric potential is not the same as electrical potential energy. Electric potential is electrical potential energy per charge.

- The energy stored in a capacitor comes from the work done to charge it.

- The voltage of a Van de Graaff generator can be increased by increasing the radius of the sphere or by placing the system in a container filled with high-pressure gas.

Key Terms ······

electric field *(p. 665)*

electrical potential energy *(p. 670)*

electric potential *(p. 670)*

volt *(p. 671)*

voltage *(p. 671)*

capacitor *(p. 672)*

think! Answers

33.2 When the charge on the plates is reversed, the electric field will be in the opposite direction, so the electron beam will be deflected upward. If the field is made to oscillate, the beam will be swept up and down. With a second set of plates and further refinements it could sweep a picture onto the screen! (Think television!)

33.3 No. Gravity can be canceled inside a planet or between planets, but it cannot be shielded by a planet or by any arrangement of masses. During a lunar eclipse, for example, when Earth is directly between the sun and the moon, there is no shielding of the sun's field to affect the moon's orbit. Even a very slight shielding would accumulate over a period of years and show itself in the timing of subsequent eclipses. Shielding requires a combination of repelling and attracting forces, and gravity only attracts.

33.5 Twice as much charge would cause the object to have twice as much electrical potential energy, because it would have taken twice as much work to bring the object to that location. But the electric potential would be the same, because the electric potential is total electrical potential energy divided by total charge. In this case, twice the energy divided by twice the charge gives the same value as the original energy divided by the original charge.

33 ASSESS

Check Concepts ......

Section 33.1

1. What is meant by the expression *action at a distance?*

2. How does the concept of a field eliminate the idea of action at a distance?

3. How are a gravitational field and an electric field similar?

Section 33.2

4. Why is an electric field considered a vector quantity?

5. **a.** What are electric field lines?
   b. How do their directions compare with the direction of the force that acts on a positive test charge in the same region?

6. How is the strength of an electric field indicated with field lines?

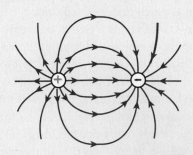

7. Describe the electric field lines in the space between a pair of parallel plates with equal and opposite charges.

Section 33.3

8. Why are occupants safe inside a car struck by lightning?

9. **a.** Can gravity be shielded?
   b. Can electric fields be shielded?

10. What happens to the electric field inside a conductor when free charges arrange themselves on its surface?

Section 33.4

11. What is the relationship between the amount of work you do on an object and its potential energy?

12. What will happen to the electrical potential energy of a charged particle in an electric field when the particle is released and free to move?

Section 33.5

13. Clearly distinguish between *electrical potential energy* and *electric potential.*

14. If you do more work to move more charge a certain distance against an electric field, and increase the electrical potential energy as a result, why do you not also increase the electric potential?

15. The SI unit for electrical potential energy is the joule. What is the SI unit for electric potential?

16. Charge must be present at a location in order for there to be electrical potential energy. Must charge also be present at a location for there to be electric potential?

17. How can electric potential be high when electrical potential energy is relatively low?

Section 33.6

18. How does the amount of charge on the plate of a charged capacitor compare with the amount of charge on the opposite plate?

Section 33.7

19. How does the amount of charge on the inside surface of the sphere of a charged Van de Graaff generator compare with the amount on the outside?

20. How much voltage can be built up on a Van de Graaff generator of 1 m radius before electric discharge occurs through the air?

Think and Rank ••••••

Rank each of the following sets of scenarios in order of the quantity of property involved. List them from left and right. If scenarios have equal rankings, separate them with an equal sign. (e.g., A = B)

21. The diagrams A, B, and C represent pairs of charges in three different arrangements. The distance from point P to the nearest charge is the same in each arrangement. Rank the arrangements A, B, and C from strongest to weakest electric field at point P.

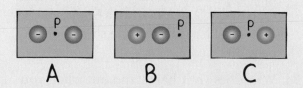

22. Rank from greatest to least the force on the following particles in the following electric fields.
(A) $6q$ in field E
(B) $4q$ in field $2E$
(C) q in field $3E$

23. Three charged particles are in an electric field E. Rank their accelerations from greatest to least:
(A) charge q, mass m
(B) charge $3q$, mass $2m$
(C) charge $2q$, mass m

24. A charged ball is suspended by a string in a uniform electric field pointing to the right. The string makes an angle θ with the vertical, as two forces act on the ball—one gravitational and the other electric.

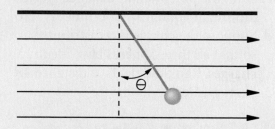

Consider the following three scenarios for the ball's mass and charge.
(A) mass = 3 g; charge = 2 nC
(B) mass = 6 g; charge = 8 nC
(C) mass = 9 g; charge = 4 nC

Rank, from greatest to least, the angle the string makes with the vertical.

25. Shown below are three hollow copper spheres. Sphere A has a radius R, Sphere B has a radius of $2R$, and Sphere C has a radius $3R$. On each sphere is a charge, as indicated, which is evenly distributed over the spheres surface. (Each sphere is independent of the others; they don't influence one another.)

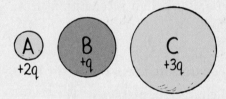

a. Rank from greatest to least the magnitude of the electric fields at a distance $4R$ from the center of the spheres.

b. Rank the field strengths at the center of the spheres.

c. Rank the potentials at distance $4R$ (assuming the potential at infinity is zero).

d. Suppose the charge is redistributed so that all three spheres have identical charges. Rank the fields at distance $4R$ from greatest to least.

Think and Explain ••••••

26. How is an electric field different from a gravitational field?

27. The vectors for the gravitational field of Earth point *toward* Earth; the vectors for the electric field of a proton point *away* from the proton. Explain.

28. Imagine an electron and a proton held midway between the plates of a charged parallel plate capacitor. If they are released, how do their accelerations and directions of travel compare? (Ignore their attraction to each other.) Which reaches a capacitor plate first?

29. Suppose that the strength of the electric field about an isolated point charge has a certain value at a distance of 1 m. How will the electric field strength compare at a distance of 2 m from the point charge? What law guides your answer?

30. When a conductor is charged, the charge moves to the outer surface of the conductor. What property of charge accounts for this spreading?

31. Suppose that a metal file cabinet is charged. How will the charge concentration at the corners of the cabinet compare with the charge concentration on the flat parts of the cabinet? Defend your answer.

32. Does an object with twice the electric potential of another have twice the electrical potential energy? Explain.

33. You are not harmed by contact with a charged balloon, even though its voltage is very high. Is the reason for this similar to why you are not harmed by the greater-than-1000°C sparks from a Fourth of July-type sparkler (like the one shown on page 404)?

34. Why does your hair stand out when you are charged by a device such as a Van de Graaff generator?

Think and Solve ••••••

35. If you put in 10 joules of work to push 1 coulomb of charge against an electric field, what will be its voltage with respect to its starting position? When released, what will be its kinetic energy if it flies past its starting position?

36. At a particular point near a second charge, a 50-μC charge experiences a force of 2.0 N. What is the electric field strength at that point? (1 μC = 10^{-6} coulomb.)

37. When placed near another charge, a 20-μC charge experiences an attractive force of 0.080 N. Show that the electric field strength at the location of the 20-μC charge is 4000 N/C.

38. A 12-μC charge is located in a 350-N/C electric field. Show that the charge experiences a force of 0.0042 N.

39. a. If you do 12 J of work to push 0.001 C of charge from point A to point B in an electric field, what is the voltage difference between points A and B?
b. When the charge is released, what will be its kinetic energy as it flies back past its starting point A? What principle guides your answer?

40. What is the voltage at the location of a 0.0001-C charge that has an electrical potential energy of 0.5 J? Both voltage and potential energy are measured relative to the same reference point.

41. a. Suppose that you start with a charge of 0.002 C in an electric field and find that it takes 24 J of work to move the charge from point A to point B. What is the voltage difference between points A and B?
b. If the charge is released, what is its kinetic energy as it flies back past point A?

42. Point A is at +10 V, point B is at +7 V, and point C is at 0 V. Show that it takes
a. 6 J of work to move 2 C of charge from point B to point A.
b. 14 J of work to move 2 C of charge from point C to point B.
c. 20 J of work to move 2 C of charge from point C to point A.

43. In a hydrogen atom, the proton and the electron ($q = 1.6 \times 10^{-19}$ C) are separated by an average distance of 5×10^{-11} m.
a. Calculate the force that the proton exerts on the electron at this distance.
b. Show that the electric field strength at the average location of the electron is an enormous 6×10^{11} N/C.

44. The potential difference between a storm cloud and the ground is 5.0×10^7 volts. During a lightning flash, 3.0 coulombs of charge are transferred to the ground.
a. How much energy is transferred to the ground in this lightning flash?
b. If this much energy were used to accelerate a 3500-kg truck from rest, how fast would the truck end up going?

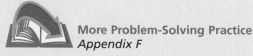

More Problem-Solving Practice
Appendix F

34 ELECTRIC CURRENT

THE BIG IDEA Electric current is related to the voltage that produces it and the resistance that opposes it.

The previous chapter discussed the concept of electric potential, or voltage, in terms of energy per charge. We'll see in this chapter that voltage can be thought of as an "electric pressure" that produces a flow of charge, or *current*, within a conductor. The flow is restrained by the *resistance* it encounters. When the flow takes place along one direction, it is called *direct current* (DC); when the charges flow to and fro, it is called *alternating current* (AC). The rate at which energy is transferred by electric current is *power*. These ideas are better understood if you know how they relate to one another. Let's begin with the flow of electric charge.

34.1 Flow of Charge

Recall that heat flows through a conductor when a difference in temperature exists between its ends. Heat flows from the end of higher temperature to the end of lower temperature. When both ends reach the same temperature, the flow of heat ceases.

Charge flows in a similar way. ☑ **When the ends of an electric conductor are at different electric potentials, charge flows from one end to the other.** Charge flows when there is a **potential difference,** or difference in potential (voltage), between the ends of a conductor. The flow of charge will continue until both ends reach a common potential. When there is no potential difference, there is no longer a flow of charge through the conductor. As an example, if one end of a wire were connected to the ground and the other end placed in contact with the sphere of a Van de Graaff generator that is charged to a high potential, a surge of charge would flow through the wire. The flow would be brief, however, for the sphere of the generator would quickly reach a common potential with the ground.

To attain a sustained flow of charge in a conductor, some arrangement must be provided to keep one end at a higher potential than the other. The situation is analogous to the flow of water from a higher reservoir to a lower one, as shown in Figure 34.1a. Water will flow in a pipe that connects the reservoirs only as long as a difference in water level exists. The flow of water in the pipe, like the flow of charge in the wire that connects the Van de Graaff generator to the ground, will cease when the "pressures" at the two ends are equal. In order that the flow be sustained, there must be a suitable pump of some sort to maintain a difference in water levels, as shown in Figure 34.1b. Then there will be a continual difference in water pressures and a continual flow of water. The same is true of electric current.

Electrons in a wire are like water in a pipe; whenever a little water enters one end, almost immediately the same amount of water exits the other end.

CONCEPT CHECK : What happens when the ends of a conductor are at different electrical potentials?

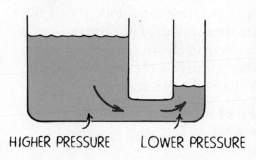

HIGHER PRESSURE   LOWER PRESSURE

a

← PUMP

b

◀ **FIGURE 34.1**
a. Water flows from higher pressure to lower pressure. The flow will cease when the difference in pressure ceases. **b.** Water continues to flow because a difference in pressure is maintained with the pump.

34.2 Electric Current

Electric current is the flow of electric charge. In solid conductors the electrons carry the charge through the circuit because they are free to move throughout the atomic network. These electrons are called *conduction electrons*. Protons, on the other hand, are bound inside atomic nuclei that are more or less locked in fixed positions within the conductor. In fluids, such as the electrolyte in a car battery, positive and negative ions as well as electrons may compose the flow of electric charge.

Measuring Current Electric current is measured in **amperes,** for which the SI unit is symbol A.[34.2] An ampere is the flow of 1 coulomb of charge per second. (Recall that 1 coulomb, the standard unit of charge, is the electric charge of 6.24 billion billion electrons.) In a wire that carries a current of 5 amperes, for example, 5 coulombs of charge pass through any cross section in the wire each second. That's a lot of electrons! In a wire that carries 10 amperes, twice as many electrons pass any cross section each second. Figure 34.2 shows a simplified view of electrons flowing in a wire.

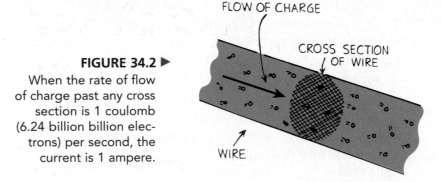

FIGURE 34.2 ▶

When the rate of flow of charge past any cross section is 1 coulomb (6.24 billion billion electrons) per second, the current is 1 ampere.

Net Charge of a Wire ⊘ **A current-carrying wire has a net electric charge of zero.** While the current is flowing, negative electrons swarm through the atomic network that is composed of positively charged atomic nuclei. Under ordinary conditions, the number of electrons in the wire is equal to the number of positive protons in the atomic nuclei. When electrons flow in a wire, the number entering one end is the same as the number leaving the other. So we see that the net charge of the wire is normally zero at every moment.

CONCEPT CHECK : What is the net flow of electric charge in a current-carrying wire?

34.3 Voltage Sources

Charges do not flow unless there is a potential difference. A sustained current requires a suitable "electric pump" to provide a sustained potential difference. Something that provides a potential difference is known as a **voltage source.**

If you charge a metal sphere positively, and another negatively, you can develop a large voltage between them. This is not a good voltage source because when the spheres are connected by a conductor, the potentials equalize in a single brief surge of moving charges. It is not practical. Batteries and generators, however, are capable of maintaining a continuous flow.

Steady Voltage Sources ☑ **Voltage sources such as batteries and generators supply energy that allows charges to move steadily.** In a battery, a chemical reaction occurring inside releases electrical energy.[34.3.1] Generators—such as the alternators in automobiles—convert mechanical energy to electrical energy, as will be discussed in Chapter 37. The electrical potential energy produced by whatever means is available at the terminals of the battery or generator. The potential energy per coulomb of charge available to electrons moving between terminals is the voltage (sometimes called the *electromotive force, or emf*). The voltage provides the "electric pressure" to move electrons between the terminals in a circuit.

Power utilities use electric generators to provide the 120 volts delivered to home outlets. The alternating potential difference between the two holes in the outlet averages 120 volts. When the prongs of a plug are inserted into the outlet, an average electric "pressure" of 120 volts is placed across the circuit connected to the prongs. This means that 120 joules of energy is supplied to each coulomb of charge that is made to flow in the circuit.

Distinguishing Between Current and Voltage There is often some confusion between charge flowing *through* a circuit and voltage being impressed *across* a circuit. To distinguish between these ideas, consider a long pipe filled with water. Water will flow *through* the pipe if there is a difference in pressure *across* the pipe or between its ends. Water flows from the high-pressure end to the low-pressure end. Only the water flows, not the pressure. Similarly, charges flow *through* a circuit because of an applied voltage *across* the circuit.[34.3.2] You don't say that voltage flows through a circuit. Voltage doesn't go anywhere, for it is the charges that move. Voltage causes current.

CONCEPT CHECK : What are two voltage sources used to provide the energy that allows charges to move steadily?

FIGURE 34.3 ▲
Each coulomb of charge that is made to flow in a circuit that connects the ends of this 1.5-volt flashlight cell is energized with 1.5 joules.

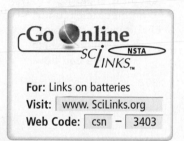

FIGURE 34.4 ▼

For a given pressure, more water passes through a large pipe than a small one. Similarly, for a given voltage, more electric current passes through a large-diameter wire than a small-diameter one.

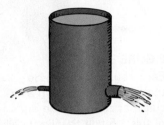

34.4 Electric Resistance

The amount of charge that flows in a circuit depends on the voltage provided by the voltage source. The current also depends on the resistance that the conductor offers to the flow of charge—the **electric resistance.** This is similar to the rate of water flow in a pipe, which depends not only on the pressure difference between the ends of the pipe but on the resistance offered by the pipe itself, as shown in Figure 34.4. ☑ **The resistance of a wire depends on the *conductivity* of the material used in the wire (that is, how well it conducts) and also on the thickness and length of the wire.**

Thick wires have less resistance than thin wires. Longer wires have more resistance than short wires. In addition, electric resistance depends on temperature. The greater the jostling about of atoms within the conductor, the greater resistance the conductor offers to the flow of charge. For most conductors, increased temperature means increased resistance.[34.4.1]

The resistance of some materials becomes zero at very low temperatures, a phenomenon known as **superconductivity.** Certain metals acquire superconductivity (zero resistance to the flow of charge) at temperatures near absolute zero. Since 1987, superconductivity at "high" temperatures (above 100 K) has been found in a variety of nonmetallic compounds. Once electric current is established in a superconductor, the electrons flow indefinitely.

Electric resistance is measured in units called **ohms,**[34.4.2] after Georg Simon Ohm (1789–1854), a German physicist who tested different wires in circuits to see what effect the resistance of the wire had on the current.

A material with a low resistance has a high *conductivity.*

CONCEPT CHECK What factors affect the resistance of a wire?

FIGURE 34.5 ▶

A simple hydraulic circuit is analogous to an electric circuit. A circuit is any complete path along which charge can flow.

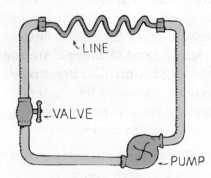

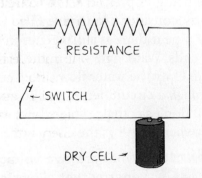

34.5 Ohm's Law

The relationship among voltage, current, and resistance is called **Ohm's law.** [34.5] ☑ **Ohm's law states that the current in a circuit is directly proportional to the voltage impressed across the circuit, and is inversely proportional to the resistance of the circuit.** In short,

$$\text{current} = \frac{\text{voltage}}{\text{resistance}}$$

Using *I* for current, *V* for voltage, and *R* for resistance, Ohm's law reads $I = V/R$.

The relationship among the units of measurement for these three quantities is as follows:

$$1 \text{ ampere} = 1\frac{\text{volt}}{\text{ohm}}$$

For a given circuit of constant resistance, current and voltage are proportional. This means that you'll get twice the current through a circuit for twice the voltage across the circuit. The greater the voltage, the greater the current. But if the resistance is doubled for a circuit, the current will be half what it would be otherwise. The greater the resistance, the less the current. Ohm's law makes good sense.

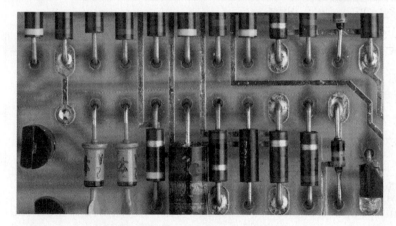

◀ **FIGURE 34.6**
The stripes on these resistors are color coded to indicate the resistance in ohms.

Using specific values, a potential difference of 1 volt impressed (imposed) across a circuit that has a resistance of 1 ohm will produce a current of 1 ampere. If a voltage of 12 volts is impressed across the same circuit, the current will be 12 amperes.

The resistance of a typical lamp cord is much less than 1 ohm, while a typical lightbulb has a resistance of about 100 ohms. An iron or electric toaster has a resistance of 15 to 20 ohms. The low resistance permits a large current, which produces considerable heat. The current inside electric devices such as radio and television receivers is regulated by circuit elements called *resistors*, whose resistance may range from a few ohms to millions of ohms.

think!

How much current is drawn by a lamp that has a resistance of 100 ohms when a voltage of 50 volts is impressed across it?
Answer: 34.5

CONCEPT CHECK ⋮ What does Ohm's law state?

VOLTAGE SUPPLIES THE PUSH

RESISTANCE OPPOSES THE PUSH

CURRENT RESULTS!

34.6 Ohm's Law and Electric Shock

What causes electric shock in the human body—current or voltage? ☑ **The damaging effects of electric shock are the result of current passing through the body.** From Ohm's law, we can see that this current depends on the voltage applied, and also on the electric resistance of the human body.

The Body's Resistance The resistance of your body depends on its condition and ranges from about 100 ohms if you're soaked with salt water to about 500,000 ohms if your skin is very dry. If you touched the two electrodes of a battery with dry fingers, the resistance your body would normally offer to the flow of charge would be about 100,000 ohms. You usually would not feel 12 volts, and 24 volts would just barely tingle. If your skin were moist, on the other hand, 24 volts could be quite uncomfortable. Table 34.1 describes the effects of different amounts of current on the human body.

Table 34.1	Effect of Various Electric Currents on the Body
Current (amperes)	**Effect**
0.001	Can be felt
0.005	Painful
0.010	Involuntary muscle contractions (spasms)
0.015	Loss of muscle control
0.070	If through the heart, serious disruption; probably fatal if current lasts for more than 1 second

The unit of electrical resistance is the ohm, Ω. Like the song of old, "Ω, Ω on the Range."

Many people are killed each year by current from common 120-volt electric circuits. If you touch a faulty 120-volt light fixture with your hand while you are standing on the ground, there is a 120-volt "electric pressure" between your hand and the ground. The soles of your shoes normally provide a very large resistance between your feet and the ground, so the current would probably not be enough to do serious harm. But if you are standing barefoot in a wet bathtub connected through its plumbing to the ground, the resistance between you and the ground is very small. Your overall resistance is lowered so much that the 120-volt potential difference may produce a harmful current through your body.

Drops of water that collect around the on/off switches of devices such as a hair dryer can conduct current to the user. Although distilled water is a good insulator, the ions in ordinary water greatly

FIGURE 34.7 ▲
Handling a wet hair dryer can be like sticking your fingers into a live socket.

FIGURE 34.8 ▲
The bird can stand harmlessly on one wire of high potential, but it better not grab a neighboring wire!

reduce the electric resistance. There is also usually a layer of salt left from perspiration on your skin, which when wet lowers your skin resistance to a few hundred ohms or less. Handling electric devices while taking a bath is extremely dangerous.

High-Voltage Wires You probably have seen birds perched on high-voltage wires like the one in Figure 34.8. Every part of the bird's body is at the same high potential as the wire, and it feels no ill effects. For the bird to receive a shock, there must be a *difference* in potential between one part of its body and another part. Most of the current will then pass along the path of least electric resistance connecting these two points.

Suppose you fall from a bridge and manage to grab onto a high-voltage power line, halting your fall. So long as you touch nothing else of different potential, you will receive no shock at all. Even if the wire is thousands of volts above ground potential and even if you hang by it with two hands, no charge will flow from one hand to the other. This is because there is no appreciable difference in electric potential between your hands. If, however, you reach over with one hand and grab onto a wire of different potential, ZAP!!

Ground Wires Mild shocks occur when the surfaces of appliances are at an electric potential different from that of the surfaces of other nearby devices. If you touch surfaces of different potentials, you become a pathway for current. To prevent this problem, the outsides of electric appliances are connected to a ground wire, which is connected to the round third prong of a three-wire electric plug, shown in Figure 34.9. All ground wires in all plugs are connected together through the wiring system of the house. The two flat prongs are for the current-carrying double wire. If the live wire accidentally comes in contact with the metal surface of an appliance, the current will be directed to ground rather than shocking you if you handle it.

FIGURE 34.9 ▼
The third prong connects the body of the appliance directly to ground. Any charge that builds up on an appliance is therefore conducted to the ground.

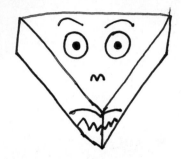

Health Effects One effect of electric shock is to overheat tissues in the body or to disrupt normal nerve functions. It can upset the nerve center that controls breathing. In rescuing victims, the first thing to do is clear them from the electric power supply with a wooden stick or some other nonconductor so that you don't get electrocuted yourself. Then apply artificial respiration.

CONCEPT CHECK What causes the damaging effects of electric shock?

think!

If the resistance of your body were 100,000 ohms, what would be the current in your body when you touched the terminals of a 12-volt battery?
Answer: 34.6.1

If your skin were very moist, so that your resistance was only 1000 ohms, and you touched the terminals of a 24-volt battery, how much current would you draw?
Answer: 34.6.2

34.7 Direct Current and Alternating Current

☑ **Electric current may be DC or AC.** By DC, we mean **direct current,** which refers to a flow of charge that *always flows in one direction.* A battery produces direct current in a circuit because the terminals of the battery always have the same sign of charge. Electrons always move through the circuit in the same direction, from the repelling negative terminal and toward the attracting positive terminal. Even if the current moves in unsteady pulses, so long as it moves in one direction only, it is DC.

Alternating current (AC), as the name implies, is electric current that repeatedly reverses direction. Electrons in the circuit move first in one direction and then in the opposite direction, alternating back and forth about relatively fixed positions. This is accomplished by alternating the polarity of voltage at the generator or other voltage source. Nearly all commercial AC circuits in North America involve voltages and currents that alternate back and forth at a frequency of 60 cycles per second. This is 60-hertz current. In some places, 25-hertz, 30-hertz, or 50-hertz current is used.

By plotting current over time, as shown in Figure 34.10, you can illustrate the difference between DC and AC. DC flows in only one direction over time; AC cycles back and forth over time.

Ventricular fibrillation may be induced by only 0.06 A through the chest for a fraction of a second from a common 120-V circuit. Inducing the same effect with direct current requires about 0.3 to 0.5 A. If the current has a direct pathway to the heart (via a cardiac catheter or other electrodes), less than 0.001 A (AC or DC) can cause fibrillation.

FIGURE 34.10 ▼
a. Direct current (DC) does not change direction over time. **b.** Alternating current (AC) cycles back and forth.

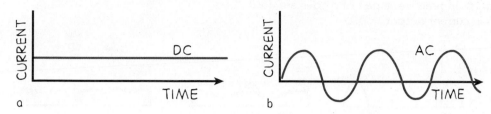

Voltage Standards

Voltage of AC in North America is normally 120 volts.[34.7.1] In the early days of electricity, higher voltages burned out the filaments of electric lightbulbs. Tradition has it that 110 volts was settled on because it made bulbs of the day glow as brightly as a gas lamp. So the hundreds of power plants built in the United States prior to 1900 adopted 110 volts (or 115 or 120 volts) as their standard. By the time electricity became popular in Europe, engineers had figured out how to make lightbulbs that would not burn out so fast at higher voltages. Power transmission is more efficient at higher voltages, so Europe adopted 220 volts as their standard. The United States stayed with 110 volts (today officially 120 volts) because of the installed base of 110-volt equipment.

Three-Wire Service

Although lamps in an American home operate on 110–120 volts, many electric stoves and other energy-hungry appliances operate on 220–240 volts. How is this possible? Because most electric service in the United States is three-wire: one wire at 120 volts positive, one wire at zero volts (neutral), and the other wire at a negative 120 volts. This is AC, with the positive and negative alternating at 60 hertz. A wire that is positive at one instant is negative 1/120 of a second later. Most home appliances are connected between the neutral wire and either of the other two wires, producing 120 volts. When the plus-120 is connected to the minus-120, a 240-volt jolt is produced—just right for electric stoves, air conditioners, and clothes dryers.[34.7.2]

The popularity of AC arises from the fact that electrical energy in the form of AC can be transmitted great distances with easy voltage step-ups that result in lower heat losses in the wires. Why this is so will be discussed in Chapter 37. The primary use of electric current, whether DC or AC, is to transfer energy quietly, flexibly, and conveniently from one place to another.

For: Links on electric current
Visit: www.SciLinks.org
Web Code: csn – 3407

CONCEPT CHECK What are the two types of electric current?

CHAPTER 34   ELECTRIC CURRENT   **689**

FIGURE 34.11 ▼
a. When input to a diode is AC, **b.** output is pulsating DC.
c. Charging and discharging of a capacitor provides continuous
and smoother current. **d.** In practice, a pair of diodes are used
so there are no gaps in current output.

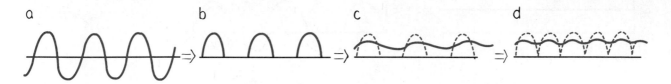

a   b   c   d

34.8 Converting AC to DC

The current in your home is AC. The current in a battery-operated
device, such as a laptop computer or cell phone, is DC. ☑ **With an
AC–DC converter, you can operate a battery-run device on AC
instead of batteries.** In addition to a transformer to lower the voltage (Chapter 37), the converter uses a **diode,** a tiny electronic
device that acts as a one-way valve to allow electron flow in only
one direction. Since alternating current vibrates in two directions,
only half of each cycle will pass through a diode (Figures 34.11a
and 34.11b). The output is a rough DC, off half the time. To maintain continuous current while smoothing the bumps, a capacitor is
used (Figure 34.11c).

Recall from the previous chapter that a capacitor acts as a storage
reservoir for charge. Just as it takes time to raise or lower the water
level in a reservoir, it takes time to add or remove electrons from the
plates of a capacitor. A capacitor therefore produces a retarding effect
on changes in current flow. It smooths the pulsed output.

A familiar diode is the
light-emitting diode
(LED) seen on clocks
and instrument panels.
A solar cell is an LED
in reverse—it absorbs
light and produces
electricity.

CONCEPT CHECK : How can you operate a battery-run device on AC?

FIGURE 34.12 ▶
Diodes are tiny devices
that allow electrons to
flow in only one direction.

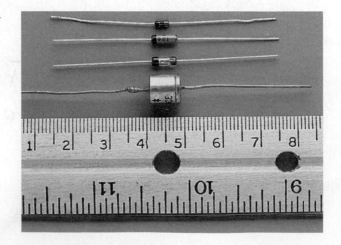

34.9 The Speed of Electrons in a Circuit

When you flip on the light switch on your wall and the circuit is completed, the lightbulb appears to glow immediately. Energy is transported through the connecting wires at nearly the speed of light. The electrons that make up the current, however, do not move at this high speed.

At room temperature, the electrons inside a metal wire have an average speed of a few million kilometers per hour due to their thermal motion. This does not produce a current because the motion is random. There is no net flow in any one direction. But when a battery or generator is connected, an electric field is established inside the wire. It is a pulsating electric field that can travel through a circuit at nearly the speed of light. The electrons continue their random motions in all directions while simultaneously being nudged along the wire by the electric field.

The conducting wire acts as a guide or "pipe" for electric field lines, as you can see in Figure 34.13. In the space outside the wire, the electric field has a pattern determined by the location of electric charges, including charges in the wire. Inside the wire, the electric field is directed along the wire. If the voltage source is DC, like the battery shown in Figure 34.13, the electric field lines are maintained in one direction in the conductor.

Caution: Don't short out the terminals of a battery as shown in Figure 34.13. If you touch both terminals with a metal wrench, for instance, you can create a spark that can ignite hydrogen gas in the battery and send pieces of battery and acid flying.

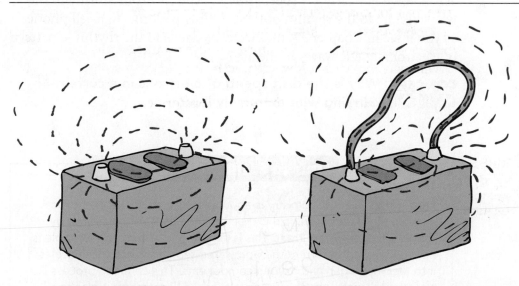

FIGURE 34.13 ▲
The electric field lines between the terminals of a battery are directed through a conductor, which joins the terminals.

FIGURE 34.14 ▶

The solid lines depict a random path of an electron bouncing off atoms in a conductor. The dashed lines show an exaggerated view of how this path changes when an electric field is applied. The electron drifts toward the right with an average speed less than a snail's pace.

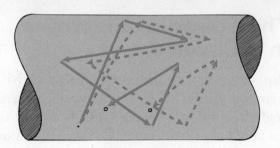

Conduction electrons are accelerated by the field. Before the electrons gain appreciable speed, they "bump into" the anchored metallic ions in their paths and transfer some of their kinetic energy to them. This is why current-carrying wires become hot. ✅ **In a current-carrying wire, collisions interrupt the motion of the electrons so that their actual *drift speed*, or *net speed* through the wire due to the field, is extremely low.** In a typical DC circuit, in the electric system of an automobile for example, electrons have a net average drift speed of about 0.01 cm/s. At this rate, it would take about three hours for an electron to travel through 1 meter of wire.

In an AC circuit, the conduction electrons don't make any net progress in any direction. In a single cycle they drift a tiny fraction of a centimeter in one direction, and then the same tiny distance in the opposite direction. Hence they oscillate rhythmically to and fro about relatively fixed positions. When you talk to your friend on a conventional telephone, it is the *pattern* of oscillating motion that is carried across town at nearly the speed of light. The electrons already in the wires vibrate to the rhythm of the traveling pattern. (In a cell phone, as you'll see in Chapter 37, the electrons dance to the rhythmic pattern of electromagnetic waves in the air.)

CONCEPT : Why is the drift speed of electrons in a current-
CHECK : carrying wire extremely low?

Link to ELECTROCHEMISTRY

Electrolysis Electrochemistry is about electrical energy and chemical change. Molecules in a liquid can be broken apart and separated by the action of electric current. This is *electrolysis*. A common example is passing an electric current through water, separating water molecules into their hydrogen and oxygen components. This common process is also at work when a car battery is recharged. Electrolysis is also used to produce metals from ores. Aluminum is a familiar metal produced by electrolysis. Aluminum is common today, but before the advent of its production by electrolysis in 1886, aluminum was much more expensive than silver or gold!

34.10 The Source of Electrons in a Circuit

In a hardware store you can buy a water hose that is empty of water. But you can't buy a piece of wire, an "electron pipe," that is empty of electrons. ☑ **The source of electrons in a circuit is the conducting circuit material itself.** Some people think that the electric outlets in the walls of their homes are a source of electrons. They think that electrons flow from the power utility through the power lines and into the wall outlets of their homes. This is not true. The outlets in homes are AC. Electrons do not travel appreciable distances through a wire in an AC circuit. Instead, they vibrate to and fro about relatively fixed positions.

When you plug a lamp into an AC outlet, *energy* flows from the outlet into the lamp, not electrons. Energy is carried by the electric field and causes a vibratory motion of the electrons that already exist in the lamp filament. If 120 volts AC are impressed on a lamp, then an average of 120 joules of energy are dissipated by each coulomb of charge that is made to vibrate. Most of this electrical energy appears as heat, while some of it takes the form of light. Power utilities do not sell electrons. They sell *energy*. You supply the electrons.

Thus, when you are jolted by an AC electric shock, the electrons making up the current in your body originate in your body. Electrons do not come out of the wire and through your body and into the ground; energy does. The energy simply causes free electrons in your body to vibrate in unison. Small vibrations tingle; large vibrations can be fatal.

CONCEPT CHECK What is the source of electrons in a circuit?

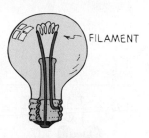

FIGURE 34.15 ▲
The conduction electrons that surge to and fro in the filament of the lamp do not come from the voltage source. They are in the filament to begin with. The voltage source simply provides them with surges of energy.

34.11 Electric Power

Unless it is in a superconductor, a charge moving in a circuit expends energy. This may result in heating the circuit or in turning a motor. **Electric power** is the rate at which electrical energy is converted into another form such as mechanical energy, heat, or light. ☑ **Electric power is equal to the product of current and voltage.**[34.11.1]

$$\text{electric power} = \text{current} \times \text{voltage}$$

If the voltage is expressed in volts and the current in amperes, then the power is expressed in watts. So, in units form,

$$1 \text{ watt} = (1 \text{ ampere}) \times (1 \text{ volt})$$

Solid-state lighting may soon make conventional lightbulbs obsolete. Watch for the progression of LEDs from flashlights to automobile headlights.

$$1W = \frac{1\ J}{1\ \mathcal{C}} \times \frac{1\ \mathcal{C}}{1\ s} = \frac{1\ J}{1\ s}$$

FIGURE 34.16 ▲

The power and voltage on the lightbulb read "60 W, 120 V." You can calculate the current that would flow through the bulb as follows:
$I = P/V = (60\ W)/(120\ V) = 0.5\ A$.

If a lamp rated at 120 watts operates on a 120-volt line, you can see that it will draw a current of 1 ampere, since 120 watts = (1 ampere) × (120 volts). A 60-watt lamp draws 0.5 ampere on a 120-volt line. This relationship becomes a practical matter when you wish to know the cost of electrical energy, which varies from 1 cent to 10 cents per kilowatt-hour depending on locality.

A *kilowatt* is 1000 watts, and a *kilowatt-hour* represents the amount of energy consumed in 1 hour at the rate of 1 kilowatt.[34.11.2] Therefore, in a locality where electrical energy costs 10 cents per kilowatt-hour, a 100-watt electric lightbulb can be run for 10 hours at a cost of 10 cents, or a cent for each hour. A toaster or iron, which draws more current and therefore more power, costs several times as much to operate for the same time.

CONCEPT CHECK : How can you express electric power in terms of current and voltage?

think!

How much power is used by a calculator that operates on 8 volts and 0.1 ampere? If it is used for one hour, how much energy does it use?
Answer: 34.11.1

Will a 1200-watt hair dryer operate on a 120-volt line if the current is limited to 15 amperes by a safety fuse? Can two hair dryers operate on this line?
Answer: 34.11.2

REVIEW

Concept Summary ......

- When the ends of an electric conductor are at different electric potentials, charge flows from one end to the other.

- A current-carrying wire has a net electric charge of zero.

- Voltage sources such as batteries and generators supply energy that allows charges to move steadily.

- The resistance of a wire depends on the conductivity of the material used in the wire and also on the thickness and length of the wire.

- Ohm's law states that the current in a circuit is directly proportional to the voltage impressed across the circuit and is inversely proportional to the resistance of the circuit.

- The damaging effects of shock are the result of current passing through the body.

- Electric current may be AD or DC.

- With an AC–DC converter, you can operate a battery-run device on AC instead of batteries.

- In a current-carrying wire, collisions interrupt the motion of the electrons so that their actual *drift speed*, or *net speed*, through the wire due to the field is extremely low.

- The source of electrons in a circuit is the conducting circuit material itself.

- Electric power is equal to the product of current and voltage.

Key Terms ......

potential
  difference (*p. 681*)

electric
  current (*p. 682*)

ampere (*p. 682*)

voltage source (*p. 683*)

electric
  resistance (*p. 684*)

superconductivity
  (*p. 684*)

ohm (*p. 684*)

Ohm's law (*p. 685*)

direct current (*p. 688*)

alternating
  current (*p. 688*)

diode (*p. 690*)

electric power (*p. 693*)

think! Answers

34.5 $\text{Current} = \dfrac{\text{voltage}}{\text{resistance}} = \dfrac{50\ \text{V}}{100\ \Omega} = 0.5\ \text{A}$

34.6.1 $\text{Current} = \dfrac{\text{voltage}}{\text{resistance}} = \dfrac{12\ \text{V}}{100{,}000\ \Omega} =$
0.00012 A (quite harmless)

34.6.2 You would draw $\dfrac{24\ \text{V}}{1000\ \Omega}$, or 0.024 A,
a dangerous amount of current!

34.11.1 Power = current × voltage = (0.1 A) × (8 V) = 0.8 W. Energy = power × time = (0.8 W) × (1 h) = 0.8 watt-hour, or 0.0008 kilowatt-hour.

34.11.2 One 1200-W hair dryer can be operated because the circuit can provide (15 A) × (120 V) = 1800 W. But there is inadequate power to operate two hair dryers of combined power 2400 W. In terms of current, (1200 W)/(120 V) = 10 A; so the hair dryer will operate when connected to the circuit. But two hair dryers will require 20 A and will blow the 15-A fuse.

34 ASSESS

Check Concepts ......

Section 34.1

1. What condition is necessary for the flow of heat? What analogous condition is necessary for the flow of charge?

2. What is meant by the term *potential*? What is meant by *potential difference*?

3. What condition is necessary for the sustained flow of water in a pipe? What analogous condition is necessary for the sustained flow of charge in a wire?

Section 34.2

4. What is electric current?

5. What is an ampere?

Section 34.3

6. What is voltage?

7. How many joules per coulomb are given to charges that flow in a 120-volt circuit?

8. Does charge flow through a circuit or into a circuit?

9. Does voltage flow through a circuit, or is voltage established across a circuit?

Section 34.4

10. What is electric resistance?

11. Is electric resistance greater in a short fat wire or a long thin wire?

Section 34.5

12. What is Ohm's law?

13. If the resistance of a circuit remains constant while the voltage across the circuit decreases to half its former value, what change occurs in the current?

14. If the voltage impressed across a circuit is constant but the resistance doubles, what change occurs in the current?

Section 34.6

15. How does wetness affect the resistance of your body?

16. Why is it that a bird can perch without harm on a high-voltage wire?

17. What is the function of the third prong in a household electric plug?

Section 34.7

18. Distinguish between DC and AC. Which is produced by a battery and which is usually produced by a generator?

Section 34.8

19. A diode converts AC to pulsed DC. What electric device smooths the pulsed DC to a smoother DC?

20. What are the roles of a diode and a capacitor in an AC–DC converter?

Section 34.9

21. What is a typical "drift" speed of electrons that make up a current in a typical DC circuit? In a typical AC circuit?

Section 34.10

22. From where do the electrons originate that flow in a typical electric circuit?

Section 34.11

23. What is power?

24. Which of these is a unit of power and which is a unit of electrical energy: a watt, a kilowatt, and a kilowatt-hour?

25. How many amperes flow through a 60-watt bulb when 120 volts are impressed across it?

Think and Rank ......

Rank each of the following sets of scenarios in order of the quantity or property involved. List them from left to right. If scenarios have equal rankings, separate them with an equal sign. (e.g., A = B)

26. Rank the circuits below according to the brightness of the bulbs, from brightest to dimmest.

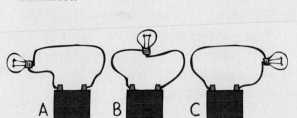

27. The bulbs shown below are identical. An ammeter is placed in different branches, as shown. Rank the current readings in the ammeter from greatest to least.

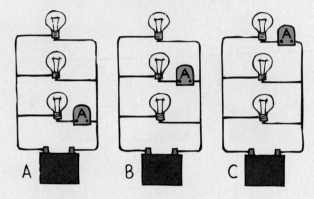

28. All bulbs are identical in the circuits shown below. An ammeter is connected next to the battery as shown. Rank the current readings in the ammeter, from greatest to least.

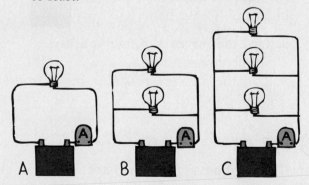

29. In each of the circuits shown below, a voltmeter is connected across a bulb to measure the voltage drop across it. Rank the voltage readings from greatest to least.

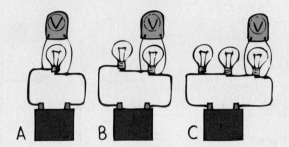

A   B   C

30. All bulbs are identical in the circuit shown to the right. The circuit consists of three parts: (A) the top branch with two bulbs; (B) the middle branch with one bulb; and (C) the battery.

a. Rank the current through A, B, and C, from greatest to least.

b. Rank the voltage across A, B, and C, from greatest to least.

Plug and Chug · · · · · ·

The key equations of the chapter are shown below in bold type.

Ohm's law: $I = \dfrac{V}{R}$

Electric power: $P = IV$

31. Calculate the current where 10 coulombs of charge pass a point in 5 seconds.

32. Calculate the current of a lightning bolt that delivers a charge of 35 coulombs to the ground in a time of 1/1000 second.

33. Calculate the current in a toaster that has a heating element of 14 ohms when connected to a 120-V outlet.

34. Calculate the current in the coiled heating element of a 240-V stove. The resistance of the element is 60 ohms at its operating temperature.

35. Electric socks, popular in cold weather, have a 90-ohm heating element that is powered by a 9-volt battery. How much current warms your feet?

36. How much current moves through your fingers (resistance: 1200 ohms) if you touch them to the terminals of a 6-volt battery?

37. Calculate the power supplied to an electric blanket that carries 1.20 A when connected to a 120-V outlet.

Think and Explain · · · · · ·

38. Is this label on a household product cause for concern? "Caution: This product contains tiny electrically charged particles moving at speeds in excess of 10,000,000 kilometers per hour."

39. Do an *ampere* and a *volt* measure the same thing, or different things? What are those things, and which is a flow and which is the cause of the flow?

40. What happens to the brightness of light emitted by a light bulb when the current in it increases?

41. In terms of heating, why are thick wires rather than thin wires used to carry large currents?

42. Why is it important that the resistance of an extension cord be small when it is used to power an electric heater?

43. Why will an electric drill operating on a very long extension cord not rotate as fast as one operated on a short cord?

44. Your tutor tells you that an ampere and a volt really measure the same thing, and the different terms only serve to make a simple concept seem confusing. Why should you consider getting a different tutor?

45. Does more current flow out of a battery than into it? Does more current flow into a lightbulb than out of it? Explain.

46. A simple lie detector consists of an electric circuit, one part of which is part of your body. A sensitive meter shows the current that flows when a small voltage is applied. How does this technique indicate that a person is lying? (And when does this technique not indicate when someone is lying?)

47. Only a small fraction of the electric energy fed into a common lightbulb is transformed into light. What happens to the rest?

48. Will a lamp with a thick filament draw more current or less current than a lamp with a thin filament made of the same material?

49. A 1-mile-long copper wire has a resistance of 10 ohms. What will be its new resistance when it is shortened by (a) cutting it in half or by (b) doubling it over and using it as if it were one wire of half the length but twice the cross-sectional area?

50. Will the current in a lightbulb connected to 220 V be more or less than when the bulb is connected to 110 V? How much?

51. Which will do more damage—plugging a 110-V toaster into a 220-V circuit or plugging a 220-V toaster into a 110-V circuit? Explain.

52. If a current of one- or two-tenths of an ampere were to flow into one of your hands and out the other, you would probably be electrocuted. But if the same current were to flow into your hand and out the elbow above the same hand, you could survive, even though the current might be large enough to burn your flesh. Explain.

53. What is the effect on current if both the voltage and the resistance are doubled? If both are halved?

54. In 60-Hz alternating current, how many times per second does an electron change its direction? (Don't say 60!)

55. If electrons flow very slowly through a circuit, why doesn't it take a noticeably long time for a lamp to glow when you turn on a distant switch?

56. What unit is represented by (a) joule per coulomb, (b) coulomb per second, and (c) watt-second?

57. Two lightbulbs designed for 120-V use are rated at 40 W and 60 W. Which lightbulb has the greater filament resistance? Why?

58. A car's headlights dissipate 40 W on low beam and 50 W on high beam. Is there more or less resistance in the high-beam filament?

Think and Solve ......

59. How much current, in amperes, is in a lightning stroke that lasts 0.05 second and transfers 100 coulombs?

60. How much charge flows in a pocket calculator each minute when the current is 0.0001 ampere?

61. How much voltage is required to make 2 amperes flow through a resistance of 8 ohms?

62. Use the relationship power = current × voltage to find out how much current is drawn by a 1200-watt hair dryer when it operates on 120 volts. Then use Ohm's law to find the resistance of the hair dryer.

63. The current driven by voltage V in a circuit of resistance R is given by Ohm's law, $I = V/R$. Show that the resistance of a circuit carrying current I and driven by voltage V is given by the equation $R = V/I$.

64. Use the equation just derived and show that when a device in a 120-V circuit draws a current of 20 A, its resistance is 6 Ω.

65. The power of an electric circuit is given by the equation $P = IV$. Use Ohm's law to express V and show that power can be expressed by the equation $P = I^2R$.

66. An electric heater has a heating element of resistance 12 Ω. It is plugged into a wall socket that provides 120 V.
a. What is the current through the heater?
b. What is the power "consumption" of the heater?

67. Calculate the resistance of the filament in a lightbulb that carries 0. 4 A when 3.0 V is impressed across it.

FILAMENT

68. A lightbulb is marked "120 V, 60 W."
a. What current flows through the filament when the bulb is turned on?
b. Show that the electrical resistance of the lightbulb filament is 240 Ω.

69. A microwave oven is marked "120 V, 1100 W."
  a. How much current does the oven draw?
  b. To heat 380 g of 20°C water to 86°C, show that you should set the timer for at least 95 s.

70. A typical car headlight may put out 50 watts at 12 volts.
  a. Show that 4.2 A is drawn by the headlight.
  b. How many electrons pass through the bulb filament each second?

71. Suppose that an ammeter inserted in series in a toaster circuit shows that the current is 5.0 amps when the toaster is plugged into a 120-volt circuit. Show that the energy dissipated by the toaster in 40 seconds is 24,000 joules.

72. The wattage marked on a lightbulb is not an inherent property of the bulb but depends on the amount of voltage to which it is connected, usually 110 V or 120 V.
  a. Calculate the current through a 40-W bulb connected to 120 V.
  b. Calculate the current through the same bulb when it is connected to 60 V.

73. The resistance of a certain wire is 10 ohms.
  a. What would the resistance of the same wire be if it were twice as long?
  b. If it had twice the diameter?

74. Calculate the power dissipated in a toaster that has a resistance of 14 ohms and is plugged into a 120-V outlet.

75. Calculate the yearly cost of running a 5-W electric clock continuously in a location where electricity costs 10 cents per kWh.

Activity ● ● ● ● ● ●

76. Batteries are made up of electric cells, which are composed of two unlike pieces of metal separated by a conducting solution. A simple 1.5-volt cell, equivalent to a flashlight cell, can be made by placing a strip of copper and a strip of zinc in a moist vegetable or piece of fruit, as shown in the figure. A lemon or banana works well. Hold the ends of the strips close together but not touching, and place the ends on your tongue. The slight tingle you feel and the metallic taste you experience result from a small electric current that flows through the cell when your moist tongue closes the circuit. Try this and compare the results for different metals and different fruits and vegetables.

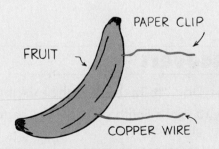

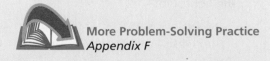

More Problem-Solving Practice
Appendix F

35 ELECTRIC CIRCUITS

THE BIG IDEA : Any path along which electrons can flow is a circuit.

Mechanical things seem to be easier to figure out for most people than electrical things. Maybe this is because most people have had experience playing with blocks and mechanical toys when they were children. If you are among the many who have had far less direct experience with the inner workings of electric devices than with mechanical gadgets, you are encouraged to put extra effort into the laboratory part of this course. You'll find hands-on laboratory experience aids your understanding of electric circuits. The experience can be a lot of fun, too!

---

discover!

What Does It Take to Light a Lightbulb?

1. Try to light a lightbulb with just a battery and a single piece of wire.
2. Now try to get the same result with different arrangements of the wire, the battery, and the lightbulb.

Analyze and Conclude

1. **Observing** Describe both successful and unsuccessful attempts to light the lightbulb.
2. **Predicting** How many possible arrangements of the wire, the battery, and the lightbulb will result in the bulb being lit?
3. **Making Generalizations** What conditions are necessary in order for the bulb to light?

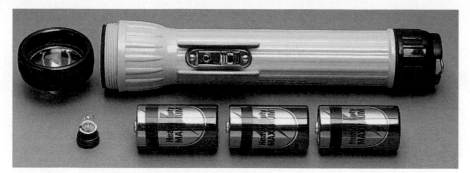

35.1 A Battery and a Bulb

Take apart an ordinary flashlight like the one shown in Figure 35.1. If you don't have any spare pieces of wire around, cut some strips from some aluminum foil that you probably have in one of your kitchen drawers. Try to light up the bulb using a single battery[35.1] and a couple of pieces of wire or foil.

Some of the ways you *can* light the bulb and some of the ways you *can't* light it are shown in Figure 35.2. The important thing to note is that there must be a complete path, or **circuit,** that includes the bulb filament and that runs from the positive terminal at the top of the battery to the negative terminal, which is the bottom of the battery. Electrons flow from the negative part of the battery through the wire or foil to the side (or bottom) of the bulb, through the filament inside the bulb, and out the bottom (or side) and through the other piece of wire or foil to the positive part of the battery. The current then passes through the interior of the battery to complete the circuit.

The flow of charge in a circuit is very much like the flow of water in a closed system of pipes. In a flashlight, or for the setups shown in Figure 35.2b, the battery is analogous to a pump, the wires are analogous to the pipes, and the bulb is analogous to any device that operates when the water is flowing. When a valve in the line is opened and the pump is operating, water already in the pipes starts to flow.

Filament resistance in a 120-V, 60-W bulb increases about 15 times from room temperature to its nearly 3000-K operating temperature in a time of about 100 milliseconds. The initial 10-A current drawn quickly decreases to a steady 0.7 A.

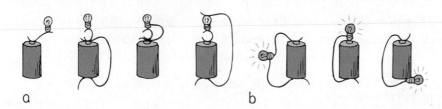

a   b

FIGURE 35.2 ▲
a. Unsuccessful ways to light a bulb. **b.** Successful ways to light a bulb.

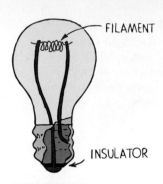

FILAMENT

INSULATOR

FIGURE 35.3 ▲

Electrons do not pile up inside a bulb, but instead flow through its filament.

☑ **In a flashlight, when the switch is turned on to complete an electric circuit, the mobile conduction electrons already in the wires and the filament begin to drift through the circuit.** The water flows *through* the pump and electrons in effect flow *through* the battery. Neither the water nor the electrons "squash up" and concentrate in certain places; they flow continuously around a loop, or circuit.

CONCEPT CHECK : What happens to the mobile conduction electrons when you turn on a flashlight?

35.2 Electric Circuits

Any path along which electrons can flow is a circuit. ☑ **For a continuous flow of electrons, there must be a complete circuit with no gaps.** A gap is usually provided by an electric switch that can be opened or closed to either cut off or allow electron flow.

The water analogy is quite useful for gaining a conceptual understanding of electric circuits, but it does have some limitations. An important one is that a break in a water pipe results in water spilling from the circuit, whereas a break in an electric circuit results in a complete stop in the flow of electricity. Another difference has to do with turning current off and on. When you *close* an electrical switch that connects the circuit, you allow current to flow in much the same way as you allow water to flow by *opening* a faucet. Opening a switch stops the flow of electricity. An electric circuit must be closed for electricity to flow. Opening a water faucet, on the other hand, starts the flow of water. Despite these and some other differences, thinking of electric current in terms of water current is a helpful way to study electric circuits.

Most circuits have more than one device that receives electrical energy. These devices are commonly connected in a circuit in one of two ways, *series* or *parallel*. When connected **in series,** the devices in a circuit form a single pathway for electron flow between the terminals of the battery, generator, or wall socket (which is simply an extension of these terminals). When connected **in parallel,** the devices in a circuit form branches, each of which is a separate path for the flow of electrons. Both series and parallel connections have their own distinctive characteristics. This chapter briefly treats circuits with these two types of connections.

CONCEPT CHECK : How can a circuit achieve a continuous flow of electrons?

After failing more than 6000 times before perfecting the first electric lightbulb, Thomas Edison stated that his trials were not failures, because he successfully discovered 6000 ways that don't work.

Electrician An electrician is called upon whenever a building is being constructed or rewired. Electricians install wiring and connect the circuits to the local power company. The first step an electrician must take is to prepare a wiring diagram that shows how the series and parallel circuits will be arranged and where the switches will be located. The next step is to install the circuits and make sure current flows through the circuits properly and safely. The electrician must also make sure that the wiring meets local codes. Builders and contractors rely on electricians for any structure that uses electricity—from tall skyscrapers to backyard lighting systems.

35.3 Series Circuits

Figure 35.4 shows three lamps connected in series with a battery. This is an example of a simple **series circuit,** or a circuit in which devices are arranged so that charge flows through each in turn. When the switch is closed, a current exists almost immediately in all three lamps. The current does not "pile up" in any lamp but flows *through* each lamp. Electrons in all parts of the circuit begin to move at once. Some electrons move away from the negative terminal of the battery, some move toward the positive terminal, and some move through the filament of each lamp. Eventually the electrons move all the way around the circuit. A break anywhere in the path results in an open circuit, and the flow of electrons ceases. Burning out of one of the lamp filaments or simply opening the switch could cause such a break.

think!

What happens to the light intensity of each lamp in a series circuit when more lamps are added to the circuit?
Answer: 35.3.1

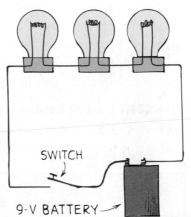

SWITCH

9-V BATTERY

Go **Online**
active art

For: Series Circuit activity
Visit: PHSchool.com
Web Code: csp – 3503

FIGURE 35.4 ▲
In this simple series circuit, a 9-volt battery provides 3 volts across each lamp.

The circuit shown in Figure 35.4 illustrates the following important characteristics of series connections:

1. Electric current has but a single pathway through the circuit. This means that the current passing through each electric device is the same.
2. This current is resisted by the resistance of the first device, the resistance of the second, and the third also, so that the total resistance to current in the circuit is the sum of the individual resistances along the circuit path.
3. The current in the circuit is numerically equal to the voltage supplied by the source divided by the total resistance of the circuit. This is Ohm's law.
4. Ohm's law also applies separately to each device. The *voltage drop*, or potential difference, across each device depends directly on its resistance. This follows from the fact that more energy is used to move a unit of charge through a large resistance than through a small resistance.
5. The total voltage impressed across a series circuit divides among the individual electric devices in the circuit so that the sum of the voltage drops across the individual devices is equal to the total voltage supplied by the source. This follows from the fact that the amount of energy used to move each unit of charge through the entire circuit equals the sum of the energies used to move that unit of charge through each of the electric devices in the circuit.

It is easy to see the main disadvantage of a series circuit. ✓ **If one device fails in a series circuit, current in the whole circuit ceases and none of the devices will work.** Some cheap party lights are connected in series. When one lamp burns out, it's "fun and games" (or frustration) trying to find which bulb to replace.

Most circuits are wired so that it is possible to operate electric devices independently of each other. In your home, for example, a lamp can be turned on or off without affecting the operation of other lamps or electric devices. This is because these devices are connected not in series but in parallel to one another.

A series circuit is like a single-lane road with no alternate path. If there is a roadblock or a cave-in, traffic will stop.

CONCEPT CHECK: What happens to current in other lamps if one lamp in a series circuit burns out?

think!

Look at the circuit shown in Figure 35.4. If the current through one of the bulbs is 1 A, can you tell what the current is through each of the other two bulbs? If the voltage across bulb 1 is 2 V, and across bulb 2 is 4 V, what is the voltage across bulb 3?
Answer: 35.3.2

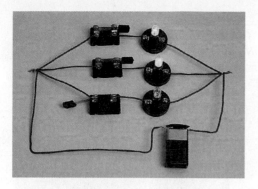

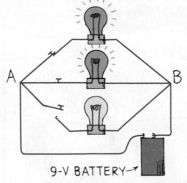

◀ **FIGURE 35.5**
In this simple parallel circuit, a 9-volt battery provides 9 volts across each activated lamp.

9-V BATTERY →

35.4 Parallel Circuits

Figure 35.5 shows three lamps connected to the same two points A and B. In a **parallel circuit,** each electric device is connected to the same two points of the circuit. Notice that each lamp has its own path from one terminal of the battery to the other. There are three separate pathways for current, one through each lamp. In contrast to a series circuit, the current in one lamp does not pass through the other lamps. Also, unlike lamps connected in series, the parallel circuit is completed whether all, two, or only one lamp is lit.

☑ **In a parallel circuit, each device operates independent of the other devices. A break in any one path does not interrupt the flow of charge in the other paths.**

The circuit shown in Figure 35.5 illustrates the following major characteristics of parallel connections:

1. Each device connects the same two points A and B of the circuit. The voltage is therefore the same across each device.
2. The total current in the circuit (that is, the total current through the battery) divides among the parallel branches. Current passes more readily into devices of low resistance, so the amount of current in each branch is inversely proportional to the resistance of the branch. Ohm's law applies separately to each branch.
3. The total current in the circuit equals the sum of the currents in its parallel branches.
4. As the number of parallel branches is increased, the total current through the battery increases. From the battery's perspective, the overall resistance of the circuit is *decreased*. This means the overall resistance of the circuit is less than the resistance of any one of the branches.

Go Online
active art

For: Parallel Circuits activity
Visit: PHSchool.com
Web Code: csp – 3504

think!

What happens to the light intensity of each lamp in a parallel circuit when more lamps are added in parallel to the circuit?
Answer: 35.4

CONCEPT CHECK : What happens if one device in a parallel circuit fails?

35.5 Schematic Diagrams

Electric circuits are frequently described by simple diagrams, called **schematic diagrams,** that are similar to those of the last two figures. Some of the symbols used to represent certain circuit elements are shown in Figure 35.6. ✅ **In a schematic diagram, resistance is shown by a zigzag line, and ideal resistance-free wires are shown with solid straight lines. A battery is represented with a set of short and long parallel lines.** The convention is to represent the positive terminal of the battery with a long line and the negative terminal with a short line. Sometimes a two-cell battery is represented with a pair of such lines, a three-cell with three, and so on. Figures 35.7a and 35.7b show schematic diagrams for the circuits of Figures 35.4 and 35.5.

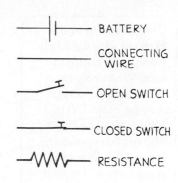

FIGURE 35.6 ▲
Symbols of some common circuit devices.

CONCEPT CHECK : What symbols are used to represent resistance, wires, and batteries in schematic diagrams?

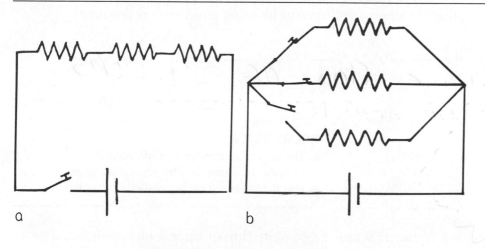

a   b

◀ **FIGURE 35.7**
These schematic diagrams represent **a.** the circuit of Figure 35.4, with three lamps in series; and **b.** the circuit of Figure 35.5, with three lamps in parallel.

Link to TECHNOLOGY

Measuring with Current A fuel gauge in an automobile uses variable resistance to measure the level in the gasoline tank. A float in the tank adjusts the resistance of a variable electric resistor. Maximum resistance occurs when the float bottoms out in the tank. Maximum resistance produces the minimum current, which barely deflects the pointer on the fuel gauge. When the tank is full, the variable resistor has its lowest resistance and the maximum current flows through the fuel gauge. For this current, the gauge is calibrated to read a full tank. Between empty and full, corresponding values of current produce appropriate deflections of the fuel gauge pointer.

The resistance in the filament of a lightbulb varies with temperature. When cold (at room temperature) it may be only 16 Ω in a 120-V, 60-W bulb, while 100 ms later when it reaches its operating temperature, filament resistance increases to a steady 240 Ω.

35.6 Combining Resistors in a Compound Circuit

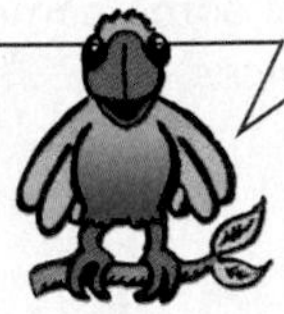

Sometimes it is useful to know the *equivalent resistance* of a circuit that has several resistors in its network. The equivalent resistance is the value of the single resistor that would comprise the same load to the battery or power source. ✓ **The equivalent resistance of resistors connected in series is the sum of their values.** For example, the equivalent resistance for a pair of 1-ohm resistors in series is simply 2 ohms.

The equivalent resistance for a pair of 1-ohm resistors in parallel is 0.5 ohm. (The equivalent resistance is *less* because the current has "twice the path width" when it takes the parallel path. In a similar way, the more doors that are open in an auditorium full of people trying to exit, the *less* will be the resistance to their departure.) ✓ **The equivalent resistance for a pair of equal resistors in parallel is half the value of either resistor.** Figure 35.8 shows how you can simplify schematic diagrams by using equivalent resistances.

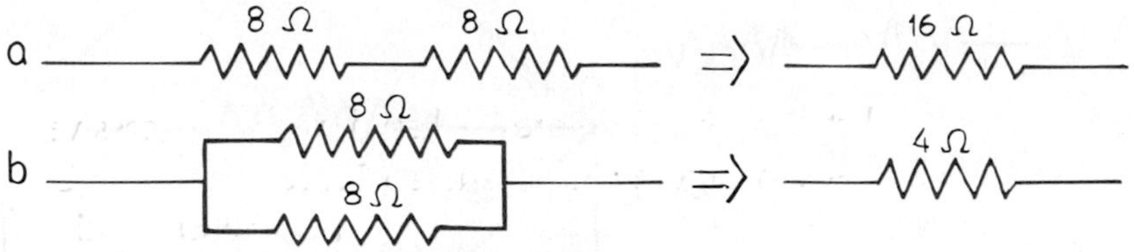

FIGURE 35.8 ▲

a. The equivalent resistance of two 8-ohm resistors in series is 16 ohms. **b.** The equivalent resistance of two 8-ohm resistors in parallel is 4 ohms.

Figure 35.9 shows a combination of three 8-ohm resistors. The two resistors in parallel are equivalent to a single 4-ohm resistor, which is in series with an 8-ohm resistor and adds to produce an equivalent resistance of 12 ohms. If a 12-volt battery were connected to these resistors, can you see from Ohm's law that the current through the battery would be 1 ampere? (In practice it would be less, for there is resistance inside the battery as well, called the battery's *internal resistance.*)

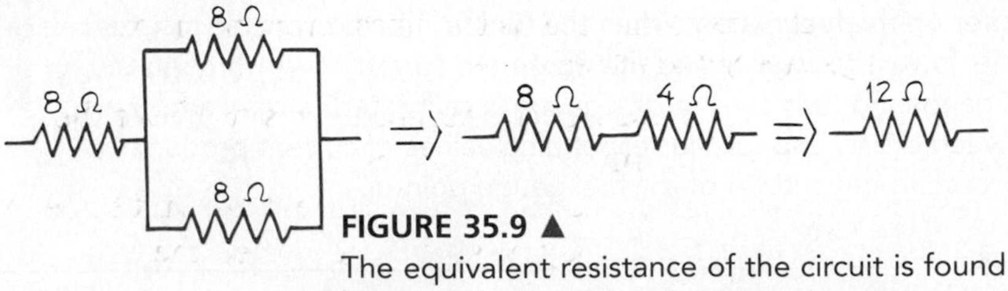

FIGURE 35.9 ▲

The equivalent resistance of the circuit is found by combining resistors in successive steps.

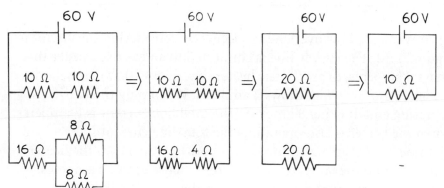

◀ **FIGURE 35.10**
The equivalent resistance of the top branch is 3 ohms, which is in parallel with the 3-ohm resistance of the lower branch. The overall equivalent resistance is 1.5 ohms.

◀ **FIGURE 35.11**
Schematic diagrams for an arrangement of various electric devices. The equivalent resistance of the circuit is 10 ohms. (The 60-V battery is for numerical convenience—most batteries are less than 60 V.)

Two more complex combinations are broken down in successive equivalent combinations in Figures 35.10 and 35.11. It's like a game: Combine resistors in series by adding; combine a pair of equal resistors in parallel by halving.[35.6] The value of the single resistor left is the equivalent resistance of the combination.

See Note 35.6 on page 908 for more on equivalent resistances.

CONCEPT CHECK : What is the equivalent resistance of resistors in series? Of a pair of equal resistors in parallel?

35.7 Parallel Circuits and Overloading

Electric current is usually fed into a home by way of two lead wires called *lines*. These lines are very low in resistance and are connected to wall outlets in each room. About 110 to 120 volts are impressed on these lines by the power company. This voltage is applied to appliances and other devices that are connected in parallel by plugs to these lines.

As more devices are connected to the lines, more pathways are provided for current. What effect do the additional pathways produce? The answer is, a lowering of the combined resistance of the circuit. Therefore, a greater amount of current occurs in the lines. Lines that carry more than a safe amount of current are said to be *overloaded*. The resulting heat may be sufficient to melt the insulation and start a fire.

think!

Use Figure 35.11 to answer the following questions.

What is the current in amperes through the battery? (Neglect the internal resistance of the battery.)
Answer: 35.6.1

What is the current in amperes through the pair of 10-ohm resistors? Through *each* of the 8-ohm resistors?
Answers: 35.6.2

How much power is provided by the battery?
Answer: 35.6.3

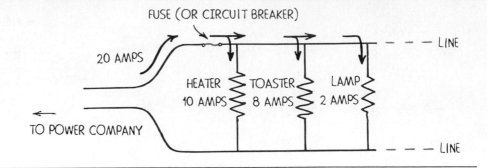

FIGURE 35.12 ▶
The more devices you connect to your household supply line, the more you increase the total line current.

FIGURE 35.13 ▼
Above a specified current, the metal ribbon in a safety fuse melts and breaks the circuit.

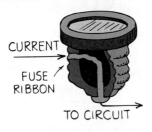

In practice, the lines in your home are not perfect conductors. With the large current used to operate a vacuum cleaner, the connecting wires do warm up. But for most cases, the resistance of the lines can be neglected.

You can see how overloading occurs by considering the circuit in Figure 35.12. The supply line is connected to an electric toaster that draws 8 amperes, to an electric heater that draws 10 amperes, and to an electric lamp that draws 2 amperes. When only the toaster is operating and drawing 8 amperes, the total line current is 8 amperes. When the heater is also operating, the total line current increases to 18 amperes (8 amperes to the toaster and 10 amperes to the heater). If you turn on the lamp, the line current increases to 20 amperes. Connecting any more devices increases the current still more.

☑ **To prevent overloading in circuits, fuses or circuit breakers are connected in series along the supply line.** In this way the entire line current must pass through the fuse. The safety fuse shown in Figure 35.13 is constructed with a wire ribbon that will heat up and melt at a given current. If the fuse is rated at 20 amperes, it will pass 20 amperes, but no more. A current above 20 amperes will melt the fuse, which "blows out" and breaks the circuit. Before a blown fuse is replaced, the cause of overloading should be determined and remedied. Often, insulation that separates the wires in a circuit wears away and allows the wires to touch. This effectively shortens the path of the circuit, and is called a *short circuit*. A short circuit draws a dangerously large current because it bypasses the normal circuit resistance.

Circuits may also be protected by *circuit breakers,* which use magnets or bimetallic strips to open the switch. Utility companies use circuit breakers to protect their lines all the way back to the generators. Circuit breakers are used instead of fuses in modern buildings because they do not have to be replaced each time the circuit is opened. Instead, the switch can simply be moved back to the "on" position after the problem has been corrected.

CONCEPT CHECK How can you prevent overloading in circuits?

35 REVIEW

Go Online
PHSchool.com
For: Self-Assessment
Visit: PHSchool.com
Web Code: csa – 3500

Concept Summary ······

- In a flashlight, when the switch is turned on to complete an electric circuit, the mobile conduction electrons already in the wires and the filament begin to drift through the circuit.

- For a continuous flow of electrons, there must be a complete circuit with no gaps.

- If one device fails in a series circuit, current in the whole circuit ceases and none of the devices will work.

- In a parallel circuit, each device operates independent of the other devices. A break in any one path does not interrupt the flow of charge in the other paths.

- In a schematic diagram, resistance is shown by a zigzag line, and ideal resistance-free wires are shown with solid straight lines.

- The equivalent resistance of resistors connected in series is the sum of their values. The equivalent resistance for a pair of equal resistors in parallel is half the value of either resistor.

- To prevent overloading, fuses or circuit breakers are connected in series along the supply line.

Key Terms ······

circuit (p. 703)

in series (p. 704)

in parallel (p. 704)

series circuit (p. 705)

parallel circuit (p. 707)

schematic diagram (p. 709)

think! Answers

35.3.1 The addition of more lamps results in a greater circuit resistance. This decreases the current in the circuit (and in each lamp), which causes dimming of the lamps.

35.3.2 Yes—it is also 1 A. (The same current passes through every part of a series circuit.) The voltage across bulb 3 is 3 V. Each coulomb of charge flowing in the wire from the battery has 9 J of electrical potential energy (9 V = 9 J/C). That energized coulomb of charge must distribute its energy among three bulbs in proportion to their resistances and return to the battery with 0 J. If it spends 2 J in one bulb and 4 in another, it must spend 3 J in the last bulb. 3 J/C = 3 V

35.4 The light intensity for each lamp is unchanged as other lamps are introduced (or removed). Although changes of resistance and current occur for the circuit as a whole, no changes occur in any individual branch in the circuit.

35.6.1 6 A. From Ohm's law: current = (voltage)/(resistance) = (60 V)/(10 Ω) = 6 A

35.6.2 The total resistance of the middle branch is 20 Ω. Since the voltage is 60 V, the current = (voltage)/(resistance) = (60 V)/(2 Ω) = 3 A. The current through the pair of 8-Ω resistors is 3 A, and the current through each is therefore 1.5 A. (The 3-A current divides equally between these equal resistances.)

35.6.3 Power = current × voltage = (6 A) × (60 V) = 360 watts

35 ASSESS

Check Concepts ......

Section 35.1

1. Are all the electrons flowing in a circuit provided by the battery?

Section 35.2

2. Why must there be no gaps in an electric circuit for it to carry current?

3. Distinguish between a series circuit and a parallel circuit.

Section 35.3

4. If three lamps are connected in series to a 6-volt battery, how many volts are impressed across each lamp?

5. If one of three lamps blows out when connected in series, what happens to the current in the other two?

Section 35.4

6. If three lamps are connected in parallel to a 6-volt battery, how many volts are impressed across each lamp?

7. If one of three lamps blows out when connected in parallel, what happens to the current in the other two?

8. **a.** In which case will there be more current in each of three lamps—if they are connected to the same battery in series or in parallel?
   b. In which case will there be more voltage across each lamp?

Section 35.6

9. What happens to the total circuit resistance when more devices are added to a series circuit? To a parallel circuit?

10. What is the equivalent resistance of a pair of 8-ohm resistors in series? In parallel?

Section 35.7

11. Why does the total circuit resistance decrease when more devices are added to a parallel circuit?

12. What does it mean when you say that lines in a home are overloaded?

13. What is the function of a fuse or circuit breaker in a circuit?

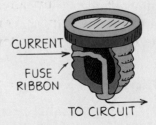

CURRENT

FUSE RIBBON

TO CIRCUIT

14. Why will too many electric devices operating at one time often blow a fuse or trip a circuit breaker?

15. What is meant by a short circuit?

Think and Rank ......

Rank each of the following sets of scenarios in order of the quantity or property involved. List them from left to right. If scenarios have equal rankings, separate them with an equal sign. (e.g., A = B)

16. The resistors in the circuits below are all identical. Rank the circuits according to the size of the equivalent resistance for each, from most resistance to least resistance.

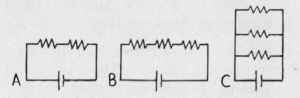

17. The circuit below contains resistors R_1, R_2, and R_3.

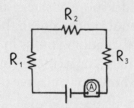

    Rank the following combinations of resistances in terms of the current measured by the ammeter, from highest to lowest.

    (A) $R_1 = 1\ \Omega, R_2 = 2\ \Omega, R_3 = 3\ \Omega$
    (B) $R_1 = 2\ \Omega, R_2 = 1\ \Omega, R_3 = 2\ \Omega$
    (C) $R_1 = 3\ \Omega, R_2 = 3\ \Omega, R_3 = 1\ \Omega$

18. The resistors in the circuits below are 10 Ω each. Each circuit is powered with a 12-V battery. Assume that the battery and connecting wires have negligible resistance.

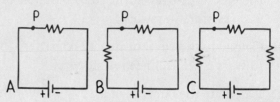

    a. Rank the circuits in terms of the amount of current passing point P in each circuit, from greatest current to least current.
    b. Suppose a voltmeter is connected between point P and the negative terminal of the battery. Rank the circuits in terms of voltmeter readings, from highest voltage to lowest voltage.

Plug and Chug ......

To answer Questions 19–24, you will need to know the following information.

The equivalent resistance of resistors in series is their sum. The equivalent resistance for resistors in parallel can be calculated as follows:

$$\frac{1}{R_{eq}} = \frac{1}{R_1} + \frac{1}{R_2} + \frac{1}{R_3} \cdots + \frac{1}{R_n}$$

In the special case of only two parallel branches with resistances R_1 and R_2, this becomes

$$R_{eq} = \frac{R_1 R_2}{R_1 + R_2}$$

The equation above is often called the "product-over-sum" rule.

19. Calculate the equivalent resistance of two 6-Ω resistors in series.

20. Calculate the equivalent resistance (using the "product-over-sum" rule) of a pair of 6-Ω resistors in parallel.

21. Calculate the current in a 12-V battery that powers a single 30-Ω resistor.

22. Calculate the current in a 12-V battery that powers three 30-Ω resistors connected in series.

23. Calculate the current in a 48-V battery that powers a pair of 30-Ω resistors connected in series.

24. Calculate the current in a 48-V battery that powers a pair of 30-Ω resistors connected in parallel.

Think and Explain ••••••

25. One example of a water system is a garden hose that waters a garden. Another is the cooling system of an automobile. Which of these exhibits behavior more analogous to that of an electric circuit? Why?

26. Sometimes you hear someone say that a particular appliance "uses up" electricity. What is it that the appliance actually "uses up," and what becomes of it?

27. Why are the wingspans of birds a consideration in determining the spacing between parallel wires in a power line?

28. Your lab partner says that a battery provides not a source of constant current, but a source of constant voltage. Do you agree or disagree, and why?

29. Will the current in a lightbulb connected to a 220-V source be greater or less than that in the same bulb when it is connected to a 110-V source?

30. To connect a pair of resistors so that their equivalent resistance will be greater than the resistance of either one, should you connect them in series or in parallel?

31. To connect a pair of resistors so that their equivalent resistance will be less than the resistance of either one, should you connect them in series or in parallel?

32. Hector says that adding bulbs in series to a circuit provides more obstacles to the flow of charge, reducing current in the circuit. Jeremy says that adding bulbs in parallel provides more paths so more current can flow. With whom do you agree or disagree?

33. Consider a pair of flashlight bulbs connected to a battery. Emily asks if they glow brighter when connected in series, or in parallel. She looks to you for an answer. What is your answer?

34. Harry asks whether a battery will run down slower or faster when it connects to a pair of bulbs in series or to the same pair in parallel. He looks to you for an answer. What is your answer?

35. As more and more lamps are connected in series to a flashlight battery, what happens to the brightness of each lamp?

36. As more and more lamps are connected in parallel to a battery, and if the current does not produce heating inside the battery, what happens to the brightness of each lamp?

37. If several bulbs are connected in series to a battery, they may feel warm to the touch even though they are not visibly glowing. What is your explanation?

38. Are automobile headlights wired in parallel or in series? What is your evidence?

39. Why are household appliances almost never connected in series?

40. In the circuit shown, how do the brightnesses of the identical bulbs compare? Which lightbulb draws the most current? What happens if bulb A is unscrewed? If bulb C is unscrewed?

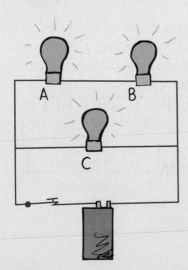

41. A number of lightbulbs are to be connected to a battery. Which will provide more overall brightness, connecting them in series or in parallel? Which will run the battery down faster, the bulbs connected in series or the bulbs connected in parallel?

42. Are these circuits equivalent to one another? Why or why not?

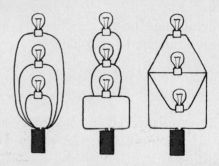

43. A battery has internal resistance, so if the current it supplies goes up, the voltage it supplies goes down. If too many bulbs are connected in parallel across a battery, will their brightness diminish? Explain.

44. A three-way bulb uses two filaments to produce three levels of illumination (50 W, 100 W, and 150 W) using a 120-V socket. When one of the filaments burns out, only one level of illumination (50 W or 100 W) is available. Are the filaments connected in series or in parallel?

45. How does the line current compare with the total currents of all devices connected in parallel?

46. Your friend says that electric current takes the path of least resistance. Why is it more accurate in the case of a parallel circuit to say that greatest current travels in the path of least resistance?

47. A 60-W bulb and a 100-W bulb are connected in series in a circuit.
   a. Which bulb has the greater current flowing in it?
   b. Which has the greater current when they are connected in parallel?

Think and Solve ••••••

48. A 30-Ω resistor is connected to a 240-V source. How much current flows in the resistor?

49. A lightbulb connected to a 3.0-V battery draws 1.2 A of current. Calculate the resistance of the bulb.

50. A lantern battery is connected to a 4-Ω device that draws 1.5 A. Calculate the battery voltage.

51. A 16-Ω loudspeaker and an 8-Ω loudspeaker are connected in parallel across the terminals of an amplifier. Assuming the speakers behave as resistors, calculate the equivalent resistance of the two speakers.

52. Consider the combination series and parallel circuit shown here.

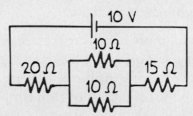

   a. Identify the parallel part of the circuit. What is the equivalent resistance of this part? In other words, what single resistance could replace this part of the circuit and not change the total current from the battery?
   b. What is the equivalent resistance of all the resistors? In other words, what single resistance could replace the whole circuit without changing the current produced by the battery?

53. How many 4-Ω resistors must be connected in parallel to create an equivalent resistance of 0.5 Ω?

54. What is the current in the battery of the circuit shown below? (What must you find before you can calculate the current?)

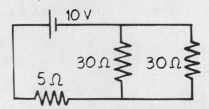

55. The rear window defrosters on automobiles are made up of several strips of heater wire connected in parallel. Consider the case of four wires, each of 6 Ω resistance, connected to 12 V.
  a. What is the equivalent resistance of the four wires? (Consider the wires to be two groups of two.)
  b. What is the total current drawn?

56. A 4-watt night light is plugged into a 120-volt circuit and operates continuously for a 30-day month.
  a. How much current does it draw?
  b. What is the resistance of its filament?
  c. How much energy does it use in the month?
  d. What is the cost of its operation for the month at the utility rate of 10 cents per kilowatt-hour?

57. The same voltage V is impressed on each of the branches of a parallel circuit. The voltage source provides a total current I_{total} to the circuit, and "sees" a total equivalent resistance of R_{eq} in the circuit. That is, $V = I_{total}R_{eq}$. The total current is equal to the sum of the currents through each branch of the parallel circuit. In a circuit with n branches, $I_{total} = I_1 + I_2 + I_3 \ldots I_n$. Use Ohm's law ($I = V/R$) and show how the equivalent resistance of a parallel circuit with n branches is given by the following equation.

$$\frac{1}{R_{eq}} = \frac{1}{R_1} + \frac{1}{R_2} + \frac{1}{R_3} \cdots + \frac{1}{R_n}$$

58. Show how the expression given in Question 57, when applied to two branches with resistances R_1 and R_2, can be written as follows.

$$R_{eq} = \frac{R_1 R_2}{R_1 + R_2}$$

Activity ● ● ● ● ● ●

59. Obtain several drinking straws. Take a deep breath and then fully exhale through one of the straws. Note the time it takes to do this. Repeat, fully exhaling through a pair of straws side by side. Can you exhale in less time? Try with three side-by-side straws. How does this relate to resistors in parallel in electric circuits?

More Problem-Solving Practice
Appendix F

36 MAGNETISM

THE BIG IDEA : A magnetic field surrounds a moving electric charge.

Electricity and magnetism were regarded as unrelated phenomena into the early nineteenth century. This changed in 1820 when a Danish science professor, Hans Christian Oersted, discovered a relationship between the two while demonstrating electric currents in front of a class of students. When electric current was passed in a wire near a magnetic compass, both Oersted and his students noticed the deflection of the compass needle. This was the connecting link that had eluded investigators for decades.[36.0] Other discoveries soon followed. Magnets were found to exert forces on current-carrying wires, which led to electric meters and motors. The stage was set for a whole new technology, which would eventually bring electric power, radio, and television.

discover!

What Does a Magnetic Field Look Like?

1. Place a bar magnet on a level surface. Cover the magnet with a thin sheet of glass, clear plastic, or cardboard.

2. Sprinkle iron filings onto the sheet in the area above the magnet. Gently tap the sheet and observe the pattern formed by the filings.

3. Repeat Steps 1 and 2 using two bar magnets. Arrange the magnets in a straight line with opposite poles facing each other. Leave a gap of 4–6 cm between the poles.

4. Rotate one of the magnets 180 degrees and observe any change in the pattern formed by the filings.

Analyze and Conclude

1. **Observing** Make sketches of the patterns produced by the single magnet and by the pair of magnets in both orientations.

2. **Predicting** What pattern do you think would be formed if you used a horseshoe magnet in Step 1?

3. **Making Generalizations** Describe some characteristics common to the patterns you observed. What do you think these patterns represent?

◀ FIGURE 36.1
Which interaction has the greater strength—the gravitational attraction between the scrap iron and Earth, or the magnetic attraction between the magnet and the scrap iron?

Beware of junk scientists who sell magnets to cure physical ailments. Claims for cures are bogus. We need a knowledge filter to tell the difference between what is true and what seems to be true. The best knowledge filter ever invented is science.

36.1 Magnetic Poles

Magnets exert forces on one another. They are similar to electric charges, for they can both attract and repel without touching, depending on which end is held near the other. Also, like electric charges, the strength of their interaction depends on the distance of separation of the two magnets. Whereas electric charges produce electrical forces, regions called **magnetic poles** produce magnetic forces.

If you suspend a bar magnet from its center by a piece of string, it will act as a compass. The end that points northward is called the *north-seeking pole,* and the end that points southward is called the *south-seeking pole.* More simply, these are called the *north* and *south poles.* All magnets have both a north and a south pole. For a simple bar magnet the poles are located at the two ends. The common horseshoe magnet is a bar magnet that has been bent, so its poles are also at its two ends.

If the north pole of one magnet is brought near the north pole of another magnet, they repel. The same is true of a south pole near a south pole. If opposite poles are brought together, however, attraction occurs.[36.1] ⊘ **Like poles repel; opposite poles attract.**

┌─ **think!** ──────────┐
Does every magnet necessarily have a north and a south pole?
Answer: 36.1
└──────────────────────┘

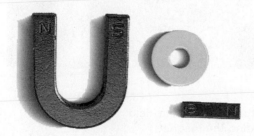

◀ FIGURE 36.2
Common magnets come in a variety of shapes.

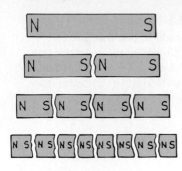

FIGURE 36.3 ▲
Magnetic poles always exist in pairs. Keep breaking a magnet in half and you will never isolate a single pole.

Magnetic poles behave similarly to electric charges in some ways, but there is a very important difference. Electric charges can be isolated, but magnetic poles cannot. Negatively charged electrons and positively charged protons are entities by themselves. A cluster of electrons need not be accompanied by a cluster of protons, and vice versa. But a north magnetic pole never exists without the presence of a south pole, and vice versa. The north and south poles of a magnet are like the head and tail of the same coin.

If you break a bar magnet in half, as shown in Figure 36.3, each half still behaves as a complete magnet. Break the pieces in half again, and you have four complete magnets. You can continue breaking the pieces in half and never isolate a single pole. Even when your piece is one atom thick, there are two poles. This suggests that atoms themselves are magnets.

CONCEPT CHECK How do magnetic poles affect each other?

36.2 Magnetic Fields

Place a sheet of paper over a bar magnet and sprinkle iron filings on the paper. The filings will tend to trace out an orderly pattern of lines that surround the magnet. The space around a magnet, in which a magnetic force is exerted, is filled with a **magnetic field.** The shape of the field is revealed by *magnetic field lines.* Magnetic field lines spread out from one pole, curve around the magnet, and return to the other pole, as shown in Figure 36.4.

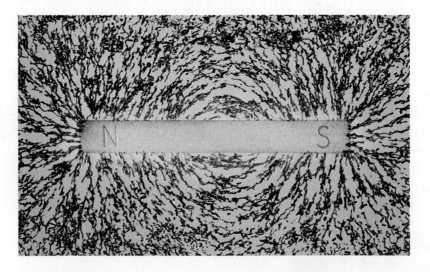

FIGURE 36.4 ▲
Iron filings trace out a pattern of magnetic field lines in the space surrounding the magnet.

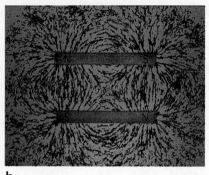

a   b

◀ **FIGURE 36.5**
You observe different magnetic field patterns for a pair of magnets when **a.** like poles are near each other, and **b.** opposite poles are near each other.

☑ **The direction of the magnetic field outside a magnet is from the north to the south pole.** Where the lines are closer together, the field strength is greater. We see that the magnetic field strength is greater at the poles. If we place another magnet or a small compass anywhere in the field, its poles will tend to line up with the magnetic field, as shown in Figure 36.6.

CONCEPT CHECK: What is the direction of the magnetic field outside a magnet?

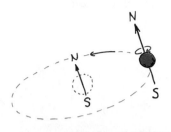

FIGURE 36.6 ▲
Like the iron filings, the compasses line up with the magnetic field lines.

36.3 The Nature of a Magnetic Field

Magnetism is very much related to electricity. Just as an electric charge is surrounded by an electric field, a moving electric charge is also surrounded by a magnetic field. This is due to the "distortions" in the electric field caused by motion, and was explained by Albert Einstein in 1905 in his theory of special relativity. This text will not go into the details, except to acknowledge that a magnetic field is a relativistic by-product of the electric field. Charges in motion have associated with them both an electric and a magnetic field. ☑ **A magnetic field is produced by the motion of electric charge.**[36.3.1]

Electrons in Motion Where is the motion of electric charges in a common bar magnet? Although the magnet as a whole may be stationary, it is composed of atoms whose electrons are in constant motion about atomic nuclei. This moving charge constitutes a tiny current and produces a magnetic field. More important, electrons can be thought of as spinning about their own axes like tops. A spinning electron constitutes a charge in motion and thus creates another magnetic field. In most materials, the field due to spinning predominates over the field due to orbital motion.

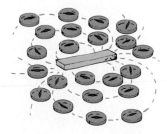

FIGURE 36.7 ▲
Both the orbital motion and the spinning motion of every electron in an atom produce magnetic fields.

Spin Magnetism Every spinning electron is a tiny magnet. A pair of electrons spinning in the same direction makes up a stronger magnet. Electrons spinning in opposite directions, however, work against one another. Their magnetic fields cancel. This is why most substances are not magnets. In most atoms, the various fields cancel one another because the electrons spin in opposite directions. In materials such as iron, nickel, and cobalt, however, the fields do not cancel one another entirely. Each iron atom has four electrons whose spin magnetism is uncanceled. Each iron atom, then, is a tiny magnet. The same is true to a lesser degree for the atoms of nickel and cobalt.[36.3.2]

CONCEPT CHECK How is a magnetic field produced?

36.4 Magnetic Domains

The magnetic fields of individual iron atoms are so strong that interactions among adjacent iron atoms cause large clusters of them to line up with one another. These clusters of aligned atoms are called **magnetic domains.** Each domain is perfectly magnetized, and is made up of billions of aligned atoms. The domains are microscopic, and there are many of them in a crystal of iron.

The difference between a piece of ordinary iron and an iron magnet is the alignment of domains. In a common iron nail, the domains are randomly oriented. When a strong magnet is brought nearby, as shown in Figure 36.9, two effects take place. One is a growth in size of domains that are oriented in the direction of the magnetic field. This growth is at the expense of domains that are not aligned. The other effect is a rotation of domains as they are brought into alignment. The domains become aligned much as electric dipoles are aligned in the presence of a charged rod. When you remove the nail from the magnet, ordinary thermal motion causes most or all of the domains in the nail to return to a random arrangement.

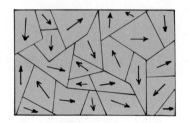

FIGURE 36.8 ▲
A crystal of iron contains microscopic clusters of aligned atoms called magnetic domains. Each domain consists of billions of aligned iron atoms.

think!

The iron filings sprinkled on the paper that covers the magnet in Figure 36.4 were not initially magnetized. Why, then, do they line up with the magnetic field of the magnet?
Answer: 36.4

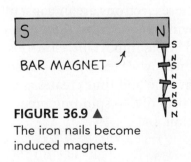

FIGURE 36.9 ▲
The iron nails become induced magnets.

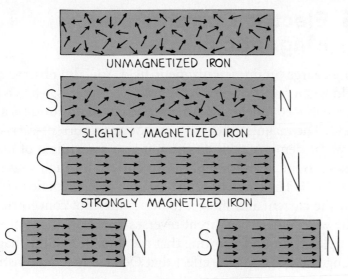

The illustrations show a piece of iron in successive stages of magnetism. The arrows represent domains, where the head is a north pole and the tail a south pole. Poles of neighboring domains neutralize one another's effects, except at the ends.

UNMAGNETIZED IRON

S · · · N
SLIGHTLY MAGNETIZED IRON

S · · · N
STRONGLY MAGNETIZED IRON

S · · N   S · · N

WHEN A MAGNET IS BROKEN
INTO TWO PIECES, EACH PIECE
RETAINS EQUALLY STRONG POLES

A magstripe on a credit card contains millions of tiny magnetic domains held together by a resin binder. Data are encoded in binary, with zeros and ones distinguished by the frequency of domain reversals.

✔ **Permanent magnets are made by simply placing pieces of iron or certain iron alloys in strong magnetic fields.** Alloys of iron differ; soft iron is easier to magnetize than steel. It helps to tap the iron to nudge any stubborn domains into alignment. Another way of making a permanent magnet is to stroke a piece of iron with a magnet. The stroking motion aligns the domains in the iron. If a permanent magnet is dropped or heated, some of the domains are jostled out of alignment and the magnet becomes weaker.

CONCEPT CHECK How can you make a permanent magnet?

---

discover!

Uncanny Magnetism?

1. Hold a magnetic compass vertically, just above the tops of some iron or steel objects in your classroom or home.

2. See if the north pole of the compass points to the tops of the objects, and the south pole points to the bottoms. If so, the objects have become magnetized by Earth's magnetic field.

3. Place the compass alongside a can of stored food in your pantry. See if the can is magnetized.

4. Turn the can over and see how many days it takes for it to lose its magnetism and then reverse its polarity.

5. **Think** Why does the can gradually lose its magnetism after you turn it over?

36.5 Electric Currents and Magnetic Fields

A moving charge produces a magnetic field. You also observe a magnetic field when many charges are in motion—that is, when a current flows through a conductor. ✅ **An electric current produces a magnetic field.** The magnetic field that surrounds a current-carrying conductor can be demonstrated by arranging an assortment of magnetic compasses around a wire and passing a current through it, as shown in Figure 36.11. The compasses line up with the magnetic field produced by the current and show it to be a pattern of concentric circles about the wire. When the current reverses direction, the compasses turn completely around, showing that the direction of the magnetic field changes also. This is the effect that Oersted first demonstrated.

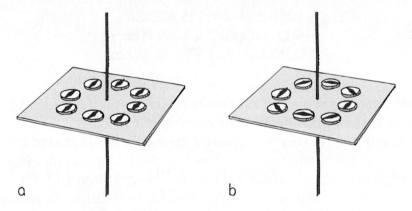

FIGURE 36.11 ▶
a. When there is no current in the wire, the compasses align with Earth's magnetic field. **b.** When there is a current in the wire, the compasses align with the stronger magnetic field near the wire.

a   b

If the wire is bent into a loop, the magnetic field lines become bunched up inside the loop, as shown in Figure 36.12. If the wire is bent into another loop, overlapping the first, the concentration of magnetic field lines inside the double loop is twice as much as in the single loop. It follows that the magnetic field intensity in this region is increased as the number of loops is increased. A current-carrying coil of wire with many loops is an **electromagnet.**

FIGURE 36.12 ▶
Magnetic field lines about a current-carrying wire crowd up when the wire is bent into a loop.

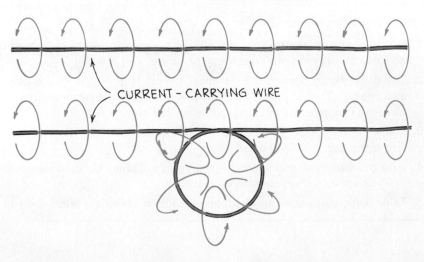

CURRENT - CARRYING WIRE

a

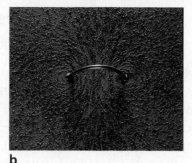
b

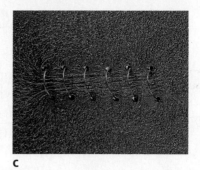
c

FIGURE 36.13 ▲
Iron filings sprinkled on paper reveal the magnetic field configurations about **a.** a current-carrying wire, **b.** a current-carrying loop, and **c.** a coil of loops.

Sometimes a piece of iron is placed inside the coil of an electromagnet. The magnetic domains in the iron are induced into alignment, increasing the magnetic field intensity. Beyond a certain limit, the magnetic field in iron "saturates," so iron is not used in the cores of the strongest electromagnets, which are made of superconducting material (see Section 34.4).

A superconducting electromagnet can generate a powerful magnetic field indefinitely without using any power. At Fermilab near Chicago, superconducting electromagnets guide high-energy particles around the four-mile-circumference accelerator. Since the substitution of superconducting electromagnets for conventional ones in 1983, monthly electric bills have been far less, even though the particles are accelerated to greater energies. Superconducting magnets can also be found in magnetic resonance imaging (MRI) devices in hospitals. They also hold much promise for high-speed transportation.

CONCEPT CHECK : Why does a current-carrying wire deflect a magnetic compass?

Science, Technology, and Society

Maglev Transportation

An exciting application of superconducting electromagnets is magnetically levitated, or "maglev," transportation. Shown here is a maglev train that shuttles passengers to and from Shanghai International Airport at speeds up to 460 km/h. It covers some 30 kilometers in less than eight minutes. The train carries superconducting coils on its underside. Moving along the aluminum track, called a guideway, the coils generate currents

in the aluminum that act as mirror-image magnets and repel the train. It floats about 10 millimeters above the guideway, and its speed is limited only by air friction and passenger comfort. Watch for the proliferation of this relatively new technology.

Critical Thinking What advantages do magnetically levitated trains have over conventional trains?

36.6 Magnetic Forces on Moving Charged Particles

In your next physics course you'll learn the "simple" right-hand rule!

A charged particle at rest will not interact with a static magnetic field. But if the charged particle *moves* in a magnetic field, the charged particle experiences a deflecting force.[36.6] This force is greatest when the particle moves in a direction perpendicular to the magnetic field lines. At other angles, the force is less; it becomes zero when the particle moves parallel to the field lines. In any case, the direction of the force is always perpendicular to both the magnetic field lines and the velocity of the charged particle, as shown in Figure 36.14. ⊘ **A moving charge is deflected when it crosses magnetic field lines but not when it travels parallel to the field lines.**

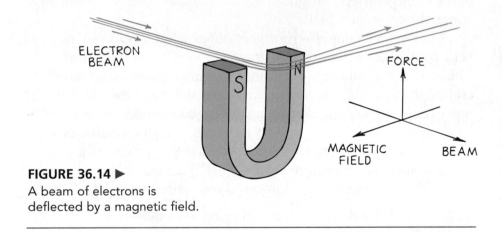

FIGURE 36.14 ▶
A beam of electrons is deflected by a magnetic field.

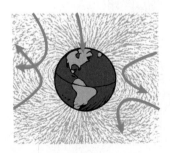

FIGURE 36.15 ▲
The magnetic field of Earth deflects many charged particles that make up cosmic radiation.

This sideways deflecting force is very different from the forces that occur in other interactions, such as the force of gravitation between masses, the electrostatic force between charges, and the force between magnetic poles. The force that acts on a moving charged particle does not act in a direction between the sources of interaction, but instead acts perpendicular to both the magnetic field and the electron velocity.

It's nice that charged particles are deflected by magnetic fields, for this fact was employed in early TV tubes to steer electrons onto the inner surface of the screens and provide a picture. This effect of magnetic fields also works on a larger scale. As shown in Figure 36.15, charged particles from outer space are deflected by Earth's magnetic field, which reduces the intensity of cosmic radiation. A much greater reduction in intensity results from the absorption of cosmic rays in the atmosphere.

CONCEPT CHECK : What happens when a charged particle moves in a magnetic field?

36.7 Magnetic Forces on Current-Carrying Wires

☑ **Since a charged particle moving through a magnetic field experiences a deflecting force, a current of charged particles moving through a magnetic field also experiences a deflecting force.** If the particles are trapped inside a wire when they respond to the deflecting force, the wire will also move as shown in Figure 36.16.

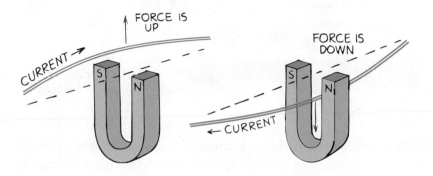

◀ **FIGURE 36.16**
A current-carrying wire experiences a force in a magnetic field.

If the direction of current in the wire is reversed, the deflecting force acts in the opposite direction. The force is maximum when the current is perpendicular to the magnetic field lines. The direction of force is along neither the magnetic field lines nor the direction of current. The force is perpendicular to both field lines and current, and it is a sideways force.

There is a symmetry here—just as a current-carrying wire will deflect a magnetic compass, a magnet will deflect a current-carrying wire. Both cases show different effects of the same phenomenon. The discovery that a magnet exerts a force on a current-carrying wire created much excitement, for almost immediately people began harnessing this force for useful purposes—with great sensitivity in electric meters, and with great force in electric motors.

think!

What law of physics tells you that if a current-carrying wire produces a force on a magnet, a magnet must produce a force on a current-carrying wire?
Answer: 36.7

CONCEPT CHECK How is current affected by a magnetic field?

36.8 Meters to Motors

The simplest meter to detect electric current is shown in Figure 36.17. It consists of a magnetic needle on a pivot at the center of a number of loops of insulated wire. When an electric current passes through the coil, each loop produces its own effect on the needle so that a very small current can be detected. A sensitive current-indicating instrument is called a *galvanometer*.[36.8]

FIGURE 36.17 ▶
You can make a very simple galvanometer with a magnetic needle and insulated wire.

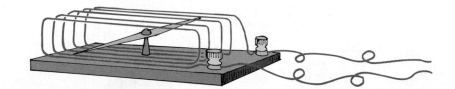

Common Galvanometers A more common design is shown in Figure 36.18a. It employs more loops of wire and is therefore more sensitive. The coil is mounted for movement and the magnet is held stationary. The coil turns against a spring, so the greater the current in its loops, the greater its deflection.

A galvanometer may be calibrated to measure current (amperes), in which case it is called an *ammeter*. Or it may be calibrated to measure electric potential (volts), in which case it is called a *voltmeter*.

FIGURE 36.18 ▶
a. A common galvanometer consists of a stationary magnet and a movable coil of wire. **b.** A multimeter can function as both an ammeter and a voltmeter. (The resistance of the instrument is made to be very low for the ammeter, and very high for the voltmeter.)

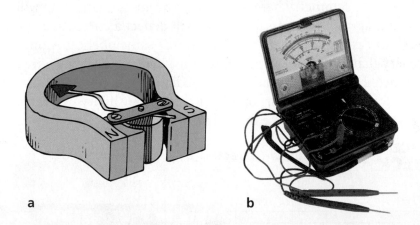

a   b

Electric Motors If the design of the galvanometer is slightly modified, you have an electric motor. ⊘ **The principal difference between a galvanometer and an electric motor is that in an electric motor, the current is made to change direction every time the coil makes a half revolution.** After it has been forced to rotate one half revolution, it overshoots just in time for the current to reverse, whereupon the coil is forced to continue another half revolution, and so on in cyclic fashion to produce continuous rotation.

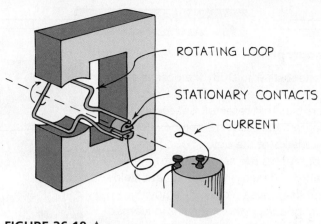

FIGURE 36.19 ▲
A simplified DC motor can be constructed from a magnet, a rotating loop of wire, and a voltage source.

ROTATING LOOP

STATIONARY CONTACTS

CURRENT

Go Online
SciLinks NSTA

For: Links on electric motors
Visit: www.SciLinks.org
Web Code: csn – 3608

A simple DC motor is shown in bare outline in Figure 36.19. A permanent magnet is used to produce a magnetic field in a region where a rectangular loop of wire is mounted so that it can turn about an axis as shown. When a current passes through the loop, it flows in opposite directions in the upper and lower sides of the loop. (It has to do this because if charge flows into one end of the loop, it must flow out the other end.) If the upper portion of the loop is forced to the left, then the lower portion is forced to the right, as if it were a galvanometer. But unlike a galvanometer, the current is reversed during each half revolution by means of stationary contacts on the shaft. The parts of the wire that brush against these contacts are called *brushes*. In this way, the current in the loop alternates so that the forces in the upper and lower regions do not change directions as the loop rotates. The rotation is continuous as long as current is supplied.

Larger motors, DC or AC, are usually made by replacing the permanent magnet with an electromagnet that is energized by the power source. Of course, more than a single loop is used. Many loops of wire are wound about an iron cylinder, called an *armature*, which then rotates when energized with electric current.

The advent of the motor made it possible to replace enormous human and animal toil by electric power in most parts of the world. Electric motors have greatly changed the way people live.

think!

How is a galvanometer similar to a simple electric motor? How do they fundamentally differ?
Answer: 36.8

A motor and a generator are the same device, with input or output reversed. The electrical device in a hybrid car operates both ways.

CONCEPT CHECK : What is the main difference between a galvanometer and an electric motor?

36.9 Earth's Magnetic Field

A compass points northward because Earth itself is a huge magnet. The compass aligns with the magnetic field of Earth. The magnetic poles of Earth, however, do not coincide with the geographic poles—in fact, they aren't even close to the geographic poles. Figure 36.20 illustrates the discrepancy. The magnetic pole in the Northern Hemisphere, for example, is located some 800 kilometers from the geographic North Pole, northwest of Sverdrup Island in northern Canada. The other magnetic pole is located just off the coast of Antarctica. This means that compasses do not generally point to true north. The discrepancy between the orientation of a compass and true north is known as the *magnetic declination*.

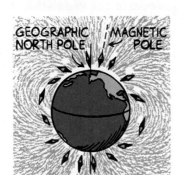

FIGURE 36.20 ▲
Earth is a giant magnet.

Moving Charges Within Earth

It is not known exactly why Earth itself is a magnet. The configuration of Earth's magnetic field is like that of a strong bar magnet placed near the center of Earth. But Earth is not a magnetized chunk of iron like a bar magnet. It is simply too hot for individual atoms to remain aligned.

Currents in the molten core of Earth provide a better explanation for Earth's magnetic field. Most geologists think that moving charges looping around within Earth create its magnetic field. Because of Earth's great size, the speed of moving charges would have to be less than one millimeter per second to account for the field.

The convection currents in Earth's molten interior, shown in Figure 36.21, are driven by rising heat from radioactive decay within Earth's core. Perhaps such convection currents combined with the rotational effects of Earth produce Earth's magnetic field. A firmer explanation awaits more study.

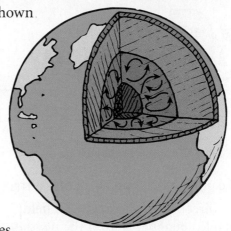

FIGURE 36.21 ▲
Convection currents in the molten parts of Earth's interior may produce Earth's magnetic field.

Magnetic Field Reversals Whatever the cause, the magnetic field of Earth is not stable; it has flip-flopped throughout geologic time. Evidence of this comes from analysis of the magnetic properties of rock strata. Iron atoms in a molten state tend to align themselves with Earth's magnetic field. When the iron solidifies, the direction of Earth's field is recorded by the orientation of the domains in the rock. The slight magnetism that results can be measured with sensitive instruments. The evidence from the rock shows that there have been times when the magnetic field of Earth has diminished to zero and then reversed itself.

This reversal of magnetic poles is clearly evident in the seafloor of the middle of the Atlantic Ocean. On the ocean floor at mid-ocean ridges, continuous eruption of lava produces new seafloor. This new rock is magnetized according to the existing magnetic field. Older seafloor is pushed away from the ridge as newer seafloor forms. Magnetic surveys of the ocean floor reveal a zebra-striped pattern centered along, and symmetrical to, the mid-ocean ridge. Because each stripe indicates magnetic direction, the alternating stripes show the change from periods of normal polarity to periods of reversed polarity.

More than twenty reversals have taken place in the past 5 million years. The most recent occurred 780,000 years ago. Prior reversals happened 870,000 and 950,000 years ago. Studies of deep-sea sediments indicate that the field was virtually switched off for 10,000 to 20,000 years just over 1 million years ago.

We cannot predict when the next reversal will occur because the reversal sequence is not regular. But there is a clue in recent measurements that show a decrease of over 5% of Earth's magnetic field strength in the last 100 years. If this change is maintained, we may well have another magnetic field reversal within 2000 years.

Like tape from a tape recorder, the ocean bottom preserves its own record in a magnetic record.

CONCEPT CHECK Why does a magnetic compass point northward?

36 REVIEW

Concept Summary ······

- Like poles repel; opposite poles attract.

- The direction of the magnetic field outside a magnet is from the north to the south pole.

- A magnetic field is produced by the motion of electric charge.

- Permanent magnets are made by simply placing pieces of iron or certain iron alloys in strong magnetic fields.

- An electric current produces a magnetic field.

- A moving charge is deflected when it crosses magnetic field lines but not when it travels parallel to the field lines.

- Since a charged particle moving through a magnetic field experiences a deflecting force, a current of charged particles moving through a magnetic field also experiences a deflecting force.

- The principal difference between a galvanometer and an electric motor is that in an electric motor, the current is made to change direction every time the coil makes a half revolution.

- A compass points northward because Earth itself is a huge magnet.

Key Terms ······

magnetic pole
(p. 721)

magnetic domain
(p. 724)

magnetic field
(p. 722)

electromagnet
(p. 726)

think! Answers

36.1 Yes, just as every coin has two sides, a "head" and a "tail." (Some "trick" magnets have more than two poles.)

36.4 Domains align in the individual filings, causing them to act like tiny compasses. The poles of each "compass" are pulled in opposite directions, producing a torque that twists each filing into alignment with the external magnetic field.

36.7 Newton's third law, which applies to all forces in nature.

36.8 A galvanometer and a motor are similar in that they both employ coils positioned in magnetic fields. When current passes through the coils, forces on the wires rotate the coils. The fundamental difference is that the maximum rotation of the coil in a galvanometer is one half turn, whereas in a motor the coil (armature) rotates through many complete turns. In the armature of a motor, the current is made to change direction with each half turn of the armature.

36 ASSESS

Check Concepts ......

Section 36.1

1. What do electric charges have in common with magnetic poles?

2. What is a major difference between electric charges and magnetic poles?

Section 36.2

3. What is a magnetic field, and what is its source?

Section 36.3

4. Every spinning electron is a tiny magnet. Since all atoms have spinning electrons, why are not all atoms tiny magnets?

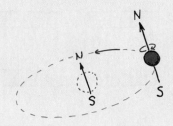

5. What is so special about iron that makes each iron atom a tiny magnet?

Section 36.4

6. What is a magnetic domain?

7. Why do some pieces of iron behave as magnets, while other pieces of iron do not?

8. How can a piece of iron be induced into becoming a magnet? For example, if you place a paper clip near a magnet, it will itself become a magnet. Why?

9. Why will heating or dropping a magnet on a hard surface weaken it?

Section 36.5

10. What is the shape of the magnetic field that surrounds a current-carrying wire?

11. If a current-carrying wire is bent into a loop, why is the magnetic field stronger inside the loop than outside?

Section 36.6

12. What must a charged particle be doing in order to experience a magnetic force?

13. With respect to an electric and a magnetic field, how does the direction of a magnetic force on a charged particle differ from the direction of the electric force?

14. What role does Earth's magnetic field play in cosmic ray bombardment?

Section 36.7

15. How does the direction in which a current-carrying wire is forced when in a magnetic field compare with the direction that moving charges are forced?

Section 36.8

16. How do the concepts of force, field, and current relate to a galvanometer?

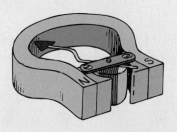

17. Why is it important that the current in the armature of a motor that uses a permanent magnet periodically change direction?

Section 36.9

18. What is meant by magnetic declination?

19. According to most geophysicists, what is the probable cause of Earth's magnetic field?

20. What are magnetic pole reversals, and what evidence is there that Earth's magnetic field has undergone pole reversals throughout its history?

Think and Rank •••••

Suppose you wrap some wire into a coil around an iron bar. When the coil carries a current, you have an electromagnet. The polarity of the electromagnet can be found using your right hand: When you curl your right-hand fingers in the direction of the current, your thumb points to the north pole. (The opposite end of the electromagnet is the south pole.)

Rank each of the following sets of scenarios in order of the quantity or property involved. List them from left to right. If scenarios have equal rankings, separate them with an equal sign. (e.g., A = B)

21. The electromagnets A, B, and C are shown below. Note the number of turns of wire and the current in each. The iron cores are identical. Rank the electromagnets in magnetic field intensity at point P (just outside each electromagnet), from strongest to weakest.

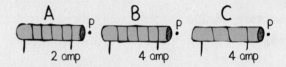

22. Three pairs of electromagnets made with identical iron cores are shown below. Note the number of turns of wire, each of which carries the same current.

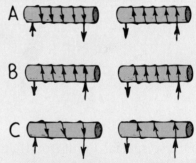

a. Rank the electromagnet pairs A, B, and C in terms of the force between the electromagnets, from most attractive to most repulsive.
b. Rank the electromagnet pairs A, B, and C in terms of the magnitude of the magnetic field at the exact midpoint between the electromagnets.

Think and Explain •••••

23. Since every iron atom is a tiny magnet, why aren't all iron materials themselves magnets?

24. "An electron always experiences a force in an electric field, but not always in a magnetic field." Defend this statement.

25. What kind of field surrounds a stationary electric charge? A moving electric charge?

26. Why can iron be made to behave as a magnet while wood cannot?

27. If you place a chunk of iron near the north pole of a magnet, attraction will occur. Why will attraction also occur if you place the iron near the south pole of the magnet?

28. A friend tells you that a refrigerator door, beneath a layer of white-painted plastic, is made of aluminum. How could you check to see if this is true (without any scraping)?

29. Since iron filings are not themselves magnets, by what mechanism do they align themselves with a magnetic field as shown in Figure 36.6?

30. We know a compass points northward because Earth is a giant magnet. Will the northward-pointing needle point northward when the compass is brought to the Southern Hemisphere?

31. A strong magnet and a weak magnet attract each other. Which magnet exerts the stronger force—the strong one or the weak one? (Could you have answered this using what you learned in Chapter 6?)

32. A strong magnet attracts a paper clip to itself with a certain force. Does the paper clip exert a force on the strong magnet? If not, why not? If so, does it exert as much force on the magnet as the magnet exerts on it? Defend your answers.

33. Why will the magnetic field strength be further increased inside a current-carrying coil if a piece of iron is placed in the coil?

34. Can an electron be set into motion with a magnetic field? With an electric field? Explain.

35. In what direction relative to a magnetic field does a charged particle travel in order to experience maximum magnetic force? Minimum magnetic force?

36. When a current-carrying wire is placed in a strong magnetic field, no force acts on the wire. What orientation of the wire is likely?

37. A magnetic field can deflect a beam of electrons, but it cannot do work on them to speed them up. Why? (*Hint:* Consider the direction of the force relative to the direction in which the electrons move.)

38. A cyclotron is a device for accelerating charged particles to high speeds in circular orbits of ever-increasing radius. The charged particles are subjected to both an electric field and a magnetic field. One of these fields increases the speed of the particles, and the other field holds them in a circular path. Which field performs which function?

39. By present-day custom, the direction of electric current is the direction in which positive charge flows. The direction of a magnetic field surrounding a current-carrying wire can be shown by what is called the "right-hand rule." Wrap your right-hand fingers around a current-carrying wire in such a way that your thumb points in the direction of the electric current; then your fingers point in the direction of the magnetic field. Suppose instead that the current direction were defined as the direction in which electrons move in the wire. Why then would a "left-hand rule" be used for identifying magnetic field direction?

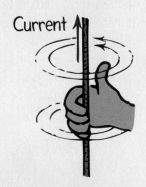

40. Pigeons have multiple-domain magnetite magnets within their skulls that are connected through a large number of nerves to the pigeon's brain. How does this aid the pigeon in navigation? (Magnetic material also exists in the abdomens of bees.)

41. How do the input and output parts of a generator and a motor compare?

42. Your friend says that if you crank the shaft of a DC motor manually, the motor becomes a DC generator. Do you agree or disagree? Defend your position.

43. Residents of northern Canada are bombarded by more intense cosmic radiation than are residents of Mexico. Why is this so?

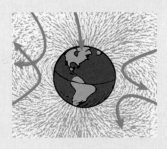

44. What changes in cosmic ray intensity at Earth's surface would you expect during periods in which Earth's magnetic field passed through a zero phase while undergoing pole reversals? (A speculation supported by fossil evidence is that the periods of no protective magnetic field may have been as effective in changing life forms as X-rays have been in the famous heredity studies of fruit flies.)

45. Earth's core is probably composed of iron and nickel, excellent metals for making permanent magnets. Why is it unlikely that Earth's core is a permanent magnet?

47. Find the direction and dip of Earth's magnetic field lines in your locality. Magnetize a large steel needle or straight piece of steel wire by stroking it a few dozen times with a strong magnet. Run the needle or wire through a cork in such a way that when the cork floats, the thin magnet remains horizontal (parallel to the water surface). Float the cork in a plastic or wooden container of water. The needle will point toward the magnetic pole. Then press unmagnetized common pins into the sides of the cork perpendicular to the needle. Rest the pins on the rims of a pair of drinking glasses so that the needle or wire points toward the magnetic pole. It should dip in line with Earth's magnetic field.

Activities ......

46. An iron bar can be easily magnetized by aligning it with the magnetic field lines of Earth and striking it lightly a few times with a hammer. This works best if the bar is tilted down to match the dip of Earth's field. The hammering jostles the domains so they can better fall into alignment with Earth's field. The bar can be demagnetized by striking it when it is in an east–west direction.

37 ELECTROMAGNETIC INDUCTION

THE BIG IDEA : Magnetism can produce electricity, and electricity can produce magnetism.

The discovery that an electric current in a wire produced magnetism was a turning point in physics and the technology that followed. The question arose as to whether magnetism could produce an electric current in a wire. In 1831, two physicists, Michael Faraday in England and Joseph Henry in the United States, independently discovered that the answer is yes. Until their discovery, the only current-producing devices were voltaic cells, which produced small currents by dissolving expensive metals in acids. These were the forerunners of our present-day batteries. The discovery of Faraday and Henry provided a major alternative to these crude devices. Their discovery was to change the world by making electricity so commonplace that it would power industries by day and light up cities by night.

discover!

Can You Create an Electric Current Without a Battery?

1. Use two lengths of wire to connect two galvanometers.
2. Shake one of the galvanometers while watching the needle of the other meter.
3. Now reverse the roles of the galvanometers by shaking the galvanometer that was originally stationary.

Analyze and Conclude

1. **Observing** Describe the reading on a stationary galvanometer as the other galvanometer is shaken.
2. **Predicting** What would happen if you moved a magnet through the wire loops connecting the galvanometers?
3. **Making Generalizations** How could you use mechanical motion to power an electronic device?

37.1 Electromagnetic Induction

Faraday and Henry both made the same discovery. ✅ **Electric current can be produced in a wire by simply moving a magnet into or out of a wire coil.** No battery or other voltage source was needed—only the motion of a magnet in a coil or in a single wire loop as shown in Figure 37.1. They discovered that voltage was induced by the relative motion of a wire with respect to a magnetic field.

The production of voltage depends only on the relative motion of the conductor with respect to the magnetic field. Voltage is induced whether the magnetic field of a magnet moves past a stationary conductor, or the conductor moves through a stationary magnetic field as shown in Figure 37.2. The results are the same for the same *relative* motion.

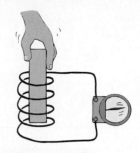

FIGURE 37.1 ▲
When the magnet is plunged into the coil, voltage is induced in the coil and charges in the coil are set in motion.

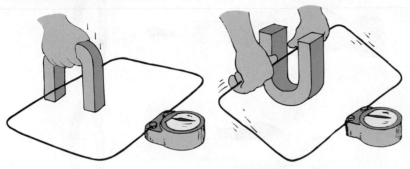

◀ **FIGURE 37.2**
Voltage is induced in the wire loop whether the magnetic field moves past the wire or the wire moves through the magnetic field.

The amount of voltage induced depends on how quickly the magnetic field lines are traversed by the wire. Very slow motion produces hardly any voltage at all. Quick motion induces a greater voltage.

The greater the number of loops of wire that move in a magnetic field, the greater are the induced voltage and the current in the wire, as shown in Figure 37.3. Pushing a magnet into twice as many loops will induce twice as much voltage; pushing it into ten times as many loops will induce ten times as much voltage; and so on.[37.1.1]

FIGURE 37.3 ▼
When a magnet is plunged into a coil of twice as many loops as another, twice as much voltage is induced. If the magnet is plunged into a coil with three times as many loops, then three times as much voltage is induced.

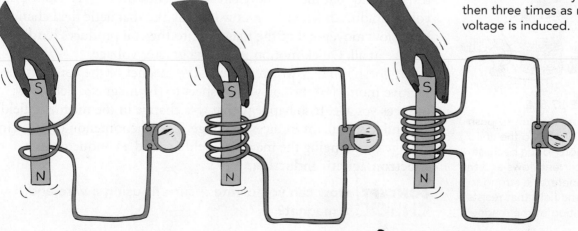

Does it seem that we get something (energy) for nothing by simply increasing the number of loops in a coil of wire? We don't. Work is done in pushing the magnet into the loop. That's because the induced current in the loop creates a magnetic field that repels the approaching magnet. For example, in Figure 37.4a the north pole of a bar magnet is pushed toward a single loop. The current induced in the loop produces a magnetic field that repels the approaching bar magnet. We see that, in Figure 37.4b, when the magnet is pulled away from the loop, the induced current produces a magnetic field that attracts the receding bar magnet. Both cases require work input. If you try to push a magnet into a coil with more loops, it requires even more work, as shown in Figure 37.5.

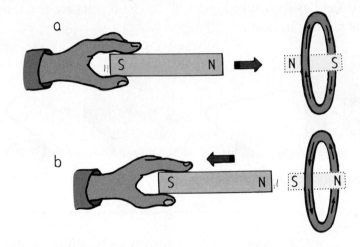

FIGURE 37.4 ▶

a. Current induced in the loop produces a magnetic field (suggested by the imaginary yellow bar magnet), which repels the approaching bar magnet. **b.** When the bar magnet is pulled away from the loop, the induced current is in the opposite direction and produces a magnetic field that attracts the receding bar magnet.

FIGURE 37.5 ▲

It is more difficult to push the magnet into the coil with more loops because more current flows and the coil generates a stronger magnetic field that resists the motion of the magnet.

The law of energy conservation applies here. In Figures 37.3 and 37.4, the force that you exert on the magnet multiplied by the distance that you move the magnet is your input work. This work is equal to the energy expended (or possibly stored) in the circuit to which the coil is connected. If the coil is connected to a resistor, for example, more induced voltage in the coil means more current through the resistor, and that means more energy expenditure.[37.1,2] The amount of voltage induced depends on how quickly the magnetic field changes. Very slow movement of the magnet into the coil produces hardly any voltage at all. Quick motion induces a greater voltage.

It doesn't matter which moves—the magnet or the coil. It is the relative motion of the coil with respect to the magnetic field that induces voltage. It so happens that any change in the magnetic field around a conductor induces a voltage. The phenomenon of inducing voltage by changing the magnetic field around a conductor is **electromagnetic induction.**

CONCEPT : How can you create a current using a wire and
CHECK : a magnet?

37.2 Faraday's Law

Faraday's law describes the relationship between induced voltage and rate of change of a magnetic field. ✅ **Faraday's law states that the induced voltage in a coil is proportional to the product of the number of loops, the cross-sectional area of each loop, and the rate at which the magnetic field changes within those loops.**

Voltage is one thing, and current is another. The amount of current produced by electromagnetic induction depends not only on the induced voltage but also on the resistance of the coil and the circuit to which it is connected.[37.2] For example, you can plunge a magnet in and out of a closed rubber loop and in and out of a closed loop of copper. The voltage induced in each is the same, providing each intercepts the same number of magnetic field lines. But the current in each is quite different—a lot in the copper but almost none in the rubber. The electrons in the rubber sense the same electric field as those in the copper, but their bonding to the fixed atoms prevents the movement of charge that occurs so freely in the copper.

CONCEPT CHECK What does Faraday's law state?

think!

If you push a magnet into a coil connected to a resistor, as shown in Figure 37.5, you'll feel a resistance to your push. For the same pushing speed, why is this resistance greater in a coil with more loops?

Answer: 37.2

37.3 Generators and Alternating Current

One way to generate a current is to plunge a magnet into and out of a coil of wire. As the magnetic field strength inside the coil is increased (magnet entering), the induced voltage in the coil is directed one way. When the magnetic field strength diminishes (magnet leaving), the voltage is induced in the opposite direction. The greater the frequency of field change, the greater the induced voltage. The frequency of the induced alternating voltage equals the frequency of the changing magnetic field within the loop.

Rather than moving the magnet, it is more practical to move the coil. This is best accomplished by rotating the coil in a stationary magnetic field, as shown in Figure 37.6. A machine that produces electric current by rotating a coil within a stationary magnetic field is called a **generator.** It is essentially the opposite of a motor. ✅ **Whereas a motor converts electrical energy into mechanical energy, a generator converts mechanical energy into electrical energy.**

FIGURE 37.6 ▼
A simple generator turns mechanical energy into electrical energy. Voltage is induced in the loop when it is rotated in the magnetic field.

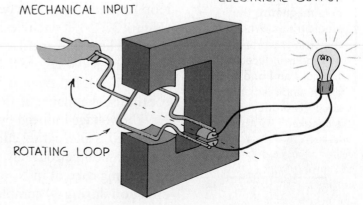

ELECTRICAL OUTPUT

MECHANICAL INPUT

ROTATING LOOP

FIGURE 37.7 ▼
As the loop rotates, there is a change in the number of
magnetic field lines it encloses.

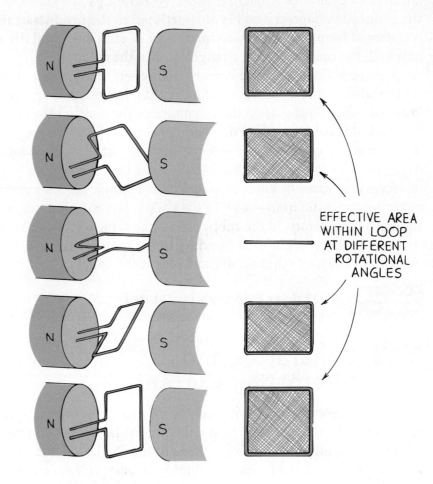

a. The loop starts by
enclosing the maximum
number of field lines.

b. As the loop rotates,
fewer field lines pass
through it.

c. In this position, the loop
encloses no field lines.

d. Now the loop encloses
more field lines again.

e. After half a turn, the loop
again encloses the maxi-
mum number of field lines.

EFFECTIVE AREA
WITHIN LOOP
AT DIFFERENT
ROTATIONAL
ANGLES

Guitar pickups are tiny
coils with magnets
inside them. The mag-
nets magnetize the
steel strings. When
the strings vibrate,
voltage is induced in
the coils and boosted
by an amplifier, and
sound is produced by
a speaker.

Simple Generators When the loop of wire is rotated in the magnetic field, there is a change in the number of magnetic field lines
within the loop, as shown in the diagram above. In Figure 37.7a, the
loop has the largest number of lines inside it. As the loop rotates
(Figure 37.7b), it encircles fewer of the field lines until it lies along
the field lines and encloses none at all (Figure 37.7c). As rotation continues, it encloses more field lines (Figure 37.7d) and reaches a maximum when it has made a half revolution (Figure 37.7e). As rotation
continues, the magnetic field inside the loop changes in cyclic fashion.

The voltage induced by the generator alternates, and the current
produced is alternating current (AC). The current changes magnitude
and direction periodically, as shown in Figure 37.8. The standard
alternating current in North America changes its magnitude and
direction during 60 complete cycles per second—60 hertz.

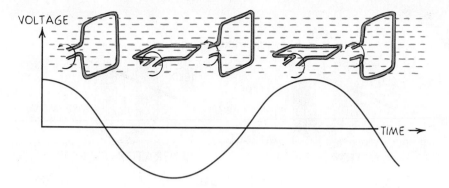

Complex Generators The generators used in power plants are much more complex than the model discussed here. Huge coils made up of many loops of wire are wrapped on an iron core, to make an armature much like the armature of a motor. They rotate in the very strong magnetic fields of powerful electromagnets. The armature is connected externally to an assembly of paddle wheels called a turbine. Energy from wind or falling water can be used to produce rotation of the turbine, but as shown in Figure 37.9, most commercial generators are driven by moving steam. At the present time, a fossil fuel or nuclear fuel is used as the energy source for the steam.

It is important to emphasize that an energy source of some kind is required to operate a generator. Some fraction of energy from the source, usually some type of fuel, is converted to mechanical energy to drive the turbine, and the generator converts most of this to electrical energy. The electricity that is produced simply carries this energy to distant places. Some people think that electricity is a source of energy. It is not. It is a *form* of energy that must have a source.[37.3]

CONCEPT CHECK How is a generator different from a motor?

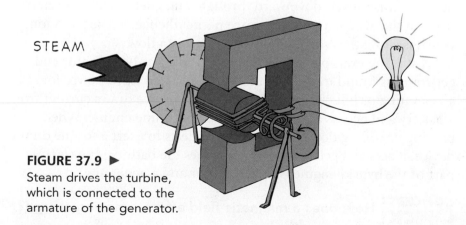

FIGURE 37.9 ▶
Steam drives the turbine, which is connected to the armature of the generator.

Link to TECHNOLOGY

Metal Detectors Walk through a metal detector in an airport, and you're walking through a coil of wire that carries a small electric current. In the opening in the coil there is a magnetic field. Any change in this field is sensed by the coil. If you carry iron into the coil, you change this magnetic field. A changing magnetic field induces a change in the current in the coil. The change sets off an alarm.

FIGURE 37.10 ▶

The figure shows the motor effect and the generator effect. **a.** When a current moves to the right, there is a force on the electrons, and the wire is tugged upward. **b.** When a wire with no current is moved downward, the electrons in the wire experience a force, creating current.

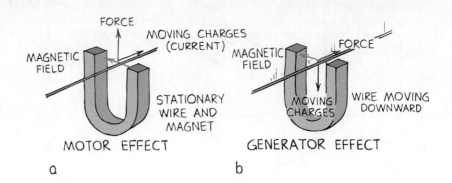

37.4 Motor and Generator Comparison

In Chapter 36 you saw how an electric current is deflected in a magnetic field, which underlies the operation of the motor. This discovery occurred about 10 years before Faraday and Henry discovered electromagnetic induction, which underlies the operation of a generator. Both of these discoveries, however, stem from the same single fact: ✅ **Moving charges experience a force that is perpendicular to both their motion and the magnetic field they traverse.** We will call the deflected wire the motor effect and the law of induction the generator effect. Each of these effects is summarized in Figure 37.10. Study them. Can you see that the two effects are related?

The motor effect occurs when a current moves through a magnetic field. In the figure, the current is moving to the right, and the magnetic field creates a perpendicular upward force on the electrons. Because the electrons can't leave the wire, the entire wire is tugged upward along with the electrons. In the generator effect, a wire with no current is moved downward through a magnetic field. The electrons in this wire experience a force perpendicular to their motion, which is along the wire. So a current begins to flow.

A striking example of a device functioning as both motor and generator is found in hybrid automobiles. When extra power for accelerating or hill climbing is needed, this device draws current from a battery and acts as a motor to assist the gasoline engine. When braking or rolling downhill causes the wheels to exert a torque on the device, it acts as a generator and recharges the battery. The electrical part of the hybrid engine is both a motor and a generator.

CONCEPT CHECK : How does a magnetic field affect a moving charge?

37.5 Transformers

Consider a pair of coils, side by side, as shown in Figure 37.11. One is connected to a battery and the other is connected to a galvanometer. It is customary to refer to the coil connected to the power source as the *primary* (input), and the other as the *secondary* (output). As soon as the switch is closed in the primary and current passes through its coil, a current occurs in the secondary also—even though there is no material connection between the two coils. Only a brief surge of current occurs in the secondary, however. Then when the primary switch is opened, a surge of current again registers in the secondary but in the opposite direction.

think!

When the switch of the primary in Figure 37.11 is opened or closed, the galvanometer in the secondary registers a current. But when the switch remains closed, no current is registered on the galvanometer of the secondary. Why?

Answer: 37.5.1

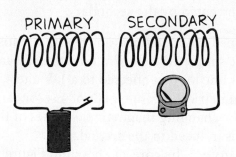

◀ **FIGURE 37.11**
Whenever the primary switch is opened or closed, voltage is induced in the secondary circuit.

The explanation is that the magnetic field that builds up around the primary extends into the secondary coil. Changes in the magnetic field of the primary are sensed by the nearby secondary. These changes of magnetic field intensity at the secondary induce voltage in the secondary, in accord with Faraday's law.

If we place an iron core inside the primary and secondary coils of the arrangement shown in Figure 37.11, the magnetic field within the primary is intensified by the alignment of magnetic domains in the iron. The magnetic field is also concentrated in the core, which extends into the secondary, so the secondary intercepts more of the field change. The galvanometer will show greater surges of current when the switch of the primary is opened or closed.

Instead of opening and closing a switch to produce the change of magnetic field, suppose that alternating current is used to power the primary. Then the rate at which the magnetic field changes in the primary (and hence in the secondary) is equal to the frequency of the alternating current. Now we have a *transformer*, as shown in Figure 37.12. A **transformer** is a device for increasing or decreasing voltage through electromagnetic induction. ☑ **A transformer works by inducing a changing magnetic field in one coil, which induces an alternating current in a nearby second coil.**

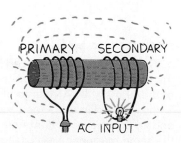

FIGURE 37.12 ▲
A simple transformer arrangement using an iron core creates greater current in the secondary coil.

FIGURE 37.13 ▶
The iron core guides the changing
magnetic field lines, which makes
a more efficient transformer.

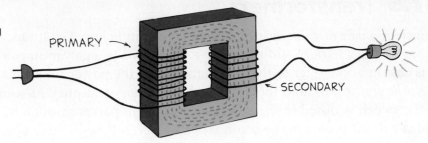
PRIMARY
SECONDARY

A more efficient arrangement for a transformer is shown in
Figure 37.13, where the iron core forms a complete loop to guide all
the magnetic field lines through the secondary. All the magnetic field
lines within the primary are intercepted by the secondary.

Voltage Voltages may be stepped up or stepped down with a transformer. To see how, consider the simple case shown in Figure 37.14a.
Suppose the primary consists of one loop connected to a 1-V alternating source. Consider the symmetrical arrangement of a secondary
of one loop that intercepts all the changing magnetic field lines of the
primary. Then a voltage of 1 V is induced in the secondary.

If another loop is wrapped around the core, as shown in Figure
37.14c, the induced voltage will be twice as much, in accord with
Faraday's law. If the secondary is wound with three times as many
loops, or turns as they are called, then three times as much voltage will be induced. If the secondary has a hundred times as many
turns as the primary, then a hundred times as much voltage will be
induced, and so on. This arrangement of a greater number of turns
on the secondary than on the primary makes up a step-up transformer. Stepped-up voltage may light a neon sign or operate the picture tube in a television receiver.

Transformers convert
voltage from high to
low (from 120 V to
6 V for your laptop)
or from low to high
(from 120 V to 220 V,
for your Hong-Kong
hair dryer).

FIGURE 37.14 ▶
a. The voltage of 1 V induced in
the secondary equals the voltage
of the primary. **b.** A voltage of
1 V is induced in the added secondary also because it intercepts
the same magnetic field change
from the primary. **c.** The voltages
of 1 V induced in each of the
two one-turn secondaries
are equivalent to a voltage of
2 V induced in a single two-turn
secondary.

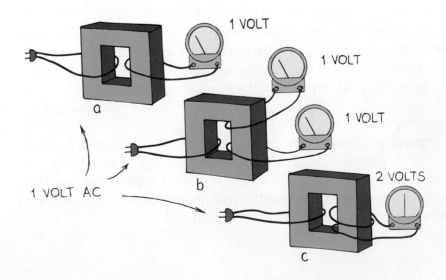
1 VOLT
1 VOLT
1 VOLT
2 VOLTS
1 VOLT AC
a
b
c

If the secondary has fewer turns than the primary, the alternating voltage produced in the secondary will be *lower* than that in the primary. The voltage is said to be stepped down. If the secondary has half as many turns as the primary, then only half as much voltage is induced in the secondary.

So electrical energy can be fed into the primary at a given alternating voltage and taken from the secondary at a greater or lower alternating voltage, depending on the relative number of turns in the primary and secondary coil windings, as shown in Figure 37.15.

The relationship between primary and secondary voltages with respect to the relative number of turns is

$$\frac{\text{primary voltage}}{\text{number of primary turns}} = \frac{\text{secondary voltage}}{\text{number of secondary turns}}$$

think!

If the voltage in a transformer is stepped up, then the current is stepped down. Ohm's law says that increased voltage will produce increased current. Is there a contradiction here, or does Ohm's Law not apply to transformers?
Answer: 37.5.2

◀ **FIGURE 37.15**
A practical transformer uses many coils. The relative numbers of turns in the coils determines how much the voltage changes.

Power It might seem that you get something for nothing with a transformer that steps up the voltage. Not so, for energy conservation always controls what can happen. The transformer actually transfers energy from one coil to the other. The rate at which energy is transferred is the power. The power used in the secondary is supplied by the primary. The primary gives no more power than the secondary uses, in accord with the conservation of energy. If the slight power losses due to heating of the core are neglected, then the power going into the primary equals the power coming out of the secondary. Electric power is equal to the product of voltage and current:

$$(\text{voltage} \times \text{current})_{\text{primary}} = (\text{voltage} \times \text{current})_{\text{secondary}}$$

You can see that if the secondary has more voltage, it will have less current than the primary. Or vice versa; if the secondary has less voltage, it will have more current than the primary. The ease with which voltages can be stepped up or down with a transformer is the principal reason that most electric power is AC rather than DC. Figure 37.16 shows a common household transformer used today.

FIGURE 37.16 ▲
This common transformer lowers 120 V to 6 V or 9 V. It also converts AC to DC by means of a *diode* inside—a tiny electronic device (shown in Chapter 34, Figure 34.12) that acts as a one-way valve.

CONCEPT CHECK: How does a transformer work?

37.6 Power Transmission

✅ **Almost all electric energy sold today is in the form of alternating current because of the ease with which it can be transformed from one voltage to another.** Power is transmitted great distances at high voltages and correspondingly low currents, a process that otherwise would result in large energy losses owing to the heating of the wires. Power may be carried from power plants to cities at about 120,000 volts or more, stepped down to about 2400 volts in the city, and finally stepped down again by a transformer such as the one shown in Figure 37.17 to provide the 120 volts used in household circuits.

FIGURE 37.17 ▶
A common neighborhood transformer, which typically steps 2400 V down to 240 V for houses and small businesses. Inside the home or business, the 240 V can be divided to a safer 120 V.

Energy, then, is transformed from one system of conducting wires to another by electromagnetic induction as shown in Figure 37.18. The same principles account for eliminating wires and sending energy from a radio-transmitter antenna to a radio receiver many kilometers away, and for the transformation of energy of vibrating electrons in the sun to life energy on Earth. The effects of electromagnetic induction are very far-reaching.

CONCEPT CHECK : Why is almost all electrical energy sold today in the form of alternating current?

FIGURE 37.18 ▼
Power transmission depends on transformers. Voltage is increased for long-distance transmission and then decreased before it reaches your home.

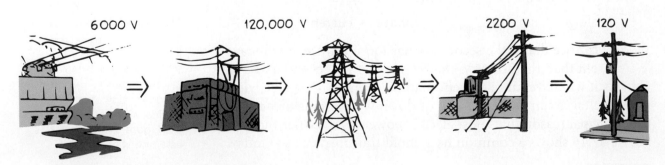

6 000 V ⟹ 120,000 V ⟹ 2200 V ⟹ 120 V

37.7 Induction of Electric and Magnetic Fields

Electromagnetic induction has thus far been discussed in terms of the production of voltages and currents. Actually, the more fundamental way to look at it is in terms of the induction of electric *fields*. The electric fields, in turn, give rise to voltages and currents. Induction takes place whether or not a conducting wire or any material medium is present. Faraday's law states that an electric field is created in any region of space in which a magnetic field is changing with time. The magnitude of the created electric field is proportional to the rate at which the magnetic field changes. The direction of the created electric field is at right angles to the changing magnetic field.

If electric charge happens to be present where the electric field is created, this charge will experience a force. For a charge in a wire, the force could cause it to flow as current, or to push the wire to one side. For a charge in an evacuated region, like in the chamber of a particle accelerator, the force can accelerate the charge to high speeds.

There is a second effect, which is the counterpart to Faraday's law. It is just like Faraday's law, except that the roles of electric and magnetic fields are interchanged. The symmetry between electric and magnetic fields revealed by this pair of laws is one of the many beautiful symmetries in nature. The companion to Faraday's law was advanced by the British physicist James Clerk Maxwell in the 1860s. **⊘ A magnetic field is created in any region of space in which an electric field is changing with time.** According to Maxwell, the magnitude of the created magnetic field is proportional to the rate at which the electric field changes. The direction of the created magnetic field is at right angles to the changing electric field.

In making a scientific discovery, being at the right place at the right time is not enough—curiosity, patience, and hard work are also important.

CONCEPT CHECK How can an electric field create a magnetic field?

Link to TECHNOLOGY

Magnetic Storage Computers store data on plastic disks that have been coated with a magnetic material. Magnetic patterns can be applied to the disk by a recording head. Coded electrical pulses that carry information are changed into magnetic pulses and stored on the disk. When a magnetically stored bit of information on the disk spins under a reading head that contains a small coil, the pulses are converted back to electrical signals again.

POWER LINES

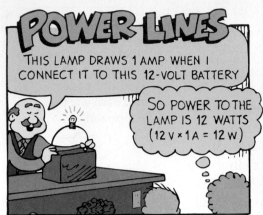

THIS LAMP DRAWS 1 AMP WHEN I CONNECT IT TO THIS 12-VOLT BATTERY

SO POWER TO THE LAMP IS 12 WATTS ($12 V \times 1 A = 12 W$)

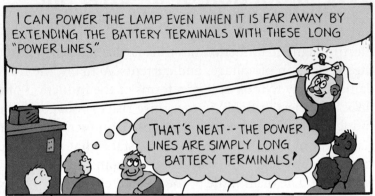

I CAN POWER THE LAMP EVEN WHEN IT IS FAR AWAY BY EXTENDING THE BATTERY TERMINALS WITH THESE LONG "POWER LINES."

THAT'S NEAT -- THE POWER LINES ARE SIMPLY LONG BATTERY TERMINALS!

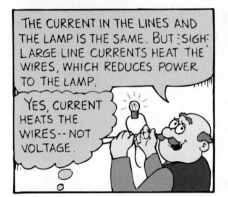

THE CURRENT IN THE LINES AND THE LAMP IS THE SAME. BUT :SIGH: LARGE LINE CURRENTS HEAT THE WIRES, WHICH REDUCES POWER TO THE LAMP.

YES, CURRENT HEATS THE WIRES -- NOT VOLTAGE.

TO SEND POWER EFFICIENTLY OVER LONG DISTANCES REQUIRES SMALL LINE CURRENTS.

BUT WON'T SMALL CURRENTS DELIVER ONLY SMALL AMOUNTS OF POWER?

WE CAN SEND A LOT OF POWER AT SMALL CURRENTS AND HIGH VOLTAGES VIA AC INSTEAD OF DC. THIS TIME I'LL CONNECT OUR LINES TO THIS 120-VOLT AC WALL OUTLET.

BUT WON'T YOU DELIVER MORE THAN 12 W AT THE HIGHER VOLTAGE?

120 VOLTS WILL BURN OUT OUR LAMP, SO I'LL PUT A TRANSFORMER BETWEEN THE LINES AND THE LAMP AND STEP THE VOLTAGE DOWN BY 10.

PHYSICS ? ? PHYSICS ? PHYSICS!

NOW WE HAVE 12 VOLTS ACROSS OUR LAMP AND AN AC OF 1 AMP!

100 TURNS   10 TURNS

AHA! 12 WATTS!

CAREFUL THOUGHT WILL SHOW THAT ONLY $\frac{1}{10}$ AMP FLOWS IN THE POWER LINES.

THAT'S RIGHT --- POWER$_{IN}$ = POWER$_{OUT}$ $120 V \times \frac{1}{10} A = 12 V \times 1 A$

NOW DO YOU SEE WHY POWER IS DELIVERED OVER LONG DISTANCES AT VERY HIGH VOLTAGES?

120,000 V   12,000 V   120 V

PHYSICS PHYSICS :SIGH:

37.8 Electromagnetic Waves

Shake the end of a stick back and forth in still water and you will produce waves on the water surface. Similarly shake a charged rod back and forth in empty space and you will produce electromagnetic waves in space, as shown in Figure 37.19. This is because the shaking charge can be considered an electric current. What surrounds an electric current? The answer is a magnetic field. What surrounds a *changing* electric current? The answer is, a changing magnetic field. What do we know about a changing magnetic field? The answer is, it will create a changing electric field, in accord with Faraday's law. What do we know about a changing electric field? The answer is, in accord with Maxwell's counterpart to Faraday's law, the changing electric field will create a changing magnetic field.

⊘ **An electromagnetic wave is composed of oscillating electric and magnetic fields that regenerate each other.** No medium is required. The oscillating fields emanate (move outward) from the vibrating charge. At any point on the wave, the electric field is perpendicular to the magnetic field, and both are perpendicular to the direction of motion of the wave, as shown in Figure 37.20.

Speed of Electromagnetic Waves How fast does the electromagnetic wave move? This is a very interesting question, and, in the history of physics, a very important one. If you ask how fast a baseball moves, or a car, or a spacecraft, or a planet, there is no single answer. It depends on how the motion got started, what forces are acting, and how fast the observer is moving. But for electromagnetic radiation, there is only one speed—the speed of light—no matter what the frequency or wavelength or intensity of the radiation.

FIGURE 37.19 ▲
Shake a charged object back and forth and you produce electromagnetic waves.

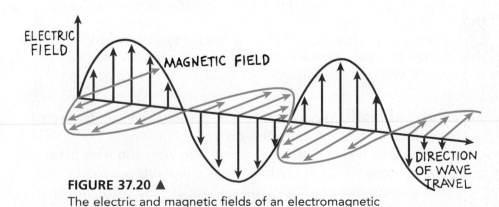

FIGURE 37.20 ▲
The electric and magnetic fields of an electromagnetic wave are perpendicular to each other.

At only one speed will the linkage between electric and magnetic fields be in perfect balance with no gain or loss of energy—exactly the speed of light!

This remarkable constancy of the speed of propagating electric and magnetic fields was discovered by Maxwell. The key to understanding it lies in the perfect balance between the two kinds of fields that must exist if they are to propagate as waves. The changing electric field induces a magnetic field. The changing magnetic field acts back to induce an electric field. The wave is continually self-reinforcing. Maxwell's equations showed that only one speed could preserve this harmonious balance of fields.

If, hypothetically, the wave traveled at less than the speed of light, the fields would rapidly die out. The electric field would induce a weaker magnetic field, which would induce a still weaker electric field, and so on. If, still hypothetically, the wave traveled at more than the speed of light, the fields would build up in a crescendo of ever greater magnitudes—clearly a no-no with respect to energy conservation. At some critical speed, however, mutual induction continues indefinitely, with neither a loss nor a gain in energy.

From his equations of electromagnetic induction, Maxwell calculated the value of this critical speed and found it to be 300,000 kilometers per second. To do this calculation, he used only the constants in his equations determined by simple laboratory experiments with electric and magnetic fields. He didn't *use* the speed of light. He *found* the speed of light!

Physics on the Job

Cellular Field Technician Wireless communication through such devices as cellular telephones and pagers depends on communications towers maintained by cellular field technicians. Signals carried by electromagnetic waves are transferred from one tower to the next. The Federal Communications Commission (FCC) determines the frequency of the waves allowed at each tower. Cellular field technicians use physics to analyze or alter the electromagnetic waves coming into a receiver or being sent out by a transmitter. Cellular field technicians are employed by companies that maintain cellular communications towers.

Nature of Light Maxwell quickly realized that he had discovered the solution to one of the greatest mysteries of the universe—the nature of light. If electric charges are set into vibration with frequencies in the range of 4.3×10^{14} to 7×10^{14} vibrations per second, the resulting electromagnetic wave will activate the "electrical antennae" in the retina of the eye. Light is simply electromagnetic waves in this range of frequencies! The lower end of this frequency range appears red, and the higher end appears violet. Maxwell realized that radiation of any frequency would propagate at the same speed as light.

This radiation includes radio waves, which can be generated and received by antennas, as shown in Figure 37.21. A rotating device in the sending antenna alternately charges the upper and lower parts of the antenna positively and negatively. The charges accelerating up and down the antenna transmit electromagnetic waves. When the waves hit a receiving antenna, the electric charges inside vibrate in rhythm with the variations of the field.

On the evening of Maxwell's discovery of the nature of light, he had a date with a young woman he was later to marry. While walking in a garden, his date remarked about the beauty and wonder of the stars. Maxwell asked how she would feel to know that she was walking with the only person in the world who knew what the starlight really was. For it was true. At that time, James Clerk Maxwell was the only person in the world to know that light of any kind is energy carried in waves of electric and magnetic fields that continually regenerate each other.

CONCEPT CHECK What makes up an electromagnetic wave?

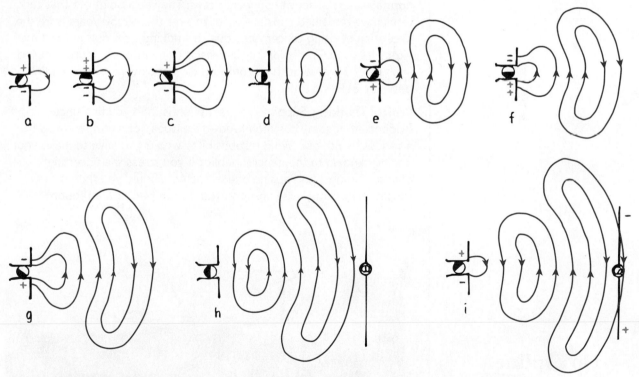

FIGURE 37.21 ▲
Electromagnetic wave emanation by a sending antenna and reception by a receiving antenna. Successive views, (a) through (i), show how acceleration of the charges up and down the antenna transmits electromagnetic waves. Only sample electric field lines of the wave are shown—the magnetic field lines are perpendicular to the electric field lines and extend into and out of the page.

Is ELF Radiation Dangerous?

We live in fear of the unsensed. Anything that exists, or is imagined to exist, yet escapes detection by our five senses, is often a source of fear.

Many people fear radiation. Some is hazardous, and some is not. No one doubts the hazards of radiation from some nuclear reactions, and no one seriously fears the low-frequency radiations of AM radio. But in recent years a series of books and magazine articles have fanned the flames of public fear by claiming that the *extremely low frequency* (ELF) *radiation* of common 60-Hz electric power causes certain forms of cancer.

Is this claim true? Some activists say yes, although the scientific consensus is that this is just one of many health scares that has no basis. Careful studies have not substantiated the claimed risk. Bioscientists point out that the electric fields due to power lines at the location of a cell in the body are thousands of times smaller than those due to the normal electrical activity of nearby cells. They also point out that cancer rates have remained constant or fallen over the last 50 years (with the exception of rising cancer rates due to smoking). Yet during this time, exposure to ELF radiation has increased tremendously. More detailed analysis of the studies that prompted the controversy shows no link between ELF and cancer.

Critical Thinking Suppose you're a scientist and you find uncertain evidence that some common food—tomatoes, for example—may be a serious health risk. What responsibility would you have to make your findings known to the general public? If you stress the uncertainty of your findings, perhaps no one will listen. Should you then make sensational claims, even unsupported, to get people's attention?

Go Online
SciLINKS NSTA

For: Links on electromagnetic induction
Visit: www.SciLinks.org
Web Code: csn – 3708

 **REVIEW**

Go **O**nline
PHSchool.com

For: Self-Assessment
Visit: PHSchool.com
Web Code: csa – 3700

Concept Summary · · · · · ·

- Electric current can be produced in a wire simply by moving a magnet into or out of a wire coil.

- Faraday's law states that the induced voltage in a coil is proportional to the product of the number of loops, the cross-sectional area of each loop, and the rate at which the magnetic field changes.

- A generator converts mechanical energy into electrical energy.

- Moving charges experience a force that is perpendicular to both their motion and the magnetic field they traverse.

- A transformer works by inducing a changing magnetic field in one coil, which induces an alternating current in a nearby second coil.

- Almost all electric energy sold today is in the form of alternating current because of the ease with which it can be transformed from one voltage to another.

- A magnetic field is created anywhere an electric field changes with time.

- An electromagnetic wave is composed of oscillating electric and magnetic fields.

Key Terms · · · · · · · · · · · · ·

electromagnetic induction (p. 742)

Faraday's law (p. 743)

generator (p. 743)

transformer (p. 747)

think! Answers

37.2 Simply put, more work is required because more turns mean that more voltage is induced, producing more current in the resistor and more energy transfer. You can also look at it this way: When the magnetic fields of two magnets (electro or permanent) overlap, the two magnets are either forced together or forced apart. When one of the fields is induced by motion of the other, the polarity of the fields is always such as to force the magnets apart. This produces the resistive force you feel. Inducing more current in more coils simply increases the induced magnetic field and thus the resistive force.

37.5.1 A current is only induced in a coil when there is a *change* in the magnetic field passing through it. When the switch remains in the closed position, there is a steady current in the primary and a steady magnetic field about the coil. This field extends into the secondary, but unless there is a *change* in the field, electromagnetic induction does not occur.

37.5.2 Ohm's law still holds, and there is no contradiction. The voltage induced across the secondary circuit, divided by the load (resistance) of the secondary circuit, equals the current in the secondary circuit. The current is stepped down in comparison with the larger current that is drawn in the *primary* circuit.

37 ASSESS

Check Concepts • • • • • •

Section 37.1

1. What did Michael Faraday and Joseph Henry discover?

2. How can voltage be induced in a wire with the help of a magnet?

3. A magnet moved into a coil of wire will induce voltage in the coil. What is the effect of moving a magnet into a coil with more loops?

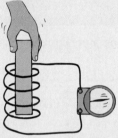

4. Why is it more difficult to move a magnet into a coil of more loops that is connected to a resistor?

Section 37.2

5. Current, as well as voltage, can be induced in a wire by electromagnetic induction. When can voltage be induced but not current?

Section 37.3

6. How does the frequency of a changing magnetic field compare with the frequency of the alternating voltage that is induced?

7. What is a generator, and how does it differ from a motor?

8. Why is the voltage induced in an alternator AC rather than DC?

9. The armature of a generator must rotate in order to induce voltage and current. What produces the rotation?

Section 37.4

10. A motor is characterized by three main ingredients: magnetic field, moving charges, and magnetic force. What are the three main ingredients that characterize a generator?

Section 37.5

11. What does a transformer actually transform—voltage, current, or energy?

12. What does a step-up transformer step up—voltage, current, or energy?

13. How does the relative number of turns on the primary and the secondary coil in a transformer affect the step-up or step-down voltage factor?

14. If the number of secondary turns is 10 times the number of primary turns, and the input voltage to the primary is 6 volts, how many volts will be induced in the secondary coil?

15. a. In a transformer, how does the power input to the primary coil compare with the power output of the secondary coil?

b. How does the product of voltage and current in the primary compare with the product of voltage and current in the secondary?

Section 37.6

16. Why is it advantageous to transmit electric power long distances at high voltages?

Section 37.7

17. What fundamental quantity underlies the concepts of voltages and currents?

18. Distinguish between Faraday's law expressed in terms of fields and Maxwell's counterpart to Faraday's law. How are the two laws symmetrical?

Section 37.8

19. How do the wave speeds compare for high-frequency and low-frequency electromagnetic waves?

20. What is light?

Think and Rank ......

Rank each of the following sets of scenarios in order of the quantity or property involved. List them from left to right. If scenarios have equal rankings, then separate them with an equal sign. (e.g., A = B)

21. The magnets are moved into the wire coils in identical quick fashion. Voltage induced in each coil causes a current to flow, as indicated on the galvanometer. Neglect the electrical resistance of the loops in the coil.

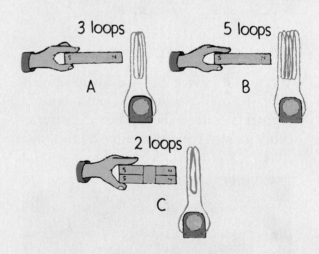

a. Rank from greatest to least the reading on the galvanometer.

b. Make the same ranking, only this time for each coil having twice as many loops as in part (a).

22. The transformers are all powered with 100 W, and all have 100 turns on the primary. The number of turns on each secondary varies as shown.

    a. Rank the voltage output of the secondaries from greatest to least.

    b. Rank the current in the secondaries from greatest to least.

    c. Rank the power output in the secondaries from greatest to least.

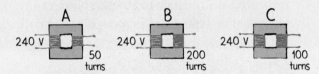

Think and Explain ••••••

23. When Tim pushes the wire down between the poles of the magnet, the galvanometer registers a pulse. When he lifts the wire, another pulse is registered. How do the pulses differ?

24. A common pickup for an electric guitar consists of a coil of wire around a permanent magnet. The permanent magnet magnetizes the nearby guitar string. When the string is plucked, it oscillates above the coil, thereby changing the magnetic field that passes through the coil. The rhythmic oscillations of the string produce the same rhythmic changes in the magnetic field in the coil, which in turn induce the same rhythmic voltages in the coil, which when amplified and sent to a speaker produce music! Why will this type of pickup not work with nylon strings?

25. Two separate but similar coils of wire are mounted close to each other, as shown below. The first coil is connected to a battery and has a direct current flowing through it. The second coil is connected to a galvanometer. How does the galvanometer respond when the switch in the first circuit is closed? When the current is steady after the switch is closed? When the switch is opened?

26. If you place a metal ring in a region in where a magnetic field is rapidly alternating, the ring may become hot to your touch. Why?

27. A magician places an aluminum ring on a table, underneath which is hidden an electromagnet. When the magician says "abracadabra" (and pushes a switch that starts current flowing through the coil under the table), the ring jumps into the air. Explain his trick.

28. How could you light a lightbulb that is near, yet not touching, an electromagnet? Is AC or DC required? Defend your answer.

29. What is the basic difference between an electric generator and an electric motor?

30. With no magnets around, why will current flow in a coil of wire waved around in the air?

31. What is the source of all electromagnetic waves?

32. Why is a generator armature more difficult to rotate when it is connected to and supplying electric current to a circuit?

33. Your classmate says that, if you crank the shaft of a conventional motor manually, the motor becomes a generator. Do you agree or disagree, and why?

34. Some bicycles have electric generators that are made to turn when the bike wheel turns. These generators provide energy for the bike's lamp. Will a cyclist coast farther if the lamp connected to the generator is turned off? Explain.

35. An electric hair drier running at normal speed draws a relatively small current. But if somehow the motor shaft is prevented from turning, the current dramatically increases and the motor overheats. Why?

36. When a piece of plastic tape coated with iron oxide that is magnetized more in some parts than others is moved past a small coil of wire, what happens in the coil? What is a practical application of this?

37. Why is it important that the core of a transformer pass through both coils?

38. Why can a hum often be heard when a transformer is operating?

39. When a strip of magnetic material, variably magnetized, is embedded in a plastic card that is moved past a small coil of wire, what happens in the coil? What is a practical application of this?

40. If a car made of iron and steel moves over a wide closed loop of wire embedded in a road surface, will the magnetic field of Earth in the loop be altered? Will this produce a current pulse? (Can you think of a practical application of this?)

41. At the security area of an airport, you walk through a metal detector that uses a weak AC magnetic field inside a large coil of wire. You are surprised that a piece of aluminum (nonmagnetic) in your pocket sounds the alarm. The security officer explains that loops of current (eddy currents) were induced in the metal. Why would eddy currents affect the net field in the detector?

42. How could you move a conducting loop of wire through a magnetic field without inducing a voltage in the loop?

43. Why does a transformer require alternating voltage?

44. How does the current in the secondary of a transformer compare with the current in the primary when the secondary voltage is twice the primary voltage?

45. In what sense can a transformer be thought of as an electrical lever? What does it multiply? What does it not multiply?

46. Can an efficient transformer step up energy? Defend your answer.

47. A friend says that changing electric and magnetic fields generate one another, and this gives rise to visible light when the frequency of change matches the frequencies of light. Do you agree? Explain.

48. Would electromagnetic waves exist if changing magnetic fields could produce electric fields but changing electric fields could not in turn produce magnetic fields? Explain.

49. When a bar magnet is dropped through a vertical length of copper pipe, it falls noticeably more slowly than it does when it is dropped through a vertical length of plastic pipe. If the copper pipe is long enough, the dropped magnet will reach a terminal falling speed. Propose an explanation.

50. What is wrong with this scheme? To generate electricity without fuel, arrange a motor to run a generator that will produce electricity that is stepped up with transformers so that the generator can run the motor and simultaneously furnish electricity for other uses.

51. An electromagnet A with a coil of 10 turns carrying 1 A interacts with electromagnet B, which has 100 turns carrying 2 A. Which electromagnet exerts the greater force on the other?

Think and Solve ••••••

52. An electric doorbell requires 12 volts to operate correctly. A transformer nicely allows it to be powered from a 120-volt outlet. If the primary has 500 turns, show that the secondary should have 50 turns.

53. A model electric train requires 6 V to operate. When connected to a 120-V household circuit, a transformer is needed. If the primary coil of the transformer has 240 windings, show that there should be 12 turns in the secondary coil.

54. If the output current for the above transformer is 1.8 amps, show that the input current is 0.09 A.

55. A transformer has an input of 9 volts and an output of 36 volts. If the input is changed to 12 volts, show that the output would be 48 volts.

56. A model electric train requires a low voltage to operate. If the primary coil of its transformer has 400 turns, and the secondary has 40 turns, how many volts will power the train when the primary is connected to a 120-volt household circuit?

57. The primary coil of a step-up transformer draws 100 W. Find the power provided to the secondary circuit.

58. An ideal transformer has 50 turns in its primary coil and 250 turns in its secondary coil. A 12-V AC source is connected to the primary. Find
   a. the AC voltage available at the secondary
   b. the current in a 10-Ω device connected to the secondary
   c. the power supplied to the primary

59. Neon signs require about 12,000 V for their operation. What should be the ratio of the number of loops in the secondary to the number of loops in the primary for a neon-sign transformer that operates off 120-V lines?

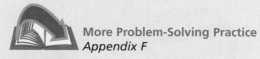

More Problem-Solving Practice
Appendix F

UNIT VI ATOMIC AND NUCLEAR PHYSICS

IT'S A FACT!

Remember that all matter is made of tiny particles called atoms. The light that we see and the heat that we feel are all a result of changes that occur within atoms. Besides the electrons, protons, and neutrons inside an atom, other small particles such as photons and neutrinos all play a role in these energetic reactions and interactions. In this unit, you will learn many interesting facts about physics on a very small scale.

The natural heat of Earth that warms this natural hot spring, or that powers a geyser or a volcano, comes from nuclear power—the radioactivity of minerals in Earth's interior. Power from the atomic nucleus has been with us since Earth was formed and is not restricted to today's nuclear reactors, or "nukes" as they are called. Opinions about nuclear power are informed opinions if we first "know nukes"!

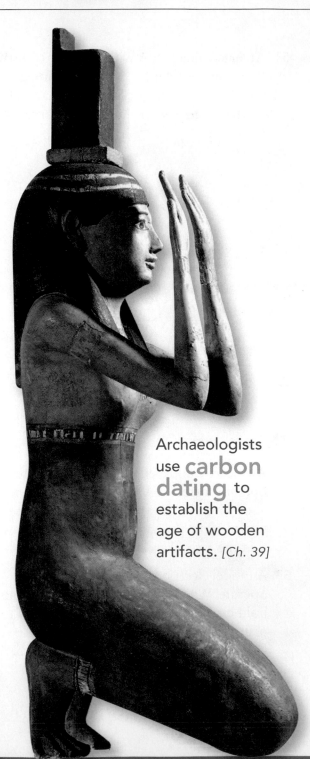

Archaeologists use **carbon dating** to establish the age of wooden artifacts. [Ch. 39]

CAUTION
RADIOACTIVE MATERIALS

All elements with an **atomic number** greater than 83 decay in one way or another. [Ch. 39]

Go Online
SCIENCE NEWS

For: Articles on atomic and nuclear physics
Visit: PHSchool.com
Web Code: cse – 6000

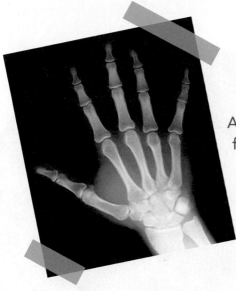

A couple of round-trip flights on an airplane expose you to as much **radiation** as a routine x-ray. [Ch. 39]

An electron microscope makes use of the wave nature of electrons. [Ch. 38]

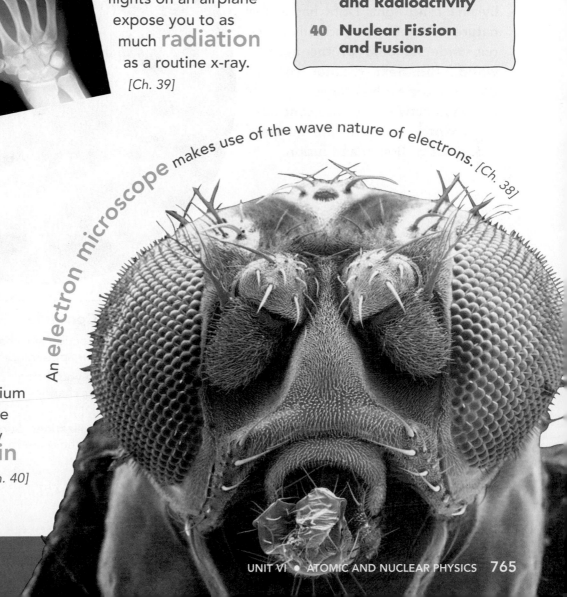

It is rare for uranium deposits in nature to spontaneously undergo a **chain reaction.** [Ch. 40]

38 THE ATOM AND THE QUANTUM

THE BIG IDEA : Material particles and light have both wave properties and particle properties.

The final unit of this book is about the realm of the unimaginably tiny atom. This chapter investigates atomic structure, which is revealed by analyzing light. Light has a dual nature, which in turn radically alters our understanding of the atomic world. The next chapter covers the structure of the atomic nucleus and radioactivity, and the concluding chapter is about the nuclear processes of fission and fusion.

discover!

How Can Waves Behave as Particles and Particles Behave as Waves?

1. Draw a square with sides of approximately 5 cm.
2. Draw a second square of the same size on top, but slightly displaced to the side, of the first square.
3. Form a cube by connecting the two squares with straight lines connected to the corresponding vertices.
4. Stare at the cube until you observe a change in the drawing.

Analyze and Conclude

1. **Observing** Describe any changes you observed in the appearance of the cube.
2. **Predicting** Do you think you would observe similar changes when viewing other figures or objects?
3. **Making Generalizations** Suggest other situations in which there are two equally valid points of view.

◀ **FIGURE 38.1**
In the old planetary model of the atom, the electrons orbit the nucleus like little planets around a tiny sun.

38.1 Models

Nobody knows what an atom's internal structure looks like, for there is no way to see it with our eyes. To visualize the processes that occur in the subatomic realm, we construct models. Figure 38.1 shows the planetary model—the one that most people think of when they picture an atom—in which the electrons orbit the nucleus like planets going around the sun. This was an early model of the atom suggested by the Danish physicist Niels Bohr in 1913. We still tend to think in terms of this simple picture, even though it has been replaced by a more complex model in which the electrons are represented as clouds spread throughout the interior of the atom, as shown in Figure 38.2. We will see that the planetary model of the atom is still useful for understanding the emission of light.

Models are assessed not in terms of their "truthfulness," but in terms of their "usefulness." Models help us to understand processes that are difficult to visualize. A useful model of the atom must be consistent with a model for light, for most of what we know about atoms we learn from the light and other radiations they emit. Most light has its source in the motion of electrons within the atom.

⊘ **Through the centuries there have been two primary models of light: the particle model and the wave model.** Isaac Newton believed light was composed of a hail of tiny particles. Christian Huygens believed that light was a wave phenomenon. The wave model was reinforced more than a century later when Thomas Young demonstrated that light exhibited constructive and destructive interference. Later, James Clerk Maxwell proposed that light is an electromagnetic wave and a part of a broader electromagnetic spectrum. The wave model gained further support when Heinrich Hertz produced radio waves that behaved as Maxwell had predicted. This seemed to verify the wave nature of light once and for all. But Maxwell's electromagnetic wave model was not the last word on the nature of light. In 1905 Albert Einstein resurrected the particle theory of light.

CONCEPT CHECK What are the two primary models of light?

FIGURE 38.2 ▲
In the current model of the atom, electrons are spread out in waves or clouds.

38.2 Light Quanta

Einstein visualized particles of light as concentrated bundles of electromagnetic energy. Einstein built on the idea of a German physicist, Max Planck, who a few years earlier had proposed that atoms do not emit and absorb light continuously, but do so in little chunks. Each chunk was considered a **quantum,** or a fundamental unit. (The plural of *quantum* is *quanta*.) Planck believed that light existed as continuous waves, just as Maxwell had asserted, but that emission and absorption occurred in quantum chunks. Einstein went further and proposed that light itself is composed of quanta. One quantum of light energy is now called a **photon.**

The idea that certain quantities are quantized—that they come in discrete (separate) units—was known in Einstein's time. Matter is quantized. The mass of a gold ring, for example, is equal to some whole-number multiple of the mass of a single gold atom. Electric charge is quantized, as all charge is some whole-number multiple of the charge of a single electron.

Other quantities such as energy and angular momentum are quantized. The energy in a light beam is quantized and comes in packets, or quanta; only a whole number of quanta can exist. The quanta of light, or of electromagnetic radiation in general, are the photons.

Photons have no rest energy. They move at one speed only—at the speed of light! The total energy of a photon is the same as its kinetic energy. ✔ **The energy of a photon is directly proportional to the photon's frequency.** This relationship is illustrated in Figure 38.3. When the energy E of a photon is divided by its frequency f, the quantity that results is known as **Planck's constant,** h. This quantity is always the same, no matter what the frequency. The energy of every photon is therefore $E = hf$.

This equation gives the smallest amount of energy that can be converted to light of frequency f. Light is not emitted continuously, but as a stream of photons, each with an energy hf.

CONCEPT CHECK How is the energy of a photon related to its frequency?

FIGURE 38.3 ▶
The energy of a photon of light is proportional to its vibrational frequency.

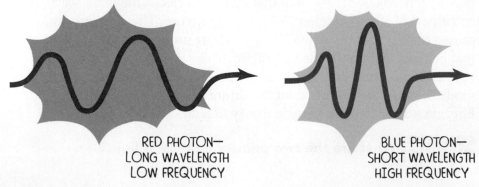

RED PHOTON—
LONG WAVELENGTH
LOW FREQUENCY

BLUE PHOTON—
SHORT WAVELENGTH
HIGH FREQUENCY

38.3 The Photoelectric Effect

Einstein found support for his quantum theory of light in the photoelectric effect. The **photoelectric effect** is the ejection of electrons from certain metals when light falls upon them. These metals are said to be *photosensitive* (that is, sensitive to light). This effect is used in electric eyes, in the photographer's light meter, and in picking up sound from the soundtracks of motion pictures.

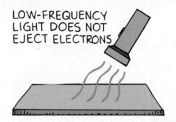
LOW-FREQUENCY LIGHT DOES NOT EJECT ELECTRONS

HIGH-FREQUENCY LIGHT DOES EJECT ELECTRONS

◀ **FIGURE 38.4**
The photoelectric effect depends on the frequency of light that shines on the metal.

Explanation of the Photoelectric Effect The photoelectric effect is illustrated in Figure 38.4. Energy from the light shining on the metal plate gives electrons bound in the metal enough energy to escape. Investigators discovered that high-frequency light, even from a dim source, was capable of ejecting electrons from a photosensitive metal surface; yet low-frequency light, even from a very bright source, could not dislodge electrons. Since bright light carries more energy than dim light, it was puzzling that dim blue or violet light could dislodge electrons from certain metals when bright red light could not.

Einstein explained the photoelectric effect by thinking of light in terms of photons. The absorption of a photon by an atom in the metal surface is an all-or-nothing process. Only one photon is absorbed by each electron ejected from the metal. The *number* of photons that hit the metal has nothing to do with whether a given electron will be ejected. If the energy in the photon is large enough, the electron will be ejected from the metal. But if the energy in the photon is too small, then the electron is not ejected. The intensity of light does not matter. From $E = hf$, the critical factor is the frequency, or color, of the light. Since each blue or violet light photon carries enough energy to free an electron from the metal, a few photons of blue or violet light can eject a few electrons. But hordes of red or orange photons cannot eject a single electron. Only high-frequency photons have the energy needed to pull loose an electron.

Support for the Particle Model of Light The energy of a wave is spread out along a broad front. For the energy of a light wave to be concentrated enough to eject a single electron from a metal surface is as unlikely as for an ocean wave to hurl a boulder off the beach with an energy equal to the energy of the whole wave.

think!

Will high-frequency light eject a greater number of electrons than low-frequency light?
Answer: 38.3

Light travels as a wave and hits as a particle.

Light quanta, electrons, and other particles all behave in some ways as if they were lumps and in other ways as if they were waves.

⊘ **The photoelectric effect suggests that light interacts with matter as a stream of particle-like photons.** The number of photons in a light beam controls the brightness of the *whole* beam, but the frequency of the light controls the energy of each *individual* photon.

Experimental verification of Einstein's explanation of the photoelectric effect was made 11 years later by the American physicist Robert Millikan. Every aspect of Einstein's interpretation was confirmed, including the direct proportionality of photon energy to frequency. It was for this (and not for his theory of relativity) that Einstein received the Nobel Prize.

CONCEPT CHECK : What does the photoelectric effect suggest about the way light interacts with matter?

38.4 Waves as Particles

⊘ **Light behaves like waves when it travels in empty space, and like particles when it interacts with solid matter.** Figure 38.5 is a striking example of the particle nature of light. The photograph was taken with exceedingly feeble light. Each frame shows the image progressing photon by photon. Note also that the photons seem to strike the film in an independent and random manner.

CONCEPT CHECK : What causes light to behave like a wave? Like a particle?

FIGURE 38.5 ▼
Stages of the exposure of film to light reveal the photon-by-photon production of a photograph. The approximate numbers of photons at each stage were **a.** 3×10^3, **b.** 1.2×10^4, **c.** 9.3×10^4, **d.** 7.6×10^5, **e.** 3.6×10^6, and **f.** 2.8×10^7.

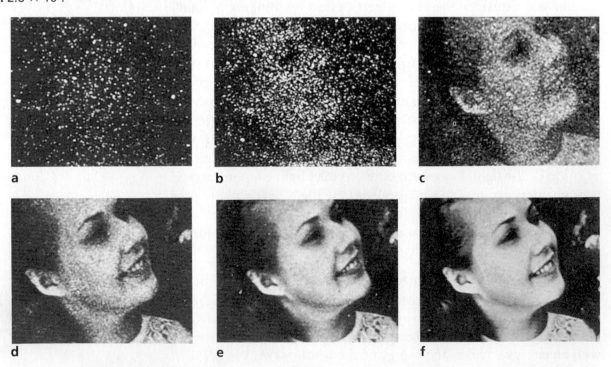

a

b

c

d

e

f

38.5 Particles as Waves

If waves can have particle properties, cannot particles have wave properties? This question was posed by the French physicist Louis de Broglie in 1924, while he was still a student. His answer to the question earned him a Ph.D. in physics, and later won him the Nobel Prize in physics.

◀ **FIGURE 38.6**
This color-enhanced image of lily pollen grains was taken with a scanning electron microscope. Unlike an optical microscope, which makes use of the wave nature of light, a scanning electron microscope makes use of the wave nature of electrons.

✅ **De Broglie suggested that all matter could be viewed as having wave properties.** All particles—electrons, protons, atoms, marbles, and even humans—have a wavelength that is related to the momentum of the particles by

$$\text{wavelength} = \frac{h}{\text{momentum}}$$

where h is, lo and behold, Planck's constant again. The wavelength of a particle is called the *de Broglie wavelength*. A particle of large mass and ordinary speed has too small a wavelength to be detected by conventional means. However, a tiny particle—such as an electron—moving at typical speed has a detectable wavelength.[38.5] It is smaller than the wavelength of visible light but large enough for noticeable diffraction. A beam of electrons, interestingly enough, behaves like a beam of light. It can be diffracted and undergoes wave interference under the same conditions that light does.

An electron microscope makes practical use of the wave nature of electrons. The wavelength of electron beams is typically thousands of times shorter than the wavelength of visible light, so the electron microscope is able to distinguish details thousands of times smaller than is possible with optical microscopes. Figures 38.6 and 38.7 show examples of images generated by scanning electron microscopes.

FIGURE 38.7 ▲
A scanning electron microscope allows you to see this fly's head in striking detail.

CONCEPT CHECK What did de Broglie suggest about all matter?

38.6 Electron Waves

FIRST SHELL

SECOND SHELL

FIGURE 38.8 ▲
In the Bohr model of the atom, the electron orbits correspond to different energy levels.

The planetary model of the atom developed by Niels Bohr, illustrated in Figure 38.8, was useful in explaining the atomic spectra of the elements and why elements emitted only certain frequencies of light. An electron has different amounts of energy when it is in different orbits around a nucleus. An electron is said to be in a different *energy level* when it is in a different orbit. The electrons in an atom normally occupy the lowest energy levels available.

Bohr Model Explanation of Atomic Spectra An electron can be boosted by various means to a higher energy level. This occurs in gas discharge tubes, like those that make up neon signs. Electric current boosts the electrons of the gas to higher energy levels. As the electrons return to lower levels, photons are emitted. The energy of a photon is exactly equal to the difference in the energy levels in the atom. The characteristic pattern of lines in the spectrum of an element corresponds to electron transitions between the energy levels of the atoms of that element. By examining spectra, physicists were able to determine the various energy levels in the atom. This was a tremendous triumph for atomic physics.

One of the difficulties of this model of the atom, however, was reconciling why electrons occupied only certain energy levels in the atom—why, in effect, they were at discrete distances from the atomic nucleus. This was resolved by thinking of the electron not as a particle whirling around the nucleus but as a wave.

De Broglie's Theory ⊘ **According to de Broglie's theory of matter waves, electron orbits exist only where an electron wave closes in on itself in phase.** The electron wave reinforces itself constructively in each cycle, just as the standing wave on a music string is constructively reinforced by its successive reflections. The electron is visualized not as a particle located at some point in the atom, but as though its mass and charge were spread throughout a standing wave surrounding the nucleus. The wavelength of the electron wave must fit evenly into the circumferences of the orbits, as illustrated in Figure 38.9.

FIGURE 38.9 ▶
De Broglie suggested electrons have a wavelength.
a. Electron orbits exist only when the circumference of the orbit is a whole-number multiple of the wavelength. **b.** When the wave does not close in on itself in phase, it undergoes destructive interference.

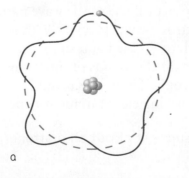

a

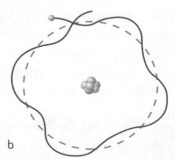

b

FIGURE 38.10 ▼

In this simplified version of de Broglie's theory of the atom, the waves are shown only in circular paths around the nucleus. In an actual atom, the standing waves make up spherical and ellipsoidal shells rather than flat, circular ones.

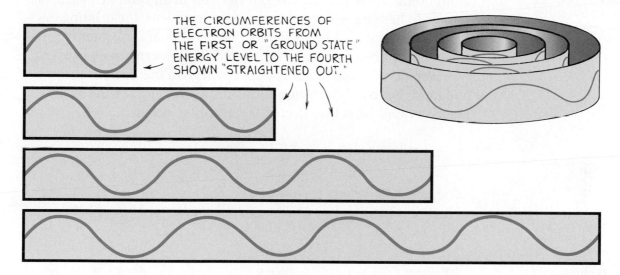

THE CIRCUMFERENCES OF ELECTRON ORBITS FROM THE FIRST OR "GROUND STATE" ENERGY LEVEL TO THE FOURTH SHOWN "STRAIGHTENED OUT."

The circumference of the innermost orbit, according to this model, is equal to one wavelength of the electron wave. The second orbit has a circumference of two electron wavelengths, the third three, and so on. This is illustrated in Figure 38.10. Orbit circumferences are whole-number multiples of the electron wavelengths, which differ for the various elements (and also for different orbits within the elements). This results in discrete energy levels, which characterize each element. You can also think of a "chain necklace" made of paper clips. No matter what size necklace is made, its circumference is equal to some multiple of the length of a single paper clip.[38.6] Since the circumferences of electron orbits are discrete, it follows that the radii of these orbits, and hence the energy levels, are also discrete.

This view explains why electrons do not spiral closer and closer to the nucleus when photons are emitted. Since each electron orbit is described by a standing wave, the circumference of the smallest orbit can be no smaller than one wavelength—no fraction of a wavelength is possible in a circular (or elliptical) standing wave.

In the still more modern wave model of the atom, electron waves move not only around the nucleus, but also in and out, toward and away from the nucleus. The electron wave is spread out in three dimensions. This leads to the picture of an electron "cloud," shown previously in Figure 38.2.

Both artists and scientists look for patterns in nature, finding connections that have always been there yet have been missed by the eye.

CONCEPT CHECK : How did de Broglie's theory of matter waves describe electron orbits?

38.7 Relative Sizes of Atoms

⊘ **The radii of the electron orbits in the Bohr model of the atom are determined by the amount of electric charge in the nucleus.** For example, the single positively charged proton in the hydrogen atom holds one negatively charged electron in an orbit at a particular radius. In helium, with two protons in the nucleus, the orbiting electron would be pulled into a tighter orbit with half its former radius since the electrical attraction is doubled. This doesn't quite happen, however, because the double-positive charge in the nucleus attracts and holds a second electron, and the negative charge of the second electron diminishes the effect of the positive nucleus.

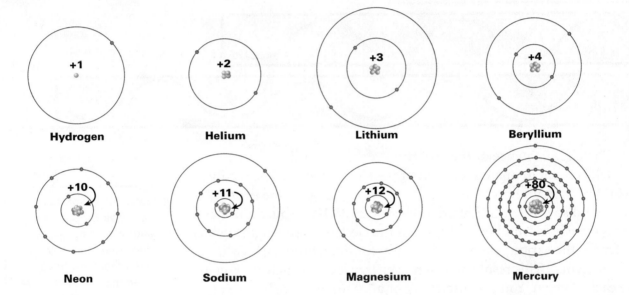

FIGURE 38.11 ▲
The orbital model of the atom is illustrated for some light and heavy atoms. Note that the heavier atoms are not appreciably larger than the lighter atoms.

This added electron makes the atom electrically neutral. The two electrons assume an orbit characteristic of helium. An additional proton added to the nucleus pulls the electrons into an even closer orbit and, furthermore, holds a third electron in a second orbit. This is the lithium atom, atomic number 3. We can continue with this process, increasing the positive charge of the nucleus and adding successively more electrons and more orbits all the way up to atomic numbers above 100, to the synthetic radioactive elements.[38.7]

As the nuclear charge increases and additional electrons are added in outer orbits, the inner orbits shrink in size because of the stronger electrical attraction to the nucleus. This means that the heavier elements are not much larger in diameter than the lighter elements. The diameter of the uranium atom, for example, is only about three hydrogen diameters even though it is 238 times more massive. The schematic diagrams in Figure 38.11 are drawn approximately to the same scale.

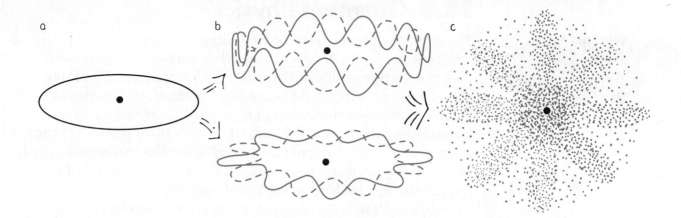

a   b   c

FIGURE 38.12 ▲
The model of the atom has evolved over time. **a.** In the Bohr model, the electrons orbit the nucleus like planets going around the sun. **b.** De Broglie's idea of a wave following along an orbit was an important stepping stone toward the current model. **c.** In the current model of the atom, the wave model, the electrons are distributed in a "cloud" throughout the volume of the atom.

Each element has an arrangement of electron orbits unique to that element. For example, the radii of the orbits for the sodium atom are the same for all sodium atoms, but different from the radii of the orbits for other kinds of atoms. When we consider all the elements, we find that each has its own distinct orbits.

The Bohr model of the atom solved the mystery of the atomic spectra of the elements. It accounted for X-rays that were emitted when electrons made transitions from outer orbits to innermost orbits. Bohr was able to predict X-ray frequencies that were later experimentally confirmed. He calculated the *ionization energy* of the hydrogen atom—the energy needed to knock the electron out of the atom completely. This also was verified by experiment. The Bohr model accounted for the general chemical properties of the elements and predicted properties of a missing element (hafnium), which led to its discovery.

The Bohr model was impressive. Nonetheless, Bohr was quick to point out that his model was to be interpreted as a crude beginning, and the picture of electrons whirling like planets about the sun was not to be taken literally (a statement to which popularizers of science paid no heed). His discrete orbits were conceptual representations of an atom whose later description involved a wave description. Still, his planetary model of the atom with electrons occupying discrete energy levels underlies the more complex models of the atom today, which are built upon a completely different structure from that built by Newton and other physicists before the twentieth century. This is the structure called *quantum mechanics*. Figure 38.12 shows how the model of the atom has evolved over time.

think!

What fundamental force dictates the size of an atom?
Answer: 38.7

CONCEPT CHECK What determines the radii of the electron orbits in the Bohr model of the atom?

A QUANTUM MECHANIC!

38.8 Quantum Physics

The more that physicists studied the atom, the more convinced they became that the Newtonian laws that work so well for large objects such as baseballs and planets (in the "macroworld") simply do not apply to events in the microworld of the atom. Whereas in the macroworld the study of motion is called *mechanics,* or sometimes classical mechanics, the study of the motion of particles in the microworld of atoms and nuclei is called **quantum mechanics.** The branch of physics that is the general study of the microworld of photons, atoms, and nuclei is simply called **quantum physics.**

While one can be quite certain about careful measurements in the macroscopic world, there are fundamental uncertainties in the measurements of the atomic domain. For the measurement of macroscopic quantities, such as the temperature of materials, the vibrational frequencies of certain crystals, and the speeds of light and sound, there is no limit in practice to the accuracy with which the experimenter can measure. But subatomic measurements, such as the momentum and position of an electron or the mass of an extremely short-lived particle, are entirely different. In this domain, the uncertainties in many measurements are comparable to the magnitudes of the quantities themselves.

✅ **The subatomic interactions described by quantum mechanics are governed by laws of probability, not laws of certainty.** This notion is difficult for many people to accept. Even Einstein did not accept this.[38.8]

If you continue to study physics, you will likely encounter quantum mechanics some time in the future. Scientists and philosophers are still pondering the real meaning of quantum mechanics. It's a fascinating subject.

CONCEPT CHECK: What laws govern the interactions described by quantum mechanics?

38.9 Predictability and Chaos

When we know the initial conditions of an orderly system we can make predictions about it. For example, in the Newtonian macroworld, knowing with accuracy the initial conditions lets us state where a planet will be after a certain time, where a launched rocket will land, and when an eclipse will occur. In the quantum microworld, we can give odds where an electron is likely to be in an atom, and calculate the probability that a radioactive particle will decay in a given time interval.

✅ **Predictability in orderly systems, both Newtonian and quantum, depends on knowledge of initial conditions.**

Some systems, however, whether Newtonian or quantum, are not orderly—they are inherently unpredictable. These are called "chaotic systems." Turbulent water flow is an example. No matter how accurately we know the initial conditions of a piece of floating wood as it flows downstream, we cannot predict its location later downstream. A feature of chaotic systems is that slight differences in initial conditions result in wildly different outcomes later. Two identical pieces of wood just slightly apart from each other at one time are vastly far apart soon thereafter.

Weather is chaotic. Small changes in one day's weather can produce big (and largely unpredictable) changes a week later. Meteorologists try their best, but they are bucking the hard fact of chaos in nature. This barrier to good prediction first led the scientist Edward Lorenz to ask, "Does the flap of a butterfly's wings in Brazil set off a tornado in Texas?" Now we talk about the *butterfly effect* when we are dealing with situations where very small effects can amplify into very big effects.

CONCEPT CHECK What determines predictability in orderly systems?

Physics of Sports

Chaos on the Slopes

If you and a friend, sitting on snowboards at the top of a perfectly smooth ski slope, push off from positions close together with about the same velocity, you'll follow similar paths and end up near each other at the bottom of the slope. This is *orderly* behavior. Small differences in conditions at the beginning result in small differences in conditions at the end. But if the ski slope is full of hundreds of moguls (bumps) you'll likely find, after bouncing and jouncing down the slope, that you and your friend wind up many meters apart—no matter how close your initial conditions. This is *chaotic* behavior. Small differences in conditions at the beginning are

likely to result in large differences in conditions at the end—so much so that you can't predict where you'll end up.

Interestingly, chaos is not all hopeless unpredictability. If you and your friend compare notes after your rides down the moguled slope, you might find that you had some very similar experiences. Maybe you skirted around the sides of many moguls in just the same way. Maybe you never went straight over the top of a mogul. So there is *order in chaos*. Scientists have learned how to treat chaos mathematically and how to find the parts of it that are orderly.

38 REVIEW

Concept Summary ······

- Through the centuries there have been two primary models of light: the particle model and the wave model.

- The energy of a photon is directly proportional to the photon's frequency.

- The photoelectric effect suggests that light interacts with matter as a stream of particle-like photons.

- Light behaves like waves when it travels in empty space and like particles when it interacts with solid matter.

- De Broglie suggested that all matter could be viewed as having wave properties.

- According to de Broglie's theory of matter waves, electron orbits exist only where an electron wave closes in on itself in phase.

- The radii of the electron orbits in the Bohr model of the atom are determined by the amount of electric charge in the nucleus.

- The subatomic interactions described by quantum mechanics are governed by laws of probability, not by laws of certainty.

- Predictability in orderly systems, both Newtonian and quantum, depends on knowledge of initial conditions.

Key Terms ······

quantum (p. 768)

photon (p. 768)

Planck's constant (p. 768)

photoelectric effect (p. 769)

quantum mechanics (p. 776)

quantum physics (p. 776)

---

think!   Answers

38.3   Not necessarily. The answer is yes if electrons are ejected by the high-frequency light but not by the low-frequency light, because its photons do not have enough energy. If the light of both frequencies can eject electrons, then the number of electrons ejected depends on the brightness of the light, not on its frequency.

38.7   The electrical force.

38 ASSESS

Check Concepts ......

Section 38.1

1. What is a model? Give two examples for the nature of light.

Section 38.2

2. What is a quantum? Give two examples.

3. What is a quantum of light called?

4. What is Planck's constant, and how does it relate to the frequency and energy of a quantum of light?

5. Which has more energy per photon—red light or blue light?

Section 38.3

6. What is the photoelectric effect?

7. Why does violet light eject electrons from a certain photosensitive surface, whereas red light has no effect on that surface?

8. Will bright violet light eject more electrons than dim light of the same frequency?

9. Does the photoelectric effect support the particle model or the wave model of light?

Section 38.4

10. What causes light to behave like a particle?

Section 38.5

11. a. Do particles of matter have wave properties?
b. Who was the first physicist to give a convincing answer to this question?

12. As the speed of a particle increases, does its associated wavelength increase or decrease?

13. Does the diffraction of an electron beam support the particle model or the wave model of electrons?

Section 38.6

14. How does the energy of a photon compare with the difference in energy levels of the atom from which it is emitted?

15. What does it mean to say that an electron occupies discrete energy levels in an atom?

16. What does wave interference have to do with the electron energy levels in an atom?

17. Does the particle view of an electron or the wave view of an electron better explain the discreteness of electron energy levels? Why?

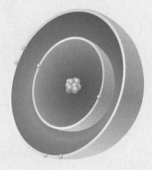

Section 38.7

18. Why is a helium atom smaller than a hydrogen atom?

19. Why are the heaviest elements not appreciably larger than the lightest elements?

Section 38.8

20. What is quantum mechanics?

21. Can the momenta and positions of electrons in an atom be measured with certainty?

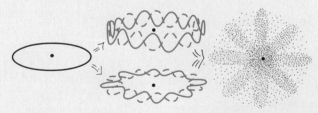

Section 38.9

22. What information is necessary to make predictions about an orderly system?

Think and Explain ......

23. What evidence can you cite for the wave nature of light? For the particle nature of light?

24. A very bright source of red light gives off much more energy than a dim source of blue light, but the red light has no effect in ejecting electrons from a certain photosensitive surface. Why is this so?

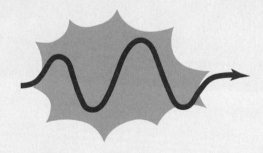

25. Why is it that for certain materials ultraviolet light induces the photoelectric effect and visible light does not?

26. Why does light striking a metal surface eject only electrons, not protons?

27. a. In the photoelectric effect, does brightness or frequency determine the kinetic energy of the ejected electrons?
b. Which determines the number of ejected electrons?

28. We speak of photons of red light and photons of green light. Can we speak of a single photon of white light? Why or why not?

29. Which laser beam carries more energy per photon—a red beam or a green beam?

30. Which photon has the most energy—one from infrared, visible, or ultraviolet light?

31. If a beam of red light and a beam of green light have exactly the same energy, which beam contains the greater number of photons?

32. If we double the frequency of light, we double the energy of each of its photons. If we instead double the wavelength of light, what happens to the photon energy?

33. Suntanning produces cell damage in the skin. Why is ultraviolet light capable of producing this damage while infrared radiation is not?

34. Electrons in one electron beam have a greater speed than those in another. Which electrons have the longer de Broglie wavelength?

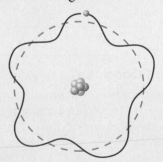

35. An electron and a proton travel at the same speed.
    a. Which has more momentum?
    b. Which has the longer wavelength?

36. Does the de Broglie wavelength of a proton become longer or shorter as its velocity increases?

37. We do not notice the wavelength of moving matter in our ordinary experience. Is this because the wavelength is extraordinarily large or extraordinarily small?

38. The equation $E = hf$ describes the energy of each photon in a beam of light. If Planck's constant, h, were larger, would photons of light of the same frequency be more energetic or less energetic?

39. When do photons behave like waves? When do they behave like particles?

40. A friend says, "If an electron is not a particle, then it must be a wave." What is your response? (Do you hear "either or" statements like this often?)

41. Why will helium leak through an inflated rubber balloon more readily than hydrogen will?

39° THE ATOMIC NUCLEUS AND RADIOACTIVITY

THE BIG IDEA : Certain elements radiate particles and turn into other elements.

From the time of the early Greek philosophers, atoms were thought to be the building blocks of matter. Atoms were considered eternal and indivisible. This idea changed in 1896 when the French physicist Henri Becquerel discovered that some unused photographic plates had been exposed by particles coming from a piece of uranium. Soon after, Pierre and Marie Curie discovered that certain elements radiate particles and turn into other elements. Investigators were introduced to what was then a new phenomenon—*radioactivity*.

Understanding how atoms can change requires looking deep into the structure of the atom—into the atomic nucleus.

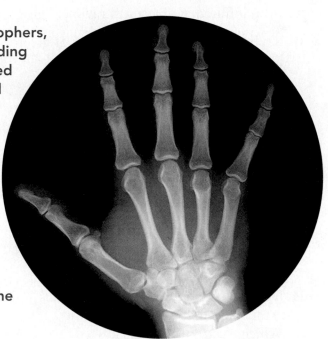

discover!

How Do You Model Exponential Growth and Decay?

1. Place a single stackable object, such as a domino, a paper cup, etc., on your desk.

2. Place a stack of two of the same objects to the right of the original object.

3. Repeat the process of creating stacks, each time doubling the number of objects in the stack. Continue the process until you have five stacks.

Analyze and Conclude

1. **Observing** Look for mathematical patterns in the array of stacked objects. For example, how does the number of objects in a given stack compare the to sum of objects in all the preceeding stacks?

2. **Predicting** Can you predict the total number of stacks you could create if you had 127 objects at your disposal?

3. **Making Generalizations** How can your array of objects be used to represent both growth and decay?

39.1 The Atomic Nucleus

It would take 30,000 carbon nuclei to stretch across a single carbon atom. The nucleus within the atom is as inconspicuous as a cookie crumb in the middle of the Rose Bowl football stadium. Despite the small size of the nucleus, much has been learned about its structure. The nucleus is composed of particles called **nucleons,** which when electrically charged are protons, and when electrically neutral are neutrons.[39.1] Neutrons and protons have close to the same mass, with the neutron's being slightly greater. Nucleons have nearly 2000 times the mass of electrons, so the mass of an atom is practically equal to the mass of its nucleus alone.

The positively charged protons in the nucleus hold the negatively charged electrons in their orbits. Each proton has exactly the same magnitude of charge as the electron, but the opposite sign. So in an electrically neutral atom, there are as many protons in the nucleus as there are electrons outside as shown in Figure 39.1. The number of protons in the nucleus therefore determines the chemical properties of that atom, because the positive nuclear charge determines the possible structures of electron orbits that can occur.

Radioactivity has been around since Earth's beginning.

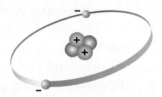

◀ **FIGURE 39.1**
The number of electrons that surround the atomic nucleus is matched by the number of protons in the nucleus.

The number of neutrons in the nucleus has no direct effect on the electron structure, and hence does not affect the chemistry of the atom. ✅ **The principal role of the neutrons in an atomic nucleus is to act as a sort of nuclear cement to hold the nucleus together.** Nucleons are bound together by an attractive nuclear force appropriately called the **strong force.**

The nuclear force of attraction is strong only over a very short distance, as shown in Figure 39.2. Whereas the electrical force between charges decreases as the inverse square of the distance, the nuclear force decreases far more rapidly. When two nucleons are just a few nucleon diameters apart, the nuclear force they exert on each other is nearly zero. This means that if nucleons are to be held together by the strong force, they must be held in a very small volume. Nuclei are tiny because the nuclear force is very short-range.

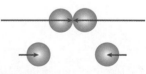

FIGURE 39.2 ▲
The nuclear strong force is a very short-range force. For nucleons very close or in contact, it is very strong (large force vectors). But a few nucleon diameters away it is nearly zero (small force vectors).

FIGURE 39.3 ▶

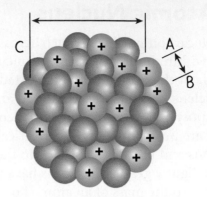

It is useful to imagine the protons and neutrons as small balls covered with hook-and-loop fasteners, some charged (protons) and some not (neutrons). Like the strong force, the hook and loop act between balls (nucleons) that are close to one another but have no effect on balls that are on the other side of the nucleus. Meanwhile, the electrical force acts as a repulsive force between protons that are not in direct contact with one another. The stability of any collection of nucleons is due to a tension between the strong force's tendency to hold the nucleus together and the electrical force's tendency to blow it apart. A nucleus needs a certain balance of neutrons and protons for stability.

It is an interesting feature of quantum mechanics that particles held close together have large kinetic energy and tend to fly apart. So, although the nuclear force is strong, it is only barely strong enough to hold a pair of nucleons together. For a pair of protons, which repel each other electrically, the nuclear force is not quite strong enough to keep them together. When neutrons are present, however, the attractive strong force is increased relative to the repulsive electric force (since neutrons have no charge). Thus, the presence of neutrons adds to the nuclear attraction and keeps protons from flying apart.

The more protons there are in a nucleus, the more neutrons are needed to hold them together, as shown in Figure 39.3. For light elements, it is sufficient to have about as many neutrons as protons. For heavy elements, extra neutrons are required. The most common form of lead, for example, has 82 protons and 126 neutrons, or about one and a half times as many neutrons as protons. For elements with more than 83 protons, even the addition of extra neutrons cannot completely stabilize the nucleus.

CONCEPT CHECK What is the role of neutrons in the nucleus?

39.2 Radioactive Decay

One factor that limits how many stable nuclei can exist is the instability of neutrons. A lone neutron, such as the one in Figure 39.4, will decay into a proton plus an electron (and also an antineutrino, a tiny particle we will not discuss here). About half of a bunch of lone neutrons will decay in 11 minutes. Particles that decay by spontaneously emitting charged particles and energy are said to be **radioactive.**

Radioactivity inside atomic nuclei is governed by the mass–energy equivalence. Particles decay spontaneously only when their combined products have less mass after decay than before. The mass of a neutron is slightly greater than the total mass of a proton plus electron (and the antineutrino). So when a neutron decays, there is less mass after decay than before. Decay will not spontaneously occur for reactions where more mass results. The reverse reaction, a proton decaying into a neutron, can occur only with external energy input.

All elements heavier than bismuth (atomic number 83) decay in one way or another. Thus, these elements are radioactive. **Radiation** is the name given to the charged particles and energy emitted by an unstable nucleus or particle. ☑ **The atoms of radioactive elements emit three distinct types of radiation called *alpha particles*, *beta particles*, and *gamma rays*.** They are named after the first three letters of the Greek alphabet, α, β, and γ. Alpha particles have a positive electric charge, beta particles are negative, and gamma rays are electrically neutral. Beams of all three of these can be separated by putting a magnetic field across their path as shown in Figure 39.5.

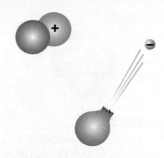

FIGURE 39.4 ▲

A neutron–proton combination is stable, but a neutron by itself is unstable and turns into a proton by emitting an electron (as well as an antineutrino—not shown).

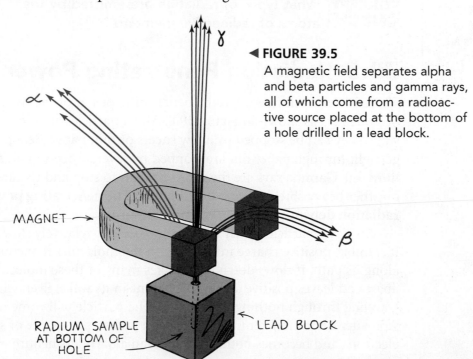

◀ **FIGURE 39.5**

A magnetic field separates alpha and beta particles and gamma rays, all of which come from a radioactive source placed at the bottom of a hole drilled in a lead block.

α

γ

β

MAGNET →

RADIUM SAMPLE AT BOTTOM OF HOLE

← LEAD BLOCK

FIGURE 39.6 ▲
An alpha particle contains two protons and two neutrons bound together and is identical to a helium nucleus.

An alpha particle is made of two protons and two neutrons and is identical to the nucleus of a helium atom, as shown in Figure 39.6. A beta particle is simply an electron ejected from the nucleus when a neutron is transformed into a proton. It may seem that the electrons are "buried" inside the neutron, but this is not true. An electron does not exist in a neutron any more than a spark exists inside a rock about to be scraped across a rough surface. The electron that pops out of the neutron, like the spark that pops out of the scraped rock, is produced during an interaction.

FIGURE 39.7 ▶
A gamma ray is simply electromagnetic radiation, much higher in frequency and energy per photon than light and X-rays.

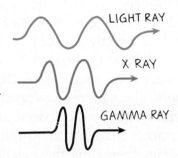

A gamma ray is massless energy. Like visible light, gamma rays are simply photons, but of much higher frequency and energy, as shown in Figure 39.7. Visible light is emitted when electrons jump from one atomic orbit to another of lower energy. Gamma rays are emitted when nucleons do a similar sort of thing inside the nucleus. There are great energy differences in nuclear energy levels, so the photons (gamma rays) emitted carry a large amount of energy.

CONCEPT CHECK : What types of radiation are emitted by the atoms of radioactive elements?

think!

The electric force of repulsion between the protons in a heavy nucleus acts over a greater distance than the attractive forces among the neutrons and protons in the nucleus. Given this fact, explain why all of the very heavy elements are radioactive. *Answer: 39.2*

39.3 Radiation Penetrating Power

There is a great difference in the penetrating power of the three types of radiation, as shown in Figure 39.8. Alpha particles are the easiest to stop. They can be stopped by a few sheets of thin paper. Beta particles go right through paper but are stopped by several sheets of aluminum foil. Gamma rays are the most difficult to stop and require lead or other heavy shielding to block them. ☑ **The penetrating power of radiation depends on its speed and its charge.**

An alpha particle is easy to stop because it is relatively slow and its double-positive charge interacts with the molecules it encounters along its path. It slows down as it shakes many of these molecules apart and leaves positive and negative ions in its wake. Even when traveling through nothing but air, an alpha particle will come to a stop after only a few centimeters. It soon grabs up a couple of stray electrons and becomes nothing more than a harmless helium atom.

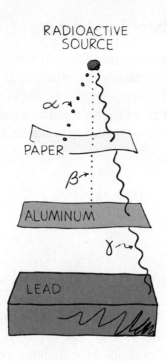

RADIOACTIVE SOURCE

α

PAPER

β

ALUMINUM

γ

LEAD

◄ FIGURE 39.8
Alpha particles penetrate least and can be stopped by a few sheets of paper; beta particles by a sheet of aluminum; gamma rays by a thick layer of lead.

A beta particle normally moves at a faster speed than an alpha particle, carries only a single negative charge, and is able to travel much farther through the air. Most beta particles lose their energy during the course of a large number of glancing collisions with atomic electrons. Except for rare direct hits, energy is lost in many small steps. Beta particles slow down until they reach the speeds of thermal motion, becoming a part of the material they are in, like any other electron.

Gamma rays are the most penetrating of the three because they have no charge. With no electrical attraction or deflection, a gamma ray photon interacts with the absorbing material only via a direct hit with an atomic electron or a nucleus. Unlike charged particles, a gamma ray photon can be removed from its beam in a single encounter. Dense materials such as lead are good absorbers mainly because of their high electron density.

Once alpha and beta particles are slowed by collisions, they become harmless. Alpha particles combine with electrons to become helium atoms.

CONCEPT CHECK: What factors determine the penetrating power of radiation?

think!

Pretend you are given three radioactive cookies—one alpha, one beta, and the other gamma. Pretend that you must eat one, hold one in your hand, and put the other in your pocket. Which would you eat, hold, and pocket, if you were trying to minimize your exposure to radiation?
Answer: 39.3

39.4 Radioactive Isotopes

In a neutral atom, the number of protons in the nucleus determines the number of electrons surrounding the nucleus. If there is a difference in the number of electrons and protons, the atom is charged and is called an *ion*. An ionized atom is one that has a different number of electrons than nuclear protons, as shown in Figure 39.9.

FIGURE 39.9 ▶
Of these three atoms, only the middle one has a net charge and is an ion.

The number of neutrons in the nucleus, however, has no bearing on the number of electrons the atom may have. This means that the number of neutrons has no direct bearing on the chemistry of an atom. Let's consider a hydrogen atom. The common form of hydrogen has a bare proton as its nucleus. Any nuclear configuration that has only one proton in its nucleus *is* hydrogen—by definition. There can be different kinds, or *isotopes*, of hydrogen, however, because there can be different numbers of neutrons in the nucleus. An **isotope** is a form of an element having a particular number of neutrons in the nuclei of its atoms. ☑ **Isotopes of an element are chemically identical but differ in the number of neutrons.** In one isotope of hydrogen, the nucleus consists of only a single proton. In a second isotope of hydrogen, the proton is accompanied by a neutron. In a third isotope of hydrogen, there are two neutrons. All the isotopes of hydrogen are chemically identical. The orbital electrons are affected only by the positive charge in the nucleus, not by its neutrons.

We distinguish between the different isotopes of hydrogen with the symbols $_1^1H$, $_1^2H$, and $_1^3H$. The lower number in each notation is the **atomic number** or the number of protons. The upper number is the **atomic mass number** or the total number of nucleons in the nucleus. You can see how this works for helium in Figure 39.10.

FIGURE 39.10 ▶
The atomic number is equal to the number of protons in the nucleus, and the atomic mass number is equal to the number of nucleons in the nucleus (both protons and neutrons).

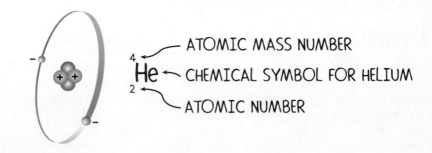

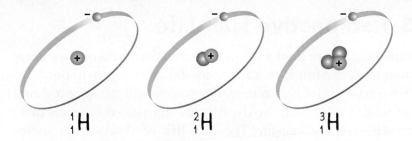

FIGURE 39.11 ▲
The three isotopes of hydrogen have different numbers of neutrons in the nucleus. Each nucleus has a single proton that holds a single orbital electron, which, in turn, determines the chemical properties of the atom. The varying number of neutrons changes the mass of the atom, but not its chemical properties.

The common isotope of hydrogen, $_1^1 H$, is a stable element. So is the isotope $_1^2 H$, called *deuterium.* "Heavy water" is the name usually given to H_2O in which the H's are deuterium atoms. The triple-weight hydrogen isotope $_1^3 H$, called *tritium,* however, is unstable and undergoes beta decay. This is the radioactive isotope of hydrogen. All three are shown in Figure 39.11. All elements have isotopes. Some are radioactive and some are not. All the isotopes of elements above atomic number 83, however, are radioactive.

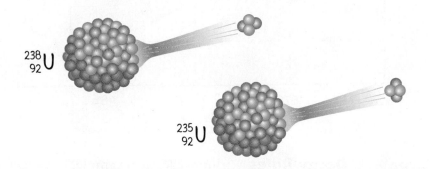

◄ **FIGURE 39.12**
All isotopes of uranium are unstable and undergo radioactive decay.

The common isotope of uranium is $_{92}^{238} U$, or U-238 for short. It has 92 protons and 146 neutrons in its nucleus. It is radioactive, but with a smaller decay rate than $_{92}^{235} U$, or U-235, with 92 protons and 143 neutrons in its nucleus. Any nucleus with 92 protons is uranium, by definition. Nuclei with 92 protons but different numbers of neutrons are simply different isotopes of uranium, as shown in Figure 39.12.

CONCEPT : **How are the isotopes of an element similar?**
CHECK : **How do they differ?**

think!

The nucleus of beryllium-8, $_4^8Be$, undergoes a special kind of radioactive decay: it splits into two equal halves. What nuclei are the products of this decay? Why is this a form of alpha decay?
Answer: 39.4

39.5 Radioactive Half-Life

Since some radioactive nuclei are more stable than others, they decay at different rates. A sample of a relatively stable isotope will decay slowly, whereas a sample of an unstable isotope will decay in a shorter period of time. The radioactive decay rate is measured in terms of a characteristic time, the *half-life*. The **half-life** of a radioactive material is the time needed for half of the radioactive atoms to decay.

FIGURE 39.13 ▶

Every 1620 years the amount of radium decreases by half.

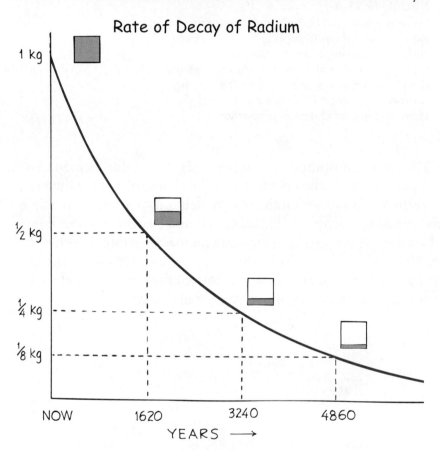

Graphing Decay Rates Radium-226, for example, has a half-life of 1620 years. This means that half of any given specimen of Ra-226 will have undergone decay by the end of 1620 years, as shown in Figure 39.13. In the next 1620 years, half of the remaining radium decays, leaving only one-fourth the original number of radium atoms. The rest are converted, by a succession of disintegrations, to lead. After 20 half-lives, an initial quantity of radioactive atoms will be diminished to about one-millionth of the original quantity.

The isotopes of some elements have a half-life of less than a millionth of a second, while U-238, for example, has a half-life of 4.5 billion years. Each isotope of a radioactive element has its own characteristic half-life.

The radioactive half-life of a material is also the time for its decay rate to reduce to half.

FIGURE 39.14 ▼
A variety of devices are used for radiation detection.
a. A Geiger counter detects incoming radiation by
its ionizing effect on enclosed gas in the tube.
b. Lab workers wear film badges to measure their
accumulated radiation exposure.

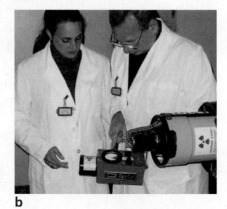

a   b

Constancy of Decay Rates ✅ Rates of radioactive decay appear to be absolutely constant, unaffected by any external conditions. High or low pressures, high or low temperatures, strong magnetic or electric fields, and even violent chemical reactions have no detectable effect on the rate of decay of an element. Any of these stresses, however severe by ordinary standards, is far too mild to affect the nucleus deep in the interior of the atom.

Measuring Decay Rates How do physicists measure radioactive half-lives? They cannot always do it by observing a specimen and waiting until the quantity decreases by half. This is often much longer than a human life span! One can determine, however, the number of atoms in a sample and the rate at which the sample decays. Figure 39.14 shows devices used for this purpose.

The half-life of an isotope is related to its rate of disintegration. In general, the shorter the half-life of a substance, the faster it disintegrates, and the more active is the substance. The half-life can be computed from the rate of disintegration, which can be measured in the laboratory.

CONCEPT CHECK : How do external conditions affect rates of radioactive decay?

think!

If a sample of a radioactive isotope has a half-life of 1 year, how much of the original sample will be left at the end of the second year? What happens to the rest of the sample?
Answer: 39.5

39.6 Natural Transmutation of Elements

⊘ **When a radioactive isotope undergoes alpha or beta decay, it changes to an isotope of a different element.** The changing of one element to another is called **transmutation.** Consider common uranium, for example. Uranium-238 has 92 protons and 146 neutrons. When an alpha particle is ejected, the nucleus loses two protons and two neutrons. (They make up the alpha particle that leaves.) The 90 protons and 144 neutrons left behind are the nucleus of a new element. This element is *thorium*. This reaction is expressed as the following equation.

$$^{238}_{92}U \rightarrow ^{234}_{90}Th + ^{4}_{2}He$$

Alpha Decay An arrow is used here to show that the $^{238}_{92}U$ changes into the other elements. When this happens, energy is released in three forms: gamma radiation, the kinetic energy of the alpha particle ($^{4}_{2}He$), and the kinetic energy of the thorium atom. Be sure to notice in the nuclear equation that the mass numbers at the top balance ($238 = 234 + 4$) and that the atomic numbers at the bottom also balance ($92 = 90 + 2$).

Beta Decay Thorium-234, the product of this reaction, is also radioactive. When it decays, it emits a beta particle, an electron ejected from the nucleus. When a beta particle is ejected, a neutron changes into a proton. In this case, the new nucleus then has 91 protons and is no longer thorium. It is the element *protactinium.* The reaction can be written as follows.[39.6.1]

$$^{234}_{90}Th \rightarrow ^{234}_{91}Pa + ^{0}_{-1}e$$

Note that although the atomic number has increased by 1 in this process, the mass number (number of nucleons) remains the same. Also note that the beta particle (electron) is written as $^{0}_{-1}e$. The −1 is the charge of the electron. The 0 indicates that its mass is insignificant when compared with the mass of the protons and neutrons that alone contribute to the mass number. Beta emission has hardly any effect on the mass of the nucleus; only the charge (atomic number) changes.

think!

Complete the following nuclear reactions.

a. $^{228}_{88}Ra \rightarrow ^{?}_{?}? + ^{0}_{-1}e$

b. $^{209}_{84}Po \rightarrow ^{205}_{82}Pb + ^{?}_{?}?$

Answer: 39.6.1

Transmutation and the Periodic Table As the example of uranium-238 decay shows, when an atom ejects an alpha particle from its nucleus, the mass number of the resulting atom decreases by 4, and its atomic number decreases by 2. The resulting atom belongs to an element two spaces back in the periodic table. (See Figure 17.12 on page 336.) When an atom ejects a beta particle from its nucleus, it loses no nucleons, so there is no change in mass number but its atomic number *increases* by 1.[39.6.2] The resulting atom belongs to an element one place forward in the periodic table. Thus, radioactive elements decay backward or forward in the periodic table. A radioactive nucleus may emit gamma radiation along with an alpha particle or a beta particle. Gamma emission has no effect on the mass number or the atomic number.

think!

What finally becomes of all the uranium-238 that undergoes radioactive decay?
Answer: 39.6.2

Radioactive Decay Series The radioactive decay of $^{238}_{92}U$ to an isotope of lead, $^{206}_{82}Pb$, is shown on the next page in Figure 39.15. The steps in the decay process are shown in the diagram, where each nucleus that plays a part in the series is shown by a burst. The vertical column that contains the burst shows the atomic number of the nucleus, and the horizontal row shows its mass number. Each arrow that slants downward toward the left shows an alpha decay. Each arrow that points to the right shows a beta decay. Notice that some of the nuclei in the series can decay either way. This is one of several similar radioactive series that occur in nature.

CONCEPT CHECK: How is the chemical identity of a radioactive isotope affected by alpha or beta decay?

Link to TECHNOLOGY

Smoke Detectors Thousands of homes each year are spared destruction in fires by smoke alarms that operate by radioactivity. A weak radioactive source, usually the transuranic element americium-241 (atomic number 95) detects the presence of smoke. Americium-241 undergoes alpha decay, according to the following equation.

$$^{241}_{95}Am \rightarrow ^{237}_{93}Np + ^{4}_{2}He$$

The alpha particles from the source hit air molecules in the chamber and eject electrons from them, creating ions that provide a small electric current. If smoke enters this chamber, the ions are disturbed and the current diminishes. Electronic sensors in the circuit detect this reduced current and sound the alarm. Radioactivity used for this purpose saves many lives. Because alpha particles have such a short range in air before becoming harmless helium, no radiation reaches you.

FIGURE 39.15 ▶
U-238 decays to Pb-206
through a series of alpha
and beta decays.

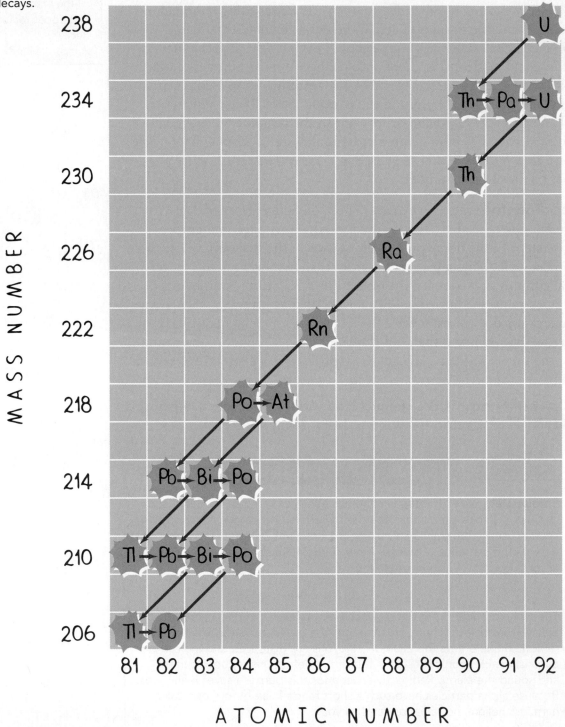

U-238 Radioactive Decay Series

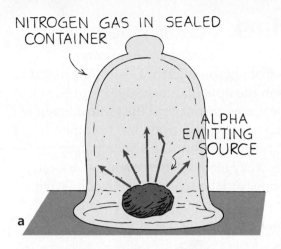

NITROGEN GAS IN SEALED CONTAINER

ALPHA EMITTING SOURCE

a

b

39.7 Artificial Transmutation of Elements

New Zealander Ernest Rutherford, in 1919, was the first physicist to succeed in artificially transmuting a chemical element. In a sealed container he bombarded nitrogen nuclei with alpha particles from a radioactive piece of ore, as shown in Figure 39.16a, and then found traces of oxygen and hydrogen that were not there before. Rutherford accounted for the presence of the oxygen and hydrogen with the nuclear equation

$$^{14}_{7}\text{N} + ^{4}_{2}\text{He} \rightarrow ^{17}_{8}\text{O} + ^{1}_{1}\text{H}$$

After Rutherford's experiment there followed many such nuclear reactions—first with natural bombarding particles from radioactive elements, and then with more energetic particles (mainly protons and alpha particles) hurled by giant atom-smashing particle accelerators, such as the one pictured in Figure 39.16b. Artificial transmutation is an everyday fact of life to the nuclear researchers of today.

☑ **The elements beyond uranium in the periodic table—the** *transuranic* **elements—have been produced through artificial transmutation.** All of these elements have half-lives that are much less than the age of Earth. Whatever transuranic elements might have existed naturally when Earth was formed have long since decayed.

CONCEPT : Which elements have been produced through
CHECK : artificial transmutation?

39.8 Carbon Dating

Earth's atmosphere is continuously bombarded by *cosmic rays*—mainly high-energy protons—from beyond Earth. This results in the transmutation of many atoms in the upper atmosphere. Protons, neutrons, and other particles are scattered throughout the atmosphere. Most of the protons quickly capture stray electrons and become hydrogen atoms in the upper atmosphere, but the neutrons keep going for long distances because they have no charge and do not interact electrically with matter. Sooner or later many of them collide with the nuclei of atoms in the lower atmosphere. If they are captured by the nucleus of a nitrogen atom, the following reaction can take place:

$$^{14}_{7}N + ^{1}_{0}n \rightarrow ^{14}_{6}C + ^{1}_{1}H$$

In this reaction, when nitrogen-14 is hit by a neutron ($^{1}_{0}n$), carbon-14 and hydrogen are produced.

Most of the carbon that exists on Earth is the stable $^{12}_{6}C$, carbon-12. In the air, it appears mainly in the compound carbon dioxide. Because of the cosmic bombardment, less than one-millionth of 1% of the carbon in the atmosphere is carbon-14. Like carbon-12, it joins with oxygen to form carbon dioxide, which is taken in by plants. This means that all plants have a tiny bit of radioactive carbon-14 in them. All animals eat plants (or eat plant-eating animals), and therefore have a little carbon-14 in them. All living things contain some carbon-14. The ratio of carbon-14 to carbon-12 in living things is the same as the ratio of carbon-14 to carbon-12 in the atmosphere.

Carbon-14 is a beta emitter and decays back into nitrogen by the following reaction:[39.8]

$$^{14}_{6}C \rightarrow ^{14}_{7}N + ^{0}_{-1}e$$

In a living plant, which continues to take in carbon dioxide, a radioactive equilibrium is reached where there is a fixed ratio of carbon-14 to carbon-12. But when a plant or animal dies, it stops taking in carbon-14 from the environment. Then the percentage of carbon-14 decreases—at a known rate. The longer an organism has been dead, the less carbon-14 that remains. ✓ **Scientists can figure out how long ago a plant or animal died by measuring the ratio of carbon-14 to carbon-12 in the remains.**

The half-life of carbon-14 is 5730 years. This means that half of the carbon-14 atoms that are now present in the remains of a body, plant, or tree will decay in the next 5730 years. Half the remaining carbon-14 atoms will then decay in the following 5730 years, and so forth. The radioactivity of once-living things therefore gradually decreases at a predictable rate as shown in Figure 39.17.

22,920 years ago   17,190 years ago   11,460 years ago   5730 years ago   Present

   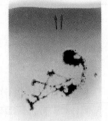 

Archeologists use the carbon-14 dating technique to establish the dates of wooden artifacts and skeletons. Because of fluctuations in the production of carbon-14 through the centuries (due partly to changes in Earth's magnetic field and the consequent changes in the cosmic ray intensity), this technique gives an uncertainty of about 15%. This means, for example, that a mastodon bone that is dated to be 10,000 years old may really be only 8500 years old on the low side, or 11,500 years old on the high side. For many purposes this is an acceptable level of uncertainty. If greater accuracy is desired, then other techniques must be employed.

FIGURE 39.17 ▲
The radioactive carbon isotopes in the skeleton diminish by one-half every 5730 years. The red arrows symbolize relative amounts of carbon-14.

CONCEPT CHECK: How can scientists determine the age of carbon-containing artifacts?

think!

An archeologist extracts a gram of carbon from an ancient bone and measures between 7 and 8 beta emissions per minute from the sample. A gram of carbon extracted from a fresh piece of bone gives off 15 betas per minute. Estimate the age of the ancient bone.

Now suppose the carbon sample from the ancient bone were found to be only one-fourth as radioactive as a gram of carbon from new bone. Estimate the age of the ancient bone.
Answer: 39.8

NEW SAMPLE AT 15 COUNTS/MIN

OLD SAMPLE AT 7 COUNTS/MIN

Archeologist

We know about animals and plants that lived thousands of years ago thanks to the work of archeologists. An archeologist is a person who studies ancient cultures. Archeologists act as detectives as they sift through artifacts, or remnants, of homes, tools, and living things in order to figure out what life was like in bygone times.

To find out how old an artifact is, archeologists use carbon-14 dating. An archeologist understands that this works only for artifacts that were once living and that are less than 50,000 years old. Archeologists work for government and university research facilities as well as for museums and privately funded organizations.

39.9 Uranium Dating

Carbon-14 dating works only on things that were once alive. ✅ **The dating of very old, nonliving things is accomplished with radioactive minerals, such as uranium.** The naturally occurring isotopes U-238 and U-235 decay very slowly and ultimately become isotopes of lead—but not the common lead isotope Pb-208. For example, U-238 decays through several stages to finally become Pb-206, whereas U-235 finally becomes the isotope Pb-207. Most of the lead isotopes 206 and 207 that exist were at one time uranium. The older the uranium-bearing rock, the higher the percentage of these lead isotopes.

From the half-lives of the uranium isotopes and the percentage of lead isotopes in uranium-bearing rock, you can calculate when the rock was formed. Rocks dated in this way have been found to be as much as 3.7 billion years old. Samples from the moon, where there has been less obliteration of early rocks than on Earth, have been dated at 4.2 billion years. This is "only" 400 million years short of the well-established 4.6-billion-year age of Earth and the solar system.

One ton of ordinary granite contains about 9 grams of uranium and 20 grams of thorium. Basalt rocks contain 3.5 and 7.7 grams of the same.

CONCEPT CHECK How do scientists date very old, nonliving things?

39.10 Radioactive Tracers

Radioactive isotopes of the elements have been produced by bombarding the elements with neutrons and other particles. These isotopes are inexpensive, quite available, and very useful in scientific research and industry. ✅ **Scientists can analyze biological or mechanical processes using small amounts of radioactive isotopes as tracers.**

For example, agricultural researchers mix a small amount of radioactive isotopes with fertilizer before applying it to growing plants. Once the plants are growing, the amount of fertilizer taken up by the plant can be easily measured with radiation detectors. From such measurements, researchers can tell farmers the proper amount of fertilizer to use.

Tracers are used in medicine to study the process of digestion and the way in which chemicals move about in the body. Food containing a tiny amount of a radioactive isotope is fed to a patient. The paths of the tracers in the food are then followed through the body with a radiation detector. Figure 39.18 shows tracers being used in both agriculture and medicine.

Engineers study how parts of an automobile test engine wear away by making the cylinder walls in the engine radioactive. While the engine is running, the piston rings rub against the cylinder walls. The tiny particles of radioactive metal that are worn away fall into the lubricating oil, where they can be measured with a radiation detector. This test is repeated with different oils. In this way the engineer can determine which oil gives the least wear and longest life to the engine.

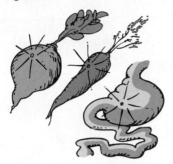

FIGURE 39.18 ▼
Radioactive isotopes are used to check the action of fertilizers in plants and the progress of food in digestion.

◀ **FIGURE 39.19**
The shelf life of fresh strawberries and other perishables is markedly increased when the food is subjected to gamma rays from a radioactive source.

There are hundreds more examples of the use of radioactive isotopes. For example, radioactive isotopes can prevent food from spoiling quickly, as shown in Figure 39.19. The strawberries on the right were treated with gamma radiation, which kills the microorganisms that normally lead to spoilage. The food is only a receiver of radiation and is in no way transformed into an emitter of radiation, as can be confirmed with a radiation detector. Radioactive isotopes can also be used to trace leaks in pipes, as shown in Figure 39.20. This technique provides a way to detect and count atoms in quantities too small to be seen with a microscope and too small to be hazardous.[39.10]

CONCEPT CHECK : How can scientists use radioactive isotopes to analyze biological or mechanical processes?

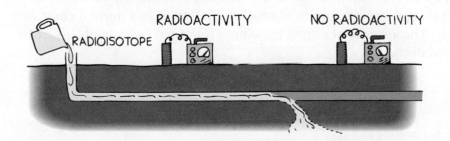

◀ **FIGURE 39.20**
Radioactive isotopes can be used to track pipe leaks.

39.11 Radiation and You

Radioactivity has been around longer than humans have. It is as much a part of our environment as the sun and the rain. It is what warms the interior of Earth and makes it molten. In fact, radioactive decay inside Earth is what heats the water that spurts from a geyser or that wells up from a natural hot spring. Even the helium in a child's balloon is the result of radioactivity. Its nuclei are nothing more than alpha particles that were once shot out of radioactive nuclei.

As Figure 39.21 shows, most radiation you encounter originates in nature. ☑ **Sources of natural radiation include cosmic rays, Earth minerals, and radon in the air.** Radiation is in the ground you stand on, and in the bricks and stones of surrounding buildings. Even the cleanest air we breathe is slightly radioactive. This natural background radiation was present before humans emerged in the world. If our bodies couldn't tolerate it, we wouldn't be here.

FIGURE 39.21 ▶

The pie chart shows origins of radiation exposure for an average individual in the United States.

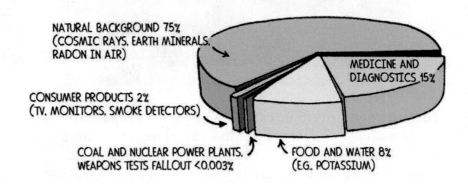

NATURAL BACKGROUND 75%
(COSMIC RAYS, EARTH MINERALS, RADON IN AIR)

MEDICINE AND DIAGNOSTICS 15%

CONSUMER PRODUCTS 2%
(TV, MONITORS, SMOKE DETECTORS)

COAL AND NUCLEAR POWER PLANTS, WEAPONS TESTS FALLOUT <0.003%

FOOD AND WATER 8% (E.G., POTASSIUM)

An average ton of coal contains 1.3 grams of uranium and 3.2 grams of thorium. That's why the average coal-burning power plant is a far greater source of airborne radioactive material than a nuclear power plant.

Cosmic Rays Much of the radiation we are exposed to is cosmic radiation streaming down through the atmosphere. Most of the protons and other atomic nuclei that fly toward Earth from outer space are deflected away. The atmosphere, acting as a protective shield, stops most of the rest. But some cosmic rays penetrate the atmosphere, mostly in the form of secondary particles such as muons. At higher altitudes, radiation is more intense. In Denver, the "mile-high city," you receive more than twice the cosmic radiation you receive at sea level. A couple of round-trip flights between New York and San Francisco exposes you to as much radiation as in a normal chest X-ray. The air time of airline personnel is limited because of this extra radiation.

Neutrinos We are bombarded most by what harms us least—neutrinos. Neutrinos are the most weakly interacting of all particles. They have near-zero mass, no charge, and are produced frequently in radioactive decays. They are the most common high-speed particles known, zapping the universe, and passing unhindered through our bodies by the billions every second. It would take a "piece" of lead 6 light-years in thickness to absorb half the neutrinos incident upon it. About once per year on the average, a neutrino triggers a nuclear reaction in your body. We don't hear much about neutrinos because they ignore us.

Gamma Rays Of the types of radiation we have focused upon in this chapter, gamma radiation is by far the most dangerous. It emanates from radioactive materials and makes up a substantial part of the normal background radiation. Exposure to gamma radiation should be minimized. The cells of living tissue are composed of intricately structured molecules in a watery, ion-rich brine. When gamma radiation encounters this highly ordered soup, it produces damage on the atomic scale. These altered molecules are often more harmful than useful to life processes. Altered DNA molecules, for example, can produce harmful genetic mutations.

Radiation Safety Cells can repair most kinds of molecular damage if the radiation they are exposed to is not too intense. This is how we are able to tolerate small radiation doses. On the other hand, people who work around high concentrations of radioactive materials must be specially trained and protected to avoid an increased risk of cancer. This applies to medical people, workers in nuclear power plants, and personnel on nuclear-powered ships. People who receive high doses of radiation (on the order of 1000 times natural background or more) run a greater risk of cancer and have a shorter life expectancy than people who are not so exposed.

Whenever possible, exposure to radiation should be avoided, as indicated by the sign in Figure 39.22. Unavoidable, however, is the natural background radiation that all living beings have always absorbed.

Go Online

SciLINKS NSTA

For: Links on radioactivity
Visit: www.SciLinks.org
Web Code: csn – 3911

FIGURE 39.22 ▼
This is the internationally used symbol to indicate an area where radioactive material is being handled or produced.

CONCEPT CHECK What are sources of natural radiation?

REVIEW

Go Online

For: Self-Assessment
Visit: PHSchool.com
Web Code: csa – 3900

PHSchool.com

Concept Summary ······

- The neutrons in an atomic nucleus hold the nucleus together.
- Radioactive elements emit *alpha* particles, *beta* particles, and *gamma* rays.
- The penetrating power of radiation depends on its speed and its charge.
- Isotopes of an element differ in the number of neutrons.
- Rates of radioactive decay appear to be absolutely constant.
- When an isotope undergoes alpha or beta decay, it changes to a different element.
- Elements beyond uranium have been produced through artificial transmutation.
- Scientists can figure out how long ago a plant or animal died by measuring the ratio of carbon-14 to carbon-12.
- The dating of very old things is accomplished with radioactive minerals.
- Scientists use radioactive isotopes as tracers.
- Sources of natural radiation include cosmic rays, Earth minerals, and radon.

Key Terms ······

nucleons (*p. 783*)
strong force (*p. 783*)
radioactive (*p. 785*)
radiation (*p. 785*)
isotope (*p. 788*)

atomic number (*p. 788*)
atomic mass number (*p. 788*)
half-life (*p. 790*)
transmutation (*p. 792*)

think! Answers

39.2 In a large nucleus, where protons such as those on opposite sides are far apart, electrical repulsion can exceed nuclear attraction. This instability makes all the heaviest atoms radioactive.

39.3 Ideally, of course, get as far from the cookies as possible. But if you must, then hold the alpha; the skin on your hand will shield you. Put the beta in your pocket; your clothing will likely shield you. Eat the gamma; it will penetrate your body anyway. (In real life always use appropriate safeguards when near radioactive materials.)

39.4 When beryllium-8 splits into equal halves, a pair of nuclei with 2 protons and 2 neutrons are created. These are nuclei of helium-4, $^4_2$He, also called alpha particles. So this reaction is a form of alpha decay.

39.5 One-quarter of the original sample will be left. The three-quarters that underwent decay became other elements.

39.6.1 a. $^{228}_{88}$Ra $\rightarrow$ $^{228}_{89}$Ac $+$ $^{0}_{-1}e$

b. $^{209}_{84}$Po $\rightarrow$ $^{205}_{82}$Pb $+$ $^{4}_{2}$He

39.6.2 All the uranium-238 will ultimately become lead. On the way to becoming lead, it will exist as a series of other elements, as indicated in Figure 39.15.

39.8 Since beta emission for the first old sample is one-half that of the fresh sample, about one half-life has passed, 5730 years. In the second case, the ancient bone is two half-lives of carbon-14 or about 11,460 years old.

 **ASSESS**

Check Concepts ......

Section 39.1

1. Which of the following are nucleons—protons, neutrons, or electrons?

2. Do electrical forces tend to hold a nucleus together or push it apart?

3. Between what kinds of particles does the nuclear strong force act?

4. Which force has a longer range, the electric force or the strong force?

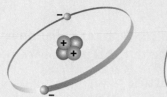

Section 39.2

5. When is a neutron unstable?

6. Distinguish among alpha particles, beta particles, and gamma rays.

Section 39.3

7. How do the penetrating powers of the three types of radiation compare?

Section 39.4

8. Distinguish between an ion and an isotope.

9. How does the number of electrons in a normal atom compare with the number of protons in its nucleus?

10. Which isotope has the greater number of neutrons, U-235 or U-238?

Section 39.5

11. What is meant by radioactive half-life?

12. If the radioactive half-life of a certain isotope is 1620 years, how much of that substance will be left at the end of 1620 years? After 3240 years?

Section 39.6

13. When an atom undergoes radioactive decay, does it become a completely different element?

14. a. What happens to the atomic number of an atom when it ejects an alpha particle?
    b. What happens to its atomic mass number?

15. a. What happens to the atomic number of an atom when it ejects a beta particle?
    b. What happens to its atomic mass number?

16. a. What element does thorium become if it emits an alpha particle?
    b. What if it emits a beta particle?

Section 39.7

17. a. What is a transuranic element?
    b. Why are there no ore deposits of transuranic elements on Earth?

Section 39.8

18. Which is radioactive, C-12 or C-14?

19. Why is more C-14 found in new bones than in ancient bones of the same mass?

20. Why would the carbon dating method be useless in dating old coins but not old pieces of adobe bricks?

Section 39.9

21. Why are there deposits of lead in all deposits of uranium ore?

22. What isotopes accumulate in old, uranium-bearing rock?

Section 39.10

23. What is a radioactive tracer?

Section 39.11

24. From where does most of the radiation you encounter originate?

25. Why is radiation more intense at high altitudes and near Earth's poles?

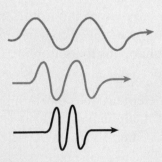

Think and Rank ••••••

Rank each of the following sets of scenarios in order of the quantity or property involved. List them from left to right. If scenarios have equal rankings, then separate them with an equal sign. (e.g., A = B)

26. Rank these three types of radiation by their ability to penetrate this page of your book:

   (A) Alpha particle

   (B) Beta particle

   (C) Gamma ray

27. Consider the following nuclei:

   (A) Th-233   (B) U-235   (C) U-238

   a. Rank these nuclei by the number of protons in the nucleus.
   b. Rank them by the number of neutrons in the nucleus.
   c. Rank them by the number of electrons that surround them.

28. Consider the following.

   (A) oxygen atom

   (B) negative fluorine ion

   (C) sulfur atom

   (D) positive sodium ion

   a. Rank these by the number of protons in the nucleus.
   b. Rank them by the number of neutrons in the nucleus.
   c. Rank them by the number of electrons that surround them.

29. Consider two 100-gram samples of radium-226 and uranium-238. Rank by the amount left of each.

    (A) radium after 1620 years

    (B) uranium after 2 half-lives

    (C) radium after 3 half-lives

    (D) uranium after 1 half-life

30. Consider these four isotopes.

    (A) Th-234 undergoes beta decay.

    (B) U-238 undergoes alpha decay.

    (C) Pa-234 undergoes beta decay.

    (D) U-234 undergoes alpha decay.

    a. Rank the isotopes by the atomic number of the final product.
    b. Rank the isotopes by the atomic mass of the final product.

Think and Explain • • • • •

31. Is radioactivity in the world something relatively new? Defend your answer.

32. In the nineteenth century, the famous physicist Lord Kelvin made measurements of heat transfer in Earth's crust and estimated Earth's age to be very much less than the present estimate. What information did Kelvin not have that might have allowed him to avoid making his erroneous estimate?

33. What experimental evidence indicates that radioactivity is a process that occurs in the atomic nucleus?

34. You and your friend journey to the mountain foothills to get closer to nature and to escape such things as radioactivity. While bathing in the warmth of a natural hot spring, your friend wonders aloud how the spring gets its heat. What is your response?

35. Does your body contain more neutrons than protons? More protons than electrons? Discuss.

36. Can it be truthfully said that, whenever a nucleus emits an alpha or beta particle, it necessarily becomes the nucleus of a different element?

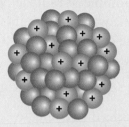

37. Why are the atomic masses of many elements in the periodic table not whole numbers?

38. How do the atomic number and atomic mass of an atom change when a proton is added to its nucleus? When a neutron is added? Which determines the chemical nature of the element?

39. What do different isotopes of a given element have in common? How are they different?

40. Why are alpha and beta rays deflected in opposite directions in a magnetic field? Would they be deflected in opposite directions in an electric field? Why are gamma rays undeflected in either field?

41. When an alpha particle leaves the nucleus, would you expect it to speed up? Defend your answer.

42. Why does an alpha particle deflect less than a beta particle in a magnetic field?

43. Exactly what is a positively charged hydrogen atom?

44. Some people say that all things are possible. Is it at all possible for a hydrogen nucleus to emit an alpha particle? Defend your answer.

45. Why is a sample of radioactive material always a little warmer than its surroundings? Why is the center of Earth so hot?

46. Why do different isotopes of the same element have the same chemical properties?

47. A friend asks if a radioactive substance with a half-life of 1 day will be entirely gone at the end of 2 days. What is your answer?

48. Coal contains minute quantities of radioactive materials, and in fact there is more total radiation outside a coal-fired power plant than outside a fission power plant. What does this tell you about the shielding that typically surrounds these power plants?

49. When we speak of dangerous radiation exposure, are we generally speaking of alpha radiation, beta radiation, or gamma radiation? Discuss.

50. When food is irradiated with gamma rays from a cobalt-60 source, does the food become radioactive? Defend your answer.

51. When the isotope bismuth-213 emits an alpha particle, it becomes a new element.
    a. What are the atomic number and atomic mass number of the new element?
    b. What element results if bismuth-213 emits a beta particle instead?

52. a. State the numbers of neutrons and protons in each of the following nuclei: $^{6}_{3}Li$, $^{14}_{6}C$, $^{56}_{26}Fe$, $^{201}_{80}Hg$, and $^{239}_{94}Pu$.
    b. How many electrons will typically surround each of these nuclei?

53. Your friend Art uses a Geiger counter to check the local background radiation. It ticks. Your other friend, Bart, who normally fears most that which is understood least, makes an effort to keep away from the region of the Geiger counter. Art asks Bart if he'd avoid a thermometer to stay cool on a hot day. Bart looks to you for advice. What do you say?

54. What element results when radium-226 decays by alpha emission? What is the atomic mass of this element?

55. How is it possible for an element to decay "forward in the periodic table"—that is, to an element of higher atomic number?

56. Elements with atomic numbers greater than that of uranium do not exist in any appreciable amounts in nature because they have short half-lives. Yet there are several elements with atomic numbers smaller than that of uranium that have equally short half-lives and that do exist in appreciable amounts in nature. How can you account for this?

57. People working around radioactivity wear film badges to monitor their radiation exposure. These badges are small pieces of photographic film enclosed in a lightproof wrapper. What kind of radiation do these devices monitor?

58. A friend says that the helium used to inflate balloons is a product of radioactive decay. Another friend disagrees. With whom do you agree?

59. The age of the Dead Sea Scrolls was found by carbon dating. Could this technique work if they were instead stone tablets? Explain.

Think and Solve ......

60. If a sample of radioactive material has a half-life of one week, how much of the original sample will be left at the end of the second week? The third week? The fourth week?

61. A product of nuclear power plants is the isotope cesium-137, which has a half-life of 30 years. How long will it take for this isotope to decay to one-sixteenth its original amount?

62. A radioisotope is placed near a radiation detector, which registers 80 counts per second. Eight hours later, the detector registers five counts per second. What is the isotope's half-life?

63. Radiation from a point source follows an inverse-square law. If a Geiger counter that is 1 m away from a small source reads 100 counts per minute, what will be its reading 2 m from the source? 3 m from it?

64. Cobalt-60 undergoes beta decay. Show that the beta decay of cobalt-60 ($_{27}^{60}$Co) results in nickel-60 ($_{28}^{60}$Ni).

65. When a target of oxygen-16 ($_{8}^{16}$O) is bombarded with protons, a target nucleus can absorb a proton and then eject an alpha particle. Show that the target material then contains nitrogen-13 ($_{7}^{13}$N).

66. Radon-212 ($_{86}^{212}$Rn) is a radioactive gas with a half-life of 24 minutes. Show that when radon-212 undergoes alpha decay, the isotope polonium-208 is formed ($_{84}^{208}$Po).

67. Uranium-238 absorbs a neutron and then emits a beta particle. Show that the result is neptunium-239.

Activity ......

68. Write a letter to a friend and explain that you've learned that radioactivity has been a part of nature from the beginning of time. Explain its benefits and its dangers, and how common sense can minimize radiation dangers.

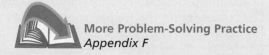

More Problem-Solving Practice
Appendix F

40 NUCLEAR FISSION AND FUSION

 **THE BIG IDEA** : Nuclear fission and nuclear fusion reactions release huge amounts of energy.

In 1939, just at the beginning of World War II, a nuclear reaction was discovered that released much more energy per atom than previously known reactions, and had the potential to be used for both explosions and power production. This was the splitting of the atom, or *nuclear fission.*

A very different nuclear reaction, *nuclear fusion*, involves joining two small nuclei together to produce a larger nucleus, and can also release huge amounts of energy. Both nuclear fission and nuclear fusion produce vastly more energy per kilogram of matter than any chemical reaction, and even more than most other nuclear reactions. The awesome release of this energy in atomic and hydrogen bombs ushered in the present "nuclear age." Out of the ashes of despair brought about by these bombs, hope grew that atoms could be used for peaceful purposes—that the energy of nuclear reactions could be used for domestic power instead of arsenals of war.

discover!

How Can You Model Nuclear Reactions?

1. Dip one of the two circular frames provided in a bubble solution and blow a bubble.
2. Catch the bubble between two circular frames.
3. Slowly move the frames apart until the single bubble separates into two bubbles.
4. After producing bubbles in both frames, slowly bring the frames together until the bubbles merge into a single bubble.

Analyze and Conclude

1. **Observing** Provide a thorough description of the bubbles you produced in Steps 3 and 4.
2. **Predicting** What do you think would happen if you were to carry out Steps 3 and 4 more rapidly?
3. **Making Generalizations** How do you think the actions of the bubbles in this activity might be used to explain the processes of nuclear fission and fusion?

40.1 Nuclear Fission

Biology students know that living tissue grows by the division of cells. The splitting in half of living cells is called *fission*. In a similar way, the splitting of atomic nuclei is called **nuclear fission.**

Nuclear fission involves the delicate balance between the attraction of nuclear strong forces and the repulsion of electrical forces within the nucleus. In all known nuclei the nuclear strong forces dominate. In uranium, however, this domination is tenuous. If the uranium nucleus is stretched into an elongated shape, as shown in Figure 40.1, the electrical forces may push it into an even more elongated shape. ✓ **Nuclear fission occurs when the repelling electrical forces within a nucleus overpower the attracting nuclear strong forces.**

The absorption of a neutron by a uranium nucleus supplies enough energy to cause such an elongation. The resulting fission process may produce many different combinations of smaller nuclei. A typical example is shown in Figure 40.2. The energy that is released by the fission of one U-235 atom is enormous—about seven million times the energy released by the explosion of one TNT molecule. This energy is mainly in the form of kinetic energy of the fission fragments, with some energy given to ejected neutrons, and the rest to gamma radiation.

FIGURE 40.1 ▼
Nuclear deformation leads to fission when repelling electrical forces dominate over attracting nuclear forces.

THE NUCLEAR FORCE IS DOMINANT

CRITICAL DEFORMATION

THE ELECTRICAL FORCE IS DOMINANT

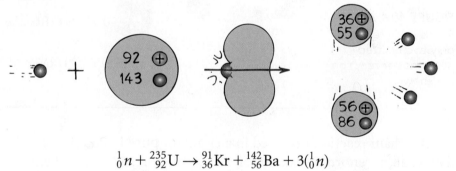

$$^1_0n + ^{235}_{92}U \rightarrow ^{91}_{36}Kr + ^{142}_{56}Ba + 3(^1_0n)$$

◀ FIGURE 40.2
In a typical example of nuclear fission, one neutron starts the fission of the uranium atom and three more neutrons are produced when the uranium fissions.

Chain Reaction Note that one neutron starts the fission of the uranium atom, and, in the example shown in Figure 40.2, three more neutrons are produced when the uranium fissions. Between two and three neutrons are produced in most nuclear fission reactions. These new neutrons can, in turn, cause the fissioning of two or three other nuclei, releasing from four to nine more neutrons. If each of these succeeds in splitting just one atom, the next step in the reaction will produce between 8 and 27 neutrons, and so on. This makes a chain reaction. A **chain reaction** is a self-sustaining reaction in which one reaction event stimulates one or more additional reaction events to keep the process going.

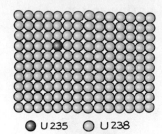

FIGURE 40.3 ▲

Only 1 part in 140 of naturally occurring uranium
is U-235.

Why do chain reactions not occur in naturally occurring uranium
ore deposits? They would if all uranium atoms fissioned so easily.
Fission occurs mainly for the rare isotope U-235. As Figure 40.3
shows, only 0.7%, or 1 part in 140, of the uranium in pure uranium
metal is U-235. When the prevalent isotope U-238 absorbs neutrons
from fission, it does not undergo fission. So a chain reaction can be
snuffed out by the neutron-absorbing U-238. It is rare for uranium
deposits in nature to spontaneously undergo a chain reaction. A
model of a chain reaction is shown in Figure 40.4.

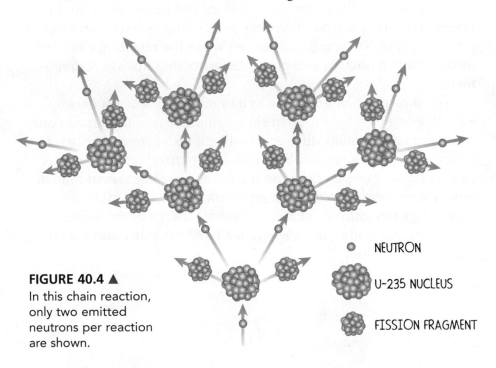

NEUTRON

U-235 NUCLEUS

FISSION FRAGMENT

FIGURE 40.4 ▲

In this chain reaction,
only two emitted
neutrons per reaction
are shown.

If a chain reaction occurred in a chunk of pure U-235 the size of
a baseball, an enormous explosion would likely result. If the chain
reaction were started in a smaller chunk of pure U-235, however, no
explosion would occur. Why? Because a neutron ejected by a fission
event travels a certain average distance through the material before
it encounters another uranium nucleus and triggers another fission
event. If the piece of uranium is too small, as in Figure 40.5a, a neutron is likely to escape through the surface before it "finds" another
nucleus. On the average, fewer than one neutron per fission will be
available to trigger more fission, and the chain reaction will die out.
As Figure 40.5b shows, in a bigger piece a neutron can move farther
through the material before reaching a surface. Then more than one
neutron from each fission event, on the average, will be available to
trigger more fission. The chain reaction will build up to enormous
energy.[40.1]

think!

Five kilograms of U-235
broken up into small
separated chunks is sub-
critical, but if the chunks
are put together in a ball
shape, it is supercritical.
Why?
Answer: 40.1

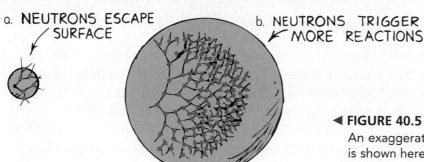

a. NEUTRONS ESCAPE SURFACE

b. NEUTRONS TRIGGER MORE REACTIONS

◀ FIGURE 40.5

An exaggerated view of a chain reaction is shown here. **a.** In a small piece of pure U-235, the chain reaction dies out. **b.** In a larger piece, a chain reaction builds up.

Critical Mass The **critical mass** is the amount of mass for which each fission event produces, on the average, one additional fission event. It is just enough to "hold even." A *subcritical* mass is one in which the chain reaction dies out. A *supercritical* mass is one in which the chain reaction builds up explosively.

In Figure 40.6 there are two pieces of pure U-235, each of them subcritical. Neutrons readily reach a surface and escape before a sizable chain reaction builds up. But if the pieces are joined together, there will be more distance available for neutron travel and a greater likelihood of their triggering fission before escaping through the surface. If the combined mass is supercritical, we have a nuclear fission bomb. A simplified diagram of an idealized uranium fission bomb is shown in Figure 40.7.

The construction of a uranium fission bomb is not a formidable task. The difficulty is separating enough U-235 from the more abundant U-238. It took Manhattan Project scientists and engineers more than two years to extract enough U-235 from uranium ore to make the bomb that was detonated over Hiroshima in 1945. Uranium isotope separation is still a difficult, expensive process today.

SHORT PATH THROUGH EACH PIECE

LONGER PATH

FIGURE 40.6 ▲

Each piece is subcritical because a neutron is likely to escape. When the pieces are combined, there is less chance that a neutron will escape. The combination may be supercritical.

CONCEPT CHECK What causes nuclear fission?

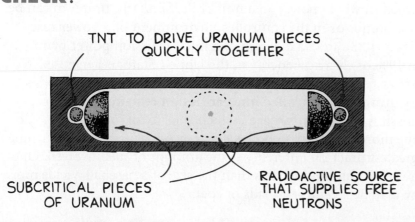

TNT TO DRIVE URANIUM PIECES QUICKLY TOGETHER

SUBCRITICAL PIECES OF URANIUM

RADIOACTIVE SOURCE THAT SUPPLIES FREE NEUTRONS

◀ FIGURE 40.7

A simplified diagram of an uranium fission bomb is shown here. (In an actual "gun-type" weapon, only one of the two pieces of uranium is fired toward the other one, which is the "target.")

40.2 Uranium Enrichment

Uranium-235 undergoes fission when it absorbs a neutron, but uranium-238 normally doesn't. ⊘ **In order to sustain a chain reaction in uranium, the sample used must contain a higher percentage of U-235 than occurs naturally.** Since atoms U-235 and U-238 are virtually identical chemically, they cannot be separated by a chemical reaction. They must be separated by physical means. *Gaseous diffusion* offers a way. Industrial-scale separation of the two isotopes takes advantage of the difference in their masses. For a given temperature, heavier molecules move more slowly on average than lighter ones.

Gaseous diffusion uses uranium hexafluoride (UF_6) gas. Molecules of the gas with U-235 move faster than molecules with U-238. The gas initially entering the chamber is 0.7% U-235. These lighter molecules hit the diffusion membrane on average 0.4% more often than any given molecule with U-238. So the gas leaving the chamber is ever-so-slightly enriched in the U-235 isotope. It requires passing the gas through thousands of interconnected stages to end up with uranium sufficiently enriched in the U-235 isotope for it to be used in a power reactor (3% U-235) or a bomb (U-235 > 90%).

A newer method of isotope separation involves gas centrifuges. The uranium hexafluoride gas is spun at high speed. The lighter molecules with U-235 tend toward the center of the centrifuge. The slightly enriched gases at the center are collected and sent forward to another centrifuge. It may require thousands of stages before the uranium is sufficiently enriched to be used as fuel.

CONCEPT CHECK What is necessary to sustain a chain reaction?

40.3 The Nuclear Fission Reactor

A liter of gasoline can be used to make a violent explosion. Or it can be burned slowly to power an automobile. Similarly, uranium can be used for bombs or in the controlled environment of a power reactor. Figure 40.8 shows a diagram of a nuclear fission power plant. About 19% of electrical energy in the United States is generated by nuclear fission reactors. ⊘ **A nuclear fission reactor generates energy through a controlled nuclear fission reaction.** These reactors are simply nuclear furnaces, which (like fossil fuel furnaces) do nothing more elegant than boil water to produce steam for a turbine. The greatest practical difference is the amount of fuel involved. One kilogram of uranium fuel, less than the size of a baseball, yields more energy than 30 freight-car loads of coal.

Components of a Fission Reactor A reactor contains three main components: the nuclear fuel combined with a moderator, the control rods, and water. The nuclear fuel is uranium, with its fissionable isotope U-235 enriched to about 3%. The moderator may be graphite, a pure form of carbon, or it may be water. Because the U-235 is so highly diluted with U-238, an explosion like that of a nuclear bomb is not possible. Control rods that can be moved in and out of the reactor control the "multiplication" of neutrons, that is, how many neutrons from each fission event are available to trigger additional fission events. The control rods are made of a material (usually the metal cadmium or the metalloid boron) that readily absorbs neutrons. Heated water around the nuclear fuel is kept under high pressure and thus brought to a high temperature without boiling. It transfers heat to a second, lower-pressure water system, which operates the electric generator in a conventional fashion.

think!

What would happen if a nuclear reactor had no control rods?
Answer: 40.3

Figure 40.8 shows one of many reactor designs for this growing technology.

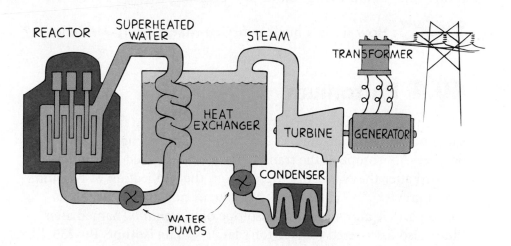

FIGURE 40.8 ▲
A nuclear fission power plant converts nuclear energy to electrical energy.

Waste Products of Fission A major drawback to fission power is the generation of radioactive waste products of fission. Recall that light atomic nuclei are most stable when composed of equal numbers of protons and neutrons, and that heavy nuclei need more neutrons than protons for stability. So there are more neutrons than protons in uranium—143 neutrons compared with 92 protons in U-235, for example. When uranium fissions into two medium-weight elements, the ratio of neutrons to protons in the product nuclei is greater than for medium-weight stable nuclei. These fission products are radioactive. Safely disposing of these waste products requires special storage casks and procedures. It is a developing technology.

American policy has been to look for ways to deeply bury radio-active wastes, but many nuclear scientists argue that "spent" nuclear fuel should first be treated in ways to derive value from it or make it less hazardous, before what is left over is finally buried. A concept called the Integral Fast Reactor, studied in the 1990s (but never built), would derive additional energy from what is now waste and reduce the chance of diversion of spent fuel to weapons. Other devices are being researched that convert long-life isotopes to ones of shorter half-life. Rather than deeply burying nuclear wastes, for many years the French have been tending and monitoring them in under-ground storage facilities. Just as the tailings of gold mines and other mines were considered worthless a century ago but are today being reworked for their commercial value, so it may well be for today's radioactive wastes. If these wastes are kept where they are accessible, it may turn out that they can be modified to be less of a danger to future generations than is thought at present.

CONCEPT CHECK How does a nuclear fission reactor generate energy?

40.4 Plutonium

When a neutron is absorbed by a U-238 nucleus, no fission results. The nucleus that is created, U-239, emits a beta particle instead and becomes an isotope of the transuranic element called *neptunium* (named after the planet discovered from the application of Newton's law of gravity).[40.4] This isotope, Np-239, in turn, very soon emits a beta particle and becomes an isotope of *plutonium* (named after Pluto, also discovered via Newton's law). ☑ **The isotope, Pu-239, like U-235, will undergo fission when it captures a neutron.** Figure 40.9 demonstrates how neutron absorption in U-238 leads to the production of Pu-239.

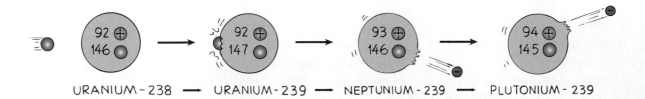

URANIUM-238 ⟶ URANIUM-239 ⟶ NEPTUNIUM-239 ⟶ PLUTONIUM-239

FIGURE 40.9 ▲
After U-238 absorbs a neutron, it emits a beta particle (and an antineutrino, not shown). The atom is no longer uranium, but neptunium. After the neptunium atom emits a beta particle, it becomes plutonium.

The half-life of neptunium-239 is only 2.3 days, while the half-life of plutonium-239 is about 24,000 years. Since plutonium is an element distinct from uranium, it can be separated from uranium by ordinary chemical methods. Unlike the difficult process of separating U-235 from U-238, it is relatively easy to separate plutonium from uranium.

The element plutonium is chemically a poison in the same sense as are lead and arsenic. It attacks the nervous system and can cause paralysis. Death can follow if the dose is sufficiently large. Fortunately, plutonium does not remain in its elemental form for long because it rapidly combines with oxygen to form three compounds, PuO, PuO_2, and Pu_2O_3, all of which are chemically relatively benign. They will not dissolve in water or in biological systems. These plutonium compounds do not attack the nervous system and have been found to be biologically harmless.

Plutonium in any form, however, is radioactively toxic. It is more toxic than uranium, although less toxic than radium. Pu-239 emits high-energy alpha particles, which kill cells rather than simply disrupting them and leading to mutations. Interestingly enough, damaged cells rather than dead cells contribute to cancer, which is why plutonium ranks low as a cancer-producing substance. The greatest danger that plutonium presents to humans is its potential for use in nuclear fission bombs. Its usefulness is in breeder reactors.

As part of its normal operation, any nuclear power plant converts some of its U-238 to Pu-239.

CONCEPT CHECK What happens when Pu-239 captures a neutron?

Physics on the Job

Nuclear Power Plant Technician Around the world, nuclear power plants use the energy of nuclear fission to produce electricity. While this process has many advantages, such as the reduction of pollution, it also has serious risks. The possibility of an accident in which radioactive materials are released into the environment makes the job of a nuclear power plant technician especially important. Nuclear power plant technicians are employed at every nuclear power plant facility. They must have a solid understanding of the process of nuclear fission and chain reactions as well as the properties of radioactive materials. Nuclear power plant technicians monitor the processes at the power plant and are trained to recognize problems and to follow containment procedures immediately in the event of an emergency.

FIGURE 40.10 ▶
Pu-239, like U-235, undergoes fission when it cap-
tures a neutron.

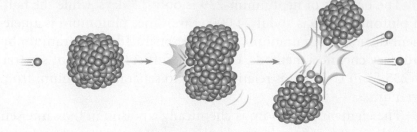

40.5 The Breeder Reactor

When small amounts of Pu-239 are mixed with U-238 in a reactor, the fissioning of plutonium liberates neutrons that convert the abundant, nonfissionable U-238 into more of the fissionable Pu-239. This process, modeled in Figure 40.10, not only produces useful energy, it also "breeds" more fission fuel. A reactor with this fuel is a breeder reactor. A **breeder reactor** is a nuclear fission reactor that produces more nuclear fuel than it consumes. ⊘ **A breeder reactor converts a non-fissionable uranium isotope into a fissionable plutonium isotope.** Using a breeder reactor is like filling a gas tank in a car with water, adding some gasoline, then driving the car, and having more gasoline after the trip than at the beginning, at the expense of common water! After the initial high costs of building such a device, this is an economical method of producing vast amounts of energy. After a few years of operation, breeder-reactor power utilities breed twice as much fuel as they start with.

Fission power has several benefits. First, it supplies plentiful electricity. Second, it conserves the many billions of tons of coal, oil, and natural gas that every year are literally turned to heat and smoke, and which in the long run may be far more precious as sources of organic molecules than as sources of heat. Third, it eliminates the megatons of sulfur oxides and other poisons that are put into the air each year by the burning of these fuels. Very important, it produces no carbon dioxide or other greenhouse gases that can contribute to global warming.

The drawbacks include the problems of storing radioactive wastes, the production of plutonium and the danger of nuclear weapons proliferation, low-level release of radioactive materials into the air and groundwater, and the risk of an accidental (or terrorist-caused) release of large amounts of radioactivity.

Reasoned judgment is not made by considering only the benefits or the drawbacks of fission power. You must also compare nuclear fission to alternate power sources. All power sources have a drawback of some kind. Fission power is a subject of much debate.

Know nukes before you say, "No nukes!"

CONCEPT CHECK: What is the function of a breeder reactor?

Airport Scanners Ion-mobility mass spectrometers are used at airports for scanning luggage and passengers. After you check in for a flight, security personnel will often swab your luggage with a small disk of paper. The paper is then placed in a device that heats it enough to expel vapors. Molecules in the vapor are ionized by exposure to beta radiation. Most of the molecules exposed become positive ions, whereas nitrogen-rich molecules characteristic of explosives become negative ions. The negative ions drift against a flow of air toward a positively charged detector. The heavier the negative ion, the longer it will take to reach the detector. In a body scan, a person stands momentarily in an enclosed region where puffs of air impinge on the body. The air is then analyzed by the same technique.

40.6 Mass–Energy Equivalence

The key to understanding why a great deal of energy is released in nuclear reactions has to do with the equivalence of mass and energy. Recall from our study of relativity in Chapter 16 that mass and energy are essentially the same—they are two sides of the same coin. Mass is like a super storage battery. It stores energy—vast quantities of energy—that can be released if and when the mass decreases.

FIGURE 40.11 ▲
Work is required to pull a nucleon from an atomic nucleus. This work goes into mass energy.

Mass Energy If you stacked up 238 bricks, the mass of the stack would be equal to the sum of the masses of the bricks. Is the mass of a U-238 nucleus equal to the sum of the masses of the 238 nucleons that make it up? Like so much ruled by relativity, the answer isn't obvious. To find the answer, we consider the work that would be required to separate all the nucleons from a nucleus.

Recall that work, which transfers energy, is equal to the product of force and distance. Imagine that you can reach into a U-238 nucleus and, pulling with a force even greater than the attractive nuclear force, remove one nucleon. That would require considerable work as shown in the cartoon in Figure 40.11. Then keep repeating the process until you end up with 238 nucleons, stationary and well separated. What happened to all the work done? You started with one stationary nucleus containing 238 particles and ended with 238 separate stationary particles. The work done shows up as *mass* energy. The separated nucleons have a total mass greater than the mass of the original nucleus. The extra mass, multiplied by the square of the speed of light, is exactly equal to your energy input: $\Delta E = \Delta mc^2$.

$E = mc^2$ says that mass and energy are two sides of the same coin.

Binding Energy One way to interpret this mass change is to say that a nucleon inside a nucleus has less mass than its rest mass outside the nucleus. How much less depends on which nucleus. The mass difference is related to the "binding energy" of the nucleus. For uranium, the mass difference is about 0.7%, or 7 parts in a thousand. The 0.7% reduced nucleon mass in uranium indicates the binding energy of the nucleus, or how much work it would take to disassemble the atom into individual nucleons.

The standard nucleus by which others are compared is carbon-12, which has a mass of exactly 12.00000 units.[40.6] In these units, a proton outside the nucleus has a mass of 1.00728, a neutron has a mass of 1.00866, and an electron has a mass of 0.00055. The masses of the pieces that make up the carbon atom—6 protons, 6 neutrons, and 6 electrons—add up to 12.0989, about 0.8% more than the mass of a C-12 atom. That difference indicates the binding energy of the C-12 nucleus. We will see shortly that binding energy per nucleon is greatest in the nucleus of iron.

FIGURE 40.12 ▶

In a mass spectrometer, ions of a fixed speed are directed into the semicircular "drum," where they are swept into semicircular paths by a strong magnetic field. Heavier ions are swept into curves of larger radii than lighter ions.

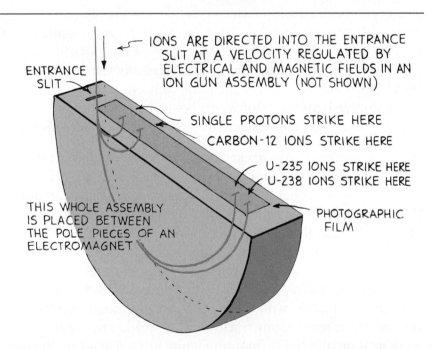

think!

If you know the mass of a particular nucleus, how do you calculate the mass per nucleon?

Answer: 40.6

Measuring Nuclear Mass The masses of ions of isotopes of various elements can be accurately measured with a *mass spectrometer*. A diagram of a mass spectrometer is shown in Figure 40.12. This important device uses a magnetic field to deflect ions into circular arcs. The ions entering the device all have the same speed. The greater the inertia (mass) of the ion, the more it resists deflection, and the greater the radius of its curved path. In this way the nuclear masses can be compared as the magnetic force sweeps heavier ions into larger arcs and lighter ions into smaller arcs.

A graph of the nuclear masses for the elements from hydrogen through uranium is shown in Figure 40.13. The graph slopes upward with increasing atomic number as expected—elements are more massive as atomic number increases. The slope curves slightly because there are proportionally more neutrons in the more massive atoms.

Nuclear Mass per Nucleon A more important graph is shown in Figure 40.14. This graph results from the plot of nuclear mass *per nucleon* from hydrogen through uranium. To obtain the nuclear mass per nucleon, simply divide the nuclear mass by the number of nucleons in the particular nucleus. (If you divided the mass of your whole class by the number of people in your class, you would get the average mass per person.) The graph indicates the different average effective masses of nucleons in atomic nuclei. A proton has the greatest mass when it is the nucleus of a hydrogen atom. None of the proton's mass is binding energy—it isn't bound to anything. Progressing beyond hydrogen, the masses of nucleons in heavier nuclei are effectively smaller. The low point of the graph occurs at the element iron. This means that pulling apart an iron nucleus would take more work per nucleon than pulling apart any other nucleus. Iron holds its nucleons more tightly than any other nucleus does. Beyond iron, the average effective mass of nucleons increases. For elements lighter than iron and heavier than iron, the binding energy per nucleon is less than it is in iron.

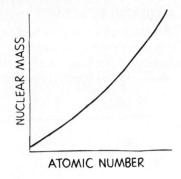

FIGURE 40.13 ▲
A graph that shows how nuclear mass increases with increasing atomic number. The curvature is somewhat exaggerated.

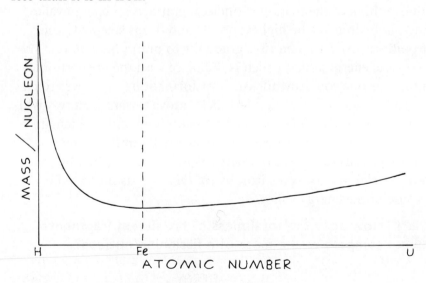

FIGURE 40.14 ▲
The graph shows that the mass per nucleon is greatest for the lightest nuclei, the least for iron, and has an intermediate value for the heaviest nuclei. (The vertical scale covers only about 1% of the mass of a nucleon.)

FIGURE 40.15 ▶

The mass of a uranium nucleus is greater than the combined masses of the fission fragments (including any ejected neutrons).

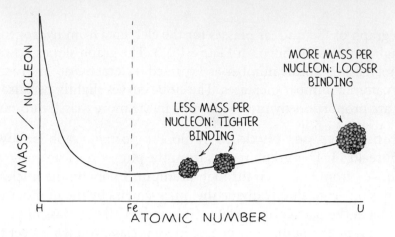

For energy release, Lose Mass is the name of the game—any game.

Figure 40.15 shows why energy is released when a uranium nucleus is split into nuclei of lower atomic number. If a uranium nucleus splits in two, the masses of the fission fragments lie about halfway between uranium and hydrogen on the horizontal scale of the graph. Note that the mass per nucleon in the fission fragments is *less than* the mass per nucleon when the same set of nucleons are combined in the uranium nucleus. When this decrease in mass is multiplied by the speed of light squared, it is equal to the energy yielded by each uranium nucleus that undergoes fission. ✅ **During fission, the total mass of the fission fragments (including the ejected neutrons) is less than the mass of the fissioning nucleus.** The missing mass is equivalent to the energy released.

You can think of the mass-per-nucleon graph as an energy valley that starts at hydrogen (the highest point) and drops steeply to the lowest point (iron), and then rises gradually to uranium. Iron is at the bottom of the energy valley, which is the place with the greatest binding energy per nucleon. Any nuclear transformation that moves nuclei toward iron releases energy. Heavier nuclei move toward iron by dividing—nuclear fission. A drawback is the fission fragments, which are radioactive because of their greater-than-normal number of neutrons.

A more promising source of energy is to be found when lighter-than-iron nuclei move toward iron by *combining*—as indicated on the left side of the energy valley.

CONCEPT CHECK: How does the total mass of the fission fragments compare to the mass of a fissioning nucleus?

FIGURE 40.16 ▶

The difference in the mass of a heavy nucleus and its fission fragments is the energy released in the fission process.

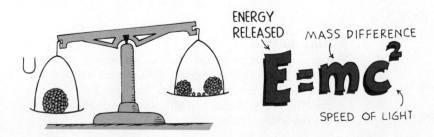

40.7 Nuclear Fusion

Inspection of the graph of Figure 40.14 will show that the steepest part of the energy hill is from hydrogen to iron. Energy is released as light nuclei *fuse*, or combine, rather than split apart. This process, in which the nuclei of light atoms fuse, is **nuclear fusion.** Nuclear fusion is the opposite of nuclear fission. Whereas energy is released when heavy nuclei split apart in the fission process, in nuclear fusion energy is released when light nuclei fuse together. ✅ **After fusion, the total mass of the light nuclei formed in the fusion process is less than the total mass of the nuclei that fused.** As the graph in Figure 40.17a shows, a proton has more mass by itself than it does inside a helium nucleus.

Atomic nuclei are positively charged. For fusion to occur, they normally must collide at very high speed in order to overcome electrical repulsion. The required speeds correspond to the extremely high temperatures found in the center of the sun and other stars. Fusion brought about by high temperatures is called **thermonuclear fusion** —that is, the welding together of atomic nuclei by high temperature. In the hot central part of the sun, approximately 657 million tons of hydrogen are converted into 653 million tons of helium each second. The missing 4 million tons of mass is discharged as radiant energy. Such reactions are, quite literally, nuclear burning.

think!

First it was stated that nuclear energy is released when atoms split apart. Now it is stated that nuclear energy is released when atoms combine. Is this a contradiction?
Answer: 40.7

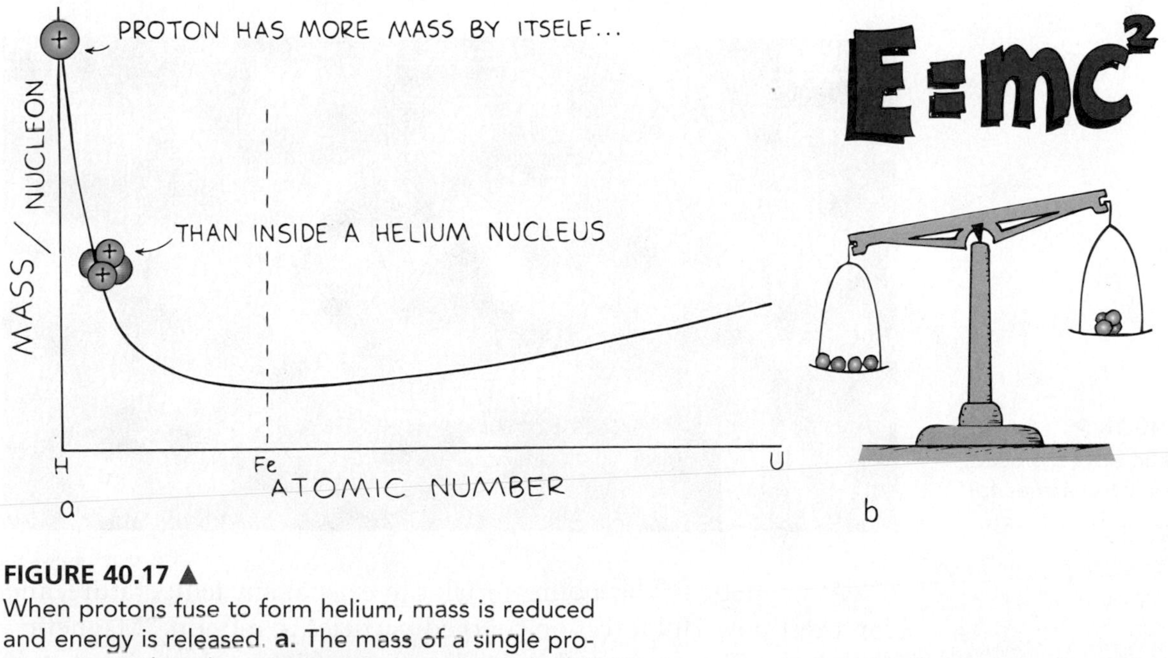

FIGURE 40.17 ▲
When protons fuse to form helium, mass is reduced and energy is released. **a.** The mass of a single proton is more than the mass per nucleon in a helium-4 nucleus. **b.** Two protons and two neutrons have more total mass when they are free than when they are combined in a helium nucleus.

The most important graphs in this book are shown in Figures 40.14, 40.15, and 40.17, which reveal the energy of the atomic nucleus—a primary source of energy in the universe.

Thermonuclear fusion is analogous to ordinary chemical combustion. In both chemical and nuclear burning, a high temperature starts the reaction; the release of energy by the reaction maintains a high enough temperature to spread the fire. The net result of the chemical reaction is a combination of atoms into more tightly bound molecules. In nuclear reactions, the net result is more tightly bound nuclei. The difference between chemical and nuclear burning is essentially one of scale.

CONCEPT CHECK : How does the total mass of the products of fusion compare to the the mass of the nuclei that fused?

40.8 Controlling Nuclear Fusion

⊘ **Producing thermonuclear fusion reactions under controlled conditions requires temperatures of hundreds of millions of degrees.** Producing and sustaining such high temperatures along with reasonable densities is the goal of much current research. There are a variety of techniques for attaining high temperatures. No matter how the temperature is produced, a problem is that all materials melt and vaporize at the temperatures required for fusion. One solution to this problem is to confine the reaction in a nonmaterial container. The magnetic bottle shown in Figure 40.18 is an example of a nonmaterial container.

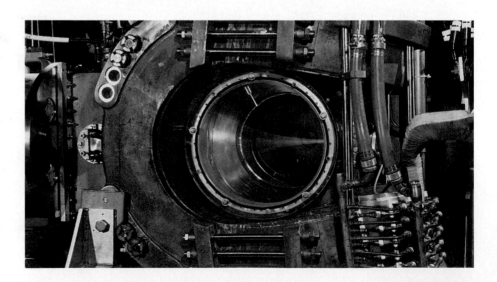

FIGURE 40.18 ▶

A magnetic bottle is used for containing plasmas for fusion research.

A magnetic field is nonmaterial, can exist at any temperature, and can exert powerful forces on charged particles in motion. "Magnetic walls" of sufficient strength provide a kind of magnetic straitjacket for hot ionized gases called *plasmas*. Magnetic compression further heats the plasma to fusion temperatures.

At a temperature of about a million degrees, some nuclei are moving fast enough to overcome electrical repulsion and slam together, but the energy output is much smaller than the energy used to heat the plasma. Even at 100 million degrees, more energy must be put into the plasma than will be given off by fusion. At about 350 million degrees, the fusion reactions will produce enough energy to be self-sustaining. At this *ignition temperature,* nuclear burning yields a sustained power output without further input of energy. A steady feeding of nuclei is all that is needed to produce continuous power.

The State of Fusion Research Fusion has already been achieved in several devices, but instabilities in the plasma have thus far prevented a sustained reaction. A big problem is devising a field system that will hold the plasma in a stable and sustained position while an ample number of nuclei fuse. A variety of magnetic confinement devices are the subject of much present-day research.

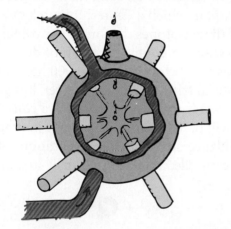

◀ **FIGURE 40.19**
In fusion with multiple laser beams, pellets of frozen deuterium are rhythmically dropped into synchronized laser crossfire.

Another promising approach bypasses magnetic confinement altogether with high-energy lasers. As Figure 40.19 shows, one technique is to aim an array of laser beams at a common point and drop solid pellets composed of frozen hydrogen isotopes through the synchronous crossfire. According to plan, the resulting heat will be carried off by molten lithium to produce steam. Figure 40.20 shows the pellet chamber at Lawrence Livermore Laboratory.

Other fusion schemes involve the bombardment of fuel pellets not by laser light but by beams of electrons, light ions, and heavy ions.

As this book goes to press, nations in Europe, China, India, Japan, Korea, the Russian Federation, and the United States have agreed to build an international fusion research center to develop nuclear fusion as a practical energy source. We are still looking forward to the great "Break-Even Day" when one of the variety of fusion schemes will sustain a yield of at least as much energy as is required to initiate it.

Fusing hydrogen releases less energy per nucleus than fissioning uranium. But since there are more atoms in a gram of hydrogen than in a gram of uranium, gram for gram, fusion releases more energy.

FIGURE 40.20 ▲

In the pellet chamber at Lawrence Livermore Laboratory, the laser source is Nova, the most powerful laser in the world, which directs 10 beams into the target region.

A Potential Energy Source Fusion power is nearly ideal. Fusion reactors cannot become "supercritical" and get out of control because fusion requires no critical mass. Furthermore, there is no air pollution because the only product of the thermonuclear combustion is helium (good for children's balloons). Except for some radioactivity in the inner chamber of the fusion device because of high-energy neutrons, the by-products of fusion are not radioactive. Disposal of radioactive waste is not a major problem.

As Figure 40.21 shows, the fuel for nuclear fusion is hydrogen—in particular, its heavier isotopes, deuterium (H-2) and tritium (H-3). Hydrogen is the most plentiful element in the universe. The thermonuclear reaction that occurs most readily at an achievable temperature is the so-called D–T reaction, in which a deuterium nucleus and a tritium nucleus fuse. Both of these isotopes are found in ordinary water. For example, 30 liters of seawater contains 1 gram of deuterium, which when fused releases as much energy as 10,000 liters of gasoline or 80 tons of TNT. Natural tritium is much scarcer, but given enough to get started (it can be made in a fission reactor), a controlled thermonuclear reactor will breed it from deuterium in ample quantities. Because of the abundance of fusion fuel, the amount of energy that can be released in a controlled manner is virtually unlimited.

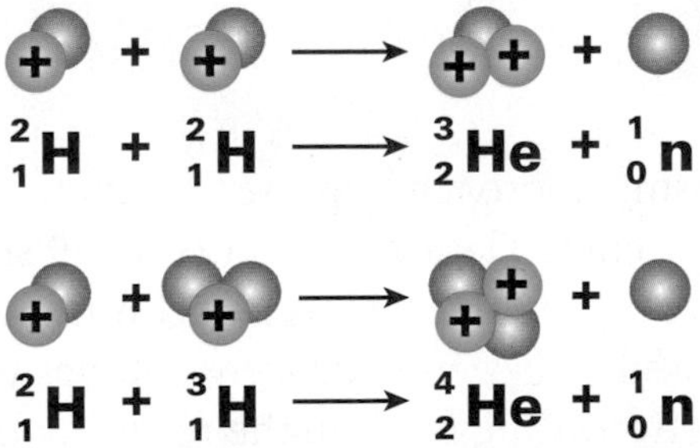

FIGURE 40.21 ▶

In the fusion reactions of hydrogen isotopes, most of the energy released is carried by the lighter-weight neutrons that fly off at high speeds.

$$^{2}_{1}\text{H} + ^{2}_{1}\text{H} \longrightarrow ^{3}_{2}\text{He} + ^{1}_{0}\text{n}$$

$$^{2}_{1}\text{H} + ^{3}_{1}\text{H} \longrightarrow ^{4}_{2}\text{He} + ^{1}_{0}\text{n}$$

The development of fusion power has been slow and difficult, already extending over fifty years. It is one of the biggest scientific and engineering challenges that we face. Our hope is that it will be achieved and will be a primary energy source for future generations.

Humans may one day travel to the stars in ships fueled by the same energy that makes the stars shine.

CONCEPT CHECK : Why are thermonuclear fusion reactions so difficult to carry out?

REVIEW

Go Online For: Self-Assessment
PHSchool.com Visit: PHSchool.com
Web Code: csd – 4000

Concept Summary

- Nuclear fission occurs when the repelling electrical forces within a nucleus overpower the attracting nuclear strong forces.

- A sustained chain reaction requires that the uranium contain a higher percentage of U-235 than occurs naturally.

- A fission reactor generates energy through a controlled fission reaction.

- The isotope Pu-239, like U-235, undergoes fission when it captures a neutron.

- A breeder reactor converts a nonfissionable uranium isotope into a fissionable plutonium isotope.

- During fission, the total mass of the fission fragments (including the ejected neutrons) is less than the mass of the fissioning nucleus. The missing mass is equivalent to the energy released.

- After fusion, the mass of the light nuclei formed is less than the total mass of nuclei that fused.

- Producing thermonuclear fusion reactions under controlled conditions requires temperatures of hundreds of millions of degrees.

think! Answers

40.1 Five kilograms of U-235 in small chunks will not support a sustained reaction because the path for a neutron in each chunk is so short that the neutron is likely to escape through the surface without causing fission. When the chunks are brought together there is sufficient material that the neutron is likely to hit a nucleus and to cause fission rather than escape.

40.3 Control rods control the number of neutrons that participate in a chain reaction. They thereby keep the reactor in its critical state. Without the control rods, the reactor could become subcritical or supercritical.

40.6 You divide the mass of the nucleus by the number of nucleons in it.

40.7 No, no, no! This is contradictory only if the same element is said to release energy by both the processes of fission and fusion. Only the fusion of light elements and the fission of heavy elements result in a decrease in nucleon mass and a release of energy.

Key Terms

nuclear fission
  (p. 809)

breeder reactor
  (p. 816)

chain reaction
  (p. 809)

nuclear fusion
  (p. 821)

critical mass
  (p. 811)

thermonuclear
  fusion (p. 821)

ASSESS

Check Concepts · · · · ·

Section 40.1

1. What is the role of electrical forces in nuclear fission?

2. What is the role of a neutron in nuclear fission?

3. Of what use are the neutrons that are produced when a nucleus undergoes fission?

4. Why does a chain reaction not occur in uranium ore?

5. **a.** Which isotope of uranium is most common?
   b. Which isotope of uranium will fission?

6. Which will leak more neutrons—two separate pieces of uranium or the same pieces stuck together?

7. Will a supercritical chain reaction be more likely in two separate pieces of U-235 or in the same pieces stuck together?

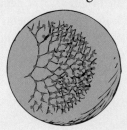

Section 40.2

8. Why must uranium be enriched so that it contains a higher percentage of U-235 in order to sustain a chain reaction?

9. Why do heavier molecules in a gas move more slowly on average than lighter ones at the same temperature?

10. Why can't U-235 and U-238 be separated by a chemical reaction?

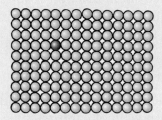

11. How is gaseous diffusion used to separate atoms of U-235 and U-238?

Section 40.3

12. What controls the chain reaction in a nuclear reactor?

13. Are the fission fragments from a nuclear reactor light, medium, or heavy elements?

14. Why are the fission-fragment elements radioactive?

Section 40.4

15. What happens when U-238 absorbs a neutron?

16. Is plutonium an isotope of uranium or is it a completely different element?

Section 40.5

17. What is the effect of putting a little Pu-239 with a lot of U-238 in a reactor?

Section 40.6

18. Is the mass per nucleon of a nucleus greater than, less than, or the same as the mass of a nucleon outside a nucleus?

19. What device can be used to measure the relative masses of ions of isotopes?

20. What is the primary difference in the graphs shown in Figures 40.13 and 40.14?

21. Distinguish between the mass of a nucleus and the mass per nucleon of the nucleus.

Section 40.7

22. Why does iron not yield energy if fused with something else or if fissioned?

23. What becomes of the loss in mass when light atoms fuse to become heavier ones?

Section 40.8

24. Why are fusion reactors not a present-day reality like fission reactors?

Think and Rank •••••

Rank each of the following sets of scenarios in order of the quantity or property involved. List them from left to right. If scenarios have equal rankings, then separate them with an equal sign. (e.g., A = B)

25. Consider the isotopes $^{238}_{92}$U, $^{239}_{90}$Th, $^{239}_{94}$Pu, and $^{239}_{93}$Np.
 a. Rank these isotopes from greatest number of protons to least number of protons.
 b. Rank these isotopes from greatest number of neutrons to least number of neutrons.

26. Consider the following nuclear reactions.
 (A) $^{238}_{92}$U emits an alpha particle.
 (B) $^{239}_{94}$Pu emits an alpha particle.
 (C) $^{239}_{90}$Th emits a beta particle.
 (D) $^{239}_{93}$N emits a beta particle.

 a. Rank the product nuclei of these reactions by atomic number from greatest to least.
 b. Rank the product nuclei by the number of neutrons from greatest to least.

27. Assume that all of the following atoms could undergo fission. Using Figure 40.14 as your guide, rank from greatest to least the reduction in mass for these nuclei after undergoing fission.
 (A) uranium
 (B) radium
 (C) gold
 (D) iron

28. Rank from greatest to least the reduction in mass that accompanies *fusion* of the following pairs of atomic nuclei.
 (A) two hydrogen nuclei
 (B) two carbon nuclei
 (C) two aluminum nuclei
 (D) two iron nuclei

Think and Explain •••••

29. Why does a neutron often make a better nuclear bullet than a proton?

30. Why does a chain reaction die out in small pieces of fissionable fuel, but not in large pieces?

31. If a piece of uranium is flattened into a pancake shape, will this make a supercritical chain reaction more or less likely? Why?

32. Why does a chain reaction not occur in uranium mines?

33. Why is lead found in all deposits of uranium ores?

34. Why are there no appreciable deposits of plutonium in Earth's crust?

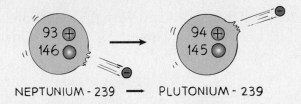

NEPTUNIUM - 239 ⟶ PLUTONIUM - 239

35. Your tutor says atomic nuclei are converted to energy in a nuclear reaction. Why should you seek a new tutor?

36. What becomes of the loss in mass of nuclei when heavy atoms split?

37. Why does helium not yield energy if fissioned?

38. Why does uranium not yield energy if fused with something else?

39. Is the mass of an atomic nucleus greater or less than the total mass of the nucleons that compose it?

40. In a nuclear fission reaction, which has more mass: the initial uranium atom or the sum of its products?

41. How does the mass per nucleon in uranium compare with the mass per nucleon in the fission fragments of uranium?

42. In a nuclear fusion reaction, which has more mass: the initial hydrogen isotopes or the fusion products?

43. To predict the approximate energy release of either a fission or a fusion reaction, explain how a physicist makes use of the curve of Figure 40.14, or a table of nuclear masses and the equation $\Delta E = \Delta mc^2$.

44. Which process, fission or fusion, would release energy from gold? From carbon? From iron?

45. If a uranium nucleus were to split into three pieces of approximately the same size instead of two, would more energy or less energy be released? Defend your answer in terms of Figure 40.14.

46. The energy release of nuclear fission is tied to the fact that the mass per nucleon of medium-weight nuclei is about 0.1% less than the mass per nucleon of the heaviest nuclei. What would be the effect on energy release if the 0.1% figure were 1%?

47. Explain how radioactive decay has always warmed Earth from the inside, and nuclear fusion has always warmed Earth from the outside.

48. The energy of fission is the kinetic energy of the nuclear fragments. What becomes of this energy in a commercial power reactor?

49. If a nucleus of $^{232}_{90}$Th absorbs a neutron, and the resulting nucleus undergoes two successive beta decays (emitting electrons), what nucleus results?

50. Mixing copper and zinc atoms produces the alloy brass. At the nuclear level, what would be produced with the fusion of copper and zinc nuclei?

51. Oxygen and hydrogen atoms combine to form water. At the nuclear level, if one oxygen and one hydrogen were fused, what element would be produced?

52. If a pair of carbon nuclei were fused, and the product emitted a beta particle, what element would be produced?

Think and Solve ·····

53. Burning one metric ton (1000 kg) of dry wood releases about 20 GJ (1 gigajoule = 10^9 J) of energy. Show that this is equivalent to converting 0.22 milligrams of mass to energy.

54. The total U.S. consumption of electricity in 2001 was approximately 4×10^{12} kilowatt-hours, or approximately 1.4×10^{19} J. Show that this much energy is equivalent to converting approximately 160 kg of mass to energy (roughly speaking, the mass of a small motorcycle).

Activities ·····

55. Make a list comparing the kinds of pollution resulting from fossil-fuel power plants and nuclear fission power plants. Share your list with somebody in your family.

56. Summarize and compare the benefits to society and the costs to society of fossil fuel plants and nuclear fission plants. Share this comparison with somebody in your family.

More Problem-Solving Practice
Appendix F

Appendix A Units of Measurement

The units of measurement primarily used in this book are those used by scientists throughout the world—the International System of Units, or SI (after the French name, Système International). SI units are the outgrowth of the metric system of units. While familiar to scientists, many SI units are not generally familiar to students in high school. The SI units used in this book are the following.

Meter

The meter (m) is the SI unit of length. The standard of length for the metric system originally was defined in terms of the distance from the North Pole to the equator. This distance is close to 10 million meters. So one meter equals approximately one ten-millionth of the distance from the North Pole to the equator. A more exact definition is that one meter equals the length of the path traveled by light in a vacuum during a time interval of 1/299,792,458 of a second.

Common SI length units based on the meter are the *centimeter*, *millimeter*, and *kilometer*.

> 1 centimeter (cm) = 1/100 meter
>
> 1 millimeter (mm) = 1/1000 meter
>
> 1 kilometer (km) = 1000 meters

One meter is a little more than a yard. It is equal to 3.28 feet, or 39.37 inches. It takes 1.609 kilometers to make one mile.

Kilogram

The kilogram (kg), the SI unit of mass, is defined as the mass of a platinum-iridium cylinder preserved at the International Bureau of Weights and Measures in France. The kilogram originally was defined as the mass of one liter (1000 cubic centimeters) of water at the temperature at which it is most dense, 4° Celsius. Other common mass units are the *gram* and *milligram*.

> 1 gram (g) = 1/1000 kilogram
>
> 1 milligram (mg) = 1/1000 gram
>
> = 1/1,000,000 kilogram

The mass of a 1-pound object is 0.4536 kilogram. One kilogram weighs about 2.2 pounds at Earth's surface.

Second

The second (s) is the SI unit of time. Until 1956, the second was defined in terms of the mean solar day, which was divided into 24 hours. Each hour was divided into 60 minutes and each minute into 60 seconds. Thus, there were 86,400 seconds per day, and the second was defined as 1/86,400 of the mean solar day. This was found to be unsatisfactory because the rate of rotation of Earth is gradually slowing. In 1956, the mean solar day of the year 1900 was chosen as the standard on which to base the second. Since 1964, the second has been officially defined as the time taken by a cesium-133 atom to make 9,192,631,770 vibrations.

Newton

The newton (N), the SI unit of force, is named after Sir Isaac Newton. One newton is the force required to give an object with a mass of one kilogram an acceleration of one meter per second squared.

One newton is a little less than a quarter of a pound—more accurately, 0.225 pound.

Joule

The joule (J), the SI unit of energy, is named after James Joule. One joule is equal to the amount of work done by a force of one newton acting over a distance of one meter.

The unit for power is derived from the unit for energy. Power is the rate at which energy is expended. Work done at the rate of one joule per second is equal to a power of one *watt* (W). The *kilowatt* (kW) equals 1000 watts. From the definition of power, it follows that energy can be expressed as the product of power and time. Electrical energy is often expressed in units of *kilowatt-hours* (kW h), where

> 1 kilowatt-hour (kWh) = 3.60×10^6 joules

The horsepower, a commonly used power unit for engines, is equal to 746 watts. A commonly used alternate energy unit for heat is the calorie. One calorie is equal to 4.184 joules.

Ampere

The ampere (A), the SI unit of electric current, is named after André-Marie Ampère. In this text the ampere is defined as the rate of flow of one coulomb of charge per second, where one coulomb is the charge of 6.24×10^{18} electrons. The official definition of the ampere is the intensity of constant electric current maintained in two parallel conductors of infinite length and negligible cross section that, when placed one meter apart in a vacuum, would produce between them a force of 2×10^{-7} N per meter of length.

Kelvin

The kelvin (K), the SI unit of temperature, is named after the scientist Lord Kelvin. The kelvin is defined as 1/273.16 of the temperature change between absolute zero (the coldest possible temperature) and the triple point of water (the fixed temperature at which, for a certain pressure, ice, liquid water, and water vapor coexist in equilibrium). Temperatures are expressed in kelvins, and not in "degrees kelvin." On the Kelvin scale, absolute zero is 0 K. The temperature of melting ice at atmospheric pressure is 273.15 K, the triple point of water is 273.16 K, and the temperature of pure boiling water at atmospheric pressure is 373.15 K. There are 100 kelvins between the melting and boiling points of water, just as there are 100 Celsius degrees between these points. So a temperature change of 1 Celsius degree is the same as a temperature change of 1 kelvin.

A Fahrenheit degree measures a smaller temperature change. It takes a temperature change of 1.8 Fahrenheit degrees to equal a change of 1 kelvin or 1 Celsius degree. So the number of Fahrenheit degrees between the melting and boiling points of water is 180 (the difference between 212 and 32).

Measurements of Area and Volume

Area   Area refers to the amount of surface. The unit of area is the surface of a square that has a standard unit of length as a side. In the SI system it is a square with sides one meter in length, which makes a unit of area of one square meter (1 m^2). A smaller unit area is represented by a square with sides one centimeter in length, which makes a unit of area of one square centimeter (1 cm^2).

The area of a rectangle equals the rectangle's length times its width. The area of a circle is equal to πr^2, where $\pi = 3.14$, and r is the radius of the circle. Formulas for the surfaces of other shapes can be found in geometry textbooks.

One square meter is equal to 10.76 square feet.

Volume   The volume of an object refers to the space it occupies. The unit volume is the space taken up by a cube that has a standard unit of length for its edge. In the SI system, it is the space occupied by a cube whose sides are one meter. This volume is one cubic meter (1 m^3) and is a relatively large volume by everyday standards. A smaller unit volume is the space occupied by a cube whose sides are one centimeter. Its volume is one cubic centimeter (1 cm^3), the space taken up by one gram of water at 4°C.

A liter (L) is equal to 1000 cm^3 and is a common measure of volume for liquids.

One liter, a little larger than a quart, is 1.057 quarts. It takes 3.785 liters to make one U.S. gallon.

Appendix B Working with Units in Physics

A quantity in science is expressed by a number and a unit of measurement. A unit (singular) may be a combination of other units. The unit of acceleration, for instance, is m/s^2. Quantities may be actual measurements, or they may be obtained by performing calculations on measurements. Quantities may be added, subtracted, multiplied, or divided. There are rules for handling both the numbers and the units of measurement during these mathematical operations.

Addition

When you add quantities, all must have the *same* unit. Add up the numbers. The sum has the same unit as well.

Example:
(4 m) + (8 m) + (3 m) = 15 m

Subtraction

When you subtract one quantity from another, both must have the *same* unit. Subtract the numbers. The difference has the same unit.

Example:
(5.2 s) − (3.8 s) = 1.4 s

Multiplication

Quantities that are multiplied together need *not* have the same unit. Multiply the numbers. Multiply the units just as if they are algebraic variables.

When full names of units are used, use a hyphen between the units that are multiplied together.

Example:
(3 newtons) × (2 meters) = 6 newton-meters

When symbols are used, you can use a centered dot between the unit symbols that are multiplied together.

Example:
(3 N) × (2 m) = 6 N·m

When the units being multiplied are the same, the product is called the square (or cubic) unit. In symbols, a raised 2 after the unit symbol is used for the square. A raised 3 after the unit symbol is used for the cubic unit. These raised numerals are known as *exponents*.

Examples:
(3 meters) × (2 meters) = 6 meter-meters

$$= 6 \text{ square meters}$$

$$(3 \text{ m}) \times (2 \text{ m}) = 6 \text{ m·m} = 6 \text{ m}^2$$

(3 meters) × (2 meters) × (4 meters)

$$= 24 \text{ meter-meter-meters}$$

$$= 24 \text{ cubic meters}$$

$$(3 \text{ m}) \times (2 \text{ m}) \times (4 \text{ m}) = 24 \text{ m·m·m} = 24 \text{ m}^3$$

Division

Quantities that are divided by each other need *not* have the same unit. Divide the numbers. Divide the units as though they are algebraic variables.

When the units are full names, use the word *per* after the unit that is being divided.

Example:
(100 kilometers) ÷ (2 hours)

$$= \frac{100 \text{ kilometers}}{2 \text{ hours}}$$

$$= 50 \text{ kilometers per hour}$$

When the units are symbols, use a slash after the unit symbol that is being divided.

Example:
$$(100 \text{ km}) \div (2 \text{ h}) = \frac{100 \text{ km}}{2 \text{ h}}$$

$$= 50 \text{ km/h}$$

When both units are the same, they "cancel" out and do not appear in the quotient.

Example:
$$(6 \text{ m}) \div (3 \text{ m}) = \frac{6 \,\cancel{m}}{3 \,\cancel{m}}$$

$$= 2$$

Complicated Multiplication and Division

In multiplication, when the quantities have units that are quotients of units, treat them as algebraic variables. Identical units in the numerator and denominator may be "canceled" out.

Example:
(25 meters per second) × (6 seconds)

$$= \left(25\,\frac{\text{meters}}{\text{second}}\right) \times 6\ \text{seconds}$$

$$= 25 \times 6\,\frac{\text{meters-\cancel{seconds}}}{\cancel{\text{second}}}$$

$$= 150\ \text{meters}$$

$$(25\ \text{m/s}) \times (6\ \text{s}) = \left(25\,\frac{\text{m}}{\text{s}}\right) \times (6\ \text{s})$$

$$= 25 \times 6\,\frac{\text{m} \cdot \cancel{s}}{\cancel{s}}$$

$$= 150\ \text{m}$$

In division, when the quantities have units that are quotients of units, it is easiest to express the division in numerator and denominator form. That is, the number to be divided is the numerator (top value) and the divisor is the denominator (bottom value). Divide the numbers. Treat units as algebraic variables.

Examples:
(8.2 meters per second) ÷ (2.0 seconds)

$$= \frac{8.2\ \text{meters per second}}{2.0\ \text{seconds}}$$

$$= \frac{8.2}{2.0}\,\frac{\text{meters}}{\text{second-second}}$$

$$= 4.1\ \text{meters per second squared}$$

$$(8.2\ \text{m/s}) \div (2.0\ \text{s}) = \frac{8.2\ \text{m/s}}{2.0\ \text{s}}$$

$$= \frac{8.2}{2.0}\,\frac{\text{m}}{\text{s} \cdot \text{s}}$$

$$= 4.1\ \text{m/s}^2$$

Note that when *second* is multiplied by itself in the denominator, it is changed to *per second squared* (and not to *per square second*). Similarly, the symbols "m/s^2" are read as "meters per second squared."

Scientific Notation

It is convenient to use a mathematical abbreviation for large and small numbers. The number 40,000,000 can be obtained by multiplying 4 by 10, and again by 10, and again by 10, and so on until 10 has been used as a multiplier seven times. The short way of showing this is to write the number 40,000,000 as 4×10^7.

The number 0.0004 can be obtained from 4 by using 10 as a divisor four times. The shorthand way of showing this is to write the number 0.0004 as 4×10^{-4}. Thus,

$$2 \times 10^5 = 2 \times 10 \times 10 \times 10 \times 10 \times 10 = 200{,}000$$

$$5 \times 10^{-3} = 5/(10 \times 10 \times 10) = 0.005$$

Numbers expressed in this shorthand manner are said to be in *scientific notation*.

$$
\begin{aligned}
1{,}000{,}000 &= 10 \times 10 \times 10 \times 10 \times 10 \times 10 = 10^6 \\
100{,}000 &= 10 \times 10 \times 10 \times 10 \times 10 = 10^5 \\
10{,}000 &= 10 \times 10 \times 10 \times 10 = 10^4 \\
1000 &= 10 \times 10 \times 10 = 10^3 \\
100 &= 10 \times 10 = 10^2 \\
10 &= 10 = 10^1 \\
1 &= 1 = 10^0 \\
0.1 &= 1/10 = 10^{-1} \\
0.01 &= 1/100 = 10^{-2} \\
0.001 &= 1/1000 = 10^{-3} \\
0.0001 &= 1/10{,}000 = 10^{-4} \\
0.00001 &= 1/100{,}000 = 10^{-5} \\
0.000001 &= 1/1{,}000{,}000 = 10^{-6}
\end{aligned}
$$

We can use scientific notation to express some of the physical data often used in physics.

Table B.1	Some Important Values in Physics
Speed of light in a vacuum	$= 2.9979 \times 10^8$ m/s
Average Earth–sun distance (1 astronomical unit (A.U.))	$= 1.50 \times 10^{11}$ m
Average Earth–moon distance	$= 3.84 \times 10^8$ m
Average radius of the sun	$= 6.96 \times 10^8$ m
Average radius of Jupiter	$= 6.99 \times 10^7$ m
Average radius of Earth	$= 6.37 \times 10^6$ m
Average radius of the moon	$= 1.74 \times 10^6$ m
Average radius of the hydrogen atom	$\approx 5 \times 10^{-11}$ m
Mass of the sun	$= 1.99 \times 10^{30}$ kg
Mass of Jupiter	$= 1.90 \times 10^{27}$ kg
Mass of Earth	$= 5.98 \times 10^{24}$ kg
Mass of the moon	$= 7.35 \times 10^{22}$ kg
Proton mass	$= 1.6726 \times 10^{-27}$ kg
Neutron mass	$= 1.6749 \times 10^{-27}$ kg
Electron mass	$= 9.11 \times 10^{-31}$ kg
Electron charge	$= 1.602 \times 10^{-19}$ C

Appendix C Graphing

Graphs—A Way to Express Quantitative Relationships

Graphs, like equations and tables, show how two or more quantities relate to each other. Since investigating relationships between quantities makes up much of the work of physics, equations, tables, and graphs are important physics tools.

Equations are the most concise way to describe quantitative relationships. For example, consider the equation $v = v_0 + gt$. It compactly describes how a freely falling object's velocity depends on its initial velocity, acceleration due to gravity, and time. Equations are nice shorthand expressions for relationships among quantities.

Tables give values of variables in list form. The dependence of v on t in $v = v_0 + gt$ can be shown by a table that lists various values v for corresponding times t. Table 4.2 on page 53 is an example. Tables are especially useful when the mathematical relationship between quantities is not known or when numerical values must be given to a high degree of accuracy. Also, tables are handy for recording experimental data.

Graphs *visually* represent relationships between quantities. By looking at the shape of a graph, you can quickly tell a lot about how the variables are related. For this reason, graphs can help clarify the meaning of an equation or table of numbers. And, when the equation is not already known, a graph can help reveal the relationship between variables. Experimental data are often graphed for this reason.

Graphs are helpful in another way. If a graph contains enough plotted points, it can be used to estimate values between the points (interpolation), or following the points (extrapolation).

Cartesian Graphs

The most common and useful graph in science is the *Cartesian* graph. On a Cartesian graph, possible values of one variable are represented on the vertical axis (called the *y-axis*) and possible values of the other variable are plotted on the horizontal axis (*x-axis*).

Figure C-1 shows a graph of two variables, x and y, that are *directly proportional* to each other. A direct proportionality is a type of *linear* relationship. Linear relationships have straight-line graphs—the easiest kinds of graphs to interpret. On the graph shown in Figure C-1, the continuous straight-line rise from left to right tells you that as x increases, y increases. More specifically, it shows that y increases at a constant rate with respect to x. As x doubles, y doubles; as x triples, y triples, etc. The graph of a direct proportionality passes through the "origin"—the point at the lower left where $x = 0$ and $y = 0$.

Figure C-2 below shows a graph of the equation $v = v_0 + gt$. Speed v is plotted along the y-axis, and time t along the x-axis. As you can see, there is a linear relationship between v and t.

Direct Proportionality Relationship

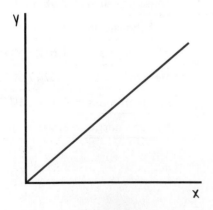

Figure C-1

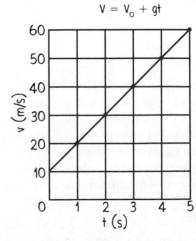

Figure C-2

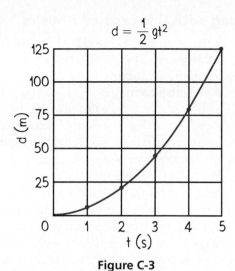

$$d = \frac{1}{2} gt^2$$

Figure C-3

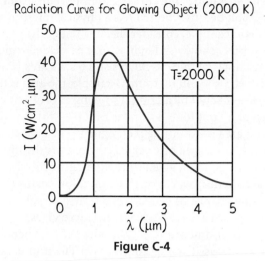

Radiation Curve for Glowing Object (2000 K)

T=2000 K

Figure C-4

Many physically significant relationships are more complicated than linear relationships, however. If you double the size of a room, the area of the floor increases four times; tripling the size of the room increases the floor area nine times, and so on. This is one example of a *nonlinear* relationship. Figure C-3 shows a graph of another nonlinear relationship: distance vs. time in the equation of free fall from rest, $d = 1/2 \, gt^2$.

Figure C-4 shows a *radiation curve*. The *curve* (or graph) shows the rather complex nonlinear relationship between intensity I and radiation wavelength λ for a glowing object at 2000 K. The graph shows that radiation is most intense when λ equals about 1.4 μm. Which is brighter, radiation at 0.5 μm or radiation at 2.0 μm? The graph can quickly tell you that radiation at 2.0 μm is appreciably more intense.

Slope and Area Under the Curve

Quantitative information can be obtained from a graph's *slope* and the *area under the curve*. The slope of the graph in Figure C-2 represents the rate at which v increases relative to t. It can be calculated by dividing a segment Δv along the y-axis by a corresponding segment Δt along the x-axis. For example, dividing Δv of 30 m/s by Δt of 3 s gives $\Delta v / \Delta t = 10$ m/s·s $= 10$ m/s^2, the acceleration due to gravity. By contrast, consider the graph in Figure C-5, which is a horizontal straight line. Its slope of zero shows zero acceleration—that is, constant speed. The graph shows that the speed is 30 m/s, acting throughout the 5-second interval. The rate of change, or slope, of the speed with respect to time is zero—there is no change in speed at all.

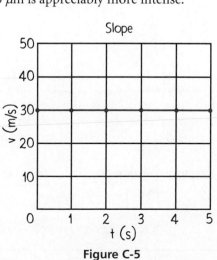

Slope

Figure C-5

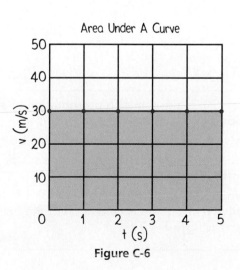

Area Under A Curve

Figure C-6

The area under the curve is an important feature of a graph because it often has a physical interpretation. For example, consider the area under the graph of v versus t shown in Figure C-6. The shaded region is a rectangle with sides 30 m/s and 5 s. Its area is 30 m/s $\times$ 5 s = 150 m. In this example, the area is the distance covered by an object moving at constant speed of 30 m/s for 5 s ($d = vt$).

The area need not be rectangular. The area beneath any curve of v versus t represents the distance traveled in a given time interval. Similarly, the area beneath a curve of acceleration versus time gives the change of velocity in a time interval. The area beneath a force-versus-time curve gives the change of momentum. (What does the area beneath a force-versus-distance curve give?) The nonrectangular areas under various curves, including rather complicated ones, can be found by way of an important branch of mathematics—*integral calculus.*

Graphing with Conceptual Physics

You will develop basic graphing skills in the laboratory part of this course. The lab *Blind as a Bat* introduces you to graphing concepts. It also gives you a chance to work with a computer and sonic-ranging device. The lab *Trial and Error* will show you the useful technique of converting a nonlinear graph to a linear one to discover a direct proportionality. The area under the curve is the basis of the lab activities *Impact Speed* and *Wrap Your Energy in a Bow.* You will learn about graphing by doing it in other labs as well.

You will also learn in the lab part of your *Conceptual Physics* course that computers can graph data for you. You are not being lazy when you graph your data with a software program. Instead of investing time and energy scaling the axes and plotting points, you spend your time and energy investigating the meaning of the graph, a high level of thinking!

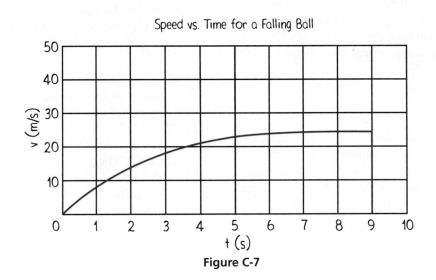

Figure C-7

think!

Figure C-7 is a graphical representation of a ball dropped into a mine shaft.

1. How long did the ball take to hit the bottom?

2. What was the ball's speed when it struck bottom?

3. What does the decreasing slope of the graph tell you about the acceleration of the ball with increasing speed?

4. Did the ball reach terminal speed before hitting the bottom of the shaft? If so, about how many seconds did it take to reach its terminal speed?

5. What is the approximate depth of the mine shaft?

Appendix D Vector Applications

Appendix D expands the concept of vectors introduced in Chapters 2 and 5. Vectors are illustrated here by two fascinating cases: a sailboat sailing into the wind, and the passage of light through polarization filters, as discussed in Chapter 27. Vector explanations for both the sailboat and the transmission of light through polarizing filters involve a blend of geometry and physics.

The Sailboat

Sailors have always known that a sailboat can sail downwind (in the same direction as the wind). The ships of Columbus were designed to sail principally downwind. Not until modern times did sailors learn that a sailboat can sail upwind (against the wind). It turns out that many types of sailboats can sail faster "cutting" upwind than when sailing directly with the wind. The old-timers didn't know this, probably because they didn't understand vectors and vector components. Luckily, we do, and today's sailboats are far more maneuverable than the sailboats of the past.

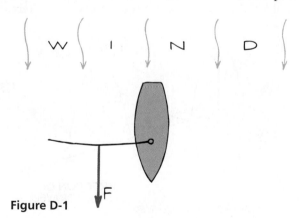

Figure D-1

To understand all this, first consider the relatively simple case of sailing downwind. Figure D-1 shows a force vector F due to the impact of the wind against the sail. This force tends to increase the speed of the boat. If it were not for resistive forces, mainly water drag, the speed of the boat would build up to nearly the speed of the wind. (It could be pushed no faster than wind speed because the wind would no longer have any speed relative to the sails. The sails would sag and the force F would shrink to zero.) It is impor-

tant to note that the faster the boat goes, the smaller the magnitude of F. So we see that a sailboat sailing directly with the wind can sail no faster than the wind.

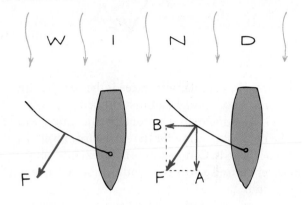

Figure D-2

If the sail is oriented as shown in Figure D-2 (left), the boat will move forward but with less speed for two reasons. First, the force F on the sail is less because the sail does not intercept as much wind at this angle. Second, the force on the sail is not in the direction of the boat's motion. It is instead perpendicular to the sail's surface. Generally speaking, whenever any fluid (liquid or gas) interacts with a smooth surface, the force of interaction is perpendicular to the smooth surface. In this case, the boat will not move in the direction of F because of its deep finlike keel, which knifes through the water and resists motion in sideways directions.

We can understand the motion of the boat by resolving F into perpendicular components, as shown in Figure D-2 (right). The important component is the one parallel to the keel and is labeled A. Component A propels the boat forward. The other component (B) is useless and tends to tip the boat over and move it sideways. The tendency to tip is offset by the heavy deep keel. Again, maximum speed can only approach wind speed.

When a sailboat's keel points in a direction other than exactly downwind and its sails are properly oriented, it can exceed wind speed. In the case of cutting across at an angular direction to the wind (Figure D-3, left), the wind continues to move relative to the sail even after the boat achieves wind speed.

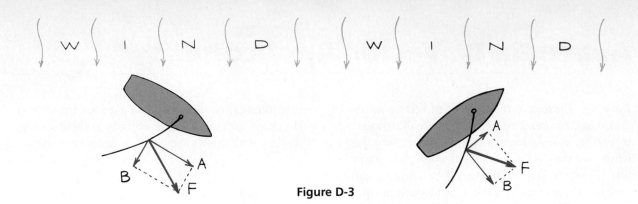

Figure D-3

A surfer, in a similar way, exceeds the speed of the propelling wave by angling the surfboard across the wave. Greater angles to the propelling medium (wind for the boat, water wave for the surfboard) result in greater speeds. Can you see why a sailcraft can sail faster cutting across the wind than it can sailing downwind?

As strange as it may seem to people who do not understand vectors, maximum speed is attained by cutting into (against) the wind—that is, by angling the sailcraft in a direction upwind (Figure D-3, right)! Although a sailboat cannot sail *directly* upwind, it can reach a destination upwind by angling back and forth in zigzag fashion. This is called *tacking*. As the speed increases, the relative speed of the wind, rather than decreasing, actually *increases*. Wind impact increases. (If you run outdoors in a slanting rain, the drops will hit you harder if you run into the rain rather than away from the rain!) The faster the boat moves as it tacks upwind, the greater the magnitude of *F*. Thus, component *A* will continue pushing the boat along in the forward direction. The boat reaches its terminal speed when opposing forces, mainly water drag, balance the force of wind impact.

Icecraft, which are equipped with runners for sliding on ice, encounter no water drag. They can travel at several times wind speed when they tack upwind. Terminal speed is reached not so much because of resistive forces, but because the wind direction shifts relative to the moving craft. When this happens, the wind finally moves parallel to the sail rather than against it. This appendix will not go into detail about this complication; nor will it discuss the curvature of the sail, which also plays an important role.

The central concept underlying sailcraft is the vector. It ushered in the era of clipper ships and revolutionized the sailing industry. Sailing, like most things, is more enjoyable if you understand what is happening.

The Vector Nature of Light

Recall from Chapter 27 that light is electromagnetic energy that travels as a transverse wave. The wave is made up of an oscillating electric field vector and an oscillating magnetic field vector that is at right angles to the electric field vector (Figure D-4). It is the orientation of the electric field vector that defines the direction of polarization of light waves.

The electric field vectors in waves of light from the sun or from a lamp are generated in all conceivable directions. Such light is nonpolarized. When the electric vectors of the waves are aligned parallel to each other, the light is considered to be *polarized*. Light can be polarized when it passes through polarizing filters.

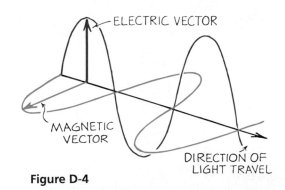

Figure D-4

The most familiar are Polaroid sunglasses. Ordinary nonpolarized light incident upon a polarizing filter emerges as polarized light.

Think of a beam of nonpolarized light coming straight toward you. Consider the electric vectors in that beam. Some of the possible directions of the vibrations are as shown in Figure D-5 (left). For this unpolarized light, there are as many vectors in any direction as in any other. These many directions of vibration can be replaced by just two directions, horizontal and vertical, since any electric vector can be

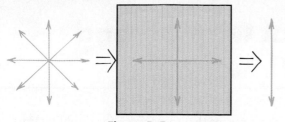

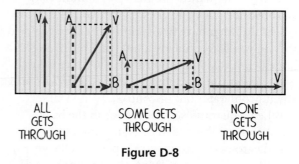

Figure D-5

resolved into horizontal and vertical components. The center sketch shows the light, with its horizontally and vertically vibrating electric vectors, falling on a polarizing filter with its polarization axis vertically oriented. Only vertical components of light pass through the filter, and the light that emerges is vertically polarized, as shown on the right.

Figure D-6 shows that no light can pass through a pair of Polaroid filters when their axes are at a right angle to each other, but some light does pass through when their axes are at any other angle. This fact can be understood with vectors and vector components.

Figure D-6

Recall from Chapter 3 that any vector can be resolved into two components at right angles to each other. The two components are often chosen to be in the horizontal and vertical directions, but they can be in *any* two perpendicular directions. In fact, the number of sets of perpendicular components possible for any vector is infinite. A few of them are shown for the vector *V* in Figure D-7. In every case, components *A* and *B* make up the sides of a rectangle that has *V* as its diagonal.

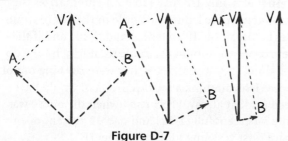

Figure D-7

You can see this somewhat differently by thinking of component *A* as always being vertical and *B* as being horizontal, and picturing vector *V* as rotating instead (Figure D-8). This time the different orientations of *V* are superimposed on a polarizing filter with its polarization axis vertical. In the first sketch on the left, when the electric field vector is vertical, all of *V* gets through. As *V* rotates, only the vertical component *A* passes through. This component *A* gets shorter and shorter until it is zero when *V* is completely horizontal.

ALL GETS THROUGH   SOME GETS THROUGH   NONE GETS THROUGH

Figure D-8

Can you now understand how light gets through the first pair of Polaroid sunglasses in Figure D-6? Look at Figure D-9, where for clarity the two crossed lenses of Figure D-6, which are one atop the other, are instead shown side by side. The vector *V* that emerges from the first lens is vertical. However, it has a component *A* in the direction of the polarization axis of the second lens. Component *A* passes through the second lens, while component *B* is absorbed.

To really appreciate this, you must toy around with a couple of polarizing filters, which you can do in a lab exercise. Rotate one above the other and see how you can regulate the amount of light that gets through. Can you think of practical uses for such a system?

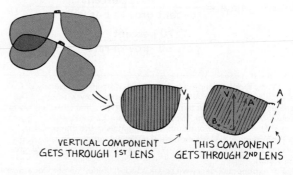

VERTICAL COMPONENT GETS THROUGH 1ST LENS   THIS COMPONENT GETS THROUGH 2ND LENS

Figure D-9

Appendix E Exponential Growth and Doubling Time*

You can't fold a piece of paper in half, then fold it again upon itself successively for 9 times. It gets too thick to keep folding. And if you could fold a fine piece of tissue paper upon itself 50 times, it would be more than 20 million kilometers thick! The continual doubling of a quantity builds up astronomically. Double one penny 30 times, so that you begin with one penny, then have two pennies, then four, and so on, and you'll accumulate a total of $10,737,418.23! One of the most important things we have trouble perceiving is the process of exponential growth and why it proliferates out of control.

When a quantity such as money in the bank, population, or the rate of consumption of a resource steadily grows at a fixed percent per year, the growth is said to be *exponential.* Money in the bank may grow at 5 or 6 percent per year; world population is presently growing at about 2 percent per year; the electric power generating capacity in the United States grew at about 7 percent per year for the first three quarters of the last century. The important thing about exponential growth is that the time required for the growing quantity to double in size (increase by 100 percent) is constant. For example, if the population of a growing city takes 10 years to double from 10,000 to 20,000 people and its growth remains steady, in the next 10 years the population will double to 40,000, and in the next 10 years to 80,000, and so on.

There is an important relationship between the percent growth rate and its *doubling time,* the time it takes to double a quantity:**

$$\text{doubling time} = \frac{69.2 \text{ percent}}{\text{percent growth per unit time}}$$

$$= \frac{70 \text{ percent}}{\text{percent growth rate}}$$

---

* This appendix is adapted from material written by University of Colorado physics professor Albert A. Bartlett, who strongly asserts, "The greatest shortcoming of the human race is man's inability to understand the exponential function." Look up Professor Bartlett's still timely and provocative article, "Forgotten Fundamentals in the Energy Crisis," in the September 1978 issue of the *American Journal of Physics,* or his revised version in the January 1980 issue of the *Journal of Geological Education.*

** For exponential decay we speak about *half-life,* the time for a quantity to reduce to half its value. An example of this case is radioactive decay, treated in Chapter 39.

This means that to estimate the doubling time for a steadily growing quantity, we simply divide 70 percent by the percentage growth rate. For example, when electric power generating capacity in the United States was growing at 7 percent per year, the capacity doubled every 10 years (since [70%]/[7%/year] = 10 years). If world population grew steadily at 2 percent per year, the world population would double every 35 years (since [70%]/[2%/year] = 35 years). A city planning commission that accepts what seems like a modest 3.5-percent-per-year growth rate may not realize that this means that doubling will occur in 20 years (since [70%]/[3.5%/year] = 20 years). That means double capacity for all municipal services every 20 years.

Steady growth in a steadily expanding environment is one thing, but what happens when steady growth occurs in a finite environment? Consider the growth of bacteria that grow by division, so that one bacterium becomes two, the two divide to become four, the four divide to become eight, and so on. Suppose the division time for a certain kind of bacterium is one minute. This is then steady growth—the number of bacteria grows exponentially with a doubling time of one minute. Further, suppose that one bacterium is put in a bottle at 11:00 a.m. and that growth continues steadily until the bottle becomes full of bacteria at 12 noon.

think!

A. When was the bottle half full?

It is startling to note that at 2 minutes before noon the bottle was only 1/4 full, and at 3 minutes before noon it was only 1/8 full. Table E.1 summarizes the amount of space left in the bottle in the last few minutes before noon. If bacteria could think, and if they were concerned about their future, at which time do you think they would sense they were running out of space? Do you think a serious problem would have been evident at, say, 11:55 a.m., when the bottle was only 3-percent full (1/32) and had 97 percent open space (just yearning for development)?

Table E.1	Bacteria in a Bottle	
Time	**Portion Full**	**Portion Empty**
11:54 a.m.	1/64 (1.5%)	63/64 (98.5%)
11:55 a.m.	1/32 (3%)	31/32 (97%)
11:56 a.m.	1/16 (6%)	15/16 (94%)
11:57 a.m.	1/8 (12%)	7/8 (88%)
11:58 a.m.	1/4 (25%)	3/4 (75%)
11:59 a.m.	1/2 (50%)	1/2 (50%)
12:00 noon	Full (100%)	None (0%)

The point is that there isn't much time between the moment the effects of growth become noticeable and the time when they become overwhelming.

Suppose that at 11:58 a.m. some farsighted bacteria see that they are running out of space and launch a full-scale search for new bottles. And further suppose they consider themselves lucky, for they find three new empty bottles. This is three times as much space as they have ever known. It may seem to the bacteria that their problems are solved—and just in time.

think!

B. If the bacteria are able to migrate to the new bottles and their growth continues at the same rate, what time will it be when the three new bottles are filled to capacity?

Table E.2 illustrates that the discovery of the new bottles extends the resource by only two doubling times. In this example the resource is space—such as land area for a growing population. But it could be coal, oil, uranium, or any nonrenewable resource.

Continued growth and continued doubling lead to enormous numbers. In two doubling times, a quantity will double twice ($2^2 = 4$), or quadruple in size;

Table E.2	Effects of the Discovery of the Three New Bottles
Time	**Effect**
11:58 a.m.	Bottle 1 is 1/4 full; bacteria divide into four bottles, each 1/16 full
11:59 a.m.	Bottles 1, 2, 3, and 4 are each 1/8 full
12:00 noon	Bottles 1, 2, 3, and 4 are each 1/4 full
12:01 p.m.	Bottles 1, 2, 3, and 4 are each 1/2 full
12:02 p.m.	Bottles 1, 2, 3, and 4 are each all full

think!

C. According to a French riddle, a lily pond starts with a single leaf. Each day the number of leaves doubles, until the pond is completely full on the thirtieth day. On what day was the pond half covered? One-quarter covered?

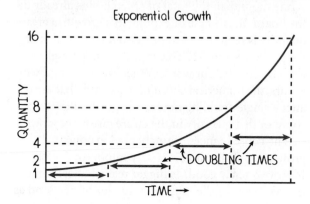

Figure E-1 Graph of a quantity that grows at an exponential rate. Notice that the quantity doubles during each of the successive equal time intervals marked on the horizontal scale. Each of these time intervals represents the doubling time.

in three doubling times, its size will increase eightfold ($2^3 = 8$); in four doubling times, it will increase sixteenfold ($2^4 = 16$); and so on. This is best illustrated by the story of the court mathematician in India who years ago invented the game of chess for his king. The king was so pleased with the game that he offered to repay the mathematician, whose request seemed modest enough. The mathematician requested a single grain of wheat on the first square of the chessboard, two grains on the second square, four on the third square, and so on, doubling the number of grains on each succeeding square until all squares had been used. At this rate there would be 2^{63} grains of wheat on the sixty-fourth square alone. The king soon saw that he could not fill this "modest" request, which amounted to more wheat than had been harvested in the entire history of Earth!

Figure E-2 A single grain of wheat placed on the first square of the chess board is doubled on the second square, and this number is doubled on the third square, and so on. There is not enough wheat in the world for this process to continue to the sixty-fourth square!

As Table E.3 shows, the number of grains on any square is one grain more than the total of all grains on the preceding squares. This is true anywhere on the board. For example, when four grains are placed on the third square, that number of grains is one more than the total of three grains already on the board. The number of grains (eight) on the fourth square is one more than the total of seven grains already on the board. In any case of exponential growth, a greater quantity is represented in one doubling time than in all the preceding growth. This is important enough to be repeated in different words: Whenever steady growth occurs, the numerical count of a quantity that exists after a single doubling time is one greater than the total count of that quantity in the entire history of growth.

The consequences of unchecked exponential growth are staggering. It is very important to ask, Is growth really good? Is bigger really better? Is the motto "Grow or die" a good guide for humankind as a whole?

Table E.3	Filling the Squares on the Chessboard	
Square Number	Grains on a Square	Total Grains Thus Far
1	1	1
2	2	3
3	$4 = 2^2$	7
4	$8 = 2^3$	15
5	$16 = 2^4$	31
6	$32 = 2^5$	63
7	$64 = 2^6$	127
64	2^{63}	$2^{64} - 1$

think!

1. In 2000, the population growth rate of the world was 1.4% per year, and the total world population was 6.1 billion. If this rate continued, how long would it take for the world population to double?

2. What annual percentage increase in world population would be required to double the world population in 100 years?

3. In an economy that has a steady inflation rate of 7% per year, in how many years does a $1 bill lose half its value?

4. At a steady inflation rate of 7%, what will be the price every 10 yr for the next 50 yr for a theater ticket that now costs $20? For a coat that now costs $200? For a car that now costs $20,000? For a home that now costs $200,000?

5. If the population of a city with one overloaded sewage treatment plant grows steadily at 5% annually, how many overloaded sewage treatment plants will be necessary 42 yr later?

6. In 2007 the population growth rate for the United States was 0.8%, for Mexico 1.2%, and for Liberia, the highest growth rate in the world, nearly 5% (taking into account births, deaths, and immigration). If these rates were steady, how long would it take for the population in each of these countries to double?

7. If world population doubles in 40 yr and world food production also doubles in 40 yr, how many people then will be starving each year compared to now?

8. Suppose you get a prospective employer to agree to hire your services for a wage of 1¢ for the first day, 2¢ the second day, and so forth. Your employer agrees to double your wage each day for a month. What will be your total wages for the month?

9. In the last question, how will your wages for only the 30th day compare to your total wages for the previous 29 days?

10. Oil has been produced in the U.S. for about 150 yr. If there remains in the country as much undiscovered oil as all that has been used, what is wrong with the argument that the remaining oil will be sufficient for another 150 yr?

11. If fusion power were harnessed today, the abundant energy resulting would likely sustain and even further encourage our present appetite for continued growth. In a relatively few doubling times, human beings on Earth could produce an appreciable fraction of the solar power input. Make an argument that the current delay in harnessing fusion is a blessing for the human race.

Appendix F Problem-Solving Practice

For many students, the major difficulty with problem solving is getting started. In most cases, start by identifying the underlying physics concept, and then express the concept in equation form. There may be more than one equation that applies, so choose the equation that incorporates the given values and the unknown value you're looking for. Rewrite the equation, solving for the unknown, and then let the terms in your equation guide you to a solution.

There are several guiding principles that will help you get organized to tackle problems. Refer frequently to the summary in each section as you work through the practice problems.

Note that the problems marked with an asterisk (*) are particularly challenging.

Chapter 2 Mechanical Equilibrium

1. Anthony weighs 300 N and holds his 90-N dog in his arms. He also holds a helium-filled party balloon that pulls him upward with a force of 2 N. Show that the support force of the floor on Anthony is 388 N.

2. John pushes horizontally with an 80-N force against a heavy desk, but the desk doesn't move. How much friction force acts horizontally between the desk and the floor?

3. Now John increases his push to 110 N, and the desk still doesn't move. How much friction force acts horizontally between the desk and the floor now?

4. Og ties a vine around a boulder and drags it horizontally across the floor of his cave. If Og is pulling horizontally on the boulder with a force of 400 N and the boulder moves across the floor at a constant speed, how much friction force acts between the boulder and the floor?

5. An airplane with a weight of 11,000 N cruises at 180 km/h in level flight 2300 m above the ground. How much upward lift force must be acting on the plane? How can you tell?

6. Gymnast Nellie weighs 300 N. She hangs from two non-vertical ropes, as shown in Figures 2.11 and 2.12 in Chapter 2. (a) How large is the resultant of the rope tensions in Figure 2.11? (b) How large is the resultant of the rope tension in Figure 2.12? (c) In which of these two figures is the horizontal component of the rope tension greater? Explain how you can tell.

7. Find the magnitude of the net force produced by a 30-N force and a 20-N force in each of the following cases: (a) Both forces act in the same direction. (b) The two act in opposite directions. (c) The two forces act at right angles to each other.

8. Nellie, who weighs 300 N, hangs suspended at the middle of a rope that makes 45° angles with the vertical. Show that the tension in each rope is about 212 N. (*Hint:* Think Pythagorean theorem.)

Chapter 3 Newton's First Law of Motion—Inertia

1. What is the weight in newtons of Lily Lightweight, who has a mass of 40 kg?

2. What is the net force on a 1000-N barrel falling in air with an air drag of 400 N?

3. When a 1000-N barrel is sinking through the water at a constant speed, what is the upward force of the water on the barrel?

4. What would be the weight of a gold crown on the moon if it has a mass of 3 kg? The acceleration due to gravity on the moon is $\frac{1}{6}$ that on Earth.

5. What is the mass of a 100-N crate of delicious candy?

6. Larry Lightweight stands on a pair of bathroom scales. Each scale reads 300 N. What is Larry's mass?

7. Suppose Larry stands with more weight on one scale than the other. If one scale reads 400 N, what does the other read?

8. Just as a 1-kg ball sitting at the edge of a table falls off the edge, it is kicked horizontally with a force of 10 N. What is the net force on the ball during the kick?

9. A high-flying jet cruises at an altitude of 30,000 feet at a constant velocity of 700 km/h. The jet engines provide 40,000 N of forward thrust. How much air drag acts on the craft?

10. A 400-kg bear grasping a vertical tree slides down at constant velocity. What is the friction force that acts on the bear?

11. Burl and Paul have a combined weight of 1200 N. They are on a scaffold supported by two vertical ropes. The tension in one rope is 800 N and the tension in the other is 630 N. Show that the weight of the scaffold is 230 N.

12. A liter of water has a mass of 1 kg. If you drink a half-liter of soda, by how much will your weight immediately increase?

13. Spaceman Bob can lift 450 N on Earth. He visits an asteroid where the surface gravity is 0.9 that of Earth's gravity, and picks up a rock sample that he can barely lift. (a) What is the weight of the rock on the asteroid? (b) How much will it weigh when he gets it back to Earth?

sample problem

Find the maximum height attained by a ball thrown straight up with an initial speed of 30 m/s. Ignore air resistance.

▶ **Step 1** Identify the underlying physics concept and write the equation that best expresses it.

In the absence of air resistance, a ball thrown straight up takes the same time going up as it does coming down. The concept here is *free fall* (any projectile under the influence of only gravity is in free fall). Height, the vertical distance, is given by $d = \frac{1}{2}gt^2$.

▶ **Step 2** Rewrite the equation so that the term whose value you're looking for is isolated on the left side of the equation.

In this case, we are looking for d, so where is no need to rewrite the equation.

▶ **Step 3** Substitute the values of the terms, with their units, for the variables in your equation. (This may involve repeating the process for unknown terms.)

$$d = \tfrac{1}{2}gt^2 = \tfrac{1}{2}(10 \text{ m/s}^2)t^2$$

We still need to find t in order to solve for d. Since the ball starts going up at 30 m/s and loses 10 m/s each second, its upward motion takes 3 s, so $t = 3$ s.

$$d = \tfrac{1}{2}(10 \text{ m/s}^2)(3 \text{ s})^2$$

▶ **Step 4** Do the necessary calculations.

$$d = \tfrac{1}{2}(10 \text{ m/s}^2)(3 \text{ s})^2 = \tfrac{1}{2}(10 \text{ m/s}^2)(9 \text{ s}^2) = 45 \text{ m}$$

▶ **Step 5** Evaluate your solution.

Note that the units of the solution are correct for distance. Also, from $d = vt$, where average velocity is $\frac{(30 \text{ m/s} + 0)}{2} = 15$ m/s, and time is 3 s, we get $d = 15$ m/s $\times$ 3 s $= 45$ m.

---

1. If humans originated in Africa and migrated to other parts of the world, some time would be required for this to occur. At the modest rate of a mere one kilometer per year, how many centuries would it take for humans originating in Africa to migrate to China, some 10,000 kilometers away?

2. A stone is thrown with enough speed straight up so that it is in the air several seconds. (a) What is the velocity of the stone when it reaches its highest point? (b) What is its velocity 1 s before it reaches its highest point? (c) What is the change in its velocity during this 1-s interval? (d) What is its velocity 1 s after it reaches its highest point? (e) What is the change in velocity during this 1-s interval? (f) What is the change in velocity during the 2-s interval? (g) What is the acceleration of the stone during any of these time intervals and at the moment the stone has zero velocity?

3. Johnny Hotfoot slams on the brakes of his car moving at 60 mph (26.7 m/s) and skids to a stop in 4 s. (a) What is the deceleration of the car? (b) How far does it skid?

4. The free-fall distance is 39 meters in the Drop-Zone experience at Paramount's Great America in California. If you can't experience such a ride, at least find the number of seconds you'd experience in this free fall. Find the speed at the end of this time.

5. You drop your pencil from your desk, which is 1.0 m above the floor. (a) How long does it take for the pencil to hit the floor? (b) How fast is it going just before it hits the floor?

6. Tara Trucker is driving at 27 m/s through a fog that limits her visibility to 30 m. She suddenly sees a car in front of her traveling in the same direction at 10 m/s. If she fails to apply the brakes, how much time does Tara have between seeing the car and crashing into it?

7. What is the acceleration of a vehicle that changes its velocity from 100 km/h to a dead stop in 10 s?

8. A car going at 30 m/s undergoes an acceleration of 2 m/s² for 4 seconds. (a) What is its final speed? (b) Show that it traveled 136 m while it was accelerating.

9. A ball is thrown straight up with an initial speed of 40 m/s. How high does it go, and how long is it in the air (neglecting air resistance)?

10. Zephram wants to know the height of a bridge, so he drops a rock off the edge. The rock lands in the stream below 3 seconds later. How high is the bridge?

11. Toss a ball upward. How high should you throw it so it will be airborne for 1 second? With no air resistance, how fast will it return to your hand (assuming the same tossing and catching distance from the ground)?

12. (a) Find the speed required to throw a ball straight up and have it return 6 seconds later. (Neglect air resistance.) (b) How high does the ball go?

*13. You drive to the city at an average speed of 40 km/h and return at an average speed of 60 km/h. Find your average speed for the entire trip. Explain why the answer is not 50 km/h.

*14. Harry Hopeless averages 40 km/h for the first half of his car trip. How fast should he drive on the remaining half of the trip to have an average speed of 80 km/h for his trip?

*15. A train moves at a constant speed of 60 km/h toward a station 30 km away. At that moment Fanny Fastbird leaves her perch on the locomotive and flies toward the station at a constant speed of 100 km/h relative to the ground. When the bird reaches the station, she immediately turns around and flies back to the train at the same speed. When reaching the train she again immediately turns around and flies back to the station, repeating the process until the train passes the station. What total distance is traveled by the bird?

16. Use the time-independent equation for uniformly accelerated motion, $v_{final}^2 - v_o^2 = 2ad$, to solve the following: A rocket traveling at 40 m/s accelerates at 2 m/s². Find its speed when it has traveled 200 m. (The equation is derived from $d = v_{average}\, t$, where $v_{average} = \frac{v_f + v_o}{2}$, solving for t, and then substituting t in the equation $d = v_o t + \frac{1}{2} at^2$).

*17. When Valerie Volleyballer jumps to spike a ball, she rises a total of 2.0 m in the air after accelerating through 0.5 m (from crouch to full extension). What is her acceleration during takeoff?

18. Lillian rides her bicycle along a straight road at an average velocity v. (a) Write an equation showing how far she travels in time t. (b) If Lillian's average speed is 7.5 m/s for a time of 5.0 minutes, show that she travels a distance of approximately 2300 m.

19. A race car races on a circular racetrack of radius r. (a) Write an equation for the car's average speed when it travels a complete lap in time t. (b) The radius of the track is 400 m and the time to make a lap is 40 s. Show that the average speed around the track is 63 m/s.

20. George drops a stone from atop a cliff of height h that overlooks the ocean. (a) Ignoring air resistance, show that the stone hits the water in time $\sqrt{\frac{2h}{g}}$. (b) If the cliff is 25 m high, show that the time of fall is 2.2 s. (c) Show that the stone will hit the water at a speed of 22 m/s.

21. A dart that starts at rest leaves the barrel of a blowgun at a speed v. The length of the blowgun barrel is L. Assume that the acceleration of the dart in the barrel is uniform. (a) Show that the dart moves inside the barrel for a time of $2L/v$. (b) If the dart's exit speed is 15.0 m/s and the length of the blowgun is 1.4 m, show that the time the dart is in the barrel is 0.19 s.

sample problem

1. In a physics lab, a 10-g marble, after rolling down a ramp, shoots off the edge of a table with a horizontal velocity of 1.2 m/s. The table is 1.0 m high. You want the marble to land in a shallow cup on the floor. How far from the edge of the table should you place the cup?

▶ **Step 1** Identify the underlying physics concept and write the equation that best expresses it.

The concept is *projectile motion* in the absence of air drag, where the horizontal component of motion remains constant while the vertical component has an acceleration of 10 m/s^2. You are looking for the horizontal distance the ball travels when it leaves the table. The main equation for this is $d = vt$.

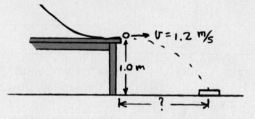

▶ **Step 2** Rewrite the equation so that the term whose value you're looking for is isolated on the left side of the equation.

In this case, you are looking for d so there is no need to rewrite the equation.

▶ **Step 3** Substitute the values of the terms, with their units, for the variables in your equation. (This may involve repeating the process for unknown terms.)

$d = vt = (1.2 \text{ m/s})t$. You must find t (the time in the air) in order to solve for d. Find the time from the formula for the vertical distance, $d = \frac{1}{2}gt^2$. Rearranging the equation to solve for t gives $t = \sqrt{2\frac{d}{g}}$. Since you are concerned with two distances, horizontal and vertical, use x for horizontal distance, and y for vertical distance. Then $x = vt = v\sqrt{2\frac{y}{g}}$.

▶ **Step 4** Do the necessary calculations.

$x = v\sqrt{\frac{2y}{g}} = 1.2 \text{ m/s}\sqrt{\frac{2(1.0 \text{ m})}{1.0 \text{ m/s}^2}} = 0.54 \text{ m}$

▶ **Step 5** Evaluate your solution.

If the cup were taller, then you'd solve the problem by letting y be the vertical distance below the tabletop to the top of the cup. (You may have to take the cup's height into account if you do this in lab!) Note that the marble's mass doesn't matter.

---

1. A plane is flying at an altitude of 8000 m at a speed of 250 m/s. At what horizontal distance ahead of its target must a water balloon be released to strike the target on the ground (neglecting air resistance)?

2. Kayla throws a rock horizontally at 12 m/s from the top of a 45-m high cliff. How far will the rock land from the base of the cliff?

3. Tyler accidentally falls out of an airplane that is traveling horizontally at 45 m/s. He plunges into the water below 3 seconds later. Assuming no air resistance, what was the horizontal distance between Tyler's falling point and the water splash?

4. Jada throws a rock horizontally from a bridge 32 m above the water, which hits the water approximately 25 m from a point immediately below the bridge. Show that Jada's tossing speed was about 10 m/s.

5. Suppose that Hotshot Harry, in moon attire, jumps a vertical distance of 8.0 m on the moon. Acceleration due to gravity there is 1.6 m/s^2. What is Harry's hang time?

6. Suppose that Harry makes the same jump from a horizontally-moving skateboard on the moon's surface. Is his hang time more, less, or the same?

7. Karen, at her third floor window, 7.2 meters above the ground, wants to toss an egg onto the head of Michael who is sunbathing below, 8.0 m away from the building. With what horizontal velocity must Karen launch the egg? (*Hint*: Think first about the time.)

8. Paul is shadow boxing when he makes a horizontal jab with his fist 1.2 m above the ground. His too-loose boxing glove comes off and lands 2.8 m away. How fast was Paul's fist going when his glove came off?

9. A rock dropped from a cliff hits the ground 2.5 s later. Another rock is thrown horizontally from the same cliff lands 20 m from the base of the cliff. What was the thrown rock's initial speed?

10. Brandon the blimp pilot drops his glasses just as he passes 61 m above the home plate of a baseball field. The blimp was moving horizontally at 7.0 m/s at the time. (a) Explain why the initial horizontal velocity of the glasses is 7.0 m/s, while their initial vertical velocity is zero. (b) Ignoring air resistance, show that it takes 3.5 seconds for the glasses to hit the ground. (c) Show that the glasses hit the ground approximately 25 m from home plate.

11. Students in a lab measure the speed of a steel ball launched horizontally from a tabletop to be v. The tabletop is distance y above the floor. They place a tall tin coffee can of height $0.1y$ on the floor to catch the ball, which enters at the top of the can.

(a) Show that the center of the can should be placed at a horizontal distance of $v\sqrt{\dfrac{2(0.9)y}{g}}$ from the base of the table. (b) If the ball leaves the tabletop at a speed of 4.0 m/s, the tabletop is 1.5 m above the floor, and the can is 0.15 m tall, show that the center of the can should be placed a horizontal distance of 2.1 m from the base of the table.

---

sample problem

2. A horizontally moving tennis ball barely clears the top of the net, a distance y above the surface of the court. To land in-bounds, the ball must not be moving too fast. The baseline of the court lies at a distance d from the bottom of the net.

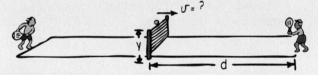

(a) Ignoring air resistance and any spin effects of the ball, show that the ball will land within the court only if its speed v over the net is no greater than $\dfrac{d}{\sqrt{\dfrac{2y}{g}}}$.
(b) Suppose that the height of the net is 1.0 m and that the baseline is 12.0 m from the bottom of the net. Use $g = 10$ m/s² and show that the horizontally moving ball will land in-bounds only if it clears the net with a speed no greater than about 27 m/s (about 60 mi/h).

Note that the solution here is the same as for Sample Problem 1. The motion of the tennis ball as it clears the net is the same as the motion of a marble rolling off a table. The time of fall is the same as the time to move horizontally. The main equation to use is $d = vt$. This time use d (instead of x) for the horizontal distance.

$$v_x = \frac{\text{horizontal distance traveled}}{\text{time to travel that distance}} = \frac{d}{t}$$

The time in the air is the same as the time it takes for the ball to fall the vertical distance y. Substituting for t gives you:

$$v_x = \frac{d}{t} = \frac{d}{\sqrt{\dfrac{2y}{g}}}$$

This equation answers part (a). Now plug and chug to answer part (b):

$$v_x = \frac{d}{\sqrt{\dfrac{2y}{g}}} = \frac{12.0 \text{ m}}{\sqrt{\dfrac{2(1.0 \text{ m})}{10 \text{ m/s}^2}}} = 27 \text{ m/s}$$

The units of the solution are correct for speed. Also note the positions of d, y, and g in the equation. If the baseline was farther away or the pull of gravity was greater, the speed would have to be greater. But if the net was taller, the speed could be less.

12. Annoying Alex slides your physics textbook of mass m off the lab table with a speed v. It meets the floor in time t. (a) Write an equation showing how high the tabletop is above the floor. (b) Write an equation showing how far the book lands from the edge of the table. (c) Calculate the numerical answers to parts (a) and (b) if the book leaves the table at 1.2 m/s, the time in the air is 0.43 s, and you don't know the mass of the book.

13. Megan rolls a ball horizontally at speed v off the edge of a lab bench. The ball lands a horizontal distance x beyond the edge of the bench. (a) Begin with the equation $v_x = x/t$ and write an equation that shows how long the ball is in the air. (b) Write an equation that shows the height of the bench. (c) Calculate the height of the bench if the ball rolls off the edge at 4.0 m/s and lands 2.0 m away.

* 14. A poodle runs at speed v off the end of a diving board. The height of the board above the water is h. (a) Write an equation that shows the horizontal distance from the end of the board that the poodle lands. (b) Write an equation showing the poodle's speed upon landing. (c) Calculate answers to parts (a) and (b) if the height of the board is 1.5 m, initial speed of the poodle is 2.0 m/s, and its mass is 1.6 kg.

* 15. A popped-up baseball follows a smooth parabolic path from home plate to the second baseman. Its time in the air is t and it reaches a maximum height h. Assume that air resistance is negligible. (a) Show that the height reached by the ball is $gt^2/8$. (b) If the ball is in the air for 4 seconds, show that the ball reaches a height of 20 m. (c) If the ball reached the same height as when batted at some other angle, would the time of flight be the same?

* 16. Vincent kicks a soccer ball, which remains in the air for 4 seconds and lands 40 m down field. Show that the ball left Vincent's foot at a speed of about 22 m/s.

* 17. Suppose that flight attendant Paula on a commercial jet moving at 230 m/s, expertly pours a cup of coffee from a pot held 28 cm above the coffee cup. Show that the coffee travels a horizontal distance of 54 meters relative to the Earth between the time it leaves the pot and the time it lands in the cup.

* 18. While running down the street at 6.0 m/s, Leslie tosses her keys straight up (relative to herself) so that she catches them again 9.0 m further along. Show that Leslie tosses the keys upward at 7.5 m/s.

Problems with Trigonometry

19. An experimental jet plane, just after takeoff, climbs with a speed of 500 km/h at an angle of 37° with the horizontal. At what rate is the plane gaining altitude?

20. A soccer ball is kicked with an initial speed of 24 m/s at an angle of 30° to the ground. Neglect air resistance. (a) Calculate the vertical component of the initial velocity. (b) What is the vertical component of velocity at the top of its upward movement? (c) What is the acceleration of the ball on the way up? (d) Show that the ball spends 1.2 s in the air on the way up. (e) Show that the ball rises to a height of 7.2 m. (f) How much total time does the ball spend in the air?

21. Benjamin throws a small coconut at 18 m/s and at a projection angle of 55° above the horizontal to his friend Junior, who is up in a tree house. Junior catches the coconut right at the top of its trajectory. (a) Show that the speed of the coconut just as Junior catches it is about 10 m/s. (b) Show that Junior's tree house is almost 11 m above the ground.

22. Skyler kicks a football. Two seconds later it hits the ground 37 m away. What was the initial speed and direction of the football?

23. A stream of water leaves a high-pressure hose at 25 m/s and makes a 57° angle with the ground. Show that the water lands 57 m away.

24. Adam is skateboarding across the gym floor at 5.5 m/s when he throws his keys straight up (relative to himself) at 7 m/s. Show that Adam has moved 7.7 m across the floor when he catches his keys again.

25. A golf ball leaves the tee at an angle of 30 degrees above the horizontal with a speed of 50 m/s. It lands at the same height from which it was hit. Ignore air resistance. (a) How long is it in the air? (b) What is the maximum height it reaches? (c) Show that the ball lands 217 m downrange.

Chapter 6 Newton's Second Law of Motion—Force and Acceleration

sample problems

1. Find the acceleration of a crate of mass m on a horizontal surface when acted upon by a net force F.

▶ **Step 1** Identify the underlying physics concept and write the equation that best expresses it.

The physics underlying this situation is Newton's second law. In equation form, the solution is:

$$a = \frac{F_{net}}{m} = \frac{F}{m}$$

This is a one-step problem. If we're given the values of F and m, the solution is a straightforward plug-and-chug.

2. Find the acceleration of a crate of mass m on a factory floor when the horizontal net force F acting on it is equal to one-half the weight of the crate.

▶ **Step 1** Identify the underlying physics concept and write the equation that best expresses it.

$$a = \frac{F_{net}}{m}$$

▶ **Step 2** Substitute and simplify.

$$a = \frac{F_{net}}{m} = \frac{\left(\frac{mg}{2}\right)}{m} = \frac{g}{2} = 0.5g$$

Note that we've simply substituted $\frac{mg}{2}$ for F_{net}. Then after cancellation of m we have our solution: $a = 0.5g = 0.5(10\ m/s^2) = 5\ m/s^2$.

---

1. Calculate the acceleration of a 100-kg cart when the net force on it is 50 N.

2. Calculate the horizontal force needed to make a 1-kg hockey puck accelerate at 1000 m/s².

3. What is the acceleration given to a 50-kg block of cement when it is pulled sideways with a net force of 800 N?

4. What is the pressure on a table when a 15-N dictionary with a 0.05-m² cover lies flat on it?

5. Heather can apply a force of 72 N to a wagon in which sits her little brother, Bryce. The combined mass of Bryce and the wagon is 48 kg. If starting from rest, how much speed will the wagon pick up after Heather has pushed the wagon for 3 s?

6. When the wagon in the previous problem reaches a speed of 8 m/s, Heather lets go and Bryce puts on the brakes. If the wagon comes to rest 6 s later, how much force did the brakes apply?

7. A golf ball leaves the tee at a speed of 170 mph (75 m/s). If the ball has a mass of 0.05 kg and gains this speed in 0.02 s, what is the average force of impact of the club on the ball?

8. A 500-kg subcompact car and a 1500-kg standard car are given equal accelerations. How much greater is the force that acts on the more massive car?

9. Scarlet Skydiver, who has a mass of 60 kg, jumps from a stationary helicopter. (a) What is the net force on her as she emerges from the helicopter? (b) What is the net force on her 10 s into the dive, when she has reached terminal speed? (c) What is her acceleration when she reaches terminal speed?

10. Suppose Scarlet then opens her parachute. Air drag on the chute and Scarlet then becomes 2000 N. (a) What is the net force on her now? (b) What is her acceleration?

11. As Scarlet and the parachute slow down, the drag decreases until it equals Scarlet's weight. At that point, what is her acceleration? Will the new terminal speed be greater than, less than, or the same as the terminal speed before the parachute was opened?

12. After being pushed and released, a 50-kg crate slides across a factory floor. Friction on the sliding crate is 200 N. What is the crate's acceleration?

13. What is the acceleration of a 20-kg container of paint pulled upward (not sideways) with a force of 300 N?

14. A firefighter of mass 80 kg slides down a vertical pole with an acceleration of 4 m/s². What is the friction force that acts on the firefighter?

15. The frictional force on Block A is half its weight. Blocks A and B have the same mass. What is the acceleration of the two blocks?

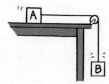

16. A 60.0-kg astronaut finds his weight to be 96.0 N on the moon. Show that the acceleration due to gravity on the moon is 1.6 m/s^2.

17. A 5.0-kg block accelerates at 0.80 m/s^2 along a horizontal surface when a horizontal 12.0-N force acts on it. Show that the force of friction on the block is 8.0 N.

18. A 1.0-kg ball traveling at a velocity of 45 m/s bounces from a wall with a velocity of –33 m/s, after an impact time of 0.20 s. Show that the average force of impact on the ball is 390 N.

19. Kayla exerts a horizontal force F on a box of mass m that sits on a frictionless horizontal surface. (a) Write an equation for the acceleration of the box. (b) Suppose her push is 15 N and the mass of the box is 10 kg. Show that the acceleration of the box is 1.5 m/s^2.

20. A toy airplane of mass m has an engine that creates a thrust F on the plane. (a) Write an equation for the acceleration of the airplane moving horizontally when air resistance is R. (b) Suppose the mass of the plane is 1.1 kg, the engine produces a forward force of 18 N, and air resistance at a particular moment is 8 N. Show that the acceleration at that moment is 9.1 m/s^2.

21. Michael wants to slow a truck of mass m from speed v_o to speed v in a time t. (a) Write an equation that shows the amount of braking force needed to slow the truck. (b) What braking force is needed for a truck of mass 3000 kg that it is slowed from 32 m/s to 12 m/s in 6.0 s?

22. The engine of a Cessna 172 airplane of mass m produces an acceleration a along the runway during takeoff. (a) Write an equation for the net force that acts on the airplane along the runway. (b) Calculate the force when the mass is 1045 kg and acceleration along the runway is 0.8 m/s^2.

23. When using a spring balance in lab you find that a force F accelerates a block across a nearly frictionless horizontal surface at acceleration a. (a) Write an equation for the mass of the block. (b) Calculate the mass of the block if a 5.0-N force accelerates it 2.5 m/s^2.

24. When a horizontal force F is applied to a box having a mass m, the box slides on a level floor, opposed by a force of friction f. (a) Write an equation showing the magnitude of acceleration of the box. (b) Calculate the acceleration if the horizontal force is 412 N, friction is 122 N, and the mass of the box is 75 kg.

25. A cart of mass m is accelerated from rest by a net force F acting for a time t. (a) What will be the speed of the cart at the end of that time? (b) Calculate the final speed of the cart of mass 5.0 kg when a 2.0 N force acts for 10 s.

26. Consider a skydiver at the moment air resistance builds up to half her weight. Show that her acceleration is 0.5g.

27. At one point during her fall, parachutist Rachel of mass m experiences an upward drag force R on her parachute. (a) Write an equation showing her resulting acceleration. (Consider downward to be the positive direction in this case.) (b) R is greater than mg when the parachute first opens. What, then, is the direction of the acceleration? How does this compare with the direction of the velocity? (c) Suppose the drag force on Rachel is 1000 N and the mass of the parachutist is 80 kg. Neglect the mass of the parachute. Show that her acceleration is an upward 2.5 m/s^2. (d) How large a drag force will produce terminal velocity?

28. During a collision, a driver of mass m in a car moving at speed v is brought to rest by an inflated air bag in time t. (a) Write an equation showing the average force the air bag exerts on the driver. (b) Suppose the mass of the driver is 55 kg, the initial speed of the car is 28 m/s, and the contact time with the air bag is 0.20 s. Show that the average force is 7700 N.

* 29. A car of mass m has a maximum acceleration a. When it pulls a trailer of mass $2m$, its acceleration is less. (a) Write an equation showing the maximum acceleration of the car and trailer together. (b) A friend says the answer is $a/2$. Why should you suggest that your friend go back and try again?

*30. Phil and his rocket-powered sled have a combined mass M and are accelerating at a rate a when the sled runs into Mala, mass m, who tumbles aboard. (a) Show that the sled now accelerates at a rate equal to $\frac{M}{M+m}a$. (b) If Phil and his sled have a combined mass of 70 kg, Mala's mass is 45 kg, and the initial acceleration of the sled was 3.6 m/s², show that when Mala joins Phil the acceleration of the sled is 2.2 m/s².

*31. A rock band's tour bus, mass M, is accelerating at rate a when a piece of heavy metal, mass $M/6$, falls onto the top of the bus and remains there. (a) Show that the bus's acceleration is now $\frac{6}{7}a$. (b) If the initial acceleration of the bus is 1.2 m/s², show that when the bus carries the metal piece with it, the acceleration will be 1.0 m/s².

Problems with Trigonometry

32. Marvin exerts 40.0 N on a chain attached to a crate. The chain remains 20° above the horizontal as the crate slides at constant velocity on a horizontal surface. (a) How much of Marvin's force is in the horizontal direction? (b) How much of Marvin's force is in the vertical direction? (c) How much friction acts on the crate? (d) By how much does Marvin's pull affect the normal force on the crate? (e) Would the friction force be greater or less if the chain were horizontal?

33. Consider the following three situations. In each case, a 1000-kg wagon is already moving to the right with negligible friction, and is pulled on with a 100-N force in the directions shown. (a) In which case does the wagon not accelerate? (b) In which case is acceleration greatest? (c) Calculate the acceleration for Case 3.

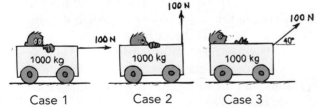

Case 1   Case 2   Case 3

34. Emile pulls a 40-kg wagon along the level sidewalk, exerting a 35-N force on the wagon handle, which makes a 37° angle with the ground. (a) What is the horizontal component of the applied force? (b) If there is no friction force acting on the wagon, what is the wagon's acceleration? (c) If the wagon is moving at a constant speed, show that 28 N of friction are acting on the cart. (d) Show that the normal force applied on the wagon by the sidewalk is almost 380 N.

35. A 10.0-kg box slides down a ramp inclined 30° to the horizontal. How great is the normal force by the ramp on the block?

36. Consider a plastic block of mass m that accelerates down a friction-free plane inclined at 42° to the horizontal. Show that its acceleration down the plane is $0.67g$.

37. Consider a block of wood of mass m resting on a surface inclined at 30°. (a) Compared with the weight of the block, mg, how large of a friction force holds the block at rest? (b) Compared with mg, how large is the normal force on the block? (c) If the surface is raised beyond 30° and the block remains at rest, what changes occur in the magnitude of the friction force? In the normal force?

sample problem

With all his might, a boxer punches a sheet of tissue paper of mass m in midair. The punch brings the paper from rest up to a speed v in time t. (a) Using Newton's second law, write an equation showing how much force the boxer exerts on the tissue paper. (b) By Newton's third law, what amount of force does the tissue paper exert on the boxer? (c) Assume the paper has mass of 0.001 kg and gains a speed of 30.0 m/s in an impact time of 0.050 s. Show that the force of impact is only 0.6 N.

(a) From Newton's second law:

$$a = \frac{F_{net}}{m}$$

$$F_{net} = ma = m\frac{\Delta v}{\Delta t} = m\frac{v}{t}$$

All the terms above are known quantities, so the solution is complete.

(b) By Newton's third law, the magnitude of the force the tissue paper exerts on the boxer and the force the boxer exerts on the tissue paper is the same:

$$F = ma = m\frac{v}{t}$$

(c) Now plug and chug to calculate the force of impact F.

$$F = m\frac{v}{t} = 0.001 \text{ kg} \left(\frac{30.0 \frac{m}{s}}{0.050 \text{ s}}\right) = 0.6 \text{ N}.$$

This is about a 2-ounce tap—hence the origin of the expression about not being able to fight your way out of a paper bag!

1. When a boxer in the gym punches a heavy bag of mass 60 kg, the bag moves from rest to a speed of 2.0 m/s in 0.50 second. Show that the force of impact on the bag is about 240 N. (Neglect the fact that the bag is suspended, and is not really a freely-moving body.)

2. A boxer punches a sheet of paper in midair, and brings it from rest up to a speed of 25 m/s in 0.050 second. The mass of the paper is 0.0030 kg. Show that the force of impact on the paper is merely 1.5 N.

3. During an underwater relay race, Sam, an octopus of mass m, pushes off horizontally from the vertical face of an undersea cliff. Sam experiences an average water resistance force R during the push. (a) Write an equation showing Sam's average acceleration during the push. (b) What does Newton's third law say about the force that Sam exerts on the cliff face and the force that the cliff face exerts on Sam?

4. A 65-kg astronaut in the space station kicks a soccer ball with a force of 13 N. Show that the astronaut accelerates backwards at 0.20 m/s^2.

5. A water skier of mass m is pulled at a constant velocity v by a boat of mass M. Tension in the rope held horizontally by the skier is T. (a) Defend the fact that the amount of resistive force from the water and air on the skier is T. (b) Defend the fact that the upward force the water exerts on the skier is mg.

6. Two ninth-graders, one with three times the mass of the other, attempt a tug-of-war on frictionless ice. Show that the heavier person will gain a speed one-third that of the lighter person.

7. Carts A and B are connected by a compressed spring. Cart A has a mass of 0.25 kg and Cart B has a mass of 1.00 kg. The spring is released. Show that Cart A initially moves four times as fast as Cart B.

8. When two identical air pucks with repelling magnets are held together on an air table and released, they end up moving in opposite directions at the same speed v. Assume the mass of one of the pucks is doubled and the procedure is repeated. (a) How does the final speed of the double-mass puck compare with the speed of the single puck? (b) Calculate the speed of the double-mass puck if the single puck moves away at 0.4 m/s.

9. Daniel (mass 40 kg) and Justin (mass 30 kg) face each other at rest while wearing roller blades. Daniel pushes Justin and accelerates him at 1.6 m/s². Show that Daniel accelerates in the other direction at 1.2 m/s².

10. Manuel, mass M, and Caillen, mass m, put on their ice skates and meet near the center of a frozen pond. While facing each other Manuel pushes Caillen away with force F, giving her an acceleration a. Assume that friction between their ice skates and the ice is negligible. (a) During the contact with Caillen, show that Manuel's acceleration is $\frac{m}{M}a$. What is the direction of his acceleration? (b) Assume Manuel's mass is 66 kg, and Caillen of mass 44 kg accelerates at 2.4 m/s². Show that Manuel accelerates at 1.6 m/s².

11. Ryan observes a tug-of-war between José (mass M) and Juanita (mass m), taking place on a quite slippery floor. José pulls on the rope and imparts an acceleration a to Juanita. (a) Write an equation for the tension in the rope. (b) Assume José's mass is 80 kg, Juanita's mass is 60 kg, and that Ryan observes Juanita accelerate across the floor at 0.10 m/s². Show that the rope tension is 6.0 N.

12. When Abigail swims to the end of the pool she wants to increase her speed after turning around by pushing against the pool wall with force F. Her mass is m, and during her push the average force of water resistance is R. (a) Write an equation showing her average acceleration. (b) Is it possible for Abigail to push against the wall without the wall simultaneously pushing on her?

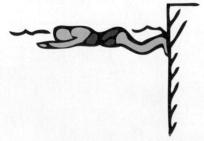

13. Two cars of mass m traveling with crash dummies at the same speed v have a head-on collision and slam to a halt. The collision occurs in a brief time t. (a) Show that the average deceleration of each car is $\frac{v}{t}$. (b) Assume each car's mass is 958 kg, initial speed is 15 m/s, and impact time is 0.20 s. Show that the magnitude of deceleration for each car is 75 m/s². (c) Show that during collision the magnitude of the average force acting on each car is 72,000 N. (d) If you simulate this with smaller carts in lab, each with a force sensor at its "front bumper," a graph of the force readings for both carts during the collision appears as shown below. Why are the two force readings symmetrical?

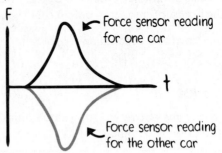

14. A giant frog of mass m is placed on a skateboard of mass M at rest. When the frog jumps in a forward direction from the skateboard, the skateboard rolls freely in the opposite direction at speed V. (a) Show that the frog's horizontal jumping speed is $\frac{M}{m}V$ relative to the ground.

(b) Assume the frog's mass is 2.0 kg, the skateboard's mass is 3.0 kg, and the skateboard recoils at 1.4 m/s immediately after the jump. Show that the frog ends up moving at 2.1 m/s relative to the ground. (c) A force of friction is needed for the frog to propel itself horizontally from the skateboard (a slippery surface won't do). Can the skateboard surface provide a friction force on the frog without an equal and opposite force of friction on the skateboard? Defend your answer.

sample problem

1. A giant frog of mass m is placed on a skateboard of mass M, initially at rest. When the frog jumps horizontally from the skateboard in a forward direction, the skateboard rolls backward at speed V. **(a)** Show that the frog's jumping speed is $\frac{MV}{m}$. **(b)** Show that the frog's horizontal jumping speed is 2.1 m/s, for a frog of mass 2.0 kg and skateboard of mass 3.0 kg that recoils at 1.4 m/s immediately after the jump.

▶ **Step 1** Identify the underlying physics concept and write the equation that best expresses it.

No horizontal external forces act on the frog + skateboard system, so the momentum of the system is conserved. Since the initial momentum of the system is zero, the final momentum of the system must also be zero. That means the momentum of the jumping frog is equal and opposite to the momentum of the recoiling skateboard.

$$m_{frog}v_{frog} = M_{board}V_{board}$$

▶ **Step 2** Rewrite the equation so the term you're looking for is on the left side of the equation.

$$v_{frog} = \frac{M_{board}V_{board}}{m_{frog}} = \frac{MV}{m}$$

The equation above answers part (a).

▶ **Step 3 and 4** Substitute values for terms and calculate.

$$v_{frog} = \frac{MV}{m} = \frac{(3.0\text{kg})(1.4\text{m/s})}{2.0 \text{ kg}} = 2.1 \text{ m/s}$$

You have now answered part (b).

▶ **Step 5** Evaluate your solution.

Note that this is a version of Problem 14 from Chapter 7! Conservation of momentum provides a quicker route to the solution.

2. A giant frog of mass m drops vertically from a tree branch onto a skateboard of mass M that is moving horizontally beneath it at speed V.

(a) Show that the speed of the skateboard right after the frog lands on it is $\frac{M}{M + m}V$.
(b) Show that the speed of the skateboard after the frog lands on it is 2.4 m/s if the frog's mass is 2.0 kg and the mass of the skateboard is 3.0 kg, which initially was moving at 4.0 m/s.
(c) When the frog lands, a force of friction keeps it on the skateboard (without friction on a slippery board, the frog would end up on the ground). Can the skateboard surface provide a friction force on the frog without an equal and opposite force of friction on the skateboard? Defend your answer.

Again, we employ the law of conservation of momentum, and again no external forces act horizontally on the skateboard + frog system. So the horizontal momentum of the skateboard before the frog lands has the same magnitude as the momentum of the skateboard + frog after the frog lands.

$$MV_{before} = (M + m)v_{after}$$

Rearrange the equation to answer part (a):

$$v_{after} = \frac{M}{M + m}V_{before}$$

Now plug and chug to answer part (b):

$$v_{after} = \frac{M}{M + m}V_{before} = \frac{3.0 \text{ kg}}{3.0 \text{ kg} + 2.0 \text{ kg}}(4.0 \text{ m/s})$$
$$= 2.4 \text{ m/s}$$

(c) No. In accord with Newton's third law, the skateboard can only supply a force (friction or otherwise) on the frog if the frog supplies an equal and opposite force on the skateboard.

1. A car of mass 1100 kg moves at 24 m/s. What braking force is needed to bring the car to a halt in 20 s?

2. What average force is exerted on a 25-g egg by a bed sheet if the egg hits the sheet at 4 m/s and takes 0.2 s to stop? (Remember to work in kilograms!)

3. A 100-kg quarterback is traveling 5 m/s and is stopped by a tackler in 1 s. Calculate (a) the initial momentum of the quarterback, (b) the impulse imparted by the tackler, and (c) the average force exerted by the tackler.

4. A 40-kg football player going through the air at 4 m/s tackles a 60-kg player who is heading toward her at 3 m/s, in the air. What is the speed and direction of the entangled players?

5. A jet engine gets its thrust by taking in air, heating and compressing it, and then ejecting it at a high speed. If a particular engine takes in 20 kg of air per second at 100 m/s, and ejects it at 500 m/s, calculate the thrust of the engine.

6. A 40-kg projectile leaves a 2000-kg launcher with a speed of 400 m/s. What is the recoil speed of the launcher?

7. A car of mass 1400 kg travels at 20 m/s and collides with a stationary truck of mass 2800 kg, with its parking brake off. The two vehicles interlock as a result of the collision and slide along the icy road. What is the velocity of the car–truck system?

8. A 10,000-kg truck moving at 10 m/s collides with a 2000-kg car moving at 30 m/s in the opposite direction. If they stick together after impact, how fast, and in what direction, will they be moving?

9. In a fireworks display a 3-kg body moving at 4 km/h due north explodes into three equal pieces: A, at 4 km/h east; B, at 5 km/h 37° south of west; and C, at 15 km/h due north. After the explosion, what is the total momentum of all the pieces?

10. Lonnie's truck of mass m moves at speed v into a headwind of speed V. The temperature of the road surface is T. (a) Write the equation for the momentum of the truck. (b) Calculate the momentum of Lonnie's 3500-kg truck moving at 18 m/s when it drives into a 5 m/s headwind, and when the temperature of the road is 24°C. (c) How does this problem show the importance of letting equations guide your thinking?

11. A block of ice, mass m, slides from rest down an inclined plane. At the bottom of the incline it slides onto the floor at speed v. (a) Show the equation for the momentum gain of the block in sliding down the incline. (b) Calculate the momentum gained by a 25-kg block of ice that starts from rest and slides off the end of an inclined plane at a speed of 6.0 m/s.

12. Soccer Sam kicks a ball initially at rest with an average force F. Sam's foot remains in contact with the ball for a brief time t. (a) Show the equation for the impulse that acts on the ball. (b) What change in momentum occurs for the ball? (c) The ball has a mass of 0.45 kg, the average force of the kick is 1620 N and the time the foot acts on the ball is 0.0050 s. Calculate the speed of the ball after the kick.

13. In the hammer throw contest at a track and field event, Rod whirls a hammer of mass m in a circle and releases it at speed v. (a) How much impulse acted on the hammer? (b) Calculate the impulse if the mass of the hammer is 7.3 kg and it is released at a speed of 28 m/s.

14. A lump of clay of mass m_1 and velocity v_1 catches up with and bumps into a slower lump of clay of mass m_2 and velocity v_2 heading in the same direction. They share a common velocity after they stick together. (a) Derive the equation for this common velocity. (b) Calculate the final velocity of the stuck-together lumps when a lump of mass 2.2 kg moving at 3.2 m/s catches up with and sticks to a 2.8-kg lump moving at 1.2 m/s.

15. Mala of mass m_1 is on roller skates and moves at speed v_1 when she crashes into and hugs Phil (mass m_2) initially at rest and also on skates. (a) Derive an equation for their velocity as they skate off together into the sunset. (b) Calculate their sunset velocity if Phil's mass is 64.0 kg, Mala's mass is 45.0 kg and she initially moves toward Phil at speed 4.5 m/s.

16. A golf ball of mass 0.045 kg traveling horizontally at 28 m/s hits a brick wall and bounces back at the same speed after a contact time of 0.040 s. Show that the average force of impact with the wall is 63 N.

17. Dotty Diver of mass m springs from a diving board and enters straight down into the water below. Dotty's speed just before striking the water is v_1. After a brief time t in the water her speed is reduced to v_2. (a) What average net force acts on Dotty to reduce her speed from v_1 to v_2? (b) Suppose her mass is 48.0 kg and she hits the water at a speed 9.9 m/s, which is reduced to 0.5 m/s in 0.60 s. Show that the average impact force on Dotty is 750 N. (c) How does this force compare with her weight?

18. A chunk of ice of mass m breaks loose from a suspension bridge and falls for time t. (a) Neglecting air resistance, what will be its momentum when it hits the water below? (b) What would be its momentum falling from a higher bridge where the falling time is $2t$?

19. A lump of putty of mass m drops vertically onto a cart of mass M that rolls horizontally at a speed v. (a) What is the speed of the cart after the putty sticks to it? (b) Calculate the speed of the cart if the putty's mass is 5.0 kg, the mass of the cart is 10.0 kg, and the initial speed of the cart is 5.0 m/s.

20. A 2.0-kg object traveling 10.0 m/s north collides with a 5.0-kg object traveling 4.0 m/s south. Show that the combined momentum after the collision is zero.

21. A 115-kg astronaut, floating next to his spacecraft in deep space, becomes untethered. In order to get back to the craft, he throws an 18-kg tool kit at 4.6 m/s away from the craft. Show that the astronaut will recoil back toward the spacecraft at a speed of 0.72 m/s.

22. A 40-kg cart rolls along a railroad track at 4.0 m/s. A dog running at 7.6 m/s to catch up with the cart jumps into the cart. Afterwards the cart is moving at 6.0 m/s. Show that the dog's mass is 50 kg.

23. A 0.50-kg clump of clay moving horizontally at 3.0 m/s has a head-on collision with a 0.6-kg cart. The final clay-cart combination is at rest immediately after the collision. Show that the speed of the cart before the collision was 2.5 m/s.

24. Diane's car of mass m moving at speed v on an icy road collides with a stationary truck of mass M. (a) What is the speed of the interlocked vehicles as they slide along the icy road? (b) Diane's car has a mass of 1500 kg and the truck's mass is 3200 kg. If Diane's initial speed was 22 m/s just before the collision, show that the interlocked vehicles initially move at 7 m/s.

Problems with Trigonometry

25. Two blobs of gooey putty travel at the same speed at right angles to each other. One blob traveling east has twice the mass of the other. The smaller blob travels north. They stick together upon collision. Show that the direction of the stuck-together blobs is 26.6° north of due east.

26. Freddy Frog jumps at a 20° angle above the horizontal from his skateboard at rest. His jumping speed is 3 m/s, his mass is 2 kg, and the mass of the skateboard is 4 kg. Show that the skateboard recoils at a speed of 1.4 m/s.

27. Rosario is standing on roller skates when she throws a 3.0-kg pumpkin into the air. The flying pumpkin takes off at 4.0 m/s, making an angle of 60° with the ground. How fast does the 60-kg Rosario roll backward?

28. An exploding hockey puck (initially at rest) breaks into three pieces of mass m, $2m$, and $3m$. The piece of mass $2m$ heads off along ice in the $+x$-axis at a speed $2v$, while the piece of mass $3m$ heads off along the $+y$-axis at a speed v. (a) What will be the momentum (magnitude and direction) of the piece of mass m? (b) How fast will the m piece be going?

sample problem

1. A simple pendulum 1 m long has a 5-kg bob. (a) Calculate the work done by an outside force in pulling the pendulum from a vertical to a horizontal position. (b) If the pendulum is then released, what will be the speed of the bob as it passes through the lowest point of its path?

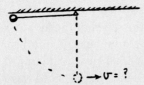

▶ **Step 1** Identify the underlying physics concept and write the equation that best expresses it.

(a) The outside force has to counteract the gravitational force mg, and it acts through a vertical distance h equal to the length of the pendulum.
$W = Fd = mgh$

▶ **Step 2** Rewrite the equation so that the term whose value you're looking for is isolated on the left side of the equation.

You are looking for W, so use the equation as it is written.

▶ **Step 3** Substitute the values of the terms, with their units, for the variables in your equation. (This may involve repeating the process for unknown terms.)

$W = Fd = mgh = (5 \text{ kg})(10 \text{ m/s}^2)(1 \text{ m})$

▶ **Step 4** Do the necessary calculations.

$W = (5 \text{ kg})(10 \text{ m/s}^2)(1 \text{ m}) = 50 \text{ J}$

▶ **Step 5** Evaluate your solution.

The units of the solution are correct for work.

(b) The underlying concept here is *conservation of energy*. The KE at the bottom will equal the PE at the top, or $KE_{bottom} = PE_{top}$. Substituting for both terms gives:

$$\tfrac{1}{2}mv^2_{bottom} = mgh_{top}$$

Now solve $\tfrac{1}{2}mv^2 = mgh$ for v:

$$v^2 = \frac{2mgh}{m} = 2gh$$

$$v = \sqrt{2gh} = \sqrt{2(10 \text{ m/s}^2)(1 \text{ m})} = 4.5 \text{ m/s}$$

The units of the solution are correct for velocity.

Notice that the speed at the bottom of the swing is the same speed the bob would acquire if it were simply dropped down the same vertical distance, and the speed doesn't depend on the mass of the bob. Further thought will show that the time taken to swing down is longer than the time taken to drop vertically. Be careful to distinguish between time and speed when solving problems using energy.

---

1. Calculate the change in kinetic energy when the speed of a 10-kg cart increases from 4 m/s to 10 m/s.

2. How much work is required to make the change in kinetic energy in the previous problem? (Why is your answer the same as in the previous problem?)

3. How much work is done by a person who picks up a 3-kg crate from the floor, raises it 2 m, and sends it flying with a speed of 4 m/s?

4. At one point in its fall, a falling object has a kinetic energy of 5 J and a potential energy of 10 J (relative to the floor). It continues to another point where its potential energy is 3 J. What is its kinetic energy at this point?

5. Calculate the efficiency of a machine that has a useful energy output of 220 J when the work input is 300 J.

6. Use the conservation of energy to find an equation for the speed of a freely falling object that falls from rest at a height h. That is, equate the loss of PE to the gain of KE and solve for velocity v.

7. A pole vaulter wishes to clear a 4-m bar. How fast must she run? (Neglect energy that heats the pole and assume that all her kinetic energy is converted into gravitational potential energy.)

8. In the hydraulic machine shown, you observe that when the small piston is pushed down a distance of 10 cm, the large piston rises 1 cm. If the small piston is pushed down with a force of 200 N, how much force is the large piston exerting?

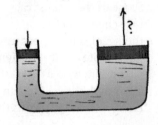

9. (a) What is the theoretical mechanical advantage of a 5-m-long inclined plane that has the high end 1 m above the ground? (b) What is the actual mechanical advantage if 100 N of effort is needed to push a block of ice that weighs 400 N up the plane? (c) What is the efficiency of the inclined plane?

10. What is the efficiency of the body when a cyclist expends 1000 watts of power to deliver mechanical energy to the bicycle at the rate of 100 watts?

11. In the pulley system shown, (a) ideally, what force is necessary to raise the 10-kg weight with a constant speed? (b) If the object rises 4 cm, how far does the puller's hand move? (c) If the system is 40% efficient, what force is necessary to raise the 10-kg block at a constant velocity?

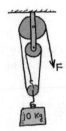

sample problems

2. Milo pushes horizontally on a crate to move it a distance *x* across a factory floor. He exerts a force equal in magnitude to half the weight of the crate. (a) How much work does he do on the crate? (b) If the crate has a mass of 30 kg, calculate the work Milo does in pushing it 12 m.

$$W = Fd = \left(\frac{mg}{2}\right)x = \frac{mgx}{2}$$

The equation above answers part (a). Plug and chug to answer part (b):

$$W = \frac{mgx}{2} = \frac{(30\,kg)(10\,m/s^2)(12\,m)}{2} = 1800\,J$$

3. Janet is cruising along a level road at speed *v* and slams on the car's non-antilock brakes and slides to a stop. The force of friction is one quarter of the car's weight. How far does Janet's car slide?

Friction does work to slow the car and bring its KE to zero. Recall the work–energy theorem, $W = \Delta KE$. Here, work W is friction f acting over a distance d. The mass of the car is m, and the car's initial speed is v. The final speed of the car will be zero, so the amount of change in KE is equal to the initial KE at speed v.

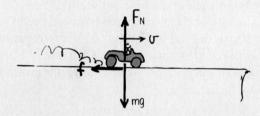

From $W = \Delta KE$, you can write:

$$fd = \frac{1}{2}mv^2 \Rightarrow d = \frac{\frac{1}{2}mv^2}{f} = \frac{\frac{1}{2}mv^2}{(mg/4)} = \frac{2v^2}{g}$$

The solution tells us that the stopping distance is proportional to speed squared, which is consistent with KE—a car going twice as fast will have four times as much KE, and so will require four times the distance for the same friction force to bring it to a stop. Note that the mass cancels in the equations, which tells us that the mass of the car doesn't matter. All cars skidding with the same initial speed and with friction equaling one quarter the car's weight will skid the same distance. And note that $2v^2/g$ has units of $\frac{m^2/s^2}{m^2/s^2} = m$, which is correct for distance.

859

12. A person atop a 30-m cliff throws a ball at 4 m/s at an angle of 37° above the horizontal. How fast does the ball hit the ground?

13. Daniel's mass is 100 kg and he climbs a 4.3-m-high flight of stairs in 5.4 seconds. Show that the average power expended by Daniel is about 796 watts.

14. A cart moving at a constant speed of 25 m/s possesses 438 J of kinetic energy. Show that the cart has a mass of 1.4 kg.

15. A steady force of friction acts on a 15.0-kg mass moving initially at 10.0 m/s on a horizontal surface. Show that if the mass is brought to rest over a distance of 12.5 m, the friction force is 60.0 N.

16. A 2.4-kg brick slides across an ice-covered pond at 5.0 m/s. (a) Show that the kinetic energy of the sliding brick is 30 J. (b) When it slows to half speed, will its kinetic energy be half as much? One-quarter as much? One-eighth as much? Defend your answer.

17. A shiny new 180-kg motorcycle sits at the edge of a 35-m cliff. The gravitational potential energy of the motorcycle at the base of the cliff is zero. (a) Show that its gravitational potential energy at the top of the cliff is 63,000 J. (b) If it were pushed over the edge by envious rascals, what would be its kinetic energy right before hitting the ground below?

18. A 0.50-kg croquet ball at the top of an incline has a potential energy of 6.0 J relative to the base of the incline. (a) What will be the ball's potential energy when it rolls halfway down the incline? (b) What will be the ball's potential energy and kinetic energy at the bottom of the incline?

19. A 20-N block falls freely from rest from a point 3.0 m above the surface of Earth. Show that after falling 1.5 m, the gravitational potential energy of the block relative to Earth's surface is 30 J.

20. A 70-kg mountain climber with 35-kg of gear climbs from his base camp to the top of Mt. Everest, a vertical distance of approximately 2400 m. Show that his change is PE is about 2.5×10^6 J (about the same as the amount of energy stored in three candy bars).

21. A chunk of ice of mass m breaks loose from a suspension bridge of height h. (a) Write an equation for the chunk's kinetic energy when it hits the water below. (b) What would be its kinetic energy if it fell from a bridge twice as high? (c) A 0.80-kg chunk of ice falls from a suspension bridge 45 m above the water. Calculate the KE of the ice right before it hits the water.

22. Some of the newest cars have a regenerative braking scheme, so that when the brakes are applied the KE of the car goes into charging batteries instead of into thermal energy in the brakes. Show that, with a 50% efficient system, a 1400-kg car moving at 24 m/s can provide 2.0×10^5 J of energy to the battery as the car slows to a stop.

23. Work is done on a cannonball by the force from gunpowder exploding in a cannon. Assume the average force on the cannonball is 3500 N while it is pushed 2.2 m inside the cannon barrel. (a) Show that the work done on the cannonball is 7700 J. (b) How does 7700 J compare with the kinetic energy gained by the cannonball?

24. Tsing does work W in moving a box of mass m, initially at rest, over a distance x on a horizontal friction-free surface. (a) Write an equation for the horizontal force that Tsing exerts on the box. (b) What is the final speed of the box? (c) Show that Tsing exerts 60 N when doing 660 J of work moving a 28-kg box from rest over a horizontal distance of 11 m. Also show that the speed of the box is nearly 7.0 m/s when it reaches the 11-m distance.

25. When an average force F is exerted over a certain distance on a system of mass m that starts from rest, the system's kinetic energy increases by $\frac{1}{2}mv^2$. (a) Derive an equation for the distance over which the force acts. (b) If twice the force is exerted over twice the distance, how does the resulting increase in kinetic energy compare with the original increase in kinetic energy?

26. A block of ice, mass m, at an initial height h slides from rest down an inclined plane. At the bottom of the incline it slides onto the floor at speed v. (a) Derive an equation for this speed, assuming friction can be ignored. (b) Calculate the speed that a 27-kg block of ice will have when it reaches the bottom of an inclined plane of height 1.5 m. Again, ignore friction.

27. A car of mass m undergoes an increase in speed from v_o to v in a time interval t. (a) Derive an equation showing the car's increase in kinetic energy. (b) Calculate the change of kinetic energy if the mass of the car is 1300 kg, its initial speed is 13 m/s, and 5.0 seconds later its speed is 19 m/s. (c) Show that the average power exerted by the car's engine is about 25 kW.

28. Ryan finds that 700 watts of power is needed to keep his boat moving through the water at a constant speed of 10 m/s. Show that the amount of force exerted by the water on the boat is 70 N.

29. A loaded elevator is lifted, starting at rest and ending at rest, a distance of h in a time t by a motor delivering power P. (a) Derive an equation for the force the motor exerts in lifting the elevator. (b) Show that 90 kN of force is exerted when the distance raised is 20 m, the time of lift is 30 s, and the power of the motor is 60 kW.

30. An electric motor lifts an elevator of mass m from ground level to the top of a building of height h in time t. (a) Derive an equation for the average power the motor delivers. (b) Show that the motor delivers 75 kW of power when it lifts a 10,000-kg elevator from ground level to the top of a 30-m building in 40 s.

31. Benjamin applies a force F over a distance x to a rope connected to a set of pulleys. This raises a block of weight w to height h above its initial level. (a) Write an equation for Benjamin's work input. (b) What work is done on the block? (c) What is the efficiency of the pulley system? (d) Calculate answers to the above questions given that the force applied is 75 N over a 12-m distance, the weight of the block is 300 N, and it is raised a vertical distance of 2.0 m.

32. A block of weight w is raised a vertical distance h by means of a device having an efficiency E. (a) What is the work output? (b) What is the work input? (c) Calculate answers to the above questions when a 300-N block is raised is 5 m and the efficiency of the device is 65%.

33. The pulley combination shown is used to lift a heavy block. (a) What is the ideal mechanical advantage of the pulley system? (b) Show that you should be able to lift up a 24-kg block by pulling on the rope with a force of 60 N. (c) If you are actually required to exert a force of 132 N to lift the block, show that the pulley system has an efficiency of 0.45.

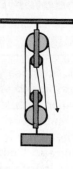

34. An acrobat of mass m stands on the left end of a seesaw. A second acrobat of mass M jumps from a height h onto the right end of the seesaw, thus propelling the first acrobat into the air. (a) Neglecting inefficiencies, how will the PE of the smaller acrobat at the top of his trajectory compare with the PE of the second acrobat just as he jumps? (b) Neglecting inefficiencies, how high does the first acrobat go? (c) Calculate the maximum height the first acrobat reaches if his mass is 40 kg, the mass of the second acrobat is 70 kg, and the initial height jumped from was 4 m.

Problems with Trigonometry

35. Phil pushes Cheryl on her sled across a snow-covered field. Cheryl and the sled together have a mass of 62 kg. Phil exerts a force $F = 116$ N at an angle $\theta = 22°$ below the horizontal to keep Cheryl moving at a constant speed of 1.0 m/s. (a) How large is the friction force acting on the sled? (b) How large is the normal force acting on the sled? (c) How much work does Phil expend in moving her 10.0 m? (d) Since speed is constant, what net work is done on the sled?

sample problem

1. Suppose you attach a ball of mass _m_ to a string and whirl it overhead in a horizontal circular path. If you keep the ball moving at constant speed _v_ and shorten the string, tension in the string increases. The string will break if you exceed a critical tension _T_. (a) What is the shortest length of string you can use so the string doesn't break? (Make the approximation that the string remains horizontal.) (b) Calculate the minimum length of string needed to keep a 250 g ball circling at a constant speed of 6 m/s if the string's breaking tension is 45 N.

The physics concept is centripetal force. Here, string tension _T_ provides the centripetal force:

$$F = T = \frac{mv^2}{L}$$

Rearrange the equation to answer part (a):

$$L = \frac{mv^2}{T}$$

To answer part (b), first convert to consistent SI units (250 g = 0.25 kg), and then substitute.

$$L = \frac{mv^2}{T} = \frac{(0.25 \text{ kg})(6.0 \text{ m/s})^2}{45 \text{ N}} = 0.20 \frac{\text{kg} \cdot \text{m}^2 \text{s}^2}{\text{kg} \cdot \text{m/s}^2}$$

$$= 0.20 \text{ m}$$

Note that the _maximum_ value for _T_ gives the _minimum_ value _L_ can have for a given mass and speed. (In reality, the string _must_ make an angle with the horizontal, as shown below. For the net force on the ball in the vertical direction to equal zero, its weight _mg_ must be countered by an equal upward force supplied by a vertical component of string tension.)

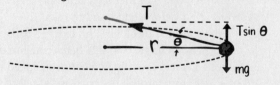

2. When an airplane flies in a vertical loop with just the right speed _v_ at the very top, the pilot can experience weightlessness. (a) For a vertical loop of radius _r_, at what critical speed will the pilot feel weightless? (b) Calculate the critical speed for achieving weightlessness at the top of a vertical loop of radius 200 m.

The underlying physics is centripetal force:

$$F = \frac{mv^2}{r}$$

Rearrange the equation for _v_:

$$v = \sqrt{\frac{Fr}{m}}$$

Two principal forces act on a pilot while executing a vertical loop: gravitational force _mg_ and the normal force _n_ from the seat pushing on the pilot's body. At the top of the loop, both forces are downward in the radial direction. Their vector sum provides the centripetal force:

$$F_{net} = mg + n = \frac{mv^2}{r}$$

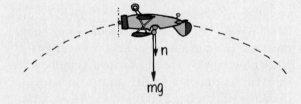

During weightlessness, _n_ = 0, so $F_{net} = mg$. Now solve for the speed for achieving weightlessness:

$$v = \sqrt{\frac{Fr}{m}} = \sqrt{\frac{mgr}{m}} = \sqrt{gr}$$

This answers part (a). (Note that the pilot's mass cancels.) Plug and chug to answer part (b):

$$v = \sqrt{gr} = \sqrt{(10 \text{m/s}^2)(200 \text{m})} = 44.7 \text{ m/s}$$

1. Find the number of revolutions of a bicycle wheel of diameter 0.7 m when the bike goes a distance of 22 m down the street.

2. Calculate the tension in a 2-m length of string that whirls a 1-kg mass at 2 m/s in a horizontal circle.

3. Answer the previous question for the case of (a) twice the mass, (b) twice the speed, (c) twice the length of string (radial distance), and (d) twice the mass, twice the speed, and twice the radial distance all at the same time.

4. Harry Hotrod rounds a corner in his sports car at 50 km/h. Fortunately, a force of friction holds him on the road. If he rounds the corner at twice the speed, how much greater must the force of friction be to prevent him from skidding off the road?

5. In the Olympic hammer-throw event, an athlete throws a 7.3-kg lead ball attached to a 1.2-m cable. The athlete swings the ball in a circle three or four times before letting it go. If the ball attains a speed of 27 m/s, how much tension is there in the cable just before it is released?

6. Spin Out is a carnival ride consisting of a large open cylinder. Riders stand inside with their backs against the cylinder wall. (a) What is the centripetal force acting on you in the ride if the radius of the cylinder is 3.5 m, your mass is 50 kg, and you are traveling at 5 m/s? (b) What force keeps you from sliding downward and how does that force relate to the above spinning speed?

7. A 50-kg ice skater moves around a bend at 8 m/s. The radius of the bend is 8 m. Centripetal force is provided by friction between the blade of the skates and the ice. Show that the amount of centripetal force is 400 N.

8. Freddie swings a 2-kg stone at the end of a thin rope of length 1.2 m. He tugs mightily, swinging the stone so fast that the rope is almost horizontal. If the string tension is 200 N, show that the stone moves at 11 m/s.

9. Suppose you tie a rock to the end of a string of length L and spin it in a vertical circle. Show that the minimum speed it can travel and "just" get around the top is given by $\sqrt{gL}$. (*Hint:* The rope will just start to go "slack" when string tension is zero and the only force acting on the rock, downward, is gravity.)

10. A centripetal force is needed to keep a block of mass m moving on a smooth floor in a circular path of radius r. The block makes a complete revolution in time t. (a) Show that the centripetal force is given by $\frac{4\pi^2 mr}{t^2}$. (b) Suppose the mass is 2.0 kg, the radial distance is 1.0 m, and each revolution takes 5.0 s. Show that the centripetal force will be 3.2 N.

11. A puck of mass m is attached to a string of length L and moves in a horizontal circle on an air table (where friction can be neglected). (a) Derive an equation that shows the speed of the puck when the centripetal acceleration equals the acceleration of gravity g. (b) Use your equation to calculate this speed for a 0.60-m-long string and a 0.20-kg puck. (c) What is the speed if the mass is 0.40 kg?

12. A sand-filled tin can is tied to the end of a wire of length L. When the can revolves around a center pole in a horizontal circle on a smooth floor at a steady speed v, the tension in the wire is T. (a) Starting with the equation for centripetal force, derive an equation showing the mass of the sand-filled can. (b) When the can moves at 15 m/s at the end of a 2.0-m-long wire, the tension in the wire is 195 N. Show that the mass of the can is 1.7 kg.

13. A centripetal force acts on an airplane of mass m flying at speed v in a horizontal circle of radius r. (a) Find the centripetal force divided by the mass (this is the force per unit mass, which is the same as the centripetal acceleration). (b) When the speed of the airplane is 200.0 m/s and the radius of its path is 12,500 m, show that the centripetal force per kilogram is 3.2 N/kg.

*14. A certain 0.80-m cord will break when a 25-kg block is suspended from it. Suppose the cord is attached to a 0.50-kg ball, which is swung so fast in a circle that the cord is nearly horizontal. (a) At what linear speed will the cord break? (b) If the ball is to be swung with a speed of 25 m/s, what is the shortest length of the same kind of cord that can be used?

*15. Evan stands on Earth's equator. He has a tangential speed due to Earth's daily spin. (a) Given that Earth has mass M and equatorial radius R, derive an equation for the tangential speed of Evan at the equator. (b) Calculate the tangential speed at Earth's equator. Earth's equatorial radius is 6.38×10^6 m. (c) How fast would Earth have to spin so that Evan and his friends would have no weight? That is, what linear speed would correspond to a normal force of zero? (d) How does this speed compare with the speed of a satellite near Earth's surface?

Problems With Trigonometry

16. Whereas friction provides the centripetal force to hold a car on a curved non-banked track, a properly-banked curve requires no friction at all. Consider a horizontal circular track of radius r banked at angle θ. (a) Inspect the sketch and compare the vertical component of the normal force n with the magnitude of mg. Why are they the same size? (b) What role does the horizontal component of n play? (c) Find the speed of a car of mass m that will enable it to remain on the track without the benefit of friction. (d) Calculate the speed of the car if the angle is 23°, radius is 125 m, and the mass of the vehicle unknown.

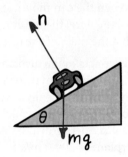

17. A 0.28-kg tetherball swings in a circular path on the end of a line that is 2.4 m long, and makes an angle of 50° with the horizontal. Show that the speed of the ball is 3.6 m/s.

*18. At a popular carnival ride Mala sits in a chair that is swung in a circular path by a cable as shown. Mala, in effect, is the bob of a conical pendulum. The mass of Mala and the chair is 184 kg, the length of the cable L is 15 m, and the angle the cable makes with the vertical is $\theta = 25°$. (a) Show that Mala's radial distance in circling is 6.3 m. (b) Show that the tension T in the cable is 2030 N. (c) Show that Mala's speed is 5.4 m/s.

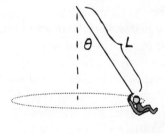

Chapter 11 Rotational Equilibrium

Use the diagram below to answer Questions 1–3. The diagram shows a meterstick placed with the fulcrum at the 50-cm mark.

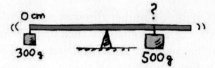

1. If a 300-g mass is placed at the 0-cm mark (50 cm from the fulcrum), at what mark should a 500-g mass be placed so that the system is balanced?

2. If a 120-g mass is placed at the 25-cm mark and a 25-g mass at the 10-cm mark, where should a 500-g mass be placed to balance the system?

3. Suppose the mass of the stick is 200 g, and a single 500-g mass is to play "solitary seesaw" at the 0-cm mark. Where should the fulcrum be located?

4. A horizontal meterstick has a 3-kg blob of clay stuck on one end, at the 0-cm mark, and a 1-kg blob stuck on the other end, at the 100-cm mark. Neglecting the mass of the stick itself, where is the center of gravity of the stick and clay system?

5. A 10,000-N vehicle is stalled one-quarter of the way across a bridge. Calculate the additional forces supplied at the supports on both ends of the bridge due to the vehicle's weight.

6. James uses a wrench to turn a stubborn bolt. (a) How much would the torque on the bolt increase if the applied force were doubled? (b) How much would the torque increase for the original force if a pipe were inserted over the wrench to make the lever arm 3 times as long?

7. José pushes perpendicular to a door with force F at the door's far edge. Marie pushes the door from the opposite side and the door doesn't turn. Her push is perpendicular to the door but at a point halfway from the hinge to the edge. (A top view of the door is seen in the sketch.) (a) How hard does she push on the door? (b) Calculate Marie's push if José pushes with a force of 10 N.

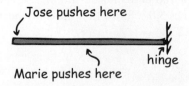

8. A boy and girl sit on a seesaw of length L balanced at its center. The girl sits at the far end. The boy is twice as heavy as the girl, and therefore sits midway between his end and the center. Then the girl is given a bag of oranges weighing 10 N and the seesaw rotates out of balance. When the boy is given a bag of apples, balance is restored. What is the weight of the bag of apples?

9. Consider two identical metersticks tied together with a loose piece of string attached to their ends. If you hold one stick horizontal, the other dangles vertically, as shown. You place your finger at an appropriate location beneath the horizontal stick so the two sticks will balance. Where along the horizontal stick should you place your finger so the metersticks will balance?

10. Consider the previous problem. If you did the same with one horizontal meterstick and two vertical metersticks dangling from its one end, where would you place your finger to balance the system?

11. Karen wants to figure out the mass of a meterstick. She suspends the meterstick by a string tied around the 20-cm mark of the meterstick. She finds that it takes a mass m tied at the 5-cm mark of the meterstick to balance it. (a) What is the mass of the meterstick? (b) The meterstick was balanced by a 70-gram mass. Find the mass of the meterstick.

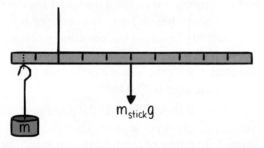

12. Mary Beth holds a meterstick horizontally with a 1-kg weight hanging from its far end. How much weight should she instead suspend from the center of the stick to feel the same torque?

13. A uniform heavy plank of mass m lies on a raised horizontal surface, with one end overhanging. The maximum overhang distance is half the length of the plank. Suppose you put your pet cat of mass $0.2\ m$ on the end of the overhung plank (with a safety net below). Of course the plank would topple, unless it is moved to the left. (a) What percentage of the plank can overhang without toppling, with the cat at its end? (b) If the cat were twice as heavy, what would be the maximum percentage of overhang distance?

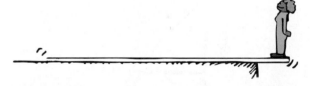

14. Lydia has a mass m and stands at the end of a uniform plank of length L and mass M that overhangs the top of a building as shown. The maximum distance of overhang for tipping to not occur is one-eighth the length of the plank. (a) How does Lydia's mass compare with the mass of the plank? (b) Calculate the mass of the plank if Lydia's mass is 45 kg.

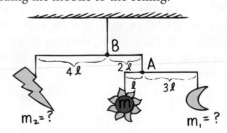

15. Michael sees this mobile hanging from the ceiling, constructed with string and two very stiff lightweight wires. (a) Compared with the central "sun" of mass m, how do the masses m_1 and m_2 compare? (b) How much tension is in the string holding the mobile to the ceiling?

Problems With Trigonometry

16. A 600-gram squirrel stands on the end of a 2.5-m-long branch that makes a 60° angle with the vertical trunk of the tree. Show that the squirrel's weight exerts an additional 13 N·m torque on the branch.

17. A 6.0-kg uniform trap door set into the floor is a square 1.0 m on a side and has its handle set 0.80 m from its hinges. Joel leans over the hinges and grabs the handle, pulling at an angle of 33° to the floor. Show that to get the door to open he must exert a force of 69 N.

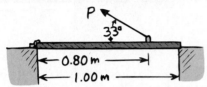

18. A 24-N lantern is suspended at the end of a 60-N horizontal bar 2.4 m long that is supported by a cable that makes an angle $\theta = 53°$ with the side of a vertical wall. Assume the weight of the bar is at its center. Calculate the tension in the supporting cable.

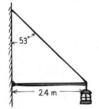

19. Garrett hinges a 3.0-m plank at the edge of his roof. The plank extends horizontally and is supported by a rope at the far end that reaches to a sturdy tree branch. The rope makes 50° to the horizontal, Garrett's mass is 52 kg, and the mass of the plank is 12 kg. (a) When Garrett stands 1.0 m from the hinge, show that the rope tension is slightly more than 300 N. (b) How much tension is in the rope when Garrett stands 2.0 m from the hinge?

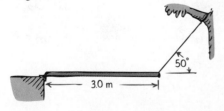

Chapter 12 Rotational Motion

1. (a) Find the angular momentum of a 5-kg iron ball swinging in a horizontal circle at 3 m/s at the end of a 4-m rope. (b) What happens to the angular momentum when both the speed and length of rope are doubled?

2. A ball of gas in outer space rotates once each month while contracting due to gravity. When it contracts to reduce its rotational inertia to one-tenth, find the number of rotations it makes per month.

3. A pendulum consists of a 1.00-kg bob suspended by a 1.20-m length of string. (a) Show that its rotational inertia about the top end of the string is 1.44 kg·m². (b) Calculate its rotational inertia if the string is shortened by half.

4. Find the change in the rotational inertia of a solid cylinder when both its mass and its radius are doubled.

5. A playground carousel is free to rotate about its center on frictionless bearings. The carousel has a mass M, radius r, and is at rest. Consider the carousel to simply be a big disk. (a) Write the equation for the rotational inertia of the carousel. (b) Write the equation for the rotational inertia of a man of mass m rotating in a circle of radius r (the same radius as the carousel). (c) It so happens that the rotational inertias of bodies add when they share the same center of rotation. What will be the combined rotational inertia of the man and carousel when the man sits at the edge of the carousel? (d) Calculate the combined rotational inertia if the diameter of the carousel is 4.0 m, its rotational inertia alone is 400 kg·m², and the mass of the man is 70.0 kg.

6. Suppose that the carousel in the previous problem makes 1 rotation per second. Then the man walks toward the center of the rotating carousel. Use the conservation of angular momentum and calculate the rotational speed of the carousel when the man gets to the carousel's center.

7. A skater rotates at 1.2 revolutions per second with arms at her side. When she raises her arms to a horizontal position, her speed decreases to 0.8 revolutions per second. Show that her rotational inertia with outstretched arms has increased by 1.5 times.

8. A ball of mass m at the end of a string moves at constant speed v_o in a horizontal circle of radius r. Assume the speed is great enough so the string remains practically horizontal. (a) If the ball is pulled into a circular path of half the radius, what will be its speed? (b) If the original tension was T_o, what is the new tension? (c) Calculate the new tension if the mass of the ball is 0.50 kg, initial speed 20 m/s, and initial radius 4.0 m.

9. A space pod circles a space station at the end of a long tether line. (a) How will the linear speed of the pod compare with its original speed when the line has been pulled in to half its length? (b) How will the linear speed compare whcn the line is pulled in to one-tenth its original length?

10. An astronaut on a space walk swings a 0.5-kg metal tool in a circular path at the end of a cable 3.6 m long. The astronaut then reels in the tool to a 1.2-m distance. Show that the speed of the tool will be three times as great at the reduced distance.

*11. Suppose you are standing within the rim of a circular space station, in outer space. The rim revolves around the center of the space station at a speed of 300 m/s. If the radius of the station is 9000 meters, what will you weigh? (*Hint:* Find v^2/r and compare it to g.)

*12. Suppose you are asked to design a space station that is 1.0 km in diameter, and is spun fast enough so that a resident standing within it at the outer circumference of the station would experience Earth-normal gravity. How fast (in RPM) would you have to spin the space station?

13. A small space telescope at the end of a tether line of length L moves at linear speed v about a central space station. (a) What will be the linear speed of the telescope if the length of the line is reduced to $0.33L$? (b) If the initial linear speed of the telescope is 1.0 m/s, what is its speed when pulled in to one-third its initial distance from the space station?

Chapter 13 Universal Gravitation

1. Find the change in the force of gravity between two planets when the distance between them is reduced to one-tenth of the original distance.

2. Consider a bright point light source located 1 m from a square opening that is 1 m^2 in area. Light passing through the opening illuminates an area of 4 m^2 on a screen 2 m from the opening. (a) Find the area illuminated if the screen is moved to distances of 3 m, 5 m, and 10 m. (b) How can the same amount of light illuminate more area as the screen is moved farther away?

3. Earth's surface is one Earth radius from its center. The gravitational force on a 1-kg object at Earth's surface is 10 N. What is the gravitational force on this object if it is moved to a point four Earth radii from the center of Earth?

4. If you stand 1 km from the center of a typical mountain of mass 5×10^{11} kg, you'll be gravitationally attracted to it (as you're attracted to everything else). Likewise, you're attracted to the moon, which has a mass of 7.4×10^{22} kg and which is 3.8×10^5 km away. Which of the two, the mountain or the moon, exerts the greater force on you?

5. Calculate the force of gravity between Earth and the sun if the mass of Earth is 6.0×10^{24} kg, the mass of the sun is 2.0×10^{30} kg, and the distance between them is 1.5×10^{11} m.

6. Suppose that the mass of a star somchow doubles without any change in its radius. Use the equation for gravitational force and show that the force of gravity on its surface also doubles.

7. Suppose that the radius of a star somehow doubles without any change in its mass. Use the equation for gravitational force and show that the force of gravity on its surface becomes one-fourth of what it was.

8. Suppose that the mass of a star and its radius both somehow double. Use the equation for gravitational force to show by what factor the force of gravity changes on its surface.

9. Newton's universal law of gravity tells us that $F = G\frac{m_1 m_2}{d^2}$. Newton's second law tells us that $a = \frac{F}{m}$. (a) With a bit of algebraic reasoning show that your gravitational acceleration toward any planet of mass M a distance d from its center is $a = G\frac{M}{d^2}$. (b) How does this equation tell you whether or not your gravitational acceleration depends on your mass?

10. The gravitational field about a massive object is defined to be the gravitational force per mass on an object in the vicinity of the massive object. The symbol for the gravitational field is bold-faced **g** (with magnitude the same as the magnitude of gravitational acceleration at that point, g). (a) Show that the gravitational field a distance d from Earth's center (with d greater than Earth's radius) is $\frac{GM}{d^2}$, where G is the universal gravitational constant and M is the mass of Earth. (b) The value of g at Earth's surface is about 10 N/kg. Show that the value of **g** at a distance of four Earth radii from Earth's center is 0.6 N/kg.

11. The mass of Mars is 0.11 that of Earth, and its radius 0.53 that of Earth. Use this information to show that your weight on the surface of Mars would be about 0.4 your weight on Earth.

12. A group of students repeat Philipp von Jolly's experiment (discussed on page 238). They record the following data: $m_1 = 5.00$ kg, $m_2 = 5775$ kg, F = the weight of 0.589 milligram (the *extra* mass needed to maintain balance after the large sphere is rolled under the smaller one), and $d = 0.569$ m, the distance between the centers of m_1 and m_2. With these data compute the universal gravitational constant, G.

*13. The mass of a certain neutron star is 3.0×10^{30} kg (1.5 solar masses) and its radius is 8,000 m (8.0 km). Show that the force of gravity at the surface of this condensed, burned-out star is about 300 billion times that on Earth.

*14. Jack climbs a beanstalk so high that his weight at the top is half that at Earth's surface. Show that Jack is 9,010 km from Earth's center.

*15. Suppose that you are standing on a very tall ladder so that you are two Earth radii above Earth's center. You give a rock a gentle toss upward. How does the distance the rock travels upward compare with the distance it would go if you gave the rock the same toss at Earth's surface?

*16. Saturn's moon Titan has a mass of 1.35×10^{23} kg and a radius of 2.58×10^6 m. (a) Show that the force that Titan would exert on a 1.0-kg ball located at its surface is 1.35 N. (b) Calculate the acceleration due to gravity on Titan. (c) If you could toss a 1.0-kg ball horizontally at 15 m/s on Titan from the top of your 20-m tall space ship, how far away from the base of the ship would it land? (Assume only the vertical component of motion changes due to gravity, but the horizontal component of motion doesn't change.) (d) Calculate your answer to (c) with the same ball tossed on Earth.

*17. In November of 2005, the Japanese space probe *Hayabusa* visited an asteroid with a mass of about 3.5×10^{10} kg. The acceleration due to gravity on the surface of the asteroid is estimated to be about 0.0001 m/s². Show that to experience the same acceleration due to Earth's gravity you'd have to be about 320 Earth radii away from Earth's center.

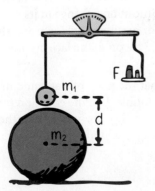

sample problem

A satellite of mass m circles Earth at a constant altitude h above Earth's surface. (a) What is the speed of the satellite? (b) The International Space Station orbits Earth in a nearly circular orbit, averaging a height of 370 km above Earth's surface. What is the speed of the ISS as it circles Earth?

(a) Since the satellite travels in a circular orbit, the gravitational force must provide a centripetal force mv^2/r. Math-wise:

$$G\frac{M_E m_{sat}}{d^2} = \frac{m_{sat}v^2}{r}$$

Three things to notice before we go any further:
(1) The term d is the distance from the center of Earth to the satellite, equal to $R_E + h$ (Earth's radius + distance above Earth's surface).
(2) The radius of the orbit (r in the mv^2/r term) is also measured from the center of Earth, and is exactly the same as d.
(3) We don't need to know the mass of the satellite (because it cancels out of the equation).

$$G\frac{M_E m_{sat}}{d^2} = \frac{m_{sat}v^2}{r} \Rightarrow$$

$$G\frac{M_E}{(R_E + h)^2} = \frac{v^2}{(R_E + h)} \Rightarrow v = \sqrt{\frac{GM_E}{(R_E + h)}}$$

(b) From part (a), $v = \sqrt{\frac{GM_E}{(R_E + h)}}$.

Two things to notice before we go any further:
(1) G has units of N·m²/kg², so all of the distances we use should be expressed in meters before we can use the equation.
(2) The mass and radius of Earth are listed in Table B.1 in Appendix B at the back of this textbook.

First let's convert the units:

height $h = 370$ km $= 3.7 \times 10^5$ m

$R_E + h = (6.37 \times 10^6 \text{ m}) + (0.37 \times 10^6 \text{ m})$
$= 6.74 \times 10^6$ m

Then

$$v = \sqrt{\frac{6.67 \times 10^{-11} \frac{\text{N·m}^2}{\text{kg}^2} (5.98 \times 10^{24} \text{ kg})}{6.74 \times 10^6 \text{ m}}}$$

$= 7690 \frac{\text{m}}{\text{s}}$

The space station moves about 25 to 30 times faster than a normal commercial jet. This high speed ensures that it falls around and around Earth, and not into its surface!

1. A satellite in circular orbit about Earth has a period T. Show that its distance from Earth's center is $\sqrt[3]{\frac{T^2 GM}{4\pi^2}}$.

2. Using the result of the previous problem, show that a satellite in geosynchronous orbit will orbit at a distance of 35,900 km above Earth's surface.

3. The moon is about 3.8×10^5 km from Earth. Use $v = \sqrt{\frac{GM}{d}}$ to show that its average orbital speed about Earth is about 1030 m/s.

*4. Write the equation for centripetal force, expressing satellite speed as $2\pi r/T$, where r is the distance between the satellite and the center of Earth of mass M and T is the period—the time for one complete revolution. Then equate centripetal force to gravitational force and derive Kepler's third law: $r^3/T^2 = GM/4\pi^2$, a constant for a particular center of force.

*5. An astronomical unit (AU) is defined as the average distance between the centers of Earth and the sun. Jupiter is on average 5.19 AU from the sun. (a) Use Kepler's third law $\left(T^2_{orbit} \sim r^3_{orbit}\right)$ to find how long it takes for Jupiter to orbit the sun. (b) How would Jupiter's orbital period be affected if Jupiter were closer to the sun?

*6. The value of r^3/T^2 is the same for all planets. Show that its value is $3.3 \times 10^{18} \text{ m}^3/\text{s}^2$.

7. Show that the constant r^3/T^2 for satellites around the moon is approximately $1.24 \times 10^{11} \text{ m}^3/\text{s}^2$.

8. Escape speed at a distance d from the center of a body of mass M is $v_{escape} = \sqrt{\frac{2\,GM}{d}}$. Calculate the escape speed from the moon's surface (moon's radius $= 1.74 \times 10^6 \text{ m}$, moon's mass $= 7.40 \times 10^{22} \text{ kg}$). Check your answer with Table 14.1.

9. Mars has a radius of $3.4 \times 10^6 \text{ m}$, and its mass is 11% the mass of Earth. Calculate the escape speed from the surface of Mars. Check your answer with Table 14.1.

10. A certain satellite has a kinetic energy of 8 billion joules at perigee (the point at which it is closest to Earth) and 5 billion joules at apogee (the point at which it is farthest from the Earth). As the satellite travels from apogee to perigee, how much work does the gravitational force do on it? Does its potential energy increase or decrease during this time, and by how much?

11. A rocket coasts in an elliptical orbit around Earth. To attain the greatest amount of KE for escape using a given amount of fuel, should it fire its engines at the apogee or at the perigee? (*Hint*: Let the formula $Fd = \Delta KE$ be your guide to thinking. Suppose the thrust F is brief and of the same duration in either case. Then consider the distance d the rocket would travel during this brief burst at the apogee and at the perigee.)

Chapter 18 Solids

1. A standard queen-size waterbed mattress is 5 feet wide, 7 feet long, and 9 inches high. Show that the water in such a mattress weighs more than 1600 pounds. (The density of water is 62.4 lb/ft^3.)

2. A 2.900-kg solid cylinder that is 0.1200 m tall has a radius of 0.0300 m. Show that the density of the cylinder is about 8550 kg/m^3.

3. A solid iron sphere ($\rho = 7874 \text{ kg/m}^3$) has a diameter of 0.040 m. Show that its mass is 0.26 kg.

4. The density of water is 1000 kg/m^3. The density of ice is 917 kg/m^3. A certain amount of water changes phase to form ice. (a) Compared with the mass of water, is the mass of ice the same, greater, or less? (b) Compared with the weight of water, is the weight of ice the same, greater, or less? (c) Compared with the volume of water, is the volume of ice the same, greater, or less? (d) Which weighs more, 1 liter of water or 1 liter of ice? (Recall 1 L $= 1000 \text{ cm}^3$.) (e) Show that water expands by a factor of 1.09 when it freezes.

5. A full half-liter aluminum can of water has a mass of 0.525 kg. Recall that the density of aluminum is 2.700 g/cm^3. Show that the volume of aluminum that composes the can is 9.3 cm^3.

6. In lab you measure a rectangular piece of aluminum foil to be 9.2 cm wide and 79 cm long and to have a mass of 4.21 g. Your book tells you that the density of aluminum is 2.70 g/cm^3. (a) Calculate the thickness of this piece of aluminum. (b) A typical roll of aluminum foil has a surface area of 18.5 cm^2. Calculate the mass of aluminum in a typical roll of aluminum foil.

7. Note the data for Earth in Table B.1 in Appendix B. (a) Show that the average density of Earth is approximately 5500 kg/m^3. (b) Interestingly, the average density of rocks at Earth's surface is about 2700–3000 kg/m^3. What does this tell you about the density of the material at Earth's center?

8. A solid copper sphere of radius 0.0150 m is suspended from a vertical spring. The density of copper is 8960 kg/m^3. (a) Show that the tension in the spring is 1.27 N. (b) Show that if the spring stretches 0.25 m, the spring constant k is approximately 5 N/m.

9. A 1.5-kg block is pulled across a frictionless horizontal surface by a spring having a spring constant $k = 15$ N/m. The block undergoes an acceleration 0.30 m/s^2. (a) Show that the net force on the block is 0.45 N. (b) Show that the spring stretches 3.0 cm.

10. A 4.8-kg block rests on a horizontal air table (friction free) and is attached to a practically massless horizontal spring with $k = 120$ N/m. When the block is pulled horizontally from rest by the spring with the spring maintaining a constant stretch, the block reaches a speed of 0.45 m/s in 1.8 seconds. (a) What is the acceleration on the block? (b) How much force does the spring exert on the block? (c) How much force does the block exert on the spring? (d) By how much does the spring stretch?

11. A 1-cm^3 cube has sides 1 cm in length. What is the length of the sides of a cube of volume 3 cm^3?

12. Show that there is 26% more crust in a 9-inch diameter pizza than in an 8-inch diameter pizza.

13. If each of the linear dimensions of a storage tank is reduced to half its former value, by how much does the overall surface area of the tank decrease? By how much does its volume decrease?

14. Mary buys some fencing to enclose a horse corral. How much can she enlarge the area of the corral if she buys twice as much fencing?

15. A bust of a famous president cast in solid brass has a mass of 12.0 kg. Show that the same bust scaled down to half size would have a mass of 1.5 kg.

16. Lucinda Landscaper decides to increase the length and width of her lawn by 25%. How much more water will this new lawn require?

17. Gillian is planning to decorate her party with helium balloons. How much more helium would Gillian need to order if she gets the 9-inch diameter balloons instead of the 7-inch diameter balloons?

18. Daniel wants to replace the one-half inch diameter pipe in his home water supply line so that the pipe can carry twice as much water as it presently does. Show that the diameter of the pipe should be about 0.7 inch.

19. A cube 2 cm on a side is cut into cubes 1 cm on a side. (a) How many cubes result? (b) What was the surface area of the original cube and what is the total surface area of the smaller cubes? What is the ratio of surface areas? (c) What are the surface-to-volume ratios of the original cube and the combination of all the smaller cubes?

20. A model steel bridge is 1/20 the exact scale of the real bridge that is to be built. Show that if the model bridge weighs 50 N that the real bridge will weigh about 400,000 N.

21. Toothpicks are made from a log that is 100 times longer and 100 times thicker than an individual toothpick. Show that the weight of the log is a million times greater than the weight of one of the toothpicks.

*22. When supported horizontally at both ends, the toothpick of the previous problem shows no noticeable sag. But the log from which it was made shows a noticeable sag when similarly supported. Show that each unit of cross-sectional area for the log supports 100 times more weight than each unit of cross section for the toothpick.

*23. Larger people at the beach need more suntan lotion than smaller people. Relative to a smaller person, show that a person twice as heavy as another uses about 1.6 times as much lotion as the smaller person uses.

*24. A 4.5 kg chunk of brass is suspended from a spring. The spring hangs from the ceiling of an elevator. The spring constant $k = 750$ N/m. How much does the spring stretch: (a) When the elevator is at rest? (b) When the elevator moves upward at a constant speed of 3.0 m/s? (c) When the elevator accelerates upward at 0.50 m/s^2? (d) When the elevator accelerates downward at 0.50 m/s^2? (e) When the elevator moves downward at a constant speed of 3.0 m/s?

Chapter 19 Liquids

1. Calculate the approximate volume of a person of mass 100 kg who can just barely float in fresh water.

2. When a 2.0-kg object is suspended in water from a spring scale, the scale reading is 1.5 kg. What is the density of the object?

3. A circus seal uses its nose to balance a long 5-kg pole on its end. The cross sectional area of the pole is 1 cm². What pressure does the pole exert on the seal's nose?

4. Assume the density of blood is nearly the same as that of water. (a) How much greater is blood pressure in your feet than in your brain when standing up? (Assume a height of 1.5 m.) (b) Why are damaged veins (such as varicose veins) common in lower legs and rare in ears?

5. A king's crown, presumed to be pure gold, has a mass of 1.000 kg. When submerged in water its apparent mass is measured to be 0.920 kg. (a) Express the buoyant force on the crown in kilograms. (b) What volume of water in liters is displaced? (c) Is the crown made of pure gold? (The density of gold is 19.3 kg/L.)

6. A scuba diver dives to a depth of 20 m in ocean water. The circular glass plate on the diver's face mask has a diameter of 16 cm. Show that the water pressure on the plate produces a force on it of 4140 N. Ignore the pressure of the atmosphere.

7. A bathyscaphe descends to a depth of 11,000 m (nearly 7 miles!) in the Mariana Trench in the Pacific Ocean. (a) Show that the pressure at that depth is 1.1×10^8 N/m². (b) Show that the force exerted by the water on a circular observation window of diameter 16 cm is 2.2×10^6 N. (c) How much greater is the force compared with the force on the diver's mask in the previous question?

8. An open U-tube contains mercury. When water is poured into one end of the tube, mercury in the other end rises 4 cm. What column height of water does this? (The density of water is 13.6 g/cm³.)

9. A 0.5-m³ cube just barely floats in water. Show that the mass of the cube is 500 kg.

10. The cross-sectional area of the output piston in a hydraulic device is ten times the input piston's area. (a) By how much will the device multiply the input force? (b) How far will the output piston move compared to the distance the input piston is moved? (Does this satisfy $F_1 d_1 = F_2 d_2$, the equation for conservation of energy?)

11. Suppose the piston in the hydraulic lift of Figure 19.20 has a cross sectional area of 0.10 m². (a) What air pressure must be produced by the air compressor to support 10,000 N, the combined weight of car and lift? (b) How does this compare with atmospheric pressure (100 kPa)? (c) Why is the area of the liquid surface in the reservoir irrelevant, yet the cross sectional area of the piston very relevant?

12. The depth of water behind the Oroville Dam on the Feather River in northern California is 234 m. (a) What is the water pressure at the base of this dam? (b) Given that atmospheric pressure is about 1.0×10^5 N/m², why can it be neglected in this case?

13. Oak is 0.83 as dense as water and therefore floats in water. (a) What weight of water will be displaced by a 50-kg floating oak beam? (b) What additional force would be required to poke the oak beneath the surface so it is completely submerged?

Chapter 20 Gases

1. Show that the total weight of air pushing down on a sheet of newspaper of area 0.20 m² is about 20,000 N.

2. The density of liquid air is about 900 kg/m³. What will be the volume of 1 m³ of liquid air when it turns to its gaseous form at 0°C and standard pressure?

3. Nitrogen and oxygen in their liquid states have densities only 0.8 and 0.9 that of water. Atmospheric pressure is due primarily to the weight of nitrogen and oxygen gas in the air. If the atmosphere liquefied, would its depth be greater or less than 10.3 m?

4. Air in a cylinder is compressed to one-fourth its original volume with no change in temperature. What happens to its pressure?

5. In the previous problem, if a valve is opened to let out enough air to bring the pressure back down to its original value, what percentage of the molecules escape?

6. A typical filled scuba tank has an internal volume of about 14 L and a pressure of 20,000 kPa. Show that at normal atmospheric pressure this air would occupy 2,800 L (about the volume of a very large hippopotamus!).

7. Professor John places a bit of dry ice in an un-inflated balloon. He ties the balloon shut and sets it on a digital balance. As the dry ice sublimes (that is, turns into gas) and the balloon inflates, the reading on the scale goes down. (a) What is your explanation for the decreased scale reading? (b) If the scale reading decreases by about 2.4 grams, show that the balloon inflates to a volume of 2.0 liters.

*8. A spherical 50.0-kg balloon filled with helium (density 0.179 kg/m³) and of volume 500.0 m³ carries a load and floats motionless in air (density 1.29 kg/m³). Show that the mass of the load is 505 kg. (Ignore the small buoyancy on the load itself.)

*9. Referring to the above problem, show that if the helium in the balloon were replaced with hydrogen (density 0.090 kg/m³), the balloon could support a 550 kg load.

*10. A 236-kg slab of lead is suspended from an air-filled rubber balloon, which floats on the surface of a lake. The balloon holds 0.450 m³ of air (assume at atmospheric pressure even though its slightly compressed due to the stretched rubber). (a) Show that if the balloon is pulled approximately 11 m beneath the surface it and the lead slab will tend to neither rise nor sink (neglect the weight of the air and the balloon but don't neglect the volume of the lead slab). (b) If the balloon is pulled a little deeper than this, what will happen?

*11. You make a barometer by attaching a tube with a 0.040 cm² cross-section to an airtight container. You place a small blob of mercury in the tube such that the volume of air trapped in the container is 250.0 cm³. If the atmospheric pressure drops by 0.20%, show that the small blob of mercury will move 12.5 cm along the tube. (Assume that temperature remains constant.)

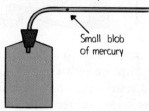

Small blob of mercury

12. The density of liquid air at standard temperature and pressure is about 900 kg/m³. What will be the volume of 1 m³ of liquid air when it turns to gaseous form?

*13. Estimate the ratio of the atmospheric buoyant force per unit of body weight for an average person.

14. Estimate the volume of a hydrogen-filled balloon that will carry a 300-kg load in air. Assume that the density of hydrogen is 0.09 kg/m³ and the density of the surrounding air is 1.30 kg/m³. (Ignore the small buoyancy on the load itself.)

*15. The air in the bicycle pump cylinder shown below is at atmospheric pressure (100 kPa) while the air in the bicycle tire is at 340 kPa. (A one-way valve prevents air from flowing out of the tire.) The cylinder is 2.6 cm in diameter. (a) Show that you'll have to push the handle down almost 40 cm before air will start to flow into the tire. (b) Show that the downward force you exert on the pump handle at this point is 130 N. (*Hint:* The outside air is also pushing down on the piston.) (c) Which (if either) of your answers would be different if the area of the pump cylinder was half as much?

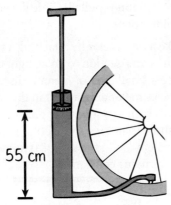

55 cm

16. How many newtons of lift are exerted on the wings of an airplane with a total top wing area of 160 m² (projected area) when the difference in air pressures below and above the wings is 6% of atmospheric pressure?

*17. The air inside a hot-air balloon is at 100°C. At this temperature the density of dry air at sea level is 0.94 kg/m³. The mass of fuel, balloon fabric, passengers, burner and basket is 720 kg. (a) Show that 2500 m³ of hot air inside the balloon would be more than sufficient to get the balloon off the ground on a morning where the outdoor air temperature is 10°C (so ρ_{air} = 1.25 kg/m³. Ignore the small buoyancy on the load itself.). (b) What happens to the amount of buoyant force on the balloon as it rises? (c) Why are balloon flights typically done in the cool of the morning?

Chapter 21 Temperature, Heat, and Expansion

1. Austin heats a 62.3-gram sample of aluminum. Show that 516 J will raise its temperature by 9.2°C.

2. David considers a piece of silver of mass 88.9 g at 93.0°C, which he places in an insulated container of 175 g of olive oil at 18.0°C. Show that the final temperature will be 22.2°C.

3. In lab you place a 355-g cold copper block into an insulated cup that contains 250 g of water at 24°C. Show that the initial temperature of the block must be −2°C to bring the final temperature of the water to 21°C.

4. Joshua puts a heat input of 35.9 J to raise the temperature of 47.0 grams of a material by 2.5°C. He claims, after calculating, that the specific heat capacity of the material is 0.306 J/g°C. Show why you agree or not.

5. You want to find the specific heat capacity of some vegetable oil. You place 65 g of oil into an insulated cup at a temperature of 23°C. After you add 57 g of 100°C aluminum into the oil and stir, the final temperature is 46°C. From this information, show that the specific heat capacity of the oil is 1.85 J/g°C.

6. Your uncle's half-finished cup of coffee has cooled to a temperature of 22°C. He'd like his coffee to be at 83°C. He puts his cup that contains 140 mL of coffee into the microwave oven. (One mL of coffee has a mass of 1 gram.) If the microwave oven delivers 750 W to the coffee, how many seconds will it take to reheat the coffee from 22°C to 83°C?

7. Some homes have "on-demand" water heaters. Rather than storing hot water in a large tank, these heaters activate when hot water is turned on, and provide hot water only when needed. (a) When taking a shower, suppose that you use 10 liters of hot water each minute. (Recall that each liter of water has a mass of 1 kg.) How much energy (in joules) is required to raise the temperature of this water from 14°C to 50°C? (b) Calculate the power rating for a perfectly efficient electric heater designed to deliver this much hot water every minute.

To solve Questions 8–14, you need to know about the average coefficient of linear expansion, α, which differs for different materials. We define α to be the change in length per unit length for a 1°C temperature change. That is, $\alpha = \Delta L/L$ per °C. For aluminum, $\alpha = 23 \times 10^{-6}/°C$, and for steel, $\alpha = 11 \times 10^{-6}/°C$. The change in length ΔL of a material is $\Delta L = L\alpha\Delta T$.

Material	Coefficient of Linear Expansion, α (°C)$^{-1}$
Steel	11×10^{-6}
Brass	19×10^{-6}
Aluminum	23×10^{-6}
Glass	10×10^{-6}
Gold	14.3×10^{-6}

8. A popular demonstration of linear expansion involves trying to push a brass ball through a brass ring of a slightly smaller diameter. The initial temperature of the ball and ring is 21°C. The ring is placed in a flame and heated until it has expanded enough for the ball to pass through. Suppose that the ball has a diameter of 2.540 cm, while the ring has a diameter of 2.530 cm. What is the minimum temperature T_f to which the ring must be heated before the ball will fit through it?

9. Before Dad goes to bed he removes his 24-karat gold ring (of inner diameter 1.90 cm) from his warm finger (at 36°C) and sets the ring on the nightstand. The following morning when the bedroom temperature is 20°C he attempts putting on the ring. By how much has the diameter of the ring shrunk overnight?

10. The Eiffel Tower in Paris stands 300.0 m tall on a day of average temperature, 22.0°C. How much taller is the steel tower on a hot summer day ($T = 40°C$)? Express your answer in centimeters.

11. Two 5.00-m strips of metal, one of aluminum and one of steel, are the same length at room temperature, 20.0°C. When heated to 200°C, how many centimeters longer is one strip than the other?

12. Your lab partner tries to place an aluminum rod 2.000 cm in diameter into a round hole 1.998 cm across. Show that the temperature of the aluminum rod must be lowered by 44°C to get it to fit.

13. Lauren's lab assignment involves a brass rod that is 2.4 m long at 21°C. Show that it will be 3.6 mm longer at 100°C.

14. Suppose that you are laying 10 km of steel railroad track on a day when the temperature is 3°C. Show that the total amount of gap you need to leave in the track to accommodate a 45°C day is 4.6 m.

15. Jessica puts 22.0 g of lead shot at 22.0°C into a cardboard tube of length $L = 1.0$ m long. She puts stoppers on both ends of the tube. She then inverts the tube 50 times. With each inversion the lead falls through the 1.0 m distance. Assume that all the PE of the lead goes into warming the lead shot. She then calculates the final temperature of the lead. You do the same. (*Hint:* 1 J = 1 kg·m^2/s^2. Be sure to express quantities in consistent units.)

Chapter 22 Heat Transfer

1. A gas water heater burns natural gas (methane, CH_4). Each gram of natural gas burned yields approximately 13,000 calories of energy. A typical water heater takes in water at about 20°C (68°F) and raises its temperature to 60°C (140°F). A typical "low-flow" shower-head might use around 10 L of water per minute (which we can estimate is 5 L of hot water and 5 L of cold water mixed), and a typical shower might last 8 min. A liter of water has a mass of 1000 g. So, how much natural gas does a typical shower require?

2. A container of hot water at 80°C cools to 79°C in 15 seconds when it is placed in a 20°C room. At 80°C, ΔT is 60° warmer than the surroundings. Show with Newton's law of cooling that is will take 30 seconds for the container to cool from 50°C to 49°C.

3. Continuing with the above problem, how much time does it take the same container of water to cool from 40°C to 39°C?

4. In a 25°C room, hot coffee in a vacuum flask cools from 75°C to 50°C in eight hours. Show that after another eight hours the temperature will be slightly more than 37°C.

5. If you wish to warm 100 kg of water by 20°C for your bath, show that the amount of heat needed is 2000 kilocalories (2000 Calories). Then show that this is equivalent to 8370 kilojoules.

6. The specific heat capacity of copper is 0.092 calories per gram per degree Celsius. Show that the amount of heat needed to raise the temperature of a 10-gram piece of copper from 0°C to 100°C is 92 calories. How does this compare with the heat needed to raise the temperature of the same mass of water through the same temperature difference?

7. In lab, you submerge 100 grams of 40°C nails in 100 grams of 20°C water. (The specific heat of iron is 0.12 cal/g°C.) Equate the heat gained by the water to the heat lost by the nails and show that the final temperature of the water becomes 22.1°C.

Chapter 23 Change of Phase

1. Water at the surface of a small pond in Toronto is at the freezing point as the sun sets on a winter day. In one hour, the water loses 5,738,000 J of thermal energy to its surroundings. How much water in the pond turns to ice in that hour? Express your answer in kilograms.

2. Consider a 0.63-kg sample of metal at room temperature of 20°C. The addition of 642,000 J increases its temperature to its melting point (782°C). An additional 59,400 J causes the sample to completely liquefy. (a) What is the specific heat capacity of the sample? (b) What is the heat of fusion of the sample?

3. A 6.0-g sample of sugar is burned in a calorimeter. The temperature of 1.0 kg of water in the calorimeter rises from 20°C to 44°C. Find the energy value of the sugar per gram.

4. Five grams of fat are burned in a calorimeter, raising the temperature of 2.0 kg of water from 20°C to 42°C. What is the energy value per kilogram of the fat?

5. When hydrogen and oxygen are burned to produce water, heat is produced at the rate of 58 kcal/mole of water. A mole contains 6.02×10^{23} molecules. How much heat energy is produced per molecule of water?

6. A concert hall has an inside volume of 12,000 m³. The air in it has a density of 1.3 kg/m³ and a specific heat of 0.24 kcal/kg°C. How much heat energy must an air conditioner remove from the air to reduce the temperature of the air by 10°C?

7. Fifty grams of hot water at 80°C is poured into a cavity in a very large block of ice at 0°C. The final temperature of the water in the cavity is then 0°C. Show that the mass of ice that melts is 50 grams.

8. A 50-gram chunk of 80°C iron is dropped into a cavity in a very large block of ice at 0°C. Show that the mass of ice that melts is 5.5 grams. (The specific heat capacity of iron is 0.11 cal/g°C.)

9. The heat of vaporization of ethyl alcohol is about 200 cal/g. Show that if 2 kg of this refrigerant were allowed to vaporize in a refrigerator, it could freeze 5 kg of 0°C water to ice.

10. A 10-kg iron ball is dropped onto a pavement from a height of 100 m. Suppose half of the heat generated goes into warming the ball. Show that the temperature increase of the ball is 1.1°C. (In SI units, the specific heat capacity of iron is 450 J/kg°C.) Why is the answer the same for an iron ball of any mass?

11. A small block of ice at 0°C is subjected to 10 g of 100°C steam and melts completely. Show that the mass of the block of ice can be no more than 80 grams.

12. If a 100-g piece of iron is heated to 100°C and then dropped into a cavity in a large block of ice at 0°C, how much ice will melt? (The specific heat capacity of iron is 0.11 cal/g°C.)

13. A block of ice at 0°C is dropped from a height that causes it to completely melt upon impact. Assume that there is no air resistance and that all the energy goes into melting the ice. Show that the height necessary for this to occur is at least 34 km. [*Hint*: Equate the joules of gravitational potential energy to the product of the mass of ice and its heat of fusion (in SI units, 335,000 J/kg). Do you see why the answer doesn't depend on mass?]

Chapter 24 Thermodynamics

1. Ramon finds that a particular gas does 250 J of work while absorbing 130 J of heat. He asks you to confirm that its change in internal energy is −120 J. Do you agree?

2. A certain system experiences an internal energy change of +670 J while absorbing 1350 J of heat. With this information, Madison says the system does 680 J of work on its surroundings. Confirm her findings.

3. During a certain thermodynamic process, a sample of gas expands and cools, reducing its internal energy by 2500 J, while no heat is added or taken away. How much work is done during this process?

4. Suppose an engine with an ideal efficiency of 25% is constructed so that the hot reservoir has a temperature of 100°C (373 K). What would the temperature of the cold reservoir be?

5. Suppose an engine with an ideal efficiency of 33% is constructed. If the temperature of the cold reservoir is 20°C (293 K), find the temperature of the hot reservoir.

6. In a foundry, a particular heat engine rated for 27% efficiency does 1400 J of work. (a) Show that the amount of heat the engine takes in is 5200 J. (b) Show that the amount of heat it exhausts to its surroundings is 3800 J.

7. In the 1990s, a 210-kW OTEC (Ocean Thermal Energy Conversion) power plant in Hawaii was designed to run between the warm ocean surface waters at 26°C and the colder deep ocean waters at 6°C. (a) What is the theoretical maximum efficiency of the power plant? (b) Theoretically, how much heat must be extracted from the warmer seawater each second to produce 210 kW of useful power?

8. Latisha finds in a lab experiment that 160 J of work is done on a gas while 50 J of heat are removed from the gas. Her lab partner says the change in the internal energy of the gas is +110 J. A second lab partner says the change in internal energy is +210 J. Which lab partner is correct?

9. Turbine generators are like jet engines—they draw in large quantities of air, then compress it and mix it with fuel. Combustion of the fuel turns the turbine, which draws in and compresses more air, and also turns a generator. Typical combustion temperatures are approximately 1100°C and typical exhaust temperatures are about 500°C. (a) If this turbine operates like an ideal Carnot heat engine, what would be the efficiency of the turbine? (b) For every 100.0 J of heat the engine takes in, how much work is done? (c) For every 100.0 J of heat the engine takes in, how much heat is rejected into the exhaust? (d) Combined-cycle turbines use the hot exhaust as a source of heat to produce steam to run a steam turbine. If the exhaust from the gas turbine (now our heat input) is at 500°C, and the steam turbine is cooled with 20°C water, what is the maximum efficiency of this second part of the cycle? (e) The amount of waste heat from the first part of the cycle [your answer to part (c)] is the heat input for the steam turbine. Use the efficiency that you calculated in part (d) to calculate how much work you get out of the steam turbine. (f) How much work is done overall in the combined-cycle turbine for every 100.0 J of heat input? [This should be the work you calculated in (b) plus the work you calculated in (e).] (g) What is the theoretical efficiency of the combined-cycle turbine?* (h) Why does using a combined-cycle turbine make more sense than using a single-cycle turbine?

10. A Stirling engine uses two joined piston-cylinder combinations to obtain work from an external heat source. Suppose it heats a confined gas to 300°C and rejects heat to its surrounding at 30°C. The heat input comes from a 3.0-m^2 solar collector illuminated by sunlight of intensity 800 W/m^2. (a) Show that the theoretical maximum efficiency of this Stirling engine is 0.47. (b) Show that the sunlight energy incident on the collector is 2400 J/s (2400 W). (c) Show that the maximum useful work we could get from this Stirling engine is 1130 J each second.

* The *real* efficiencies of combined-cycle turbines run about 55–60%.

Chapter 25 Vibrations and Waves

1. What is the frequency, in hertz, that corresponds to each of the following periods? (a) 0.10 s (b) 5 s (c) $\frac{1}{60}$ s (d) 24 h

2. What is the period, in seconds, that corresponds to each of the following frequencies? (a) 10 Hz (b) 0.2 Hz (c) 60 Hz (d) 1.1574×10^{-5} Hz

3. A metronome is set so that it makes ten complete vibrations in 12 s. Find the frequency of the metronome.

4. Carmen notices that a cork floating in water bobs up and down four times each second as a small wave passes. She measures the wave peaks to be 0.5 m apart. From this information he can calculate the speed of the waves. What's your answer?

5. Michael is working on a lab project and wishes to know the frequency of ultraviolet light that will have a wavelength of 360 nanometers (1 nm = 10^{-9} m). His assistant calculates the answer and finds it to be 8.33×10^{14} Hz. Should Michael believe his assistant?

6. Microwave ovens typically cook food by using microwaves with frequency 2.45 GHz (gigahertz, 10^9 Hz). What is the wavelength of these microwaves?

7. While sitting on a pier, Carlos notices that incoming waves are 2.0 m between crests. If the waves lap against the pier every 0.5 s, find (a) the frequency and (b) the speed of the waves.

8. Light travels at a speed of 3×10^8 m/s in a vacuum, and for practical purposes, through air as well. The wavelength of a shade of yellow light is 5.80×10^{-7} m. Find the frequency of this light.

9. A gamma ray is high-frequency light. Find the wavelength of a gamma ray with a frequency of 10^{22} Hz.

10. If the speed of a longitudinal sound wave is 340 m/s, and the frequency is 1000 Hz, what is the wavelength of the wave?

11. Refer to Figure 25.14 on page 501. What is the longest wavelength of a standing wave that can be produced on an 80-cm-long string when properly plucked? What are the next two longest wavelengths of standing waves that can be produced?

12. The world's most accurate "clocks" use the vibrations of cesium-133 atoms for timekeeping. In such clocks, microwaves are tuned to the vibrations of radiation emitted and absorbed in a particular transition between energy states in the atom at a frequency of 9,192,631,770 Hz. (a) What is the period of the radiation (to 4 significant figures)? (b) What is the wavelength of the microwaves used to excite the cesium atoms (to 3 significant figures)?

13. Brandon makes a 78-cm-long simple pendulum. He is asked to predict how many seconds it will take to make 20 complete oscillations. He predicts 35 seconds. Do you agree, or disagree? Show your calculation.

14. An astronaut on the moon attaches a small brass ball to a 1.00-m length of string and makes a simple pendulum. She times 15 complete swings in a time of 75 seconds. From this measurement she calculates the acceleration due to gravity on the moon. What is her result?

15. The above astronaut knows that the radius of the moon is 1740 km. Combine her finding of the acceleration due to gravity on the moon with Newton's law of gravity ($F = GM_{moon}m/d^2$) and $W = mg$ to determine the moon's mass.

16. In lab, you want to double the period of a certain pendulum. Gary says you'll have to make the pendulum twice as long. Madison says you'll have to make a pendulum four times as long. Do you agree with Gary, Madison, or neither?

Chapter 26   Sound

1. We know that speed v = distance/time. Show that when the distance traveled is one wavelength λ and the time of travel is the period T (which equals 1/frequency), you get $v = \lambda f$.

2. You hear the chirp of a cricket. When you move twice as close to the cricket, how much louder is the sound?

3. Find the wavelength of a 680-Hz tone in air, where the wave speed is 340 m/s.

4. Find the wavelength of a 68,000-Hz ultrasound wave in air.

5. Find the frequency of a sound wave that has a wavelength of 1.50 m. Could you hear this sound?

6. Your teacher says "Hello" to you from across the gym, 34 m away. How long does it take the sound to reach you?

7. Imagine a hiker camping in the mountains. Just before going to sleep he yells "WAKE UP," and the sound echoes off the nearest mountain, returning 8 h later. How far away is that mountain?

8. For years, scientists were mystified by sound waves picked up by underwater microphones in the Pacific Ocean. These so-called T-waves were among the purest sounds in nature. Eventually they traced the source to underwater volcanoes whose rising columns of bubbles resonated like organ pipes. What is the wavelength of a typical T-wave whose frequency is 7 Hz? (The speed of sound in sea water is 1530 m/s.)

9. Suppose that you put your left ear down against a railroad track, and your friend 1.00 km away strikes the track with a hammer. How much sooner will the sound get to your left ear than to your right ear? (The speed of sound is about 5950 m/s in steel and 340 m/s in air.)

10. You watch a carpenter down the street hammering nails in a roof and note that the sound and sight are synchronized perfectly. Then when he stops hammering you hear one more hammer blow. (a) If the time delay is 1 second, what is the distance between you and the carpenter? (b) If you hear two blows after seeing the last blow, what is the distance between you and the carpenter?

Chapter 27 Light

1. The wavelength of green light from an argon ion laser is 0.000000488 m. Express this wavelength in micrometers (μm) and nanometers (nm).

2. Convert the following wavelengths to frequencies in hertz: 300 nm, 533 nm, 623 nm, 974 nm.

3. The wavelength of light emitted by a CO_2 laser is 10.6 μm. What frequency light is this, and in what part of the spectrum is it?

4. Laser pointers emit light waves with a wavelength of 670 nm. What is the frequency of this light?

5. The wavelength of green light is about 500 nm. How many wavelengths thick is a $\frac{1}{2}$ mm-thick thumbnail? A 100-μm thick hair?

6. When Mars is 90 million km from Earth, how long would it take for a radio wave from a video camera mounted on the back of a Mars Rover to tell people on Earth that the Rover is about to go over a cliff? How long would it take for a radio signal from Earth to reach the Rover saying "Stop"? Why do our Mars Rovers have to be "intelligent" enough to figure out how to deal with obstacles themselves?

7. Lillian listens to her favorite radio station broadcasting at 101 MHz. What is the wavelength of the radio waves? How does the wavelength of these waves compare with the 10-ft-tall walls in her room?

8. Rick uses a cutting laser in his engraving business. The frequency associated with the laser light is 2.40×10^{14} Hz. (a) What is the wavelength of the cutting laser's light? (b) Is this light inside or outside the range of visible light?

9. Light of wavelength 560 nm travels through a 1-cm vacuum gap. (a) How many wavelengths fit into the gap? (b) What is the time taken for light to travel the gap?

10. A particle accelerator is used to accelerate a proton to a speed of 6×10^7 m/s. What fraction of the speed of light is this?

11. The average speed of light slows to $0.75c$ when it refracts through a particular piece of plastic. (a) What change is there in the light's frequency in the plastic? (b) In its wavelength?

12. Suppose that you wish to draw Figure 27.11 (page 541, an eclipse of the sun) to scale on a roll of butcher paper, and you decide to use a scale of 1 cm = 1000 km on the paper. How large would the moon be (3500 km diameter)? Earth (12,800 km diameter)? The sun (1,400,000 km diameter)? How far away from Earth would you have to draw the sun (Earth–sun distance is 150,000,000 km)?

13. In one of Michelson's experiments, a beam of light from a revolving mirror traveled 15.0 km to a stationary mirror. Find the round-trip time for the beam returning to the revolving mirror.

14. If the revolving mirror in Problem 13 has eight sides, how rapidly, in rev/s must the mirror revolve so that light initially reflecting from one face is received by the adjoining next face?

Chapter 29 Reflection and Refraction

1. Angelina is 1.5 m tall and stands 10 m in front of a flat mirror. How far behind the mirror is her image?

2. Rita walks at a speed of 2 m/s toward a mirror. What is the relative speed of Rita with respect to her image?

3. You are in an almost dark room and put a tiny light bulb on the floor, 2 m from a wall. You place a 50-cm-tall bowling pin on the floor, halfway between the light and the wall. How tall will the shadow of the pin be on the wall? (You may find it helpful to draw a diagram.)

4. In the previous problem, how will the area of the shadow on the wall compare with the cross-sectional area of the bowling pin?

5. No glass is perfectly transparent. Mainly because of reflections, about 92% of light passes through an average sheet of clear windowpane. The 8% loss is not noticed through a single sheet, but through several sheets it is apparent. How much light is transmitted by two sheets?

The following problems require using Snell's law, which involves sine functions. Snell's law states that $n \sin \theta_i = n' \sin \theta_r$ where θ_i and θ_r are the angles of incidence and refraction, respectively, and n and n' are the indices of refraction in the corresponding two media.

6. A light beam in air ($n = 1.00$) makes an angle of 45° with the normal to a glass window pane ($n' = 1.44$). (a) What is the angle to the normal of the light beam after it is refracted into the glass? (b) What is the angle to the normal of the light beam after it exits the other side of the glass into air?

7. A light beam strikes a glass plate normal to the surface of the plate. What is the angle of the beam to the normal within the glass? (Use $n = 1.0$, $n' = 1.4$.)

8. (a) A fish looks upward in water ($n = 1.33$) at an angle of 25° to the vertical (i.e., 25° to the normal to the water's surface). Can the fish see out into the air? If so, at what angle to the vertical is the fish's line of sight outside the water? (b) Answer the same questions if the fish looks upward at an angle of 50° to the vertical.

9. The fish described in Problem 8 is wondering what the greatest angle to the vertical is at which she can look and see out into the air. What is that angle?

10. The critical angle in diamond (the angle within the diamond beyond which total internal reflection occurs) is 24.6°. Calculate the index of refraction of diamond.

11. Use the results of the previous problem to calculate the speed of light inside a diamond.

Chapter 30 Lenses

Use the equation $\frac{1}{o} + \frac{1}{i} = \frac{1}{f}$ to solve the following problems. Object distance is o, image distance is i, and focal length is f.

1. When you focus on a newspaper page, the lens in your eye forms a real image of the paper on the retina in the back of your eye. The light-sensitive retina then translates the patterns of light and dark areas to your brain, which in turn interprets them as words. If your newspaper is 28.0 cm from your eye, and the focal length of your eye is 2.7 cm, what is the diameter of your eye from front to back? (The diameter of your eye is the image distance.)

2. A far-sighted eye whose comfortable reading distance is 80 cm is to be supplied a corrective lens to enable reading at a normal distance of 40 cm. So the object distance is 80 cm and image distance is 40 cm. What is the focal length of the corrective lens?

3. A near-sighted eye sees close objects clearly at 15 cm. A corrective lens will provide a normal viewing distance of 40 cm. Hence the object distance is 15 cm and image distance is 40 cm. What is the focal length of the corrective lens?

4. An image of a candle appears in sharp focus on a screen that is 60 cm from a lens whose focal length is 20 cm. How far is the candle from the lens (i.e., what is the object distance)?

5. Poke a very small hole in a piece of card and hold it in the sunlight. When the card is 1 meter above the ground, a round 1-centimeter diameter image of the sun is cast on the ground. If you hold the card 2 meters above the ground, the solar image has a diameter of 2 centimeters. In a similar way, sunlight passing through small openings between leaves at the top of a tree casts solar images on the ground below. Sophia notices that sun images on a sidewalk beneath a tree have diameters averaging 5 centimeters. About how high is the tree?

Chapter 31 Diffraction and Interference

1. Two friends, Daniel and Martin, set up a pair of speakers as shown. Both speakers in phase play a tone having a wavelength of 1 m. (a) How many wavelengths occur between Speaker 1 and Daniel? Between Speaker 2 and Daniel? (b) When the waves arrive at Daniel's ears, will they be in phase or out of phase with one another? Will Daniel hear a loud sound or a quiet sound? Explain. (c) How many wavelengths are between Speaker 1 and Martin? Between Speaker 2 and Martin? (d) When the waves arrive at Martin's ears, will they be in phase or out of phase with one another? Will Martin hear a loud sound or a quiet sound? Why?

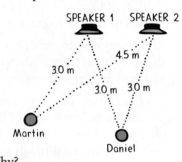

2. Refer to the diagram above: If the tone frequency were doubled so that the wavelength is now 0.5 m, what would each listener hear?

3. Also refer to the diagram above: What does each listener hear when the frequency is lowered to produce a wavelength of 3.0 m?

4. When you shine a laser through a pair of slits, an interference pattern is formed on a far-away screen. (Refer to Figure 31.15 on page 630.) A helium-neon laser emits coherent (in phase) light with a wavelength of 633 nm. Suppose that the distance between the slits and the screen is 4.0 m, and that the centers of two adjacent bright lines on the screen are 4.0 cm apart. (a) Show that there are 6.3 million wavelengths of this light between the slits and the screen. (b) The "central" bright line of the screen is equidistant from both slits. The next line above or below it on the screen represents a path length difference of one wavelength; that is, the distance between one slit and the screen is one wavelength more than the distance between the other slit and the screen. Show that the ratio of wavelength of light to the total number of wavelengths between the slits and the screen is 0.00000016.

Chapter 32 Electrostatics

1. Two point charges are separated by 6 cm. The attractive force between them is 20 N. Show that when they are separated by 12 cm the force between them is 5 N. (Why can you solve this problem without knowing the magnitudes of the charges?)

2. If the charges attracting each other in the preceding problem have equal magnitudes, show that the magnitude of each charge is 2.8 μC.

3. Show that 26 μC is the charge on 1.6×10^{14} electrons.

4. In accord with Coulomb's law, a force of attraction or repulsion occurs between pairs of charged particles. (a) Calculate the force between a particle with charge -5.0 μC and a particle with charge $+3.0$ μC separated by a distance of 0.50 m. (b) Calculate the force between a particle with charge $+5.0$ μC and a particle with charge -3.0 μC separated by a distance of 0.50 m. (c) Does the magnitude of calculated forces depend on the signs of the charges? Explain.

5. One charge exerts a force of 1.6 N on a second charge located 15 cm (0.15 m) away. (a) How much force docs the second charge exert on the first charge? (b) How much force is it if you double the distance between the charges? (c) How much force is it if you triple the distance between charges?

6. Assuming that the two charges above are of equal magnitude, what is the magnitude of each charge?

7. A penny is made up of zinc and copper atoms. Each penny contains about 110,000 C of positive charge and 110,000 C of negative charge. (a) If you could somehow leave all of the penny's positive charges on Earth but take all of its negative charges to the Moon, 384,000 km (3.84×10^8 m) away, how much force would these charges cxert on each other? (b) Compare this to the weight of a 70-kg (154-lb) person on Earth's surface.

8. A 30 μC charge is held 35 cm away from a 12 μC charge. Show that the charges exert a force of 26 N on each other.

9. A 25 μC charge experiences a 28-N attraction to a second charge held 42 cm away. Show that the second charge is 22 μC.

10. A $+15$ μC charge exerts a 4.5 N attractive force on a -20 μC charge. Show that the charges are separated by 77 cm.

11. A pair of 10-cent coins are electrically charged, one with a charge of $+20$ μC (0.000020 C) and the other a charge of -10 μC (-0.000010 C). When they are brought together, what is the charge on each after contact?

12. If 50 μC of positive charge is transferred to a body, which is then found to have a charge of -10 μC, what was its original charge?

13. What is the electrostatic force between a pair of electrons 1.0 m apart?

14. If the force between a pair of electrons is 1.0 N, how far are they from each other?

15. Consider two charged objects. One carries a charge of 18 μC (0.000018 C). When the two are separated by a distance of 0.9 m, there is a force of 2.7 N between them. What is the charge on the second object?

16. You want one of your 90-gram gym socks to float 1.0 m off the ground, so you put equal charges on it and on your Earth-bound gym shoe. Show that you need to put 10 μC of charge on both sock and shoe.

Chapter 33 Electric Fields and Potential

1. What is the electric field 1.0 m from an isolated proton?

2. What is the electric field 1.0 m from an isolated helium nucleus (an alpha particle)?

3. What is the electric field 1.0 m from an isolated electron?

4. What is the electric field 1.0 m from an isolated hydrogen atom?

5. The electric field 1.0 m from a charged Van de Graaff generator is 2500 N/C. Calculate the charge on the generator.

6. Earth may be considered as a huge sphere that is negatively charged. The magnitude of the electric field at the surface is 100 N/C. Calculate the charge of Earth. (The radius of Earth is 6.4×10^6 m.)

7. British scientist J. J. Thomson was the first to measure the ratio of an electron charge to its mass, and expressed surprise at the value he found. (a) Calculate the ratio. (The mass of an electron is 9.1×10^{-31} kg.) (b) Using the result from Problem 6, compare your answer with the charge-to-mass ratio for Earth. (Earth's mass is 6.0×10^{24} kg.)

8. An alpha particle has twice the charge of a proton, and about four times its mass. Calculate the ratio of charge to mass for an alpha particle. (The mass of a proton is 1.67×10^{-27} kg.)

9. When a 0.0040-C charge is near a charged Van de Graaff generator, it experiences an electrostatic force of 12 N. What is the strength of the electric field in that region of space?

10. How much electrostatic force would a 0.060-C charge experience in a 2400 N/C electric field?

11. A charged object experiences 36 N of electrostatic force when placed in a 5800 N/C electric field. What is the charge on the object?

12. How much potential energy is converted to kinetic energy when 1.0 C of charge is allowed to flow between two points separated by a potential difference of 115 V?

13. How much energy is stored when 7.2 C of charge is moved through a potential difference of 1.5 V?

14. During a particular thunderstorm, an electric potential difference of 48,000,000 V is established between a cloud and the ground. If a lightning bolt transfers 32 C between the cloud and ground, how much energy is released?

15. How much charge is driven through a circuit by a 9.0-V battery delivering 3.0 J of energy?

16. A 9-V battery gives 9 joules of energy to each coulomb of charge that circulates through a circuit. If 0.20 C of charge circulate through a light bulb circuit every second, how much energy is the battery providing to the circuit each second?

17. The potential at point A is 30 volts higher than at point B. How much work would you do moving 4.0 C of charge from B to A?

18. The potential at the positive terminal of a 9-V battery is 9 V higher than at the negative terminal. How much potential energy does +1 C of charge "lose" as it travels through an external circuit from the positive terminal to the negative terminal of the battery? How much energy does +3 C "lose"?

19. A proton (charge $= 1.60 \times 10^{-19}$ C, mass $= 1.67 \times 10^{-27}$ kg) is released from the positive side of a capacitor and accelerates to the negative side of the capacitor. The potential across the capacitor is 12 volts. (a) How much work does the electric field between the capacitors do on the proton? (b) How much kinetic energy does the proton have when it reaches the negative side of the capacitor? (c) Show that the speed of the proton when it gets there is 4.8×10^4 m/s.

20. The electric field at a particular point in space has strength of 3500 N/C. How much force is experienced there by (a) a 10-μC charge? (b) a 20-μC charge? (c) a 50-μC charge?

*21. A tiny, positively charged oil drop 2.2 μm in diameter floats in a 39,000 N/C electric field. Gravity pulls down on the drop, while an equal electrical force acts upward on the drop. The density of the drop is 0.89 g/cm^3 (890 kg/m^3). (a) What is the mass of the drop? (b) What is the charge on the drop? (c) How many electrons are missing from the drop? (d) If another same-sized drop floats motionless in a 78,000 N/C electric field, how many electrons must be missing from it? (e) Is it possible for a same-sized drop to float motionless in a 48,000 N/C field? Explain.

Chapter 34   Electric Current

1. What is the current if 26 coulombs of charge pass a point in a wire in 4.0 seconds?

2. A total charge of 220 C moves through a light bulb when the current is 500 mA. For how many seconds has the light bulb been on?

3. A DC circuit has a 5.3 A current flowing through it. How many electrons pass by a point in the circuit each second?

4. A car's starter motor draws 50 A. How much charge flows if the motor runs for 0.75 s?

5. How long does it take for 52 C to pass through a wire carrying a current of 8.0 A?

6. How much current passes through a person whose resistance is 100,000 Ω and to whom 120 V is applied? If resistance is lowered to 1000 Ω?

7. A current of 4 A flows when a resistor is connected across a 12-V battery. What is the resistance of this resistor?

8. What is the resistance of a clothes iron that draws 8 A when connected to 120 V?

9. How much energy is expended in lighting a 100-W bulb for 30 min?

10. A motor connected to 120 V draws a current of 10 A. What power is being consumed? How much energy does the motor use in 8 h of operation?

11. What current flows in a 60-W bulb in a 120-V circuit? What is the resistance of the filament?

12. How much does it cost to operate a 100-W lamp continuously for one week if the power utility rate is 10 cents per kilowatt-hour?

13. A 1500-W hair dryer connected to a 120-V outlet runs for 3 min (180 s). (a) How much current does the hair dryer draw? (b) How much energy does it use? (c) How many kWh of energy were used? (1 kWh = 3,600,000 J)

14. A current of 2.0 amps flows through a resistor, and the voltage across the resistor is 6.0 volts. (a) Show that the power dissipated by the resistor is 12 watts. (b) Show that the energy dissipated by the resistor in 30 seconds is 360 joules. (c) Show that 46 coulombs of charge flow through the resistor in 23 seconds. (d) Show that the resistor has a resistance of 3.0 Ω.

15. A three-way light bulb designed for a 220-V circuit is marked "50 W/100W/150 W." Compared to the current when the bulb puts out 50 W, how much more current flows through the bulb when it is putting out 150 W?

16. A current of 4.0 amps flows through a resistor, and the voltage across the resistor is 32 volts. (a) What is the power dissipated by the resistor, in watts? (b) How much energy is dissipated by the resistor in 20 seconds? (c) What is the resistance of the resistor?

17. Suppose that you double the potential difference across the resistor above. (a) What happens to the current? (b) What happens to the power? (c) What happens to the resistance?

18. Show that when you triple the voltage across a resistor, the current through the resistor triples and the power increases by a factor of nine.

19. A person in good shape and working hard can put out around 100 watts on a bicycle. Show that you would have to pedal for 2.5 hours in order to provide enough energy to run a 1500-W hair dryer for 10 minutes.

20. You may have noticed that some cities are replacing their traditional incandescent traffic light bulbs with lights made up of arrays of LEDs (light emitting diodes). Suppose that a normal traffic light bulb uses 100 watts, and an LED array uses, say, 20 watts. Suppose that a traffic intersection has 8 traffic signals, and at least one light (red, yellow, or green) is on in each signal all of the time. (a) Show that the normal light bulbs for one intersection consume 19.2 kilowatt-hours (kWh) per day. (b) Show that the LED lights consume 3.84 kWh per day. (c) Suppose that a city pays 15¢ per kWh for electricity. Show that the city will reduce its annual electricity consumption by about 5600 kWh, and save about $840 a year on electricity bills alone for one intersection by replacing its incandescent bulbs with LEDs.

21. A compact fluorescent outdoor floodlight is labeled "19 W = 85 W incandescent bulb." Suppose that you have the bulb on 8 hours each night for one year. (a) Show that this bulb is on for 2920 hours each year. (b) Show that the compact fluorescent bulb uses 193 fewer kilowatt-hours each year than the equivalent incandescent bulb. (c) Show that if you pay 15¢ per kWh, you would save about $29 a year on your electric bill.

22. Some motorcyclists have electrically heated vests. The vest plugs into the motorcycle battery, and wires sewn into the vest keep the motorcyclist warm. (a) If the motorcycle battery has a voltage of 12 V and the vest is rated at 36 W, what is the current through the vest? (b) Show that the resistance of the heating element in the vest is 4 Ω.

23. The current in a motor is 4.0 A when a voltage of 32 V is applied. (a) Show that the power dissipated in the motor is 128 W. (b) Show that the motor is energized with approximately 2600 J every 20 seconds. (c) Show that the motor's resistance is 8.0 Ω.

24. You have a battery-powered electric bicycle that, with you on it, has a mass of 90 kg. You want to accelerate the bicycle from rest to a final speed of 8.0 m/s. (a) How much work must the motor do to accelerate the bicycle? (b) If the bike has a 24-V battery, how much charge has to pass through the electric motor (assuming that the motor is 100% efficient)?

*25. The wire leading to a car's headlights is typically 1.0 mm in diameter. A 1-m length of this contains about 8×10^{22} copper atoms, each with a free conduction electron. (a) If the current in the wire is 4 A, how many electrons are flowing past a point in the wire every second? (b) How many seconds will it take for the number of free electrons in 1 meter of wire to flow past that point? (c) What is the average drift speed of the electrons in the wire?

Chapter 35 Electric Circuits

For resistors in parallel, the equivalent resistance can be calculated by using the following equation.

$$\frac{1}{R_{equivalent}} = \frac{1}{R_1} + \frac{1}{R_2} + \frac{1}{R_3} + \ldots$$

For two resistors in parallel, this rule can be simplified as follows:

$$R_{equivalent} = \frac{R_1 R_2}{R_1 + R_2}$$

1. What single resistor connected to a battery would result in the same current as you'd get from two 12-Ω resistors connected in series to the same battery? (In other words, what is the equivalent resistance of a pair of 12-Ω resistors connected in series?)

2. What is the equivalent resistance of a 6-Ω and 9-Ω resistor connected in series?

3. What is the equivalent resistance of two 12-Ω resistors connected in parallel?

4. What is the equivalent resistance of a 6-Ω and 9-Ω resistor connected in parallel?

5. You're given three 10-Ω resistors. Find (a) the maximum equivalent resistance of the three when connected and (b) the minimum equivalent resistance of the three when connected. Describe each circuit.

6. Find the equivalent resistance of three 10-Ω resistors when one is connected in series to two that are connected in parallel.

7. If a flashlight has four 1.5-V D cells in series with a bulb having a resistance of 18 Ω, find the current in the circuit.

8. A string of 50 party lights operates at 120 V. (a) In series, what is the voltage across each bulb? (b) What is the resistance of each bulb if 0.1 A flows through the string of bulbs?

9. Six identical lamps are connected in series across a 120-V line. (a) What is the voltage across each one? (b) If the current is 0.50 A, calculate the resistance of each lamp. (c) Calculate the power dissipated by each lamp.

10. Six identical lamps are connected in parallel in a 120-V circuit. (a) What is the voltage across each lamp? (b) If the total current in the circuit is 5.0 A, calculate the resistance of each lamp. (c) Calculate the power dissipated by each lamp.

11. A certain light bulb with a resistance of 95 ohms is labeled "150 W." Was this bulb designed for use in a 120-V circuit or a 220-V circuit?

12. In periods of peak demand, power companies lower their voltage. This saves them power (and saves you money)! To see the effect, consider a 1200-W toaster that draws 10 A when connected to 120 V. Suppose the voltage is lowered by 10 percent to 108 V. By how much does the current decrease? By how much does the power decrease? (*Caution:* The 1200-W label is valid only when 120 V is applied. When the voltage is lowered, it is the resistance of the toaster, not its power, that remains constant.)

13. (a) Find the equivalent resistance of the circuit below. (b) What current will be in the 10-Ω resistor if 12 V is impressed across points A and B?

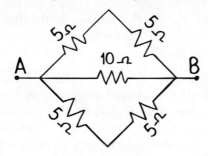

14. (a) Find the equivalent resistance of the circuit below. (b) Then calculate the amount of current in the battery. (c) What power is supplied by the battery?

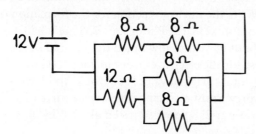

Chapter 37 Electromagnetic Induction

1. Power of 100 kW is delivered to the other side of a city by a pair of power lines between which the voltage is 12,000 V. (a) What current flows in the lines? (b) Each of the two lines has a resistance of 10-Ω. What is the voltage change along *each* line? (c) What power is expended in the form of heat in both lines together (as distinct from power delivered to customers)? (d) State why it is so important to step voltages up with transformers for long-distance transmission.

2. One day, if fusion energy becomes practical, garbage dumps may become a thing of the past. Solid waste may be completely vaporized in the star-hot flame of a "fusion torch" and sent through a magnetic field to be separated into raw material. Consider an ion-separation chamber with a uniform magnetic field of strength B. Elements including iron are sent into the chamber at velocity *v*. The mass of an iron ion is *m*, and its charge is *q*. (a) How great is the force acting on the iron ion in the magnetic field? (b) Equate this force to centripetal force and write an equation for the radius of the curvature of the ion in the magnetic field. (c) Which ion would have the largest radius of curvature in the chamber, iron or gold? Why?

Chapter 39 The Atomic Nucleus and Radioactivity

1. Suppose that you want to find out how much gasoline is in an underground storage tank. You add 1 gallon of gasoline that contains some long half-life radioactive material that gives off 50,000 decays each minute. You pour this radioactive gallon into the underground tank and let it mix. One day later you remove a gallon of gasoline from the underground tank, and measure its radioactivity. You detect 20 radioactive decays each minute. How much gasoline is in the tank?

2. Iodine-131$(^{131}_{53}\text{I})$ undergoes beta decay. What nucleus is formed?

3. Nuclear reactors are sometimes started up with neutrons originating from a beryllium-9 $(^{9}_{4}\text{Be})$ target that has been bombarded by alpha particles. This produces a new nucleus and an ejected neutron. What is the identity of the new nucleus?

4. Radon gas is a natural decay product from radium present in soils. It percolates up from the ground. High levels of radon gas in a home can be a health hazard. (a) Radon-222 $(^{222}_{86}\text{Rn})$ gas in your lungs undergoes an alpha decay to become what metallic element? (b) This element has a half-life of only 3 minutes. It goes through an alpha decay, two beta decays, and another alpha decay to become what element?

5. Strontium-90 (half-life, 29 years) was produced as part of the nuclear fallout from atomic bomb tests conducted in the 1950s. How much of the strontium-90 produced in 1955 will remain in 2042?

6. Iodine-131 has a half-life of 8 days. It is given to patients to study how well their thyroid gland is functioning. If you anticipate that 16 days from now you will need an iodine-131 sample to produce 1.0×10^{12} decays per second, how many decays per second should your sample be producing today?

7. A piece of flesh from a frozen mammoth discovered in Siberia was recently sampled for carbon-14. It contained one-fourth as much carbon-14 as a same-mass piece of flesh taken from a recently-deceased elephant. (a) Approximately how long ago did the mammoth live? (b) If instead the mammoth's flesh had only $\frac{1}{16}$ as much carbon-14 as does the flesh of a living elephant, how long ago did the mammoth die?

8. Amanda does some baking and has an interesting idea on how to tell when her cookies have passed their "sell-by" date and should be taken off of the shelf. She plans to bake her cookies using iodized salt, where some of the added iodine is radioactive iodine-133 with a half-life of 21 hours. (a) If Amanda's cookies originally contain enough iodine-133 to each give off 200 decays per minute, about how many decays per minute will she measure from a cookie that remains on the shelf 2.5 days later? (b) What will be the decay count after twice this time?

9. Plutonium-238 $(^{238}_{94}\text{Pu})$ is useful as a power source for heart pacemakers and for spacecraft. Heat from nuclear decay of plutonium-238 is used by specialized semiconductor chips to produce electric current in a device called a Radioisotope Thermoelectric Generator (RTG). Plutonium-238 is manufactured in nuclear reactors by bombarding neptunium-237 with neutrons. The neptunium-237 nucleus absorbs a neutron and then undergoes beta decay to form the plutonium-238. (a) Write the nuclear reaction for the formation of plutonium-238. (b) Plutonium-238 has a half-life of about 88 years. How much time would have to elapse for the electric current in your RTG to fall to $\frac{1}{16}$ of its original value? (c) Would you have to worry about replacing the power source of a plutonium-238 powered pacemaker? Why or why not?

10. Plutonium-239 has a half-life of approximately 24,000 years. Show that about 190,000 years are required for the amount of plutonium-239 to decrease to $\frac{1}{256}$ of its present amount.

Use the table below to help you answer the problems that follow. Note that 1 amu converted to energy is equivalent to 1.494×10^{-10} J.

Particle	Mass (amu)	Particle	Mass (amu)
electron $\left(_{-1}^{0}e\right)$	0.000549	lithium-6 $\left(_{3}^{6}Li\right)$	6.015122
proton $\left(_{1}^{1}p\right)$	1.007276	carbon-12 $\left(_{6}^{12}C\right)$	12.00000
neutron $\left(_{0}^{1}n\right)$	1.008665	magnesium-24 $\left(_{12}^{24}Mg\right)$	23.985042
hydrogen-1 $\left(_{1}^{1}H\right)$	1.007825	krypton-91 $\left(_{36}^{91}Kr\right)$	90.92344
deuterium $\left(_{1}^{2}H\right)$	2.014102	strontium-94 $\left(_{38}^{94}Sr\right)$	93.915361
tritium $\left(_{1}^{3}H\right)$	3.016049	xenon-140 $\left(_{54}^{140}Xe\right)$	139.92164
helium-3 $\left(_{2}^{3}He\right)$	3.016029	barium-142 $\left(_{56}^{142}Ba\right)$	141.916448
helium-4 $\left(_{2}^{4}He\right)$	4.002603	uranium-235 $\left(_{92}^{235}U\right)$	235.043923

sample problem

A neon-22 $\left(_{12}^{24}Ne\right)$ atom has a mass of 21.991385 amu. (a) Calculate the mass defect of a neon-22 atom. (b) How much energy would be released if you could assemble a neon-22 atom from 10 protons, 12 neutrons, and 10 electrons?

(a) Neon-22 has 10 protons, 12 neutrons, and 10 electrons. Its mass defect is equal to the difference in mass between the protons and neutrons and electrons that make it up, and the mass of the final atom. That is

Mass defect $= \left[(10m_{proton} + 12m_{neutron} + 10m_{electron}) - m_{Ne\text{-}22\ atom}\right]$

Mass defect $= \left[10(1.007276 \text{ amu}) + 12(1.008665 \text{ amu}) + 10(0.000549 \text{ amu})\right.$

$\left. -21.991385 \text{ amu}\right] = 0.190845 \text{ amu}$

(b) In effect, we fuse the individual nucleons to form the neon nucleus and add the electrons. The amount of energy is equal to the corresponding mass defect.

$$\Delta mc^2 = 0.190845 \text{ amu} \times \frac{1.494 \times 10^{-10} \text{ J}}{\text{amu}} = 2.851 \times 10^{-11} \text{ J}$$

This may not seem like much energy, but the energy released to produce just one kilogram of neon-22 in this way is about 7.8×10^{14} J, enough to melt a cube of ice over 130 m on each side!

1. The difference between the mass of a nucleus and the sum total of the masses of its constituent nucleons is called the *mass defect*. Show that the mass defect for magnesium-24 $\left(^{24}_{12}\text{Mg}\right)$ is 0.212838 amu.

2. Amanda sees that the element lithium comes before iron in the periodic table, and hence is to the left of the bottom of the curve of Figure 40.14. (a) Would lithium be a candidate for releasing energy by fission, or by fusion? (b) Calculate the mass defect for a lithium-6 $\left(^{6}_{3}\text{Li}\right)$ atom.

3. Within the sun, three helium atoms can fuse to form carbon-12:
$$^4_2\text{He} + ^4_2\text{He} + ^4_2\text{He} \rightarrow ^{12}_6\text{C}$$
Show that this fusion reaction releases 1.17×10^{-12} J for each carbon-12 atom formed.

4. One possible fusion reaction is the combination of two deuterium (hydrogen-2) nuclei to form helium-3 and a neutron:
$$^2_1\text{H} + ^2_1\text{H} \rightarrow ^3_2\text{He} + ^1_0 n$$
Show that this reaction produces 5.24×10^{-13} J per fusion.

5. One of the many ways uranium-235 can fission when it is hit with a neutron is to form xenon-140 $\left(^{140}_{54}\text{Xe}\right)$ and strontium-94 $\left(^{94}_{38}\text{Sr}\right)$ as daughter nuclei. (a) Write this nuclear fission reaction. (Remember to include the neutron at the beginning, and the appropriate number of neutrons at the end). (b) Calculate the energy released in one fission reaction.

6. One reaction scheme for running a fusion reactor (also a hydrogen bomb) involves firing a neutron at a lithium-6 nucleus to produce tritium (hydrogen-3) and then fusing the tritium to a deuterium (hydrogen-2) nucleus to form helium and another neutron:
$$^1_0 n + ^6_3\text{Li} \rightarrow ^3_1\text{H} + ^4_2\text{He}$$
$$^3_1\text{H} + ^2_1\text{H} \rightarrow ^4_2\text{He} + ^1_0 n$$
How much energy is required or produced in each step?

7. In a typical fission reaction, a slow neutron strikes a U-235 nucleus to produce two daughter nuclei and three neutrons. One such fission reaction is shown below:
$$^1_0 n + ^{235}_{92}\text{U} \rightarrow ^{91}_{36}\text{Kr} + ^{142}_{56}\text{Ba} + 3(^1_0 n)$$
(a) How many joules of energy are released in this fission reaction? (b) There are 2.56×10^{21} U-235 nuclei in one gram of U-235. How much energy is released when 1 gram of U-235 is fissioned? (c) How fast would a fully-laden 50,000 kg truck have to be going to have this much kinetic energy?

8. The biggest fusion bomb detonated to date was the *Tsar Bomba*, exploded on July 10, 1961, in a test by the former Soviet Union. The bomb had an explosive yield of about 50 megatons of TNT (each megaton is 4.2×10^{15} joules). The bomb itself was about 8 meters long and 2 meters in diameter. (It was a one-of-a-kind bomb rather than one of a family of bombs.) (a) How much mass was converted to energy in this bomb? (b) If an asteroid moving at 18 km/s were to have this much kinetic energy in striking the Earth, what would be the approximate mass of the asteroid?

9. A "kiloton" is the amount of energy released when 1000 tons of TNT explodes, about 4.2×10^{12} J. Suppose that a single uranium fission reaction releases about 3.0×10^{-11} J. (a) Approximately how many uranium nuclei had to fission in the 14-kiloton bomb that was dropped on Hiroshima? (b) There are about 2.6×10^{21} uranium nuclei in a gram of uranium. How many grams of uranium fissioned in the Hiroshima bomb?

Appendix G Notes

Notes to the text are listed by section number. In sections containing more than one note, the reference numbers for the notes contain an additional digit. For example, Note 2.1.1 is the first note that appears in Section 2.1, and Note 2.1.2 is the second.

Chapter 1

1.2   Although mathematics is very important to scientific mastery, it will not be the main focus in this book. This book focuses instead upon what should come first: the basic ideas and concepts of physics—in familiar language. For example, the *Think and Explain* exercises at the ends of each chapter outnumber the *Think and Solve* problems requiring elementary algebra. The *Plug and Chugs* familiarize you with equations, requiring minimal math skills. You'll see the mathematical structure of physics evident in these equations, which serve as *guides to thinking* about how concepts connect—and only secondarily as recipes for solving algebraic problems. Comprehension first, then computation!

1.4   In your education it is not enough to be aware that other people may try to fool you, but mainly to be aware of your own tendency to fool yourself.

Chapter 2

2.1.1   The scientific system of units is called SI, for the French name, *Le Système International d'Unités*. The SI unit for force is the newton, N. 1 N is 0.22 lb, about the weight of a quarter-pound hamburger *after* it's been cooked. 1 lb is about 4.5 N.

2.1.2   If you ever happen to sit next to a physicist on a bus, in a cafeteria, or at a train station, you'll likely see doodles in his or her writing. You'll see arrows, pictorial representations of physics ideas that are useful for analyzing many situations—physics and otherwise. We will see how vectors nicely describe forces in this chapter, then to represent velocity in Chapter 4, projectile motion in Chapter 5, and momentum in Chapter 8. Vectors are treated in Appendix C at the back of this book and in the *Concept-Development Practice Book*. Although the learning curve for vectors can be a bit steep at first, after some study and practice, vectors can become a comfortable tool for analyzing everything that is described by amount and direction.

2.1.3   I am forever indebted to Burl Grey for the stimulation he provided, for when I continued with my formal education, it was with enthusiasm. I lost touch with Burl for 40 years. A student in my class, Jayson Wechter, doing some detective work, located him in 1998 and put us in contact. Friendship renewed, we once again continue our spirited conversations.

2.2   We'll see in Chapter 11 that another condition for mechanical equilibrium is that the net torque equals zero.

2.3.1 This force acts at right angles to the surface. When we say "normal to," we are saying "at right angles to," which is why this force is called a normal force.

2.3.2 Support force can be used to *define* weight. With this definition, as we'll see in Chapter 13, an astronaut floating freely in a spacecraft with no support force is truly weightless—even though he or she is not free from gravity.

2.5 A parallelogram is a four-sided figure having opposite sides parallel to each other. Familiar examples of parallelograms are rectangles and squares.

Chapter 3

3.5.1 The metric system was originally established in France in the 1790s, and in 1960 was incorporated in the International System of Units (abbreviated SI). The short forms of the SI units are called *symbols* rather than *abbreviations*.

3.5.2 We will see in Chapter 6 that *weight = mass × acceleration due to gravity*, or simply, *weight = mg*.

Chapter 4

4.4.1 The Greek letter delta, Δ, is often used as a symbol for "change in" or "difference in." In delta notation, $a = \dfrac{\Delta v}{\Delta t}$ where Δv is the change in velocity and Δt is the change in time (the time interval).

4.4.2 When we divide $\dfrac{\text{km}}{\text{h}}$ by s $\left(\dfrac{\text{km}}{\text{h}} \div \text{s}\right)$, we can express this as $\dfrac{\text{km}}{\text{h}} \times \dfrac{1}{\text{s}} = \dfrac{\text{km}}{\text{h}\cdot\text{s}}$ (some textbooks express this as km/h/s, which is confusing notation). Or when we divide $\dfrac{\text{m}}{\text{s}}$ by s $\left(\dfrac{\text{m}}{\text{s}} \div \text{s}\right)$, we can express this as $\dfrac{\text{m}}{\text{s}} \times \dfrac{1}{\text{s}} = \dfrac{\text{m}}{\text{s}\cdot\text{s}} = \dfrac{\text{m}}{\text{s}^2}$ (which can also be written as ms^{-2}, or m/s/s).

4.5 This relationship follows from the definition of acceleration when the acceleration is g and the initial speed is zero. If the object is initially moving downward at speed v_o, the speed v after any elapsed time t is $v = v_o + gt$. This book will not focus on such added complications. You can learn a lot from even the simplest cases!

4.6.1 Distance = average speed × time interval
$$= \frac{\text{beginning speed} + \text{final speed}}{2} \times \text{time}$$
$$= \frac{0 + gt}{2} \times t$$
$$= \tfrac{1}{2}gt^2$$

4.6.2 If the object has an initial speed v_o, some thought will show that the equations for velocity and distance traveled become $v = v_o + at$ and $d = v_o t + \tfrac{1}{2}at^2$.

4.9 The value of 1.25 m for d represents the maximum height of the jumper's center of gravity. The height gained by the jumper's center of gravity is what's important in determining jumping ability. You will learn about center of gravity in Chapter 11.

Chapter 5

5.2.1 Whenever a pair of vectors are at right angles (90°), their resultant can be found by the Pythagorean Theorem, a well-known tool of geometry. It states that the square of the hypotenuse of a right-angle triangle is equal to the sum of the squares of the other two sides. Note that two right triangles are present in the rectangle in Figure 5.3. From either one of these triangles we get

$$\text{resultant}^2 = (60 \text{ km/h})^2 + (80 \text{ km/h})^2$$
$$= 3600 \ (\text{km/h})^2 + 6400 \ (\text{km/h})^2$$
$$= 10{,}000 \ (\text{km/h})^2$$

The square root of 10,000 $(\text{km/h})^2$ is 100 km/h, as expected.

5.2.2 An important property of vectors is that they can be moved around as long as their length and direction are not changed. Vectors can be rearranged into a chain, tail-to-head in any order. A vector drawn from the tail of the first vector to the head of the last vector represents the resultant of the entire chain of vectors.

Chapter 7

7.0 The terms *push* and *pull* usually invoke the idea of a living thing exerting a force. So, strictly speaking, to say "the wall pushes on you" is to say "the wall exerts a force as though it were pushing on you." As far as these mutual forces are concerned, there is no observable difference between the force exerted by you, a living being, and the force exerted by a wall, a nonliving object.

7.5 In both cases we consider the football to be the system. In the first case, the foot (A) exerts a force on the ball (B). The force exerted by A is the net force on the system (the ball), so the ball accelerates. In the second case, there are two forces on the ball—A on B, and C on B. Note two things: A doesn't interact with C and vice versa—so A and C do not make up an action-reaction pair of forces. Also note there are three objects involved, not just two. Read on to the horse-cart problem, which may make this clearer.

Chapter 8

8.2 This relationship is derived by rearranging Newton's second law to make the time factor more evident. If we equate the formula for acceleration, $a = F/m$, with what acceleration actually is, $a = \Delta v / \Delta t$, we get $F/m = \Delta v / \Delta t$. From this we derive $F \Delta t = \Delta(mv)$.

Chapter 9

9.1 For the more general case, work is the product of the *component* of force acting in the direction of motion and the distance moved. (No work is done when force and distance are perpendicular to each other.)

9.3 Strictly speaking, that which enables an object to do work is called its *available energy,* because not all the energy of an object can be transformed into work.

9.5 This formula is derived algebraically as follows. Multiply both sides of $F = ma$, which is Newton's second law, by d to get $Fd = mad$. Recall that for motion in a straight line at constant acceleration, $d = \frac{1}{2}at^2$. So $Fd = ma\left(\frac{1}{2}at^2\right) = \frac{1}{2}maat^2 = \frac{1}{2}m(at)^2$. Substituting $v = at$, we get $Fd = \frac{1}{2}mv^2$.

9.8 The number-of-strands rule applies only to simple pulleys, where same-size pulleys are on the same shaft. The chain hoist popular in auto repair shops, for example, gets its mechanical advantage from different-size pulleys on the same shaft.

9.9.1 Energy of atomic or molecular motion is actually thermal energy, not heat. We'll see in Chapter 21 that heat is transferred from one place to another by atomic and molecular motion. Heat is analogous to work; both involve energy transfer by motion.

9.9.2 To raise a load by 2 mm, the handle has to be turned once, through a distance equal to the circumference of the circular path of the 16-cm radius. This distance is 100 cm (since the circumference is $2\pi r = 2 \times 3.14 \times 16$ cm $= 100$ cm). A simple calculation will show that the 100-cm work-input distance is 500 times greater than the work-output distance of 2 mm. If the jack were 100% efficient, then the input force would be multiplied by 500 times. The theoretical mechanical advantage of the jack is 500.

9.10 Even complex organisms living near geothermal vents deep in the ocean that need neither sunlight nor oxygen are powered by the energy of heat and nourished by various inorganic compounds.

Chapter 10

10.1.1 Can you see the reason for leap years? Since Earth takes $\frac{1}{4}$ day more than 365 days to circle the sun, an extra day is added to the calendar every fourth year.

10.1.2 Relative to the sun, Earth rotates once each 24-hour period. A 24-hour day is the time required for a point on Earth that is located directly under the sun to rotate and reach that point again. But relative to the stars, a complete rotation of Earth takes 23 hours and 56 minutes. Why? Because while Earth rotates, it revolves about one degree around the sun in its orbit.

10.2.1 Rotation rate is described as turns per unit of time, or as the angle turned (degrees or radians) per unit of time. Examples of units for rotational speed are RPM, degrees per second, or radians per second. One degree is $\frac{1}{360}$ of a full turn. One radian is about $\frac{1}{6}$ of a full turn—precisely, it is $\frac{1}{2}\pi$ times 360 degrees, or 57.3 degrees. You might learn more about radians in a follow-up course.

10.2.2 If you take a follow-up physics course you'll learn that when the proper units are used for tangential speed v, rotational speed ω, and radial distance r, the direct proportion of v to r and ω becomes the exact equation $v = r\omega$. This relationship applies only to a rotating system wherein all parts simultaneously have the same ω, like a rigid disk or rigid rod. It does not apply to a system of planets, for example, where each planet has a different rotational speed ω. (We will learn later that the innermost planets in a planetary system have both the greatest rotational speed *and* the greatest linear speed as they orbit the sun.)

10.3.1 An object undergoing a change in tangential velocity, speeding up or slowing down, also undergoes *tangential acceleration,* which is in the direction of tangential velocity. For brevity, we'll not treat cases of tangential acceleration.

10.3.2 Centripetal force can also be expressed as $F_c \sim mr\omega^2$, where $r\omega$ is substituted for v (from $v \sim r\omega$). When ω is in SI units, radians/second, $v = r\omega$ and $F_c = mr\omega^2$.

Chapter 11

11.1 The unit of a torque is a newton-meter. Work is also measured in newton-meters (the same as joules), but work and torque are very different. What contributes to work is the force along or parallel to the direction of motion; what contributes to torque is the force *perpendicular* to the lever arm.

Chapter 12

12.4 Whereas the impulse to change linear momentum involves force, the impulse to change angular momentum involves torque. Torque × time = change in angular momentum.

12.6 At the risk of stating the obvious, this preparation can well begin by taking your study of physics very seriously.

Chapter 13

13.2.1 Or working backward, $(0.0014 \text{ m}) \times (60)^2 = 5 \text{ m}$.

13.2.2 Compare Newton's painstaking effort to get everything right and nailed down mathematically with the lack of "doing one's homework," the hasty judgments, and the absence of cross-checking that so often characterize the pronouncement of less-than-scientific theories.

13.4.1 In previous chapters we have treated mass as a measure of inertia, which is called inertial mass. Now we see mass as a measure of gravitational force, which in this context is called gravitational mass. Experiments show that the two are equal, and as a matter of principle, the equivalence of inertial and gravitational mass is the foundation of Einstein's general theory of relativity (Chapter 16).

13.4.2 The numerical value of G depends entirely on the units of measurement we choose for mass, distance, and time. Using SI units, the choice is mass in kilograms, distance in meters, and time in seconds. Scientific notation is discussed in Appendix B at the end of this book.

13.6 The strength of the gravitational field at any point is equal to the force F per unit mass placed there. Bold letter g denotes field strength. Then $g = F/m$, and its units are N/kg. Letting F be the force of gravity, $g = F/m = (Gmm/d^2) \div m = Gm/d^2$. The field g also equals the free-fall acceleration of gravity g. The units N/kg and m/s^2 are equivalent.

13.7 Curiously, you'd gain acceleration during the first few kilometers beneath Earth's surface, because the density of surface material is much less than the density of the condensed center. This means the force of gravity on you would be slightly more for the first few kilometers beneath Earth's surface. Farther in, the force would decrease and would diminish at Earth's center.

13.9 While Earth spins, the moon moves along its orbit and appears at the same position in our sky every 24 hours and 50 minutes. Hence, the cycle of two high tides is actually of 24 hour and 50 minute intervals. This means tides do not occur at the same time every day. In addition, tides in any area are affected by the local coastline.

13.10 Astrophysicists don't yet have an exact number for the least massive star that will inevitably become a black hole. They believe it to be at least two solar masses.

Chapter 14

14.2 If you continue with your study of physics and take a follow-up course, you'll learn that the tangential speed v of a satellite in circular orbit is given by $v = \sqrt{\frac{GM}{d}}$, and the period T of satellite motion is given by $T = 2\pi\sqrt{\frac{d^3}{GM}}$, where G is the universal gravitational constant (see Chapter 13), M is the mass of Earth (or whatever body the satellite orbits), and d is the altitude of the satellite measured from the center of Earth or parent body.

14.5 It is not easy to look at familiar things through the new insights of others. We tend to see only what we have learned to see or wish to see. Galileo reported that many of his colleagues were unable or refused to see the moons of Jupiter when they peered skeptically through his telescopes. Galileo's telescopes were a boon to astronomy, but more important than a new instrument to see things better was a new way of understanding what is seen. Isn't this still true today?

14.6.1 Escape speed from any planet or any body is given by $v = \sqrt{2\frac{GM}{d}}$, where G is the universal gravitational constant, M is the mass of the attracting body, and d is the distance from its center. (At the surface of the body, d would simply be the radius of the body.) For a bit more mathematical insight, compare this formula with the one for orbital speed in Note 14.2.

14.6.2 Interestingly enough, this might well be called the *maximum falling speed*. Any object, however far from Earth, released and allowed to fall to Earth only under the influence of Earth's gravity would not exceed 11.2 km/s. (With air friction, it would be less.)

Chapter 15

15.0 The concerns of Albert Einstein (1879–1955) were not limited to physics. As a German citizen in Nazi Germany, he spoke out against Hitler's racial and political policies, which prompted his resignation from the University of Berlin. He fled Germany in 1933 and became an American citizen in 1940.

15.1 In 1887, two American physicists, A. A. Michelson and E. W. Morley, performed an experiment to determine differences in the speed of light in different directions. They thought that the motion of Earth in its orbit about the sun would cause shifts in the speed of light. They thought that the speed of light should have been faster when it was going in the direction Earth was moving and slower when it was going opposite to the direction Earth was moving. Using a device called an *interferometer*, they found that the speed seemed to be the same in all directions. For Michelson's many experiments on the speed of light, he was the first American honored with a Nobel Prize.

15.3 The presently accepted value for the speed of light is 299,792 km/s, which we round off to 300,000 km/s. This corresponds to 186,000 mi/s.

15.4 The mathematical derivation of this equation for time dilation is included here mainly to show that it involves only a bit of geometry and elementary algebra. It is not expected that you master it! (If you take a follow-up physics course, you can master it then.)

15.5 A light-year is the distance that light travels in one year (9.46×10^{12} km).

15.6 This equation is simply stated as a "guide to thinking" about the length contraction. The equation is given here without any explanation as to how it is derived.

Chapter 16

16.5.1 Don't get discouraged if you cannot visualize four-dimensional space-time. Einstein himself often told his friends, "Don't try. I can't do it either." Perhaps we are not too different from the great thinkers in Galileo's time who couldn't think of a moving Earth!

16.5.2 Straining to balance equations in his relativity theory, Einstein decided in 1917 that an unknown cosmological force was counteracting gravity—an idea he later called his greatest blunder. Then in 1988, two studies showed that the expansion of the universe is accelerating—and hence that some new cosmological force (now called dark energy) must indeed be acting against gravity!

16.6 In the late 1950s, shortly after Einstein's death, the German physicist Rudolph Mössbauer discovered a way to use atomic nuclei to measure incredibly small frequency changes. For this *Mössbauer effect,* he was awarded the Nobel Prize. In 1960, Robert Pound and Glen Rebka at Harvard University used the Mössbauer effect to perform an experiment that detected Earth's gravitational effect on light.

Chapter 17

17.0 The word *atom* comes from a Greek word meaning "indivisible." But atoms are not truly indivisible. Under extreme conditions, such as in particle accelerators or in the center of the sun, atoms can be further broken down into smaller, "subatomic" particles.

17.5 An exception is DNA, a macromolecule that can be seen with an optical microscope. More dramatically, a diamond may be regarded as one huge carbon molecule, and this can be seen with the naked eye!

17.7 Nucleons are composed of still smaller particles called *quarks,* which are discussed in Note 39.1.

Chapter 18

18.2.1 Densities in kg/m^3 are 1000 times greater. For instance, the density of water is $1000 \ kg/m^3$ and the density of osmium is $22,600 \ kg/m^3$.

18.2.2 Weight density is common to British units, where one cubic foot of fresh water (almost 7.5 gallons) weighs 62.4 pounds. So fresh water has a weight density of $62.4 \ lb/ft^3$. Salt water is a bit denser, $64 \ lb/ft^3$.

Chapter 19

19.1.1 Pressure may be measured in any unit of force divided by any unit of area. The standard international (SI) unit for pressure is newtons per square meter, called the *pascal* (Pa), named after the seventeenth-century theologian and scientist Blaise Pascal. A pressure of 1 Pa is very small, about that of a dollar bill resting flat on a table. Scientists more often use kilopascals (1 kPa = 1000 Pa).

19.1.2 This relationship is derived from the definitions of pressure and density. Consider an area at the bottom of a container of liquid. Pressure is produced by the weight of the column of liquid directly above this area. From the definition of density as mass divided by volume, this weight of liquid can be expressed as density times g times volume. The volume of the column is simply the area multiplied by the depth. Then we get

$$\text{pressure} = \frac{\text{force}}{\text{area}} = \frac{\text{weight}}{\text{area}} = \frac{\text{density} \times g \times \text{volume}}{\text{area}}$$
$$= \frac{\text{density} \times g \times \text{area} \times \text{depth}}{\text{area}} = \text{density} \times g \times \text{depth}$$

19.1.3 What would that pressure be? The density of fresh water is 1 gram per cubic centimeter, which equals 1000 kilograms per cubic meter in SI units. Since the weight (*mg*) of 1000 kilograms is $(1000 \ kg) \times (10 \ N/kg) = 1000 \ N$, the weight density of water is 1000 newtons per cubic meter ($1000 \ N/m^3$). Water pressure in a pool or lake is simply equal to the product of the weight density of fresh water and the depth in meters. So at a depth of 1 meter, water pressure in a large lake or small pool is $(1000 \ N/m^3) \times (1 \ m) = 1000 \ N/m^2$. In SI units, pressure is measured in pascals ($1 \ Pa = 1 \ N/m^2$), so our result would be 1000 Pa or, in the frequently used unit of kilopascals, 10 kPa. For the *total pressure* in these cases, add the pressure of the atmosphere, 101.3 kPa.

19.3 Water is practically incompressible. A liter of water under great pressure far below the surface still weighs almost the same as a liter of water near the surface, approximately 10 N.

19.4 Interestingly enough, the people who can't float are, 9 times out of 10, males. Most males are more muscular and slightly denser than females.

19.5 Note that this is a general statement for all fluids rather than just liquids. As the next chapter shows, the same principle applies to gases as well.

Chapter 20

20.2 The average pressure at sea level used to be called one *atmosphere*. This term is still commonly used, but it is no longer acceptable with SI units. In British units, the average atmospheric pressure at sea level is 14.7 pounds/inch^2.

20.5.1 Air is composed of a mixture of gases—mainly nitrogen and oxygen, with some argon and a little carbon dioxide. When we speak of *molecules of air,* we are referring to any of the different kinds of molecules found in air.

20.5.2 A general law that takes temperature changes into account is $P_1 V_1/T_1 = P_2 V_2/T_2$, where T_1 and T_2 represent the initial and final *absolute temperatures,* measured in SI units called *kelvins* (Chapter 21).

20.7 In mathematical form: $\frac{1}{2}mv^2 + pV + mgh =$ constant (along any particular streamline), where m is the mass of some small volume V, v its speed, p its internal pressure, g the acceleration due to gravity, and h its elevation. If mass m is expressed in terms of density ρ, where $\rho = m/V$, and each term is divided by V, Bernoulli's equation takes the form $\frac{1}{2}\rho v^2 + p + \rho gh =$ constant. Then all three terms have units of pressure. If h does not change, then an increase in v means a decrease in p, and vice versa.

20.8 Pressure differences are only one way to understand wing lift. Another way uses Newton's third law. The wing forces air downward (action) and the air forces the wing upward (reaction). Air is deflected downward by the wing tilt, called the *angle of attack.* When riding in a car, place your hand out the window and pretend it's a wing. Tip it up slightly so air is forced downward. Up goes your hand! Air lift provides a nice example to remind us that often there is more than one way to explain the way nature behaves.

Chapter 21

21.1 The Celsius scale is named in honor of the man who first suggested it, the Swedish astronomer Anders Celsius (1701–1744). It used to be called the centigrade scale, from *centi* ("hundredth") and *gradus* ("degree"). The Fahrenheit scale is named after the German physicist Gabriel Fahrenheit (1686–1736), and the Kelvin scale, after the British physicist Lord Kelvin (1824–1907).

21.2 Similarly, work is also energy in transit. A body does not *contain* work. It *does* work or has work done on it. Matter has internal energy. When that energy flows we call it heat.

21.5 Still another unit of heat is the British thermal unit (Btu). The Btu is defined as the quantity of heat required to change the temperature of 1 pound of water by 1°F. One Btu is equal to 1054 J.

21.8 This rule is valid if the solid, liquid, and gas expand against constant pressure. A gas in a container can be prevented from expanding, but then its pressure is not constant.

Chapter 22

22.2 Where does the energy go in this case? We will see in Chapter 24 that it goes into work done on the surrounding air as the expanding air pushes outward.

22.3.1 The word *radiation* derives from the Latin word *radius*, which means "the spoke of a wheel." Anything that spreads out from some center we call *radiation*. Do not confuse heat radiation with radioactive radiation, which is given off by the nuclei of radioactive atoms such as uranium and radium.

22.3.2 Infrared (below-the-red) radiation has longer wavelengths than those of visible light. The longest visible wavelengths are for red light, and the shortest are for violet light. Ultraviolet (beyond-the-violet) radiation has shorter wavelengths. (More on wavelength in Chapter 25, and electromagnetic waves in Chapters 27 and 37.)

22.5 Outdoors on a hot day, thermal equilibrium is not reached when black materials such as pavements or automobile bodies remain hotter than their surroundings—until evening, when they cool faster!

22.7 Interestingly, in the florist's greenhouse, heating is mainly due to the ability of glass to prevent convection currents from mixing the cooler outside air with the warmer inside air. So the greenhouse effect plays a bigger role in global warming than it does in the warming of greenhouses.

Chapter 23

23.2.1 Some solids, such as solid carbon dioxide (dry ice) and naphthalene crystals (moth balls), go directly to the gaseous phase in a process called sublimation. Snow and ice in dry weather and direct sunlight do the same. The reverse happens as H_2O molecules in cold air form snow.

23.2.2 What keeps the droplets of water in a cloud or fog from falling to Earth? If they're very small, like dust, they have small terminal velocities, typically about 1 cm/s. This means it takes 100 s to fall 1 m. A slow 1-cm/s updraft keeps the droplets in suspension. As drops grow, their terminal velocity increases, and when terminal velocity is more than updraft velocity, drops do fall. This is rain!

23.8.1 The value 540 calories per gram (in SI units, 2.26 megajoules/kilogram) required for vaporization or condensation is known as the *heat of vaporization* of water. The 80 calories per gram (in SI units, 0.335 MJ/kg) required for melting or freezing is known as the *heat of fusion* of water. These are energies per mass required to break intermolecular bonds during vaporization or melting, or equivalently, are energies released when bonds are formed during condensation or freezing. They vary with temperature and pressure.

23.8.2 Hot water will not freeze before cold water does, but it will freeze before lukewarm water does. Water at 100°C, for example, will freeze before water warmer than 60°C, but not before water cooler than 60°C. What's the "trick"? The hot water freezes first because more of it evaporates leaving less of it to freeze. Try it and see!

Chapter 24

24.1 It was found that any gas at 0°C, regardless of its initial pressure or volume, changes by $\frac{1}{273}$ of its initial volume for each 1°C change in temperature, when pressure is held constant. For example, when the temperature is reduced to −100°C, the volume of gas is reduced by $\frac{100}{273}$. More striking, if a gas at 0°C were cooled to −273°C, its volume would be reduced by $\frac{273}{273}$ and become zero. Clearly, we cannot have a substance with zero volume. It was also found that the pressure of any gas in any container of fixed volume would change by $\frac{1}{273}$ for each 1°C change. So gas in a container of fixed volume cooled to −273°C would have no pressure whatsoever. In practice, every gas liquefies before it gets this cold. Nevertheless, these decreases of volume and pressure by increments of $\frac{1}{273}$ suggested the idea of the lowest temperature: −273°C (more precisely, −273.15°C, and −459.69° on the Fahrenheit scale). Interestingly, even at absolute zero, atoms still have a small kinetic energy, called the *zero-point energy*. Helium, for example, has enough motion at absolute zero to keep it from freezing. The explanation involves quantum theory.

24.2.1 Popular ideas, when proven wrong, are seldom suddenly discarded. People tend to identify with the ideas that characterize their time; hence, it is often the young who are more prone to discover and accept new ideas and push the human adventure forward.

24.2.2 When no heat is added, Δ Heat is zero. Then

Δ Heat = Δ internal energy + work
0 = Δ internal energy + work

Then we can say

−Work = Δ internal energy

24.3 Interestingly enough, when you're flying at high altitudes where outside air temperature is typically −35°C, you're quite comfortable in your warm cabin—but not because of heaters. The process of compressing outside air to near sea-level cabin pressure would normally heat the air to a roasting 55°C (131°F). So air conditioners must be used to extract heat from the pressurized air.

24.5.1 It can be difficult to abandon our way of looking at the world when a newer method comes along to replace established ways. Physicist Victor Weisskopf illustrates this with a story: An engineer explains the operation of a steam engine to a curious peasant. After hearing the detailed explanation of the engine's steam cycle, the peasant asks, "Yes, I understand all that, but where's the horse?"

24.5.2 The ideal efficiency of an ordinary gasoline-powered automobile engine is somewhat more than 50%, but in practice the actual efficiency is about 25%. Engines of higher operating temperatures (compared with low-temperature reservoir temperatures) would be more efficient, but the melting point of engine materials limits the upper temperatures at which they can operate. Higher efficiencies await engines made with new materials with higher melting points—such as ceramic engines.

24.7.1 Entropy can be expressed as a mathematical equation, stating that the increase in entropy, ΔS, in an ideal thermodynamic system is equal to the amount of heat added to a system, ΔQ, divided by the temperature, T, of the system: $\Delta S = \Delta Q/T$.

24.7.2 The American writer Ralph Waldo Emerson, who lived when the second law of thermodynamics was the new science topic of the day, philosophically speculated that not everything becomes more disordered with time. He cited the example of human thought. Ideas about the nature of things grow increasingly refined and organized as they pass through the minds of succeeding generations. Human thought is evolving toward more order.

Chapter 25

25.1 The exact relationship for the period T of a simple pendulum is

$$T = 2\pi\sqrt{\frac{L}{g}}$$

where L is the length of the pendulum, and g is the acceleration of gravity.

25.2 The condition for simple harmonic motion, met for many kinds of vibrations, is that the restoring force is proportional to the displacement from equilibrium. The component of weight that restores a displaced pendulum to its equilibrium position is directly proportional to the pendulum's displacement (for small angles)—likewise for a weight attached to a spring. Recall from Section 18.3, Hooke's law for a spring: $F = k\Delta x$, where the force that stretches (or compresses) a spring is directly proportional to the distance the spring is stretched (or compressed).

Chapter 26

26.4 You may be surprised that steel is considered elastic and putty inelastic. After all, that stretchy material that keeps our socks up is called elastic, and putty is more stretchy than steel. But elasticity is not "stretchability;" it's the tendency of a material to resume its initial shape after having been exposed to a distorting force. Some very stiff materials are elastic!

Chapter 27

27.2 Roemer's estimate was not quite correct. The correct value is 17 minutes, or about 1000 seconds.

27.6 People are cautioned not to look at the sun at the time of a solar eclipse because the brightness and ultraviolet radiation of direct sunlight is damaging to the eyes. This good advice is often misunderstood by those who then think that sunlight is more damaging at this special time. But staring at the sun when it is high in the sky is harmful whether or not an eclipse occurs. In fact, staring at the bare sun is more harmful than when part of the moon blocks it! The reason for special caution at the time of an eclipse is simply that more people are interested in looking at the sun during an eclipse.

Chapter 28

28.5 On a black-and-white television set, the black we see in the darkest scenes is simply the color of the tube face itself, which is more a light gray than black. Our eyes are sensitive to the contrast with the illuminated parts of the screen, and we see the light gray as black. In our minds, we make it black.

28.7 Note that magenta, yellow, and cyan are used to make other colors by *subtraction,* as when colored paints or dyes are mixed. When colors are mixed by *addition,* as when colored light is mixed, red, green, and blue are the most useful colors to mix.

28.11.1 When the frequency of any photon is divided by its energy, $\frac{f}{E}$, the same number always results: 6.67×10^{-34} joule·second, which is Planck's constant, h. Then we can say that $E = hf$.

28.11.2 Although a *diffraction grating* works differently from a prism, it too spreads light into a spectrum. It is more commonly used than a prism in spectroscopes. A *spectrometer* is similar to a spectroscope except that it also measures the wavelengths of a spectrum and records the spectrum (on film for example).

Chapter 29

29.6 Wave fronts can also represent the positions of different troughs—or any continuous portions of the wave that are all vibrating the same way at the same time.

29.8 The ratio *n* of the speed of light in a vacuum to the speed in a given material is called the *index of refraction* of that material.

$$\text{index of refraction } n = \frac{\text{speed of light in vacuum}}{\text{speed of light in material}}$$

The quantitative law of refraction, called *Snell's law,* is credited to Willebrod Snell, a seventeenth-century Dutch astronomer and mathematician. According to Snell's law,

$$n \sin \theta = n' \sin \theta'$$

where *n* and *n'* are the indices of refraction of the media on either side of the boundary, and θ and θ' are the respective angles of incidence and refraction. If three of these values are known, the fourth can be calculated from this relationship.

Chapter 30

30.3 The mathematical relationship between object distance *o*, image distance *i*, and focal length *f* is given by

$$\frac{1}{o} + \frac{1}{i} = \frac{1}{f}$$

This is called the *thin-lens equation.*

30.6 The hole of the pupil usually looks black because light is going in but not coming out. Sometimes in flash photos, the light from the flashbulb enters the eye at just the right angle to reflect off the retina at the back of the eye. That's why flash photographs sometimes show the pupils to be reddish.

Chapter 31

31.2.1 On the other hand, a framework of connected steel girders in a building or bridge can act as a "polished" surface for long-wavelength radio waves, reflecting them away from the structure. That's why you lose reception when you drive onto a steel bridge while listening to an AM station. So although long waves get *around* a steel structure, they don't get *into* it.

31.2.2 Most TV channels have wavelengths shorter than FM wavelengths, and therefore have even less diffraction than FM, but some (channels 2–6) have wavelengths longer than FM wavelengths.

31.2.3 The primary sense of the dolphin is acoustic, for vision is not a very useful sense in the often murky and dark depths of the ocean. Whereas sound is a passive sense for us, it is an active sense for the dolphin, which sends out sounds and then perceives its surroundings on the basis of the echoes that come back. Distance is sensed by the time delay between sending sound and receiving its echo, and direction is sensed by differences in time or phase for echoes reaching its two ears. A dolphin's main diet is fish and, since hearing in fish is limited to fairly long wavelength sound, they are not alerted to the fact they are being hunted. What's more interesting, the dolphin can reproduce the sonic signals that paint the image of its surroundings; therefore, the dolphin probably communicates its experience to other dolphins by communicating the full acoustic image of what is "seen," placing it directly in the minds of other dolphins. The dolphin needs no word or symbol for "fish," for example, but communicates an image of the real thing—maybe with emphasis highlighted by selective filtering, as we similarly communicate a musical concert to others through various means of sound reproduction. Is it any wonder that the language of the dolphin is very different from ours?

31.4 Young read fluently at the age of two; by four, he had read the Bible twice; by fourteen, he knew eight languages. During his adult life he contributed to an understanding of fluids, work and energy, and the elastic properties of materials. He was also the first person to make progress in deciphering Egyptian hieroglyphics. No doubt about it: Thomas Young was smart—very smart.

31.6 A word constructed from the initials of a phrase is called an *acronym*.

Chapter 32

32.1 Why don't protons pull the oppositely charged electrons into the nucleus? Interestingly enough, the reason is *not* the same as the reason that planets orbit the sun. Within the atom, different laws of physics apply. This is the domain of *quantum physics*, which we come to in Chapter 38. According to quantum physics, an electron behaves like a wave and has to occupy a certain amount of space related to its wavelength. The size of an atom is set by the minimum amount of "elbow room" that an electron requires.

Why is it that the protons in the nucleus do not fly apart from one another? What holds the nucleus together? The answer is that in addition to electrical forces in the nucleus, there are even stronger forces that are nonelectrical in nature. These are *nuclear forces* and are discussed in Chapter 39.

32.2 Within the atomic nucleus, however, elementary particles called *quarks* carry charges $\frac{1}{3}$ and $\frac{2}{3}$ the magnitude of the electron's charge. Each proton and each neutron is made up of three quarks. Since quarks always exist in such combinations and have never been found as separate individual particles, the whole-number-multiple rule of electron charge holds for nuclear processes as well.

32.3.1 Contrast this with the gravitational force of attraction between two masses of 1 kg, each a distance 1 m apart: 6.67×10^{-11} N. This is an extremely small force. For the force to be 1 N, two masses 1 m apart would have to be about 122,000 kilograms each! Gravitational forces between ordinary objects are much too small to be detected except in delicate experiments. Electrical forces (noncanceled) between ordinary objects are large enough to be commonly experienced.

32.3.2 The similarities between these two forces have made some physicists think they may be different aspects of the same thing. Albert Einstein was one of these people; he spent the later part of his life searching with little success for a "unified field theory." In recent years, the electrical force has been unified with the nuclear *weak force*, which plays a role in radioactive decay. Physicists are still looking for a way to unify electrical and gravitational forces.

32.6 Benjamin Franklin was most fortunate that he was not electrocuted, as others were who attempted to duplicate his experiment. In addition to being a great statesman, Franklin was a first-rate scientist. He introduced the terms *positive* and *negative* as they relate to electricity but nevertheless supported the "one-fluid theory" of electric currents. He also contributed to our understanding of grounding and insulation. As Franklin approached the height of his scientific career, a more compelling task was presented to him—helping to form the system of government of the newly independent United States. A less important undertaking would not have kept him from spending more of his energies on his favorite activity—the scientific investigation of nature.

Chapter 33

33.1 The strength of an electric field is a measure of the force exerted on a small test charge placed in the field. (The test charge must be small enough that it doesn't push the original charge around and thus alter the field we are trying to measure.) If a test charge q experiences a force F at some point in space, then the electric field E at that point is

$$E = \frac{F}{q}$$

Electric field strength can be measured in units of newtons per coulomb (N/C), or equivalently, volts per meter (V/m).

33.5 It is common practice to assign a zero electric potential to places infinitely far away from any charges. As the next chapter discusses, for electric currents, the value zero is assigned to the potential of the ground.

33.7 The electric field strength for arc discharge is directly proportional to the radius of the conducting sphere. Hence we see that the large-radius sphere of a Van de Graaff generator holds considerable charge before arc discharge occurs, while the sharp points of lightning rods readily leak charge. The sharp points behave as small-radius spheres. The greater the radius, the greater the charge that can be stored before arc discharge occurs.

34.2 The SI symbol for ampere is A. However, an older symbol still in common usage is amp. People often speak of a current of, say, "5 amps."

34.3.1 A description of the chemical reactions occurring inside a battery can be found in almost any chemistry textbook.

34.3.2 It is conceptually simpler to say that current flows through a circuit, but don't say this around somebody who is "picky" about grammar, for the expression current flows is redundant. More properly, charge flows, which *is* current.

34.4.1 Carbon is an interesting exception. At high temperatures, electrons are shaken from the carbon atom, which increases electric current. Carbon's resistance decreases with increasing temperature. This behavior, along with its high melting temperature, accounts for the use of carbon in arc lamps.

34.4.2 The Greek letter capital Ω (omega) is usually used as a symbol for ohm.

34.5 Many texts use V for voltage, I for current, and R for resistance, and express Ohm's law as $V = IR$. It then follows that $I = V/R$, or $R = V/I$, so if any two variables are known, the third can be found.

34.7.1 120 volts refers to the "root-mean-square" average of the voltage. The actual voltage in a 120-volt AC circuit varies between $+170$-volt and -170-volt peaks. It delivers the same power to an iron or a toaster as a 120-volt DC circuit.

34.7.2 The "plus" and "minus" are arbitrary, because they alternate. The important thing is that they are opposite.

34.11.1 Note that this follows from the definitions of current and voltage:

$$\text{current} \times \text{voltage} = \frac{\cancel{\text{charge}}}{\text{time}} \times \frac{\text{energy}}{\cancel{\text{charge}}} = \frac{\text{energy}}{\text{time}} = \text{power}$$

34.11.2 Since power = energy/time, simple rearrangement gives energy = power × time; hence, energy can be expressed in units of kilowatt-hours.

Physicists measure energy in *joules,* but utility companies customarily sell energy in units of *kilowatt-hours* (kW·h), where 1 kW·h = 3.6×10^6 J. This duplication of units added to an already long list of units can make the study of physics more difficult. You should at least become familiar with, and be able to distinguish among, the units *coulombs, volts, ohms, amperes, watts, kilowatts,* and *kilowatt-hours* here. An understanding of electricity takes considerable time and effort, so be patient with yourself if you find this material difficult.

Chapter 35

35.1 Strictly speaking, a battery consists of two or more cells. What most people call a flashlight battery is more properly called a flashlight dry cell. To conform with popular usage, this chapter uses the term *battery* to mean either a single cell or series of cells.

35.6 For a pair of equal or nonequal resistors in parallel, the equivalent resistance is found by taking the product of the pair and dividing by the sum of the pair:

$$R_{\text{equivalent}} = \frac{R_1 R_2}{R_1 + R_2}$$

This rule of "product divided by sum" holds only for two resistors in parallel. For three or more parallel resistors, you can do a pair at a time (as is done in Figures 35.10 and 35.11), or use the more general formula

$$\frac{1}{R_{\text{equivalent}}} = \frac{1}{R_1} + \frac{1}{R_2} + \frac{1}{R_3} \quad \text{and so on.}$$

Chapter 36

36.0 We can only speculate about how often such relationships become evident when they "aren't supposed to" and are dismissed as "something wrong with the apparatus." Oersted, however, had the insight characteristic of a good scientist to see that nature was revealing another of its secrets.

36.1 The force of interaction between magnetic poles is given by

$$F \sim \frac{pp'}{d^2}$$

where p and p' represent magnetic pole strengths, and d represents the separation distance between them. Note the similarity of this relationship to Coulomb's law and Newton's law of gravity.

36.3.1 Interestingly enough, since motion is relative, the magnetic field is relative. For example, when a charge moves by you, there is a definite magnetic field associated with the moving charge. But if you move along with the charge so that there is no motion relative to you, there is no magnetic field associated with the charge. Magnetism is relativistic.

36.3.2 Most common magnets are made from alloys containing iron, nickel, cobalt, and aluminum in various proportions. In these metals, the electron spin contributes virtually all the magnetic properties. In the rare earth metals, such as gadolinium, the orbital motion is more significant.

36.6 When particles of electric charge q and speed v move perpendicular to a magnetic field of strength B, the force F on each particle is simply the product of the three variables: $F = qvB$. For nonperpendicular angles, v in this relationship must be the component of velocity perpendicular to the field.

36.8 The galvanometer is named after Luigi Galvani (1737–1798), who discovered while dissecting a frog's leg that electric charge caused the leg to twitch. This chance discovery led to the invention of the chemical cell and the battery.

Chapter 37

37.1.1 Multiple loops of wire must be insulated, for bare wire loops touching each other make a short circuit. Interestingly, Joseph Henry's wife tearfully sacrificed part of the silk in her wedding gown to cover the wires of Henry's first electromagnets.

37.1.2 If the coil is not connected to anything, it takes no work to plunge the magnet into the coil, regardless of its number of turns. In this sense, you do get something for nothing—an induced voltage, but it doesn't "do" anything. There is no current flow and no transfer of energy.

37.2 Current also depends on the "reactance" of the coil. Reactance is similar to resistance and is important in AC circuits; it depends on the number of loops in the coil and on the frequency of the AC source, among other things.

37.3 The conversion of mechanical energy to electrical energy can be close to 100% efficient, but because of the laws of thermodynamics, the conversion of heat to either mechanical energy or electrical energy is much less efficient. In a typical thermal power plant, only 35% to 40% of the fuel energy leaves the plant as electrical energy. Hence we look to sources of energy that are not chemical fuels.

Chapter 38

38.5 A ball bearing of mass 0.02 kg traveling at 330 m/s, for example, has a de Broglie wavelength of $h/mv = (6.6 \times 10^{-34} \text{ J·s})/[(0.02 \text{ kg}) \times (330 \text{ m/s})] = 10^{-34}$ m, an incredibly small size that is a million million million millionth the diameter of a hydrogen atom. An electron traveling at 2% the speed of light, on the other hand, has a wavelength of 10^{-10} m, which is equal to the diameter of the hydrogen atom. Diffraction effects for electrons are measurable, but diffraction effects for ball bearings are not.

38.6 Electron wavelengths are successively longer for orbits of increasing radii; so for a more accurate analogy, the construction of longer necklaces requires using not only *more* paper clips, but *larger* paper clips as well.

38.7 There is a maximum number of electrons that each orbit may hold. A rule of quantum mechanics states that an orbit is filled when it contains a number of electrons given by $2n^2$, where n is 1 for the first orbit, 2 for the second orbit, 3 for the third orbit, and so on. For $n = 1$, there are 2 electrons; for $n = 2$, there are $2(2^2)$, or 8 electrons; for $n = 3$, there are a maximum of $2(3^2)$, or 18 electrons, and so on. The number n is called the *principal quantum number*. Because of complexities that arise in heavy atoms, the $2n^2$ rule is strictly valid only for the lighter atoms.

38.8 This prompted his often-quoted statement, "I cannot believe that God plays dice with the universe." To Einstein, who practiced no religion, God was nature itself.

Chapter 39

39.1 Protons and neutrons are themselves composed of subnuclear particles called *quarks*. There is no evidence or theoretical reason for thinking that quarks are made up of still smaller particles. Theoretical physicists say today that quarks are the elementary particles of which all nucleons and other strongly interacting particles are made.

39.6.1 Beta emission is accompanied by the ejection of an antineutrino, not shown here. Antineutrinos are the antiparticles of neutrinos, and are extremely swift (moving at or close to the speed of light) and extremely plentiful. Whether they have mass is still questionable. If they do, it is thousands of times less than the mass of the electron. Neutrinos have no charge and seldom interact with matter. As you are reading this sentence, a thousand billion neutrinos emanating from the sun pierce through your body. This is true day or night, since at nighttime the solar neutrinos travel through Earth and pierce you from below. A cause for concern? No, that's just nature in action!

39.6.2 Sometimes a nucleus emits a *positron*, which is the antiparticle of an electron. A positron has a charge of +1 and the same mass as the electron. In this case, a proton in the nucleus becomes a neutron, and the atomic number is decreased by 1 with no change in mass number.

39.8 The accompanying antineutrino is not shown.

39.10 The use of intense radiation in treating cancer is different. The quantity of radioactive material is then far greater than in research using radioactive tracers, but the benefit is reckoned to outweigh the risk.

Chapter 40

40.1 Another way to understand this is geometrically. Recall the concept of scaling in Chapter 18. Small pieces of material have more surface area relative to volume than large pieces (there is more skin on a kilogram of small potatoes than on a single 1-kilogram large potato). The larger the piece of fission fuel, the less surface area it has relative to its volume.

40.6 These units are called *atomic mass units* and are the units for atomic mass used in chemistry.

Glossary

A

aberration (ab-er-RAY-shun) Distortion in an image produced by a lens. (30.8)

absolute zero The temperature at which a substance has no kinetic energy per particle (thermal) to give up. This temperature corresponds to 0 K, or to −273°C. (21.1, 24.1)

acceleration (ak-sel´-er-RAY-shun) The rate at which velocity is changing. The change may be in magnitude, direction, or both. (4.4)

action force One of the pair of forces described in Newton's third law. (7.2)

additive primary colors Red, blue, and green light. These colors when added together produce white light. (28.5)

adiabatic (ay-dee-ah-BAT-ik) Term applied to expansion or compression of a gas occurring without gain or loss of heat. (24.3)

air resistance Friction, or drag, that acts on something moving through air. (6.4)

alternating current (AC) Electric current that repeatedly reverses direction, twice each cycle. Usually at 60 cycles per second, or hertz (Hz), in North America, or 50 hertz elsewhere. (34.7)

ampere (AM-peer) SI unit of electric current. A flow of one coulomb of charge per second is one ampere (symbol A). (34.2)

amplitude (AMP-lih-tewd) The distance from the midpoint to the maximum (crest) of a wave or, equivalently, from the midpoint to the minimum (trough). (25.2)

aneroid barometer (AN-er-oyd buh-ROM-uh-ter) An instrument used to measure atmospheric pressure; based on the movement of the lid of a metal box. (20.4)

angle of incidence (IN-sih-dens) Angle between an incident ray and the normal to a surface (see Figure 29.3). (29.2)

angle of reflection Angle between a reflected ray and the normal to a surface (see Figure 29.3). (29.2)

angular momentum (mo-MEN-tum) Product of rotational inertia and rotational velocity. (12.4)

antinodes The positions on a standing wave where the largest amplitudes occur. (25.8)

apogee (AP-uh-jee) The point in a satellite's elliptical orbit farthest from the center of Earth. (14.4)

Archimedes' principle (ark-uh-MEE-deez) The relationship between buoyancy and displaced fluid: An immersed object is buoyed up by a force equal to the weight of the fluid it displaces. (19.3)

astigmatism (uh-STIG-muh-tizm) A defect of the eye caused when the cornea is curved more in one direction than in another. (30.7)

atom The smallest particle of an element that can be identified with that element. Consists of protons and neutrons in a nucleus surrounded by electrons. (17.1)

atomic mass number Total number of nucleons (neutrons and protons) in the nucleus of an atom. (39.4)

atomic number Number of protons in the nucleus of an atom. (17.7, 39.4)

average speed Path distance divided by time interval. (4.2)

axis (AK-sis) (a) The straight line around which an object may rotate or revolve. (10.1) (b) A horizontal or vertical reference line in a graph. (Appendix C)

B

barometer An instrument used to measure the pressure of the atmosphere. (20.3)

beats A periodic variation in the loudness of sound caused by interference when two tones of slightly different frequencies are sounded together. (26.10)

Bernoulli's principle (ber-NOO-leez) The statement that the pressure in a fluid decreases as the speed of the fluid increases. (20.7)

bimetallic strip (bi´-meh-TAL´-ik) Two strips of different metals, such as one of brass and one of iron, welded or riveted together into one strip. Because the two substances expand at different rates, when heated or cooled the strip bends. Used in thermostats. (21.8)

black hole   A mass that has collapsed to so great a density that its enormous local gravitational field prevents light from escaping. (13.10)

blue shift   An increase in the measured frequency of light from an approaching source; called the blue shift because the apparent increase is toward the high-frequency, or blue, end of the color spectrum. Also occurs when an observer approaches a source. (25.9)

boiling   The change of phase from liquid to gas that occurs beneath the surface in the liquid. The gas forms bubbles that rise to the surface and escape. (23.4)

bow wave   The V-shaped wave produced by an object moving on a liquid surface faster than the wave speed. (25.10)

Boyle's law   For a constant number of molecules of gas at constant temperature, the product of pressure and volume is constant. (20.5)

breeder reactor   A nuclear fission reactor that not only produces power but produces more nuclear fuel than it consumes by converting a nonfissionable uranium isotope into a fissionable plutonium isotope. (40.5)

Brownian motion   The perpetual random movement of microscopic particles suspended in a fluid medium. (17.4)

buoyancy (BOY-un-see)   The apparent loss of weight of an object immersed or submerged in a fluid. (19.2)

buoyant force (BOY-unt)   The net upward force exerted by a fluid on a submerged or immersed object. (19.2)

C

calorie (KAL-er-ee)   A unit of heat. One calorie (symbol cal) is the heat required to raise the temperature of one gram of water one Celsius degree. One Calorie (with a capital C) is equal to one thousand calories and is the unit used in describing the energy available from food. (1 cal = 4.186 J, or 1 J = 0.24 cal) (21.5)

capacitor (kuh-PAS-ih-ter)   A device used to store charge in a circuit. (33.6)

Carnot efficiency (KAR-no)   The ideal maximum percentage of input energy that can be converted to work in a heat engine. (24.5)

Celsius scale (SEL-see-us)   A temperature scale with 0 as the melt-freeze temperature for water and 100 as the boil-condense temperature of water at standard pressure (one atmosphere at sea level). (21.1)

center of gravity   The point at the center of an object's weight distribution, where the force of gravity can be considered to act. Abbreviated CG. (11.4)

center of mass   The point at the center of an object's mass distribution, where all its mass can be considered to be concentrated. For everyday conditions, it is the same as the center of gravity. (13.3)

centrifugal force (sen-TRIH-fuh-gul)   An apparent outward force on a rotating or revolving body. It is fictitious in the sense that it is not part of an interaction but is due to the tendency of a moving body to move in a straight-line path. (10.4)

centripetal force (sen-TRIH-peh-tul)   A center-directed force that causes an object to move in a curved (sometimes circular) path. (10.3)

chain reaction   A self-sustaining reaction in which one reaction event stimulates one or more additional reaction events to keep the process going. (40.1)

charge   The fundamental electrical property to which the mutual attractions or repulsions between electrons or protons is attributed. (32.1)

chemical formula   A description that uses numbers and symbols of elements to describe the proportions of elements in a compound or reaction. (17.6)

circuit (SER-kit)   Any complete path along which charge can flow. (35.1)

coherent (ko-HEER-ent)   As applied to light waves, having identical frequency and identical phase, and traveling in the same direction. Lasers produce coherent light. (31.6)

complementary colors (kom´-pluh-MENT´-uh-ree)   Two colors of light beams that when added together appear white. (28.6)

component (kom-PO-nent)   One of the vectors, often mutually perpendicular, whose sum is a resultant vector. Any resultant vector may be regarded as the combination of two or more components. (See resultant.) (5.3)

compound   A chemical substance made of atoms of two or more different elements combined in a fixed proportion. (17.6)

compression   (kom-PRE-shun) (a) In mechanics, the act of squeezing material and reducing its volume. (18.4) (b) In sound, a pulse of compressed air (or other matter); opposite of rarefaction. (26.2)

concave lens   A lens that is thinnest in the middle and that causes parallel rays of light to diverge. Also known as a *diverging lens.* (30.1)

condensation   (kon´-den-SAY´-shun) The change of phase of a gas into a liquid; the opposite of evaporation. (23.2)

conduction   (a) In heat, energy transfer from particle to particle within certain materials, or from one material to another when the two are in direct contact. (22.1) (b) In electricity, the flow of charge through a conductor. (32.4)

conductor   (a) Material through which heat can be transferred. (22.1) (b) Material, usually a metal, through which electric charge can flow. Good conductors of heat are generally good charge conductors. (32.4)

conservation of charge   The principle that net electric charge is neither created nor destroyed but is transferable from one material to another. (32.2)

conserved   Term applied to a physical quantity, such as momentum, energy, or electric charge, that remains unchanged during interactions. (8.4)

constructive interference   Addition of two or more waves when wave crests overlap to produce a resulting wave of increased amplitude. (25.7)

convection   A means of heat transfer by movement of the heated substance itself, such as by currents in a fluid. (22.2)

converging lens   A lens that is thickest in the middle, causing parallel rays of light to converge to a focus. Also known as a *convex lens.* (30.1)

convex lens   A lens that is thickest in the middle, causing parallel rays of light to converge or focus. Also known as a *converging lens.* (30.1)

cornea (KOR-nee-uh)   The transparent covering over the eyeball. (30.6)

correspondence principle   If a new theory is valid, it must account for the verified results of the old theory in the region where both theories apply. (16.3)

coulomb (KOO-lom)   SI unit of charge. One coulomb (symbol C) is equal to the total charge of 6.24×10^{18} electrons. (32.3)

Coulomb's law   The relationship among electrical force, charges, and distance: The electrical force between two charges varies directly as the product of the charges and inversely as the square of the distance between them. (32.3)

crest   One of the places in a wave where the wave is highest or the disturbance is greatest. (25.2)

critical angle   The minimum angle of incidence for which a light ray is totally reflected within a medium. (29.12)

critical mass   The minimum mass of fissionable material in a nuclear reactor or nuclear bomb that will sustain a chain reaction. (40.1)

crystal (KRIS-tul)   A regular geometric shape found in a solid in which the component particles are arranged in an orderly, three-dimensional, repeating pattern. (18.1)

current   See *electric current.*

 D

density (DEN-sih-tee)   A property of a substance, equal to its mass per volume. (18.2)

destructive interference   Combination of waves where crests of one wave overlap troughs of another, resulting in a wave of decreased amplitude. (25.7)

diode (DY-ohd)   An electronic device that restricts current to flow in a single direction in an electric circuit. (34.8)

diffraction (dih-FRAK-shun)   The bending of a wave around a barrier, such as an obstacle or the edges of an opening. (31.2)

diffraction grating   A series of closely spaced parallel slits or grooves that are used to separate colors of light by interference. (31.4)

diffuse reflection (dih-FYOOS)   The reflection of waves in many directions from a rough surface (see Figure 29.7). (29.4)

direct current (DC)   Electric current whose flow of charge is always in one direction. (34.7)

dispersion (dih-SPER-zhun)   The separation of light into colors arranged according to their frequency, by interaction with a prism or diffraction grating, for example. (29.10)

diverging lens   A lens that is thinnest in the middle and that causes parallel rays of light to diverge. Also known as a *concave lens*. (30.1)

Doppler effect (DOP-ler)   The apparent change in frequency of a wave due to the motion of the source or of the receiver. (25.9)

E

eddy   Changing, curling paths in turbulent flow of a fluid. (20.7)

efficiency   In a machine, the ratio of useful energy output to total energy input, or the percentage of the work input that is converted to work output. (9.9)

elapsed time   The time that has passed since the beginning of an event. (4.5)

elastic   Term applied to a material that returns to its original shape after it has been stretched or compressed. (18.3)

elastic collision   Collision in which colliding objects rebound without lasting deformation or heat generation. (8.5)

elastic limit   The distance of stretching or compressing beyond which an elastic material will not return to its original shape. (18.3)

elasticity (ih-las-TIH-sih-tee)   The property of a solid wherein a change in shape is experienced when a deforming force acts on it, with a return to its original shape when the deforming force is removed. (18.3)

electric charge   See *charge*.

electric current   The flow of electric charge; measured in amperes (C/s). (34.2)

electric field   A force field that fills the space around every electric charge or group of charges. Measured by force per charge (N/C). (33.1)

electric potential   Electrical potential energy per coulomb (J/C) at a location in an electric field; measured in volts and often called voltage. (33.5)

electric power   The rate at which electrical energy is converted into another form, such as light, heat, or mechanical energy (or converted from another form into electrical energy). (34.11)

electric resistance   The resistance of a material to the flow of electric current through it; measured in ohms (symbol Ω). (34.4)

electrical force   A force that one charge exerts on another. When the charges are the same sign, they repel; when the charges are opposite, they attract. (32.1)

electrical potential energy   Energy a charge has due to its location in an electric field. (33.4)

electrically polarized   Term applied to an atom or molecule in which the charges are aligned so that one side is slightly more positive or negative than the opposite side. (32.7)

electromagnet   (ih-lek´-tro-MAG´-net) Magnet with a field produced by electric current; usually in the form of a wire coiled around a piece of iron. (36.5)

electromagnetic induction   (ih-lek´-tro-mag-NET´-ik in-DUK-shun) The phenomenon of inducing a voltage in a conductor by changing the magnetic field near the conductor. (37.1)

electromagnetic spectrum   The range of electromagnetic waves extending from radio waves to gamma rays. (27.3)

electromagnetic wave   A wave that is partly electric and partly magnetic and carries energy. Emitted by vibrating electric charges. (27.3)

electrostatics   (ih-lek´-tro-STAT´-iks) The study of electric charges at rest. (32.0)

element   A substance made of only one kind of atom. Examples of elements are carbon, hydrogen, oxygen, and nitrogen. (17.1)

ellipse   (ih-LIPS) An oval-shaped curve that is the path of a point that moves such that the sum of its distances from two fixed points (foci) is constant (see Figure 14.8). (14.3)

energy   The property of an object or a system that enables it to do work; measured in joules. (9.3)

entropy   A measure of the amount of disorder in a system. (24.7)

equilibrium   (ee-kwih-LIH-bree-um) See *mechanical equilibrium* or *equilibrium rule*.

equilibrium rule   An object is in mechanical equilibrium whenever the net force on the object is zero. (2.2).

escape speed The minimum speed necessary for an object to escape permanently from a gravitational field that holds it. (14.5)

evaporation (ih-vap´-or-AY´-shun) The change of phase from liquid to gas that takes place at the surface of a liquid. (23.1)

excited state A state with greater energy than an atom's lowest state. (28.11)

eyepiece Lens of a telescope closest to the eye; enlarges the real image formed by the first lens. (30.5)

F

fact A close agreement by competent observers of a series of observations of the same phenomena. (1.4)

Fahrenheit scale (FA-ren-hit) The temperature scale in common use in the United States. The number 32 is assigned to the freezing point of water and the number 212 to the boiling point of water (at standard atmospheric pressure). (21.1)

Faraday's law (FA-ruh-dayz) Induced voltage in a coil is proportional to the product of the number of loops and the rate at which the magnetic field changes within those loops. (37.2) In general, an electric field is induced in any region of space in which a magnetic field is changing with time. The magnitude of the induced electric field is proportional to the rate at which the magnetic field changes. (37.7)

farsighted Term applied to a person who has trouble focusing on nearby objects because the eyeball is so short that images form behind the retina. (30.7)

field See *force field*.

first law of thermodynamics Heat added to a system is transformed to an equal amount of some other form of energy; a version of the law of conservation of energy. (24.2)

first postulate of special relativity All the laws of nature are the same in all uniformly moving reference frames. (15.2)

fission See *nuclear fission*.

fluid Anything that flows; in particular, any liquid or gas. (6.4, 19.6)

focal length The distance between the center of a lens and either focal point. (30.1)

focal plane A plane passing through either focal point of a lens that is perpendicular to the principal axis. For a converging lens, any incident parallel beam of light converges to a point somewhere on a focal plane. For a diverging lens, such a beam appears to come from a point on a focal plane. (30.1)

focal point For a converging lens, the point at which a beam of light parallel to the principal axis converges. For a diverging lens, the point from which such a beam appears to come. (30.1)

focus (FO-kus); pl. **foci** (FO-si) (a) For an ellipse, one of the two points for which the sum of the distances to any point on the ellipse is a constant. A satellite orbiting Earth moves in an ellipse that has Earth at one focus. (14.3) (b) For optics, the point where parallel light rays converge. (30.1)

force Any influence that tends to accelerate an object; a push or pull; measured in newtons. A vector quantity. (2.1)

forced vibration The vibration of an object that is made to vibrate by another vibrating object that is nearby. The sounding board in a musical instrument amplifies the sound through forced vibration. (26.7)

force field That which exists in the space surrounding a mass, electric charge, or magnet, so that another mass, electric charge, or magnet introduced to this region will experience a force. Examples of force fields are gravitational fields, electric fields, and magnetic fields. (13.1)

free-body diagram A diagram showing all the forces acting on an object. (6.4)

free fall Motion under the influence of the gravitational force only. (4.5)

freezing Change in phase from liquid to solid. (23.5)

frequency (FREE-kwen-see) The number of events (cycles, vibrations, oscillations, or any repeated event) per time; measured in hertz (or events per time). Inverse of period. (25.2)

friction The force that acts to resist the relative motion (or attempted motion) of objects or materials that are in contact. (3.3)

fuel cell A device in which hydrogen and oxygen are compressed at electrodes to produce water and electric current. (9.10)

fulcrum (FOOL-krum) The pivot point of a lever. (9.8)

fusion See *nuclear fusion*.

G

geodesics   Lines of shortest distance between two points in curved space. (16.5)

general theory of relativity   Einstein's generalization of special relativity, where gravity causes space to become curved and time to slow down. (16.3)

generator   A machine that produces electric current by rotating a coil within a stationary magnetic field. (37.3)

global warming   See *greenhouse effect.*

gravitational field   (grav´-ih-TAY´-shun-ul) A force field that exists in the space around every mass or group of masses. (13.1)

gravitational shift   A slight decrease in the frequency of light due to the effect of strong gravitational fields, such as those of stars. (16.6)

gravitational waves   Ripples that travel outward from gravitational sources at the speed of light. (16.5)

greenhouse effect   The warming effect whose cause is that short-wavelength radiant energy from the sun can enter the atmosphere and be absorbed by Earth more easily than long-wavelength energy from Earth can leave. (22.7)

grounding   Allowing charges to move freely along a connection between a conductor and the ground. (32.6)

group   Elements in the same column of the periodic table. (17.8)

H

half-life   The time required for half the atoms of a radioactive isotope of an element to decay. Also used for decay processes in general. (39.5)

heat   Energy transfer from one object to another because of a temperature difference. (21.2)

heat engine   A device that changes internal energy to mechanical work. (24.5)

heat pump   A device that moves heat. (23.8)

hertz   (HERTS) The SI unit of frequency. One hertz (Hz) is one cycle per second. (25.2)

hologram   (HOL-uh-gram) A three-dimensional version of a photograph produced by interference patterns of laser beams. (31.7)

Hooke's law   The distance of stretch or squeeze (extension or compression) of an elastic material is directly proportional to the applied force. (18.3)

Huygens' principle   (HI-gunz) Every point on any wave front can be regarded as a new point source of secondary waves. (31.1)

hypothesis   (hi-POTH-uh-sis) An educated guess; a reasonable explanation of an observation or experimental result that is not fully accepted as factual until tested over and over again by experiment. (1.4)

I

impulse   (IM-puls) Product of force and time interval during which the force acts. Impulse equals momentum change. (8.2)

incoherent   (in´-ko-HEER´-ent) As applied to light waves, having a jumbled mixture of frequency, phase, and possibly direction. (31.6)

induced   (in-DEWSD) (a) Term applied to electric charge that has been redistributed on an object because of the presence of a charged object nearby. (32.6) (b) Term applied to a voltage, electric field, or magnetic field that is created due to a change in or motion through a magnetic field or electric field. (37.1, 37.7)

induction   (in-DUK-shun) The charging of an object without direct contact. (32.6) See also *electromagnetic induction.*

inelastic   Term applied to a material that does not return to its original shape after it has been stretched or compressed. (Also called plastic.) (18.3)

inelastic collision   A collision in which the colliding objects become tangled or coupled together, distorted and/or generate heat during the collision. (8.5)

inertia   (ih-NER-shuh) The property of any body to resist changes in its state of motion. Mass is the measure of inertia. (3.3)

infrared   Electromagnetic waves of frequencies lower than the red of visible light. (27.3)

infrasonic   (in´-fruh-SON´-ik) Term applied to sound pitch too low to be heard by the human ear, that is, below 20 hertz. (26.1)

in parallel Term applied to portions of an electric circuit that are connected at two points and provide alternative paths for the current between those two points. (35.2)

in phase (FAYZ) Term applied to two or more waves whose crests (and troughs) arrive at a place at the same time, so that their effects reinforce each other. (25.7)

in series Term applied to portions of an electric circuit that are connected in a row so that the current that goes through one must go through all of them. (35.2)

instantaneous speed (in-stan-TAY-nee-us) Speed at any instant of time. (4.2)

insulator (IN-suh-lay-ter) (a) A material that is a poor conductor of heat and that delays the transfer of heat. (22.1) (b) A material that is a poor conductor of electricity. (32.4)

interaction A mutual action between objects where each object exerts an equal and opposite force on the other. (7.1)

interference pattern (in´-ter-FEER´-ens) A pattern formed by the overlapping of two or more waves that arrive in a region at the same time. (25.7)

internal energy The total energy stored in the atoms and molecules within a substance. (21.4)

inverse-square law A physical quantity varies inversely as another quantity squared. Example: Illumination varies inversely as the square of the distance from the source. (3.5)

inversely When two values change in opposite directions, so that if one increases the other decreases. (6.2)

ion (I-un) An atom (or group of atoms bound together) with a net electric charge, which is due to the loss or gain of electrons. (17.8)

iridescence (ih-rih-DES-ens) The phenomenon whereby interference of light waves of mixed frequencies reflected from the top and bottom of thin films produces a spectrum of colors. (31.5)

iris (I-ris) The colored part of the eye that surrounds the black opening through which light passes. The iris regulates the amount of light entering the eye. (30.6)

isotope (I-suh-top) A form of an element having a particular number of neutrons in the nuclei of its atoms. Different isotopes of a particular element have the same atomic number but different atomic mass numbers. (17.7, 39.4)

J

joule (JOOL) The SI unit of work and of all other forms of energy. One joule (symbol J) of work is done when a force of one newton is exerted on an object moved one meter in the direction of the force. (9.1)

K

kelvin (KEL-vin) The SI unit of temperature. A temperature measured in kelvins (symbol K) indicates the number of units above absolute zero. Since the divisions on the Kelvin scale and Celsius scale are the same size, a change in temperature of one kelvin equals a change in temperature of one Celsius degree. (21.1)

Kelvin scale A temperature scale whose zero (called absolute zero) is assigned to the lowest temperature possible. 0 K = −273°C. There are no negative temperatures on the Kelvin scale. (21.1)

kilocalorie (KIL-o-kal-er-ee) A unit of heat. One kilocalorie equals 1000 calories, or the amount of heat required to raise the temperature of one kilogram of water by 1°C. (21.5)

kilogram (KIL-o-gram) The fundamental SI unit of mass. One kilogram (symbol kg) is the amount of mass in one liter of water at 4°C. See *Appendix A*. (3.5)

kinetic energy (kih-NET-ik) Energy of motion, equal to half the mass multiplied by the speed squared. (9.5)

L

laser (LAY-zer) An optical instrument that produces a beam of coherent light—that is, having the waves all the same frequency, phase, and direction. (31.6)

law A general hypothesis or statement about the relationship of natural quantities that has been tested over and over again and has not been contradicted. Also known as a principle. (1.4)

law of conservation of angular momentum An object or system of objects will maintain a constant angular momentum unless acted upon by an unbalanced external torque. (12.5)

law of conservation of energy Energy cannot be created or destroyed. It may be transformed from one form into another, but the total amount of energy never changes. (9.6)

law of conservation of momentum   In the absence of a net external force, the momentum of an object or system of objects is unchanged. (8.4)

law of inertia   Every body continues in its state of rest, or of motion in a straight line at constant speed, unless acted upon by a nonzero force. Also known as *Newton's first law*. (3.4)

law of reflection   The angle of incidence for a wave that strikes a surface is equal to the angle of reflection. This is true for both partially and totally reflected waves. (29.2)

law of universal gravitation   For any pair of objects, each object attracts the other object with a force that is directly proportional to the product of the masses of the objects, and inversely proportional to the square of the distance between their centers of mass. (3.4)

length contraction   The observable shortening of objects moving at speeds approaching the speed of light. (15.6)

lens (LENZ)   A piece of glass (or other transparent material) that can bend parallel rays of light so that they cross, or appear to cross, at a single point. (30.1)

lever (LEH-ver, LEE-ver)   A simple machine, made of a bar that turns about a fixed point. (9.8)

lever arm   The perpendicular distance between an axis and the line of action of a force that tends to produce rotation about that axis. (11.1)

lift   In application of Bernoulli's principle, the net upward force produced by the difference between upward and downward pressures. When lift equals weight, horizontal flight is possible. (20.8)

light-year   The distance light travels through a vacuum during one year. (27.2)

line spectrum   A pattern of distinct lines of color, corresponding to particular wavelengths, that are seen in a spectroscope when a hot gas is viewed. (28.11)

linear momentum   Product of the mass and the velocity of an object. Also called momentum. (This definition applies at speeds much less than the speed of light.) (12.4)

linear speed   The path distance moved per unit of time. Also called simply speed. (10.2)

longitudinal wave (lon-jih-TEWD-ih-nul)   A wave in which the vibration is in the same direction as that in which the wave is traveling, rather than at right angles to it. (25.6)

M

machine   A device for increasing (or decreasing) a force or simply changing the direction of a force. (9.8)

magnetic domain   A microscopic cluster of atoms with their magnetic fields aligned. (36.4)

magnetic field   A force field that fills the space around every magnet or current-carrying wire. (36.2)

magnetic pole   One of the regions on a magnet that produces magnetic forces. (36.1)

mass   A measure of an object's inertia; also a measure of the amount of matter in an object. Depends only on the amount of and kind of particles that compose an object—not on its location (as weight does). (3.5)

mechanical advantage   The ratio of output force to input force for a machine. (9.8)

mechanical energy   The energy due to the position or the movement of something; potential or kinetic energy (or a combination of both). (9.3)

mechanical equilibrium   A state wherein no physical change occurs. (2.2)

mirage (mih-RAHZH)   A floating image that appears in the distance and is due to the refraction of light in Earth's atmosphere. (29.9)

molecule (MOL-uh-kyool)   The smallest particle of substance consisting of two or more atoms of the same or different elements bonded together. (17.5)

momentum   The product of the mass and the velocity of an object (provided the speed is much less than the speed of light). Has magnitude and direction (a vector quantity). Also called linear momentum. (8.1)

monochromatic (mon´-o-kro-MAT´-ik)   Having a single color or frequency. (31.4)

N

natural frequency   A frequency at which an elastic object, once energized, will vibrate. Minimum energy is required to continue vibration at that frequency. Also called resonant frequency. (26.6)

neap tide   A tide that occurs when the moon is halfway between a new moon and a full moon, in either direction. The tides due to the sun and the moon partly cancel, so that the high tides are lower than average and the low tides are not as low as average. (13.9)

nearsighted Term applied to a person who can clearly see nearby objects but not clearly see distant objects. The eyeball is elongated so that images focus in front of rather than on the retina. (30.7)

net force The combination of all the forces that act on an object. (2.1)

neutral equilibrium The state of an object balanced so that any small movement neither raises nor lowers its center of gravity. (11.7)

neutron An electrically neutral particle that is one of the two kinds of particles that compose an atomic nucleus. (17.7)

newton SI unit of force. One newton (N) is the force applied to a one-kilogram mass that will produce an acceleration of one meter per second per second. (3.5)

Newton's first law See *law of inertia.*

Newton's law of cooling The rate of cooling of an object—whether by conduction, convection, or radiation—is approximately proportional to the temperature difference between the object and its surroundings. (22.6)

Newton's second law The acceleration produced by a net force on a body is directly proportional to the magnitude of the net force, is in the same direction as the net force, and is inversely proportional to the mass of the body. (6.3)

Newton's third law Whenever one body exerts a force on a second body, the second body exerts an equal and opposite force on the first. (7.2)

node Any part of a standing wave that remains stationary. (25.8)

normal A line perpendicular to a surface. (29.2)

normal force For an object resting on a horizontal surface, the upward force that balances the weight of the object; also called the support force. (2.3)

nuclear fission (FIH-shun) The splitting of an atomic nucleus, particularly that of a heavy element such as uranium-235, into two main parts accompanied by the release of much energy. (40.1)

nuclear fusion (FEW-zhun) The combining of nuclei of light atoms, such as hydrogen, into heavier nuclei accompanied by the release of much energy. (40.7)

nucleon (NEW-klee-on) The principal building block of the nucleus; a neutron or a proton. (17.7, 39.1)

nucleus The positively charged center of an atom, which contains protons and neutrons and has almost all the mass of the entire atom but only a tiny fraction of the volume. (17.7)

neutron An electrically neutral particle that is one of the two kinds of particles found in the nucleus of an atom. (17.7)

 O

objective lens In an optical device using compound lenses, the lens closest to the object observed. (30.5)

ohm (OM) The SI unit of electric resistance. One ohm (symbol Ω) is the resistance of a device that draws a current of one ampere when a voltage of one volt is impressed across it. (34.4)

Ohm's law The statement that the current in a circuit is directly proportional to the voltage impressed across the circuit, and is inversely proportional to the resistance of the circuit. (34.5)

opaque Term applied to materials that absorb light without reemission, and consequently do not allow light through them. (27.5)

optical fiber A transparent fiber, usually of glass or plastic, that can transmit light down its length by means of total internal reflection. (29.12)

out of phase Term applied to two waves for which the crest of one wave arrives at a point at the same time that a trough of the second wave arrives. Their effects cancel each other. (25.7)

 P

parallel circuit An electric circuit in which devices are connected to the same two points of the circuit, so that any single device completes the circuit independently of the others. (35.4)

pascal (pas-KAL) The SI unit of pressure. One pascal (symbol Pa) of pressure exerts a normal force of one newton per square meter. (6.5)

Pascal's principle Changes in pressure at any point in an enclosed fluid at rest are transmitted undiminished to all points in the fluid and act in all directions. (19.6)

penumbra A partial shadow that appears where light from part of the source is blocked and light from another part of the source is not blocked. (27.6)

perigee (PEH-rih-jee) The point in a satellite's elliptical orbit where it is nearest the center of Earth. (14.4)

period (a) The time required for a complete orbit. (14.2) (b) The time required for a pendulum to make one to-and-fro swing. In general, the time required to complete a single cycle. (25.1)

periodic table A chart that lists elements by atomic number and by electron arrangements, so that elements with similar chemical properties are in the same column (Figure 17.12). (17.8)

perturbation The deviation of an orbiting object from its path around a center of force caused by the action of an additional center of force. (13.11)

phase One of the four possible forms of matter: solid, liquid, gas, and plasma. Often called state. (23.0)

photoelectric effect The ejection of electrons from certain metals when exposed to certain frequencies of light. (38.3)

photon (FO-ton) In the particle model of electromagnetic radiation, a particle that travels only at the speed of light and whose energy is related to the frequency of the radiation in the wave model. (27.1, 38.2)

pigment A material that selectively absorbs colored light. (28.3)

pitch Term that refers to how high or low sound frequencies appear to be. (26.1)

Planck's constant A fundamental constant of quantum theory that determines the scale of the small-scale world. Planck's constant (symbol h) multiplied by the frequency of radiation gives the energy of a photon of that radiation. (38.2)

plasma (PLAZ-muh) A fourth phase of matter, in addition to solid, liquid, and gas. In the plasma phase, which exists mainly at high temperature, matter consists of positively charged ions and free electrons. (17.9)

polarization (po-ler-ih-ZAY´-shun) The aligning of vibrations in a transverse wave, usually by filtering out waves of other directions. (27.7)

postulate (POS-tyoo-lit) A fundamental assumption. (15.1)

potential See *electric potential*.

potential difference The difference in electric potential (voltage) between two points. Free charge flows when there is a difference and will continue until both points reach a common potential. (34.1)

potential energy Energy of position, usually related to the relative position of two things, such as a stone and Earth, or an electron and a nucleus. (9.4)

power Rate at which work is done or energy is transformed, equal to the work done or energy transformed divided by time; measured in watts. (8.2)

pressure Force per unit of surface area where the force is perpendicular to the surface; measured in pascals. (6.5)

principal axis The line joining the centers of curvature of the surfaces of a lens. (30.1)

principle A general hypothesis or statement about the relationship of natural quantities that has been tested over and over again and has not been contradicted; also known as a law. (1.4)

principle of equivalence Local observations made in an accelerated frame of reference cannot be distinguished from observations made in a Newtonian gravitational field. (16.4)

projectile Any object that moves through the air or through space, acted on only by gravity (and air resistance, if any). (5.4)

proton A positively charged particle that is one of the two kinds of particles found in the nucleus of an atom. (17.7)

pulley A type of lever that is a wheel with a groove in its rim, which is used to change the direction of a force exerted by a rope or cable. A pulley or system of pulleys can also multiply forces. (9.8)

pupil The opening in the eyeball through which light passes. (30.6)

 Q

quantum (pl. quanta) (KWONT-um) The fundamental "size" unit; the smallest amount of anything. One quantum of light energy is called a photon. (38.2)

quantum mechanics The branch of physics that is the study of the motion of particles in the microworld of atoms and nuclei. (38.8)

quantum physics The branch of physics that is the general study of the microworld of photons, atoms, and nuclei. (38.8)

R

radiant energy   Any energy, including heat, light, and X-rays, that is transmitted by radiation. It occurs in the form of electromagnetic waves. (22.3)

radiation   (a) Energy transmitted by electromagnetic waves. (22.3) (b) The charged particles and energy given off by radioactive atoms such as uranium. (39.2)

radioactive   Term applied to an atom with a nucleus that is unstable and that can spontaneously emit a particle and become the nucleus of another element. (39.2)

rarefaction (rayr-uh-FAK-shun)   A disturbance in air (or matter) in which the pressure is lowered. Opposite of compression. (26.2)

ray   A thin beam of light. (27.6)

ray diagram   A diagram showing rays that can be drawn to determine the size and location of an image formed by a mirror or lens. (30.3)

reaction force   The force that is equal in strength and opposite in direction to the action force, which acts simultaneously on whatever is exerting the action force. (7.2)

real image   An image that is formed by converging light rays and that can be displayed on a screen. (30.2)

red shift   A decrease in the measured frequency of light (or other radiation) from a receding source; called the red shift because the decrease is toward the low-frequency, or red, end of the color spectrum. (25.9)

reflection   The bouncing back of a particle or wave that strikes the boundary between two media. (29.1)

refraction   The change in direction of a wave as it crosses the boundary between two media in which the wave travels at different speeds. (29.6)

regelation   The phenomenon of ice melting under pressure and freezing again when the pressure is reduced. (23.7)

relative   Regarded in relation to something else. Depends on point of view, or frame of reference. Sometimes referred to as "with respect to." (4.1)

relative humidity   A ratio between how much water vapor is in the air and the maximum amount of water vapor that could be in the air at the same temperature. (23.2)

relativistic momentum   Momentum at very high speeds approaching the speed of light. (16.1)

resolution (rez-uh-LOO-shun)   (a) The process of resolving a vector into components. (5.3) (b) In optics, a measure of how well closely adjacent optical images are distinguished.

resonance (REZ-uh-nuns)   A phenomenon that occurs when the frequency of forced vibrations on an object matches the object's natural frequency, and a dramatic increase in amplitude results. (26.8)

rest energy   The "energy of being," given the equation $E = mc^2$. (16.2)

rest mass   The intrinsic mass of an object, a fixed property independent of speed or energy. (16.1)

resultant (rih-ZUL-tunt)   The vector sum of two or more component vectors. (2.5)

retina (RET-ih-nuh)   The layer of light-sensitive tissue at the back of the eye. (30.6)

reverberation (rih-verb-er-AY-shun)   Persistence of a sound, as in an echo, due to multiple reflections. (29.5)

revolution   Motion of an object turning around an axis outside the object. (10.1)

rotation   The spinning motion that takes place when an object rotates about an axis located within the object (usually an axis through its center of mass). (10.1)

rotational inertia   The resistance of an object to changes in its state of rotation, determined by the distribution of the mass of the object and the location of the axis of rotation or revolution. (12.1)

rotational speed   The number of rotations or revolutions per unit of time; often measured in rotations or revolutions per second or per minute (RPM). (10.2)

rotational velocity   Rotational speed together with a direction for the axis of rotation or revolution. (12.4)

S

satellite   An object that falls around Earth or some other body rather than falling into it. (14.1)

saturated   Term applied to a substance, such as air, that contains the maximum amount of another substance, such as water vapor, at a given temperature and pressure. (23.2)

scalar quantity   A quantity in physics, such as mass, volume, and time, that can be completely specified by its magnitude, and has no direction. (2.1)

scaling   The study of how size affects the relationship among weight, strength, and surface area. (18.5)

scattering   A process in which sound or light is absorbed and reemitted in all directions. (28.8)

schematic diagram   A diagram that describes an electric circuit, using special symbols to represent different devices in the circuit. (35.5)

scientific method   An orderly method for gaining, organizing, and applying new knowledge. (1.3)

second law of thermodynamics   Heat will never of itself flow from one object to another of higher temperature. (24.4)

second postulate of special relativity   The speed of light in empty space always has the same value regardless of the motion of the source or the motion of the observer. (15.3)

semiconductor   Material that can be made to behave as either a conductor or an insulator of electricity. (32.4)

series circuit   An electric circuit in which devices are arranged so that charge flows through each in turn. If one part of the circuit should stop the current, it will stop throughout the circuit. (35.3)

shadow   A shaded region that results when light falls on an object and thus cannot reach into the region on the far side of the object. (27.6)

shell model of the atom   A model in which the electrons of an atom are pictured as grouped in concentric shells around the nucleus. (17.8)

shock wave   A cone-shaped wave produced by an object moving at supersonic speed through a fluid. (25.11)

simple harmonic motion   The back-and-forth vibratory motion of a swinging pendulum. (25.2)

sine curve   A curve whose shape represents the crests and troughs of a wave, as traced out by a swinging pendulum that drops a trail of sand over a moving conveyor belt. (25.2)

sonic boom   The sharp crack heard when the shock wave that sweeps behind a supersonic aircraft reaches the listener. (25.11)

space-time   A combination of space and time, which are viewed in special relativity as two parts of one whole. (15.1)

special theory of relativity   The theory, introduced in 1905 by Albert Einstein, that describes how time is affected by motion in space at a constant velocity, and how mass and energy are related. (15.1)

specific gravity   The ratio of the mass (or weight) of a substance to the mass (or weight) of an equal volume of water. (18.2)

specific heat capacity   The quantity of heat required to raise the temperature of a unit mass of a substance by one degree Celsius. Often simply called "specific heat," or "heat capacity." (21.6)

spectroscope   An instrument used to separate the light from a hot gas or other light source into its constituent frequencies. (28.11)

spectrum   For sunlight and other white light, the spread of colors seen when the light is passed through a prism or diffraction grating. In general, the spread of radiation by frequency, so that each frequency appears at a different position. (28.1)

speed   How fast something is moving; the path distance moved per time. The magnitude of the velocity vector. (4.2)

spring tide   A high or low tide that occurs when the sun, Earth, and the moon are all lined up so that the tides due to the sun and moon coincide, making the high tides higher than average and the low tides lower than average. (13.9)

stable equilibrium   The state of an object balanced so that any small displacement or rotation raises its center of gravity. (11.7)

standing wave   Wave in which parts of the wave remain stationary and the wave appears not to be traveling. The result of interference between an incident (original) wave and a reflected wave. (25.8)

stellar radiation   The radiant energy emitted by the stars. (22.4)

streamline   The smooth path of a small region of fluid in steady flow. (20.7)

strong force   The force that attracts nucleons to one another within the nucleus; a force that is very strong at close distances but decreases rapidly as the distance increases. (39.1)

subtractive primary colors   The colors of magenta, yellow, and cyan. These are the three colors most useful in color mixing by subtraction. (28.7)

superconductivity   A property of a material that has infinite conductivity at very low temperatures, so that charge flows through it without resistance. (34.4)

support force   The upward force that balances the weight of an object on a surface; also called normal force. (2.3)

T

tangential speed   The speed of an object moving along a circular path. (10.2)

temperature   The property of a material that tells how warm or cold it is relative to some standard. In an ideal gas, the molecular kinetic energy per molecule. (21.1)

terminal speed   The speed at which the acceleration of a falling object is zero because friction balances the weight. (6.7)

terminal velocity   Terminal speed together with the direction of motion (down for falling objects). (6.7)

terrestrial radiation   Radiant energy emitted from Earth. (22.7)

theory   A synthesis of a large body of information that encompasses well-tested and verified hypotheses about aspects of the natural world. (1.4)

thermal contact   The state of two or more objects or substances in contact such that it is possible for heat to flow from one object or substance to another. (21.2)

thermal equilibrium   The state of two or more objects or substances in thermal contact when they have reached the same temperature. (21.3)

thermodynamics   The study of heat and its transformation to mechanical energy. (24.0)

thermonuclear fusion   Nuclear fusion brought about by extremely high temperatures. (40.7)

thermostat   A type of valve or switch that responds to changes in temperature and that is used to control the temperature of something. (21.8)

third law of thermodynamics   No system can reach absolute zero. (24.4)

time dilation   An observable stretching, or slowing, of time in a frame of reference moving past the observer at a speed approaching the speed of light. (15.4)

torque (TORK)   The rotational analog of force; the product of force and the lever arm (measured in newton-meters). Torque tends to produce rotational acceleration. (11.1)

total internal reflection   The 100% reflection (with no transmission) of light that strikes the boundary between two media at an angle greater than the critical angle. (29.12)

transformer   A device for increasing or decreasing voltage through electromagnetic induction. (37.5)

transmutation   The changing of one element into another element through a loss or gain in the number of protons. (39.6)

transparent   Term applied to materials that allow light to pass through them in straight lines. (27.4)

transverse wave   A wave with vibration at right angles to the direction the wave is traveling. (25.5)

trough (TRAWF)   One of the places in a wave where the wave is lowest, or the disturbance is greatest, in the opposite direction from a crest. (25.2)

U

ultrasonic   Term applied to sound frequencies above 20,000 hertz, the normal upper limit of human hearing. (26.1)

ultraviolet   Electromagnetic waves of frequencies higher than those of violet light. (27.3)

umbra   The darker part of a shadow where all the light is blocked. (27.6)

unstable equilibrium   The state of an object balanced so that any small displacement or rotation lowers its center of gravity. (11.7)

universal gravitational constant   The constant G in the equation for Newton's law of universal gravitation; measures the strength of gravity. (3.4)

V

vector   An arrow whose length represents the magnitude of a quantity and whose direction represents the direction of the quantity. (2.1)

vector quantity A quantity in physics, such as force, that has both magnitude and direction. (2.1)

velocity Speed together with the direction of motion. (4.3)

vibration An oscillation, or repeating back-and-forth motion, about an equilibrium position. (25.0)

virtual image An image formed through reflection or refraction that can be seen by an observer but cannot be projected on a screen because light from the object does not actually come to a focus. (29.3, 30.2)

volt The SI unit of electric potential. One volt (symbol V) is the electrical potential difference across which one coulomb of charge gains or loses one joule of energy. (33.5)

voltage (VOL-tij) (a) Electric potential; measured in volts. (33.5) (b) Potential difference; measured in volts. (34.1)

voltage source A device, such as a battery or generator, that provides a potential difference. (34.3)

watt (WAT) The SI unit of power. One watt is expended when one joule of work is done in one second. (9.2)

wave A disturbance that repeats regularly in space and time and that is transmitted progressively from one place to the next with no actual transport of matter. (25.0)

wave front The crest, trough, or any continuous portion of a two-dimensional or three-dimensional wave in which the vibrations are all the same way at the same time (see Figure 29.14). (29.6)

wavelength The distance from the top of the crest of a wave to the top of the following crest, or equivalently, the distance between successive identical parts of the wave. (25.2)

weight The force on a body due to the gravitational attraction of another body (commonly Earth). (3.5)

weightlessness The condition of free fall toward or around Earth, in which an object experiences no support force (and exerts no force on a scale). (13.8)

weight density The weight of a substance divided by its volume. (18.2)

white light Light, such as sunlight, that is a combination of all the colors. Under white light, white objects appear white and colored objects appear in their individual colors. (28.1)

work The product of the force on an object and the distance through which the object is moved (when force is constant and motion is in a straight line in the direction of the force); measured in joules. (9.1)

work–energy theorem The theorem that states that whenever work is done, energy changes. (9.5)

Index

Bernoulli, Daniel, 392

Bernoulli's principle, 392–395

Beta particle, 785–787

Big Bang theory, 253

Bimetallic strips, 417, 419

Binoculars, 611

Biology, 1

Black, as absence of light, 555

Black dwarf star, 249

Black holes, 249–250

Blind spot, 613, 626

Blue shift, 503

Bohr, Niels, 645, 767, 775

Boiling, 454–457

Bouncing, 129–130

Bow waves, 504

Boyle, Robert, 390

Boyle's law, 389–390

Breeder reactor, 816

British thermal unit (Btu), 900

Brown, Robert, 328

Brownian motion, 328

Buoyancy, 366–367
    of air, 391
    Archimedes' principle and, 367–368

Buoyant force, 366–367
    principle of flotation and, 371–372
    volume and, 369

C

Caloric, 470

Calorie, 411, 412

Cameras, parts and function of, 610

Capacitor, 672–673, 690

Carbon dating, 796–798

Carbon dioxide, and terrestrial
    radiation, 441–443

Careers
    astronaut, 343
    astronomer, 254
    civil engineer, 350
    electrician, 705
    firefighter, 461
    oceanographer, 732
    photographer, 614

Carnot, Sadi, 476

Carnot efficiency, 476–478

Catenary, 352

Cavendish, Henry, 238

Cellular field technician, 754

Celsius, Anders, 899

Celsius scale, 407, 469

Center of gravity, 195–204
    defined, 195
    locating, 195–196
    of people, 199–200

Center of mass, 192–195, 198

Centrifugal force, 178–180, 223–224

Centripetal force, 175–179

Chain reactions, 809

Chaos, 777

Charge, 645
    conductors of, 651–652
    conservation of, 646–647
    by contact, 652
    Coulomb's law and, 648–650
    electrical potential energy per, 670
    flow of, 681–682
    by friction, 652
    by induction, 653–654
    negative, 333, 645–647
    polarization of, 655–657
    positive, 333, 645–647
    types of, 645–647

Chemical energy, 148

Chemical formula, 331

Chemist, 333

Chemistry, 1

Chinooks, 474

Chromatic aberration, 616

Ciliary muscle, 613

Circuit. *See* Electric circuits

Circuit breakers, 712

Circular motion, 170–180

Circular orbits, 265–266, 269

Civil engineer, 350

Climate, and specific heat of water,
    415–416

Clock, light, 287–288

Clouds, 453

Coal, formation of, 154

Coherent light, 633

Collisions, 132–134
    elastic, 132
    heat generated by, 132, 134
    inelastic, 133
    net momentum before and after, 133

Color, 554–573
    complementary, 562–563

effect of light source on, 557
    of light emitted by elements, 571–573
    by reflection, 556–558
    of sky, 566–567
    of sunset, 568–569
    by transmission, 558
    of water, 570–571

Color addition, 561, 565

Color mixing, 560–561, 564–565, 568

Color separation
    by diffraction grating, 572, 630
    by prism, 555, 572
    by thin film, 631

Color spectrum, 555–556. *See also*
    Spectrum

Color subtraction, 555–556, 564–565

Communications satellites, 275

Complementary colors, 562–563

Components of vectors, 72

Compound microscope, 612

Compounds, 331
    interaction of elements in forming, 334
    molecular, 331

Compression, 350–352, 516, 522–523

Condensation, 452–453
    in atmosphere, 452–453
    in cooling process, 459–460
    rate of, 454

Conduction, heat, 431–432

Conduction electrons, 682, 692

Conductivity, 684

Conductors, 651–652
    charge by induction and, 653–655
    electric field within, 668–669
    heat, 431–432
    superconductors, 684

Conservation
    of angular momentum, 221–222
    of charge, 646–647
    of energy, 153–154
    of momentum, 110–111

Constant speed, 50

Constant velocity, 50

Constructive interference, 498, 628

Contact
    charging by, 652
    thermal, 409

Contraction, length, 294–295

Convection, 433–435
    Earth's magnetic field as effect of, 733
    winds as effect of, 434

Converging lens, 603–604

Electromagnetic induction, 740–755
    Faraday's law and, 743

Electromagnetic spectrum, 536

Electromagnetic waves, 436, 493, 536, 753–755

Electron, 334–335
    charge of, 645
    conduction, 682, 691–692
    configuration of, in shell model of atom, 335
    diffraction of, 771
    electric forces of repulsion in, 334
    excitation of, 573
    as magnet, 723–724
    source of, in circuit, 693
    speed of, in circuit, 691–692

Electron beam, 329

Electron microscopes, 329, 330, 627, 771

Electron orbits, differences in, 774–775

Electron waves, 772–773

Electrostatics, 644–657

Elements, 325–326
    artificial transmutation of, 795
    natural transmutation of, 792–793
    periodic table of, 335–336

Elliptical orbits, 267–269

Emerson, Ralph Waldo, 902

Emitters, heat, 438–440

Empedocles, and concept of light, 533

Energy, 144–163
    available, 147
    body's output of, computational example, 412
    changes of phase and, 458–461
    chemical, 148
    conservation of, 153–154, 163
        Bernoulli's principle and, 393
        law of, 153
    defined, 147
    disordered, 479
    dissipation of, 158
    electric, 672–673, 693–694
    generator source of, 745
    gravitational potential, 148–149
    heat, 409
    heating process and, 458–459
    internal, 411
    ionization, 775
    kinetic. See Kinetic energy
    for life, 160
    light, 536
    machines and, 115–117
    mass and, 305–306
    mechanical, 147

potential. See Potential energy
    radiant. See Radiant energy
    release of, and freezing, 459–460
    rest, 305–306
    satellite motion and, 269–270
    sound, 493–494
    thermal. See Kinetic energy
    transfer by wave, 436, 443, 493–494
    transformation of, 153–154
        in car engine, 159
        to heat, 159–160
        in pendulum, 153
    units of
        calorie, 411–412
        joule, 146
    useful, 160
    wave, reflection of, 579
    zero-point, 901

Energy levels, 772–773

Engines
    efficiency of, 159–160
    heat, 475–478
    internal combustion, 472
    steam turbine, 477–478

Entropy, 480–481

Equilibrium
    Equilibrium rule, 16
    of condensation and evaporation, 454
    net force of zero in, 15–19
    neutral, 201
    rotational, 188–204
    stable, 201–202
    thermal, 410
    unstable, 201

Equivalence, mass–energy, 816

Equivalence, principle of, 309–311

Equivalent resistance, 710

Escape speed, 272–275

Ethyl alcohol, density of, 347

Euclid, and concept of light, 533

Evaporation, 451
    as cooling process, 459–460
    rate of, 454

Evolution, Darwin's theory of, 5

Excitation of electrons, 571

Expansion. See Thermal expansion

Eye, 612–613

Eyeglasses, polarizing, 544, 545

Eyepiece, 611, 612

Extremely low frequency (ELF) radiation, 756

F

Fact, defined, 2

Fahrenheit, Gabriel, 899

Fahrenheit scale, 407

Fall, free. See Free fall

Falling, around versus into, 263–265

Faraday, Michael, 740–741

Faraday's law, 743, 751
    electromagnetic induction and, 743

Farsightedness, 614

Fibers, optical, 595

Field, 242. See also Electric field; Gravitational field; Magnetic field

Field lines, 242, 666–667
    magnetic, 722–723, 728

Films, thin
    iridescence from, 631–632

Firefighter, 461

Fission, nuclear, 809–812

Flanges, 351

Floating, and density, 369–370

Flotation, 371–372

Flow, steady, and Bernoulli's principle, 393

Fluid
    buoyancy in, 366–367, 391
    flotation in, 371–372
    friction of, 90
    pressure in, 363–365, 392

Focal length, 604

Focal plane, 604

Focal point, 604

Foci, elliptical, 267

Fog, 453

Food, energy value of, 442

Force, 13–22
    acceleration and, 87
    action, 108
    action and reaction, 116
    in action–reaction pair, 112–113
    applied, 91–92. See also Pressure
    buoyant, 366–368, 371
    centrifugal, 178–180
    centripetal, 175–179
    electrical. See Electrical forces
    friction, 18, 30–32
    fundamental, 238
    gravitational. See Gravitational force; Gravity
    in impulses, 125–129
    interaction as producer of, 107

generated by collisions, 132, 134
internal energy and, 411
measurement of, 411–412
poor conductors of, 431–442
transmission of, 430–443
useful energy as, 160

Heat engines, 475–478

Heating process, and energy, 458–459

Heat of fusion, 458

Heat of vaporization, 459

Heat pump, 460

Heat transfer, 460–461

Heavy water, 789

Helium
density of, 384
model of atom of, 645

Henry, Joseph, 740–741

Hertz, Heinrich, 492, 767

Hertz (unit of frequency), 492

Hologram, 634, 635–636

Hooke, Robert, 349

Hooke's law, 349, 902

Horse–cart problem, 114–115

Human body
center of gravity of, 199–200
cooling through perspiration, 451
effect of electric current on, 686–688
energy output of, computational
example, 412
principal axes of rotation of, 216–217

Humidity, relative, 452

Huygens, Christian, 534, 623, 767

Huygens' principle, 623–624

Hydraulic press, and Pascal's
principle, 373–374

Hydrogen
atoms of, 325
density of, 384

Hypothesis
in scientific method, 2
testable nature of, 4

I

I-beams, 351

Ice
density of, 347
expansion of, 419–421
formation of, and energy release,
458–459
melting of, 458–459

Ice crystals, 420–422, 456

Ignition temperature, 823

Illusions, optical, 516

Image
constructing, through ray diagrams,
606–609
formation of, by lens, 604–606, 610
real, 605
virtual, 581, 605, 606

Impact, force of, 127–129

Impulse
as change in momentum, 125–129
defined, 126
effects of bouncing on, 129–130
forces involved in, 126

Incidence, angle of, 580

Inclined plane, 158

Incoherent light, 633

Index of refraction, 904

Induction
charge by, 653–654
electromagnetic, 741–742

Inelastic collisions, 133

Inelasticity, 348

Inertia, 32–34, 36–37
defined, 32
demonstrations of, 33–34
Earth's motion and, 38–39
mass as measure of, 36–38
Newton's law of, 33–34
rotational, 213–218
See also Momentum

Infrared radiation, 436, 536, 538

Infrasonic sound waves, 515

In phase, 499

Instantaneous speed, 49, 53–55

Insulators, 431–432, 651

Interactions, 107

Interference, 498–499
color separation and, 630–631
constructive, 498, 522, 628
destructive, 498, 522, 628
for measurement of light wavelengths, 632
sound waves and, 522–523
water waves and, 628
Young's experiment with, 629–630

Interference fringes, 629–630, 635–636,
771

Interference pattern, 498, 622, 628,
629–630

Interferometer, 632

Internal combustion engines,
159–160, 472

Internal energy, 411, 413

Internal force, 130–131

Internal resistance, 710

International System of Units, 38, 412

Inverse proportion, 87

Inverse-square law, 240–241

Ion, 334–335, 646, 788

Ionization energy, 775

Iridescence from thin films, 631–632

Iris, 612

Iron
flotation and, 371–372
magnetic domains in, 724–725

Isotopes, 333
radioactive, 788–789

J

Jack, 159

Jolly, Philipp von, 238

Joule, 146

Jumping, 60, 78, 128

K

Kelvin, Lord, 469

Kelvin (unit of temperature), 407, 899

Kelvin scale, 407, 469

Kilocalorie, 412

Kilogram, 36

Kilowatt, 146, 694

Kilowatt-hour, 694

Kinetic energy, 150
defined, 150
increasing, 406
satellite motion and, 269–270
temperature and, 407, 451

L

Laser, 633

Laser light, 626, 633–634

Laws, 2
Boyle's, 389–390
conservation
of angular momentum, 221–222
of charge, 646–647

Acknowledgments

I am thankful to the four contributors listed on the title page of this book. Chris Chiaverina, recently retired from New Trier High School in Winnetka, Illinois, authored all the Discover features that open each chapter. Chris nicely directs students to a hands-on activity to begin each chapter. Ken Ford, my physics mentor, has added clarity to many of the explanations in this (and my college) book. Ken's help spans many years, from when he was CEO of The American Institute of Physics to his most recent position as a part-time teacher of ninth graders at Germantown Academy, Germantown, Pennsylvania. Diane Riendeau, Deerfield High School, Deerfield, Illinois, in addition to class testing chapter backmatter with her students, authored many of the Think and Rank exercises. These were inspired by the book *Ranking Task Exercises in Physics* by Thomas L. O'Kuma, David P. Maloney, and Curtis J. Hieggelke, to whom Diane and I are grateful for their permission to draw freely from their stimulating book. Phil Wolf, community college physics teacher at Mt. San Antonio College in Walnut, California, authored many of the Think and Solve and Appendix F problems in this and the previous edition. Phil also provided great feedback about material new to this edition. Chris, Ken, Diane, and Phil have been the backbone of what's new in this edition.

Marshall Ellenstein, recently retired Chicago physics teacher, was also a great resource, providing valuable feedback to both the Think and Solves and Think and Ranks. Marshall is the editor and producer of the DVDs of my physics lectures. New Zealand physics teacher David Housden also supplied major input to both Think and Solves and the problem sets in Appendix F. Evan Jones checked solutions to most of these, for which I am grateful. I credit Marshall, David, and Evan for many of the improvements in this edition.

Teachers who have contributed to new Think and Solves and problems for Appendix F include Dean Baird, Lonnie Grimes, Rog Lucido, Diane Goldstein, Fred Myers, Gene Pere, Les Sawyer, and David Williamson.

For valued feedback and suggestions, I am grateful to Tsing and Keith Bardin, Bob Bauman, Dale Beamers, Howie Brand, Ernie Brown, George Curtis, Jeff Drake, Paul Hammer, Jim Hicks, Vonnie Hicks, John Hubisz, Dan Johnson, Griff Jones, David Kagan, Don Kanner, Jules Layugan, Mark Linnenburger, Suzanne Lyons, Iain MacInnes, Jesse MacKinnon, Will Maynez, Steve Mozzer, Alan Pepper, Ray Serway, Les Sawyer, John Suchocki, Larry Weinstein, Joe Wesney, Lynda Williams, and Erik Wong.

For their insightful feedback as content reviewers for this edition, I am grateful to Sylvia Angelo, Ann M. W. Brandon, Martha Dickinson, Paul Doherty, Barry Feierman, Howard Glasser, Chuck Stone, Martin Teachworth, and Dean Zollman.

For being a local resource, I am grateful to Anne Cox.

For helping at every stage of this book, I am enormously grateful to my wife Lillian. At Pearson, I have been fortunate to have Caroline Power, the best physics editor in my career, guiding the production of this book. Assisting her has been Ken Chang. I credit these three people for the overall quality of this book.

Staff Credits

Joyce Barisano, Brittany Betts, Peggy Bliss, Michael A. Burstein, Ken Chang, Frederick Fellows, Jonathan Fisher, Kathryn Fobert, Etta Jacobs, Greg Lam, Russ Lappa, Mary Ellen Leahy, Caroline Power-Dolan, Marcy Rose, Malti Sharma, Lisa Smith-Ruvalcaba, Emily Soltanoff, Cheryl Steinecker, Amanda Watters

Additional Credits
Vassia Alaykova, Ernie Albanese, Bob Doron, Paula Gogan-Porter, Adam Groffman, Amy Hamel, Kerri Hoar, Gillian Kahn, Cheryl Mahan, Michelle Reyes, Stephen Rider, Jewel Simmons

Photo Credits

Cover & Title Page roller coaster, Jeremy Sutton-Hibbert/Alamy; **background,** Shutterstock

Table of Contents v l, Getty Images, Inc.; **v r,** istockphoto; **vi l,** Worth Canoy/Icon SMI/Corbis; **vi r,** Morgan Howarth/IPN; **vii,** istockphoto; **viii l, viii tr,** Getty Images, Inc.; **viii br, x,** istockphoto; **xii,** Getty Images, Inc.; **xiii,** Cheryl Fenton

Front Matter xvi t, Getty Images, Inc.; **xvi m,** Kent Wood/Photo Researchers, Inc.; **xvi b,** Pearson Scott Foresman; **xix,** Paul Hewitt

Unit Openers

Unit 1 10 bl, Paul Hewitt; **10 r,** Getty Images, Inc.; **b,** Shutterstock; **11 l,** istockphoto; **11 tr,** Morgan Howarth/IPN; **11 m,** Getty Images, Inc.; **11 b,** Shutterstock

Unit 2 322 t, Getty Images, Inc.; **322 bl,** Paul Hewitt; **322 br,** Michael Dalton/Fundamental Photographs; **323 t,** Radius Images/Masterfile Corporation; **323 m,** NASA/Photo Researchers, Inc.; **323 b,** Getty Images, Inc.

Unit 3 404 t, Photolibrary.com; **404 bl,** Paul Hewitt; **405 t,** Mark Boulton/Photo Researchers, Inc.; **405 ml,** Phil Degginger/Alamy; **405 mr,** Tad Denson/Dreamstime.com; **404–405 b,** Veer

Unit 4 488 t, istockphoto; **488 bl,** Paul Hewitt; **488 br,** Getty Images, Inc.; **489 t,** Corbis; **489 m,** Getty Images, Inc.; **489 bl,** Getty Images, Inc.; **489 br,** Clayton J. Price/Corbis

Unit 5 642 t, Dieter Spannknebel/Getty Images, Inc.; **642 bl,** Paul Hewitt; **643 t,** Tony Freeman/PhotoEdit; **643 m,** PictureNet/Corbis; **643 br,** Ryan Mcvay/photolibrary.com; **642–643 b,** Virgo Productions/zefa/Corbis

Unit 6 764 l, Paul Hewitt; **764 r,** Erich Lessing/Art Resource, NY; **765 t,** Image Farm Inc./Alamy; **765 m,** Neil Borden/Photo Researchers, Inc.; **765 bl,** Science Photo Library; **765 br,** Oliver Meckes/Photo Researchers, Inc.

Chapter 1 xx, istockphoto; **2 both,** Corbis; **4,** Paul Hewitt; **7,** Roger Ressmeyer/Starlight

Chapter 2 12, Getty Images, Inc.; **14,** Jim Stith, Collection of Paul Hewitt

Chapter 3 28, Mike Powell/Getty Images, Inc.; **29,** Corbis; **30,** Erich Lessing/Art Resource, NY; **32,** Alinari/Art Resource, NY; **34,** Ken Karp; **35,** Giraudon/Art Resource, NY; **37,** Digital Vision; **43,** Paul Hewitt

Chapter 4 46, istockphoto; **47,** Jello5700/iStockphoto; **48,** Shutterstock; **49,** Cheryl Fenton; **60,** Tim Davis/Photo Researchers, Inc.

Chapter 5 68, 74, Richard Megna/Fundamental Photographs; **78 t,** David Madison; **78 b,** David Madison/Duomo

Chapter 6 86, Worth Canoy/Icon SMI/Corbis; **89,** Simon Bruty/Getty Images, Inc.; **92 both,** Colin Vinnard; **96 t,** F. Rickard-Artdia, Agence Vandystadt/Photo Researchers, Inc.; **96 b,** Stephen Dalton/NHPA; **97,** Fundamental Photographs

Chapter 7 106, Neil Rabinowitz/Corbis; **107,** David Madison/Bruce Coleman Inc.; **116, 121,** Paul Hewitt

Chapter 8 124, Getty Images, Inc.; **126,** © The Harold E. Edgerton 1992 Trust, courtesy Palm Press, Inc.; **129, 130 t,** Paul Hewitt; **130 b,** Benjamin Alexander, Collection of Paul Hewitt; **134,** Paul Hewitt; **136,** Dan McCoy/Rainbow

Chapter 9 144, istockphoto; **145,** William R. Sallaz/Duomo; **146,** Roger Ressmeyer/Starlight; **150,** AP Photo/Al Behrman; **151 both,** Michael Vollmer; **153,** Paul Hewitt; **154,** Richard Megna/Fundamental Photographs; **161,** Martin Bond/Peter Arnold, Inc.; **163 t,** Mark A Leman/Getty Images, Inc.; **163 b,** Macarena Minguell/AFP/Getty Images, Inc.

Chapter 10 170, Getty Images, Inc.; **171,** Guenther Fuernsteiner/age fotostock

Chapter 11 188, Gerald Lacz/NHPA; **190,** Ken Karp; **193,** Richard Megna/Fundamental Photographs; **197,** London Transport Museum; **198,** Paul Hewitt; **199 t,** David Madison; **199 b,** Denise Tackett/Tom Stack & Associates; **202,** Owaki-Kulla; **204,** Larry Brownstein/Rainbow

Chapter 12 212, Morgan Howarth/IPN; **214,** Deanne Fitzmaurice; **219 t,** Richard Megna/Fundamental Photographs; **219 b,** Paul Hewitt; **220,** Jonathan Nourok/PhotoEdit; **222,** Gerald Lacz/NHPA; **223,** Bill & Sally Fletcher/Tom Stack & Associates; **225,** NASA; **230,** Paul Hewitt

Chapter 13 232, Getty Images, Inc.; **243,** NASA; **248,** Bill Brooks/Alamy Images; **252,** NASA Jet Propulsion Laboratory

Chapter 14 262, Getty Images, Inc.; **266,** NASA; **271 l,** Royal Observatory, Edinburgh/Photo Researchers, Inc.; **271 r,** Erich Lessing/Art Resource, NY; **274,** NASA

Chapter 15 282, istockphoto; **283,** Roger Ressmeyer/Starlight; **289,** Paul Hewitt; **293,** NASA

Chapter 16 302, European Space Agency/Photo Researchers, Inc.; **306,** Manfred Gottschalk/Tom Stack & Associates

Chapter 17 324, istockphoto; **326,** Paul Hewitt; **329 t,** Enrico Fermi Institute/University of Chicago; **329 b,** Dr. Mitsuo Ohtsuki/SPL/Photo Researchers, Inc.; **330,** NIBSC/SPL/Photo Researchers, Inc.; **337,** Ken Graham/Getty Images, Inc.

Chapter 18 344, istockphoto; **352 t,** Barrie Rokeach; **352 b,** Paul Hewitt; **356,** Joe Bensen/Stock Boston

Chapter 19 362, Getty Images, Inc.; **364,** Michael A. Keller/Index Stock Imagery, Inc.; **371,** Michael Townsend

Chapter 20 382, istockphoto; **384,** Anthony Nettle/Alamy Images; **387,** Paul Hewitt; **388 t all,** Getty Images, Inc.; **388 b,** Paul Silverman/Fundamental Photographs; **390,** Stephen Frink/Getty Images, Inc.; **391,** Francis Lepine/Earth Scenes; **394,** Liza Loeffler

Chapter 21 406, Tad Denson/Dreamstime.com; **408,** Jose Fuste Raga/age fotostock; **412,** GHP Studio; **416,** AP/Wide World Photos; **417,** Breck P. Kent/Earth Scenes; **419,** Ken Karp; **421,** Claude Nuridsany & Marie Perennou/Photo Researchers, Inc.

Chapter 22 430, Getty Images, Inc.; **432,** John Coletti/Stock Boston; **437,** Paul Hewitt; **439 both,** Anne Dowie; **440,** Cheryl Fenton

Chapter 23 450, Getty Images, Inc.; **451 t,** Liza Loeffler; **451 b,** Pat Crowe/Animals Animals; **452,** Cheryl Fenton; **461,** Bill Stormont/Corbis

Chapter 24 468, istockphoto; **472,** Paul Hewitt; **474,** Dan McCoy/Rainbow; **479,** Michael J. Howell/Stock Boston; **480,** Cory Wolinsky/Stock Boston; **481,** David Gould/Getty Images, Inc.

Chapter 25 490, Pearson Scott Foresman; **491 both,** Paul Hewitt; **493,** Carl Newman/Alamy Images; **494,** Kim Taylor/Bruce Coleman Inc.; **499 all,** Education Development Center, Inc., Newton, MA. PSSC PHYSICS, 2nd Edition, 1965

Chapter 26 514, istockphoto; **515,** Richard Megna/Fundamental Photographs; **516,** Paul Hewitt; **518,** P. Saada/Eurelios/SPL/Photo Researchers, Inc.; **520,** Paul Hewitt; **522 all,** AP/Wide World Photos; **524,** Paul Hewitt; **525,** Cheryl Fenton; **526,** George W. Disario

Chapter 27 532, istockphoto; **540 all,** Cheryl Fenton; **541,** The Exploratorium; **543 all,** Anne Dowie

Chapter 28 554, istockphoto; **555 t,** Bettman/Corbis; **555 b,** © Matthias Kulka/Corbis; **556 t,** Cheryl Fenton; **556 b,** James H. Carmichael/Getty Images, Inc.; **562 all,** Fundamental Photographs; **563,** Dave Vasquez; **564,** Paul Hewitt; **565 all,** Paul Hewitt; **566,** Charlie Ott/Photo Researchers, Inc.; **567,** Triff/Shutterstock; **569,** Katrina Brown/Shutterstock; **570,** Don & Uysa King/Getty Images, Inc.; **572,** © sciencephotos/Alamy images; **573,** © 1994 Wabash Instrument Corp./Fundamental Photographs

Chapter 29 578, Sean Bolton/Alamy Images; **581,** Paul Hewitt; **583,** Dr. Jeremy Burgess/SPL/Photo Researchers, Inc.; **584,** Jane Lidz; **585,** Education Development Center, Inc., Newton, MA. PSSC PHYSICS, 2nd Edition, 1965; **589,** John M. Dunay IV/Fundamental Photographs; **590,** Marc Romanelli/Getty Images, Inc.; **593,** Paul Hewitt; **595,** Bill Pierce/Rainbow Fundamental Photographs; **599 t,** Barbara Thomas; **599 b,** Launch McKenzie, Collection of Paul Hewitt; **600,** Cheryl Fenton

Chapter 30 602, t, cardiae/Shutterstock: **b,** Yobidaba/Shutterstock; **606,** Renee Lynn; **611,** istockphoto; **614,** David Young-Wolff/PhotoEdit; **620,** Milo Patterson

Chapter 31 622, Getty Images, Inc.; **623 t both,** Burndy Library; **625 all,** Education Development Center, Inc., Newton, MA PSSC PHYSICS, 2nd Edition, 1965; **626,** Richard Megna/Fundamental Photographs; **627,** © Jeff Rotman/Alamy Images; **628 all,** Educational Development Center, Inc., Newton, MA, PSSC PHYSICS, 2nd Edition, 1965; **629,** Richard Megna/Fundamental Photographs; **630,** Fedorov Oleksiy/Shutterstock; **631,** GHP Studio; **632,** Paul Hewitt; **634,** Ken Karp; **635,** David Muench; **637,** Burndy Library

Chapter 32 644, Kent Wood/Photo Researchers, Inc.; **648,** © Roy Lawe/Alamy; **651,** © Mark Lavin Art Photo/Alamy Images

Chapter 33 664, © Nicholas Vasilakes/Alamy Images; **667 all,** Harold Waage/Princeton University; **668,** © Bettmann/Corbis; **669, 672,** Ken Karp; **673,** Ahmed Eid; **674,** Paul Hewitt

Chapter 34 680, Russ Lappa; **683, 685, 690,** Ken Karp; **694,** Cheryl Fenton

Chapter 35 702, Ryan Mcvay/photolibrary.com; **703,** Cheryl Fenton; **705, 707, 709,** Ken Karp

Chapter 36 720, Getty Images, Inc.; **721 t,** Eunice Harris/Photo Researchers, Inc.; **721 b,** Cheryl Fenton; **722, 723 both,** Richard Megna/Fundamental Photographs; **724,** Lori Patterson; **727 top all,** Richard Megna/Fundamental Photographs; **727 b,** Reuters/China Photo/Corbis; **729,** Dave Wilhelm/Corbis; **730,** Ken Karp; **732,** Stephen Rose/Rainbow

Chapter 37 740, D. Hurst/Alamy Images; **745,** Chuck Fishman/Woodfin Camp & Associates; **749 t,** Cheryl Fenton; **749 b, 750,** Paul Hewitt; **751,** Corbis; **756,** Pearson Education/PH College; **760,** Diane Riendeau

Chapter 38 766, Paul Freytag/Zefa/Corbis; **770 all,** Albert Rose; **771 t,** Susumu Nishinaga/Photo Researchers, Inc.; **771 br,** Nuridsany et Perennou/Photo Researchers, Inc.; **777,** Phil Schermeister/Getty Images, Inc.

Chapter 39 782, Neil Borden/PhotoResearchers, Inc.; **791 l,** CNRI/SPL/Photo Researchers, Inc.; **791 r,** Jerry Nulk and Joshua Baker; **795,** Stanford Linear Accelerator Center; **799,** International Atomic Energy Agency; **801,** Jose Fernandez/Woodfin Camp & Associates

Chapter 40 808, Cheryl Fenton; **817,** AP Photo/Joe Giblin; **822, 824,** Lawrence Livermore National Laboratory

End Matter 839, Ken Karp